CASES AND MATERIALS

FUNDAMENTALS OF BUSINESS ENTERPRISE TAXATION

FOURTH EDITION

by

STEPHEN A. LIND
Albert R. Abramson Distinguished Professor of Law
University of California, Hastings College of the Law

STEPHEN SCHWARZ
Professor of Law Emeritus
University of California, Hastings College of the Law

DANIEL J. LATHROPE
Professor of Law
University of California, Hastings College of the Law

JOSHUA D. ROSENBERG
Professor of Law
University of San Francisco School of Law

FOUNDATION PRESS
75TH ANNIVERSARY

THOMSON
WEST

395 Hudson Street
New York, NY 10014
Phone Toll Free 1–877–888–1330
Fax (212) 367–6799
foundation–press.com

Printed in the United States of America

ISBN 978–1–59941–385–3

TEXT IS PRINTED ON 10% POST CONSUMER RECYCLED PAPER

To our students

*

PREFACE

Developments over the past two decades have profoundly influenced the legal structure and taxation of business enterprises. The rise of limited liability companies, more permissive tax classification regulations, flatter and lower individual tax rates, repeal of the *General Utilities* doctrine, and the greater availability of Subchapter S, all have contributed to the growth of pass-through entities as a favored form for conducting a closely held business. At the same time, C corporations remain the inevitable choice for virtually all publicly traded companies and continue as a viable alternative for many private firms whose owners now enjoy the advantage of a lower tax rate on qualified dividends.

These developments have influenced the teaching of business enterprise taxation, particularly at the J.D. level. Many law schools now offer a three or four-unit course combining corporate and partnership tax. Adherents of this approach point to the virtues of studying business enterprise taxation as an integrated unit. A combined course, so the argument goes, provides a better and more efficient vantage point for students to compare and contrast the major taxing models, enabling them to emerge with a real-world perspective on issues confronting the small to mid-size businesses that they are most likely to encounter in practice.

The combined course has its detractors, ranging from professors who believe that separate courses are a more pedagogically sound approach, to overwhelmed students who complain that combining corporate and partnership tax in one class is far too demanding for the units that appear on their transcripts. The authors of this text have taken various sides in this ongoing debate. Twenty-five years ago, when we embarked on the project that culminated in discrete texts on corporate and partnership tax, we intended to publish a combined casebook but then convinced ourselves that separate books were preferable or at least more marketable. We later saw a need for an alternative single volume that accommodates a J.D.-level course on business enterprise taxation. Publication of this Fourth Edition offered another opportunity to refine this combined text and incorporate recent legislation, several important new regulations projects, and the usual trickle of published rulings.

For this revision, we continue to resist the temptation merely to join our separate books at the hip, republishing them under one cover with new chapter numbers. Although substantial material has been incorporated without change, this text has been custom tailored for a course on business enterprise taxation. To that end, we have pruned considerably, removing entire chapters (e.g., Subchapter C anti-avoidance provisions and affiliated corporations), and condensing or eliminating topics (e.g., advanced corporate acquisition issues), cases, and problems that cannot realistically be covered in a combined course or have lost their relevance as a result of recent tax legislation. This text also includes comprehensive problems with a planning orientation in several areas to facilitate more efficient coverage.

We remain mindful, however, that instructors approach an integrated business enterprise tax course with different goals and interests. And we are human and found it hard to delete a few favorite topics that perhaps should not be covered in a sensible survey offering. So we warn instructors that it would be imprudent to cover all the material in this text, even in a four-unit course. Some choices still must be made, and a few topics should be left for an advanced follow-up course or business planning seminar.

This text remains faithful to the problem-oriented "fundamentals" approach used in our companion volumes. Some level of detail is unavoidable, but we pause once again to remind ourselves and others of the importance of teaching the "fundamentals" by the problem method. As we have said in earlier Prefaces:

> * * * [In] our collective experience, we have been troubled by a common denominator in the many fine * * * casebooks and texts: their sheer bulk. * * * [W]e attempt to chart a different course by bringing the "fundamentals" philosophy to the teaching of taxation of the business enterprise. * * * [T]he fundamentals approach involves selectivity of subject matter, emphasis on basic concepts, avoidance of esoteric detail and realistic depth of coverage. To those ends, this volume is the product of self-restraint — although perhaps not enough. At times, we opted for over inclusion to accommodate the varied teaching biases and favorite cases and topics of experienced instructors (including ourselves). We have continued, however, to select and edit cases with care. Lengthy citations, obscure questions, and meanderings into minutia have been avoided. Throughout the book, we have made an effort to remember what it was like when we were students; this volume is designed as a teaching book, not the definitive treatise. And so, of course, we expect students to do the reading!
>
> We also believe that the most effective way to teach and learn tax fundamentals is by the problem method. This book thus contains a comprehensive yet manageable set of problems to accompany every major topic. The problems are designed to help students decipher the statute and apply it in a wide variety of alternative fact situations. Some are "building block" problems with specific answers. We are mindful, however, of the tendency to become pre-

occupied with technical trivia and have also included some more sophisticated (and realistic) problems with a planning orientation.

The primary sources in any tax course are the Code and Regulations. But the statute is frequently unintelligible when read out of context. To provide a foundation of understanding, this book includes extensive explanatory text to accompany the problems and a selection of cases, rulings, legislative history and other materials. The goal of the text is not merely to paraphrase the Code. In addition to describing the *workings* of the statute, we have attempted to explain *why* it works the way it does. If presented as a purely mechanical exercise, the problem method can degenerate into a mindless series of computations, leaving one without insights into the function of the statute, the relationship between sections and the broad principles * * *. By first explaining the "why" and well as the "how," we hope that even the computational problems will serve as launching pads for the discussion of more important policy and planning issues.

Turning to organization, Chapter 1 offers an introductory "perspective" that can be covered in the first few hours of class when students are not quite ready (or prepared?) for total immersion in the Internal Revenue Code. It provides a comparative overview of the major taxing models for taxing business enterprises and an expanded introduction to choice of entity, including the planning implications of the current rate structure. Chapter 1 also discusses the Service's flexible check-the-box classification regulations; previews the relevant tax policy issues; and introduces students to the pervasive judicial doctrines that have influenced interpretation of Subchapters C and K.

The text then proceeds systematically to examine the complex partnership pass-through regime of Subchapter K, then the double-tax regime of Subchapter C, and lastly the simpler alternative pass-through model of Subchapter S. Students find all of this to be very challenging material. We considered the arguments for integrated coverage of Subchapters K, S and C rather than examining them as discrete subjects. Based on many years of experience, we concluded that the most pedagogically proven approach is to cover each taxing model separately, using a "cradle to grave" organization. Although the text begins with Subchapter K and ends with Subchapter S, each Part is freestanding, and instructors easily can begin with C corporations and end with partnerships.

The decision—not yet permanent—to tax qualified dividends and long-term capital gains at the same reduced rate, has altered the tax stakes for many corporate-shareholder transactions and complicated the teaching of Subchapter C. Where the historical agenda was to avoid dividend treatment and "bail out" corporate earnings at capital gains rates, now the major advantage of a successful bailout is recovery of basis. As we await the outcome, if any, of the long-promised "fundamental tax reform," the materials on C corporations do their best to address the planning implications of the current (transitional?) regime. But mindful that nothing is certain, many of the traditional materials have been retained, except for a few cases that no longer seemed to be worth the time and effort. It will be up to instructors to decide how much emphasis to give to corporate tax characterization issues in view of these altered stakes.

As for matters of style, we assume the text will be assigned with the most recent edition of the Code and Regulations. Suggested assignments to these sources are provided for each topic. Instructors may wish to review these assignments, editing when necessary to ensure they are consistent with the desired level of coverage. Deletions from cases and other authorities have been made freely, with asterisks used to denote substantive omissions, but citations and internal cross references in excerpted materials have been deleted without so indicating. Editorial additions are in brackets. Footnotes to the original text are numbered consecutively within each section, and many footnotes have been deleted from cases without renumbering those that remain. In general, coverage is current as of April 1, 2008.

We are indebted to our colleagues, Steve Lind and Josh Rosenberg, who no longer actively participate as co-authors, and express here our gratitude for their contributions to the development of this text and its many previous editions. We also thank the administration of Hastings College of the Law for its research support.

STEPHEN SCHWARZ
DANIEL J. LATHROPE

San Francisco, California
May, 2008

ACKNOWLEDGEMENTS

We gratefully acknowledge the permission extended by the following authors and publishers to reprint excerpts from the material listed below:

William B. Brannan, "The Subchapter K Reform Act of 1997," 75 Tax Notes 121, 122–124 (April 7, 1997). Reprinted with permission. Copyright © 1997 Tax Analysts.

Heather M. Field, "Fiction, Form, and Substance in Subchapter K: Taxing Partnership Mergers, Divisions, and Incorporations," 44 San Diego L. Rev. 259, 296–297 (2007). Copyright © 2007 San Diego Law Review. Reprinted with permission of the San Diego Law Review.

*

SUMMARY OF CONTENTS

*

TABLE OF CONTENTS

*

TABLE OF INTERNAL REVENUE CODE SECTIONS

UNITED STATES

UNITED STATES CODE ANNOTATED

26 U.S.C.A.—Internal Revenue Code

UNITED STATES CODE ANNOTATED

26 U.S.C.A.—Internal Revenue Code

UNITED STATES CODE ANNOTATED
26 U.S.C.A.—Internal Revenue Code

UNITED STATES CODE ANNOTATED
26 U.S.C.A.—Internal Revenue Code

UNITED STATES CODE ANNOTATED

26 U.S.C.A.—Internal Revenue Code

UNITED STATES CODE ANNOTATED

26 U.S.C.A.—Internal Revenue Code

UNITED STATES CODE ANNOTATED

26 U.S.C.A.—Internal Revenue Code

UNITED STATES CODE ANNOTATED

26 U.S.C.A.—Internal Revenue Code

UNITED STATES CODE ANNOTATED

26 U.S.C.A.—Internal Revenue Code

UNITED STATES CODE ANNOTATED
26 U.S.C.A.—Internal Revenue Code

UNITED STATES CODE ANNOTATED
26 U.S.C.A.—Internal Revenue Code

UNITED STATES CODE ANNOTATED

26 U.S.C.A.—Internal Revenue Code

UNITED STATES CODE ANNOTATED
26 U.S.C.A.—Internal Revenue Code

UNITED STATES CODE ANNOTATED
26 U.S.C.A.—Internal Revenue Code

UNITED STATES CODE ANNOTATED
26 U.S.C.A.—Internal Revenue Code

UNITED STATES CODE ANNOTATED
26 U.S.C.A.—Internal Revenue Code

UNITED STATES CODE ANNOTATED

26 U.S.C.A.—Internal Revenue Code

UNITED STATES CODE ANNOTATED

26 U.S.C.A.—Internal Revenue Code

UNITED STATES CODE ANNOTATED

26 U.S.C.A.—Internal Revenue Code

UNITED STATES CODE ANNOTATED
26 U.S.C.A.—Internal Revenue Code

UNITED STATES CODE ANNOTATED
26 U.S.C.A.—Internal Revenue Code

UNITED STATES CODE ANNOTATED
26 U.S.C.A.—Internal Revenue Code

UNITED STATES CODE ANNOTATED
26 U.S.C.A.—Internal Revenue Code

UNITED STATES CODE ANNOTATED

26 U.S.C.A.—Internal Revenue Code

UNITED STATES CODE ANNOTATED

26 U.S.C.A.—Internal Revenue Code

UNITED STATES CODE ANNOTATED
26 U.S.C.A.—Internal Revenue Code

UNITED STATES CODE ANNOTATED
26 U.S.C.A.—Internal Revenue Code

UNITED STATES CODE ANNOTATED
26 U.S.C.A.—Internal Revenue Code

UNITED STATES CODE ANNOTATED
26 U.S.C.A.—Internal Revenue Code

UNITED STATES CODE ANNOTATED
26 U.S.C.A.—Internal Revenue Code

UNITED STATES CODE ANNOTATED
26 U.S.C.A.—Internal Revenue Code

UNITED STATES CODE ANNOTATED

26 U.S.C.A.—Internal Revenue Code

UNITED STATES CODE ANNOTATED

26 U.S.C.A.—Internal Revenue Code

UNITED STATES CODE ANNOTATED

26 U.S.C.A.—Internal Revenue Code

UNITED STATES CODE ANNOTATED

26 U.S.C.A.—Internal Revenue Code

UNITED STATES CODE ANNOTATED

26 U.S.C.A.—Internal Revenue Code

UNITED STATES CODE ANNOTATED

26 U.S.C.A.—Internal Revenue Code

UNITED STATES CODE ANNOTATED

26 U.S.C.A.—Internal Revenue Code

UNITED STATES CODE ANNOTATED

26 U.S.C.A.—Internal Revenue Code

UNITED STATES CODE ANNOTATED

26 U.S.C.A.—Internal Revenue Code

UNITED STATES CODE ANNOTATED

26 U.S.C.A.—Internal Revenue Code

*

TABLE OF TREASURY REGULATIONS

TEMPORARY TREASURY REGULATIONS

PROPOSED TREASURY REGULATIONS

PROPOSED TREASURY REGULATIONS

PROPOSED TREASURY REGULATIONS

TREASURY REGULATIONS

TREASURY REGULATIONS

TREASURY REGULATIONS

TREASURY REGULATIONS

TREASURY REGULATIONS

TREASURY REGULATIONS

TREASURY REGULATIONS

TREASURY REGULATIONS

TREASURY REGULATIONS

TREASURY REGULATIONS

TREASURY REGULATIONS

TREASURY REGULATIONS

TREASURY REGULATIONS

TREASURY REGULATIONS

TREASURY REGULATIONS

TREASURY REGULATIONS

TREASURY REGULATIONS

TREASURY REGULATIONS

TREASURY REGULATIONS

*

TABLE OF REVENUE RULINGS

REVENUE RULINGS

REVENUE RULINGS

TABLE OF MISCELLANEOUS RULINGS

REVENUE PROCEDURES

Rev.Proc.	This Work Page
74–33	892
77–37	442
77–37	721
77–37	734
77–37	812
81–70	769
84–35	91
89–12	11
90–56	721
91–13	11
93–27	61
93–27	**79**
93–27	80
93–27	81
93–27	82
93–27	84
93–27	233
96–30	797
96–30	812
96–30	817
96–30	819
96–30	820
96–30	840
2001–43	82
2002–69	13
2004–48	889
2005–43	83
2005–43	85
2005–43	86
2005–43	86
2006–46	109
2006–46	892
2007–62	889
2008–3	491
2008–3	578
2008–3	597
2008–3	721

*

TABLE OF CASES

Principal cases are in bold type. Non-principal cases are in roman type. References are to Pages.

*

TABLE OF AUTHORITIES

Abrams, A Close Look at the Carried Interest Legislation, 117 Tax Notes 961 (2007), 245

Abrams, "Taxation of Carried Interests," 116 Tax Notes 183 (2007), 245

Alexander, "The Questionable Continued Flourishing of S Corporations," 87 Tax Notes 577 (2000), 30

American Law Institute, Federal Income Tax Project, Subchapter C (1986), 850

American Law Institute, Federal Income Tax Project—Subchapter C 341–355 (1982), 8

American Law Institute, Federal Income Tax Project—Subchapter K 47–55 (1984), 317

American Law Institute, Federal Income Tax Project—Taxation of Pass–Through Entities, Memorandum No. 2 96–105 (1996), 930

Anderson, "Blackstone Founders Prepare to Count Their Billions," N.Y. Times (2007), 23

Andrews, "Comment: Estate Waiver of the Estate–Beneficiary Attribution Rules in Nonliquidating Redemptions Under Section 302 and Related Matter: The *Rickey* Case in the Fifth Circuit," 35 Tax L.Rev. 147 (1979), 580

Andrews, " 'Out of Its Earnings and Profits': Some Reflections on the Taxation of Dividends," 69 Harv.L.Rev. 1403 (1956), 511

Andrews, "Tax Neutrality Between Equity Capital and Debt," 30 Wayne L.Rev. 1057 (1984), 485

Aprill, Tax Shelters, Tax Law, and Morality: Codifying Judicial Doctrines, 54 SMU L. Rev. 9 (2001), 35

Arlen & Weiss, "A Political Theory of Corporate Taxation," 105 Yale L.J. 325 (1995), 426

Aron–Dine, The Effects of the Capital Gains and Dividend Tax Cuts on The Economy and Revenues, Center on Budget and Policy Priorities (2007), 515

Aron–Dine & Friedman, The Capital Gain and Dividend Tax Cuts and the Economy, Center on Budget and Policy Priorities (2006), 515

Asimow, "Applying the Assignment of Income Principle Correctly," 54 Tax Notes 607 (1992), 108

"Attorneys Question Ruling That Transaction Wasn't a D Reorganization," 111 Tax Notes 241 (2006), 780

August, "Benefits and Burdens of Subchapter S in a Check-in-the-Box World," 4 Fla. Tax Rev. 287 (1999), 9

Bagley & Dauchy, The Entrepreneur's Guide to Business Law 64–68 (3d ed. 2007), 24

Bank, "Codifying Judicial Doctrines: No Cure for Rules But More Rules?," 54 SMU L. Rev. 37 (2001), 35

Bank "Is Double Taxation a Scapegoat for Declining Dividends: Evidence from History," 56 Tax L.Rev. 463 (2003), 513

Bank, "Taxing Divisive and Disregarded Mergers," 34 Geo. L.Rev. 1523 (2000), 723

Bankman, "The Economic Substance Doctrine," 74 S.Cal. L. Rev. 5 (2000), 35

Bankman, "The Structure of Silicon Valley Start-ups," 42 UCLA L.Rev. 1737 (1994), 29

Banks–Golub, "Recent Amendments to Code Sec. 357: Congress Responds to Artificial Basis Creation," 78 Taxes 19 (2000), 471

Banoff, "Guaranteed Payments for the Use of Capital: Schizophrenia in Subchapter K," 70 Taxes 820 (1992), 244

Banoff, Long, Steele & Smith, "Family Partnerships: Capital as a Material Income–Producing Factor," 37 Tax Lawyer 275 (1984), 220

Birnbaum & Murray, Showdown at Gucci Gulch 229–232 (1987), 126

Bishop & Kleinberger, Limited Liability Companies: Tax and Business Law (2003), 3

Bittker & Eustice, Federal Income Taxation of Corporations and Shareholders (3rd ed. 1971), para. 4.05, p. 494

Bittker & Eustice, Federal Income Taxation of Corporations and Shareholders (4th ed. 1979), para. 4.04, p. 491

Bittker & Eustice, Federal Income Taxation of Corporations and Shareholders (5th ed. 1987), para. 1.02, p. 405; para. 11.45, p. 699

Bittker & Eustice, Federal Income Taxation of Corporations and Shareholders (7th ed. 2000), para. 3.14, p. 505; para. 7.07, p. 485; para. 7.20, p. 408; para. 8.02[3], p. 510; para. 8.05, p. 528; para. 8.20[2], p. 523; para. 8.40[1], p. 641; para. 9.01, p. 557; para. 9.24[4], p. 626; para. 10.03[2], p. 660; para. 11.01, p. 796; para. 11.05[2][a], p. 816; para. 11.12[1], p. 832; para. 11.15[3], p. 835; para. 12.01[4], p. 718; para. 12.21, p. 726; para. 12.27[4][c], p. 775; para. 12.27[5][d], p. 777

Bittker & Lokken, Federal Taxation of Income, Estates and Gifts (3d ed. 1999), para. 4.3.1, p. 32; para. 5.7.1, p. 481

Block, "Liquidations Before and After Repeal of *General Utilities,*" 21 Harv.J.Legis. 307 (1984), 524

Bloom, "Taxpayers Have More Planning Flexibility in Reorganizations After Seagram If It Survives," 82 Tax'n 334 (1995), 732

Eustice, "Alternatives for Limiting Loss Carryovers," 22 San Diego L.Rev. 149 (1985), 850
Eustice, "Subchapter S Corporations and Partnerships: A Search for the Pass Through Paradigm," 39 Tax L.Rev. 345 (1989), 9, 927
Eustice and Kuntz, Federal Income Taxation of Subchapter S Corporations (4th ed. 2001), 880
Eustice & Kuntz, Federal Income Taxation of S Corporations (4th ed. 2001), para. 6.03[1], p. 918, para. 11.02[2], p. 923

Federal Income Tax Project, Subchapter C, American Law Institute (1982), 718
Feld, "Dividends Reconsidered," 101 Tax Notes 1117 (2003), 533
Ferguson & Ginsburg, "Triangular Reorganizations," 28 Tax L.Rev. 159 (1973), 748
Field, "Fiction, Form, and Substance in Subchapter K: Taxing Partnership Mergers, Divisions, and Incorporations" 44 San Diego L.Rev. 259 (2007), 371
Fleischer, "The Rational Exuberance of Structuring Venture Capital Start-ups," 57 Tax L.Rev. 137 (2003), 29
Fleischer, "Two and Twenty: Taxing Partnership Profits in Private Equity Funds," 83 N.Y.U. L.Rev. 1 (2008) 245
Fowler, "Practical Transactional Aspects of Rev. Rul. 2001–46," 93 Tax Notes 963 (2001), 758
Freeland, Lathrope, Lind & Stephens, Fundamentals of Federal Income Taxation (Foundation Press, 14th ed. 2006), Ch. 17E, p. 123; Ch. 24E, p. 381

Gergen, "Pooling or Exchange: The Taxation of Joint Ventures Between Labor and Capital," 44 Tax L.Rev. 519 (1989), 64, 71
Gergen, "Reforming Subchapter K: Special Allocations," 46 Tax L.Rev. 1 (1990), 132
Ginsburg, "Taxing Corporate Acquisitions," 38 Tax L.Rev. 171 (1983), 598
Ginsburg & Levin, "Integrated Corporate Acquisitions: Comments on Rev. Rul. 2001–46," 93 Tax Notes 553 (2001), 758
Ginsburg & Levin, Mergers, Acquisitions & Buyouts, § 610.2 (2008), 727, 820
Goode, The Corporate Income Tax (1951), 8
Graetz & Warren, "Integration of Corporate and Individual Income Taxes: An Introduction," 84 Tax Notes 1767 (1999), 418
Gunn, "Partnership Interest for Services: Partnership Gain and Loss?" 47 Tax Notes 699 (May 7, 1990), 64
Gunn, "The Use and Misuse of Antiabuse Rules: Lessons from the Partnership Antiabuse Regulations," 54 SMU L.Rev. 159 (2001), 36
Guth & Thurm, Microsoft to Dole Out its Cash Hoard, Wall St. Journal, (2004), 514

Hamill, "The Limited Liability Company: A Catalyst Exposing The Corporate Integration Question," 95 Mich.L.Rev. 393, p. 9
Hamilton, Business Basics for Law Students: Essential Concepts and Applications (4th ed. 2006), 513, 696
Hanna, "A Partnership's Business Purpose Taxable Year: A Deferred Provision Whose Time Has Passed," 45 Tax Lawyer 685 (1992), 109
Hanna, "Partnership Distributions: Whatever Happened to Nonrecognition," 82 Kentucky Law J. 465 (1993), 308
Harberger, "The Incidence of the Corporation Income Tax," 70 J.Pol.Econ. 215 (1962), 8
Hariton, "Distinguishing Between Equity and Debt in the New Financial Environment," 49 Tax L.Rev. 499 (1994), 492, 497
Henderson, "Federal Tax Techniques for Asset Redeployment Transactions," 37 Tax L.Rev. 325 (1982), 598, 602
Henkel, Estate Planning and Wealth Preservation, Ch. 16 (1997), 381
Herman, "Tax Report," Wall St.J. at A–1 (1999), 410

Jackson, Johnson, Surrey, Tenen & Warren, "The Internal Revenue Code of 1954: Partnerships," 54 Colum.L.Rev. 1183 (1954), 5, 321
Jacobs, "Tax Treatment of Corporate Net Operating Losses and Other Tax Attribute Carryovers," 5 Va.Tax Rev. 701 (1986), 850
Jewett, "Characterization of Income: Compensation vs. Dividends," 103 Tax Notes 1501 (2004), 533
Jickling & Marples, "Taxation of Hedge Funds and Private Equity Managers," Congressional Research Service Report for Congress (2007), 246
Johnston, Perfectly Legal (2004), 411
Joint Committee on Taxation, Background and Present Law Relating to Tax Shelters (JCX–19–02), (2002), 409
Joint Committee on Taxation, Federal Income Tax Aspects of Corporate Financial Structures, 101st Cong., 1st Sess. 53–58 (1989), 486
Joint Committee on Taxation, Impact of Small Business of Replacing the Federal Income Tax 5 (J.C.S. 3–96, 1996), 26
Joint Committee on Taxation, Present Law and Analysis Relating to Tax Treatment of Partnership Carried Interests (JCX–41–07) (2007), 246
Joint Committee on Taxation, Review of Selected Entity Classification and Partner-

ship Tax Issues 47 (JCS–6–97), (1997), 244

Joint Committee on Taxation, Tax Shelter Proposals and Other Tax-Motivated Transactions, 98th Cong., 2d Sess. 39–40 (1984), 536

Kaden & Wolfe, "Spin-offs, Split-offs, and Split-ups: A Detailed Analysis of Section 355," 44 Tax Notes 565 (1989), 821

Kahn, "Closely Held Stocks—Deferral and Financing of Estate Tax Costs through Sections 303 and 6166," 35 Tax Lawyer 639 (1982), 636

Kalinka, "Hubert Enterprises: LLC Members, Partners Deficit Restoration Obligations, and the At–Risk Rules," 112 Tax Notes 137 (2006), 121

Kalinka, "In Light of Depreciation Recapture Regs, Plan Allocation Carefully," 77 Tax Notes 1387 (1997), 162

Kalinka, "Proposed Regulations Would Provide Guidance, but Add Complexity for Making Code Sec. 704(c) Allocations After an Assets-over Merger–Part I," 86 Taxes 11 (2008), 363

Kalinka, "Rev. Proc. 2001–43 and the Transfer of a Nonvested Partnership Profits Interest," 79 Taxes 11 (2001), 82

Klein, "The Incidence of the Corporation Income Tax: A Lawyer's View of a Problem in Economics," 65 Wisc.L.Rev. 576 (1965), 8

Klein & Coffee, Business Organization and Finance, Legal and Economic Principles 352–385 (10th ed. 2007), 484, 513

Klein & Zolt, "Business Form, Limited Liability, and Tax Regimes: Lurching Toward a Coherent Outcome," 66 Colo.L.Rev. 1001 (1995), 10

Kuntz, "Stock, Redemptions Following Stock Transfers—An Expanding 'Safe Harbor,' Under Section 302(c)(2)(B)," 58 Taxes 29 (1980), 565

Lane, "Sol Diamond: The Tax Court Upsets the Service Partner," 46 S.Cal.L.Rev. 239 (1973), 77

Larvick, "Noncompensatory Partnership Options: The Proposed Regulations," 99 Tax Notes 271 (2003), 45

Lathrope, The Alternative Minimum Tax (1994), 402

Lazar, "*Lessinger*, *Peracchi*, and the Emperor's New Clothes; Covering a Section 357(c) Deficit with Invisible (or Nonexistent) Property," 58 Tax Law. 41 (2004), 468

Lee, "A Populist Political Perspective of the Business Tax Entities Universe: Hey the Stars Might Lie But the Numbers Never Do," 78 Texas L.Rev. 885 (2000), 30

Lee, "Choice of Small Business Tax Entity: Facts and Fiction," 87 Tax Notes 417 (2000), 30

Levin & Bowen, "The Section 385 Regulations Regarding Debt Versus Equity: Is the Cure Worse than the Malady?" 35 Tax Lawyer 1 (1981), 496

Lewis, "A Proposal for a Corporate Level Tax on Major Stock Sales," 37 Tax Notes 1041 (1987), 710

Lewis, "A Proposed New Treatment for Corporate Distributions and Sales in Liquidations," 86th Cong., 1st Sess., 3 Tax Revision Compendium 1643 (1959), 668

Lind, Schwarz, Lathrope & Rosenberg, Fundamentals of Corporate Taxation (7th ed. 2008), 6

Lind, Schwarz, Lathrope & Rosenberg, Fundamentals of Partnership Taxation (8th ed. 2008), 6

Lipton, "Proposed Regulations on Built–In Gain and Partnership Mergers: The Service Refuses to Budge," 107 J.Tax'n 324 (2007), 363

Little, Federal Income Taxation of Partnerships (1952), 5

Lockhart, "IRS Concedes Tax Treatment of a Partnership Profits Interest Received for Services," 10 J.P'ship Tax'n 283 (1993), 81

Lokken, "Partnership Allocations," 41 Tax L.Rev. 545 (1986), 141

Lokken, "Taxation of Private Business Firms: Imagining a Future Without Subchapter K," 4 Fla. Tax Rev. 249 (1999), 9

Luttrell, S Corporation Returns, 2003, 25 SOI Bulletin 91 (2006), 31, 882

McKee, "Partnership Allocations: The Need For an Entity Approach," 66 Va.L.Rev. 1039 (1980), 138

McKee, Nelson & Whitmire, Federal Taxation of Partnerships and Partners (4th ed. 2007), para. 4.03[3], p. 58; para. 5.02[1], p. 77; para. 5.08[2][b], p. 64; para. 5.09, p. 63; para. 11.06[2][c], p. 119; para. 11.08[3][a], p. 124; para. 12.03[3], p. 213; para. 14.02[4][a], p. 252; para. 14.03[2], p. 237; para. 17.05, p. 273; para. 19.03[2], p. 288; para. 19.06, p. 323; para. 21.01[4][b], p. 312; para. 22.01[1], p. 349; para. 22.02[4], p. 339; para. 23.02[2][a], p. 383; para. 23.02[2][b], p. 383

McKinnon, "Congressional Probe to Examine Enron's Tax–Avoidance Strategies" (2002), 499

McLure, "Integration of the Personal and Corporate Income Taxes: The Missing Element in Recent Tax Reform Proposals," 88 Harv.L.Rev. 532 (1975), 8, 418

McMahon, "Random Thoughts on Applying Judicial Doctrines to Interpret the Internal Revenue Code," 54 SMU L.Rev. 195 (2001), 36

Thompson, "Despite Widespread Opposition, Congress Should Codify the ESD," 110 Tax Notes 781 (2006), 35
Treubert & Janquet, "Corporation Income Tax Returns, 1998," 21 SOI Bulletin 66 (2001), 30

U.S. Treasury Dept., A Recommendation for Integration of the Individual and Corporate Income Tax Systems (1992), 425
U.S. Treasury Dept., Investing in America's Future: Report of the Department of the Treasury on the Economic Effects of Cutting Dividend and Capital Gains Taxes in 2003 ("2006 Treasury Study") (2006), 515
U.S. Treasury Dept., Technical Explanation of Treasury Tax Reform Proposals: Hearings Before the House Comm. on Ways and Means, 91st Cong., 1st Sess. 5228–5275 (1969), 881

Walter, " 'Preferred Stock' and 'Common Stock': The Meaning of the Terms and the Importance of the Distinction for Tax Purposes," 5 J.Corp.Tax'n 211 (1978), 651
Warren, "Integration of the Individual and Corporate Income Taxes," Reporter's Study of Corporate Tax Integration (American Law Institute, 1993), 425
Weidner, "Partnership Allocations and Capital Account Analysis," 42 Ohio St.L.Rev. 467 (1981), 138
Wheeler & Shumofsky, Partnership Returns, 2005, 27 SOI Bulletin 69 (2007), 31
Willens, "Dividends, Capital Gains, and Spinoffs Affected by Increase, Prevention and Reconciliation Act," 104 J. Tax'n 327 (2006), 827
Willens, "IRS Clarifies Contours of D Reorganizations," 114 Tax Notes 227 (2007), 780
Willens, "Some Observations on the Tax Court's Seagram Decision," 66 Tax Notes 1465 (1995), 732
Willis, Little & McDonald, "Problems on Death, Retirement, or Withdrawal of a Partner," 17 N.Y.U. Inst. on Fed. Tax'n 1033 (1959), 383
Willis, Pennell & Postlewaite, Partnership Taxation (6th ed. 1997), para. 1.02[8], p. 20; para. 4.05[5][a], p. 64; para. 12.01[12], p. 273; para. 15.05, p. 329; para. 15.06, p. 329
Willis, Pennell & Postlewaite, Partnership Taxation (4th ed. 1989), ? 46.04, p. 78
Wolfman, "Subchapter C and the 100th Congress," 33 Tax Notes 669 (1986), 406, 764
Wolfman, "Why Economic Substance is Better Left Uncodified," 104 Tax Notes 445 (2004), 35

Yin, "A Carryover Basis Regime? A Few Words of Caution," 37 Tax Notes 415 (1987), 710
Yin, "General Utilities Repeal: Is Tax Reform Really Going to Pass it By?" 31 Tax Notes 1111 (1986), 525, 668
Yin, "Getting Serious About Corporate Tax Shelters: Taking a Lesson from History," 54 SMU L.Rev. 209 (2001), 410
Yin, "The Future Taxation of Private Business Firms," 4 Fla. Tax Rev. 141 (1999), 10

Zaffino, "Projections of Returns to be Filed in Calendar Years 1995–2005," 18 SOI Bulletin 178 (1999), 30
Zolt, "Corporate Taxation After the Tax Reform Act of 1986: A State of Disequilibrium," 66 N.C.L.Rev. 839 (1988), 8
Zolt, "The *General Utilities* Doctrine: Examining the Scope of Repeal," 65 Taxes 819 (1987), 710
Zuckerman, "Climb of Corporate Debt Trips Analysts' Alarm" (2001), 484

*

Fundamentals of Business Enterprise Taxation

*

PART ONE

INTRODUCTION

CHAPTER 1

AN OVERVIEW OF BUSINESS ENTERPRISE TAXATION

A. LEGAL FORMS OF BUSINESS ENTERPRISE

One of the most critical decisions facing the founders of a new business venture involves the legal form in which they will conduct their enterprise. The available choices are initially dictated by state law. They include the classic organizational forms—sole proprietorships, general and limited partnerships, and corporations—as well as newer alternatives, most notably the limited liability company. The selection of a legal form for a particular business venture will depend upon a variety of factors, including organizational convenience, familiarity with the form and a recognized body of law, the desired management and governance structure, compensation and fringe benefits for key executives, estate planning considerations of major shareholders, and the future capital needs of the enterprise. The extent to which investors in the business will be personally liable for debts and claims against the venture may be a particularly important consideration. And inevitably, the topic of this text—federal income taxes—will prove to be a significant if not determinative factor in making the choice of entity decision.

This introductory chapter provides an overview of the business enterprise taxation landscape. It previews the major conceptual taxing models used in the Internal Revenue Code, summarizes the tax factors that influence the choice of entity decision, describes the current system for classifying business entities for federal tax purposes, and introduces the "common law" doctrines that have helped shape this dynamic and challenging area of the law. To set the stage, the chapter begins with a brief description of the state-law characteristics of the principal legal forms for business organizations.

Sole Proprietorship. A sole proprietorship is a business owned and controlled by a single individual. Sole proprietors are personally liable for debts and claims against the business and must report their business income and expenses, along with other items, on their individual tax returns.

Partnership. The Uniform Partnership Act defines a partnership as "an association of two or more persons to carry on as co-owners a business for profit."[1] Partnerships formed for a particular project or transaction often are referred to as joint ventures. In a general partnership, every

1. Uniform Partnership Act § 6(1).

partner is an agent of the firm for purposes of its business, and the act of every partner in apparently carrying on the partnership business generally binds the partnership.[2] Each general partner has a right to participate in partnership management, as well as a right to share in profits of the partnership and an undivided interest in partnership property.[3] General partners ordinarily are also jointly and severally liable for all debts and obligations of the partnership.[4]

A limited partnership has both a general partner (or partners) and limited partners. The general partners of a limited partnership have the same rights, powers, and liabilities that they would have in a general partnership.[5] Limited partners, however, generally do not participate in management and are not personally liable for debts and obligations of the partnership.[6] The creation of a limited partnership also requires more legal formalities, such as the execution and filing of a certificate of limited partnership with the appropriate state officials.[7]

Every state now permits the creation of a limited liability partnership ("LLP"). An LLP basically is operated as a general partnership, but all the partners obtain full or partial limited liability by filing a registration and complying with other statutory requirements.[8] A partner of an LLP is protected, in varying degrees depending on state law, from vicarious liability for acts (e.g., professional malpractice) of the other partners. Not surprisingly, many large law and accounting firms are organized as LLPs. Some states[9] also permit the formation of limited liability limited partnerships ("LLLPs"), which are traditional limited partnerships in form but extend limited liability to the general partners much like an LLP.

Limited Liability Company. A limited liability company ("LLC") is an unincorporated entity in which the owners, called "members," have limited liability for the enterprise's debts and claims even if they participate in management. Members of an LLC have great flexibility in structuring the management of their venture through the LLC's governing document, known as an "operating agreement." LLCs have emerged rapidly since the late 1980's and they are now authorized in every state.[10]

2. Uniform Partnership Act § 9(1).

3. Uniform Partnership Act §§ 9, 18(e), 24, 25 and 26.

4. Uniform Partnership Act § 15.

5. Revised Uniform Limited Partnership Act § 403. The general partner can be an individual or, as is the norm in more sophisticated limited partnerships, a legal entity such as an S corporation or a limited liability company.

6. Revised Uniform Limited Partnership Act § 303.

7. Revised Uniform Limited Partnership Act §§ 201–209.

8. See Ely, Grissom & Houser, "State Tax Treatment of Limited Liability Companies and Limited Liability Partnerships," 112 Tax Notes 45 (July 3, 2006), for citations to LLP acts in all 50 states.

9. See, e.g., Del. Code Ann., tit. 6, § 1553.

10. See generally Ribstein & Keatinge, Limited Liability Companies (2003); Bishop & Kleinberger, Limited Liability Companies: Tax and Business Law (2003). See also Ely, Grissom & Houser, supra note 8, for citations to the various state LLC acts.

Corporation. A corporation is a legal entity formed under state law. Corporations have long been the most commonly used legal form for operating virtually all publicly held businesses and many closely held companies. Management authority in a corporation is vested in the board of directors. The owners of the corporation, its shareholders, do not participate in management of the enterprise and are not personally liable for its debts. State "close corporation" statutes also may permit the owners of a corporation to combine the limited liability of a corporation with partnership-type owner-management structure.[11]

B. Business Enterprise Taxation Models

1. Conceptual Models

In designing a model for taxing the income of a business enterprise, a threshold conceptual question is whether the business should be treated as an aggregate of its underlying owners, as a separate taxable entity, or as an aggregate/entity hybrid.

Under a pure aggregate concept, the business organization itself is not treated as a separate taxable entity. Instead, each owner is taxed directly on his or her respective "distributive share" of the organization's income and deductions. Because the existence of the entity is disregarded for tax purposes, contributions to and distributions from the entity generally are not taxable events. The aggregate/entity hybrid is a variation from the pure aggregate approach. Under one hybrid model, the organization's income is *taxed* under an aggregate theory but the entity is recognized for purposes of calculating the tax results of its operations, filing informational tax returns, making tax elections, and for certain other purposes.

Under an entity concept, a business organization is a separate taxable person that must determine and pay tax on its annual taxable income. Transactions between the entity and its owners generally are treated as if they were between unrelated entities. Once a decision is made to adopt an entity approach, a host of additional questions follow. For example, what rates should be applied to the income of the enterprise? Should they resemble the graduated rates applicable to individuals or is a flat rate more appropriate? If the entity already has been taxed on its earnings, should those earnings be taxed again when they are distributed to the owners? The answers to these and many other questions are previewed in this introductory chapter and will be developed in great detail throughout the text.

2. Taxing Regimes Under the Internal Revenue Code

The three principal business enterprise taxing regimes in the Internal Revenue Code are found in Subchapters K (Sections 701–777), C (Sections 301–385), and S (Sections 1361–1378).

11. See, e.g., Ribstein & Keatinge, supra note 10, at § 1:2 (2004).

Subchapter K. The partnership has long served as a business and investment vehicle, but for many years the taxation of partnerships was little more than a primitive backwater province in the Internal Revenue Code. Prior to 1954, only a small number of special sections dealt specifically with the taxation of partnerships.[1] It was not until the enactment of Subchapter K,[2] which at the time was lauded as one of the more "notable achievements of the 1954 Internal Revenue Code,"[3] that Congress provided a detailed statutory scheme to govern the federal income taxation of partnerships and partners. Both Congressional tax-writing committees explained the legislative objectives underlying the enactment of Subchapter K as follows:[4]

> The existing tax treatment of partners and partnerships is among the most confused in the entire income tax field. The present statutory provisions are wholly inadequate. The published regulations, rulings and court decisions are incomplete and frequently contradictory. As a result, partners today cannot form, operate or dissolve a partnership with any assurance as to tax consequences.
>
> This confusion is particularly unfortunate in view of the great number of business enterprises and ventures carried on in the partnership form. It should also be noted that the partnership form of organization is much more commonly employed by small businesses and in farming operations than the corporate form.
>
> Because of the vital need for clarification, your committee has undertaken the first comprehensive treatment of partners and partnerships in the history of the income tax laws. In establishing a broad pattern applicable to partnerships generally, the principal objectives have been simplicity, flexibility, and equity as between the partners.

The business enterprises potentially subject to Subchapter K include general and limited partnerships, LLPs, LLLPs, and LLCs.[5] The study of partnership tax is challenging (some might even say fun) because Subchapter K does not exclusively employ either the aggregate or the entity model of taxation. Instead, partnerships are considered to be aggregates of their owners for some tax purposes and entities for others. On the one hand, partnerships are treated as pass-through entities that do not pay federal income tax. The partners include their respective shares of partnership income, deductions, losses and other items when determining their tax

1. I.R.C. (1939) Supplement F. See generally Little, Federal Income Taxation of Partnerships (1952).

2. I.R.C. §§ 701–761.

3. Jackson, Johnson, Surrey, Tenen & Warren, "The Internal Revenue Code of 1954: Partnerships," 54 Colum.L.Rev. 1183, 1235 (1954).

4. H.R.Rep. No. 1337, 83d Cong., 2d Sess. 65 (1954); S.Rep. No. 1622, 83d Cong., 2d Sess. 89 (1954).

5. With some notable exceptions, most partnerships that are "publicly traded" on a securities exchange are treated as corporations for tax purposes. See I.R.C. § 7704 and Section C2c of this chapter, infra.

liability,[6] except that a partner's share of partnership losses for a taxable year are deductible only to the extent of the partner's basis in her partnership interest[7] and those pass-through losses also may be subject to other timing limitations.[8] Ongoing adjustments to the basis of a partner's interest in the partnership ensure that income and losses are not taxed (or deducted) twice.[9]

Partnerships are treated as entities, however, for purposes of selecting a taxable year, computing and characterizing partnership income, filing information returns, making elections, undergoing an audit by the Internal Revenue Service and in several substantive contexts, such as formation and termination, transactions between partners and partnerships, and sales of partnership interests.[10] This mixture of approaches contributes to substantial complexity and tax avoidance opportunities, which are compounded by the fact that Subchapter K affords partners considerable flexibility in determining their individual tax consequences from partnership operations.

Subchapter C. Congress made a markedly different policy decision in the case of corporations, which have been treated as separate taxable entities ever since the first modern corporate income tax was enacted in 1909. The Payne–Aldrich Tariff Act of 1909 imposed a modest one percent tax on corporate net income over $5,000. When Congress added an individual income tax four years later, it gave birth to what we will come to know as the "double tax regime." Under current law, a corporate tax is imposed annually, at the rates set forth in Section 11, on the taxable income of a corporation. That income is effectively taxed again if it is distributed to the shareholders in the form of dividends, which are not deductible by the distributing corporation.[11] Because a corporation is treated as a separate taxable entity, transactions between corporations and their shareholders are taxable events.[12] The tax consequences of these transactions and other major changes and adjustments in a corporation are governed by Subchapter C of the Code. Corporations subject to the double tax regime also draw their identity (and monogram) from Subchapter C. Collectively, the Code refers to them as "C corporations."[13]

Subchapter S. The partnership pass-through system and the double tax regime generally applicable to corporations represent the Code's two fundamental alternatives for taxing business enterprises. They also are the main focus of this text. To level the playing field and respond to special problems of unique industries, Congress occasionally has enacted other tax regimes. For example, to minimize the role of taxes on the choice of form for smaller

6. I.R.C. § 701.

7. I.R.C. § 704(d).

8. See, e.g., I.R.C. §§ 465; 469.

9. I.R.C. § 705.

10. I.R.C. §§ 721; 707; 741. See generally, Lind, Schwarz, Lathrope & Rosenberg, Fundamentals of Partnership Taxation (8th ed. 2008).

11. Some relief from a potential triple tax is provided to corporate shareholders, who qualify for a 70, 80 or 100 percent dividends received deduction under Section 243.

12. See generally, Lind, Schwarz, Lathrope & Rosenberg, Fundamentals of Corporate Taxation (7th ed. 2008).

13. I.R.C. § 1361(a)(2).

businesses, certain closely held corporations may elect under Subchapter S of the Internal Revenue Code to be taxed under a conduit approach similar to the taxation of partnerships.[14] Corporations making that election are referred to as "S corporations."[15]

The principal obstacle to making an S election is found in the Code's definition of "small business corporation" in Section 1361, which sets forth strict eligibility requirements for S corporation status. In general, a corporation may make an S election only if it has not more than 100 shareholders who must be individuals other than nonresident aliens, estates or certain trusts,[16] and an S corporation may not have more than one class of stock.[17]

The income of an S corporation generally is subject to a single, shareholder-level tax.[18] The corporation's income, losses, deductions and credits pass through to its shareholders, but the character of those items is determined at the corporate level.[19] Basis and distribution rules are designed to assure that the shareholders may receive previously taxed income without paying additional tax.[20] While the taxation of S corporations and their shareholders is quite similar to the taxation of partners, the two systems are not identical. In general, the provisions of Subchapter K offer partners much greater flexibility in fashioning their tax results. For example, partnerships have far greater freedom to make special allocations of income and losses among different investors, and S corporation shareholders, unlike partners, may not include their pro rata share of the firm's liabilities in the basis of their stock.[21]

Finally, even though S corporations and their shareholders are taxed under a special regime, S corporations remain "corporations" for purposes of Subchapter C.[22] Thus, the two corporate subchapters often operate in tandem when an S corporation engages in transactions, such as distributions of appreciated property, stock redemptions and liquidations, that are subject to Subchapter C,[23] or when an S corporation formerly was a C corporation.[24]

Other Taxing Regimes. The Code taxes other types of hybrid entities under a pass-through model if they satisfy requirements designed to limit the nature of their business operations. For example, Subchapter M of the Code taxes regulated investment companies (i.e., mutual funds) and real estate investment trusts as conduits. Corporations in certain discrete industries, such as insurance and banking, and tax-exempt organizations

14. See Chapter 20, infra.

15. I.R.C. § 1361(a)(1).

16. I.R.C. § 1361(b)(1)(A), (B), (C). For purposes of the 100–shareholder limit, members of one "family," broadly defined, are treated as one shareholder. I.R.C. § 1361(c)(1).

17. I.R.C. § 1361(b)(1)(D).

18. But see note 24, infra.

19. I.R.C. § 1366(a), (b).

20. I.R.C. §§ 1367(a); 1368(a), (b).

21. See I.R.C. §§ 704(b); 752; 1366(d).

22. I.R.C. § 1371(a)(1).

23. See Chapter 20G, infra.

24. See, e.g., I.R.C. §§ 1374 and 1375, which impose a corporate-level tax on certain S corporations that previously were C corporations.

and cooperatives, also are governed by their own taxing regimes.[25] These specialized regimes are beyond the scope of this text.

3. TAX POLICY ISSUES

The business tax policy debate has revolved around the concept at the heart of Subchapter C—the double taxation of corporate income. The earnings of C corporations are taxed once at the corporate level when earned and again when distributed as dividends to shareholders.[1] This decision to treat corporations as separate taxable entities has been controversial.[2] Some of the debate is over the incidence of the corporate tax—whether it is borne by shareholders, employees, corporate managers, consumers of the company's goods or services, or investors in general.[3] Critics also point to the adverse impact of the tax on the allocation of economic resources; its complexity; and many other evils, including three distinct biases: (1) against corporate as opposed to noncorporate investment (because only corporate capital is subject to a second tax); (2) in favor of excessive debt financing for businesses organized as C corporations; and (3) in favor of retention of earnings at the corporate level as opposed to distribution of dividends.[4] Advocates for reform argue that the double tax regime should be replaced by a system that "integrates" the individual and corporate tax systems and imposes only one level of tax.[5]

If a double tax is accepted as the appropriate taxing model, the discussion then turns to the "integrity" of the corporate-level tax. For example, should the corporate income tax apply not only to operating profits but also to distributions of appreciated property and sales in connection with corporate liquidations? The outcome of this controversy will unfold as these and other transactions are studied in Part 3 of this text. For now, it is sufficient to observe that in the Tax Reform Act of 1986 the defenders of the corporate income tax largely prevailed on these

25. See, e.g., Subchapter L (insurance companies), Subchapter H (banks and trust companies), and Subchapter F (tax-exempt organizations and cooperatives).

1. Of course, many shareholders, such as pension funds and nonprofit organizations, generally do not pay taxes on the dividends they receive, and many C corporations do not distribute their earnings as dividends.

2. See generally Goode, The Corporate Income Tax (1951); McLure, "Integration of the Personal and Corporate Income Taxes: The Missing Element in Recent Tax Reform Proposals," 88 Harv. L. Rev. 532 (1975).

3. See e.g., Harberger, "The Incidence of the Corporation Income Tax," 70 J.Pol.Econ. 215 (1962); Klein, "The Incidence of the Corporation Income Tax: A Lawyer's View of a Problem in Economics," 65 Wisc. L.Rev. 576 (1965). Lest there be any suspense, economists have concluded that they are unable to ascertain who bears the burden of the corporate tax. See generally Break, "The Incidence and Economic Effects of Taxation," in The Economics of Public Finance (Brookings 1974).

4. See generally American Law Institute, Federal Income Tax Project—Subchapter C 341–355 (1982). Commentators also point to the "compensating biases" in the individual income tax, such as the rate structure, the capital gains preference, and the ability of individuals to obtain a stepped-up basis in property held at death. See Zolt, "Corporate Taxation After the Tax Reform Act of 1986: A State of Disequilibrium," 66 N.C.L.Rev. 839 (1988).

5. See Chapter 10F, infra.

theoretical questions. The results were a strengthened double tax regime, an increase in the tax costs of operating a profitable business as a C corporation, and greater pressure on techniques to reduce these costs. More recently, the pendulum has shifted in the other direction, most notably with the reduction in the tax rate on dividends.[6] The enactment of various business tax incentives also has softened the impact of the corporate income tax for those fortunate industries targeted for tax relief.[7]

The desire to avoid the double tax on corporate profits while obtaining limited liability for all the owners of a business fueled the emergence of new legal forms, such as the LLC. Entities similar to the LLC have long been used in other countries. Examples include the Latin American *limitada* and the German *Gesellschaft mit besechrankter Haftung* ("GmbH").[8] The origins of the LLC in the United States can be traced to the search by foreign investors in the oil and gas industry for a U.S. business entity that would combine limited liability protection for all owners with one level of taxation. Because nonresident aliens may not own stock in an S corporation, the investors' objectives could not be met using the corporate form. So they began lobbying state legislatures, and by the late 1970's Wyoming had enacted the first domestic limited liability company statute.[9] LLCs were not practically viable, however, until the Internal Revenue Service ruled, first privately and then in a 1989 published ruling, that a Wyoming LLC would be treated as a partnership rather than a corporation for tax purposes.[10]

The explosive growth of the LLC as a "best of all worlds" legal form breathed new life into the business enterprise tax policy debate. Consider the following questions. Why do Subchapter K and Subchapter S continue to coexist in the Internal Revenue Code? Why should the Code have two separate pass-through tax regimes for closely held business enterprises, each with different qualification standards and operative provisions?[11] If a single pass-through regime were adopted, would Subchapter K be preferable to Subchapter S, or would some combination of the two be the best approach?[12] Why are C corporations singled out for a double tax regime? Is

6. I.R.C. § 1(h)(11)(A). Until at least through 2010, qualified dividends received by noncorporate shareholders are generally taxed at the same 15 percent maximum rate as long-term capital gains. See Chapter 12A2, infra.

7. See, e.g., § 199, providing a special tax deduction for domestic production activities.

8. See Carney, "Limited Liability Companies: Origins and Antecedents," 66 U.Colo. L.Rev. 855 (1995).

9. See Hamill, "The Limited Liability Company: A Catalyst Exposing The Corporate Integration Question," 95 Mich. L. Rev. 393, 399 (1996), for a history of LLC's rise from obscurity to its current position as a mainstream form of business entity.

10. Rev. Rul. 88–76, 1988–2 C.B. 360. See Section C1 of this chapter, infra.

11. See Lokken, "Taxation of Private Business Firms: Imagining a Future Without Subchapter K," 4 Fla. Tax Rev. 249 (1999); Schwidetzky, "Is it Time to Give the S Corporation a Proper Burial?", 15 Va. Tax Rev. 591 (1996); Rands, "Passthrough Entities and Their Unprincipled Differences Under Federal Tax Law," 49 SMU L. Rev. 15 (1995).

12. See Eustice, "Subchapter S Corporations and Partnerships: A Search for the Passthrough Paradigm," 39 Tax L. Rev. 345 (1989); August, "Benefits and Burdens of Subchapter S in a Check-the-Box World," 4 Fla. Tax Rev. 287 (1999).

it because they enjoy limited liability under state law? Presumably not, because LLCs are not subject to Subchapter C. Does the rise of the LLC undermine the policy underlying the double tax and threaten to destroy the corporate tax base? Would it make more sense to limit Subchapter C to large corporations (based on revenues) or publicly traded entities? Or should there be a single one-tier tax regime for all business income without regard to the organizational form?[13]

This is enough food for thought at this early juncture. The remaining chapters offer ample opportunity to reconsider these issues as you study the Code's three business taxation regimes in greater depth.

C. TAX CLASSIFICATION OF BUSINESS ENTERPRISES

1. IN GENERAL

Code: §§ 761(a), 7701(a)(3).

It should be apparent by now that the classification of a business organization may have profound tax consequences. The tax classification area has a rich and textured history, as the stakes have changed in response to shifting tax incentives to utilize one form of business entity over another. After decades of strife, much confusion, and reams of boilerplate classification opinion letters issued by high-priced counsel, there is good news. Beginning in 1997, the Internal Revenue Service simplified this topic considerably (and shortened your reading assignment) by adopting a classification system that as a practical matter permits a closely held unincorporated business to elect its taxing regime. Because of the importance of the issue, we begin with a brief overview of the historical classification standards and their background.

For tax purposes, Section 7701 defines a corporation to include "associations, joint-stock companies, and insurance companies." Thus, if an entity is an unincorporated "association," it will be classified as a corporation. The longstanding, pre–1997 classification regulations did not define the term "association." Instead, they listed six characteristics ordinarily found in a "pure" corporation: (1) associates (i.e., two or more persons joining together in shared control and ownership of the venture); (2) an objective to carry on business and divide the gains therefrom; (3) continuity of life (a corporation continues in existence despite the death or withdrawal of one or more shareholders); (4) centralization of management (i.e., management responsibility is vested in directors and is not exercised directly by the shareholders); (5) limited liability (shareholders are not personally liable for corporate debts); and (6) free transferability of interests (i.e., shareholders may dispose of their shares).[1] The regulations then explained that "an

13. See, e.g., Yin, "The Future Taxation of Private Business Firms," 4 Fla. Tax Rev. 141 (1999); Klein & Zolt, "Business Form, Limited Liability, and Tax Regimes: Lurching Toward a Coherent Outcome," 66 Colo.L.Rev. 1001 (1995).

1. Reg. § 301.7701–2(a)(1) (pre–1997).

organization will be treated as an association if the corporate characteristics are such that the organization more nearly resembles a corporation than a partnership or trust."[2] Under those regulations, characteristics common to corporations and partnerships (associates and a business objective) were disregarded in classifying an entity as an association or a partnership. The remaining characteristics (continuity of life, centralized management, limited liability, and free transferability of interests) were then weighted equally and an organization was classified as an association only if it had three of the remaining corporate characteristics.[3]

The pre–1997 regulations were issued at a time when professional service providers (e.g., doctors and lawyers), forbidden from incorporating under state law, attempted to form entities that qualified as "associations" taxable as corporations. Their tax planning agenda was to qualify for tax advantages, such as qualified retirement plans and tax-free fringe benefits, that were then available to corporations and their employees but not to partnerships and partners.[4] The Treasury's mission was to make it more difficult for unincorporated entities to qualify as corporations for federal tax purposes, but its efforts were undercut by the subsequent willingness of state legislators to permit the formation of professional corporations.[5]

One result of this early fray was that the old regulations reflected an anti-association, pro-partnership bias. This redounded to the benefit of high-income taxpayers seeking to shelter their compensation, dividends, or interest income with losses from strategically structured investment activities in real estate and other tax-favored industries. Limited partnerships became the vehicle of choice for these "tax shelters" because they permitted losses to pass through to investors, allowed the partners to maximize those losses by including their share of partnership debt in the basis of their partnership interests, and provided protection for the limited partners against personal liability for debts of the enterprise. These goals could not be achieved in a C or S corporation. The Service's effort to convince the courts that limited partnerships should be classified as "associations" was unsuccessful.[6] Even after tax shelters were derailed by the Tax Reform Act of 1986, the Service continued to issue stringent guidelines for limited partnerships seeking a favorable classification ruling.[7] Most tax advisors bypassed the ruling process, and the well informed easily were able to structure a limited partnership that would avoid "association" classification.

2. Id.

3. Reg. § 1.7701–2(a) (pre–1997).

4. United States v. Kintner, 216 F.2d 418 (9th Cir.1954). Cf. Morrissey v. Commissioner, 296 U.S. 344, 56 S.Ct. 289 (1935). Virtually all of the advantages of corporate classification in the retirement plan context have been eliminated.

5. See, e.g., West's Ann. Cal. Corp. Code §§ 13400–13410; Maryland Code, Corporations and Associations, Title 5, Subtitle 1 (1999); West's Florida Statutes Annotated, ch. 621.

6. See Larson v. Commissioner, 66 T.C. 159 (1976).

7. See, e.g., Rev. Proc. 89–12, 1989–1 C.B. 798; Rev. Proc. 91–13, 1991–1 C.B. 477.

In the 1980's, limited liability companies (LLCs) emerged on the scene and quickly became touted as the "best of all worlds" alternative for conducting a closely held business. The Internal Revenue Service gave a major boost to the LLC movement in 1988 by classifying a Wyoming LLC as a partnership for federal tax purposes.[8] That ruling was followed by others making it clear that an LLC could be structured as either an association or a partnership depending on the flexibility provided by state law and the desires of the members.[9]

2. Corporations vs. Partnerships

a. "CHECK–THE–BOX" REGULATIONS

Code: § 7701(a)(3).

Regulations: §§ 301.7701–1(a)(1) & (2); –2(a), (b)(1)–(3), (c)(1) & (2); –3(a), (b)(1).

The pre–1997 classification regulations were based on the traditional state-law differences between a pure corporation and other types of organizations, such as partnerships.[1] State law developments, however, largely blurred the classic distinctions between corporations and the unincorporated forms for doing business. For example, the increasingly popular LLC offers all its investors (including those involved in management) limited liability for obligations of the venture—a characteristic traditionally available only in a corporation—along with classification as a partnership for federal tax purposes.

The Service eventually concluded that the state law differences between corporations and partnerships had narrowed to such a degree that the venerable corporate resemblance test for classifying unincorporated entities should be abandoned in favor of a simpler classification regime that is generally elective.[2] To that end, the regulations have discarded the four-factor classification system, which was de facto elective for individuals with skilled tax advisors, and replaced it with a "check-the-box" system in which most new unincorporated entities automatically will be classified as partnerships for federal tax purposes unless the entity elects to be an association taxable as a C corporation.

General Classification Rules. The regulations only apply to entities that are treated for federal tax purposes as being separate from their owners.[3] If an organization recognized as a separate entity for federal tax purposes is not a trust, it is a "business entity" under the regulations.[4]

8. Rev. Rul. 88–76, 1988–2 C.B. 360.

9. See Rev. Rul. 93–38, 1993–1 C.B. 233, where LLCs formed under the Delaware statute were classified as an association or a partnership depending on the terms of the LLC agreement.

1. Reg. § 301.7701–2(a)(1) (pre–1997).

2. Preamble to Final Regulations on Simplification of Entity Classification Rules, 61 Fed. Reg. 66584 (Dec. 18, 1986). The elective regime became effective as of January 1, 1997. Reg. § 301.7701–1(f).

3. See Section C2b of this chapter, infra.

4. Reg. § 301.7701–2(a).

Certain business entities are automatically classified as corporations.[5] Most importantly, a business entity organized under a federal or state statute that refers to the entity as "incorporated" or as a "corporation," "body corporate," or "body politic," is treated as a corporation for federal tax purposes,[6] as are other business entities taxable as corporations under other Code provisions, such as publicly traded partnerships which are treated as corporations under Section 7704.[7]

Under the regulations, a noncorporate business entity (an "eligible entity") with at least two members is classified as a partnership unless an election is made for the entity to be classified as an association. Thus, partnership status is the default classification for unincorporated entities with two or more members.[8]

Single–Owner Organizations. The regulations treat a noncorporate business entity that has a single owner as a "tax nothing." A single-owner entity is disregarded for tax purposes and treated as an extension of its owner unless the entity elects to be classified as an association and thus taxed as a C corporation.[9] Consequently, if no such election is made, the entity is treated for federal tax purposes as if it were a sole proprietorship (if owned by an individual), or a branch or division (if owned by another business entity, such as a C corporation)[10] This rule is particularly useful in the vast majority of states which permit single-member LLCs.

An entity that is solely owned by a husband and wife as community property may be treated by its owners as either a disregarded entity or a partnership unless the entity elects to be taxed as a C corporation.[11]

Foreign Organizations. The regulations list certain business entities formed in specific jurisdictions (e.g., a public limited company formed in Hong Kong) that will be automatically classified as a corporation.[12] In the absence of a contrary election, other foreign entities are classified as: (1) a partnership if the entity has two or more members and at least one member does not have limited liability, (2) an association if all members have limited liability, or (3) disregarded as an entity separate from its owner if the entity has a single owner that does not have limited liability.[13]

Existing Entities. Under the "check-the-box" system, an existing business entity generally retains the same classification that it claimed under

5. Reg. § 301.7701–2(b)(1) through (8).

6. Reg. § 301.7701–2(b)(1).

7. Reg. § 301.7701–2(b)(7). See Section B2c of this chapter, infra, for a discussion of publicly traded partnerships.

8. Reg. §§ 301.7701–2(c)(1), 301.7701–3(a), 301.7701–3(b)(1)(i).

9. Reg. §§ 301.7701–2(c)(2), 301.7701–3(a), 301.7701–3(b)(1)(ii).

10. Reg. § 1.301.7701–2(a). See Miller, "The Strange Materialization of the Tax Nothing," 87 Tax Notes 685 (May 5, 2000).

11. Rev. Proc. 2002–69, §§ 3.02, 4.01–4.02, 2002–2 C.B. 831. If such an entity changes its classification for tax purposes, the change is treated as a conversion of the entity. Id. at § 4.03.

12. Reg. § 301.7701–2(b)(8).

13. Reg. § 301.7701–3(b)(2)(i). Limited liability generally exists if the member has no personal liability for the debts of or claims against the entity by reason of being a member. Reg. § 301.7701–3(b)(2)(ii).

the prior regulations unless it elects otherwise. An exception is provided for an entity with a single owner that claimed to be a partnership under the earlier regulations but which is disregarded as an entity separate from its owner under the current version.[14]

Election. A classification election under the regulations may be designated as effective up to 75 days before or twelve months after the election is filed.[15] The election generally must be signed either by (1) each member of the electing entity, including prior members affected by a retroactive election, or (2) by an officer, manager, or member authorized to make the election.[16] If an entity makes a classification election, a new classification election generally cannot be made for 60 months, unless the Service allows such an election and more than 50 percent of the ownership interests in the entity are owned by persons that did not own any interests when the first election was made.[17]

Change in Number of Members of an Entity. The regulations provide that the classification of an eligible entity as an association generally is not affected by any change in the numbers of members of the entity.[18] But if an eligible entity (such as a limited liability company) is classified as a partnership and its membership is reduced to one member, it becomes a disregarded entity.[19] A single-member disregarded entity also is classified as a partnership if it gains more than one member.[20]

Elective Changes in Classification. The regulations also prescribe the tax consequences when an entity makes a valid election to change its tax classification. If a partnership elects to be reclassified as an association, it is deemed to contribute all of its assets and liabilities to the association for stock and then to liquidate by distributing the stock to its partners.[21] If an association elects to be classified as a partnership, it is deemed to liquidate by distributing all of its assets and liabilities to its shareholders, who then contribute the assets and liabilities to a newly formed partnership.[22] If an association with one owner elects to be classified as a disregarded entity, it is deemed to liquidate by distributing all of its assets and liabilities to the single owner.[23] Finally, if a disregarded entity elects to be classified as an association, the owner is deemed to contribute all of the assets and liabilities of the entity to the association for stock in the association.[24]

14. Reg. § 301.7701–3(b)(3).

15. Reg. § 301.7701–3(c)(1)(iii).

16. Reg. § 301.7701–3(c)(2).

17. Reg. 301.7701–3(c)(1)(iv).

18. Reg. § 301.7701–3(f)(1).

19. Reg. § 301.7701–3(f)(2).

20. Id.

21. Reg. § 301.7701–3(g)(1)(i). See, e.g., Rev. Rul. 2004–59, 2004–1 C.B. 1050 (partnership that converts to a state law corporation under a local "formless conversion statute" is treated as having elected to be reclassified as an association).

22. Reg. § 301.7701–3(g)(1)(ii).

23. Reg. § 301.7701–3(g)(1)(iii). If an association is deemed to liquidate under Section 332 (relating to complete liquidations of certain corporate subsidiaries), the election to change classification is considered to be the adoption of a plan of liquidation. Reg. § 301.7701–3(g)(2)(ii).

24. Reg. § 301.7701–3(g)(1)(iv).

The tax treatment of a change in classification is determined under all relevant provisions of the Internal Revenue Code and general principles of tax law, including the step transaction doctrine.[25] An election to change the classification of an eligible entity is treated as occurring at the start of the day for which the election is effective.[26]

b. EXISTENCE OF A "SEPARATE ENTITY" FOR FEDERAL TAX PURPOSES

Code: § 761(a).

Regulations: §§ 1.761–1(a); 301.7701–1(a)(1) & (2).

The check-the-box regulations only apply to an entity that is treated as separate from its owners. Whether a separate entity exists is a matter of federal tax law and does not depend on the organization's status under local law.[27] A joint venture or other contractual arrangement may create a separate entity for federal tax purposes if the participants carry on a trade, business, financial operation, or venture and divide the profits therefrom.[28] For example, because a separate entity is not created in an expense-sharing relationship or when mere co-owners maintain, repair, and rent their property, no classification issue is raised in those situations. But a separate entity does exist for federal tax purposes if co-owners of property lease space and also provide services to the tenants either directly or through an agent.[29] The two cases that follow illustrate the issues and tax stakes in deciding whether a separate tax entity exists.

Podell v. Commissioner

United States Tax Court, 1970.
55 T.C. 429.

■ QUEALY, JUDGE.

* * *

OPINION

In this case, during each of the years 1964 and 1965, petitioner entered into an oral agreement with Young for the purchase, renovation, and sale of certain residential real estate. Profit and loss realized on the sale of such property was shared equally by petitioner and Young.

Section 1221, which defines "capital asset," provides in pertinent part: [Section 1221 is omitted. Ed.]

25. Reg. § 301.7701–3(g)(2).

26. Reg. § 301.7701–3(g)(3)(i). Transactions deemed to occur as a result of the election are treated as occurring immediately before the close of the day before the election is effective. Id.

27. Reg. § 301.7701–1(a)(1).

28. Reg. § 301.7701–1(a)(2).

29. Id.

Petitioner maintains that the properties sold were capital assets and that any gains on those sales should be taxed as capital gains.

Respondent argues that the oral agreements between petitioner and Young established a partnership or joint venture for the purposes of purchasing, renovating, and selling real estate in the ordinary course of business, and that consequently, the gains arose from the sale of noncapital assets and are to be treated as ordinary income.

We have found as an ultimate fact that the agreement between petitioner and Young gave rise to a joint venture. Under section 761(a), a joint venture is included within the definition of a "partnership" for purposes of the internal revenue laws (henceforth in this opinion, the terms are used interchangeably). Section 761(a) provides:

> (a) PARTNERSHIP.—For purposes of this subtitle, the term "partnership" *includes* a syndicate, group, pool, *joint venture* or other unincorporated organization through or by means of which any business, financial operation, or venture is carried on, and which is not, within the meaning of this title [subtitle], a corporation or a trust or estate. * * * [Emphasis supplied.]

A joint venture has been defined as a "special combination of two or more persons, where in some specific venture a profit is jointly sought without any actual partnership or corporate designation." * * *

The elements of a joint venture are: (a) A contract (express or implied) showing that it was the intent of the parties that a business venture be established; (b) an agreement for joint control and proprietorship; (c) a contribution of money, property, and/or services by the prospective joint venturers; and (d) a sharing of profits, but not necessarily of losses (although some jurisdictions require that there be a sharing of losses). * * *

In many respects, the concept of joint venture is similar to the concept of partnership, and many of the principles of partnership law are applicable to joint ventures. Blackner v. McDermott, 176 F.2d 498 (C.A.10, 1949). A primary distinction between the two concepts is that a joint venture is generally established for a single business venture (even though the business of managing the venture to a successful conclusion may continue for a number of years) while a partnership is formed to carry on a business for profit over a long period of time. Fishback v. United States, 215 F.Supp. 621 (D.S.Dak.1963).

It is undisputed that petitioner and Young joined in an agreement establishing a joint business venture to acquire, improve, and resell residential property at a profit, and it is immaterial that the petitioner was motivated, in part, by social objectives. There was a contribution to the business of property, services, or money by each of the parties involved. Petitioner and Young also agreed to share equally in any resulting gain or loss.

The fact that petitioner did not exercise as much managerial control over the day-to-day activities relating to the purchase, renovation, and sale of the real estate as Young is not sufficient reason for this Court to find against the existence of a joint venture. While petitioner gave Young discretion with respect to all aspects of the purchase, renovation, and sale of the real estate in question, petitioner retained the power to approve of the steps undertaken by Young to execute their agreement through his control over his continued contributions of funds to the venture. *Fishback v. United States*, supra; and *Flanders v. United States*, supra.

The real estate acquired by the joint venture is to be considered partnership property for purposes of taxation. [The court went on to conclude that the partnership's gains were ordinary income. See Chapter 3A. Ed.]

Allison v. Commissioner

United States Tax Court, 1976.
35 T.C.M. 1069.

■ STERRETT, JUDGE.

* * *

OPINION

This consolidated case presents for our determination several issues involving the business relationships and practices of Acceptance, Mortgage, Allison, and Krikac. The first issue concerns the nature of the business relationship between Acceptance and Investment with respect to their Goose Lake activities and the attendant tax consequences of Acceptance's receipt of property in December, 1969.

Acceptance's position is that it entered into a joint venture with Investment to develop the property and that its receipt of the 75 lots represents a nontaxable distribution by a partnership to a partner. Respondent contends that the parties did not enter into a joint venture and that Acceptance's receipt of the 75 lots and the residual property represents ordinary income received for financial services rendered. We find the question a close one, but it is our responsibility to resolve the issue one way or the other.

A joint venture has been defined as a "special combination of two or more persons, where in some specific venture a profit is jointly sought without any actual partnership or corporate designation". The term "joint venture" is included within the definition of the term "partnership" as found in section 761(a) with the former to be considered under the same concepts as the latter.

The question of whether a joint venture has been created by the parties is essentially factual with special emphasis placed upon the intention of the parties. In sifting through the facts and circumstances of each case it is well established that they are to be applied against a framework of four basic attributes that are indicative of a joint venture. These attributes include: a contract, express or implied, that a joint venture be formed; the contribution of money, property and/or services by the venturers; an agreement for joint proprietorship and control; and an agreement to share profits.

Acceptance has recognized these principles and has argued that their application in this case leads to the conclusion that a joint venture was formed. Acceptance points to the October, 1969 agreement executed by the parties and the testimony of Allison and McCoy in support of its position. However, our interpretation of the agreement and the other related events leads us to come down on the respondent's side of the arguments.

In October, 1969 Acceptance and Investment entered into an agreement that established certain rights and obligations between them with respect to the Goose Lake property. Acceptance argues that this agreement represents the intentions of the parties in that it memorializes the various discussions held during which the project was discussed. The agreement, which is reproduced in relevant part in the findings of fact, is entitled "Joint Venture Agreement" and does contain some indicia of a joint venture as that term is used in tax law. However, the form of the agreement is only one factor to be considered, and further we do not believe that it comports with the agreement's substance.

In the opening part the project is described as being limited to the purchase and subdivision of the property. There is no indication that the parties contemplated the subsequent joint sale of the lots or agreed to a procedure of dividing the possible profits. From the description of their endeavor and despite a "Pro Forma Profit and Loss Statement" attached to the agreement, it does not appear that the parties jointly sought a profit or that there was any agreement to pursue a business venture and to divide the profits as such therefrom. We believe that an analysis of the remaining portions of the agreement supports this conclusion.

In the next paragraph Acceptance was obligated to provide a $53,000 loan to Investment and to arrange for Investment the $80,000 secured loan from the Sierra National Bank. As noted previously, Acceptance was licensed as a property loan broker to deal in commercial finance. It appears that Acceptance's obligations with respect to this project fit within its primary business activity.

In a subsequent paragraph the agreement provides that the 75 lots were to be deeded to Acceptance "free and clear of any encumbrances * * * ". There is no indication that Investment would have any control over the ultimate disposition of these lots or that Acceptance would have any control over the property retained by Investment. This conclusion is supported by the method, which will be discussed infra, by which Acceptance attempted to dispose of these lots. Further, in the same paragraph it provides that these lots were to be deeded to Acceptance "for and in consideration of the efforts, services and liabilities specifically assumed by [Acceptance] * * * ". We find the specificity and certainty, as distinguished from a proportion of an unknown quantity, of the amount to be distributed significant. Between the parties Acceptance was entitled to the 75 lots in all events. Finally the agreement closed with the provision that it would terminate when the lots were distributed. The lack of a profit motive we find fatal to Acceptance's position.

The manner in which the agreement was implemented supports our conclusion. Acceptance fulfilled its obligations by providing and arranging for the financial requirements of the project. Pursuant to the agreements the loans were made directly to Investment. McCoy testified that his company, Investment, was directly liable for these loans. It is true that, when the venture terminated, Acceptance assumed and subsequently paid the outstanding indebtedness, but this fact indicates to us that Acceptance was merely financing Investment's project and was to receive part of the property for its trouble.

Acceptance did in fact, pursuant to the agreement, receive the 75 lots in December, 1969. Even before they were actually received, Acceptance or its subsidiaries had negotiated with Pacific States, Seckel, and the Starretts for the disposition of all but three of these lots. Even though these sales agreements did not mature, due to the inability to resell the lots at a predetermined price, we believe this clearly indicates that Acceptance had no intention of being in the real estate development business. Further, it appears these transactions were independently negotiated by Acceptance without any influence by Investment. Finally we do not agree that the president of McCoy testified that a joint venture had been formed.

Acceptance has cited several cases in support of its position, but we find that they only emphasize the distinctions upon which we are relying. In Hyman Podell, 55 T.C. 429 (1970), this Court found that a joint venture was created based upon an agreement to acquire, rehabilitate, and resell residential real estate. We have found the last element to be lacking in the case at bar. In Clarence A. Luckey, 41 T.C. 1 (1963), affd. 334 F.2d 719 (9th Cir.1964), we found the existence of a joint venture where the invested capital was to be repaid from the first profits of the business. In the case at bar we have found that Investment was primarily liable for the outstanding debts which apparently were intended to be repaid from its own profits.

We recognize that there are instances where Acceptance and Investment worked together towards the development of the property. However, when compared to the other elements in this case, they seem relatively insignificant. We find that the second agreement, executed by the parties in February, 1970, provides some insight into the nature and extent of these joint activities. From our review, the agreement appears merely to be a recitation of the rights and obligations of the parties with respect to the events that had transpired. Finally we note that neither partnership books were kept nor tax returns filed to record and report these events, an omission which can be fairly described as an admission against interest.

After a careful review of the evidence we hold that Acceptance and Investment did not enter into a joint venture to develop the Goose Lake property. We find that Acceptance received the 75 lots and its interest in the residual property on December 18, 1969 in return for financial services with respect to the property. Having made that determination we must now determine the fair market value of this property as of the above date so that Acceptance's income can be properly measured.

NOTE

Electing Out of Partnership Status. Section 761(a) permits all the members of an unincorporated organization to elect to be excluded from the application of Subchapter K if the organization is availed of: (1) for investment purposes only and not for the active conduct of a business; (2) for the joint production, extraction, or use of property but not for the purpose of selling services or property produced or extracted; or (3) by securities dealers who engage in a short-term joint venture to underwrite, sell or distribute a particular issue of securities.[1] In all cases, the members of the organization must be able to determine their income adequately without the computation of "partnership taxable income." The regulations amplify the statutory requirements[2] and describe the time and method for making the Section 761 election.[3]

When might a Section 761 election be desirable? Co-owners of property held solely for investment purposes might make the election to assure that their arrangement is not governed by Subchapter K in the event the activity is classified as a partnership.[4] Members of joint operating arrangements also make Section 761 elections in order to make inconsistent tax elections to suit their individual tax situations.[5] For example, joint venturers engaged in drilling for oil may make a Section 761 election in order to permit inconsistent elections with respect to the tax treatment of intangible drilling and development costs.[6] Although a Section 761 election removes an unincorporated entity from the application of Subchapter K, the organization nonetheless is considered a partnership for purposes of other provisions of the Code.[7]

Husband and Wife Business Partnerships. Section 761(f) provides that an unincorporated business conducted by a married couple filing a joint return and each of whom "materially participates"[8] in the business (a "qualified joint venture") may elect not to be treated as a partnership for federal tax purposes. In that event, the spouses must divide the items of income, gain, loss, deduction and credit of the business in accordance with

1. See generally McMahon, "The Availability and Effect of Election Out of Partnership Status Under Section 761(a)," 9 Va.Tax. Rev. 1 (1989).

2. Reg. § 1.761–2(a)(2) & (3).

3. Reg. § 1.761–2(b).

4. Willis, Pennell & Postlewaite, Partnership Taxation ¶ 1.02[8] (6th ed. 1997).

5. Cf. I.R.C. § 703(b).

6. Cf. Rev.Rul. 83–129, 1983–2 C.B. 105. See generally Burke and Meyer, "Federal Income Tax Classification of Natural Resource Ventures: Co–Ownership, Partnership or Association?," 37 S.W.L.J. 859, 865–72 (1984).

7. Cokes v. Commissioner, 91 T.C. 222 (1988).

8. Material participation status is determined by importing the definition from the passive loss limitation rules in Section 469(h). See Chapter 3C3, infra. In general, a taxpayer is treated as materially participating in an activity only if she is involved in its operations on a basis that is regular, continuous and substantial. I.R.C. § 469(h)(1).

their respective interests in the venture, and each spouse's share of such items is taken into account as if the items were attributable to a trade or business conducted by such spouse as a sole proprietor.[9] Only businesses that are owned and operated by spouses as co-owners, rather than in the name of state law entities (such as general or limited partnerships or LLCs), qualify to make this election.

The purpose of the Section 761(f) election is to allow co-owner spouses to avoid the burden of filing a partnership tax return and, more importantly, to permit each spouse to receive separate credit for his or her respective share of self-employment income from the venture for social security and medicare coverage purposes.[10] Spouses make the election on their joint income tax return by filing a separate Schedule C (or, for farm businesses, Schedule F) and, if required, a separate Schedule SE (self-employment tax form) on which they report their respective shares of tax items from the business.

PROBLEMS

1. Which of the following relationships are likely to constitute a separate entity for federal tax purposes?

(a) A, B and C purchase a single parcel of land as tenants-in-common and hold the land as an investment.

(b) Same as (a), above, except the land is subdivided and A, B and C sell the lots.

(c) Litigator and Negotiator are attorneys who share an office and a secretary. Each attorney services and bills his own individual clients.

(d) Doctor will locate and purchase a suitable four unit building. Architect will remodel it. When the work is done, the renovated building will be sold by the Doctor–Architect real estate company and Architect will receive 25% of the net profits.

(e) Would the result in (d), above, be different if Doctor and Architect agreed that Doctor will retain three of the units as rental property and Architect will receive one unit to hold as rental property?

(f) Fisher will purchase and operate a fishing boat. Lender will provide 10–year nonrecourse financing to Fisher. The arrangement will be evidenced by a note, secured by the boat, which will require repayment of the principal sum ratably over the 10–year period. In addition, Lender will receive 15% of Fisher's net profits from the fishing operation each year of the arrangement.

9. I.R.C. § 761(f)(1).

10. See I.R.C. § 1402(a)(17), under which each spouse's share of income or loss from a qualified joint venture is taken into account in determining net earnings from self-employment.

2. The provisions of Section 7701 that define corporations and partnerships do not explicitly describe an elective tax classification regime. The definition of a partnership in Section 7701(a)(2) provides that it "includes a syndicate, group, pool, joint venture, or other unincorporated organization, through or by means of which any business, financial operation, or venture is carried on, and which is not, within the meaning of [the Code], a trust or estate or a corporation." The statutory definition of a corporation (section 7701(a)(3)) provides that it "includes associations, joint-stock companies, and insurance companies." Moreover, in Morrissey v. Commissioner, 296 U.S. 344, 56 S.Ct. 289 (1935), the Supreme Court endorsed the corporate resemblance approach reflected in the prior classification regulations. Against this background, did the Treasury have the authority to issue the check-the-box regulations? See Section 7805. Is it likely that anyone would challenge the Treasury's authority? Should Congress codify the regulations by specific legislation?

c. PUBLICLY TRADED PARTNERSHIPS

Code: § 7704.

For a brief time after enactment of the Tax Reform Act of 1986, the publicly traded partnership ("PTP") surfaced as a refuge from the costly double tax regime of Subchapter C. Unlike an S corporation, a PTP could have an unlimited number of shareholders. It could register its limited partnership interests, known as "units," with the Securities and Exchange Commission, and the units were freely tradable on a securities exchange or in the over-the-counter market. A profitable PTP thus avoided the corporate income tax and passed through its income to noncorporate limited partners at the lower individual rates.

Alarmed at the proliferation of PTPs and the potential erosion of the corporate tax base, Congress responded by enacting Section 7704, which classifies certain PTPs as corporations for tax purposes. As defined, a "publicly traded partnership" is any partnership whose interests are: (1) traded on an established securities market, or (2) readily tradable on a secondary market (or its substantial equivalent).[11] The regulations generally provide that an interest is "readily tradable" if "taking into account all of the facts and circumstances, the partners are readily able to buy, sell, or exchange their partnership interests in a manner that is comparable, economically, to trading on an established securities market."[12]

An important exception from reclassification is provided for partnerships if 90 percent or more of their gross income consists of certain passive-type income items (e.g., interest, dividends, real property rents, gains from the sale of real property and income and gains from certain natural resources activities).[13] These excepted PTPs continue to be treated as pass-through entities for federal tax purposes. The scope of this narrow escape hatch came under scrutiny after several large private investment firms

11. I.R.C. § 7704(b).

12. Reg. § 1.7704–1(c)(1).

13. I.R.C. § 7704(c).

"went public" in 2007 using a PTP structure under which they offered publicly traded units representing limited partnership interests. One of the largest IPO transactions involved The Blackstone Group, a global asset firm with approximately $88.4 billion under management. In addition to providing advisory services, Blackstone manages a variety of investment pools, including private equity and venture capital funds, real estate partnerships, and hedge funds. Before it went public, Blackstone easily qualified for pass-through tax treatment, and it sought to continue avoiding the corporate-level tax as a public company by employing the PTP structure and qualifying for the passive income exception even though the bulk of its profits are derived from an active money management business.[14]

In response to news reports about the lavish compensation and expensive birthday party of Blackstone's CEO and critical commentary about financial service firm IPOs, Senate Finance Committee chair Max Baucus and ranking Republican Charles Grassley introduced legislation providing generally that the Section 7704(c) exception will not apply in the case of a PTP that directly or indirectly derives income from investment adviser or related asset management services. Their stated goal was to preserve the integrity of the corporate tax base for firms that seek access to public markets and to curtail any special treatment for the lucrative asset management business.

Although this proposal enjoyed bipartisan support when it was introduced, it failed to gain traction and had not become law as of early 2008 when this edition went to press. It thus remains "on the shelf" and ready to be resuscitated if and when Congress decides to reconsider the issue.

3. TRUSTS

Regulations: § 301.7701–4(a), (b).

Trusts, like corporations, may be taxpaying entities, but the income taxation of trusts differs from the taxation of corporations in several important respects. First, a corporation is taxed on its profits as they are earned under the relatively flat rates in Section 11. If it later distributes the remaining after-tax earnings as dividends, the shareholders are subject to a second tax. But there is no double tax on trust income. Under the complex rules of Subchapter J, trust income currently distributed to beneficiaries is generally not taxed to the trust. Rather, the income is taxed to the recipient beneficiaries to the extent of the trust's "distributable net income." If, however, trust income is accumulated, it is taxed to the trust when earned under the rates in Section 1(e) but normally not taxed again when distributed to the beneficiaries. Also, corporate shareholders who receive dividends are taxable at ordinary income rates, regardless of the character of the corporation's earnings. By contrast, trust income retains its tax character in the hands of the beneficiaries.

14. For press coverage of this transaction, see Anderson, "Blackstone Founders Prepare to Count Their Billions," N.Y. Times, June 12, 2007, at C1.

The regulations distinguish between "ordinary trusts" created to take title to property for the purpose of protecting and conserving it for the beneficiaries, and "business" or "commercial" trusts which are created to carry on a business for profit. An ordinary trust is classified as a "trust" and taxed under Subchapter J.[1] A business trust, on the other hand, is a business entity that is classified under the check-the-box regulations.[2] Because a business trust is an unincorporated entity, it will be classified as a partnership for federal tax purposes if it has two or more members and does not make an election to be classified as a corporation.[3]

D. INTRODUCTION TO CHOICE OF BUSINESS ENTITY

The choice of entity for a business enterprise depends on a wide variety of tax and nontax considerations. In some instances, necessities of the particular business may drive the decision. For example, if public trading of ownership interests is desired, a C corporation almost always is the entity of choice.[1] Access to venture capital investors, a preference for executive compensation techniques such as stock options, or an exit strategy that anticipates a public offering or merger with a public company all may dictate use of the corporate form.

In many cases, however, the nontax objectives of the parties can be adequately satisfied in a variety of legal forms. For example, where limited liability is a critical concern, it can be achieved in a corporation, limited liability company, or limited partnership with a corporate general partner. In the many situations where state law provides flexibility to achieve these and other nontax goals, tax considerations often will be controlling or at least a paramount factor in deciding what legal form to select. In evaluating the choices, three critical questions are: (1) who will own the business and what type of economic relationship among them is contemplated, (2) how and when do the owners intend to realize a return on their investment, and (3) is the business initially expected to generate losses and for how long?[2] In making the choice, the threshold tax question often will be whether to use a C corporation or a pass-through entity and, if the latter, whether it should be a partnership, LLC or S corporation.

The choice of entity stakes and strategies have changed dramatically as the federal tax system has experienced a sustained period of instability since the mid–1980's. The discussion that follows provides an overview of the most significant tax considerations in making the decision, looking back

1. Reg. § 301.7701–4(a).

2. Reg. § 301.7701–4(b).

3. Reg. § 301.7701–2(c)(1);–3(a), (b)(1)(i).

1. Except in a few specialized industries, such as natural resources, virtually all publicly traded partnerships are classified as corporations for tax purposes. As a result, there is rarely any tax incentive to use that legal form instead of a corporation. See I.R.C. § 7704 and Section B2c of this chapter, supra.

2. See generally Bagley & Dauchy, The Entrepreneur's Guide to Business Law 64–68 (3d ed. 2007).

briefly at tax history to place the current state of affairs into proper perspective. Throughout the discussion, remember that individuals, trusts and C corporations are separate taxable entities, while S corporations, partnerships and limited liability companies are generally not subject to an entity-level tax but pass through their income, losses, credits and other tax items to the owners of the business.

Rates on Ordinary Income. For C corporations with significant taxable income, the corporate income tax is essentially a 34 or 35 percent flat rate tax with no preferential rate for long-term capital gains.[3] Corporations with smaller amounts of income, however, can take advantage of lower rates (15 and 25 percent) on their first $75,000 of taxable income.[4] Individuals pay tax at graduated rates beginning at 10 percent of taxable income and peaking at a nominal rate of 35 percent.[5] And profits of C corporations are potentially taxed both at the corporate and shareholder levels when they are distributed as dividends or when the shareholders sell their stock.

At first glance, the highest individual and corporate rates appear to be the same, but a true comparison is a bit more complex. The effective marginal rate for some individuals may be higher than 35 percent on some income because of the disallowance of itemized deductions and the phase-out of personal exemptions for high-income taxpayers.[6] Beginning in 2003 and continuing at least until the end of 2010, dividends received by noncorporate shareholders are taxed at the same preferential 15 percent rate as long-term capital gains.[7] Other variables that may affect the overall tax burden include the corporate and individual alternative minimum taxes; a long list of corporate tax benefits, ranging from accelerated depreciation to targeted subsidies for particular industries, that lower the effective corporate tax rate; employment taxes imposed on owners who also perform services for the business; and the impact of state and local taxes.

At one time, when the maximum individual tax rate on ordinary income peaked at 70 percent or higher and the top corporate rate was 46 percent, C corporations served as a refuge from the steeper individual rates. This rate differential prompted privately held firms to conduct their business and investment activities as C corporations rather than pass-through entities because their income was taxed at lower rates and could remain in corporate solution to compound at the these tax-preferred rates until the business was sold or liquidated. In the meantime, shareholders who wished to withdraw earnings utilized tax efficient strategies to avoid the sting of the double tax. For example, owner-employees of a C corporation typically have distributed profits in the form of salary and fringe

3. I.R.C. §§ 11; 1201(a).

4. I.R.C. 11(b). Certain corporations with major shareholders who render personal services, such as professional corporations of lawyers, accountants, architects, and the like, are not entitled to the lower marginal corporate rates. I.R.C. §§ 11(b)(2); 448(d)(2).

5. I.R.C. § 1.

6. See I.R.C. §§ 68; 151(d)(3). The phase-outs are themselves being phased out, however, and are scheduled for repeal by 2010, but just for one year unless Congress makes the repeal permanent.

7. I.R.C. § 1(h)(11).

benefits that are tax-deductible by the corporation and, in the case of many fringe benefits, excludable by the owner-employee. Shareholders also can loan funds or lease property to a C corporation and withdraw earnings in the form of tax-deductible interest or rent.

To be sure, the Service had weapons to combat these self-help strategies. Payments of salary or interest could be attacked as unreasonable compensation or disguised dividends but usually these arguments were reserved for the most egregious cases. Congress also enacted penalty taxes to patrol against excessive accumulations or avoidance of the individual progressive rates.[8] With foresight and good planning, however, an active business that paid reasonable compensation and justified any accumulations of earnings on the basis of reasonable business judgment could avoid constructive dividends and the corporate penalty taxes with relative ease.

For many C corporations, these tax saving strategies have withstood the test of time. A study by the Joint Committee on Taxation revealed that in 1993, 61 percent of all C corporations reported no taxable income and another 37 percent reported taxable income of less than $355,000.[9] More recent data indicates that in 2005, 48.4 percent of all C corporations filing returns reported no taxable income, and only 33.5 percent of C corporations had any corporate tax liability after tax credits were taken into account.[10]

Along with the tax rates, some of the key variables also have changed. Today, with individuals and C corporations subject to the same top rate and with dividends and long-term capital gains generally taxed at a maximum rate of 15 percent, the C-corporation-earnings-accumulation strategy is much less compelling than when corporations enjoyed a significant tax rate advantage over individuals. This rate parity, together with the prospect of two levels of tax when a C corporation is sold, provides a greater incentive to use a pass-through entity instead of a C corporation, particularly if the business intends to distribute its earnings currently, does not have owners who work for the firm, or holds assets that are likely to appreciate in value over a relatively short time horizon. It would be rare, for example, for a venture investing in real estate or financial assets for current income or capital appreciation (or both) to operate as a C corporation because the costs of doing so would be prohibitive in light of the double tax. In some cases, however, C corporations still offer tax savings, especially for businesses that pay out most of their earnings as compensation to their high-income owners.

Preferential Capital Gains Rates. The decision to tax long-term capital gains at substantially lower rates than ordinary income is another feature of the tax system that historically eased the tax burden of conducting a business as a C corporation. Rather than paying dividends, tax advisors

8. See I.R.C. § 531 et seq. (accumulated earnings tax); § 541 (personal holding company tax).

9. Joint Committee on Taxation, Impact of Small Business of Replacing the Federal Income Tax 5 (J.C.S., 3–96, April 23, 1996).

10. Statistics of Income—2005, Returns of Active Corporations, Other than Forms 1120S, 1120–REIT, and 1120–RIC, Table 22.

devised techniques to "bail out" earnings at capital gains rates. A "bailout" is a distribution of earnings in a transaction, such as a redemption of stock, that qualifies as a "sale or exchange," enabling the shareholder to recover all or part of her stock basis and to benefit from preferential capital gain treatment on any realized gain.[11] In some cases, such as where the shareholder has died and the basis of her stock has been stepped up to its date-of-death value, the bailout may be accomplished tax-free.[12] Over the years, Congress responded with complex anti-bailout provisions to ensure that distributions resembling dividends would be taxed as ordinary income.[13]

As long as dividends and capital gains are taxed at the same preferential rates, the traditional incentive for a bailout has just about disappeared. Under the new rate regime, the tax goal of a bailout will not be to convert dividend income to capital gain but rather to enable shareholders to recover all or part of the basis in their stock. It is unlikely that this will tip the scales in favor of using a C corporation but this new type of bailout continues to raise challenging tax issues for the many closely held businesses that currently operate as C corporations.

Pass–Through of Losses. Investors often anticipate losses in the early years of a new venture and desire to deduct those losses against income from other sources as quickly as possible. A pass-through tax regime permits the losses to pass through to the owners who devote their time and energy to the business, but the ability of investors to deduct those losses is often delayed by an array of Code provisions designed to curtail tax shelters.[14]

A C corporation is not able to pass through start-up losses to its shareholders, but corporations may deduct losses against their taxable income and carry any excess back or forward as net operating losses.[15] For start-up companies that raise capital from outside investors, these tax rules are among several factors that may weigh in favor of a C corporation. Although the start-up losses do not pass through as they are realized, most taxable investors would be unable to deduct them currently in any event, and nontaxable investors, such as pension funds and charities, are indifferent. The losses may be used more efficiently as carryforwards to shelter income earned during the early years of a C corporation's profitability.[16]

11. Subchapter C includes many provisions to patrol against bailout transactions that are essentially equivalent to dividend distributions. See, e.g., I.R.C. §§ 302; 304; 306.

12. The date-of-death basis rule in Section 1014 is scheduled to be replaced by a carryover basis regime (with some exceptions) in 2010 (but for one year only) in the unlikely event that the estate tax is repealed. See I.R.C. § 1022.

13. See, e.g., I.R.C. §§ 302; 304; 306.

14. See, e.g., I.R.C. §§ 465; 469; 704(d); 1366(d).

15. See I.R.C. § 172.

16. In some cases, however, the use of loss carryovers by a C corporation may be limited after a significant change of ownership. See I.R.C. § 382.

Subchapter K vs. Subchapter S. If a pass-through tax regime is desired, the owners of the business must decide whether to employ a partnership (or LLC taxed as a partnership) or an S corporation. The ownership and capital structure restrictions imposed on S corporations may require use of a partnership or LLC. S corporations are limited to 100 shareholders (although members of a "family," broadly defined, are counted as one shareholder), and they may not have more than one class of stock.[17] Subchapter K is much more flexible. To accommodate different types of owners, partnerships and LLCs may make special allocations of partnership income and deduction items, while shareholders of an S corporation must include corporate income and loss on a pro rata share basis.[18] Thus, partners may agree to share certain income or deductions disproportionately, and the agreement will be respected for tax purposes if it reflects their economic business deal. In most cases, partnerships and LLCs (but not S corporations) also can distribute appreciated property in kind without immediate recognition of taxable gain.

Unlike S corporation shareholders, partners may increase the basis of their partnership interests by their allocable share of entity-level debts.[19] That additional "basis credit" may be important for maximizing the ability to deduct losses realized by the enterprise—e.g., in ventures that own leveraged real estate—or avoiding gain on distributions.[20] For these and other reasons, the conventional wisdom is that Subchapter K is more taxpayer-friendly than Subchapter S. In fact, much of the popularity of the LLC is attributable to the fact that LLCs offer limited liability to all investors combined with the more flexible partnership tax regime.

In some situations, however, the goals of business owners may be better achieved with an S corporation. For example, an S corporation may be the entity of choice for a business with only a few owners because the flexibility of Subchapter K is not necessary. Moreover, many entrepreneurs prefer to conduct their business as a state law corporation instead of a partnership or limited liability company because they (or their advisors) are more comfortable with the corporate governance structure. Subchapter S provides these owners with a relatively simple pass-through tax regime. As discussed below, S corporations also are often used by service providers to minimize their exposure to employment taxes.

On the other hand, S corporations are not a viable choice in many situations—for example, a business with foreign investors, who are not permissible S corporation shareholders. Many institutional investors (e.g., tax-exempt pension funds and charitable organizations) are discouraged by the tax system from investing in any type of active business that is operated as a pass-through entity.[21] Venture capital funds, which provide a

17. I.R.C. § 1361(b).

18. Compare I.R.C. § 704(b)(2) with I.R.C. § 1366(a).

19. See I.R.C. §§ 722; 752(a).

20. See I.R.C. §§ 704(d); 731(a)(1); 1366(d)(1); 1368(b).

21. Stripped of detail, pension funds and other tax-exempt organizations are potentially subject to the "unrelated business income tax" on income passing through from

large source of capital for start-up companies, appear to be more comfortable using the familiar C corporation capitalized with several classes of stock, a structure not available in an S corporation.[22] These are just a few illustrations of the types of additional factors influencing the choice of entity decision.

Employment Tax Considerations. Where a principal owner also is a service provider for the business, employment taxes can be an influential factor. In addition to income taxes, social security and medicare taxes must be paid on income from self-employment and wages of employees.[23] Net earnings from self-employment include a sole proprietor or partner's gross income derived from any trade or business.[24] Assume, for example, that Trial Lawyer has $500,000 of net earnings from self-employment. Her self-employment tax (using the 2008 wage base and rates) will be $27,148, consisting of 12.4 percent on the first $102,000 of self-employment income ($12,648) and 2.9 percent on the entire $500,000 ($14,500). Assume Trial Lawyer incorporates her practice using an S corporation which nets the same $500,000, pays the lawyer a salary of $150,000, and either retains the $350,000 balance or distributes it as a dividend. Some tax advisors take the position that as long as the compensation paid by the S corporation is within a reasonable range, the 2.9 percent medicare tax can be avoided on any remaining S corporation income.[25] If this is correct, Trial Lawyer would save $10,150 (the 2.9 percent medicare tax on the $350,000). Whether or not this S corporation strategy should succeed is debatable, although anecdotal evidence suggests that it is widely used and often goes unchallenged. But the strategy clearly would fail if Trial Lawyer conducted her practice as a single member limited liability company (assuming state law allowed that form for lawyers) which, as a disregarded entity, would be treated as a sole proprietorship for tax purposes.

Employment taxes also may influence the choice between a limited partnership and an LLC. Unlike general partners, limited partners generally are not subject to self-employment tax on their distributive share of

an operating business conducted as a partnership or S corporation, but they are generally not taxable on income from "portfolio" investments, such as dividends and interest received from an equity or debt interest in a C corporation. See generally I.R.C. § 511 et seq.

22. See Bankman, "The Structure of Silicon Valley Start-ups," 42 UCLA L. Rev. 1737 (1994), which observes that venture capitalists are foregoing valuable tax benefits (e.g., current deductibility of start-up losses) by using C corporations rather than a business form eligible for pass-through tax treatment. See also Fleischer, "The Rational Exuberance of Structuring Venture Capital Start-ups," 57 Tax L. Rev. 137 (2003).

23. I.R.C. § 1401.

24. I.R.C. § 1402(a). Self-employment taxes include a 12.4 percent "social security" tax on self-employment income up to $102,000 (in 2008; the cap is indexed annually) and a 2.9 percent medicare tax on the entire amount of self-employment income. Self-employed taxpayers may take an above-the-line deduction for one-half of self-employment tax paid. I.R.C. § 164(f).

25. In egregious cases, such as where little or no compensation is paid and the S corporation distributes a large dividend to its sole owner, the Service likely will reclassify all or part of the dividend as wages for employment tax purposes. See Chapter 11H, infra.

partnership income (apart from salary-like guaranteed payments), while the employment tax treatment of LLC members (who are classified as neither general nor limited partners under state law) is uncertain.[26] The unsettled state of the law has created an opportunity for abuse by LLC members who are active in the business. In 1997, the Service issued proposed regulations to clarify these issues,[27] but Congress imposed a moratorium[28] after a storm of protest and no final regulations had been issued as of early 2008.

State Tax Issues. State tax considerations may also play a role in the choice of entity decision. For example, in some states LLCs may be subject to taxes or charges that are not imposed on partnerships, or S corporations may be taxed adversely compared to partnerships.[29]

Existing Entities: Change of Form. If an existing entity wants to change its legal form or tax status, it may confront significant tax impediments. For example, converting a C corporation to a partnership or LLC will require the corporation to liquidate, which may trigger significant corporate and shareholder tax liability.[30] Alternatively, a C corporation may make an election to become an S corporation with no immediate tax consequences, but asset appreciation and other income accruing prior to the conversion still may be subject to a corporate-level tax when those gains are ultimately realized.[31] Incorporating a partnership or LLC, and converting a partnership into an LLC or an LLP, generally may be accomplished without adverse tax consequences.

Choice of Entity Trends. The choice of entity landscape continues to evolve, and some interesting trends have developed. Despite the advent of limited liability companies, corporate formations outnumbered LLC formations in most jurisdictions during the 1990's by a healthy 2:1 margin.[32] Contrary to predictions of their demise, S corporations have shown surprising vitality. In 1997, for the first time, a majority of corporate tax returns were filed by S corporations,[33] and it was estimated that they would be the fastest growing type of business entity from 1999 through 2005.[34] These forecasts have proven to be true. Between 1997 and 2001, there was a 29.5

26. I.R.C. § 1402(a)(13).

27. Prop. Reg. § 1.1402(a)–2(h).

28. Pub. L. No. 105–34, § 935, 111 Stat. 788 (1997).

29. See generally Ely, Grissom & Houser, "State Tax Treatment of Limited Liability Companies and Limited Liability Partnership," 112 Tax Notes 45 (July 3, 2006).

30. See Chapter 15, infra.

31. See I.R.C. § 1374, discussed in Chapter 20F, infra.

32. See Lee, "Choice of Small Business Tax Entity: Facts and Fiction," 87 Tax Notes 417 (2000) (herein cited as "Lee I"), for data and analysis concerning the trends in formations of small business entities. See also Lee, "A Populist Political Perspective of the Business Tax Entities Universe: Hey the Stars Might Lie But the Numbers Never Do," 78 Texas L. Rev. 885 (2000) (herein cited as "Lee II").

33. Treubert & Janquet, "Corporation Income Tax Returns, 1998," 21 SOI Bulletin 66, 67 (2001).

34. Lee I, supra note 32, citing Zaffino, "Projections of Returns to be Filed in Calendar Years 1995–2005," 18 SOI Bulletin 178 (1999). For a view questioning this projection, see Alexander, "The Questionable Continued Flourishing of S Corporations," 87 Tax Notes 577 (April 24, 2000).

percent increase in S corporations and, by 2003, S corporations accounted for 61.9 percent of the 5.4 million corporate returns filed.[35]

Legislation increasing the number and type of permissible S corporation shareholders does not appear to have had much influence on this growth pattern. The available data confirms that S corporations are most widely used by firms with very concentrated ownership. Approximately 34 percent of all S corporations filing returns in 2003 had only one shareholder, 99.4 percent of all S corporations had 10 or fewer shareholders, and only 3,150 S corporations (out of the approximately 3.3 million S corporations filing returns) had more than 30 shareholders.[36]

The number of businesses filing partnership tax returns has grown modestly, increasing at an average annual rate of 5.7 percent between 1995 and 2005, but the mix of entities within the partnership tax universe has changed dramatically.[37] The number of LLCs increased 1,136 percent between 1995 and 2005, from 118,559 to 1,465,223. LLCs now outnumber limited partnerships by more than 2:1, and beginning in 2002, the number of LLCs surpassed general and limited partnerships combined.[38] In 2005, LLCs represented 53 percent of all partnerships, although limited partnerships reported the largest share of overall partnership profits.[39] This data suggests that the explosive growth of LLCs is coming more at the expense of entities that would have been general or limited partnerships rather than from C or S corporations, which remain alive and well for closely held businesses.[40]

It is apparent from this introductory discussion that a good grounding in the fundamentals of business enterprise and individual taxation is essential to make a competent choice of entity decision. That study has just begun. When it ends, the many issues and options confronting the founders of a new business, which may seem quite intimidating at this point, should come into sharper focus.

PROBLEM

Betty and Emil are two single, cash method taxpayers interested in beginning a new shoe manufacturing business. The business, which Betty and Emil call "Boots", is expected to produce about $1 million of taxable income per year.

(a) Assuming Boots is formed as a C corporation, determine its regular tax liability on $1 million of taxable income. See § 11.

(b) What will be the result to Betty and Emil in part (a), above, if Boots distributes $330,000 to each of them as qualified dividends? Assume that both Betty's and Emil's taxable income for the year

35. Luttrell, S Corporation Returns, 2003, 25 SOI Bulletin 91 (2006).

36. Id. at 97–98.

37. Wheeler & Shumofsky, Partnership Returns, 2005, 27 SOI Bulletin 69 (2007).

38. Id. at 75.

39. Id.

40. See Lee I, supra note 32.

will be $330,000. For convenience, assume that Emil and Betty are taxable at a combined federal and state flat rate of 40% on ordinary income and a combined flat rate of 20% on qualified dividends and long-term capital gains.

(c) What result in (a), above, if instead of paying dividends Boots pays Betty and Emil salaries of $500,000 each? What other strategies could Betty and Emil employ to reduce the impact of the corporate "double tax"? In general, what are the risks of these strategies? See, e.g., §§ 79; 105(a), (b); 106; 118; 162(a)(3); 163.

(d) How much total tax will Betty and Emil pay if Boots is formed as a limited partnership, an LLC taxed as a partnership, or an S corporation?

(e) In general, what other factors should Betty and Emil consider in deciding the legal form for Boots?

E. THE "COMMON LAW" OF BUSINESS ENTERPRISE TAXATION

1. JUDICIAL DOCTRINES

Although the study of business enterprise taxation principally involves the application of complex statutes to particular transactions, the Code is not the only analytical tool. In scrutinizing taxpayer behavior, the courts at an early date went beyond the literal statutory language and began to formulate a set of doctrines that have become the "common law" of federal taxation. Some of these principles, such as the assignment of income doctrine, were encountered in the basic income tax course. Unlike the Code, which often provides bright-line rules for solving problems, the judicial doctrines are imprecise. The very vagueness of these pronouncements, however, has contributed to their influence. When the system is working, they loom large in the tax advisor's conscience and serve to thwart aggressive schemes that literally comply with the statute but are incompatible with its intended purpose.[1] This introductory survey is intended to preview some of the reasoning that lies at the heart of this tax jurisprudence.

Viewed most broadly, these overlapping judicial doctrines ask a simple question that is central to almost every case in this text. Have the taxpayers actually done what they, and their documents, represent, or are the economic realities of the transaction—and the attendant tax consequences—other than what the taxpayers purports them to be? The tests used to resolve this question bear many labels which are often used interchangeably. What follows is a summary of the terminology that soon will become familiar.

1. See generally Bittker & Lokken, Federal Taxation of Income, Estates and Gifts ¶ 4.3.1 (3d ed. 1999).

Sham Transaction and Economic Substance Doctrines. If a transaction is a "sham," it will not be respected for tax purposes. A "sham" is best defined as a transaction that never actually occurred but is represented by the taxpayer to have transpired—with favorable tax consequences of course.[2] One court has colorfully described a sham as an "attempt by a taxpayer to ward off tax blows with paper armor,"[3] in a purported transaction that "gives off an unmistakably hollow sound when it is tapped."[4]

Because a "sham" often connotes near fraudulent behavior, the courts tend to reserve this doctrine in its purest form for the more egregious cases. But the pejorative term also is used to describe the kinds of transactions that are challenged under the related economic substance doctrine. In one typically overlapping formulation, the Fourth Circuit articulated the following two-part test to define a sham:[5]

> To treat a transaction as a sham, the court must find that the taxpayer was motivated by no business purpose other than obtaining tax benefits in entering the transaction, and that the transaction has no economic substance because no reasonable possibility of a profit exists.

The economic substance doctrine has become one of the IRS's principal weapons in its assault on abusive tax shelters. Its essence is that claimed tax benefits should be denied if the transactions that give rise to them lack economic substance apart from tax considerations even if the purported activity actually occurred. Most courts have been receptive to the doctrine, but they disagree over its proper formulation.[6] Some apply a conjunctive two-part test requiring a taxpayer first to establish the presence of economic substance (an objective inquiry) and then a business purpose (a subjective test).[7] Others use a narrower disjunctive approach that respects a

2. See, e.g., Knetsch v. United States, 364 U.S. 361, 81 S.Ct. 132 (1960).

3. Waterman Steamship Corp. v. Commissioner, 430 F.2d 1185 (5th Cir.1970), cert. denied, 401 U.S. 939, 91 S.Ct. 936 (1971).

4. Id. at 1196, quoting United States v. General Geophysical Co., 296 F.2d 86, 89 (5th Cir.1961), cert. denied, 369 U.S. 849, 82 S.Ct. 932 (1962).

5. Rice's Toyota World, Inc. v. Commissioner, 752 F.2d 89, 91 (4th Cir.1985). See also Winn–Dixie Stores, Inc. v. Commissioner, 254 F.3d 1313 (11th Cir. 2001); Kirchman v. Commissioner, 862 F.2d 1486 (11th Cir. 1989). For cases where courts have declined to characterize a questionable transaction as a sham, see Compaq v. Commissioner, 277 F.3d 778 (5th Cir.2001); IES Industries, Inc. v. United States, 253 F.3d 350 (8th Cir.2001).

6. For a hostile view, see Coltec Industries v. United States, 62 Fed. Cl. 716, 752–756 (Ct. Fed. Cl. 2004), where the court held that the economic substance doctrine was unconstitutional because it violated separation of powers principles. This outlier decision was reversed on appeal by the Federal Circuit, which described the trial court's decision as "untenable" and upheld the doctrine as a permissible tool of construction that allowed courts to look beyond the literal language of a statute if a strict construction would violate legislative intent. Coltec Industries v. United States, 454 F.3d 1340, 1352 (Fed. Cir. 2006), cert. denied, 127 S.Ct. 1261 (2007) (2007). The court then applied a set of principles and determined that the transaction under scrutiny lacked economic substance because it did not effect "any real change in the flow of economic benefits, provide ... any real opportunity to make a profit, or appreciably affect [the taxpayer's] beneficial interest aside from creating a tax advantage." Id. at 1360.

7. See, e.g., Pasternak v. Commissioner, 990 F.2d 893, 898 (6th Cir. 1993).

transaction if it has either a business purpose or economic substance.[8] Still others treat economic substance and business purpose as "precise factors" to consider rather than a rigid test.[9] The courts also disagree regarding the type of non-tax economic benefit that a taxpayer must establish to demonstrate economic substance.[10]

Substance Over Form. The form of a transaction frequently is determinative of its tax consequences. Since the early days of the income tax, however, the courts have been willing to go beyond the formal papers and evaluate the "substance" of a transaction. A familiar example is the proper classification of a business arrangement as a sale or a lease.[11] The documents used by the taxpayer may use one label, but the courts are not inhibited from examining the arrangement and restructuring it for tax purposes to comport with the economic realities.

The tension between form and substance will be evident throughout the chapters that follow. Did a retiring partner sell her partnership interest to the remaining partners or was the interest liquidated by the partnership? Is a corporate instrument "debt," as the taxpayer contends, or "equity," as the Service usually will assert? Is a payment to a shareholder-employee really "compensation" or is it a disguised dividend? Who, in substance, made a sale of corporate assets—the corporation or its shareholders? It is impossible to generalize as to when and how this doctrine will be applied. Individual cases turn on the particular facts and the court's attitude toward tax avoidance.

Despite the influence of this doctrine over time, some courts have shown reluctance to accept recent attempts by the Service to restructure legitimate transactions to reach a result that will produce more revenue. The Tax Court, for example, has been wary of extending the judicial doctrines where Congress has mandated that particular results shall flow from a given form and the taxpayers have carefully structured an otherwise legitimate transaction to comply with the statutory requirements.[12]

Business Purpose. The business purpose doctrine is conceptually linked to the sham and substance-versus-form tests. A transaction motivated by a business purpose usually is compared to one that has no substance, purpose or utility apart from tax avoidance. As originally formulated by Judge

8. Black & Decker Corp. v. United States, 436 F.3d 431 (4th Cir. 2006); Rice's Toyota World v. Commissioner, supra note 5.

9. See, e.g., ACM Partnership v. Commissioner, 157 F.3d 231 (3d Cir. 1998), cert. denied, 526 U.S. 1017, 119 S.Ct. 1251 (1999); Sacks v. Commissioner, 69 F.3d 982, 985 (9th Cir. 1995).

10. One widely used formulation requires an objective determination of whether a "reasonable possibility of profit" exists or, put differently, finds no economic substance if there is no reasonable expectation of a pre-tax profit for the transaction under scrutiny. See, e.g,. Dow Chemical Co. v. United States, 435 F.3d 594 (6th Cir. 2006); Rice's Toyota World v. Commissioner, supra note 5.

11. See, e.g., Frank Lyon Co. v. United States, 435 U.S. 561, 98 S.Ct. 1291 (1978).

12. See, e.g., Esmark, Inc. v. Commissioner, 90 T.C. 171 (1988), affirmed, 886 F.2d 1318 (7th Cir.1989). See also United Parcel Service of America, Inc. v. Commissioner, 254 F.3d 1014 (11th Cir.2001), rev'g 78 T.C.M. (CCH) 262 (1999).

Learned Hand,[13] the business purpose doctrine was applied to deny tax-free status to a transaction that would not have been consummated but for the tax savings that would result if its form were respected. The doctrine took hold and has become an independent requirement for tax recognition of many transactions.[14]

Codification of Judicial Doctrines. As the courts struggle over how to apply these case law principles, proposals to codify the economic substance doctrine have become an annual ritual in Congress. Advocates of codification believe it would be desirable to settle on a consistent formulation for the courts to apply and to buttress the doctrine by imposing penalties for transactions that fail to meet the statutory test. Codification also is attractive because it is a "revenue raiser" that can be used to offset projected losses from other pro-taxpayer provisions when the goal is to enact revenue-neutral tax legislation. Opponents, including the Treasury Department, the IRS and a coalition of practitioners and academics, argue that codification is impractical and would interfere with bona fide business transactions. They believe that the courts have sufficient flexibility under current law to disallow tax benefits in appropriate cases.[15] The codification proposals have been included in final versions of several tax bills passed by the Senate, but they have not yet survived House–Senate conference committees, leaving the courts to grapple with how and when the doctrine should be applied.[16]

Step Transaction Doctrine. When courts apply the step transaction doctrine, they combine (or "step") formally distinct transactions to determine the tax treatment of the single integrated series of events. The doctrine frequently is applied in conjunction with the other judicial tests.

The courts disagree on the standard to be employed in applying the step transaction doctrine. Some require a binding legal commitment to complete all the steps from the outset before combining them, while others require only a "mutual interdependence" of steps or a preconceived intent to reach a particular end result.[17]

13. See Helvering v. Gregory, 69 F.2d 809 (2d Cir.1934).

14. See, e.g., Reg. § 1.355–2(b), requiring a corporate business purpose to qualify as a tax-free corporate division under Section 355; Reg. § 1.701–2(a), providing that business purpose is implicit in the intent of Subchapter K.

15. For academic commentary pro and con, see Bankman, "The Economic Substance Doctrine," 74 S.Cal. L. Rev. 5 (2000); Wolfman, "Why Economic Substance is Better Left Uncodified," 104 Tax Notes 445 (July 26, 2004); Thompson, "Despite Widespread Opposition, Congress Should Codify the ESD," 110 Tax Notes 781 (Feb. 13, 2006); Aprill, Tax Shelters, Tax Law, and Morality: Codifying Judicial Doctrines, 54 SMU L. Rev. 9 (2001); Bank, "Codifying Judicial Doctrines: No Cure for Rules But More Rules?," 54 SMU L. Rev. 37 (2001). For a practitioner's view, see Canellos, "A Tax Practitioner's Perspective on Substance, Form and Business Purpose in Structuring Business Transactions and in Tax Shelters," 54 SMU L. Rev. 47 (2001).

16. For more extended coverage of the judicial doctrines and the codification proposals in the context of corporate tax shelters, see Chapter 10D, infra.

17. This doctrine is analyzed in some detail in connection with corporate liquidations and corporate reorganizations. See,

The meaning and scope of all this common law tax jurisprudence has befuddled (and yet challenged) tax advisors for decades. Our goal here is to identify the principal terminology and give fair warning that literal compliance with the Code may not be enough for a transaction to pass muster. Students should not expect to master a precise or consistent explanation of the judicial doctrines. It will be enough simply to develop a sense of smell for the kinds of cases in which the doctrines might be invoked.[18]

2. Partnership Anti-Abuse Regulations

The history of business enterprise taxation is replete with skirmishes between taxpayers and their advisers on one side, and the government on the other. The goal of the taxpayers is simple enough. They want to reduce their tax liability to the greatest extent possible. Their advisers often pursue that objective by craftily constructing transactions that "push the envelope" in order to achieve optimum tax results. The government typically responds by asserting its interpretation of the Code or by advocating a "common law" principle in an effort to upset the taxpayers' plans. If all else fails, the government may raise a cry of "loophole" and seek the assistance of Congress by amending the Code.

The Internal Revenue Service has also begun to attack aberrant taxpayer behavior through enactment of "anti-abuse" regulations. Subchapter K has been a particular focus of this regulatory effort.[1] In general, each anti-abuse regulation authorizes the Service to recast transactions, as appropriate, in order to achieve tax results that are consistent with the intent of a particular Code provision.

The most ambitious of the anti-abuse regulations is Section 1.701–2, which contains two main provisions. The first allows the Service to recast a transaction as appropriate to achieve tax results that are consistent with Subchapter K.[2] Those rules invoke the principles of business purpose, substance over form, and clear reflection of income from Section 482.[3] An all facts and circumstances test is also employed to determine whether a partnership is formed or availed of to reduce tax liability in a manner inconsistent with Subchapter K.[4] The second anti-abuse rule permits the Service to disregard the partnership entity and treat it as an aggregate of the partners when that approach is appropriate to carry out the purposes of any Code provision or the regulations.[5]

e.g., Commissioner v. Court Holding Co., infra p. 663.

18. For an analysis of the state of the judicial doctrines, see McMahon, "Random Thoughts on Applying Judicial Doctrines to Interpret the Internal Revenue Code," 54 SMU L. Rev. 195 (2001).

1. See Reg. §§ 1.701–2, 1.704–4(f), 1.737–4. The partnership anti-abuse rules are analyzed in Gunn, "The Use and Misuse of Antiabuse Rules: Lessons from the Partnership Antiabuse Regulations," 54 SMU L. Rev. 159 (2001).

2. Reg. § 1.701–2(a)–(c).

3. Reg. § 1.701–2(a).

4. Reg. § 1.701–2(c).

5. Reg. § 1.701–2(e).

The partnership anti-abuse rules are illustrated by several examples. The examples generally assume the reader has advanced knowledge of the workings of Subchapter K. It is sufficient to note here that the examples are fact specific and hedged by the caveat that they "do not delineate the boundaries of either permissible or impermissible types of transactions."[6] Thus, a tax adviser who becomes too adventurous in Subchapter K does so at the peril of running afoul of the anti-abuse regulations.

6. Reg. § 1.701–2(d).

*

PART TWO

PARTNERSHIPS

CHAPTER 2

FORMATION OF A PARTNERSHIP

A. CONTRIBUTIONS OF PROPERTY

1. GENERAL RULES

Code: §§ 721; 722; 723. Skim §§ 453B(a), (b); 704(c)(1)(A); 724; 1223(1) & (2); 1245(b)(3).

Regulations: §§ 1.453–9(c)(2); 1.721–1; 1.722–1; 1.723–1; 1.1223–3(a), (b)(1).

Although the study of Subchapter K may become a "distressingly complex and confusing" enterprise,[1] it begins with a reassuring review of the fundamental tax concept of nonrecognition. Under general principles of Section 1001(a), a partner who contributes property to a newly formed partnership in exchange for a partnership interest would appear to *realize* gain or loss in an amount equal to the difference between the fair market value of the partnership interest and the adjusted basis of the transferred property.[2] But Section 721(a) comes to the rescue in a manner closely paralleling Section 351, its corporate tax counterpart, by providing that no gain or loss shall be *recognized* to a partnership or to any of its partners on a "contribution of property to the partnership in exchange for an interest in the partnership."[3] The rationale for nonrecognition is familiar. The transfer of property to a partnership is considered to be a mere change in the form of the partner's investment and is viewed as a business transaction that should not be impeded by the imposition of a tax. The general rule of Section 721, equally applicable whether the contribution is to a newly formed or preexisting partnership, is accompanied by the usual corollary provisions governing basis and holding period.[4]

1. See Judge Arnold Raum's gloomy appraisal of Subchapter K in Foxman v. Commissioner, 41 T.C. 535, 551 note 9 (1964), affirmed, 352 F.2d 466 (3d Cir.1965).

2. But see Helvering v. Walbridge, 70 F.2d 683 (2d Cir.1934), cert. denied, 293 U.S. 594, 55 S.Ct. 109 (1934), which held even prior to the enactment of Section 721, that a transfer of property to a partnership was not a taxable event.

3. This general nonrecognition rule is subject to a narrow exception in Section 721(b), which provides for recognition of gain when a partner transfers property to a "partnership which would be treated as an investment company (within the meaning of Section 351) if the partnership were incorporated." See Section 351(e)(1) and Reg. § 1.351–1(c) for the definition of "investment company." This exception is designed to preclude the tax-free diversification of a portfolio by a group of taxpayers through the transfer of appreciated securities and certain other investment assets to a partnership.

4. Compare I.R.C. §§ 721, 722 and 723 with I.R.C. §§ 351, 1032(a), 358 & 362(a), and see I.R.C. § 1223(1) & (2).

The principal requirement for nonrecognition under Section 721 is that "property" must be contributed in exchange for an interest in the partnership. Since there is no statutory definition of property, the courts have been guided by analogous interpretations under Section 351, which provides for nonrecognition treatment on the transfer of property to a controlled corporation in exchange for stock. For purposes of both sections, the term is broadly defined to embrace money, goodwill, and even intangible service-flavored assets such as accounts receivable, patents, unpatented technical know-how and favorable loan or lease commitments embodied in a letter of intent secured through the efforts of the contributing partner.[5] But "property" does not include services rendered to the partnership,[6] and a partner who receives a partnership interest in exchange for services generally realizes ordinary income under Section 61.[7] While Section 721 and Section 351 are similar in many respects, the analogy is not perfect. Unlike Section 351, Section 721 does not require the transferors of property to be in "control" of the partnership immediately after the exchange.

If Section 721 applies to a transfer, any gain or loss realized by the partner is not currently recognized, but several related sections preserve to the contributing partner the amount and sometimes the character of any gain or loss inherent in the contributed property. The amount of gain initially is preserved by Section 723, which provides that the partner's basis in the contributed property is transferred to the partnership.[8] Section 1223(2) similarly provides that the partner's holding period in the property carries over to the partnership. The precontribution character of the contributed property sometimes is preserved by Section 724, which provides that, in certain situations, the partnership will recognize the same character of gain or loss that the contributing partner would have recognized on a sale of the property. Finally, Section 704(c)(1) generally prevents the precontribution gain or loss from being shifted to the other partners by requiring the partnership to allocate that gain or loss solely to the contributing partner when it subsequently disposes of the property or distributes it to another partner.[9]

5. For examples of this breadth, see Hempt Brothers, Inc. v. United States, 490 F.2d 1172 (3d Cir.1974), cert. denied, 419 U.S. 826, 95 S.Ct. 44 (1974) (a Section 351 case involving accounts receivable); United States v. Stafford, 727 F.2d 1043 (11th Cir. 1984) (a legally unenforceable "letter of intent" arranged by a developer to finance the construction of a hotel); and United States v. Frazell, 335 F.2d 487 (5th Cir.1964), rehearing denied, 339 F.2d 885 (5th Cir.1964), cert. denied, 380 U.S. 961, 85 S.Ct. 1104 (1965) (geophysical maps created by the personal efforts of the taxpayer).

6. See Reg. § 1.721–1(b)(1) and compare I.R.C. § 351(d)(1).

7. The timing of the income is governed by Section 83. These issues are discussed in Section C of this chapter.

8. See I.R.C. § 7701(a)(43)–(44) for the appropriate basis terminology ("transferred basis" and "exchanged basis"). The transferred basis is increased by any gain recognized by the partner on the transfer under Section 721(b).

9. Sections 724 and 704(c), both of which govern the tax consequences on a subsequent sale or distribution of the property, are discussed in Chapter 4C, infra.

To complete the statutory scheme, Section 722 provides that a partner's basis in his partnership interest is equal to the sum of the cash and adjusted basis of any property contributed to the partnership.[10] This ensures that the contributing partner may not avoid recognizing the gain that went unrecognized on the contribution by selling his interest before the partnership disposes of the contributed property. The partner's holding period in the partnership interest is determined by Section 1223(1), which permits the partner to tack his holding period for the contributed property if that property was a capital or Section 1231 asset. To the extent the contributed property consists of cash or ordinary income assets, the holding period begins on the date of the exchange. If a partner contributes a mix of assets (e.g., cash plus capital, Section 1231, and ordinary income assets), the holding period in the partnership interest is fragmented in proportion to the fair market value of the portion of the interest received for the property to which the holding period relates, divided by the fair market value of the entire interest.[11] For this purpose, recapture gain (e.g., under Section 1245) is treated as a separate asset which is not a capital or Section 1231 asset.[12]

A partner's basis in his partnership interest is commonly referred to as the "outside basis" and the partnership's basis in its assets is known as the "inside basis." These terms will be used throughout this book as shorthand references to distinguish the two concepts, which play an important role in the taxation of partnerships and partners.

The following Revenue Ruling illustrates the operation of the Code's general rules for determining the tax consequences of a contribution of property to a partnership.

Revenue Ruling 99–5

1999–1 Cum. Bull. 434.

ISSUE

What are the federal income tax consequences when a single member domestic limited liability company (LLC) that is disregarded for federal tax purposes as an entity separate from its owner under § 301.7701–3 of the Procedure and Administration Regulations becomes an entity with more than one owner that is classified as a partnership for federal tax purposes?

FACTS

In each of the following two situations, an LLC is formed and operates in a state which permits an LLC to have a single owner. Each LLC has a single owner, A, and is disregarded as an entity separate from its owner for federal tax purposes under § 301.7701–3. In both situations, the LLC would not be treated as an investment company (within the meaning of

10. Once again, this basis is increased by any gain recognized by the partner on the transfer under Section 721(b).

11. Reg. §§ 1.1223–3(a)(2), (b)(1).

12. Reg. § 1.1223–3(e).

§ 351) if it were incorporated. All of the assets held by each LLC are capital assets or property described in § 1231. For the sake of simplicity, it is assumed that neither LLC is liable for any indebtedness, nor are the assets of the LLCs subject to any indebtedness.

Situation 1. B, who is not related to A, purchases 50% of A's ownership interest in the LLC for $5,000. A does not contribute any portion of the $5,000 to the LLC. A and B continue to operate the business of the LLC as co-owners of the LLC.

Situation 2. B, who is not related to A, contributes $10,000 to the LLC in exchange for a 50% ownership interest in the LLC. The LLC uses all of the contributed cash in its business. A and B continue to operate the business of the LLC as co-owners of the LLC.

After the sale, in both situations, no entity classification election is made under § 301.7701–3(c) to treat the LLC as an association for federal tax purposes.

LAW AND ANALYSIS

Section 721(a) generally provides that no gain or loss shall be recognized to a partnership or to any of its partners in the case of a contribution of property to the partnership in exchange for an interest in the partnership.

Section 722 provides that the basis of an interest in a partnership acquired by a contribution of property, including money, to the partnership shall be the amount of the money and the adjusted basis of the property to the contributing partner at the time of the contribution increased by the amount (if any) of gain recognized under § 721(b) to the contributing partner at such time.

Section 723 provides that the basis of property contributed to a partnership by a partner shall be the adjusted basis of the property to the contributing partner at the time of the contribution increased by the amount (if any) of gain recognized under § 721(b) to the contributing partner at such time.

Section 1001(a) provides that the gain or loss from the sale or other disposition of property shall be the difference between the amount realized therefrom and the adjusted basis provided in § 1011.

Section 1223(1) provides that, in determining the holding period of a taxpayer who receives property in an exchange, there shall be included the period for which the taxpayer held the property exchanged if the property has the same basis in whole or in part in the taxpayer's hands as the property exchanged, and the property exchanged at the time of the exchange was a capital asset or property described in § 1231.

Section 1223(2) provides that, regardless of how a property is acquired, in determining the holding period of a taxpayer who holds the property, there shall be included the period for which such property was held by any other person if the property has the same basis in whole or in part in the taxpayer's hands as it would have in the hands of such other person.

HOLDING(S)

Situation 1. In this situation, the LLC, which, for federal tax purposes, is disregarded as an entity separate from its owner, is converted to a partnership when the new member, B, purchases an interest in the disregarded entity from the owner, A. B's purchase of 50% of A's ownership interest in the LLC is treated as the purchase of a 50% interest in each of the LLC's assets, which are treated as held directly by A for federal tax purposes. Immediately thereafter, A and B are treated as contributing their respective interests in those assets to a partnership in exchange for ownership interests in the partnership.

Under § 1001, A recognizes gain or loss from the deemed sale of the 50% interest in each asset of the LLC to B.

Under § 721(a), no gain or loss is recognized by A or B as a result of the conversion of the disregarded entity to a partnership.

Under § 722, B's basis in the partnership interest is equal to $5,000, the amount paid by B to A for the assets which B is deemed to contribute to the newly-created partnership. A's basis in the partnership interest is equal to A's basis in A's 50% share of the assets of the LLC.

Under § 723, the basis of the property treated as contributed to the partnership by A and B is the adjusted basis of that property in A's and B's hands immediately after the deemed sale.

Under § 1223(1), A's holding period for the partnership interest received includes A's holding period in the capital assets and property described in § 1231 held by the LLC when it converted from an entity that was disregarded as an entity separate from A to a partnership. B's holding period for the partnership interest begins on the day following the date of B's purchase of the LLC interest from A. See Rev. Rul. 66–7, 1966–1 C.B. 188, which provides that the holding period of a purchased asset is computed by excluding the date on which the asset is acquired. Under § 1223(2), the partnership's holding period for the assets deemed transferred to it includes A's and B's holding periods for such assets.

Situation 2. In this situation, the LLC is converted from an entity that is disregarded as an entity separate from its owner to a partnership when a new member, B, contributes cash to the LLC. B's contribution is treated as a contribution to a partnership in exchange for an ownership interest in the partnership. A is treated as contributing all of the assets of the LLC to the partnership in exchange for a partnership interest.

Under § 721(a), no gain or loss is recognized by A or B as a result of the conversion of the disregarded entity to a partnership.

Under § 722, B's basis in the partnership interest is equal to $10,000, the amount of cash contributed to the partnership. A's basis in the partnership interest is equal to A's basis in the assets of the LLC which A was treated as contributing to the newly-created partnership.

Under § 723, the basis of the property contributed to the partnership by A is the adjusted basis of that property in A's hands. The basis of the property contributed to the partnership by B is $10,000, the amount of cash contributed to the partnership.

Under § 1223(1), A's holding period for the partnership interest received includes A's holding period in the capital and § 1231 assets deemed contributed when the disregarded entity converted to a partnership. B's holding period for the partnership interest begins on the day following the date of B's contribution of money to the LLC. Under § 1223(2), the partnership's holding period for the assets transferred to it includes A's holding period.

NOTE

A partnership may acquire the capital it uses in its business ventures in a variety of ways. The simplest and most direct way is for the partners to contribute property in exchange for their partnership interests. In more complex transactions, the partnership may issue options that allow the holder to purchase an equity interest in the partnership. Similarly, a partnership may borrow funds in exchange for convertible debt that allows the holder to acquire an equity interest in the partnership through the instrument's conversion feature. How should Section 721 apply in these more complex transactions?

The Service has issued proposed regulations that govern the tax consequences of "noncompensatory" options to acquire a partnership interest—i.e., an option that is not issued in connection with the performance of services.[1] A noncompensatory option includes a call option or warrant to acquire a partnership interest, the conversion feature in a partnership debt instrument, and the conversion feature in a preferred equity interest in a partnership.[2] Under the regulations, Section 721 does not apply to the transfer of property to a partnership in exchange for a noncompensatory option, but it does apply to the exercise of the option.[3] For example, assume an individual transfers property with a basis of $600 and a fair market value of $1,000 to a partnership in exchange for an option to buy a one-third partnership interest for $5,000 at any time during the next three years. On the transfer for the option, the individual recognizes $400 of gain. If the individual later exercises the option by transferring property with a $3,000 basis and $5,000 fair market value to the partnership for a partnership interest, that transfer is protected by Section 721. The proposed regulations permit the partnership to use open transaction principles

1. Prop. Reg. § 1.721–2(d).

2. Prop. Reg. § 1.721–2(e)(1). For an extensive analysis of the proposed regulations, see Larvick, "Noncompensatory Partnership Options: The Proposed Regulations," 99 Tax Notes 271 (April 14, 2003).

3. Prop. Reg. § 1.721–2(a) & (b).

on the transfer of property for the option so it generally does not recognize any income until the option is exercised or lapses and it takes a $1,000 basis in the property transferred for the option. Under Section 723 the partnership has a $3,000 basis in the property contributed for the partnership interest.[4] Section 721 does not apply to the lapse of a noncompensatory option.[5]

Generally, an individual holding a noncompensatory option to acquire a partnership interest is not treated as a partner for purposes of allocating partnership income but if the option provides the holder with rights substantially similar to the rights afforded a partner, then the option holder is treated as a partner in allocating income.[6]

PROBLEM

A, B, C and D (all individuals) form a general partnership in which they each have an equal interest in capital and profits. All the partners and the partnership are cash method taxpayers. In exchange for their respective partnership interests, each partner transfers the following assets, all of which have been held more than two years:

Partner	Asset	Adjusted Basis	Fair Mkt. Value
A	Land	$ 30,000	$ 70,000
	Goodwill	0	30,000
B	Equipment (all § 1245 gain)	25,000	45,000
	Installment note from the sale of land	20,000	25,000
	Inventory	5,000	30,000
C	Building	25,000	60,000
	Land	25,000	10,000
	Receivables for services rendered to E	0	30,000
D	Cash	100,000	100,000

(a) What are the tax consequences (consider only gain or loss realized and recognized, basis and holding period) to each of the partners?

(b) What are the tax consequences (consider only gain recognized, basis and holding period) to the partnership?

4. This example is Prop. Reg. § 1.721–2(f) Example.

5. Prop. Reg. § 1.721–2(c). Thus, if the option in the example lapsed without being exercised, the partnership would have $1,000 of gross income and the individual would be entitled to a $1,000 loss deduction.

6. Prop. Reg. 1.761–3(a). Special rules also apply to capital account adjustments and allocations on the exercise of a noncompensatory option. Prop. Reg. §§ 1.704–1(b)(2)(iv)*(d)(4)*, 1.704–1(b)(2)(iv)*(s)*; see Prop. Reg. 1.704–1(b)(5) Examples 20–24. These rules are designed to account for any shifts in capital that result from the exercise of noncompensatory options.

(c) Although each of the partners contributes property of equal value, D transfers only cash while the other partners transfer property. Section 704(c)(1)(A) requires the partnership to allocate the precontribution gain or loss solely to the contributing partner when the partnership subsequently disposes of the property. What is the objective of that section? See also § 724.

2. INTRODUCTION TO PARTNERSHIP ACCOUNTING

Regulations: § 1.704–1(b)(2)(iv)(*b*)–(*d*), (*f*), (*h*).

The partners' interests in the assets of the partnership, their responsibility for partnership liabilities, and their respective rights to profits and losses and to operating and liquidating distributions, are determined by the partnership agreement. The financial condition of a partnership on formation and each partner's ownership interest in the firm are depicted on an opening day "balance sheet" which lists the partnership's assets on the left side and the liabilities and partners' capital on the right side. Under the venerable accounting principle known as the "Fundamental Equation," the two sides always must be equal—that is, Assets = Liabilities + Net Worth. This makes sense because the partners' equity interest necessarily equates with the net worth of the partnership which in turn is the difference between the partnership's assets and its liabilities. Because this text often presents problems (or asks for answers) in the form of a partnership balance sheet, a basic introduction to partnership accounting is in order.

Assume that Alison ("A"), Bill ("B") and Carol ("C") join forces and agree to do business as the ABC Partnership. A contributes securities worth $60,000, B contributes land worth $30,000 and C contributes $10,000 cash. At the inception of the business, the ABC Partnership balance sheet is as follows:

Assets		**Liabilities and Partners' Capital**	
Cash	$ 10,000	Liabilities:	
Securities	60,000	None	
Land	30,000	Capital:	
		A	$ 60,000
		B	30,000
		C	10,000
Total	$100,000		$100,000

Some elaboration is necessary. On the left side of the balance sheet, partnership assets are recorded at their "book value," which is sometimes called "historical cost." During the life of the partnership, book value is not necessarily the same as fair market value and, in some cases, it may differ from the tax basis of the asset. But book value is considered to be a more reliable figure for balance sheet purposes, and it will not change until some event occurs that warrants a revaluation of the partnership's assets.

Moving to the right side, each partner's interest in partnership assets is reflected on the balance sheet by what is known in accounting lexicon as the partner's "capital account." The capital account represents a partner's equity in the firm. At any point in time during the life of a partnership, it generally identifies what each partner would be entitled to receive upon liquidation of his or her interest in the partnership.[1] A partner's capital account begins with the amount of money and the fair market value of any property contributed to the partnership by the partner, is increased by the partner's share of the profits of the firm and is decreased by the partner's share of partnership losses and the amount of cash and the fair market value of any property distributed to the partner.[2]

The tax regulations governing partnership allocations provide detailed rules for the maintenance of capital accounts.[3] Capital accounts maintained in accordance with these requirements do not always accurately reflect the current fair market value of a partner's investment. In order to stay in balance with the asset side of the balance sheet, capital accounts must track the historical cost of assets as reported on the partnership's books; thus, they ordinarily do not take into account the appreciation or decline in value of partnership property until that gain or loss has been realized and recognized.[4]

The intrusion of tax concepts adds some complications to partnership accounting. Because the tax consequences of any disposition of property depend, in part, on the tax basis of that property, both the partnership's inside bases in its assets and the partners' outside bases in their partnership interests are important elements in the equation. To keep the example simple, assume that the land contributed by B has a tax basis equal to its value but that A has a $40,000 basis for the contributed securities. The "book/tax"[5] balance sheet of the partnership will be as follows:

1. A partner also may have an interest in partnership assets as a creditor. If so, the value of that interest will not be reflected in the partner's capital account. Rather, partner loans will be reflected as such on the partnership's books as a liability, along with the interests of the partnership's other creditors. Under the Uniform Partnership Act, debts to partners have a lower priority than debts to third party creditors if a partnership's assets are insufficient to discharge all of its liabilities. Uniform Partnership Act § 40(b).

2. Reg. § 1.704–1(b)(2)(iv)(*b*).

3. Reg. § 1.704–1(b)(2)(iv). See Chapter 4B2, infra.

4. In certain situations a partnership may restate its capital accounts at current value. See Reg. § 1.704–1(b)(2)(iv)(*f*). Moreover, in the case of depreciation or cost depletion, the balance sheet will reflect certain changes in the book value of assets (and corresponding changes to partners' capital accounts) prior to disposition of the asset. These changes are based on cost recovery principles and are not intended to mirror the real life changes in value of depreciable or depletable property.

5. "Book/Tax" balance sheet means a financial statement that shows both the book value of the partnership's assets and the partners' capital accounts and the adjusted bases of those assets as used for tax purposes.

Assets	**A.B.**[6]	**Bk. Val.**	**Liabilities and Partners' Capital**	**A.B.**	**Bk. Val.**
Cash	$ 10,000	$ 10,000	Liabilities:		
Securities	40,000	60,000	None		
Land	30,000	30,000	Capital:		
			A	$ 40,000	$ 60,000
			B	30,000	30,000
			C	10,000	10,000
Total	$ 80,000	$100,000		$ 80,000	$100,000

Now that the ABC Partnership is off and running, the partners will become keenly interested in their share of partnership profits or losses—an amount that we will come to know as a partner's "distributive share."[7] Absent an agreement among the partners, the Uniform Partnership Act provides that profits will be shared equally,[8] but the flexibility of the partnership form allows partners to agree to share profits in any other manner they see fit. Partners frequently will agree to allocate profits in proportion to their respective interests in partnership capital. Other common approaches are to allocate to each partner a specific percentage of the overall profit or to assign a specific number of partnership "units."[9] No particular profit allocation method is required, and allocations in some partnerships may vary over the life of the enterprise.[10] Indeed, for both tax and business reasons, lawyers have concocted more profit sharing formulas than ever could be devised by the human mind (assuming, of course, that the legal community is an altogether different species).[11]

6. On the left side of the balance sheets in the text, "A.B." signifies the partnership's adjusted basis of an asset for tax purposes; on the right side, "A.B." signifies the partner's basis in his partnership interest. See I.R.C. §§ 722; 723.

7. The term "distributive" is somewhat misleading in that it suggests that a distribution may be imminent. Profits may or may not be distributed, depending on the agreement of the partners. For tax and accounting purposes, "distributive" connotes an allocation of the tax burdens and benefits arising from partnership operations which, to be respected for tax purposes, must correspond to the economic burdens and benefits that are reflected on the partners' capital accounts. See I.R.C. § 704(a), (b); Chapter 4B2, infra.

8. Uniform Partnership Act § 18(a).

9. The use of units to represent ownership and, correspondingly, profit sharing ratios, is typical in larger partnerships where the interests of the partners may vary frequently as new partners are admitted and others retire. For example, the profit share of a senior partner in a large law firm may be represented by eight units and a new junior partner may be assigned only two units. This method obviates the need to recalculate profit percentages and simplifies accounting for the entry or departure of partners and for the change in a partner's relative share of the firm. See Siegel & Siegel, Accounting and Financial Disclosure 90 (West, 1983).

10. For example, in more complex limited partnerships, the limited partner investors are often allocated virtually all of the losses and profits during the early years of the venture; but once the investors have recouped their initial contributions, the profit-sharing ratio often "flips" to a more equal division between the promoters (usually general partners) and the investors.

11. Because a partner's capital account represents the partner's equity investment, it would seem that when profits are shared in any manner other than in proportion to the relative capital account balances, any partner with a larger capital account is receiving a smaller percentage return on his investment and thus would be dissatisfied with the allocation. We will see, however, that there are many reasons, both tax and nontax, for "special allocations." See Chapter 4B, infra.

To observe the effects of ABC's operations on its balance sheet, assume that during year one it has a $10,000 net profit from its operations and sells the land for $40,000. Assume further that the partners have agreed to allocate profits according to their capital account balances. The $10,000 operating profit and the $10,000 gain on the sale of the land ($20,000 total income) will be allocated 60 percent ($12,000) to A, 30 percent ($6,000) to B and 10 percent ($2,000) to C. At the end of year one, the balance sheet will look like this:

Assets			**Liabilities and Partners' Capital**		
	A.B.	**Bk. Val.**		**A.B.**	**Bk. Val.**
Cash	$ 60,000	$ 60,000[12]	Liabilities:		
Securities	40,000	60,000	None		
			Capital:		
			A	$ 52,000	$ 72,000
			B	36,000	36,000
			C	12,000	12,000
Total	$100,000	$120,000		$100,000	$120,000

You may have noticed one strikingly unrealistic aspect of the ABC Partnership and therefore its balance sheet. It is devoid of any debt! Many partnerships, of course, need to borrow money to finance operations, either from the partners or outside lenders. To fill this gap in the liability column (and our knowledge of partnership accounting), assume that ABC borrows $30,000 from Bank at the beginning of year two. The bookkeeper will record this transaction by adding $30,000 to the asset side of the balance sheet and placing a corresponding entry on the right side under "Liabilities." The partners' capital accounts are unaffected by the loan,[13] but the bank's right to repayment takes priority over any return of capital to the partners. After the borrowing, ABC's balance sheet will look like this:

Assets			**Liabilities and Partners' Capital**		
	A.B.	**Bk. Val.**		**A.B.**[14]	**Bk. Val.**
Cash	$ 90,000	$ 90,000	Liabilities:		$ 30,000
Securities	40,000	60,000	Capital:		
			A	$ 70,000	$ 72,000
			B	45,000	36,000
			C	15,000	12,000
Total	$130,000	$150,000		$130,000	$150,000

The time will come when the partners wish to withdraw some funds from the business. As with the allocation of profits and losses, the timing

12. This $60,000 of cash represents the original $10,000 cash contributed by C, the $40,000 proceeds from the sale of the land and the $10,000 of net profits earned during year one.

13. As we will see later in this chapter, however, each partner's *tax* basis in his partnership interest is increased by the partner's share of partnership liabilities on the theory that the partners ultimately will be responsible for paying that debt. I.R.C. § 752(a). The result is that the borrowed funds become an asset ($30,000 cash) having a basis of $30,000 to the partnership, and the resulting liability to repay that cash increases the partners' outside bases by that same amount in a ratio of 6:3:1, or $18,000 to A, $9,000 to B and $3,000 to C.

14. See note 13, supra.

and method of distributions is determined by the partnership agreement. Distributions may be made as profits are earned, before they are earned (in the form of "draws" against anticipated profits), or even in the absence of any profits (e.g., if the partners desire the return of some or all of their invested capital). Alternatively, the partners may elect to defer making any distributions until they dissolve the partnership or liquidate a particular partner's interest. Whatever the format, a distribution will affect the partnership balance sheet, and the distributee partner's capital account must be adjusted to reflect the removal of all or part of his or her investment in the firm.

To illustrate the effect of a distribution, assume that ABC realizes no net income or loss from operations during year two. But with its coffers still awash with cash from the land sale and bank loan, the partners agree to make a distribution of $60,000 in proportion to their respective capital account balances. A thus receives $36,000 (60%), B receives $18,000 (30%) and C receives $6,000 (10%). The balance sheet at the end of year two will then look like this:[15]

Assets			**Liabilities and Partners' Capital**		
	A.B.	**Bk. Val.**		**A.B.**	**Bk. Val.**
Cash	$ 30,000	$ 30,000	Liabilities:		$ 30,000
Securities	40,000	60,000	Capital:		
			A	$ 34,000	$ 36,000
			B	27,000	18,000
			C	9,000	6,000
Total	$ 70,000	$ 90,000		$ 70,000	$ 90,000

At this point, it is worth noting that the value of the securities may have changed from the time they were acquired. The securities nonetheless continue to be shown on the balance sheet at their historical cost ("book value").[16] When the securities are sold and the appreciation (or, in bear markets, the decline in value) is realized, any gain or loss will be reflected on the partnership balance sheet because, of course, the securities will have been converted into cash.

Assume, for example, that the partnership sells the securities for $160,000. Since the securities had appreciated in value between the time they were acquired by A and contributed to the partnership, Section 704(c)(1)(A) requires that the precontribution gain must be allocated solely to the contributing partner when the partnership sells the securities. Thus, the first $20,000 of tax gain will be allocated to A, but A's capital account is not similarly adjusted[17] because the gain is already reflected in the value of

15. Note that the distribution causes the cash to be reduced by $60,000 on the asset side of the balance sheet. The partners' capital accounts are reduced by a corresponding amount. Reg. § 1.704–1(b)(2)(iv)(*b*)(*4*).

16. The partners might wish to present a more accurate picture of the partnership's net worth to potential lenders or outside investors, and they are free to do so for that purpose.

17. See Reg. § 1.704–1(b)(2)(iv)(*b*)(*3*), 1.704–1(b)(2)(iv)(*d*)(*3*), 1.704–1(b)(2)(iv)(*g*).

the securities on the partnership's books and in A's capital account. The $100,000 of postcontribution gain, however, has not yet been reflected in the capital accounts and is allocated to the partners based on their capital account balances, which are increased accordingly.[18] The balance sheet after the sale would look like this:

Assets			**Liabilities and Partners' Capital**		
	A.B.	**Bk. Val.**		**A.B.**	**Bk. Val.**
Cash	$190,000	$190,000	Liabilities:		$ 30,000
			Capital:		
			A	$114,000	$ 96,000
			B	57,000	48,000
			C	19,000	16,000
Total	$190,000	$190,000		$190,000	$190,000

Now assume the sale of securities does not occur and that, instead, a new partner arrives on the scene, or the relative interests of the partners change, or an asset is distributed to one of the partners. For example, assume that at the beginning of year three, the securities again are worth $160,000 and Dan ("D") desires to join the partnership as a 10 percent partner. If the parties simply look at the balance sheet, D might be expected to base his contribution on the $60,000 aggregate book value of the partnership.[19] In fact, however, the partnership has a net worth of $160,000 ($190,000 assets less $30,000 of liabilities) because the securities are worth $100,000 more than their reported book value. In this situation, the partners may wish to readjust their capital accounts to reflect the current economic condition of the partnership.[20] The securities (and any other partnership assets) then would be reflected on the partnership's books at their current fair market value ($160,000 for the securities), and each partner's capital account should be increased by his or her share of the unrealized postcontribution appreciation inherent in the securities.[21] After such a revaluation (and before D is admitted), the balance sheet would be as follows:

18. Reg. § 1.704–1(b)(2)(iv)(*b*)(*3*). Thus, A's capital account is increased by $60,000 to $96,000, B's is increased by $30,000 to $48,000, and C's is increased by $10,000 to $16,000. The partners' outside bases also are increased by their respective shares of tax gain—$80,000 to A, $30,000 to B and $10,000 to C. I.R.C. § 705(a)(1).

19. See the balance sheet accompanying note 15, supra.

20. Such a revaluation is permitted in this situation by the regulations governing partnership allocations. Reg. § 1.704–1(b)(2)(iv)(*f*). It may not be appropriate, however, under conventional accounting principles.

21. Similar adjustments are permitted if one or more existing partners changes his or her percentage interest in the partnership or if an asset is distributed to one of the partners. See, e.g., Reg. § 1.704–1(b)(2)(iv)(*e*)(*1*).

Assets			**Liabilities and Partners' Capital**		
	A.B.	**Bk. Val.**		**A.B.**	**Bk. Val.**
Cash	$ 30,000	$ 30,000	Liabilities:		$ 30,000
Securities	40,000	160,000	Capital:		
			A	$ 34,000	$ 96,000
			B	27,000	48,000
			C	9,000	16,000
Total	$ 70,000	$190,000		$ 70,000	$190,000

Finally, what happens when a partnership dissolves? Moving back to the original ABC partnership, assume that at the beginning of year three, the partnership sells the securities for $160,000, repays its $30,000 bank loan and liquidates. The $120,000 gain on the sale will be allocated to the partners in accordance with Section 704(c) and their interests in partnership profits and capital: $80,000 to A, $30,000 to B and $10,000 to C.[22] Immediately prior to the liquidation, the partnership balance sheet will look like this:

Assets			**Liabilities and Partners' Capital**		
	A.B.	**Bk. Val.**		**A.B.**	**Bk. Val.**
Cash	$160,000	$160,000	Liabilities:		
			None		
			Capital:		
			A	$ 96,000[23]	$ 96,000
			B	48,000	48,000
			C	16,000	16,000
Total	$160,000	$160,000		$160,000	$160,000

Liquidating distributions of cash then will be made in accordance with the partners' final capital accounts.

PROBLEM

A, B and C are equal general partners in the ABC Partnership. On formation of the partnership, A contributes $50,000 cash, B contributes land (Parcel #1) with a basis of $40,000 and a fair market value of $50,000, and C contributes securities with a basis and fair market value of $50,000. Prepare the partnership's opening balance sheet and then reconstruct the balance sheet to account for each of the following (cumulative) subsequent events:

(a) The partnership leases Parcel #1 for $15,000 and sells the securities for $50,000.

(b) The partnership borrows $300,000 and then buys more land (Parcel #2) for $330,000.

(c) The partnership distributes $20,000 each to A, B and C.

22. See notes 17 and 18, supra.

23. This figure represents A's adjusted basis of $34,000 at the beginning of year three decreased by his $18,000 (i.e., 60%) share of the liabilities (see I.R.C. §§ 752(b) and 733) and increased by his $80,000 share of the gain on the securities. Similar adjustments are made for B and C.

(d) The partnership sells Parcel #1 for $65,000.

(e) When Parcel #2 has a value of $420,000, the assets and capital accounts are restated to current value, and new partner D contributes $70,000 cash to the partnership in exchange for a 25% general partnership interest.

B. Treatment of Liabilities: The Basics

1. Impact of Liabilities on Partner's Outside Basis

Code: § 752(a)–(c). Skim §§ 705(a); 722; 733.

Regulations: § 1.752–1(a)(1), (2), & (4), (b), (c); –2(a), (b); –3(a).

The general rules discussed in the preceding section closely parallel nonrecognition principles that recur throughout the study of the income tax. But they presuppose a world without debt—a fiscal utopia that has yet to be achieved. In reality, leverage pervades the partnership world, and many partnership formations involve the borrowing of money by the partnership or the contribution of encumbered property by a partner. These liabilities have a significant impact on a partner's outside basis.[1] Moreover, when property subject to a liability is transferred to a partnership or when a partnership incurs or pays off a liability, a mechanism must be found to allocate the liability among the partners and reflect that allocation in each partner's outside basis.

The solution adopted by Subchapter K to the treatment of partnership liabilities is intricate and requires an understanding of an amalgam of Code sections and complex regulations.[2] For these reasons, a detailed study of this topic is deferred until later in the text.[3] This early discussion will be confined to an overview of the general principles that relate to partnership formations. The starting point is Section 752, a broad provision that governs the treatment of partnership liabilities in many different contexts, including formations.[4] Section 752(a) treats any increase in a partner's share of partnership liabilities as if it were a cash contribution by the partner to the partnership, increasing the partner's outside basis under Section 722. Section 752(b) treats any decrease in a partner's share of liabilities, including the partnership's assumption of a partner's liability, as if it were a cash distribution to the partner, decreasing his outside basis under Sections 705(a) and 733. For purposes of Section 752, liabilities that would be deductible when paid (e.g., accounts payable of a cash basis

1. The outside basis is significant because, among other functions, it limits the amount of partnership losses which may be deducted by a partner and is used in determining the amount of gain or loss recognized by a partner on the receipt of certain partnership distributions and on the sale or liquidation of a partnership interest.

2. See Reg. § 1.752–2,–3.

3. See Chapter 4D, infra.

4. Section 752 applies, for example, when a partnership incurs or pays off a liability, distributes property subject to a liability, admits a new partner, or distributes property in liquidation of a partner's interest.

taxpayer) are disregarded.[5] This is consistent with the treatment of deductible liabilities in the corporate formation context under Section 357(c)(3)(A) and for purposes of cancellation of indebtedness under Section 108(e).

These rules are consistent with the teachings of the celebrated *Crane* case.[6] Under *Crane*, taxpayers who acquire property subject to a debt, whether or not there is personal liability, include the amount of the debt in their cost basis, just as if they had paid cash, on the assumption that the loan ultimately will be paid. Taxpayers who sell encumbered property must include the debt relief in the amount realized, just as if they had received additional cash. For the same reasons, a partner's outside basis includes his share of a partnership's liabilities on the assumption that the debt will be satisfied in due course and, similarly, the partner is treated as receiving the equivalent of cash when a partnership liability is extinguished. Also in keeping with *Crane*, Section 752(c) provides that a liability to which property is subject shall be treated as a liability of the owner, at least to the extent of the fair market value of the property.[7]

A partner's share of partnership liabilities for purposes of Section 752 generally depends on the status of the partner (general or limited) and the nature of the liability (recourse or nonrecourse). A partnership liability is a recourse liability to the extent that any partner bears the economic risk of loss for the liability.[8] If no partner bears the economic risk of loss, the liability is classified as nonrecourse.[9]

A partner's share of recourse liabilities equals the portion of the liability for which the partner bears the economic risk of loss.[10] A partner bears the economic risk of loss to the extent that the partner (or a person related to the partner) would be required to pay the liability if the partnership were unable to do so. This determination is made by asking who would be obligated to pay the liability if all of the partnership's liabilities are payable in full and all of the partnership's assets, including cash, are worthless.[11] Statutory and contractual obligations relating to the partnership liability, such as guarantees, obligations to restore a deficit capital account balance or obligations imposed by state law, are taken into account in deciding who bears the economic risk of loss.[12] Under these principles, equal partners in a general partnership ordinarily will share the economic risk of loss for a partnership recourse debt equally because that is

5. Reg. § 1.752–1(a)(4); see Rev.Rul. 88–77, 1988–2 C.B. 128.

6. Crane v. Commissioner, 331 U.S. 1, 67 S.Ct. 1047 (1947).

7. The fair market value limitation in Section 752(c) applies only to contributions to and distributions from a partnership. On the sale of a partnership interest, nonrecourse liabilities are included in the amount realized even if they exceed the fair market value of the property. See I.R.C. § 752(d); Commissioner v. Tufts, 461 U.S. 300, 103 S.Ct. 1826 (1983), rehearing denied, 463 U.S. 1215, 103 S.Ct. 3555 (1983).

8. Reg. § 1.752–1(a)(1).

9. Reg. § 1.752–1(a)(2).

10. Reg. § 1.752–2(a).

11. Reg. § 1.752–2(b)(1).

12. Reg. § 1.752–2(b)(3). The methodology employed by the regulations to determine who bears the economic risk of loss for a recourse liability is discussed in more detail in Chapter 4D, infra.

how they share the economic burden to pay the debt under state law. Since a limited partner ordinarily bears no risk of loss beyond his original capital contributions to the partnership and any additional contributions that he is committed to make under the partnership agreement, a limited partner's share of recourse liabilities generally may not exceed the amount which he is obligated to contribute to the partnership in the future.[13]

In the case of nonrecourse partnership liabilities, none of the partners has any personal liability. Since general and limited partners all enjoy limited liability with respect to nonrecourse debts, those liabilities generally are allocated among the partners in accordance with each partner's share of partnership profits rather than losses.[14]

PROBLEM

A, B, C and D each contribute $25,000 to the ABCD partnership, which then acquires a $1,000,000 building, paying $100,000 cash and borrowing $900,000 on a nonrecourse basis.

(a) If the parties are equal general partners, what is each partner's outside basis?

(b) What result if the partnership is a limited partnership, A is the sole general partner and all the partners share profits and losses equally?

(c) What result in (b), above, if the partnership were personally liable for the debt?

2. Contributions of Encumbered Property

Code: §§ 704(c)(1)(A); 731(a)(1); 752(a)–(c). Skim §§ 705(a); 722; 733; 734(b)(1)(A).

Regulations: § 1.752–1(b), (c) and (f); –2(a), (b); –3(a).

General Rules. Additional sections of the Code come into play in determining the tax consequences of a contribution of encumbered property to a partnership. The regulations under Section 722, incorporating the approach taken by Section 752, recharacterize such a contribution as a cash transaction.[1] To the extent that a contributing partner is relieved of a liability, he is treated as having received a distribution of cash from the partnership. This constructive distribution in turn triggers the rules governing operating distributions by a partnership.[2] Under Sections 731 and 733, a distribution of cash is considered a return of capital, which reduces the partner's outside basis (but not below zero) by the amount of the distribution. The portion of the debt from which the contributing partner is

13. Reg. § 1.752–2(b)(3)(ii).

14. Reg. § 1.752–3(a).

1. Reg. § 1.722–1; See Reg. § 1.752–1(b) and (c).

2. See I.R.C. §§ 731–734. These rules will be covered in depth in Chapter 7, infra.

relieved is then allocated to the other partners, who are considered to have contributed cash to the partnership, and the outside basis of each is increased accordingly. Section 752 works with the basic rules of Section 722 and the operating distribution provisions to reallocate the liabilities among the partners and properly adjust each partner's outside basis.

Recourse Liabilities: In General. The operation of these general rules is best illustrated by an example where the contributed property is encumbered by a recourse liability. Assume that Partner A contributes a parcel of land with a fair market value of $150,000, an adjusted basis of $50,000, and encumbered by a recourse mortgage of $30,000 in exchange for a 50 percent interest in the newly formed AB general partnership. B, the other partner, contributes $120,000 in cash. The partnership has a net worth of $240,000 and the value of each partner's interest is $120,000. If the partnership assumes the mortgage, A and B, as equal general partners, are each considered to bear the risk of loss for $15,000 of the $30,000 liability transferred by A.[3] A thus is considered to have $15,000 of debt relief and, under Section 752(b), is treated as receiving a $15,000 cash distribution from the partnership. A's outside basis would then be determined as follows:

Adjusted basis of parcel contributed by A	$ 50,000
Less: Portion of liability treated under § 752(b) as cash distribution to A (½ of $30,000)	(15,000)
Equals: A's outside basis	$ 35,000

B's outside basis would be determined as follows:

Cash contributed by B	$120,000
Plus: Portion of liability allocated to B and treated under § 752(a) as a cash contribution by B (½ of $30,000)	15,000
Equals: B's outside basis	$135,000

Recourse Liabilities in Excess of Basis. The plot thickens, however, if we assume the same facts except that the adjusted basis of the parcel contributed by A is $10,000 instead of $50,000 and the liability is recourse. A's outside basis under Section 722 initially is $10,000, the adjusted basis of the parcel. A's outside basis is then decreased (and B's is increased) by the net amount of debt that is allocated away from A and over to B.[4] Thus, $15,000 of the liability is reallocated from A to B,[5] and A is deemed to receive a constructive cash distribution of $15,000 (the net amount of the recourse debt that is allocated to B). A's outside basis under Section 722

3. Reg. § 1.752–2(b)(3)(iii). The example in the text assumes that A does not remain personally liable to the creditor. If A does remain personally liable, then B does not bear the economic risk of loss under state law.

4. See Reg. § 1.752–1(f).

5. In effect, A is relieved of $30,000 of debt and assumes as a general partner $15,000 of partnership debt, resulting in a net reduction of $15,000. See Reg. § 1.752–1(f).

initially is $10,000, the adjusted basis of the parcel. It then would appear to be reduced by the $15,000 constructive distribution, seemingly yielding the impossible—a $5,000 negative basis. Section 733 precludes this tax taboo by providing that a distribution may not reduce a partner's basis below zero, and Section 731(a)(1) balances the books by treating the excess of the constructive cash distribution over A's outside basis as gain from the sale or exchange of A's newly acquired partnership interest.[6] This gain is treated as capital gain under Section 741.[7]

Returning to the example, A thus would recognize $5,000 of capital gain on the constructive cash distribution of $15,000. A's outside basis would be determined as follows:

Adjusted basis of parcel (§ 722)	$10,000
Less: Portion of liability treated as cash distribution to A (½ of $30,000)	(15,000)
Equals: A's outside basis (may not be less than zero under § 733)	–0–

Keep in mind that any gain recognized because of the contribution of property with recourse liabilities in excess of basis results from the constructive cash distribution from the partnership—not from the contribution of property by the partner.[8] This point is significant in light of the language in both Sections 722 and 723 permitting an increase in basis "by the amount (if any) of gain recognized under Section 721(b) to the contributing partner *at such time*" (emphasis added). The clause "at such time" refers to the time of the contribution as distinguished from the time of the subsequent hypothetical cash distribution. Consequently, neither Partner A nor the AB Partnership in the example above is entitled to a basis increase for the $5,000 of gain recognized under Section 731.[9] An increase to outside and inside bases under Sections 722 and 723 is only allowed in the narrow situation where a partner recognizes gain under Section 721(b) on a

6. See Reg. § 1.722–1 Example (2). This also is the result when a partner receives actual cash distributions in excess of his outside basis. This example predates the Section 752 regulations and does not accurately illustrate how partners share nonrecourse liabilities. See notes 16–20, infra, and accompanying text.

7. I.R.C. § 731(a), flush language. Reg. § 1.731–1(a)(3). Gain from the sale or exchange of a partnership interest generally is treated as capital gain under Section 741 except to the extent that the amount realized is attributable to certain ordinary income assets (known as "Section 751 assets"). See I.R.C. § 751 and Chapter 6A, infra. In addition, Section 751(b) treats certain distributions of partnership property (including cash) in exchange for Section 751 property as a transaction resulting in ordinary income to the partner. See Chapter 7E, infra. Detailed consideration of these concepts is premature, other than to note that these rules appear not to apply to any Section 731(a)(1) gain recognized on the contribution of encumbered property to a partnership by a new partner. See McKee, Nelson & Whitmire, Federal Taxation of Partnerships and Partners ¶ 4.03[3] at note 111 (4th ed. 2007). Cf. Rev.Rul. 84–102, 1984–2 C.B. 119.

8. But see Reg. § 1.1245–4(c)(4) Example (3), which inappropriately treats the gain as arising from a contribution of the property rather than a constructive distribution of cash by the partnership.

9. See Rev.Rul. 84–15, 1984–1 C.B. 158.

contribution of an asset to a partnership that would be treated as an "investment company" within the meaning of Section 351 if the partnership were incorporated.[10]

Nonrecourse Liabilities: In General. In the basic example above, A contributes a parcel of land with a fair market value of $150,000, an adjusted basis of $50,000, and the property is encumbered by a $30,000 mortgage. In exchange for the property, A receives a 50 percent interest in the partnership. Assume now that the mortgage is a nonrecourse liability. Determining how the $30,000 debt is allocated in this case begins with the general principle that nonrecourse liabilities are allocated among the partners in proportion to their respective shares of partnership profits.[11] In the case of contributed property, however, the determination of the partners' profit-sharing ratios may become more complex.

Recall that when a partner contributes appreciated property to a partnership, precontribution gain is allocated to the contributing partner under section 704(c)(1)(A) to the extent it is realized by the partnership on a subsequent disposition. One difficulty in determining how future profits of the partnership will be shared is that it is impossible to know whether any of the potential built-in gain in the contributed property will ever be recognized. For example, if the parcel of land is only worth $30,000 when it is sold by the partnership, the result would be a $20,000 loss.[12] Perhaps because of this uncertainty, the regulations give partners a great deal of flexibility to determine their share of profits for purposes of allocating nonrecourse liabilities. Under the regulations, a partner's interest in partnership profits is determined by taking into account all facts and circumstances relating to the economic arrangement of the partners.[13] The partnership agreement for sharing profits and the partner's share of built-in gain in partnership property are factors to be considered in determining the partners' interests in profits.[14] The regulations also allow the partners to specify their interests in partnership profits for purposes of allocating nonrecourse liabilities, and those interests will be respected if they are reasonably consistent with allocations of other significant items of partnership income or gain that are respected for tax purposes.[15] Thus, in the example, if it is determined that A and B each have a 50 percent interest in partnership profits, A would be considered to have $15,000 of debt relief and a $15,000 cash distribution from the partnership. A's outside basis in the partnership interest would be $35,000. The other $15,000 of the liability would be allocated to B, and B's outside basis would be $135,000. A

10. See I.R.C. § 351(e)(1); Reg. § 1.351-1(c)(1).

11. Reg. § 1.752-3(a)(3).

12. In that case, the partnership's amount realized would consist of the $30,000 debt relief. Commissioner v. Tufts, 461 U.S. 300, 103 S.Ct. 1826 (1983), rehearing denied, 463 U.S. 1215, 103 S.Ct. 3555 (1983).

13. Reg. § 1.752-3(a)(3).

14. Rev. Rul. 95-41, 1995-1 C.B. 132.

15. Reg. § 1.752-3(a)(3). The regulations also permit nonrecourse liabilities to be allocated (1) in accordance with the manner in which it is reasonably expected that the deductions attributable to those nonrecourse liabilities will be allocated, or (2) to a partner up to the amount of the built-in gain allocable to the partner on section 704(c) property that is in excess of any gain attributable to the liability exceeding the property's basis. Id. See Chapter 4D3, infra.

and B might want to specify that they share partnership profits equally for purposes of allocating the nonrecourse liability to ensure that result. Alternatively, A and B might want to specify some other profits-sharing arrangement (e.g., 60 percent to A and 40 percent to B) for purposes of allocating liabilities, and that arrangement will be respected if it is reasonably consistent with allocations of some other significant item of partnership income or gain that is respected for tax purposes.

Nonrecourse Liabilities in Excess of Basis. The analysis changes if contributed property is encumbered by nonrecourse liabilities that exceed the property's adjusted basis. Assume again that in the ongoing example Partner A contributes a parcel of land with a fair market value of $150,000, an adjusted basis of $10,000, and the property is encumbered by a $30,000 nonrecourse liability. Under the Supreme Court's decision in the *Tufts* case,[16] the amount realized by the partnership on the disposition of the land subject to nonrecourse debt includes at least the amount of the debt relief even if the debt exceeds the value of the property. As a result, whenever the partnership disposes of the land contributed by A, the amount realized at least will include the $30,000 of debt relief regardless of the actual value the land. On these facts, where the $30,000 nonrecourse debt exceeds the $10,000 basis of the land, the partnership is assured of recognizing at least $20,000 of gain when it sells the parcel even if its value should plummet, and under section 704(c)(1)(A) that gain must be allocated to contributing partner A. In keeping with the principle that nonrecourse debt is allocated in accordance with the partners' shares of partnership profits, the section 752 regulations provide that a partner who contributes property encumbered by nonrecourse debt is first allocated that portion of the liability equaling the gain that would be allocated to that partner under section 704(c) if the property were sold at the time of the contribution for an amount equal to the liability.[17] The balance of the liability is allocated under the flexible general rule—that is, in accordance with the partners' share of partnership profits.[18]

Applying these rules to the last example, when A contributes land with a basis of $10,000 subject to a $30,000 nonrecourse liability, $20,000 of that liability is allocated to A. The remaining $10,000 of liability is allocated according to A's and B's shares of partnership profits. Assuming they share partnership profits equally, the remaining $10,000 would be allocated $5,000 to each partner. The net effect is that $5,000 of the debt is reallocated from A to B. As a result, A's outside basis is decreased from $10,000 to $5,000,[19] and B's outside basis is increased by $5,000.[20]

PROBLEMS

1. A and B each contribute $30,000 cash to the ABC partnership and C contributes land held for more than one year, worth $60,000 and subject to

16. Commissioner v. Tufts, supra note 12.

17. Reg. § 1.752–3(a)(2).

18. Reg. § 1.752–3(a)(3).

19. I.R.C. §§ 733; 752(b).

20. I.R.C. §§ 722; 752(a).

a recourse debt of $30,000. A, B and C are all general partners with a one-third interest in the profits and losses of ABC.

(a) What are the tax consequences to A, B, C and ABC if the land has a basis to C of $40,000 and the partnership assumes the debt?

(b) Same as (a), above, except that the land has a basis to C of $10,000. What could C do to avoid this result?

(c) Same as (a), above, except that the debt is nonrecourse, and the partners agree that for purposes of allocating nonrecourse liabilities they each have a one-third interest in profits.

(d) Same as (b), above, except that the debt is nonrecourse and the partners agree that for purposes of allocating nonrecourse liabilities they each have a one-third interest in profits.

2. Attorney, a cash method unincorporated sole practitioner, joins a cash method partnership of three other attorneys all of whom own an equal one-quarter interest in the partnership after Attorney joins the firm. Attorney transfers some accounts receivable for services with a zero basis and a $20,000 face value to the partnership as part of her contribution in exchange for her partnership interest. The partnership also assumes $6,000 of Attorney's accounts payable. What are the tax consequences of the transaction to attorney? See § 704(c)(3).

C. CONTRIBUTIONS OF SERVICES

1. INTRODUCTION

Section 721 provides nonrecognition of gain or loss only when a partner contributes "property" in exchange for an interest in the partnership. "Property" for this purpose does not include services—and properly so, because they are ephemeral and do not leave behind an identifiable continuing capital investment in the business. A partner who receives a partnership interest in exchange for services, whether they be past, present or future, is being compensated and should realize ordinary income under Section 61(a). In that event, the partner takes a Section 1012 "tax cost" basis in the partnership interest equal to the amount that is included in income.

The timing of the service partner's income, the valuation of the interest received and the tax consequences to the partnership raise more difficult questions. Because their resolution may turn on the nature of the interest received by the partner, a few definitions are in order at the outset. A service partner may receive a capital interest, which generally is defined as an interest in both the future earnings and the underlying assets (i.e., the "capital") of the partnership. A partner who has a capital interest will be entitled to a share of the partnership's net assets in the event the partner withdraws or the partnership is liquidated.[1] Alternatively, a part-

1. See Rev.Proc. 93–27, 1993–2 C.B. 343, which defines a capital interest as "an interest that would give the holder a share of the proceeds if the partnership's assets were

ner may receive merely a profits interest, which entitles him to a share of future earnings (including, perhaps, gain on the sale of property) but gives him no current right to a distribution of a share of the partnership's capital in the event of a withdrawal or liquidation.

To illustrate, assume Proprietor, Investor and Manager join forces to form a partnership. Proprietor and Investor each contribute $60,000 but Manager contributes nothing except his agreement to provide needed expertise to the business. The partners agree to share profits and losses equally. If Manager also is credited with a one-third interest in the partnership's capital (⅓ of $120,000, or $40,000), he has received a capital interest, and the other partners have relinquished $20,000 each of their capital accounts—presumably to compensate Manager for his services. But if Manager's capital account is zero, he has received only a "profits interest" and would receive nothing on a subsequent liquidation apart from his share of undistributed earnings of the business.[2]

2. Receipt of a Capital Interest for Services

Code: §§ 83(a)–(c), (h); 721. Skim §§ 706(d)(1); 707(a).

Regulations: § 1.83–6(b).

A service partner who receives a capital interest realizes ordinary income in an amount equal to the value of the interest received less the amount, if any, paid for the interest. The timing of that income is determined under Section 83, which broadly applies to all transfers of property in connection with the performance of services. If the interest is received without restrictions, income is realized upon its receipt. But if the interest is transferred subject to substantial restrictions, Section 83(a) provides that its fair market value is included in gross income when the restrictions lapse—i.e., in the first taxable year in which the service partner's rights are "transferable or are not subject to a substantial risk of forfeiture."[1] Thus, a partner whose interest will be forfeited unless he continues to manage the partnership's business for five years may defer

sold at fair market value and then the proceeds were distributed in a complete liquidation of the partnership." See also Reg. § 1.704–1(e)(1)(v) which, for purposes of the family partnership provisions, defines a "capital interest" as "an interest in the assets of the partnership, which is distributable to the owner of the capital interest upon his withdrawal from the partnership or upon liquidation of the partnership," as distinguished from a "mere right to participate in the earnings and profits of a partnership * * *".

2. The example is no doubt oversimplified because many partnership agreements are ambiguous or silent as to the precise nature of the interest received by a service partner.

1. Section 83(c)(1) provides that a person's rights to property are subject to a substantial risk of forfeiture if their full enjoyment is "conditioned upon the future performance of substantial services by any individual." Section 83(c)(2) provides that "[t]he rights of a person in property are transferable only if the rights in such property of any transferee are not subject to a substantial risk of forfeiture." Proposed regulations would change the analysis and some of the tax results when a partner contributes services for a capital interest. See Chapter 2C4, infra.

any inclusion of income until the interest is free of restrictions. The amount to be included in income is the excess of the fair market value of the interest at the time the partner's rights have vested over the amount, if any, paid for the interest.[2]

A transferee of restricted property is permitted to elect under Section 83(b) to include the value of the property in income at the time of its receipt.[3] If a Section 83(b) election is made, the transferee may not take any deduction (except for the amount actually paid) if the property is subsequently forfeited.[4] The service partner receiving a restricted interest is thus faced with a "gambler's choice." Where a partnership interest has minimal value upon receipt but is expected to appreciate by the time the restrictions lapse, service partners usually are motivated to make the election in the hope that the future appreciation in the property will be taxed at preferential capital gains rates at a later date when the property is sold.

The tax consequences to the service partner are only one side of the transaction. To return to our introductory example, assume that Proprietor and Investor each contribute $60,000 cash to the partnership and Manager, who contributes solely his expertise, receives an unrestricted one-third interest in capital and profits with a value of $40,000. Is the partnership entitled to deduct this $40,000?

One's initial reaction might be to permit the partnership to take a $40,000 ordinary and necessary business deduction, which would flow through to the partners (but which partners?),[5] reducing their distributive share of taxable income or increasing their loss, and in either event also reducing their outside bases under Section 705. But allowance of this deduction depends on the nature of Manager's services. If Manager is the company lawyer who received his interest for services rendered in connection with the formation of the partnership or the construction manager for the partnership's new hotel, an ordinary and necessary deduction for the entire $40,000 would be inappropriate.[6] Rather, the payment to Manager

2. The Section 83 regulations also provide that property received with substantial restrictions is not regarded as owned by the transferee but rather by the person for whom the services are performed until the restrictions lapse. Reg. § 1.83–1(a)(1). Does that make the service partner a nonpartner until his rights have fully vested? For a discussion of the problems raised by this position, see McKee, Nelson & Whitmire, Federal Taxation of Partnerships and Partners ¶ 5.09 (4th ed. 2007).

3. The election must be made within thirty days of the transfer. I.R.C. § 83(b)(2).

4. I.R.C. § 83(b)(1), last sentence; Reg. § 1.83–2(a).

5. The logical result would be to pass through any deduction connected with the admission of a service partner to the other partners. This approach is supported by Section 706(d)(1) (a provision governing the computation of the partners' distributive shares when there is a change in partnership interests during the year; see Chapter 4E, infra), which would allocate the deduction to the other partners because the expense was incurred prior to the service partner's admission to the partnership. This result could be assured by a special allocation in the partnership agreement. See I.R.C. § 704(b).

6. The attorney's fee is an organizational expense, the first $5,000 of which could be deducted and the remainder of which would be amortizable over 180 months if the

would be a capital expenditure, and the partnership's deduction must be partially or totally deferred despite any realization of income by the partner.[7]

The transfer of a capital interest for services also may cause the partnership to recognize gain. Suppose, for example, that Manager receives a one-third capital interest in a partnership previously formed by Proprietor and Investor, and the partnership's sole asset is land with a value of $120,000 and an adjusted basis of $45,000. The transfer of the capital interest to Manager likely is viewed as a two-step transaction: (1) the transfer of a one-third undivided interest in the land from the partnership to Manager as compensation for his services and (2) the contribution of that interest back to the partnership by Manager. The first step involves the transfer of appreciated property (i.e., a one-third interest in the land, having a basis of $15,000 and a value of $40,000) in a Section 83 compensatory transfer to Manager and thus is a taxable event resulting in $25,000 of capital gain to the partnership (i.e., to Proprietor and Investor).[8] The second step is a tax-free contribution of Manager's $40,000 interest in the land back to the partnership under Section 721, and Manager's $40,000 "tax cost" basis is transferred to the partnership under Section 723.[9]

The preceding example involved the transfer of a capital interest to a partner in exchange for past or future services rendered to an ongoing partnership. The *McDougal* case, which follows, illustrates that the tax

partnership so elects under Section 709(b). See Section D of this chapter, infra. Amounts paid to the construction manager would be capitalized and added to the partnership's basis in the building. Cf. Commissioner v. Idaho Power Co., 418 U.S. 1, 94 S.Ct. 2757 (1974).

7. This result is required by Reg. § 1.83–6(a)(4), which provides that no deduction is allowed under Section 83(h) to the extent that a transfer of property constitutes a capital expenditure or an item of deferred expense. If the service partner's interest is subject to substantial restrictions, any deduction allowable to the partnership is determined at the time the service partner recognizes income. See I.R.C. § 83(h); Reg. § 1.83–6(a)(4).

8. Reg. § 1.83–6(b); cf. United States v. Davis, 370 U.S. 65, 82 S.Ct. 1190 (1962), rehearing denied, 371 U.S. 854, 83 S.Ct. 14 (1962) (the transfer of property to satisfy an obligation constitutes a taxable disposition). The leading treatises agree that a partnership must recognize gain in this situation. McKee, Nelson & Whitmire, Federal Taxation of Partnerships and Partners ¶ 5.08[2][b] (4th ed. 2007); Willis, Pennell & Postlewaite, Partnership Taxation ¶ 4.05[5][a] (6th ed. 1997). See also Gergen, "Pooling or Exchange: The Taxation of Joint Ventures Between Labor and Capital," 44 Tax L.Rev. 519 (1989). For a contrary view, see Gunn, "Partnership Interest for Services: Partnership Gain and Loss?" 47 Tax Notes 699 (May 7, 1990). Proposed regulations, however, would permit the partnership to avoid recognizing this gain. See Chapter 2C4, infra.

9. To preserve their equal one-third partnership arrangement and prevent the shifting of taxable gain to Manager, the partnership also should ensure that the remaining $50,000 appreciation in the land at the time Manager becomes a partner will be allocated to Proprietor and Investor when the property is sold. This may be accomplished by applying the principles of Section 704(c) in the context of a special allocation of the built-in gain under Section 704(b). Absent such an agreement, the gain would be shared equally among the three partners and would upset the equality of their capital accounts. See Reg. § 1.704–1(b)(2)(iv)*(f)(5)(iii),* Reg. § 1.704–1(b)(5) Example (14)(i)–(iv), and Chapter 4C4, infra. The shifting of capital interests among the partners could have other tax consequences. See Reg. § 1.704–1(b)(1)(iii) & (iv).

consequences are similar when a partner receives a capital interest in a newly formed partnership in exchange for past services rendered. In reading *McDougal*, consider what steps the parties might have taken to minimize the adverse tax consequences that resulted upon the formation of the partnership.

McDougal v. Commissioner

United States Tax Court, 1974.
62 T.C. 720.

■ FAY, JUDGE. * * *

FINDINGS OF FACT

Certain facts have been stipulated by the parties and are found accordingly. The stipulation of facts and exhibits attached thereto are incorporated herein by this reference.

F.C. and Frankie McDougal are husband and wife, as are Gilbert and Jackie McClanahan. Each couple filed joint Federal income tax returns for the years 1968 and 1969 with the district director of internal revenue in Austin, Tex. Petitioners were all residents of Berino, N. Mex., when they filed their petitions with this Court.

F.C. and Frankie McDougal maintained farms at Lamesa, Tex., where they were engaged in the business of breeding and racing horses. Gilbert McClanahan was a licensed public horse trainer who rendered his services to various horse owners for a standard fee. He had numbered the McDougals among his clientele since 1965.

On February 21, 1965, a horse of exceptional pedigree, Iron Card, had been foaled at the Anthony Ranch in Florida. Title to Iron Card was acquired in January of 1967 by one Frank Ratliff, Jr., who in turn transferred title to himself, M. H. Ratliff, and John V. Burnett (Burnett). The Ratliffs and Burnett entered Iron Card in several races as a 2-year-old; and although the horse enjoyed some success in these contests, it soon became evident that he was suffering from a condition diagnosed by a veterinarian as a protein allergy.

When, due to a dispute among themselves, the Ratliffs and Burnett decided to sell Iron Card for whatever price he could attract, McClanahan (who had trained the horse for the Ratliffs and Burnett) advised the McDougals to make the purchase. He made this recommendation because, despite the veterinarian's prognosis to the contrary, McClanahan believed that by the use of home remedy Iron Card could be restored to full racing vigor. Furthermore, McClanahan felt that as Iron Card's allergy was not genetic and as his pedigree was impressive, he would be valuable in the future as a stud even if further attempts to race him proved unsuccessful.

The McDougals purchased Iron Card for $10,000 on January 1, 1968. At the time of the purchase McDougal promised that if McClanahan trained and attended to Iron Card, a half interest in the horse would be his once the McDougals had recovered the costs and expenses of acquisition. This promise was not made in lieu of payment of the standard trainer's fee; for from January 1, 1968, until the date of the transfer, McClanahan was paid $2,910 as compensation for services rendered as Iron Card's trainer.

McClanahan's home remedy proved so effective in relieving Iron Card of his allergy that the horse began to race with success, and his reputation consequently grew to such proportion that he attracted a succession of offers to purchase, one of which reached $60,000. The McDougals decided, however, to keep the horse and by October 4, 1968, had recovered out of their winnings the costs of acquiring him. It was therefore on that date that they transferred a half interest in the horse to McClanahan in accordance with the promise which McDougal had made to the trainer. A document entitled "Bill of Sale," wherein the transfer was described as a gift, was executed on the following day.

Iron Card continued to race well until very late in 1968 when, without warning and for an unascertained cause, he developed a condition called "hot ankle" which effectively terminated his racing career. From 1970 onward he was used exclusively for breeding purposes. That his value as a stud was no less than his value as a racehorse is attested to by the fact that in September of 1970 petitioners were offered $75,000 for him; but after considering the offer, the McDougals and McClanahan decided to refuse it, preferring to exploit Iron Card's earning potential as a stud to their own profit.

On November 1, 1968, petitioners had concluded a partnership agreement by parol to effectuate their design of racing the horse for as long as that proved feasible and of offering him out as a stud thereafter. Profits were to be shared equally by the McDougals and the McClanahans, while losses were to be allocated to the McDougals alone.

* * *

OPINION

Respondent contends that the McDougals did not recognize a $25,000 gain on the transaction of October 4, 1968, and that they were not entitled to claim a $30,000 business expense deduction by reason thereof. He further contends that were Iron Card to be contributed to a partnership or joint venture under the circumstances obtaining in the instant case, its basis in Iron Card at the time of contribution would have been limited by the McDougals' cost basis in the horse, as adjusted. Respondent justifies these contentions by arguing that the transfer of October 4, 1968, constituted a gift.

In the alternative, respondent has urged us to find that at some point in time no later than the transfer of October 4, 1968, McDougal and McClanahan entered into a partnership or joint venture to which the McDougals contributed Iron Card and McClanahan contributed services. Respondent contends that such a finding would require our holding that the McDougals did not recognize a gain on the transfer of October 4, 1968, by reason of section 721, and that under section 723 the joint venture's basis in Iron Card at the time of the contribution was equal to the McDougals' adjusted basis in the horse as of that time.

We dismiss at the outset respondent's contention that the transfer of October 4, 1968, constituted a gift, and we are undeterred in so doing by the fact that petitioners originally characterized the transfer as a gift, Bogardus v. Commissioner, 302 U.S. 34 (1937). A gift has been defined as a transfer motivated by detached and disinterested generosity, Commissioner v. Duberstein, 363 U.S. 278 (1960). The presence of such motivation is belied in this instance by two factors. The relationship of the parties concerned was essentially of a business nature, and the transfer itself was made conditional upon the outcome of an enterprise which McDougal had undertaken at McClanahan's suggestion and in reliance upon McClanahan's ability to render it profitable. These factors instead bespeak the presence of an arm's-length transaction.

With respect to respondent's alternative contention, we note firstly that the law provides no rule easy of application for making a determination as to whether a partnership or joint venture has been formed but rather directs our attention to a congeries of factors relevant to the issue, of which none is conclusive, Hubert M. Luna, 42 T.C. 1067 (1964).

A joint venture is deemed to arise when two or more persons agree, expressly or impliedly, to enter actively upon a specific business enterprise, the purpose of which is the pursuit of profit; the ownership of whose productive assets and of the profits generated by them is shared; the parties to which all bear the burden of any loss; and the management of which is not confined to a single participant, * * *.

While in the case at bar the risk of loss was to be borne by the McDougals alone, all the other elements of a joint venture were present once the transfer of October 4, 1968, had been effected. Accordingly, we hold that the aforesaid transfer constituted the formation of a joint venture to which the McDougals contributed capital in the form of the horse, Iron Card, and in which they granted McClanahan an interest equal to their own in capital and profits as compensation for his having trained Iron Card. We further hold that the agreement formally entered into on November 1, 1968, and reduced to writing in April of 1970, constituted a continuation of the original joint venture under section 708(b)(2)(A). Furthermore, that McClanahan continued to receive a fee for serving as Iron Card's trainer after October 4, 1968, in no way militates against the soundness of this holding. See sec. 707(c), and sec. 1.707–1(c), example 1, Income Tax Regs. However, this holding does not result in the tax consequences which respondent has contended would follow from it. See sec. 1.721–1(b)(1), Income Tax Regs.

When on the formation of a joint venture a party contributing appreciated assets satisfies an obligation by granting his obligee a capital interest in the venture, he is deemed first to have transferred to the obligee an undivided interest in the assets contributed, equal in value to the amount of the obligation so satisfied. He and the obligee are deemed thereafter and in concert to have contributed those assets to the joint venture.

The contributing obligor will recognize gain on the transaction to the extent that the value of the undivided interest which he is deemed to have transferred exceeds his basis therein. The obligee is considered to have realized an amount equal to the fair market value of the interest which he receives in the venture and will recognize income depending upon the character of the obligation satisfied.[12] The joint venture's basis in the assets will be determined under section 723 in accordance with the foregoing assumptions. Accordingly, we hold that the transaction under consideration constituted an exchange in which the McDougals realized $30,000, United States v. Davis, 370 U.S. 65 (1962); Kenan v. Commissioner, 114 F.2d 217 (C.A.2, 1940), affirming 40 B.T.A. 824 (1939).

In determining the basis offset to which the McDougals are entitled with respect to the transfer of October 4, 1968, we note the following: that the McDougals had an unadjusted cost basis in Iron Card of $10,000; that they had claimed $1,390 in depreciation on the entire horse for the period January 1 to October 31, 1968; and that after an agreement of partnership was concluded on November 1, 1968, depreciation on Iron Card was deducted by the partnership exclusively.

Section 704(c) [pre–1984. Ed.] allows partners and joint venturers some freedom in determining who is to claim the deductions for depreciation on contributed property. As is permissible under the statute, petitioners clearly intended the depreciation to be claimed by the common enterprise once it had come into existence, an event which they considered to have occurred on November 1, 1968. Consistent with their intent and with our own holding that a joint venture arose on October 4, 1968, we now further hold that the McDougals were entitled to claim depreciation on Iron Card only until the transfer of October 4, 1968. Thereafter depreciation on Iron Card ought to have been deducted by the joint venture in the computation of its taxable income.

In determining their adjusted basis in the portion of Iron Card on whose disposition they are required to recognize gain, the McDougals charged all the depreciation which they had taken on the horse against their basis in the half in which they retained an interest. This procedure was improper. As in accordance with section 1.167(g)–1, Income Tax Regs., we have allowed the McDougals a depreciation deduction with respect to Iron Card for the period January 1 to October 4, 1968, computed on their entire cost basis in the horse of $10,000; so also do we require that the said deduction be charged against that entire cost basis under section 1016(a)(2)(A).

12. For example, if the obligation arose out of a loan, the obligee will recognize no income by reason of the transaction; if the obligation represents the selling price of a capital asset, he will recognize a capital gain to the extent that the amount he is deemed to have realized exceeds his adjusted basis in the asset; if the obligation represents compensation for services, the transaction will result in ordinary income to the obligee in an amount equal to the value of the interest which he received in the joint venture.

As the McDougals were in the business of racing horses, any gain recognized by them on the exchange of Iron Card in satisfaction of a debt would be characterized under section 1231(a) provided he had been held by them for the period requisite under section 1231(b) as it applies to livestock acquired before 1970. In that as of October 4, 1968, Iron Card had been used by the McDougals exclusively for racing and not for breeding, we do now hold that they had held him for a period sufficiently long to make section 1231(a) applicable to their gain on the transaction. This is the case although the McDougals may have intended eventually to use Iron Card for breeding purposes, Anderson Fowler, 37 T.C. 1124 (1962).

The joint venture's basis in Iron Card as of October 4, 1968, must be determined under section 723 in accordance with the principles of law set forth earlier in this opinion. In the half interest in the horse which it is deemed to have received from the McDougals, the joint venture had a basis equal to one-half of the McDougals' adjusted cost basis in Iron Card as of October 4, 1968, i.e., the excess of $5,000 over one-half of the depreciation which the McDougals were entitled to claim on Iron Card for the period January 1 to October 4, 1968. In the half interest which the venture is considered to have received from McClanahan, it can claim to have had a basis equal to the amount which McClanahan is considered to have realized on the transaction, $30,000. The joint venture's deductions for depreciation on Iron Card for the years 1968 and 1969 are to be determined on the basis computed in the above-described manner.

When an interest in a joint venture is transferred as compensation for services rendered, any deduction which may be authorized under section 162(a)(1) by reason of that transfer is properly claimed by the party to whose benefit the services accrued, be that party the venture itself or one or more venturers, sec. 1.721–1(b)(2), Income Tax Regs. Prior to McClanahan's receipt of his interest, a joint venture did not exist under the facts of the case at bar; the McDougals were the sole owners of Iron Card and recipients of his earnings. Therefore, they alone could have benefited from the services rendered by McClanahan prior to October 4, 1968, for which he was compensated by the transaction of that date. Accordingly, we hold that the McDougals are entitled to a business expense deduction of $30,000, that amount being the value of the interest which McClanahan received. Respondent has contended that a deduction of $30,000 would be unreasonable in amount in view of the nature of the services for which McClanahan was being compensated. But having found that the transaction under consideration was not a gift but rather was occasioned by a compensation arrangement which was entered upon at arm's length, we must reject this contention. See sec. 1.162–7(b)(2), Income Tax Regs.

* * *

PROBLEM

C is offered a capital interest in a partnership whose sole asset is a commercial building with a fair market value of $150,000 and an adjusted basis of $90,000. The building has been depreciated on the straight line method. A and B have $45,000 outside bases in their respective partnership interests. C has performed real estate management services for the partnership over the past year and has agreed to perform additional services in the future.

(a) What are the tax consequences to C and to the partnership (i.e., A and B) if in year one C receives a one-tenth capital interest in the partnership as compensation for his management services over the past year?

(b) What result in (a), above, if C receives his capital interest in exchange for legal services performed in connection with the acquisition of the building?

(c) What result in (a), above, if C receives his interest as compensation for services to be rendered in the succeeding three years provided, however, that if C ceases to render services before the end of year three, C or any transferee of C must relinquish his interest in the partnership. Assume for this problem that the building will have a value of $450,000 and an adjusted basis of $90,000 at the end of year three.

(d) What result in (a), above, if C is promised that if he renders services until the end of year three, the partnership interest will be transferred to him at that time? Again assume that the building will have a value of $450,000 and an adjusted basis of $90,000 at the end of year three.

3. Receipt of a Profits Interest for Services

Regulations: § 1.83–3(e).

The principles considered above would seem to apply to the receipt of a profits interest for services. Returning to the example in the preceding section, if Manager receives only an interest in the future profits of the partnership, he nonetheless is being compensated for his services and theoretically has realized ordinary income. But what is the value of his interest, which measures the *amount* of his income? And should the income be considered realized at the time the interest is received, when the amount is speculative, or only when the profits are actually earned by the partnership? If the interest is taxed upon its receipt, will the service partner be taxed again when the profits are actually earned? And does it matter whether the service provider receives the interest for past or future services, or in what capacity (e.g., partner or employee) those services were performed? Because of the practical problems raised by these questions, it had long been assumed that the receipt of a profits interest was not a taxable event.[1] And then along came Sol Diamond, whose clumsy attempt

1. This assumption was based, in part, on Reg. § 1.721–1(b)(1), which states that, "To the extent that any of the partners gives up any part of his right to be repaid his contributions (as distinguished from a share in partnership profits) in favor of another

to convert ordinary income to capital gain on a routine real estate venture called the conventional wisdom into question. The Tax Court, affirmed by the Seventh Circuit in the opinion below, held that a service partner is currently taxable on receipt of a profits interest—provided that the interest is susceptible of valuation at the time of its receipt. In reading the *Diamond* opinion, consider whether Mr. Diamond was in fact a partner and whether the court might have reached the same result on narrower grounds.

Diamond v. Commissioner

United States Court of Appeals, Seventh Circuit, 1974.
492 F.2d 286.

■ FAIRCHILD, CIRCUIT JUDGE.

This is an appeal from a decision of the Tax Court upholding the commissioner's assessment of deficiencies against Sol and Muriel Diamond for the years 1961 and 1962. The deficiencies for each year were consolidated for trial, but are essentially unrelated. The Tax Court concluded that Diamond realized ordinary income on the receipt of a right to a share of profit or loss to be derived from a real estate venture (the 1962 partnership case) * * *. The facts in both cases appear in Diamond v. Commissioner, 56 T.C. 530 (1971). Unnecessary repetitions will be avoided.

The 1962 Partnership Case

During 1961, Diamond was a mortgage broker. Philip Kargman had acquired for $25,000 the buyer's rights in a contract for the sale of an office building. Kargman asked Diamond to obtain a mortgage loan for the full $1,100,000 purchase price of the building. Diamond and Kargman agreed that Diamond would receive a 60% share of profit or loss of the venture if he arranged the financing.

Diamond succeeded in obtaining a $1,100,000 mortgage loan from Marshall Savings and Loan. On December 15, 1961 Diamond and Kargman entered into an agreement which provided:

(1) The two were associated as joint venturers for 24 years (the life of the mortgage) unless earlier terminated by agreement or by sale;

(2) Kargman was to advance all cash needed for the purchase beyond the loan proceeds;

(3) Profits and losses would be divided, 40% to Kargman, 60% to Diamond;

partner as compensation for services ... section 721 does not apply." See, e.g., Hale v. Commissioner, 24 T.C.M. 1497 n. 3 (1965) (the "mere receipt of a partnership interest in future profits does not create any tax liability"). See also Gergen, "Pooling or Exchange: The Taxation of Joint Ventures Between Labor and Capital," 44 Tax L.Rev. 519 (1989), which analyzes the Code's treatment of exchanges of labor for capital.

(4) In event of sale, proceeds would be devoted first to repayment to Kargman of money supplied by him, and net profits thereafter would be divided 40% to Kargman, 60% to Diamond.

Early in 1962, Kargman and Diamond created an Illinois land trust to hold title to the property. The chief motivation for the land trust arrangement was apparently to insulate Diamond and Kargman from personal liability on the mortgage note.

The purchase proceeded as planned and closing took place on February 18, 1962. Kargman made cash outlays totalling $78,195.33 in connection with the purchase. Thus, under the terms of the agreement, the property would have to appreciate at least $78,195.33 before Diamond would have any equity in it.

Shortly after closing, it was proposed that Diamond would sell his interest and one Liederman would be substituted, except on a 50–50 basis. Liederman persuaded Diamond to sell his interest for $40,000. This sale was effectuated on March 8, 1962 by Diamond assigning his interest to Kargman for $40,000. Kargman in turn then conveyed a similar interest, except for 50–50 sharing, to Liederman for the same amount.

On their 1962 joint return, the Diamonds reported the March 8, 1962 $40,000 sale proceeds as a short term capital gain. This gain was offset by an unrelated short term capital loss. They reported no tax consequences from the February 18 receipt of the interest in the venture. Diamond's position is that his receipt of this type of interest in partnership is not taxable income although received in return for services. He relies on § 721 and Reg. § 1.721–1(b)(1). He further argues that the subsequent sale of this interest produced a capital gain under § 741. The Tax Court held that the receipt of this type of interest in partnership in return for services is not within § 721 and is taxable under § 61 when received. The Tax Court valued the interest at $40,000 as of February 18, as evidenced by the sale for that amount three weeks later, on March 8.

Both the taxpayer and the Tax Court treated the venture as a partnership and purported to apply partnership income tax principles. It has been suggested that the record might have supported findings that there was in truth an employment or other relationship, other than partnership, and produced a similar result, but these findings were not made. See Cowan, The Diamond Case, 27 Tax Law Review 161 (1972). It has also been suggested (and argued, alternatively, by the government) that although on the face of the agreement Diamond appeared to receive only a right to share in profit (loss) to be derived, the value of the real estate may well have been substantially greater than the purchase price, so that Diamond may really have had an interest in capital, if the assets were properly valued. This finding was not made. The Tax Court, 56 T.C. at 547, n. 16, suggested the possibility that Diamond would not in any event be entitled to capital gains treatment of his sale of a right to receive income in the future, but did not decide the question.[3]

3. Because of the decision we reach, it is also unnecessary for us to consider this possibility and we express no conclusions concerning it.

Taking matters at face value, taxpayer received, on February 18, an interest in partnership, limited to a right to a share of profit (loss) to be derived. In discussion we shall refer to this interest either as his interest in partnership or a profit-share.

The Tax Court, with clearly adequate support, found that Diamond's interest in partnership had a market value of $40,000 on February 18. Taxpayer's analysis is that under the regulations the receipt of a profit-share February 18, albeit having a market value and being conferred in return for services, was not a taxable event, and that the entire proceeds of the March 8 sale were a capital gain. The Tax Court analysis was that the interest in partnership, albeit limited to a profit-share, was property worth $40,000, and taxpayer's acquisition, thereof on February 18 was compensation for services and ordinary income. Assuming that capital gain treatment at sale would have been appropriate, there was no gain because the sale was for the same amount.

There is no statute or regulation which expressly and particularly prescribes the income tax effect, or absence of one, at the moment a partner receives a profit-share in return for services. The Tax Court's holding rests upon the general principle that a valuable property interest received in return for services is compensation, and income. Taxpayer's argument is predicated upon an implication which his counsel, and others, have found in Reg. § 1.721–1(b)(1), but which need not, and the government argues should not, be found there.

26 U.S.C. § 721 is entitled "Nonrecognition of gain or loss on contribution," and provides: "No gain or loss shall be recognized to a partnership or to any of its partners in the case of a contribution of property to the partnership in exchange for an interest in the partnership." Only if, by a strained construction, "property" were said to include services, would § 721 say anything about the effect of furnishing services. It clearly deals with a contribution like Kargman's of property, and prescribes that when he contributed his property, no gain or loss was recognized. It does not, of course, explicitly say that no income accrues to one who renders services and, in return, becomes a partner with a profit-share.

Reg. § 1.721–1 presumably explains and interprets § 721, perhaps to the extent of qualifying or limiting its meaning. Subsec. (b)(1), particularly relied on here, reads in part as follows:

> "Normally, under local law, each partner is entitled to be repaid his contributions of money or other property to the partnership (at the value placed upon such property by the partnership at the time of the contribution) whether made at the formation of the partnership or subsequent thereto. To the extent that any of the partners gives up any part of his right to be repaid his contributions (as distinguished from a share in partnership profits) in favor of another partner as compensation for services (or in satisfaction of an obligation), section 721 does not apply. The value of an interest

in such partnership capital so transferred to a partner as compensation for services constitutes income to the partner under section 61. * * * "

The quoted portion of the regulation may well be read, like § 721, as being directly addressed only to the consequences of a contribution of money or other property. It asserts that when a partner making such contributions transfers to another some part of the contributing partner's right to be repaid, in order to compensate the other for services or to satisfy an obligation to the other, § 721 does not apply, there is recognition of gain or loss to the contributing partner, and there is income to the partner who receives, as compensation for services, part of the right to be repaid.

The regulation does not specify that if a partner contributing property agrees that, in return for services, another shall be a partner with a profit-share only, the value of the profit-share is not income to the recipient. An implication to that effect, such as is relied on by taxpayer, would have to rest on the proposition that the regulation was meant to be all inclusive as to when gain or loss would be recognized or income would exist as a consequence of the contribution of property to a partnership and disposition of the partnership interests. It would have to appear, in order to sustain such implication, that the existence of income by reason of a creation of a profit-share, immediately having a determinable market value, in favor of a partner would be inconsistent with the result specified in the regulation.

We do not find this implication in our own reading of the regulation. It becomes necessary to consider the substantial consensus of commentators in favor of the principle claimed to be implied and to look to judicial interpretation, legislative history, administrative interpretation, and policy considerations to determine whether the implication is justified.

The Commentators: There is a startling degree of unanimity that the conferral of a profit-share as compensation for services is not income at the time of the conferral, although little by way of explanation of why this should be so, or analysis of statute or regulation to show that it is prescribed. See publications cited pp. 181–2 of Cowan, The Diamond Case.[4]

One of the most unequivocal statements, with an explanation in terms of practicality or policy, was made by Arthur Willis in a text:

> "However obliquely the proposition is stated in the regulations, it is clear that a partner who receives only an interest in future profits of the partnership as compensation for services is not required to report the receipt of his partnership interest as taxable income. The rationale is twofold. In the first place, the present value of a right to participate in future profits is usually too conjectural to be subject to valuation. In the second place, the

4. See also Halperin & Tucker, Low Income Housing (FHA 236) Programs: One of Few Tax Shelter Opportunities Left, 36 J. Taxation 2, 5–6 (1972); Research Institute of America, Tax Coordinator B–1210.1, Developments 15,010; Surrey & Warren, Federal Income Taxation: Cases and Materials (1964 Supp. to 1960 ed.), p. 146.

service partner is taxable on his distributive share of partnership income as it is realized by the partnership. If he were taxed on the present value of the right to receive his share of future partnership income, either he would be taxed twice, or the value of his right to participate in partnership income must be amortized over some period of time."[5]

Judicial Interpretation: Except for one statement by the Tax Court no decision cited by the parties or found by us appears squarely to reach the question, either on principle in the absence of the regulations, or by application of the regulations. In a footnote in Herman M. Hale, 24 T.C.M. 1497, 1502 (1965) the Tax Court said: "Under the regulations, the mere receipt of a partnership interest in future profits does not create any tax liability. Sec. 1.721–1(b), Income Tax Regs." There was no explanation of how this conclusion was derived from the regulations.

Legislative History: The legislative history is equivocal.

An advisory group appointed in 1956 to review the regulations evidently felt concern about whether the provision of Reg. § 1.721–1 that the value of an interest in capital transferred to a partner in compensation for services constitutes income had a statutory basis in the light of § 721 providing that there shall be no recognition of gain or loss in the case of a contribution of property. The group proposed enactment of a new section to provide such basis, and legislation introduced into the 86th Congress in 1959 incorporated this recommendation. The bill, H.R. 9662, would have created a new § 770 providing specifically for the taxation of a person receiving an interest in partnership capital in exchange for the performance of services for the partnership. However, neither proposed § 770 nor anything else in H.R. 9662 dealt with the receipt merely of a profit-share. The lack of concern over an income tax impact when only a profit-share was conferred might imply an opinion that such conferring of a profit-share would not be taxable under any circumstances, or might imply an opinion that it would be income or not under § 61 depending upon whether it had a determinable market value or not.

Several statements in the course of the hearings and committee reports paralleled the first parenthetical phrase in Reg. § 1.721–1(b) and were to the effect that the provision did not apply where a person received only a profit-share.[6] There was, however, at least one specific statement by the chairman of the advisory group (Mr. Willis) that if the service partner "were to receive merely an interest in future profits in exchange for his services, he would have no immediate taxable gain because he would be taxed on his share of income as it was earned."[7] H.R. 9662 passed the House of Representatives, and was favorably reported to the Senate by its

5. Willis on Partnership Taxation 84–85 (1971). See Cowan, The Diamond Case, 27 Tax Law Review 181 n. 56 (1972).

6. See, e.g., Senate Rep. No. 1616, 86th Cong., 2d Sess. 117 (1960).

7. See Hearings on Advisory Group Recommendations on Subchapters C, J, and K of the Internal Revenue Code before the House Comm. on Ways and Means, 86th Cong., 1st Sess. 53 (1959).

finance committee, but never came to a vote in the Senate. Even had the bill become law, it would not have dealt expressly with the problem at hand.

Administrative Interpretation: We are unaware of instances in which the Commissioner has asserted delinquencies where a taxpayer who received a profit-share with determinable market value in return for services failed to report the value as income, or has otherwise acted consistently with the Tax Court decision in *Diamond*. Although the consensus referred to earlier appears to exist, the Commissioner has not by regulation or otherwise acted affirmatively to reject it, and in a sense might be said to have agreed by silence.

Consideration of partnership principles or practices: There must be wide variation in the degree to which a profit-share created in favor of a partner who has or will render service has determinable market value at the moment of creation. Surely in many if not the typical situations it will have only speculative value, if any.

In the present case, taxpayer's services had all been rendered, and the prospect of earnings from the real estate under Kargman's management was evidently very good. The profit-share had determinable market value.

If the present decision be sound, then the question will always arise, whenever a profit-share is created or augmented, whether it has a market value capable of determination. Will the existence of this question be unduly burdensome on those who choose to do business under the partnership form?

Each partner determines his income tax by taking into account his distributive share of the taxable income of the partnership. 26 U.S.C. § 702. Taxpayer's position here is that he was entitled to defer income taxation on the compensation for his services except as partnership earnings were realized. If a partner is taxed on the determinable market value of a profit-share at the time it is created in his favor, and is also taxed on his full share of earnings as realized, there will arguably be double taxation, avoidable by permitting him to amortize the value which was originally treated as income. Does the absence of a recognized procedure for amortization militate against the treatment of the creation of the profit-share as income?

Do the disadvantages of treating the creation of the profit-share as income in those instances where it has a determinable market value at that time outweigh the desirability of imposing a tax at the time the taxpayer has received an interest with determinable market value as compensation for services?

We think, of course, that the resolution of these practical questions makes clearly desirable the promulgation of appropriate regulations, to achieve a degree of certainty. But in the absence of regulation, we think it sound policy to defer to the expertise of the Commissioner and the Judges of the Tax Court, and to sustain their decision that the receipt of a profit-share with determinable market value is income.

* * *

NOTE

The Scope of Diamond. The scope of *Diamond* has been widely debated. Although the decision reasonably can be read to apply whenever a service partner receives a profits interest that is readily susceptible of valuation, the facts of the case suggest a narrower holding. The Seventh Circuit assumed that Diamond received an interest in future partnership profits. Several weeks after receiving the interest, however, Diamond sold it for $40,000. This indicates that whatever he received was initially worth $40,000—that is, it was really a *capital* interest, which everyone agrees is taxable. It is likely that the building was worth more than the $1,100,000 option price, and what Diamond actually received was an interest of 60 percent of any amount realized in excess of that $1,100,000 plus Kargman's $80,000 cash investment. It also is significant that Diamond received his interest for past services rendered for Kargman, not future services to be performed for the partnership. Indeed, there is some question whether Diamond was even a partner.

Subsequent Developments. Since the opinion in *Diamond* was far from narrow, the case shocked the tax bar, which routinely had been advising clients that the receipt of a profits interest for services was not a taxable event. After making the obligatory calls to their malpractice carriers, partnership tax specialists authored reams of commentary urging the Service to reconsider its position, or at least narrow the *Diamond* holding.[1] In the ensuing debate, Section 83 assumed center stage. Recall that Section 83, which was enacted after the taxable year in *Diamond*, applies to any transfer of "property" (whether or not subject to restrictions) in connection with the performance of services. For this purpose, the regulations define "property" to include all real and personal property, excluding only money or "an unfunded and unsecured promise to pay money or property in the future."[2] The Section 83 regulations make no reference to partnership interests, or to property received in a partner capacity. But in view of the sweeping definition of "property" and the Congressional policy to include all forms of nonmonetary compensation within the scope of Section 83, it seemed theoretically correct, albeit impractical and unwise from a policy standpoint, to treat a profits interest as Section 83 "property."[3] The pro-

1. The leading article was Cowan, "Receipt of an Interest in Partnership Profits in Consideration for Services: The *Diamond* Case," 27 Tax L.Rev. 161 (1972). See also Lane, "Sol Diamond: The Tax Court Upsets the Service Partner," 46 S.Cal.L.Rev. 239 (1973).

2. Reg. § 1.83–3(e).

3. But see McKee, Nelson & Whitmire, Federal Taxation of Partnerships and Partners ¶ 5.02[1] (4th ed. 2007). The authors argue that when the Section 721 and Section 83 regulations are read together, transfers of a profits interest are not directly covered by Section 83.

taxpayer commentators argued that a profits interest, being contingent on the future economic success of the partnership, is tantamount to an "unfunded and unsecured promise to pay money or property in the future." They pointed to the practical problems of timing and valuation that would result from extending Section 83 to service partners and urged that the revenue would be adequately protected by taxing the service partner on the profits as they are earned.[4]

The Service's initial response to *Diamond* was a mix of ambiguity and ambivalence. While the case was pending, it issued proposed regulations under Section 721 which obliquely implied that the receipt of a profits interest might not be a taxable event by providing that transfers of *capital* interests for services do come within Section 83 while remaining silent on the status of a profits interest as Section 83 "property."[5]

The Service later intimated, in an internal Chief Counsel's legal memorandum, that it would not follow *Diamond* to the extent that it held that the receipt of an interest in future partnership profits as compensation was a taxable event.[6] Tax advisors also were reassured by the few cases decided after *Diamond*, where the courts generally held that, whether or not Section 83 applied, a profits interest received for services had no value for tax purposes because the taxpayer would not be entitled to any interest in partnership capital on liquidation and the future profits of the partnership were speculative.[7]

This period of calm was abruptly interrupted in 1990 when the Tax Court held in Campbell v. Commissioner[8] that the receipt of profits interests in real estate limited partnerships by a taxpayer who had performed services for the syndicator of the ventures was taxable even though the taxpayer would not have been entitled to receive anything of value on an immediate liquidation of his interest. The court valued the interests by looking to the present value of the projected future tax benefits and cash distributions of the partnerships. On appeal, the Eighth Circuit reversed, holding that the profits interests had no value because the projected future benefits were wholly speculative.[9] The court of appeals decision in *Campbell* was principally a valuation holding. In the course of its opinion, however, the court appeared to leave open the possibility that a profits interest received by a service partner acting in a partner capacity would be taxable if it were susceptible of valuation. At the same time, it suggested that, irrespective of valuation concerns, the receipt of a profits interest by a

4. See generally Willis, Pennell & Postlewaite, Partnership Taxation § 46.04 (4th ed. 1989).

5. Prop.Reg. § 1.721–1(b)(1). These proposed regulations were issued in 1971 and were withdrawn in 2005.

6. G.C.M. 36346 (July 23, 1975).

7. See, e.g., St. John v. United States, 84–1 USTC ¶ 9158 (C.D.Ill.1983); Kenroy, Inc. v. Commissioner, 47 T.C.M. 1749 (1984).

8. 59 T.C.M. 236 (1990).

9. Campbell v. Commissioner, 943 F.2d 815 (8th Cir.1991). On appeal, the *Campbell* case was complicated by the government's argument that the taxpayer had received the profits interest in his capacity as an employee of his corporate employer rather than as a partner. The court declined to consider this argument because it was raised for the first time on appeal.

partner might not be taxable as a matter of law because Sections 61 and 83 were preempted by other provisions of Subchapter K that govern the taxation of compensatory payments to partners for services rendered in their partner and nonpartner capacities.[10]

The Eighth Circuit decision in *Campbell* settled the jangled nerves of tax advisors, but students of Subchapter K continued to debate the scope of the decision and its conceptual basis.[11] In the midst of this discussion, the Service finally announced a formal position on the taxation of profits interests in Revenue Procedure 93–27, which follows.

Revenue Procedure 93–27

1993–2 Cum.Bull. 343.

SEC. 1. PURPOSE

This revenue procedure provides guidance on the treatment of the receipt of a partnership profits interest for services provided to or for the benefit of the partnership.

SEC. 2. DEFINITIONS

The following definitions apply for purposes of this revenue procedure.

.01 A capital interest is an interest that would give the holder a share of the proceeds if the partnership's assets were sold at fair market value and then the proceeds were distributed in a complete liquidation of the partnership. This determination generally is made at the time of receipt of the partnership interest.

.02 A profits interest is a partnership interest other than a capital interest.

SEC. 3. BACKGROUND

Under section 1.721–1(b)(1) of the Income Tax Regulations, the receipt of a partnership capital interest for services provided to or for the benefit of the partnership is taxable as compensation. On the other hand, the issue of whether the receipt of a partnership profits interest for services is taxable has been the subject of litigation. Most recently, in Campbell v. Commissioner, 943 F.2d 815 (8th Cir.1991), the Eighth Circuit in dictum suggested that the taxpayer's receipt of a partnership profits interest received for

10. See, e.g., I.R.C. § 707, which governs transactions between partners and partnerships and provides in effect that a partner may not receive taxable compensation from a partnership while acting in a *partner* capacity unless it is in the form of a fixed "guaranteed payment." See I.R.C. § 707(c). Other forms of compensatory payments to partners are included in the partner's distributive share of partnership profits and generally are taxed when those profits are realized. Section 707 is examined in detail in Chapter 5, infra.

11. See, e.g., Cunningham, "Taxing Partnership Interests Exchanged for Services," 47 Tax L.Rev. 247 (1991); Castleberry, "*Campbell*—A Simpler Solution," 47 Tax L.Rev. 277 (1991); Schmolka, "Taxing Partnership Interests Exchanged for Services: Let *Diamond/Campbell* Quietly Die," 47 Tax L.Rev. 287 (1991).

services was not taxable, but decided the case on valuation. Other courts have determined that in certain circumstances the receipt of a partnership profits interest for services is a taxable event under section 83 of the Internal Revenue Code. See, e.g., Campbell v. Commissioner, T.C.M. 1990–162, rev'd, 943 F.2d 815 (8th Cir.1991); St. John v. United States, No. 82–1134 (C.D.Ill. Nov.16, 1983). The courts have also found that typically the profits interest received has speculative or no determinable value at the time of receipt. See Campbell, 943 F.2d at 823; St. John. In Diamond v. Commissioner, 56 T.C. 530 (1971), aff'd, 492 F.2d 286 (7th Cir.1974), however, the court assumed that the interest received by the taxpayer was a partnership profits interest and found the value of the interest was readily determinable. In that case, the interest was sold soon after receipt.

SEC. 4. APPLICATION

.01 Other than as provided below, if a person receives a profits interest for the provision of services to or for the benefit of a partnership in a partner capacity or in anticipation of being a partner, the Internal Revenue Service will not treat the receipt of such an interest as a taxable event for the partner or the partnership.

.02 This revenue procedure does not apply:

(1) If the profits interest relates to a substantially certain and predictable stream of income from partnership assets, such as income from high-quality debt securities or a high-quality net lease;

(2) If within two years of receipt, the partner disposes of the profits interest; or

(3) If the profits interest is a limited partnership interest in a "publicly traded partnership" within the meaning of section 7704(b) of the Internal Revenue Code.

NOTE

Revenue Procedure 93–27 goes a long way toward clarifying the tax treatment of a partner who receives a profits interest for services. In a typical situation, where a partner with managerial or technical expertise receives a share of future profits upon joining a partnership, the receipt of the profits interest will not be a taxable event as long as the three exceptions in Revenue Procedure 93–27 are avoided.

The Service's tolerant policy applies, however, only if the services are performed for the partnership "in a partner capacity or in anticipation of being a partner." Thus, if a profits interest is received for services performed in a nonpartner capacity (e.g., as an independent contractor or employee), the service provider is taxable. Section 707(a), which is covered in Chapter 5, provides principles for determining the capacity in which a partner is acting in a particular transaction with the partnership.[1]

1. See Chapter 5A, infra.

The exceptions in Revenue Procedure 93–27 raise a few additional issues. For example, when will a service partner be taxable because the stream of income from partnership assets is sufficiently "certain and predictable?" Does *every* disposition of a profits interest within two years of receipt trigger taxation? What if the partner disposes of the interest by gift, at death, or exchanges the interest for stock in a newly formed corporation in a nonrecognition transaction under Section 351? These and other lingering issues may need to be addressed in the future.[2]

If a partner is taxable under one of the exceptions in Revenue Procedure 93–27, several more thorny questions are raised. For example, is the profits interest taxable as "property" received in connection with the performance of services under Section 83? If so, what are the consequences to the partnership? If Section 83 applies, a profits interest that is freely transferable and not subject to a substantial risk of forfeiture would be taxable on receipt in an amount equal to the fair market value of the interest. After Revenue Procedure 93–27, the rare taxable profits interest would be susceptible of valuation, presumably based on the present value of the predictable income stream. The partner's outside basis in the profits interest would be the amount included in income.

As for the partnership, recall that upon transfer of a capital interest for services, the partnership may take an ordinary and necessary business deduction or must capitalize the expenditure, depending on the nature of the services rendered. The transfer of a capital interest also was a taxable event to the partnership—i.e., the other partners—on the theory that they were transferring an undivided interest in partnership assets that in turn was recontributed by the service partner to the partnership. A similar approach may apply if the transfer of a profits interest is taxable. First, the partnership would either deduct or capitalize an amount equal to the value of the profits interest transferred. Then, the transaction could be treated as the partnership's transfer of a right to future profits which, under the assignment of income doctrine, should result in immediate taxation of the other partners on the value of this assigned interest in future income.[3] Since the service partner is treated as transferring the right to future profits back to the partnership, the partnership should take a transferred inside basis equal to the amount that the service partner included in gross income upon receipt.[4] Finally, to avoid double taxation of the same profits, the partnership should be able to amortize this basis and reduce its taxable income in the future. To claim this deduction, however, the partnership would be required to demonstrate that the profits interest has a determinable useful life. This amortization deduction should be allocated to the service partner, who was already taxed when he received the profits interest and should not be taxed again.[5]

2. See Lockhart, "IRS Concedes Tax Treatment of a Partnership Profits Interest Received for Services," 10 J.P'ship Tax'n 283 (1993) for a discussion of these and other issues raised by Revenue Procedure 93–27.

3. Cf. Stranahan's Estate v. Commissioner, 472 F.2d 867 (6th Cir.1973).

4. I.R.C. § 723.

5. This type of allocation could be made under Section 704(b). See Chapter 4B, infra.

Still more questions would arise if a service provider received a taxable profits interest that was not substantially vested upon receipt. For example, unless the partner makes a Section 83(b) election, he would not be considered as the owner of the property until the restrictions lapse.[6] That may mean that the service provider is not a partner until the interest vests, but in that case it is unclear how the service provider and the other partners would be taxed in the meantime. Having raised all of these technical teasers, it is important to remember that they only arise when a partner is taxable on the receipt of a profits interest.

Revenue Procedure 2001–43[7] clarifies Revenue Procedure 93–27 on a few technical points. First, it provides that the determination of whether an interest granted to a service provider is a profits interest is tested at the time the interest is granted, even if that interest is not substantially vested under Section 83. Second, the Service will not treat the grant of a nontaxable profits interest, or the event that causes the interest to be substantially vested under Section 83, as a taxable event. Thus, a Section 83(b) election would not be needed if such a partnership interest were not substantially vested at the time it was granted. For these rules to apply, Revenue Procedure 2001–43 requires that: (1) the partnership and the service provider must treat the service provider as the owner of the interest from the date of its grant, and the service provider must take into account the distributive share of all items associated with the interest for the entire period during which the service provider has the interest, (2) neither the partnership nor any partner may deduct any amount for the fair market value of the interest either upon the grant of the interest or when it becomes substantially vested, and (3) all the other requirements of Revenue Procedure 93–27 must be satisfied.

PROBLEMS

1. The AB partnership is a law firm. C, an associate in the firm, is offered a one-third partnership interest in the future profits of the partnership. C is not required to make any capital contribution. Is C taxable upon his admission to the partnership?

2. C, an experienced real estate manager, receives a nonforfeitable one-tenth profits interest in the AB general partnership, whose sole asset is a commercial building with a value of $1,000,000 in return for his agreement to render management services in his capacity as a partner. Net rentals from the building recently have been averaging $100,000 per year. C has been asked to manage the building in the hope that his expertise will

Alternatively, the regulations permit a revaluation of partnership property, adjustments to capital accounts, and application of Section 704(c) principles when a partnership interest (that is not de minimis) is transferred to a partner as consideration for the provision of services. See Reg. § 1.704–1(b)(2)(iv)*(f)(5)(iii)*.

6. Reg. § 1.83–1(a)(1).

7. 2001–2 C.B. 191. For an analysis of Rev. Proc. 2001–43, see Kalinka, "Rev. Proc. 2001–43 and the Transfer of a Nonvested Partnership Profits Interest," 79 Taxes 11 (2001).

increase the rental income and ultimately lead to a profitable sale of the property.

(a) What are the tax consequences to C upon receipt of the profits interest?

(b) What are the tax consequences to C upon receipt of the profits interest if C, prior to becoming a partner, rendered services to the partnership in connection with obtaining financing and soliciting tenants for the building?

(c) What result in (a), above, if C sells his profits interest for $50,000 within one year of acquiring the interest and prior to receiving any profits?

(d) What results in (c), above, to the partnership (and to A and B)?

(e) What result to C and to the partnership in (a), above, if C's profits interest was subject to forfeiture until C rendered services for the partnership for a period of five years?

4. PROPOSED REGULATIONS

The saga of the services partner who is compensated with a partnership interest never seems to rest. The Internal Revenue Service has issued proposed regulations[1] and a proposed revenue procedure[2] that adopt a new approach for taxing a transfer of a partnership interest in connection with the performance of services. The proposed regulations provide that a partnership interest is "property" for purposes of Section 83 and do not distinguish between partnership capital and profits interests.[3] Their key features are a safe harbor election for valuation of a transferred partnership interest and nonrecognition of gain or loss for the partnership in connection with the transfer.

Safe Harbor Election. Under the proposed regulations, a partnership and all of its partners may elect a safe harbor under which the fair market value of a partnership interest that is transferred in connection with the performance of services is treated as being equal to the liquidation value of the partnership interest.[4] "Liquidation value" generally is the amount of cash that the service partner would receive if, immediately after the transfer, the partnership sold all of its assets (including goodwill, going concern value, and any other intangibles associated with the partnership's operations) for cash equal to the fair market value of those assets and then liquidated.[5] Thus, under the safe harbor, a service partner who receives a partnership interest that is substantially vested under Section 83 will

1. REG–105346–03, 70 Fed. Reg. 29675 (May 24, 2005).

2. I.R.S. Notice 2005–43, 2005–1 C.B. 1221.

3. Prop. Reg. § 1.83–3(e); Preamble to Proposed Regulations, 70 Fed. Reg. 29675 (May 24, 2005).

4. Prop. Reg. § 1.83–3(*l*)(1).

5. Prop. Rev. Proc. 2005–43, § 4.02, 2005–1 C.B. 1221.

recognize compensation income equal to the liquidation value of the transferred partnership interest less any amount paid for the interest. If the partnership interest that is received for services is not substantially vested (i.e., it is subject to a substantial risk of forfeiture and not transferable) and the partner does not make a Section 83(b) election, the service partner will recognize as compensation income the liquidation value of the interest when it vests under Section 83 less any amount paid for the interest. Finally, if the partnership interest is not substantially vested and the service partner makes a Section 83(b) election, then the partner includes as compensation income the liquidation value of the interest at the time of the election less any amount paid for the partnership interest.[6] It is important to recognize that the definition of liquidation value for measuring the amount of compensation income generally will produce a zero value for any profits interest that is received by a service partner because a partner who only has a profits interest would not receive any cash upon sale of all of the partnership's assets immediately after the transfer. Thus, while the proposed regulations adopt a new analytical framework and new terminology, the bottom-line result to a services partner generally does not change. In most situations, a services partner will be able to receive a profits interest tax free.

The safe harbor election is available only in the case of a "safe harbor partnership interest." Borrowing from Revenue Procedure 93–27, the Service defines a safe harbor partnership interest as any partnership interest provided that it is not: (a) related to a substantially certain and predictable stream of income from partnership assets, such as income from high-quality debt securities or a high-quality net lease, (b) transferred in anticipation of a subsequent disposition, or (c) an interest in a publicly traded partnership interest within the meaning of Section 7704(b). If a partnership interest is sold or disposed of within two years of receipt, it is presumed to have been transferred in anticipation of a subsequent disposition unless the contrary is established by clear and convincing evidence.[7]

Required Conditions for the Safe Harbor Election. In order to effect and maintain a safe harbor election, the partnership must: (1) prepare a document, executed by a partner who has responsibility for federal income tax reporting, stating that the partnership is electing, on behalf of the partnership and each of its partners, to have the safe harbor apply irrevocably, and (2) include in the partnership agreement provisions that are legally binding on all of the partners that (a) the partnership is authorized and directed to elect the safe harbor, and (b) the partnership and each of its partners agrees to comply with all of the requirements of the safe harbor.[8]

6. Id. at § 5.01.

7. Id. at § 3.02. Rights to buy or sell the partnership interest created within two years of receipt also are treated as equivalent to a sale or disposition and exceptions are provided for sales and dispositions by reason of death or disability. Id.

8. Prop. Reg. § 1.83–3(*l*)(1)(i) & (ii). If the partnership agreement does not satisfy these requirements, then each partner must execute a document that satisfies the require-

Service Partner's Capital Account. The capital account of the service partner is the amount of money contributed by the partner to the partnership plus the amount included in income under Section 83.[9]

Recognition of Gain or Loss by the Partnership. Under the proposed regulations, a partnership generally does not recognize gain or loss on the transfer or substantial vesting of a compensatory partnership interest.[10] The Service concluded that a nonrecognition rule for the partnership "is more consistent with the policies underlying section 721—to defer recognition of gain and loss when persons join together to conduct a business—than would be a rule requiring the partnership to recognize gain on the transfer of these types of interests."[11] The historic partners will be required to recognize any built-in income or loss in the partnership's assets when those assets are later sold or depreciated.[12] The nonrecognition rule does not apply, however, in the case of a transfer of property that results in the creation of a partnership. Thus, in the *McDougal* case at page 65 of the text, the McDougals' transfer of one-half of Iron Card to McClanahan is still a taxable transaction to the McDougals under the proposed regulations.[13]

Deduction for the Partnership. Assuming that the partnership is entitled to a deduction for the services that the partner performed in exchange for the partnership interest (e.g., the expenditure does not have to be capitalized), the deduction generally is allowed for the taxable year of the partnership in which or with which ends the taxable year of the service partner in which the amount is included in gross income as compensation.[14] Any deduction allowed to the partnership generally is allocated to the historic partners.[15]

Characterization of Transferee Partner. The proposed regulations provide that the holder of a partnership interest that is substantially nonvested under section 83 is not treated as a partner unless the holder makes a Section 83(b) election.[16]

Forfeiture of Compensatory Partnership Interest. If the holder of a nonvested partnership interest makes a section 83(b) election, the holder

ments of the safe harbor. Prop. Reg. § 1.83–3(*l*)(1)(iii). A safe harbor election terminates if: (1) a condition or requirement for the election is not satisfied, (2) the partnership or a partner reports the tax effects of the transfer of a partnership interest in a manner inconsistent with the proposed revenue procedure, or (3) the partnership affirmatively terminates the election. Prop. Rev. Proc. 2005–43, supra note 5, § 3.04. If an election terminates, the partnership is not eligible to make another election for five years without the consent of the Service. Id. at § 3.05.

9. Prop. Reg. § 1.704–1(b)(2)(iv)(*b*)(1).

10. Prop. Reg. §§ 1.83–6(b); 1.721–1(b)(1).

11. Preamble to Proposed Regulations, supra note 3.

12. Id. See generally Chapter 4C.

13. Preamble to Proposed Regulations, supra note 3.

14. The transfer is treated as a guaranteed payment under Section 707(c) but the timing of the deduction is determined under Section 83(h). Prop. Reg. §§ 1.707–1(c); 1.721–1(b)(4)(i).

15. I.R.C. § 706(d)(1); Prop. Reg. § 1.706–3; see generally Chapter 4E.

16. Prop. Reg. § 1.761–1(b).

will be treated as a partner and may be allocated items of partnership income, gain, loss or deduction. But keep in mind that the holder of a partnership interest that is nonvested may not satisfy the conditions for retaining the interest and the interest may later be forfeited. The proposed regulations provide that allocations of income, gain, loss, and deduction to the holder of a nonvested partnership interest who has made a Section 83(b) election generally will be respected if the partnership agreement requires that the partnership will make forfeiture allocations if the interest is forfeited.[17] Forfeiture allocations basically offset prior allocations of income or loss and distributions that were made to the holder of the forfeited interest.[18] Upon forfeiture of the partnership interest by the holder, the partnership must also include in income an amount equal to any deduction that was allowable when the holder made the section 83(b) election.[19]

Examples. The proposed Revenue Procedure includes several examples, some of which are reproduced in the excerpt below, to illustrate the fundamental principles of the proposed regulations.[20] Each of the examples assumes that the partnership, its members, and the service providers qualify for and make the safe harbor election.

Excerpt from Proposed Revenue Procedure 2005–43

2005–1 C.B. 1221.

(1) Example 1: Substantially Vested Profits Interest

Facts: PRS has two partners, A and B, each with a 50% interest in PRS. On March 1, 2005, SP agrees to perform services for the partnership in exchange for a partnership interest. Under the terms of the partnership agreement, SP is entitled to 10% of the future profits and losses of PRS, but is not entitled to any of the partnership's capital as of the date of transfer. Although SP must surrender the partnership interest upon termination of services to the partnership, SP will not surrender any share of the profits accumulated through the end of the partnership taxable year preceding the partnership taxable year in which SP terminates services.

Conclusion: * * * SP's interest in PRS is treated as substantially vested at the time of transfer. [T]he fair market value of the interest for purposes of § 83 is treated as being equal to its liquidation value (zero). Therefore, SP does not recognize compensation income under § 83(a) as a result of the transfer, PRS is not entitled to a deduction, and SP is not entitled to a capital account balance.

17. Allocations of partnership items generally will be respected if such allocations have substantial economic effect. See Chapter 4B. The special rule respecting allocations to the holder of a nonvested partnership interest is in Prop. Reg. § 1.704–1(b)(4)(xii). The special rule does not apply if at the time the Section 83(b) election was made there is a plan that the interest will be forfeited. Prop. Reg. § 1.704–1(b)(4)(xii)(e).

18. Prop. Reg. §§ 1.704–1(b)(4); 1.706–3(b).

19. Reg. § 1.83–6(c).

20. Prop. Rev. Proc. 2005–43, supra note 5, § 6.

(2) Example 2: Substantially Vested Interest

Facts: PRS has two partners, A and B, each with a 50% interest in PRS. On March 1, 2005, SP pays the partnership $10 and agrees to perform services for the partnership in exchange for a 10% partnership interest that is treated as substantially vested * * *. Immediately before SP's $10 payment to PRS and the transfer of the partnership interest to SP in connection with the performance of services, the value of the partnership's assets (including goodwill, going concern value, and any other intangibles associated with the partnership's operations) is $990.

Conclusion: [T]he fair market value of SP's interest in PRS at the time the interest becomes substantially vested is treated as being equal to its liquidation value at that time for purposes of § 83. Therefore, in 2005, SP includes $90 ($100 liquidation value less $10 amount paid for the interest) as compensation income under § 83(a), PRS is entitled to a deduction of $90 under § 83(h), and SP's initial capital account is $100 ($90 included in income plus $10 amount paid for the interest).

* * *

(4) Example 4: Substantially Nonvested Interest; No § 83(b) Election

Facts: PRS has two partners, A and B, each with a 50% interest in PRS. On December 31, 2004, SP pays the partnership $10 and agrees to perform services for the partnership in exchange for a 10% partnership interest. Under the terms of the partnership agreement, if SP terminates services on or before January 1, 2008, SP forfeits any rights to any share of accumulated, undistributed profits, but is entitled to a return of SP's $10 initial contribution. SP's partnership interest is not transferable and no election is made under § 83(b). SP continues performing services through January 1, 2008. PRS earns $500 of taxable income in 2005, and $1,000 in each of 2006 and 2007. A and B each receive distributions of $225 in 2005, but neither A nor B receive distributions in 2006 and 2007. PRS transfers $50 to SP in 2005, but does not make any transfers to SP in 2006 or 2007. On January 1, 2008, SP's partnership interest has a liquidation value of $300 (taking into account the unpaid partnership income credited to SP through that date).

Conclusion: * * * SP's partnership interest is treated as substantially nonvested at the time of transfer. Because a § 83(b) election is not made, SP does not include any amount as compensation income attributable to the transfer and, correspondingly, PRS is not entitled to a deduction under § 83(h). Under proposed § 1.761–1(b), SP is not a partner in PRS; therefore, none of PRS's taxable income for the years in which SP's interest is substantially nonvested may be allocated to SP. Rather, PRS's taxable income is allocated exclusively to A and B. In addition, the $50 paid by PRS to SP in 2005 is compensation income to SP, and PRS is entitled to a deduction of $50 under § 162 in accordance with its method of accounting.

On January 1, 2008, SP's interest in PRS is treated as becoming substantially vested * * *. * * * [T]he fair market value of the interest at the time the interest becomes substantially vested is treated as being equal to its liquidation value at that time for § 83 purposes. Therefore, in 2008, SP includes $290 ($300 liquidation value less $10 amount paid for the interest) as compensation income under § 83(a), PRS is entitled to a $290 deduction, and SP's capital account is increased to $300 ($290 included in income plus $10 amount paid for the interest).

(5) Example 5: Substantially Nonvested Interest; § 83(b) Election

Facts: The facts are the same as in Example 4, except that SP makes an election under § 83(b) with respect to SP's interest in PRS. The liquidation value of the interest is $100 at the time the interest in PRS is transferred to SP. SP continues performing services through January 1, 2008.

Conclusion: [T]the fair market value (disregarding lapse restrictions) of SP's interest in PRS at the time of transfer is treated as being equal to its liquidation value (disregarding lapse restrictions) at that time for § 83 purposes. Because a § 83(b) election is made, in 2004 SP includes $90 ($100 liquidation value less $10 amount paid for the interest) as compensation income, PRS is entitled to a $90 deduction, and SP's initial capital account is $100 ($90 included in SP's income plus $10 amount paid for the interest). Under proposed § 1.761–1(b), as a result of SP's election under § 83(b), SP is treated as a partner starting from the date of the transfer of the interest to SP. Accordingly, SP includes in 2005 taxable income SP's $50 distributive share of PRS income, and the $50 payment to SP by PRS in 2005 is a partnership distribution under § 731. SP includes in 2006 and 2007 taxable income SP's $100 distributive shares of PRS income for those years.

(6) Example 6: Substantially Nonvested Interest; § 83(b) Election; Forfeiture; Net Profit

Facts: The facts are the same as in Example 5, except that SP terminates services on September 30, 2007, and is repaid the $10 that SP paid for the PRS interest in 2004. The partnership agreement provides that if SP's partnership interest is forfeited, SP's distributive share of all partnership items (other than forfeiture allocations) will be zero with respect to the interest for the taxable year of the partnership in which the interest is forfeited.

Conclusion: The tax consequences for 2004 through 2006 are the same as in Example (5). As a result of the forfeiture in 2007, PRS is required under § 1.83–6(c) to include in gross income $90 (the amount of the allowable deduction on the transfer of the interest to SP). In accordance with the partnership agreement, PRS also makes forfeiture allocations in 2007 to offset partnership income and loss that was allocated to SP and partnership distributions to SP prior to the forfeiture. Cumulative net income of $150 was allocated to SP prior to the forfeiture ($50 in 2005 and

$100 in 2006) and SP received a total of $60 of distributions from PRS ($50 in 2005 and $10 in 2007 (the repayment of SP's initial contribution to PRS)). Under proposed § 1.704–1(b)(4)(xii), the total forfeiture allocations to SP is $100 of partnership loss and deduction, the difference between $50 ($60 of distributions to SP less $10 of contributions to PRS by SP) and $150 (cumulative net income allocated to SP). Pursuant to the partnership agreement, none of the partnership income for the year 2007 is allocated to SP. In accordance with § 83(b)(1) (last sentence), SP does not receive a deduction or capital loss for the amount ($90) that was included as SP's compensation income as a result of the election under § 83(b).

* * *

D. ORGANIZATION AND SYNDICATION EXPENSES

Code: § 709.

Regulations: § 1.709–1, –2.

A wide variety of expenses is incurred on the organization of a partnership. In keeping with the approach in the corporate area,[1] Section 709(a) provides that organizational expenses and expenses in connection with the promotion and sale of partnership interests (i.e., syndication fees) are not deductible. Under Section 709(b), however, a partnership may elect to deduct up to $5,000 of organizational expenses in the taxable year in which it begins business. The $5,000 amount is reduced (but not below zero) by the amount of the partnership's organizational expenses in excess of $50,000.[2] Organizational expenses that are not deducted in the year in which the partnership begins business may be amortized ratably over the 180–month period beginning with the month in which the business begins.[3] If the partnership liquidates before the end of the 180–month amortization period, it may deduct the unamortized portion of its organizational expenses (but not capitalized syndication expenses) as a loss under Section 165.[4]

"Organizational expenses" are defined in Section 709(b)(3) as expenditures that are: (1) incident to the creation of the partnership; (2) chargeable to capital account; and (3) of a character which, if expended to create a partnership having an ascertainable life, would be amortizable over that life. Examples are legal fees incident to the organization of the partnership, including negotiation and preparation of the partnership agreement; fees

1. See I.R.C. § 248.

2. I.R.C. § 709(b)(1)(A).

3. I.R.C. § 709(b)(1)(B). The 180–month period corresponds to the amortization period for intangibles in Section 197.

4. I.R.C. § 709(b)(2). If the partnership did not elect to amortize its organizational expenses, it may not deduct those costs on liquidation under Section 165. Rev.Rul. 87–111, 1987–2 C.B. 160. But because the costs ordinarily are reflected in the partners' outside bases, they should decrease the capital gain, increase the capital loss, or increase the basis of distributed property when the partnership liquidates. See Chapter 8D, infra.

for establishing an accounting system; and filing fees.[5] Specifically excluded are expenses connected with acquiring assets or transferring assets to the partnership; expenses connected with a contract relating to the operation of the partnership's trade or business; and syndication expenses.[6]

The flat ban against deducting or amortizing syndication expenses is intended to preclude the typical investment limited partnership from deducting payments made for services rendered with respect to the promotion of the venture. "Syndication expenses" are defined broadly to include brokerage and registration fees; legal fees of the underwriter and the general partner for securities advice; accounting fees for preparation of representations to be included in the offering materials; and printing costs of all selling and promotional material.[7] The Service also has ruled that fees paid by a syndicated limited partnership for the tax opinion used in its prospectus is a syndication expense that is neither deductible under Section 212(3) nor amortizable under Section 709(b).[8]

5. Reg. § 1.709–2(a).

6. Id.

7. Reg. § 1.709–2(b). See Flowers v. Commissioner, 80 T.C. 914 (1983); Rev.Rul. 85–32, 1985–1 C.B. 186.

8. Rev.Rul. 88–4, 1988–1 C.B. 264. See Surloff v. Commissioner, 81 T.C. 210 (1983).

CHAPTER 3

Operations of a Partnership: General Rules

A. Tax Consequences to the Partnership: Aggregate and Entity Principles

1. The Partnership as an Entity

Code: §§ 701; 702(b); 703. Skim §§ 179(d)(8); 442; 702(a); 6031.

Regulations: §§ 1.701–1; 1.702–1(b); 1.703–1(a), (b)(1); 1.6031–1(e)(2).

The rules in Subchapter K for the taxation of partnership operations are a mixture of aggregate and entity principles. Section 701 adopts an aggregate approach by providing that a partnership is not a taxable entity. Instead, it is a conduit through which the income, deductions, credits and other tax attributes generated by partnership activities flow to the partners, who separately report their distributive shares of these items. But imagine a pure pass-through approach where each partner would independently determine partnership accounting methods, the availability of deductions, tax elections affecting the computation of taxable income and the many other issues that arise in computing the tax liability of a business enterprise. If each partner were left to his own devices, the results would be chaotic.

To bring order and uniformity to the taxation of partnership operations, Congress wisely chose to treat partnerships as entities for purposes of reporting and determining partnership income or loss. A partnership thus is required to file an informational tax return[1] and is essentially treated as an entity for purposes of administrative and judicial procedures.[2] Section 703(a) requires a partnership to determine its own taxable income and provides rules designed to preserve the character of capital gains, charitable contributions, foreign taxes and other items that may be subject to special treatment in the hands of the partners.[3] Section 702(b) similarly

1. I.R.C. § 6031. The return is to be filed on or before the 15th day of the fourth month after the close of the partnership's taxable year. Reg. § 1.6031–1(e)(2). Failure to file can lead to civil or criminal penalties. I.R.C. §§ 6698; 7203. Rev.Proc. 84–35, 1984–1 C.B. 509, provides that in certain limited situations, partnerships with 10 or fewer partners will not be penalized for failing to file partnership tax returns.

2. I.R.C. §§ 6221–6234.

3. Section 702(a) lists certain items which must be separately stated so that they are properly reflected on the partners' returns, and Section 703(a)(2) disallows certain deductions in computing partnership taxable income. The mechanics of these computations

provides that the character of a partnership item taxed to the partners is to be determined "as if such item were realized directly from the source from which realized by the partnership, or incurred in the same manner as incurred by the partnership." As a result, questions involving the holding period of property[4] or the characterization of gains and losses[5] are determined at the partnership level.

In harmony with the entity approach, Section 703(b) provides, with limited exceptions, that the partnership will select its accounting method[6] and make various elections affecting the computation of taxable income. The partnership also will have its own taxable year, which may be separate from the taxable years of some of its partners.[7] The ruling and case that follow illustrate Subchapter K's application of entity principles to the characterization of partnership income and loss and partnership tax elections.

Revenue Ruling 68–79

1968–1 Cum.Bull. 310.

Advice has been requested whether a partner's distributive share of partnership capital gains resulting under the circumstances described below is long-term capital gain. [Under the 1954 Code, as applicable to the years involved in this ruling, the required holding period for long-term capital gain or loss treatment was more than six months. Eds.]

A, B and *C* were equal partners in *ABC* partnership. On June 1, 1966, the partnership acquired 300 shares of *X* corporation stock as an investment. On February 1, 1967, *A* sold his partnership interest to new partner *D*. On May 1, 1967, the partnership sold at a gain the 300 shares of *X* stock (at which time *D*'s holding period for his partnership interest was not more than six months).

Section 1222(1) of the Internal Revenue Code of 1954 defines the term "short-term capital gain" as gain from the sale or exchange of a capital asset held for not more than six months, if and to the extent such gain is taken into account in computing gross income.

Section 1222(3) of the Code defines the term "long-term capital gain" as gain from the sale or exchange of a capital asset held for more than six months, if and to the extent that such gain is taken into account in computing gross income.

Section 702(a) of the Code provides that in determining his income tax, each partner shall take into account separately his distributive share of the

and their impact on the partners is discussed in Section B of this chapter.

4. See Rev.Rul. 68–79, below.

5. McManus v. Commissioner, 65 T.C. 197 (1975), affirmed 583 F.2d 443 (9th Cir. 1978), cert. denied, 440 U.S. 959, 99 S.Ct. 1501 (1979); Podell v. Commissioner, 55 T.C. 429 (1970).

6. Reg. § 1.703–1(b)(1). But see I.R.C. § 448(a)(2), (b).

7. See Section A3 of this chapter, infra.

partnership's gains and losses from sales or exchanges of capital assets held for more than six months.

Section 702(b) of the Code provides that the character of any item of income, gain, loss, deduction, or credit included in a partner's distributive share under paragraphs (1) through (8) of subsection (a) shall be determined as if such item were realized directly from the source from which realized by the partnership, or incurred in the same manner as incurred by the partnership.

The character of any item of income, gain, loss, deduction, or credit included in a partner's distributive share under paragraphs (1) through (8) of section 702(a) of the Code is determined at the partnership level. Compare Revenue Ruling 67–188, C.B. 1967–1, 216.

Since the *ABC* partnership held the *X* stock for more than six months, the gain realized by the partnership is long-term capital gain.

Accordingly, in computing his gross income, *D* should take into account separately in his return, as long-term capital gain, his distributive share of the partnership's long-term capital gain arising from the sale by the partnership of *X* corporation stock held by it as an investment for more than six months, notwithstanding that *D* has a holding period for his partnership interest of not more than six months.

Demirjian v. Commissioner

United States Court of Appeals, Third Circuit, 1972.
457 F.2d 1.

■ VAN DUSEN, CIRCUIT JUDGE.

The petitioning taxpayers, Anne and Mabel Demirjian, have filed a timely petition for review of an adverse decision of the Tax Court affirming a finding of tax deficiencies for 1962 by the Commissioner of Internal Revenue. The tax deficiencies were based on the failure to report $54,835.00 in gain for the taxable year 1962. Plaintiffs maintain that the gain in question is covered by the nonrecognition provisions of Code Section 1033. As pointed out below, we agree with the ruling of the Tax Court that § 703 of the Internal Revenue Code requires that the nonrecognition of gain election and replacement under § 1033 be made by Kin–Bro Realty, a partnership, and that the replacements by plaintiffs individually were thus ineffective.

The facts, as stipulated in the proceedings before the Tax Court, show that Anne and Mabel Demirjian each owned 50% of the stock of Kin–Bro Realty Corporation, which had acquired title to a three-story office building in Newark, New Jersey, in October 1944. On November 3, 1960, the corporation was dissolved and its chief asset, the office building, was conveyed by deed to "Anne Demirjian * * * and Mabel Demirjian * * * partners trading as Kin–Bro Real Estate Company." Although no formal partnership agreement was executed, Anne and Mabel did file a trade name certificate indicating that they intended to conduct a real estate investment business at the Newark office building under the name of Kin–Bro Real Estate Company. The office building, which constituted Kin–Bro's sole operating asset, was conveyed to the Newark Housing Authority on September 12, 1962, after an involuntary condemnation proceeding. In the deed of conveyance the grantors are listed as "Anne Demirjian and Mabel Demirjian, partners trading as Kin–Bro Real Estate Company." The net proceeds of the sale were distributed to Anne and Mabel in amounts equal to approximately 50% of the total sale price. At this point, both Anne and Mabel apparently elected to replace the property with equivalent property in order to take advantage of the nonrecognition of gain provision contained in § 1033 of the Internal Revenue Code. Normally gain resulting from the sale or exchange of investment real property is taxable, but § 1033 provides that if property is involuntarily converted and the proceeds are used to replace it with substantially equivalent property within one year [now two years, Ed.] then gain is recognized only to the extent that the amount received due to the conversion exceeds the purchase price of the replacement property. The reinvestments, however, were made by Anne and Mabel as individuals and not through the partnership. On April 15, 1963, Anne invested $40,934.05 of her share of the proceeds in property which was similar to the condemned property. Mabel was unable to find suitable replacement property within the one-year replacement period, and, by letter of October 17, 1963, she made a written application to the District Director of Internal Revenue, Newark, New Jersey, for an extension of time in which to make such a replacement. In a letter dated January 16, 1964, the District Director stated:

> "In a letter dated October 17, 1963 received from Mr. Ralph Niebart and subsequent correspondence, an extension of time was requested for the purpose of replacing your share of the partnership property that was owned by Kin–Bro Real Estate Company (a partnership). The property was sold to the Housing Authority of the City of Newark on September 12, 1962 under threat of condemnation.
>
> "You have stated that although you have made a continued effort to replace the converted property, you have not been successful to date.
>
> * * *
>
> "Based on the information submitted, together with the data already in our file, extension is hereby granted until December 31, 1964, within which to complete the replacement of the converted property."

On February 7, 1964, Mabel invested $45,711.17 in similar real estate. Neither Anne nor Mabel reported any portion of the gain realized on the condemnation sale in their initial returns for the 1962 tax year. In 1964 Anne and Mabel filed amended 1962 joint returns with their husbands, reporting the excess of their distributive share from the condemnation sale over the cost of their respective replacement property as long-term capital gains. The Commissioner of Internal Revenue disagreed with these computations and assessed deficiencies, reasoning that the § 1033 election for nonrecognition of gain and replacement with equivalent property could only be made by the partnership under the terms of § 703(b) of the Code. The Tax Court affirmed the Commissioner's finding of deficiencies and plaintiffs here appeal that decision.

In reviewing a decision of the Tax Court, this court is normally limited in its scope of review by the clearly erroneous test of Rule 52(a), F.R.Civ.P. However, in cases such as the instant action, where the facts have been fully stipulated and no testimony was taken, the Court of Appeals may, within certain limits, substitute its factual conclusions and inferences for those of the Tax Court.

Petitioners' first contention on this appeal is that the Newark office building was owned by Anne and Mabel as tenants in common, not as partners, and that, therefore, the § 1033 nonrecognition of gain election and replacement was properly made by them in their individual capacities as co-tenants. On the basis of the record before the Tax Court, we find that the property in question was owned by Kin–Bro Realty, a partnership, composed of Anne and Mabel Demirjian. It is noted that several federal cases have ruled that taxpayers such as petitioners who represent, in their dealings with the Internal Revenue Service, that property is owned by a partnership are bound by such representations.

Petitioners next contend that even if the office building was owned by the partnership, the election and replacement with equivalent property under 26 U.S.C. § 1033[(a)(2)(A), Ed.] were properly made by them in their capacity as individual partners. We agree with the Tax Court's determination that 26 U.S.C. § 703(b) requires that the election and replacement under § 1033 be made by the partnership and that replacement by individual partners of property owned by the partnership does not qualify for nonrecognition of the gain. Section 703(b) provides, with exceptions not relevant here, that any election which affects the computation of taxable income derived from a partnership must be made by the partnership. The election for nonrecognition of gain on the involuntary conversion of property would affect such computation and is the type of election contemplated by § 703(b). The partnership provisions of the Internal Revenue Code treat a partnership as an aggregate of its members for purposes of taxing profits to the individual members and as an entity for purposes of computing and reporting income. In light of this entity approach to reporting income, Congress included § 703(b) to avoid the possible confusion which might result if each partner were to determine partnership income separately only on his own return for his own purposes. To avoid the possible confusion which could result from separate elections under § 1033(a), the election must be made by the partnership as an entity, and the failure of the partnership to so act results in the recognition of the gain on the sale of partnership property.

Petitioners' final contention is that the Commissioner is estopped from denying that a valid election and replacement were made under § 1033.

Two separate grounds for estoppel are alleged. The first ground, that the petitioners have conformed their conduct to existing interpretations of the law and the Commissioner may not "invoke a retroactive interpretation to the taxpayer's detriment," is clearly without merit. The second alleged ground is that the Commissioner is estopped by the implicit approval of the individual partner's election and replacement by the District Director for Newark in his letter of January 16, 1964. Even if we were to accept the letter as a justifiable basis for detrimental reliance, petitioners have demonstrated no such reliance and, furthermore, the doctrine of estoppel does not prevent the Commissioner from correcting errors of law.

For the foregoing reasons, the September 1, 1970, orders of the Tax Court, in accordance with its opinion of that date, will be affirmed.

2. Assignment of Income

Schneer v. Commissioner

United States Tax Court, 1991.
97 T.C. 643.

■ Gerber, Judge: * * *

[The taxpayer, Mr. Schneer, was an associate in a law firm ("BSI"). BSI paid Schneer a salary and a percentage of fees generated by the clients he referred to the firm. When Schneer resigned from BSI, he was entitled to receive a percentage of the fees from clients he had referred to that firm and fees for other consulting services that he was obligated to perform for BSI with respect to those clients. Schneer subsequently became a partner in two different law firms ("B & K" and "SSG & M"). Under the partnership agreements of those firms, he was required to turn over the fees that he received from BSI. The new firms treated the fees as partnership income and allocated them to each partner, including Schneer, according to the partners' respective share of partnership profits. Ed.]

We consider here basic principles of income taxation. There is agreement that the amounts paid to petitioner by his former employer-law firm are income in the year of receipt. The question is whether petitioner (individually) or the partners of petitioner's partnerships (including petitioner) should report the income in their respective shares.

The parties have couched the issue in terms of the anticipatory assignment-of-income principles. See Lucas v. Earl, 281 U.S. 111 (1930). Equally important to this case, however, is the viability of the principle that partners may pool their earnings and report partnership income in amounts different from their contribution to the pool. See sec. 704(a) and (b). The parties' arguments bring into focus potential conflict between these two principles and compel us to address both.

First, we examine the parties' arguments with respect to the assignment-of-income doctrine. Respondent argues that petitioner earned the income in question before leaving BSI, despite the fact that petitioner did not receive that income until he was a partner in B & K and, later, SSG &

M. According to respondent, by entering into partnership agreements requiring payment of all legal fees to his new partnerships, petitioner anticipatorily assigned to those partnerships the income earned but not yet received from BSI. * * *

Petitioner contends that the income in question was not earned until after he left BSI and joined B & K and SSG & M. He argues that the income received from BSI is reportable by the partners of the B & K and SSG & M partnerships (including petitioner) in their respective shares. Petitioner also points out that partnership agreements, which like the ones in issue allocate and redistribute partners' income, have received the approval of respondent in Rev.Rul. 64–90, 1964–1 (Part 1) C.B. 226. Petitioner argues that he was obligated to consult with BSI in order to be entitled to the BSI fees. Petitioner concedes that, for some of the income in question, no consultation was performed or requested. He emphasizes, however, that a substantial amount (about 90 percent) of the fees involved clients of BSI for whom consultation was performed. Finally, petitioner believes that his failure to consult would have resulted in loss of the fees.

The principle of assignment of income, in the context of Federal taxation, first arose in Lucas v. Earl, supra, where the Supreme Court, interpreting the Revenue Act of 1918, held that income from a husband-taxpayer's legal practice was taxable to him, even though he and his wife had entered into a valid contract under State law to split all income earned by each of them. In so holding, Justice Holmes, speaking for the Court, stated:

> There is no doubt that the statute could tax salaries to those who earned them and provide that the tax could not be escaped by anticipatory arrangements and contracts however skillfully devised to prevent the salary when paid from vesting even for a second in the man who earned it. [281 U.S. at 114–115.]

From that pervasive and simply stated interpretation, a plethora of cases and learned studies have sprung forth. Early cases reflected the use of the assignment-of-income principle only with respect to income not yet earned. The theory behind those interpretations was that income not yet earned is controlled by the assignor, even if assigned to another. Such income is necessarily generated by services not yet performed. Because the assignor may refuse to perform services, he necessarily has control over income yet to be earned. * * * This early rationale left open the possibility of successful assignments, for tax purposes, of income already earned. That possibility was foreclosed in Helvering v. Eubank, 311 U.S. 122 (1940), where the Supreme Court held that income already earned would also fall within the assignment-of-income doctrine of Lucas v. Earl, supra.

* * *

In this case, petitioner was not entitled to the referral fees unless the work for the referred clients had been successfully completed. On the other hand, petitioner would be entitled to the fees if the work was completed or if at the time of the assignment there was nothing contingent in petitioner's right to collect his percentage of the fees. Additionally, the majority of the services had not been performed prior to petitioner's leaving BSI. In this regard services had been performed with respect to $1,250 prior to 1984. With respect to $3,325 of the $21,329 of fees received in 1984, petitioner did not consult and was not required to do anything subsequent to leaving BSI to be entitled to those fees. With respect to the remainder of the $21,329 for 1984 and all of the 1985 fees, petitioner was called upon to and did consult while he was a partner of B & K or SSG & M.

We must decide whether petitioner had earned the fees in question prior to assigning them to the B & K or the SSG & M partnerships. Although petitioner was on the cash method, the principles that control use of the cash method are not suited to this inquiry. For purposes of the assignment-of-income doctrine, it must be determined whether the income was earned prior to an assignment. * * *

The record in this case reflects that, with the exception of $1,250 of services performed in prior years, the billings and payments in question were performed and collected subsequent to the time of assignment of the income. * * *

With these principles as our guide, we hold that petitioner had not earned the fees in question prior to leaving BSI, with the exception of the $1,250 received for services performed in an earlier year. More specifically, we hold that petitioner earned the income in question while a partner of a partnership to which he had agreed to pay such income. With respect to substantially all of the fees in issue, BSI records reflect that clients were billed and payment received during the years in issue. Moreover, if petitioner had refused a request for his consultation, it was, at the very least, questionable whether he would have received his share of the fee if the work had been successfully completed without him. Petitioner was requested to and did provide further services with regard to clients from which about 90 percent of the fees were generated. We note that BSI did not request consultation with respect to $3,325 remitted during 1984. However, that amount was not earned as of the time of the assignment because the work had not yet been performed for the BSI clients (irrespective of whether or not petitioner would be called upon to consult). Accordingly, with the exception of $1,250 for petitioner's 1984 taxable year, we hold that petitioner had not earned the income in question prior to leaving BSI and did not make an anticipatory assignment of income which had been earned.

Two additional related questions remain for our consideration. First, respondent argues that irrespective of when petitioner earned the income from BSI, "there was no relationship * * * [between] the past activity of introducing a client to * * * [BSI], and the petitioner's work as a partner with * * * [B & K or SSG & M]." According to respondent, petitioner should not be allowed to characterize as partnership income fees that did not have a requisite or direct relationship to a partnership's business. In making this argument, respondent attempts to limit and modify his long-standing and judicially approved position in Rev.Rul. 64–90, 1964–1 C.B. (Part 1) 226. * * * Second, while we generally hold that petitioner did not make an assignment of income already earned, the possibility that this was an assignment of unearned income was not foreclosed.

These final two questions bring into focus the true nature of the potential conflict in this case—between respondent's revenue ruling and the assignment-of-income doctrine. Both questions, in their own way, ask whether any partnership agreement—under which partners agree in advance to turn over to the partnership all income from their individual efforts—can survive scrutiny under the assignment-of-income principles.

Rev.Rul. 64–90, 1964–1 (Part 1) C.B. at 226–227, in pertinent part, contains the following:

> Federal income tax treatment of compensation received by a partner and paid over to a partnership where the partner, who uses the cash receipts and disbursements method of accounting, files his returns on a calendar year basis and the partnership, which also uses the cash method, files its returns on a fiscal year basis. * * *
>
> Advice has been requested regarding the Federal income tax consequences of a change in the terms of a partnership agreement to provide that all compensation received by the partners will be paid over to the partnership immediately upon receipt.
>
> In the instant case, several individuals formed a partnership for the purpose of engaging in the general practice of law. Aside from the partnership business, each of the partners has performed services from time to time in his individual capacity and not as a partner. The several partners have always regarded the fees received for such services as compensation to the recipient as an individual.
>
> The partnership which was formed in 1954 and uses the cash receipts and disbursements method of accounting files its Federal income tax returns for fiscal years ending January 31, and the partners file their individual returns on the cash method for calendar years. Each partner reports his distributive share of the partnership income, gain, loss, deduction or credit for the partnership fiscal year ending within the calendar year for which his individual return is filed. All compensation received by each partner for services performed in his individual capacity is reported in that partner's return for the calendar year when received.
>
> It is proposed to amend the partnership agreement as of the beginning of the partnership's next fiscal year to provide that all compensation received by the partners be paid over to the partnership immediately upon receipt.
>
> The question in the instant case is whether compensation remitted to the partnership pursuant to this provision will constitute partnership income.

> Similar inquiries were previously considered by the Internal Revenue Service. * * * In both instances, it was pointed out that a partnership could not exist for the purpose of performing the services for which the compensation and allowances were received, and, thus, the recipient partner would be required to report the taxable portion of the compensation and allowances in his individual return, even though these items were pooled with partnership earnings. * * *
>
> *In the instant case, the general practice of the partnership consists of rendering legal advice and services. Consequently, fees received by a partner for similar services performed in his individual return capacity will be considered as partnership income if paid to the partnership in accordance with the agreement. Those fees need not be reported separately by the partner on his individual return. However, the partner's distributive share of the partnership's taxable income which he must report on his individual return will include a portion of such fees.* [Emphasis supplied.]

A key requirement of this ruling is that the services for which fees are received by individual partners must be SIMILAR to those normally performed by the partnership. * * * Respondent now attempts to add to this requirement by arguing that the fees here in question were earned through activity, which was admittedly legal work, but was not sufficiently related to the work of petitioner's new partnerships. In other words, respondent argues that the income here was earned in BSI's business activity and not B & K's or SSG & M's business activity.

* * *

There is no need for us to adopt a broader view of petitioner's partnership in this case. His referral fee income was clearly earned through activities "within the ambit" of the business of his new partnerships. Their business was the practice of law as was petitioner's consulting activity for BSI. His work was incident to the conduct of the business of his partnerships. We decline to adopt respondent's more narrow characterization of the business of petitioner's new partnerships. Neither the case law nor respondent's rulings support such a characterization.

Thus, we arrive at the final question in this case. We have already held that petitioner had not yet earned the majority of the income in question when he joined his new partnerships. Additionally, petitioner's fee income from his BSI clients qualifies, under the case law and respondent's rulings, as income generated by services sufficiently related to the business conducted by petitioner's new partnerships. If we decide that petitioner's partnerships should report the income in question, petitioner would be taxable only to the extent of his respective partnership share. This would allow petitioner, through his partnership agreements with B & K and SSG & M, to assign income not yet earned from BSI. Thus, the case law and respondent's rulings permit (without explanation), in a partnership setting, the type of assignment addressed by Lucas v. Earl, 281 U.S. 111 (1930). We must reconcile the principle behind Rev.Rul. 64–90, 1964–1 C.B. (Part 1) 226, with Lucas v. Earl, supra. The question is whether income not yet earned and anticipatorily assigned under certain partnership agreements are without the reach of the assignment-of-income principle.

The Internal Revenue Code of 1954 provided the first comprehensive statutory scheme for the tax treatment of partners and partnerships. No section of the 1954 Code, successive amendments or acts, nor the legislative history specifically addresses the treatment of income earned by partners in their individual capacity but which is pooled with other partnership income. It is implicit in subchapter K, however, that the pooling of income and losses of partners was intended by Congress. This question is more easily answered where the partnership contracts with the client for services which are then performed by the partner. The question becomes more complex where the partner contracts and performs the services when he is a partner.

Moreover, no opinion contains a satisfactory rationale as to why partnership pooling agreements do not come within the holding of Lucas v. Earl, supra. * * *

The fundamental theme penned by Justice Holmes provides that the individual who earns income is liable for the tax. It is obvious that the partnership, as an abstract entity, does not provide the physical and mental activity that facilitates the process of "earning" income. Only a partner can do so. The income earned is turned over to the partnership due solely to a contractual agreement, i.e., an assignment, in advance, of income.

The pooling of income is essential to the meaningful existence of subchapter K. If partners were not able to share profits in an amount disproportionate to the ratio in which they earned the underlying income, the partnership provisions of the Code would, to some extent, be rendered unnecessary. * * *

The provisions of subchapter K tacitly imply that the pooling of income is permissible. Said implication may provide sufficient reason to conclude that a partnership should be treated as an entity for the purpose of pooling the income of its partners. Under an entity approach, the income would be considered that of the partnership rather than the partner, even though the partner's individual efforts may have earned the income. If the partnership is treated as an entity earning the income, then assignment-of-income concepts would not come into play.

In this regard, an analysis of personal service corporations (PSC's) may provide, by way of analogy, some assistance in reconciling the principles inherent in Rev.Rul. 64–90, 1964–1 C.B. (Part 1) at 226, with those underlying Lucas v. Earl, supra. Keeping in mind Justice Holmes' desire to tax the "earner" of the income, we consider the assignment-of-income doctrine in the context of personal service corporation cases. In partnerships and personal service corporations an individual performs the services that earn income. In both, a separate entity—the partnership or personal service corporation—is cast as the "earner" for tax purposes. That characterization in both situations is, in essence, an assignment of income.[9] If, in either situation, the transfer to the entity is of income earned before an agreement to turn it over is entered into, the assignment-of-income doctrine will serve to invalidate the transfer.[10] In both the context of a PSC or partnership, transfers prior to the performance of a partner's services may be subject to the partner's or employee's control—in that either may refuse to perform.

In analyzing the status of personal service corporations, courts have relied upon the rationale that:

> the realities of the business world present an overly simplistic application of the Lucas v. Earl rule whereby the true earner may be identified by merely pointing to the one actually turning the spade or dribbling the ball. Recognition must be given to corporations as taxable entities which, to a great extent, rely upon the personal services of their employees to produce corporate income. When a corporate employee performs labors which give rise to income, it solves little merely to identify the actual laborer. Thus, a tension has evolved between the basic tenets of Lucas v. Earl and recognition of the nature of the corporate business form. [Fn. ref. omitted.]

Johnson v. Commissioner, 78 T.C. 882, 890 (1982). * * * Thus, an employee of a personal service corporation, or other corporate entity, is outside the holding of Lucas v. Earl, supra, to some degree because of the "entity concept." The business entity is cast as the earner of the income, obviating the need to analyze whether there has been an assignment of income.[11]

The same type of approach may be used with respect to partners of a partnership. In the same manner that a corporation is considered the earner of income gained through the labor of its employees, a partnership, with an appropriate partnership agreement, may be considered the earner

9. The same could be said of the normal corporate entity as well. The analogy only to PSC's, however, is slightly more apt because, as discussed below, the influence of the assignment-of-income doctrine depends to a large extent on the presence and status of the business form as an entity. In this regard, the corporate form and the partnership are at opposite ends of the spectrum. PSC's fall somewhere in between. This becomes clear through an analysis of the cases where the issue is whether the business form should be disregarded for tax purposes. Compare Moline Properties, Inc. v. Commissioner, 319 U.S. 436, 438–439 (1943) (regular corporation remains separate taxable entity so long as business activity conducted); Keller v. Commissioner, 77 T.C. 1014 (1981), affd. 723 F.2d 58 (10th Cir.1983) (PSC entity form respected because of contractual employment agreement); United States v. Basye, 410 U.S. 441, 448 (1973) (partnership an "independently recognizable entity" for reporting purposes but entity disregarded when determining partner's own tax liabilities).

10. Note that in some cases the act of incorporation itself will ostensibly act as the agreement to turn over all income earned.

11. It should be noted that in all of these cases, the assignment to the corporation was of income not yet earned. That is, in situations where the entity was validly cast as the earner of the income, the factual pattern involved an incorporation and subsequent earnings by the incorporator. Situations involving contrary facts are usually considered assignments of income.

of income.[12] Income earned prior to such an agreement, of course, remains within the principles and holding of Lucas v. Earl, supra. The link between respondent's Rev. Rul. 64–90, 1964–1 C.B. (Part 1) 226, and Lucas v. Earl, supra, must be the entity concept as it relates to partnerships.

The theory concerning partnerships as entities is not easily defined. It is well established that the partnership form is a hybrid—part separate entity, part aggregate. * * * The difficulty lies in deciding whether a particular set of circumstances relate to one end or the other of the partnership hybrid spectrum. The Supreme Court in *Basye* stated that "partnerships are entities for purposes of calculating and filing informational returns but * * * they are conduits through which the taxpaying obligation passes to the individual partners in accord with their distributive shares." 410 U.S. at 448 n. 8. This analysis provides some foundation for the idea that partners should report their distributive share, rather than the fruits of their personal labors. But it does not provide any guidance concerning the type of income or service that should be brought within the entity concept as it relates to partnerships.

The principle we must analyze in this case involves the role of the partnership with respect to the function of earning income. A general partnership[13] is "an association of two or more persons to carry on as co-owners a business for profit." Uniform Partnership Act sec. 6(1). Either a partnership or a corporation may enter into a contract with clients to perform services. In a partnership, however, either the entity or the individual may enter into contracts. The question we seek to answer is whether this distinction should be treated differently.

For purposes of an entity concept approach to partnerships, we must consider the type and source of income which should be included. Because we have already determined that the type of activity generating the income is relevant to an assignment-of-income analysis in the partnership setting, we focus our analysis of partnerships as entities on situations where the income is of a type normally earned by the partnership. Only in such situations has a partner acted as part of the partnership entity.

The entity concept as it relates to partnerships is based, in part, on the concept that a partner may further the business of the partnership by performing services in the name of the partnership or individually. The

12. We recognize that in a personal service corporation setting the person performing the service is an employee and that the contract to perform may be with the corporate entity. In a general partnership, the partners are principals and agents and not generally considered employees of the partnership. Partnerships, in the same manner as corporations, however, have employees who perform services contracted for by the partnership. That aspect draws a closer parallel between partnerships and personal service corporations for purposes of our analogy. This aspect does not answer the question concerning income of a partner becoming income of the partnership, but is concerned with the partnership's being treated as an entity for purposes of this issue.

13. Our discussion focuses upon professional partnerships composed of general partners who are actively engaged in a business venture. The principles here may not apply to limited or general partners who are mere passive investors and are not involved in the income earning process of the partnership.

name and reputation of a professional partnership plays a role in the financial success of the partnership business. If the partners perform services in the name of the partnership or individually they are, nonetheless, associated with the partnership as a partner. This is the very essence of a professional service partnership, because each partner, although acting individually, is furthering the business of the partnership. * * * The lack of structure inherent in the partnership form does not lend itself to easy resolution of the assignment-of-income question. A partnership's characteristics do, however, militate in favor of treating a partner's income from services performed in an individual capacity, which are contractually obligated to the partnership for allocation in accord with the pre-established distributive shares, in the same manner as income earned through partnership engagement.

Accordingly, in circumstances where individuals are not joining in a venture merely to avoid the effect of Lucas v. Earl, supra, it is appropriate to treat income earned by partners individually, as income earned by the partnership entity, i.e., partnership income, to be allocated to partners in their respective shares.[14] To provide the essential continuity necessary for the use of an entity concept in the partnership setting, the income should be earned from an activity which can reasonably be associated with the partnership's business activity. In the setting of this case, with the exception of $1,250 in 1984, petitioner was a partner of B & K or SSG & M when the fees were earned. Additionally, about 90 percent of the fees were, in part, earned through petitioner's efforts while he was a partner of B & K or SSG & M.

There is no apparent attempt to avoid the incidence of tax by the formation or operation of the partnerships in this case. Petitioner, in performing legal work for clients of another firm, was a partner with the law firms of B & K and SSG & M. In view of the foregoing, we hold that, with the exception of $1,250 for 1984, the fee income from BSI was correctly returned by the two partnerships in accord with the respective partnership agreements. * * *

■ BEGHE, J., concurring: I generally try to apply Occam's razor to the solution of legal problems as well as logic problems. In this case, however, I believe a two-step journey along the right-angle sides of the triangle follows a clearer path to the correct result. The path along the hypotenuse is beset with the obstacles and pitfalls of the assignment-of-income doctrine, if it isn't led to a dead-end by the disquisition on the law of agency.

14. In following this approach we can also look to the safeguards that are observed in the corporate setting where the entity is being misused. "The assignment of income doctrine * * * continues to be an essential tool * * * where the corporation is not respected by the taxpayer/shareholders as a separate entity which carries on business activities." Keller v. Commissioner, 77 T.C. at 1033. (Fn. ref. omitted.) Moreover, while geared primarily toward the family partnership area, there is a body of partnership-oriented case law involving safeguards which may be similarly applicable to the type of circumstances considered here. See Commissioner v. Culbertson, 337 U.S. 733, 742 (1949), where a facts and circumstances approach was used to determine the intent of parties in forming a partnership.

I reach the majority result in the following two steps. Even if the assignment-of-income doctrine requires petitioner to include in his gross income the amounts of the fees he earned and received from BSI after he became a partner in B & K and in SSG & M, his payments of those amounts to B & K and SSG & M, pursuant to his agreements with those firms, entitled him to equivalent concurrent deductions as ordinary and necessary business expenses under section 162(a). * * * Those amounts thereby became partnership income distributable to all the partners, including petitioner, in accordance with the partnership agreements.

■ JACOBS, J., agrees with this concurring opinion.

■ WELLS, J., dissenting: With due respect, I cannot agree with the majority's analysis and conclusion with respect to the primary issue to be decided in the instant case. Consequently, I must dissent.

The critical threshold issue framed by the majority is whether the fees were paid to petitioner for services he performed prior to leaving BSI or for services he performed after he left BSI. If the fees were for services performed by petitioner prior to the time he left BSI, they are "past services" which should be taxed to petitioner under the rule of Helvering v. Eubank, 311 U.S. 122 (1940).[1] On the other hand, if the fees were paid to petitioner for services to be performed by him after he left BSI, they are future services, Eubank does not apply, and the income should be taxed to the partners of petitioner's subsequent law firms.

To decide the issue, we must ask what petitioner did to earn the fees in question. The analysis necessary to such an inquiry should be made by examining the agreement and course of dealing between petitioner and BSI. * * * When the agreement and course of dealing between petitioner and BSI are examined closely, I am impelled to conclude that the fees in question actually were paid on account of petitioner's services in bringing or referring the clients to BSI, or at the very least, that petitioner failed to carry his burden of proving that the fees were not paid for such services.

* * *

Petitioner must show that the subsequent performance of services was the act giving rise to his right to the fees in order to put his case beyond the scope of *Eubank*. In my view, not only has he failed to do so, the majority's findings concerning the nature of the relationship between petitioner and BSI shows that the actual event giving rise to the right to the fees was the past services of petitioner in securing the clients for BSI. Accordingly, I would hold that the fee income was taxable to petitioner under assignment of income principles, as required by *Eubank*.

1. Helvering v. Eubank, 311 U.S. 122 (1940), involved an insurance agent who assigned the right to receive future renewal commissions paid on account of services he had rendered in selling insurance policies. The Supreme Court held that the commission income should be taxed to the agent, reasoning that an assignment of the right to receive income paid on account of past services was insufficient to shift the incidence of taxation on such income from the earner.

■ HALPERN, J., dissenting. The majority perceives a conflict between the anticipatory assignment-of-income doctrine, see Lucas v. Earl, 281 U.S. 111 (1930), and the principle that partners may pool their earnings and report partnership income in amounts different from their contribution to the pool. With respect, I believe the conflict to be illusory, except insofar as the majority here today creates one where heretofore none existed.

According to the majority, the mere redistribution of income within a partnership is inconsistent with the assignment-of-income doctrine. "In partnerships and personal service corporations an individual performs the services that earn income. In both, a separate entity—the partnership or personal service corporation—is cast as the 'earner' for tax purposes. That characterization in both situations is, in essence, an assignment of income." * * *

This analysis wholly ignores the doctrine of agency. When a partner, *acting as agent for the partnership*, performs services for a client, the partnership is the earner of the income: the instrumentality (in this case the partner) through which the partnership has earned its fee is of no consequence. Therefore, the focus of the anticipatory assignment-of-income analysis ought to be on whether the partner acted for himself individually or as agent of the partnership. This is entirely consistent with the latitude accorded partnerships to disproportionately distribute partnership income: the pertinent requirement is merely that the partnership income so distributed have been earned *by the partnership*. In this case, it is quite clear that petitioner earned the fees in question pursuant to an agreement he entered into, on his own behalf, with [BSI]—an agreement that was consummated before petitioner's relationship with [B & K].[2] Consequently, petitioner is the true earner of the income and should not escape taxation by means of an anticipatory assignment. Lucas v. Earl, 281 U.S. 111 (1930).

The majority's "resolution" of the perceived conflict is unsatisfactory, The majority considers the determinative question to be whether the income is "of a type normally earned by the partnership. Only in such situations has the partner acted as part of the partnership entity." * * * The majority requires merely that income "be earned from an activity which can reasonably be associated with the partnership's business activity." * * * Thus, the majority would allow a partner to assign fees to the partnership if the work performed for such fees is similar to that performed by the partnership, but not if the work is different. * * *

The majority's distinction is unprincipled.[3] The majority observes that "The name and reputation of a professional partnership plays a role in the

2. Had there been a novation, substituting the partnership for petitioner, then the partnership could properly be considered the earner of the income. In this case, however, there is no basis set forth in the majority opinion for concluding that a novation has taken place or that a substitution of [B & K] for petitioner had been even discussed with [BSI]. We are not privileged to simply assume a novation, since petitioner bears the burden of proof. Rule 142(a).

3. The majority fails to explain why the similarity of the work done by the partner to earn the fees to the work of the partnership is determinative. That failure not only casts doubt upon the correctness of this decision,

financial success of a partnership business" suggesting that partners, even acting individually, can further the business of the partnership by adding to its reputation. * * * But, that may be so even if the partner acts individually, doing work entirely dissimilar to that normally performed by the partnership. In any event, the majority fails to explain why such an obviously incidental benefit to the partnership should permit us to frustrate the assignment-of-income doctrine. The majority asserts that "The lack of structure inherent in the partnership form does not lend itself to easy resolution of the assignment-of-income question." * * * I must respectfully disagree. The lack of structure of the partnership form is irrelevant. All that matters is whether the partner has acted on his own behalf or on behalf, and as agent of, the partnership. Moreover, even if the lack of structure were relevant, the majority fails to explain why such would mandate the distinction between the type of income normally earned by the partnership and the type of income that is not. It would make far more sense to ask, with agency principles in mind, whether the income in question was earned by the partnership or by the partner acting as an individual.

Furthermore, I must disagree with Judge Beghe's concurring opinion on several grounds. First, section 721 would seem to prohibit any deduction for petitioner's contribution of money to the partnership. Second, the issue of a deduction under section 162 was not raised by the parties and thus is an inappropriate basis for decision. Third, the majority opinion does not set forth sufficient facts to determine, under the theory of the concurring opinion, the timing of any available deduction.

For the foregoing reasons, I respectfully dissent.

NOTE

The Tax Court's opinion in *Schneer* sparked a great deal of controversy, with the commentators being split in as many directions as the judges on the Tax Court. One observer labeled the decision "exquisitely wrong, so misguided at every turn, that it becomes a wayward sort of achievement."[1] Subscribing to Judge Halpern's view, this writer concludes that the critical fact for assignment of income purposes was that Schneer earned the income in his individual capacity and not as a partner of B & K and SSG & M. Further, when Schneer earned the fees he was not jointly carrying on a business enterprise with the new partnerships. Rather, he was conducting a separate business of servicing former clients and that enterprise should not have been pooled with B & K and SSG & M.

but foreshadows the difficulty future courts will have in resolving the question: how similar is similar enough? Without any inkling of why similarity has been deemed important, future courts will lack any effective guidelines for answering that question.

1. Sheppard, "Partnership Mysticism and the Assignment of Income Doctrine," 54 Tax Notes 8 (Jan. 6, 1992).

Defenders of the result in *Schneer* have offered varying alternative rationales to support the decision.[2] One commentator suggests that *Schneer* represents a proper compromise between the assignment of income doctrine and the policy of Section 721 against impeding the formation of partnerships.[3] The purpose of the assignment of income doctrine is to preserve the integrity of the progressive rates by preventing easy tax avoidance through income shifting strategies. The transaction in *Schneer* is fairly common among law partners, who typically agree to pool all of their income from the practice of law, including royalties from writings and other related earnings. Further, it is reasonable to assume that the partners of B & K and SSG & M were taxed at the same marginal tax rate as Mr. Schneer. Since the arrangement in *Schneer* posed no real abuse, the writer concludes that assignment of income doctrine is inapplicable. And if the doctrine does not apply because the transaction is not tax motivated, related issues, such as whether the income-generating activity is sufficiently similar to the business of the partnership, are no longer relevant.[4]

3. The Taxable Year

Code: § 706(b). Skim § 444.

Regulations: § 1.706–1(b)(1), (2) & (3)(i).

Section 706(a) requires a partner to include his share of partnership income, losses and other items in his tax return for the taxable year in which the partnership's year ends. To preclude partnerships from using fiscal years to achieve a deferral of the partners' tax liability, Section 706(b)(1)(B) generally requires a partnership to determine its taxable year by reference to a series of mechanical rules related to the taxable years of its partners unless the partnership can establish a "business purpose" for using a different taxable year.[1] Under the mechanical rules, if one or more partners having a majority (i.e., greater than 50 percent) interest in partnership profits and capital have the same taxable year, the partnership also must use that year.[2] Thus, if a partnership has two 30 percent individual partners who use a calendar year and a 40 percent corporate partner which uses a June 30 fiscal year, the partnership must adopt a calendar year. If partners owning a majority interest in partnership profits

2. See Asimow, "Applying the Assignment of Income Principle Correctly," 54 Tax Notes 607 (Feb. 3, 1992); Cowan, "Tax Court Leaves Confusion in Wake of Decision on Assignment of Income to Partnership," 55 Tax Notes 1535 (June 15, 1992); Raby, "Outside Income of Professionals in Practice," 54 Tax Notes 423 (Jan. 27, 1992); Raby, "More on Assignment of a Partner's Outside Income," 54 Tax Notes 991 (Feb. 24, 1992).

3. Asimow, supra note 2.

4. Id. at 608.

1. I.R.C. § 706(b)(1)(C). See infra notes 5–7 and accompanying text. Even more restrictive rules apply to S corporations (see Chapter 20, infra) and personal service corporations. See I.R.C. §§ 441(i); 1378.

2. I.R.C. § 706(b)(1)(B)(i) & (b)(4)(A)(i). Except as provided by regulations, any partnership forced to change to a "majority interest taxable year" by Section 706(b)(1)(B)(i) can not be required to change to another year for either of the two taxable years following the year of change. I.R.C. § 706(b)(4)(B).

and capital do not have the same taxable year, the partnership must use the same taxable year as all of its "principal partners" (i.e., those having a 5 percent or more interest in profits or capital).[3] If neither of these first two rules applies, the regulations require the partnership to use the taxable year that results in the least aggregate deferral of income to the partners.[4]

Alternatively, a partnership may use a year not prescribed by the mechanical tests described above if it establishes to the satisfaction of the Treasury a "business purpose" for doing so.[5] Deferral of income to partners, however, is not treated as a business purpose.[6] A business purpose for a different year may be established under either of two different tests. First, there is a business purpose for a partnership to use a natural business year if it satisfies a 25–percent test.[7] Under the test, a natural business year exists if 25 percent or more of the partnership's gross receipts for the selected year are earned in the last two months. The 25–percent test must be satisfied in each of the preceding three 12–month periods that correspond to the requested fiscal year.

If a taxpayer cannot satisfy the 25–percent test, the business purpose for a year must be established under an all facts and circumstances test, which considers the tax consequences of the proposed year.[8] Congress has identified certain nontax factors that ordinarily will not be sufficient to satisfy the business purpose requirement. Those factors are: (1) the use of a particular year for regulatory or accounting purposes; (2) the seasonal hiring patterns of a business; (3) the use of a particular year for administrative purposes, such as retirements, promotions, or salary increases; and (4) the fact that a business involves the use of price lists, a model year, or other items that change annually.[9] Because these factors all relate to taxpayer convenience, the Service has concluded that a taxpayer must demonstrate compelling reasons in order to establish a business purpose for a requested year.[10] For example, the Service found that a taxpayer established a business purpose to use a June 30 tax year, where the taxpayer could not satisfy the 25–percent test for a June 30 natural business year because a labor strike had closed the business during its normal peak season. The taxpayer also had data from prior years that demonstrated that the 25–percent test would have been met if the strike had not occurred.[11]

When the mechanical rules in Section 706(b)(1)(B) were enacted, adversely affected fiscal year entities and their tax advisors greeted the

3. I.R.C. § 706(b)(1)(B)(ii) & (b)(3). Note that this rule does not apply unless all of the "principal partners" have the same taxable year.

4. I.R.C. § 706(b)(1)(B)(iii). Reg. § 1.706–1(b)(2)(C). For a formula to determine "the least aggregate deferral," see Reg. § 1.706–1(b)(3)(i).

5. I.R.C. § 706(b)(1)(C). For a critique of the business purpose taxable year, see Hanna, "A Partnership's Business Purpose Taxable Year: A Deferral Provision Whose Time Has Passed," 45 Tax Lawyer 685 (1992).

6. I.R.C. § 706(b)(1)(C).

7. Rev. Proc. 2006–46; §§ 2.02, 2.06, 5.07; 2006–2 C.B. 859.

8. Rev. Rul. 87–57, 1987–2 C.B. 117.

9. H.R. Rep. No. 99–841, 99th Cong., 2d Sess. II–319 (1986).

10. Rev. Rul. 87–57, 1987–2 C.B. 117.

11. Id. (Situation 6).

more restrictive taxable year rules with cries of outrage. In an effort to reduce the calendar year tax return preparation workload of the accounting industry without reopening the door to deferral, Congress agreed to permit some flexibility. Under Section 444, partnerships may elect a taxable year other than the year required by the mechanical tests in Section 706(b)(1)(B) under certain conditions, including the payment of an entity-level tax designed to eliminate the benefits of deferral at the partner level.[12] When elected, Section 444 thus provides an escape from the Section 706(b)(1)(B) mechanical rules, but the election does not apply to partnerships using a taxable year for which they have established a business purpose under Section 706(b)(1)(C).[13] Thus, a partnership which has established a business purpose for a fiscal year may continue to use that year without having to make a Section 444 election or to pay an entity-level tax under Section 7519.[14]

Although Section 444 is hardly a model of clarity, it was intended to permit a newly formed partnership that does not come within the business purpose exception to elect to use a taxable year other than that required by Section 706(b)(1)(B) provided that the year elected results in no more than a three-month deferral of income to the partners.[15] Reconfirming the adage that there is no free lunch, Congress provided that partnerships (and S corporations) making the Section 444 election would be subject to a new tax imposed by Section 7519.[16] Computation of this "required payment" is highly complex and we will dispense with many of the details,[17] but at least the concept should be understood. Congress is attempting to require an electing partnership to pay (and in effect keep "on deposit") an amount of tax roughly approximating the tax that the partners would have paid on their income for any deferral period if a Section 444 election had not been made. Thus, if a partnership whose partners all used calendar years elected a fiscal year ending September 30, it would be required to pay a tax that supposedly equalled the benefit of three months' deferral received by the

12. I.R.C. §§ 444(a), (e); 7519. Similar relief was provided to S corporations and personal service corporations.

13. I.R.C. § 444(a), (e).

14. Although the statute is not crystal clear on this point, the legislative history suggests this is what Congress intended (see H.R.Rep. No. 100–495, 100th Cong., 1st Sess. 938 (1987)), and the Service has announced that it concurs with this interpretation (I.R.S. Notice 88–10, 1988–1 C.B. 478). But if the only business purpose for a previously approved fiscal year was an automatic three-month deferral, which was permitted prior to 1987, a Section 444 election will be required to retain that fiscal year.

15. I.R.C. § 444(a), (b)(1). Thus, if the mechanical rules would have required a calendar year, the partnership nonetheless may elect a fiscal year ending September 30 because the "deferral period" (I.R.C. § 444(b)(4)) does not exceed three months.

16. I.R.C. § 444(c)(1).

17. In general, the "required payment" under Section 7519(b) is an amount equal to the highest individual tax rate plus one percent multiplied by the partnership's "net base year income" (generally defined by Section 7519(d)(1) as the net income of the partnership for the year preceding the election multiplied by a "deferral ratio" based on the relationship of the number of months in the deferral period of the preceding taxable year to the total number of months in that year) less the amount of any "required" payment for the preceding election year. So much for reducing the accountants' workload.

partners.[18] Under a de minimis rule, no payment is required if the amount due is less than $500.[19]

PROBLEM

What taxable year must Partnership adopt under § 706(b) in each of the following alternatives? Unless stated to the contrary, assume Partnership is a newly formed partnership.

(a) All partners of Partnership are calendar year taxpayers? If the partners believe that the partnership will have substantial income and they are free to choose, what taxable year should they select for the partnership? What if they expect the partnership to have substantial losses?

(b) Partnership has a 20% corporate general partner which uses a July 31 fiscal year and 20 individual 4% limited partners all of whom are on a calendar year?

(c) What result in (b), above, if 10 of the limited partners use a September 30 fiscal year and the other 10 use a calendar year?

(d) What result in (b), above, if Partnership wants to adopt a September 30 fiscal year under § 706(b) in order to have sufficient time to gather tax information for its calendar year partners? May Partnership adopt a September 30 fiscal year in some other manner? If so, with what cost?

(e) What result in (b), above, if over the prior five years Partnership has been in the retail business and does 20% of its annual business in December and 10% of its business in January in post-Christmas sales. Partnership has been using a calendar year. It wishes to change to a January 31 fiscal year. May it do so? If so, is a § 444 election and a § 7519 "required payment" necessary?

B. TAX CONSEQUENCES TO THE PARTNERS

1. GENERAL RULES

Code: §§ 701; 702; 703(a); 705; 706(a).

Regulations: §§ 1.702–1(a), (c); 1.705–1(a); 1.706–1(a).

18. We say "supposedly" because the Section 7519 required payment is determined mechanically, without regard to amounts actually deferred by the partners. If the partnership receives income evenly throughout its taxable year, the required payment eventually will approximate what the partners would have paid without the deferral. But if the partnership's income is bunched in a particular period (e.g., the first or last three months of the taxable year), the payment may be greater or lesser than the actual deferral benefits enjoyed by the partners.

19. I.R.C. § 7519(a)(2).

Under the aggregate theory of Section 701, each partner is taxed on his or her share of partnership income or loss,[1] but the entity approach requires that the income, deductions and other tax items must be computed at the partnership level in order to determine the amounts that flow through to the partners. For this purpose, Section 703(a) provides that a partnership computes its "taxable income" in the same manner as an individual except that certain items described in Section 702(a) must be separately stated and certain deductions are disallowed.

The items listed in Section 702(a) must be separately stated because they may have potentially varying tax consequences to the different partners. The most common separately stated items are capital and Section 1231 gains and losses,[2] tax-exempt interest, dividends taxed as net capital gain, charitable contributions, and foreign taxes. Each partner's share of items subject to special treatment at the partner level (e.g., income or losses from passive activities, alternative minimum tax adjustment and preference items) also must be separately stated. The character of these items must be preserved so that they can be passed through and combined with any similar items derived by the partners from other activities for purposes of applying various special rules and limitations on the partner's tax return.

To illustrate, assume that the equal ABC partnership has a $30,000 Section 1231 gain[3] in the current year. If the partnership simply netted its Section 1231 gains and losses and then determined the ultimate result as if it were an individual, each partner would report his one-third share of the $30,000 gain, or $10,000 of long-term capital gain each. But if each partner were required to report his one-third share of the Section 1231 gain, preserving its character as such, the results might differ substantially. One partner might have a $20,000 Section 1231 loss from another source, winding up with a net ordinary loss from Section 1231 transactions, while another partner might have no Section 1231 gains or losses and end up with simply a $10,000 long-term capital gain. Because the tax treatment of the partnership's Section 1231 gains and losses may have varying effects among the partners, depending upon each partner's individual Section 1231 gains and losses, the Subchapter K pass-through scheme requires the partnership's Section 1231 gains and losses (among other items) to be

1. Section 702(c) provides that where it is necessary to determine a partner's gross income (e.g., for purposes of determining the need to file a return) that amount will include the partner's distributive share of the partnership's gross income. See the examples in Reg. § 1.702–1(c)(1) and (2).

2. The different capital gains rates for individuals have expanded the list of separately stated items. Section 1(h)(9) authorizes the Service to issue regulations implementing the capital gains regime in the case of sales and exchanges by partnerships. See Reg. § 1.1(h)–1. Form 1065, Schedule K–1 (see Appendix) now includes separate lines for reporting long-term capital gains, Section 1231 gains, and collectibles gains that are subject to a 28 percent maximum rate. See infra note 5.

3. For convenience, assume that all long-term capital gains and Section 1231 gains in this and later illustrations are from the sale of assets held for more than one year and qualify for the 15 percent maximum long-term capital gains rate applicable to noncorporate taxpayers. See I.R.C. § 1(h).

separately reported by the partners.[4] Any items of partnership income or loss which may have potentially different tax consequences to the partners, or any other person, are commonly referred to as "separately stated" or "variable effect" items, and each partner must separately take into account his or her distributive share of such items.[5] The regulations also require that any specially allocated items under Sections 704(b) or (c)[6] must be separately stated by the partners.[7] All the remaining partnership items of income or loss (i.e., the nonseparately stated items) are combined into one aggregate income or loss amount, and each partner reports his or her distributive share of that lump sum amount.[8]

A partner is taxed on his distributive share of partnership income or loss in his taxable year in which the partnership's tax year ends. Consequently, Section 705(a) requires that adjustments be made to the partner's outside basis to reflect the tax results from partnership operations. In general, a partner's outside basis is *increased* by his share of the partnership's (1) taxable income,[9] and (2) tax-exempt income,[10] and *decreased* (but not below zero) by (1) distributions from the partnership as provided in Section 733,[11] (2) the partner's share of partnership loss,[12] and (3) his share of partnership expenditures which are not deductible in arriving at taxable income and are not properly capitalized.[13]

The rationale for most of the Section 705 adjustments is straightforward. A partner is taxed on partnership income whether or not it is currently distributed to him, and he is permitted an upward basis adjustment for his share of partnership income to prevent that income from being taxed again on a subsequent distribution or sale of his partnership interest.[14] When the income is distributed, the statute logically requires a corresponding downward basis reduction.[15] When a partner deducts his share of partnership losses, Section 705 requires a downward basis adjustment to prevent the partner from effectively recognizing the loss a second

4. I.R.C. § 702(a)(3); Reg. § 1.702–1(a)(3).

5. I.R.C. § 702(a)(1)–(7); Reg. § 1.702–1(a)(8)(i), (ii). For example, Rev. Rul. 92–97, 1992–2 C.B. 124, holds that cancellation of indebtedness income is a separately stated item under Section 702(a). In preparing its information return (Form 1065), the partnership is required to complete and send to each partner a schedule known as a "K–1," on which the partners are advised of their respective shares of income and loss items, separately stated deductions, credits, tax preference items, investment interest, foreign taxes and a few other specialized items. See Appendix, infra.

6. See Chapter 4, infra.

7. Reg. § 1.702–1(a)(8)(i).

8. I.R.C. § 702(a)(8).

9. I.R.C. § 705(a)(1)(A).

10. I.R.C. § 705(a)(1)(B).

11. I.R.C. § 705(a)(2).

12. I.R.C. § 705(a)(2)(A).

13. I.R.C. § 705(a)(2)(B). The regulations provide that the Section 705(a)(2)(B) decrease in basis for nondeductible expenses is made before any Section 705(a)(2)(A) decrease for the partner's share of losses. Reg. § 1.704–1(d)(2). Section 705(b) adds an alternative rule under which, in limited circumstances, a partner's outside basis will be determined by his share of the inside bases of partnership assets upon a termination of the partnership. See Reg. § 1.705–1(b).

14. See Chapters 6 and 7, infra.

15. I.R.C. § 733.

time in the form of less gain or more loss on a subsequent disposition of his partnership interest.

The rationale for the basis adjustments for tax-exempt income and nondeductible noncapitalized items is less obvious. Even though a partner is not taxed on his share of the partnership's tax-exempt income, the Section 705(a)(1)(B) upward adjustment is necessary to prevent the partner from being taxed on the income when it is distributed or when the partner sells his partnership interest. For example, assume that a partner has a $1,000 outside basis and his share of the partnership's tax-exempt interest for the year is $200. The partner will not be taxed on the exempt interest. But if the $200 of interest is not distributed to the partner, his partnership interest will be worth $200 more than it was at the beginning of the year. Without a $200 upward basis adjustment, the partner would recognize $200 of additional income attributable to the tax-exempt interest on a subsequent sale of his partnership interest because the partner's outside basis would remain $1,000. The same rationale underlies the Section 705(a)(2)(B) downward basis adjustment for nondeductible or noncapitalized items. Without this adjustment, a partner would realize less gain or more loss on a subsequent sale of his partnership interest because the nondeductible item would have decreased the value of his interest (also decreasing his amount realized on disposition of the interest) without changing his outside basis.

PROBLEM

A and B, both calendar year noncorporate taxpayers, are equal partners in the AB Partnership, which had the following income and expenses during its (business purpose) taxable year that ended on July 31 of the current year:

Gross receipts from inventory sales	$100,000
Cost of goods sold	30,000
Salaries paid to nonpartners	10,000
Depreciation	12,000
Advertising expenses	8,000
Interest expense paid on investment margin account maintained by AB (see § 163(d))	6,000
Gain from the sale of machine held for two years:	
§ 1245 gain	8,000
§ 1231 gain	2,000
Dividends	7,000
Charitable contributions	800
Tax-exempt interest	500
STCG on a sale of stock	6,000
LTCG on a sale of stock held for two years	4,000
LTCL on a sale of stock held for two years	2,000
§ 1231 gain on a casualty to machine held for two years	1,000

(a) How and when will AB, A and B report the income and who will be liable for the taxes?

(b) Assume this is the first year of partnership operations, A's basis in his partnership interest is $70,000 and B's basis in her partnership interest is $40,000. What will be the tax consequences of AB's first year of operations to A and B?

(c) What would be the result in (b), above, if the partnership distributed $20,000 in cash to each partner at the end of the year?

(d) Would it matter if the § 1231 gain on the sale of the machine would have been ordinary income if A had sold it individually?

2. ELECTING LARGE PARTNERSHIPS

Code: §§ 771; 772(a), (b), (c)(1); 773(a), (b); 775.

The Subchapter K pass-through rules are simple enough to apply in most situations, but they can become an accounting and paperwork nightmare for a partnership with a large number of passive investors. In connection with its ongoing study of tax simplification, the staff of the Joint Committee on Taxation described the problems confronting a large partnership:[1]

> The requirement that each partner take into account separately his distributive share of a partnership's income, gain, loss, deduction and credit can result in the reporting of a large number of items to each partner. The Schedule K–1, on which such items are reported, contains space for more than 40 items. Reporting so many separately stated items is burdensome for individual investors with relatively small, passive interests in large partnerships. In many respects such investments are indistinguishable from those made in corporate stock or mutual funds, which do not require reporting of numerous separate items.
>
> In addition, the number of items reported under the current regime makes it difficult for the Internal Revenue Service to match items reported on the K–1 against the partner's income tax return. Matching is also difficult because items on the K–1 are often modified or limited at the partner level before appearing on the partner's tax return.

The Joint Committee's proposed solution was to ease the reporting and audit burden by reducing the number of separately stated items and to develop a simpler Form K–1 for certain large partnerships. The proposals were trapped in legislative gridlock for several years but finally were added to Subchapter K in 1997.

The large partnership regime applies to an electing large partnership ("ELP") and its partners. An ELP generally is any partnership with 100 or

1. Staff of the Joint Committee on Taxation, Technical Explanation of the Tax Simplification Act of 1993 (H.R. 13) (J.C.S–1–93) 55–56 (Jan. 8, 1993).

more partners in the preceding taxable year that makes an election to apply the simplified rules.[2] The number of partners is determined by counting only persons directly holding partnership interests in the taxable year, including persons holding through nominees, but persons holding interests indirectly (e.g., through another partnership) are not counted.[3] Once made, an ELP election applies to all subsequent taxable years unless it is revoked with the consent of the Service.[4] Significantly, service partnerships, such as law and accounting firms, may not make an ELP election.[5]

Each partner in an ELP separately takes into account his or her distributive share of the partnership's: (1) taxable income or loss from passive loss limitation activities, (2) taxable income or loss from other activities (e.g., portfolio income or loss), (3) net capital gain or loss separated into amounts allocable to passive activities and other activities,[6] (4) tax-exempt interest, (5) a net alternative minimum tax adjustment separately computed for passive activities and other activities, (6) various general and specialized tax credits, (7) foreign income taxes, and (8) other items to the extent the Treasury determines that separate treatment is appropriate.[7] The taxable income of an ELP generally is computed in the same manner as an individual except that the items identified above must be separately stated.[8] An ELP is not allowed deductions for personal exemptions, net operating losses, or certain itemized deductions other than Section 212 expenses (e.g., investment expenses).[9] All elections affecting the computation of an ELP's taxable income or tax credits generally are made by the partnership.[10] Similarly, all limitations and other provisions affecting the computation of the taxable income or tax credits of an ELP are applied at the partnership level, other than: (1) the Section 68 overall limitation on itemized deductions, (2) the at-risk limitations, (3) the passive activity loss limitations, and (4) any other provision specified in the regulations.[11] Finally, the Service is given broad regulatory authority to prescribe regulations necessary to carry out the purposes of the new ELP rules.[12]

2. I.R.C. §§ 771; 775(a). The Service may issue regulations under which a partnership will cease to be treated as an ELP in any taxable year in which it has fewer than 100 partners. I.R.C. § 775(a)(1).

3. H.R. Rep. No. 105–148, 105th Cong., 1st Sess. 576 (1997).

4. I.R.C. § 775(a)(2).

5. I.R.C. § 775(b)(2).

6. For example, if an ELP has an excess of net short-term capital gain over net long-term capital loss, the excess is consolidated with the ELP's other taxable income and is not separately stated. Also, Section 1231 gains and losses are netted at the partnership level and any net gain is treated as long-term capital gain. Net Section 1231 loss is treated as ordinary loss and consolidated with the ELP's other taxable income. H.R. Rep. No. 105–148, supra note 3, at 573.

7. I.R.C. § 772(a). See Notice 2004–5, 2004–1 C.B. 489, which requires a partner in an ELP to take into account separately the partner's distributive share of qualified dividend income under Section 1(h)(11)(B).

8. I.R.C. § 773(a)(1)(A).

9. I.R.C. §§ 773(b)(1).

10. I.R.C. § 773(a)(2). Elections under Sections 901 (the foreign tax credit) and 108 (discharge of indebtedness) are made individually by the partners. Id.

11. I.R.C. § 773(a)(3).

12. I.R.C. § 777.

Two special rules apply to an ELP's deductions. First, miscellaneous itemized deductions are not separately reported to the partners. At the partnership level, the two percent floor in Section 67 does not apply, but 70 percent of such deductions are disallowed as a form of rough justice "payback."[13] Second, an ELP's charitable contributions are not separately stated, but a charitable deduction is allowed at the partnership level in determining taxable income, subject to the ten-percent-of-taxable income limitation applicable to C corporations.[14] Several other special provisions are either industry specific or designed to prevent abuse.[15] For example, if an ELP has discharge of indebtedness income, such income is separately reported to the partners and the provisions of Section 108 are applied at the partner level.[16] Finally, ELPs are subject to a special procedural regime which includes an audit system and accelerated due date (March 15 for calendar year partnerships) for providing tax information to the partners.[17]

C. LIMITATIONS ON PARTNERSHIP LOSSES

1. BASIS LIMITATIONS

Code: § 704(d).

Regulations: § 1.704–1(d).

Section 704(d) provides that a partner's distributive share of partnership loss, including capital loss, is allowable as a deduction only to the extent of the partner's outside basis at the end of the partnership's taxable year in which the loss occurred. This is appropriate because the partner's outside basis is reduced by his share of partnership losses under Section 705(a)(2)(A) and may not be reduced below zero. Section 704(d) merely defers deductions; if the limitation applies, any excess loss may be carried forward indefinitely and utilized when the partner acquires additional outside basis. For example, assume that a partner's basis in his partnership interest is $1,000 and his share of partnership loss is $1,200. Section 704(d) will limit the partner's allowable loss to $1,000, unless the partner somehow obtains an increase in his outside basis (for example, by contributing cash or property, or by increasing his share of partnership liabilities).[1] The $200 of disallowed loss will be suspended and may be used in later years when the partner has additional basis. If the partnership has both ordinary and capital losses, the regulations provide that the partner's loss is allocated to reflect the composition of the partnership's loss.[2] In the example, if

13. I.R.C. § 773(b)(3).

14. I.R.C. § 773(b)(2).

15. See, e.g., I.R.C. § 776 (special rules for partnerships holding oil and gas properties).

16. I.R.C. § 773(c). Computations at the partnership level disregard reductions in tax attributes under Section 108(b), but the partners' distributive shares are adjusted to reflect such reductions. I.R.C. § 774(a).

17. I.R.C. §§ 6031(b), 6240 et seq.

1. I.R.C. § 752(a). The allocation of partnership liabilities is introduced in Chapter 2B, supra, and discussed in depth in Chapter 4D infra.

2. Reg. § 1.704–1(d)(4) Example (3).

the $1,200 of loss consists of $900 of ordinary loss and $300 of short-term capital loss, the partner's $1,000 allowable loss will be characterized as follows:

$$\frac{\$900}{\$1,200} \times \$1,000 = \$750 \text{ ordinary loss}$$

$$\frac{\$300}{\$1,200} \times \$1,000 = \$250 \text{ short-term capital loss}$$

The $200 of carryover loss will consist of $150 of ordinary loss and $50 of short-term capital loss.

While not free from doubt, it is likely that the carryover loss is generally personal to each individual partner. Thus, if a partner sells his partnership interest, the seller's previously deferred losses will disappear and not carry over to the buyer.[3] The carryover loss also apparently terminates if a partner dies,[4] but it is not totally certain whether a carryover loss may be used by a donee partner.[5]

PROBLEM

C and D are partners who share income and losses equally. C has an outside basis of $5,000 in his partnership interest and D has an outside basis of $15,000 in her partnership interest.

(a) During the current year the partnership has gross income of $40,000 and expenses of $60,000. What are the tax results to C and D?

(b) What are the results to C and D in the succeeding year when the partnership has $20,000 of net profits?

(c) How might C have alleviated his problem in the first year?

(d) What result in (a), above, if the net $20,000 loss consists of $15,000 of ordinary loss and $5,000 of long-term capital loss?

(e) What result to S, C's son, in (a), above, if C gives his interest in the partnership to S on the first day of a year in which the partnership has profits of $20,000?

2. AT-RISK LIMITATIONS

Code: §§ 49(a)(1)(D)(iv) & (v); 465(a)(1) & (2), (b), (c)(1) & (3), (d), (e).

3. Cf. Sennett v. Commissioner, 80 T.C. 825 (1983), where the Tax Court held that Section 704(d) contemplates that a taxpayer will be a partner at the end of the year in which the carryover loss is utilized. In that case, a partner who sold his partnership interest to the partnership was not allowed to utilize suspended losses when he repaid the losses to the partnership in a later year pursuant to a sale contract. Instead, the payment was treated as a reduction in gain from the sale of the partnership interest.

4. Capital loss carryovers also terminate at death. Rev.Rul. 74–175, 1974–1 C.B. 52.

5. Problem (e), below, raises this issue.

General Rules. Individuals (including individual partners) and certain closely held corporations are subject to the Section 465 at-risk rules, which seek to limit a taxpayer's deductible losses from a broad range of business and investment activities to the amount that the taxpayer is "at risk"[1] with respect to those activities. In the partnership setting, the at-risk rules are applied on a partner-by-partner basis rather than at the partnership level.[2] In general, the rules are applied separately to each "activity" in which a partnership is engaged,[3] but exceptions may require certain trade or business activities to be aggregated.[4]

A taxpayer's initial at-risk amount generally includes: (1) his cash contributions to the activity; (2) the adjusted basis of other property contributed by the taxpayer to the activity; and (3) amounts borrowed for use in the activity for which the taxpayer is personally liable or which are secured by property of the taxpayer (not otherwise used in the activity) to the extent of the fair market value of the encumbered property.[5] The most important distinction between the Section 704(d) basis limitation and the at-risk limitation is that nonrecourse liabilities of the partnership will increase a partner's outside basis[6] but, except with respect to certain real estate activities,[7] a taxpayer is not considered at risk with respect to nonrecourse loans and similar arrangements where the taxpayer has no economic risk.[8] As a result, a loss allowable after application of Section 704(d) nonetheless may be disallowed (or, more accurately, deferred) by Section 465. Any loss disallowed by Section 465 may be carried over and deducted when either the taxpayer becomes at risk, the partnership disposes of the activity, or the taxpayer disposes of his partnership interest.[9] If a partner's loss is deferred by Section 465, the partner's outside basis is nonetheless reduced by the amount of the loss.[10]

A partner is considered at risk with respect to his share of partnership recourse debt.[11] For a debt to be considered "recourse," the regulations require that a creditor must be able to sue the partner under state law, and the funds must be borrowed from a person who has no interest (other than as a creditor) in the activity in which those funds are used.[12]

1. See I.R.C. § 465(b)(1) & (2).

2. I.R.C. § 465(a)(1); Prop.Reg. § 1.465–41 Example (1). Cf. Prop.Reg. § 1.465–42(c)(2).

3. I.R.C. § 465(c)(2)(A) & (3)(A).

4. I.R.C. § 465(c)(2)(B), (3)(B), and (C). See McKee, Nelson & Whitmire, Federal Taxation of Partnerships and Partners ¶ 11.06[2][c] (4th ed. 2007).

5. Id. The initial at-risk amount is generally increased by the taxpayer's share of income and decreased by the taxpayer's share of losses and distributions from the activity. I.R.C. § 465(b)(5). But see I.R.C. § 465(b)(3), which provides that a taxpayer is not at risk with respect to recourse borrowings if the lender or a person related to the lender has an interest in the activity other than as a creditor.

6. I.R.C. §§ 722; 752(a).

7. See I.R.C. §§ 465(b)(6); 49(a)(1)(D)(iv) & (v) and infra notes 13–20 and accompanying text.

8. I.R.C. § 465(b)(2) & (4).

9. I.R.C. § 465(a)(1); Prop.Reg. § 1.465–66.

10. Prop.Reg. § 1.465–1(e).

11. I.R.C. § 465(b)(1)(B), (b)(2)(A). See Prop.Reg. § 1.465–24. Compare Reg. § 1.752–2, discussed in Chapter 4D, infra.

12. Reg. § 1.465–8(a); Prop. Reg. § 1.465–24(a)(2); I.R.C. § 465(b)(3)(A) & (B)(i).

Qualified Nonrecourse Financing Exception. Although Congress extended the at-risk rules to real estate activities in the 1986 Code, it included an important escape hatch. Taxpayers are still considered at risk with respect to certain nonrecourse loans secured by real property which constitute "qualified nonrecourse financing."[13] In broad outline, this exception is available for nonrecourse financing obtained from commercial lenders or the government but not with respect to seller or promoter-financed debt. Nonrecourse financing is "qualified" if it is nonconvertible debt[14] for which no person is personally liable[15] and which is incurred by the taxpayer with respect to the holding of real estate[16] and is borrowed from a "qualified person" or from certain government instrumentalities. A "qualified person" is any person actively and regularly engaged in the business of lending money who is not related to the borrower and is not the seller of the property, a relative of the seller or a person who receives a fee (e.g., a promoter or a broker) with respect to the taxpayer's investment in the real property, or a relative of such a fee recipient.[17] A typical qualified person would be a bank, savings and loan association, insurance company or pension fund. These distinctions arose out of Congress's effort to limit the opportunity for taxpayers to inflate deductions by overvaluing depreciable real estate.[18] Unrelated lenders were viewed as less likely to make loans which exceed the true value of the encumbered property, while sellers, promoters and lenders related to the borrower were assumed to have little incentive to limit the financing to the value of the property.[19] Even related persons (other than sellers or promoters) will be treated as qualified, however, if they are regular money lenders and the loan is commercially reasonable and on substantially the same terms as loans to unrelated persons.[20]

In the case of a partnership, a partner's share of any qualified nonrecourse financing is determined on the basis of the partner's share of partnership liabilities under Section 752,[21] provided the financing is quali-

13. I.R.C. § 465(b)(6)(A); Reg. § 1.465–27.

14. I.R.C. § 465(b)(6)(B)(iv).

15. I.R.C. § 465(b)(6)(B)(iii). Congress authorized the Treasury to set forth circumstances in which guaranties, indemnities, or personal liability of a person other than the taxpayer will not prevent the debt from being treated as qualified nonrecourse financing. Staff of the Joint Committee on Taxation, General Explanation of the Tax Reform Act of 1986 (hereinafter "1986 Act General Explanation"), 100th Cong., 1st Sess. 258 (1987).

16. I.R.C. § 465(b)(6)(B)(i).

17. I.R.C. § 49(a)(1)(D)(iv). For this purpose, "related persons" are defined by a chain of statutory cross-references, beginning in Section 49(a)(1)(D) and snake dancing through Section 465(b)(3)(C) and on to Sections 267(b) and 707(b)(1). In general, related persons include certain family members, trusts and corporations or partnerships in which a person has at least a 10 percent interest. Relationships are determined at the close of the taxable year. I.R.C. § 49(a)(1)(D)(v).

18. 1986 Act General Explanation, supra note 15, at 256.

19. Id. at 257.

20. I.R.C. § 465(b)(6)(D)(ii). For when the terms of a nonrecourse loan are considered commercially reasonable, see 1986 Act General Explanation, supra note 15, at 258–259.

21. I.R.C. § 465(b)(6)(C). See Reg. § 1.752–3 and Chapter 4D, infra.

fied nonrecourse financing with respect to both the partner and the partnership. The amount for which partners may be treated at risk, however, may not exceed the total amount of qualified nonrecourse financing at the partnership level.[22]

Effect of Deficit Capital Account Restoration Obligation. A recent court case raised the question of how the at-risk rules apply in the case of a partner's obligation to restore a deficit capital account balance. Hubert Enterprises, Inc. v. Commissioner[23] involved a limited liability company, called LCL, which was classified as a partnership for tax purposes. LCL's operating agreement provided that no member would be liable for the firm's liabilities. The agreement, however, was amended to include a provision that required a member with a deficit capital account balance following liquidation of the membership interest to restore the deficit balance at that time. A member of the LCL sought to take deductions under Section 465, arguing that the deficit restoration obligation in the amended agreement made it "at-risk" with respect to its share of LCL's recourse liabilities. The Tax Court, agreeing with the IRS that LCL's members were not at risk for the recourse liabilities, stated:[24]

> The aspect of petitioners' dispute with respondent's application of the at-risk rules rests on whether LCL's members may take into account any part of LCL's recourse obligations. We agree with respondent that they may not. The recourse notes signed by LCL were not personally guaranteed by LCL's members, and applicable State (Wyoming) law provides that the members of a limited liability company are not personally liable for the debts, obligations, or liabilities of the company. See Wyo. Stat. Ann. sec. 17–15–113 (LexisNexis 2005). The agreements of LCL also contain no provisions obligating its members to pay LCL's debts, obligations, or expenses. Because LCL's members did not assume personal liability for the notes, the members are not at risk under section 465(b)(1)(B) and (2)(A) with respect to LCL's recourse obligations. Cf. Emershaw v. Commissioner, 949 F.2d 841 (6th Cir.1991), affg. T.C. Memo.1990–246.
>
> Petitioners seek a contrary result, focusing on the deficit capital account restoration provision in section 7.7 of the revised LCL operating agreement. Petitioners argue that this provision made LCL's members personally liable for LCL's recourse obligations for purposes of applying the at-risk rules. We disagree. As observed by respondent, section 7.7 contains a condition that must be met before the deficit capital account restoration obligation arises. In accordance with that condition, an LCL member must

22. 1986 Act General Explanation, supra note 15, at 260.

23. 125 T.C. 72 (2005).

24. For a discussion of the Tax Court decision, see Kalinka, "Hubert Enterprises: LLC Members, Partners Deficit Restoration Obligations, and the At–Risk Rules," 112 Tax Notes 137 (July 10, 2006); and Rubin, Whiteway, & Finkelstein, "The Effect of a 'DRO' on a Partner's At–Risk Amount and Share of Liabilities: *Hubert Enterprises v. Commissioner*," 111 Tax Notes 1031 (May 29, 2006).

first liquidate its interest in LCL before the member has any obligation to the entity. Neither * * * [member, Ed.] liquidated its interest in LCL during the relevant years.

On appeal, the Sixth Circuit remanded the case back to the Tax Court.[25] In so doing, it cited Emershaw v. Commissioner[26] as establishing the standard for whether a taxpayer is liable for a debt under Section 465. Under *Emershaw*, the Sixth Circuit said "a taxpayer is personally liable if, in the worst case, he or she will be the 'payor of last resort.' " The Sixth Circuit concluded that the Tax Court had not reached that issue and remanded the case to develop the record on whether the taxpayer was the payor of last resort.[27] On remand, the Tax Court concluded that the partner was not personally liable for the repayment of any of the partnership's recourse liabilities because its obligation to contribute additional capital funds was avoidable simply by not liquidating the partnership.[28]

PROBLEMS

1. LP is a limited partner in a newly formed partnership which is engaged in the following activities:

(i) A research and development activity to which LP contributed $10,000 cash; LP's share of partnership nonrecourse liability attributable to this activity is $10,000. LP's share of loss from the research and development activity is $12,000 for the current year.

(ii) A motion picture production activity to which LP contributed $20,000 cash; LP's share of income from this activity for the current year is $25,000.

LP's outside basis at the beginning of the year was $40,000, and his share of net gain for the year was $13,000. What are the tax consequences to LP under § 465.

2. The ABC equal limited partnership (in which A is a general partner and B and C are limited partners) purchased an apartment building for $540,000, paying $90,000 of cash (contributed equally by the partners to the partnership) and financing the balance with a $450,000 nonrecourse loan secured by the building. Assume that A, B and C are all unrelated and that the partnership holds no other assets. To what extent are each of the partners at risk if the loan is:

(a) From a commercial bank in which none of the parties owns an interest.

(b) From the seller of the apartment complex.

25. Hubert Enterprises, Inc. v. Commissioner, 230 Fed. Appx. 526 (6th Cir. 2007).

26. 949 F.2d 841 (6th Cir. 1991).

27. For an analysis of the Sixth Circuit's decision and the issues in *Hubert Enterprises*, see Burke, "Illusory DROs: At-Risk Lessons From *Hubert*," 118 Tax Notes 405 (Jan. 21, 2008).

28. Hubert Enterprises, Inc. v. Commissioner, 95 T.C.M. (CCH) 1194 (2008).

(c) From B's brother, who is in the money lending business and makes the loan at a rate of interest 25% below comparable rates charged to unrelated borrowers.

(d) The same as (c), above, except the loan is at regular commercial rates of interest.

3. PASSIVE LOSS LIMITATIONS

Code: § 469(a), (b), (c), (d)(1), (e)(1)(A), (g)(1), (h)(1), (2) and (5), (i)(1), (2), (3) and (6), (k); 772(a)(1) & (2), (c)(2) & (3), (d)(1), (f).

Temporary Regulations: § 1.469–5T(a), (b)(2), (c), (d), (e), (f)(1) & (4).

Overview. Just as the Section 704(d) basis limitation was demoted upon the arrival of the at-risk rules, so it is that both those curbs on allowable losses were largely pushed to the sidelines with the enactment of the Section 469 passive loss limitations in the Tax Reform Act of 1986. Section 469 is broadly applicable and is likely to have been studied in a basic income tax course. Our coverage here will be selective, beginning with an overview and then focusing on the application of the passive loss limitations to partnerships and their interaction with Sections 704(d) and 465.

Section 469 was enacted to restrict taxpayers from using deductions and other losses generated from certain passive investment activities to "shelter" income from other sources (e.g., a taxpayer's regular business income, compensation, dividends and interest).[1] The Section 704(d) basis and Section 465 at-risk limitations are bottomed on similar objectives, but they were ineffective in curbing the proliferation of tax shelters. The ability of limited partners to include nonrecourse debt in their outside bases contributed to the impotence of Section 704(d). Although the at-risk rules were successful in limiting the pass-through of losses from some of the more exotic tax avoidance vehicles, the pre–1987 exemption of real estate from Section 465 permitted that most conventional of tax shelters to flourish. By 1986, Congress concluded that decisive action was needed to curb the tax shelter market and restore public confidence in the fairness of the tax system.

Section 469 goes well beyond its earlier counterparts by disallowing the current deductibility of losses and the use of credits from "passive activities."[2] The income and losses from each of a taxpayer's passive activities are first computed and then all are combined; in any taxable year, passive activity losses can be deducted only to the extent of the taxpayer's income from passive activities for that year.[3] To the extent that losses from passive activities for the taxable year exceed the taxpayer's passive income, that

1. See generally Staff of the Joint Committee on Taxation, General Explanation of the Tax Reform Act of 1986 (hereinafter "1986 Act General Explanation"), 100th Cong., 1st Sess. 209–254 (1987). For another detailed discussion of Section 469, see Freeland, Lathrope, Lind & Stephens, Fundamentals of Federal Income Taxation Ch. 17E (Foundation Press, 14th ed. 2006).

2. I.R.C. § 469(a)(1).

3. I.R.C. § 469(a)(1)(A) & (d)(1).

excess may be carried forward and deducted (subject to the same limitation) against future net income from passive activities.[4] Similar rules are applicable to credits from passive activities.[5] Disallowed losses from a particular activity (but not credits)[6] may be deducted in full on a taxable disposition of the entire activity.[7] In short, Section 469 does not forever disallow excess passive losses; it merely postpones them. This delayed gratification is enough to destroy any after-tax economic benefits of the typical leveraged tax shelter.

Section 469 applies to individuals (including partners), estates, trusts, personal service corporations and certain other closely held corporations.[8] As in the case of the at-risk rules, the passive loss limitations are applied on a partner-by-partner basis, not at the partnership level. The limitations are applied only after application of the Section 704(d) and Section 465 limitations.[9]

The "Material Participation" Standard. In considering the proper form of attack and the appropriate targets of reform, Congress determined that limitations should not be imposed on taxpayers who were actively involved in a business activity. Rather, the restrictions are aimed squarely at tax shelters by focusing on the passive investor, who is viewed as less likely to approach an activity with a significant nontax economic motive.[10] In keeping with these objectives, "passive activity" is defined by reference to a "material participation" standard. A "passive activity" is any activity involving the conduct of any trade or business (including nonbusiness profit-motivated activities within the ambit of Section 212) in which the taxpayer does not "materially participate."[11] Under the statute, a taxpayer

4. I.R.C. § 469(b).

5. I.R.C. § 469(a)(1)(B). The limitation applies to the extent that credits from passive activities for the year exceed tax liability for the year attributable to such activities. I.R.C. § 469(d)(2). Credits also may be carried forward. I.R.C. § 469(b).

6. Disallowed credits are not allowed on the sale of a passive activity. Cf. I.R.C. § 469(g). See 1986 Act General Explanation, supra note 1, at 228.

7. I.R.C. § 469(g)(1)(A). This rule applies to a disposition of a limited partnership interest. The loss is allowed on the disposition by the partnership of a passive activity or on the disposition of the partnership interest, whichever occurs first. See 1986 Act General Explanation, supra note 1, at 227–229 and McKee, Nelson & Whitmire, Federal Taxation of Partnerships and Partners ¶ 11.08[3][a] (4th ed. 2007). Special rules apply to installment sale dispositions (I.R.C. § 469(g)(3)), dispositions to related parties (I.R.C. § 469(g)(1)(B)), dispositions at death (I.R.C. § 469(g)(2)), and dispositions by gift (I.R.C. § 469(j)(6)).

8. I.R.C. § 469(a)(2).

9. Temp.Reg. § 1.469–2T(d)(6). As in the case of the at-risk limitations (see Prop. Reg. § 1.465–1(e)), a partner's outside basis is reduced for losses which are allowed under Section 704(d) even though such losses are disallowed by Section 469. Id.

10. 1986 Act General Explanation, supra note 1, at 211–212.

11. I.R.C. § 469(c)(1) & (6). For the Service's flexible facts and circumstances approach to defining an "activity," see Prop. Reg. § 1.469–4. Section 469 does not apply to working interests in oil and gas properties, ostensibly in order to attract investors to this beleaguered industry, at least if they are willing to accept the financial risk of a working interest. I.R.C. § 469(c)(3)(A). See 1986 Act General Explanation, supra note 1, at 213–214.

materially participates in an activity only if he is involved on a regular, continuous and substantial basis in the operation of the activity.[12]

The regulations elaborate on the material participation standard by defining "participation" and setting forth seven separate situations in which a taxpayer's participation in an activity will be considered material. "Participation" generally includes work done by the taxpayer in all capacities except as an investor in the activity unless the taxpayer is directly involved in day-to-day management or operations.[13] A taxpayer is treated as materially participating in an activity for a taxable year[14] if any one of these tests is met:[15] (1) the taxpayer participates in the activity for more than 500 hours during the year; (2) the taxpayer's participation in the activity constitutes substantially all of the participation in the activity by any individual for the year; (3) the taxpayer devotes more than 100 hours to the activity during the year and his participation is not less than that of any other person; (4) the activity is a "significant participation" activity—that is, a trade or business activity in which the taxpayer participates for more than 100 hours and the taxpayer does not satisfy any of the other tests for material participation[16]—and the individual's aggregate participation in all "significant participation" activities for the year exceeds 500 hours; (5) the taxpayer materially participated in the activity for any five of the ten taxable years immediately preceding the taxable year; (6) the activity is a "personal service activity"—that is, an activity principally involving the performance of services in fields such as health, law, engineering, architecture and accounting[17]—and the taxpayer materially participated in the activity for any three taxable years preceding the taxable year; or (7) based on all the facts and circumstances, the taxpayer's participation in the activity during the taxable year is regular, continuous and substantial.[18] Notably, the regulations do not impose any particular recordkeeping requirements, but they suggest that appointment books, calendars and narrative summaries may help establish the approximate hours devoted to an activity.[19]

Rental Activities. Congress concluded that the material participation standard was inappropriate in the case of most rental activities, which were historically used as tax shelters and generally require less personal involvement than other business pursuits. For example, a taxpayer engaged full-time in one profession easily might provide all the necessary management activities for a rental property in her spare time and still meet the material participation test because she was the only person involved in managing

12. I.R.C. § 469(h)(1). See 1986 Act General Explanation, supra note 1, at 235–245.

13. Temp.Reg. § 1.469–5T(f)(2)(ii).

14. Where the taxpayer is a partner, the "taxable year" is the partnership's year rather than the partner's if the two are different. Temp.Reg. § 1.469–2T(e)(1).

15. Temp.Reg. § 1.469–5T(a)(1)–(7).

16. Temp.Reg. § 1.469–5T(c).

17. Temp.Reg. § 1.469–5T(d).

18. The regulations do not yet identify what facts and circumstances may be relevant, but they state that taxpayers will not meet this fallback test unless they participate in the activity for more than 100 hours. Temp.Reg. § 1.469–5T(b)(2)(iii).

19. Temp.Reg. § 1.469–5T(f)(4).

the property.[20] With a few limited exceptions, Section 469 presumes that all rental activities are "passive" regardless of the extent of participation by the taxpayer.[21] Modest relief is provided for middle-income taxpayers who invest in rental property—for example, "Mom and Pop," who own and manage one duplex apartment to provide financial security rather than to shelter a substantial amount of other income. Under Section 469(i), these individual taxpayers may deduct up to $25,000 of losses attributable to rental real estate activities if they "actively participate"[22] and own at least a 10 percent interest in the activity.[23] Beginning in 1994, the real estate rental activities of taxpayers other than closely held C corporations are treated as active trades or businesses if more than half of the personal services performed by the taxpayer in all trades or businesses during the year, and more than 750 hours, are in real property trades or businesses in which the taxpayer materially participates.[24] This rule, which was intended to provide relief to developers and other active real estate entrepreneurs, generally does not apply to limited partnership interests.[25]

Working Interests. Regardless of the taxpayer's material participation, a passive activity does not include a working interest in any oil or gas well which the taxpayer holds directly or through an entity that does not limit the taxpayer's liability with respect to the drilling or operation of the property.[26] Even though passive investors commonly have owned working interests, this exception was included in Section 469 at the behest of legislators from oil producing states.[27] The exception does not apply to a limited partnership in which the taxpayer is not a general partner.[28]

Portfolio Income. Without some refinement, the broad definition of passive activity would embrace all of a taxpayer's portfolio investments, such as stocks and bonds. As a result, a taxpayer could shelter the classic forms of investment income (dividends, interest, capital gains from the sales of securities) with passive losses. The Senate Finance Committee recognized that "[t]o permit portfolio income to be offset by passive losses or credits would create the inequitable result of restricting sheltering by individuals dependent for support on wages or active business income, while permitting sheltering by those whose income is derived from an

20. Temp.Reg. § 1.469–5T(a)(2). See S.Rep. No. 99–313, 99th Cong., 2d Sess. 718 (1986).

21. I.R.C. § 469(c)(2). "Rental activity" is broadly defined by Section 469(j)(8) as any activity where payments are made for the use of tangible property.

22. "Active" participation requires something less than "material" participation. Except as provided in regulations (not yet issued), limited partners are not treated as actively participating. I.R.C. § 469(i)(6)(C).

23. I.R.C. § 469(i)(1), (2) and (6). The $25,000 allowance is phased out by 50 percent of the amount by which the taxpayer's adjusted gross income (without regard to this deduction) exceeds $100,000. I.R.C. § 469(i)(3).

24. I.R.C. § 469(c)(7).

25. I.R.C. § 469(c)(7)(A). For some other narrowing exceptions and safe harbors from the rental activity rule, see Temp.Reg. § 1.469–1T(e)(3)(ii).

26. I.R.C. § 469(c)(3).

27. See Birnbaum & Murray, Showdown at Gucci Gulch 229–232 (1987).

28. Temp.Reg. § 1.469–1T(e)(4)(v)(A)(*i*).

investment portfolio."[29] Section 469 thus provides that "portfolio income" (interest, dividends, annuities, royalties not derived in the ordinary course of a trade or business and gains or losses from assets that produce such income, less related expenses) shall not be considered as arising from a passive activity.[30] To prevent investors from skirting these rules by investing in limited partnerships that generate dividends, interest, and capital gains, portfolio income earned by a partnership is separately stated and retains its character when it passes through to the partners.[31] Moreover, Section 469(*l*)(3) authorizes the Treasury to prescribe regulations to require certain income from limited partnerships or from other passive activities to be reclassified as not arising from a passive activity.[32]

General Partners. Whether or not a *general* partner's share of income or loss is treated as derived from a passive activity requires a separate analysis of each general partner and of each separate activity in which the partnership engages. The critical issues narrow to: (1) when are different pursuits of the partnership classified as separate "activities" in which a partner must materially participate in order to avoid the passive loss limitations, and (2) what degree of participation by a partner in an activity is "material?"

The legislative history states that "[t]he determination of what constitutes a separate activity is intended to be made in a realistic economic sense" by looking to whether the "undertakings consist of an integrated and interrelated economic unit, conducted in coordination with or reliance upon each other, and constituting an appropriate unit for the measurement of gain or loss."[33] The regulations make it clear that a single partnership may engage in more than one activity.[34] When a partnership's separate activities are identified, the partner's participation in each activity must be analyzed to determine whether or not it is "material," employing the seven tests discussed above.[35] Apart from material participation, the definition of "activity" is significant because previously suspended losses from a passive activity become currently deductible upon the taxpayer's disposition of his entire interest in the activity.[36]

Limited Partners. Congress was aware of the widespread use of syndicated limited partnerships as tax shelters, and it also recognized that limited partners were restricted in their ability to manage partnership activities. Section 469 thus presumes, except as may be provided otherwise

29. S.Rep. No. 99–313, supra note 20, at 728.

30. I.R.C. § 469(e)(1).

31. Temp.Reg. § 1.469–2T(c)(3)(i), 1.469–2T(c)(3)(iv) Example (2). Cf. Temp. Reg. § 1.469–2T(e)(1). See also Form 1065, Schedule K–1, reproduced in Appendix A, infra.

32. For examples of the Treasury's exercise of this regulatory authority, see Temp. Reg. § 1.469–2T(f).

33. S.Rep. No. 99–313, supra note 20, at 739.

34. See generally Reg. § 1.469–4, especially 4(c), which adopts a flexible facts and circumstances approach to define an "activity."

35. See supra notes 13–19 and accompanying text.

36. I.R.C. § 469(g)(1)(A).

in regulations, that all limited partnership interests are activities in which a taxpayer does not materially participate.[37] Under the regulations, limited partners are considered to materially participate only if: (1) they participate in the activity for more than 500 hours during the taxable year, (2) they materially participated in the activity for any five tax years during the ten years preceding the taxable year, or (3) the activity is a "personal service activity" and the limited partner materially participated in the activity for any three tax years (whether or not consecutive) preceding the taxable year.[38] A limited partner who is also a general partner and who meets one of the seven tests for material participation is treated as materially participating with respect to both the limited and general partnership interests.[39] A limited partner's share of income received for the performance of services (e.g., by way of salary, guaranteed payment or allocation of partnership income) is not treated as income from a passive activity.[40]

Electing Large Partnerships. A partner in an electing large partnership takes into account separately the partner's share of taxable income or loss from (1) passive loss limitation activities, and (2) other activities.[41] A passive loss limitation activity is any partnership activity which involves the conduct of a trade or business and any rental activity.[42] A partner's distributive share of an ELP's taxable income or loss from passive loss limitation activities is treated as being from a single passive activity.[43] Thus, an ELP generally does not have to separately report items from its different activities.

A partner's distributive share of an ELP's taxable income or loss from activities that are not passive loss limitation activities is treated as income or expense from property held for investment.[44] Thus, an ELP's portfolio income is reported separately and reduced by portfolio deductions.[45]

A special rule applies to the passive loss limitation in the case of a general partner in an ELP. If a partner holds an interest in an ELP other than a limited partnership interest, the partner's distributive share of any items are taken into account separately to the extent necessary to comply with the passive loss rules.[46] For example, income from an ELP is not treated as passive income to a general partner who materially participates in the partnership's trade or business.[47]

Publicly Traded Partnerships. As soon as the passive limitations were enacted, taxpayers began maneuvering to avoid their impact by seeking out sources of passive income against which passive losses might be deducted. Because a limited partner's share of partnership income is presumptively

37. I.R.C. § 469(h)(2).

38. Temp.Reg. § 1.469–5T(e)(1) and (2).

39. Temp.Reg. § 1.469–5T(e)(3)(ii).

40. I.R.C. § 469(e)(3). See 1986 Act General Explanation, supra note 1, at 236–237.

41. I.R.C. §§ 772(a)(1), 772(a)(2).

42. I.R.C. § 772(d)(1).

43. I.R.C. § 772(c)(2).

44. I.R.C. § 772(c)(3)(A).

45. H.R. Rep. No. 105–148, 105th Cong., 1st Sess. 574 (1997).

46. I.R.C. § 772(f).

47. H.R. Rep. No. 105–148, supra note 45, at 574–75.

passive,[48] the publicly traded partnership ("PTP") emerged as a promising passive income generator. Although the Treasury might have attacked this strategy with regulations classifying a PTP's income as "portfolio income,"[49] Congress concluded that specific legislation was preferable to ensure that income from a PTP would be treated on a par with other investment income for purposes of the passive loss limitations.[50]

We have seen that Congress first addressed the broader classification problem by enacting Section 7704, which provides that a PTP generally is taxed as a corporation.[51] A PTP is defined for this purpose as a partnership whose interests are traded on an established securities market or are readily tradable on a secondary market.[52] If, however, 90 percent of the gross income of a PTP is "qualifying income" (generally passive investment income, such as dividends, interest, real property rents and natural resources royalties[53]), the PTP is not taxed as a corporation.[54]

For those PTPs still taxed as partnerships, net income that passes through to partners is treated as portfolio income which may not be offset by losses from passive activities.[55] A partner's passive losses from a PTP that is taxed as a partnership may be deducted only against passive income from the same PTP. Unused losses are suspended and carried forward until that PTP has passive income or until the partner completely disposes of his interest in the partnership.

PROBLEMS

1. Producer owns both a 40% interest as a general partner and a 20% interest as a limited partner in PG–13 Associates, a motion picture production partnership which also pays Producer a $100,000 annual salary for her services as a full-time (1,500 hours per year) producer. After deducting Producer's salary, the partnership has a $300,000 net loss in the current year. Producer's aggregate outside basis for her partnership interests at the beginning of the year is $350,000. Producer's outside basis is attributable to cash contributed to PG–13 Associates.

(a) What are the tax consequences to Producer from her interests in PG–13 Associates for the current year?

(b) What result in (a), above, if Producer spends most of her time farming and only devotes 300 hours during the year to PG–13?

(c) What result in (b), above, if Producer had devoted 1,500 hours to PG–13 during each of the previous five years?

48. I.R.C. § 469(h)(2).

49. I.R.C. § 469(*l*).

50. See S.Rep. No. 100–76, 100th Cong., 1st Sess. 185–186 (1987).

51. I.R.C. § 7704(a). See Chapter 1D, supra.

52. I.R.C. § 7704(b).

53. I.R.C. § 7704(d).

54. I.R.C. § 7704(c). The 90 percent test must be met for each year beginning after December 31, 1987 during which the partnership is in existence. I.R.C. § 7704(c)(1).

55. I.R.C. § 469(k). See S.Rep. No. 100–76, supra note 50, at 186–187.

(d) What result in (b), above, if the partnership's loss for the year is only $200,000 because it also realizes $60,000 of dividend income and $40,000 of net gains from sales of marketable securities?

(e) What result in (b), above, if Producer also has $75,000 of income from an interest in a "burned out" real estate limited partnership interest?

(f) What result in (b), above, if Producer also has a $25,000 loss from a rental real estate limited partnership interest?

(g) What result in (b), above, if Producer also has a $50,000 loss from an investment in a general partnership that owns a working interest in an oil and gas property?

(h) Same as (g), above, except Producer holds her interest in the oil and gas partnership as a limited partner?

2. During the current year LP has investments in four limited partnerships as follows:

(i) A motion picture production limited partnership in which LP has an outside basis of $10,000 attributable to LP's cash contribution to the partnership. LP's distributive share of loss in this partnership for the current year is $25,000.

(ii) An equipment leasing limited partnership in which LP has a $100,000 outside basis (attributable to a $15,000 cash contribution and an $85,000 nonrecourse liability). LP's share of loss for the year is $20,000.

(iii) A real estate limited partnership in which LP has a positive outside basis and his share of partnership income is $30,000 for the year.

(iv) A research and development limited partnership in which LP has an outside basis of $60,000, attributable to his $60,000 cash contribution to the partnership. LP's share of the partnership's loss for the year is $40,000.

Consider to what extent LP may deduct his share of losses from these partnerships for the current year, assuming he has no carryovers under Sections 704(d), 465 or 469.

CHAPTER 4

PARTNERSHIP ALLOCATIONS

A. INTRODUCTION

One of the critical nontax differences between partnerships and corporations is the greater flexibility for partners to custom tailor their economic arrangements. Through their partnership agreement, partners have considerable latitude to structure allocations of profits and losses (both generally and as to specific income and expense items), the amount and timing of distributions of cash or property, and the compensation paid to partners who render services to the enterprise. The partnership agreement can provide priority returns to partners on their invested capital or for services, and it can specify how much each partner is entitled to receive on a liquidation of the firm.

Despite what this chapter may come to suggest, the vast majority of allocation provisions in partnership agreements are not tax driven. Rather, they are influenced by economic considerations that would be present even without an income tax system. Consider, for example, a typical "money and brains" partnership where investor partners contribute cash and other forms of capital, and manager partners contribute their expertise and entrepreneurial skills. With or without the intrusion of an income tax, a manager partner ordinarily will demand some form of base compensation for her efforts, while the investors may seek a preferred return on their invested capital and an allocation mechanism that provides for a recovery of their investment before profits are shared with the manager partners. If and when the enterprise becomes profitable, the managers usually will insist upon a priority allocation of a stated percentage of net profits (e.g., the first 20 percent), with the remaining profits to be shared among all partners in proportion to their capital investments. Additional allocation provisions may address such matters as the amount and timing of operating distributions of cash, payments to partners who retire, and distributions on liquidation.

Since its enactment, Subchapter K has largely accommodated for tax purposes the flexible economic arrangements that long have been the hallmark of the partnership under state law. The Code itself is remarkably terse on this important topic. Section 704(a) provides that a partner's "distributive share" of income, gain, loss, deduction or other tax items shall be determined by the partnership agreement, and Section 761(c) defines the partnership agreement as including any modifications up to the time for filing the partnership's tax return. This permits partners to make what are called "special allocations," which are allocations that differ from the partners' respective interests in partnership capital. If there is no allocation agreement, Section 704(b) provides that distributive shares are determined for tax purposes "in accordance with the partner's interest in the partnership," taking into account "all facts and circumstances."

Without more, this permissive special allocation regime would offer taxpayers the opportunity to engage in a variety of tax saving maneuvers that might not be attainable outside the partnership setting. For example, the partnership could be used to shift income or losses between partners in high and low marginal income tax brackets and to allocate the character of income or losses among partners with different tax profiles. These arrangements, all scrupulously memorialized in the partnership agreement, might or might not be related to the partners' economic bargain.

As previewed in Chapter 2, additional income and character shifting opportunities are presented when a partner makes a tax-free contribution of an asset with a built-in gain or loss to a newly formed or ongoing partnership, and the contributed property is later sold or distributed, or where the contributed asset is depreciable. And because of the relationship between partnership liabilities and outside basis, the plot thickens even further when a partnership seeks to allocate its liabilities among the partners to inflate the outside bases of partners who may be seeking to increase their distributive shares of partnership losses. Still more temptations to exploit the system are presented by partnerships that consist primarily of members of the same family.

It took a while for Congress and the Treasury to appreciate these problems.[1] The statutory provisions governing partnership allocations are still brief—but with brevity comes ambiguity. Many of the gaps have been filled by a complex regulatory scheme that is the primary subject of this chapter. The starting point is Section 704(b) which, in addition to governing allocations where the partnership agreement fails to do so, provides that particular items or the entire amount of partnership income or loss will be allocated in accordance with the partners' interests in the partnership if an agreed allocation lacks substantial economic effect. The *Orrisch* case, which follows, sets the stage with a homely but fairly typical fact pattern illustrating the type of tax avoidance that Section 704(b) seeks to regulate.

B. Special Allocations Under Section 704(b)

1. Background: The Substantial Economic Effect Concept

Code: § 704(b).

1. Commentators continue to debate whether Congress got it right. For a provocative argument to abolish all special allocations, see Gergen, "Reforming Subchapter K: Special Allocations," 46 Tax L.Rev. 1 (1990).

Orrisch v. Commissioner

United States Tax Court, 1970.
55 T.C. 395, affirmed per curiam in unpublished opinion (9th Cir. 1973).

■ FEATHERSTON, JUDGE. * * *

[The Crisafis and the Orrisches formed a partnership to purchase and rent two apartment houses. The purchases were financed principally by approximately $385,000 in secured loans. In addition, from 1963 to 1965 the Orrisches contributed $35,300 cash and the Crisafis contributed $21,300. The parties had an oral partnership agreement in which they initially agreed to share profits and losses equally.

From 1963 to 1965, the partnership realized ordinary losses, principally as a result of accelerated depreciation deductions taken on the apartment buildings. As the partners had agreed, the losses were divided equally. The Orrisches were able to deduct their share of partnership losses against income that they realized from other business sources. The Crisafis, on the other hand, did not report any taxable income during the years in question because of large losses generated by their other real estate holdings. As a result, they did not receive any current tax benefit from their share of losses from the partnership with the Orrisches. It was against this background that, in early 1966, the partners agreed that for 1966 and subsequent years all the partnership's depreciation deductions would be allocated to the Orrisches, and any other gain or loss would be divided equally. They agreed further that, if the partnership sold the buildings, any gain attributable to the specially allocated depreciation deductions would be allocated ("charged back") to the Orrisches, and any remaining gain would be divided equally.

In 1966 and 1967, the partnership allocated all its depreciation deductions to the Orrisches. This special allocation, along with the original cash contributions of the partners and other partnership income and loss, was reflected in the partners' capital accounts. By the end of 1967, the Orrisches had a $25,187 capital account deficit, and the Crisafis had a positive capital account of $406.

The Service, applying a test imposed by the pre–1976 version of Section 704(b), determined that the special allocation of depreciation deductions to the Orrisches should be disregarded because it "was made with the principal purpose of avoidance of income." Ed.]

OPINION

The only issue presented for decision is whether tax effect can be given the agreement between petitioners and the Crisafis that, beginning with 1966, all the partnership's depreciation deductions were to be allocated to petitioners for their use in computing their individual income tax liabilities. In our view, the answer must be in the negative, and the amounts of each of the partners' deductions for the depreciation of partnership property must be determined in accordance with the ratio used generally in computing their distributive shares of the partnership's profits and losses.

Among the important innovations of the 1954 Code are limited provisions for flexibility in arrangements for the sharing of income, losses, and deductions arising from business activities conducted through partnerships. The authority for special allocations of such items appears in section 704(a), which provides that a partner's share of any item of income, gain, loss, deduction, or credit shall be determined by the partnership agreement. That rule is coupled with a limitation in [pre–1976] section 704(b),[4] however, which states that a special allocation of an item will be disregarded if its "principal purpose" is the avoidance or evasion of Federal income tax. See Smith v. Commissioner, 331 F.2d 298 (C.A.7, 1964), affirming a Memorandum Opinion of this Court; Jean v. Kresser, 54 T.C. 1621 (1970). In case a special allocation is disregarded, the partner's share of the item is to be determined in accordance with the ratio by which the partners divide the general profits or losses of the partnership. Sec. 1.704–1(b)(2), Income Tax Regs.

The report of the Senate Committee on Finance accompanying the bill finally enacted as the 1954 Code (S.Rept. No. 1622, to accompany H.R. 8300 (Pub.L. No. 591), 83d Cong., 2d Sess., p. 379 (1954)) explained the tax-avoidance restriction prescribed by section 704(b) as follows:

> Subsection (b) * * * provides that if the principal purpose of any provision in the partnership agreement dealing with a partner's distributive share of a particular item is to avoid or evade the Federal income tax, the partner's distributive share of that item shall be redetermined in accordance with his distributive share of partnership income or loss described in section 702(a)(9) [i.e., the ratio used by the partners for dividing general profits or losses]. * * *
>
> Where, however, a provision in a partnership agreement for a special allocation of certain items has substantial economic effect and is not merely a device for reducing the taxes of certain partners without actually affecting their shares of partnership income, then such a provision will be recognized for tax purposes. * * *

This reference to "substantial economic effect" did not appear in the House Ways and Means Committee report (H.Rept. No. 1337, to accompany H.R. 8300 (Pub.L. No. 591), 83d Cong., 2d Sess., p. A223 (1954)) discussing section 704(b), and was apparently added in the Senate Finance Committee

4. SEC. 704 [prior to 1976 amendment Ed.]. PARTNER'S DISTRIBUTIVE SHARE.

(b) DISTRIBUTIVE SHARE DETERMINED BY INCOME OR LOSS RATIO.—A partner's distributive share of any item of income, gain, loss, deduction, or credit shall be determined in accordance with his distributive share of taxable income or loss of the partnership, as described in section 702(a)(9), for the taxable year, if—

(1) the partnership agreement does not provide as to the partner's distributive share of such item, or

(2) the principal purpose of any provision in the partnership agreement with respect to the partner's distributive share of such item is the avoidance or evasion of any tax imposed by this subtitle.

to allay fears that special allocations of income or deductions would be denied effect in every case where the allocation resulted in a reduction in the income tax liabilities of one or more of the partners. The statement is an affirmation that special allocations are ordinarily to be recognized if they have business validity apart from their tax consequences. Driscoll, "Tax Problems of Partnerships—Special Allocation of Specific Items," 1958 So. Cal. Tax Inst. 421, 426.

In resolving the question whether the principal purpose of a provision in a partnership agreement is the avoidance or evasion of Federal income tax, all the facts and circumstances in relation to the provision must be taken into account. Section 1.704–1(b)(2), Income Tax Regs., lists the following as relevant circumstances to be considered:

> Whether the partnership or a partner individually has a business purpose for the allocation; whether the allocation has "substantial economic effect", that is, whether the allocation may actually affect the dollar amount of the partners' shares of the total partnership income or loss independently of tax consequences; whether related items of income, gain, loss, deduction, or credit from the same source are subject to the same allocation; whether the allocation was made without recognition of normal business factors and only after the amount of the specially allocated item could reasonably be estimated; the duration of the allocation; and the overall tax consequences of the allocation. * * *

Applying these standards, we do not think the special allocation of depreciation in the present case can be given effect.

The evidence is persuasive that the special allocation of depreciation was adopted for a tax-avoidance rather than a business purpose. Depreciation was the only item which was adjusted by the parties; both the income from the buildings and the expenses incurred in their operation, maintenance, and repair were allocated to the partners equally. Since the deduction for depreciation does not vary from year to year with the fortunes of the business, the parties obviously knew what the tax effect of the special allocation would be at the time they adopted it. Furthermore, as shown by our Findings, petitioners had large amounts of income which would be offset by the additional deduction for depreciation; the Crisafis, in contrast, had no taxable income from which to subtract the partnership depreciation deductions, and, due to depreciation deductions which they were obtaining with respect to other housing projects, could expect to have no taxable income in the near future. On the other hand, the insulation of the Crisafis from at least part of a potential capital gains tax was an obvious tax advantage. The inference is unmistakably clear that the agreement did not reflect normal business considerations but was designed primarily to minimize the overall tax liabilities of the partners.

Petitioners urge that the special allocation of the depreciation deduction was adopted in order to equalize the capital accounts of the partners, correcting a disparity ($14,000) in the amounts initially contributed to the partnership by them ($26,500) and the Crisafis ($12,500). But the evidence does not support this contention. Under the special allocation agreement, petitioners were to be entitled, in computing their individual income tax liabilities, to deduct the full amount of the depreciation realized on the partnership property. For 1966, as an example, petitioners were allocated a sum ($18,904) equal to the depreciation on the partnership property ($18,412) plus one-half of the net loss computed without regard to depreciation ($492). The other one-half of the net loss was, of course, allocated to the Crisafis. Petitioners' allocation ($18,904) was then applied to reduce their capital account. The depreciation specially allocated to petitioners ($18,412) in 1966 alone exceeded the amount of the disparity in the contributions. Indeed, at the end of 1967, petitioners' capital account showed a deficit of $25,187.11 compared with a positive balance of $405.65 in the Crisafis' account. By the time the partnership's properties are fully depreciated, the amount of the reduction in petitioners' capital account will approximate the remaining basis for the buildings as of the end of 1967. The Crisafis' capital account will be adjusted only for contributions, withdrawals, gain or loss, without regard to depreciation, and similar adjustments for these factors will also be made in petitioners' capital account. Thus, rather than correcting an imbalance in the capital accounts of the partners, the special allocation of depreciation will create a vastly greater imbalance than existed at the end of 1966. In the light of these facts, we find it incredible that equalization of the capital accounts was the objective of the special allocation.[5]

Petitioners rely primarily on the argument that the allocation has "substantial economic effect" in that it is reflected in the capital accounts of the partners. Referring to the material quoted above from the report of the Senate Committee on Finance, they contend that this alone is sufficient to show that the special allocation served a business rather than a tax-avoidance purpose.

According to the regulations, an allocation has economic effect if it "may actually affect the dollar amount of the partners' shares of the total partnership income or loss independently of tax consequences." The agreement in this case provided not only for the allocation of depreciation to petitioners but also for gain on the sale of the partnership property to be "charged back" to them. The charge back would cause the gain, for tax purposes, to be allocated on the books entirely to petitioners to the extent of the special allocation of depreciation, and their capital account would be correspondingly increased. The remainder of the gain, if any, would be

5. We recognize that petitioners had more money invested in the partnership than the Crisafis and that it is reasonable for the partners to endeavor to equalize their investments, since each one was to share equally in the profits and losses of the enterprise. However, we do not think that sec. 704(a) permits the partners' prospective tax benefits to be used as the medium for equalizing their investments, and it is apparent that the economic burden of the depreciation (which is reflected by the allowance for depreciation) was not intended to be the medium used.

This case is to be distinguished from situations where one partner contributed property and the other cash; in such cases sec. 704(c) may allow a special allocation of income and expenses in order to reflect the tax consequences inherent in the original contributions.

shared equally by the partners. If the gain on the sale were to equal or exceed the depreciation specially allocated to petitioners, the increase in their capital account caused by the charge back would exactly equal the depreciation deductions previously allowed to them and the proceeds of the sale of the property would be divided equally. In such circumstances, the only effect of the allocation would be a trade of tax consequences, i.e., the Crisafis would relinquish a current depreciation deduction in exchange for exoneration from all or part of the capital gains tax when the property is sold, and petitioners would enjoy a larger current depreciation deduction but would assume a larger ultimate capital gains tax liability. Quite clearly, if the property is sold at a gain, the special allocation will affect only the tax liabilities of the partners and will have no other economic effect.

To find any economic effect of the special allocation agreement aside from its tax consequences, we must, therefore, look to see who is to bear the economic burden of the depreciation if the buildings should be sold for a sum less than their original cost. There is not one syllable of evidence bearing directly on this crucial point. We have noted, however, that when the buildings are fully depreciated, petitioners' capital account will have a deficit, or there will be a disparity in the capital accounts, approximately equal to the undepreciated basis of the buildings as of the beginning of 1966.[6] Under normal accounting procedures, if the building were sold at a gain less than the amount of such disparity petitioners would either be required to contribute to the partnership a sum equal to the remaining deficit in their capital account after the gain on the sale had been added back or would be entitled to receive a proportionately smaller share of the partnership assets on liquidation. Based on the record as a whole, we do not think the partners ever agreed to such an arrangement. On dissolution, we think the partners contemplated an equal division of the partnership assets which would be adjusted only for disparities in cash contributions or withdrawals.[7] Certainly there is no evidence to show otherwise. That being true, the special allocation does not "actually affect the dollar amount of the partners' share of the total partnership income or loss independently of tax consequences" within the meaning of the regulation referred to above.

Our interpretation of the partnership agreement is supported by an analysis of a somewhat similar agreement, quoted in material part in our Findings, which petitioners made as part of a marital property settlement agreement in 1968. Under this agreement, Orrisch was entitled to deduct all the depreciation for 1968 in computing his income tax liability, and his wife was to deduct none; but on the sale of the property they were to first reimburse Orrisch for "such moneys as he may have advanced," and then divide the balance of the "profits or proceeds" of the sale equally, each party to report one-half of the capital gain or loss on his income tax return.

6. This assumes, of course, that all partnership withdrawals and capital contributions will be equal.

7. We note that, in the course of Orrisch's testimony, petitioners' counsel made a distinction between entries in the taxpayer's capital accounts which reflect actual cash transactions and those relating to the special allocation which are "paper entries relating to depreciation."

In the 1969 amendment to this agreement the unequal allocation of the depreciation deduction was discontinued, and a provision similar to the partnership "charge back" was added, i.e., while the proceeds of the sale were to be divided equally, only Orrisch's basis was to be reduced by the depreciation allowed for 1968 so that he would pay taxes on a larger portion of the gain realized on the sale. Significantly, in both this agreement and the partnership agreement, as we interpret it, each party's share of the sales proceeds was determined independently from his share of the depreciation deduction.

In the light of all the evidence we have found as an ultimate fact that the "principal purpose" of the special allocation agreement was tax avoidance within the meaning of section 704(b). Accordingly, the deduction for depreciation for 1966 and 1967 must be allocated between the parties in the same manner as other deductions.

Decision will be entered for the respondent.

NOTE

Although the *Orrisch* case is not a model of clarity, it is regarded as a major milestone in the interpretation of Section 704(b). The litigated allocations occurred in a year prior to 1977, at a time when Section 704(b) required special allocations to be tested by determining whether the principal purpose of the allocation was the avoidance or evasion of income tax.[1] As *Orrisch* illustrates, the regulations interpreting that test looked to whether the allocation had "substantial economic effect"—i.e., "whether the allocation may actually affect the dollar amount of the partners' shares of the total partnership income or loss independently of tax consequences."[2] In the Tax Reform Act of 1976,[3] Congress incorporated the "substantial economic effect" test in Section 704(b), in effect codifying the prior regulations.[4]

Under prior law, there was authority that Section 704(b) applied to "*items*" of income, loss, etc., but not to allocations of total or "bottom line" income or loss.[5] Nevertheless, the courts had applied a test to determine the propriety of bottom line allocations which is virtually identical to the Section 704(b) test.[6] As a second amendment in the 1976 Act, Congress provided that the propriety of bottom line allocations also would be

1. Reg. § 1.704–1(b)(2) (pre–1977).

2. Id.

3. Pub.L. No. 94–455, 90 Stat. 1520, reprinted in 1976–3 C.B. (Vol. 1) 1.

4. See generally Cowan, "Substantial Economic Effect—The Outer Limits for Partnership Allocations," 39 N.Y.U.Inst. on Fed. Tax'n 23–1 (1981); McKee, "Partnership Allocations: The Need for an Entity Approach," 66 Va.L.Rev. 1039 (1980); Weidner, "Partnership Allocations and Capital Account Analysis," 42 Ohio St. L.Rev. 467 (1981).

5. Holladay v. Commissioner, 72 T.C. 571 (1979).

6. Hamilton v. United States, 687 F.2d 408 (Ct.Cl.1982). At page 414 of the opinion, the Court states: "that standard [for bottom line items] differs only slightly from the standard found in section 704(b)(2) and the use of one rather than the other should have little effect on the outcome of [a] case."

evaluated under the substantial economic effect test. Both of the 1976 amendments were essentially house-cleaning measures to conform the statute to the approach being taken by the courts. The Joint Committee General Explanation of amended Section 704(b) describes the 1976 changes as follows:[7]

Prior law

> A limited (or a general) partnership agreement may allocate income, gain, loss, deduction, or credit (or items thereof) among the partners in a manner that is disproportionate to the capital contributions of the partners. These are sometimes referred to as "special allocations" and, with respect to any taxable year, may be made by amendment to the partnership agreement at any time up to the initial due date of the partnership tax return for that year (sec. 761(c)).
>
> A special allocation was not recognized under prior law (sec. 704(b)(2)) if its principal purpose was to avoid or evade a Federal tax. In determining whether a special allocation had been made principally for the avoidance of tax, the regulations focused upon whether the special allocation had "substantial economic effect," that is, whether the allocation may actually affect the dollar amount of the partner's share of the total partnership income or loss independently of tax consequences (Regs. § 1.704–1(b)(2)). The regulations also inquired as to whether there was a business purpose for this special allocation, whether related items from the same source were subject to the same allocation, whether the allocation ignored normal business factors and was made after the amount of the specially allocated item could reasonably be estimated, the duration of the allocation, and the overall tax consequences of the allocation.
>
> By its terms, the tax avoidance provisions of prior law section 704(b)(2) applied to allocations of *items* of income, gain, loss, deduction, or credit. It was thus argued that these provisions did not apply to and would not preclude allocations of taxable income or loss, as opposed to specific items of income, gain, deduction, loss, or credit.

* * *

Reasons for change

> Congress believed that an overall allocation of the taxable income or loss for a taxable year (described under section 702(a) [8]) should be subject to disallowance in the same manner as allocations of items of income or loss.

7. Staff of the Joint Comm. on Internal Revenue Taxation, 94th Cong., 2d Sess., General Explanation of the Tax Reform Act of 1976 at 94, reprinted in 1976–3 C.B. (Vol. 2) 106.

Also, allocations of special items and overall allocations should be restricted to those situations where the allocations have substantial economic effect.

Explanation of provisions

The Act provides that an allocation of overall income or loss (described under Section 702(a) [8]), or of any item of income, gain, loss, deduction, or credit (described under section 702(a)(1)–[7]), shall be controlled by the partnership agreement if the partner receiving the allocation can demonstrate that it has "substantial economic effect", i.e., whether the allocation may actually affect the dollar amount of the partners' share of the total partnership income or loss, independent of tax consequences.* Other factors that could possibly relate to the determination of the validity of an allocation are set forth under the present regulations (Regs. § 1.704–1(b)(2)).

If an allocation made by the partnership is set aside, a partner's share of the income, gain, loss, deduction or credit (or item thereof) will be determined in accordance with his interest in the partnership.

In determining a "partner's interest in the partnership", all the relevant facts and circumstances are to be taken into account. Among the relevant factors to be taken into account are the interest of the respective partners in profits and losses (if different from that in taxable income or loss), cash flow, and their rights to distributions of capital upon liquidation.

As amended by the 1976 legislation, Section 704(b) is deceptively brief, stating merely that a special allocation will not be respected if it lacks "substantial economic effect." Congress delegated to the Treasury the arduous task of formulating guidelines for the application of the substantial economic effect concept to the innumerable and intricate partnership arrangements emanating from the business, investment and tax shelter communities.

Building upon the Tax Court's primitive analysis in *Orrisch* and other cases,[8] the Section 704(b) regulations are a lengthy and sophisticated response to the ingenuity of the tax advisors. They have been accurately described by one leading commentator as "a creation of prodigious complexity * * * essentially impenetrable to all but those with the time, talent

* The determination of whether an allocation may actually affect the dollar amount of the partners' shares of total partnership income or loss, independent of tax consequences, will to a substantial extent involve an examination of how these allocations are treated in the partners' capital accounts for financial (as opposed to tax) accounting purposes; this assumes that these accounts actually reflect the dollar amounts to which the partners would be entitled upon the liquidation of the partnership.

8. See, e.g., Ogden v. Commissioner, 84 T.C. 871 (1985), affirmed per curiam 788 F.2d 252 (5th Cir.1986); Allison v. United States, 701 F.2d 933 (Fed.Cir.1983); Holladay v. Commissioner, 72 T.C. 571 (1979), affirmed 649 F.2d 1176 (5th Cir.1981).

and determination to become thoroughly prepared experts on the subject."[9] Such a gloomy characterization prompts one to ask: is mastering these regulations worth the trouble, especially considering that one of the Treasury's principal targets—tax shelters—has been rendered virtually extinct?

It would be tempting to gloss over Section 704(b) but for the fact that drafters of partnership agreements have continued spawning diverse profit and loss sharing arrangements as the economy adapts to the altered tax landscape. In keeping with the philosophy of this text, the focus will be on the fundamentals, looking first at the basic rules for special partnership allocations under Section 704(b) and the consequences if an allocation is set aside,[10] and then turning to allocations attributable to nonrecourse debt.[11]

2. The Section 704(b) Regulations: Basic Rules

Code: § 704(b).

Regulations: § 1.704–1(b)(1)(i), (iii) & (vii);–1(b)(2)(i)–(iii), (iv)(*a*)–(*c*), (*f*), (*h*), (*n*);–1(b)(3);–1(b)(5) Examples (1), (2), (3), (5), (6), (7), & (15)(i), (ii).

a. INTRODUCTION

At the heart of the Section 704(b) regulations is a two-part test to determine if a partnership allocation has substantial economic effect. To be respected for tax purposes, an allocation first must have "economic effect," meaning generally that the allocation must be consistent with the economic business deal of the partners.[1] The economic effect test is objective and is satisfied if the partnership agreement complies with a series of mechanical requirements to be described below. The "substantiality" test is more subjective and thus harder to apply. In general, for the economic effect of an allocation to be substantial, there must be a reasonable possibility that the allocation will affect substantially the dollar amounts to be received by the partners from the partnership apart from tax consequences; insubstantiality results when the economic effect of an allocation is likely to be eliminated by one or more contemporaneous or later allocations and the overall tax liability of the partners is reduced.[2]

If the partnership agreement is silent as to the partners' distributive shares of income, losses and other tax items, or if a special allocation is found wanting because it lacks substantial economic effect, then the partners' respective shares of income, loss and other items are determined in accordance with the partners' respective "interests in the partnership."[3]

9. Lokken, "Partnership Allocations," 41 Tax L.Rev. 545, 621 (1986). See also Close & Kusnetz, "The Final Section 704(b) Regulations: Special Allocations Reach New Heights of Complexity," 40 Tax Lawyer 307 (1987).

10. See Reg. § 1.704–1(b)(1), (2), (3) and (5) and Section B2 of this chapter, infra.

11. See Reg. § 1.704–1(b)(4)(iv) and Section B3 of this chapter, infra.

1. Reg. § 1.704–1(b)(2)(ii)(*a*).

2. Reg. § 1.704–1(b)(2)(iii)(*a*).

3. I.R.C. § 704(b). See Reg. §§ 1.704–1(b)(1)(i), 1.704–1(b)(3).

A partner's interest in the partnership is determined by taking into account "all the facts and circumstances;" the regulations elaborate by providing a few broad rules and examples for making this essentially factual (and often elusive) determination.[4]

The Section 704(b) regulations have a broad scope. They apply to all allocations of specific items of income, gain, loss, deductions and credits (e.g., depreciation, tax-exempt income) as well as to allocations of partnership net (i.e., "bottom line") taxable income and loss.[5] The substantial economic effect test is applied on an annual basis to determine the validity of an allocation for the year involved.[6] An allocation that is valid in one year may fail to pass muster in a subsequent year, and in any one year, a portion of an allocation may be valid while other portions are invalid.[7]

The regulations include 19 examples illustrating practical applications of the rules.[8] In the explanation to follow, we borrow generously from these examples, but this discussion is not intended to relieve students from the obligation of reading and engaging in direct combat with the language of the regulations.

b. MAINTENANCE OF PARTNERS' CAPITAL ACCOUNTS

A critical precept of the substantial economic effect test is that an allocation is valid for tax purposes only if it is "consistent with the underlying economic arrangement of the partners."[9] The reference point employed by the regulations for testing whether allocations are sufficiently linked to the partners' economic deal is the capital account. Recall[10] that a capital account essentially represents a partner's equity in the partnership; at any point during the life of the firm, it identifies the amounts the partners would be entitled to receive if and when their interests in the partnerships were liquidated. The regulations go to great lengths to ensure that the capital accounts employed to test partnership allocations are an accurate measure of these economic entitlements. In so doing, the rules depart in some respects from generally accepted accounting principles. Our coverage here will be limited to the basic capital account maintenance rules; discussion of certain other capital account adjustments will be deferred until the transactions that trigger those adjustments are examined.[11]

From the standpoint of an attorney drafting a partnership agreement, the message of the regulations is that the capital account rules must be incorporated in the partnership agreement if an allocation is to have

4. Reg. § 1.704–1(b)(3).

5. Reg. § 1.704–1(b)(1)(vii).

6. Reg. § 1.704–1(b)(2)(i).

7. See, e.g., Reg. § 1.704–1(b)(5) Examples (1)(iv), (v), (vi) & (15)(ii).

8. See Reg. § 1.704–1(b)(5).

9. Reg. § 1.704–1(b)(2)(ii)(*a*).

10. See Chapter 2A2, supra.

11. See, e.g., Chapters 4C (contributed property), 6B (sales of partnership interests), 7C (operating distributions) and 8A (liquidating distributions).

economic effect. At the very least, a typical broad definition of "capital account" in an agreement would read:[12]

> The "Capital Account" of a partner shall mean the capital account of that partner from the inception of the partnership as determined in accordance with Section 1.704–1(b)(2)(iv) of the Treasury Regulations or any successor provision.

For this purpose, the "partnership agreement" includes all agreements among the partners, or between one or more partners and the partnership, whether oral or written and whether or not embodied in a document referred to by the partners as their "agreement."[13] Once the magic words are inserted in the document, it is primarily up to the partnership's accountant to ensure that capital accounts are properly maintained in accordance with the regulations throughout the life of the partnership.[14]

Capital accounts are considered properly determined and maintained only if each partner's capital account is increased by:[15]

(1) the amount of money contributed to the partnership by the partner;[16]

(2) the fair market value of property contributed by the partner to the partnership (net of liabilities securing the property that the partnership is considered to assume or take subject to under Section 752);[17] and

(3) allocations to the partner of partnership income and gain, including tax-exempt income;

and is decreased by:[18]

(1) the amount of money distributed to the partner by the partnership;

(2) the fair market value of property distributed to the partner by the partnership (net of liabilities secured by the property that the partner is considered to assume or take subject to under Section 752);[19]

12. This and later sample clauses have been adapted from partnership agreements made available to the authors by practitioners.

13. Reg. § 1.704–1(b)(2)(ii)(*h*). If a partner has more than one type of interest in the partnership—e.g., as both a general and a limited partner—the regulations require that one single capital account must be maintained reflecting all of those interests, whenever they were acquired. Reg. § 1.704–1(b)(2)(iv)(*b*).

14. Reg. § 1.704–1(b)(2)(iv)(*a*).

15. See Reg. § 1.704–1(b)(2)(iv)(*b*).

16. For this purpose, "money" includes the amount of any partnership liabilities assumed by the partner to the extent that the assuming partner is primarily and personally liable with respect to the obligation and the creditor is aware of the assumption and can directly enforce the assuming partner's obligation. Reg. § 1.704–1(b)(2)(iv)(*b*), (*c*).

17. See Reg. § 1.704–1(b)(2)(iv)(*c*). Special rules are provided for contributions of promissory notes. See Reg. § 1.704–1(b)(2)(iv)(*d*)(*2*).

18. Reg. § 1.704–1(b)(2)(iv)(*b*).

19. Special rules are provided for distributions of promissory notes. See Reg. § 1.704–1(b)(2)(iv)(*e*)(*2*).

(3) allocations to the partner of partnership expenditures that are neither deductible in computing taxable income nor properly chargeable to capital account, including Section 705(a)(2)(B) items (e.g., gambling losses, bribes, charitable contributions), Section 709 organizational and syndication expenses that are not amortized under Section 709(b) and losses disallowed under Section 267(a)(1);[20] and

(4) allocations of partnership loss and deduction (excluding the items listed in (3), above).

Stepping back from the detail for a moment, it should be apparent that these rules are designed to determine, throughout the life of the partnership, the "book value" of each partner's interest in the firm. Thus, a partner's capital account may differ markedly from his outside basis, especially where the partnership has liabilities.[21] Moreover, the regulations seek a truer measure of a partner's equity by reflecting all contributions and distributions of property in the partners' capital accounts at their fair market value when contributed or distributed rather than at their adjusted tax basis. In the case of contributed property with built-in gain or loss, this treatment often will create a "book/tax" disparity—i.e., a difference between the adjusted basis of the asset for tax purposes and its value as reported on the partnership's books (and reflected in the partners' capital accounts).[22] These book/tax differences raise challenging issues, some of which will be examined in more detail later in this chapter.[23] For now, it is important to keep in mind that because capital accounts reflect the *value* of contributed property rather than its tax basis,[24] further adjustments may be required to ensure that capital accounts are adjusted by book income rather than taxable income.[25]

To patrol against inflated valuations, the regulations provide that a fair market value reasonably agreed to among the partners in arm's length negotiations will control if the partners have sufficiently adverse interests.[26] The theory is that if the valuation is hammered out between genuinely adverse parties, abuse is unlikely.[27] Fair market value is otherwise determined under "general tax principles," which in theory means a "willing buyer/willing seller" test and in practice degenerates into a battle

20. Reg. § 1.704–1(b)(2)(iv)(*i*).

21. For example, Section 752(a) treats an increase in a partner's share of partnership liabilities as a contribution of money, which results in an increase to the partner's outside basis under Section 705. Similarly, Section 752(b) treats a decrease of a partner's share of partnership liabilities as a distribution of money, resulting in a decrease in the partner's outside basis. See Section D of this chapter, infra. Neither of these adjustments is appropriate for capital account purposes, however, because liabilities obviously are not "capital" and they do not represent what the partners would be entitled to receive on liquidation. See Reg. § 1.704–1(b)(2)(iv)(*c*).

22. See I.R.C. § 723 and Chapter 2A, supra.

23. See Section C of this chapter, infra.

24. Reg. § 1.704–1(b)(2)(iv)(*g*).

25. See, e.g., Reg. § 1.704–1(b)(2)(iv)(*d*)(*1*).

26. Reg. § 1.704–1(b)(2)(iv)(*h*).

27. Query whether valuation agreements among members of the same family will be respected?

of expert appraisers followed by a Solomonic compromise. If these conditions are not met, the capital account rules are considered to have been violated if "the value assigned to such property is overstated or understated (by more than an insignificant amount)."[28] The effect of a valuation error could be potentially devastating because, if capital accounts are improperly maintained, all allocations in the partnership agreement will be set aside and result in a reallocation in accordance with the partners' interests in the partnership.[29]

The regulations also allow partnerships to restate assets at their current fair market value on certain occasions, such as the admission of a new partner to the partnership, a distribution in complete or partial liquidation of a partner's interest in the firm, or the grant of a partnership interest as consideration for the provision of services to the partnership, provided the adjustments are made for a "substantial non-tax business purpose."[30] In these circumstances, restatements are permissible only if the partnership agreement so provides and a set of detailed rules are followed in making the adjustments.[31]

c. ECONOMIC EFFECT

The Big Three. In providing that an allocation will have economic effect only if it is consistent with the underlying economic arrangement of the partners, the regulations mean that if there is an economic benefit or burden corresponding to the allocation, the partner to whom the allocation is made must receive the benefit or bear the burden.[32] Fortunately, this standard is not as vague as it first appears. The regulations test "economic effect" mechanically, first providing a three-pronged primary test, then a more flexible alternate test and finally a narrowly applicable fallback test of "economic effect equivalence."

Under the primary test, an allocation will have economic effect if, and only if, throughout the life of the partnership, the partnership agreement provides that:

(1) Capital accounts must be determined and maintained in accordance with the rules of Section 1.704–1(b)(2)(iv) of the regulations;[33]

28. Reg. § 1.704–1(b)(2)(iv)(*h*).

29. See Reg. § 1.704–1(b)(2)(ii)(*b*). But see Reg. § 1.704–1(b)(2)(ii)(*i*) and infra p. 155 for situations where an allocation nonetheless will be respected if it has "economic effect equivalence."

30. Reg. § 1.704–1(b)(2)(iv)(*f*). A fourth situation where an optional restatement is permitted is where "substantially all of the partnership's property (excluding money)" consists of marketable securities. Reg. § 1.704–1(b)(2)(iv)(*f*)(*5*)(*iv*). In these circumstances, periodic "mark-ups to market" are permitted provided that "generally accepted industry accounting practices" are observed. Id.

31. See Reg. § 1.704–1(b)(2)(iv)(*f*). See Section C of this chapter and Chapter 7C, infra, for circumstances in which a restatement of capital accounts may be desirable.

32. Reg. § 1.704–1(b)(2)(ii)(*a*).

33. Reg. § 1.704–1(b)(2)(ii)(*b*)(*1*). Only minor, accidental departures made in good faith will be tolerated. Reg. § 1.704–1(b)(2)(iv)(*p*).

(2) Upon a liquidation of the partnership, or of any partner's interest, liquidating distributions must be made in accordance with the positive capital account balances of the partners;[34]

(3) If a partner has a deficit balance in his capital account following the liquidation of his interest in the partnership, he must be unconditionally obligated to restore the deficit by the later of: (a) the end of the taxable year of the liquidation of the partner's interest, or (b) 90 days after the date of the liquidation.[35]

Because we will mention these three parts of the primary test frequently in the ensuing discussion, they collectively will be referred to for convenience as "The Big Three."

From a mechanical standpoint, satisfying The Big Three is a straightforward matter. The requirements are easily met simply by including the requisite provisions relating to maintenance of capital accounts, distributions on liquidation and restoration of deficit capital accounts in the partnership agreement and by adhering to them for the duration of the partnership.[36] Provisions that would satisfy the second and third requirements might read as follows:

> *Distributions on Liquidation.* All distributions in liquidation of the partnership or of any partner's interest in the partnership shall be in an amount equal to the positive balance in the Capital Account of each partner whose interest is being liquidated as that account is determined after all adjustments to such account for the taxable year of the partnership during which the liquidation occurs as are required by Treasury Regulations § 1.704–1(b). Such adjustments shall be made within the time specified in such Regulations.
>
> *Restoration of Deficit Capital Account.* Any partner whose Capital Account has a deficit balance after the liquidation of such partner's partnership interest shall restore such deficit to the partnership no later than the end of the partnership taxable year in which such liquidation occurs, or, if later, within 90 days after the date of such liquidation.

The rationale for The Big Three should be apparent. Unless tax allocations of income or loss are accompanied by increases or decreases to the partner's capital accounts, there is no way to assure that the tax

34. Reg. § 1.704–1(b)(2)(ii)(*b*)(*2*). This determination is made after taking into account all capital account adjustments for the partnership taxable year during which the liquidation occurs. Id. For when a "liquidation" occurs, see Reg. § 1.704–1(b)(2)(ii)(*g*). A liquidation may include a constructive termination of the partnership under Section 708(b)(1)—e.g., where there are sales and exchanges of 50 percent or more of the interests of the partnership within a 12–month period. See Close & Kusnetz, "The Final Section 704(b) Regulations: Special Allocations Reach New Heights of Complexity," 40 Tax Lawyer 307 (1987), and Chapter 8D2, infra.

35. Reg. § 1.704–1(b)(2)(ii)(*b*)(*3*). Any amounts restored must be paid to creditors of the partnership or distributed to other partners in accordance with their positive capital account balances. Id.

36. Reg. § 1.704–1(b)(2)(ii)(*b*).

consequences ever will reflect the partners' economic business deal. For example, a special allocation of $100 of extra income can be respected for tax purposes only if the partners eventually will receive the economic benefit of that income. And since the partners' ultimate economic stakes in the partnership are measured by their capital accounts, all allocations (and other significant financial events in the life of the partnership) must be reflected in those capital accounts. The second and third requirements ensure the validity of this premise by requiring that the amounts partners will receive on liquidation are determined by their positive capital accounts. Because a negative capital account indicates that the partner is in debt to the partnership (i.e., to creditors or the other partners), the regulations require that the partner must satisfy that debt (by restoring the deficit) on or before a liquidation.

An example or two (adapted from the regulations)[37] may be helpful at this point. Assume a situation very similar to the *Orrisch* case, where A and B, each contributing $40,000 cash, form the AB general partnership to purchase and lease depreciable equipment. A and B thus each begin with a $40,000 capital account. The partnership agreement provides that: (1) the partners equally will share taxable income (without regard to Section 168 cost recovery deductions) and cash flow except that all cost recovery deductions are specially allocated to A; (2) capital accounts will be maintained in accordance with the regulations; and (3) on liquidation all distributions will be made equally between A and B. Neither partner, however, has any obligation to restore a deficit in his capital account. Something is awry here! Although A and B assiduously maintain capital accounts, they agree to ignore them upon liquidation. More facts are necessary to identify the flaw.

For convenience, assume that apart from cost recovery deductions, AB breaks even (i.e., operating income equals operating expenses) for its first taxable year, but a $20,000 cost recovery deduction is allocated to A pursuant to the agreement.[38] A's capital account is thus reduced to $20,000 while B's stays at $40,000. Assume further, as the regulations generally require,[39] that the fair market value of the equipment (the partnership's only asset) equals its adjusted basis ($60,000 here, after the first year's cost recovery deductions). In that event, if the partnership were to sell the equipment for $60,000 and liquidate, the agreement would require the proceeds to be divided equally ($30,000 each). The flaw thus is revealed because, if the special allocation of cost recovery deductions to A is to have economic effect, A must bear the full risk of economic loss corresponding to that allocated deduction. A does not bear that loss if the capital account balances—which are designed to reflect the economic entitlements of the partners—are ignored on liquidation. For this allocation to have economic

37. See Reg. § 1.704–1(b)(5) Example (1)(i).

38. Section 168 technicians should not be distracted by our computation of cost recovery deductions. Like the example in the regulations, we conveniently assume for illustration a four-year straight line recovery period, with no half-year convention or other complications.

39. See Reg. § 1.704–1(b)(2)(iii)(*c*).

effect, the agreement should have provided for distributions in liquidation to be made in accordance with the positive capital accounts of the partners—i.e., $20,000 to A and $40,000 to B. Only then would the tax allocation match the economics. Because the allocation lacks economic effect, the $20,000 cost recovery deduction must be reallocated in accordance with the partners' interests in the partnership—50/50 in this example.[40]

Now assume the same basic facts except that A and B agreed from the outset to make distributions in accordance with the partners' positive capital account balances, but their agreement still fails to include a deficit restoration requirement. Assume further that apart from cost recovery deductions the partnership continues to break even in years two and three, and $20,000 of cost recovery deductions are allocated to A in each of those three years. Again assuming that the economic decline in value matches tax depreciation, the equipment is now presumed to be worth $20,000 ($80,000 cost less $60,000 cost recovery deductions for years one through three). The capital accounts of the partners are thus:

	A	B
On formation	$40,000	$40,000
Less: cost recovery deductions (years 1–3)	(60,000)	0
Capital account at end of year 3	($20,000)	$40,000

If the partnership sells the equipment for $20,000 and liquidates at the end of year three, the agreement would entitle B to the entire $20,000, which is all there is to distribute. Shouldn't that be enough for the allocation to have economic effect? The regulations answer "No!" because B—who enjoyed none of the cost recovery deductions associated with the equipment—should be entitled to fully recover her $40,000 investment, while A, whose $60,000 of cost recovery deductions ostensibly were coupled with an equivalent economic burden, has only lost $40,000 under the arrangement described above. For A's economic burden to correspond to the allocation, A must be obligated to restore the $20,000 deficit balance in his capital account so that B is not short-changed.[41] After such a restoration, the economics are respected because A will have lost $60,000 and B will have recouped her entire $40,000 investment—satisfying the command that "in the event there is an economic benefit or an economic burden that corresponds to an allocation, the partner to whom the allocation is made must receive such economic benefit or bear such economic burden."[42] Consequently, without such a deficit restoration obligation, the allocation fails The Big Three for all the years involved and must be reallocated in accordance with the partners' interests in the partnership.

40. See Reg. § 1.704–1(b)(5) Example (1)(i).

41. But why should the absence of a deficit restoration obligation cause allocations to lack economic effect in the earlier years when A did *not* have a negative capital account? See infra pp. 149–155 for a possible answer.

42. Reg. § 1.704–1(b)(2)(ii)(*a*).

The deficit restoration requirement is the most troublesome of The Big Three in the case of limited partnerships and limited liability companies because investors with limited liability (limited partners and members of an LLC) invariably are unwilling to make such an open-ended commitment. As we are about to see, however, the regulations provide an alternate test to avoid this problem and preserve special allocations of losses as long as they do not reduce a partner's capital account below zero.

Alternate Economic Effect: Basic Rules. If a partnership agreement satisfies the first two requirements of The Big Three but fails to include an unconditional deficit make-up provision, the regulations provide an alternate test for economic effect. This more flexible standard looks to both the effect of an allocation on a partner's capital account and the extent of any partial obligation by the partner to restore a deficit or make additional capital contributions to the partnership. An allocation will have economic effect under the alternate test to the extent that it does not create or increase a deficit in the partner's capital account (in excess of any limited deficit restoration obligation that the partner may have)[43] and the agreement includes a provision known as a "qualified income offset."[44] The test makes sense because, even without an unlimited obligation to restore a deficit, a partner who receives an allocation of losses still suffers a corresponding economic burden as long as the allocation does not create a capital account deficit or exceed any additional amounts that the partner has agreed to contribute to the partnership in the future. If an allocation of loss does create or increase a deficit (in excess of any limited deficit make-up obligation), the loss will be reallocated in accordance with the partners' interests in the partnership.[45]

In the revenue ruling that follows, the Service illustrates the operation of the alternate test for economic effect in a situation where a partner has a limited deficit restoration obligation.

43. This test thus recognizes a partner's *limited* obligation to restore a deficit. For this purpose, the regulations provide that a partner will be treated as obligated to restore a deficit to the extent of: (1) the outstanding principal balance of any promissory note contributed by the partner to the partnership (Reg. § 1.704–1(b)(2)(ii)(*c*)(*1*)) and (2) the amount of any unconditional obligation (whether imposed by the partnership agreement or local law) of the partner to make subsequent contributions to the partnership (Reg. § 1.704–1(b)(2)(ii)(*c*)(*2*)). The note or obligation must have economic substance and payment must not be unduly deferred. Reg. § 1.704–1(b)(2)(ii)(*c*). See Reg. § 1.704–1(b)(2)(ii)(*g*). Despite the location of these rules in the regulations, it is clear from later examples that they do not apply to The Big Three primary test but are applicable only to the alternate test for economic effect. See, e.g., Reg. § 1.704–1(b)(5) Examples (1)(viii) and (ix). See also Rev. Rul. 92–97, 1992–2 C.B. 124, for a situation where the partners' limited deficit restoration obligation under a recourse liability of the partnership supported allocations under the alternate test for economic effect.

44. Reg. § 1.704–1(b)(2)(ii)(*d*).

45. See Reg. §§ 1.704–1(b)(3)(iii) & 1.704–1(b)(5) Example (1)(iv)–(vi).

Revenue Ruling 97–38

1997–2 Cum. Bull. 69.

ISSUE

If a partner is treated as having a limited deficit restoration obligation under § 1.704–1(b)(2)(ii)(c) of the Income Tax Regulations by reason of the partner's liability to the partnership's creditors, how is the amount of that obligation calculated?

FACTS

In year 1, GP and LP, general partner and limited partner, each contribute $100x to form limited partnership LPRS. In general, GP and LP share LPRS's income and loss 50 percent each. However, LPRS allocates to GP all depreciation deductions and gain from the sale of depreciable assets up to the amount of those deductions. LPRS maintains capital accounts according to the rules set forth in § 1.704–1(b)(2)(iv), and the partners agree to liquidate according to positive capital account balances under the rules of § 1.704–1(b)(2)(ii)(*b*)(*2*).

Under applicable state law, GP is liable to creditors for all partnership recourse liabilities, but LP has no personal liability. GP and LP do not agree to unconditional deficit restoration obligations as described in § 1.704–1(b)(2)(ii)(*b*)(*3*) (in general, a deficit restoration obligation requires a partner to restore any deficit capital account balance following the liquidation of the partner's interest in the partnership); GP is obligated to restore a deficit capital account only to the extent necessary to pay creditors. Thus, if LPRS were to liquidate after paying all creditors and LP had a positive capital account balance, GP would not be required to restore GP' s deficit capital account to permit a liquidating distribution to LP. In addition, GP and LP agree to a qualified income offset, thus satisfying the requirements of the alternate test for economic effect of § 1.704–1(b)(2)(ii)(*d*). GP and LP also agree that no allocation will be made that causes or increases a deficit balance in any partner's capital account in excess of the partner's obligation to restore the deficit.

LPRS purchases depreciable property for $1,000x from an unrelated seller, paying $200x in cash and borrowing the $800x balance from an unrelated bank that is not the seller of the property. The note is recourse to LPRS. The principal of the loan is due in 6 years; interest is payable semi-annually at the applicable federal rate. GP bears the entire economic risk of loss for LPRS's recourse liability, and GP's basis in LPRS (outside basis) is increased by $800x. See § 1.752–2.

In each of years 1 through 5, the property generates $200x of depreciation. All other partnership deductions and losses exactly equal income, so that in each of years 1 through 5 LPRS has a net loss of $200x.

LAW AND ANALYSIS

Under § 704(b) of the Internal Revenue Code and the regulations thereunder, a partnership's allocations of income, gain, loss, deduction, or credit set forth in the partnership agreement are respected if they have substantial economic effect. If allocations under the partnership agreement would not have substantial economic effect, the partnership's allocations are determined according to the partners' interests in the partnership. The fundamental principles for establishing economic effect require an allocation to be consistent with the partners' underlying economic arrangement. A partner allocated a share of income should enjoy any corresponding economic benefit, and a partner allocated a share of losses or deductions should bear any corresponding economic burden. See § 1.704–1(b)(2)(ii)(*a*).

To come within the safe harbor for establishing economic effect in § 1.704–1(b)(2)(ii), partners must agree to maintain capital accounts under the rules of § 1.704–1(b)(2)(iv), liquidate according to positive capital account balances, and agree to an unconditional deficit restoration obligation for any partner with a deficit in that partner's capital account, as described in § 1.704–1(b)(2)(ii)(*b*)(*3*). Alternatively, the partnership may satisfy the requirements of the alternate test for economic effect provided in § 1.704–1(b)(2)(ii)(*d*). LPRS's partnership agreement complies with the alternate test for economic effect.

The alternate test for economic effect requires the partners to agree to a qualified income offset in lieu of an unconditional deficit restoration obligation. If the partners so agree, allocations will have economic effect to the extent that they do not create a deficit capital account for any partner (in excess of any limited deficit restoration obligation of that partner) as of the end of the partnership taxable year to which the allocation relates. Section 1.704–1(b)(2)(ii)(*d*)(*3*) (flush language).

A partner is treated as having a limited deficit restoration obligation to the extent of: (1) the outstanding principal balance of any promissory note contributed to the partnership by the partner, and (2) the amount of any unconditional obligation of the partner (whether imposed by the partnership agreement or by state or local law) to make subsequent contributions to the partnership. Section 1.704–1(b)(2)(ii)(c).

LP has no obligation under the partnership agreement or state or local law to make additional contributions to the partnership and, therefore, has no deficit restoration obligation. Under applicable state law, GP may have to make additional contributions to the partnership to pay creditors. However, GP's obligation only arises to the extent that the amount of LPRS's liabilities exceeds the value of LPRS's assets available to satisfy the liabilities. Thus, the amount of GP's limited deficit restoration obligation each year is equal to the difference between the amount of the partnership's recourse liabilities at the end of the year and the value of the partnership's assets available to satisfy the liabilities at the end of the year.

To ensure consistency with the other requirements of the regulations under § 704(b), where a partner's obligation to make additional contributions to the partnership is dependent on the value of the partnership's assets, the partner's deficit restoration obligation must be computed by reference to the rules for determining the value of partnership property contained in the regulations under § 704(b). Consequently, in computing

GP's limited deficit restoration obligation, the value of the partnership's assets is conclusively presumed to equal the book basis of those assets under the capital account maintenance rules of § 1.704–1(b)(2)(iv). See § 1.704–1(b)(2)(ii)(*d*) (value equals basis presumption applies for purposes of determining expected allocations and distributions under the alternate test for economic effect); § 1.704–1(b)(2)(iii) (value equals basis presumption applies for purposes of the substantiality test); § 1.704–1(b)(3)(iii) (value equals basis presumption applies for purposes of the partner's interest in the partnership test); § 1.704–2(d) (value equals basis presumption applies in computing partnership minimum gain).

The LPRS agreement allocates all depreciation deductions and gain on the sale of depreciable property to the extent of those deductions to GP. Because LPRS's partnership agreement satisfies the alternate test for economic effect, the allocations of depreciation deductions to GP will have economic effect to the extent that they do not create a deficit capital account for GP in excess of GP's obligation to restore the deficit balance. At the end of year 1, the basis of the depreciable property has been reduced to $800x. If LPRS liquidated at the beginning of year 2, selling its depreciable property for its basis of $800x, the proceeds would be used to repay the $800 principal on LPRS's recourse liability. All of LPRS's creditors would be satisfied and GP would have no obligation to contribute to pay them. Thus, at the end of year 1, GP has no obligation to restore a deficit in its capital account.

Because GP has no obligation to restore a deficit balance in its capital account at the end of year 1, an allocation that reduces GP's capital account below $0 is not permitted under the partnership agreement and would not satisfy the alternate test for economic effect. An allocation of $200x of depreciation deductions to GP would reduce GP's capital account to negative $100x. Because the allocation would result in a deficit capital account balance in excess of GP's obligation to restore, the allocation is not permitted under the partnership agreement, and would not satisfy the safe harbor under the alternate test for economic effect. Therefore, the deductions for year 1 must be allocated $100x each to GP and LP (which is in accordance with their interests in the partnership).

The allocation of depreciation of $200x to GP in year 2 has economic effect. Although the allocation reduces GP's capital account to negative $200x, while LP's capital account remains $0, the allocation to GP does not create a deficit capital account in excess of GP's limited deficit restoration obligation. If LPRS liquidated at the beginning of year 3, selling the depreciable property for its basis of $600x, the proceeds would be applied toward the $800x LPRS liability. Because GP is obligated to restore a deficit capital account to the extent necessary to pay creditors, GP would be required to contribute $200x to LPRS to satisfy the outstanding liability. Thus, at the end of year 2, GP has a deficit restoration obligation of $200x, and the allocation of depreciation to GP does not reduce GP's capital account below its obligation to restore a deficit capital account.

This analysis also applies to the allocation of $200x of depreciation to GP in years 3 through 5. At the beginning of year 6, when the property is fully depreciated, the $800x principal amount of the partnership liability is due. The partners' capital accounts at the beginning of year 6 will equal negative $800x and $0, respectively, for GP and LP. Because value is conclusive presumed to equal basis, the depreciable property would be worthless and could not be used to satisfy LPRS's $800x liability. As a result, GP is deemed to be required to contribute $800x to LPRS. A contribution by GP to satisfy this limited deficit restoration obligation would increase GP's capital account balance to $0.

HOLDING

When a partner is treated as having a limited deficit restoration obligation by reason of the partner's liability to the partnership's creditors, the amount of that obligation is the amount of money that the partner would be required to contribute to the partnership to satisfy partnership liabilities if all partnership property were sold for the amount of the partnership's book basis in the property.

NOTE

Alternate Economic Effect: Special Rules. The drafters of the regulations were mindful that partners might attempt to manipulate the alternate test for economic effect by careful timing of distributions and other events that could be anticipated at the time of the allocation under scrutiny. To prevent such gambits, the regulations require that, for purposes of the alternate test, partners must reduce their capital accounts by distributions that are reasonably expected (to the extent those distributions exceed reasonably expected offsetting increases, other than recognized gains) as of the end of the partnership year in which the loss allocation was made.[1]

A return to the earlier example will illustrate the purpose of these rules. Recall that A and B each contributed $40,000 to the AB general partnership, which used the funds to acquire $80,000 of depreciable equipment. Assume that the first two prongs of The Big Three are satisfied, but the agreement does not include a deficit restoration requirement. A and B share all profits and losses equally, except all cost recovery deductions are allocated to A. As before, the partnership breaks even apart from the $20,000 annual cost recovery deduction. Finally, the partnership agreement contains a "qualified income offset" and neither distributions nor the other items specified in the regulations are expected to cause or increase a deficit balance in A's capital account.

In these circumstances, the $20,000 cost recovery deduction allocated to A for year one will have economic effect under the alternate test.[2]

1. Reg. § 1.704–1(b)(2)(ii)(*d*).

2. See Reg. § 1.704–1(b)(5) Example (1)(iii).

Assuming the partnership otherwise continues to break even apart from cost recovery deductions, a $20,000 allocation to A in year two also has economic effect because A's capital account has not yet fallen below zero. But if the cost recovery deduction allocated to A in year two were $25,000, only $20,000 (A's remaining capital account) would have economic effect; the $5,000 balance would be reallocated to B, who bears the economic burden in the absence of any deficit restoration agreement by A.[3] In short, under the alternate test, an allocation will be sustained to the extent of a partner's positive capital account plus any limited obligation to restore a deficit. That principle is simple enough to absorb, but students who are still conscious and the least bit inquisitive may be asking where the "reasonably anticipated distributions" and "qualified income offset" fit into this scheme.

Returning to the basic facts, assume it is near the end of year two. The partners need cash, and the partnership—holding only the equipment (presumed to be worth $40,000)—raises the funds by borrowing $40,000, using the equipment as security. The plan is to distribute the cash equally to the partners, but when? If $20,000 cash were distributed to A before the end of year two, it would reduce his capital account to zero and A would not be entitled to any further cost recovery deductions under the alternate test. But if the partnership waited until early in year three to make the distribution, A's capital account at the end of year two still would be $20,000, enabling the $20,000 special allocation to pass muster for that year. To preclude this maneuver, the regulations require A's capital account to be reduced by distributions that are reasonably expected to be made in future years to the extent they exceed reasonably expected capital account increases during the same period.[4] On these facts, then, with the partnership expected to break even in year three, the allocation to A must be tested under the alternate test by first reducing A's capital account by the $20,000 anticipated year three distribution. As a result, his capital account falls to zero, and the $20,000 year two cost recovery deduction will be reallocated to B.

Finally, return to the end of year two and assume no distributions are on the horizon. In that event, the $20,000 special allocation to A in year two will be respected under the alternate test. What happens if in year three, the partnership *unexpectedly* distributes cash to A, driving his capital account below zero, without any corresponding increase? Here is where the "qualified income offset" assumes center stage. A qualified income offset ("QIO") is a provision in the partnership agreement stating that any partner who has a deficit capital account as a result of unexpectedly receiving a distribution (or the other specialized adjustments listed in the regulations) must be allocated items of future income or gain in an amount

3. Reg. § 1.704–1(b)(3)(iii). See Reg. § 1.704–1(b)(5) Example (1)(iv).

4. If the partnership reasonably expected $10,000 of operating income over operating expenses for year two, A's $5,000 share of the resulting capital account increase could be taken into account and the anticipatory reduction to his capital account at the end of year two would only be $15,000 ($20,000 distribution less $5,000 anticipated income).

and manner sufficient to eliminate any remaining deficit balance as quickly as possible.[5] The allocation triggered by a QIO must consist of a pro rata share of each item of partnership income and gain for the taxable year;[6] the regulations deem such an allocation to be in accordance with the partner's interest in the partnership.[7] A QIO is only needed, then, when an event such as an unexpected distribution pushes a partner's capital account below zero. To preserve the economic effect of prior allocations, it requires partners with positive capital accounts to shift income otherwise allocable to them to the partners with deficit capital accounts until those deficits are eliminated.

Economic Effect Equivalence. If an allocation fails to meet either the primary or alternate tests for economic effect, the regulations offer relief if the allocation has "economic effect equivalence." Under this final fallback, allocations are deemed to have economic effect if the partnership agreement, interpreted by reference to applicable state law, ensures that a liquidation of the partnership as of the end of each partnership taxable year will produce the same economic results as if The Big Three were satisfied.[8] To illustrate, assume the partnership agreement commits a technical foot fault by failing to provide for the maintenance of capital accounts. The agreement allocates all income, losses, deductions and distributions among the partners in specified percentages and the partners are liable under state law in the same ratios for partnership debts. In these circumstances, the result on liquidation will be the same as if capital accounts were maintained and thus the allocations will be considered to have economic effect.[9]

d. SUBSTANTIALITY

In General. The second major test under the regulations looks to whether the economic effect of an allocation is "substantial," both in the year of the allocation[1] and over the life of the partnership.[2] The economic effect of an allocation is considered to be substantial if there is a reasonable possibility that the allocation will affect substantially the dollar amounts to

5. Reg. § 1.704–1(b)(2)(ii)(*d*). A typical qualified income offset provision would read:

> In the event that at the end of any partnership taxable year any partner's capital account is adjusted for, or such partner is allocated, or there is distributed to such partner, any item described in § 1.704–1(b)(2)(ii)(*d*)(*4*), (*5*) or (*6*) in an amount not reasonably expected at the end of such year, and such treatment creates a deficit balance in that partner's capital account, then such partner shall be allocated all items of income and gain of the partnership for such year and for all subsequent taxable years of the partnership until such deficit balance has been eliminated.

6. A qualified income offset seemingly requires an allocation of gross income in situations where the partnership has no taxable income—e.g., in a real estate partnership that realizes gross rental income but has no taxable income because of offsetting deductions.

7. Reg. § 1.704–1(b)(2)(ii)(*d*).

8. Reg. § 1.704–1(b)(2)(ii)(*i*).

9. See Reg. § 1.704–1(b)(5) Examples (4)(ii) & (iii).

1. Reg. § 1.704–1(b)(2)(i).

2. Cf. Reg. § 1.704–1(b)(2)(iii)(*c*).

be received by the partners from the partnership, independent of tax consequences.[3] Perhaps recognizing that this general rule is not very informative, the regulations elaborate by stating that, notwithstanding the above rule, the economic effect of an allocation is not substantial if, at the time the allocation becomes part of the partnership agreement:[4]

(1) the after-tax economic consequences of at least one partner may, in present value terms, be enhanced compared to such consequences if the allocation were not contained in the partnership agreement; and

(2) there is a strong likelihood that the after-tax economic consequences of no partner will, in present value terms, be substantially diminished compared to such consequences if the allocation were not contained in the partnership agreement.

In other words, an allocation fails the substantiality test if its effect is to benefit one or more partners after taxes and not to affect adversely any partner—in both cases, comparing the effect of the allocation to the result if no allocation had been contained in the agreement. In determining the after-tax economic benefit or detriment to a partner, tax consequences that result from the interaction of the allocation with other tax attributes of the partner unrelated to the partnership must be taken into account.[5]

To illustrate the general rule, assume the AB general partnership invests in income-producing securities. Partner A expects to be in the 30 percent marginal tax bracket in the current year[6] and Partner B expects to be in the 15 percent marginal bracket. Assume further that the partnership faithfully satisfies The Big Three and thus all of its allocations will have economic effect. Finally, assume that the partnership structures its investments so that it will earn relatively equal amounts of tax-exempt interest and taxable dividends and the partnership agreement allocates the tax-exempt interest 90% to A and 10% to B and the dividends 100% to B. Although the allocation has economic effect, the substantiality test is failed at the time the allocation is made because A is expected to enhance his after-tax economic consequences as a result of the allocation, and there is a strong likelihood that neither A nor B will substantially diminish his after-tax consequences.[7]

To illustrate more precisely, assume the partnership earns $10,000 each of tax-exempt interest and taxable dividends. The interest is allocated $9,000 to A and $1,000 to B; the dividends are allocated $10,000 to B. Before taxes are considered, A is allocated a total of $9,000 and B is allocated $11,000. After taxes, and taking the partners' individual tax brackets into account, the results are as follows:

3. Reg. § 1.704–1(b)(2)(iii)(*a*).

4. Id.

5. Id.

6. We adopt this fictional tax bracket for computational convenience.

7. This illustration is adapted from Reg. § 1.704–1(b)(5) Example (5).

	A	B
Interest	$9,000	$ 1,000
Dividends	0	10,000
Pre–Tax Income	$9,000	$11,000
Tax on Dividends	0	(1,500)
After–Tax	$9,000	$ 9,500

If there had been no special allocation and the equal partners had shared the interest and dividends 50/50, the results would be as follows:

	A	B
Interest	$ 5,000	$ 5,000
Dividends	5,000	5,000
Pre–Tax Income	$10,000	$10,000
Tax on Dividends	(1,500)	(750)
After–Tax	$ 8,500	$ 9,250

The effect of the special allocation is to benefit both partners after-taxes (A nets $9,000 rather than $8,500; B nets $9,500 rather than $9,250). The allocation thus fails the substantiality test because the after-tax consequences of at least one partner are enhanced relative to the consequences if there had been no such allocation, and there is a strong likelihood that the after-tax consequences of no partner will be substantially diminished. Under the partnership agreement, A's capital account is increased by $9,000 (45 percent of total partnership income) and B's is increased by $11,000 (55 percent). Since the special allocation fails the substantial test, the dividends and tax-exempt interest are reallocated 45 percent to A and 55 percent to B.[8]

Shifting and Transitory Allocations. The regulations elaborate on the general "substantiality" standard by highlighting two special situations where the economic effect of an allocation will be considered insubstantial: shifting allocations and transitory allocations.[9] In each case, the Treasury's concern is that an initial allocation will be offset by one or more later allocations, resulting in no significant economic consequences to the partners (i.e., no net impact on their capital accounts) but reducing their total tax liability. The effect of offsetting allocations is "shifting" if they occur within the same taxable year; it is "transitory" if the allocations span two or more taxable years.

Consider first a "shifting" allocation. The regulations provide that the economic effect of an allocation (or allocations) within one partnership taxable year is not substantial if, at the time the allocation becomes part of the partnership agreement, there is a "strong likelihood" that the capital accounts of the partners will be unaffected by the allocation (normally because of an equal and offsetting allocation in the same year),[10] and the total tax liability of the partners will be less than if there had been no such allocations, taking into account any tax consequences that result from the

8. Reg. § 1.704–1(b)(3). See Reg. § 1.704–1(b)(5) Example (5)(ii).

9. Reg. § 1.704–1(b)(2)(iii)(*b*), (*c*).

10. For this purpose, "unaffected" means that the net increases and decreases to the respective capital accounts of the partners as a result of the allocation do not differ significantly from the net increases and decreases that would have been recorded without the special allocations. Reg. § 1.704–1(b)(2)(iii)(*b*)(*1*).

interaction of the allocation with tax attributes of the partner that are unrelated to the partnership.[11] It should be apparent that this is but an illustration of the general insubstantiality scenario discussed above—i.e., the partners know that the allocation will benefit one or more of them (after taxes) and nobody will suffer.

To illustrate,[12] assume that the AB equal general partnership acquires and leases Section 1231 real property and invests in marketable securities. The partnership agreement faithfully adheres to The Big Three. At the beginning of the current year, the partnership anticipates incurring a $100,000 loss on the sale of Section 1231 property, and it is in a position to realize a $100,000 capital loss on the sale of stock. It otherwise expects to break even. Partner A expects to have $500,000 of ordinary income and no Section 1231 gains for the same taxable year. Partner B expects to have $300,000 of ordinary income and a $200,000 Section 1231 gain from a sale unrelated to the partnership.[13] To maximize tax benefits resulting from the interaction of the partnership's expected losses with the individual tax attributes of the partners, A and B amend their partnership agreement and allocate up to $100,000 of Section 1231 loss to A and an equivalent amount of capital loss to B; all other losses in excess of these allocations will be divided equally between the partners.

Since each partner is allocated a total of $100,000 of partnership losses, their respective capital accounts at the end of the year are the same as if the Section 1231 loss and capital loss had been divided equally between A and B. The partners' agenda is revealed by comparing the after-tax consequences of the special allocation with the results in the current year if there had been an equal division of the two $100,000 losses:

	Special Allocation	**Equal Division**
Partner A		
Ordinary income	$500,000	$500,000
Partnership losses:		
§ 1231 loss	(100,000)	(50,000)
Capital loss	0	(3,000)[14]
Net taxable income	$400,000	$447,000

11. Reg. § 1.704–1(b)(2)(iii)(*b*). Thus, items such as a partner's net operating losses and Section 1231 gains and losses outside the partnership are taken into account.

12. This example is adapted from Reg. § 1.704–1(b)(5) Example (6).

13. To understand this example, you may need to review the operation of Section 1231. Keep in mind that Section 1231 gains and losses retain their character as they are passed through from the partnership to the partners (see Chapter 3A1, supra), and that net Section 1231 losses are treated as ordinary losses which may offset ordinary income without limitation (see I.R.C. § 1231(a)). But see I.R.C. § 1231(c).

14. Only $3,000 of the capital loss passed through to A from the partnership is available to offset ordinary income in the current year. The $47,000 balance must be carried forward. See I.R.C. §§ 1211(b); 1212(b).

	Special Allocation	Equal Division
Partner B		
Ordinary income	$300,000	$300,000
§ 1231 Gain	200,000	200,000
Partnership losses:		
§ 1231 loss	0	(50,000)
Capital loss	(100,000)	(50,000)[15]
Net taxable income	$400,000	$400,000

Because of A's ability to fully utilize the Section 1231 loss in the current year to offset ordinary income, A's net income is reduced by $47,000 as a result of the allocation, while B's net income is unaffected. In addition, there was a strong likelihood[16] that these results would occur at the time the allocation became part of the agreement. Consequently, the economic effect of the allocation is insubstantial, and the losses must be reallocated in accordance with the partners' 50/50 interests in the partnership.[17]

Transitory allocations are simply a variation on the same theme. They lack substantial economic effect if the partnership agreement provides for the "possibility," over two or more taxable years, that an "original allocation" will be largely offset by one or more "offsetting allocations" and, at the time the allocations became part of the agreement, there is a "strong likelihood" that the partners' capital accounts will emerge unaffected by the allocations (relative to what would have occurred had there been no allocations) and the partners enjoy a reduction in their total tax liability for the period involved.[18] Once again, to relieve the Service from proving that the partners knew all of this was likely to occur when they agreed on the allocation, the regulations presume the requisite "strong likelihood" if the allocations in fact resulted in no material change to the partners' capital accounts and taxes were reduced relative to what would have occurred if there had been no special allocation.[19]

To illustrate,[20] assume the equal three-person ABC partnership has a reliable and relatively fixed flow of income (e.g., its only activity is the

15. Both with and without the special allocation, B uses the capital loss and the Section 1231 loss in the same manner—i.e., they may be deducted against B's $200,000 Section 1231 gain. I.R.C. §§ 1231(a); 1211(b).

16. Keep in mind that the regulations, recognizing the problems of proving the requisite "strong likelihood," presume that if the conditions for a shifting allocation are in fact met, there was a strong likelihood that they would occur. Reg. § 1.704–1(b)(2)(iii)(*b*).

17. For what would happen in a more complex situation where the losses were not exactly equal, see supra note 8 and accompanying text. Reg. § 1.704–1(b)(5) Example (6).

18. Reg. § 1.704–1(b)(2)(iii)(*c*). In determining whether there is a reduction in tax liability, tax consequences resulting from the interaction of the allocation with partner tax attributes that are unrelated to the partnership, such as net operating losses and Section 1231 gains and losses, are taken into account. Reg. § 1.704–1(b)(2)(iii)(*c*)(*2*).

19. Reg. § 1.704–1(b)(2)(iii)(*c*).

20. This example is adapted from Reg. § 1.704–1(b)(5) Example (8)(i).

rental of property subject to a long-term lease). At the beginning of year one, Partner A knows for certain that he has an expiring net operating loss deduction from activities unrelated to the partnership, while B and C are in the highest marginal tax brackets. To help A but burden neither B nor C, the partners agree to allocate 100 percent of the partnership income to A in year one; the trade-off is that 100 percent of the income will be divided equally between B and C in the succeeding two years, after which the partners will revert back to an equal three-way division of profits. At all times, the partnership agreement adheres to The Big Three so that all allocations have economic effect. But is the economic effect of this allocation substantial? Viewing year one in isolation, it is substantial because A benefits economically from the allocation and the other partners suffer.[21] But viewing all three years together, the economic effect of the deal is a "wash" because the partners are well aware from the start that the net increases and decreases in their capital accounts resulting from the allocations will be the same at the end of year three as they would have been in the absence of the allocations. Moreover, because the allocation enables A to apply his expiring net operating loss deduction against the year one partnership income, the total taxes of A, B and C over the three-year period are reduced.

The regulations contain an additional rule which is helpful to taxpayers in situations where an offsetting allocation is likely but will not occur for a while. An allocation and a subsequent offsetting allocation will not be considered transitory (and thus will not fail the substantiality test) if there is a strong likelihood that the offsetting allocation will not, in large part, be made within five years from the original allocation.[22] In addition, the regulations presume for purposes of the substantiality test that the adjusted tax basis of partnership property will be equal to its fair market value and that adjustments to the tax basis of the property will be matched by corresponding changes in its fair market value.[23] This presumption may be helpful in validating special allocations of cost recovery deductions to one partner (or partners) in situations where subsequent gains on the sale of the property are allocable to that partner in an amount equal to the prior cost recovery deductions.[24] As the problems below will illustrate, this type of special allocation scheme would be "transitory" were it not for the presumption that fair market value always equals adjusted basis. Using that assumption, even if it is plainly wrong, there cannot be a strong likelihood that the original cost recovery deductions will be offset in large part by the later offsetting allocations of gain on sale.[25]

21. For example, if the partnership were liquidated at the end of year one, A would come out ahead because the allocation of 100 percent of the year one income would increase his capital account (and thus his share on liquidation) relative to the capital accounts of B and C.

22. Reg. § 1.704–1(b)(2)(iii)(*c*).

23. Reg. § 1.704–1(b)(2)(iii)(*c*).

24. This type of provision is known as a "gain chargeback" and was illustrated in the *Orrisch* case supra at page 133.

25. See Reg. § 1.704–1(b)(5) Example (1)(xi) and Problem 1(c), infra.

e. DEFAULT REALLOCATIONS: THE PARTNERS' INTEREST IN THE PARTNERSHIP

If a partnership agreement is silent as to the partners' distributive shares or an allocation lacks substantial economic effect, then the partners' share of gain, loss, deduction or credit is determined in accordance with "the partners' interest in the partnership."[26] Once again, the standard here is the economic arrangement of the partners. The term "partners' interest in the partnership" refers to "the manner in which the partners have agreed to share the economic benefit or burden * * * corresponding to the [item] that is allocated," taking into account all the facts and circumstances relating to the economic arrangement of the partners.[27] The regulations open the bidding with a presumption of equality—i.e., all the partners' interests are presumed to be equal, determined on a per capita basis.[28] In practice, this arbitrary presumption is little more than a last resort. It is rebuttable by either the taxpayer or the Service by establishing facts and circumstances that show that the partners' interest in the partnership are otherwise.[29] Among the factors to be considered in making this determination are:[30]

(1) The relative contributions of the partners to the partnership;

(2) The interests of the partners in economic profits and losses if they differ from their interests in taxable income or loss;

(3) The interests of the partners in cash flow and other nonliquidating distributions; and

(4) The rights of the partners to distributions of capital upon liquidation.

These factors are simple enough to apply if the agreement clearly specifies one method of sharing profits and losses throughout the life of the partnership. Thus, if a two-person partnership agreement provides for an equal division of profits and losses and liquidating distributions (without regard to capital accounts), but allocates cost recovery deductions only to one partner, we know that the special allocation lacks economic effect.[31] Because the arrangement clearly demonstrates that the partners intended to equally share risk and rewards, the cost recovery deduction would be split equally between the two partners. In more complex cases, however, the partners may have varying profit and loss sharing arrangements over the life of the partnership. Despite their length, the regulations offer little guidance as to how the partners' interests would be determined in such cases, an uncertainty which makes it all the more important to ensure that special allocations are structured to comply with the substantial economic effect safe harbor.

26. I.R.C. § 704(b); Reg. § 1.704-1(b)(3)(i).

27. Reg. § 1.704-1(b)(3)(i).

28. Id.

29. Id.

30. Reg. § 1.704-1(b)(3)(ii).

31. See, e.g., Reg. § 1.704-1(b)(5) Example (1)(i).

The regulations include a special rule if an allocation is upset because the partnership agreement fails to include an unlimited deficit make-up provision.[32] If the first two requirements of The Big Three are met and the substantiality rules have not been breached, this rule provides that the partners' interests in the partnership with respect to the disallowed portion of the allocation are to be determined by comparing:

(1) the manner in which distributions (and contributions) would be made if all partnership property were sold at book value and the partnership were liquidated following the end of the taxable year in which the allocation relates with,

(2) the manner in which distributions (and contributions) would be made if all partnership property were sold at book value and the partnership were liquidated immediately following the end of the prior taxable year.[33]

The purpose of this formula is to reallocate items lacking economic effect to the partner who bears the economic loss corresponding to the item. Several examples in the regulations illustrate the application of this special rule.[34]

f. ALLOCATIONS OF DEPRECIATION RECAPTURE

Allocations of depreciation recapture cannot have substantial economic effect because classifying a portion of the gain as recapture merely changes its tax character. Also, if depreciation recapture can be allocated in the same manner as total gain, it is more likely that a partner may receive an allocation of recapture gain in excess of the partner's share of depreciation from the property.[35] For example, if a partner acquires an interest in a partnership that has fully depreciated a property and the partnership later sells that property at a gain, the partner may be allocated a portion of the total gain and a portion of the recapture gain, despite the fact that the partnership did not pass through any depreciation deductions from the property to the partner.[36]

The regulations attempt to minimize the mismatching of depreciation and recapture allocations.[37] Under the regulations, a partner's share of recapture gain generally is equal to the lesser of (1) the partner's share of the total gain from the disposition of the property, or (2) the total amount of depreciation previously allocated to the partner with respect to the

32. Reg. § 1.704–1(b)(3)(iii).

33. Id. The result then must be adjusted for the reasonably expected future distributions (in excess of anticipated offsetting positive capital account adjustments) and the other specialized items that are taken into account in determining a partner's capital account for purposes of the alternate test for economic effect. See Reg. § 1.704–1(b)(2)(i)(*d*).

34. See Reg. § 1.704–1(b)(5) Examples (1)(iv)–(vi), (15)(i)–(ii).

35. 61 Fed. Reg. 65371 (Dec. 12, 1996).

36. Id. But if the partnership had made a Section 754 election, this distortion would be eliminated. See Chapter 6B, infra.

37. See Reg. §§ 1.704–3(a)(11); 1.1245–1(e)(2); 1.1250–1(f). See Kalinka, "In Light of Depreciation Recapture Regs, Plan Allocations Carefully," 77 Tax Notes 1387 (Dec. 22, 1997).

property.[38] For example, assume A and B each contribute $5,000 to form the AB partnership. A and B agree that depreciation deductions will be allocated 90 percent to A and 10 percent to B. Gain on the sale of depreciable property will first be allocated as necessary to equalize the partners' capital accounts, and any remaining gain will be allocated equally between A and B. In its first year, AB purchases depreciable equipment for $5,000. Assume that AB depreciates the equipment over a 5–year recovery period using the straight-line method and has $1,000 of depreciation on the equipment each year.[39] Assume further that except for depreciation, AB's operating income equals its expenses in the first year. Under the partnership agreement, $900 of the depreciation is allocated to A and $100 is allocated to B. If at the end of the year the partnership sells the equipment for $5,200, there will be a total gain of $1,200 ($5,200 amount realized less $4,000 basis), of which $1,000 is Section 1245 recapture gain. Under the partnership agreement, the first $800 of gain is allocated to A to equalize the partner's capital accounts, and the remaining $400 of gain is allocated $200 each to A and B. Under the regulations, each partner's share of the Section 1245 gain is the lesser of the partner's share of total gain recognized on the sale of the equipment or the partner's share of total depreciation with respect to the equipment. Thus, A's share of Section 1245 gain is $900 (A's share of total gain is $1,000 and A's share of depreciation is $900) and B's share of Section 1245 gain is $100 (B's share of total gain is $200 and B's share of depreciation is $100).[40]

Under the regulations, a partner's allocation of recapture gain may be limited by that partner's share of total gain. Returning to the example, assume the same facts except that the partners agree that gains from the sale of depreciable property will be allocated equally between them. On the sale of the equipment for $5,200, the $1,200 gain would be allocated $600 each to A and B. A's share of the Section 1245 gain would be limited to $600 (the total gain allocated to A) even though A's share of depreciation from the equipment was $900. The remaining $400 of Section 1245 gain therefore must be allocated to B. Thus, all $600 of A's total gain is characterized as ordinary income and $400 of B's $600 of total gain is characterized as ordinary income.[41]

g. ALLOCATIONS OF TAX CREDITS

Allocations of tax credits are generally not reflected in the partners' capital accounts and, therefore, they cannot have economic effect.[42] As a result, tax credits and recapture of tax credits generally must be allocated in accordance with the partners' interests in the partnership. The regulations provide that if a partnership expenditure (whether or not deductible)

38. Reg. §§ 1.1245–1(e)(2)(i) & (ii); 1.1250–1(f).

39. For convenience, the example disregards the first-year depreciation convention.

40. See Reg. § 1.1245–1(e)(2)(iii) Example 1.

41. See Reg. § 1.1245–1(e)(2)(iii) Example 2(i) & (ii).

42. Reg. § 1.704–1(b)(4)(ii).

that gives rise to a tax credit also gives rise to valid tax allocations of loss or deduction, then the partners' interests in the partnership with respect to such credit shall be in the same proportion as the partner's distributive share of the loss or deduction.[43]

PROBLEMS

1. A and B each contribute $100,000 upon formation of a limited partnership. A is a general partner and B is a limited partner. The partnership purchases an office building on leased land for $200,000 and elects straight-line cost recovery. Assume (for simplicity) that the property has a 10–year recovery period. The partnership agreement allocates all items of income and loss equally with the exception of the cost recovery deductions, which are allocated entirely to B. Assume (perhaps unrealistically) that both partners are unconditionally obligated to restore a deficit to their capital accounts upon a liquidation of the partnership.

(a) Assume that apart from cost recovery deductions, the partnership's rental income is equal to its operating expenses. What must the partners' respective capital account balances be at the end of year one if the allocation of cost recovery deductions is to have economic effect?

(b) Assume the partnership sells the building on January 1 of year two and immediately liquidates. Again, with an eye toward qualifying the allocation, how must the proceeds be distributed if the building is sold for $180,000? For $200,000?

(c) Assume the agreement further provides that gain on disposition will be allocated to B to the extent of the cost recovery deductions specially allocated to her. What result when the partnership sells the building on January 1 of year two for $200,000?

(d) Assume that B is not required to restore a deficit in her capital account, but the partnership agreement includes a "qualified income offset." If the partnership continues to operate the building, what is the result to A and B in year one? In year six?

(e) What results in both years under the facts of (d), above, if in addition B has contributed her promissory note for $100,000 to the partnership?

(f) What results under the facts in (e), above, if in year six the building has a $400,000 fair market value, and A and B, acting as partners, agree that they will borrow $200,000 on a recourse basis, using the building as security, and distribute the proceeds equally to themselves early in year seven?

(g) What result under the facts in (e), above, if in year six the value of the building is $300,000, and A and B, acting as partners, agree

43. Reg. § 1.704–1(b)(4)(ii). See Reg. § 1.704–1(b)(5) Example (11), illustrating this principle in the context of the targeted jobs credit.

that when its value reaches $400,000 they will take out a $200,000 recourse mortgage and distribute the proceeds equally?

(h) Assume that B is not required to restore a deficit in her capital account and that the partnership agreement does not contain a "qualified income offset." If the partnership continues to operate the building, what is the result to A and B in year one? In year six?

(i) What results in both years under the facts of (h), above, if in addition B has contributed her promissory note for $100,000 to the partnership?

2. C and D are equal partners in a general partnership formed to design and produce clothing for sale to retailers located throughout Europe and the United States. D is a nonresident alien. At the beginning of the tax year, the relative dollar amounts of United States and foreign source income cannot be predicted. Any foreign source income allocated to D is exempt from United States taxation. Assume that all of the following allocations have economic effect.

(a) What result if the partnership agreement provides that all U.S. source income will be allocated to C, and all foreign source income will be allocated to D?

(b) What result if the agreement provides that all income will be shared equally but that D will be allocated all the foreign source income up to the dollar amount of her 50% share of income?

(c) Assume, instead, that at the beginning of the tax year it can be predicted that the relative dollar amounts of U.S. and foreign source income will be roughly equal. What result if the agreement provides, as in (a), above, that all U.S. source income shall be allocated to C, and all foreign source income shall be allocated to D?

3. E and F form a limited partnership to purchase and lease a computer for $1,000,000. E, the limited partner, contributes $990,000, and F, the general partner, contributes $10,000. The agreement provides that § 168 cost recovery deductions will be allocated entirely to E and that all other items of income or loss will be allocated 99% to E until he has been allocated income equal to his share of cost recovery deductions and partnership losses. Thereafter, E and F will share income and loss equally. Assuming the capital account, liquidating distribution, and deficit restoration tests are met, will the allocations be respected? See Reg. § 1.704–1(b)(5) examples (2) and (3).

3. ALLOCATIONS ATTRIBUTABLE TO NONRECOURSE DEBT

Regulations: §§ 1.704–2(b), (c), (d)(1), (e), (f)(1)–(3) & (6), (g), (j)(2) & (m) Examples 1(i)–(iv) & 3(i).

Overview. The preceding discussion was limited to situations where partnership activities were financed with partner contributions of cash or property, or with recourse borrowings. Many partnerships, however, finance their acquisitions of property largely with nonrecourse debt. Although the *Crane* case has long permitted taxpayers to include the amount of a nonrecourse mortgage acquisition debt in the cost basis of the encumbered property,[1] the economic risk of those taxpayers is limited to their cash investment and any loans for which they are personally liable. If the value of the property declines below the amount of the debt, the owner is free to walk away, leaving the creditor to bear the economic loss to the extent that the property does not satisfy the debt.[2]

It follows that when a partnership finances depreciable property with nonrecourse debt, the economic burden of the resulting cost recovery deductions is borne by the partners only to the extent of their investments of cash and other property or their shares of recourse debt. Cost recovery deductions in excess of the partnership's equity and recourse borrowings are attributable to the nonrecourse debt, and the economic risk resulting from any equivalent decline in value of the property is borne by the lender. Because an allocation of deduction or loss lacks economic effect unless it reflects a corresponding economic burden to the partner, the regulations properly acknowledge that no allocation of deductions attributable to nonrecourse debt can have substantial economic effect.[3] To illustrate, assume that the AB partnership finances the purchase of a $100,000 building (on leased land) by borrowing the entire $100,000 on a nonrecourse basis from Lender. Assume further that the partnership's first year cost recovery deduction is $5,000. In these circumstances, no allocation of the deduction has substantial economic effect because, if the property declines in value by $5,000, the partnership could default on the loan and Lender would sustain the $5,000 economic loss.

Although borrowers can avoid the economic burden of repaying nonrecourse debt, they cannot escape the *tax* burden of including the full amount of the debt in their amount realized on a disposition (including a foreclosure) of the encumbered property. Under the Supreme Court's holding in Commissioner v. Tufts,[4] a taxpayer recognizes gain on a disposition at least to the extent that the nonrecourse debt exceeds the adjusted basis of the property, regardless of the actual value of the asset. For example, on a disposition of the building in the example above at the end of year one, the partnership's minimum amount realized would be $100,000 (the debt relief), and it would recognize at least $5,000 of gain (the excess of the $100,000 amount realized over the $95,000 adjusted basis of the building). Under the regulations, the gain represented by this excess of nonrecourse debt over basis is known as "partnership minimum gain." This is the amount of gain that the partnership would realize if it disposed of partnership property subject to a nonrecourse liability in full satisfaction of the

1. Crane v. Commissioner, 331 U.S. 1, 67 S.Ct. 1047 (1947). See also Parker v. Delaney, 186 F.2d 455 (1st Cir.1950), cert. denied, 341 U.S. 926, 71 S.Ct. 797 (1951).

2. On dispositions of property in these circumstances, the taxpayer recognizes gain to the extent that the outstanding indebtedness exceeds the taxpayer's adjusted basis in the property regardless of the fair market value of the property. See Commissioner v. Tufts, 461 U.S. 300, 103 S.Ct. 1826 (1983), rehearing denied, 463 U.S. 1215, 103 S.Ct. 3555 (1983).

3. Reg. § 1.704–2(b)(1).

4. See note 2, supra.

debt and for no other consideration.[5] Deductions that create or increase partnership minimum gain (e.g., by reducing the adjusted basis of an asset that secures nonrecourse debt below the amount of the debt) are called "nonrecourse deductions."[6] Although an allocation of nonrecourse deductions cannot have economic effect, the regulations nonetheless generally permit a partnership to allocate those deductions to partners to whom the related minimum gain will be allocated. This tax payback is accomplished by a "minimum gain chargeback,"[7] which is a provision in the partnership agreement that requires the partnership to allocate minimum gain to those partners to whom the nonrecourse deductions were previously allocated. These matching allocations of nonrecourse deductions and partnership minimum gain eventually neutralize each other in the partners' capital accounts.[8] And since an allocation of nonrecourse deductions must be accompanied by a minimum gain chargeback, the regulations treat a partner's share of partnership minimum gain as an increase to the partner's obligation to restore a deficit capital account balance for purposes of the alternate test for economic effect.[9] That deficit restoration obligation will be made up when partnership minimum gain is reduced—for example, on a disposition of the property or a repayment of the liability.

The regulations incorporate these concepts into a four-part safe harbor test. If the test is satisfied, allocations of nonrecourse deductions are deemed to be made in accordance with the partners' interests in the partnership.[10] If an allocation fails to meet the test, nonrecourse deductions are allocated "according to the partners' overall economic interests in the partnership."[11] For planning purposes, it is highly desirable to draft a partnership agreement that complies with the safe harbor.

Before examining the four-part test, it is necessary to master the technical vocabulary employed by the regulations. Those who are successful in this endeavor can reasonably add a new foreign language skill to their resumes. The critical terms of art are: "partnership minimum gain;" "nonrecourse deductions;" "distribution of nonrecourse liability proceeds allocable to an increase in minimum gain;" "partner's share of partnership minimum gain;" and "minimum gain chargeback."

Partnership Minimum Gain. "Partnership minimum gain" is the amount of gain that a partnership would realize if it disposed of each of its properties that is subject to a nonrecourse liability for no consideration other than satisfaction of the debt—i.e., the excess of the nonrecourse liability over the adjusted basis of the property securing the debt.[12] Clients

5. Reg. § 1.704–2(d)(1).

6. Reg. § 1.704–2(c).

7. Reg. § 1.704–2(f)(1).

8. Nonrecourse deductions generally may be allocated to any partner provided that the allocations are "reasonably consistent with allocations that have substantial economic effect of some other significant partnership item attributable to the property securing the nonrecourse liabilities * * *." Reg. § 1.704–2(e)(2). See infra notes 31–33 and accompanying text.

9. Reg. § 1.704–2(g)(1). See Reg. § 1.704–1(b)(2)(ii)(*d*).

10. Reg. § 1.704–2(b)(1) & (e).

11. Id. See Reg. § 1.704–1(b)(3).

12. Reg. § 1.704–2(d)(1). If a partnership has more than one nonrecourse liability, total partnership minimum gain is the aggre-

and others who do not understand the economics of leveraged transactions often describe this income as "phantom gain." Partnership minimum gain is created in two situations: (1) as the adjusted basis of the encumbered property is reduced below the amount of the nonrecourse liability (e.g., by cost recovery deductions), or (2) as the amount of the nonrecourse liability is increased in excess of the adjusted basis of the property (e.g., on a refinancing).

To illustrate, assume that Developer (the general partner) and Investor (the limited partner) form a limited partnership to acquire and rent out a $100,000 commercial building on leased land. Developer contributes $1,000 and Investor contributes $9,000 to the partnership, which finances the balance of the purchase price with a $90,000 nonrecourse loan secured by the building. No principal payments on the loan are due for ten years. The partnership agreement requires capital accounts to be maintained in accordance with the Section 704(b) regulations, and liquidating distributions must be made in accordance with the positive capital account balances of the partners. Developer is obligated to restore a deficit. Investor has no such obligation, but the partnership agreement contains a qualified income offset and a minimum gain chargeback provision. The partnership allocates all partnership income, deductions and losses 90 percent to Investor and 10 percent to Developer until aggregate partnership income offsets previously incurred losses, at which time all further items (except as otherwise provided by a qualified income offset or minimum gain chargeback provision) will be divided equally between the partners. Assume that the expenses of operating the building always equal the rental income; the partnership is entitled to straight-line cost recovery deductions of $5,000 per year[13] and the value of the building always equals its adjusted basis.

On these facts, the partnership will take $10,000 of cost recovery deductions in the first two years, reducing its adjusted basis in the building to $90,000. The losses, allocated 90 percent to Investor and 10 percent to Developer, reduce each partner's capital account to zero.[14] By the end of year three, the adjusted basis of the building is reduced to $85,000 (below the $90,000 nonrecourse debt), and the partners each have negative capital accounts ($4,500 for Investor and $500 for Developer) as a result of the allocation of year three cost recovery deductions. If the partnership disposed of the building at the end of year three in full satisfaction of the debt, the amount realized would include the $90,000 of debt relief, and the partnership would realize $5,000 of gain ($90,000 amount realized less $85,000 adjusted basis). That $5,000 is "partnership minimum gain"—i.e., the amount of gain that the partnership would realize if it disposed of

gate of minimum gain on all properties of the partnership encumbered by nonrecourse debt. Id.

13. This simplified cost recovery system has been adopted for convenience.

14. Investor's initial capital account of $9,000 (his cash contribution) is reduced by his $9,000 share of cost recovery deductions. Similarly, Developer's initial capital account of $1,000 is reduced by his $1,000 share of cost recovery deductions.

property subject to a nonrecourse liability in full satisfaction of the debt.[15] There was no minimum gain at the end of years one or two because, if the partnership had disposed of the building for no consideration other than full satisfaction of the nonrecourse debt in either of those years, its $90,000 amount realized would not have exceeded the building's adjusted basis—hence, no gain and no minimum gain. In year three, there was a $5,000 increase in partnership minimum gain.

An increase in partnership minimum gain also results when a partnership incurs a nonrecourse liability that exceeds the adjusted basis of the property encumbered by the new debt.[16] Returning to the example, assume it is the first day of year four, and the building (with an adjusted basis of $85,000 and subject to a nonrecourse liability of $90,000) has increased in value to $150,000. If the partnership then incurs an additional $20,000 nonrecourse loan secured by the property, partnership minimum gain would increase by $20,000, from $5,000 to $25,000.

Nonrecourse Deductions. Generally speaking, "nonrecourse deductions" are deductions that relate to a net increase[17] in partnership minimum gain.[18] They most commonly are cost recovery deductions that reduce the adjusted basis of depreciable property below the amount of nonrecourse debt secured by the property.[19] In our example with Developer and Investor, the partnership had no nonrecourse deductions in years one and two because there was no net increase in partnership minimum gain in those years. In year three, however, there was a $5,000 net increase in partnership minimum gain and thus nonrecourse deductions of $5,000.

A Partner's Share of Partnership Minimum Gain. A central premise of the regulations is that, even in the absence of a deficit restoration provision, nonrecourse deductions may reduce a partner's capital account below zero to the extent of a partner's share of partnership minimum gain. This is because those deductions will be "recaptured" and charged back to the partner to whom they were allocated and increase that partner's capital account when the partnership disposes of the property. Consistent with this policy, partners must keep track of their respective shares of partnership minimum gain in order to: (1) determine the extent to which they may have a capital account deficit without triggering a qualified income offset; (2) ensure that they are allocated their appropriate share of partnership minimum gain when it is recognized by the partnership; and (3) properly

15. Reg. § 1.704–2(d)(1).

16. Reg. § 1.704–2(b)(2). Such subsequent borrowing is not a currently taxable event. See Woodsam Associates, Inc. v. Commissioner, 198 F.2d 357 (2d Cir.1952). The *Woodsam* case held that a taxpayer does not realize income on incurring an additional liability on property because he has a corresponding obligation to repay the loan, and no upward basis adjustment is allowed unless the taxpayer uses the loan proceeds to make capital improvements to the property.

17. All of a partnership's increases and decreases in minimum gain during a taxable year are netted to determine if there is a net increase in minimum gain. Both nonrecourse deductions and nonrecourse distributions only arise if there is a *net* increase in partnership minimum gain during the year. See Reg. §§ 1.704–2(d)(1), (g)(1).

18. Reg. § 1.704–2(c).

19. Reg. § 1.704–2(b)(2).

determine their share of partnership nonrecourse liabilities under Section 752.[20]

A partner's share of partnership minimum gain at the end of any taxable year is equal to the sum of the nonrecourse deductions allocated to the partner throughout the life of the partnership and the partner's share of distributions of nonrecourse liability proceeds allocable to an increase in minimum gain,[21] reduced by the partner's share of any prior net decreases in partnership minimum gain.[22]

Minimum Gain Chargeback. We have seen that the regulations permit an allocation of nonrecourse deductions and certain other events to reduce a partner's capital account below zero to the extent of that partner's share of minimum gain. This is permitted, even though the allocations do not have economic effect, because at some time in the future the partner will be taxable on his share of that minimum gain, and the partner's capital account will be increased accordingly. That point may be best described as "payback time." It follows that if there is a decrease in a partner's share of minimum gain, something must be done to allocate gain to the partner and to make a corresponding increase in that partner's capital account. To that end, the regulations generally require that, for any taxable year in which there is a net decrease in a partner's share of minimum gain, that partner must be allocated, by a provision in the partnership agreement known as a "minimum gain chargeback," income and gain in an amount equal to the net decrease in the partner's share of minimum gain.[23]

The most obvious transaction that triggers a decrease in partnership minimum gain is the disposition of property subject to nonrecourse debt. Returning to the example, assume that it is the beginning of year four. The partnership's adjusted basis in the property is now $85,000 ($100,000 original cost less $15,000 of cost recovery deductions in years 1–3), and the minimum gain is thus $5,000 ($90,000 of total nonrecourse debt less $85,000 adjusted basis). Assume that the partners have the following shares of minimum gain and capital accounts:

	Developer	**Investor**
Cash Investment	$1,000	$ 9,000
Cost Recovery Deductions	($1,500)	($13,500)
Capital Account (and Min. Gain)	($ 500)	($ 4,500)

If during year four the property is foreclosed without the receipt of any cash, the partnership nonetheless recognizes a taxable gain of $5,000

20. See Reg. § 1.752–3(a)(1) and Section D of this chapter, infra.

21. If a partnership distributes the proceeds of a nonrecourse liability allocable to an increase in partnership minimum gain, the partners receiving the distribution add the additional share of partnership minimum gain to their restoration obligation to satisfy the alternate test for economic effect. Reg. §§ 1.704–2(g)(1) & (h)(1).

22. Reg. § 1.704–2(g)(1).

23. Reg. § 1.704–2(f)(1). A partner's share of the net decrease in partnership minimum gain is the partner's percentage share of the partnership minimum gain at the end of the immediately preceding year multiplied by the total net decrease in partnership minimum gain. Reg. § 1.704–2(g)(2).

($90,000 debt relief less $85,000 adjusted basis). The foreclosure also triggers a $5,000 net decrease in partnership minimum gain because the partnership no longer holds any property with minimum gain potential.[24] The minimum gain chargeback requires the partnership to allocate the $5,000 net decrease in minimum gain on the foreclosure to the partners to the extent of their respective shares of partnership minimum gain. In the example, that means that $500 (10 percent) of the gain is allocated to Developer and $4,500 (90 percent) is allocated to Investor.[25] In keeping with the principle of the *Tufts* case, the purpose of the minimum gain chargeback is to "balance the books" by recapturing, for tax purposes, the nonrecourse deductions previously allocated to a partner that did not result in a corresponding economic burden.

A decrease in partnership minimum gain also can occur when the principal amount due on a nonrecourse liability is reduced or when a partnership liability is converted from nonrecourse to recourse. In those situations, the minimum gain chargeback rule operates differently.

If a partner contributes capital to the partnership that is used to pay all or part of the partnership's nonrecourse debt, that partner's share of partnership minimum gain will decrease, but the partner's capital contribution increases his capital account in an amount equal to the total decrease in minimum gain. In that event, there is no need to allocate additional income to the partner in order to make an appropriate restoration of his negative capital account. The regulations reflect these realities by providing that a partner is not subject to a minimum gain chargeback to the extent that the decrease in the partner's share of minimum gain is attributable to the partner's own capital contribution that is used to pay the partnership's nonrecourse debt.[26]

A similar policy applies when partnership debt is converted in whole or in part from nonrecourse to recourse as a result of a guarantee, refinancing or a comparable arrangement. In that case, there is no minimum gain chargeback to a partner to the extent that the partner bears the economic risk of loss[27] for the new recourse liability.[28]

Under a final exception, a minimum gain chargeback is not triggered if it would cause a distortion in the economic arrangement among the partners and there is insufficient other income to correct the distortion.[29]

24. The minimum gain was $5,000 at the beginning of the year and zero at the end of the year.

25. Reg. § 1.704–2(g)(2). The regulations provide that any minimum gain chargeback consists first of gains recognized from the disposition of partnership property subject to a nonrecourse liability. Only where the gain from the disposition of the property is less than the decrease in partnership minimum gain for the year does the partnership need to allocate income or gain from other sources as part of an allocation of partnership minimum gain. Reg. § 1.704–2(f)(6). If the amount of the minimum gain chargeback exceeds the partnership's income and gain for the year, the excess carries over. Id. See Reg. § 1.704–2(j)(2)(i) & (iii).

26. Reg. § 1.704–2(f)(3). See Reg. § 1.704–2(m) Example (1)(iv).

27. Reg. § 1.752–2.

28. Reg. § 1.704–2(f)(2).

29. Reg. § 1.704–2(f)(4). For an example of such a situation, see Reg. § 1.704–2(f)(7) Example 1. The Commissioner is au-

Safe Harbor Test. Having mastered the glossary, we finally can turn to the safe harbor test—an experience that gives new definition to the term "anticlimax." Allocations of "nonrecourse deductions" will be respected if the following four requirements are satisfied:

(1) Throughout the life of the partnership, the partnership agreement must satisfy the requirements of either The Big Three test or the alternative test for economic effect.[30]

(2) Beginning in the first taxable year in which the partnership has nonrecourse deductions and thereafter for the life of the partnership, nonrecourse deductions must be allocated in a manner that is reasonably consistent with allocations (having substantial economic effect) of some other significant partnership item attributable to the property securing the nonrecourse liabilities of the partnership (other than allocation of minimum gain).[31]

The second part of the test requires allocation of nonrecourse deductions to be "reasonably consistent" with allocations of some other "significant partnership item" attributable to the property. The agreement in our example provides that all income, deductions and losses are allocated 90 percent to Investor and 10 percent to Developer until aggregate profits from the venture exceed previously incurred losses, at which time all profits are split 50:50. In that situation, the regulations sanction either a 90:10 allocation or a 50:50 allocation of the nonrecourse deductions (or any ratio between 90:10 and 50:50), because either allocation would be "reasonably consistent" with the allocation of a different partnership item attributable to the property.[32] On the other hand, an allocation of 99 percent of nonrecourse deductions to Investor would not be treated as reasonably consistent with a 90:10 or 50:50 division of other partnership items.[33]

(3) Beginning in the first year in which the partnership has nonrecourse deductions or makes a distribution of proceeds of a nonrecourse liability allocable to an increase in partnership minimum gain,[34] the partnership agreement must contain a minimum gain chargeback.[35]

Although the concept is complex, it is simple enough to include a minimum gain chargeback provision in a partnership agreement. Moreover, the application of a minimum gain chargeback is usually quite routine because the partnership likely will realize enough gain on a disposition

thorized to provide additional exceptions to the minimum gain chargeback rule. Reg. § 1.704–2(f)(5).

30. Reg. § 1.704–2(e)(1).

31. Reg. § 1.704–2(e)(2).

32. Reg. § 1.704–2(m) Example (1)(i). The example in the regulations assumes that, at the time of the agreed allocation, there was a reasonable likelihood that the partnership would recognize amounts of income and gain significantly in excess of amounts of loss and deduction (other than nonrecourse deductions). Reg. § 1.704–2(m) Example (1).

33. Reg. § 1.704–2(m) Example (1)(iii).

34. See note 21, supra, regarding the treatment of a distribution of proceeds of a nonrecourse liability allocable to an increase in partnership minimum gain.

35. Reg. § 1.704–2(e)(3).

(including a foreclosure) of the encumbered property to eliminate the deficit capital accounts of partners who enjoyed the tax benefits flowing from nonrecourse deductions.[36]

(4) All other material allocations and capital account adjustments under the partnership agreement must comply with the basic Section 704(b) regulations.[37]

The fourth and final prong of the safe harbor test is purely mechanical. It simply requires that allocations of other material items (other than nonrecourse deductions) must have substantial economic effect. Because limited partners are averse to unlimited deficit restoration obligations, limited partnerships typically will seek to validate allocations of other partnership items under the alternate economic effect test.[38] As a result, a properly drafted agreement for a partnership with nonrecourse debt should include both a qualified income offset for the limited partners and a minimum gain chargeback that complies with the regulations governing nonrecourse deductions.[39]

PROBLEM

G and L form a limited partnership. G, the general partner, contributes $80,000 and L, the limited partner, contributes $320,000. The partnership purchases commercial real estate on leased land, paying $400,000 cash and borrowing $1,600,000 on a nonrecourse basis from a commercial lender. The terms of the loan require payment of interest only for the first five years. The GL partnership agreement allocates all income, gain, loss and deductions 20% to G and 80% to L until the first time that the partnership has recognized items of income and gain that exceed the items of loss and deduction recognized over its life, and then all further partnership items are to be allocated equally between G and L. At the time the partnership agreement is entered into, there is a reasonable likelihood that, over the partnership's life, it will recognize amounts of income and gain significantly in excess of losses and deductions. The partnership agreement requires that all allocations are to be reflected in appropriate adjustments to the partners' capital accounts and liquidation proceeds are to be distributed in accordance with positive capital account balances. Only G is required to restore a capital account deficit. The partnership agreement contains a qualified income offset for L and a minimum gain chargeback provision. Finally, the agreement provides that all nonliquidating distributions will be made 20% to G and 80% to L until a total of $400,000 (equal to the partners' original cash contributions) has been distributed, and thereafter all distributions will be made equally to G and L. The partner-

36. It is important to remember that any tax benefits from allocations of nonrecourse deductions also are subject to the at-risk and passive loss limitations, which in many cases may postpone the deduction until the property is sold. See Chapter 3C, supra.

37. Reg. § 1.704–2(e)(4).

38. Reg. § 1.704–1(b)(2)(ii)(*d*).

39. See, e.g., Reg. § 1.704–2(m) Example (1)(i).

ship depreciates its property using the straight-line method over a valid (you may assume) 10–year recovery period.

(a) Assume that rental income from the property of $150,000 equals operating expenses (including interest on the nonrecourse debt) of $150,000. Determine the allocation of the partnership's cost recovery deductions in each of the first three years of operations and determine the partners' capital accounts at the end of each year.

(b) Same as (a), above, except the partnership agreement provides that L will be allocated 99% and G 1% of all the partnership's cost recovery deductions.

4. Policy Considerations

The Section 704(b) regulations are among the most complex rules that a student (or practitioner) will ever encounter. Anyone with the fortitude and perspective to master the technical details will discover that the allocation rules are quite permissive. It is relatively easy to anchor a partnership allocation within the liberal safe harbors if the partnership agreement includes certain magic language and the partners maintain their capital accounts properly throughout the life of their enterprise. The regulations even provide some guidance for those who fail to satisfy the safe harbors. If flexibility and certainty of result are desirable goals, the Section 704(b) regulations have much to offer.

But are the regulations too permissive? The excerpt below addresses these questions, focusing on allocations attributable to nonrecourse debt and the substantiality requirement. The author provides helpful insights on the deficiencies of the partnership allocation regulations and offers possible legislative solutions. The discussion is presented in the form of a congressional committee report on a hypothetical Subchapter K Reform Act. Keep in mind that this proposal has not yet been enacted into law, but it may be influential if Congress ever should summon the courage to engage in a comprehensive review of Subchapter K.

Excerpt From William B. Brannan, The Subchapter K Reform Act of 1997

75 Tax Notes 121, 122–124 (April 7, 1997).

1. Partnership Tax Allocation Provisions

a. Prohibit Special Allocations Attributable to Nonrecourse Debt

Present Law

Under section 704(b) and Treasury regulation section 1.704–1(b), partnerships have great flexibility in allocating income and loss among their partners. In general, partnership tax allocations will be respected if either (i) such allocations have substantial economic effect by complying with the detailed rules set forth in Treasury regulation section 1.704–1(b)(2) regarding the maintenance of capital accounts (as described below) or (ii) such allocations are in accordance with the economic interests of the partners in the partnership (as determined under the facts and circumstances test set forth in Treasury regulation section 1.704–1(b)(3)).

It appears that in practice most partnerships now rely on the capital account rules to validate their tax allocations. Under those rules, allocations of partnership tax items generally will be respected if such allocations satisfy the following three mechanical requirements that are intended to cause allocations to have economic effect: (i) the partnership maintains capital accounts for its partners in accordance with the principles of Treasury regulation section 1.704–1(b)(2)(ii) so as to reflect all partnership tax allocations, (ii) distributions upon liquidation of the partnership (or upon the liquidation of a partner's interest in the partnership) are made in accordance with such capital accounts, and (iii) any partner with a deficit balance in his capital account upon the liquidation of the partnership (or upon the liquidation of his interest in the partnership) must make a capital contribution to the partnership to eliminate such deficit balance. In addition to the foregoing mechanical requirements, the economic effect of the partnership's tax allocations must be "substantial" within the meaning of Treasury regulation section 1.704–1(b)(2)(iii).

As indicated by Treasury regulation section 1.704–2(b)(1), allocations of losses, deductions, or section 705(a)(2)(B) expenditures attributable to the nonrecourse debt of a partnership cannot have economic effect through capital account adjustments, because the economic risk of loss associated with such tax items is borne by the nonrecourse lender.[6] Thus, the normal substantial economic effect rules do not apply to such allocations. Instead, Treasury regulation section 1.704–2(b) generally allows a partnership to allocate tax items attributable to nonrecourse debt however the partnership chooses, provided that such allocation corresponds to the allocation of some other significant partnership tax item that itself has substantial economic effect and the partnership agreement contains a so-called "minimum gain chargeback" to ensure that such allocations will be reversed by income allocations when the property securing the debt is sold or the debt is paid down.[7] The one important exception to that rule is for tax items attributable to nonrecourse debt where the lender is a partner or an affiliate of a partner, in which case such tax items generally must be allocated exclusively to that partner.[8]

6. As a broad generalization, tax items attributable to nonrecourse debt arise in any taxable year in which the ending debt balance exceeds the section 704(b) book value of the property securing such debt and such items usually consist of the depreciation or amortization deductions attributable to such property for such year (reduced by the amount of any amortization of the debt balance, or the amount of any capitalized expenditures with respect to such property, during such year). See Treas. reg. sections 1.704–2(c) and 1.704–2(i)(2). If such deductions were matched by a corresponding decline in the economic value of such property, the lender would bear such loss on a foreclosure.

7. In the parlance of the section 704(b) regulations, such allocations of tax items attributable to nonrecourse debt are "deemed" to be in accordance with economic interests of the partners.

8. See Treas. reg. section 1.704–2(i). Such debt is referred to in the section 704(b) regulation as "partner nonrecourse debt."

Since most partnership agreements provide for "flips" in their allocations over time, special allocations of particular tax items or other complexities in their allocations, the above-stated limitation on allocations of tax items attributable to third-party nonrecourse debt often leaves a partnership with a wide range of choices in making such allocations. Even if the desired allocation of tax items attributable to third-party nonrecourse debt is not supported by the other allocations that naturally would occur by reason of the business arrangement of the partners, it is possible in many circumstances to provide for a special allocation of a significant partnership tax item in order to support the desired allocation of tax items attributable to third-party nonrecourse debt.

The foregoing discussion has focused on allocations of the items attributable to nonrecourse debt in the context of partnerships that rely on the capital account rules to validate their tax allocations. It should be noted that it is not clear how much latitude partnerships that rely upon the alternative test based upon the economic interests of the partners have to allocate tax items attributable to nonrecourse debt, since there is no regulation that specifically addresses that issue. In the case of third-party nonrecourse debt, the spirit of the section 704(b) regulations appears to be that such allocations should be based upon the overall economic interests of the partners in the partnership.[9] In the case of partner nonrecourse debt, it is arguable that the fact that the partner (or its affiliate) bears the economic risk of loss on the debt should be taken into account in allocating tax items attributable to that debt, although it is by no means clear that economic risk of loss borne in a lender capacity (particularly if the lender is not a partner) is relevant for that purpose.

Reasons for Change

The committee generally believes that partnerships should have the flexibility in allocating tax items to reflect the economic arrangement of their partners and that section 704(b) should provide as much certainty as possible regarding the validity of such allocations, which objectives are facilitated by the mechanical capital account rules under section 704(b). However, the committee believes that it is inappropriate to allow partnerships to specially allocate losses, deductions and section 705(a)(2)(B) expenditures attributable to third-party nonrecourse debt as permitted under current law. As indicated above, such allocations, by definition, have no

See Treas. reg. section 1.704–2(b)(4). In the discussion below, the term "third-party nonrecourse debt" is used to distinguish partner nonrecourse debt from nonrecourse debt that is not subject to Treas. reg. section 1.704–2(i). * * *

9. The general approach of the alternate test in the section 704(b) regulations is to treat the overall economic interests of the partners as the basis for tax allocations, except where there is a special arrangement for sharing the economic benefit or burden corresponding to a particular item, in which event that tax item should be specially allocated to reflect such arrangement. See Treas. reg. section 1.704–1(b)(3)(i). Cf. Treas. reg. section 1.704–2(b)(1) (tax items attributable to the nonrecourse debt of a partnership that is attempting to follow the capital account rules must be allocated in accordance with "the partners' overall economic interests" if the requirements of that regulation are not satisfied).

economic effect on the partners. While it is true that other partnership tax allocations may not, in practice, have actual economic effect in many circumstances because of offsetting allocations or other events that occur later, there is at least a potential for actual economic effect that usually necessitates that such allocations follow the economic arrangement of the partners. In contrast, allocations of tax items attributable to third-party nonrecourse debt often are highly tax-motivated.

The current system imposes no meaningful limitation on the ability of partnerships to make tax-motivated allocations of tax items attributable to third-party nonrecourse debt. Indeed, one professional group has equated the ability to shift tax benefits among partners afforded by the current rules governing the allocation of tax items attributable to non-recourse debt with the old safe harbor leasing rules.[10]

Explanation of Provision

Under the act, section 704(b) is amended to provide that partnership tax [items] attributable to third-party nonrecourse debt, as determined under the principles of Treasury regulation section 1.704–2, generally must be allocated in accordance with the overall economic interests of the partners in the partnership. The overall economic interests of the partners in the partnership shall be determined in accordance with the principles of Treasury regulations section 1.704–1(b)(3). However, to provide some certainty in making this determination, partnerships generally may elect to determine the economic interests of the partners based on the partners' relative capital contributions.[11] The foregoing provisions apply to both partnerships that rely on capital accounts to validate their tax allocations and to partnerships that rely on the partners' economic interests in the partnership approach.

The provisions of the act do not affect the current rules regarding allocations of losses, deductions, or section 705(a)(2)(B) expenditures attributable to so-called "partner nonrecourse liabilities" set forth in Treasury regulation section 1.704–2(i). Accordingly, such items generally must continue to be allocated to the partner that bears the economic risk of loss with respect to such tax items. However, the act expressly provides that

10. New York State Bar Association Tax Section, Report on Proposed Treasury Regulations Under Internal Revenue Code Section 704(b) (May 12, 1983) at 36–7. That comment was made with reference to the original 1983 proposed section 704(b) regulations, which did not even include the requirement that the allocation of tax items attributable to nonrecourse debt be consistent with the allocation of some other partnership tax item that does have substantial economic effect. * * * However, as indicated above, the committee does not view that as an adequate limitation.

11. The determination of the economic interests of the partners based on relative capital contributions may be challenged by the Service in any case where (i) the capital contributions by the partners represent an insubstantial part of the total capitalization of the partnership or (ii) the partners expect that the partnership will earn substantial profits in excess of a reasonable return on such capital contributions and such residual profits will be shared on a basis that is substantially different from the relative capital contributions of the partners.

this rule also applies to partnerships that rely on the economic interests of the partners approach to validate their tax allocations.

b. Strengthen the Substantiality Requirement

Present Law

As indicated above, the substantial economic effect test in Treasury regulations section 1.704–1(b)(2) is not satisfied unless the economic effect of that allocation is "substantial."

The basic test for determining whether the economic effect of an allocation is substantial is set forth in Treasury regulation section 1.704–1(b)(2)(iii). Under that test, the economic effect of an allocation is not substantial if, at the time the allocation becomes part of the partnership agreement, (i) the economic consequences to at least one partner, as determined on a present value, after-tax basis, may be enhanced as compared to the case where such allocation is not made, and (ii) there is a strong likelihood that the economic consequences to no partner, as so determined, will be substantially diminished as compared to the case where such allocation is not made. To provide certainty in applying the test, the fair market value of partnership property is presumed to be equal to its adjusted book value as determined for section 704(b) purposes. As a result, the substantiality of allocations is tested on the assumption that there will be no gain on the sale of partnership property that might reverse the effect of prior allocations.

In addition to the basic substantiality test, Treasury regulation section 1.704–1(b)(2)(iii) contains specific rules preventing shifting and transitory allocations.

Reasons for Change

The committee believes the "value equals basis" presumption that applies in testing the substantiality of an allocation, while often economically unrealistic, generally is appropriate for two reasons. First, it makes the substantiality test relatively simple to apply, thereby avoiding the burdensome financial forecasting that would be necessary if partnerships were required to use a more economically realistic model. Second, it provides a reasonable degree of certainty in testing allocations, thereby facilitating taxpayer planning and minimizing controversies on audit.[12]

However, at the same time, the "value equals basis" presumption usually makes it fairly easy for a partnership to satisfy the substantiality test, even in a tax-motivated situation. That follows because the "value equals basis" presumption effectively means that each dollar of loss or deduction specially allocated to a partner generally will reduce the amount

12. The substantiality test does involve some uncertainties, such as what the allocations of the partnership would be in the absence of the special allocation being tested (an issue that is considerably more difficult than might first appear) and how to make assumptions about asset holding periods, annual operating income, and other relevant facts.

such partner will receive on liquidation of the partnership, and so the only question is whether the present value of the tax benefit created by that allocation is fully offset by the present value of the lost dollar of liquidating distributions. At the same time, it is perfectly rational for the parties to make such special allocations if, as is often the case, the economic value of partnership property is not expected to decline at the same rate as its adjusted book basis declines to reflect book depreciation or amortization. In such cases, the potential economic effect of the special allocation can be offset by specially allocating gain on the sale of the property (or other partnership income).

In some extreme cases, it is possible that an allocation would be vulnerable to challenge under the anti-abuse rule in Treasury regulation section 1.701–2 or some general principle of law.[13] However, as a practical matter, it is very unlikely that any such general principle would be used to attack an abusive partnership tax allocation. First, the audit rate for partnerships is extremely low.[14] Second, it is unlikely that an auditor would seek to apply general principles to situations that facially seem to satisfy the capital account rules, since auditors usually have difficulty just understanding complex partnership tax allocations and there is no decided case or ruling that applies general principles in the section 704(b) context. Third, it is quite possible that a court would conclude that the extremely detailed capital account rules occupy the field (except in cases involving a total sham), thereby precluding the application of general principles.[15] While Congress wants to maintain the basic framework of the current rules, it does not want the substantiality test to be easily satisfied in cases of tax-motivated allocations where there is some objective indication that the allocations are not expected to have economic effect.

Explanation of Provision

Under the act, a special allocation of income or loss will be treated as not having substantial economic effect if the parties believe that there is only a remote possibility that such allocation will actually have economic effect. Whether a special allocation is expected to have economic effect for this purpose is to be evaluated on a present value, after-tax basis.

13. The section 704(b) regulations actually contain an express statement that allocations that satisfy the mechanical rules of the regulations may still be vulnerable to challenge under general tax principles. See Treas. reg. section 1.704–1(b)(1)(iii).

14. According to a recent General Accounting Office report, the audit rate for partnerships, which has never been high, has been dropping steadily in recent years and is now about 0.5 percent (versus 2.89 percent for corporations). See General Accounting Office, Report to the Joint Committee on Taxation, GGD–95–151 (June 16, 1995).

15. With respect to the section 701 anti-abuse rule [discussed in Chapter 1, supra, Ed.], the regulations contain examples that strongly suggest that the anti-abuse rule may not be used to challenge allocations that satisfy the section 704(b) rules (see Treasury reg. section 1.701–2(d) (Examples 5 and 6)). In addition, it may be significant that the Treasury did not amend the section 704(b) regulation referred to in note 13, supra, to provide a specific cross-reference to the antiabuse rule.

The Service shall have the burden of proof under this provision, and must satisfy that burden with clear and convincing evidence. Such burden of proof generally will be satisfied if the offering documents or other promotional materials for the transaction do not disclose the potential economic effect of the special allocation or, if they do disclose the potential economic effect, they characterize the risk of such effect actually occurring in a manner such that a reasonable person would conclude that the risk is not significant.

C. ALLOCATIONS WITH RESPECT TO CONTRIBUTED PROPERTY

1. INTRODUCTION

Code: §§ 704(a), (c)(1)(A) & (3).

Regulations: §§ 1.704–3(a)(1)–(5) & (10),–3(e)(1); 1.704–1(b)(1)(vi),–1(b)(2)(iv)(*d*)(*1*) & (*3*).

Background. When partners contribute property to a partnership in exchange for an interest in the firm,[1] they recognize neither gain nor loss[2] and their basis in the contributed property carries over to the partnership.[3] If the general rule in Section 704(a) applied to this transaction, gain or loss on the disposition of the contributed property would be allocated in accordance with the partnership agreement. This approach would provide a convenient method for shifting precontribution gains or losses among the partners. For example, assume the AB equal partnership is formed with A contributing Gainacre, a capital asset, with an adjusted basis of $12,000 and a fair market value of $20,000, and B contributing $20,000 in cash. Although Gainacre is recorded on the partnership's books at its fair market value,[4] the partnership takes over A's $12,000 adjusted basis for tax purposes.[5] If A and B agree to allocate profits according to their equal 50 percent interests in the partnership, any gain or loss on a subsequent sale of Gainacre would be allocated equally to A and B under Section 704(a). Thus, if the partnership sold Gainacre for $20,000, it would not realize any book gain and the capital accounts of the partners would be unaffected,[6] but $4,000 of the $8,000 *tax* gain realized on the sale would be allocated to B even though that entire gain is attributable to the period when A held the property. Half of the precontribution gain would be shifted to B simply because the AB partnership, rather than A, sold the property. Similarly, a tax loss could be shifted if A contributed property with an adjusted basis exceeding its fair market value.

1. See Chapter 2A, supra.
2. I.R.C. § 721. See I.R.C. § 722.
3. I.R.C. § 723.
4. Reg. §§ 1.704–1(b)(2)(iv)(*b*), (*d*)(*1*); 1.704–1(b)(5) Example (13)(i).
5. I.R.C. § 723. The effect is to create a book/tax disparity of $8,000.
6. Reg. §§ 1.704–1(b)(2)(iv)(*b*)(*3*); 1.704–1(b)(4)(i).

The shift of precontribution gain to B is not permanent, but it may last for many years—perhaps as long as the AB partnership remains in existence. After the partnership's $8,000 tax gain is allocated equally to A and B, their outside bases are increased to $16,000 and $24,000, respectively.[7] If the partnership then were liquidated with A and B each receiving $20,000 in cash, A would recognize his remaining $4,000 gain and B would recognize a $4,000 loss. Even though B eventually recognizes a $4,000 loss to offset his earlier gain on the sale of Gainacre, substantial time may have elapsed before the loss is recognized. Moreover, if the contributed property were depreciable, the character of the gain and the later offsetting loss may differ. B's loss on a liquidation or sale of his partnership interest would be a capital loss[8] while the gain on the sale of the depreciable property might be ordinary as a result of depreciation recapture.[9]

The example illustrates a problem with applying the general allocation rule in Section 704(a) to gain or loss on the disposition of contributed property. That rule would enable partners to shift income or loss for tax purposes without any corresponding economic benefit or burden,[10] and cause distortions in the timing and character of future income or loss.[11] Similar distortions would result from depreciation deductions with respect to contributed property.

A tempting solution to the income shifting problem might be for the partnership to make a special allocation of the $8,000 of tax gain to contributing partner A under Section 704(b). But remember that the property was recorded on the books of the partnership at its $20,000 fair market value when it was contributed by A. As a result, there is no book gain (or capital account adjustment) on its sale for $20,000, and a special allocation of the $8,000 tax gain thus would not have substantial economic effect under the now familiar principles of Section 704(b).

General Section 704(c) Allocation Principles. The Congressional response to these and related concerns is Section 704(c)(1)(A), which provides, under regulations promulgated by the Service,[12] that items of income, gain, loss and deduction with respect to property contributed by a partner to a partnership shall be shared among the partners "so as to take account of the variation between the basis of the property to the partnership and its fair market value at the time of contribution."[13] Because this is

7. I.R.C. § 705(a)(1)(A).

8. I.R.C. §§ 731(a); 741. See Chapters 6 & 8, infra.

9. I.R.C. §§ 1245; 1250.

10. Even when marginal tax rates are compressed, incentives remain for shifting income and losses in the partnership setting. For example, it might be desirable to shift taxable income to a tax-exempt partner or to a partner with an expiring net operating loss carryover.

11. In the event of a partner's death, even the amount of loss could be affected. I.R.C. § 1014.

12. See Reg. § 1.704–3.

13. Section 704(c)(1)(A) is patterned after its predecessor, Section 704(c)(2), which was wholly or partially elective by the partners. It also applies to contributions by cash method taxpayers of accounts payable and other accrued but unpaid cash basis items, such as zero basis accounts receivable. I.R.C. § 704(c)(3); Reg. § 1.704–3(a)(4). See Chap-

a tax allocation that lacks substantial economic effect, it is not accompanied by any change to the partners' capital accounts.

Typically, Congress did not grovel in the details of how these tax allocations would be made, delegating that arduous task to the regulations writers at the Treasury. The regulations apply to allocations with respect to "Section 704(c) property," which is defined as property that at the time of its contribution to the partnership has a fair market (book) value that differs from contributing partner's adjusted tax basis.[14] If the property's book value is greater than its adjusted basis, the difference is a "built-in gain," and if the adjusted basis exceeds the book value, the difference is a "built-in loss."[15] In determining whether property has a built-in gain or loss, the Service generally will accept the valuation determined by the arm's lengths dealings of the partners as reflected in their capital accounts if the parties have sufficiently adverse interests.[16]

In keeping with the Service's policy to "simplify" and provide "flexibility" to taxpayers, the regulations permit a partnership to make allocations using any reasonable method that is consistent with the purpose of Section 704(c).[17] The regulations give their blessing to three methods: the "traditional method,"[18] the "traditional method with curative allocations,"[19] and the "remedial method."[20] Each is subject to a general anti-abuse rule under which an allocation method is not reasonable if the contribution of property and the corresponding allocation of tax items are made with a view to shifting the tax consequences of the built-in gain or loss among the partners in a manner that substantially reduces the present value of their aggregate tax liability.[21]

No more than one allocation method may be used with respect to each item of Section 704(c) property and, although a different method may be used with respect to different items of property, a partner and partnership must use a method or combination of methods that is reasonable under the facts and circumstances.[22] In general, Section 704(c) must be applied on a

ter 2B, supra, and Problem 2 at page 61 supra.

14. Reg. § 1.704–3(a)(3)(i).

15. Reg. § 1.704–3(a)(3)(ii). Built-in gains and losses are determined at the time of the contribution. They are reduced thereafter by any decreases in the difference between the property's adjusted basis and book value. Id.

16. This determination will be respected except in abuse cases. See Staff of the Joint Committee on Taxation, General Explanation of the Revenue Provisions of the Deficit Reduction Act of 1984 (hereinafter "1984 Act General Explanation"), 98th Cong., 2d Sess. 213 (1984). Cf. Reg. § 1.704–1(b)(2)(iv)(*h*).

17. Reg. § 1.704–3(a)(1).

18. Reg. § 1.704–3(b).

19. Reg. § 1.704–3(c).

20. Reg. § 1.704–3(d).

21. Reg. § 1.704–3(a)(10). For examples of unreasonable allocations, see Reg. §§ 1.704–3(b)(2) Example 2 and 1.704–3(c)(4) Example 1(iii). The abuses identified in the examples are reminiscent of the types of manipulation that may violate the "substantiality" test of the Section 704(b) regulations. See Reg. § 1.704–1(b)(2)(iii).

22. Reg. § 1.704–3(a)(2). The regulations indicate that it may be unreasonable to use one method for appreciated property and another method for depreciated property. Whatever method is elected must be consistently applied by both the partner and the partnership in each year. Id.

property-by-property basis except that property with identical tax characteristics (e.g., depreciable property, inventory) may be aggregated for purposes of determining whether built-in gains and losses exist.[23]

A partnership may disregard or defer the application of Section 704(c) in a single year if there is a "small disparity" between the book value and the adjusted basis of the contributed property.[24] A "small disparity" exists if the total fair market value of all property contributed by a partner during the taxable year does not differ from the total adjusted basis of the property by more than 15 percent of the adjusted basis, and the total gross disparity does not exceed $20,000.[25] To illustrate, assume that the AB partnership is formed with A contributing $100,000 cash and B contributing land with an adjusted basis of $90,000 and a fair market value of $100,000. The partnership may disregard Section 704(c) with respect to the land because the $10,000 difference between its fair market value and basis does not differ from the adjusted basis by more than 15 percent of that basis (i.e., 15% × $90,000 = $13,500, which is more than $10,000), and the disparity does not exceed $20,000.

Against the background of these general rules and exceptions, we turn next to the application of the three allocation methods to the two most typical situations that arise under Section 704(c): sales and exchanges, and depreciation of contributed property.

2. Sales and Exchanges of Contributed Property

a. SECTION 704(c) ALLOCATION METHODS

Code: § 704(c)(1)(A).

Regulations: § 1.704–3(b)(1);–3(c)(1)–(3);–3(d)(1), (3), (4), (5), and (7) Example 2.

The Traditional Method. The "traditional method" is based on the approach used when Section 704(c) allocations were elective and during the period between the enactment of current Section 704(c)(1)(A) in 1984 and the effective date of the regulations. As applied to sales of contributed property, the traditional method generally requires a partnership to allocate any built-in gain or loss to the contributing partner.[1]

Return again to the example in which A and B form the AB partnership with A contributing Gainacre (basis—$12,000, value—$20,000), and B contributing $20,000 cash. If the partnership sells Gainacre for $20,000, the traditional method allocates the entire $8,000 of built-in gain to A.[2] If

23. Reg. §§ 1.704–3(a)(2) & (e)(2).

24. Reg. § 1.704–3(e)(1)(i).

25. Reg. § 1.704–3(e)(1)(ii). In determining whether a disparity is "small," the partner can aggregate properties with similar tax characteristics. Id.

1. Reg. § 1.704–3(b)(1). If the partnership disposes of Section 704(c) property in a nonrecognition transaction, such as a like-kind exchange, the new property is treated as Section 704(c) property with the same built-in gain or loss as the property disposed of by the partnership. Reg. § 1.704–3(a)(8).

2. The same rule would apply to any successor in interest to A (e.g., a donee). See I.R.C. § 704(c)(3), last sentence.

the partnership sells Gainacre for $35,000, resulting in $23,000 of taxable gain, of which $8,000 accrued prior to A's contribution and $15,000 accrued while Gainacre was held by the partnership, the $8,000 precontribution gain is allocated to A under Section 704(c)(1)(A), and the $15,000 postcontribution gain is divided equally between A and B.[3]

The Section 704(b) regulations elaborate on the relationship between Section 704(c) allocations and the rules governing maintenance of capital accounts. The difference between the tax basis and the fair market (book) value of contributed property at the time of the contribution requires a partnership to keep two sets of accounts—one for "book" (including capital account) purposes and the other for "tax" purposes. The "book" items, which reflect the economic arrangement of the partners, are used in testing the substantial economic effect of an allocation. The "tax" items—i.e., the amounts reported on the partnership's tax return that pass through to the partners—must be determined with reference to the partners' distributive shares of the corresponding book items.[4]

In the example, Gainacre would be recorded on the partnership's books at its $20,000 fair market value,[5] but the partnership takes over A's $12,000 adjusted basis for tax purposes,[6] creating an initial book/tax disparity of $8,000. A and B each have a $20,000 capital account upon formation of the partnership,[7] but A's initial outside basis for tax purposes is $12,000 while B's outside basis is $20,000.[8] When Gainacre is sold for $35,000 (and assuming the partnership otherwise breaks even), the bookkeeper must do double duty, separately computing a $15,000 book gain ($35,000 amount realized less $20,000 book value) and a $23,000 tax gain ($35,000 amount realized less $12,000 adjusted basis). Under the partnership agreement, the book gain is allocated $7,500 each to A and B, and their capital accounts are adjusted accordingly.[9] For tax purposes, the partners are allocated their respective shares of this book gain and, in addition, the traditional method allocates the $8,000 difference between the book and tax gains to A, the contributing partner, to take into account the variation between the tax basis and the fair market value of Gainacre at the time of the contribution and to eliminate to the extent possible any book/tax disparity.[10] After recovering from this computational binge, the bookkeeper will be gratified to discover that the book and tax capital accounts of the partners are back in balance:

3. Cf. Reg. § 1.704–1(b)(5) Example (13)(i).

4. Reg. § 1.704–1(b)(1)(vi).

5. Reg. § 1.704–1(b)(2)(iv)(*b*),–1(b)(2)(iv)(*d*)(*1*),–1(b)(5) Example (13)(i).

6. I.R.C. § 723.

7. Reg. § 1.704–1(b)(2)(iv)(*b*).

8. I.R.C. § 722.

9. The allocation of the book gain has substantial economic effect under Section 704(b). See Reg. § 1.704–1(b)(5) Example (13)(i).

10. Reg. § 1.704–1(b)(4)(i).

	A		B	
	Tax	**Book**	**Tax**	**Book**
On Formation	$12,000	$20,000	$20,000	$20,000
Gain on Sale	15,500	7,500	7,500	7,500
Balance	$27,500	$27,500	$27,500	$27,500

The Ceiling Rule. Suppose that the partnership sells Gainacre for $15,000—an amount less than its $20,000 book value but more than its $12,000 adjusted tax basis. On the sale, the partnership has a tax gain of $3,000 but a book loss of $5,000. Under the partnership agreement, the partners share the book loss equally, but what about the tax gain? A sensible approach might be to allocate the $8,000 precontribution gain to A and then to allocate the $5,000 postcontribution loss equally to A and B so that A ends up with a $5,500 net taxable gain and B ends up with a $2,500 tax loss. Each partner's outside basis then would be reconciled with his share of inside basis, and any book/tax disparity would be eliminated.[11]

The traditional method, however, imposes a "ceiling rule," under which the total gain or loss allocated to the partners may not exceed the tax gain or loss realized by the partnership.[12] As a result, no tax loss can be allocated to B despite his economic loss of $2,500 because the partnership did not realize a loss for tax purposes. And although A has a precontribution gain of $8,000 and a postcontribution loss of $2,500, for a net gain of $5,500, the ceiling rule allows only $3,000 of tax gain to be allocated to A because that is all of the tax gain recognized by the partnership. This deprives B of his rightful share of the loss on Gainacre while it was held by the partnership and understates the gain accruing to A during the entire time he held Gainacre—the very shifting of income or loss that Section 704(c)(1)(A) was designed to prevent! As the following summary of the partners' book (capital) and tax accounts reveals, the ceiling rule perpetuates the partnership's book/tax disparities:[13]

	A		B	
	Tax	**Book**	**Tax**	**Book**
On Formation	$12,000	$20,000	$20,000	$20,000
Tax Gain on Sale	3,000			
Book Loss on Sale		(2,500)		(2,500)
Balance	$15,000	$17,500	$20,000	$17,500

11. A's outside basis under this approach would be $17,500 ($12,000 on formation + $8,000 allocable gain − $2,500 allocable loss); B's outside basis also would be $17,500 ($20,000 on formation − $2,500 allocable loss). I.R.C. §§ 722; 705. The partners' outside bases would equal their respective shares of the inside bases of the partnership's assets (the $35,000 cash, representing B's $20,000 initial cash contribution plus the $15,000 proceeds on the sale of Gainacre). The outside bases of the partners also would equal their $17,500 capital accounts after the sale ($20,000 minus $2,500 book loss).

12. Reg. § 1.704–3(b)(1).

13. This distortion is not necessarily permanent. Assume, for example, that the partnership liquidates after the sale, distributing $35,000 of cash equally to A and B. On the liquidation, A would recognize $2,500 gain and B would recognize $2,500 loss. I.R.C. § 731. As discussed earlier, however, this adjustment still results in distortions of timing or character.

Apart from a nostalgic adherence to tradition, it is not clear why the Service continues to sanction an allocation method that incorporates the ceiling rule and its resulting distortions. The regulations authorize two additional methods, however, that use different approaches to cure (or remedy) the ceiling rule malady.

Traditional Method With Curative Allocations. The traditional method with curative allocations permits a partnership to make reasonable "curative allocations" of other partnership tax items of income, gain, loss or deduction to correct ceiling rule distortions.[14] A curative allocation is an allocation made solely for tax purposes that differs from the partnership's allocation of the corresponding book item. As such, a curative allocation has no economic effect and is not reflected in the partners' capital accounts.

A curative allocation is reasonable only if (1) it does not exceed the amount necessary to offset the effect of the ceiling rule[15] and (2) the income or loss allocated is of the same character and has the same tax consequences as the tax item affected by the ceiling rule.[16] Curative allocations may be made to correct ceiling rule distortions from a prior taxable year if they are made over a "reasonable period of time" (e.g., the economic life of the property) and were authorized by the partnership agreement in effect for the year that the property was contributed.[17]

Curative allocations are best explained by returning to the example, where the AB partnership sells Gainacre for $15,000, realizing a $5,000 book loss ($20,000 book value less $15,000 amount realized) and a $3,000 tax gain ($15,000 amount realized less $12,000 tax basis). As before, the book loss is allocated equally to A and B, and the tax gain is allocated entirely to A. Assume further that the partnership invested the $20,000 cash contributed by B in stock that it has held long-term and the partnership sells the stock for $30,000, realizing a book and tax gain of $10,000. The book gain is allocated $5,000 to each partner. In addition, since the gain on the sale of Gainacre and the stock are of the same character (long-term capital gain), the partnership may make a curative allocation of $2,500 of B's tax gain on the stock to A. Thus, instead of allocating to A $5,000 capital gain on the stock sale to match his book gain, A is allocated a $7,500 capital gain, and B is allocated only a $2,500 capital gain. The net result cures the ceiling rule distortion that caused not enough gain to be allocated to A and not enough loss to be allocated to B on the sale of Gainacre. And all is well. After these allocations, the partners' tax and book (capital) accounts would be as follows:

14. Reg. § 1.704–3(c)(1).

15. Reg. § 1.704–3(c)(3)(i). Cf. Reg. § 1.704–3(c)(4) Examples 1(ii) & (iii).

16. Reg. § 1.704–3(c)(3)(ii).

17. Reg. § 1.704–3(c)(3)(ii).

	A		B	
	Tax	Book	Tax	Book
On Formation	$12,000	$20,000	$20,000	$20,000
Gainacre—Tax Gain	3,000			
Gainacre—Book Loss		(2,500)		(2,500)
Stock—Tax Gain	7,500		2,500	
Stock—Book Gain		5,000		5,000
Balance	$22,500	$22,500	$22,500	$22,500

Remedial Method. The traditional method with curative allocations cures ceiling rule distortions only if the partnership has enough recognized tax gain or loss of the appropriate type from another source. If the partnership had not sold the stock in the example, there would have been no tax gain to allocate to A, and the pernicious impact of the ceiling rule would linger. The remedial allocation method allows the partnership to restore its books to good health by creating the tax gain or loss of the appropriate type needed to offset ceiling rule distortions. Like their curative cousins, remedial allocations are solely tax allocations that have no effect on the partnership's book capital accounts.[18]

Under the remedial method, if the ceiling rule results in a book allocation to a noncontributing partner that differs from the partner's corresponding tax allocation, the partnership may make a remedial allocation to the noncontributing partner equal to the full amount of the disparity and a simultaneous offsetting remedial allocation to the contributing partner.[19] A remedial allocation must have the same effect on each partner's tax liability as the item limited by the ceiling rule—for example, if the tax item limited by the ceiling rule is a loss from the sale of a contributed capital asset, the offsetting remedial allocation to the contributing partner must be capital gain.[20]

Returning to the example, assume again that the partnership sells Gainacre for $15,000 and has no other taxable transactions during the year. If it adopts the remedial allocation method, it may create and then allocate $2,500 of capital gain to A, and make an offsetting remedial allocation of $2,500 of capital loss to B.[21] Note that this has the same effect as allocating to A the entire $8,000 precontribution gain on Gainacre less A's share ($2,500) of postcontribution loss (for a net gain of $5,500), and of allocating to B his rightful $2,500 share of postcontribution loss.

Planning Aspects. Although the remedial method assures that ceiling rule distortions are corrected regardless of other income or loss realized by the partnership, the regulations do not make it mandatory. The partnership may adopt any reasonable method in making Section 704(c) allocations, including the traditional method with its potential for book/tax disparities. The regulations thus offer taxpayers some flexibility in dealing with contributed property. They even permit the partnership to use different methods for different properties. What method would A and B prefer in our continuing example? The answer may depend on the tax profiles of the partners outside the partnership. In the case where the partnership sells

18. Reg. § 1.704–3(d)(4)(ii).

19. Reg. § 1.704–3(d)(1).

20. Reg. § 1.704–3(d)(3).

21. See Reg. § 1.704–3(d)(7) Example 2.

Gainacre for $15,000, the method of choice might be the traditional method and its ceiling rule (which understates A's gain and delays B's use of his $2,500 economic loss for tax purposes) if A were in a high tax bracket and B had no use for the deduction, perhaps because he had an expiring net operating loss from another source or was subject to the $3,000 limitation on capital losses. This assumes that use of the traditional method is reasonable on these facts. If it were not, the allocation would violate the anti-abuse rule of the regulations and cause the Service to intervene.[22] Alternatively, if B were in a high tax bracket relative to A, the partners might prefer to use the traditional method with curative allocations or the remedial method so that B could use the loss more rapidly.

b. CHARACTERIZATION OF GAIN OR LOSS ON DISPOSITION OF CONTRIBUTED PROPERTY

Code: §§ 724; 751(c), (d). Skim §§ 7701(a)(42)–(44).

We must take a brief detour from Section 704(c) to address the related issue of characterization of the gain or loss when a partnership disposes of contributed property. In addition to income shifting, taxpayers historically have sought to alter the tax character of gain or loss—converting ordinary income into capital gains and capital losses into ordinary losses. Partnerships were useful vehicles for this pastime because the character of income or loss from the disposition of partnership property was generally determined at the partnership level, without regard to the prior status of the property in the hands of the contributing partner. For example, a partner who was a dealer in land might transfer an appreciated parcel to a partnership with no prior real estate dealings and cause the partnership to sell the property at some later time. If the partnership aged the real estate sufficiently to withstand scrutiny under the step transaction doctrine or other judicially created barriers to tax avoidance, it might successfully contend that it realized a capital gain on the sale. Similarly, a taxpayer might attempt to convert a built-in capital loss on contributed property (e.g., securities) into an ordinary loss. We have seen how Section 704(c)(1)(A) prevents income *shifting* in this context by allocating any built-in gain or loss to the contributing partner. Section 724 seeks to prevent the *conversion* of gain or loss through contributions of property to a new or existing partnership.[1]

Section 724 applies to three categories of contributed property: unrealized receivables, inventory items and capital loss property. Different rules are provided for each category. "Unrealized receivables" are generally defined in Section 751(c) as rights (contractual or otherwise) to payment for goods or services that have not been previously included in income, provided in the case of goods that the sales proceeds would be treated as

22. See, e.g., Reg. § 1.704–3(b)(2) Example 2.

1. Congress also has acted to prevent altering the character of gain or loss through distributions in kind by a partnership followed by a sale by the distributee partner. See I.R.C. § 735 and Chapter 7A2, infra.

received from the sale or exchange of noncapital assets.[2] Because unrealized receivables essentially represent ripe transactions that will produce ordinary income or loss, Section 724(a) provides that any gain or loss recognized by the partnership on the disposition of unrealized receivables will be ordinary.[3]

The term "inventory items" is broadly defined in Section 751(d)(2) to include not only the familiar category of noncapital assets described in Section 1221(1) (i.e., inventory and other dealer property) but also any other property which, upon sale by the contributing partner, would not be considered as a capital or Section 1231 asset.[4] Inventory items retain their ordinary income taint under Section 724(b) for five years after their contribution to the partnership.[5] After that period, the character of contributed inventory items is determined at the partnership level.

"Capital loss property" includes any capital asset held by the contributing partner which had an adjusted basis in excess of its fair market value immediately before it was contributed to the partnership.[6] If the partnership sells capital loss property at a loss, Section 724(c) requires the built-in loss at the time of the contribution to retain its character as a capital loss for a period of five years from the date of the contribution. Any additional loss accruing while the property is held by the partnership is characterized at the partnership level.

A partnership might attempt to remove the taint inflicted by Section 724 by exchanging the contributed asset for other property in a nonrecognition transaction (e.g., a like-kind exchange). Section 724(d)(3) prevents this opportunity by making it clear that the Section 724 taint applies to any "substituted basis property"[7] resulting from such a transaction, whether held by the transferor-partnership or a transferee[8] unless that property is stock of a C corporation[9] acquired in an exchange governed by Section 351

2. I.R.C. §§ 724(d)(1); 751(c). For certain other purposes, "unrealized receivables" also include certain assets to the extent that their disposition at fair market value would result in recapture of depreciation. But the Section 751(c) definition of unrealized receivables does not include recapture income for purposes of Section 724. See I.R.C. § 751(c), last paragraph, which applies only to Sections 731 and 741.

3. It is not necessary for Section 724 to apply to recapture income because the lurking recapture gain on contributed property carries over to the partnership, which recognizes ordinary income to that extent on a subsequent disposition of the property. This is accomplished through the definitions of "recomputed basis," (I.R.C. § 1245(a)(2)) and "depreciation adjustments" (I.R.C. § 1250(b)(3)).

4. I.R.C. §§ 724(d)(2); 751(d). In determining whether an asset is Section 1231 property, the Section 1231(b) holding period requirement is disregarded. I.R.C. § 724(d)(2). The definitions of both unrealized receivables and inventory items are considered in more depth in connection with sales of partnership interests. See Chapter 6A, infra.

5. For purposes of measuring the five-year time period, the holding period of the partner does not tack.

6. I.R.C. § 724(c).

7. See I.R.C. § 7701(a)(42)–(44).

8. See Staff of the Joint Committee on Taxation, General Explanation of the Tax Reform Act of 1984 (hereinafter "1984 Act General Explanation"), 98th Cong., 2d Sess. 235 (1984).

9. A "C corporation" is any corporation which is not an "S corporation." See I.R.C. § 1361(a)(2) and Chapter 20, infra.

(relating to certain transfers of property to 80 percent or more controlled corporations). In the case of substituted basis property, the five-year taint period commences as of the date that the original property was contributed to the partnership.[10]

3. Depreciation of Contributed Property

Regulations: § 1.704–3(b)(1), (2) Examples 1(i) and 2; –3(c)(1)–(3), (4) Example 1; –3(d)(1)–(5), (7) Example 1.

Section 704(c)(1)(A) also applies to the allocation of depreciation, amortization, and depletion deductions with respect to contributed property. In the typical case where a partner contributes depreciable property with a tax basis that is less than the property's book value, a general goal of Section 704(c) is to ensure that the noncontributing partners are not deprived of their legitimate share of the partnership's tax depreciation. As with sales or exchanges, this policy (and students of partnership tax) can be frustrated by the ceiling rule.

Traditional Method. Under the traditional method, tax depreciation on contributed property is allocated first to the noncontributing partner in an amount equal to his share of book depreciation, and the balance of tax depreciation is allocated to the contributing partner.[1] Book and tax depreciation must be computed using the same depreciation method and recovery period.[2] To illustrate, assume that the AB partnership is formed by A contributing depreciable equipment with an adjusted basis of $12,000 and a fair market value of $20,000, and B contributing $20,000 cash. Assume that the equipment, which is 10–year property and depreciable under the straight line method, was purchased by A for $24,000 and has five years remaining on its recovery period.[3] The equipment is recorded on the books of the partnership at its $20,000 fair market value, and each partner has a $20,000 capital account,[4] but the partnership takes over A's $12,000 adjusted tax basis and remaining five-year recovery period.[5]

The partnership is entitled to $4,000 of book depreciation each year, allocated $2,000 each to A and B. Tax depreciation is $2,400 per year, of which $2,000 is allocated to B (the amount equal to his book depreciation) and the balance of $400 is allocated to A. Note that the tax depreciation is allocated so as to reduce to the extent possible the disparity between the

10. 1984 Act General Explanation, supra note 8, at 235.

1. Reg. § 1.704–3(b)(1) and –3(b)(2) Example 1(ii).

2. The Section 704(b) regulations require that book depreciation be an amount which bears the same relationship to the book value of the property as the tax depreciation bears to the adjusted basis of the property. This relationship can be maintained only if the book and tax depreciation are computed in similar fashion. Reg. § 1.704–1(b)(2)(iv)(*g*)(*3*). If the property has a zero adjusted basis, book depreciation may be determined under any reasonable method. Id.

3. The depreciation methods, which ignore the half-year convention prescribed by Section 168, are being made for convenience of illustration.

4. Reg. § 1.704–1(b)(2)(iv)(*b*)(*2*) & (*d*).

5. See I.R.C. § 168(i)(7); Prop.Reg. § 1.168–5(b).

partners' book and tax accounts. If the equipment is held for its entire remaining recovery period, the $8,000 built-in gain at the time of the contribution results in an $8,000 reduction of depreciation deductions for A. At the end of the recovery period, the tax and capital accounts are brought into balance:

	A		B	
	Tax	**Book**	**Tax**	**Book**
On Formation	$12,000	$20,000	$20,000	$20,000
Depreciation	(2,000)	(10,000)	(10,000)	(10,000)
Balance	$10,000	$10,000	$10,000	$10,000

Allocation of depreciation under Section 704(c)(1)(A) using the traditional method also can be affected by the ceiling rule. Assume that A contributes $20,000 of equipment with an adjusted basis of $8,000 and 5–year remaining recovery period, and B contributes $20,000 cash to the AB partnership. Because B's share of book depreciation is still $2,000, B should be allocated $2,000 of tax depreciation, but the ceiling rule limits the partnership's tax depreciation to $1,600 per year, all of which is allocated to B.[6] At the end of the first year, the book value of the equipment is $16,000 ($20,000 less the $4,000 book depreciation), its adjusted tax basis is $6,400 ($8,000 less the $1,600 tax depreciation), and A's built-in gain decreases from $12,000 to $9,600 ($16,000 book value less $6,400 tax basis).

If the partnership sells the equipment at the beginning of AB's second year for $16,000, the partnership realizes tax gain of $9,600 ($16,000 amount realized less $6,400 adjusted basis), but no book gain. Under the traditional method, the entire tax gain is allocated to A because the contributed equipment has that much built-in gain remaining. If the tax gain had exceeded the remaining built-in gain, the excess would be allocated equally to A and B under the partnership agreement. If the tax gain had been less than the remaining built-in gain (e.g., on sale for $14,000, yielding tax gain of only $7,600), the ceiling rule again would intervene by limiting the gain allocable to A to the partnership's tax gain.[7]

Traditional Method With Curative Allocations. In the example where A contributes equipment with an adjusted basis of $8,000, a fair market value of $20,000, and a 5–year remaining straight-line recovery period, the ceiling rule limited B's tax depreciation to $1,600 per year even though his book depreciation was $2,000. If the partnership elects the traditional method with curative allocations, it may make a curative allocation to B of up to $400 per year of tax depreciation from another partnership asset or allocate an extra $400 of ordinary income to A (and away from B) to correct the distortion.[8]

6. Reg. § 1.704–3(b)(3) Example 1(ii).

7. Reg. § 1.704–3(b)(2) Example 1(iii).

8. See Reg. § 1.704–3(c) especially—3(c)(4) Example 1(i) and (ii). Compare Reg. § 1.704–3(c)(4) Example 1(iii) involving an unreasonable curative allocation. The partners' shares of depreciation with respect to contributed property must be adjusted to account for any curative allocations. See Prop. Reg. § 1.1245–1(e)(2)(iii)(B). The adjust-

The Remedial Method. Under the remedial method, ceiling rule distortions from depreciation of contributed property are corrected by a tax allocation of additional depreciation to the noncontributing partner in an amount equal to the full amount of the limitation caused by the ceiling rule and a simultaneous offsetting allocation of ordinary income to the contributing partner.[9] The timing of the remedial allocations is the tricky part. For this purpose, the calculation of book depreciation differs from the method authorized by the Section 704(b) regulations and used for purposes of the traditional methods.[10] Under the remedial method, the portion of the partnership's book basis in contributed property that equals the tax basis of the property at the time of contribution is depreciated under the same method used for tax depreciation—generally over the property's remaining recovery period at the time of contribution. The amount by which the book basis exceeds the tax basis ("the excess book basis") is depreciated using any applicable recovery period and depreciation method available to the partnership for newly acquired property.[11]

Return one last time to the example where A contributes depreciable equipment with an adjusted basis of $8,000, a fair market value of $20,000, and five years remaining on its 10–year recovery period, and B contributes $20,000 cash. The partnership's tax depreciation is still $1,600 per year. Under the remedial method,[12] the partnership's book depreciation for the next five years consists of two components: $1,600 ($8,000 tax basis divided by remaining 5 years in recovery period) plus $1,200 ($12,000 excess of book value over tax basis divided by a new 10–year recovery period), or a total of $2,800 per year. Under the partnership agreement, A and B are each allocated $1,400 of the book depreciation, B is allocated $1,400 of tax depreciation, and A is allocated the remaining $200 of tax depreciation. No remedial allocations are made because the ceiling rule has not yet caused a book allocation of depreciation to the noncontributing partner that differs from the tax allocation. For years 6 through 10, however, the partnership has $1,200 of annual book depreciation ($12,000 excess book basis divided by new 10–year recovery period), allocated $600 each to A and B, but it has no more tax depreciation. Since B is allocated $600 of book depreciation but not tax depreciation, the partnership must make a remedial allocation of $600 of tax depreciation to B and an offsetting allocation of $600 of ordinary income to A for each of years 6 through 10. At the end of year 10, the partnership's tax and book accounts are as follows:

ments are important for allocations of Section 1245 recapture gain. See Section B2 of this chapter, supra.

9. Reg. § 1.704–3(d)(1). Once again, the partners' shares of depreciation with respect to contributed property must be adjusted to account for any remedial allocations. See Prop. Reg. § 1.1245–1(e)(2)(iii)(C).

10. See, e.g., Reg. § 1.704–1(b)(2)(iv)(*g*)(*3*) for the generally applicable rules for determining book depreciation.

11. Reg. § 1.704–3(d)(2).

12. See Reg. § 1.704–3(d)(7) Example 1.

	A		B	
	Tax	Book	Tax	Book
On Formation	$ 8,000	$20,000	$20,000	$20,000
Depreciation (Yrs. 1–5)	(1,000)	(7,000)	(7,000)	(7,000)
Depreciation (Yrs. 6–10)		(3,000)		(3,000)
Remedial Allocations	3,000		(3,000)	
Balance	$10,000	$10,000	$10,000	$10,000

4. OTHER APPLICATIONS OF SECTION 704(c) PRINCIPLES

Regulations: § 1.704–1(b)(4)(i),–1(b)(5) Examples (14)(i)–(iv).

A problem analogous to allocations with respect to contributed property may arise when a new partner is admitted to an existing partnership. The Section 704(b) regulations require application of "Section 704(c) principles" in those situations.[1]

For example, assume partners X and Y each contribute $10,000 cash to the XY partnership, which purchases $20,000 of securities with the contributed funds. Assume further that the XY partnership agreement requires proper maintenance of capital accounts, liquidation according to positive capital account balances and restoration of deficit capital account balances upon liquidation. Finally, assume that after the securities have appreciated in value to $30,000, new partner Z makes a $15,000 cash contribution in exchange for a one-third interest in the partnership. Section 704(c) does not directly apply here because there is no contribution of property to the partnership. But the Section 704(b) regulations require application of similar principles so that the $10,000 of gain attributable to the appreciation in the securities prior to Z's entering the firm will be taxed equally to partners X and Y.[2] Allocation of the built-in gain in this manner may be accomplished by a revaluation of the securities at the time of Z's admission to the partnership along with a corresponding upward adjustment to X and Y's capital accounts.[3] If such a revaluation is made, the rules of the regulations applicable to Section 704(c) property once again come into play[4] allowing the partnership to use any reasonable method of allocation.[5]

To illustrate, assuming the partnership uses the traditional method[6] and has no other assets, the securities would be restated at their $30,000

1. Reg. §§ 1.704–1(b)(4)(i),–1(b)(5) Examples (14)(i)–(iv) & (18)(ii)–(xiii).

2. See Reg. § 1.704–1(b)(5) Example (14)(i). For a similar but far more complex example involving depreciation, see Reg. § 1.704–1(b)(5) Example (18).

3. Reg. §§ 1.704–1(b)(2)(iv)(*f*); 1.704–1(b)(4)(i). The regulations permit a revaluation of partnership property in connection with: (1) contributions of money or property, (2) the liquidation of the partnership or a distribution of money or property to a partner, and (3) the grant of a partnership interest in exchange for services for the benefit of the partnership. Reg. § 1.704–1(b)(2)(iv)(*f*)(*5*).

4. Reg. § 1.704–3.

5. Reg. § 1.704–3(a)(6). Partnerships are generally not required to use the same allocation method for reverse Section 704(c) allocations as for Section 704(c) property or to use the same allocation method each time the partnership revalues its property. Id. However, each method used must be reasonable. Id. See Rev. Rul. 2004–49, 2004–1 C.B. 939 (discussing allocation of amortization with respect to a Section 197 intangible following a revaluation of an asset upon entry of a new partner).

6. Reg. § 1.704–3(b).

current value when Z joins the partnership, and each partner's capital account will be recorded at $15,000 to reflect their equal one-third interests. The "book" gain on any subsequent sale of the securities will be shared equally among the partners, and any difference between the book gain or loss and the tax gain or loss will be allocated only to X and Y. Thus, if the securities are later sold for $36,000, the $6,000 book gain is allocated $2,000 to each of the three partners for both book and tax purposes, and the remaining $10,000 of tax gain is equally divided between X and Y.[7]

The same result can be accomplished without a revaluation by a special allocation of the precontribution gain to X and Y under Section 704(b). Thus, if the securities are sold for $36,000, resulting in both a tax and book gain of $16,000, an allocation of the first $10,000 of gain to X and Y will have substantial economic effect.[8] But what if the partnership's assets are not revalued and the agreement lacks a special allocation of the built-in gain at the time of Z's admission, so that the $16,000 tax and book gain is allocated equally among the three partners? In that case, Z's capital account (and thus his entitlement in the event of a liquidation) is increased by $5,333 even though his share of appreciation is only $2,000, effectively shifting a portion of the tax gain and economic benefit of the prior appreciation from X and Y to Z. In this situation, the regulations warn that other tax consequences may arise from this capital shift, depending on its origins—e.g., the amount shifted may be treated as compensation or a gift to Z.[9]

5. Distributions of Contributed Property

Code: § 704(c)(1)(B). Skim § 737.

As originally enacted, Section 704(c) was limited to partnership sales of contributed property. As a result, a contributing partner could avoid an allocation of built-in gain or loss if the partnership distributed the contributed property to another partner rather than selling it. Since a partnership generally does not recognize gain or loss on a distribution of property,[1] the contributing partner was not taxed on the distribution, and any built-in gain was shifted to the distributee partner through a transferred basis mechanism.[2] Similarly, because a distribution of property can generally be made tax free to a contributing partner, a contributing partner also could

7. Reg. § 1.704–1(b)(5) Example (14)(i)–(ii). If the securities dropped in value after Z's admission to the partnership and are sold at less than book value but more than their tax basis, the book loss is allocated equally among the partners but the tax gain is shared by X and Y. This is another example of the ceiling rule, which results in Z bearing an economic loss without a corresponding tax loss, understates X and Y's tax gain and fails to cure disparities between the partners' tax and book accounts. See Reg. § 1.704–1(b)(5) Example (14)(iii). Cf. Reg. § 1.704–1(b)(5) Example (18)(vi).

8. Reg. § 1.704–1(b)(5) Example (14)(iv).

9. Reg. § 1.704–1(b)(5) Example (14)(iv). See Reg. § 1.704–1(b)(1)(iv).

1. I.R.C. § 731. See Chapters 7B & 7C, infra.

2. I.R.C. § 732. See Chapter 7B, infra.

postpone an allocation of built-in gain or loss but end up with substitute property if the partnership distributed property other than the contributed property to the contributing partner. Both of these strategies—commonly referred to as mixing bowl transactions—are now precluded by Section 704(c)(1)(B) and Section 737, respectively, if the transactions occur within seven years of the contribution of the property. Since mixing bowl transactions are interrelated with the operating distribution rules, in-depth consideration of those sections is deferred until Chapter 7.[3]

6. Anti-Abuse Rules for Loss Property

Code: § 704(c)(1)(C).

If a partner contributes property with a built-in loss to a partnership, that transaction may set the stage for shifting the loss to another partner or result in the partners benefiting more than once from the loss. Even though Section 704(c)(1)(A) requires precontribution loss to be allocated to the contributing partner, that provision has no effect if the contributing partner leaves the partnership. In fact, the regulations provide that if a partner transfers a partnership interest, built-in gain or loss must be allocated to the transferee partner as it would have been allocated to the transferor partner.[1] Thus, while Section 704(c)(1)(A) prevents the shift of a precontribution loss to the other partners, the current regulations *require* that a precontribution loss be shifted to a transferee of the contributing partner. Moreover, once you have mastered the intricacies of the Code provisions dealing with transfers of a partnership interest and partnership distributions,[2] you will discover that it was possible for a partner who contributed a built-in loss to a partnership, in effect to recognize the loss and also permit the remaining partners to employ the contributed property to defer their tax liability.[3]

Eventually, Congress decided to attack these tax avoidance strategies. Section 704(c)(1)(C) provides that if contributed property has a built-in loss (i.e., an excess of adjusted basis over fair market value at the time of the contribution) then (1) the built-in loss is to be taken into account only in determining the amount of items allocated to the contributing partner, and (2) in determining the amount of items allocated to other partners, the partnership's basis in the contributed property shall be treated as being the fair market value of the property at the time of contribution.[4] This rule will

3. See Chapter 7D, infra.

1. Reg. § 1.704–3(a)(7).

2. See Chapters 6, 7, 8, and 9, *infra*.

3. The basic strategy involved a transfer of a partnership interest or distribution where the partnership did not make a Section 754 election to reduce the inside basis of the partnership's property under Section 734 or Section 743. See generally, Chapters 6B and 7C, infra.

4. The regulations may provide exceptions to this rule. The legislative history indicates that an exception should be created for a corporation succeeding to the tax attributes of a corporate partner under Section 381. H. Rep. No. 108–548, 108th Cong., 2d Sess. 283 note 312 (2004).

prevent partners (even a transferee partner) from benefiting from a built-in loss in property contributed by another partner.[5]

PROBLEMS

1. A, B and C form an equal partnership. A contributes accounts receivable for services rendered (A.B.—$0, F.M.V.—$10,000); B, a real estate dealer, contributes lots held primarily for sale (A.B.—$5,000, F.M.V.—$10,000); and C, an investor, contributes land (A.B.—$20,000, F.M.V.—$10,000). Unless otherwise stated, the partnership is not a dealer in receivables or land, all contributed assets have been held long-term by the partners prior to contribution, and the traditional method of allocation is applied with respect to all contributed property. What tax results in the following alternative transactions:

(a) The partnership sells the receivables contributed by A for $10,000?

(b) The partnership sells the lots contributed by B for $10,600?

(c) The partnership sells the lots contributed by B for $9,100?

(d) Same as (c), above, except the partnership elects to use the remedial method of allocation.

(e) The partnership is a real estate dealer and sells the land contributed by C for $17,000?

(f) Same as (e), above, except the sale is for $7,000?

(g) Would the result in any of the above transactions change if all sales had occurred six years after the property was contributed?

2. A contributes $100,000 cash to the AB partnership and B contributes a building with an adjusted basis of $50,000 and a fair market value of $100,000. Unless otherwise stated, apply the traditional method with respect to all contributed property.

(a) If the building is depreciable, has a ten-year remaining recovery period and is depreciated under the straight-line method, how much tax and book depreciation will be allocated to each partner?

(b) Same as (a), above, except that B's basis in the building is $60,000?

(c) Same as (a), above, except that B's basis in the building is $40,000?

(d) Same as (a), above, except that B's basis in the building is $120,000?

(e) If in (a), above, the building is sold for $90,000 after it has been held (and depreciated) by the partnership for two years, how must the partnership allocate the tax gain on the sale?

(f) Same as (e), above, except the building is sold for $60,000?

5. Sections 734 and 743 were also modified to require a reduction in the inside basis of partnership property in certain situations. See I.R.C. §§ 734(b) & (d), 743(a) & (d). These provisions address situations that may not involve contributed property.

(g) What result in (c), above, if the recovery period for the building is 20 years and the partnership elects the remedial method of allocation?

3. A and B, both dealers in real estate, find a parcel of land to purchase for $100,000 as an investment. They believe it can be sold in two years for $200,000. They either will buy the land as tenants-in-common for $100,000 and jointly contribute it to a partnership or contribute $50,000 each to an equal partnership, which then will buy the land.

(a) How should they structure the transaction?

(b) Assume the AB partnership purchased the land for $100,000 in year one and it appreciated in value to $200,000 by the beginning of year three. At that point, C joins the partnership as an equal partner by contributing $100,000 cash to be used by the partnership to improve the land and sell it. The partners believe they can sell the land for $450,000. What results for tax and book purposes if the partnership sells the improved parcel of land for $450,000 and allocates the gain to reflect the appreciation at the time of C's entry into the partnership?

(c) What results to the partners under the facts of (b), above, if they elect to use a reverse § 704(c) allocation under Reg. § 1.704–1(b)(2)(iv)(*f*)(*5*) and they apply the traditional method of allocation.

(d) What results on a sale of land for $450,000 if the capital accounts of the partners are not adjusted when C joins the partnership and the agreement does not include any special allocation to reflect the built-in gain at the time C became a partner?

D. ALLOCATION OF PARTNERSHIP LIABILITIES

Code: §§ 704(c)(1)(A), 752(a)–(c).

Regulations: § 1.752–1, –2(a), (b), (c)(1), (f) Examples (1)–(5), (g)(1), (h), (j)(1), –3, –4(a), (b)(1), (c), (d).

1. INTRODUCTION

Background. We have seen that Section 704(d) limits the deductibility of a partner's share of partnership losses to the partner's outside basis in her partnership interest.[1] A partner's outside basis also measures the extent to which a cash distribution results in the recognition of gain or loss[2], as well as a partner's gain or loss on the sale of her partnership interest.[3] We also know that each partner's outside basis depends, in part, on her share of partnership liabilities.[4] It now is appropriate to explore in

1. See Chapter 3C1, supra.

2. See I.R.C. § 731; Chapters 7B1 & 8B1, infra.

3. See I.R.C. § 741; Chapter 6A, infra.

4. See I.R.C. § 752; Chapter 2B, supra.

greater detail the rules that govern the allocation of partnership liabilities among the partners.

Since the Code itself provides no guidance, the allocation question historically has been answered in regulations and rulings issued by the Treasury. Under the regulations, recourse liabilities generally are allocated in proportion to the partners' respective shares of partnership losses[5] on the theory that loss-sharing ratios are the best indication of which partners would be responsible for paying the liabilities if the partnership is unable to do so. Nonrecourse liabilities generally are allocated by reference to the partners' respective shares of partnership profits on the assumption that those debts will be paid, if at all, from profits or assets of the partnership.[6] These rules become more complex in the case of limited partners, who by definition are not liable for partnership losses beyond their original capital contribution and any additional contributions that they are required to make under the partnership agreement. Thus, while both general and limited partners share in partnership nonrecourse liabilities, limited partners generally are not allocated partnership recourse liabilities beyond the amounts they are obligated to contribute to the partnership or pay to the creditor in the future.[7]

A laudable feature of the Section 752 regulations is their relationship to the rules governing allocations of income and losses under Section 704(b) and the rule in Section 704(d) limiting a partner from deducting losses in excess of her outside basis. The regulations allocate recourse liabilities by using the same kind of economic risk of loss analysis that is employed in testing partnership allocations under Section 704(b);[8] and in generally allocating nonrecourse liabilities by reference to the partners' profit-sharing ratios, they take into account partnership minimum gain and Section 704(c) minimum gain.[9] Coordinating these rules makes sense because a principal reason for including liabilities in a partner's outside basis is to support the deductions claimed by the partner for items attributable to those liabilities. This natural synergy will become evident soon enough. For now, it is sufficient to observe that familiarity with the Section 704(b) regulations and the treatment of contributed property under Section 704(c)(1)(A) is essential to understanding the liability allocation rules. That is why detailed coverage of Section 752 has been deferred until this point.

Liability Defined. An obligation is a "liability" for Section 752 purposes if, when, and to the extent that incurring the obligation (1) creates or increases the basis of any of the obligor's assets (including cash), (2) gives rise to an immediate deduction to the obligor, or (3) gives rise to an expense that is not deductible in computing the obligor's taxable income and is not properly chargeable to capital.[10] Under this definition, a liability

5. Reg. § 1.752–2(a); Reg. § 1.752–1(e).

6. Reg. § 1.752–3(a)(3); Reg. § 1.752–1(e).

7. Reg. § 1.752–2(a), (b).

8. Reg. § 1.752–2(b).

9. Reg. § 1.752–3(a).

10. Reg. § 1.752–1–(a)(4).

of a cash method taxpayer that is deductible when paid is disregarded.[11] Certain contingent or contested liabilities or obligations that are devoid of economic reality also are disregarded.[12]

2. Recourse Liabilities

Economic Risk of Loss Concept. A partnership liability is a recourse liability only to the extent that a partner or any person related to a partner[1] bears the economic risk of loss with respect to that debt.[2] To the extent that no partner or related person bears the economic risk of loss, the liability is treated as nonrecourse.[3] Thus, the economic risk of loss concept is critical in classifying a liability as recourse or nonrecourse. In the case of recourse liabilities, the extent to which a partner bears the economic risk of loss also must be determined in order to allocate the debt.[4] In general, a partner bears the economic risk of loss for a partnership liability to the extent that he ultimately would be obligated to pay the debt if all partnership assets were worthless and all partnership liabilities were due and payable.[5] In determining the risk of loss, the regulations take into account not only each partner's obligations under the partnership agreement to pay the creditor or to contribute funds to the partnership, but also all other economic arrangements or legal obligations (such as guarantees, indemnification agreements, etc.) between partners and between any partners and the partnership's creditors.[6] As a result, funds borrowed on a nonrecourse basis but personally guaranteed by a partner who has no right of reimbursement from another partner, subject the guaranteeing partner to an economic risk of loss and are recourse liabilities under the regulations.[7] Similarly, nonrecourse liabilities for which a partner or related person has pledged his own property as security subject that partner to an economic risk of loss and are recourse liabilities to the extent of the value of the security.[8] Finally, nonrecourse loans from a partner to the partnership are

11. See e.g., Rev Rul. 88–77, 1988–2 C.B. 128.

12. See, e.g., Reg. § 1.752–2(b)(4) and Franklin v. Commissioner, 64 T.C. 752 (1975), affirmed, 544 F.2d 1045 (9th Cir. 1976).

1. Under the regulations, related persons are defined by reference to the relationships specified in Sections 267(b) and 707(b)(1), with some modifications. Reg. § 1.752–4(b)(1). It should be assumed that all references to a "partner" in the textual discussion of the economic risk of loss concept also encompass persons related to the partner.

2. Reg. § 1.752–1(a)(1).

3. Reg. § 1.752–1(a)(2).

4. Reg. § 1.752–2(b)–(j).

5. Reg. § 1.752–2(b)(1).

6. Reg. § 1.752–2(b)(3), (5).

7. Reg. § 1.752–2(b)(3)(i). Cf. Reg. § 1.752–2(f) Example 3. In addition, if one or more partners guarantee the payment of more than 25 percent of the total interest that accrues on an otherwise nonrecourse liability of the partnership, the loan is treated as recourse to the guaranteeing partners to the extent of the present value of the guaranteed future interest payments. Reg. §§ 1.752–2(e)(1); 1.752–2(f) Example 7. Under a safe harbor, this rule does not apply to a guarantee of interest for a period that does not exceed the lesser of five years or one-third of the term of the loan. Reg. § 1.752–2(e)(3).

8. Reg. § 1.752–2(h)(1).

treated as recourse liabilities because they expose the lending partner to an economic risk of loss.[9]

Constructive Liquidation. At the heart of the economic risk of loss analysis is the concept of a constructive liquidation of the partnership. Adopting a worst case scenario, the regulations assume that all of the partnership's liabilities become due and payable in full, any separate property pledged (directly or indirectly) by a partner to secure a partnership liability is transferred to the creditor in full or partial satisfaction of that liability,[10] and all the rest of the partnership's assets (including cash) become worthless.[11] The partnership is deemed to dispose of all of its now worthless assets in a taxable transaction for no consideration (other than the relief of any nonrecourse debt to which any asset is subject).[12] The gains and losses on these deemed dispositions, along with any actual income or loss items as of the date of the constructive liquidation, are then allocated among the partners in accordance with the partnership agreement; the partnership books and capital accounts are adjusted accordingly; and the partnership is deemed to liquidate.[13]

This doomsday scenario employed by the regulations assumes that a partner bears the economic risk of loss for the net amount that he must pay directly to creditors or contribute to the partnership at the time of the deemed liquidation. In determining a partner's payment obligation, the regulations take into account all the facts and circumstances, including contractual obligations outside the partnership agreement (such as guarantees, indemnities and reimbursement agreements running directly to creditors or to other partners, or to the partnership),[14] obligations imposed by the partnership agreement (such as obligations to make capital contributions and to restore a deficit capital account upon liquidation of the partnership),[15] obligations imposed by state law,[16] and the value of any property pledged (directly or indirectly) by the partner to secure any partnership liability.[17] The amount of a partner's gross payment obligation is reduced to the extent of any right to reimbursement, leaving the

9. Reg. § 1.752–2(c)(1). Under a de minimis rule, a partner who makes a nonrecourse loan to a partnership does not bear the economic risk of loss with respect to the loan if the partner owns a ten percent or less interest in each item of partnership income, gain, loss, deduction or credit, and the loan constitutes "qualified nonrecourse financing" as defined for purposes of the at-risk limitations. Reg. § 1.752–2(d)(1). See I.R.C. § 465(b)(6) and Section 3C2 of this chapter, supra.

10. Reg. § 1.752–2(h). Property is considered to be pledged indirectly the extent of the value of any property that the partner contributes to the partnership solely for the purpose of securing a partnership liability. Reg. § 1.752–2(h)(2).

11. Reg. § 1.752–2(b)(1)(i)–(ii).

12. Reg. § 1.752–2(b)(1)(iii). The exception for assets that secure nonrecourse liabilities is consistent with Commissioner v. Tufts, 461 U.S. 300, 103 S.Ct. 1826 (1983), rehearing denied, 463 U.S. 1215, 103 S.Ct. 3555 (1983).

13. Reg. § 1.752–2(b)(1)(iv), (v).

14. Reg. § 1.752–2(b)(3)(i).

15. Reg. § 1.752–2(b)(3)(ii).

16. Reg. § 1.752–2(b)(3)(iii).

17. The value of property pledged by a partner is deemed to be the value of the property at the time of the pledge. Reg. § 1.752–2(h)(3).

partner's *net* payment obligation as the ultimate measure of his potential economic risk of loss.[18] The regulations in essence seek to determine where the buck stops with respect to the responsibility for any recourse liability.

The regulations assume that recourse liabilities actually will be paid by the partners to the extent that they are personally obligated to do so even if the partner's net worth is less than the amount of the obligation, unless the facts and circumstances indicate a plan to circumvent or avoid the obligation.[19] In determining both the partner's payment obligations and rights to reimbursement, obligations that are subject to contingencies that make it unlikely that the obligation will ever be discharged are disregarded.[20] If an obligation need not be satisfied within a reasonable period of time, only its discounted present value is taken into account.[21]

Examples. The regulations elaborate on all these principles with several examples and, for the same reason, some examples are appropriate here. Assume that A and B are equal partners in the AB general partnership, which has an agreement that satisfies the primary test for economic effect ("The Big Three") in the Section 704(b) regulations.[22] Each partner contributes $20,000 cash, and the partnership purchases a building for $50,000, consisting of a $40,000 cash down payment and a $10,000 recourse note to the seller. In order to determine how the $10,000 liability is allocated between A and B, we must assume that the building becomes worthless and is sold for no consideration in a taxable transaction, the $10,000 debt is immediately due in full, and the partnership books are adjusted accordingly. On the sale of the worthless building, the partnership recognizes a $50,000 loss, which is allocated equally between A and B, reducing each partner's capital account by $25,000, to negative $5,000. The resulting balance sheet reveals that each partner must contribute $5,000 to the partnership to bring their respective capital accounts back to zero, and it is assumed that the partnership will use these contributions to pay off the debt. Based on these deficit restoration obligations, each partner bears a $5,000 payment obligation and thus a $5,000 economic risk of loss with respect to the liability.[23] If the partnership agreement had failed to satisfy The Big Three in these circumstances but A and B were equal general partners, each partner still would be allocated $5,000 of the liability, but their payment obligation would arise by operation of state law.[24]

The example provides a rather circuitous route to the general rule that where partners share partnership losses according to a fixed ratio (50:50 in the example) and their initial capital accounts reflect that same ratio, recourse debt will be allocated accordingly. But what if the loss sharing

18. Reg. § 1.752–2(b)(5).

19. Reg. § 1.752–2(b)(6); see Reg. § 1.752–2(j).

20. Reg. §§ 1.752–2(b)(4), –2(f) Example 8.

21. Reg. § 1.752–2(g). There is no discount if interest that equals or exceeds the Section 1274(d) "applicable federal rate" must be paid on the obligation. Reg. § 1.752–2(g)(2).

22. See Reg. § 1.704–1(b)(2)(ii)(*b*) and Section B2 of this chapter, supra.

23. Cf. Reg. § 1.752–2(f) Examples 1 and 2.

24. Reg. § 1.752–2(b)(3)(iii).

ratios do not match the ratios of the initial capital accounts? To illustrate, assume that the facts are the same as above except that losses are allocated 60 percent to A and 40 percent to B. In this situation the $50,000 loss on the deemed disposition is allocated $30,000 to A and $20,000 to B, causing A's capital account to be negative $10,000 and B's capital account to be zero. Because A would be required to contribute $10,000 to the partnership to bring his capital account to zero, A bears the economic risk of loss with respect to the liability.[25]

Now assume the same equal profit and loss sharing ratios as in the first example except that A's initial contribution and capital account was $30,000 and B's was $10,000. The constructive liquidation mandated by the regulations would generate the same $50,000 loss, allocated equally between A and B, and the allocation would reduce A's capital account to $5,000 and B's to negative $15,000. As a result, B would be required to make a contribution to the partnership of $15,000 in order to bring his capital account back to zero. Since two-thirds of this contribution would be used to pay the $10,000 partnership debt and one-third would be used to pay A his positive capital account balance on liquidation, B's payment obligation is $10,000. A has no payment obligation because his capital account is positive. Accordingly, the $10,000 liability is allocated entirely to B.[26]

The synergy between the Section 752 regulations and Section 704 should now be apparent. Although A and B divided losses equally, B began with a lower capital account and outside basis. Because B was ultimately responsible for paying the liability, the regulations consider him to be entitled to the extra basis provided by the partnership debt, which in turn supports his share of deductions under Section 704(d).

The analysis changes where at least one of the partners is a limited partner. Assume that A and B each contribute $20,000 to their equal partnership; that B is a limited partner who has no obligation to restore a capital account deficit; and the partnership agreement complies with the alternate test for economic effect.[27] As in the earlier example, the partnership purchases a $50,000 building, paying $40,000 cash and financing the $10,000 balance with a recourse note. Although losses are generally allocated equally between the two partners, only $20,000 of losses (the extent of B's initial capital account) can be allocated to B because more losses would result in an impermissible capital account deficit.[28] If the building were sold for nothing, generating a loss of $50,000, only $20,000 of that loss could be

25. Cf. Reg. § 1.752–2(f) Examples 1 and 2. If the partnership agreement did not include The Big Three, the allocation of the liability would depend on where the ultimate economic responsibility for the debt lies under state law. The result would be the same as described in the text if, taking the partnership agreement and applicable state law into account, A would be required to contribute $10,000 to the partnership upon liquidation. But if state law required A and B each to contribute $5,000 on the deemed liquidation, the liability would be allocated $5,000 to each partner.

26. Cf. Reg. § 1.752–2(f) Example 1.

27. See Reg. § 1.704–1(b)(2)(ii).

28. Reg. § 1.704–1(b)(2)(ii)(*d*)(3).

allocated to B and the remaining $30,000 loss would be allocated to A (the general partner with a deficit restoration obligation), bringing A's capital account to negative $10,000 and requiring A to make a contribution of $10,000 to the partnership on the constructive liquidation. This $10,000 would be used to pay the partnership liability. As a result, the $10,000 liability is allocated entirely to A, who bears the economic risk of loss.[29]

The preceding example illustrates the broader general rule that recourse debt is ordinarily allocated only among the general partners and not to any limited partners. The analysis changes to the extent that a limited partner contributes a promissory note to the partnership, pledges property as security, or is otherwise obligated to contribute additional unreimbursed amounts or make unreimbursed payments directly to the creditor. Assume, for example, that limited partner B contributes a $4,000 promissory note to the partnership.[30] The note does not increase B's capital account.[31] But since it represents an obligation to contribute an additional $4,000 to the partnership, B may be allocated losses that create a capital account deficit of up to $4,000.[32] On the constructive liquidation, $24,000 of the partnership's $50,000 loss can be allocated to B under Section 704(b), bringing B's capital account to negative $4,000, and B is obligated to contribute $4,000 to the partnership to pay off his note.[33] The remaining $26,000 of the partnership's loss on the deemed sale of the building must be allocated to A, giving A a capital account deficit and a payment obligation of $6,000. As a result, the $10,000 partnership liability is allocated $6,000 to A and $4,000 to B.

A final example applies the regulations to a guarantee of a nonrecourse loan by a general partner. Assume, as above, that B is a limited partner and A is the general partner in the AB partnership, and that A and B share income equally and share losses equally up to the point that B's capital account is reduced to zero. The partnership again purchases a $50,000 building, secured by a $10,000 debt that is nonrecourse as to the partnership but personally guaranteed by A. Under the now familiar doomsday liquidation scenario, the building becomes worthless and the $10,000 debt is fully due and payable. As guarantor, A is obligated to pay the debt, resulting in a $10,000 payment obligation if A has no right to reimbursement, directly or indirectly, from B.[34] A thus bears a $10,000 economic risk of loss, and the debt is treated as a recourse liability allocated entirely to A. The result would be the same if A did not personally guarantee the

29. Cf. Reg. § 1.752–2(f) Example 3. The result would be the same if A's obligation arose by operation of law.

30. Assume the note is due in the year the partnership liquidates so that discounting it to present value is not required. See Reg. § 1.752–2(g)(1)(i).

31. Reg. § 1.704–1(b)(2)(iv)(*d*)(*2*).

32. Reg. §§ 1.704–1(b)(2)(ii)(*c*)(*1*), (*d*).

33. See Reg. § 1.752–2(b)(3)(ii). Although the regulations disregard a partner's promissory note for certain other purposes unless they are readily tradeable on an established securities market (see Reg. § 1.752–2(g)(3), (h)(4)), a partner's promissory note to a partnership should be recognized as a payment obligation for purposes of the economic risk of loss test. See Reg. § 1.752–2(b)(3)(ii).

34. Cf. Reg. § 1.752–2(f) Example 3.

obligation but instead contributed property worth $10,000 to be used solely as security.[35]

If B rather than A had personally guaranteed the debt, the result would depend on whether or not B was entitled to reimbursement from the partnership for payments made to the creditor in satisfaction of the debt. If B were not entitled to reimbursement, he would have a $10,000 net payment obligation, and the debt would be allocated to him in its entirety. But if B were entitled to reimbursement from the partnership for payments made to the creditor, B's payment obligation would be zero ($10,000 payment obligation minus $10,000 reimbursement). The reimbursement would come from the $10,000 that A would be required to contribute as a result of operation of law or the partnership agreement.[36] Thus, A would have a $10,000 net contribution obligation, and the liability would be allocated entirely to A.[37]

3. Nonrecourse Liabilities

Overview. To the extent that no partner bears the economic risk of loss for a partnership liability, the liability is classified as nonrecourse.[1] Nonrecourse liabilities generally are allocated among the partners in accordance with their respective shares of partnership profits.[2] This general rule would suffice were it not for the complications resulting from special allocations, partnership minimum gain and Section 704(c) built-in gain.

To accommodate the more complex realities of modern partnerships, the regulations adopt a three-step approach under which a partner's share of nonrecourse liabilities is the sum of: (1) the partner's share of partnership minimum gain determined in accordance with the Section 704(b) regulations,[3] (2) in the case of nonrecourse liabilities secured by contributed property, the amount of gain that the partner would recognize under Section 704(c) if the partnership disposed of that property in a taxable transaction in full satisfaction of the liabilities and no other consideration;[4] and (3) the partner's share of any remaining ("excess") nonrecourse liabilities, determined in accordance with his share of partnership profits.[5] The third part of the formula, although labelled as the rule for "excess nonrecourse liabilities," actually governs the vast majority of situations and thus is the appropriate place to begin this discussion.

Partner's Share of Partnership Profits. The general rule for the allocation of nonrecourse liabilities is straightforward: nonrecourse liabilities are

35. Reg. § 1.752–2(h)(2).

36. A would be required to contribute $10,000 to make up the $10,000 capital account deficit that would result from the allocation to A of $30,000 of the partnership's $50,000 loss. B, as a limited partner, would have no such obligation.

37. See Reg. § 1.752–2(f) Example 3.

1. Reg. § 1.752–1(a)(2).

2. Reg. § 1.752–3(a)(3).

3. Reg. § 1.752–3(a)(1). See Reg. § 1.704–2(g)(1).

4. Reg. § 1.752–3(a)(2).

5. Reg. § 1.752–3(a)(3).

allocated in proportion to the partners' interests in partnership profits.[6] Absent any special allocations, nonrecourse liabilities simply are allocated in accordance with the partners' interests in the partnership. The possibilities expand considerably when the partnership agreement provides for special allocations of profits. For example, assume that A and B are equal partners, but their agreement includes allocations (that have substantial economic effect) of one significant profits item exclusively to A, and of another significant profits item exclusively to B. If the partnership purchases an asset subject to a nonrecourse liability, the regulations provide that any specification of the partners' interests in the partnership agreement will be respected for Section 752 purposes as long as it is reasonably consistent with an allocation (having substantial economic effect) of any significant item of partnership income or gain.[7] As a result, the AB partnership may allocate the nonrecourse liability exclusively to A, exclusively to B, or equally to A and B, merely by specifying "the partners' interests in partnership profits for Section 752 purposes" in the partnership agreement. Absent such a direction, the partners' interests in partnership profits are determined by taking into account all the facts and circumstances relating to the economic arrangement of the partners.[8]

The regulations also provide some alternative methods for allocating nonrecourse liabilities. Excess nonrecourse liabilities may be allocated in accordance with the manner in which it is reasonably expected that the deductions attributable to those liabilities will be allocated.[9] Additionally, in the case of contributed property subject to a nonrecourse liability, the partnership may first allocate an excess nonrecourse liability to the contributing partner to the extent that Section 704(c) gain on the property is greater than the gain resulting from the liability exceeding the basis of the property.[10] Finally, the regulations provide that the method selected for allocating excess nonrecourse liabilities may vary from year to year.[11]

Partners' Share of Partnership Minimum Gain. Where the partnership has generated minimum gain, the rule for allocation of nonrecourse liabilities directly follows the rule for allocation of the deductions and distributions attributable to those liabilities. The liabilities are first allocated in accordance with each partner's share of partnership minimum gain.[12] To illustrate, assume that A and B each contribute $500 cash to the AB equal partnership. The partnership purchases an asset worth $10,000 by paying $1,000 cash and taking the asset subject to a $9,000 nonrecourse liability payable in full after five years. Assume further that there is a valid special

6. Id.

7. Id.

8. Id.

9. Id. See Reg. § 1.752–3(b) Example 2.

10. Id. If the entire amount of the excess nonrecourse liability is not allocated to the contributing partner, the remaining amount must be allocated under one of the other methods. This allocation method is also available in the case of property for which reverse Section 704(c) allocations are applicable under Reg. § 1.704–3(a)(6)(i), but it does not apply for purposes of Reg. § 1.707–5(a)(2)(ii) (disguised sales of property). Id.

11. Id.

12. Reg. § 1.752–3(a)(1). See Reg. § 1.704–2(g)(1).

allocation of all depreciation, income, gain or loss with respect to this asset to A for the first four years,[13] followed by an equal split over the remaining life of the asset. The asset is depreciable on a straight-line basis at the rate of $500 per year. For the first two years, the partnership has no minimum gain, and the liability is allocated between A and B according to their overall interests in partnership profits, or as otherwise specified in the partnership agreement provided that agreed allocation is either reasonably consistent with: (1) some other valid allocation of a significant item of partnership income or gain, or (2) the manner in which it is reasonably expected that the deductions attributable to those nonrecourse liabilities will be allocated.[14] If we assume that the partnership agreement provides for an equal division of profits for Section 752 purposes, the liability will be allocated equally, increasing each partner's outside basis by $4,500 to $5,000.

At the end of year three, with the basis of the asset reduced to $8,500 and the liability remaining at $9,000, there is $500 of partnership minimum gain. Since all of the nonrecourse deductions that gave rise to the partnership minimum gain are allocated to A,[15] there also must be a minimum gain chargeback to A. And since A's share of partnership minimum gain is now $500, $500 of the partnership nonrecourse liability must be allocated to A.[16] The remainder of the nonrecourse liability continues to be allocated in the same proportion as it was during the first two years. As a result, the nonrecourse liability allocated to A at the end of year three will be equal to A's $500 share of partnership minimum gain plus half of the remaining $8,500, for a total of $4,750. The balance (i.e., half of $8,500, or $4,250) is allocated to B. To ensure that A has enough outside basis to be able to use the $500 nonrecourse deduction allocated to him, the basis increase attributable to the allocation of the nonrecourse liability should be deemed to occur immediately before the allocation to A of the nonrecourse deductions which caused the increase in minimum gain. This rule reflects the fact that one of the principal purposes for including partnership liabilities in the partners' outside bases is to support the deductions that will be claimed by the partners for items attributable to those liabilities.[17]

13. See Reg. § 1.704–2(e).

14. See supra notes 6–9 and accompanying text.

15. See Section B3 of this chapter, supra.

16. Reg. § 1.752–3(a)(1).

17. See Reg. § 1.752–3(b) Example 1. The allocation guarantees that A's outside basis is increased just when A is likely to need additional outside basis to take the deductions allocated to him. Each year that more nonrecourse deductions and minimum gain is allocated to A, more of the partnership's nonrecourse liability (and a corresponding amount of outside basis) also is allocated to A and away from B. A possibly disruptive side effect of this approach is that each partner's outside basis must be recalculated each year that partnership minimum gain is generated. If the partnership wishes to avoid this annual shifting of the liability allocation, it may elect to initially allocate the nonrecourse liability according to the manner in which it expects that the deductions attributable to that liability will be allocated—i.e., $5,500 ($2,000 plus $3,500) to A and $3,500 to B.

The minimum gain allocation rule also applies where the minimum gain is triggered by a distribution of the proceeds of a nonrecourse loan. In that event, the distributee partner, to whom the minimum gain is allocated under the Section 704(b) regulations, is the partner to whom the nonrecourse liability that generates the minimum gain will be allocated. To return to the example, assume that the AB partnership borrows another $10,000 on a nonrecourse basis secured by the asset at the end of year two (when the asset's basis was $9,000 and the asset was already encumbered by a $9,000 nonrecourse liability) and immediately distributes the loan proceeds to B. Under the Section 704(b) and Section 752 regulations, the $10,000 of partnership minimum gain generated by the borrowing is allocated to B,[18] and the $10,000 liability also is allocated to B. To ensure that the distribution of the loan proceeds does not result in the recognition of gain to B (as it would if B's outside basis were below $10,000 at the time of the cash distribution), the increase in basis that results from the allocation of partnership nonrecourse liabilities should occur before the decrease in basis from the distribution.

Partners' Shares of Section 704(c) Gain. When property contributed to a partnership is subject to a nonrecourse liability in excess of its adjusted basis, the property has a built-in gain (equal to the excess of liabilities over basis) similar to partnership minimum gain. Under the regulations, however, the built-in gain is not partnership minimum gain under Section 704(b) but instead is potential Section 704(c) gain.[19] The regulations provide that, to the extent of the minimum Section 704(c) gain, the nonrecourse liability secured by the contributed property is allocated to the same partner to whom this minimum built-in gain is allocated under Section 704(c).[20]

For example, assume that A and B form the equal AB partnership with A contributing $1,000 cash, and B contributing property with a value of $3,500, a basis of $1,000 and subject to a nonrecourse debt of $2,500. Also, assume A and B agree they will use the traditional method to allocate Section 704(c) gain.[21] Since a disposition of B's property for no consider-

18. Reg. § 1.704–2(h).

19. There is partnership minimum gain only to the extent that a nonrecourse liability to which an asset is subject exceeds the book value of the asset. Reg. § 1.704–2(d)(3). Under the regulations, contributed property is entered on the partnership's books at its fair market value at the time of the contribution. Reg. § 1.704–1(b)(2)(iv)(*d*)(*1*). As a result, there is no partnership minimum gain at the time of the contribution.

20. Reg. § 1.752–3(a)(2). If a partnership holds multiple properties subject to a single nonrecourse liability, it may allocate the liability among those properties under any reasonable method, and then the portion of the liability allocated to each property is treated as a separate loan for purposes of determining the minimum built-in gain in the property. Reg. § 1.752–3(b)(1). An allocation method is not reasonable if it allocates an amount of liability that, when combined with other liabilities allocated to the property, is in excess of the property's fair market value. The method of allocating a single nonrecourse liability can not be changed. But if a property becomes no longer subject to the liability, the portion of the liability allocated to that property must be reallocated to the other properties. Id. Principal payments on the liability are allocated among the multiple properties in the same proportion that the liability was allocated. Reg. § 1.752–3(b)(2).

21. Alternatively, the partnership could use the traditional method with curative allocations or the remedial method. If the tradiation other than debt relief would generate $1,500 of gain under Section 704(c), $1,500 of the nonrecourse liability is allocated to B. The remaining $1,000 of the nonrecourse liability could be allocated between A and B in accordance with their interests in partnership profits—in this case $500 to each.[22] In these circumstances, B is relieved of $2,500 of debt but also is allocated $2,000 of the partnership's liability. The regulations allow these amounts to be netted, resulting in a net decrease in B's liabilities of $500.[23] A's share of partnership liabilities is $500.

Finally, there may be a minimum amount of gain built into an asset (as a result of nonrecourse liabilities in excess of basis) which is neither minimum gain nor Section 704(c) gain. For example,[24] when a new partner joins an ongoing partnership, the book value of partnership assets may be restated to reflect their current fair market value.[25] Thus, if the XY partnership has a building with a basis of zero and a value of $10,000 when Z becomes a partner, the building may be revalued on the partnership books at $10,000.[26] If the partnership later borrows $5,000 on a nonrecourse basis secured by the building, the partnership will have no minimum gain because the debt will not exceed the building's *book* value even though the debt exceeds the tax basis of the building by $5,000. This built-in minimum amount of gain is treated the same as Section 704(c) gain under the regulations.[27] Thus, X and Y are each allocated $2,500 of the Section 704(c)-type gain which would result if there were a sale of the property, and each is also allocated $2,500 of the $5,000 nonrecourse liability.[28]

Part–Recourse, Part–Nonrecourse Liabilities. The rules for allocating part-recourse, part-nonrecourse liabilities are straightforward. After properly bifurcating the debt, the recourse portion is allocated under the rules for recourse liabilities, and the nonrecourse portion is allocated separately under the rules for nonrecourse liabilities.[29]

To illustrate, assume that G and L form a limited partnership in which G is the general partner and L is the limited partner. Each partner contributes $20,000 and the partners agree to share profits and losses

tional method with curative allocations is selected, the Service takes the position that curative allocations are disregarded for Section 752 purposes because those allocations cannot be determined solely from the hypothetical sale of the contributed property. Thus, there would be no difference between the traditional method and traditional method with curative allocations. See Rev. Rul. 95–41, 1995–1 C.B. 132.

22. The regulations also would permit the partnership to allocate all $1,000 of the remaining excess nonrecourse liability to B because there is an additional $1,000 of Section 704(c) gain in the property. Reg. § 1.752–3(a)(3).

23. Reg. § 1.752–1(f).

24. See Section C4 of this chapter, supra.

25. Reg. § 1.704–1(b)(2)(iv)(*f*).

26. Id.

27. Reg. § 1.752–3(a)(2). See Reg. § 1.704–1(b)(2)(iv)(*f*)(*4*).

28. If the partnership does not revalue its assets when Z becomes a partner, the regulations require that Section 704(c) principles must nonetheless be applied in order to reach the same result. Reg. § 1.704–1(b)(2)(iv)(*f*) (flush language).

29. Reg. § 1.752–1(i). See also Rev.Rul. 84–118, 1984–2 C.B. 120, where the Service took the same position prior to the proposed Section 752 regulations.

equally, except that L is not liable for losses beyond his original contribution. GL purchases a building worth $40,000, paying $5,000 down and taking the building subject to a $35,000 nonrecourse liability. G personally guarantees $15,000 of the partnership liability, and G is not entitled to reimbursement from the partnership for any part of this amount. With respect to the $15,000 of the liability which G has personally guaranteed, G will be required to pay $15,000 to the creditor if the partnership's assets are worthless. As a result, G bears the economic risk of loss with respect to $15,000 of the partnership liability. To that extent, the liability is a recourse liability and is allocated to G.[30]

With respect to the remaining $20,000, the creditor will bear the economic risk of loss if all partnership assets become worthless. As a result, the liability is a nonrecourse liability which is allocated between G and L in proportion to their equal shares of partnership profits.[31]

4. TIERED PARTNERSHIPS

The regulations provide special rules for allocation of liabilities of tiered partnerships. To illustrate, assume that A and B form the AB general partnership and agree to share profits and losses equally. A and B each contribute $5,000 to AB, which has no liabilities, and AB then contributes $10,000 cash to the ABCDEF general partnership in exchange for a one-third interest in partnership profits and losses. ABCDEF borrows $120,000 on a nonrecourse basis in order to purchase land. AB's basis in its ABCDEF partnership interest equals its $10,000 cash contribution plus its one-third share of partnership debt ($40,000), for a total outside basis of $50,000. The regulations provide that the liabilities of a subsidiary partnership that are properly allocated to an upper-tier ("parent") partnership are treated as liabilities of the upper-tier partnership for purposes of again applying Section 752 to the partners of the parent.[1] As a result, AB's $40,000 share of ABCDEF's liability is reallocated $20,000 each to A and B, increasing each partner's outside basis by $20,000 to $25,000.

PROBLEMS

1. A, B and C each contribute $20,000 to form the ABC general partnership. The partnership agreement satisfies the primary test for economic effect under Section 704(b). Partnership profits and losses are allocated 40% to A, 40% to B and 20% to C. The partnership uses its $60,000 cash and borrows an additional $40,000 on a recourse basis and purchases land for $100,000.

(a) How will the $40,000 liability be allocated and what will be each partner's outside basis?

30. See Reg. § 1.752–2(f) Example 5.

31. Id.

1. Reg. § 1.752–4(a). See also Reg. § 1.752–2(i). This result is consistent with the law prior to the proposed regulations. See Rev.Rul. 77–309, 1977–2 C.B. 216.

(b) What result in (a), above, if A, B and C had contributed $10,000, $20,000 and $30,000, respectively, to the ABC partnership?

(c) What result in (a), above, if A and B are limited partners who are not obligated to restore a capital account deficit but the partnership agreement includes a qualified income offset?

(d) What result in (c), above, if A contributes $15,000 of stock to the partnership as security for the liability and all income, gain or loss on the stock is allocated to A? What result if A contributes his $15,000 note as security for the liability?

(e) What result in (c), above, if A personally guarantees the $40,000 liability?

2. G and L form a limited partnership. G, the general partner, contributes $10,000 and L, the limited partner, contributes $90,000. The partnership purchases a building on leased land, paying $100,000 cash and borrowing $900,000 on a nonrecourse basis from a commercial lender, securing the loan with a mortgage on the building. The terms of the loan require the payment of market rate interest and no principal for the first ten years. Assume for convenience that the building is depreciable at the rate of $50,000 per year for twenty years, and that other partnership income equals expenses for the years in question. The partnership agreement contains a qualified income offset, and G is required to make up any capital account deficit. Except as otherwise required by a minimum gain chargeback provision, the agreement allocates profit and loss 90% to L and 10% to G until such time as the partnership recognizes items of income and gain that exceed the items of deduction and loss that is has recognized over its life. Subsequent partnership income and losses are allocated equally between G and L. Assume that it is reasonably anticipated that the equal allocation will begin after ten years. The partnership agreement states that G and L each has a 50% interest in partnership profits for purposes of § 752.

(a) How is the $900,000 liability allocated in year one?

(b) How will the liability be allocated at the end of year three?

(c) How will the liability be allocated at the end of years one and three if excess nonrecourse liabilities are allocated in a ratio of 90% to L and 10% to G?

(d) What result in (a), above, if the debt is guaranteed by G, who has no right to reimbursement from the partnership? Does the result change if G has a right to reimbursement from the partnership? What if G has a gross assets of only $6,000?

(e) What result in (a), above, if the debt is guaranteed by L, and L has a right to reimbursement from the partnership?

(f) What result in (a), above, if G is the lender?

3. The equal AB partnership's only asset is Building #1, which has a fair market value of $800,000 and an adjusted basis of $300,000. C becomes a one-third partner by contributing Building #2 with a fair market value of

$700,000 and an adjusted basis of $150,000 and which is subject to a $300,000 recourse liability which the partnership assumes. At the time of C's contribution, the partnership revalues its assets under Reg. § 1.704–1(b)(2)(iv)(*f*).

(a) How is the $300,000 liability allocated?

(b) What result in (a), above, if the liability is a nonrecourse debt secured by Building #2 and the partners agree to use the traditional method to allocate § 704(c) gain?

(c) If C, instead of contributing Building #2, contributes $400,000 cash and shortly thereafter the partnership incurs a $500,000 nonrecourse loan secured by Building #1, how is the $500,000 liability allocated?

E. ALLOCATIONS WHERE PARTNERS' INTERESTS VARY DURING THE YEAR

Code: § 706(c)(2)(B) & (d).

Regulations: § 1.706–1(c)(4).

We have assumed up to now that the interests of all the partners in the partnership are the same throughout the partnership's taxable year. But if a partner sells part of his interest during the year, or if the proportionate interests of the partners change as a result of the entry of a new partner, a capital contribution by an existing partner, a partial liquidation, a gift, or for some other reason, a method must be found to determine each partner's respective share of income, losses, deductions and other partnership items.

Section 706(c)(2)(B) initially provides that if a partner disposes of less than his entire partnership interest, the partnership taxable year will not close with respect to that partner.[1] When partners' interests change during a taxable year, however, Section 706(d)(1) provides that each partner's distributive share of partnership income or loss is determined by taking into account the partners' varying interests in the partnership during the year. In general, this means that if A is a one-third partner in the ABC Partnership for the first half of the year and a one-quarter partner for the balance, A generally must be allocated one-third of each partnership item for the first six months and one-quarter of those items for the second half of the year.[2] These rules are intended to preclude a partner who acquires

1. The partnership year will close, however, with respect to a partner whose entire interest in the partnership terminates (whether by reason of death, liquidation, or otherwise). I.R.C. § 706(c)(2)(A). See Chapters 6A & 8A, infra.

2. Of course, if the partnership agreement contains a special allocation that is valid under Section 704(b), the partners do not have to be allocated amounts corresponding exactly to their percentage interests in the partnership. See Section B2 of this chapter, supra. But an allocation that passes muster under Section 704(b) may be reallocated under Section 706(d) and related assignment of income principles in appropriate cases. See infra note 8.

his interest toward the end of the year from receiving the benefits of a retroactive allocation of deductions and losses incurred prior to his admission to the partnership.[3]

When the interests of partners change during the year, a partnership may use either of two methods to determine the distributive shares of the partners: (1) the "interim closing of the books" method, or (2) the "proration" method.[4] The interim closing method traces income and deduction items to the particular segment of the taxable year during which they are paid or incurred. Thus, a one-third partner admitted to a calendar year partnership on December 1 would be allocated only his one-third share of items paid or incurred during December. The proration method is simpler but more arbitrary. Partnership items are prorated throughout the year, and a partner's share is based on the number of days during which he was a partner. Applying the proration method to the above example, the new one-third partner admitted on December 1 would be allocated $\frac{1}{12}$ of his hypothetical one-third share of partnership items for the entire taxable year regardless of when those expenses were paid or incurred.

In response to attempts by partnerships to circumvent these general rules, Congress enacted a complex set of anti-avoidance provisions designed to prevent retroactive allocations by cash method partnerships and tiered partnership arrangements. A typical target of the reforms was the taxpayer who joined a cash method partnership toward the end of the year and sought to deduct expenses incurred prior to her admission to the firm. To illustrate, assume that B becomes a 10 percent partner in Loss Associates, a calendar year partnership, on December 1, and that Loss has a $120,000 net loss which has accrued ratably through the year. Since B has been a 10 percent partner for one-twelfth of the year, she should be entitled to deduct 10 percent of the loss accruing during her one month as a partner, or a total of $1,000 ($120,000 × $\frac{1}{12}$ × $\frac{1}{10}$). If B wished to deduct more than $1,000, and the other partners were agreeable, the partnership might allocate to B 10 percent of its losses for the entire year, including the eleven months when she was not a partner. Because Section 706 prevented such a straightforward approach, resourceful tax advisors concocted more creative techniques to achieve the effect of a retroactive allocation without

3. See generally Staff of the Joint Committee on Taxation, General Explanation of Tax Reform Act of 1976, 94th Cong., 2d Sess. 91–94 (1976). Section 761(c), however, defines a "partnership agreement" to include any modifications made prior to the due date for filing the partnership return and, under Section 704(a), a partner's distributive share is determined by the partnership agreement. This suggests that retroactive allocations may be permissible through an amendment to the agreement. This result clearly was not intended (cf. I.R.C. § 761(f)), but the legislative history of the Tax Reform Act of 1984 makes it clear that Section 761(c) still permits retroactive modifications to a partnership agreement that result in shifts of interests among partners who are members of the partnership for the entire taxable year, provided those shifts are not attributable to additional capital contributions. See Staff of the Joint Committee on Taxation, General Explanation of the Revenue Provisions of the Deficit Reduction Act of 1984 (hereinafter "1984 Act General Explanation"), 98th Cong., 2d Sess. 219 (1984). See Lipke v. Commissioner, 81 T.C. 689 (1983).

4. See 1984 Act General Explanation, supra note 3, at 217. Cf. Reg. § 1.706–1(c)(2)(ii).

its appearance. For example, with careful advance planning and an eye toward attracting year-end investors craving tax losses, Loss Associates, as a cash method taxpayer, could adopt the interim closing of the books method of allocation and simply defer payment of its deductible expenses until late in the year. In that event, even if the last minute investors were allocated only the losses incurred during the time they were partners, their allocable share would be disproportionately large in the typical case where the expenses economically accrued before the new investors became partners.[5]

To curtail this technique, Section 706(d)(2)(A) requires cash method partnerships[6] to allocate certain specified cash basis items to the time during the taxable year that these items are economically attributable, regardless of when they are paid. At the expense of simplicity, this provision puts cash basis partnerships on an accrual basis with respect to the specified items for purposes of determining distributive shares when the interests of the partners vary during the year. For this purpose, "allocable cash basis items"[7] are defined as interest, taxes, payments for services or for the use of property, and any other items specified by the Service.[8] Thus, in the example above, even if the partnership did not pay the expenses giving rise to the $120,000 loss until after B became a partner,

5. Prior to the enactment of Section 706(d) in the Tax Reform Act of 1984, these techniques met with mixed success. Compare Richardson v. Commissioner, 76 T.C. 512 (1981), affirmed on other issues, 693 F.2d 1189 (5th Cir.1982) (retroactive allocation upheld where payment of deductible items by cash method partnership occurred after taxpayer's admission to the partnership and interim closing of books method used) with Williams v. United States, 680 F.2d 382 (5th Cir.1982) (similar retroactive allocation rejected in an accrual method partnership).

6. Because this avoidance technique was not available to accrual method partnerships, Congress singled out cash method partnerships for special scrutiny. Section 706(d)(2), however, applies whether the interim closing or the proration method is used. If the partnership's "planning" involved only a single year, as in the example in the text, the rule could be further limited to partnerships using the interim closing method because the proration method would result in an automatic accrual of the items. But if the planning extended over more than a single year (see the discussion of Section 706(d)(2)(C) below), an anti-avoidance rule is needed under both the interim and proration methods. The statute is thus not limited to interim closings.

7. Although Congress seemingly intended to single out *deductible* cash basis items, the statutory language seems broad enough to embrace cash method income items as well. Thus, Section 706(d)(2) might be applied to require cash method partnerships to allocate prepaid income items (e.g., interest or rent) to those who were partners at the time the item was accrued regardless of when the income was received. The relationship of Section 706(d)(2) to income items is unclear and raises enough troublesome issues to suggest that Congress should have explicitly limited application of that section to the deduction setting. See McKee, Nelson & Whitmire, Federal Taxation of Partnerships and Partners ¶ 12.03[3] (4th ed. 2007).

8. I.R.C. § 706(d)(2)(B). Because Section 706(d) would be ineffective if it could be overridden by a special allocation of the relevant cash basis items under Section 704, the regulations provide that an allocation valid under Section 704(b) nonetheless is subject to reallocation under Section 706(d). Reg. § 1.704–1(b)(1)(iii). Cf. Hawkins v. Commissioner, 713 F.2d 347 (8th Cir.1983) and Prop. Reg. § 1.168–2(k), both holding that depreciation accrues on a pro rata basis throughout the year.

Section 706(d)(2) would limit B's allowable loss to $1,000 if the postponed expense was an allocable cash basis item (e.g., a rent payment).[9]

The workings of Section 706(d)(2) become more complex if the partnership pays a deductible expense in a year other than that to which the item is economically attributable. A partnership using the cash method generally may deduct an expense[10] in the year of payment. Because the deduction is ultimately passed through to the partners, it must flow to those persons who are partners in the year that the expense is deductible to the partnership. If the identity or proportionate interests of the partners in the year of payment (and, correspondingly, the year of deduction) are not identical to those that exist in the year of accrual, the deductions cannot simply be allocated according to the partners' proportionate interests at the time of accrual. Instead, they somehow must be allocated to those who are partners in the year in which the payments are deductible under the cash method.

To alleviate these problems, Section 706(d)(2)(C) provides that any allocable cash basis item which is attributable to a period before or after the year of the payment is to be assigned entirely to the first day of the year (if the payment is attributable to a prior year)[11] or entirely to the final day of the year (if the payment is attributable to a future year).[12] In addition, if the payment is attributable to a prior year and is a deductible item, the payment will be allocated to those who were partners at the time the deduction accrued in proportion to their interests at that time.[13] To the extent that some or all of the deduction would be allocable to persons who are no longer partners at the time the expense becomes deductible, that part of the payment cannot be deducted but instead must be capitalized[14] and added to the basis of partnership assets.[15]

To illustrate what is going on here, assume the equal cash method ABC partnership incurs deductible interest expense of $12,000 in year one which it fails to pay until year two. Assume further that on December 31 of year one, the partnership liquidates partner A's one-third interest, and partner B buys half of one-third partner C's interest so that on January 1 of year two B owns a 75 percent interest in the partnership and C owns a 25 percent interest. Under Sections 706(d)(2)(C)(i) and (D), the $12,000 inter-

9. In addition, the General Explanation of the Tax Reform Act of 1984 allows the Service to promulgate regulations which adopt conventions for determining the date of the month that a partnership interest change is deemed to occur. Use of such conventions is not permitted when the occurrence of a significant discrete event (e.g., an extraordinary gain or loss) results in significant tax avoidance. See 1984 Act General Explanation, supra note 3, at 221–222.

10. But see infra note 12.

11. I.R.C. § 706(d)(2)(C)(i).

12. I.R.C. § 706(d)(2)(C)(ii). This is a rare occurrence in light of current requirements of capitalization for most prepaid expenses. See Reg. § 1.263–4; compare Commissioner v. Boylston Market Ass'n, 131 F.2d 966 (1st Cir.1942), with Zaninovich v. Commissioner, 616 F.2d 429 (9th Cir.1980). See also I.R.C. § 461(i).

13. I.R.C. § 706(d)(2)(D)(i).

14. I.R.C. § 706(d)(2)(D)(ii).

15. See I.R.C. § 755; Chapter 6B, infra.

est payment made in year two is allocated $4,000 to both B and C.[16] A cannot deduct his $4,000 share of the expense because he is no longer a partner. Instead, that $4,000 must be capitalized, added to the basis of partnership assets and allocated among them according to their relative appreciation under the principles of Section 755.[17]

Tiered partnerships also have been used to avoid the prohibition against retroactive allocations. To illustrate, assume that Loss Associates ("Loss") expects to have substantial tax losses during the year and it wishes to make those losses available to Nupartner, who will not enter the firm until just before the close of the year. The rules of Section 706(d) described above are generally adequate to prevent the parties from fulfilling their objectives. But if the promoters of Loss form new Upper Partnership ("Upper"), which in turn becomes a 95 percent partner in Loss, it may be possible to avoid Section 706(d). If both partnerships use calendar years, 95 percent of Loss's loss for the year will flow through to Upper on December 31 of Loss's taxable year. If Nupartner becomes a 50 percent partner in Upper on December 29, she will be a partner as of the time that Upper's share of Loss's loss passes through, so that a full one-half of that loss could be allocated to her if the interim closing method is used. Section 706(d)(3)[18] prohibits such arrangements by treating Upper (the "upper tier partnership")[19] as if it accrued each item of income or loss that flows through to it from Loss on the day that the item was actually accrued by Loss (the "lower tier partnership").[20] Of course, this type of allocation is necessary, and Section 706(d)(3) is applicable, only if there is a change in the proportionate ownership of the upper tier partnership during the year.

PROBLEMS

1. The ABC partnership has three partners, A, B, and C, who each has an equal interest in partnership capital, profits, and losses. To pay off losses incurred by the partnership, C contributed additional capital on October 31 of the current year. As a result of C's contribution, the partners' interests in partnership capital, profits, and losses changed to 25% for A, 25% for B, and 50% for C. The partnership is an accrual method, calendar year taxpayer.

16. I.R.C. § 706(d)(2)(D)(i).

17. See Chapter 6B, infra.

18. Section 706(d)(3) essentially codifies the Service's prior position in Rev.Rul. 77–311, 1977–2 C.B. 218.

19. Note that Section 706(d)(3) appropriately applies regardless of whether Upper is a cash or accrual method partnership.

20. The 1984 Act General Explanation, supra note 3, at 221, explains this provision as follows:

Effectively, under this rule, the existence of the tiered partnership arrangement is ignored for allocation purposes and the items of the lower-tier partnership "flow through" to the partners in the upper-tier partnership in accordance with their effective interests in the lower tier partnership as of the close of each day.

(a) If the partnership loses $24,000 in the current year and the partners use the proration method of allocation, how will the losses be allocated?

(b) What results if the facts are the same as in (a), above, except that the entire $24,000 loss was incurred during the first half of the year but the expenses that created that loss were paid on November 15 with cash contributed to the partnership by C, all other income and deductions of the partnership accrued ratably throughout the year, and the partnership uses the interim closing of the books method of allocation?

(c) Assume the facts are the same as in (a), above, except that the partnership is a cash method taxpayer, the partnership uses the interim closing of the books method of allocation, and all income and deduction items, other than the $24,000 loss, were received or incurred ratably throughout the year. What result if:

(i) The loss is the result of payment on November 15 of $24,000 to rent an office for the entire year?

(ii) The partnership breaks even for the year, but the loss is the result of a settlement of a breach of contract suit brought by Plaintiff. Settlement is made on June 1 and payment is made on November 15?

(iii) The loss in (i), above, is the result of the payment on March 1 of the current year of $24,000 rent past due from the previous year?

2. The AB partnership is a 75% partner in the ABC partnership, in which C owns the other 25%. Both partnerships use the calendar year as their taxable year. The ABC partnership has a tax loss of $16,000 for the year. D becomes a one-third partner in the AB partnership (with A and B owning the other two-thirds equally) on December 1 by making a cash contribution on that date. How will the ABC loss be allocated if the AB (now ABD) partnership uses the proration method? The interim closing method (assuming all income and deductions other than the $16,000 loss accrued ratably throughout the year)?

F. THE FAMILY PARTNERSHIP RULES

Code: § 704(e).

Regulations: § 1.704–1(e)(1) & (3)(i)(b). Skim § 1.704–1(e)(2) & (3).

Section 704(e) governs what are commonly referred to as family partnerships. Although family limited partnerships have become a popular estate planning technique and raise many challenging wealth transfer tax issues, this discussion is limited to income tax rules that codify familiar assignment of income principles. Section 704(e)(1) utilizes those principles to determine whether a person will be recognized as a partner in a partnership and Section 704(e)(2) applies the same principles to ascertain whether the income generated by a donated partnership interest is being taxed to the appropriate partner. For the most part, the application of these sections is straightforward but inevitably there may be some surprises.

Section 704(e)(1). To put Section 704(e)(1) into its proper perspective, we must glance backward at its historical development. In 1946, the Supreme Court held in two cases that a partnership would be recognized as such for federal tax purposes if the parties had a bona fide intent to create a partnership.[1] The Court added that if a party provided either "original capital" or "vital services" to the partnership, that fact would be indicative of an intent to become a member of a partnership. In the succeeding few years, the Tax Court misinterpreted the Supreme Court's message by *requiring* "original capital" or "vital services" in order to form a valid partnership.[2] As a result, the Supreme Court again discussed the issue in the *Culbertson* case,[3] where it redelivered its message:[4]

> * * * We turn next to a consideration of the Tax Court's approach to the family partnership problem. It treated as essential to membership in a family partnership for tax purposes the contribution of either "vital services" or "original capital". Use of these "tests" of partnership indicates, at best, an error in emphasis. It ignores what we said is the ultimate question for decision, namely, "whether the partnership is real within the meaning of the federal revenue laws" and makes decisive what we described as "circumstances [to be taken] into consideration" in making that determination.
>
> The *Tower* case thus provides no support for such an approach. We there said that the question whether the family partnership is real for income-tax purposes depends upon
>
>> "whether the partners really and truly intended to join together for the purpose of carrying on business and sharing in the profits or losses or both. And their intention in this respect is a question of fact, to be determined from testimony disclosed by their 'agreement, considered as a whole, and by their conduct in execution of its provisions.' Drennen v. London Assurance Corp., 113 U.S. 51, 56, 5 S.Ct. 341 [343] 344; Cox v. Hickman, 8 H.L.Cas. 268. We see no reason why this general rule should not apply in tax cases where the Government challenges the existence of a partnership for tax purposes." 327 U.S. at page 287, 66 S.Ct. at page 536.

1. Commissioner v. Tower, 327 U.S. 280, 66 S.Ct. 532 (1946); Lusthaus v. Commissioner, 327 U.S. 293, 66 S.Ct. 539 (1946).

2. Scherf v. Commissioner, 7 T.C. 346 (1946), affirmed, 161 F.2d 495 (5th Cir.1947), cert. denied, 332 U.S. 810, 68 S.Ct. 111 (1947); Monroe v. Commissioner, 7 T.C. 278 (1946).

3. Commissioner v. Culbertson, 337 U.S. 733, 69 S.Ct. 1210 (1949).

4. 337 U.S. at 741, 69 S.Ct. at 1213. (Footnotes omitted.)

The question is not whether the services or capital contributed by a partner are of sufficient importance to meet some objective standard supposedly established by the *Tower* case, but whether, considering all the facts—the agreement, the conduct of the parties in execution of its provisions, their statements, the testimony of disinterested persons, the relationship of the parties, their respective abilities and capital contributions, the actual control of income and the purposes for which it is used, and any other facts throwing light on their true intent—the parties in good faith and acting with a business purpose intended to join together in the present conduct of the enterprise. There is nothing new or particularly difficult about such a test. Triers of fact are constantly called upon to determine the intent with which a person acted. The Tax Court, for example, must make such a determination in every estate tax case in which it is contended that a transfer was made in contemplation of death, for "The question, necessarily, is as to the state of mind of the donor." United States v. Wells, 283 U.S. 102, 117, 51 S.Ct. 446, 451 (1931). See Allen v. Trust Co. of Georgia, 326 U.S. 630, 66 S.Ct. 389 (1946). Whether the parties really intended to carry on business as partners is not, we think, any more difficult of determination or the manifestations of such intent any less perceptible than is ordinarily true of inquiries into the subjective.

But the Tax Court did not view the question as one concerning the bona fide intent of the parties to join together as partners. Not once in its opinion is there even an oblique reference to any lack of intent on the part of respondent and his sons to combine their capital and services "for the purpose of carrying on the business." Instead, the court, focusing entirely upon concepts of "vital services" and "original capital," simply decided that the alleged partners had not satisfied those tests when the facts were compared with those in the *Tower* case. The court's opinion is replete with such statements as "we discern nothing constituting what we think is a requisite contribution to a real partnership," "we find no son adding 'vital additional service' which would take the place of capital contributed because of formation of a partnership," and "the sons made no capital contribution, within the sense of the *Tower* case." 6 CCH TCM 698, 699.

Unquestionably a court's determination that the services contributed by a partner are not "vital" and that he has not participated in "management and control of the business" or contributed "original capital" has the effect of placing a heavy burden on the taxpayer to show the bona fide intent of the parties to join together as partners. But such a determination is not conclusive, and that is the vice in the "tests" adopted by the Tax Court. It assumes that there is no room for an honest difference of opinion as to whether the services or capital furnished by the alleged partner are of sufficient importance to justify his inclusion in the partnership. If, upon a consideration of all the facts, it is found that the partners joined together in good faith to conduct a business having agreed that the services or capital to be contributed presently by each is of such value to the partnership that the contributor should participate in the distribution of profits, that is sufficient. The *Tower* case did not purport to authorize the Tax Court to substitute its judgment for that of the parties; it simply furnished some guides to the determination of their true intent. Even though it was admitted in the *Tower* case that the wife contributed no original capital, management of the business, or other vital services, this Court did not say as a matter of law that there was no valid partnership. We said, instead, that "There was, thus, more than ample evidence to support the Tax Court's finding that no genuine union for partnership business purposes *was ever intended* and that the husband earned the income." 327 U.S. at page 292, 66 S.Ct. at page 538. (Italics added.)

Third. The Tax Court's isolation of "original capital" as an essential of membership in a family partnership also indicates an erroneous reading of the *Tower* opinion. We did not say that the donee of an intra-family gift could never become a partner through investment of the capital in the family partnership, any more than we said that all family trusts are invalid for tax purposes in Helvering v. Clifford, supra. The facts may indicate, on the contrary, that the amount thus contributed and the income therefrom should be considered the property of the donee for tax, as well as general law, purposes. In the *Tower* and *Lusthaus* cases this Court, applying the principles of Lucas v. Earl, supra; Helvering v. Clifford, supra; and Helvering v. Horst, 311 U.S. 112, 61 S.Ct. 144, found that the purported gift, whether or not technically complete, had made no substantial change in the economic relation of members of the family to the income. In each case the husband continued to manage and control the business as before, and income from the property given to the wife and invested by her in the partnership continued to be used in the business or expended for family purposes. We characterized the results of the transactions entered into between husband and wife as "a mere paper reallocation of income among the family members," noting that "The actualities of their relation to the income did not change." [327 U.S. at 292, 66 S.Ct. at 538.] This, we thought, provided ample grounds for the finding that no true partnership was intended; that the husband was still the true earner of the income.

But application of the *Clifford–Horst* principle does not follow automatically upon a gift to a member of one's family, followed by its investment in the family partnership. It if did, it would be necessary to define "family" and to set precise limits of membership therein. We have not done so for the obvious reason that existence of the family relationship does not create a status which itself determines tax questions, but is simply a warning that things may not be what they seem. It is frequently stated that transactions between members of a family will be carefully scrutinized. But, more particularly, the family relationship often makes it possible for one to shift tax incidence by surface changes of ownership without disturbing in the least his dominion and control over the subject of the gift or the purposes for which the income from the property is used. He is able, in other words, to retain "the substance of full enjoyment of all the rights which previously he had in the property." Helvering v. Clifford, supra [at 336.] * * *

The fact that transfers to members of the family group may be mere camouflage does not, however, mean that they invariably are. The *Tower* case recognized that one's participation in control and management of the business is a circumstance indicating an intent to be a bona fide partner despite the fact that the capital contributed originated elsewhere in the family. If the donee of property who then invests it in the family partnership exercises dominion and control over that property—and through that control influences the conduct of the partnership and the disposition of its income—he may well be a true partner. Whether he is free to, and does, enjoy the fruits of the partnership is strongly indicative of the reality of his participation in the enterprise. In the *Tower* and *Lusthaus* cases we distinguished between active participation in the affairs of the business by a donee of a share in the partnership on the one hand, and his passive acquiescence to the will of the donor on the other. This distinction is of obvious importance to a determination of the true intent of the parties. It is meaningless if "original capital" is an essential test of membership in a family partnership.

The cause must therefore be remanded to the Tax Court for a decision as to which, if any, of respondent's sons were partners with him in the operation of the ranch during 1940 and 1941. As to which of them, in other words, was there a bona fide intent that they be partners in the conduct of the cattle business, either because of services to be performed during those years, or because of contributions of capital of which they were the true owners, as we have defined that term in the *Clifford, Horst*, and *Tower* cases? No question as to the allocation of income between capital and services is presented in this case, and we intimate no opinion on that subject.

In 1951 Congress enacted Section 704(e)(1), which provides statutory guidance to validating a partnership.[5] Nevertheless, this statutory provision is not exclusive and the *Culbertson* case may still come to a taxpayer's assistance if the requirements of Section 704(e)(1) are not satisfied.

5. See generally Banoff, Long, Steele & Smith, "Family Partnerships: Capital as a Material Income–Producing Factor," 37 Tax Lawyer 275 (1984).

Section 704(e)(2). This subsection attempts to guarantee that income generated by a family partnership is not assigned among the partners. It requires that the donor partner's services be adequately compensated and that the rate of return on the donee's capital not exceed the rate of return on the donor's capital. The section applies to all gift situations (not just family gifts) and to any interest in a partnership acquired from a "family" member by purchase.[6] Similar to Section 704(e)(1), Section 704(e)(2) is not exclusive and general assignment of income principles may apply to reallocate income.[7]

PROBLEMS

1. Section 704(e)(1) recognizes a partner if he "owns a capital interest in a partnership in which capital is a material income-producing factor." Consider whether the statutory requirement is satisfied in the following situations:

(a) Father is a lawyer who makes Son (a contractor) and Daughter (a student) partners in his sole practitioner law firm.

(b) Father is a lawyer who makes Daughter (a law-school graduate who has recently passed the bar) a partner in his sole practitioner law firm.

(c) Father owns a building subject to a 10 year lease and he transfers the building along with the lease to a partnership with Son and Daughter.

(d) Father transfers just the lease in part (c), above, to the partnership.

(e) Same as part (c), above, except Father retains the right in any year to allocate the income to any of the partners and to give the building to Mother.

2. Father owns a group of commercial rental properties which he transfers to a partnership with Son and Daughter, who provide no consideration for their ⅓ interest in the partnership. The income from the partnership is $90,000.

(a) What result if Father renders services worth $30,000 to the partnership but the partnership agreement merely calls for splitting the income ⅓ each and each partner actually receives $30,000?

(b) What result if Father renders no services but the agreement provides the income is to be divided 20% to Father and 40% to Son and Daughter?

(c) What result if Father renders services worth $30,000 and the agreement is the same as in part (b), above?

6. Section 704(e)(3) defines "family" to include one's spouse, ancestors, lineal descendants and any trusts for the primary benefit of such persons.

7. See Reg. § 1.704–1(e)(3)(i)(*b*); Woodbury v. Commissioner, 49 T.C. 180 (1967).

(d) What result if Son renders services worth $30,000 and the agreement is the same as in part (a), above? See Reg. § 1.704–1(e)(3)(i)(b).

(e) What results in parts (a)–(d), above, if Son and Daughter purchased their ⅓ interests from Father for fair market value?

3. The AB cash method, calendar year partnership is owned equally by unrelated partners A and B. During the current year, the partnership has $40,000 of net ordinary income after deductions and $20,000 of long-term capital gains. The partnership agrees to compensate B with 10% of its profits each year for his ongoing services in managing the partnership's operations. On July 1, B gives one-half of his interest in the partnership to his son, S, together with the right to all of B's non-services income from the partnership for the entire year. However, B retains the right to all of his one-half share of the partnership's depreciation deductions. Assume that the requirements of § 704(e)(1) are met and that all of the partnership's special allocations are reflected in capital accounts and satisfy the substantial economic effect standard in the § 704(b) regulations. Discuss B and S's income from the partnership for the current year as well as the allocation of the depreciation to B.

CHAPTER 5

TRANSACTIONS BETWEEN PARTNERS AND PARTNERSHIPS

A. PAYMENTS FOR SERVICES AND THE USE OF PROPERTY

1. INTRODUCTION

Code: Skim § 707(a)(1) & (c).

Regulations: § 1.707–1(a) & (c) (omit the examples).

Up to now, we have been examining how partners are taxed by focusing exclusively on their "distributive shares" of partnership income and deductions, as determined by the partnership agreement[1] and subject to the limitations of Sections 704(b), 704(c) and 706(d). Distributive shares represent the partners' annual return on their interests in the partnership and generally are based on their contributed capital and the services they may render in their capacities as partners. But partners can wear many different hats when they engage in business dealings with their partnerships. Consider, for example, Realtor, who is the general partner in a limited partnership organized to acquire and lease an apartment building. If Realtor also is a mortgage broker who helps arrange financing for the project and is paid a $50,000 fee by the partnership for his services, he may be acting other than in his capacity as a partner. To what extent should the nature of his relationship affect the tax consequences of this transaction to Realtor and the partnership? Should his fee simply be part of his distributive share (an aggregate approach), or should the transaction be treated as if it occurred between the partnership and an unrelated third party (an entity approach)?

Suppose that Realtor also performs ongoing management services for the partnership. The partnership might offer to compensate Realtor with an allocation of the first $100,000 of partnership income, leaving any remaining income or loss to be divided as agreed by all of the partners. But Realtor understandably may balk at a salary that is dependent on partnership profits, demanding instead a fixed annual fee of $100,000, payable up-front, without regard to the income of the partnership. As a general partner with day-to-day management responsibilities, Realtor likely is acting in either case as a partner, not a stranger, and even his guaranteed fee more closely resembles a distributive share than a salary paid to an

1. I.R.C. § 704(a).

unrelated third party. Once again, the questions are how and when should Realtor be taxed and how should that treatment affect the partnership.

Sorting out the tax consequences of payments by a partnership for services rendered by partners and a number of other partner-partnership transactions[2] has presented Congress and the courts with a conceptual challenge and offers students of Subchapter K yet another opportunity to witness the tension between the aggregate and entity theories of partnership taxation. Prior to 1954, the cases were in conflict, with a minority of courts applying an entity theory in the interests of simplicity and a majority opting for an aggregate approach.[3] In enacting the 1954 Code, Congress veered toward the entity approach by dividing partner-partnership transactions for services and the use of property into the following three broad categories:

(1) transactions between a partnership and a partner who is not acting in his capacity as a partner—treated by Section 707(a)(1) for all purposes as transactions between the partnership and an unrelated third party;

(2) "guaranteed payments"—i.e., payments to a partner in his partner capacity for services or for the use of capital, if determined without regard to the income of the partnership—treated by Section 707(c) for some purposes as payments of compensation or interest to an unrelated third party but for other purposes (principally timing) as a distributive share; and

(3) any other payments to partners in their capacity as such—e.g., payments for services rendered as a partner which are based on a percentage of partnership profits—which fall outside the ambit of Section 707 and thus are treated as part of a partner's distributive share and, when paid to the partner, are governed by the distribution rules of Section 731.[4]

Over the years, Congress has buttressed this statutory structure with rules to prevent partners from exploiting the flexibility of the partnership form by engaging in maneuvers to defer income, accelerate deductions, convert the character of income and losses and the like.[5] These anti-abuse provisions add to the challenge of planning transactions between a partnership and its partners.

2. Some other examples are sales and exchanges, loans and leases.

3. Compare Wegener v. Commissioner, 119 F.2d 49 (5th Cir.1941), cert. denied, 314 U.S. 643, 62 S.Ct. 84 (1941) (entity approach) with Lloyd v. Commissioner, 15 B.T.A. 82 (1929) (aggregate approach). Advocates of the aggregate approach rejected the entity theory on the ground that partners could not engage in transactions (even in part) with themselves. Those courts thus treated salaries to partners as distributive shares, an approach that engendered confusion when the salaries exceeded the income of the partnership. See, e.g., Appeal of Estate of Tilton, 8 B.T.A. 914 (1927).

4. See Chapter 7, infra.

5. See, e.g., I.R.C. § 707(a)(2)(A).

2. PARTNER ACTING IN NONPARTNER CAPACITY

Code: §§ 267(a)(2), (e)(1) & (2); 707(a)(1).

Pratt v. Commissioner

United States Tax Court, 1975.
64 T.C. 203, affirmed in part, reversed in part 550 F.2d 1023 (5th Cir.1977).

■ SCOTT, JUDGE:

[The taxpayers were general partners of two limited partnerships formed to develop and operate a shopping center. Under the partnership agreements, they were paid management fees based on a percentage of gross rentals. The Tax Court found that the fees were reasonable in amount and comparable to fees that would have been paid if an unrelated party had been employed to manage the shopping center. The partners were cash method taxpayers, but the partnership used the accrual method. The fees were accrued and deducted by the partnership but they were not actually paid to the partners during the taxable years in controversy. The issue was the proper tax classification of the fees. The parties' tax agenda was deferral—i.e., the partnership was attempting to claim a current business expense deduction when the fees were accrued but the cash method general partners wished to defer reporting the fees in income until they were received. The Service contended that the fees were for services performed as partners and thus were properly included in the partners' distributive share of partnership income. In rejecting the taxpayers' argument that they received their fees in a nonpartner capacity, the Tax Court discussed the types of transactions that are encompassed by Section 707(a)(1). Ed.]

Section 1.707–1(a) of the Income Tax Regulations with respect to a "partner not acting in capacity as partner" states that "In all cases, the substance of the transaction will govern rather than its form." Here, the record indicates that in managing the partnership petitioners were acting in their capacity as partners. They were performing basic duties of the partnership business pursuant to the partnership agreement. Although we have been unable to find cases arising under the 1954 Code concerning when a partner is acting within his capacity as such, a few cases arising under the provisions of the 1939 Code dealt with whether a payment to a partner should be considered as paid to him in a capacity other than as a partner. See Leif J. Sverdrup, 14 T.C. 859, 866 (1950); Wegener v. Commissioner, 119 F.2d 49 (5th Cir.1941), affg. 41 B.T.A. 857 (1940), cert. denied 314 U.S. 643 (1941). In *Wegener*, a joint venture was treated as a partnership for limited purposes, and the taxpayer-partner was found to be acting outside the scope of his partnership duties and in an individual capacity as an oil well drilling contractor, so that payments he received from the "partnership" for carrying out this separate and distinct activity were income to him individually as if he were an outsider. In the *Sverdrup* case, we recognized a payment to a taxpayer by a joint venture between a partnership of which the taxpayer was a member and a third party as compensation for work done on contracts being performed by the joint venture since "This sum was not a part of the income of the partnership of which he was a member, but was paid to him as an individual for services rendered to the joint venture."

Petitioners in this case were to receive the management fees for performing services within the normal scope of their duties as general partners and pursuant to the partnership agreement. There is no indication that any one of the petitioners was engaged in a transaction with the partnership other than in his capacity as a partner. * * *

Armstrong v. Phinney

United States Court of Appeals, Fifth Circuit, 1968.
394 F.2d 661.

■ DYER, CIRCUIT JUDGE.

Appealing from an adverse judgment in the court below, taxpayer, Tobin Armstrong, presents a novel question for our determination: Under the Internal Revenue Code of 1954 is it legally possible for a partner to be an employee of his partnership for purposes of section 119 of the Code? In granting the government's motion for summary judgment, the District Court answered this question in the negative. We disagree and reverse.

Taxpayer is the manager of the 50,000 acre Armstrong ranch located in Armstrong, Texas. Beef cattle are raised and some of the land contains certain mineral deposits. The ranch is owned by a partnership in which taxpayer has a five percent interest. In addition to his share of the partnership profits and a fixed salary for his services as manager of the ranch, the partnership provides taxpayer certain other emoluments which are the subject of this controversy. The partnership provides a home at the ranch for taxpayer and his family, most of the groceries, utilities and insurance for the house, maid service and provides for the entertainment of business guests at the ranch. Taxpayer did not include the value of these emoluments in his gross income for the years 1960, 1961 or 1962. The Internal Revenue Service determined that these items should have been included and therefore increased his taxable income by approximately $6,000 for each year involved. Taxpayer paid the assessed deficiencies, filed a refund claim, and no action having been taken thereon within the requisite period taxpayer brought this suit seeking to recover the paid deficiencies on the ground that he is an employee of the ranch and that, as such, he comes within the provisions of section 119 of the Internal Revenue Code of 1954 and is therefore entitled to exclude the value of the items in question from his gross income. Taxpayer filed an affidavit in support of his allegations and his deposition was taken. Each side moved for a summary judgment. The court granted the government's motion without an opinion and this appeal ensued.

The case law interpreting the 1939 Internal Revenue Code held that a partner could not be an employee of his partnership under any circumstances, and that therefore no partner could take advantage of the "living expense" exclusion promulgated in the regulations and rulings under the 1939 Code. Commissioner of Internal Revenue v. Robinson, 3 Cir.1959, 273 F.2d 503, 84 A.L.R.2d 1211; United States v. Briggs, 10 Cir.1956, 238 F.2d 53; Commissioner of Internal Revenue v. Moran, 8 Cir.1956, 236 F.2d 595; Commissioner of Internal Revenue v. Doak, 4 Cir.1956, 234 F.2d 704. The earlier cases, *Doak* and *Moran*, followed with little discussion by the later cases, were grounded on the theory, present throughout the 1939 Code, that a partnership and its partners are one inseparable legal unit. However, in 1954 Congress rejected this "aggregate theory" in favor of the "entity theory" in cases where "a partner sells property to, or performs services for the partnership." H.R.Rep. No. 1337, 83d Cong., 2d Sess. 67 (1954), U.S.Code Cong. & Admin.News 1954, pp. 4025, 4093. Under the entity approach "the transaction is to be treated in the same manner as though the partner were an outsider dealing with the partnership." Id. This solution to the problem of the characterization of a partner's dealings with his partnership was codified as section 707(a) of the 1954 Code, 26 U.S.C.A. § 707(a).

Considering the legislative history and the language of the statute itself, it was manifestly the intention of Congress to provide that in any situation not covered by section 707(b)–(c), where a partner sells to or purchases from the partnership or renders services to the partnership and is not acting in his capacity as a partner, he is considered to be "an outsider" or "one who is not a partner." The terms "outsider" and "one who is not a partner" are not defined by Congress; neither is the relationship between section 707 and other sections of the Code explained. However, we have found nothing to indicate that Congress intended that this section is not to relate to section 119. Consequently, it is now possible for a partner to stand in any one of a number of relationships with his partnership, including those of creditor-debtor, vendor-vendee, *and* employee-employer. Therefore, in this case the government is not entitled to a judgment as a matter of law.

Our reversal of the District Court is not dispositive of the issues upon which rest taxpayers ultimate right of recovery. On the record before us we cannot resolve these issues, nor do we express any opinion on the final outcome of the case. Among the questions which must be answered are whether taxpayer is, in fact, an employee of the partnership; whether meals and lodging are provided for the convenience of the employer; whether living at the ranch is a condition of taxpayer's employment; whether taxpayer's wife and children are also employees and, if not, how much of the $6,000 must be allocated to their meals and lodging. These questions are not meant to be exhaustive, but are merely intended to give an indication of the nature of the inquiry into the merits which must be held on remand.

Reversed and remanded.

NOTE

The questionable holding in Armstrong v. Phinney suggests that, at least for purposes of Section 119, it is possible for partners to render services to their partnerships in an employee capacity.[1] It is more common for partners who render services to partnerships in a nonpartner capacity under Section 707(a)(1) to do so as independent contractors. Similarly, partners may loan money or lease property to their partnerships in a nonpartner capacity in exchange for payments of interest or rent. In adopting an entity approach, Section 707(a)(1) encompasses not only these types of outbound payments by partnerships to partners but also inbound payments by partners to partnerships for services, or for the use of property or money.[2]

There is a dearth of authority on the question of when a partner is or is not acting in his capacity as such. In *Pratt*, the Tax Court held that a partner is acting as a partner when he performs services that are ongoing and integral to the business of the partnership.[3] Nonpartner status is more likely to exist when a partner is acting in an independent capacity, rendering services of a limited technical nature (e.g., a partner who also is an accountant prepares the partnership's tax returns) or in connection with a specific transaction. The only example of a Section 707(a)(1) transaction in the regulations involves the use by a partnership of a partner's separately owned property to obtain credit or as collateral for a partnership loan.[4] In all other cases, the regulations merely admonish that "the substance of the transaction will govern rather than its form."[5]

Does it make any difference if a payment is classified under Section 707(a)(1) or if it is treated as a distributive share? In the rare case where a partner performing services in a nonpartner capacity is able to attain employee status, exclusions from gross income for certain employee benefits may be available under Code sections outside of Subchapter K.[6] More importantly, the timing and character of the partner's and the partner-

1. But see Wilson v. United States, 376 F.2d 280 (Ct.Cl.1967), which reached a different conclusion. See also Rev. Rul. 69–184, 1969–1 C.B. 256 (partner may render services to partnership either as a partner or an independent contractor but not as an employee).

2. Section 707(a)(1) also applies to sales of property between partners and partnerships. Sales are covered in Section B of this chapter, infra.

3. Compare Wegener v. Commissioner, 119 F.2d 49 (5th Cir.1941), affirming 41 B.T.A. 857 (1940), cert. denied, 314 U.S. 643, 62 S.Ct. 84 (1941). See also Rev. Rul. 81–301, 1981–2 C.B. 144, where a partner was determined to be providing investment advisor services in a nonpartner capacity.

4. Reg. § 1.707–1(a).

5. Id. Cf. I.R.C. § 707(a)(2)(A), which codifies the substance over form approach in the case of certain payments for property or services that are disguised as allocations coupled with distributions. See Section A3 of this chapter, infra.

6. For example, in addition to the Section 119 meals and lodging exclusion addressed in Armstrong v. Phinney, employee status may entitle a partner to receive excludable group life insurance. See I.R.C. §§ 79(a). In the more common situation where partners are not treated as employees, they may be deemed to have employee status for purposes of some excludable fringe benefits. See, e.g., I.R.C. § 401(c)(1) (qualified retirement plans); Reg. § 1.132–1(b)(1) (no additional cost service fringe benefit).

ship's income or losses may be affected. The character of items that are classified as a distributive share is determined at the partnership level[7] and those items pass through to the partners in the year in which the partnership's taxable year ends.[8] In contrast, if Section 707(a)(1) applies, the partner and the partnership generally determine their character and timing consequences as if they were dealing as unrelated parties. Thus, Section 707(a)(1) payments for services or for the use of property or money are always ordinary income to the recipient and are taxed according to the recipient's method of accounting—when received or accrued, depending on whether the recipient is a cash or accrual method taxpayer. The payor ordinarily may deduct such payments as a business expense in accordance with its method of accounting subject to the capitalization requirement of Section 263.[9]

In some cases, these technical differences between Section 707(a)(1) payments and distributive shares are inconsequential. To illustrate, assume that A, B and C, all accrual method taxpayers, are equal partners in an accrual method partnership that has $10,000 of net operating income (all ordinary income) for the year. A allows the partnership to use some of her personally owned property and, in return, the partners agree to allocate $2,500 of partnership income to A and allocate any remaining net income equally among all three partners. If the $2,500 allocated to A (whether or not currently paid) is part of A's distributive share, the taxable income of the partnership is $10,000, allocated $5,000 to A and $2,500 each to B and C. But if A in substance is leasing her property in a nonpartner capacity and the $2,500 is thus a Section 707(a)(1) rent payment, the partnership's taxable income is only $7,500 ($10,000 minus $2,500 rent paid to A), of which $2,500 will be allocated to each partner, and A also must include the $2,500 rent as ordinary income. When the smoke clears, the net tax consequences are essentially the same in either case.

In more complex situations, the tax distinctions between Section 707(a)(1) payments and allocations of distributive shares may shift the character of income among the partners. For example, assume that the ABC partnership's net income for the year consisted of $6,000 long-term capital gains and $4,000 ordinary income. The effect of a $2,500 allocation to A on these facts is to increase A's distributive share of partnership net income from one-third to one-half and to correspondingly decrease the distributive shares of the other partners from one-third to one-quarter each. This results in an allocation to A of $3,000 of capital gains and $2,000 ordinary income, and allocations to B and C of $1,500 capital gains and $1,000 ordinary income. On the other hand, if A received a Section 707(a)(1) rent payment of $2,500 and each partner received an equal one-third share of partnership profits, A would recognize $2,500 of ordinary income under Section 707(a)(1), and the partnership would take a corre-

7. I.R.C. § 702(b).

8. I.R.C. § 706(a).

9. But see I.R.C. § 267(a)(2) & (e), which alter the timing of partnership deductions in certain situations where the partner and the partnership use different methods of accounting. See infra text accompanying notes 10–11.

sponding deduction. A, B and C then each would be taxed on one-third of the partnership's remaining $1,500 of ordinary income and $6,000 capital gain, for a net result of $3,000 ordinary income and $2,000 capital gains for A and $500 ordinary income and $2,000 capital gains to B and C.

To illustrate the timing differences between Section 707(a)(1) payments and distributive shares, assume that Partner A in the example is now a cash method, calendar year taxpayer while the partnership continues to use the accrual method. If the $2,500 payment for the use of A's property were subject to Section 707(a)(1), she would not be required to include the $2,500 until she received it. But if the $2,500 were treated as an allocation, A would be taxable in full at the close of the partnership's year even if actual payment (by a partnership distribution to A) were deferred until the following year.[10]

At one time, taxpayers enjoyed additional timing advantages by classifying certain payments under Section 707(a)(1) when the partnership and the partner used different accounting methods. If partner A in the example were a cash method taxpayer and the partnership used the accrual method, the partnership could accrue and deduct the $2,500 in year one but delay actual payment (and thus inclusion in A's income) until year two. To prevent taxpayers from exploiting this mismatching of income and deductions in the partnership setting, Congress extended the timing restraints of Section 267 to transactions between partners and partnerships.[11] Section 267(a)(2), in conjunction with Section 267(e), now provides that a deduction may not be taken prior to the year in which the amount is includible in the gross income of the payee. Thus, an accrual method partnership may not deduct an item owed to a cash method partner prior to the year in which the item is paid and properly included in the payee's income.[12]

PROBLEMS

1. Armstrong v. Phinney holds that a partner who is compensated for services under § 707(a)(1) can achieve "employee" status outside of Subchapter K.

(a) What types of services are within § 707(a)(1)? Are they normally the types of services rendered by "employees?"

(b) What Code sections may come into play if a partner attains "employee" status or is deemed to be an employee?

10. The timing results are similar in the case of guaranteed payments under Section 707(c). See Section A4 of this chapter, infra.

11. Section 267 previously did not apply to these transactions because partnerships and partners were not treated as related parties for this purpose.

12. I.R.C. § 267(a)(2). Section 267 likewise would apply to defer a partner's deduction when a partner accrued an otherwise deductible expense payable to a cash method partnership in which he was a partner. If Section 707 applies to a payment of deferred compensation for services (other than pursuant to a qualified plan), Section 404(a) would defer the payor's deduction until such time as the payee included the amount in income, whether or not the parties were related.

2. The AB partnership is in the real estate development business. The partnership recently was involved in a lawsuit concerning the legal title to a parcel of land it acquired. The partnership paid partner B, who is a lawyer, a $5,000 fee to represent it in the legal proceedings. How should the partnership and B treat the payment for tax purposes?

3. DISGUISED PAYMENTS

Code: § 707(a)(2)(A).

If a partnership pays a partner for services or the use of property in a transaction governed by Section 707(a)(1) and the expense is capital in nature (e.g., organizational fees),[1] the partnership must treat the payment for tax purposes as if it were made to an unrelated third party—i.e., as a capital expenditure which, at best, may be deducted or amortized over the applicable recovery period. The timing ramifications of structuring a payment to a partner for services or property as an allocation rather than as a payment governed by Section 707(a)(1) would be dramatic if parties could convert a capital expenditure into a currently deductible expense. Section 707(a)(2)(A) prevents taxpayers from disguising payments for services or property in order to achieve this timing advantage.[2]

To illustrate, assume the equal ABC partnership has net income of $30,000 before compensating partner A for $30,000 of services rendered in A's nonpartner capacity in connection with the acquisition of a nondepreciable asset for the firm. Because the expenditure directly relates to the creation of an asset with a life extending substantially beyond the taxable year, the partnership would be required to capitalize the payment under Section 263, and its taxable income would remain at $30,000, resulting in a $10,000 distributive share to each partner and an additional $30,000 of ordinary income to A under Section 707(a)(1).

If the parties restructured the arrangement by specially allocating $30,000 to A and followed up with a distribution of that same amount, the tax consequences would differ dramatically if the form of the arrangement were respected. The partnership's $30,000 of net income all would pass through to A, reducing A's total income from $40,000 to $30,000[3] and leaving B and C with no income. If this technique were successful, the partnership would be allowed the equivalent of a current deduction for an expense that should have been capitalized. The parties similarly might circumvent the capitalization requirement using comparable arrangements under which a partner transfers the use of property to the partnership in return for a share of profits in circumstances where the partnership would

1. I.R.C. § 709.

2. A companion provision, Section 707(a)(2)(B), attacks the related device of disguised sales. Sales between partners and partnerships are examined in Section C2 of this chapter, infra.

3. The $10,000 difference is somewhat deceptive. If A were taxed on a $10,000 distributive share, he would increase his outside basis by that amount and eventually would have $10,000 less income on a sale or liquidation of his partnership interest.

be required to capitalize the payment if it were rent paid to an unrelated third party.[4]

To be sure, these maneuvers are not easily accomplished. The risk-averse service partner or lessor of property might be unwilling to accept compensation in the form of a distributive share that is dependent on partnership profits. But resourceful tax advisors devised techniques to assure partners that what might resemble a mere profit share was actually devoid of risk and thus practically guaranteed. The Service's chances of recasting these transactions[5] were impeded by the hazy line dividing the various forms of partner/partnership transactions.

Congress removed these planning opportunities when it enacted Section 707(a)(2)(A). The following excerpt from the legislative history explains the operation of this provision and surveys the factors that Congress considered most important in enforcing it:[6]

> The Act provides that, under Treasury regulations, if (1) a partner performs services for, or transfers property to, a partnership, (2) there is a related direct or indirect partnership allocation and distribution to the partner, and (3) when viewed together, the performance of such services (or the transfer of such property) and the allocation/distribution are properly characterized as a transaction between the partnership and a partner acting in a non-partner capacity, the transaction is to be treated as a transaction between the partnership and a person who is not a partner. In such a case, the amount paid to the partner in consideration for the property or services is treated as a payment for services or property provided to the partnership (as the case may be), and, where appropriate, the partnership must capitalize these amounts (or otherwise treat such amounts in a manner consistent with their recharacterization). The partnership must also treat the purported allocation to the partner performing services or transferring property to the partnership as a payment to a non-partner in determining the remaining partners' shares of taxable income or loss.
>
> Congress did not intend that this provision apply in every instance in which a partner acquires an interest in a partnership and also performs services for or transfers property to the partnership. In particular, Congress did not intend to repeal the general rule under which gain or loss is not recognized on a contribution of

4. For example, if property leased by a partner to a partnership were used by the partnership to create or acquire an asset which was capital in nature (e.g., equipment leased to construct a building), the rent payment would not be currently deductible but would be added to the basis of the created or acquired asset. See Commissioner v. Idaho Power Co., 418 U.S. 1, 94 S.Ct. 2757 (1974).

5. See, e.g., Rev.Rul. 81–301, 1981–2 C.B. 144.

6. Staff of the Joint Committee on Taxation, General Explanation of the Revenue Provisions of the Deficit Reduction Act of 1984, 98th Cong., 2d Sess. 226–229 (1984).

property in return for a partnership interest (section 721),[7] or to apply this new provision in cases in which a partner receives an allocation (or an increased allocation) for an extended period to reflect his contribution of property or services to the partnership and the facts and circumstances indicate that the partner is receiving the allocation in his capacity as a partner. However, Congress did intend that the provision apply to allocations which are determined to be related to the performance of services for, or the transfer of property to, the partnership and which, when viewed together with distributions, have the substantive economic effect of direct payments for such property or services under the facts and circumstances of the case.

The Act authorizes the Treasury Department to prescribe such regulations as may be necessary or appropriate to carry out the purposes of the provision. In prescribing these regulations, the Treasury should be mindful that Congress is concerned with transactions that work to avoid capitalization requirements or other rules and restrictions governing direct payments and not with nonabusive allocations that accurately reflect the various economic contributions of the partners. These regulations may apply the provision both to one-time transactions and to continuing arrangements which utilize purported partnership allocations and distributions in place of direct payments. Congress specifically intended that the provision apply to allocations used to pay partnership organization or syndication fees, subject to the general principles above.

The regulations will provide, when appropriate, that the purported partner performing services for or transferring property to the partnership is not a partner at all for tax purposes. If it is determined that the service performer or property transferor actually is a partner (because of other transactions), Congress believed that the factors described below should be considered in determining whether the partner is receiving the putative allocation and distribution in his capacity as a partner.

The first, and generally the most important, factor is whether the payment is subject to an appreciable risk as to amount. Partners extract the profits of the partnership with reference to the business success of the venture, while third parties generally receive payments which are not subject to this risk. Thus, an allocation and distribution provided for a service partner under the partnership agreement which subjects the partner to significant entrepreneurial risk as to both the amount and the fact of payment generally should be recognized as a distributive share and a partnership distribution, while an allocation and distribution pro-

7. Of course, if a partner received an interest in a partnership in exchange for services, he may recognize income upon that receipt; however, this issue arises only in situations where Rev.Proc. 93–27 does not apply. See Chapter 2C3, supra.

vided to a service partner under the partnership agreement which involve limited risk as to amount and payment should generally be treated as a fee under section 707(a). Examples of allocations that limit a partner's risk include both "capped" allocations of partnership income (i.e., percentage or fixed dollar amount allocations subject to an annual maximum amount when the parties could reasonably expect the cap to apply in most years) and allocations for a fixed number of years under which the income that will go to the partner is reasonably certain. Similarly, continuing arrangements in which purported allocations and distributions (under a formula or otherwise) are fixed in amount or reasonably determinable under all the facts and circumstances and which arise in connection with services also shield the purported partner from entrepreneurial risk. Although short-lived gross income allocations are particularly suspect in this regard, gross income allocations may, in very limited instances, represent an entrepreneurial return, which is classifiable as a distributive share under section 704. Similarly, although net income allocations appear generally to constitute distributive shares, some net income allocations may be fixed as to amount and probability of payment and should, if coupled with a distribution or payment from the partnership, be characterized as fees.

The second factor is whether the partner status of the recipient is transitory. Transitory partner status (which limits the duration of a purported joint undertaking for profit) suggests that a payment is a fee or is in return for property. The fact that partner status is continuing, however, is of no particular relevance in establishing that an allocation and distribution are received in an individual's capacity as a partner.

The third factor is whether the allocation and distribution that are made to the partner are close in time to the partner's performance of services for or transfer of property to the partnership. An allocation close in time to the performance of services, or the transfer of property, is more likely to be related to the services or property. In the case of continuing arrangements, the time at which income is scheduled to be allocated to the partner may be a factor indicating that an allocation is, in fact, a disguised payment. When the income subject to allocation arises over an extended period or is remote in time from the services or property contributed by a partner, the risk of not receiving payment (the first factor described above) may also increase.

The fourth factor is whether, under all the facts and circumstances, it appears that the recipient became a partner primarily to obtain tax benefits for himself or the partnership which would not have been available if he had rendered services to the partnership in a third party capacity. The fact that a partner also has significant non-tax motivations in becoming a partner is of no particular relevance.

The fifth factor, which relates to purported allocations/distributions for services, is whether the value of the recipient's interest in general and continuing partnership profits is small in relation to the allocation in question (thus suggesting that the purported allocation is, in fact, a fee). This is especially significant if the allocation for services is for a limited period of time. The fact that the recipient's interest in general and continuing partnership profits is substantial does not, however, suggest that the purported partnership allocation/distribution arrangement should be recognized.

The sixth factor, which relates to purported allocations/distributions for property [see Section B3 of this chapter, infra. Ed.] is whether the requirement that capital accounts be respected under section 704(b) (and the proposed regulations thereunder) makes income allocations which are disguised payments for capital economically unfeasible and therefore unlikely to occur. This generally will be the case unless (i) the valuation of the property contributed by the partner to the partnership is below the fair market value of such property (thus improperly understating the amount in such partner's capital account), or (ii) the property is sold by the partner to the partnership at a stated price below the fair market value of such property, or (iii) the capital account will be respected at such a distant point in the future that its present value is small and there is to be no meaningful return on the capital account in the intervening period.

Congress anticipated that the Treasury Department may describe other factors that are relevant in evaluating whether a purported allocation and distribution should be respected. In applying these various factors, the Treasury and the courts should be careful not to be misled by possibly self-serving assertions in the partnership agreement as to the duties of a partner in his partner capacity but should instead seek to determine the substance of the transaction.

In the case of allocations which are only partly determined to be related to the performance of services for, or the transfer of property to, the partnership, the provision applies to that portion of the allocation which is reasonably determined to be related to the property or services provided to the partnership. Finally, it was anticipated that Treasury regulations will provide for the coordination of this provision with the preexisting rules of section 707 and other provisions of subchapter K such as section 736.

Congress did not intend to create any inference regarding the tax treatment of the transactions described above under prior law.

PROBLEMS

1. A (a cash method taxpayer) is an equal partner in the ABCD partnership (an accrual method taxpayer) and has a $10,000 outside basis in her partnership interest. A owns depreciable personal property (adjusted basis—$2,000; fair market value—$15,000; fair rental value—$1,000 per year) which the partnership will use in its business. Before any of the transactions described below, the partnership has $10,000 of net income each year. What result in the following alternatives?

(a) A leases the property to the partnership for three years. The partnership will pay A $1,000 per year for three years for the use of the property.

(b) What result in (a), above, if the rental payments are made on January 31 of the year following accrual?

(c) A transfers the property to the partnership, which will use it for three years and transfer it back to A at the end of that period. The partnership makes a special allocation of its first $1,000 of net income to A. What result to A? What if, instead, the first $3,000 of the first year's net income and no subsequent income in excess of her one-quarter share is allocated to A?

2. Consider the following example adapted from the legislative history of § 707(a)(2)(A):

> A commercial office building constructed by a partnership is projected to generate gross income of at least $100,000 per year indefinitely. Architect, whose normal fee for architectural services is $40,000, contributes cash for a 25% interest in the partnership and receives both a 25% distributive share of net income for the life of the partnership and an allocation of $20,000 of partnership gross income for the first two years of partnership operations after the property is leased. The partnership expects to have sufficient cash available to distribute $20,000 to Architect in each of the first two years, and the agreement requires such a distribution.

What factors are most important in determining whether the $20,000 allocation of gross income to Architect is a share of profits or a § 707(a)(2)(A) payment?

4. GUARANTEED PAYMENTS

Code: § 707(c).

Regulations: § 1.707–1(c).

Guaranteed payments are payments by a partnership to a partner for services or for the use of capital which are determined without regard to partnership income. In the services context, a guaranteed payment resembles a salary. For example, if a real estate partnership paid its general partner a fixed annual amount for ongoing management services, irrespective of partnership profits, the fee would be classified as a guaranteed payment. A typical guaranteed payment for the use of capital would be a preferred return (e.g., 10 percent of a partner's initial cash contribution) on a partner's equity investment, payable in all events before any allocation of income or losses among the partners.

Guaranteed payments have some of the characteristics of Section 707(a)(1) payments in that they are fixed payments for services or the use of property. But they resemble distributive shares in that they relate to services or contributed capital that are an integral part of the partnership's ongoing activities. They are thus made to partners in their capacity as partners rather than as unrelated third parties. Guaranteed payments also are a hybrid for tax purposes. Like Section 707(a)(1) payments, they are treated for some purposes as made to a person who is not a member of the partnership. As such, they are taxable to the partner as ordinary income regardless of the amount or character of the partnership's taxable income, and they are deductible by the partnership under Section 162, subject to the capitalization requirement of Section 263.[1] For timing purposes, however, guaranteed payments resemble distributive shares in that they are included in income for a partner's taxable year "within or with which ends the partnership taxable year in which the partnership deducted such payments as paid or accrued under its method of accounting."[2] The partner thus must include them in income whether or not they are received.

Since a guaranteed payment is taxable whether or not it has been received, a mechanism is necessary to ensure that the partner is not taxed a second time when the payment is actually received. Perhaps the partner simply takes a tax cost basis in the guaranteed payment and thus has no further income when the payment is received.[3] On the other hand, footnote 16 of the *Gaines* case suggests that when the partner is taxed on a guaranteed payment, he simply increases his outside basis in his partnership interest, as he would when he reports his distributive share. If that is the case, receipt of the payment, like receipt of a partner's distributive share, simply would reduce the partner's outside basis under Section 705. While the language of Section 707(c) seems to imply that a guaranteed payment is treated as a distributive share for all purposes other than characterization of the partner's income and allowance of a deduction to the partnership, the section has not been construed quite so broadly by the Service. The regulations[4] state that the recipient of a guaranteed payment is treated as a partner rather than as an employee for fringe benefit purposes and also provide that a guaranteed payment is not treated as an interest in the partnership for purposes of several sections whose application varies depending on the size of the partner's interest.[5] Regrettably, there is no definitive authority on many of these issues.

1. I.R.C. § 707(c). Gaines v. Commissioner, infra. See also Cagle v. Commissioner, 63 T.C. 86 (1974), affirmed, 539 F.2d 409 (5th Cir.1976), the result of which was codified in Section 707(c) by the Tax Reform Act of 1976.

2. Reg. § 1.707–1(c).

3. See McKee, Nelson & Whitmire, Federal Taxation of Partnerships and Partners ¶ 14.03[2] (4th ed. 2007).

4. Reg. § 1.707–1(c).

5. The regulations provide that guaranteed payments are not treated as a profit share for purposes of Section 706(b)(3) (adop-

Gaines v. Commissioner

United States Tax Court, 1982.
45 T.C.M. 363.

■ PARKER, JUDGE.

* * *

Issue No. 2: Guaranteed Payments

Findings of Fact

On their partnership returns for the year 1973, Lincoln Manor, Brookwood, Gaines Realty, and Riverbend each claimed as deductions certain guaranteed payments to partners. Gaines Properties was a general partner in each of these partnerships. The amounts claimed by the limited partnerships as deductions for guaranteed payments to partners and Gaines Properties' share of those guaranteed payments were as follows:

Partnership	Amount Claimed	Gaines Properties' Share
Lincoln Manor	$ 74,131.26	$ 23,750.00
Brookwood	109,666.00	88,666.00
Gaines Realty	125,881.00	91,006.00
Riverbend	216,087.00	104,168.50

Each of the four limited partnerships accrued and claimed deductions for these guaranteed payments. Lincoln Manor, Brookwood, Gaines Realty, and Riverbend all used the accrual method of accounting on their 1973 partnership returns. Gaines Properties reported its income using the cash receipts and disbursements method of accounting. Gaines Properties never received any of the guaranteed payments and did not report them in its income.

Respondent determined that Gaines Properties should have reported as income the guaranteed payments accrued and deducted by the four limited partnerships. Respondent, however, disallowed portions of the deductions that the four limited partnerships claimed for these guaranteed payments, on the ground that some portions were capital expenditures and not currently deductible.

Issue No. 2: Guaranteed Payments

Opinion

Lincoln Manor, Brookwood, Riverbend, and Gaines Realty accrued and claimed deductions on their partnership returns for certain "guaranteed payments," including guaranteed payments to Gaines Properties, a general partner of each limited partnership. Gaines Properties never received these guaranteed payments. Respondent disallowed to the limited partnership

tion of a partnership taxable year), Section 707(b) (disallowance of certain losses and characterization of gains) and Section 708(b) (forced termination of a partnership).

portions of the claimed deductions for guaranteed payments, including some of the deductions attributable to the guaranteed payments to Gaines Properties. Notwithstanding this partial disallowance of deductions at the partnership level, respondent determined that the *entire amount* of the guaranteed payments to Gaines Properties, including the portion disallowed as deductions at the partnership level, should be included in Gaines Properties' income. Petitioners argue that the guaranteed payments that Gaines Properties did not receive, or at least such payments to the extent that the deductions therefor were disallowed at the partnership level, were not includable in Gaines Properties' income. Respondent argues that Gaines Properties' share of these guaranteed payments was includable in its income regardless of the fact that the deduction was partially disallowed at the partnership level and regardless of the fact that Gaines Properties, which used the cash method of accounting, never received the payments. We agree with respondent.

Section 707(c), as in effect in 1973, provided:

> To the extent determined without regard to the income of the partnership, payments to a partner for services or the use of capital shall be considered as made to one who is not a member of the partnership, but only for the purposes of section 61(a) (relating to gross income) and section 162(a) (relating to trade or business expenses).

This case does in fact involve "guaranteed payments" to a partner within the meaning of section 707(c) of the Code. The fact that no actual payments were made does not affect the status of these transactions as section 707(c) guaranteed payments. "[D]espite the use of the word 'payments' in both § 707(c) and the Regulations thereunder, it is clear that no actual payment need be made; if the partnership deducts the amount under its method of accounting, the 'recipient' partner must include the amount in income in the appropriate year." W. McKee, W. Nelson and R. Whitmire, Federal Taxation of Partnerships and Partners (hereinafter McKee, Nelson and Whitmire), par. 13.03[2], pp. 13–16. See also Pratt v. Commissioner, 64 T.C. 203, 213 (1975), affd. on this point and revd. on other grounds 550 F.2d 1023 (5th Cir.1977); sec. 1.707–1(c), Income Tax Regs. The parties stipulated that each of the four limited partnerships deducted "guaranteed payments." The partnership agreements of Brookwood and Gaines Realty expressly stated that certain payments to partners "shall constitute guaranteed payments within the meaning of section 707(c) of the Code." While the descriptions of such payments in the partnership agreements are not binding upon us (Doyle v. Mitchell Bros. Co., 247 U.S. 179, 187 (1918)), the payments referred to in those two partnership agreements are clearly fixed sums determined without regard to partnership income. See Sec. 707(c); Sec. 1.707–1(c), Income Tax Regs. Furthermore, it is equally clear that the payments to the partners were for services in their capacities as partners. Respondent in his notices of deficiency determined that these payments were in fact guaranteed payments under section 707(c), and petitioners did not dispute this determination. Accordingly, we hold that the payments here were guaranteed payments within the meaning of section 707(c).

The statutory language of section 707(c) addresses only the character of the guaranteed payments and not the timing. Respondent's regulation under section 707(c), section 1.707–1(c), Income Tax Regs., addresses the timing question, as follows:

> Payments made by a partnership to a partner for services or for the use of capital are considered as made to a person who is not a partner, to the extent such payments are determined without regard to the income of the partnership. However, a partner must include such payments as ordinary income for his taxable year within or with which ends the partnership taxable year in which the partnership deducted such payments as paid or accrued under its method of accounting. See section 706(a) and paragraph (a) of § 1.706–1.

As the regulation makes clear, the statutory authority for the timing of the inclusion of these guaranteed payments is section 706(a), which provides:

> In computing the taxable income of a partner for a taxable year, the inclusions required by section 702 and section 707(c) with respect to a partnership shall be based on the income, gain, loss, deduction, or credit of the partnership for any taxable year of the partnership ending within or with the taxable year of the partner.

The separate reference of section 707(c) guaranteed payments in the timing provisions of section 706(a) was explained by the Senate Report as simply—

> to make clear that payments made to a partner for services or for the use of capital are includible in his income at the same time as his distributive share of partnership income for the partnership year when the payments are made or accrued * * *. (S.Rept. No. 1622, to accompany H.R. 8300 (Pub.L. No. 591), 83d Cong., 2d Sess. 385 (1954)).

In Cagle v. Commissioner, 63 T.C. 86 (1974), affd. 539 F.2d 409 (5th Cir.1976), we held that includability and deductibility of guaranteed payments are two separate questions, and specifically that guaranteed payments are not automatically deductible simply by reason of their being included in the recipient's income. In *Cagle*, we stated 63 T.C. at 95:

> We think that all Congress meant was that guaranteed payments should be included in the recipient partner's income in the partnership taxable year ending with or within which the partner's taxable year ends and in which the tax accounting treatment of the transaction is determined at the partnership level. S.Rept. No. 1622, supra at pp. 94, 385, 387.

We believe our statement in *Cagle* is an accurate description of the Congressional intent. We have found nothing in the statutory language, regulations, or legislative history to indicate that includability in the recipient partner's income was intended to be dependent upon deductibility at the partnership level.

Petitioners seem to argue that there is a patent unfairness in taxing them on nonexistent income, namely income that they have neither received nor benefitted from (e.g. through a tax deduction at the partnership level). Their argument has a superficial appeal to it, but on closer analysis must fail. Except for certain very limited purposes, guaranteed payments are treated as part of the partner's distributive share of partnership income and loss. Sec. 1.707–1(c), Income Tax Regs. For timing purposes guaranteed payments are treated the same as distributive income and loss. Sec. 706(a); sec. 1.706–1(a) and sec. 1.707–1(c), Income Tax Regs. A partner's distributive share of partnership income is includable in his taxable income for any partnership year ending within or with the partner's taxable year. Sec. 706(a). As is the case with a partner's ordinary distributive share of partnership income and loss, any unfairness in taxing a partner on guaranteed payments that he neither receives nor benefits from results from the conduit theory of partnerships, and is a consequence of the taxpayer's choice to do the business in the partnership form.[16] We find no justification in the statute, regulations, or legislative history to permit these petitioners to recognize their income pro rata as deductions are allowed to the partnership. See also Pratt v. Commissioner, 64 T.C. 203, 213 (1975), affd. on this ground 550 F.2d 1023 (5th Cir.1977). We hold for respondent on the guaranteed payments issue.

Revenue Ruling 69–180

1969–1 Cum. Bull. 183.

Advice has been requested as to the proper method for computing the partners' distributive shares of the partnership's ordinary income and capital gains under the circumstances described below.

F and *G* are partners in *FG*, a two-man partnership. The partnership agreement provides that *F* is to receive 30 percent of the partnership income as determined before taking into account any guaranteed amount, but not less than 100*x* dollars. The agreement also provides that any guaranteed amount will be treated as an expense item of the partnership in any year in which *F*'s percentage of profits is less than the guaranteed amount. The partnership agreement makes no provision for sharing capital gains.

For the taxable year in question the partnership income before taking into account any guaranteed amount, is 200*x* dollars, and consists of 120*x* dollars of ordinary income and 80*x* dollars of capital gains.

Section 707(c) of the Internal Revenue Code of 1954 provides that, to the extent determined without regard to the income of the partnership,

16. As part of a partner's distributive share of profit and loss, the guaranteed payments included in his income increase the partner's basis in his partnership interest. Sec. 705(a)(1) and (2).

payments to a partner for services or the use of capital shall be considered as made to one who is not a member of the partnership, but only for the purpose of section 61(a) (relating to gross income) and section 162(a) of the Code (relating to trade or business expenses). Section 1.707–1(c) of the Income Tax Regulations provides that for purposes of section 61(a) of the Code guaranteed payments are regarded as a partner's distributive share of ordinary income. Thus, a guaranteed payment is includible in gross income of the recipient as ordinary income, and is deductible by the partnership from its ordinary income as a business expense.

For Federal income tax purposes, *F's* guaranteed payment, as defined under section 707(c) of the Code is 40x dollars, 100x dollars (minimum guarantee) less 60x dollars distributive share (30 percent of partnership income of 200x dollars). See Example 2 of section 1.707–1(c) of the regulations and Revenue Ruling 66–95, C.B. 1966–1, 169.

After the guaranteed payment is taken into account, the partnership's ordinary income is 80x dollars (120x dollars of ordinary income less the 40x dollars guaranteed payment which is deductible by the partnership as a business expense under section 162 of the Code).

For Federal income tax purposes, the taxable income of the partnership amounts to 160x dollars (80x dollars of ordinary income and 80x dollars of capital gains).

Section 704(b) of the Code and section 1.704–1(b)(1) of the regulations provide that if the partnership agreement does not specifically provide for the manner of sharing a particular item or class of items of income, gain, loss, deduction, or credit of the partnership, a partner's distributive share of any such item shall be determined in accordance with the manner provided in the partnership agreement for the division of the general profits or losses (that is, the taxable income or loss of the partnership as described in section 702(a)[8] of the Code). In applying this rule, the manner in which the net profit or loss (computed after excluding any item subject to a recognized special allocation) is actually credited on the partnership books to the accounts of the partners will generally determine each partner's share of taxable income or loss as described in section 702(a)[8] of the Code. Thus, *F* and *G* share the capital gains in the same ratio in which they share the general profits from business operations.

The partnership income for the taxable year, after deduction of the guaranteed payment, is 160x dollars. Of this amount, *F's* distributive share, as determined above under the partnership agreement is 60x dollars. Therefore, *G's* distributive share is 100x dollars. Hence, the effective profit sharing ratio for the year in question is 6/16 for *F* and 10/16 for *G*. Thus, as provided by section 704(b) of the Code, the partnership capital gains as well as the partnership ordinary income are to be shared in the ratio of 6/16 for *F* and 10/16 for *G*.

Accordingly, the amounts of ordinary income and capital gains to be reported by the partners in this case are as follows:

	F	G	Total
Ordinary income	30x dollars	50x dollars	80x dollars
Guaranteed payment	40x dollars		40x dollars
Total ordinary income	70x dollars	50x dollars	120x dollars
Capital gains	30x dollars	50x dollars	80x dollars
Total	100x dollars	100x dollars	200x dollars

Revenue Ruling 2007–40

2007–1 Cum. Bull. 1426.

ISSUE

Is a transfer of partnership property to a partner in satisfaction of a guaranteed payment under section 707(c) a sale or exchange under section 1001, or a distribution under section 731?

FACTS

Partnership purchased Blackacre for $500x. A, a partner in Partnership, is entitled to a guaranteed payment under section 707(c) of $800x. Subsequently, when the fair market value of Blackacre is $800x and Partnership's adjusted basis in Blackacre is $500x, Partnership transfers Blackacre to A in satisfaction of the guaranteed payment to A.

LAW AND ANALYSIS

Section 731(b) provides that no gain or loss shall be recognized to a partnership on a distribution to a partner of property, including money.

Section 707(c) provides that, to the extent determined without regard to the income of the partnership, payments to a partner for services or for the use of capital are considered as made to one who is not a member of the partnership, but only for the purposes of § 61(a) (relating to gross income) and, subject to § 263, for purposes of § 162(a) (relating to trade or business expenses).

Section 61(a)(3) provides the general rule that gross income includes gains derived from dealings in property. In addition, section 1001(a) provides that the gain from the sale or other disposition of property shall be the excess of the amount realized over the adjusted basis provided in section 1011 for determining gain, and the loss shall be the excess of the adjusted basis over the amount realized.

Section 1001(b) further provides, in part, that the amount realized from the sale or other disposition of property shall be the sum of any money received plus the fair market value of the property (other than money) received.

A taxpayer that conveys appreciated or depreciated property in satisfaction of an obligation, or in exchange for the performance of services, recognizes gain or loss equal to the difference between the basis in the distributed property and the property's fair market value. See, e.g., International Freighting Corp., Inc. v. Commissioner, 135 F.2d 310 (2d Cir. 1943), United States v. General Shoe Corp., 282 F.2d 9 (6th Cir. 1960).

A transfer of partnership property in satisfaction of a partnership's obligation to make a guaranteed payment under section 707(c) is a sale or exchange under section 1001. Because the transfer is a sale or exchange under section 1001, it is not a distribution within the meaning of section 731. Accordingly, the nonrecognition rule in section 731(b) does not apply to the transfer. Partnership realizes a $300x gain when Partnership transfers Blackacre in satisfaction of its section 707(c) guaranteed payment to A, the difference between the adjusted basis of the property ($500x) to the partnership and the property's fair market value ($800x).

HOLDING

A transfer of partnership property to a partner in satisfaction of a guaranteed payment under section 707(c) is a sale or exchange under section 1001, and not a distribution under section 731.

NOTE

Section 707(c) apparently was enacted to make it clear that a partner realizes income as a result of receiving payments for services or capital in his partner capacity. Section 707(a) makes the same conceptual point for partners who receive similar payments while acting in a nonpartner capacity. The two provisions operate similarly except that, for timing purposes, guaranteed payments are treated as a distributive share of partnership profits. Do these differences make sense? Do they justify the need to distinguish between payments made to an individual in his partner or nonpartner capacity?

These strange distinctions have prompted commentators to urge Congress to take a closer look at Section 707(c) and possibly even repeal it.[1] In its 1997 review of partnership tax issues, the Joint Committee on Taxation floated the following proposal, which is likely to be considered if Congress should ever engage in a comprehensive review of Subchapter K:[2]

> The [Joint Committee staff's] proposal would repeal the present-law provisions governing guaranteed payments made to a partner for capital. Thus, a guaranteed payment to a partner with respect to capital would be treated according to its substance either as a deemed non-partner payment (sec. 707(a)), or as an allocation of partnership income to the recipient partner combined with a distribution (sec. 704(b)). It is expected that most guaran-

1. See Brannan, "The Subchapter K Reform Act of 1997," 75 Tax Notes 121, 126–129 (April 7, 1997); Banoff, "Guaranteed Payments for the Use of Capital: Schizophrenia in Subchapter K," 70 Taxes 820 (1992); Postlewaite & Cameron, "Twisting Slowly in the Wind: Guaranteed Payments After the Tax Reform Act of 1984," 40 Tax Lawyer 649 (1986).

2. Joint Committee on Taxation, Review of Selected Entity Classification and Partnership Tax Issues 47 (JCS–6–97), April 8, 1997.

teed payments for capital would qualify as deemed non-partner payments that would be characterized as interest on debt for Federal tax purposes.

The proposal would retain the present-law concept of guaranteed payments for services, but would amend the treatment of such payments to conform with non-partner service payments. For service payments, the proposal would retain the present-law concepts of both guaranteed payments for services and payments for services that are performed in a non-partner capacity. However, the proposal would treat both types of payments in the same manner, applying the present-law rules for deemed non-partner payments under section 707(a), such as inclusion of such payments in gross income under the recipient's method of accounting.

5. Policy Issues: Taxation of "Carried Interests"

The taxation of a partner who provides services to a partnership presents an array of issues. Earlier, the saga of the *Diamond* case and the taxation of the transfer of a profits interest in exchange for services were covered.[1] Following the post-*Diamond* truce declared by the IRS, a services partners generally is able to receive a profits interest as compensation for services and avoid being immediately taxed on the value, if any, of the interest. This chapter has examined the tax results from alternative methods for compensating a partner who provides services to a partnership. In general, such a partner will receive a guaranteed payment, a distributive share of partnership profits, or a combination of both, in exchange for the work performed for the partnership.

These relatively well-settled rules for taxing a partner who provides services to a partnership have come under greater scrutiny as they are applied in the world of 21st century finance.[2] Hedge funds, private equity funds and other types of alternative investment pools have raised large amounts of capital from institutional investors and wealthy individuals while protecting their privacy and avoiding SEC regulation. Typically, these vehicles invest in stocks, bonds, commodities, currencies, etc., and virtually all them are structured as partnerships, with the investment manager acting as the general partner and the investors as limited partners.

The general partners of hedge funds and private equity funds generally are compensated with both a flat fee (a guaranteed payment), which is usually 1 to 2 percent of the assets under management, and they also are allocated a percentage of the fund's profits (a distributive share). The profits share may be payable in all events or, in some structures, only after

1. See Chapter 2C3, supra.

2. See, e.g., Fleischer, "Two and Twenty: Taxing Partnership Profits in Private Equity Funds," 83 N.Y.U L. Rev. 1 (2008); Abrams, "Taxation of Carried Interests," 116 Tax Notes 183 (July 16, 2007); Abrams, A Close Look at the Carried Interest Legislation, 117 Tax Notes 961 (Dec. 3, 2007).

the fund has returned a specific return (known as a "hurdle rate") to investors. The profits allocations, which have come to be known as "carried interests," often are characterized as tax-preferred capital gains because they represent a portion of the gains realized when the funds sell their investment assets. In addition to the preferential capital gains rates that apply to the carried interest, remember that the manager-general partner is not taxed on receipt of the carried interest and will not pay tax until the gains are recognized by the partnership. Thus, income from the carried interest is deferred until assets are sold and then the income is taxable at capital gains rates.

The amount of capital invested (estimated to be in the trillions of dollars), the amount of compensation paid to general partners (billions of dollars), and the fact that many hedge funds and private equity funds are organized offshore, are all factors that have increased Congressional scrutiny of these investment vehicles.[3] In 2007, as the political parties formulated their tax policy positions in anticipation of the 2008 Presidential election, some members of Congress identified taxation of "carried interests" as an appealing way to generate revenue by raising taxes on the generous compensation packages of the fund managers. The critical tax issue has become whether Subchapter K should be amended to tax all or part of carried interest as compensation (ordinary income) rather than as a distributive share of recognized capital gains. A secondary issue, with interesting political consequences, is whether any change should be narrowly tailored to cover only investment managers dealing in investments like stocks and other securities, or whether the new approach should be extended and applied more broadly to services partners in other investment fields, like real estate.

A lively debate has been ongoing concerning the taxation of carried interests.[4] But the complexity of the issues, heavy industry lobbying, and the ambivalence of some key legislators, who coincidently raise considerable sums from the investment community, suggest that the debate will not be resolved quickly.

PROBLEMS

1. The AB equal partnership is in a highly speculative business in which profits fluctuate widely. For the current year the partnership has profits of $20,000, of which $12,000 is ordinary income and $8,000 is long-term capital gain. A and B share profits and losses equally unless otherwise provided. A renders services to the partnership which are continuous,

3. For background on these issues, see Jickling & Marples, "Taxation of Hedge Funds and Private Equity Managers," Congressional Research Service Report for Congress (July 5, 2007).

4. For a comprehensive resource on the area, see Joint Committee on Taxation, Present Law and Analysis Relating to Tax Treatment of Partnership Carried Interests (JCX–41–07), July 10, 2007, available at www.house.gov/jct.

related to the function of the partnership and not in the nature of a capital expenditure.

(a) What result to A, B, and AB if A worked for the partnership and was required to be paid $15,000 per year for his services regardless of the income of the partnership?

(b) What result in (a), above, if A's services relate to improvements on land owned by the partnership?

(c) What results if A renders the services under an agreement that he will receive $15,000 or 50% of the profits before taking into account any guaranteed payments, whichever is greater, and the profits are $20,000, consisting of $12,000 of ordinary income and $8,000 of long-term capital gain?

(d) What result in (a) and (c), above, if A's compensation is not for services but is received as a guaranteed return on A's contributed capital to the partnership?

2. G, a cash method taxpayer, is a one-third partner in the FGH accrual method partnership. G is employed by the partnership and is entitled to a guaranteed payment of $10,000 for year one. G's outside basis during year one is zero. G's agreement with the partnership specifies that he will receive the $10,000 guaranteed payment on June 1 of year three. On January 1 of year two, the partnership sells an asset (basis $15,000, fair market value $15,000) and distributes $5,000 cash to each partner. What result to G?

3. In a situation similar to that in Revenue Ruling 69–180, supra p. 241, is it possible for amounts paid to a partner in excess of the guaranteed payment to be classified as a Section 707(a)(1) payment?

4. Partner renders services worth $10,000 to Partnership in which he is a partner. Without regard to Partner's services, Partnership has $75,000 of ordinary income and $25,000 of long-term capital gain for the year. Both Partner and Partnership are calendar year taxpayers, but Partner uses the cash method of accounting and Partnership uses the accrual method. Partnership makes no payment to Partner during the year, but where permitted it accrues the expense, which is currently deductible under Section 162. Determine the tax consequences of the following alternative transactions to Partner and Partnership:

(a) In recognition of his services, Partner is allocated the first $10,000 of partnership profits, which is treated as part of his distributive share.

(b) Section 707(a)(1) applies because the services are unrelated to the everyday conduct of Partnership's activities and are not continuous. See § 267(a)(2) and (e).

(c) Section 707(c) applies because the services are ongoing services related to Partnership's activities but are paid without regard to Partnership income.

(d) Partner is allocated $10,000, which is treated under § 707(a)(2)(A) as a § 707(a)(1) payment.

B. Sales and Exchanges of Property Between Partners and Partnerships

Code: §§ 267(a)(1), (c), (d); 453(g); 707(a), (b); 1239(a).

Regulations: § 1.707–1(b); –3(a), (b), (c), (d); –5(a)(1), (6) & (7).

Sales and exchanges of property between partners and their partnerships raise classification issues similar to those previously encountered with services and the use of money or property. In general, a bona fide sale or exchange of property by a partner to a partnership, or vice versa, is treated for tax purposes as a Section 707(a)(1) transaction between unrelated parties. Opportunities for collusion, however, have prompted Congress to enact a number of anti-avoidance provisions which are discussed in this section.

1. Sales and Exchanges With Respect to Controlled Partnerships

Partners, like family members and other related taxpayers, may seek to sell a loss asset to their partnerships in order to recognize a paper loss without parting with effective control of the asset. Section 267(a)(1), which disallows losses with respect to many transactions between related parties, does not apply to partner/partnership sales or exchanges, but Section 707(b)(1) fills the statutory gap by disallowing losses on sales or exchanges of property between partnerships and partners who own directly or indirectly[1] a more than 50 percent interest in partnership capital or profits.[2]

Partners also might be motivated to sell a depreciable asset to a related partnership to give the buyer a stepped-up basis while the selling partner defers gain recognition under Section 453[3] or recognizes capital gain rather than ordinary income on the sale. To prevent these abuses, Sections 707(b)(2) and 1239(a) both characterize gain on sales and exchanges of property between partners and controlled (i.e., more than 50 percent) partnerships as ordinary income. In addition, Section 453(g) disallows installment sale treatment on such sales if the property is depreciable to the transferee unless the seller can establish to the satisfaction of the Secretary that the sale did not have tax avoidance as one of its principal purposes.

1. For this purpose, Section 707(b) incorporates attribution rules from Section 267(c).

2. Section 707(b) also applies to sales or exchanges of property between two partnerships in which the same persons own, directly or indirectly, more than 50 percent of the capital or profits interests. I.R.C. § 707(b)(1)(B).

3. But see I.R.C. § 453(i), which accelerates gain recognition of ordinary recapture income on deferred payment sales of depreciable property.

2. DISGUISED SALES

The provisions discussed above were aimed at timing and conversion strategies. More adventuresome taxpayers went one step further, seeking complete nonrecognition of gain by turning a sale or exchange into a contribution of property followed or preceded by a related partnership distribution. To illustrate, assume that A is an equal partner in the AB partnership and has a $100,000 outside basis. Assume further that A owns a parcel of land with a $10,000 adjusted basis and a $50,000 fair market value. A wishes to sell the land to the partnership without altering his interest in the firm. If he sells the property to the partnership for its fair market value in a transaction governed by Section 707(a)(1), A recognizes $40,000 of gain. If instead A contributes the property, he does not recognize any gain, and his outside basis is increased to $110,000.[1] If the partnership then distributes $50,000 to A and the form of the transactions is respected,[2] A would receive the cash tax-free because the amount of the distribution does not exceed his outside basis.[3]

Section 707(a)(2)(B) responds to this potential for abuse by providing that if a partner transfers money or other property to a partnership and the partnership makes a related transfer of money or other property to that partner (or another partner), the two transfers, when appropriate, shall be treated as a sale or exchange of property between the partnership and the partner acting in a nonpartner capacity, or between two partners acting as outsiders. Congress granted the Treasury broad authority to uncover disguised sales without reclassifying "non-abusive transactions that reflect the various economic contributions of the partners."[4]

The Service has issued a detailed set of regulations under Section 707(a)(2)(B). Their guiding principle is that a contribution and related distribution should be recast as a sale only when their combined effect is to allow a partner to withdraw all or part of his equity in the transferred property. In the case of simultaneous transfers where it is clear that the partnership would not have made a distribution if the partner had not made a contribution, the transactions are likely to be viewed as a sale.[5] But a transfer will not be treated as the first step in a disguised sale if, based on all the facts and circumstances, the transferring partner is converting equity in the property into an interest in partnership capital and the transfer is subject to the entrepreneurial risks of the enterprise.[6]

In enacting Section 707(a)(2)(B), Congress suggested that the temporal proximity of the contribution and distribution should be a significant factor

1. See I.R.C. §§ 721; 722; Chapter 2A, supra.

2. But see Reg. §§ 1.721–1(a) & 1.731–1(c)(3), which provide that similar transactions may be characterized as sales under a substance over form analysis. See also Rev. Rul. 57–100, 1957–1 C.B. 546. The Service met with little success, however, in applying these regulations to disguised sales.

3. I.R.C. § 731. See, e.g., Otey v. Commissioner, 70 T.C. 312 (1978), affirmed per curiam, 634 F.2d 1046 (6th Cir.1980).

4. H.R.Rep. No. 98–432, 98th Cong., 2d Sess. 1220 (1984).

5. Reg. § 1.707–3(b)(1).

6. Id.

in identifying a disguised sale.[7] Adopting this mechanical test of time, the regulations provide that nonsimultaneous transfers between a partnership and a partner (e.g., a contribution by a partner and a subsequent distribution by the partnership to that partner) that are made within two years of each other are presumed to be a sale[8] while transfers made more than two years apart are presumed not to be a sale.[9] Both presumptions are rebuttable based on clearly established contrary facts and circumstances.[10] The presumptions do not apply to four types of partnership distributions that historically have not been used as disguised sale vehicles.[11]

Since the presumptions are rebuttable based on facts and circumstances, the regulations provide a list of factors that may tend to prove the existence of a disguised sale. The Service is urged to raise its eyebrows, for example, if the timing and amount of a subsequent transfer are determinable with reasonable certainty at the time of an earlier transfer; if the transferring partner has a legally enforceable right to a subsequent distribution; or if that partner's right to receive money or other property for his contribution is secured.[12]

The typically compulsive drafters of the regulations included countless examples of disguised sales. In general, if the consideration treated as transferred to a partner in a sale is less than the fair market value of the property transferred to the partnership, the transaction is treated as a part sale/part contribution, and the transferring partner must pro rate his basis in the property between the sale and contribution portions. The following excerpt from the regulations illustrates the operation of this rule in the simple case of a disguised sale resulting from simultaneous transfers:[13]

> A transfers property X to partnership AB on April 9, 1992, in exchange for an interest in the partnership. At the time of the transfer, property X has a fair market value of $4,000,000 and an adjusted tax basis of $1,200,000. Immediately after the transfer, the partnership transfers $3,000,000 in cash to A. Assume that, under the section, the partnership's transfer of cash to A is treated as part of a sale of property X to the partnership. Because the amount of cash A receives on April 9, 1992, does not equal the fair market value of the property, A is considered to have sold a portion of property X with a value of $3,000,000 to the partnership in exchange for the cash. Accordingly, A must recognize $2,100,000 of gain ($3,000,000 amount realized less $900,000 adjusted tax basis ($1,200,000 multiplied by $3,000,000/$4,000,000)). Assuming

7. See Staff of the Joint Committee on Taxation, General Explanation of the Revenue Provisions of the Deficit Reduction Act of 1984 (hereinafter "1984 Act General Explanation"), 98th Cong., 2d Sess. 232 (1984).

8. Reg. § 1.707–3(c)(1).

9. Reg. § 1.707–3(d).

10. Reg. § 1.707–3(c)(1), (d).

11. See generally Reg. § 1.707–4. Broadly categorized, the exceptions benefit guaranteed payments and other types of preferred returns on contributed capital that are reasonable in amount and payments to reimburse partners for costs they incurred prior to the formation of the partnership.

12. Reg. § 1.707–3(b)(2).

13. Reg. § 1.707–3(f) Example 1.

A receives no other transfers that are treated as consideration for the sale of the property under this section, A is considered to have contributed to the partnership, in A's capacity as a partner, $1,000,000 of the fair market value of the property with an adjusted tax basis of $300,000.[14]

The legislative history of Section 707(a)(2)(B) also warned the Treasury to be on the lookout for situations where a partner or the partnership borrows against property in connection with a transfer and related distribution.[15] When the borrowed funds end up in the transferring partner's pocket, the overall transaction may be equivalent to a sale, at least to the extent that the other partners (through the partnership) assume primary responsibility for repayment of the loan. The regulations respond to the Congressional challenge with an elaborate set of special rules relating to liabilities.[16] In general, if a liability incurred by a partner in anticipation of a transfer is assumed (or taken subject to) by a partnership, the partnership is treated as transferring consideration to the partner (as part of a sale) to the extent that responsibility for repayment of the transferred liability is shifted to the other partners.[17] Liabilities incurred within two years of a transfer are presumed to be in anticipation of the transfer.[18] Liabilities incurred by a partner more than two years before a transfer are called "qualified liabilities" by the regulations.[19] The assumption of these and certain other qualified liabilities[20] are treated as consideration paid in a sale only to the extent that the transferring partner is otherwise treated as having sold a portion of the property.[21]

To illustrate, assume that on the formation of the equal AB partnership A transfers a building which has a fair market value of $100,000 and is subject to a $80,000 recourse liability that A incurred immediately before the transfer, and B contributes $20,000 cash. A uses the loan proceeds to pay personal expenses. The partnership assumes the liability, which is classified as recourse under the 752 regulations,[22] and thus $40,000 of the debt is allocated to B. On these facts, the regulations treat the partnership as transferring $40,000 of consideration (the amount of the liability shifted to B) to A in connection with a sale of the property. As a result, A is treated as having sold a 40 percent interest in the building to the partnership for $40,000 and having contributed the remaining 60 percent.[23]

14. For examples of nonsimultaneous transfers and the operation of the two-year presumption, see Reg. § 1.707-3(f) Examples 2-8.

15. 1984 General Explanation, supra note 7 at 232.

16. See generally Reg. § 1.707-5.

17. Reg. § 1.707-5(a)(1). For rules on a partner's share of recourse and nonrecourse liabilities for this purpose, see Reg. § 1.707-5(a)(2).

18. Reg. § 1.707-5(a)(7).

19. Reg. § 1.707-5(a)(6)(i)(A).

20. See Reg. § 1.707-5(a)(6).

21. Reg. § 1.707-5(a)(7). See Reg. § 1.707-5(e).

22. For Section 707(a)(2) purposes, a partner's share of recourse liabilities is determined by reference to the Section 752 regulations. Reg. § 1.707-5(a)(2)(ii). See Chapter 4D supra. Special rules are provided for allocation of nonrecourse liabilities under Section 707. See Reg. § 1.707-5(a)(2)(iii).

23. Reg. § 1.707-5(a). See Reg. § 1.707-5(f) Example 2.

Finally, to give the Service a fighting chance to uncover disguised sales, the regulations require disclosure on a prescribed form when a partnership transfers money or property to a partner within two years of a transfer of property by the partner to the partnership and the partner has treated the transfer as other than a sale for tax purposes.[24]

3. Transfers of Property and Related Allocations

Unlike the rendering of services or the use of property, a contribution of property to a partnership is not likely to be accompanied by an *allocation* of partnership income to the contributing partner, at least where capital accounts are maintained in accordance with the Section 704(b) regulations. Since those regulations require that a partner's capital account must be increased by the fair market value of contributed property,[1] an allocation of additional income to the contributing partner would result in double capital account credit for the contribution. This type of double dipping by the contributing partner alters the partners' economic business deal and is not likely to be accepted by the other partners.

Congress nonetheless feared that a contribution of property might be coupled with an allocation and distribution in a manner designed to avoid the capitalization requirement. For example, if the contributing partner's capital account were not properly adjusted to take account of the contribution, or the partner sells the property to the partnership at a price well below its true value, then the other partners might agree to compensate that partner through an increased allocation of partnership income. To illustrate, assume that A owns a building with a zero basis and a $10,000 fair market value. If A sells the building to the partnership, he recognizes a $10,000 gain, and the partnership takes a $10,000 basis in the building. On the other hand, assume A contributes the building to the partnership and it is reflected on the partnership books (including A's capital account) at its zero basis. If the first $10,000 of partnership income is allocated and distributed to A, A would have $10,000 of income (as on a straight sale), but the form of the transaction allows the remaining partners to escape tax on that $10,000 (resulting in the economic equivalent of a current deduction of the $10,000 paid for the building). In such an unusual[2] case, Section 707(a)(2)(A) will recast the contribution/allocation transaction into a sale between unrelated parties under Section 707(a)(1). As with payments for services or the use of property, Section 707(a)(2)(A) requires capitalization

24. Reg. §§ 1.707–3(c)(2), 1.707–8. Similar disclosure requirements apply when debt is incurred within two years of a transfer of property that secures the debt and in a few other specialized situations. See, e.g., Reg. §§ 1.707–5(a)(7)(ii), 1.707–8.

1. Reg. § 1.704–1(b)(2)(iv)(*b*)(*2*).

2. The operative word here may be "unusual." Although the fact pattern in the text is one of the few situations where Section 707(a)(2)(A) might apply to a contribution of property, it is an unlikely scenario in light of the capital account rules in the Section 704(b) regulations. Most disguised sales will be scrutinized under Section 707(a)(2)(B). See McKee, Nelson & Whitmire, Federal Taxation of Partnerships and Partners ¶ 14.02[4][a] (4th ed. 2007).

of an item that the partners were seeking to immediately expense through the ruse of an allocation of income.

PROBLEMS

1. Partnership is owned 25% each by A, his wife, his wife's father and X Corporation, in which A is a 50% shareholder. What are the tax consequences to the parties involved in the following sales?

(a) During the year the partnership sells A some land in which it has a basis of $50,000 for its fair market value of $40,000. In the succeeding year, A sells the land to B for $45,000.

(b) Same as (a), above, except that the first sale is to a second partnership also owned by the same parties except that an unrelated party owns a 25% interest and X Corporation owns no interest in the second partnership. The second partnership then resells the land to B for $45,000.

(c) A sells depreciable equipment in which he has an adjusted basis of $20,000 to the partnership for $30,000.

(d) A's wife sells residential rental property held by A as a capital asset to the partnership for $120,000. She had a $100,000 basis in the property. The partnership is in the housing rental business.

(e) Same as (d), above, except that the partnership is in the real estate sales business.

2. Partnership CD is owned 50% by C and 50% by D. If C sells an asset to CD and recognizes a $1,000 loss on the sale, will the loss be disallowed under § 707(b)(1)? What difference would it make if C's father, F, sells an asset to CD and recognizes a $1,000 loss? See Reg. § 1.267(b)–1(b).

3. A (a cash method taxpayer) is a 25% partner in the ABCD partnership (an accrual method taxpayer) and has a $30,000 outside basis in her partnership interest. A owns depreciable equipment with an adjusted basis of $1,000 and a fair market value of $20,000. Before any of the following transactions, the partnership has $60,000 of net income each year. What are the tax consequences in the following alternatives?

(a) A sells the equipment to the partnership for $20,000.

(b) A contributes the equipment to the partnership. A is not allocated any additional income, but her capital account is increased by the value of the contributed property. Later in the year, A receives a distribution of $20,000.

(c) Same as (b), above, except that the distribution to A is only $15,000.

(d) Suppose the partnership does not need A's equipment in its business but A nevertheless transfers it to the partnership. Partner B transfers similar depreciable property (adjusted basis—4,000; fair market value—$18,000) and $2,000 cash to the partnership. Two months later, the ABCD partnership distributes A's old property to B and B's old property together with $2,000 to A.

CHAPTER 6

SALES AND EXCHANGES OF PARTNERSHIP INTERESTS

A. CONSEQUENCES TO THE SELLING PARTNER

1. THE OPERATION OF SECTION 751(a)

Code: §§ 705(a); 706(c); 741; 751(a), (c), (d), (f); 752(d). Skim §§ 64; 453(b), (i), (*l*)(1); 708; 1031(a)(2)(D); 1060; 1245(a)(1), (2), (3)(A).

Regulations: §§ 1.706–1(c)(1), (2), (4) & (5); 1.741–1; 1.751–1(a), (c)(1)–(3), (d)(2), (g) Example (1); 1.752–1(h).

The sale or exchange of a partnership interest provides another opportunity to examine the tension between the aggregate and entity concepts of partnership taxation. The transaction might be fragmented into sales of the partner's undivided fractional interest in each asset of the partnership—an aggregate approach identical to the treatment of the sale of a sole proprietorship.[1] Alternatively, it could be viewed as the disposition of a capital asset without regard to the character of the underlying partnership assets—an entity approach resembling the treatment of sales of corporate stock. Congress settled this debate by enacting a statutory hybrid falling between these two extremes: a modified entity approach.[2] An aggregate approach would have required a cumbersome asset-by-asset fragmentation of the sale, while a pure entity approach would have facilitated the conversion of ordinary income into capital gain, forcing the Commissioner to retaliate with the usual array of vague doctrines designed to uncover and correct tax avoidance. The Congressional solution is a sensible compromise that is reminiscent of several characterization issues encountered in the basic income tax course.

Examination of the statutory scheme begins with Section 741, which provides that gain or loss from the sale or exchange of an interest in a partnership shall be considered as gain or loss from the sale of a capital asset. But unqualified capital gain treatment on the sale of a partnership interest historically led to abuse if the partnership held assets, such as inventory and accounts receivable, that gave rise to ordinary income if sold by the partnership. To curb this potential for conversion of partnership

1. Williams v. McGowan, 152 F.2d 570 (2d Cir.1945).

2. In adopting this approach, Congress essentially codified the result reached in litigation prior to the 1954 Code. Most courts had analogized a partnership interest to a capital asset irrespective of the underlying partnership assets. See, e.g., Commissioner v. Shapiro, 125 F.2d 532 (6th Cir.1942); Rev. Rul. 67–406, 1967–2 C.B. 420.

ordinary income into partner capital gain, Section 741 yields to Section 751(a) to the extent that the amount received by a selling partner is attributable to "unrealized receivables" or "inventory items." Working in tandem, Sections 741 and 751(a) apply whether the selling partner disposes of his entire interest or only some portion of it.[3]

The interaction between Sections 741 and 751(a) is familiar. It strongly resembles the relationship of the depreciation recapture provisions to Sections 1221 and 1231. Section 751(a) overrides Section 741 and converts what otherwise would be capital gain or loss into ordinary gain or loss. And like its recapture counterparts, Section 751(a) has priority—first carving out an appropriate amount as ordinary gain or loss and then leaving Section 741 to characterize the balance.[4]

In applying this modified entity approach to the sale of a partnership interest, the selling partner first must apply the general rules of Section 1001(a) and compute the total realized gain or loss on the sale. This requires a determination of the difference between the amount realized by the partner on the sale and the adjusted basis of the partnership interest sold. For this purpose, Section 752(d) incorporates the teachings of *Crane*[5] by including in the amount realized the selling partner's share of all partnership liabilities along with the cash and fair market value of other property received by the seller. The adjusted basis of the seller's interest is his outside basis under Section 705(a), adjusted to reflect the seller's pro-rata share of partnership income or loss from the beginning of the current taxable year up to the date of sale.

Although a partnership's taxable year generally does not close when a partner sells an interest,[6] it closes with respect to a partner immediately upon the sale or exchange of his entire interest in the partnership.[7] The income or loss arising from that short taxable period then passes through to the partner and is reflected in his outside basis. The partnership's year does not close with respect to a partner who sells only a portion of his interest. Rather, at the end of the partnership's year, the selling partner's distributive share of income or loss is determined by taking into account

3. Rev.Rul. 59–109, 1959–1 C.B. 168. See also Rev.Rul. 84–53, 1984–1 C.B. 159.

4. The recapture provisions, however, only characterize realized *gain* as ordinary income while Section 751(a), by considering a portion of the amount realized as resulting from the sale of a noncapital asset, encompasses both gains and losses.

5. Crane v. Commissioner, 331 U.S. 1, 67 S.Ct. 1047 (1947); cf. I.R.C. § 7701(g), which attempts to codify the principle of Commissioner v. Tufts, 461 U.S. 300, 103 S.Ct. 1826 (1983), rehearing denied, 463 U.S. 1215, 103 S.Ct. 3555 (1983), which holds that the full amount of the selling partner's share of partnership nonrecourse liabilities are included in the amount realized even if they exceed the fair market value of the encumbered property at the time of disposition.

6. I.R.C. § 706(c)(1); but see I.R.C. § 708(b)(1)(B), considered in Chapter 8B2 infra, which terminates a partnership if there is a sale or exchange of 50 percent or more of the total capital and profits interests within a 12 month period.

7. I.R.C. § 706(c)(2)(A). The regulations do not require an actual closing of the partnership's books; rather, they permit the partners to estimate the selling and buying partners' share of income based on a proration using elapsed time before and after the sale or any other reasonable method. Reg. § 1.706–1(c)(2)(ii).

the partner's varying interests in the partnership during the taxable year.[8] However, the regulations require an appropriate adjustment to the outside basis of the portion sold to reflect the partner's distributive share as of the date of the exchange.[9]

The next step is to determine what portion, if any, of the seller's total realized gain or loss is characterized as ordinary income under Section 751(a).[10] Before discussing the mechanics of that computation, the categories of Section 751 assets must be defined more precisely.

Section 751 assets include "unrealized receivables" and "inventory items," as defined in Sections 751(c) and (d), respectively. Unrealized receivables generally include rights (contractual or otherwise) to payment for goods and services which have not previously been included in income, provided, in the case of goods, that the sales proceeds would be treated as received from the sale or exchange of non-capital assets.[11] In addition, unrealized receivables include certain short-term debt obligations and an array of assets to the extent that their disposition at fair market value would trigger recapture of cost recovery and certain other prior deductions.[12] Since the recapture portion would be characterized as ordinary income on a sale or other disposition of these assets, they are appropriately included in Section 751 even though it is somewhat odd to label them as "receivables."

The term "inventory items" is defined broadly, embracing not only the familiar category of non-capital assets described in Section 1221(1) but also any property which, upon sale by the partnership or the selling partner, would not be considered a capital asset or Section 1231 asset.[13] As a result of the broad definition of "inventory," an asset may constitute both an unrealized receivable and an inventory item.[14] If an asset falls within both Section 751(a)(1) and (a)(2), it will be taxed only once.[15]

Having defined the critical terms, we now may return to the computation of the selling partner's gain or loss. If part of the amount realized is attributable to Section 751 assets, the tax consequences of the sale must be

8. I.R.C. § 706(d)(1); Reg. § 1.706–1(c)(4).

9. Reg. § 1.705–1(a)(1).

10. Sales or exchanges of interests in partnerships which have Section 751 assets must be reported by the transferor partner to the partnership (I.R.C. § 6050K(c)(1)) and then by the partnership to the Service, the transferor partner and the transferee partner (I.R.C. § 6050K(a), (b) and (c)(2)). Failure to report will result in penalties. See I.R.C. §§ 6721–6724.

11. I.R.C. § 751(c).

12. The regulations generally treat a selling partner's share of recapture gain as a separate unrealized receivable with a zero basis and a value equal to the selling partner's share of recapture gain. Reg. § 1.751–1(c)(4) & (5).

13. I.R.C. § 751(d). Prior to August 6, 1997, inventory items were treated as "ordinary income" property under Section 751(a) only if they were "substantially appreciated"—i.e., only if the aggregate fair market value of the items exceeded 120 percent of their adjusted basis to the partnership. Cf. I.R.C. § 751(b)(3).

14. Reg. § 1.751–1(d)(2)(ii).

15. If unrealized receivables fall within both Section 751(c) and (d), they are treated as Section 751(c) assets under other Code provisions. See I.R.C. §§ 735(a); 736.

bifurcated by determining the amount of income or loss from Section 751 property that would have been allocated to the selling partner if the partnership had sold all of its property in a fully taxable transaction for cash in an amount equal to the fair market value of such property.[16] The selling partner's share of income or loss from Section 751 property in this hypothetical sale takes into account special allocations and allocations required under Section 704(c), including any remedial allocations.[17] The gain or loss attributable to Section 751 property will be ordinary gain or loss.

After determining the gain or loss under Section 751(a), the final step is to determine the difference between the selling partner's total gain or loss and the ordinary gain or loss determined under section 751(a). That difference is the selling partner's section 741 capital gain or loss on the sale of the partnership interest.[18] Since this is a netting process, it is possible for the seller to have a gain under section 751(a) and a loss under Section 741 or vice versa. In keeping with the entity approach, the long or short-term character of the Section 741 capital gain or loss depends upon the partner's holding period for the partnership interest and not the partnership's holding period for its assets.[19]

The prospect of ordinary income treatment on the sale of a partnership interest has motivated sophisticated taxpayers to devise strategies to avoid the taint caused by the presence of unrealized receivables and inventory items on the partnership's balance sheet. One technique was the creation of a separate second-tier partnership to hold the "parent" partnership's Section 751 assets. A partner selling an interest in the parent then would claim that none of its assets were tainted by Section 751(a) because they were limited to the retained Section 741 assets and the parent's interest in the second partnership, which was not itself a Section 751 asset irrespective of its underlying holdings. Congress put a halt to the use of multi-tiered partnerships to avoid Section 751(a) gain by adopting an aggregate theory in Section 751(f). That section provides that in determining a partnership's Section 751 assets, the partnership "shall be treated as

16. Reg. § 1.751–1(a)(2). The determination of "fair market value" is made by taking into account Section 7701(g), which provides that the fair market value of property shall not be less than the amount of any nonrecourse debt to which the property is subject. Id. At one time, the regulations allowed the selling partner and the buyer to allocate the total purchase price for the partnership interest among the partnership's assets for purposes of the Section 751 calculations. The regulations no longer permit such an allocation to control the determination of the value of the partnership's assets. The selling partner's amount realized apparently must be allocated first to Section 751 properties based on their relative fair market values and then to the other assets. Cf. I.R.C. § 1060.

A partner selling or exchanging any part of a partnership interest in a partnership holding Section 751 property is required to report the circumstances of the sale in a statement attached to the income tax return for the year in which the sale or exchange occurs. Reg. § 1.751–1(a)(3).

17. Reg. § 1.751–1(a)(2).

18. Id.

19. Gray v. Commissioner, 11 T.C.M. 17 (1952); see Section A3 of this chapter, infra., for special holding period rules in the case of a sale of a partnership interest.

owning its proportionate share of the property of any other partnership in which it is a partner." This rule applies regardless of the number of tiers between the selling partner and the ordinary income property.

The relationship of Sections 741 and 751(a) to other judicial doctrines and Code sections has evolved gradually. For example, although there once was substantial controversy over whether an exchange of partnership interests could qualify as a like-kind exchange,[20] Congress silenced the debate by disallowing nonrecognition on such exchanges.[21] Transfers of partnership interests to a controlled corporation normally qualify for nonrecognition under Section 351, but problems may arise in determining the nature of the incorporation transaction.[22] The application of the Section 453 installment sales rules to the sale of a partnership interest has been somewhat hazy, but the Service has helped to clear the air with a published ruling.[23] Finally, because of the difference in tax treatment, it sometimes is necessary to distinguish the sale of a partnership interest from the liquidation of an interest. Some of these thorny questions are explored in the materials which follow; the sale vs. liquidation and incorporation issues are discussed in a later chapter.[24]

Ledoux v. Commissioner

United States Tax Court, 1981.
77 T.C. 293, affirmed per curiam 695 F.2d 1320 (11th Cir.1983).

■ STERRETT, JUDGE. * * *

After concessions, the sole issue remaining for our decision is whether any portion of the amount received by petitioner John W. Ledoux pursuant to an agreement for the sale of a partnership interest was attributable to an unrealized receivable of the partnership and thus was required to be characterized as ordinary income under section 751, I.R.C. 1954.

FINDINGS OF FACT

* * *

[John Ledoux was a 25% partner in the Collins–Ledoux partnership, which was formed on October 1, 1955 to manage and operate a greyhound

20. See Newman, "Like Kind Exchanges of Partnership Interests Under Section 1031," 18 Wake Forest L.Rev. 663 (1982) and Brier, "Like-Kind Exchanges of Partnership Interests: A Policy Oriented Approach," 38 Tax L.Rev. 389 (1983).

21. I.R.C. § 1031(a)(2)(D). See Reg. § 1.1031(a)–1(a)(1). The legislative history states that Congress does not intend this provision to apply to exchanges of interests in the same partnership. H.Rep. No. 98–432, 98th Cong., 2d Sess. 1234 (1984). See Rev. Rul. 84–52, 1984–1 C.B. 157, holding that a conversion of a general partnership interest into a limited partnership interest in the same partnership is treated for tax purposes as a distribution of the new partnership interest to the converting partner under Section 731 and a contribution of the old interest to the partnership under Section 721. See also I.R.C. § 1031(a)(2), flush language, making it clear that an interest in a partnership which elects under Section 761 to be excluded from Subchapter K shall be treated as an interest in each of the assets of the partnership for purposes of Section 1031.

22. See Rev.Rul. 84–111, infra at page 354.

23. See Section A3 of this chapter, infra.

24. See Chapters 8C and 8D1b, infra.

dog racing track in Seminole County, Florida. The track was owned by the Sanford–Orlando Kennel Club, Inc. and previously had been managed by a related partnership, also known as Sanford–Orlando Kennel Club. Collins–Ledoux had the right to operate the track for a period of 20 years; in return, it agreed to pay the Sanford–Orlando partnership the first $200,000 of net annual profit from track operations.

From October 1, 1955 to September 30, 1972, the Collins–Ledoux partnership operated the track pursuant to the agreement with the Sanford–Orlando group. Ledoux managed the operations of the track and received a salary along with a share of the net profits of Collins–Ledoux. During this period, Collins–Ledoux made extensive improvements to the property and acquired adjacent land for use in connection with the operation of the track. The efforts were quite successful. From 1955 to 1972, the gross income of the partnership increased from $3.6 million to $23.6 million and the net income increased from $72,000 to over $550,000.

After setting forth this background, the Tax Court went on to describe the sale of John Ledoux's 25% partnership interest. Ed.]

After the 1972 racing season two of the partners, Jerry Collins and Jack Collins, decided to purchase petitioner's 25–percent partnership interest. They agreed to allow Ledoux to propose a fair selling price for his interest. Ledoux set a price based on a price-earnings multiple of 5 times his share of the partnership's 1972 earnings. This resulted in a total value for his 25–percent interest of $800,000. There was no valuation or appraisal of specific assets at the time, and the sales price included his interest in all of the assets of the partnership.

* * *

On his 1972 Federal income tax return, petitioner properly elected to report the gain from the sale of his partnership interest under the installment method as prescribed in section 453. Petitioner calculated the total gain on such sale to be as follows:

Sales price	$800,000.00
Basis in partnership interest	62,658.70
Total gain on sale	737,341.30

During 1972, 1973, and 1974, petitioner received payments in accordance with the October 17, 1972, agreement of sale. In each of those years, he characterized the reported gain, calculated pursuant to the installment sales method, as capital gain.

After consummation of the sale of petitioner's interest in the Collins–Ledoux partnership, the remaining partners continued to operate the dog track under the agreement of July 9, 1955, as amended.

Respondent, in his notice of deficiency, did not disagree with petitioner's calculation of the total gain. However, he determined that $575,392.50

of the gain was related to petitioner's interest in the dog track agreement and should be subject to ordinary income treatment pursuant to section 751.[2]

OPINION

The sole issue presented is whether a portion of the amount received by petitioner on the sale of his 25–percent partnership interest is taxable as ordinary income and not as capital gain. More specifically, we must decide whether any portion of the sales price is attributable to "unrealized receivables" of the partnership.

Generally, gain or loss on the sale or exchange of a partnership interest is treated as capital gain or loss. Sec. 741. Prior to 1954, a partner could escape ordinary income tax treatment on his portion of the partnership's unrealized receivables by selling or exchanging his interest in the partnership and treating the gain or loss therefrom as capital gain or loss. To curb such abuses, section 751 was enacted to deal with the problem of the so-called "collapsible partnership."

* * *

Petitioner contends that the dog track agreement gave the Collins–Ledoux partnership the right to manage and operate the dog track. According to petitioner, the agreement did not give the partnership any contractual rights to receive future payments and did not impose any obligation on the partnership to perform services. Rather, the agreement merely gave the partnership the right to occupy and use all of the corporation's properties (including the racetrack facilities and the racing permit) in operating its dog track business; if the partnership exercised such right, it would be obligated to make annual payments to the corporation based upon specified percentages of the annual mutuel handle. Thus, because the dog track agreement was in the nature of a leasehold agreement rather than an employment contract, it did not create the type of "unrealized receivables" referred to in section 751.

Respondent, on the other hand, contends that the partnership operated the racetrack for the corporation and was paid a portion of the profits for its efforts. As such, the agreement was in the nature of a management employment contract. When petitioner sold his partnership interest to the Collinses in 1972, the main right that he sold was a contract right to receive income in the future for yet-to-be-rendered personal services. This, respondent asserts, is supported by the fact that petitioner determined the sales price for his partnership interest by capitalizing his 1972 annual

2. Respondent determined that the value of petitioner's proportionate share of partnership assets other than the dog track agreement was as follows:

Asset	Value
Escrow deposit	$ 12,500.00
Sanford–Seminole Development Co. stock	1,000.00
Fixed assets	211,107.50
	224,607.50

The difference between this value and the total purchase price ($800,000) was treated by respondent as having been received by petitioner in exchange for his rights in the dog track agreement.

income (approximately $160,000) by a factor of 5. Therefore, respondent contends that the portion of the gain realized by petitioner that is attributable to the management contract should be characterized as an amount received for unrealized receivables of the partnership. Consequently, such gain should be characterized as ordinary income under section 751.

The legislative history is not wholly clear with respect to the types of assets that Congress intended to place under the umbrella of "unrealized receivables." The House report states:

> The term "unrealized receivables or fees" is used to apply to any rights to income which have not been included in gross income under the method of accounting employed by the partnership. The provision is applicable mainly to cash basis partnerships which have acquired a contractual or other legal right to income for goods or services. * * * [H.Rept. 1337, 83d Cong., 2d Sess. 71 (1954).]

Essentially the same language appears in the report of the Senate committee. S.Rept. 1622, 83d Cong., 2d Sess. 98 (1954). In addition, the regulations elaborate on the meaning of "unrealized receivables" as used in section 751. Section 1.751–1(c), Income Tax Regs., provides:

> Sec. 1.751–1(c) *Unrealized receivables.* (1) The term "unrealized receivables", * * * means any rights (contractual or otherwise) to payment for—
>
> (i) Goods delivered or to be delivered (to the extent that such payment would be treated as received for property other than a capital asset), or
>
> (ii) Services rendered or to be rendered, to the extent that income arising from such rights to payment was not previously includible in income under the method of accounting employed by the partnership. Such rights must have arisen under contracts or agreements in existence at the time of sale or distribution, although the partnership may not be able to enforce payment until a later time. For example, the term includes trade accounts receivable of a cash method taxpayer, and rights to payment for work or goods begun but incomplete at the time of the sale or distribution.
>
> * * *
>
> (3) In determining the amount of the sale price attributable to such unrealized receivables, or their value in a distribution treated as a sale or exchange, any arm's length agreement between the buyer and the seller, or between the partnership and the distributee partner, will generally establish the amount or value. In the absence of such an agreement, full account shall be taken not only of the estimated cost of completing performance of the contract or agreement, but also of the time between the sale or distribution and the time of payment.

The language of the legislative history and the regulations indicates that the term "unrealized receivables" includes any contractual or other right to payment for goods delivered or to be delivered or services rendered or to be rendered. Therefore, an analysis of the nature of the rights under the dog track agreement, in the context of the aforementioned legal framework, becomes appropriate. A number of cases have dealt with the meaning of "unrealized receivables" and thereby have helped to define the scope of the term. Courts that have considered the term "unrealized receivables" generally have said that it should be given a broad interpretation. Cf. Corn Products Co. v. Commissioner, 350 U.S. 46, 52 (1955) (the term "capital asset" is to be construed narrowly, but exclusions from the definition thereof are to be broadly and liberally construed). For instance, in Logan v. Commissioner, 51 T.C. 482, 486 (1968), we held that a partnership's right in quantum meruit to payment for work in progress constituted an unrealized receivable even though there was no express agreement between the partnership and its clients requiring payment.

In Roth v. Commissioner, 321 F.2d 607 (9th Cir.1963), affg. 38 T.C. 171 (1962), the Ninth Circuit dealt with the sale of an interest in a partnership which produced a movie and then gave a 10–year distribution right to Paramount Pictures Corp. in return for a percentage of the gross receipts. The selling partner claimed that his right to a portion of the payments expected under the partnership's contract with Paramount did not constitute an unrealized receivable. The court rejected this view, however, reasoning that Congress "meant to exclude from capital gains treatment any receipts which would have been treated as ordinary income to the partner if no transfer of the partnership interest had occurred." 321 F.2d at 611.* Therefore, the partnership's right to payments under the distribution contract was in the nature of an unrealized receivable.

A third example of the broad interpretation given to the term "unrealized receivable" is United States v. Eidson, 310 F.2d 111 (5th Cir.1962), revg. an unreported opinion (W.D.Tex.1961). The court there considered the nature of a management contract which was similar to the one at issue in the instant case. The case arose in the context of a sale by a partnership of all of its rights to operate and manage a mutual insurance company. The selling partnership received $170,000 for the rights it held under the management contract, and the Government asserted that the total amount should be treated as ordinary income. The Court of Appeals agreed with the Government's view on the ground that what was being assigned was not a capital asset whose value had accrued over a period of years; rather, the right to operate the company and receive profits therefrom during the remaining life of the contract was the real subject of the assignment. 310 F.2d at 116. The Fifth Circuit found the Supreme Court's holding in Commissioner v. P.G. Lake, Inc., 356 U.S. 260 (1958), to be conclusive:

* [The court, quoting 6 Mertens, Federal Income Taxation § 35.85 at 326, added: "The broad scope of the term unrealized receivables is limited only by the fact that it is confined to legal rights to income." Ed.]

> The substance of what was assigned was the right to receive future income. The substance of what was received was the present value of income which the recipient would otherwise obtain in the future. In short, consideration was paid for the right to receive future income, not for an increase in the value of the income-producing property. [356 U.S. at 266, cited in 310 F.2d at 115.]

In United States v. Woolsey, 326 F.2d 287 (5th Cir.1963), revg. 208 F.Supp. 325 (S.D.Tex.1962), the Fifth Circuit again faced a situation similar to the one that we face herein. The Fifth Circuit considered whether proceeds received by taxpayers on the sale of their partnership interests were to be treated as ordinary income or capital gain. There, the court was faced with the sale of interests in a partnership which held, as one of its assets, a 25–year contract to manage a mutual insurance company. As in the instant case, the contract gave the partners the right to render services for the term of the contract and to earn ordinary income in the future. In holding that the partnership's management contract constituted an unrealized receivable, the court stated:

> When we look at the underlying right assigned in this case, we cannot escape the conclusion that so much of the consideration which relates to the right to earn ordinary income in the future under the "management contract," taxable to the assignee as ordinary income, is likewise taxable to the assignor as ordinary income although such income must be earned. Section 751 has defined "unrealized receivables" to include any rights, contractual or otherwise, to ordinary income from "services rendered, *or to be rendered*," (emphasis added) to the extent that the same were not previously includable in income by the partnership, with the result that capital gains rates cannot be applied to the rights to income under the facts of this case, which would constitute ordinary income had the same been received in due course by the partnership. * * * It is our conclusion that such portion of the consideration received by the taxpayers in this case as properly should be allocated to the present value of their right to earn ordinary income in the future under the "management contract" is subject to taxation as ordinary income. * * * [326 F.2d at 291.]

Petitioner attempts to distinguish United States v. Woolsey, supra, and United States v. Eidson, supra, from the instant case by arguing that those cases involved a sale or termination of contracts to manage mutual insurance companies in Texas and that the management contracts therein were in the nature of employment agreements. After closely scrutinizing the facts in those cases, we conclude that petitioner's position has no merit. The fact that the *Woolsey* case involved sale of 100 percent of the partnership interests, as opposed to a sale of only a 25–percent partnership interest herein, is of no consequence. In addition, the fact that *Eidson* involved the surrender of the partnership's contract right to manage the insurance company, as opposed to the continued partnership operation in the instant case, also is not a material factual distinction.

The dog track agreement at issue in the instant case is similar to the management contract considered by the Fifth Circuit in *Woolsey*. Each gives the respective partnership the right to operate a business for a period of years and to earn ordinary income in return for payments of specified amounts to the corporation that holds the State charter. Therefore, based on our analysis of the statutory language, the legislative history, and the regulations and relevant case law, we are compelled to find that the dog track agreement gave the petitioner an interest that amounted to an "unrealized receivable" within the meaning of section 751(c).

Petitioner further contends that the dog track agreement does not represent an unrealized receivable because it does not require or obligate the partnership to perform personal services in the future. The agreement only gives, the argument continues, the Collins–Ledoux partnership the right to engage in a business.

We find this argument to be unpersuasive. The words of section 751(c), providing that the term "unrealized receivable" includes the right to payment for "services rendered, or to be rendered," do not preclude that section's application to a situation where, as here, the performance of services is not required by the agreement. As the Fifth Circuit said in United States v. Eidson, supra:

> The fact that * * * income would not be received by the [partnership] unless they performed the services which the contract required of them, that is, actively managed the affairs of the insurance company in a manner that would produce a profit after all of the necessary expenditures, does not, it seems clear, affect the nature of this payment. It affects only the amount. That is, the fact that the taxpayers would have to spend their time and energies in performing services for which the compensation would be received merely affects the price at which they would be willing to assign or transfer the contract. * * * [310 F.2d at 115.]

Consequently, a portion of the consideration received by Ledoux on the sale of his partnership interest is subject to taxation as ordinary income.

Having established that the dog track agreement qualifies as an unrealized receivable, we next consider whether all or only part of petitioner's gain in excess of the amount attributable to his share of tangible partnership assets should be treated as ordinary income. Petitioner argues that this excess gain was attributable to goodwill or the value of a going concern.

With respect to goodwill, we note that petitioner's attorney drafted, and petitioner signed, the agreement for sale of partnership interest, dated October 17, 1972, which contains the following statement in paragraph 7:

> 7. In the determination of the purchase price set forth in this agreement, the parties acknowledge no consideration has been given to any item of goodwill.

The meaning of the words "no consideration" is not entirely free from doubt. They could mean that no thought was given to an allocation of any of the sales price to goodwill, or they could indicate that the parties agreed that no part of the purchase price was allocated to goodwill. The testimony of the attorney who prepared the document indicates, however, that he did consider the implications of the sale of goodwill and even did research on the subject. He testified that he believed, albeit incorrectly, that, if goodwill were part of the purchase price, his client would not be entitled to capital gains treatment.

Petitioner attempts to justify this misstatement of the tax implications of an allocation to goodwill not by asserting mistake, but by pointing out that his attorney "is not a tax lawyer but is primarily involved with commercial law and real estate." We find as a fact that petitioner agreed at arm's length with the purchasers of his partnership interest that no part of the purchase price should be attributable to goodwill. The Tax Court long has adhered to the view that, absent "strong proof," a taxpayer cannot challenge an express allocation in an arm's-length sales contract to which he had agreed. See, e.g., Major v. Commissioner, 76 T.C. 239, 249 (1981), appeal pending (7th Cir., July 7, 1981); Lucas v. Commissioner, 58 T.C. 1022, 1032 (1972). In Spector v. Commissioner, 641 F.2d 376 (5th Cir. 1981), revg. 71 T.C. 1017 (1979), the Fifth Circuit, to which an appeal in this case will lie, appeared to step away from its prior adherence to the "strong proof" standard and move toward the stricter standard enunciated in Commissioner v. Danielson, 378 F.2d 771, 775 (3d Cir.1967), remanding 44 T.C. 549 (1965), cert. denied 389 U.S. 858 (1967). However, in this case, we need not measure the length of the step since we hold that petitioner has failed to introduce sufficient evidence to satisfy even the more lenient "strong proof" standard.

We next turn to petitioner's contention that part or all of the purchase price received in excess of the value of tangible assets is attributable to value of a going concern. In VGS Corp. v. Commissioner, 68 T.C. 563 (1977), we stated that—

> Going-concern value is, in essence, the additional element of value which attaches to property by reason of its existence as an integral part of a going concern. * * * [T]he ability of a business to continue to function and generate income without interruption as a consequence of the change in ownership, is a vital part of the value of a going concern. * * * [68 T.C. at 591–592; citations omitted.]

However, in the instant case, the ability of the dog racing track to continue to function after the sale of Ledoux's partnership interest was due to the remaining partners' retention of rights to operate under the dog track agreement. Without such agreement, there would have been no continuing right to operate a business and no right to continue to earn income. Thus, the amount paid in excess of the value of Ledoux's share of the tangible assets was not for the intangible value of the business as a going concern but rather for Ledoux's rights under the dog track agreement.

Finally, we turn to petitioner's claim that a determination of the value of rights arising from the dog track agreement has never been made and no evidence of the value of such rights was submitted in this case. We note that the $800,000 purchase price was proposed by petitioner and was accepted by Jack Collins and Jerry Collins in an arm's-length agreement of sale evidenced in the memorandum of agreement of July 19, 1972, and the agreement for sale of partnership interest of October 17, 1972. In addition, the October 17, 1972, sales agreement, written by petitioner's attorney, provided in paragraph 1 that the "Seller [Ledoux] sells to buyer [Jerry Collins and Jack Collins] all of his interest in [the partnership] * * * including but not limited to, *the seller's right to income* and to acquire the capital stock of The Sanford–Orlando Kennel Club, Inc." (Emphasis added.) Section 1.751–1(c)(3), Income Tax Regs., provides that an arm's-length agreement between the buyer and the seller generally will establish the value attributable to unrealized receivables.

Based on the provision in the agreement that no part of the consideration was attributable to goodwill, it is clear to us that the parties were aware that they could, if they so desired, have provided that no part of the consideration was attributable to the dog track agreement. No such provision was made.[8] Furthermore, the agreement clearly stated that one of the assets purchased was Ledoux's rights to future income. Considering that petitioner calculated the purchase price by capitalizing future earnings expected under the dog track agreement, we conclude that the portion of Ledoux's gain in excess of the amount attributable to tangible assets was attributable to an unrealized receivable as reflected by the dog track agreement.

Decision will be entered for the respondent.

PROBLEMS

1. Partner A owns a one-third interest in the ABC cash method, calendar year general partnership, which manufactures and sells inventory. A, B and C, the original partners, each made initial cash contributions of $75,000. All income has been distributed as earned. On January 1st, A sells his interest in the partnership to D. Consider the tax consequences of the sale to A, assuming he has owned his partnership interest for several years. The balance sheet of the ABC partnership (which is to be used in all parts of this problems unless the facts indicate to the contrary) is as follows:

Assets	A.B.	F.M.V.	Partners' Capital	A.B.	F.M.V.
Cash	$ 45,000	$ 45,000	A	$ 75,000	$135,000
			B	75,000	135,000
Inventory	75,000	90,000	C	75,000	135,000
Accounts Receivable	0	45,000			
Capital Asset	105,000	225,000			
	$225,000	$405,000		$225,000	$405,000

8. We do not mean to imply that an opposite holding would automatically pertain if a provision had been made with respect to the dog track agreement.

Consider the tax consequences to A on his sale in each of the following alternative situations:

(a) A sells his interest for $135,000 cash.

(b) Each partner originally contributed $150,000 cash (and assume each has an outside basis of $150,000), and the capital asset has a basis to the partnership of $330,000. A sells his interest to D for $135,000 cash.

(c) Each partner originally contributed only $45,000 cash instead of $75,000, and the capital asset was purchased and held subject to a $90,000 liability. A sells his interest to D for $105,000 cash.

(d) The sale occurs on March 31, one quarter of the way through the year, at a time when A's share of partnership income through March 31 (all ordinary income) is $30,000. It is agreed that D will pay A $165,000 for his interest and also will acquire A's right to income.

2. Assume the same basic facts as in Problem 1, except the ABC partnership is an accrual method partnership so that the accounts receivable have an adjusted basis of $45,000 and A has an outside basis of $90,000. For each part, determine only the amount of A's Section 751(a) ordinary income:

(a) A sells his interest to D on January 1.

(b) What result in (a), above, if the partnership held the inventory as a capital asset, but A is a dealer in that type of property?

(c) What result in (a), above, if the partnership owns no inventory but has a 50% interest in another partnership (partnership #2), whose only assets are inventory with a basis of $150,000 and a value of $180,000?

(d) What result in (a), above, if in addition the partnership had a contract worth $30,000 to perform real estate management services for the next ten years?

2. CAPITAL GAINS LOOK-THROUGH RULE

Code: §§ 1(h)(5)(B), (9), (10).

Regulations: §§ 1.1(h)–1(a), (b)(1), (2), (3)(i) & (ii).

In order to apply the Code's different rates for taxing long-term capital gains, the regulations apply a "look-through rule" for sales or exchanges of interests in a partnership, an S corporation, or a trust.[1] As a result, a partner who sells a partnership interest held for more than one year may recognize Section 751 ordinary income and up to three different types of long-term capital gains: collectibles gain (taxable at rates up to 28 percent),

1. Reg. § 1.1(h)–1.

unrecaptured Section 1250 gain (taxable at a 25 percent maximum rate), and "residual" capital gain (taxable at a 15 percent maximum rate).[2]

Under Section 1(h)(5)(B), any gain from the sale of a partnership interest held for more than one year that is attributable to unrealized appreciation in the value of the partnership's collectibles is treated as gain from the sale or exchange of a collectible. The regulations provide that the selling partner's share of collectibles gain is the amount of the net collectibles gain (but not net loss) that would be allocated to that partner (including any residual allocation under Section 704(c)) if the partnership transferred all of its collectibles for cash equal to the fair market value of such assets in a fully taxable transaction immediately before the transfer of the partnership interest.[3] The same hypothetical sale approach is used to determine a selling partner's share of unrecaptured Section 1250 capital gain.[4] The selling partner's residual capital gain is the amount of the Section 741 long-term capital gain or loss minus the partner's shares of collectibles and unrecaptured Section 1250 gains.[5] Thus, the approach of the look-through rule for capital gains is quite similar to the method used to identify the amount of a selling partner's Section 751(a) gain and Section 741 gain.[6]

The following problems are adapted from examples in the regulations.[7] Use them to see if you can apply Section 751(a) in conjunction with the look-through rule for capital gains.

PROBLEM

A and B are equal partners in a personal services partnership. Each partner acquired her partnership interest for cash several years ago. None of the partnership's assets is Section 704(c) property. The partnership has the following balance sheet:

Assets	**A.B.**	**F.M.V.**	**Liabilities and Partners' Capital**	**A.B.**	**F.M.V.**
Cash	$13,000	$13,000	Liabilities:		$ 2,000
Capital Assets:			Capital:		
Collectibles	1,000	3,000	A	$10,000	15,000
Other	6,000	2,000	B	10,000	15,000
Subtotal	7,000	5,000			
Receivables	0	14,000			
Total	$20,000	$32,000		$20,000	$32,000

2. Reg. § 1.1(h)–1(a). See I.R.C. § 1(h).

3. Reg. § 1.1(h)–1(b)(2)(ii). If less than all of the realized gain in the partnership interest is recognized, a proportionate amount of the gain in the collectibles is taxed. Id.

4. Reg. § 1.1(h)–1(b)(3)(ii).

5. Reg. § 1.1(h)–1(c).

6. Reg. § 1.1(h)–1(e) provides that reporting rules similar to the reporting rules under Section 751(a) apply when a seller of a partnership interest recognizes collectibles gain or Section 1250 capital gain.

7. See Reg. § 1.1(h)–1(f) Examples 1, 2, & 3.

Consider the tax consequences to B on her sale in each of the following alternative situations:

(a) B sells her interest for $15,000 cash.

(b) B sells her interest for $16,000 cash and under the partnership agreement all gain from the sale of the collectibles is allocated to B.

(c) Same as (a), above, except that the collectibles have a basis of $3,000 and a fair market value of $1,000, and the other capital asset has a basis of $4,000 and a fair market value of $4,000.

3. COLLATERAL ISSUES

a. HOLDING PERIOD

Regulations: §§ 1.1(h)–1(f) Example 5; 1.1223–3(a), (b), (c).

A partner may have a divided holding period in a partnership interest.[1] For example, assume a partner has held his partnership interest more than one year and the partner makes a cash contribution to the partnership. For the next year the partner will have a short-term holding period in the portion of the partnership interest attributable to the cash contribution.[2] Thus, if the partner sells all or a part of the partnership interest within one year of the cash contribution, any capital gain or loss has to be divided between long-term and short-term capital gain or loss in the same proportion as the long-term and short-term holding periods for the partnership interest.[3] The regulations integrate the holding period rule and the look-through rule for capital gains by first identifying the portions of the selling partner's Section 741 capital gain or loss that are long-term or short-term capital gain or loss. Then a proportionate amount of any collectibles or unrecaptured Section 1250 gain is deemed to be part of the long-term capital gain or loss. For example, assume a partner's partnership interest has a basis of $7,000 and a holding period that is 50 percent long-term and 50 percent short-term. Assume further that the partner's Section 751 ordinary income is $2,000 and the partner's allocable share of the partnership's collectibles gain is also $2,000. If the partner sells the partnership interest for $14,000, his total gain is $7,000 ($14,000 amount realized less $7,000 basis). Section 751(a) would characterize $2,000 of that gain as ordinary income and the remaining $5,000 of Section 741 capital gain would be characterized as $2,500 long-term capital gain and $2,500 short-term capital gain (50 percent each per the holding periods). The gain attributable to the collectibles that is allocable to the portion of the interest sold with a long-term holding period is $1,000 (again, 50 percent per the holding periods allocation). Thus, the partner would recognize $1,000 of collectibles gain, $1,500 of residual (i.e., 15 percent) long-term capital gain

1. Reg. § 1.1223–3(a).

2. Reg. § 1.1223–3(b)(1).

3. Reg. § 1.1223–3(c)(1),(2)(ii).

and $2,500 of short-term capital gain, in addition to $2,000 of Section 751(a) ordinary income.[4]

The regulations contain a few special rules for determining the holding period of a partner selling a partnership interest. First, if a partner both makes cash contributions and receives cash distributions during the one-year period before the sale or exchange of the partnership interest, the partner may reduce the cash contributions made during the year by the cash distributions on a last-in-first-out basis, treating all cash distributions as if they were received immediately before the sale or exchange.[5] Also, contributions of Section 751(c) unrealized receivables and Section 751(d) inventory items within one year of a sale or exchange of a partnership interest are disregarded for purposes of determining the holding period of the partnership interest if the partner recognizes ordinary income or loss on such Section 751 assets in a fully taxable transaction.[6] The taxable transaction can be either a sale of all or a part of the partnership interest or a sale by the partnership of the contributed section 751 asset.[7] The theory of this exception is that the contributed section 751 asset should not both produce ordinary income to the selling partner and result in a short-term holding period in the partnership interest.

b. INSTALLMENT SALES OF PARTNERSHIP INTERESTS

Revenue Ruling 89–108

1989–2 Cum.Bull. 100.

ISSUE

If the property of a partnership includes inventory, to what extent may the installment method of reporting income under section 453 of the Internal Revenue Code be used to report income on the sale of an interest in that partnership?

FACTS

P was a partner in a partnership that held substantially appreciated inventory within the meaning of section 751(d) of the Code. A portion of this property constituted inventory within the meaning of section 453(b)(2)(B). The partnership did not hold any unrealized receivables within the meaning of section 751(c). *P* sold *P*'s partnership interest in

4. See Reg. § 1.1(h)–1(f) Example 5.

5. Reg. § 1.1223–3(b)(2); see Reg. § 1.1223–3(f) Example 3. The cash distributions are treated as made at the time of the distribution if gain or loss is recognized under Section 731. Id. Deemed contributions of cash under Section 752(a) and deemed distributions of cash under Section 752(b) are disregarded to the extent they are disregarded in determining the selling partner's capital account. Reg. §§ 1.1223–3(b)(3); 1.704–1(b)(2)(iv)(c).

6. Reg. § 1.1223–3(b)(4). This exception is not available if the partner would not otherwise be treated as holding any portion of the interest long-term (e.g., because the partner's only contributions to the partnership are Section 751 assets or Section 751 assets within the one year period). Id.

7. Id.

exchange for an installment note. The gain *P* recognized from the sale was, in part, attributable to the partnership inventory. Interests in the partnership were not traded on an established market, and therefore the provisions of section 453(k) did not make the sale ineligible for installment method reporting.

LAW AND ANALYSIS

Section 453(a) of the Code states that, except as otherwise provided, income from an installment sale shall be taken into account under the installment method. Section 453(b)(1) defines an installment sale as a disposition of property where at least one payment is to be received after the close of the taxable year in which the disposition occurs. Section 453(c) defines the installment method as a method under which the income recognized for any taxable year from a disposition is that proportion of the payments received in that year which the gross profit (realized or to be realized when payment is completed) bears to the total contract price. Section 453(b)(2)(B) precludes installment method reporting in the case of a sale of personal property that is required to be included in inventory of the taxpayer if on hand at the close of the taxable year.

Section 741 of the Code provides that, in the case of a sale or exchange of a partnership interest, gain or loss recognized to the transferor is considered gain or loss from the sale or exchange of a capital asset, except as otherwise provided in section 751.

Section 751(a) of the Code provides that the amount received by a transferor partner in exchange for all or a part of a partnership interest shall be considered as an amount realized from the sale or exchange of property other than a capital asset, to the extent such an amount is attributable to unrealized receivables or inventory items that have appreciated substantially in value.

Section 751(d) of the Code provides that inventory items shall be considered to be substantially appreciated if the fair market value of the inventory exceeds 120 percent of the adjusted basis to the partnership of the inventory * * *. Under section 751(d)(2)(A), inventory items include property of the partnership described in section 1221(1). Section 1221(1) refers to property which would properly be included in the inventory of the taxpayer if on hand at the close of the taxable year, and property held by the taxpayer primarily for sale to customers in the ordinary course of his trade or business. Under section 751(d)(2)(D), inventory items also include any property held by the partnership that, if held by the selling or distributee partner, would be considered property of the type described in section 751(d)(2)(A).

Under section 741 of the Code, the sale of a partnership interest generally is treated as the sale of a single capital asset without regard to the nature of the underlying partnership property. See H.R.Rep. No. 1337, 83d Cong., 2d Sess. 70 (1954). In this respect, the tax treatment of the sale of a partnership interest differs from that accorded the sale of a sole proprietorship. See, e.g., Williams v. McGowan, 152 F.2d 570 (2d Cir.1945), which held that the sale of an entire business as a going concern was the sale of the individual assets of the business. See also Rev.Rul. 68–13, 1968–1 C.B. 195, which holds that the installment sale of a sole proprietorship is generally considered to be a sale of individual assets of the proprietorship for purposes of applying section 453.

Section 751 of the Code was enacted to prevent the conversion of certain potential ordinary income into capital gain upon the sale or exchange of a partnership interest. This section, in effect, severs certain income items from the partnership interest. H.R.Rep. No. 1337, supra, at 70, 71, and S.Rep. No. 1622, 83d Cong., 2d Sess. 99 (1954). Thus, to the extent a partnership interest represents substantially appreciated inventory or unrealized receivables described in section 751, the tax consequences to the transferor partner are "the same tax consequences which would be accorded an individual entrepreneur." H.R.Rep. No. 1337 at 71, and S.Rep. 1622, supra, at 99. In effect, the transferor partner is treated as disposing of the property described in section 751 "independently of the rest of his partnership interest." S.Rep. No. 1622 at 98, 99. * * *

Gain recognized under section 741 of the Code on the sale of a partnership interest is reportable under the installment method. See Rev. Rul. 76–483, 1976–2 C.B. 131. However, because section 751 effectively treats a partner as if the partner had sold an interest in the section 751 property of the partnership, the portion of the gain that is attributable to section 751 property is reportable under the installment method only to the extent that income realized on a direct sale of the section 751 property would be reportable under such method. Because the installment method of reporting income would not be available on a sole proprietor's sale of the inventory, the installment method is not available for reporting income realized on the sale of a partnership interest to the extent attributable to the substantially appreciated inventory which constitutes inventory within the meaning of section 453(b)(2)(B).

Accordingly, *P*'s income from the sale of the partnership interest may not be reported under the installment method to the extent it represents income attributable to the partnership's substantially appreciated inventory which would not be eligible for installment sale treatment if sold directly. The balance of the income realized by *P* from the sale of the partnership interest is reportable under the installment method.

HOLDING

Under section 453 of the Code, the income from the sale of a partnership interest may not be reported under the installment method to the extent it represents income attributable to the partnership's substantially appreciated inventory (within the meaning of section 751(d) of the Code) which would not be eligible for the installment sale treatment if sold directly. This holding is not to be construed as an interpretation of sections 453(k) and 453A(e).

NOTE

The relationship of the installment sales provisions of Section 453 to the sale of a partnership interest raises a number of intriguing questions.[1] At the heart of the issue is whether an entity or aggregate approach, or some blend of the two, should be adopted in determining whether deferral of gain is permissible. The only statutory answer is found in Section 453(i)(2), which expressly denies installment sale treatment to Section 1245 and Section 1250 recapture income. "Recapture income," for this purpose, includes "so much of section 751 as relates to section 1245 or 1250."[2] This definition makes it clear that Section 751 gain on the sale of a partnership interest that is attributable to depreciation recapture must be recognized in the year of sale. In Revenue Ruling 89–108, the Service began to unravel some additional questions when it used a modified aggregate approach in ruling that installment sale reporting is not available for gain attributable to inventory that would not be eligible for installment sale treatment if the inventory were sold directly.

An interesting aspect of Revenue Ruling 89–108 is that the partnership did not own any unrealized receivables. In its analysis, however, the Service states broadly that the portion of any gain on the sale of a partnership interest that is attributable to "section 751 property" may be reported under the installment method only to the extent that the income could have been so reported on a direct sale of the property. It follows that gain attributable to unrealized receivables, other than depreciation recapture,[3] must be analyzed to determine what portion (if any) would be eligible for installment reporting if sold directly.[4] The Service's next project should be a ruling illustrating the application of the installment reporting rules on a sale of an interest in a partnership that holds unrealized receivables.[5] In keeping with its middle ground approach in Revenue Ruling 89–108, the Service presumably would rule that installment sale treatment is generally not available with respect to Section 751 gain attributable to unrealized receivables except in the rare case where a direct sale of the receivables would qualify for installment reporting under Section 453.

Revenue Ruling 89–108 also did not discuss the impact of Section 453(k)(2), which denies the installment method of reporting on the sale of stock, securities and other property regularly traded on an established securities market. Since the ruling states that Section 741 gain may be

1. This Note assumes that the seller has not elected out of installment sale treatment under Section 453(d). For discussions of this area, see McKee, Nelson & Whitmire, Federal Taxation of Partnerships and Partners ¶ 17.05 (4th ed. 2007); Willis, Pennell & Postlewaite, Partnership Taxation ¶ 12.01[12] (6th ed. 1997).

2. I.R.C. § 453(i)(2).

3. See supra note 2 and accompanying text.

4. See Town and Country Food Co. v. Commissioner, 51 T.C. 1049 (1969), acq. 1969–2 C.B. xxv, denying Section 453 treatment to a sale of receivables for inventory and services. Compare the *Ledoux* case, supra p. 258, where the taxpayer reported his gain under Section 453. Even though the partnership held unrealized receivables for services, the Service did not question the extent to which Section 453 applied to the sale.

5. See I.R.C. § 453(b)(2), (*l*).

reported under the installment method, it implies that the sale of an interest in a nonpublicly traded partnership would qualify for installment reporting even if the partnership itself owned some publicly traded stock or securities. Query whether this treatment is consistent with Congress's directive to the Treasury to issue regulations disallowing use of the installment method where the rules in Section 453(k) "would be avoided through the use of related parties, pass-thru entities, or intermediaries."[6]

PROBLEM

The ABC partnership operates a hotel and has the following balance sheet:

Assets	A.B.	F.M.V.	Partners' Capital	A.B.*	F.M.V.
Hotel (no recapture)	$ 30,000	$300,000	A	$ 38,000	$150,000
Furniture (all gain is § 1245)	30,000	90,000	B	38,000	150,000
Inventory (products sold by hotel shops)	54,000	60,000	C	38,000	150,000
	$114,000	$450,000		$114,000	$450,000

*Basis figures represent each partner's outside basis including their shares of liabilities.

Disregarding any application of §§ 483 and 1274, what are the tax consequences to A if he sells his interest for $150,000, to be paid $50,000 per year over three years? A does not use § 453(d) to elect out of § 453 treatment.

B. CONSEQUENCES TO THE BUYING PARTNER

Code: §§ 742; 743; 752(a); 754; 755. Skim §§ 732(d); 734(b); 761(e); 774(a); 1060.

Regulations: §§ 1.743–1(a)–(e), (j)(1)–(3)(i); 1.754–1; 1.755–1(a), (b)(1)–(3); 1.755–1(a)(2)–(5).

Introduction. The general statutory rules governing the tax consequences to purchasers of partnership interests adopt the entity approach to

6. I.R.C. § 453(k), flush language. In reporting its version of the Tax Reform Act of 1986, the Senate Finance Committee stated that these regulations should not deny use of the installment method if the selling partner could not have sold or caused the sale of the publicly traded securities directly. In an example, the Finance Committee indicated that a retiring partner in a large investment partnership could report a sale of his partnership interest on the installment method even though a substantial portion of the value of the interest was attributable to publicly traded stock held by the partnership, provided that the partner could not have sold or caused the sale of the partnership's assets directly. S.Rep. No. 99–313, 99th Cong., 2d Sess. 131 (1986). But this language was not included in the Conference Report or the Joint Committee on Taxation's General Explanation of the 1986 Act. The Service also has not issued regulations under Section 453A(e)(2), which permits an aggregate approach to be used when the special rules for nondealers in Section 453A are applied to a partnership interest.

partnership taxation. Section 742 provides that a partner takes a cost basis for a partnership interest acquired by purchase; for this purpose, cost includes the partner's share of any partnership liabilities.[1]

So far, so good.... But the above rule involves only the partner's outside basis. The rule with respect to the inside basis is initially quite surprising. Assume Buyer purchases a one-third interest in a cash method, calendar year service partnership which has as its primary asset $90,000 of accounts receivable with a zero basis and $30,000 of other assets. On December 20, Buyer pays $40,000 for the interest and thus has an outside basis of $40,000. In effect, he has paid $30,000 for his one-third interest in the receivables and $10,000 for his one-third interest in other assets. On January 1 of the following year all the receivables are collected by the partnership. One's initial reaction is to say that Buyer has no income with respect to this collection. After all, Buyer paid $30,000 for his interest in the receivables, and their collection simply results in a return of capital. Right? ... Wrong!!! Section 743(a) generally provides that "[t]he basis of partnership property shall not be adjusted as the result of a transfer of an interest in a partnership by sale or exchange * * *." Thus, the partnership has $90,000 of ordinary income when the receivables are collected, and each partner, including Buyer, is taxed on his one-third distributive share, or $30,000 of ordinary income. This result occurs even though Buyer paid $30,000 for his share of the receivables and has no real gain on their collection. In addition, Seller was taxed under Section 751(a) on the $30,000 of ordinary income attributable to the receivables when he sold his partnership interest to Buyer.

In searching for relief from this result, Buyer may find solace in the fact that he may increase his outside basis by his $30,000 distributive share of partnership income under Section 705(a)(1)(A). If he later sells his partnership interest for $40,000 (still its fair market value), Buyer will have a $30,000 loss, and all will be well. Right? * * * Wrong!!! To be sure, Buyer will realize a $30,000 loss on the sale; but it will be a capital loss under Section 741, not an ordinary loss, and the timing of the loss may occur much later than when the receivables were included in income.

If you are upset and somewhat baffled by these anomalous results, join the crowd.[2] But the Code provides relief, demonstrating once again that tax equity often breeds complexity. To avoid taxing the buying partner on the appreciation of his proportionate share of partnership assets prior to the

1. I.R.C. § 752(d). Apart from tax consequences, the purchaser of a partnership interest steps into the shoes of the selling partner. To evidence the fact that the buyer has acquired the rights to partnership assets and assumed the liabilities previously attributed to the seller, the selling partner's capital account carries over to the buyer. See Reg. § 1.704–1(b)(2)(iv)(*l*).

2. One federal district judge was equally upset. In a burst of questionable judicial legislation, he refused to allow this result to occur. See Barnes v. United States, 253 F.Supp. 116 (S.D.Ill.1966).

date of purchase, the partnership may elect under Section 754[3] to adjust the basis of its assets under Section 743(b). In the example above, a Section 743(b) adjustment places Buyer in the same position as if he had purchased his proportionate share of partnership assets for their fair market value at the time the partnership interest was acquired, and it gives Buyer a $30,000 inside "cost" basis in his share of the receivables. When the receivables are collected, the other partners each will be taxed on $30,000, just as they would be in the absence of an election, but Buyer realizes no income because of the upward adjustment of his personal inside basis.[4]

The Section 743(b) basis adjustment was desirable in the example above because it eliminated the gain that otherwise would have been realized by Buyer on the collection of the accounts receivable. But the statute works in both directions. A Section 754 election also may require a *downward* adjustment to the bases of partnership assets which have declined in value as of the time of the sale or exchange of the partnership interest. Specifically, Section 743(b)(2) requires that the partnership must decrease the adjusted bases of its assets with respect to any partner if that partner's proportionate share of the partnership's total inside basis in its assets exceeds the buying partner's outside basis. The amount of the downward adjustment is the excess of that partner's proportionate share of the partnership's inside bases over the partner's outside basis in his partnership interest. The buying partner's distributive share thus will not reflect any increase or decline in value of partnership assets occurring prior to his purchase of an interest in the firm.

Mandatory Inside Basis Adjustment for Partnership with Substantial Built-in Loss. The Section 754 election provides a buying partner with a beneficial tax avoidance strategy. If the partnership's assets have appreciated and have built-in gains, the election will eliminate the potentially disadvantageous distortions in the timing and characterization of partnership income. But if the partnership's assets have depreciated in value and would produce losses, a savvy buyer would prefer the partnership not to make the election in order to reap the tax benefit of deducting those losses.[5] In order to reduce the "heads-I-win, tails-you-lose" aspect of the election, Section 743 *requires* an adjustment to the basis of partnership property on the transfer of a partnership interest if the partnership has a "substantial built-in loss" immediately after the transfer.[6] A partnership has a substantial built-in loss if the adjusted basis in its property exceeds the property's

3. See Reg. § 1.754–1(b) for the time and method of making the Section 754 election. A Section 754 election triggers both the Section 743(b) basis adjustment discussed in this chapter and the basis adjustment under Section 734(b) on a distribution of partnership property. Section 734(b) is considered in Chapter 7C, infra. Once a Section 754 election is made, it applies to all subsequent partnership distributions and transfers of partnership interests unless the Service consents to revocation of the election.

4. Buyer's outside basis, however, would remain at $40,000.

5. Of course, the recognition of partnership losses reduces the partner's outside basis and will produce more income or loss on a later sale of the partner's interest, but the distortion in the timing of income works in favor of the partner.

6. I.R.C. §§ 743(a), (b).

fair market value by more than $250,000.[7] In patrolling the $250,000 threshold for abuse, the Service has the authority to aggregate related partnerships or disregard acquisitions of property designed to avoid the limit.[8]

A special rule is provided for an "electing investment partnership,"[9] such as venture capital and buyout funds formed to raise capital from investors pursuant to a private offering and to make and hold investments for capital appreciation. Congress concluded that these types of investment partnerships "would incur administrative difficulties" if they were required to make partnership-level basis adjustments when their interests were transferred.[10] To ease the burden, an electing investment partnership is allowed to use a partner-level loss limitation instead of making basis adjustments to its assets. Under the limit, a transferee partner's share of losses (without regard to gains) from the sale or exchange of partnership property is not allowed except to the extent it is established that such losses exceed any loss recognized by the transferor on the transfer of the partnership interest.[11]

Calculating the Section 743(b) Adjustment. The purpose of the Section 743(b) adjustment is straightforward. It is designed to give new partners a special inside basis in their share of partnership assets and in so doing place them in roughly the same position as if they had purchased those assets directly. The mechanics of computing and allocating the adjustment are more complicated. The new partner first must determine the amount of the overall basis adjustment, which is the difference between the partner's outside basis (generally, the partner's cost plus his share of partnership liabilities) and his share of the partnership's inside basis in its assets.[12] The partner is then shuttled to Section 755, which prescribes a multi-step process for allocating the adjustment among the various partnership assets.

Keeping in mind that the basic purpose of the Section 743(b) adjustment is to produce the equivalent of a cost basis in the new partner's share of the partnership's assets, the amount of the overall Section 743(b) adjustment normally should be the difference between the new partner's outside basis and his proportionate share of the partnership's inside basis. In the garden variety partnership, one devoid of the complications presented by special allocations and Section 704(c) allocations with respect to contributed property, that intuitive formula generally will be accurate. But

7. I.R.C. § 743(d)(1).

8. I.R.C. § 743(d)(2).

9. An electing investment partnership must satisfy a long list of requirements set forth in Section 743(e)(6).

10. H. Rep. No. 108–548, 108th Cong. 2d Sess. 283 (2004).

11. I.R.C. § 743(e)(1), (2). Another special rule is provided for "securitization partnerships," which generally are partnerships whose sole business is to issue securities backed by the cash flow of receivables or other financial assets. Such partnerships are deemed to not have a substantial built-in loss and thereby avoid both adjustments to the bases of property and the loss-limitation rule in Section 743(e). See I.R.C. § 743(f).

12. I.R.C. § 743(b). For the rules to determine a partner's share of the adjusted basis of partnership property, see Reg. § 1.743–1(d).

the workings of Subchapter K are not always intuitive and seldom are simple.

The regulations provide a complex formula for determining the transferee partner's share of the partnership's inside basis of its assets. A transferee partner's share of the adjusted basis to the partnership of its property is equal to the sum of the transferee's interest in the partnership's "previously taxed capital," plus the transferee's share of partnership liabilities. The transferee's interest in the partnership's previously taxed capital is determined by considering a hypothetical disposition by the partnership of all of its assets in a fully taxable transaction for cash equal to the fair market value of the assets. The transferee's interest in the partnership's previously taxed capital generally is equal to the cash the transferee would receive on a liquidation following the hypothetical transaction, increased by the amount of tax loss and decreased by the amount of tax gain that would be allocated to the transferee from the transaction.[13] Returning to a variation of the earlier example, assume Buyer purchases for $30,000 a one-third interest in a partnership with $90,000 of accounts receivable having a zero basis. If the partnership has a Section 754 election in effect, the Section 743(b) adjustment is equal to the difference between Buyer's outside basis ($30,000) and Buyer's share of the adjusted basis to the partnership of its property. If there were a hypothetical disposition of all the partnership's assets, Buyer would receive $30,000 cash and Buyer would be allocated $30,000 tax gain from the transaction. Buyer's interest in the partnership's previously taxed capital and his share of the adjusted basis to the partnership of its property would be zero ($30,000 of cash received if the partnership had liquidated immediately after the hypothetical transaction, less the $30,000 of tax gain allocable to the partner on the sale of the accounts receivable). Thus, the Section 743(b) adjustment is equal to $30,000, the difference between Buyer's $30,000 outside basis and his zero share of the adjusted basis to the partnership of its property. Note that the intuitive approach was correct here; the total Section 743(b) adjustment is equal to the difference between Buyer's outside basis and his proportionate share of the partnership's zero inside basis.

The formula in the regulations is complex because it accommodates the situation where the partnership holds contributed property subject to Section 704(c). If a partner contributes appreciated or depreciated property to the partnership and later transfers his partnership interest, built-in gain or loss is allocated to the transferee partner as it would have been allocated to the transferor partner.[14] This principle is incorporated in the calculation of the transferee's share of the adjusted basis to the partnership of its property. For example, assume A contributes land worth $1,000 with an adjusted basis of $400 in exchange for a one-third interest in the ABC partnership. B and C each contribute $1,000 cash. After the land has appreciated in value to $1,300, A sells his one-third partnership interest to T for $1,100, when a Section 754 election is in effect. The amount of the

13. Reg. § 1.743–1(d)(1) & (2); see Reg. § 1.743–1(d)(3) Example 1.

14. Reg. § 1.704–3(a)(7).

tax gain allocated to T as a result of a hypothetical disposition of the partnership's assets would be $700 ($600 of Section 704(c) gain, plus one-third of the additional $300 of gain). Thus, T's interest in the partnership's previously taxed capital is $400 ($1,100, the cash T would receive on a liquidation, decreased by $700, T's share of gain from the hypothetical disposition). T's Section 743(b) adjustment to partnership property will be $700 ($1,100, T's cost for the partnership interest, less $400, T's share of the adjusted basis to the partnership of its property).[15]

Allocation of the Adjustment under Section 755. Once the total Section 743(b) adjustment is determined, that adjustment must be allocated among the partnership's assets under Section 755.[16] The Section 755 regulations provide that the partnership first must determine the value of its assets.[17] Next, the partnership's assets are first divided into two classes; (1) capital assets and Section 1231(b) property (capital gain property), and (2) any other property (ordinary income property).[18] The basis adjustment is then allocated between those classes of property and within each class based on the allocations of income, gain, or loss (including remedial allocations) that the transferee partner would receive if, immediately after the transfer, all of the partnership's assets were disposed of in a fully taxable transaction for fair market value.[19] The regulations specifically permit an increase to be made to one class or one property while a decrease is made to the other class or a different property within the class.[20] Basis is first allocated to the class of ordinary income property and then to the class of capital gain property. A decrease in basis allocated to capital gain property may not produce a negative basis in any asset. Thus, if the entire decrease allocated to capital gain property reduces the basis of those assets to zero, any excess reduces the basis of the class of ordinary income property.[21] Once again, keep in mind that the adjustment to each item of property within a class of property is designed to produce the equivalent of a cost basis for the transferee partner via the Section 743(b) adjustment.[22]

An example may be helpful in illustrating the application of these rules. Assume N buys for $90,000 a one-third interest in a partnership and is entitled to a $30,000 Section 743(b) adjustment at a time when the partnership has the following assets:[23]

15. See Reg. § 1.743–1(d)(3) Example 2.

16. I.R.C. § 743(c).

17. Reg. § 1.755–1(a)(1). See the text at notes 25–28 for discussion of the valuation process.

18. Reg. § 1.755–1(a). For this purpose, potential recapture gain that would be treated as an unrealized receivable under Section 751(c) is treated as separate ordinary income property. Id.

19. Reg. § 1.755–1(b)(1).

20. Id.

21. Reg. § 1. 755–1(b)(2)(i).

22. See Reg. § 1.755–1(b)(3).

23. Assume that none of the assets were contributed to the partnership by the partners and that the valuation of the assets is accurate.

Assets	A.B.	F.M.V.
Accounts Receivable	$ 0	$ 45,000
Inventory	90,000	105,000
Capital Asset	30,000	45,000
Depreciable Asset (no recapture)	60,000	75,000
	$180,000	$270,000

Under Section 755, the $30,000 Section 743(b) adjustment is first allocated between the two classes of property. If the partnership sold all of its assets in a fully taxable transaction immediately after the transfer of the interest to N, the total amount of ordinary income that would be allocated to N would be $20,000 ($15,000 in the receivables and $5,000 in the inventory) and the total amount of capital or Section 1231 gain that would be allocated to N would be $10,000 ($5,000 in the capital asset and $5,000 in the depreciable asset). Thus, the amount of the adjustment that would be allocated to the ordinary income property would be $20,000 and the amount of the adjustment allocated to the capital gain property would be $10,000.

Assuming the partnership's calculator is still functioning, the next step is to allocate the adjustments to each class of property within the class based on the amount of gain or loss that would be allocated to N from the hypothetical sale of the item.[24] In the class of ordinary income property, N would be allocated $15,000 of gain from the accounts receivable and $5,000 of gain from the inventory in the hypothetical transaction. Therefore, the amount of the adjustment to the accounts receivable is $15,000 and the amount of the adjustment to the inventory is $5,000. In the class of capital gain property, N would be allocated $5,000 of gain from the capital asset and $5,000 of gain from the depreciable asset. Therefore, the amount of the adjustment to each of those assets is $5,000. After these adjustments, N's personal inside basis in the assets is determined as follows:

Asset	N's Original Share of Inside Basis	+	§ 743(b) Adjustment	=	New Inside Basis
Accounts Receivable	$ 0		$15,000		$15,000
Inventory	30,000		5,000		35,000
Capital Asset	10,000		5,000		15,000
Depreciable Asset	20,000		5,000		25,000
Total	$60,000		$30,000		$90,000

The preceding example is relatively simple because all of the assets have appreciated in value. Problem 2 below illustrates these rules in more complicated situations.

A more practical complication results from the valuation of partnership assets that is required in the process of allocating a basis adjustment under section 755. If the assets of the partnership constitute a trade or business, the regulations provide that the valuation generally is done in accordance

24. Reg. § 1.755–2(b)(3). The hypothetical gain or loss is adjusted in some specialized situations not implicated by this example.

with the rules under Section 1060 for "applicable asset acquisitions."[25] The value of the partnership's assets other than Section 197 intangibles is first determined under an "all facts and circumstances" test.[26] The partnership then determines the gross value of all its assets, generally with reference to the basis of the transferee partner.[27] If the partnership's gross value is greater than the aggregate value of partnership property other than Section 197 intangibles, the excess is (1) first allocated to Section 197 intangibles other than goodwill and going concern value, and (2) then to goodwill and going concern value.[28]

Effect of the Section 743(b) Adjustment. The regulations provide that a basis adjustment under Section 743(b) is personal to the transferee partner. No adjustment is made to the common basis of the partnership property and a Section 743(b) adjustment has no effect on the partnership's computation of any Section 703 item.[29] A partnership first computes all partnership items at the partnership level and each partner, including the transferee, is allocated those items under Section 704. The partnership then adjusts the transferee's distributive share of partnership income, gain, loss or deduction to reflect the Section 743(b) basis adjustment. These basis adjustments do not affect the transferee's capital account.[30]

If depreciable or amortizable property acquires an upward basis adjustment under Section 743(b), the property generally is treated as two separate assets for depreciation or amortization purposes. The first asset retains the original depreciation remaining in the depreciable or amortizable property prior to the adjustment. The amount of the adjustment is treated as being attributable to a newly purchased asset for depreciation or amortization purposes.[31]

Relationship to Section 704(c). A principal goal of the regulations is to coordinate Sections 704(c) and 743. To that end, they generally provide that a transferee's income, gain, or loss from the sale or exchange of a partnership asset in which the transferee has a basis adjustment is equal to

25. Reg. § 1.755–1(a)(1) & (2). The definition of a "trade or business" for this purpose is borrowed from the active trade or business requirement under Section 355 (relating to tax-free corporate divisions). Reg. §§ 1.755–1(a)(2), 1.1060–1(b)(2). Alternatively, assets represent a trade or business if "goodwill or going concern value could under any circumstances" attach to them. Id. Although the definition is quite broad, it should not embrace partnerships engaged in purely passive investment activities.

26. Reg. § 1.755–1(a)(3).

27. Reg. § 1.755–1(a)(4).

28. Reg. § 1.755–1(a)(5). The buyer and seller also must comply with certain information reporting requirements. See Reg. § 1.755–1(d).

29. Reg. § 1.743–1(j)(1).

30. Reg. § 1.743–1(j)(2).

31. Reg. § 1.743–1(j)(4)(i)(B)(1). The legislative history of Section 197 makes it clear that these same rules apply to Section 197 property, such as goodwill. H.R. Rep. No. 2141, 103d Cong., 1st Sess. 336–37 (1993). If, however, the partnership elects to use the remedial allocation method in Section 1.704–3(d) with respect to recovery property, then any Section 743(b) increase attributable to Section 704(c) built-in gain is recovered over the remaining recovery period for the partnership's excess book basis in the property under the remedial method. Reg. § 1.743–1(j)(4)(i)(B)(2); see also Reg. § 1.743–1(j)(4)(i)(C) Examples.

the transferee's share of the partnership's gain or loss from the sale of the asset (including any remedial allocations of gain or loss), minus the amount of any positive Section 743(b) basis adjustment or plus the amount of any negative Section 743(b) adjustment.[32] For example, assume A and B form an equal partnership with A contributing nondepreciable property ($100 fair market value, $50 adjusted basis) and B contributing $100 cash. The partnership uses the traditional method for making Section 704(c) allocations. A later sells her partnership interest to T for $100 when the partnership has a Section 754 election in effect. T will receive a $50 basis adjustment that is allocated to the nondepreciable property. If the partnership sells the nondepreciable property for $90 it will have a $10 book loss and a $40 tax gain. T will receive an allocation of all $40 of tax gain under Section 704(c). Because T has a $50 basis adjustment in the property, she recognizes a $10 loss from the partnership's sale of the property.[33]

In the preceding example, T stepped into A's shoes with respect to the contributed property and the ceiling rule applied under the traditional method when the partnership sold that property for a book loss.[34] Assume instead that the partnership uses the remedial method for making Section 704(c) allocations. If the partnership again sells the property for $90, the $10 book loss will be allocated equally between the partners, and the $40 of tax gain will be allocated to T under Section 704(c). To match his $5 share of book loss, B will be allocated $5 of remedial loss and T will be allocated an offsetting $5 of remedial gain. Thus, T will be allocated a total of $45 of tax gain with respect to the property. Because T has a $50 basis adjustment, she recognizes a $5 loss from the partnership's sale of the property if the remedial method is used.[35]

One other aspect of Section 704(c) may also come into play in connection with the transfer of a partnership interest. Section 704(c)(1)(C) provides that in the case of property that was contributed to a partnership with a built-in loss, no other partner may be allocated that precontribution loss.[36] Thus, the purchaser of a partnership interest may not obtain the benefit of a built-in loss contributed by the seller of the interest.

PROBLEMS

1. On January 1 of year one, Nupartner purchased a one-third interest in a partnership for $40,000. At the time of purchase the partnership had the following assets:

	A.B.	F.M.V.
Accounts Receivable	$ 0	$30,000
Land	60,000	90,000

32. Reg. § 1.743–1(j)(3)(i).

33. See Reg. § 1.743–1(j)(3)(ii) Example 2.

34. See Chapter 4C, supra.

35. See Reg. § 1.743–1(j)(3)(ii) Example 3.

36. See Chapter 4C6, supra.

(a) If § 754 had not been elected by the partnership, what result to Nupartner upon collection of the receivables?

(b) What result to Nupartner in (a), above, if the partnership had made a § 754 election?

(c) Who makes a § 754 election? When and how must the election be made?

(d) Should Nupartner have conditioned his purchase of the partnership interest upon a § 754 election?

(e) Will Nupartner's purchase and the § 754 election have any immediate tax impact on the remaining old partners?

(f) Will the § 743(b) basis adjustment affect Nupartner in situations other than on collection of partnership income or sales of partnership property?

(g) At the end of year three, the partnership had earnings, all of which had been distributed, and it continued to hold the identical accounts receivable and land, each of which had the same basis and fair market value. Assuming no § 754 election, what result to Nupartner if, before the receivables are collected, he sells his partnership interest to Buyer for $40,000?

(h) What result to Nupartner in (g), above, if the partnership had made a § 754 election?

(i) What is Buyer's inside basis in (h), above?

(j) If the partnership properly maintained capital accounts and the selling partner's capital account prior to the sale of his interest was $20,000, what is Nupartner's capital account upon purchase of his one-third interest for $40,000 if:

(i) a § 754 election were in effect;

(ii) a § 754 election were not in effect.

See Reg. § 1.704–1(b)(2)(iv)(*l*), (*m*)(*1*) and (*2*).

(k) If a § 754 election is in effect, will each new purchasing partner create havoc for the partnership's accountant?

2. The ABC cash method general partnership, which has made a § 754 election, had the following balance sheet at the time D purchased C's interest for $60,000. None of the partnership's assets were contributed by a partner:

Assets	A.B.	F.M.V.	Liabilities and Partners' Capital	A.B.*	F.M.V.
			Liabilities:		$ 30,000
			Capital:		
Accounts Receivable	$ 0	$ 30,000	A	$30,000	60,000
Inventory	30,000	60,000	B	30,000	60,000
Land (§ 1231 asset)	30,000	15,000	C	30,000	60,000
Building (§ 1231 asset; no depreciation recapture)	30,000	105,000			
	$90,000	$210,000		$90,000	$210,000

* Basis figures represent each partner's outside basis including their share of liabilities

(a) What is D's personal inside basis in each of the assets?

(b) What is D's personal inside basis in the assets if he paid $70,000 (rather than $60,000) for C's interest?

(c) Same as (a), above (i.e., D buys C's interest for $60,000), except that C contributed the accounts receivable to the partnership at a time when the fair market value of the receivables was $30,000 and their basis was zero.

3. The DEF cash method general partnership, which has not made a § 754 election, had the following balance sheet at the time G purchased D's interest for $50,000. D contributed the inventory to the partnership at a time when the value of the inventory was $15,000.

Asset	A.B.	F.M.V.	Liabilities and Partners' Capital	A.B.	F.M.V.
Cash	$ 50,000	$ 50,000	D	$100,000	$ 50,000
Inventory	30,000	10,000	E	125,000	50,000
Land	270,000	90,000	F	125,000	50,000
	$350,000	$150,000		$350,000	$150,000

(a) Will the basis of the partnership's assets be adjusted under § 743 as a result of D's sale to G? Should G urge the partnership to make a § 754 election?

(b) Assuming no adjustments are made to the basis of the partnership's assets, what will be the result to G if the partnership sells the inventory for $10,000? What result to G if the partnership sells the land for $90,000?

CHAPTER 7

OPERATING DISTRIBUTIONS

A. INTRODUCTION

At this point in the study of partnership taxation, a normal student might feel entrapped in an intricate jigsaw puzzle, anxiously awaiting the moment when the pieces begin to fit together. The study of operating distributions[1] provides an opportunity for that crucial breakthrough, but the promised land is attainable only by carefully dissecting the statute while keeping the broad concepts of Subchapter K clearly in focus.

Consider, at the outset, two principles that have emerged in previous chapters. Under the aggregate approach to partnership taxation, a partner is taxed on his distributive share of partnership income whether or not it is distributed.[2] A partner's outside basis includes his share of those previously taxed profits in addition to his capital contribution to the firm.[3] It follows that, to the extent of that outside basis, a partner should not be required to recognize gain on a current distribution of cash. But if a cash distribution exceeds his outside basis, the partner has received something more than his investment in the partnership and his share of previously taxed income and thus should be required to recognize gain to the extent of the excess. If a distribution consists of property other than cash, a different approach is possible. A transferred basis mechanism can be used to preserve any unrecognized gain for reckoning at a later time. We are about to discover that the treatment of partnership distributions is consistent with these principles. Congress has gone to great lengths to provide nonrecognition of gain or loss on an operating distribution by a partnership and to preserve any unrecognized gain or loss through appropriate adjustments to basis.

Another important goal of the Code has been to prevent taxpayers from converting ordinary income into capital gain. To forestall that type of potential tax avoidance in the partnership distribution setting, it is necessary to preserve the ordinary income character of certain assets in the hands of the distributee partner. Section 735 implements this policy for distributed property in a manner mirroring the treatment of contributed property under Section 724.

1. "Operating" (sometimes called "current") distributions are any distributions by the partnership which are not liquidating distributions. Liquidating distributions are discussed in Chapter 8, supra.

2. I.R.C. § 701.

3. I.R.C. §§ 705; 722. Cf. I.R.C. § 752(a).

A third theme was introduced in the preceding chapter, where we saw that the failure to adjust the basis of partnership assets after the sale of a partnership interest may distort the tax treatment of the buying partner.[4] In the case of operating distributions, similar distortions may affect all the remaining partners. This chapter provides another opportunity to study a set of rules aimed at curing this imbalance through adjustments to the bases of partnership assets.

And no area of partnership tax is complete without a few complex anti-abuse provisions. Because Congress made every effort to defer the recognition of gain or loss on partnership distributions, it should come as no surprise that taxpayers have attempted to exploit these rules to achieve favorable results indirectly that could not be reached in a more straightforward manner. The final sections of this chapter examine the Congressional response to several sophisticated forms of taxpayer misbehavior. Sections 704(c)(1)(B) and 737 override the general nonrecognition rules in order to combat the "mixing bowl transaction," a strategy where a partner transfers appreciated property to a partnership and, within a seven-year period, the partnership either distributes the contributed property to another partner or distributes other property to the contributing partner. In either case, the agenda is to shift or defer the recognition of the contributing partner's precontribution gain. The purpose of Section 751(b), which also overrides the general nonrecognition rules previewed above, is to curb the potential shifting of the character of income that may result from distributions that alter the partners' interests in partnership property. Studying these provisions will be a memorable experience but the occasional pain should be accompanied by a greater appreciation of how different parts of the Subchapter K puzzle relate to one another.

Finally, while studying these *tax* rules governing partnership distributions, one must not lose sight of the attendant economic consequences. Because an operating distribution results in the withdrawal of part of a partner's equity in the partnership, the value of that partner's interest obviously is reduced. And if an operating distribution is not in accordance with the partners' respective interests in the partnership, it also will alter their future economic relationship. To properly account for these effects, the partnership allocation regulations logically require that a partner's capital account must be decreased by the amount of money and the fair market value of any property distributed to the partner.[5] If the partnership distributes property with a fair market value that differs from its book value, other adjustments—such as a restatement of the partnership assets and partner capital accounts at their current fair market values—also may be necessary to reflect accurately the respective economic interests of the partners after the distribution.[6]

4. See Chapter 6B, supra.

5. Reg. § 1.704–1(b)(2)(iv)(*b*)(*4*) and (*5*).

6. See Reg. § 1.704–1(b)(2)(iv)(*f*)(*5*) and Section C of this chapter, infra.

B. CONSEQUENCES TO THE DISTRIBUTEE PARTNER

1. NONRECOGNITION RULES ON THE DISTRIBUTION

Code: §§ 731; 732(a), (c) & (d); 733.

Regulations: §§ 1.731–1(a)(1) & (3), (c); 1.732–1(a), (c), (d)(1) & (4); 1.733–1.

Distributions of Cash. Section 731(a) generally provides that a partner will recognize neither gain nor loss on a current distribution of cash, and Section 733 provides that the partner's outside basis will be reduced, but not below zero, by the amount of the distribution. We have seen that the partner's outside basis represents his original investment in the partnership, adjusted upwards (or downwards) for the partner's share of profits (or losses). Consequently, to the extent of the partner's outside basis, an operating distribution represents earnings previously taxed to the partner or a return of capital. Thus, it is appropriate to confer nonrecognition of gain to the distributee partner and to require a corresponding downward adjustment to basis. On the loss side, an operating distribution does not represent a closed transaction and thus is a premature occasion for determining whether a loss has been sustained by the distributee partner.

If, however, cash distributions exceed a partner's outside basis, the partner is receiving something more than previously taxed income or a return of capital. Section 731(a)(1) thus provides, in a manner comparable to other nonrecognition provisions,[1] that the excess of cash received over the distributee partner's outside basis is treated as gain from the sale or exchange of a partnership interest—normally capital gain, unless Section 751 applies.[2] This statutory solution avoids the tax taboo of a negative basis and ensures that the partner's gain will not escape the tax collector.

The foregoing rules embrace both actual cash distributions and transactions that are treated as cash distributions. For example, recall that any reduction of a partner's share of partnership liabilities is treated as a distribution of cash to the partner.[3] Such reductions occur not only as partnership liabilities are paid off but also on various other types of transactions such as an abandonment of property,[4] a reconveyance or foreclosure,[5] a condemnation[6] or another partner's assumption of a share of liability on property.[7] A further example is provided in Revenue Ruling 79–205, which follows at page 293 in the text.

1. See, e.g., I.R.C. §§ 301(c)(3); 357(c).

2. See I.R.C. §§ 731(d); 751(b).

3. I.R.C. § 752(b).

4. Middleton v. Commissioner, 77 T.C. 310 (1981), affirmed per curiam, 693 F.2d 124 (11th Cir.1982); cf. O'Brien v. Commissioner, 77 T.C. 113 (1981).

5. Freeland v. Commissioner, 74 T.C. 970 (1980).

6. Rev.Rul. 81–242, 1981–2 C.B. 147.

7. Stilwell v. Commissioner, 46 T.C. 247 (1966). Cf. Rev.Rul. 74–40, 1974–1 C.B. 159.

The operating distribution rules do not apply if cash received from a partnership is not in fact a distribution. For example, if the cash is received as a loan, the transaction is governed by Section 707(a)(1) rather than Section 731(a)(1).[8] A discharge of the obligation to repay the loan, however, is treated as a distribution of cash.[9] Similarly, if the cash is a mere advance or draw against a partner's distributive share of income, it is equivalent to a loan and is not treated as a distribution until the last day of the partner's year.[10] A leading treatise suggests that the nature of the distribution as an advance or a draw will be assured if the partner is under an obligation to repay any distribution in excess of his share of partnership income for the year.[11]

Distributions of Property. Neither the partnership nor the distributee partner will recognize gain or loss on an operating distribution of property,[12] unless Section 704(c)(1)(B), Section 737,[13] or Section 751(b) applies,[14] or the distribution is of marketable securities. This is because a distribution of property, unlike a cash distribution, provides an opportunity for the deferral of gain. Any gain inherent in the distributed property is preserved by assigning the distributee a transferred basis under Section 732(a). Any gain inherent in the partner's interest in the partnership is preserved by Section 733, which reduces the partner's outside basis by his transferred basis in the distributed property. This scheme ensures that the sum of the partner's basis in the distributed property and his outside basis remains constant. But if the partnership's basis in the distributed assets[15] exceeds the partner's outside basis, less any cash distributed in the same transaction, the partner could not maintain his total basis unless he emerged from the distribution with a negative outside basis. Consequently, Section 732(a)(2) provides that if the partner's share of the inside basis in the distributed property exceeds his outside basis, reduced by any cash distributed in the same transaction, the transferred basis is limited to that outside basis, which then would be reduced to zero under Section 733.[16]

8. Reg. § 1.731–1(c)(2).

9. Id.

10. Reg. § 1.731–1(a)(1)(ii).

11. McKee, Nelson & Whitmire, Federal Taxation of Partnerships and Partners ¶ 19.03[2](4th ed. 2007).

12. I.R.C. § 731(a); but see I.R.C. § 731(a)(2), providing for the recognition of loss in very limited circumstances on a liquidating distribution. Section 732(f) also contains special rules for the situation where a partnership distributes corporate stock to a corporate partner who, after the distribution, controls (under Section 1504(a)(2)) the distributed corporation. The basis of the distributed corporation's assets may be reduced and the corporate partner may recognize gain. I.R.C. § 732(f)(1), (4).

13. Sections 704(c)(1)(B) and 737 are considered in Section D of this chapter.

14. See I.R.C. § 751(b), which is considered in Section E of this chapter.

15. This includes any special basis in the asset—for example, a Section 743(b) inside basis. In general, the holding period of the property also is tacked. See I.R.C. § 735(b), discussed in Section B2 of this chapter, infra.

16. In this situation, the partner's gain is preserved but the gain inherent in the distributed asset is not. Since the asset does not take a full transferred basis, the partner will recognize more gain on a sale of the asset than the partnership would have recognized had it made the sale, but this can be corrected if a Section 754 election is in effect. See

Allocation of Basis to Distributed Properties. If the special basis limitation rule in Section 732(a)(2) applies and several assets are distributed, the basis to be allocated (i.e., the partner's outside basis less cash received in the transaction) must be allocated among the distributed properties under Section 732(c)[17] using a multi-step process. First, any distributed unrealized receivables and inventory items are tentatively assigned a basis equal to the partnership's basis in each of those assets.[18] If the sum of the partnership's bases in the unrealized receivables and inventory items exceeds the basis to be allocated, then the partnership's bases in those properties must be decreased by the amount of the excess.[19] The reduction is achieved by first allocating basis decreases among the properties with built-in loss (i.e., properties with an assigned basis greater than their value) in proportion to the amounts of such loss and only to the extent of each property's built-in loss.[20] If needed, additional decreases are allocated in proportion to the remaining adjusted basis of the unrealized receivables and inventory items.[21] If the basis to be allocated exceeds the partnership's basis in the distributed unrealized receivables and inventory items, then each other distributed property is tentatively assigned a basis equal to the partnership's basis in that asset.[22] The partnership's bases in those properties then must be reduced so that the sum of their basis is equal to the remaining basis to be allocated.[23] Again, the reduction is accomplished by first allocating basis decreases in proportion to the built-in loss in the properties (but only to the extent of such loss) and then in proportion to the remaining adjusted bases of the properties.[24] This method of allocation is designed to preserve the partnership's basis for the unrealized receivables and inventory items and thus ensures that the partner will recognize at least the same amount of gain upon the disposition of those assets as the partnership would have recognized had they been sold at the partnership level.[25] As we will discover shortly, Section 735 preserves the ordinary income character of this gain.

Section 732(d). Section 732(d) provides an exception to the foregoing basis rules by permitting certain distributee partners to elect to treat any distributed properties as though the partnership had a Section 754 election

I.R.C. § 734(b)(1)(B) and Section C of this chapter.

17. Section 732(c) also applies to the allocation of outside basis to property received by a partner in a liquidating distribution. See I.R.C. § 732(b) and Chapter 8B, infra.

18. I.R.C. § 732(c)(1)(A)(i).

19. I.R.C. § 732(c)(1)(A)(ii).

20. I.R.C. § 732(c)(3)(A). These allocation rules apply to distributions after August 5, 1997. For prior distributions, basis was first allocated to any unrealized receivables and inventory items in an amount equal to the partnership's basis in each of those assets (or, if the basis to be allocated was less than the sum of such properties' basis, in proportion to such bases) and, to the extent of any remaining basis, to any other distributed properties in proportion to their adjusted bases to the partnership.

21. I.R.C. § 732(c)(3)(B).

22. I.R.C. § 732(c)(1)(B)(i).

23. I.R.C. § 732(c)(1)(B)(ii).

24. I.R.C. § 732(c)(3).

25. When the Section 732(a)(2) basis limitation rule applies, the allocation method under Section 732(c) prevents to the extent possible any decrease in the basis of the ordinary income assets.

in effect when the partner purchased or inherited his interest. As a result, assets distributed to the new partner are eligible for a Section 743(b) adjustment,[26] and a special inside basis then may be used to determine the partner's basis in the distributed assets under Sections 732(a) and (c). This election is available only if the distribution is made within two years of the distributee partner's acquisition of his interest by purchase, exchange or inheritance and the partnership had no Section 754 election in effect at the time of the acquisition of his interest. The Section 732(d) election is the partner's last chance to avoid some of the distortions which may have resulted from the partnership's failure to make a Section 754 election.[27]

There are some critical differences between the effects of a Section 732(d) and Section 754 election. Section 732(d) only applies for purposes of determining the bases of distributed assets. And unlike a Section 754 election, a Section 732(d) election does not apply for purposes of partnership depreciation, depletion, or gain or loss on disposition.[28]

A Section 732(d) adjustment may be required by the Commissioner, whether or not the distribution occurs within two years from the partner's acquisition of his partnership interest, if the fair market value of the partnership property (other than money) at the time the partner acquired his interest exceeds 110 percent of its adjusted basis to the partnership.[29] The regulations limit application of this rule to cases where lack of a Section 732(d) election would cause a shift in basis from nondepreciable to depreciable property.[30]

Distributions of Marketable Securities. Because marketable securities are easily valued and as liquid as cash, Section 731(c) generally provides that for purposes of both Sections 731(a)(1) and 737,[31] a distribution of marketable securities is treated as a distribution of money to the extent of the fair market value of the securities at the time of the distribution.[32] "Marketable securities" are financial instruments and foreign currencies which are actively traded, including interests in a common trust fund, a mutual fund, and any financial instrument convertible into money or

26. A Section 732(d) election also is permitted with respect to liquidating distributions (I.R.C. § 732(d); see Chapter 8B1, infra) and distributions under Section 751(b) (Reg. § 1.751–1(b)(2)(iii) and (b)(3)(iii); see Section E of this chapter, infra).

27. The regulations permit an adjustment under Section 732(d) to be made to property which is not the same property which would have received the adjustment (e.g., property not in hand when the transferee acquired the partnership interest) if the property received is like property and the transferee, in exchange for the distributed property, relinquishes his interest in the property which would have had the special basis adjustment. Reg. § 1.732–1(d)(1)(v).

28. Reg. § 1.732–1(d)(1)(vi) Example. Thus, the amount of the adjustment is not reduced by depletion or depreciation because the partnership is only allowed to take depletion or depreciation if a Section 743(b) adjustment is in effect.

29. I.R.C. § 732(d), last sentence.

30. Reg. § 1.732–1(d)(4)(ii).

31. Section 737 may require a partner to recognize precontribution gain in contributed property when property (other than money) is distributed to the partner. See Section D2 of this chapter, infra.

32. I.R.C. § 731(c)(1).

marketable securities.[33] Any gain recognized by the distributee partner normally will be capital gain.[34] If a partner recognizes gain on the distribution of a marketable security, the partner's basis in the security will be its basis under Section 732, increased by the amount of gain recognized by the partner.[35]

To illustrate the operation of Section 731(c), assume A and B form the AB partnership as equal partners. A contributes property with a $1,000 fair market value and $250 basis and B contributes $1,000 cash. The partnership later purchases a marketable security for $500 and immediately distributes the security to A when A's outside basis is $250. The distribution of the security is treated as a distribution of $500 of cash, and A recognizes $250 of capital gain.[36] A's basis in the security will be its $250 basis under Section 732(a), increased by the $250 of recognized gain, for a total basis of $500.

The general rule in Section 731(c) is subject to several exceptions. For example, a distribution of a marketable security to the partner who contributed the security to the partnership generally is not subject to Section 731(c).[37] An exception is also provided for a distribution by an investment partnership to a partner who did not contribute any property to the partnership other than money or securities.[38] A partner's gain under Section 731(c) is also reduced by the excess of (1) the partner's distributive share of the net gain if all the partnership's marketable securities had been sold immediately before the distribution for their fair market value, over (2) the partner's distributive share of the net gain attributable to the partnership's marketable securities immediately after the distribution.[39] Thus, a distributee partner reduces the amount of the Section 731(c) distribution by the amount of the decrease in the partner's distributive share of the net gain in the partnership's marketable securities. For example, assume A and B form the AB partnership as equal partners. The partnership distributes marketable security X to A in a current distribution. Before the distribution, AB held marketable securities with the following fair market values, bases, and unrecognized gain or loss:

Security	**F.M.V.**	**A.B.**	**Gain (Loss)**
X	$100	$ 70	$30
Y	100	80	20
Z	100	110	(10)

33. I.R.C. § 731(c)(2).

34. If the marketable security is an unrealized receivable or inventory item, the gain will be ordinary income. I.R.C. § 731(c)(6).

35. I.R.C. § 731(c)(4). A basis increase attributable to gain recognized is allocated to marketable securities in proportion to their respective amounts of unrealized appreciation. Reg. § 1.731–2(f)(1)(i).

36. See Reg. § 1.731–2(j) Example 1.

37. I.R.C. § 731(c)(3)(A)(i).

38. I.R.C. §§ 731(c)(3)(A)(iii), 731(c)(3)(C). The Service has also provided exceptions for certain securities acquired in a nonrecognition transaction and securities that were not marketable securities on the date acquired by the partnership. Reg. §§ 1.731–2(d)(1)(ii) & (iii).

39. I.R.C. § 731(c)(3)(B).

If AB had sold all the securities for their fair market value immediately before the distribution to A, the partnership would have recognized $40 of net gain and A's distributive share of that gain would have been $20. If AB sold the remaining securities immediately after the distribution of security X to A, there would be $10 of net gain and A's distributive share of that gain would have been $5. The distribution reduced A's distributive share of the partnership's net gain in marketable securities by $15 ($20 net gain before distribution minus $5 net gain after distribution). Thus, the distribution of security X to A is treated as a distribution of $85 of money to A ($100 fair market value of security X minus $15 reduction).[40]

Revenue Ruling 94–4

1994–1 Cum.Bull. 195.

ISSUE

If a deemed distribution of money under § 752(b) of the Internal Revenue Code occurs as a result of a decrease in a partner's share of the liabilities of a partnership, is the deemed distribution taken into account at the time of the distribution or at the end of the partnership taxable year?

LAW

Under § 752(b), a decrease in a partner's share of partnership liabilities is considered a distribution of money to the partner by the partnership. The partner will recognize gain under § 731(a)(1) if the distribution of money exceeds the adjusted basis of the partner's interest immediately before the distribution.

Section 1.731–1(a)(1)(ii) of the Income Tax Regulations provides that for purposes of §§ 731 and 705, advances or drawings of money or property against a partner's distributive share of income are treated as current distributions made on the last day of the partnership taxable year with respect to that partner.

Rev. Rul. 92–97, 1992–2 C.B. 124, treats a deemed distribution of money to a partner resulting from a cancellation of debt as an advance or drawing under § 1.731–1(a)(1)(ii) against that partner's distributive share of cancellation of indebtedness income.

HOLDING

A deemed distribution of money under § 752(b) resulting from a decrease in a partner's share of the liabilities of a partnership is treated as an advance or drawing of money under § 1.731–1(a)(1)(ii) to the extent of the partner's distributive share of income for the partnership taxable year. An amount treated as an advance or drawing of money is taken into account at the end of the partnership taxable year. A deemed distribution

40. Reg. § 1.731–2(j) Example 2.

of money resulting from a cancellation of debt may qualify for advance or drawing treatment under this revenue ruling and under Rev. Rul. 92–97.

Revenue Ruling 79–205

1979–2 Cum.Bull. 255.

ISSUES

When a partnership makes a nonliquidating distribution of property, (1) is a partner permitted to offset the increase in the partner's liabilities against the decrease in the partner's liabilities in determining the extent of recognition of gain or loss, and (2) is partnership basis adjusted before or after the property distribution?

FACTS

A and *B* are general partners in *M*, a general partnership, which was formed for the purposes of owning and operating shopping centers.

On December 31, 1977, *M* made nonliquidating distributions in a single transaction of a portion of its property to *A* and *B*. *A* and *B* are equal partners in *M*. *M*, *A* and *B* are calendar year taxpayers. No assets of the type described in section 751(a) of the Internal Revenue Code of 1954 were distributed by *M* to either *A* or *B*.

Immediately prior to the distribution *A* had an adjusted basis for *A*'s interest in *M* of 1,000*x* dollars, and *B* had an adjusted basis for *B*'s interest in *M* of 1,500*x* dollars. The property distributed to *A* had an adjusted basis to *M* of 2,000*x* dollars, and was subject to liabilities of 1,600*x* dollars. The property distributed to *B* had an adjusted basis to *M* of 3,200*x* dollars and was subject to liabilities of 2,800*x* dollars. *A*'s individual liabilities increased by 1,600*x* dollars by reason of the distribution to *A*. *B*'s individual liabilities increased by 2,800*x* dollars by reason of the distribution to *B*. *A*'s share and *B*'s share of the liabilities of *M* each decreased by 2,200*x* dollars (½ of 1,600*x* + ½ of 2,800*x* dollars) by reason of the distributions. The basis and fair market value of the properties distributed were greater than the liabilities to which they were subject.

LAW

Section 705(a) of the Code provides, in part, that the adjusted basis of a partner's interest in a partnership shall be the basis of such interest determined under section 722 decreased (but not below zero) by partnership distributions as provided in section 733.

Section 722 of the Code provides, in part, that the basis of a partnership interest acquired by a contribution of money shall be the amount of such money.

Section 731(a)(1) of the Code provides that in the case of a distribution by a partnership to a partner gain shall not be recognized to such partner, except to the extent that any money distributed exceeds the adjusted basis of such partner's interest in the partnership immediately before the distribution.

Section 732(a)(1) of the Code provides that the basis of property (other than money) distributed by a partnership to a partner other than in liquidation of the partner's interest shall, except as provided in section 732(a)(2), be its adjusted basis to the partnership immediately before such distribution.

Section 732(a)(2) of the Code provides that the basis to the distributee partner of property to which section 732(a)(1) is applicable shall not exceed the adjusted basis of such partner's interest in the partnership reduced by any money distributed in the same transaction.

Section 733 of the Code provides that in the case of a distribution by a partnership to a partner other than in liquidation of a partner's interest, the adjusted basis to such partner of the interest in the partnership shall be reduced (but not below zero) by the amount of any money distributed to such partner and the amount of the basis to such partner of distributed property other than money, as determined under section 732.

Section 752(a) of the Code provides that any increase in a partner's share of the liabilities of a partnership, or any increase in a partner's individual liabilities by reason of the assumption by such partner of partnership liabilities, shall be considered as a contribution of money by such partner to the partnership.

Section 752(b) of the Code provides that any decrease in a partner's share of the liabilities of a partnership, or any decrease in a partner's individual liabilities by reason of the assumption by the partnership of such individual liabilities, shall be considered as a distribution of money to the partner by the partnership.

Section 752(c) of the Code provides that for purposes of section 752 a liability to which property is subject shall, to the extent of the fair market value of such property, be considered as a liability of the owner of the property.

ANALYSIS AND HOLDING

In general, partnership distributions are taxable under section 731(a)(1) of the Code only to the extent that the amount of money distributed exceeds the distributee partner's basis for the partner's partnership interest. This rule reflects the Congressional intent to limit narrowly the area in which gain or loss is recognized upon a distribution so as to remove deterrents to property being moved in and out of partnerships as business reasons dictate. See S.Rep.No. 1622, 83rd Cong., 2nd Sess., page 96 (1954). Here, since partner liabilities are both increasing and decreasing in the same transaction offsetting the increases and decreases tends to limit recognition of gain, thereby giving effect to the Congressional intent. Consequently, in a distribution of encumbered property, the resulting liability adjustments will be treated as occurring simultaneously, rather than occurring in a particular order. Therefore, on a distribution of encumbered property, the amount of money considered distributed to a partner for purposes of section 731(a)(1) is the amount (if any) by which the decrease in the partner's share of the liabilities of the partnership under section 752(b) exceeds the increase in the partner's individual liabilities under section 752(a). The amount of money considered contributed by a partner for purposes of section 722 is the amount (if any) by which the increase in the partner's individual liabilities under section 752(a) exceeds the decrease in the partner's share of the liabilities of the partnership under section 752(b). The increase in the partner's individual liabilities occurs by reason of the assumption by the partner of partnership liabilities, or by reason of a distribution of property subject to a liability, to the extent of the fair market value of such property.

Because the distribution was part of a single transaction, the two properties are treated as having been distributed simultaneously to *A* and *B*. Therefore, all resulting liability adjustments relating to the distribution of the two properties will be treated as occurring simultaneously, rather than occurring in a particular order.

TREATMENT OF PARTNER A

A will be deemed to have received a net distribution of 600*x* dollars in money, that is, the amount by which the amount of money considered distributed to *A* (2,200*x* dollars) exceeds the amount of money considered contributed by *A* (1,600*x* dollars). Since 600*x* dollars does not exceed *A*'s basis for *A*'s interest in *M* immediately before the distribution (1,000*x* dollars), no gain is recognized to *A*.

Under section 732(a) of the Code, the basis to *A* of the property distributed to *A* is the lesser of (i) the adjusted basis of the property to the partnership (2,000*x* dollars), or (ii) the adjusted basis of *A*'s partnership interest (1,000*x* dollars) reduced by the amount of money deemed distributed to *A* (600*x* dollars). Therefore, the basis of the property in *A*'s hands is 400*x* dollars. Under section 733, the adjusted basis of *A*'s partnership interest (1,000*x* dollars) is reduced by the amount of money deemed distributed to *A* (600*x* dollars) and by the basis to *A* of the distributed property (400*x* dollars). The adjusted basis of *A*'s partnership interest is therefore reduced to zero.

TREATMENT OF PARTNER B

B will be deemed to have made a net contribution of 600*x* dollars, that is, the amount by which the amount of money considered contributed by *B* (2,800*x* dollars) exceeds the amount of money considered distributed to *B* (2,200*x* dollars). In applying sections 732(a) and 733 of the Code to *B*, the adjustment to *B*'s basis in *B*'s partnership interest attributable to the liability adjustments resulting from the distributions will be treated as occurring first, and the distribution of property to *B* as occurring second. By so doing, *B*'s basis for the distributed property is increased and *B*'s basis in *B*'s partnership interest is decreased. This allocation gives greater effect to the general rule of section 732(a)(1), which provides for the partner to have the same basis in distributed property as the partnership had for that property.

Therefore, the first step is that *B's* basis for *B's* partnership interest (1,500*x* dollars) is increased under section 722 and 705(a) by the amount of the net contribution deemed made by *B* (600*x* dollars), and is equal to 2,100*x* dollars. Next, under section 732(a) of the Code, the basis to *B* of the property distributed to *B* is the lesser of (i) the adjusted basis of the property to the partnership (3,200*x* dollars), or (ii) the adjusted basis of *B's* partnership interest (2,100*x* dollars) reduced by the amount of money deemed distributed to *B* (zero). Therefore, the basis of the property in *B's* hands is 2,100*x* dollars. Under section 733, the adjusted basis of *B's* partnership interest (2,100*x* dollars) is reduced by the amount of money deemed distributed to *B* (zero) and by the basis to *B* of the distributed property (2,100*x* dollars). The adjusted basis of *B's* partnership interest is therefore zero.

PROBLEMS

1. On July 1, the ABC Partnership, a calendar year partnership, distributes to each of its equal partners $10,000 cash and land with a value of $10,000 and a basis of $5,000. A, B and C have outside bases of $20,000, $10,000 and $5,000 respectively. The partnership has the following assets prior to the distribution:

Assets	**A.B.**	**F.M.V.**
Cash	$50,000	$50,000
Accounts Receivable	0	20,000
Inventory	20,000	30,000
Land	30,000	60,000
Building	10,000	50,000

(a) Discuss the tax consequences of the distribution to A, B, and C, each of whom has owned his partnership interest for several years.

(b) What result to C if he receives the land first and the cash in a subsequent separate distribution on October 1?

(c) What result to C in (b), above, if the cash distribution on October 1 is a draw against his share of partnership income, which is $20,000 for the year?

2. Partner has a $40,000 outside basis in her partnership interest. In a pro rata operating distribution to the partners, Partner receives two assets. Asset #1 has a value of $10,000 and a basis to the partnership of $40,000. Asset #2 has a value of $10,000 and a basis to the partnership of $20,000. What basis will partner take in each property under § 732(c) if:

(a) Asset #1 is an inventory item and Asset #2 is a capital asset?

(b) Asset #2 is an inventory item and Asset #1 is a capital asset?

(c) Both properties are inventory items?

(d) Both properties are capital assets?

(e) Suppose Asset #1 has a value of $60,000 and a basis of $40,000 to the partnership and Asset #2 has a value of $50,000 and a basis of $20,000 to the partnership. What basis will Partner take in each property under § 732(c) if she receives both properties in a pro rata operating distribution and both properties are inventory items?

3. Nupartner purchases a one-third interest in the following three-person equal partnership for $40,000. At the time of the purchase the partnership has the following assets:

	A.B.	**F.M.V.**
Accounts Receivable	$ 0	$30,000
Land (capital asset)	60,000	90,000

The partnership has made no § 754 election. It immediately distributes $10,000 of receivables to each of the three partners.

(a) What result to Nupartner on the collection of the receivables if Nupartner makes no § 732(d) election?

(b) What result to Nupartner on the collection of the receivables if he makes a § 732(d) election?

(c) If Nupartner elects § 732(d), what is his outside basis immediately after the distribution?

(d) Must the partnership approve Nupartner's election under § 732(d)?

(e) Will the § 732(d) election have any immediate effect on the basis of Nupartner's interest in the land remaining in the partnership?

2. Consequences on Subsequent Sales of Distributed Property

Code: §§ 735; 1245(b)(5).

Regulations: §§ 1.735–1; 1.1245–4(f)(2) & (3) Example (1).

The characterization of gain or loss on the disposition of property is generally determined by the character of the asset in the hands of the taxpayer who disposes of the property. But property acquired in a nonrecognition transaction is often subject to special rules that govern not only its basis and holding period but also the tax character of the asset.[1] So it is with property received by a partner in a distribution from a partnership. We already have seen how the Section 732 basis rules apply on an operating distribution to limit the distributee's basis for ordinary income assets to the partnership's basis in those assets. To complete the grand design and prevent the conversion of partnership ordinary income into partner capital gain, Section 735 provides additional rules to govern the character of gain or loss on the disposition of ordinary income property received by the partner in a distribution. In this respect, Section 735 is similar to Section 724, which preserved the ordinary income character of

1. See, e.g., I.R.C. §§ 351; 358; 362(a); 1032; 1223(1) & (2); 1245(a)(2) & (b)(3).

certain property contributed to a partnership in appropriate cases. Section 735 also provides for the tacking of the partnership's holding period in the distributed property.

Characterization. Under Section 735(a), gains or losses recognized by a distributee partner on the disposition of "unrealized receivables" received in a distribution are treated as ordinary income or loss,[2] and gains or losses on the sale or exchange of distributed inventory items suffer a similar character taint if they are sold or exchanged by the partner within five years from the date of their distribution.[3] In the case of unrealized receivables, the character taint remains with the assets as long as they are held by the distributee partner.[4] Since the taint is not permanent with inventory, a patient partner who holds these items as capital assets may avoid ordinary income characterization on the sale or exchange of the inventory by delaying any disposition until the expiration of five years from the date of distribution.[5] If an item is both an unrealized receivable and an inventory item, the more stringent rules governing receivables are applicable. The Section 735 taint cannot be removed in a nonrecognition transaction or a series of such transactions.[6] Except in the case of C corporation stock received in a Section 351 corporate formation, the taint carries over to the exchanged basis property received in the transaction.[7]

The Section 735(a) taint rules do not apply to recapture property.[8] But the recapture gain which the partnership would have recognized on a sale of the property carries over to the distributee partner, who recognizes ordinary income on a subsequent sale or exchange. This is accomplished through the definitions of "recomputed basis" and "additional depreciation" in the applicable recapture provisions. For example, where Section 1245 property is distributed by a partnership to a partner, the amount of Section 1245(a) ordinary income which the partnership would have recognized had it sold the recapture property at its fair market value on the date of the distribution is generally added to the distributee's adjusted basis in the property in determining his recomputed basis.[9] The legislative history of Section 1245 illustrates the rule as follows:[10]

2. I.R.C. § 735(a)(1). "Unrealized receivables" are as defined in Section 751(c) except that recapture items are not included in the definition for purposes of Section 735(a).

3. I.R.C. § 735(a)(2). In defining inventory items under Section 735(a)(2), the long-term holding period requirement for Section 1231 property is disregarded. I.R.C. § 735(c)(1). Thus, if property would be Section 1231 property but for the fact that the partnership did not hold it long-term, it nonetheless is treated as Section 1231 property and not as an inventory item. Cf. I.R.C. § 751(d)(2).

4. Query whether a gift of the unrealized receivables purges the ordinary income to the donee? See I.R.C. §§ 735(c)(2)(A) & 7701(a)(42), (43) & (45) and Problem 1(b), infra. Cf. Reg. § 1.267(d)–1(a)(3) & (4) Example (3).

5. For purposes of measuring this period, the holding period in the hands of the partnership does not tack. I.R.C. § 735(b), parenthetical clause.

6. I.R.C. § 735(c)(2)(A).

7. I.R.C. § 735(c)(2)(B).

8. See supra note 2.

9. I.R.C. § 1245(b)(5)(B)(i). See I.R.C. § 1245(a)(2) for the definition of "recomputed basis." Cf. § 1245(a)(1)(A). The recomputed basis must be reduced by any Section 751(b) gain recognized with respect to the property on the distribution. See Section E of this chapter, infra.

10. S.Rep. No. 1881, 87th Cong., 2d Sess. (1962), reprinted in 1962–3 C.B. 984.

The application of this provision is illustrated as follows: A, B, and C are equal partners in a partnership whose assets consist of three pieces of section 1245 property, assets X, Y, and Z, each with a fair market value of $100,000. Asset X has an adjusted basis of $60,000 and a recomputed basis of $85,000; asset Y has an adjusted basis of $85,000 and a recomputed basis of $110,000; and asset Z has an adjusted basis of $95,000 and a recomputed basis of $100,000. Asset Y is distributed to B in complete liquidation of his partnership interest. B's basis in his partnership interest is $75,000, and under section 732 this basis is allocated to asset Y. If B later sells asset Y for [$100,000] at a time when the adjusted basis is still $75,000 and if B has not taken any depreciation deductions with respect to asset Y since the distribution, the gain to which section 1245(a) applies would be $15,000, since the recomputed basis of the property is only $90,000, that is, the adjusted basis of the property ($75,000) increased by the amount of gain ($15,000) which would have been recognized to the partnership if the asset had been sold for its fair market value at the time of distribution ($100,000 minus $85,000).[11]

Tacked holding periods. Section 735(b) allows the distributee partner to tack the partnership's holding period[12] with respect to property with a transferred basis from the partnership,[13] and also any distributed property which has some special type of basis.[14] Tacking is not permitted, however, in measuring the five-year taint applicable to distributed "inventory items."[15]

PROBLEMS

1. A, a partner in the ABC cash method partnership, has an outside basis of $10,000. In a pro rata operating distribution to the partners, A receives a parcel of land held as inventory by the partnership with a basis of $2,000 and a value of $3,000 and zero basis accounts receivable with a value of $3,000. Both properties become capital assets in her hands. Six years later, she collects the receivables and sells the parcel for $3,000.

(a) What are the tax consequences to A on the distribution and on the collection of the receivables and the sale of the parcel? What is the justification for the different results?

11. Similar rules apply to other types of recapture property. Ed. See, e.g., I.R.C. § 1250(d)(5).

12. Tacking is not permitted, however, on property received on a Section 751(b) purchase rather than a Section 731 distribution.

13. Cf. I.R.C. § 1223(2).

14. See, e.g., I.R.C. §§ 732(a)(2), (c); 732(d); 743(b).

15. I.R.C. § 735(b), parenthetical clause.

(b) What result if, immediately after the distribution, A gives the parcel to her daughter, D, who promptly sells the parcel for $3,000? Assume the parcel is a capital asset in D's hands.

2. A and B operate a taxi business as partners. In the current year the partnership distributes to A a taxi purchased over one year ago for $5,000, which has an adjusted basis of $2,000 and a value of $3,000 when distributed. A's outside basis is $1,000. (To make § 751(b), which is considered later in the chapter, inapplicable, assume an identical distribution to B). The disposition of the taxi is not a taxable event to the partnership. see §§ 731(b) and 1245(b)(3). What are the tax consequences to A if he immediately sells the cab for $3,000?

C. CONSEQUENCES TO THE DISTRIBUTING PARTNERSHIP

Code: §§ 731(b); 734; 754; 755; 1245(b)(3).

Regulations: §§ 1.731–1(b); 1.734–1; 1.755–1(a) & (c).

Nonrecognition Rule. We have seen that Congress has done almost everything possible to ensure that a distributee partner does not recognize gain or loss on the receipt of partnership property.[1] Section 731(b) similarly provides that no gain or loss is recognized by a partnership on the distribution of money or property to a partner. Even the recapture provisions bow to nonrecognition under Section 731(b),[2] but nothing (except time) is lost because the potential ordinary income lurking in the asset carries over to the distributee partner along with its transferred basis.[3]

Impact on Inside Basis. Turning to the partnership's balance sheet, Section 734(a) sets forth the general rule that distributions of property do not affect the inside basis of property retained by the partnership. This "no adjustment" rule applies even though the distributee partner recognizes gain on the distribution[4] or is required to take a basis in the distributed property which differs from its basis to the partnership.[5] In these circumstances, the no adjustment rule may create distortions resembling those which occur on the sale of a partnership interest.

For example, assume the ABC partnership is an equal three-person partnership with the following balance sheet:

Assets	A.B.	F.M.V.	Partners' Capital	A.B.	F.M.V.
Cash	$6,000	$ 6,000	A	$3,000	$ 6,000
			B	3,000	6,000
Capital Asset	3,000	12,000	C	3,000	6,000
	$9,000	$18,000		$9,000	$18,000

1. I.R.C. § 731(a).

2. See, e.g., I.R.C. § 1245(b)(3).

3. See I.R.C. §§ 735(a); 1245(b)(5); and the discussion in Section B2 of this chapter, supra.

4. I.R.C. § 731(a)(1).

5. I.R.C. § 732(a)(2), (c).

If the partnership distributes $6,000 cash to A in liquidation of her entire partnership interest, A recognizes $3,000 of gain,[6] representing the previously unrealized appreciation in A's share of the capital asset, which had an inside basis of $1,000 and a fair market value of $4,000. Under the no adjustment rule, however, the partnership's basis in that one-third portion of the asset remains $1,000, and B and C each would have a $4,500 gain on a subsequent sale of the asset for $12,000. Thus, even though A realized her $3,000 pro rata share of the gain, that same amount is left behind in the partnership to be taxed to the other partners when the asset is sold. Is this double taxation? Not necessarily. If the partnership sells the capital asset for $12,000, B and C increase their outside bases under Section 705 to reflect their respective $4,500 taxable gains, and on a subsequent liquidation of the partnership they together will recognize an offsetting $3,000 loss.[7] But a liquidation may be years away, if at all. In the meantime, B and C have a total outside basis for their partnership interests which does not equal their inside basis in the partnership's capital asset, resulting in the following distorted balance sheet:

Assets	**A.B.**	**F.M.V.**	**Partners' Capital**	**A.B.**	**F.M.V.**
Capital Asset	$3,000	$12,000	B	$3,000	$ 6,000
			C	3,000	6,000
	$3,000	$12,000		$6,000	$12,000

You are on the right track if you have a sense of deja vu. We have seen a similar imbalance resulting from the failure to adjust the basis of partnership property on the acquisition of a partnership interest. In the case of appreciated partnership assets, a Section 754 election allowed the partnership to make a basis adjustment under Section 743(b) and provided relief for the buying partner. In the case of both operating and liquidating distributions, a Section 754 election triggers a similar inside basis adjustment under Section 734(b) which benefits all the remaining partners and corrects the imbalance illustrated above.[8] And like Section 743, Section 734 may require a downward adjustment in the partnership's basis in its assets in order to prevent inappropriate deferral of taxes by partners following a

6. I.R.C. § 731(a)(1).

7. For example, if the capital asset is sold for $12,000, B and C each would have a $4,500 distributive share of the gain and the outside basis of each would increase by $4,500 to $7,500. If the partnership then were liquidated and the $12,000 proceeds were distributed, B and C each would receive $6,000 cash and recognize a $1,500 capital loss under Section 731(a)(2). The net effect would be a $3,000 net long-term capital gain to B and C ($4,500 gain on the sale of the capital asset less $1,500 capital loss on the liquidation of the partnership). Although the specter of double taxation is removed, this example too conveniently assumes a prompt termination of the partnership.

8. In the case of an operating distribution, the adjustment benefits all the partners, including the continuing distributee partner, unless the partnership agreement provides a special allocation of the benefits of a basis increase to the nondistributee partners who otherwise would bear the burden of the lost basis. I.R.C. § 704(b). Cf. Reg. § 1.704–1(b)(5) Example (14)(i).

liquidating distribution.[9]

Returning to the example, Section 734(b)(1)(A) permits the partnership to increase the basis of the capital asset by the $3,000 gain recognized by A, leaving the partnership with the following balance sheet:

Assets	A.B.	F.M.V.	Partners' Capital	A.B.	F.M.V.
Capital Asset	$6,000	$12,000	B	$3,000	$ 6,000
			C	$3,000	$ 6,000
	$6,000	$12,000		$6,000	$12,000

Section 734(b) determines the overall adjustment. The action then shifts to Section 755, which governs the allocation of the adjustment among the partnership assets. As with Section 743(b) adjustments, the initial step is to value the partnership's assets. Next the assets of the partnership are divided into two classes: capital gain property (capital assets and Section 1231(b) property) and other property.[10] Because in the example the character of gain recognized by the distributee was capital, the regulations require the adjustment to be made only to the basis of the partnership's capital gain property.[11] At the next step, the allocation mechanism differs from the rules governing Section 743(b) adjustments, where the adjustment resulted in a special personal inside basis only for the acquiring partner. In contrast, the Section 734(b) adjustment benefits all continuing partners unless a special allocation to the contrary is made.[12]

Section 734(b) also permits an adjustment when the basis of the distributed property is limited under Section 732(a)(2) to the distributee partner's outside basis.[13] To illustrate the purpose for this second type of adjustment, assume that the ABC partnership has the following balance sheet:

Assets	A.B.	F.M.V.	Partners' Capital	A.B.	F.M.V.
Cash	$ 3,000	$ 3,000	A	$ 5,000	$ 5,000
Capital Asset #1	9,000	3,000	B	5,000	5,000
Capital Asset #2	3,000	9,000	C	5,000	5,000
	$15,000	$15,000		$15,000	$15,000

At this point, each partner has a $2,000 unrealized loss represented by the decline in value of capital asset #1 and a $2,000 unrealized gain represented by the appreciation of capital asset #2. If capital asset #1 is distributed to A, A's basis in the asset will be limited to her outside basis of $5,000. When A sells the asset, she will recognize her $2,000 share of the loss, but the remaining $4,000 of predistribution capital loss inherent in the asset will disappear because $4,000 of basis evaporated at the time of distribu-

9. I.R.C. § 734(a) & (d); see Chapter 6B, supra and Chapter 8B, infra.

10. Reg. § 1.755–1(a).

11. Reg. § 1.755–1(c)(1)(ii).

12. See Problem (c), below.

13. I.R.C. § 734(b)(1)(B).

tion. Without an adjustment, the partners as a group will recognize only $2,000 of the loss on asset #1 but the entire $6,000 of gain on asset #2. To cure this distortion, Section 734(b) permits the partnership to increase its bases in the remaining assets by an amount equal to the difference between the partnership's basis in the distributed property and the basis taken by the distributee partner in that property.[14]

Section 755 once again governs the allocation of the adjustment. In order to preserve both the proper amount and character of total gain or loss, the adjustment is made to property in the same class as the distributed property whose basis was changed as a result of the distribution.[15] If there is an increase in basis allocated within a class of property, it is first allocated to properties with unrealized appreciation in proportion to their appreciation. Any remaining increase is allocated in proportion to the fair market values of the properties.[16] A decrease in basis allocated within a class of property is first allocated to properties based upon their respective amounts of unrealized depreciation before the decrease and then in proportion to the adjusted bases of the properties (after adjustment for unrealized depreciation).[17] In no event can the basis of property be reduced below zero.[18] If a partnership does not have property of the character to be adjusted or if the basis of all property of like character has been reduced to zero, the adjustment is held in abeyance until the partnership acquires property in the class to be adjusted.[19]

For purposes of cost recovery under Section 168, if the basis of a partnership's recovery property is increased under Section 734 as a result of a distribution, the increased portion of the basis is treated as newly purchased recovery property placed in service when the distribution occurs.[20] Thus, any applicable recovery period and method may be used with respect to the increased portion of the basis. No change is made in determining the cost recovery allowance for the portion of the basis for which there is no increase.[21] If a distribution triggers a decrease in the basis of a partnership's cost recovery property, the decrease is accounted for over the property's remaining recovery period, beginning with the recovery period in which the basis is decreased.[22] If a distributing partnership has a large number of assets affected by these rules, it is likely to have considerable personnel turnover in its accounting department.

14. Id. The last sentence of Section 734(b) prohibits a partnership from adjusting the basis of its property following a distribution of an interest in another partnership if the second partnership does not have a Section 754 election in effect. This provision is intended to prevent taxpayers from achieving a net step-up in the basis of its assets by means of inconsistent elections under Section 754. For an example illustrating the type of abuse which this provision is designed to prevent, see H.R.Rep. No. 98–432, 98th Cong., 2d Sess. 1230 (1984).

15. Reg. § 1.755–1(c)(1)(i).

16. Reg. § 1.755–1(c)(2)(i).

17. Reg. § 1.755–2(c)(2)(ii). A decrease in the bases of partnership assets can result from a distribution that liquidates a partner's interest. See I.R.C. § 734(b) and Chapter 8B1, infra.

18. Reg. § 1.755–1(c)(3).

19. Reg. § 1.755–1(c)(4).

20. Reg. § 1.734–1(e)(1).

21. Id.

22. Reg. § 1.734–1(e)(2).

Impact on Capital Accounts. In studying the tax treatment of partnership allocations, we saw that an agreed allocation will not be respected unless, among other requirements, the partnership agreement requires "capital accounts" to be maintained throughout the life of the partnership in accordance with detailed regulations.[23] Nonliquidating distributions are among the many partnership transactions that necessitate capital account adjustments.[24]

Because a distribution reduces the distributee partner's equity in the partnership and because the function of a capital account is to measure a partner's interest in the firm at any given point in time, the regulations logically require that a partner's capital account must be reduced by any money distributed to the partner and by the fair market value of any distributed property.[25] Recall, however, that the partnership does not recognize gain or loss on distributions of property.[26] As a result, the reduction of a distributee partner's capital account by the fair market value of the distributed property would distort the partnership's balance sheet unless an additional adjustment is made to reflect the unrealized appreciation or decline in value of the property. The regulations address this problem by providing that the capital accounts of all the partners must be adjusted by their respective shares of the gain or loss that the partnership would have recognized if it had sold the distributed property for its fair market value on the date of distribution.[27]

To illustrate, assume the ABC equal partnership distributes to partner A land with a value of $10,000 and an adjusted tax basis and book value to the partnership of $4,000. For tax purposes, the partnership recognizes no gain on the distribution.[28] On the balance sheet, however, the $6,000 gain inherent in the land is treated as recognized and is allocated equally among the partners, increasing each partner's capital account by $2,000, just as if the land had been sold by the partnership for its fair market value.[29] The distributee partner (A) then reduces his capital account by $10,000, the full value of the land. When the smoke clears, A's capital account suffers a net decrease of $8,000, and the capital accounts of B and C are increased by $2,000 each.[30]

23. Reg. § 1.704–1(b)(2)(ii)(*b*). See Reg. § 1.704–1(b)(2)(iv) & Chapter 4B, supra.

24. See generally Reg. § 1.704–1(b)(2)(iv)(*b*).

25. Id. For special rules on the distribution of promissory notes, see Reg. § 1.704–1(b)(2)(iv)(*e*)(*2*). If the distributee partner assumes a liability connected to the property or takes the property subject to a liability, his capital account is reduced by the full value of the property less the liability. Reg. § 1.704–1(b)(2)(iv)(*b*).

26. I.R.C. § 731(b).

27. Reg. § 1.704–1(b)(2)(iv)(*e*)(*1*). The adjustment for unrealized gain or loss is only to the extent that it was not previously reflected in capital accounts. Reg. § 1.704–1(b)(2)(iv)(*f*). For example, the built-in gain on contributed property is already reflected because the property was recorded on the partnership's books at its fair market value at the time of contribution. If the asset is later distributed, the built-in gain should not be reflected again. See Chapter 4C, supra.

28. I.R.C. § 731(b).

29. The example assumes that the partners have agreed to share profits and losses equally.

30. See Reg. § 1.704–1(b)(5) Example (14)(v). Note that the net decrease of $4,000 ($8,000 – $2,000 – $2,000) equals the partnership's book value for the land.

In addition, if a distribution is more than a de minimis amount and is in exchange for any portion of a partners' interest in the partnership, the partnership may elect to restate on its books all remaining assets at their current fair market value and correspondingly restate the partners' capital accounts.[31]

PROBLEM

The ABC partnership has three equal partners, A, B, and C, and the following balance sheet:

Assets	A.B.	F.M.V.	Partners' Capital	A.B.	F.M.V.
Cash	$ 60,000	$ 60,000	A	$ 70,000	$ 80,000
Capital Asset #1	90,000	60,000	B	70,000	80,000
Capital Asset #2	40,000	60,000	C	70,000	80,000
Capital Asset #3	20,000	60,000			
	$210,000	$240,000		$210,000	$240,000

A receives capital asset #1 in an operating distribution. A has a one-ninth interest worth $20,000 in the partnership capital and profits after the distribution.

(a) What results to A and the partnership if there is no § 754 election? Reconstruct the balance sheet after the distribution.

(b) What results to A and the partnership if the partnership has made a § 754 election? Reconstruct the balance sheet after the distribution.

(c) How should any basis adjustment be allocated among the partners?

D. MIXING BOWL TRANSACTIONS

Code: §§ 704(c)(1)(B) & (c)(2); 737.

Although Subchapter K does almost everything possible to provide nonrecognition of gain or loss to partners and partnerships on distributions of property,[1] Congress has enacted several exceptions to combat abuse of this lenient policy. Sections 704(c)(1)(B) and 737, the two related provisions discussed in this section, are aimed at "mixing bowl transactions," an income-shifting strategy where a partner transfers appreciated property to a partnership and the partnership later either distributes the contributed

31. Reg. § 1.704–1(b)(2)(iv)(*f*)(*5*). These adjustments must be made principally for a substantial non-tax business purpose. Id. Even absent such a revaluation, a distribution also may require adjustments to the book value of the partnership's remaining assets and the capital account of the distributee partner if the partnership adjusts the basis of its remaining property under Section 734(b) pursuant to a Section 754 election. See Reg. § 1.704–1(b)(2)(iv)(*m*)(*1*), (*4*) and (*5*).

1. See Sections B and C of this chapter, supra.

property to another partner or distributes substitute property to the contributing partner. The tax planning goal of this strategy is to shift or defer recognition of the contributing partner's precontribution gain by exploiting the nonrecognition rules that apply to contributions to and distributions by a partnership.[2]

1. Distributions of Contributed Property to Another Partner

Under the now familiar general rule of Section 704(c)(1)(A), a partner contributing property with a built-in gain or loss to a partnership is generally allocated that gain or loss when the partnership subsequently disposes of the property.[3] As originally enacted, Section 704(c) was limited to partnership sales of contributed property. As a result, a contributing partner could avoid an allocation of precontribution gain if the partnership distributed the contributed property to another partner rather than selling it. Since a partnership generally does not recognize gain or loss on a distribution of property,[4] the contributing partner was not taxed on the distribution, and any built-in gain was shifted to the distributee partner through a transferred basis mechanism.[5]

To preclude this type of mixing bowl transaction, Section 704(c)(1)(B) provides that if property contributed by one partner is distributed to another partner within seven years of its contribution to the partnership, the contributing partner (or her successor)[6] is treated as recognizing Section 704(c) gain or loss as if the partnership had sold the property for its fair market value at the time of the distribution.[7] The character of the gain or loss is the same as if the partnership had sold the contributed property to the distributee partner.[8] Appropriately, the contributing partner's outside basis is increased or decreased by the amount of gain or loss recog-

2. See I.R.C. §§ 721; 731.

3. Reg. § 1.704–3 and Chapter 4C, supra.

4. I.R.C. § 731. See Section C of this chapter, supra.

5. I.R.C. § 732.

6. I.R.C. § 704(c)(3). Successor partners (e.g., purchasers, donees, or legatees) thus may recognize gain under Section 704(c)(1)(B) if the contributed property is distributed to another partner within seven years of the original contribution. Section 704(c)(1)(C), however, would prevent successor partners from recognizing loss from property that was contributed with a built-in loss because the property's basis would be deemed to be equal to its fair market value at the time it was contributed to the partnership. See also I.R.C. §§ 754 and 743(b) and Section C of this chapter, supra, for the possible basis adjustments that will eliminate built-in gain or loss on certain transfers of partnership interests.

7. The seven-year time period in Section 704(c)(1)(B) applies to property contributed after June 8, 1997. The same rule, but with a five-year threshold, applies to property contributed to a partnership before June 9, 1997.

8. I.R.C. § 704(c)(1)(B)(ii). As a result, Section 724 would apply in determining the character of gain or loss on contributed unrealized receivables, inventory items and capital loss property. Also, the special characterization rule in Section 707(b)(2) for a sale or exchange of property between a partnership and a more–than–50–percent partner applies. See Reg. § 1.704–4(b)(2) Example.

nized as a result of the distribution.[9] To avoid double recognition of that gain or loss, the partnership's inside basis in the property is increased or decreased prior to the distribution to reflect the gain or loss recognized by the contributing partner.[10]

To illustrate, return to the familiar example[11] where A contributes Gainacre with an adjusted basis of $12,000 and a fair market value of $20,000 and B contributes $20,000 cash to the equal AB partnership. Assume that three years later the partnership distributes Gainacre, then worth $23,000, to B. Under Section 704(c)(1)(B), A is allocated the $8,000 precontribution gain just as if the partnership had sold the property instead of distributing it,[12] and A would increase his outside basis by $8,000. In addition, Gainacre's basis would be increased to $20,000 prior to the distribution to B, who ordinarily would take the property with a $20,000 transferred basis.[13]

The general rule of Section 704(c)(1)(B) is subject to two statutory exceptions. First, it does not apply if the contributed property is distributed back to the contributing partner or her successor.[14] There is no abuse in this situation because the precontribution gain continues to lurk in the contributing partner's transferred basis in the distributed property.[15] Second, Section 704(c)(2) provides relief to a contributing partner who receives a distribution of like-kind property (within the meaning of Section 1031) within 180 days after the contributed property is distributed to another partner.[16] In that case, the contributing partner is allowed by the statute and regulations to reduce the amount of gain or loss recognized under Section 704(c)(1)(B) by the amount of built-in gain or loss in the distributed like-kind property. The effect of this exception may be to exempt from Section 704(c)(1)(B) distributions of property contributed by a partner who receives a timely distribution of like-kind property.[17] The policy here is that the contributing partner should not have to recognize gain under Section 704(c)(1)(B) if she would have qualified for nonrecognition if the transaction had taken place outside the partnership. To return to the example, where Gainacre (basis—$12,000, value—$20,000) is distributed to B three years later when it is worth $23,000, Section 704(c)(1)(B) would not apply if

9. I.R.C. § 704(c)(1)(B)(iii). See I.R.C. § 705(a)(1)(A) & (2)(A).

10. I.R.C. § 704(c)(1)(B)(iii). See I.R.C. §§ 732, 733.

11. See Chapter 4C1, supra.

12. If the property had been worth less than $20,000 at the time of the distribution to B and the partnership used the traditional method of making Section 704(c) allocations, A's gain would be limited by the ceiling rule. See Reg. § 1.704–3(b).

13. I.R.C. § 732. This assumes that B's outside basis is at least $20,000 at the time of the distribution. I.R.C. § 732(a)(1), (b).

14. I.R.C. § 704(c)(1)(B), second parenthetical.

15. I.R.C. § 732(a).

16. The time period is shortened to the due date for the contributing partner's tax return (with regard to extensions) if that date falls within the 180–day period. I.R.C. § 704(c)(2)(B)(ii).

17. In these circumstances, the general rules of Sections 731–733 are applicable.

the partnership distributed like-kind property with at least $8,000 of built-in gain to A within 180 days of the distribution of Gainacre to B.[18]

The regulations under Section 704(c)(1)(B) also contain an anti-abuse provision under which the statute and regulations must be applied in a manner consistent with the purpose of the section and the Service can recast a transaction for federal tax purposes to achieve appropriate tax results.[19] For example, the regulations apply Section 704(c)(1)(B) to a distribution that actually takes place after the statute's time limitation (i.e., more than seven years after the contribution of property), but where the partners took steps that were the functional equivalent of a distribution before the end of that period.[20]

2. Distributions of Other Property to the Contributing Partner

A second potential abuse identified by Congress was a transaction where a partner contributes appreciated property to a partnership and later receives a distribution of other property while the partnership retains the contributed property. If the normal contribution and distribution rules applied in that situation, the contributing partner would be able to exchange the contributed property in a nonrecognition transaction when a similar swap outside the partnership would not have qualified for nonrecognition.[1] Section 737 prevents this type of mixing bowl transaction by requiring a contributing partner to recognize gain if she contributes appreciated property to a partnership and within seven years[2] of the contribution receives property other than money as a distribution from the partnership.[3] The amount of gain is the lesser of (1) the fair market value of the distributed property (other than money) less the partner's outside basis immediately before the distribution (reduced, but not below zero, by the amount of money received in the distribution) or (2) the "net precontribution gain" of the partner.[4] "Net precontribution gain" is the net gain that

18. See Reg. § 1.704–4(d)(3) & (4) Example. Note that while Section 704(c)(2) refers to the "value" of the distributed like-kind property the regulations base the test on the built-in gain or loss in such property. Section 704(c)(1)(B) is also inapplicable if there is a constructive termination of the partnership under Section 708(b)(1)(B). Reg. § 1.704–4(c)(3). The regulations also provide some more specialized exceptions to the application of Section 704(c)(1)(B). See Reg. § 1.704–4(c). Section 708(b)(1)(B) is considered in Chapter 8D2, infra. The interrelationship of Section 704(c)(1)(B) and 708(b)(1)(B) is considered in Hanna, "Partnership Distributions: Whatever Happened to Nonrecognition," 82 Kentucky Law J. 465 (1993), which concludes that both Sections 704(c)(1)(B) and 737 along with some other provisions of the Code are unnecessary.

19. Reg. § 1.704–4(f).

20. Reg. § 1.704–4(f)(2) Example 1.

1. I.R.C. §§ 731(a) 732(a), 733. But see I.R.C. § 707(a)(2)(B) considered at Chapter 5B2, supra, which would likely apply if the distribution occurred within a two-year period. Cf. Reg. § 1.704–3(a)(3).

2. The seven-year time period in Section 737 applies to property contributed after June 8, 1997.

3. I.R.C. § 737(a). The gain is in addition to any gain recognized under Section 731. Id.

4. For purposes of Section 737, marketable securities are treated as money to the extent of their fair market value on the date of the distribution. I.R.C. § 731(c)(1).

would have been recognized by the distributee partner under Section 704(c)(1)(B) if all of the property contributed by that partner within seven years of the current distribution had been distributed to another partner at the time of the distribution to the contributing partner.[5] The character of the gain is determined by reference to the contributed property.[6]

As under Section 704(c)(1)(B), appropriate concurrent basis adjustments are triggered when Section 737 applies. The contributing (now distributee) partner may increase her outside basis by the amount of gain recognized under Section 737.[7] This adjustment is made after measurement of the amount of Section 737(a) gain but before the distribution of the property.[8] The partnership also increases its inside basis in the contributed property by the amount of any Section 737 gain.[9]

To illustrate the operation of Section 737, assume that A again contributes Gainacre with an adjusted basis of $12,000 and a fair market value of $20,000 to the equal AB partnership. B contributes cash of $5,000 and Capital Asset with an adjusted basis and value of $15,000.[10] Within seven years of A's contribution (when A's outside basis is still $12,000), A receives the Capital Asset (still valued at $15,000) in an operating distribution. In these circumstances, A would recognize a $3,000 gain, which is the lesser of (1) $3,000, the fair market value of the Capital Asset reduced by A's outside basis ($15,000 less $12,000) or (2) $8,000, A's net precontribution gain. A also would increase his outside basis by $3,000, to $15,000, immediately prior to the distribution.[11] A would take a $15,000 transferred basis in the Capital Asset,[12] and A's outside basis after the distribution would be reduced to zero.[13] To avoid double taxation, the partnership may increase its adjusted basis in Gainacre by $3,000, to $15,000.[14]

The general rule of Section 737(a) is subject to two statutory exceptions. First, if any portion of the distributed property consists of property that was contributed by the distributee partner, that property is not taken into account in determining gain under Section 737(a)(1) or measuring the net precontribution gain under Section 737(b).[15] Second, Section 737 does not apply to the extent that Section 751(b) applies.[16]

5. I.R.C. §§ 737(a) & (b).

6. I.R.C. § 737(a); Reg. § 1.737–1(d). Section 724 also would apply in determining the character of gain on contributed unrealized receivables and inventory items.

7. I.R.C. § 737(c)(1).

8. Id.

9. I.R.C. § 737(c)(2).

10. If the property had been appreciated or depreciated at the time of B's contribution, Section 704(c)(1)(B) also would apply to B.

11. I.R.C. § 737(c)(1). The increase is after the measurement of Section 737 gain and before the distribution of the property. Id.

12. I.R.C. § 732(a)(1).

13. I.R.C. § 733.

14. I.R.C. § 737(c)(2).

15. I.R.C. § 737(d)(1). However, if the property distributed consists of an interest in an entity that the distributee partner contributed to the partnership, the exception is inapplicable to the extent that the value of the entity is attributable to property contributed to the entity after its contribution to the partnership. Id. For example, assume A contributed C corporation stock with an adjusted basis of $12,000 and a fair market value of $20,000 to a partnership and the partnership subsequently contributed property worth

16. See note 16 on page 310.

Section 737 is also subject to an anti-abuse rule contained in the regulations.[17] That provision requires that the rules of Section 737 and the regulations be applied in a manner consistent with the purpose of the section. The Service is also empowered to recast a transaction for federal tax purposes as appropriate to achieve tax results consistent with the purpose of Section 737. For example, the regulations disregard the basis increase attributable to a temporary contribution of property undertaken to avoid gain under Section 737.[18]

One of the most challenging aspects of Section 737 is its interrelationship with other parts of Subchapter K. Both Section 704(c)(1)(B) and Section 737 can apply to different contributing partners when there is a single distribution of contributed property. In addition, if either Section 707(a)(2)(B) or Section 704(c)(2) applies to a transaction also covered by Section 737, those sections take precedence.[19] Finally, as noted above, Section 737 does not apply to the extent that Section 751(b) overrides it. Some of these statutory interrelationships are explored in the problem below.

PROBLEM

A, B, and C form the equal ABC partnership by contributing the following real properties, all of which are held as an investment by both the partners and the partnership:

Partner	**Property**	**A.B.**	**F.M.V.**
A	#1	$ 2,000	$10,000
B	#2	5,000	10,000
C	#3	10,000	10,000

Assume that ABC uses the "traditional method" of allocation under Reg. § 1.704–3(b). What are the tax consequences to the partners in the following transactions, assuming the partners' outside bases and ABC's inside basis in the land are unchanged at the time of each transaction, if the ABC partnership:

(a) Sells property #1 for $10,000.

(b) Distributes property #1 to C six years after formation of the partnership.

$10,000 to the C corporation. If the C corporation stock is now worth $30,000 and it is distributed to A, the distribution of $10,000 of the C corporation stock would be subject to Section 737(a).

16. I.R.C. § 737(d)(2). See Section E of this chapter for coverage of Section 751(b). Section 737 also does not apply to a constructive termination of a partnership under Section 708(b)(1)(B). Reg. § 1.737–2(a). Section 708(b)(1)(B) is considered in Chapter 8D2, infra. The regulations also provide some more specialized exceptions to the application of Section 737. See Reg. § 1.737–2.

17. Reg. § 1.737–4.

18. Reg. § 1.737–4(b) Example 1.

19. Reg. § 1.704–3(a)(5).

(c) Distributes property #3 to A six years after formation of the partnership.

(d) Distributes property #2 to A six years after formation of the partnership.

(e) Distributes property #2 to A one year after formation of the partnership.

(f) Simultaneously distributes property #1 to B and property #2 to A six years after formation of the partnership and the properties are like kind properties.

(g) Distributes property that is like kind to property #1 to A six years after formation of the partnership.

E. DISTRIBUTIONS WHICH ALTER THE PARTNERS' INTERESTS IN ORDINARY INCOME PROPERTY

Code: §§ 731(d); 732(e); 751(b). Skim § 751(a), (c) & (d).

Regulations: § 1.751–1(b). Skim § 1.751–1(g) Example (2).

Introduction. The operating distribution rules considered up to now reflect a typical nonrecognition scheme. Historically, life was not that simple in the partnership tax forest, where avaricious taxpayers prowled in search of the opportunity to shift ordinary income into a lower bracket or, better still, to convert ordinary income into capital gain. Congress understandably reacted by planting an imposing array of statutory trees designed to prevent income shifting and conversion. And so just as you feel that you have mastered an area, Section 751(b) appears on the scene to complicate this chapter as well as your life.

Section 751(b) overrides the nonrecognition and substituted basis rules of Section 731 and Section 732.[1] This occurs when a distribution has the effect of altering the partners' interests in Section 751 property—i.e., generally the same ordinary income assets (unrealized receivables and inventory items) that were singled out by Section 751(a) for special treatment in connection with the sale of a partnership interest but with one important caveat.[2] For purposes of Section 751(b), inventory items are treated as Section 751 property only if they have "appreciated substantially in value."[3] Section 751(b), which applies to both operating and liquidating distributions,[4] is the second feature of this ongoing horror show.

1. See I.R.C. §§ 731(d) & 732(e), which in essence provide that the Section 751(b) rules are to be applied prior to application of the general distribution rules. See also Reg. § 1.751–1(b)(1)(iii).

2. See Chapter 6A, supra. For convenience, partnership assets that do not constitute Section 751 property will be referred to in this discussion as "Section 741 property."

3. I.R.C. § 751(b)(1)(A)(ii).

4. This includes distributions to a retiring partner as well as a liquidation of the partnership itself. See Rev. Rul. 77–412, 1977–2 C.B. 223 and Chapter 8D, infra.

Substantially Appreciated Inventory Items. Inventory items are not treated as Section 751 property for purposes of Section 751(b) unless they are substantially appreciated—i.e., unless their aggregate fair market value (meaning total value, not merely equity) exceeds 120 percent of the adjusted basis of the inventory items in the hands of the partnership.[5] This test is intended to limit the application of Section 751(b) to cases where there is a significant potential conversion of ordinary income to capital gain. Thus, in measuring appreciation, any inventory acquired for the principal purpose of avoiding the 120 percent test is excluded from consideration.[6]

Recall that the definition of inventory items includes Section 1221(1) "dealer" property as well as any property which, upon sale by the partnership or the distributee partner, would not be considered a capital asset or a Section 1231 asset.[7] As a result of the broad definition of "inventory," an asset may constitute both an unrealized receivable and an inventory item.[8] The inclusion of receivables in the inventory category is significant because they are then combined with other inventory items in determining whether those items are substantially appreciated.[9] If the aggregate inventory items are substantially appreciated, they are all treated as Section 751 assets. If an asset falls within both Section 751(b)(1)(A)(i) and (b)(1)(A)(ii), it will be taxed only once.[10] But if the inventory items, augmented by the receivables, are not substantially appreciated, then under Section 751(b)(1)(A) only the unrealized receivables (including those which also are inventory items) are treated as Section 751 assets.

The prospect of ordinary income treatment has motivated sophisticated taxpayers to devise strategies to avoid the taint caused by the presence of substantially appreciated inventory items on the partnership's balance sheet. Historically, one popular technique was to manipulate the partnership's inventory items so they would not be classified as substantially appreciated.[11] The strategy was derailed, however, by the enactment of an "anti-stuffing" rule under which any inventory acquired for "a principal purpose" of avoiding the 120 percent test is excluded in measuring appreciation.[12]

Operation of Section 751(b). The most productive way to master a Code section is first to understand its rationale, and that will be our approach to Section 751(b). Assume that the ABC partnership has three equal partners and the following balance sheet:

5. I.R.C. § 751(b)(3)(A). The test is applied to the partnership's basis and, in making the computation, special basis adjustments of any partner are disregarded. Reg. § 1.751–1(d)(1). Cf. I.R.C. §§ 732(d); 743(b).

6. I.R.C. § 751(b)(3)(B).

7. I.R.C. § 751(d).

8. Reg. § 1.751–1(d)(2)(ii).

9. I.R.C. § 751(b)(3).

10. If unrealized receivables fall within both Section 751(c) and (d), they are treated as Section 751(c) assets under other Code provisions. See I.R.C. §§ 735(a); 736.

11. See Problem 2(c), below, and McKee, Nelson & Whitmire, Federal Taxation of Partnership and Partners ¶ 21.01[4][b] (4th ed. 2007).

12. I.R.C. § 751(b)(3)(B).

Assets	A.B.	F.M.V.	Partners' Capital	A.B.	F.M.V.
Cash	$15,000	$15,000	A	$ 9,000	$15,000
Inventory	9,000	15,000	B	9,000	15,000
Capital Asset	3,000	15,000	C	9,000	15,000
	$27,000	$45,000		$27,000	$45,000

Assume further that the partnership has held the capital asset for several years and that A receives the inventory in liquidation of his interest in the partnership.[13]

Disregarding for the moment Section 751(b), consider the tax consequences to A, B and C under the general nonrecognition rules that we have previously studied. On the distribution, A receives the inventory[14] with a $9,000 basis[15] and a $15,000 value. In effect, B and C are left with the $15,000 cash and the appreciated capital asset with a $3,000 basis and a $15,000 value. When the smoke clears from this nonrecognition transaction, A, B and C each end up with $6,000 of potential gain (A's gain lurks in the inventory, and B and C would share the $12,000 gain inherent in the capital asset). So what's the problem? It is the characterization of these potential gains. If A immediately were to sell the inventory, he would recognize $6,000 of ordinary income,[16] but if the capital asset were sold, B and C each would have $6,000 of long-term capital gain.[17] The result is an assignment of the character of the income—the very evil that Section 751(b) was designed to curb.[18] Consequently, if a current or liquidating distribution to a partner has the effect of altering the interests of the partners in Section 751 property, Section 751(b) comes into play to make things right.[19]

The *why* of Section 751(b) is perhaps easier to understand than the *how*—the mechanics of its operation. But the how also must be understood, so . . . we return to the example above. Under an aggregate approach, before the distribution of inventory, A in essence held the following one-third interest in each of the partnership's assets.

13. Do not be concerned that this is a liquidating distribution. Section 751(b) and the other provisions discussed in this example apply with respect to both operating and liquidating distributions, and it is easier to illustrate the purpose and operation of Section 751(b) in this simplified liquidation setting.

14. The inventory is "substantially appreciated," as it must be for Section 751(b) to apply. I.R.C. § 751(b)(1)(A)(ii).

15. Under Section 732(b), which applies to liquidating distributions, the inventory receives the same substituted basis it would have under Section 732(a)(1) in the case of an operating distribution.

16. I.R.C. § 735(a)(2).

17. This is the result whether B and C sell their partnership interests, the partnership distributes the assets and B and C sell them individually (assuming they remain capital assets to B and C), or the partnership sells the assets, liquidates and distributes the proceeds.

18. As you will discover in Problem 4, below, Section 751(b) does not always achieve its apparent objective. It is not concerned with the *amount* of income within a class, merely assignments between classes.

19. Several exceptions to Section 751(b) are discussed below.

Assets	A.B.	F.M.V.
Cash	$5,000	$ 5,000
Inventory	3,000	5,000
Capital Asset	1,000	5,000
	$9,000	$15,000

By receiving all the substantially appreciated inventory, A in effect exchanged his interest in the Section 741 property—the cash and capital asset—for the remaining partners' interests in the inventory.[20] Section 751(b) requires the distributee partner to engage in this constructive exchange with the partnership, i.e., the other partners, for purposes of determining the tax consequences of the transaction to all the parties.[21]

In order for A to engage in an exchange with the partnership, A must receive property to transfer in the exchange. This is achieved under Section 751(b) by the mechanism of a phantom distribution to A of the class of property in which A was short changed on the actual distribution. Under the facts in our example, A received no Section 741 assets at a time when he had a $10,000 interest in those assets. At the same time, A received $15,000 worth of inventory when he had only a $5,000 pro rata interest prior to the distribution. He thus received too much Section 751 property to the extent of $10,000 and not enough Section 741 property to the same extent. To correct the imbalance, the partnership makes a phantom distribution to A of Section 741 property with a value of $10,000. The regulations permit the partners to specify property within the class of nondistributed assets (i.e., all cash or all capital asset in our example) but, in the absence of a specific agreement among the partners as to the properties deemed to be distributed, the phantom distribution is pro rata among the assets within the class.[22] Assuming no such agreement here, the phantom distribution to A consists of $5,000 cash and $5,000 of the capital asset.

The regular operating distribution rules of Sections 731, 732 and 733 are applied to determine the tax consequences of the phantom distribution. Recall that A receives $5,000 cash and $5,000 of the capital asset with a $1,000 basis. A recognizes no gain on the distribution[23] but reduces his outside basis by $6,000 (the amount of cash and the basis in the capital asset received).[24] The value of his interest in the partnership is reduced by the amount of the distribution ($10,000) from $15,000 to $5,000. After the phantom distribution, the ABC partnership balance sheet is as follows:

20. Keep in mind that Section 751(b) is only concerned with disproportionate distributions between Section 741 and 751 assets, not assets within a class. Thus, if in a subsequent liquidating distribution, B received all the cash and C received the capital asset, Section 751(b) would not apply. See Problem 4, below.

21. Although we say that A engages in the transaction with the partnership, the exchange is really with the other partners. This is so whether the distribution is an operating or a liquidating distribution. Reg. §§ 1.751–1(b)(2)(ii) & 1.751–1(b)(3)(ii).

22. Reg. § 1.751–1(g) Examples 3(c) & 4(c).

23. I.R.C. § 731.

24. I.R.C. § 733.

Assets	A.B.	F.M.V.	Partners' Capital	A.B.	F.M.V.
Cash	$10,000	$10,000	A	$ 3,000	$ 5,000
Inventory	9,000	15,000	B	9,000	15,000
Capital Asset	2,000	10,000	C	9,000	15,000
	$21,000	$35,000		$21,000	$35,000

The phantom distribution provides A with the property to transfer to the partnership in exchange for the excess Section 751 property that he received on the actual distribution. On this fictional exchange, A transfers the cash and capital asset, worth $10,000, back to the partnership, which in turn transfers inventory worth $10,000 to A. A has $4,000 of capital gain on the exchange, representing the difference between his $10,000 amount realized (the fair market value of the inventory) and his $6,000 aggregate adjusted basis in the capital asset and the cash. He takes a $10,000 cost basis in the inventory. The partnership passes through $4,000 of ordinary income to B and C on the taxable exchange of the inventory ($10,000 amount realized less a $6,000 basis), and it acquires $5,000 of cash and takes a $5,000 cost basis in the capital asset. B and C thus both recognize $2,000 of ordinary income,[25] and they each increase their respective outside bases by $2,000.[26] Even if this had been an operating rather than a liquidating distribution, the gain or loss recognized by the partnership on the fictional exchanges would be allocated only to partners other than the distributee partner.[27]

After the Section 751(b) transaction, the partnership balance sheet is as follows:

Assets	A.B.	F.M.V.	Partners' Capital	A.B.	F.M.V.
Cash	$15,000	$15,000	A	$ 3,000	$ 5,000
Inventory	3,000	5,000	B	11,000	15,000
Capital Asset	7,000	15,000	C	11,000	15,000
	$25,000	$35,000		$25,000	$35,000

As noted above, A has acquired $10,000 of inventory with a $10,000 cost basis.

The constructive transactions described above are only part of the picture. Section 751(b) overrides the normal distribution rules to the extent that the distribution is disproportionate. On completion of the Section 751(b) transaction, the remaining portion of A's distribution is taxed under the general rules of Sections 731, 732 and 733. A recognizes no gain on receipt of the remaining $5,000 of inventory and takes a $3,000 transferred

25. I.R.C. § 702(a)(8). Reg. §§ 1.751–1(b)(2)(ii) & 1.751–1(b)(3)(ii). These regulations require that this gain be allocated entirely to the nondistributee partners in accordance with their postdistribution interests in partnership profits and losses.

26. I.R.C. § 705(a)(1)(A).

27. Reg. §§ 1.751–1(b)(2)(ii) & 1.751–1(b)(3)(ii).

basis.[28] He thus emerges with total inventory with a value of $15,000 and an adjusted basis of $13,000 ($10,000 cost basis from the constructive exchange and $3,000 transferred basis on the normal distribution). This makes sense because A started with an outside basis of $9,000 in his $15,000 partnership interest, recognized $4,000 of gain on the fictional exchange and ended up with a total basis of $13,000. The partnership balance sheet after the distribution is as follows:

Assets	A.B.	F.M.V.	Partners' Capital	A.B.	F.M.V.
Cash	$15,000	$15,000	B	$11,000	$15,000
Capital Asset	7,000	15,000	C	11,000	15,000
	$22,000	$30,000		$22,000	$30,000

The Section 751(b) rules do not apply to distributions of property which the distributee partner previously contributed to the partnership, presumably on the theory that such a distribution merely restores the status quo.[29] They also do not apply to payments governed by Section 736(a)[30] (this exception will be explained in the next chapter),[31] draws or advances received by the partner against his distributive share[32] and distributions which are gifts, payments for services or for the use of capital.[33]

Having introduced a simple Section 751(b) transaction, it is time to turn to more complex issues. The problems below, involving as they do disproportionate distributions of both Section 751 and Section 741 property, present a greater challenge because it usually is more difficult to determine the extent to which a distribution is disproportionate if it is an operating rather than a liquidating distribution. The determination is made by comparing the distributee partner's interest in either the Section 741 or 751 assets both before and after the distribution. For example, assume that the equal ABC partnership has the following balance sheet:

Assets	A.B.	F.M.V.	Partners' Capital	A.B.	F.M.V.
Cash	$36,000	$ 36,000	A	$18,000	$ 36,000
Inventory	0	36,000	B	18,000	36,000
Capital Asset	18,000	36,000	C	18,000	36,000
	$54,000	$108,000		$54,000	$108,000

If A receives an operating distribution of $18,000 cash, he will emerge with a one-fifth interest in the partnership, and the disproportionate effect of the distribution can be measured in two different ways, either of which yields the same result. A can compare his interest in Section 751 assets

28. I.R.C. § 732(b), although under these facts this also would be A's Section 732(a)(1) carryover basis if this had been an operating distribution.

29. I.R.C. § 751(b)(2)(A). Cf. I.R.C. § 704(c).

30. I.R.C. § 751(b)(2)(B).

31. See Chapter 8B2, infra.

32. Reg. § 1.751–1(b)(1)(ii).

33. Id.

before and after the distribution or he can make a similar comparison of his interest in Section 741 assets. After the distribution, the balance sheet is as follows:

Assets	A.B.	F.M.V.	Partners' Capital	A.B.	F.M.V.
Cash	$18,000	$18,000	A	$ 0	$18,000
Inventory	0	36,000	B	18,000	36,000
Capital Asset	18,000	36,000	C	18,000	36,000
	$36,000	$90,000		$36,000	$90,000

A's comparative interest in Section 751 assets is as follows:

Before the distribution:	⅓ of $36,000 =	$12,000
After the distribution:	⅕ of $36,000 =	7,200
Disproportionate share:		($ 4,800)

A similar result occurs from the following comparison of A's interest in Section 741 assets:

Before the distribution:	⅓ of $72,000 =	$24,000
After the distribution:	⅕ of $54,000 =	($10,800)
	plus $18,000 =	28,800
Disproportionate share:		$ 4,800

These comparisons demonstrate that A ends up with $4,800 more than his share of Section 741 assets and $4,800 less than his share of Section 751 assets. Consequently, A must receive a phantom distribution of $4,800 of Section 751 assets. A then engages in a constructive exchange of the excess Section 751 property for an equal amount of Section 741 property. Finally, the normal distribution rules must be applied to the remainder of the distribution.

Policy Considerations. The purpose of Section 751(b) is to prevent shifting of the character of gain or loss among partners. To do so, it constructs hypothetical exchanges of capital and noncapital assets where no exchanges actually occurred. The complexity of Section 751(b) is so mind boggling that, even though it potentially affects many partnership distributions, it is widely believed that actual compliance is rare.

Over 50 years ago, an advisory group studying Subchapter K recommended repeal of Section 751(b), as did the American Law Institute in its 1984 partnership tax project.[1] The case for repeal is well articulated in the statement below made by a leading practitioner (and former law professor) at a 1986 House Ways and Means Committee hearing on issues relating to pass-through entities. The statement was made at a time when the distinction between capital gain and ordinary income had diminished considerably. In reading the excerpt, consider whether Mr. Rabinovitz's argument

1. See American Law Institute, Federal Income Tax Project—Subchapter K 47–55 (1984).

is still as compelling in light of the resurrection of a significant rate preference for long-term capital gains recognized by individuals.

Excerpt from Statement of Joel Rabinovitz, Esq., at Hearings Before the Subcommittee on Select Revenue Measures of the House Ways and Means Committee, Issues Relating to Pass-Through Entities

99th Cong., 2d Sess. 58–65 (1986).

Repeal of IRC 751(b)

Section 751(b) of the Internal Revenue Code should be repealed. It is not necessary to prevent one of the perceived abuses at which it is apparently aimed and ineffective to prevent the other. Moreover it is generally overlooked, frequently ignored by those aware of its application, and often applied incorrectly by those, including the Internal Revenue Service, perceptive and honest enough to make the attempt.

Apparently IRC 751(b) is intended to address two potential abuses—conversion of ordinary income to capital gain and shifting of income from high bracket to low bracket taxpayers. The first of these potential abuses, to the extent that it arises on the distribution of partnership assets to a partner, is adequately addressed by IRC 735, and to the extent that it arises on a redemption of all or part of a partner's interest for cash could be adequately dealt with by a relatively simple extension of IRC 751(a). Moreover, if the pending elimination of capital gains for individuals is enacted [as it was in the Tax Reform Act of 1986, but beginning in 1993 a significant capital gains preference began to reappear, Ed.] the abuse potential itself will largely disappear. With respect to the second perceived abuse, IRC 751(b) in its present form does nothing to prevent shifting income by distributing high basis ordinary income assets to some partners and low basis ordinary assets to others. There is no evidence, however, that this possibility is currently abused enough to justify the complexity necessary to fashion an adequate curb, and a general reduction in tax rates will reduce the likelihood of abuse still further.

In numerous situations to which IRC 751(b) applies its relevance goes unrecognized. It is likely that the vast majority of small businesses operating in partnership form are not even aware that IRC 751(b) is applicable to almost any non-pro rata distribution which they make. They are even less likely to recognize its application to the admission of a new partner to a cash method partnership. Furthermore, many large professional partnerships, aware of IRC 751(b)'s application in this situation, simply close their eyes to IRC 751(b) to avoid the disproportionate complexity and expense of having to make a large number of insignificant adjustments. And the Internal Revenue Service which, at least at the national office level, is aware of the application of IRC 751(b) to the admission of a new partner to a cash basis partnership, has applied it incorrectly in its most recent public effort to provide guidance to taxpayers. See Revenue Ruling 84–102, 84–2

Cum.Bul. 119. There is little to be said for a statutory provision which is frequently ignored, is incapable of being applied by either the people affected by it or those charged with administering it and which is, at the same time, unnecessary or ineffective to prevent the perceived abuses at which it is purportedly aimed.

PROBLEMS

1. The ABC equal partnership has the following balance sheet:

Assets	A.B.	F.M.V.	Partners' Capital	A.B.	F.M.V.
Cash	$6,000	$ 6,000	A	$3,000	$ 6,000
Accounts Receivable	0	3,000	B	3,000	6,000
Capital Asset	3,000	9,000	C	3,000	6,000
	$9,000	$18,000		$9,000	$18,000

The partnership distributes the accounts receivable to A in an operating distribution. After the distribution, A has a one-fifth interest worth $3,000 in the remaining partnership assets.

(a) What results to A, B, C and the partnership as a result of the distribution? Reconstruct the partnership balance sheet at the end of the transaction.

(b) If the distribution results in an increase to the partnership's inside basis, how should that increase be allocated?

2. A, B and C are equal partners in the ABC partnership which has the following balance sheet:

Assets	A.B.	F.M.V.	Partners' Capital	A.B.	F.M.V.
Cash	$ 6,000	$ 6,000	A	$12,000	$18,000
Accounts Receivable	0	9,000	B	12,000	18,000
Inventory	18,000	18,000	C	12,000	18,000
Land & Building	6,000	12,000			
Equipment	6,000	9,000			
	$36,000	$54,000		$36,000	$54,000

The partnership distributes the $9,000 worth of accounts receivable to A and $18,000 worth of inventory equally ($9,000 each) to B and C.

(a) Is § 751(b) applicable to this operating distribution?

(b) What does this tell you about § 751(b)?

3. Should § 751(b) be repealed?

CHAPTER 8

Liquidating Distributions and Terminations

A. Introduction

Code: §§ 736; 761(d). Skim §§ 706(c)(1) & (2)(A); 731; 732(b), (c), (d) & (e).

Our study of Subchapter K parallels the life cycle of a partner's interest in a partnership, moving from cradle to grave. Having mastered the rigors of operating distributions, we have survived the inevitable mid-life crisis and may now proceed to the closing ceremonies. The end begins with a study of liquidating distributions to a "retiring partner." For this purpose, liquidation of a partner's interest means "the termination of a partner's entire interest in a partnership by means of a distribution, or a series of distributions, to the partner by the partnership,"[1] and a "retiring partner" is one who "ceases to be a partner under local law."[2] This chapter also considers the tax consequences of partnership terminations, including complete liquidations and other events that cause a partnership to terminate for tax purposes. The special problems raised by the liquidation of a deceased partner's interest are deferred until Chapter 9.

To introduce the tax treatment of liquidating distributions, consider the choices faced by Retiring Partner ("RP"), who desires to terminate her interest in a partnership that will continue to operate after RP's withdrawal. One option would be for RP to sell her interest to the remaining partners or to a third party. As we have seen,[3] the tax consequences of the sale of a partnership interest are governed by Sections 741 and 751, and RP generally will recognize capital gain or loss except to the extent of her share of Section 751 assets. Alternatively, RP could liquidate her interest in the partnership, a transaction resembling a corporation's redemption of a shareholder's stock. In exchange, RP might receive payments for a variety of items, including her pro rata share of unrealized receivables, partnership goodwill and other assets of the partnership and perhaps an additional premium in the nature of "mutual insurance" provided by the partnership

1. I.R.C. § 761(d); Reg. § 1.761–1(d).

2. Reg. § 1.736–1(a)(1)(ii). The liquidation of a partner's interest in a continuing partnership does not close the partnership's taxable year where there is not a complete liquidation of the partnership (I.R.C. § 706(c)(2), see I.R.C. § 708(b)(1) and Section C of this chapter, infra), but completion of the liquidation will result in the closing of the partnership year as to the liquidated partner (I.R.C. § 706(c)(2)(A)). These results are similar to the rules applicable to a partner who sells his partnership interest. Reg. § 1.706–1(c)(2).

3. See Chapter 6A, supra.

agreement. The tax consequences to RP and the remaining partners may differ depending on the manner in which RP structures her withdrawal from the partnership. A major goal of this chapter is to convey an understanding of the tax consequences involved in classifying and timing liquidating distributions and in distinguishing sales from liquidations.

Prior to the 1954 Code, the tax treatment of liquidating distributions was unsettled.[4] Congress ended much of the confusion by enacting Section 736, which in general classifies payments in liquidation of a retiring partner's interest in a continuing partnership by dividing them into two broad categories: (1) payments for the partner's interest in partnership property[5] and (2) all other payments.[6] Payments in the first category are treated by Section 736(b) as distributions in liquidation of the retiring partner's interest and thus are governed by the distribution provisions,[7] including the overriding disproportionate distribution rules in Section 751(b). Payments in the second category are characterized by Section 736(a) as either a distributive share of partnership income, if based on profits of the firm,[8] or as guaranteed payments under Section 707(c), if determined without reference to partnership income.[9]

In proceeding through this chapter, keep the function of Section 736 clearly in focus. It merely classifies payments, leaving the determination of the specific tax consequences to other provisions that you have previously encountered. Also note that the parties may have some flexibility to shape the tax consequences of a partner's withdrawal from a partnership by selecting the form of the transaction and classifying the payments in an arm's length agreement. For example, there may be significant differences in tax treatment with respect to "premium payments" (i.e., payments that exceed the value of the retiring partner's share of partnership property) if the transaction is structured as a liquidation rather than a sale, or if the payments in either type of transaction are made in installments.

Apart from tax consequences, also keep in mind that liquidations are inextricably linked to the capital account concept that pervades the partnership allocation regulations.[10] Capital accounts determine the amounts partners are entitled to receive on a liquidation of their interests in the partnership.[11] To properly carry out this function, they must be adjusted to reflect the book gain or loss inherent in any property distributed in liquidation of a partner's interest in a manner similar to that used in the case of operating distributions.[12]

4. See Jackson, Johnson, Surrey, Tenen & Warren, "The Internal Revenue Code of 1954: Partnerships," 54 Colum.L.Rev. 1183, 1223–1224 (1954).

5. I.R.C. § 736(b).

6. I.R.C. § 736(a).

7. See I.R.C. §§ 731; 732; 734; 735; and Chapter 7B, 7C & 7E, supra.

8. I.R.C. § 736(a)(1).

9. I.R.C. § 736(a)(2).

10. See Chapter 3B1, supra.

11. Cf. Reg. § 1.704–1(b)(2)(ii)(*b*)(*2*).

12. See Reg. § 1.704–1(b)(2)(iv)(*e*)(*1*) and Chapter 7C, supra. The liquidation of a partner's interest also is an appropriate occasion for a partnership to restate the book values of all of its remaining property and to make corresponding adjustments to the capital accounts of the continuing partners. See Reg. § 1.704–1(b)(2)(iv)(*f*).

B. LIQUIDATION OF A PARTNER'S INTEREST

1. SECTION 736(b) PAYMENTS

Code: §§ 731; 732(b), (c), (d) & (e); 736(b). Skim §§ 734; 735; 736(a); 751(b); 754; 755.

Regulations: §§ 1.731–1(a)(2); 1.732–2(b) & (c); 1.736–1(b)(4).

The Scope of Section 736(b). Section 736(b) payments are liquidating distributions that are attributable to the retiring partner's interest in most types of partnership property. Two categories of property are specifically excluded from Section 736(b) and thus are taxed under Section 736(a). In the case of a retiring general partner in a partnership where capital is not a material income producing factor (e.g., a services partnership), Section 736(b) does not apply to payments for (1) the partner's share of unrealized receivables, and (2) partnership goodwill if the partnership agreement does not expressly provide for such payments.[1] For purposes of Section 736(b), recapture gain is excluded from the definition of unrealized receivables.[2] Thus, amounts paid to a retiring partner for the recapture potential in partnership property are Section 736(b) payments. The tax consequences of Section 736(b) payments are determined, with a few limited exceptions, by the same statutory scheme applicable to operating distributions. This section thus provides an opportunity to review much of the material covered in the preceding chapter.

Tax Consequences to the Retiring Partner. As with operating distributions, a retiring partner recognizes gain on a liquidating distribution only to the extent that the cash received exceeds the partner's outside basis.[3] If both cash and other property are distributed, Sections 731 and 732 work in tandem to treat the distribution as a nonrecognition transaction. First, the partner reduces his outside basis by the cash received[4] and then, in effect, he exchanges his remaining partnership interest for the other assets received in the distribution. Section 731 provides nonrecognition treatment to the partner and the partnership on the distribution, and Section 732(b) provides the partner with an aggregate basis in the distributed property equal to his predistribution outside basis less any cash received in the liquidation. This exchanged basis mechanism preserves any gain or loss inherent in the partner's interest for recognition when the partner disposes of the distributed assets.

If more than one asset is distributed, Section 732(c) once again prescribes the method for allocating the aggregate exchanged basis to the distributee partner.[5] If inventory items or unrealized receivables have been

1. I.R.C. § 736(b)(2) & (3).
2. I.R.C. § 751(c), flush language.
3. I.R.C. § 731(a)(1).
4. I.R.C. § 733.
5. If the retiring partner received cash in excess of his outside basis, he would recognize capital gain to the extent of the excess,

distributed, those properties are first tentatively assigned a basis equal to the basis of each such property to the partnership.[6] If the sum of the partnership's bases in the distributed unrealized receivables and inventory items exceeds the basis to be allocated (the partner's outside basis less cash received in the transaction), then the partnership's bases in those properties must be reduced by the amount of the excess.[7] The reduction is achieved by first allocating basis decreases among the properties with unrealized built-in loss (i.e., properties with an assigned basis greater than their value) in proportion to the amounts of such loss and only to the extent of the built-in loss of each property.[8] If needed, additional decreases are allocated in proportion to the remaining adjusted bases of the unrealized receivables and inventory items.[9] If the basis to be allocated exceeds the partnership's basis in the distributed unrealized receivables and inventory items, then each other distributed property is next assigned a basis equal to the partnership's basis in that property.[10] Basis increases or decreases then must be allocated to the other distributed properties if the partner's remaining basis (i.e., the basis remaining after any unrealized receivables or inventory items are assigned basis equal to their bases in the hands of the partnership) is greater or less than the sum of the partnership's bases in those properties.[11] If an overall increase is required, the increase is accomplished by first allocating basis increases among the properties with unrealized appreciation in proportion to such appreciation and only to the extent of each property's unrealized appreciation.[12] Any additional increases are allocated in proportion to the respective fair market values of the properties.[13] If an overall decrease is required, the decrease is accomplished by first allocating basis decreases in proportion to the unrealized built-in loss in the properties (again, only to the extent of such loss) and then in proportion to the remaining adjusted bases of the properties.[14] In keeping with the treatment of operating distributions, the distributee partner may tack the partnership's holding period under Section 735(b), and Section 735(a) preserves the ordinary income character in the hands of the partner indefinitely for any unrealized receivables and five years for inventory items.

and any distributed assets would take a zero basis in the partner's hands.

6. I.R.C. § 732(c)(1)(A)(i).

7. I.R.C. § 732(c)(1)(A)(ii).

8. I.R.C. § 732(c)(3)(A). These allocation rules apply to distributions after August 5, 1997. For prior distributions, basis was first allocated to any unrealized receivables and inventory items in an amount equal to the partnership's basis in those assets (or, if the basis to be allocated was less than the sum of the bases of such properties, in proportion to such bases), and to the extent of any remaining basis, to any other distributed properties in proportion to their adjusted bases to the partnership. The prior rules, by failing to take account of the fair market value of distributed property, could lead to anomalous results and put a high premium on strategic tax planning. See McKee, Nelson & Whitmire, Federal Taxation of Partnerships and Partners ¶ 19.06 (3d ed. 1996).

9. I.R.C. § 732(c)(3)(B).

10. I.R.C. § 732(c)(1)(B)(i).

11. I.R.C. § 732(c)(1)(B)(ii).

12. I.R.C. § 732(c)(2)(A).

13. I.R.C. § 732(c)(2)(B).

14. I.R.C. § 732(c)(3).

But consider the partner who receives solely cash, unrealized receivables and inventory items in a liquidating distribution.[15] In that event, unlike the case with operating distributions, Section 731(a)(2) provides that the partner recognizes a loss to the extent that his outside basis exceeds the sum of the cash distributed plus the partner's Section 732 transferred basis in the receivables and inventory items. The loss is considered as incurred on the sale or exchange of a partnership interest and thus is a capital loss under Section 741. Where a partner receives only cash, any realized gain or loss must be recognized because the partner may not defer recognition by way of an exchanged basis. If the partner also receives ordinary income assets, immediate recognition of loss is required to prevent the partner from converting a capital loss into an ordinary loss on the sale of the distributed assets.

To illustrate, assume that a retiring partner with an outside basis of $60 receives $20 cash and ordinary income assets with an inside basis of $25 in a liquidating distribution to which Sections 736(a) and 751(b) do not apply.[16] The partner first reduces his outside basis by the $20 cash received and, without more, he would be left with a $40 exchanged basis to spread among the ordinary income assets, which would result in less ordinary income or more ordinary loss when the partner sells those assets. But recall that Section 732(c)(1)(A) limits the partner's basis in ordinary income assets to the partnership's predistribution inside basis—$25 in this example. As a corollary to this rule, Section 731(a)(2) provides that the partner recognizes a $15 capital loss—the excess of his $60 outside basis over the sum of the $20 cash received and the $25 transferred basis in the ordinary income assets.

Tax Consequences to the Partnership. Disregarding for the moment the impact of Sections 736(a) and 751(b), a partnership generally recognizes neither gain nor loss on a liquidating distribution of property,[17] and under Section 734(a) the basis of partnership property generally is not adjusted as a result of the distribution. But as with operating distributions, a partnership with a Section 754 election in effect may adjust the basis of its assets to prevent the distortions that result from a liquidating distribution. We have seen that on certain liquidating distributions, a partner may recognize gain or loss. If gain is recognized, the partnership may increase the basis of capital assets or Section 1231 property it retains by the amount of the gain.[18] If the retiring partner recognizes a loss while a Section 754 election is in effect, Section 734(b) conversely requires the partnership to decrease the inside basis of its retained capital assets and Section 1231 property by the amount of the loss.[19] In addition, if the liquidating partner's exchanged basis in distributed capital assets or Section 1231 property exceeds the

15. This assumes no application of Sections 736(a) or 751(b).

16. Sections 736(a) and 751(b) are both inapplicable if the retiring partner receives a pro rata distribution of partnership properties.

17. I.R.C. § 731(b).

18. I.R.C. § 734(b)(1)(A). See Chapter 7C, supra.

19. I.R.C. § 734(b)(2)(A).

partnership's inside basis in those assets and a Section 754 election is in effect, the partnership must decrease its basis in retained assets of a similar class in an amount equal to the increase in the basis of the distributed assets in the hands of the retiring partner.[20]

A partnership also must decrease its basis in retained assets even if a Section 754 election has not been made whenever a liquidating distribution results in a "substantial basis reduction."[21] A substantial basis reduction occurs if the downward basis adjustment that would have been made to the partnership's assets if a Section 754 election had been made exceeds $250,000.[22] For example, if a liquidated partner recognizes a loss on the distribution that is greater than $250,000, the partnership is required to decrease the basis in its retained assets even if it has never made a Section 754 election. Similarly, a basis reduction in a partnership's retained assets is required if the basis of capital assets or Section 1231 assets that are distributed in a liquidating distribution is increased by more than $250,000 above the partnership's basis in those assets.[23] The rules for allocation of Section 734(b) basis adjustments were discussed in Chapter 7, supra.[24]

Section 751(b). We have seen that the disproportionate distribution rules in Section 751(b) override the general rules of Sections 731 and 732 on a partnership's operating distributions.[25] In general, Section 751(b) plays an identical role with respect to liquidating distributions. But recall that payments received by a retiring general partner for her interest in unrealized receivables or unstated goodwill of a services partnership are governed by Section 736(a). In that situation, the partner's share of unrealized receivables is disregarded in determining the partner's predistribution share of Section 751 assets,[26] and the partner's predistribution share of unstated goodwill is disregarded in determining her share of Section 741 assets.[27] As a corollary to these rules, any payments received by the partner in exchange for her share of partnership unrealized receivables or unstated goodwill or any "premium" payments received (i.e., amounts paid in excess of the fair market value of the partner's share of partnership property) are governed by Section 736(a) and thus are similarly disregarded in determining the partner's postdistribution share of Section 751 or 741 assets. Section 751(b) still applies, however, with respect to disproportionate

20. I.R.C. § 734(b)(2)(B).

21. I.R.C. § 734(a).

22. I.R.C. § 734(b)(2), (d).

23. The IRS is authorized to issue regulations to carry out these provisions, including regulations aggregating related partnerships and disregarding property acquired to avoid the rules. I.R.C. § 734(d)(2), 743(d)(2). A special rule exempts securitization partnerships from required downward inside basis adjustments under Section 734(a). I.R.C. § 734(e).

24. See I.R.C. § 755; Reg. § 1.755–1(c); Chapter 7C, supra. See also Reg. § 1.755–1(c)(2)(ii), relating to adjustments for decreases in basis.

25. See Chapter 7E, supra.

26. Remember, however, that unrealized receivables are treated as inventory items under Section 751(d) but solely for the purpose of determining whether the inventory is substantially appreciated in value.

27. I.R.C. § 751(b)(2)(B); Reg. § 1.751–1(b)(4)(ii). See the discussion of the scope of Section 736(a) in Section B2 of this chapter, infra.

distributions between the remaining Section 751 assets (i.e., recapture gain and substantially appreciated inventory) and Section 741 assets.

To illustrate the operation of Section 751(b) in this context, assume the ABC services partnership has three equal general partners and the following balance sheet:[28]

Assets	A.B.	F.M.V.	Partners' Capital	A.B.	F.M.V.
Cash	$45,000	$45,000	A	$15,000	$30,000
Accounts Receivable	0	15,000	B	15,000	30,000
Inventory	0	15,000	C	15,000	30,000
Goodwill	0	15,000			
	$45,000	$90,000		$45,000	$90,000

Assume partner A's interest is liquidated and he receives a $30,000 cash payment from the partnership with no designation that $5,000 is paid for goodwill. A would be taxed on $10,000 (the payment for A's share of the receivables and unstated goodwill) as ordinary income characterized under Section 736(a). A's share of Section 736(b) assets prior to the distribution is $15,000 of cash and $5,000 of inventory. After the distribution, A has $20,000 of cash (disregarding the $10,000 payment governed by Section 736(a)) and no further interest in the partnership inventory.[29] Under Section 751(b), A is deemed to have received a phantom distribution of $5,000 of inventory with a transferred basis of zero and to have sold the inventory to the partnership for $5,000 cash, realizing $5,000 of ordinary income on the constructive sale. The final step is to determine the tax consequences of the remaining actual distribution of $15,000 cash.[30] Since A's outside basis is $15,000, the cash distribution merely reduces his basis to zero and no gain or loss is recognized under Section 731.

If the partnership were not a services partnership or A were not a general partner, Section 736(a) would not apply and A's interest in the Section 751 assets would have been $10,000 prior to the distribution and

28. The authors know that inventory should not have a zero basis. But a zero basis for noncash assets simplifies the example and, hopefully, aids comprehension of the concepts that are being illustrated.

29. Using the formula above, in determining the extent of the application of § 751(b) we disregard the $10,000 of § 736(a) payments as well as the § 736(a) property being compensated—the receivables and goodwill. A's interest in the § 751 assets (other than those under § 736(a)) prior to the transaction is $5,000 and afterwards it is zero, while his interest in the § 741 assets (other than those under § 736(a)) prior to the transaction is $15,000 (one-third of the $45,000 cash) and afterwards it is $20,000. Thus, A receives $5,000 too few § 751 assets and $5,000 too many § 741 assets.

30. If A had received $35,000 for his interest (the same as above except with a $5,000 premium), we would reduce the § 741 amount actually received by the $15,000 of § 736(a) payment, and we would disregard the $5,000 accounts receivable, the $5,000 for unstated goodwill and the $5,000 premium. Once again, A's interest in the cash is $15,000, and he actually receives $20,000, and his interest in the inventory is $5,000, but he actually receives no inventory. As before, § 751(b) results in a phantom distribution of $5,000 of inventory with a zero basis to A, who realizes $5,000 of ordinary income on the constructive exchange.

zero afterwards, while his interest in the Section 741 assets would have been $20,000 before and $30,000 after the distribution. Thus, A would have a $10,000 phantom distribution of Section 751 property with a zero basis, and A would realize $10,000 of ordinary income on the constructive sale and $5,000 of long-term capital gain under Section 731(a)(1).

This concludes the interlude of reminiscences. Test your understanding of these principles, with some new liquidation twists, by solving the following problems.

PROBLEMS

1. The ABC partnership, which has not made a § 754 election, has the following balance sheet:

Assets	A.B.	F.M.V.	Partners' Capital	A.B.	F.M.V.
Cash	$ 90,000	$ 90,000	A	$ 85,000	$ 70,000
Inventory	15,000	30,000	B	85,000	70,000
Land (Parcel #1)	100,000	60,000	C	85,000	70,000
Land (Parcel #2)	50,000	30,000			
	$255,000	$210,000		$255,000	$210,000

(a) In liquidation of his interest, A receives one-third of the inventory and Parcel #1. What are the tax consequences of this distribution to A and the partnership?

(b) In liquidation of his interest, A again receives one-third of the inventory and also receives $60,000 cash. What are the tax consequences of this distribution to A and the partnership?

(c) Why is recognized loss under § 731(a)(2) limited to liquidating distributions and further restricted with regard to the nature of the distribution?

(d) What result to A in (b), above, if the inventory were worth $120,000 rather than $30,000, A's interest were worth $100,000 and A received $60,000 of cash and his one-third of the inventory?

2. The regulations (Reg. § 1.734–1(b)(2)) intimate that a § 734(b)(2) downward adjustment applies only to distributions in complete liquidation of a partner's interest, whereas a § 734(b)(1) upward adjustment may be applicable to both operating and liquidating distributions. Is this so? Why or why not?

2. SECTION 736(a) PAYMENTS

Code: § 736. Skim § 707(c).

Regulations: § 1.736–1(a), (b)(1)–(4).

Background. We have just seen that Section 736(b) embraces payments for a retiring partner's interest in partnership assets with some limited exceptions. To the extent that Section 736(b) is inapplicable, Section 736(a) applies. In that event, amounts received by the retiring partner are treated as Section 707(c) guaranteed payments or distributive shares of partnership income, generally resulting in ordinary income to the retiring partner and a current partnership deduction (or the equivalent) that benefits the remaining partners.

The Scope of Section 736(a). Section 736(a) payments are defined as all payments not falling within Section 736(b). As a practical matter, however, most payments made in liquidation of a partner's interest fall within Section 736(b), and thus the scope of Section 736(a) is very limited. Because of the exclusions in Section 736(b), Section 736(a) applies to payments received by a general partner in a partnership in which capital is not a material income-producing factor,[1] for: (1) the partner's share of unrealized receivables (not including recapture or similar gain,)[2] and (2) partnership goodwill if the partnership agreement does not expressly provide for such payments.[3] Capital is not a material income-producing factor where substantially all of the gross income of the business consists of fees, commissions, or other compensation for personal services.[4] Thus a legal, medical, dentistry, accounting, architectural or other service partnership falls within this classification even though there is a substantial investment in office plant or equipment, if that investment is merely incidental to the rendering of services.[5] Section 736(a) also applies to a third type of payment. Any premium payment in excess of payments for a partner's interest in partnership property is a Section 736(a) payment regardless of the type of partnership.[6]

Payments for Unrealized Receivables. Section 736(b) applies to most payments for unrealized receivables. Section 736(a), however, embraces payments to compensate a liquidated general partner in a services partnership for his interest in the partnership's receivables that have not been included in income.[7] Although one would never know it from reading the statute, the regulations make it clear that only payments in excess of the partner's basis (including any special personal inside basis) in the unrealized receivables are encompassed by Section 736(a).[8] To the extent of the partner's share of the inside basis, receivables are considered as already realized and thus covered by Section 736(b).[9] Moreover, Section 736(a) only applies to *payments* for unrealized receivables. To the extent that the receivables are distributed in kind, there is no "payment," and the partner's receipt of the receivables is taxed under the Section 736(b) regime. The term "payment" does not require a cash transfer, and thus a distribution of other assets, such as land or stock, in exchange for a general

1. I.R.C. § 736(b)(3).

2. I.R.C. § 751(c) flush language.

3. I.R.C. § 736(b)(2).

4. See I.R.C. §§ 401(c)(2); 911(d).

5. WMCP Prt. No. 103–11, 103d Cong., 1st Sess. 345 (1993).

6. Reg. § 1.736–1(a)(3).

7. I.R.C. § 736(b)(2)(A) & (3).

8. Reg. § 1.736–1(b)(2). Cf. §§ 736(d); 743(b).

9. Reg. § 1.736–1(b)(1) and (2).

partner's interest in unrealized receivables in a services partnership also is governed by Section 736(a).[10]

The scope of unrealized receivables qualifying for Section 736(a) treatment is further limited by the provision in Section 751(c) that eliminates recapture gain and other similar property held by any services or capital partnership from the definition of an unrealized receivable for purposes of Section 736.[11] Thus, payments for recapture gain automatically fall within Section 736(b).[12]

Payments for Goodwill. Similar to the treatment of unrealized receivables, Section 736(b) generally applies to payments for goodwill. But Section 736(a) still applies to payments to a retiring general partner for her share of goodwill in a services partnership to the extent that the payments exceed the partner's inside basis, if any, in the goodwill,[13] and the liquidation agreement does not specifically state that the payment is for goodwill.[14] Thus, the parties in this situation may remove goodwill from Section 736(a) and include it in Section 736(b) by including a specific provision in the agreement governing the liquidation.[15] The "agreement," for this purpose, includes any written and oral modifications to the original partnership agreement made in any year prior to the date of filing an income tax return for the year of the liquidation.[16] To fall within Section 736(b), payments allocated to goodwill must be "reasonable," but a valuation normally will be accepted by the Service if it is the product of an arm's length agreement between the parties.[17] It should now be apparent that the flexibility in classifying payments for goodwill places a premium on careful drafting. The *Smith* and *Jackson Investment* cases, which follow in the text, consider the issue of whether a partnership agreement sufficiently "provides for" a payment for goodwill.

10. See Willis, Pennell & Postlewaite, Partnership Taxation ¶ 15.06 (6th ed. 1997). When Section 736(a) liquidating "payments" are made with property other than cash, the usual Subchapter K distribution rules do not apply and thus the partnership is required to recognize gain or loss if the property is appreciated or has declined in value.

11. I.R.C. § 751(c) flush language.

12. Recapture gain continues to be an unrealized receivable for purposes of the distribution rules in Section 731, and the partnership sale provisions of Sections 741 and 751, including the infamous Section 751(b) regime. See I.R.C. § 751(c) flush language.

13. Reg. § 1.736–1(b)(3). Again, any special basis adjustment of the retiring partner is used to determine his share of appreciation. Cf. I.R.C. §§ 732(d), 743(b). Goodwill normally would have a zero basis unless the partnership previously acquired a business and allocated a portion of the purchase price to goodwill or unless the basis of goodwill was increased under Sections 743(b) or 734(b).

14. I.R.C. §§ 736(b)(2)(B) & (3).

15. I.R.C. § 736(b)(2)(B); Reg. § 1.736–1(b)(3). Cf. I.R.C. § 197.

16. I.R.C. § 761(c); Reg. § 1.761–1(c); Commissioner v. Jackson Investment Co., 346 F.2d 187 (9th Cir.1965).

17. Reg. § 1.736–1(b)(1) & (3). If the agreed allocation reflects only the partner's net interest in the Section 736(b) property (i.e., total assets less liabilities), it must be adjusted so that both the value of the partner's interest in the property and the basis for his interest take into account the partner's share of partnership liabilities. Reg. § 1.736–1(b)(1).

Premium Payments. In addition, because Section 736(b) applies only to payments for a retiring partner's interest in partnership *assets* (other than payment for unrealized receivables and unstated goodwill made to a general partner of a services partnership), any premium payments to a liquidated partner (in either a services or capital partnership) also are taxed under Section 736(a).[18] To determine whether there is a premium, one must first determine the amount of the partner's share of the partnership's property. Any payments in excess of that amount in the form of cash or other property are governed by Section 736(a), regardless of the nature of the partnership. These payments often are in the nature of mutual insurance provided by a separate buy-sell agreement or in the partnership agreement itself.

The Method of Taxing Section 736(a) Payments. Section 736(a) payments are taxed either as a distributive share of partnership income or as a guaranteed payment, depending upon whether they are determined with or without regard to the income of the partnership.[19] To the extent that the payments are based on income of the firm, they are treated as a distributive share of partnership income to the recipient and correspondingly reduce the distributive shares of partnership income allocable to the remaining partners.[20] To the extent that Section 736(a) payments are determined without regard to partnership income, they are considered to be guaranteed payments under Section 707(c) and are taxed as ordinary income to the retiring partner and are deductible in computing the partnership's taxable income.[21] Whether or not the payments are made with regard to partnership income is determined in the same manner used to resolve this issue for purposes of Section 707(c).[22]

Smith v. Commissioner

United States Court of Appeals, Tenth Circuit, 1962.
313 F.2d 16.

■ HILL, CIRCUIT JUDGE.

This case is here on the Smiths' Petition To Review a decision of the Tax Court of the United States which was adverse to them.

18. Reg. § 1.736–1(a)(3).

19. I.R.C. § 736(a)(1) & (2).

20. Reg. § 1.736–1(a)(3)(i) & (a)(4). The retiring partner must include a Section 736(a)(1) distributive share in his taxable year with or within which ends the partnership taxable year for which the payment is a distributive share irrespective of when actual distributions are made. Reg. § 1.736–1(a)(5). If the payment is made by a distribution in kind, the partnership will recognize gain or loss.

21. Reg. § 1.736–1(a)(3)(ii), (4) & (5). Guaranteed payments are taxable to the distributee for his taxable year with or within which the partnership is entitled to deduct the payment. Reg. § 1.736–1(a)(5). The partnership always may deduct Section 736(a)(2) payments; they never are treated as capital expenditures. The partnership will recognize gain or loss if it uses appreciated or depreciated property to make a guaranteed payment.

22. See Chapter 5A4, supra.

The facts necessary for our disposition of the case are not in dispute. In January, 1947, V. Zay Smith (petitioner) and three other individuals formed a partnership known as Geophoto Services (Geophoto) for the purpose of engaging in the business of evaluating geological structures based upon aerial photography, which was to be used in the search for petroleum and petroleum reserves. Petitioner, at the time of World War II, was a geologist and, from his experience as a photo intelligence officer in the Navy, conceived the idea of using aerial photography for evaluating geological structures in the search for oil and petroleum.

The original partnership agreement was for a period of five years. Immediately prior to its expiration and on December 31, 1952, the articles of partnership were revised to provide a means of expelling one of the partners.

The partnership prospered during the next four years of the 5 year period of the partnership agreement, with petitioner receiving substantial net income for his share. In January, 1957, the other three partners voted to expel petitioner as a partner in Geophoto. In accordance with paragraph 25 of the revised articles, petitioner received the consideration agreed upon therein. The total amount of $77,000.00 was paid to petitioner in the form of a check for $72,740.71 and an automobile of an agreed upon value of $4,259.29. It was stipulated, however, that the book value of petitioner's interest in the partnership on the date in question was $53,264.61, thereby leaving a payment to him of $2,045.45 as salary and a payment of $21,689.94 as a "premium", for a total payment over and above his partnership interest of $23,735.39.

In their income tax return for the year 1957, petitioners reported the excess over and above his partnership interest in the amount of $23,735.39 as a capital gain—this figure includes the salary payment of $2,045.45. The Commissioner of Internal Revenue determined that the entire excess of $23,735.39 was ordinary income and, accordingly, made a deficiency assessment of $6,992.20 in their income tax for 1957.

Petitioners thereafter filed a petition with the Tax Court alleging that the Commissioner, in determining taxable income for the year 1957, erroneously included the $23,735.39 payment as ordinary income and requested the Tax Court to determine that there was no deficiency due on the 1957 income tax. The Commissioner's position before the Tax Court was that the $23,735.39 payment to petitioner was in liquidation of his interest in the partnership and, accordingly, it was taxable as ordinary income under Section 736(a) of the Internal Revenue Code of 1954, 26 U.S.C. § 736(a). Specifically, the Commissioner contended that the $2,045.45 salary payment should be taxed as a guaranteed payment under paragraph (2) of subsection (a) and the remainder as a distributive share of partnership income under paragraph (1) thereof.

Petitioners argued that the questioned amount was a payment for "good will" and should be treated as a capital gain under Section 736(b) of the Act, 26 U.S.C. § 736(b). Specifically, they urged that paragraph (2)(B) of subsection (b) applied. Beyond any question, the $2,045.45 was ordinary income and no further discussion of that item is necessary.

The Tax Court rejected petitioners' contention and, in holding that the questioned amount should be treated as ordinary income, acknowledged this was a case of first impression. The provisions of Section 736 first became embodied in the tax law by the enactment of the 1954 Internal Revenue Code. This was the first time the Congress attempted to specifically cover by statute the tax situation arising when a partnership interest is in fact liquidated by payments from the partnership to the retiring or withdrawing partner. The situation here is not that of a partner selling his interest to another partner or a third party. If that was the situation, the government concedes, and we agree, that Section 741 of the Internal Revenue Code of 1954, 26 U.S.C. § 741, would be applicable, as contended by the taxpayer. We agree with the Tax Court that under the facts Section 736 provides the proper tax treatment.

From a careful reading of Section 736 and consideration of the Senate Finance Report[7] made at the time the new legislation was before the Congress, the intended scope of such Section appears clear. Paragraph (2)(B) of subsection (b) exempts from ordinary income treatment payments made for good will only when the partnership agreement so provides specifically and does not permit an intent to compensate for good will to be drawn from the surrounding circumstances as the taxpayer here urges us to do. In fact, the partnership agreement here specifically states "* * * In determining the value or the book value of a deceased or retiring partner's interest, no value shall be assigned to good will, * * *."

The discussion in 6 Mertens, Law of Federal Income Taxation, § 35.81, pp. 232–233, of the questioned statute supports the position of the government:

> "Partnership good will has an ambivalent character under Section 736 of the 1954 Code. Because of the difficulties on the one hand of valuing good will and on the other hand the inequities which might result if good will were required to be disregarded in every case, Section 736(b)(2), in effect, permits an election as to the treatment of partnership good will.
>
> "If the partnership agreement provides for a specific payment as to good will and such amount is not in excess of the reasonable value of the partner's share of good will, good will is considered a partnership asset and payments with respect thereto are treated as

7. 3 U.S.Cong. & Adm.News (1954) p. 5037 states:

"Special rules are provided in subsection (b)(2) so as to exclude certain items from the application of subsection (b). Thus, payments for an interest in partnership property under subsection (b) do not include amounts paid for unrealized receivables of the partnership. Also excluded from subsection (b) are payments for an interest in partnership goodwill, except to the extent that the partnership agreement provides for payments with respect to goodwill. Where the partnership agreement provides for payments with respect to goodwill, such payments may not exceed the reasonable value of the partner's share of partnership goodwill."

'Section 736(b) Payments.' The capitalizing of good will may be desirable from the point of view of the retiring partner or deceased partner's successor. The retiring partner is entitled to capital gain treatment on the amount of the payments allocable to good will. The deceased partner's successor will have a basis equal to the date of death valuation for payments allocable to good will. While this treatment is beneficial to the retiring partner or deceased partner's successor, the continuing partners will not be allowed a deduction or exclusion for such payments.

"On the other hand, if the partnership agreement does not treat good will as partnership property under Section 736(b), the payments relating thereto fall under Section 736(a). Such payments are taxable as ordinary income to the recipient, and may be excluded from the current income of the partnership or deducted therefrom. The treatment of good will under Section 736(a) is favorable to continuing partners since they are permitted to expense the cost of acquiring the withdrawing partner's interest in partnership good will.

"The treatment of good will under the 1954 Code would appear to be one of the principal tax factors to be taken into account in drafting partnership agreements. In most cases it would be desirable for the partners to agree in advance as to whether partnership good will is to be capitalized or not. If the partnership agreement fails to provide for the treatment of good will, the agreement may be so amended at the time of termination of an interest. Section 761(d) of the 1954 Code also permits a partnership agreement to be modified up to the time for filing the partnership return for the taxable year. It is doubtful, however, that the remaining partners could act adversely to the interest of the withdrawing partner after he had left the partnership."

* * *

The case of Commissioner of Internal Revenue v. Lester, 366 U.S. 299, 81 S.Ct. 1343, 6 L.Ed.2d 306, is analogous to this case. It involved a situation where a divorced taxpayer and his former wife entered into a written agreement for periodic payments by him to his former wife. The agreement provided that in the event any of the parties' three children should marry, become emancipated or die, the payments should "be reduced in a sum equal to one-sixth of the payments which would thereafter otherwise accrue." The taxpayer deducted the whole of these periodic payments in the taxable years of 1951 and 1952. The government sought to recover tax deficiencies for those years equal to one-half of the periodic payments made contending that the quoted language of the written agreement sufficiently identified ½ of the periodic payments as having been "payable for the support" of the taxpayer's minor children under § 22(k)[8]

8. The pertinent portion of § 22(k) reads as follows:

"* * * This subsection [allowing deductions] shall not apply to that part of any such

of the Internal Revenue Code of 1939 and therefore, not deductible by him under § 23(u) of the Code. The Supreme Court held "that the Congress intended that, to come within the exception portion of § 22(k), the agreement providing for the periodic payments must specifically state the amounts or parts thereof allocable to the support of the children" (366 U.S. at page 301, 81 S.Ct. at page 1345) and said that by this statute "the Congress was in effect giving the husband and wife the power to shift a portion of the tax burden from the wife to the husband by the use of a simple provision in the settlement agreement which fixed the specific portion of the periodic payment made to the wife as payable for the support of the children. Here the agreement does not so specifically provide." (366 U.S. at 304, 81 S.Ct. at 1347). The court also noted that "It [the statute] does not say that 'a sufficiently clear purpose' on the part of the parties would satisfy" but "It says that the written instrument must 'fix' that amount, or 'portion of the payment' which is to go to the support of the children." (366 U.S. at page 305, 81 S.Ct. at page 1347).

This reasoning would appear to be particularly applicable here and we think the payment in question should be treated as ordinary income rather than capital gain since the articles of partnership do not specifically provide that the payment is for good will. If intent is to be determined by something other than the plain language of the partnership agreement, uncertainty and confusion will becloud the issue and the efforts of Congress to clarify a complex situation will go for naught. Important, also, is the fact that this result treats fairly both the expelled partner and the remaining partners as the tax consequences are determined in advance by the contract to which they all agreed.

The decision of the Tax Court is Affirmed.

Commissioner v. Jackson Investment Co.

United States Court of Appeals, Ninth Circuit, 1965.
346 F.2d 187.

■ BARNES, CIRCUIT JUDGE.

The Commissioner of Internal Revenue has brought this petition to review decisions of the Tax Court (41 T.C. 675 (1964)) involving federal income taxes for the taxable years 1956 through 1958. The amounts in controversy involve distributions made by respondents, Jackson Investment Company and West Shore Company, partners in George W. Carter Company, to a retiring partner, Ethel M. Carter. Petitioner concluded that the distributions were not deductible expenses, and, consequently, assessed deficiencies against Jackson in the aggregate amount of $9,848.18 and against West Shore in the aggregate amount of $15,577.85. The Tax Court,

periodic payment *which the terms of the* * * * *written instrument fix*, in terms of * * * a portion of the payment, as a sum which is payable for the support of minor children of such husband. * * * " (Emphasis supplied.)

however, rendered a decision adverse to the Commissioner. The Commissioner subsequently petitioned for review, invoking this court's jurisdiction under Section 7482 of the Internal Revenue Code of 1954.

The question presented for our consideration involves the construction of Section 736 of the Internal Revenue Code of 1954.

* * *

The intended purpose of this provision was to permit the participants themselves to determine whether the retiring partner or the remaining partners would bear the tax burdens for payments in liquidation of a retiring partner's interest. Thus, under the general approach of subsection (a), the tax burden is borne by the retiring partner—he recognizes the payments as taxable income, and the remaining partners are allowed a commensurate deduction from partnership income. Under subsection (b), the general rule conceives an approach of nonrecognition of ordinary income to the retiring partner, but places the tax burden on the partnership by denying a deduction from income for the payments. This latter subsection, however, adopts a special rule—(b)(2)(B)—in an express effort to assist the participants to decide *inter sese* upon the allocation of the tax burden. This special rule lies at the heart of the present controversy. Under this rule, payments for the good will of the partnership are deductible by the partnership (and hence recognizable as ordinary income to the retiring partner) "except to the extent that the partnership agreement provides for a payment with respect to good will." If the partnership agreement provides for a payment with respect to good will, the tax burden is allocated to the partnership—no deduction is allowed and the retiring partner need not recognize the payments as ordinary income. In the present case, petitioner contends that this exception under Section 736(b)(2)(B) applies, and thus the deductions taken by the partnership should be disallowed. We must determine, therefore, whether the parties intended to place the tax burden on the partnership by expressly incorporating into the partnership agreement a provision for payment to the retiring partner with respect to good will.

It is undisputed that the original Partnership Agreement did not contain a provision for partnership good will or a payment therefor upon the withdrawal of a partner. On May 7, 1956, however, the three partners executed an instrument entitled "Amendment of Limited Partnership Agreement of George W. Carter Co." * * * This instrument provided for Ethel Carter's retirement, and bound the partnership to compensate Ethel in the amount of $60,000.00 in consideration for her withdrawal. After the necessary adjustment of the figures, it was determined that $19,650.00 of the amount was in return for Ethel's "15% interest in the fair market value of all the net assets of the partnership." The other $40,350.00, the amount in controversy here, was referred to as "a guaranteed payment, or a payment for good will." * * * The $40,350.00 was paid by the partnership in three annual parts, and deductions were made for good will expense in the partnership net income for each of the years. It is these deductions that petitioner challenges.

The decision of the Tax Court (six judges dissenting), concluded that the document entitled "Amendment of Limited Partnership Agreement of George W. Carter Co." was not a part of the partnership agreement, and therefore, the exception of Section 736(b)(2)(B) was not applicable. As a result, the court held that the amounts in question were legitimate deductions from the partnership income under the terms of Section 736(a)(2). The court founded its conclusion on the fact that the "Amendment" was solely designed to effect a withdrawal of one of the partners; it was not at all concerned with any continued role for Ethel in the partnership affairs.

We cannot agree with the interpretation of the majority of the Tax Court. We find this view unduly interferes with the clear objective of the statute, i.e., to permit and enable the partners to allocate the tax burdens as they choose, and with a minimum of uncertainty and difficulty. If a partnership agreement such as the one involved here, had no provision regarding the withdrawal of a partner, and the partners negotiated to compensate the retiring partner with payments that could be treated by the recipient at capital gain rates, the statutory scheme should not be read to frustrate the parties' efforts. An amendment to the partnership agreement which incorporates the plan of withdrawal and which designates the amount payable as being in consideration for the partnership good will seems clearly to be an attempt to utilize Section 736(b)(2)(B), affording capital gain rates to the retiring partner but precluding an expense deduction for the partnership. Simply because the subject matter of the amendment deals only with the liquidation of one partner's interest, we should not thwart whatever may be the clear intent of the parties by holding the amendment is not part of the partnership agreement. The Internal Revenue Code of 1954 expressly touches upon modifications of partnership agreements, and it gives no support to the thesis that an amendment dealing with the withdrawal of a partner cannot be considered a part of the partnership agreement. Section 761(c) provides:

> "*Partnership Agreement.*—For purposes of this subchapter, a partnership agreement includes any modifications of the partnership agreement made prior to, or at, the time prescribed by law for the filing of the partnership return for the taxable year (not including extensions) which are agreed to by all the partners, or which are adopted in such other manner as may be provided by the partnership agreement."

We hold, therefore, in harmony with the intent of the parties to the partnership, that the "Amendment of Limited Partnership Agreement of George W. Carter Co." was a modification of the partnership agreement within the meaning of Section 761(c). As such, the requirement of a provision in the partnership agreement as specified in Section 736(b)(2)(B) is satisfied.

There remains, however, an additional requirement to call into operation Section 736(b)(2)(B), viz., that the provision for payment in the partnership agreement be *with respect to good will*. As noted above, the payment of the $40,350.00 was inartistically described in the Amendment as a "guaranteed payment, or a payment for good will." The "guaranteed payment" terminology seems to expressly incorporate Section 736(a)(2), which would permit an expense deduction to the partnership, while recognizing the payments as ordinary income to the retiring partner. The "good will" language, on the other hand, would appear directed to Section 736(b)(2)(B), which results in the opposite tax consequences. In resolving this conflict, we feel the most helpful guide is to pay deference to what we may determine was the revealed intent of the parties. An examination of the entire amendment leads us to conclude that, notwithstanding the use of the words "guaranteed payment," the parties intended to invoke Section 736(b)(2)(B), not Section 736(a)(2). The Amendment expressly states the following (which we find impossible to harmonize with the majority opinion of the Tax Court or the arguments advanced by respondents in their brief):

> "It is recognized by all the parties hereto that the prior agreements among the partners do not provide for any payment to any partner *in respect to good will* in the event of the retirement or withdrawal of a partner, but George W. Carter Company will nevertheless make a payment to Ethel M. Carter *in respect to good will* as herein provided in consideration of her entering into this agreement and her consent to retire from the partnership upon the terms herein expressed." (Tr. 66.) (Emphasis added.)

The meaning of this language as well as the words chosen to express it leads to the conclusion that the $40,350.00 was to be a payment "in respect to good will," with the parties intending to be governed by the tax consequences of Section 736(b)(2)(B). The concluding paragraph of Judge Raum's dissenting opinion in the Tax Court, joined in by five other judges, expresses in our judgment sound reasoning, and we incorporate it here as a summary statement of our viewpoint:

> "To fail to give effect to the plain language thus used by the parties is, I think, to defeat the very purpose of the pertinent partnership provisions of the statute, namely, to permit the partners themselves to fix their tax liabilities *inter sese*. Although the May 7, 1956, agreement may be inartistically drawn, and indeed may even contain some internal inconsistencies, the plain and obvious import of its provisions in respect of the present problem was to amend the partnership agreement so as to provide specifically for a goodwill payment. This is the kind of thing that section 736(b)(2)(B) dealt with when it allowed the partners to fix the tax consequences of goodwill payments to a withdrawing partner. And this is what the partners clearly attempted to do here, however crude may have been their effort. I would give further effect to that effort, and would not add further complications to an already overcomplicated statute." (41 T.C. at 685.)

The decision of the Tax Court is reversed, and the matter is remanded to that court for further proceedings consistent with this opinion.

3. ALLOCATION AND TIMING OF SECTION 736 PAYMENTS

Regulations: § 1.736–1(b)(5)–(7).

If a retiring partner receives a single lump sum liquidating distribution, the Section 736 tax consequences occur in the year of payment. It is more typical, however, to receive a series of installment payments over more than one year. In that event, the aggregate payments first must be allocated between Sections 736(a) and (b) and then each year's installment payments similarly must be allocated.[1]

Absent an agreed allocation between the parties, the rules for reporting installment payments under Section 736 differ depending on whether or not the payments are fixed in amount. If the retiring partner receives a fixed amount over a fixed number of years, the portion of each annual payment allocated to Section 736(b) is determined by the following formula:[2]

$$\S\ 736(b)\ \text{Portion} = \begin{array}{c}\text{Total Fixed Agreed}\\ \text{Payments for}\\ \text{Taxable year}\end{array} \times \frac{\text{Total Fixed } \S\ 736(b)\ \text{Payments}}{\text{Total Fixed } \S\ 736(a) \text{ and } (b)\ \text{Payments}}$$

The balance, if any, of the amount received is treated as a Section 736(a) payment.[3] If the retiring partner receives payments which are not fixed (e.g., contingent payments), the payments are first treated as Section 736(b) payments to the full extent of the partner's interest in partnership property and thereafter as Section 736(a) payments.[4]

Alternatively, the parties may avoid all this trouble by negotiating an agreement apportioning Section 736(a) and (b) payments, provided that the total amount allocated to Section 736(b) property may not exceed its total value at the date of the partner's retirement.[5] This once again illustrates the latitude accorded the parties to tailor the tax treatment of Section 736 payments to their own needs and objectives.[6]

The foregoing allocation rules are accompanied by an equally awesome array of timing options for Section 736 payments. Section 736(a) payments are taxable to the distributee in his taxable year with or within which ends the partnership's taxable year for which the payment is a distributive share

1. Reg. § 1.736–1(b)(5) & (6).

2. Reg. § 1.736–1(b)(5)(i). Note that the Section 736(b) ratio is applied to the total fixed agreed payments for the year as distinguished from the amount actually received. If less than the agreed payment is made in any year, the amount actually paid is first deemed to be a Section 736(b) payment to the extent such payment is due. Id.

3. Id.

4. Reg. § 1.736–1(b)(5)(ii). The regulations also prescribe the consequences of receiving some fixed and some contingent payments. See Reg. § 1.736–1(b)(5)(i).

5. Reg. § 1.736–1(b)(5)(iii).

6. All the parties must agree. To avoid controversies, the agreement should include covenants that all the parties will report the liquidation payments consistently with their agreed allocation. Query, should the partners retain independent counsel in negotiating such an agreement?

or in which the partnership may deduct the amount as a guaranteed payment.[7] The treatment of Section 736(b) payments is far more flexible. Under the general rule, each installment is treated as a separate distribution decreasing the partner's outside basis. The partner does not recognize gain until he receives actual and constructive distributions of cash in excess of his outside basis.[8] This gives the partner the advantage of reporting the distribution as an open transaction, a method that normally is unavailable for deferred payment arrangements.[9] Recognition of loss, if any, is deferred until the year in which the final distribution is made.[10] Alternatively, a partner who is to receive a fixed amount of Section 736(b) payments may elect to annually report a pro rata portion of his gain or loss over the distribution period, in effect treating the transaction in a manner similar to the installment method under Section 453.[11]

At the risk of turning this note into one of the first published excerpts on the intersection of tax law and cosmology, consider the timing rules applicable to Section 751(b) disproportionate distribution transactions which fall within Section 736(b). The nature of this transaction is different because each installment distribution by the partnership, when viewed in isolation, may be disproportionate even if the entire transaction is not.[12] The Section 751(b) consequences presumably should be determined as if all the payments were made at one time, and all the resulting gain or loss then should be prorated over the life of the payments.[13]

PROBLEM

A has owned a one-third general partnership interest in the ABC partnership for several years. The partnership is one in which capital is a material income-producing factor. A has an outside basis of $12,000. The partnership, which has not made a § 754 election, has the following balance sheet:

7. Reg. § 1.736–1(a)(5).

8. I.R.C. § 731(a)(1); Reg. §§ 1.731–1(a)(1), 1.736–1(b)(6), (7) Example (1).

9. Open transaction treatment is available because Section 736(b) payments are treated as distributions. The result arguably would be different if there were a "disposition," in which event the installment sale rules in Section 453 would apply and ordinarily foreclose open transaction reporting.

10. Reg. § 1.731–1(a)(2).

11. Reg. § 1.736–1(b)(6).

12. For example, assume a retiring partner has an interest in $100 worth of Section 751 assets and $100 worth of Section 741 assets. He will receive his proportionate share of both by taking $100 of Section 751 assets in year one and $100 of Section 741 assets in year two. Although the entire distribution is proportionate, if we look at each year separately the partner has received too many Section 751 assets in year one and too few in year two, resulting in the application of the Section 751(b) disproportionate distribution rule in both years!

13. For a discussion of this question and other timing issues under Section 736(b), see McKee, Nelson & Whitmire, Federal Taxation of Partnerships and Partners ¶ 22.02[4] (4th ed. 2007) and Willis, Pennell & Postlewaite, Partnership Taxation ¶ 15.05 (6th ed. 1997).

Assets	A.B.	F.M.V.	Partners' Capital	A.B.	F.M.V.
Cash	$24,000	$24,000	A	$12,000	$18,000
Accounts Receivable	0	9,000	B	12,000	18,000
Capital Assets	9,000	15,000	C	12,000	18,000
Goodwill	3,000	6,000			
	$36,000	$54,000		$36,000	$54,000

(a) What tax consequences to A and the partnership (i.e., B and C) if A receives a $20,000 cash payment for his interest and the agreement makes no provision as to goodwill? Assume the goodwill is not an amortizable § 197 intangible.

(b) What result to A and the partnership in (a), above, if substantially all of the income of the partnership consists of fees for personal services rendered by the partners?

(c) What result to A and the partnership in (b), above, if A agrees to receive $10,000 cash in year one and $1,000 cash per year in each of the next ten years?

(d) What different result in (c), above, if A has an outside basis of $16,000?

(e) What result in (c), above, if A receives $10,000 cash and one-tenth of each year's profits in each of the next ten years, assuming profits are $10,000 per year?

(f) What result in (b), above, if the agreement provides that $2,000 is being received for A's interest in partnership goodwill? Would A prefer to include this provision in the agreement?

C. Liquidation vs. Sale of a Partnership Interest

Code: Skim §§ 731; 732; 736; 741; 751.

Foxman v. Commissioner

United States Court of Appeals, Third Circuit, 1965.
352 F.2d 466.

■ WILLIAM F. SMITH, CIRCUIT JUDGE.

This matter is before the Court on petitions to review decisions of the Tax Court, 41 T.C. 535, in three related cases consolidated for the purpose of hearing. The petitions of Foxman and Grenell challenge the decision as erroneous only as it relates to them. The petition of the Commissioner seeks a review of the decision as it relates to Jacobowitz only if it is determined by us that the Tax Court erred in the other two cases.

The cases came before the Tax Court on stipulations of fact, numerous written exhibits and the conflicting testimony of several witnesses, including the taxpayers. The relevant and material facts found by the Tax Court are fully detailed in its opinion. We repeat only those which may contribute to an understanding of the narrow issue before us.

As the result of agreements reached in February of 1955, and January of 1956, Foxman, Grenell and Jacobowitz became equal partners in a commercial enterprise which was then trading under the name of Abbey Record Manufacturing Company, hereinafter identified as the Company. They also became equal shareholders in a corporation known as Sound Plastics, Inc. When differences of opinion arose in the spring of 1956, efforts were made to persuade Jacobowitz to withdraw from the partnership. These efforts failed at that time but were resumed in March of 1957. Thereafter the parties entered into negotiations which, on May 21, 1957, culminated in a contract for the acquisition of Jacobowitz's interest in the partnership of Foxman and Grenell. The terms and conditions, except one not here material, were substantially in accord with an option to purchase offered earlier to Foxman and Grenell. The relevant portions of the final contract are set forth in the Tax Court's opinion.

The contract, prepared by an attorney representing Foxman and Grenell, referred to them as the "Second Party," and to Jacobowitz as the "First Party." We regard as particularly pertinent to the issue before us the following clauses:

"Whereas, the parties hereto are equal owners and the sole partners of ABBEY Record Mfg. Co., a partnership, * * *, and are also the sole stockholders, officers and directors of SOUND PLASTICS, INC., a corporation organized under laws of the State of New York; and

"WHEREAS, the first party is desirous of selling, conveying, transferring and assigning all of his right, title and interest in and to his one-third share and interest in the said ABBEY to the second parties; and

"WHEREAS, the second parties are desirous of conveying, transferring and assigning all of their right, title and interest in and to their combined two-thirds shares and interest in SOUND PLASTICS, INC., to the first party;

"Now, Therefore, It Is Mutually Agreed as Follows:

"*First*: The second parties hereby purchase all the right, title, share and interest of the first party in ABBEY and the first party does hereby sell, transfer, convey and assign all of his right, title, interest and share in ABBEY and in the moneys in banks, trade names, accounts due, or to become due, and in all other assets of any kind whatsoever, belonging to said ABBEY, for and in consideration of the following. * * * "

The stated consideration was cash in the sum of $242,500; the assignment by Foxman and Grenell of their stock in Sound Plastics; and the transfer of an automobile, title to which was held by the Company. The agreement provided for the payment of $67,500 upon consummation of the contract and payment of the balance as follows: $67,500 on January 2, 1958, and $90,000 in equal monthly installments, payable on the first of each month after January 30, 1958. This balance was evidenced by a series of promissory notes, payment of which was secured by a chattel mortgage on the assets of the Company. This mortgage, like the contract, referred to a sale by Jacobowitz of his partnership interest to Foxman and Grenell. The notes were executed in the name of the Company as the purported maker and were signed by Foxman and Grenell, who also endorsed them under a guarantee of payment.

The down payment of $67,500 was by a cashier's check which was issued in exchange for a check drawn on the account of the Company. The first note, in the amount of $67,500, which became due on January 2, 1958, was timely paid by a check drawn on the Company's account. Pursuant to the terms of an option reserved to Foxman and Grenell, they elected to prepay the balance of $90,000 on January 28, 1958, thereby relieving themselves of an obligation to pay Jacobowitz a further $17,550, designated in the contract as a consultant's fee. They delivered to Jacobowitz a cashier's check which was charged against the account of the Company.

In its partnership return for the fiscal year ending February 28, 1958, the Company treated the sum of $159,656.09, the consideration received by Jacobowitz less the value of his interest in partnership property, as a guaranteed payment made in liquidation of a retiring partner's interest under § 736(a)(2) of the Internal Revenue Code of 1954, Title 26 U.S.C.A. This treatment resulted in a substantial reduction of the distributive shares of Foxman and Grenell and consequently a proportionate decrease in their possible tax liability. In his income tax return Jacobowitz treated the sum of $164,356.09, the consideration less the value of his partnership interest, as a long term capital gain realized upon the sale of his interest. This, of course, resulted in a tax advantage favorable to him. The Commissioner determined deficiencies against each of the taxpayers in amounts not relevant to the issue before us and each filed separate petitions for redetermination.

The critical issue before the Tax Court was raised by the antithetical positions maintained by Foxman and Grenell on one side and Jacobowitz on the other. The former, relying on § 736(a)(2), supra, contended that the transaction, evidenced by the contract, constituted a liquidation of a retiring partner's interest and that the consideration paid was accorded correct treatment in the partnership return. The latter contended that the transaction constituted a sale of his partnership interest and, under § 741 of the Code, 26 U.S.C.A., the profit realized was correctly treated in his return as a capital gain. The Tax Court rejected the position of Foxman and Grenell and held that the deficiency determinations as to them were not erroneous; it sustained the position of Jacobowitz and held that the deficiency determination as to him was erroneous. The petitioners Foxman and Grenell challenge that decision as erroneous and not in accord with the law.

It appears from the evidence, which the Tax Court apparently found credible, that the negotiations which led to the consummation of the contract of May 21, 1957, related to a contemplated sale of Jacobowitz's partnership interest to Foxman and Grenell. The option offered to Foxman and Grenell early in May of 1957, referred to a sale and the execution of "a bill of sale" upon completion of the agreement. The relevant provisions of the contract were couched in terms of "purchase" and "sale." The contract was signed by Foxman and Grenell, individually, and by them on behalf of the Company, although the Company assumed no liability thereunder. The obligation to purchase Jacobowitz's interest was solely that of Foxman and Grenell. The chattel mortgage on the partnership assets was given to secure payment.

Notwithstanding these facts and the lack of any ambiguity in the contract, Foxman and Grenell argue that the factors unequivocally determinative of the substance of the transaction were: the initial payment of $67,500 by a cashier's check issued in exchange for a check drawn on the account of the Company; the second payment in a similar amount by check drawn on the Company's account; the execution of notes in the name of the Company as maker; and, the prepayment of the notes by cashier's check charged against the Company's account.

This argument unduly emphasizes form in preference to substance. While form may be relevant "[t]he incidence of taxation depends upon the substance of a transaction." Commissioner of Internal Revenue v. Court Holding Co., 324 U.S. 331, 334, 65 S.Ct. 707, 708, 89 L.Ed. 981 (1945); United States v. Cumberland Pub. Serv. Co., 338 U.S. 451, 455, 70 S.Ct. 280, 94 L.Ed. 251 (1950). The "transaction must be viewed as a whole, and each step, from the commencement of negotiations" to consummation, is relevant. Ibid. Where, as here, there has been a transfer and an acquisition of property pursuant to a contract, the nature of the transaction does not depend solely on the means employed to effect payment. Ibid.

It is apparent from the opinion of the Tax Court that careful consideration was given to the factors relied upon by Foxman and Grenell. It is therein stated, 41 T.C. at page 553:

> "These notes were endorsed by Foxman and Grenell individually, and the liability of [the Company] thereon was merely in the nature of security for their primary obligation under the agreement of May 21, 1957. The fact that they utilized partnership resources to discharge their own individual liability in such manner can hardly convert into a section 736 'liquidation' what would otherwise qualify as a section 741 'sale'."
>
> * * *
>
> "* * * the payments received by Jacobowitz were in discharge of their [Foxman's and Grenell's] obligation under the agreement, and not that of [the Company.] It was they who procured those payments in their own behalf from the assets of the partnership which they controlled. The use of [the Company] to make payment was wholly within their discretion and of no concern to Jacobowitz; his only interest was payment."

We are of the opinion that the quoted statements represent a fair appraisal of the true significance of the notes and the means employed to effect payment.

When the members of the partnership decided that Jacobowitz would withdraw in the interest of harmony they had a choice of means by which his withdrawal could be effected. They could have agreed inter se on either liquidation or sale. On a consideration of the plain language of the contract, the negotiations which preceded its consummation, the intent of the parties as reflected by their conduct, and the circumstances surrounding the transaction, the Tax Court found that the transaction was in substance a sale and not a liquidation of a retiring partner's interest. This finding is amply supported by the evidence in the record. The partners having employed the sale method to achieve their objective, Foxman and Grenell cannot avoid the tax consequences by a hindsight application of principles they now find advantageous to them and disadvantageous to Jacobowitz.

The issue before the Tax Court was essentially one of fact and its decision thereon may not be reversed in the absence of a showing that its findings were not supported by substantial evidence or that its decision was not in accord with the law. Cleveland v. C.I.R., 335 F.2d 473, 477 (3d Cir.1964), and the cases therein cited. There has been no such showing in this case.

The decisions of the Tax Court will be affirmed.

Revenue Ruling 93–80

1993–2 Cum.Bull. 239.

ISSUE

Is a loss incurred on the abandonment or worthlessness of a partnership interest a capital or an ordinary loss?

FACTS

Situation 1. PRS is a general partnership in which *A, B*, and *C* were equal partners. During 1993, *PRS* became insolvent, and *C* abandoned *C*'s partnership interest. *C* took all steps necessary to effect a proper abandonment, including written notification to *PRS*. *PRS*'s partnership agreement was amended to indicate that *C* was no longer a partner. At the time *C* abandoned the partnership interest, *PRS*'s only liabilities were nonrecourse liabilities of 120x dollars, shared equally by *A, B*, and *C*. *C* had a remaining adjusted basis in the partnership interest of 180x dollars. *C* did not receive any money or property on leaving the partnership.

Situation 2. LP is a limited partnership in which *D* and *E* were general partners and *F* was one of the limited partners. During 1993, *LP* became insolvent, and *F* abandoned *F*'s limited partnership interest. *F* took all steps necessary to effect a proper abandonment, including written notification to *LP*. *LP*'s partnership agreement was amended to indicate that *F* was no longer a partner. At the time *F* abandoned the partnership interest, *F* had a remaining adjusted basis of 200x dollars in the partnership interest. *F* did not bear the economic risk of loss for any of the partnership liabilities and was not entitled to include a share of the partnership liabilities in the basis of *F*'s partnership interest. *F* did not receive any money or property on leaving the partnership.

LAW

Section 165(a) of the Internal Revenue Code allows a deduction for any loss sustained during the taxable year and not compensated for by insurance or otherwise. Section 165(b) provides that the basis for determining the amount of a deduction for any loss is the adjusted basis provided in section 1011 for determining the loss from the sale or other disposition of property. Section 1.165–1(b) of the Income Tax Regulations provides that a loss must be evidenced by closed and completed transactions, fixed by identifiable events, and actually sustained during the taxable year.

Section 165(f) of the Code provides that losses from sales or exchanges of capital assets are allowed only to the extent allowed in sections 1211 or 1212. Under section 1.165–2 of the regulations, however, absent a sale or exchange a loss that results from the abandonment or worthlessness of non-depreciable property is an ordinary loss even if the abandoned or worthless asset is a capital asset (such as a partnership interest).

To establish the abandonment of an asset, a taxpayer must show an intent to abandon the asset, and must overtly act to abandon the asset. CRST, Inc. v. Commissioner, 92 T.C. 1249 (1989), aff'd, 909 F.2d 1146 (8th Cir.1990); Dezendorf v. Commissioner, T.C.Memo. 1961–280, aff'd, 312 F.2d 95 (5th Cir.1963). An asset is worthless when it in fact has no value. Laport v. Commissioner, 671 F.2d 1028 (7th Cir.1982); Boehm v. Commissioner, 326 U.S. 287 (1945).

Section 731(a) of the Code provides that in the case of a distribution by a partnership to a partner, loss is recognized by the partner only upon distribution in liquidation of the interest in a partnership, and only where no property other than money, unrealized receivables, and inventory is distributed to that partner. Loss is recognized by the partner to the extent the adjusted basis of the partner's partnership interest exceeds the money distributed and the basis to the distributee partner in any unrealized receivables and inventory items distributed. Any loss recognized under section 731(a) is considered a loss from the sale or exchange of the partnership interest of the distributee partner.

Section 741 of the Code provides that in the case of a sale or exchange of a partnership interest, gain or loss is recognized to the transferor partner. The gain or loss is considered gain or loss from the sale or exchange of a capital asset, except as otherwise provided in section 751 (relating to inventory items that have appreciated substantially in value and unrealized receivables).

Section 752(b) of the Code provides that any decrease in a partner's share of the liabilities of a partnership, or any decrease in a partner's individual liabilities by reason of the assumption by the partnership of the individual liabilities, is considered a distribution of money to the partner by the partnership.

In Rev.Rul. 70–355, 1970–2 C.B. 51, a taxpayer paid cash for an interest as a limited partner in a partnership, and the taxpayer's capital account was credited with an amount less than the cash paid. The partnership agreement provided that losses would first be allocated against each partner's capital account and any balance would be shared only by the general partners. In a subsequent taxable year, the partnership sustained a loss in its business operations, entered into bankruptcy, and dissolved. The taxpayer's distributive share of the partnership loss for the taxable year reduced the taxpayer's capital account to zero. In addition, the taxpayer's adjusted basis in the partnership interest, which was greater than the taxpayer's capital account, was reduced by the taxpayer's distributive share of the loss. However, the taxpayer's adjusted basis in the partnership interest was not reduced to zero. The taxpayer did not receive any cash or other consideration in liquidation of the taxpayer's partnership interest.

Rev.Rul. 70–355 concludes that the taxpayer's loss is deductible as an ordinary loss under section 165(a) of the Code. The taxpayer's loss was composed of the taxpayer's distributive share of the partnership loss equal to the taxpayer's capital account and the balance of the taxpayer's adjusted basis in the partnership interest.

In Rev.Rul. 76–189, 1976–1 C.B. 181, *D* purchased a one-third interest in the *ABC* partnership from taxpayer *A*. *ABC* sustained a net loss from its business operations for the taxable year and terminated at the end of that taxable year. At termination, *ABC* had no remaining assets or liabilities. *D*'s distributive share of the partnership loss did not reduce *D*'s basis in *D*'s partnership interest to zero.

Rev.Rul. 76–189 concludes that *D* has an ordinary loss deduction for *D* 's distributive share of the partnership loss under section 702(a) of the Code and a capital loss deduction for any remaining adjusted basis in *D*'s partnership interest under section 731(a) on the date the partnership terminated. This was so even though there was no actual or deemed distribution from the partnership.

ANALYSIS

The abandonment or worthlessness of a partnership interest may give rise to a loss deductible under section 165(a) of the Code. Whether a loss from the abandonment or worthlessness of a partnership interest is capital or ordinary depends on whether or not the loss results from the sale or exchange of a capital asset.

Sections 731 and 741 of the Code apply to any transaction in which the partner receives an actual distribution of money or property from the partnership. These provisions likewise apply to any transaction in which a partner is deemed to receive a distribution from the partnership (*e.g.*, section 752(b)). Thus, whether there is an actual distribution or a deemed distribution, the transaction is treated as a sale or exchange of the partnership interest, and any loss resulting from the transaction is capital (except as provided in section 751(b)). Such a transaction is not treated for tax purposes as involving a loss from the abandonment or worthlessness of a partnership interest regardless of the amount of the consideration actually received or deemed received in the exchange.

Any decrease in a partner's share of partnership liabilities is deemed to be a distribution of money to the partner under section 752(b). The section 752(b) deemed distribution triggers the distribution on liquidation rule of section 731(a) for recognition of loss. For purposes of determining whether or not section 752(b) applies to create a deemed distribution upon abandonment or worthlessness, liability shifts that take place in anticipation of such event are treated as occurring at the time of the abandonment or worthlessness under general tax principles. See also section 1.731–1(a)(2) of the regulations providing that the liquidation of a partner's interest in a partnership may take place by means of a series of distributions.

A loss from the abandonment or worthlessness of a partnership interest will be ordinary if there is neither an actual nor a deemed distribution to the partner under the principles described above. Even a *de minimis* actual or deemed distribution makes the entire loss a capital loss. Citron v. Commissioner, 97 T.C. 200, 216 n. 14 (1991). In addition, the loss will be ordinary only if the transaction is not otherwise in substance a sale or exchange. For example, a partner's receipt of consideration from another partner (or a party related thereto) may, depending upon the facts and circumstances, establish that a purported abandonment or worthlessness of a partnership interest is in substance a sale or exchange.

Partner *D* in Rev.Rul. 76–189 satisfied all of the requirements for ordinary loss treatment. Partner *D* did not receive any actual distributions, and *D* was not deemed to receive any distributions under section 752(b) of the Code as a result of liability shifts. Nevertheless, Rev.Rul. 76–189 denied *D* ordinary loss treatment because the Service concluded that for partnership terminations section 731 applied as if an actual distribution had taken place. The Service will no longer follow Rev.Rul. 76–189.

The taxpayer in Rev.Rul. 70–355 also satisfied all of the requirements for ordinary loss treatment. Unlike Rev.Rul. 76–189, however, Rev.Rul. 70–355 concludes that the taxpayer's loss is ordinary without discussing the relevance of partnership liabilities in determining whether a partner has an ordinary loss under section 165(a) of the Code upon the abandonment or worthlessness of a partnership interest. Further, some taxpayers have interpreted the partnership's bankruptcy as an essential fact in Rev.Rul. 70–355. Thus, although the conclusion in Rev.Rul. 70–355 is consistent with the conclusion in this revenue ruling, to avoid further confusion, Rev.Rul. 70–355 is clarified and superseded.

In *Situation 1*, when *C* abandons the interest in *PRS*, which has liabilities in which *C* shares, a deemed distribution of $40x$ dollars is made to *C* under section 752(b) of the Code. The deemed distribution reduces the basis of *C*'s interest to $140x$ dollars ($180x - 40x = 140x$). Because there is a deemed distribution to *C*, section 731(a) applies and any loss allowed is capital. Thus, *C*'s entire $140x$ dollars loss from abandoning the *PRS* interest is a capital loss even though the deemed distribution under section 752(b) is only $40x$ dollars. The results would be the same if *C*'s interest in

PRS were found to be worthless. Because *C* shares in the liabilities of *PRS*, a deemed distribution is made to *C* on a finding of worthlessness, section 731 applies, and any loss allowed is capital.

In *Situation 2, F* permanently abandons *F*'s interest in *LP*. Section 731 of the Code does not apply because *F* did not receive any actual or deemed distribution from the partnership. *F* received nothing in exchange for *F*'s interest in *LP*. Accordingly, *F* realizes an ordinary loss of 200x dollars for the adjusted basis of *F*'s partnership interest, which may be deducted under section 165(a) as an ordinary loss subject to all other applicable rules of the Code. The results would be the same if *F*'s partnership interest in *LP* had become worthless.

HOLDING

A loss incurred on the abandonment or worthlessness of a partnership interest is an ordinary loss if sale or exchange treatment does not apply. If there is an actual or deemed distribution to the partner, or if the transaction is otherwise in substance a sale or exchange, the partner's loss is capital (except as provided in section 751(b)).

* * *

NOTE

Revenue Ruling 93–80 is a variation of the liquidation vs. sale issue where the tax stakes (ordinary vs. capital loss) may be high. The effect of the ruling is that any partner whose share of partnership liabilities is reduced on abandonment of a partnership interest will recognize a capital loss. Otherwise, if the partner takes all steps necessary to effect a proper abandonment, the transaction will yield a more valuable ordinary loss.

PROBLEM

The ABC general partnership, a law firm, has the following unusual but pedagogically useful balance sheet:

Assets	**A.B.**	**F.M.V.**	**Partners' Capital**	**A.B.**	**F.M.V.**
Cash	$60,000	$ 60,000	A	$20,000	$ 50,000
Goodwill	0	90,000	B	20,000	50,000
			C	20,000	50,000
	$60,000	$150,000		$60,000	$150,000

A is leaving the firm and retiring. He will receive $50,000 cash, which will be his only income for the year.

(a) What results if the transaction is structured as a sale of A's interest to B and C?

(b) What results if the transaction is structured as a sale of A's interest to B and C but the payment is made by the partnership rather than by B and C?

(c) What result if the transaction is structured as a liquidation? Should goodwill be stated?

(d) How can the parties be sure that their chosen structure will be respected by the Service so that they can avoid litigation?

D. LIQUIDATION OF A PARTNERSHIP

1. VOLUNTARY LIQUIDATION

a. IN GENERAL

Code: Skim §§ 708(b)(1)(A); 731; 732; 736; 751(b).

Up to this point, we have been considering the liquidation of a retiring partner's interest in a continuing partnership. If the entire partnership is liquidated, the tax consequences are somewhat different. Section 736(a) is inapplicable when there is a single distribution of assets to the parties on a complete dissolution of the partnership.[1] The essence of Section 736(a) is that payments are made by the partnership, but the partnership is hardly in a position to make payments if it no longer exists. This is distinguishable from a situation where a partner receives a series of payments and then, upon termination of the payments, the partnership is liquidated. Section 736(a) would apply to the first partner on liquidation of his interest, but it would not apply to the remaining partners on liquidation of the partnership.[2]

Since Section 736(a) is inapplicable to a liquidation of the entire partnership, the next question is whether Section 751(b) applies on a disproportionate distribution in connection with a complete liquidation. Revenue Ruling 77–412, which follows in the text, answers this question in the affirmative. It involves a two-person firm, but its principles also apply to larger partnerships.

If a liquidation of a partnership results in a pro rata or at least a nondisproportionate distribution of all the partnership assets to the partners, Sections 736(a) and 751(b) are both inapplicable, and the Sections 731, 732 and 735 distribution rules apply.[3]

1. Cf. Yourman v. United States, 277 F.Supp. 818 (S.D.Cal.1967). See McKee, Nelson & Whitmire, Federal Taxation of Partnerships and Partners ¶ 22.01 [1] (4th ed. 2007).

2. The Service applies Section 736(a) to the first partner even in the case of a two-person partnership. Reg. § 1.736–1(a)(6). But see Phillips v. Commissioner, 40 T.C. 157 (1963), and Swihart, "Tax Problems Raised by Liquidations of Partnership Interests," 44 Texas L.Rev. 1209, 1235 (1966), questioning the validity of this regulation. See also I.R.C. § 708(b)(1)(A) and Reg. § 1.708–1(b)(1)(i).

3. See Problem 1 at page 327 of the text for an example of such a situation.

Revenue Ruling 77–412

1977–2 Cum. Bull. 223.

Advice has been requested concerning the Federal income tax consequences upon the complete liquidation of a two person partnership involving the non-pro rata distribution of "section 751 property" to the partners.

Section 751 of the Internal Revenue Code of 1954 governs the treatment of unrealized receivables of the partnership (as defined in section 751(c)) and inventory items of the partnership that have appreciated substantially in value (as defined in section 751(d)), insofar as they affect sales or exchanges of partnership interests and certain distributions by a partnership. Unrealized receivables and substantially appreciated inventory items are referred to as "section 751 property."

Under section 751(a) of the Code, the amount of any money, or the fair market value of any property, received by a transferor partner in exchange for all or a part of such partner's interest in the partnership attributable to section 751 property, is considered an amount realized from the sale or exchange of property other than a capital asset. Thus, any gain or loss attributable to the sale or exchange of section 751 property would be ordinary income or loss.

Section 751(b)(1) of the Code provides that where a partner receives, in a distribution, partnership section 751 property in exchange for all or a part of such partner's interest in other partnership property (including money), or receives other partnership property (including money) in exchange for all or a part of an interest in partnership section 751 property, such transaction shall be considered as a sale or exchange of such property between the distributee and the partnership (as constituted after the distribution). Consequently, section 751(b) of the Code applies to that part of the distribution to a partner that consists of the non-pro rata distribution of the partnership section 751 property in exchange for other property, or the non-pro rata distribution of other partnership property in exchange for section 751 property.

In Yourman v. United States, 277 F.Supp. 818 (S.D.Calif.1967), the court held that section 751 of the Code applied to a non-pro rata distribution of section 751 property of a partnership even though the partnership did not continue in existence after the distribution.

Accordingly in the case of a two person partnership, to the extent that a partner either receives section 751 property in exchange for relinquishing any part of such partner's interest in other property, or receives other property in exchange for relinquishing any part of the interest in section 751 property, the distribution is treated as a sale or exchange of such properties between the distributee partner and the partnership (as constituted after the distribution), even though after the distribution the partnership consists of a single individual.

For example, the non-pro rata distribution by a two person partnership of section 751 property to its partners, *A* and *B*, as part of a distribution resulting in a complete liquidation of the partnership, can be viewed in two ways, both of which result in the same tax consequences to each party to the transaction. In the non-pro rata distribution, partner *A* receives more partnership section 751 property than *A*'s underlying interest in such property, while partner *B* receives more partnership other property than *B*'s interest in such property. Partner *A* may be treated as the distributee partner who has exchanged part of an interest in partnership property other than section 751 property with the partnership as constituted after the distribution (partner *B*) for section 751 property. Partner *A* would be treated as realizing gain or loss on a sale or exchange of the property other than section 751 property, and the partnership as constituted after the distribution would realize ordinary income or loss on the exchange of the section 751 property.

Partner *B* may be treated as the distributee partner who has exchanged part of an interest in the partnership section 751 property with the partnership as constituted after the distribution (partner *A*) for other property. Partner *B* would be treated as realizing ordinary income or loss on the exchange of the section 751 property, and the partnership as constituted after the distribution would realize gain or loss on a sale or exchange of the other property. However, regardless of which partner is considered to be the distributee and which is considered to be the remaining partner, the Federal income tax consequences are the same to each partner.

Revenue Ruling 99–6

1999–1 Cum. Bull. 432.

ISSUE

What are the federal income tax consequences if one person purchases all of the ownership interests in a domestic limited liability company (LLC) that is classified as a partnership under § 301.7701–3 of the Procedure and Administration Regulations, causing the LLC's status as a partnership to terminate under § 708(b)(1)(A) of the Internal Revenue Code?

FACTS

In each of the following situations, an LLC is formed and operates in a state which permits an LLC to have a single owner. Each LLC is classified as a partnership under § 301.7701–3. Neither of the LLCs holds any unrealized receivables or substantially appreciated inventory for purposes of § 751(b). For the sake of simplicity, it is assumed that neither LLC is liable for any indebtedness, nor are the assets of the LLCs subject to any indebtedness.

Situation 1. A and B are equal partners in AB, an LLC. A sells A's entire interest in AB to B for $10,000. After the sale, the business is continued by the LLC, which is owned solely by B.

Situation 2. C and D are equal partners in CD, an LLC. C and D sell their entire interests in CD to E, an unrelated person, in exchange for $10,000 each. After the sale, the business is continued by the LLC, which is owned solely by E.

After the sale, in both situations, no entity classification election is made under § 301.7701–3(c) to treat the LLC as an association for federal tax purposes.

LAW

Section 708(b)(1)(A) and § 1.708–1(b)(1) of the Income Tax Regulations provide that a partnership shall terminate when the operations of the partnership are discontinued and no part of any business, financial operation, or venture of the partnership continues to be carried on by any of its partners in a partnership.

Section 731(a)(1) provides that, in the case of a distribution by a partnership to a partner, gain is not recognized to the partner except to the extent that any money distributed exceeds the adjusted basis of the partner's interest in the partnership immediately before the distribution.

Section 731(a)(2) provides that, in the case of a distribution by a partnership in liquidation of a partner's interest in a partnership where no property other than money, unrealized receivables (as defined in § 751(c)), and inventory (as defined in § 751(d)(2)) is distributed to the partner, loss is recognized to the extent of the excess of the adjusted basis of the partner's interest in the partnership over the sum of (A) any money distributed, and (B) the basis to the distributee, as determined under § 732, of any unrealized receivables and inventory.

Section 732(b) provides that the basis of property (other than money) distributed by a partnership to a partner in liquidation of the partner's interest shall be an amount equal to the adjusted basis of the partner's interest in the partnership, reduced by any money distributed in the same transaction.

Section 735(b) provides that, in determining the period for which a partner has held property received in a distribution from a partnership (other than for purposes of § 735(a)(2)), there shall be included the holding period of the partnership, as determined under § 1223, with respect to the property.

Section 741 provides that gain or loss resulting from the sale or exchange of an interest in a partnership shall be recognized by the transferor partner, and that the gain or loss shall be considered as gain or loss from a capital asset, except as provided in § 751 (relating to unrealized receivables and inventory items).

Section 1.741–1(b) provides that § 741 applies to the transferor partner in a two-person partnership when one partner sells a partnership interest to the other partner, and to all the members of a partnership when they sell their interests to one or more persons outside the partnership.

Section 301.7701–2(c)(1) provides that, for federal tax purposes, the term "partnership" means a business entity (as the term is defined in § 301.7701–2(a)) that is not a corporation and that has at least two members.

In Edwin E. McCauslen v. Commissioner, 45 T.C. 588 (1966), one partner in an equal, two-person partnership died, and his partnership interest was purchased from his estate by the remaining partner. The purchase caused a termination of the partnership under § 708(b)(1)(A). The Tax Court held that the surviving partner did not purchase the deceased partner's interest in the partnership, but that the surviving partner purchased the partnership assets attributable to the interest. As a result, the surviving partner was not permitted to succeed to the partnership's holding period with respect to these assets.

Rev. Rul. 67–65, 1967–1 C.B. 168, also considered the purchase of a deceased partner's interest by the other partner in a two-person partnership. The Service ruled that, for the purpose of determining the purchaser's holding period in the assets attributable to the deceased partner's interest, the purchaser should treat the transaction as a purchase of the assets attributable to the interest. Accordingly, the purchaser was not permitted to succeed to the partnership's holding period with respect to these assets. See also Rev. Rul. 55–68, 1955–1 C.B. 372.

ANALYSIS AND HOLDINGS

Situation 1. The AB partnership terminates under § 708(b)(1)(A) when B purchases A's entire interest in AB. Accordingly, A must treat the transaction as the sale of a partnership interest. Reg. § 1.741–1(b). A must report gain or loss, if any, resulting from the sale of A's partnership interest in accordance with § 741.

Under the analysis of McCauslen and Rev. Rul. 67–65, for purposes of determining the tax treatment of B, the AB partnership is deemed to make a liquidating distribution of all of its assets to A and B, and following this distribution, B is treated as acquiring the assets deemed to have been distributed to A in liquidation of A's partnership interest.

B's basis in the assets attributable to A's one-half interest in the partnership is $10,000, the purchase price for A's partnership interest. Section 1012. Section 735(b) does not apply with respect to the assets B is deemed to have purchased from A. Therefore, B's holding period for these assets begins on the day immediately following the date of the sale. See Rev. Rul. 66–7, 1966–1 C.B. 188, which provides that the holding period of an asset is computed by excluding the date on which the asset is acquired.

Upon the termination of AB, B is considered to receive a distribution of those assets attributable to B's former interest in AB. B must recognize gain or loss, if any, on the deemed distribution of the assets to the extent required by § 731(a). B's basis in the assets received in the deemed liquidation of B's partnership interest is determined under § 732(b). Under § 735(b), B's holding period for the assets attributable to B's one-half interest in AB includes the partnership's holding period for such assets (except for purposes of § 735(a)(2)).

Situation 2. The CD partnership terminates under § 708(b)(1)(A) when E purchases the entire interests of C and D in CD. C and D must report gain or loss, if any, resulting from the sale of their partnership interests in accordance with § 741.

For purposes of classifying the acquisition by E, the CD partnership is deemed to make a liquidating distribution of its assets to C and D. Immediately following this distribution, E is deemed to acquire, by purchase, all of the former partnership's assets. Compare Rev. Rul. 84–111, 1984–2 C.B. 88 (Situation 3), which determines the tax consequences to a corporate transferee of all interests in a partnership in a manner consistent with McCauslen, and holds that the transferee's basis in the assets received equals the basis of the partnership interests, allocated among the assets in accordance with § 732(c).

E's basis in the assets is $20,000 under § 1012. E's holding period for the assets begins on the day immediately following the date of sale.

PROBLEM

The AB partnership has the following balance sheet:

Assets	**A.B.**	**F.M.V.**	**Partners' Capital**	**A.B.**	**F.M.V.**
Cash	$20,000	$ 20,000	A	$35,000	$ 60,000
Accounts Receivable	0	20,000	B	35,000	60,000
Inventory	20,000	40,000			
Capital Asset	30,000	40,000			
	$70,000	$120,000		$70,000	$120,000

A and B liquidate the partnership. A receives the accounts receivable and the capital asset, while B receives the cash and the inventory. Consider the tax consequences to A, B and the partnership on the liquidation.

b. INCORPORATION OF A PARTNERSHIP

Revenue Ruling 84–111

1984–2 Cum.Bull. 88.

ISSUE

Does Rev.Rul. 70–239, 1970–1 C.B. 74, still represent the Service's position with respect to the three situations described therein?

FACTS

The three situations described in Rev.Rul. 70–239 involve partnerships *X*, *Y*, and *Z*, respectively. Each partnership used the accrual method of accounting and had assets and liabilities consisting of cash, equipment, and accounts payable. The liabilities of each partnership did not exceed the adjusted basis of its assets. The three situations are as follows:

Situation 1

X transferred all of its assets to newly-formed corporation *R* in exchange for all the outstanding stock of *R* and the assumption by *R* of *X*'s liabilities. *X* then terminated by distributing all the stock of *R* to *X*'s partners in proportion to their partnership interests.

Situation 2

Y distributed all of its assets and liabilities to its partners in proportion to their partnership interests in a transaction that constituted a termination of *Y* under section 708(b)(1)(A) of the Code. The partners then transferred all the assets received from *Y* to newly-formed corporation *S* in exchange for all the outstanding stock of *S* and the assumption by *S* of *Y*'s liabilities that had been assumed by the partners.

Situation 3

The partners of *Z* transferred their partnership interests in *Z* to newly-formed corporation *T* in exchange for all the outstanding stock of *T*. This exchange terminated *Z* and all of its assets and liabilities became assets and liabilities of *T*.

In each situation, the steps taken by *X*, *Y*, and *Z*, and the partners of *X*, *Y*, and *Z*, were parts of a plan to transfer the partnership operations to a corporation organized for valid business reasons in exchange for its stock and were not devices to avoid or evade recognition of gain. Rev.Rul. 70–239 holds that because the federal income tax consequences of the three situations are the same, each partnership is considered to have transferred its assets and liabilities to a corporation in exchange for its stock under section 351 of the Internal Revenue Code, followed by a distribution of the stock to the partners in liquidation of the partnership.

LAW AND ANALYSIS

Section 351(a) of the Code provides that no gain or loss will be recognized if property is transferred to a corporation by one or more persons solely in exchange for stock * * * in such corporation and immediately after the exchange such person or persons are in control (as defined in section 368(c)) of the corporation.

Section 1.351–1(a)(1) of the Income Tax Regulations provides that, as used in section 351 of the Code, the phrase "one or more persons" includes individuals, trusts, estates, partnerships, associations, companies, or corporations. To be in control of the transferee corporation, such person or persons must own immediately after the transfer stock possessing at least 80 percent of the total combined voting power of all classes of stock entitled to vote and at least 80 percent of the total number of shares of all other classes of stock of such corporation.

Section 358(a) of the Code provides that in the case of an exchange to which section 351 applies, the basis of the property permitted to be received under such section without the recognition of gain or loss will be the same as that of the property exchanged, decreased by the amount of any money received by the taxpayer.

Section 358(d) of the Code provides that where, as part of the consideration to the taxpayer, another party to the exchange assumed a liability of the taxpayer or acquired from the taxpayer property subject to a liability, such assumption or acquisition (in the amount of the liability) will, for purposes of section 358, be treated as money received by the taxpayer on the exchange.

Section 362(a) of the Code provides that a corporation's basis in property acquired in a transaction to which section 351 applies will be the same as it would be in the hands of the transferor.

Under section 708(b)(1)(A) of the Code, a partnership is terminated if no part of any business, financial operation, or venture of the partnership continues to be carried on by any of its partners in a partnership. Under section 708(b)(1)(B), a partnership terminates if within a 12–month period there is a sale or exchange of 50 percent or more of the total interest in partnership capital and profits.

Section 732(b) of the Code provides that the basis of property other than money distributed by a partnership in a liquidation of a partner's interest shall be an amount equal to the adjusted basis of the partner's interest in the partnership reduced by any money distributed. Section 732(c) of the Code provides rules for the allocation of a partner's basis in a partnership interest among the assets received in a liquidating distribution.

Section 735(b) of the Code provides that a partner's holding period for property received in a distribution from a partnership (other than with respect to certain inventory items defined in section 751(d)(2)) includes the partnership's holding period, as determined under section 1223, with respect to such property.

Section 1223(1) of the Code provides that where property received in an exchange acquires the same basis, in whole or in part, as the property surrendered in the exchange, the holding period of the property received includes the holding period of the property surrendered to the extent such surrendered property was a capital asset or property described in section 1231. Under section 1223(2), the holding period of a taxpayer's property, however acquired, includes the period during which the property was held by any other person if that property has the same basis, in whole or in part, in the taxpayer's hands as it would have in the hands of such other person.

Section 741 of the Code provides that in the case of a sale or exchange of an interest in a partnership, gain or loss shall be recognized to the transferor partner. Such gain or loss shall be considered as a gain or loss from the sale or exchange of a capital asset, except as otherwise provided in section 751.

Section 751(a) of the Code provides that the amount of money or the fair value of property received by a transferor partner in exchange for all or part of such partner's interest in the partnership attributable to unrealized receivables of the partnership, or to inventory items of the partnership that have appreciated substantially in value, shall be considered as an amount realized from the sale or exchange of property other than a capital asset.

Section 752(a) of the Code provides that any increase in a partner's share of the liabilities of a partnership, or any increase in a partner's individual liabilities by reason of the assumption by the partner of partnership liabilities, will be considered as a contribution of money by such partner to the partnership.

Section 752(b) of the Code provides that any decrease in a partner's share of the liabilities of a partnership, or any decrease in a partner's individual liabilities by reason of the assumption by the partnership of such individual liabilities, will be considered as a distribution of money to the partner by the partnership. Under section 733(1) of the Code, the basis of a partner's interest in the partnership is reduced by the amount of money received in a distribution that is not in liquidation of the partnership.

Section 752(d) of the Code provides that in the case of a sale or exchange of an interest in a partnership, liabilities shall be treated in the same manner as liabilities in connection with the sale or exchange of property not associated with partnerships.

The premise in Rev.Rul. 70–239 that the federal income tax consequences of the three situations described therein would be the same, without regard to which of the three transactions was entered into, is incorrect. As described below, depending on the format chosen for the transfer to a controlled corporation, the basis and holding periods of the various assets received by the corporation and the basis and holding periods of the stock received by the former partners can vary.

Additionally, Rev.Rul. 70–239 raises questions about potential adverse tax consequences to taxpayers in certain cases involving collapsible corporations defined in section 341 of the Code, personal holding companies described in section 542, small business corporations defined in section 1244, and electing small business corporations defined in section 1371. Recognition of the three possible methods to incorporate a partnership will enable taxpayers to avoid the above potential pitfalls and will facilitate flexibility with respect to the basis and holding periods of the assets received in the exchange.

HOLDING

Rev.Rul. 70–239 no longer represents the Service's position. The Service's current position is set forth below, and for each situation, the methods described and the underlying assumptions and purposes must be satisfied for the conclusions of this revenue ruling to be applicable.

Situation 1

Under section 351 of the Code, gain or loss is not recognized by *X* on the transfer by *X* of all its assets to *R* in exchange for *R*'s stock and the assumption by *R* of *X*'s liabilities.

Under section 362(a) of the Code, *R*'s basis in the assets received from *X* equals their basis to *X* immediately before their transfer to *R*. Under section 358(a), the basis to *X* of the stock received from *R* is the same as the basis to *X* of the assets transferred to *R*, reduced by the liabilities assumed by *R*, which assumption is treated as a payment of money to *X* under section 358(d). In addition, the assumption by *R* of *X*'s liabilities decreased each partner's share of the partnership liabilities, thus, decreasing the basis of each partner's partnership interest pursuant to sections 752 and 733.

On distribution of the stock to *X*'s partners, *X* terminated under section 708(b)(1)(A) of the Code. Pursuant to section 732(b), the basis of the stock distributed to the partners in liquidation of their partnership interests is, with respect to each partner, equal to the adjusted basis of the partner's interest in the partnership.

Under section 1223(1) of the Code, *X*'s holding period for the stock received in the exchange includes its holding period in the capital assets and section 1231 assets transferred (to the extent that the stock was received in exchange for such assets). To the extent the stock was received in exchange for neither capital nor section 1231 assets, *X*'s holding period for such stock begins on the day following the date of the exchange. See Rev.Rul. 70–598, 1970–2 C.B. 168. Under section 1223(2), *R*'s holding period in the assets transferred to it includes *X*'s holding period. When *X* distributed the *R* stock to its partners, under sections 735(b) and 1223, the partners' holding periods included *X*'s holding period of the stock. Furthermore, such distribution will not violate the control requirement of section 368(c) of the Code.

Situation 2

On the transfer of all of *Y*'s assets to its partners, *Y* terminated under section 708(b)(1)(A) of the Code, and, pursuant to section 732(b), the basis of the assets (other than money) distributed to the partners in liquidation of their partnership interests in *Y* was, with respect to each partner, equal to the adjusted basis of the partner's interest in *Y*, reduced by the money distributed. Under section 752, the decrease in *Y*'s liabilities resulting from the transfer to *Y*'s partners was offset by the partners' corresponding assumption of such liabilities so that the net effect on the basis of each partner's interest in *Y*, with respect to the liabilities transferred, was zero.

Under section 351 of the Code, gain or loss is not recognized by *Y*'s former partners on the transfer to *S* in exchange for its stock and the assumption of *Y*'s liabilities, of the assets of *Y* received by *Y*'s partners in liquidation of *Y*.

Under section 358(a) of the Code, the basis to the former partners of *Y* in the stock received from *S* is the same as the section 732(b) basis to the former partners of *Y* in the assets received in liquidation of *Y* and transferred to *S*, reduced by the liabilities assumed by *S*, which assumption is treated as a payment of money to the partners under section 358(d).

Under section 362(a) of the Code, *S*'s basis in the assets received from *Y*'s former partners equals their basis to the former partners as determined under section 732(c) immediately before the transfer to *S*.

Under section 735(b) of the Code, the partners' holding periods for the assets distributed to them by *Y* includes *Y*'s holding period. Under section 1223(1), the partners' holding periods for the stock received in the exchange includes the partners' holding periods in the capital assets and section 1231 assets transferred to *S* (to the extent that the stock was received in exchange for such assets). However, to the extent that the stock received was in exchange for neither capital nor section 1231 assets, the holding period of the stock began on the day following the date of the exchange. Under section 1223(2), *S*'s holding period of the *Y* assets received in the exchange includes the partner's holding periods.

Situation 3

Under section 351 of the Code, gain or loss is not recognized by *Z*'s partners on the transfer of the partnership interests to *T* in exchange for *T*'s stock.

On the transfer of the partnership interests to the corporation, *Z* terminated under section 708(b)(1)(A) of the Code.

Under section 358(a) of the Code, the basis to the partners of *Z* of the stock received from *T* in exchange for their partnership interests equals the basis of their partnership interests transferred to *T*, reduced by *Z*'s liabilities assumed by *T*, the release from which is treated as a payment of money to *Z*'s partners under sections 752(d) and 358(d).

T's basis for the assets received in the exchange equals the basis of the partners in their partnership interests allocated in accordance with section 732(c). *T*'s holding period includes *Z*'s holding period in the assets.

Under section 1223(1) of the Code, the holding period of the *T* stock received by the former partners of *Z* includes each respective partner's holding period for the partnership interest transferred, except that the holding period of the *T* stock that was received by the partners of *Z* in exchange for their interests in section 751 assets of *Z* that are neither capital assets nor section 1231 assets begins on the day following the date of the exchange.

* * *

NOTE

Revenue Ruling 84–111 announces that for tax purposes the Service will respect the form adopted to incorporate a partnership. But what if the incorporation does not follow one of the patterns described in Revenue Ruling 84–111? For example, some states have laws that permit the conversion of a partnership into a corporation without the actual transfer of the partnership's assets or interests. How should the basis and holding period issues be sorted out in that type of incorporation? In Revenue Ruling 2004–59,[1] the Service analogizes an incorporation under such a statute to the situation where a partnership elects to be classified as a corporation for federal tax purposes. Thus, the transaction is taxed like Situation 1 in Revenue Ruling 84–111—i.e., the partnership is deemed to contribute all of its assets and liabilities to the corporation for stock and immediately thereafter, the partnership liquidates by distributing the stock to its partners.[2]

PROBLEM

The AC partnership has the following balance sheet:

Assets	**A.B.**	**F.M.V.**	**Partners' Capital**	**A.B.**	**F.M.V.**
Inventory	$ 80,000	$100,000	A	$ 60,000	$100,000
Capital Asset	40,000	100,000	C	100,000	100,000
	$120,000	$200,000		$160,000	$200,000

The difference between the partnership's aggregate inside basis in its assets and the partners' outside bases in their interests is attributable to the fact that C purchased her interest from B three years ago. For convenience, assume that the balance sheet remained unchanged over that period of time.

A and C wish to incorporate the partnership. Several alternative forms of incorporation are available: (1) the partnership could distribute its assets in complete liquidation, and A and C could transfer those assets to the corporation in exchange for its stock; (2) A and C could transfer their partnership interests to the corporation in exchange for its stock and the corporation would in essence liquidate the partnership; or (3) the partnership could transfer its assets to the corporation in return for stock and the partnership then could liquidate, distributing the stock to A and C.

(a) Consider the tax consequences of each alternative approach to incorporation of the partnership. See §§ 351, 358, 362.

(b) Does Revenue Ruling 84–111 correctly conclude that the results are different?

c. PARTNERSHIP MERGERS AND DIVISIONS

Code: § 708(b)(2)

Partnership Mergers. Section 708(b)(2)(A) provides that if two or more partnerships merge or consolidate into one partnership, the resulting

1. 2004–2 C.B. 1050.

2. See Reg. § 301.7701–3(g)(1)(i).

partnership is considered the continuation of the merging or consolidating partnership whose members own an interest of more than 50 percent in the capital and profits of the resulting partnership.[1] When partnerships merge or combine, the transaction may take one of three forms: (1) the terminated partnership may transfer its assets and liabilities to the resulting partnership in exchange for a partnership interest which is distributed to the partners of the terminated partnership (assets-over form); (2) the terminating partnership may liquidate by distributing its assets and liabilities to its partners who then contribute the assets and liabilities to the resulting partnership (assets-up form); or (3) the partners in the terminating partnership may transfer their partnership interests to the resulting partnership in exchange for interests in that partnership, and the terminating partnership liquidates into the resulting partnership (interest-over form).[2]

The tax results of a merger of partnerships may vary depending upon the form selected for the transaction. For example, the adjusted basis of assets contributed to the resulting partnership may vary depending upon the form of transaction selected when the partners' aggregate outside bases do not equal the terminating partnership's inside basis. In an assets-over transaction, the resulting partnership's basis in the assets will be the same as the terminating partnership's basis under Section 723. In contrast, in an assets-up transaction the adjusted basis of the assets will first be determined under Section 732 on the liquidation of the terminating partnership and then under Section 723 on the contribution to the resulting partnership.

The regulations under Section 708 provide partners with a great deal of flexibility when they merge partnerships. Under those regulations, the form of the merger will be respected if the partners select the assets-over or assets-up form for the transaction.[3] If the merger is accomplished without undertaking a particular form or takes an interest-over form, the merger is treated as undertaking the assets-over form for federal tax purposes.[4]

1. If the resulting partnership can be considered a continuation of more than one partnership under this rule, it is considered a continuation of the partnership contributing the assets with the greatest fair market value (net of liabilities), unless the Service permits otherwise. If the members of none of the merging or consolidated partnerships have an interest of more than 50 percent in the capital and profits of the resulting partnership, all of the merged or consolidated partnerships are terminated, and a new partnership results. Reg. § 1.708–1(c)(1).

2. A similar choice is presented when partners decide to incorporate a partnership. See Rev. Rul. 84–111, at page 354 of the text; see also Preamble to Proposed Regulations on Partnership Mergers and Divisions (hereinafter "Preamble"), 2000–1 C.B. 455.

3. Reg. § 1.708–1(c)(3).

4. Reg. § 1.708–1(c)(3)(i). The assets-over form is selected for an interest-over transaction to avoid application of Sections 704(c) and 737. Since the resulting partnership receives all of the partnership interests in the terminated partnership in an interest-over transaction, it is the sole member and would be deemed to receive the assets (a partnership cannot have one partner), thereby potentially bringing Sections 704(c) and 737 into play. Characterization of an interest-over merger as an assets-over transaction avoids this potential problem. Preamble.

Two special rules relating to mergers of partnerships deserve a brief mention. The regulations provide that increases and decreases in partnership liabilities associated with a merger or consolidation are netted by the partners in the terminating partnership and the resulting partnership to determine the effect of the merger under Section 752.[5] This rule prevents the terminating partnership from recognizing gain under section 752 when it becomes a momentary partner in the resulting partnership in an assets-over transaction.[6] Another potential problem is raised if a partner in the terminating partnership does not want to become a partner in the resulting partnership and wishes to receive money or property instead of a partnership interest. If to facilitate the buyout, the resulting partnership transfers money or other consideration to the terminating partnership in addition to the resulting partnership interests in an assets-over transaction, the terminating partnership could be treated as selling part of its property under Section 707(a)(2)(B).[7] The regulations, however, provide that the partner's sale of the interest will be respected as a sale if the merger agreement (or similar document) specifies (1) that the resulting partnership is purchasing an interest from a particular partner in the merging partnership, and (2) the consideration that is transferred for each interest sold.[8]

Partnership Divisions. Section 708(b)(2)(B) provides that if a partnership divides into two or more partnerships, a resulting partnership shall be considered a continuation of the prior partnership if members of the resulting partnership had a more than 50 percent interest in the capital and profits of the prior partnership.[9] Partnership divisions, like mergers, may be accomplished using either an assets-over or assets-up form. The regulations respect for federal tax purposes whichever of these two forms that is selected for the transaction.[10] If, however, the division takes place without a form or does not employ the assets-up form, it will be characterized under the assets-over form for federal tax purposes.[11]

Application of the Mixing–Bowl Rules. The operation of the mixing bowl rules, Sections 704(c)(1)(B) and 737, is an important issue when partnerships merge or divide. How will preexisting built-in gains and losses be treated? Will a merger trigger the beginning of a new seven-year period under the mixing bowl rules? Revenue Ruling 2004–43,[12] which follows, expresses the Service's views on how the mixing bowl rules apply to a partnership merger following the assets-order form. When it was issued,

5. Reg. § 1.752–1(f); see Reg. § 1.752–1(g) Example 2.

6. Preamble, supra note 2.

7. Id.

8. Reg. § 1.708–1(c)(4). The resulting partnership and its partners thus inherit the selling partner's capital account and Section 704(c) liability. If the terminating partnership has a Section 754 election in effect, the resulting partnership will have a special basis adjustment under Section 743. Preamble, supra note 2.

9. Any other resulting partnership is considered a new partnership. Reg. § 1.708–1(d)(1).

10. Reg. § 1.708–1(d)(3). The regulations permit the momentary ownership by the prior partnership of all interests in the new partnership when the assets-over form is used. Preamble, supra note 2.

11. Reg. 1.708–1(d)(3)(i).

12. 2004–1 C.B. 842.

Revenue Ruling 2004–43 was controversial. The Service later revoked the ruling but announced that it would issue regulations implementing its principles.[13] Proposed regulations were issued in 2007,[14] and those regulations are consistent with Revenue Ruling 2004–43. So the ruling still provides the best guidance that is available on the IRS's view of the issues.[15] Read it carefully to see if you agree with the government's analysis.

A partnership division also potentially raises issues under Sections 704(c)(1)(B) and 737. In a division following the assets-up form, the distribution of partnership assets to the partners could trigger either of those sections. In an assets-over division, the partnership interest in the resulting partnership is treated as Section 704(c) property to the extent that the interest is received in exchange for Section 704(c) property.[16] Thus, the distribution of interests in the resulting partnership will trigger Section 704(b)(1)(B) to the extent that interests are received by partners other than the partner who contributed the Section 704(c) property. Section 737 also may be triggered if a partner who contributed Section 704(c) property receives an interest in the resulting partnership that is not attributable to Section 704(c) property.[17]

Revenue Ruling 2004–43

2004–1 Cum. Bull. 842.

ISSUES

1) Does § 704(c)(1)(B) of the Internal Revenue Code apply to § 704(c) gain or loss that is created in an assets-over partnership merger?

2) For purposes of § 737(b), does net precontribution gain include § 704(c) gain or loss that is created in an assets-over partnership merger?

13. Rev. Rul. 2005–10, 2005–1 C.B. 492.

14. REG–144397–05 (Aug. 22, 2007). For analysis of the proposed regulations, see Susan Kalinka, "Proposed Regulations Would Provide Guidance, but Add Complexity for Making Code Sec. 704(c) Allocations After an Assets-over Merger–Part I," 86 Taxes 11 (2008); Richard Lipton, "Proposed Regulations on Built–In Gain and Partnership Mergers: The Service Refuses to Budge," 107 J.Tax'n 324 (2007).

15. The proposed regulations provide exceptions for situations where the ownership of the two merged partnerships is identical or the difference in ownership is de minimis (97% of ownership is the same). See Prop. Reg §§ 1.704–4(c)(4)(ii)(E), 1.737–2(b)(1)(ii)(E).

16. Reg. 1.704–4(d)(1).

17. Preamble, supra note 2. The Section 737 regulations contain one exception for a partnership division. Section 737 does not apply when a partnership transfers all of the Section 704(c) property contributed by a partner to a second partnership, followed by a distribution of an interest in the second partnership in complete liquidation of the interest of the partner who originally contributed the section 704(c) property. Reg. § 1.737–2(b)(2). No similar rule is available under Section 704(c)(1)(B). The Service has asked for comments on whether the exceptions to Sections 704(c)(1)(B) and 737 should be expanded in certain circumstances relating to divisive transactions. Preamble, supra note 2.

FACTS

Situation 1. On January 1, 2004, A contributes Asset 1, with a basis of $200x and a fair market value of $300x to partnership AB in exchange for a 50 percent interest. On the same date, B contributes $300x of cash to AB in exchange for a 50 percent interest. Also on January 1, 2004, C contributes Asset 2, with a basis of $100x and a fair market value of $200x to partnership CD in exchange for a 50 percent interest. D contributes $200x of cash to CD in exchange for a 50 percent interest.

On January 1, 2006, AB and CD undertake an assets-over partnership merger in which AB is the continuing partnership and CD is the terminating partnership. At the time of the merger, AB's only assets are Asset 1, with a fair market value of $900x, and $300x in cash, and CD's only assets are Asset 2, with a fair market value of $600x and $200x in cash. After the merger, the partners have capital and profits interests in AB as follows: A, 30 percent; B, 30 percent; C, 20 percent; and D, 20 percent.

The partnership agreements for AB and CD provide that the partners' capital accounts will be determined and maintained in accordance with § 1.704–1(b)(2)(iv) of the Income Tax Regulations, distributions in liquidation of the partnership (or any partner's interest) will be made in accordance with the partners' positive capital account balances, and any partner with a deficit balance in the partner's capital account following the liquidation of the partner's interest must restore that deficit to the partnership (as set forth in § 1.704–1(b)(2)(ii)(b)(2) and (3)). AB and CD both have provisions in their partnership agreements requiring the revaluation of partnership property upon the entry of a new partner. AB would not be treated as an investment company (within the meaning of § 351) if it were incorporated. Neither partnership holds any unrealized receivables or inventory for purposes of § 751. AB and CD do not have a § 754 election in place. Asset 1 and Asset 2 are nondepreciable capital assets.

On January 1, 2012, AB has the same assets that it had after the merger. Each asset has the same value that it had at the time of the merger. On this date, AB distributes Asset 2 to A in liquidation of A's interest in AB.

Situation 2. The facts are the same as in Situation 1, except that on January 1, 2012, Asset 1 has a value of $275x, and AB distributes Asset 1 to C in liquidation of C's interest in AB.

LAW

Under § 704(b) and the regulations thereunder, allocations of a partnership's items of income, gain, loss, deduction, or credit provided for in the partnership agreement will be respected if the allocations have substantial economic effect. Allocations that fail to have substantial economic effect will be reallocated according to the partners' interests in the partnership.

Section 1.704–1(b)(2)(iv)(*f*) provides that a partnership may, upon the occurrence of certain events (including the contribution of money to the partnership by a new or existing partner), increase or decrease the partners' capital accounts to reflect a revaluation of the partnership property.

Section 1.704–1(b)(2)(iv)(*g*) provides that, to the extent a partnership's property is reflected on the books of the partnership at a book value that differs from the adjusted tax basis, the substantial economic effect requirements apply to the allocations of book items. Section 704(c) and § 1.704–1(b)(4)(i) govern the partners' distributive shares of tax items.

Section 1.704–1(b)(4)(i) provides that if partnership property is, under § 1.704–1(b)(2)(iv)(*f*), properly reflected in the capital accounts of the partners and on the books of the partnership at a book value that differs from the adjusted tax basis of the property, then depreciation, depletion, amortization, and gain or loss, as computed for book purposes, with respect to the property will be greater or less than the depreciation, depletion, amortization, and gain or loss, as computed for federal tax purposes, with respect to the property. In these cases the capital accounts of the partners are required to be adjusted solely for allocations of the book items to the partners (see § 1.704–1(b)(2)(iv)(*g*)), and the partners' shares of the corresponding tax items are not independently reflected by further adjustments to the partners' capital accounts. Thus, separate allocations of these tax items cannot have economic effect under § 1.704–1(b)(2)(ii)(*b*)(*1*), and the partners' distributive shares of tax items must (unless governed by § 704(c)) be determined in accordance with the partners' interests in the partnership. These tax items must be shared among the partners in a manner that takes account of the variation between the adjusted tax basis of the property and its book value in the same manner as variations between the adjusted tax basis and fair market value of property contributed to the partnership are taken into account in determining the partners' shares of tax items under § 704(c).

Section 704(c)(1)(A) provides that income, gain, loss, and deduction with respect to property contributed to the partnership by a partner shall be shared among the partners so as to take account of the variation between the basis of the property to the partnership and its fair market value at the time of contribution.

Section 1.704–3(a)(2) provides that, except as provided in § 1.704–3(e)(2) and (3), § 704(c) and § 1.704–3 apply on a property-by-property basis.

Section 1.704–3(a)(3)(i) provides that property contributed to a partnership is § 704(c) property if at the time of contribution its book value differs from the contributing partner's adjusted tax basis. For purposes of § 1.704–3, book value is determined as contemplated by § 1.704–1(b). Therefore, book value is equal to fair market value at the time of contribution and is subsequently adjusted for cost recovery and other events that affect the basis of the property.

Section 1.704–3(a)(3)(ii) provides that the built-in gain on § 704(c) property is the excess of the property's book value over the contributing partner's adjusted tax basis upon contribution. The built-in gain is thereafter reduced by decreases in the difference between the property's book value and adjusted tax basis.

Section 1.704–3(a)(6) provides that the principles of § 1.704–3 also apply to "reverse § 704(c) allocations" which result from revaluations of partnership property pursuant to § 1.704–1(b)(2)(iv)(*f*).

Section 1.704–3(a)(7) provides that, if a contributing partner transfers a partnership interest, built-in gain or loss must be allocated to the transferee partner as it would have been allocated to the transferor partner. If the contributing partner transfers a portion of the partnership interest, the share of built-in gain or loss proportionate to the interest transferred must be allocated to the transferee partner.

Section 704(c)(1)(B) provides that if any property contributed to the partnership by a partner is distributed (directly or indirectly) by the partnership (other than to the contributing partner) within seven years of being contributed: (i) the contributing partner shall be treated as recognizing gain or loss (as the case may be) from the sale of the property in an amount equal to the gain or loss which would have been allocated to the partner under § 704(c)(1)(A) by reason of the variation described in § 704(c)(1)(A) if the property had been sold at its fair market value at the time of the distribution; (ii) the character of the gain or loss shall be determined by reference to the character of the gain or loss which would have resulted if the property had been sold by the partnership to the distributee; and (iii) appropriate adjustments shall be made to the adjusted basis of the contributing partner's interest in the partnership and to the adjusted basis of the property distributed to reflect any gain or loss recognized under § 704(c)(1)(B).

Section 1.704–4(c)(4) provides that § 704(c)(1)(B) and § 1.704–4 do not apply to a transfer by a partnership (transferor partnership) of all of its assets and liabilities to a second partnership (transferee partnership) in an exchange described in § 721, followed by a distribution of the interest in the transferee partnership in liquidation of the transferor partnership as part of the same plan or arrangement. Section 1.704–4(c)(4) also provides that a subsequent distribution of § 704(c) property by the transferee partnership to a partner of the transferee partnership is subject to § 704(c)(1)(B) to the same extent that a distribution by the transferor partnership would have been subject to § 704(c)(1)(B).

Section 1.704–4(d)(2) provides that the transferee of all or a portion of the partnership interest of a contributing partner is treated as the contributing partner for purposes of § 704(c)(1)(B) and § 1.704–4 to the extent of the share of built-in gain or loss allocated to the transferee partner.

Section 708(a) provides that, for purposes of subchapter K, an existing partnership shall be considered as continuing if it is not terminated.

Section 708(b)(2)(A) provides that in the case of the merger or consolidation of two or more partnerships, the resulting partnership shall, for purposes of § 708, be considered the continuation of any merging or consolidating partnership whose members own an interest of more than 50 percent in the capital and profits of the resulting partnership.

Section 1.708–1(c)(3)(i) provides that when two or more partnerships merge or consolidate into one partnership under the applicable jurisdictional law without undertaking a form for the merger or consolidation, or undertake a form for the merger or consolidation that is not described in § 1.708–1(c)(3)(ii), any merged or consolidated partnership that is considered terminated under § 1.708–1(c)(1) is treated as undertaking the assets-over form for federal income tax purposes. Under the assets-over form, the merged or consolidated partnership that is considered terminated under § 1.708–1(c)(1) contributes all of its assets and liabilities to the resulting partnership in exchange for an interest in the resulting partnership, and immediately thereafter, the terminated partnership distributes interests in the resulting partnership to its partners in liquidation of the terminated partnership.

Section 737(a) provides that, in the case of any distribution by a partnership to a partner, the partner shall be treated as recognizing gain in an amount equal to the lesser of (1) the excess (if any) of (A) the fair market value of property (other than money) received in the distribution over (B) the adjusted basis of the partner's interest in the partnership immediately before the distribution reduced (but not below zero) by the amount of money received in the distribution, or (2) the net precontribution gain of the partner. Gain recognized under the preceding sentence shall be in addition to any gain recognized under § 731. The character of the gain shall be determined by reference to the proportionate character of the net precontribution gain.

Section 737(b) provides that for purposes of § 737, the term "net precontribution gain" means the net gain (if any) which would have been recognized by the distributee partner under § 704(c)(1)(B) if all property which (1) had been contributed to the partnership by the distributee partner within seven years of the distribution, and (2) is held by the partnership immediately before the distribution, had been distributed by the partnership to another partner.

Section 1.737–1(c)(1) provides that the distributee partner's net precontribution gain is the net gain (if any) that would have been recognized by the distributee partner under § 704(c)(1)(B) and § 1.704–4 if all property that had been contributed to the partnership by the distributee partner within seven years of the distribution and is held by the partnership immediately before the distribution had been distributed by the partnership to another partner other than a partner who owns, directly or indirectly, more than 50 percent of the capital or profits interest in the partnership.

Section 1.737–1(c)(2)(iii) provides that the transferee of all or a portion of a contributing partner's partnership interest succeeds to the transferor's net precontribution gain, if any, in an amount proportionate to the interest transferred.

Section 1.737–2(b)(1) provides that § 737 and § 1.737–2 do not apply to a transfer by a partnership (transferor partnership) of all of its assets and liabilities to a second partnership (transferee partnership) in an exchange described in § 721, followed by a distribution of the interest in the transferee partnership in liquidation of the transferor partnership as part of the same plan or arrangement.

Section 1.737–2(b)(3) provides that a subsequent distribution of property by the transferee partnership to a partner of the transferee partnership that was formerly a partner of the transferor partnership is subject to § 737 to the same extent that a distribution from the transferor partnership would have been subject to § 737.

ANALYSIS

Section 1.704–4(c)(4) describes the effect of an assets-over partnership merger on pre-existing § 704(c) gain or loss for purposes of § 704(c)(1)(B). Under § 1.704–4(c)(4), if the transferor partnership in an assets-over merger holds contributed property with § 704(c) gain or loss, the seven year period in § 704(c)(1)(B) does not restart with respect to that gain or loss as a result of the merger. Section 1.704–4(c)(4) does not prevent the creation of new § 704(c) gain or loss when assets are contributed by one partnership to another partnership in an assets-over merger. Section 704(c)(1)(B) applies to this newly created § 704(c) gain or loss if the assets contributed in the merger are distributed to a partner other than the contributing partner (or its successor) within seven years of the merger.

Section 1.737–2(b)(1) and (3) describes the effect of an assets-over partnership merger on net precontribution gain that includes pre-existing § 704(c) gain or loss. Under § 1.737–2(b)(3), if the transferor partnership in an assets-over merger holds contributed property with § 704(c) gain or loss, the seven year period in § 737(b) does not restart with respect to that gain or loss as a result of the merger. Section 1.737–2(b)(3) does not prevent the creation of new § 704(c) gain or loss when assets are contributed by one partnership to another partnership in an assets-over merger. This gain or loss must be considered in determining the amount of net precontribution gain for purposes of § 737 if the continuing partnership distributes other property to the contributing partner (or its successor) within seven years of the merger.

Section 1.704–3(a)(6)(i) provides that the principles of § 1.704–3 apply to reverse § 704(c) allocations. In contrast, the regulations under § 704(c)(1)(B) and § 737 contain no similar rule requiring that the principles of § 704(c)(1)(B) and § 737 apply to reverse § 704(c) allocations. Under those regulations, § 704(c)(1)(B) and § 737 do not apply to reverse § 704(c) allocations.

In both of the situations described above, on the date of the partnership merger, CD contributes cash and Asset 2 to AB in exchange for an interest in AB. Immediately thereafter, CD distributes, in liquidation, interests in AB to C and D. Asset 2 has a basis of $100x and a fair market value of $600x upon contribution. Of the $500x of built in gain in Asset 2,

$100x is pre-existing § 704(c) gain attributable to C's contribution of Asset 2 to CD, and $400x is additional § 704(c) gain created as a result of the merger. As the transferees of CD's partnership interest in AB, C and D each succeed to one-half of CD's $400x of § 704(c) gain in Asset 2 (each $200x). Section 1.704–3(a)(7). Thus, C's share of § 704(c) gain is $300x, and D's share of § 704(c) gain is $200x.

The entry of CD as a new partner of AB causes partnership AB to revalue its property. When CD enters as a new partner of AB, Asset 1 has a basis of $200x and a fair market value of $900x. Of the $700x of built-in gain in Asset 1, $100x is pre-existing § 704(c) gain attributable to the contribution of Asset 1 by A. The revaluation results in the creation of $600x of reverse § 704(c) gain in Asset 1. This layer of reverse § 704(c) gain is shared equally by A and B ($300x each). Thus, A's share of § 704(c) gain is $400x, and B's share of § 704(c) gain is $300x. The calculation of § 704(c) gain in each asset is summarized in the following table.

	Adjusted Tax Basis	**Value on Date of Contribution**	**§ 704(c) Gain on Date of Contribution**	**Value on Date of Merger**	**§ 704(c) Gain Created by Merger**	**Total § 704(c) Gain After Merger**
Asset 1	$200x	$ 300x	$100x	$ 900x	$ 600x	$ 700x
Asset 2	$100x	$ 200x	$100x	$ 600x	$ 400x	$ 500x
Cash	$500x	$ 500x	$ 0x	$ 500x	$ 0x	$ 0x
Total	$800x	$1,000x	$200x	$2,000x	$1,000x	$1,200x

The partners' share of § 704(c) gain in each of AB's assets after the merger is summarized in the following table.

	A's Share of § 704(c) Gain	**B's Share of § 704(c) Gain**	**C's Share of § 704(c) Gain**	**D's Share of § 704(c) Gain**	**Total § 704(c) Gain**
Asset 1	$400x	$300x	$ 0x	$ 0x	$ 700x
Asset 2	$ 0x	$ 0x	$300x	$200x	$ 500x
Cash	$ 0x	$ 0x	$ 0x	$ 0x	$ 0x
Total	$400x	$300x	$300x	$200x	$1,200x

In Situation 1, the distribution of Asset 2 to A occurs more than seven years after the contribution of Asset 2 to CD. Therefore, § 704(c)(1)(B) does not apply to the $100x of pre-existing § 704(c) gain attributable to that contribution. However, the distribution of Asset 2 to A occurs within seven years of the contribution of Asset 2 by CD to AB. The contribution of Asset 2 by CD to AB creates § 704(c) gain of $400x. As the transferees of CD's partnership interest in AB, C and D each succeed to one-half of the $400x of § 704(c) gain created by the merger. Section 1.704–3(a)(7). Section 704(c)(1)(B) applies to that § 704(c) gain, causing C and D each to recognize $200x of gain.

The distribution of Asset 2 to A occurs more than seven years after the contribution of Asset 1 to AB, and A made no subsequent contributions to AB. Therefore, A's net precontribution gain for purposes of § 737(b) at the time of the distribution is zero. AB's $600x of reverse § 704(c) gain in Asset 1, resulting from a revaluation of AB's partnership property at the time of the merger, is not net precontribution gain. Accordingly, A will not recognize gain under § 737 as a result of the distribution of Asset 2.

In Situation 2, § 704(c)(1)(B) does not apply to the distribution by the continuing partnership of Asset 1 to C on January 1, 2012. The distribution of Asset 1 to C occurs more than seven years after the contribution of Asset 1 to AB, and § 704(c)(1)(B) does not apply to the reverse § 704(c) gain in Asset 1 resulting from a revaluation of AB's partnership property at the time of the merger. Accordingly, neither A nor B will recognize gain under § 704(c)(1)(B) as a result of the distribution of Asset 1 to C.

The distribution of Asset 1 to C occurs more than seven years after the contribution of Asset 2 to CD. Therefore, C's net precontribution gain at the time of the distribution does not include C's $100x of pre-existing § 704(c) gain attributable to that contribution. However, the distribution of Asset 1 to C occurs within seven years of the contribution of Asset 2 by CD to AB. The contribution of Asset 2 by CD to AB creates net precontribution gain of $400x. As the transferees of CD's partnership interest in AB, C and D each succeed to one-half of CD's $400x of net precontribution gain in Asset 2. Section 1.737–1(c)(2)(iii). Thus, C's portion of CD's net precontribution gain created by the merger is $200x. The excess of Asset 1's fair market value, $275x, over the adjusted tax basis of C's interest in AB immediately before the distribution, $100x, is $175x, which is less than C's $200x of net precontribution gain. Therefore, C will recognize $175x of capital gain under § 737 as a result of the distribution. Because no property is distributed to D and none of the property treated as contributed by D is distributed to another partner, D recognizes no gain under § 737 or § 704(c)(1)(B).

HOLDINGS

1) Section 704(c)(1)(B) applies to newly created § 704(c) gain or loss in property contributed by the transferor partnership to the continuing partnership in an assets-over partnership merger, but does not apply to newly created reverse § 704(c) gain or loss resulting from a revaluation of property in the continuing partnership.

2) For purposes of § 737(b), net precontribution gain includes newly created § 704(c) gain or loss in property contributed by the transferor partnership to the continuing partnership in an assets-over partnership merger, but does not include newly created reverse § 704(c) gain or loss resulting from a revaluation of property in the continuing partnership.

d. POLICY

The preceding sections of this chapter illustrate that partnership incorporations, mergers, and divisions may take a variety of forms. The basic policy question underlying the application of Subchapter K to these transactions is whether the form selected by the taxpayer for the transaction should be respected for tax purposes. Or, alternatively, should the tax law disregard the formal steps selected by the taxpayer, seek to determine the "substance" of the transaction, and tax it accordingly? The authorities governing these areas of partnership taxation adopt inconsistent answers to this "form versus substance" dichotomy. For example, in an incorporation of a partnership, Revenue Ruling 84–111 will respect the form selected for the transaction. Compare that approach to the taxation of partnership mergers and divisions where the rules vary as to when the form selected by the taxpayer will be respected and when a hypothetical construct will be applied to determine the tax results.

Remember also that the form utilized for a partnership restructuring may be influenced by nontax factors. Restrictions in the partnership agreement, protection of the partners from personal liability, limitations included in credit agreements and debt covenants, the administrative burden of required filings in an actual asset transfer, and regulatory restrictions on transfers of assets such as permits and licenses, may all be factors in selecting the actual steps undertaken to accomplish the transaction. These "real world" concerns and the lack of coherence in the current tax regime, have led one scholar to advocate for a new approach to the taxation of partnership incorporations, mergers, and divisions. As you read the proposal, consider whether the suggested "restructuring election" would be an improvement over the present approach for taxing these transactions.

Excerpt from Heather M. Field, "Fiction, Form, and Substance in Subchapter K: Taxing Partnership Mergers, Divisions, and Incorporations"

44 San Diego L. Rev. 259, 296–297 (2007).

* * *

IV. Picking a Side: A Proposal to Allow Taxpayers to Elect a Fiction

A. Choosing Fiction

1. The Partnership Restructuring Election—A Proposal

In order to address the issues raised in Part III, partnerships should be allowed to make an explicit election of which construct applies to their merger, division, or incorporation, regardless of the actual form of the transaction.[126] The election, which is referred to in this Article as the "Partnership Restructuring Election," would work as follows.

126. In the context of formless incorporations, others have similarly suggested allowing partnerships to elect the tax construct applicable.

> Why is the latitude available to taxpayers on actual conversions not extended to actual conversions involving "formless" incorporations as well as elective conversions? . . .
>
> . . . Parties should decide their preferred tax treatment, they should agree to report the transactions consistently both for themselves and the partnership, and the IRS should accord their choice controlling governance.

Philip F. Postlewaite, *The Transmogrification of Subchapter K*, 83 TAXES 189, 201 (2005). *But see* Banoff, *supra* note 3 (general-

Taxpayers would implement the form of merger, division, or incorporation most preferable from a business perspective. Regardless of the form of transaction chosen, the entities involved in the transaction could elect which construct would apply to the transaction for federal income tax purposes.[127] For incorporations and mergers, the parties would choose among the assets-over, assets-up, and interests-over constructs; for divisions, they would choose between the assets-over and assets-up constructs.[128] If no election were made, the assets-over construct would apply as a default. The merger buyout rule would be made available in conjunction with any merger construct.

In order to make the election of construct, the entities involved in the transaction would jointly file a form of transaction election with the IRS no later than the due date for the terminated partnership's return for the year of the transaction, including extensions.[129] The Partnership Restructuring Election would be required to be filed jointly by the relevant entities,[130] which in an incorporation are the pre-incorporation partnership and the post-incorporation corporation, in a merger are the terminated partnership and the resulting partnership, and in a division are the divided partnership (or if none, the prior partnership) and the recipient partnership (or if none, the resulting partnerships). Like many other partnership tax elections,[131] this election would be made at the partnership, and not the partner, level; however, partners are, of course, free to incorporate into the partnership agreement limitations on the partnership's ability to make certain tax elections without partner consent. The partnerships would be bound to report the transaction in a manner consistent with the election, including on the Schedule K–1s that the partnership issues to the partners. Accordingly, as long as the partners report their income in a manner consistent with the K–1s that they receive, the partners would effectively be bound by the election as well.

ly endorsing an approach that adheres to form).

127. Note that there are a number of potential structures pursuant to which a merger, division, or incorporation can be effectuated, but in an effort to ensure that this proposal is sufficiently simple and administrable, this proposal suggests that taxpayers only have a choice of three constructs. That said, taxpayers are still free to effectuate transactions in any manner that they see fit, as it is only for purposes of the tax analysis that they are limited to these three choices.

128. Recall that for divisions, there is no interests-over construct. ** *

129. This is consistent with the due dates for Section 754 elections (elections made with respect to the tax consequences of sales or exchanges of interests in partnerships). See, e.g., Treas. Reg. § 1.754–1(b) (as amended in 2000).

130. This requirement is analogous to the requirement imposed in connection with the making of a Section 338(h)(10) election. *See* Treas. Reg. § 1.338(h)(10)–1(c)(3) (as amended in 2006). In addition, requiring a joint filing obligates the relevant entities to agree to treat the transaction consistently, thereby avoiding the risk of government whipsaw.

131. *See, e.g.*, Treas. Reg. § 1.754–1 (as amended in 2000) (stating Section 754 elections are made by the partnership); AICPA Tax Division's P'ship Taxation Technical Res. Panel, *Partnership Elections Grid*, 36 TAX ADVISER 200 (2005) (detailing a number of partnership elections).

The current anti-abuse rule for mergers and divisions would remain in place and would be expanded to cover incorporations. This would give the IRS the ability to recast a transaction in accordance with its substance if the transaction is part of a larger series of transactions and the substance of the larger series of transactions is inconsistent with following the fiction elected.

* * *

2. Partnership Terminations Forced by Statute

Code: § 708(b)(1)(B). Skim §§ 721; 722; 723; 731; 732; 743(b); 755; 761(e)(1); 774(c).

Regulations: § 1.708–1(b)(2), (4), (5).

Introduction. A partnership is considered to continue for tax purposes if it is not "terminated," but termination does not result solely from the cessation of business activity. Section 708(b)(1)(B) provides that a partnership, other than an electing large partnership, is terminated if "within a 12–month period there is a sale or exchange of 50 percent or more of the total interest in partnership capital and profits."[1] The regulations make it clear that this requires a sale of different interests of 50 percent or more of partnership capital and profits within the period and not a sale of the same 25 percent interest twice.[2] Sales between partners are considered for purposes of the 50 percent test. The section does not apply, however, to dispositions by gift, inheritance or liquidation of a partnership interest.[3]

The regulations also prescribe the consequences of a Section 708(b)(1)(B) termination. A termination occurs on the date of the sale of an interest that puts sales at or over the 50 percent level,[4] and on that date the partnership year closes.[5] The regulations further provide that if a partnership is terminated by a sale or exchange of an interest, it is deemed to contribute all of its assets and liabilities to a new partnership in exchange for an interest in that new entity.[6] The terminated partnership is then deemed to liquidate by distributing interests in the new partnership to the purchasing partner and the other remaining partners, either for the continuation of the business of the new partnership or for its dissolution

1. The regulations provide that this requires a sale or exchange of 50 percent or more of the total interest in partnership capital plus 50 percent or more of the total interest in partnership profits. Reg. § 1.708–1(b)(2). Section 774(c) excludes electing large partnerships from application of Section 708(b)(1)(B).

2. Reg. § 1.708–1(b)(2).

3. Id. It also would appear that Section 708 is inapplicable to a charitable contribution of a partnership interest, at least if it is not converted into a part gift/part sale as a result of relief of the partner's share of liabilities. Changes of ownership as a result of contributions to capital also do not constitute a sale or exchange. Id. See Rev.Rul. 75–423, 1975–2 C.B. 260. However, corporate distributions of partnership interests are treated as exchanges of those interests for purposes of Section 708. I.R.C. § 761(e)(1).

4. Reg. § 1.708–1(b)(3)(ii).

5. Reg. § 1.708–1(b)(3).

6. Reg. § 1.708–1(b)(4).

and winding up.[7] Because the reconstituted partnership is treated as a new entity, it must make new elections relating to accounting methods, depreciation, and other matters.

In order to prevent an involuntary termination of a partnership resulting from a sale or exchange, many carefully drafted partnership agreements include a provision forbidding any sale or exchange that would cause a termination. If the partners balk at such a restriction, another technique to avoid a termination is for a selling partner to dispose of his interest over more than a 12 month period or to sell only a portion of his interest (e.g., in capital but not profits) and defer the sale of the remaining portion beyond the 12–month statutory window.

Collateral Consequences of a Section 708(b)(1)(B) Termination. The regulations go to great lengths to make a termination of a partnership under Section 708(b)(1)(B) as painless as possible from a tax perspective. First, the capital account of any transferee partner and the capital accounts of the other partners of the terminated partnership carry over to the new partnership and the constructive liquidation of the terminated partnership is disregarded in the maintenance and computation of the partners' capital accounts.[8] If the terminated partnership has a Section 754 election (including one made on its final return) in effect for the taxable year in which the sale occurs, the election applies to any incoming partner. Therefore, the bases of the partnership assets are adjusted pursuant to Sections 743 and 755 before the deemed contribution to the new partnership.[9] In addition, a partner with a special basis adjustment in property held by the terminated partnership continues to have the same special basis adjustment with respect to property deemed contributed to the new partnership, regardless of whether that partnership makes its own Section 754 election.[10] Subchapter K's "mixing bowl" provisions (Sections 704(c)(1)(B) and 737) are also applied with some mercy. Because a Section 708(b)(1)(B) termination does not result in a distribution of partnership properties to the partners, the mixing bowl rules do not apply to the deemed distribution of interests in the new partnership caused by the termination.[11] Also, the regulations say that a new seven-year period under Sections 704(c)(1)(B) and 737 does not begin with respect to the built-in gain and built-in loss property contributed to the new partnership.[12] However, a later distribution of Section 704(c) property by the new partnership is subject to both Sections 704(c)(1)(B)

7. Id.

8. Reg. §§ 1.704–1(b)(2)(iv)(*l*),–1(b)(5) Example 13(v). Because the termination and deemed contribution do not change capital accounts or the books of the partnership, the deemed contribution does not create new book/tax disparities under Section 704(c).

9. Reg. § 1.708–1(b)(5).

10. Reg. § 1.743–1(h)(1). Additionally, a downward inside basis adjustment could be required under Section 743(a) if the partnership has a substantial built-in loss.

11. Reg. §§ 1.704–4(c)(3); 1.737–2(a); see Reg. § 1.708–1(b)(4) Example.

12. Reg. §§ 1.704–4(a)(4)(ii); 1.737–2(a). The new partnership is not required to use the same method as the terminated partnership with respect to Section 704(c) property. Reg. § 1.704–3(a)(2).

and 737 to the same extent that a distribution by the terminated partnership would have been subject to those sections.[13]

Tiered Partnerships. The Section 708 regulations prescribe special rules for tiered partnerships. If the sale of an upper-tier partnership results in its termination, the upper-tier partnership is treated as exchanging its entire interest in the capital and profits of any lower-tier partnership.[14] This deemed exchange could terminate the lower-tier partnership or be combined with actual sales or exchanges of interests in the lower-tier partnership to cause a termination. But if a sale or exchange of an interest in an upper-tier partnership does not result in a termination, the transaction is not treated as a sale or exchange of a proportionate share of the upper-tier partnership's interest in the lower-tier partnership.[15]

Revenue Ruling 95–37

1995–1 Cum. Bull. 130.

ISSUES

(1) Do the federal income tax consequences described in Rev. Rul. 84–52, 1984–1 C.B. 157, apply to the conversion of an interest in a domestic partnership into an interest in a domestic limited liability company (LLC) that is classified as a partnership for federal tax purposes?

(2) Does the taxable year of the converting domestic partnership close with respect to all the partners or with respect to any partner?

(3) Does the resulting domestic LLC need to obtain a new taxpayer identification number?

LAW AND ANALYSIS

In Rev. Rul. 84–52, a general partnership formed under the Uniform Partnership Act of State M proposed to convert to a limited partnership under the Uniform Limited Partnership Act of State M. Rev. Rul. 84–52 generally holds that (1) under section 721 of the Internal Revenue Code, the conversion will not cause the partners to recognize gain or loss under sections 741 or 1001, (2) unless its business will not continue after the conversion, the partnership will not terminate under section 708 because the conversion is not treated as a sale or exchange for purposes of section 708, (3) if the partners' shares of partnership liabilities do not change, there will be no change in the adjusted basis of any partner's interest in the partnership, (4) if the partners' shares of partnership liabilities change and cause a deemed contribution of money to the partnership by a partner under section 752(a), then the adjusted basis of such a partner's interest will be increased under section 722 by the amount of the deemed contribution, (5) if the partners' shares of partnership liabilities change and cause a deemed distribution of money by the partnership to a partner under section

13. Reg. §§ 1.704–4(c)(3); 1.737–2(a).

14. Reg. § 1.708–1(b)(2).

15. Id.

752(b), then the basis of such a partner's interest will be reduced under section 733 (but not below zero) by the amount of the deemed distribution, and gain will be recognized by the partner under section 731 to the extent the deemed distribution exceeds the adjusted basis of the partner's interest in the partnership, and (6) under section 1223(*l*), there will be no change in the holding period of any partner's total interest in the partnership.

The conversion of an interest in a domestic partnership into an interest in domestic LLC that is classified as a partnership for federal tax purposes is treated as a partnership-to-partnership conversion that is subject to the principles of Rev. Rul. 84–52.

Section 706(c)(1) provides that, except in the case of a termination of a partnership and except as provided in section 706(c)(2), the taxable year of a partnership does not close as the result of the death of a partner, the entry of a new partner, the liquidation of a partner's interest in the partnership, or the sale or exchange of a partner's interest in the partnership.

Section 706(c)(2)(A)(i) provides that the taxable year of a partnership closes with respect to a partner who sells or exchanges the partner's entire interest in a partnership. Section 706(c)(2)(A)(ii) provides that the taxable year of a partnership closes with respect to a partner whose interest is liquidated, except that the taxable year of a partnership with respect to a partner who dies does not close prior to the end of the partnership's taxable year. [Section 706(c)(2) has been amended with respect to a partner who dies. Ed.]

In the present case, the conversion of an interest in a domestic partnership into an interest in a domestic LLC that is classified as a partnership for federal tax purposes does not cause a termination under section 708. See Rev. Rul. 84–52. Moreover, because each partner in a converting domestic partnership continues to hold an interest in the resulting domestic LLC, the conversion is not a sale, exchange, or liquidation of the converting partner's entire partnership interest for purposes of section 706(c)(2)(A). See Rev. Rul. 86–101, 1986–2 C.B. 94 (the taxable year of a partnership does not close with respect to a general partner when the partnership agreement provides that the general partner's interest converts to a limited partnership interest on the general partner's death because the decedent's successor continues to hold an interest in the partnership). Consequently, the conversion does not cause the taxable year of the domestic partnership to close with respect to all the partners or with respect to any partner.

Because the conversion of an interest in a domestic partnership into an interest in a domestic LLC that is classified as a partnership for federal tax purposes does not cause a termination under section 708, the resulting domestic LLC does not need to obtain a new taxpayer identification number.

HOLDINGS

(1) The federal income tax consequences described in Rev. Rul. 84–52 apply to the conversion of an interest in a domestic partnership into an interest in a domestic LLC that is classified as a partnership for federal tax purposes. The federal tax consequences are the same whether the resulting LLC is formed in the same state or in a different state than the converting domestic partnership.

(2) The taxable year of the converting domestic partnership does not close with respect to all the partners or with respect to any partner.

(3) The resulting domestic LLC does not need to obtain a new taxpayer identification number.

The holdings contained herein would apply in a similar manner if the conversion had been of an interest in a domestic LLC that is classified as a partnership for federal tax purposes into an interest in a domestic partnership. The holdings contained herein apply regardless of the manner in which the conversion is achieved under state law.

This revenue ruling does not address the federal tax consequences of a conversion of an organization that is classified as a corporation into an organization that is classified as a partnership for federal tax purposes. See, e.g., sections 336 and 337.

EFFECT ON OTHER REVENUE RULINGS

Rev. Rul. 84–52 and Rev. Rul. 86–101 are amplified.

NOTE

The Service has extended the principles of Revenue Ruling 95–37 to the conversion of a general partnership into a limited liability partnership. Revenue Ruling 95–55[1] holds that: (1) a New York general partnership registered as a New York limited liability partnership is a partnership for federal tax purposes, and (2) the registration does not terminate the partnership under Section 708(b).

PROBLEM

The ABCD partnership has been operating for several years. Each partner has an equal interest in capital and profits. On January 1 of the current year, C sold his interest to E, and on July 1 of the current year, D sold her interest to F. At the time of both sales, the asset side of the partnership balance sheet was as follows:

Cash	$ 4,000	$ 4,000
Accounts Receivable	8,000	8,000
Inventory	8,000	12,000
	$20,000	$24,000

1. 1995–2 C.B. 313.

The partnership at no time had any liabilities and has never filed an election under § 754. At all relevant times, A and B each had a $4,000 basis for their respective partnership interests, and the bases of E and F, representing in each instance the price paid to C and D, respectively, were each $6,000.

Discuss the tax consequences to Partners A, B, E and F and the partnership. Reconstruct the ABEF partnership balance sheet after D's sale in the following alternative situations:

(a) Assume no elective basis adjustments.

(b) Assume a § 754 election had been made by the partnership.

(c) Assume no § 754 election had been made but E and F both invoked § 732(d).

(d) Does § 708(b)(1)(B) apply if, instead of selling her interest to F, D liquidates the interest for $6,000 cash, and F contributes $6,000 to the partnership for a ⅙ interest?

CHAPTER 9

THE DEATH OF A PARTNER

A. INTRODUCTION

When a partner dies, there is no repose for her partnership interest, which remains in the purgatory that we have come to know as Subchapter K. At a partner's death, her interest in the partnership can: survive and be acquired by her successor in interest; be sold pursuant to a buy-sell agreement taking effect at the partner's death; or be liquidated by the partnership under a preexisting agreement. There are different tax consequences applicable to each of these alternatives.[1]

This chapter examines the special tax problems that arise on the death of a partner, focusing on: (1) the treatment of the deceased partner's distributive share of partnership income or loss for the year of death; (2) the inclusion and valuation of the partnership interest in the decedent's gross estate for federal estate tax purposes and the collateral basis and income in respect of a decedent consequences to the decedent's successor in interest; and (3) the tax consequences of a sale or liquidation of the deceased partner's interest at her death.

B. TREATMENT OF INCOME IN YEAR OF PARTNER'S DEATH

Code: §§ 706(c); 708(b).

In general, a partnership's taxable year does not close on the death of a partner.[1] As to the deceased partner, however, the partnership year closes at the date of the decedent's death under each of the three scenarios described above.[2] As a result, a partner's distributive share of income or loss for all or part of any partnership year is included on the decedent's final income tax return. In addition, a partner's distributive share of partnership income or loss from a partnership year ending prior to her death and within the decedent's final taxable year is included on the decedent's final return.[3] For example, assume Partner, a calendar-year taxpayer, has an interest in a partnership with a fiscal year ending April

1. It is possible that the successor in interest will enter into a sale or liquidation agreement *subsequent* to the decedent's death. In that event, the tax consequences of the first alternative will be governed by the general principles of Sections 741 and 751 (on a sale) or Section 736 (on a liquidation).

1. I.R.C. § 706(c)(1).

2. I.R.C. § 706(c)(2)(A).

3. I.R.C. § 706(a).

30. Partner dies on October 31 of year one. The distributive share of partnership income or loss for the fiscal year ending April 30 of year one must be included on Partner's final income tax return, which will cover the period from the beginning of the calendar year through the date of death. Partner's year also terminates on October 31 of year one, with the result that income for both years is bunched on Partner's final income tax return.[4]

The foregoing rules apply even if the decedent was a member of a two-person partnership, provided that her successor continues to share in the profits and losses of the firm.[5] Moreover, the partnership does not terminate under Section 708(b) even if the decedent was a 50 percent or more partner because a disposition by gift, bequest, or inheritance is not considered a "sale or exchange" for purposes of triggering a partnership termination.[6] But the partnership year does close with respect to the 50–percent–or–more deceased partner at the time of death if, as a result of a pre-existing buy-sell agreement, a sale of the deceased partner's entire interest occurs at the time of death.[7]

C. Estate Taxation of Partnership Interests, Treatment of "IRD" Items and Basis Consequences

Code: §§ 691(a)–(c); 753; 1014(a) & (c); 2033.

Regulations: §§ 1.742–1; 1.753–1(a).

Inclusion in Gross Estate and Valuation. The fair market value of a decedent's interest in a partnership, including the partner's distributive share of income earned prior to death, is included in the decedent's gross estate for federal estate tax purposes.[1] As with other closely held businesses, the valuation of a partnership interest is an inexact science. In theory, the fair market value is what a willing buyer would pay to a willing seller, neither being compelled to buy or sell and both having reasonable knowledge of the relevant facts.[2] More certainty can be achieved if the decedent enters into a bona fide, arm's length buy-sell or liquidation agreement that is binding both during the decedent's life and at death. In that event, the sale or liquidation price, which often is determined by a

4. Since all of the income is taxed on Partner's final income tax return, none of it constitutes income in respect of a decedent. See I.R.C. § 691 and Chapter 9B, infra.

5. Reg. § 1.708–1(b)(1)(i); Estate of Skaggs v. Commissioner, 75 T.C. 191 (1980). However, if the decedent's successor in interest does not continue to share in profits and losses, a two-person partnership is considered to terminate upon the death of one partner.

6. Reg. § 1.708–1(b)(2).

7. I.R.C. § 706(c)(2)(A); Reg. § 1.706–1(c)(3)(iv) & (vi) Example (2).

1. I.R.C. §§ 2031; 2033.

2. Reg. § 20.2031–3. The valuation may include discounts for a minority interest or for lack of marketability, or a premium for control. See Bogdanski, Federal Tax Valuation, Ch. 4 (Warren, Gorham & Lamont, 1996).

formula in the agreement, may determine the value of the partnership interest for estate tax purposes.[3]

Even a brief discussion of valuation of partnership interests for wealth transfer tax purposes would be incomplete without mentioning two fashionable estate planning vehicles, the family limited partnership ("FLP") and the family limited liability company ("FLLC").[4] Many legitimate nontax goals may motivate a family to form an FLP or FLLC to conduct an operating business or hold family investment assets such as real estate or securities. Centralized management, protection from the claims of creditors or ex-spouses, and achieving economies of scale are among the well-accepted business purposes for these popular vehicles. Most FLPs and FLLCs, however, are created primarily to obtain substantial wealth transfer tax valuation discounts. These entities are typically structured to maximize discounts for minority interests and illiquidity, causing value to disappear from the transfer tax base. The Service has mounted challenges in the most egregious cases, with increasing success, but legislative proposals to curtail aggressive valuation strategies have not been embraced by Congress. Detailed consideration of the ongoing transfer tax policy debate over FLPs and FLLCs is well beyond the scope of this text, but it is worth noting that the proliferation of these business and investment entities has stimulated greater interest in some of the income tax issues discussed in this chapter.

Income in Respect of a Decedent ("IRD"). Fundamental to a thorough understanding of the tax consequences of a partner's death is some familiarity with an income tax concept known as income in respect of a decedent ("IRD"). A brief explanation of IRD is included here for the uninitiated.[5]

In general, property owned at death is included in the decedent's gross estate and takes a "date-of-death" basis in the hands of the successor in interest equal to its fair market value on the date of the decedent's death.[6] The date-of-death basis rule creates special problems in connection with items that have been earned but not yet taxed as of the date of death. For example, assume that Attorney, a cash method taxpayer, dies holding a $3,000 receivable for services rendered. Attorney would not have been taxed on this amount during his life because he never received cash or its equivalent. If the basis of the receivable were stepped-up to its $3,000 date-of-death value, the decedent's successor in interest would realize no income on its subsequent sale or collection. Compare the treatment of Physician, an accrual method taxpayer, who dies holding a similar $3,000 claim for

3. See I.R.C. § 2703 (especially § 2703(b)); Reg. § 20.2031–2(h); Reg. § 25.2703–1(b)(3); Stephens, Maxfield, Lind & Calfee, Federal Estate and Gift Taxation ¶ 19.04 (8th ed. 2002).

4. See generally Henkel, Estate Planning and Wealth Preservation ch. 16 (1997).

5. For a more detailed discussion, see Freeland, Lathrope, Lind and Stephens, Fundamentals of Federal Income Taxation, Chapter 24E (14th ed. 2006).

6. At least until the new carryover basis regime of Section 1022 goes into effect in 2010 (if it does), the basis of property acquired from a decedent is its fair market value on the date of death or the Section 2032 alternate valuation date. I.R.C. §§ 1014; 2033. Cf. I.R.C. §§ 2032, 2032A.

services rendered. Since the right to receive the amount was fixed, Physician would have included the $3,000 in income prior to her death. Thus, the "ripe" income of a cash method decedent would be exempt from the income tax while similar items held by an accrual method taxpayer would be taxed. A cash *or* accrual method decedent reporting a deferred payment transaction under Section 453 would enjoy a similar advantage over a decedent who elected out of installment sale reporting under Section 453(d).

To correct these inequities, Congress devised the present "neutralization" approach under which several sections of the Code combine to require the decedent's successor in interest eventually both to report the amount and to retain the character of income which previously escaped tax in the hands of the decedent. First, Section 451(a) provides that amounts included in income on the decedent's final return are determined by his regular accounting method. Consequently, a cash method taxpayer who dies holding a $3,000 account receivable for services would not include the $3,000 on his final income tax return.[7] To preserve the income for later recognition by the decedent's successor in interest, Section 1014(c) denies a date-of-death basis to IRD items and instead requires the successor to take a transferred basis—zero in the case of a cash method decedent's receivables. Finally, Section 691(a)(1) provides that the IRD item will be taxable when it is actually received or collected by the decedent's estate or distributees,[8] and Section 691(a)(3) completes the picture by characterizing the IRD items to the recipient in the same manner as if they had been received by the decedent. Applying these provisions to the example above, the decedent's successor in interest would realize $3,000 of ordinary income on collection of the receivables.

The IRD concept is more involved than this brief introduction suggests, but the additional nuances are not essential for an understanding of this chapter.[9] It is sufficient to recall that IRD typically includes income items that already have been earned by, but not yet taxed to, the decedent prior to death, such as cash method receivables and Section 453 obligations. On the other hand, mere asset appreciation, including the built-in recapture income, generally is not subject to the IRD regime.

Outside Basis Consequences. In general, the basis of a partnership interest in the hands of the successor is the fair market value of the interest as of the date of death, increased by the successor's share of

7. Under Section 443(a)(2), the taxable year of a deceased taxpayer closes as of the date of death. The decedent's final return covers the period from the beginning of the taxable year through the date of death.

8. But see I.R.C. § 691(a)(2), which treats the transfer of a right to receive an IRD item by the successor in interest as an event triggering immediate recognition of income. Compare I.R.C. § 453B, which triggers similar recognition of gain on the disposition of an installment obligation.

9. For example, Section 691(b) passes through certain deductions of the decedent related to the IRD items which were not deductible on the decedent's final return, and Section 691(c) allows the recipient of an IRD item to take an income tax deduction for the federal estate tax attributable to the item.

partnership liabilities and decreased by any IRD items.[10] The relationship of the IRD concept to the decedent's interest in partnership assets is somewhat more complex. The consequences vary, depending on whether the partnership interest continues in the hands of the decedent's successor, is sold, or is liquidated.

Treatment of IRD Items. If the decedent's interest is liquidated pursuant to an agreement effective as of the date of death, Section 753 provides that amounts classified under Section 736(a) are considered IRD under Section 691.[11] The role of Section 753 is limited to characterizing Section 736(a) payments received by a deceased partner's successor in interest as IRD. It does not apply if the partner's interest continues in the hands of a successor or is sold pursuant to a pre-existing buy-sell agreement. In both those situations, however, the decedent may have an interest in the partnership's zero basis accounts receivables. These receivables would constitute IRD if the decedent held them directly, and there is no logical reason for treating them otherwise if they are held by a partnership. To the consternation of strict constructionists of the Code,[12] the Service has contended that Section 753 is not the exclusive means of classifying the decedent's interest in partnership assets as IRD. Applying an aggregate theory, the courts have concurred with the Service, in effect creating an additional category of IRD that is not specifically contemplated by Section 753. The *Quick's Trust* and *Woodhall* cases, below, adopted this approach with respect to a continuation of a partnership interest and a sale situation, respectively. This judicially created category of IRD should be extended to other types of partnership assets[13] and to zero basis accounts receivable of a liquidated partnership interest that are within Section 736(b).[14]

Property Contributed by the Decedent with a Built–In Loss. If the deceased partner had contributed property to the partnership with a built-in loss (i.e., the property's basis exceeded its fair market value at the time of contribution), Section 704(c)(1)(C) provides that (1) the built-in loss can only be allocated to the contributing partner and (2) the property's basis is deemed to be its fair market value at the time of contribution for purposes

10. Reg. § 1.742–1. See I.R.C. § 1014(c).

11. Reg. § 1.753–1(a). Recall that Section 736(a) payments are payments to a general partner in a services partnership for appreciation on the partner's share of unrealized receivables and unstated goodwill as well as any premium payments to any liquidated partner of either a services or capital partnership. See Chapter 8B, supra. Also keep in mind that Section 753 should apply only to Section 736(a) payments made pursuant to a liquidation agreement in effect at the decedent partner's death and not to payments negotiated by the executor or beneficiary after the date of death. See McKee, Nelson & Whitmire, Federal Taxation of Partnerships and Partners ¶ 23.02[2][a] (4th ed. 2007). But see Rev.Rul. 66–325, below, which suggests that a post-death liquidation agreement also is subject to Section 753.

12. See, e.g., Willis, Little & McDonald, "Problems on Death, Retirement, or Withdrawal of a Partner," 17 N.Y.U. Inst. on Fed. Tax'n 1033, 1042 (1959).

13. For example, a partnership Section 453 installment sales obligation should be treated as an IRD item. See McKee, Nelson & Whitmire, Federal Taxation of Partnerships and Partners ¶ 23.02[2][b] (4th ed. 2007).

14. See I.R.C. § 736(b)(2) and (3).

of making allocations to other partners. Thus, the built-in loss is eliminated when the partnership interest passes from the decedent.

Inside Basis Consequences. The death of a partner also may have an impact on the inside bases of partnership assets. Since the decedent's successor in interest takes a date-of-death outside basis (except for IRD items), the successor's outside basis may not be the same as his share of the inside basis. To correct the imbalance, Sections 743(b) and 732(d) are potentially applicable to allow an adjustment to the inside bases of partnership assets if there is a Section 754 election in effect or if a liquidation occurs within two years of the decedent's death and the successor in interest makes a Section 732(d) election.[15] The question whether a portion of the adjustment may be allocated to IRD items is considered in Revenue Ruling 66–325, which follows the cases below. Additionally, Section 743 will require a downward adjustment to the inside basis of partnership assets if the partnership has a substantial built-in loss (i.e., the adjusted basis of its assets exceeds the fair market value of those assets by more than $250,000) immediately after the transfer of the decedent's partnership interest.[16]

Quick's Trust v. Commissioner

United States Tax Court, 1970.
54 T.C. 1336, affirmed per curiam, 444 F.2d 90 (8th Cir.1971).

■ TANNENWALD, JUDGE:

* * *

OPINION

When Quick died he was an equal partner in a partnership which had been in the business of providing architectural and engineering services. In 1957, the partnership had ceased all business activity except the collection of outstanding accounts receivable. These receivables, and some cash, were the only assets of the partnership. Since partnership income was reported on the cash basis, the receivables had a zero basis.

Upon Quick's death in 1960, the estate became a partner with Maguolo and remained a partner until 1965 when it was succeeded as a partner by petitioner herein. The outstanding accounts receivable were substantial in amount at that time. In its 1960 return, the partnership elected under section 754 to make the adjustment in the basis of the partnership property provided for in section 743(b) and to allocate that adjustment in accordance with section 755. On the facts of this case, the net result of this adjustment was to increase the basis of the accounts receivable to the partnership from zero to an amount slightly less than one-half of their face value. If such treatment was correct, it substantially reduced the amount of the taxable

15. An adjustment under Section 732(d) applies only for purposes of distributions and not for purposes of gain or loss on a disposition. See Reg. § 1.732–1(d)(1)(vi) Example.

16. I.R.C. § 743(a), (d).

income to the partnership from the collection of the accounts receivable under section 743(b) and the estate and the petitioner herein were entitled to the benefit of that reduction.

The issue before us is whether the foregoing adjustment to basis was correctly made. Its resolution depends upon the determination of the basis to the estate of its interest in the partnership, since section 743(b)(1) allows only an "increase [in] the adjusted basis of the partnership property by the excess of *the basis to the transferee partner of his interest in the partnership* over his proportionate share of the adjusted basis of the partnership property." (Emphasis added.) This in turn depends upon whether, to the extent that "the basis to the transferee partner" reflects an interest in underlying accounts receivable arising out of personal services of the deceased partner, such interest constitutes income in respect of a decedent under section 691(a)(1) and (3). In such event, section 1014(c) comes into play and prohibits equating the basis of Quick's partnership interest with the fair market value of that interest at the time of his death under section 1014(a).

Petitioner argues that the partnership provisions of the Internal Revenue Code of 1954 adopted the entity theory of partnership, that the plain meaning of those provisions, insofar as they relate to the question of basis, requires the conclusion that the inherited partnership interest is separate and distinct from the underlying assets of the partnership, and that, therefore, section 691, and consequently section 1014(c), has no application herein.

Respondent counters with the assertion that the basis of a partnership interest is determined under section 742 by reference to other sections of the Code. He claims that, by virtue of section 1014(c), section 1014(a) does not apply to property which is classified as a right to receive income in respect of a decedent under section 691 and that the interest of the estate and of petitioner in the proceeds of the accounts receivable of the partnership falls within this classification. He emphasizes that, since the accounts receivable represent money earned by the performance of personal services, the collections thereon would have been taxable to the decedent, if the partnership had been on the accrual basis, or to the estate and to petitioner if the decedent had been a cash basis sole proprietor. Similarly, he points out that if the business had been conducted by a corporation, the collections on the accounts receivable would have been fully taxable, regardless of Quick's death. Respondent concludes that no different result should occur simply because a cash basis partnership is interposed.

The share of a general partner's successor in interest upon his death in the collections by a partnership on accounts receivable arising out of the rendition of personal services constituted income in respect of a decedent under the 1939 Code. United States v. Ellis, 264 F.2d 325 (C.A.2, 1959); Riegelman's Estate v. Commissioner, 253 F.2d 315 (C.A.2, 1958), affirming 27 T.C. 833 (1957). Petitioner ignores these decisions, apparently on the ground that the enactment of comprehensive provisions dealing with the taxation of partnerships in the 1954 Code and what it asserts is "the plain meaning" of those provisions render such decisions inapplicable in the instant case. We disagree.

The partnership provisions of the 1954 Code are comprehensive in the sense that they are detailed. But this does not mean that they are exclusive, especially where those provisions themselves recognize the interplay with other provisions of the Code. Section 742 specifies: "The basis of an interest in a partnership acquired other than by contribution shall be determined under part II of subchapter O (sec. 1011 and following)." With the exception of section 722, which deals with the basis of a contributing partner's interest and which has no applicability herein, this is the only section directed toward the question of the initial determination of the basis of a partnership interest. From the specification of section 742, one is thus led directly to section 1014 and by subsection (c) thereof directly to section 691. Since, insofar as this case is concerned, section 691 incorporates the provisions and legal underpinning of its predecessor (sec. 126 of the 1939 Code), we are directed back to a recognition, under the 1954 Code, of the decisional effect of *United States v. Ellis*, supra, and *Riegelman's Estate v. Commissioner*, supra.

Thus, to the extent that a "plain meaning" can be distilled from the partnership provisions of the 1954 Code, we think that it is contrary to petitioner's position.[11] In point of fact, however, we hesitate to rest our decision in an area such as is involved herein exclusively on such linguistic clarity and purity. See David A. Foxman, 41 T.C. 535, 551 fn. 9 (1964), affd. 352 F.2d 466 (C.A.3, 1965). However, an examination of the legislative purpose reinforces our reading of the statute. Section 751, dealing with unrealized receivables and inventory items, is included in subpart D of subchapter K, and is labeled "Provisions Common to Other Subparts." Both the House and Senate committee reports specifically state that income rights relating to unrealized receivables or fees are regarded "as severable from the partnership interest and as subject to the same tax consequences which would be accorded an individual entrepreneur." See H. Rept. No. 1337, 83d Cong., 2d Sess., p. 71 (1954); S. Rept. No. 1622, 83d Cong., 2d Sess., p. 99 (1954). And the Senate committee report adds the following significant language.

> *The House bill provides that a decedent partner's share of unrealized receivables are* [sic] *to be treated as income in respect of a decedent.* Such rights to income are to be taxed to the estate or heirs when collected, with an appropriate adjustment for estate taxes. * * * *Your committee's bill agrees substantially with the House in the treatment described above* but also provides that other income apart from unrealized receivables is to be treated as income in respect of a decedent. [See S. Rept. No. 1622, supra at 99; emphasis added.]

11. We note that petitioner's position has been the subject of extensive legal analysis and that it has some support among the legal pundits. See Willis, Handbook of Partnership Taxation, 389–395 (1957); Ferguson, "Income and Deductions in Respect of Decedents and Related Problems," 25 Tax L.Rev. 5, 100 et seq.

In light of the foregoing, the deletion of a provision in section 743 of the House bill which specifically provided that the optional adjustment to basis of partnership property should not be made with respect to unrealized receivables is of little, if any, significance. H.R. 8300, 83d Cong., 2d Sess., sec. 743(e) (1954) (introduced print). The fact that such deletion was made without comment either in the Senate or Conference Committee reports indicates that the problem was covered by other sections and that such a provision was therefore unnecessary. Similarly, the specific reference in section 753 to income in respect of a decedent cannot be given an exclusive characterization. That section merely states that certain distributions in liquidation under section 736(a) shall be treated as income in respect of a decedent. It does not state that no other amounts can be so treated.

Many of the assertions of the parties have dealt with the superstructure of the partnership provisions—assertions based upon a technical and involuted analysis of those provisions dealing with various adjustments and the treatment to be accorded to distributions after the basis of the partnership has been determined. But, as we have previously indicated * * *, the question herein involves the foundation, not the superstructure, i.e., what is the basis of petitioner's partnership interest?

Petitioner asserts that a partnership interest is an "asset separate and apart from the individual assets of the partnership" and that the character of the accounts receivable disappears into the character of the partnership interest, with the result that such interest cannot, in whole or in part, represent a right to receive income in respect of a decedent. In making such an argument, petitioner has erroneously transmuted the so-called partnership "entity" approach into a rule of law which allegedly precludes fragmentation of a partnership interest. But it is clear that even the "entity" approach should not be inexorably applied under all circumstances. See H. Rept. No. 2543, 83d Cong., 2d Sess., p. 59 (1954). Similarly, the fact that a rule of nonfragmentation of a partnership interest (except to the extent that the statute otherwise expressly provides) may govern sales of such an interest to third parties (cf. Donald L. Evans, 54 T.C. 40 (1970)) does not compel its application in all situations where such an interest is transferred. In short, a partnership interest is not, as petitioner suggests, a unitary res, incapable of further analysis.

A partnership interest is a property interest, and an intangible one at that. A property interest can often be appropriately viewed as a bundle of rights. Indeed, petitioner suggests this viewpoint by pointing out that the partnership interest herein is "merely a right to share in the profits and surplus of the Partnership." That partnership interest had value only insofar as it represented a right to receive the cash or other property of the partnership. Viewed as a bundle of rights, a major constituent element of that interest was the right to share in the proceeds of the accounts receivable as they were collected. This right was admittedly not the same as the right to collect the accounts receivable; only the partnership had the latter right. But it does not follow from this dichotomy that the right of the estate to share in the collections merged into the partnership interest.

Nothing in the statute compels such a merger. Indeed, an analysis of the applicable statutory provisions points to the opposite conclusion.

Accordingly, we hold that section 691(a)(1) and (3) applies and that the right to share in the collections from the accounts receivable must be considered a right to receive income in respect of a decedent. Consequently, section 1014(c) also applies and the basis of the partnership interest must be reduced from the fair market value thereof at Quick's death. The measure of that reduction under section 1014 is the extent to which that value includes the fair market value of a one-half interest in the proceeds of the zero basis partnership accounts receivable. See sec. 1.742–1, Income Tax Regs. It follows that the optional adjustment to basis made by the partnership under section 743(b) must be modified accordingly and that respondent's determination as to the amount of additional income subject to the tax should be sustained.[14] See Rev.Rul. 66–325, 1966–2 C.B. 249.

Petitioner would have us equate the absence of statutory language specifically dealing with the problem herein and purported inferences from tangential provisions with an intention on the part of Congress entirely to relieve from taxation an item that had previously been held subject to tax. We would normally be reluctant to find that Congress indirectly legislated so eccentrically. See separate opinion in Henry McK. Haserot, 46 T.C. 864, 877 (1966), affirmed sub nom. Commissioner v. Stickney, 399 F.2d 828 (C.A.6, 1968). In any event, as we have previously indicated, we think the enacted provisions prevent us from so doing herein.

* * *

Woodhall v. Commissioner

United States Court of Appeals, Ninth Circuit, 1972.
454 F.2d 226.

■ CHOY, CIRCUIT JUDGE.

W. Lyle Woodhall died on January 20, 1964, leaving Mrs. Woodhall as his sole heir and executrix. For 1964, Mrs. Woodhall filed a joint income tax return as surviving spouse. She also filed a fiduciary income tax return for the estate for part of 1964. For 1965, she filed an individual tax return and a fiduciary return.

The Commissioner of Internal Revenue determined deficiencies against Mrs. Woodhall for the years 1964 and 1965. The ground was that she had not declared as income certain amounts which came to her from the sale of her husband's interest in a partnership. Mrs. Woodhall petitioned the Tax Court for a declaration that she did not owe the deficiencies. The Tax Court upheld the Commissioner's determination and Mrs. Woodhall appeals. We affirm.

14. We reached a similar result in Chrissie H. Woodhall, T.C.Memo. 1969–279; that case involved a sale of the partnership interest by the decedent's successor in interest.

From January 1958 until his death, Woodhall was equal partner with his brother, Eldon Woodhall, in a lath and plaster contracting business known as Woodhall Brothers.

In December 1961, the brothers executed a written buy-sell agreement, which provided that "upon the death of either partner the partnership shall terminate and the survivor shall purchase the decedent's interest in the partnership." The price was to be determined according to a formula set out in the agreement. The formula defined accounts payable and included certain valuations for fixed assets, inventory, accounts receivable and other assets. It is the accounts receivable item that generates this controversy over Mrs. Woodhall's income for 1964 and 1965.

Because the partnership reported income on a cash basis, Woodhall had not paid taxes on his share of the accounts receivable which were outstanding at the time of his death. Mrs. Woodhall, in filing her tax returns as an individual and as executrix of her husband's estate, did not report as income the amounts allocated to the accounts receivable. Instead Mrs. Woodhall's tax returns stated that no gain had been realized by the sale of her husband's partnership interest because the tax basis of the interest was the fair market value at the time of death and this was the same as the sale price.

The issue presented is whether portions of payments received by Mrs. Woodhall, as executrix of the estate and as surviving spouse, constitute income in respect of a decedent under § 691(a)(1) of the Internal Revenue Code and are therefore subject to income taxes to the extent that such portions are allocable to unrealized receivables.

Generally, the sale of a partnership interest is an occasion for determining the character of gain or loss "to the transferor partner" as provided by § 741. In the case at bar, however, there was technically no "transferor partner" to accomplish the sale. The Woodhall Brothers partnership terminated automatically upon the death of Woodhall by operation of the buy-sell agreement, as well as under common law. Mrs. Woodhall, as executrix of the estate and as holder of a community property interest, was the transferor.

A tax regulation [Reg. § 1.741–1(b). Ed.] recognizes that § 741 applies when the sale of the partnership interest results in a termination of the partnership. The question arises whether a termination of the partnership by operation of a written agreement of the parties upon the death of one partner has the same effect.

The legislative history of § 741 explicitly deals with this question. The House report reads as follows:

"Transfer of an interest in a partnership (§§ 741–743, 751)

(1) General rules.—Under present decisions the sale of a partnership interest is generally considered to be a sale of a capital asset, and any gain or loss realized is treated as capital gain or loss. It is not clear whether the sale of an interest whose value is attribut-

> able to uncollected rights to income gives rise to capital gain or ordinary income * * *.
>
> * * *
>
> (2) Unrealized receivables or fees * * * In order to prevent the conversion of potential ordinary income into capital gain by virtue of transfers of partnership interests, certain rules have been adopted * * * which will apply to *all* dispositions of partnership interests.
>
> * * *
>
> A decedent partner's share of unrealized receivables and fees will be treated as income in respect of a decedent. Such rights to income will be taxed to the estate or heirs when collected * * *.
>
> * * *
>
> The term 'unrealized receivables or fees' is used to apply to any rights to income which have not been included in gross income under the method of accounting employed by the partnership. The provision is applicable mainly to cash basis partnerships which have acquired a contractual or other legal right to income for goods or services." House Report No. 1337, to accompany H.R. 8300 (Pub.L. 591), 83rd Cong., 2d Sess., pp. 70–71 (1954) (emphasis added); U.S.Code Cong. & Admin.News, p. 4096.

The Senate report is similar, with only technical amendments which do not alter the basic statement of purpose in the House report. Senate Report No. 1622, to accompany H.R. 8300 (Pub.L. 591), 83rd Cong., 2d Sess., p. 396 (1954).

Mrs. Woodhall's approach to the issue was much different. On the sale of her husband's partnership interest, she attempted to elect to establish the tax basis as the fair market value on the date of her husband's death. By this means, the sale price would be the same as the fair market value; there would be no gain and so no income to be taxed.

Mrs. Woodhall contends that the payments she received for the accounts receivable do not come within § 691(a), pertaining to income in respect of a decedent. Section 691(f) [now (e), Ed.] she points out, makes cross-reference to § 753, for application of § 691 to income in respect of a deceased partner. Section 753, in turn, refers to § 736 which provides that payments by a partnership for a deceased partner's interest in unrealized receivables shall be considered income in respect of a decedent under § 691. Mrs. Woodhall argues that a payment by a surviving partner is distinct from a payment by a partnership. Thus, she would have us interpret § 753, in conjunction with § 736, exclusively. In effect, this means that no payment other than one by a partnership which continues after one partner's death could constitute income in respect of a deceased partner. We reject this reading of the statutes.

The approach suggested by Mrs. Woodhall is not an appropriate characterization of the transfer of funds to her. Reading § 691 in the light of § 741, it is clear that Congress intended that the money Mrs. Woodhall received as an allocation from the unrealized accounts receivable be treated as income in respect of a decedent.

The Court of Appeals for the Eighth Circuit has just recently ruled that accounts receivable of a partnership shared in by a successor in interest of a deceased partner constituted income in respect of a decedent. Quick's Trust v. Commissioner of Internal Revenue, 444 F.2d 90 (8th Cir.1971.) The instant case is substantially the same.

We hold that the Commissioner rightly determined deficiencies against Mrs. Woodhall in the tax years 1964 and 1965.

* * *

Revenue Ruling 66–325

1966–2 Cum. Bull. 249.

Advice has been requested whether, in the circumstances described below, sections 754 and 743 of the Internal Revenue Code of 1954 may be applied so as to give the estate of a deceased member of a personal service partnership the benefit of an adjustment to the basis of the partnership's accounts receivable existing at the date of the decedent's death.

The decedent was a member of a two-man partnership engaged in the practice of medicine. The partnership reported its income on the cash basis method of accounting. At the time of the decedent's death, the firm had a substantial amount of accounts receivable, a small bank account and in addition, furniture and fixtures having only a nominal value. The partnership was continued in existence for well over a year after the decedent's death for the purpose of collecting its accounts receivable, paying its debts, and liquidating the interests of the two partners.

Under the terms of the liquidation agreement executed by the surviving partner and the estate of the deceased partner, after the payment of the firm's debts, the surviving partner was to receive a specified amount in cash and the estate was to receive the remaining proceeds of the partnership bank account and collections on the accounts receivable, together with the partnership furniture and fixtures.

The partnership filed a timely election under section 754 of the Code in respect to optional adjustment to basis of partnership property provided by section 743 of the Code.

Under the circumstances involved, the partnership is considered as having continued in existence during the liquidation period until the winding up of its affairs was completed. (See sections 1.708–1(b)(1)(i)(*a*) and 1.708–1(b)(1)(iii)(*a*) of the Income Tax Regulations.) Furthermore, since under the terms of the liquidation agreement payments were made to the deceased partner's estate in liquidation of the decedent's partnership interest, section 736 of the Code is applicable. Section 1.736–1(a)(6) of the regulations states that if a partner in a two-man partnership dies, and his estate or other successor in interest receives payments under section 736 of the Code the partnership shall not be considered to have terminated upon the death of the partner but shall terminate as to both partners only when the entire interest of the decedent is liquidated.

Since the payments to the decedent's estate which were attributable to the collection of the firm's accounts receivable were determined with reference to the income of the partnership, such payments must be considered as a distributive share to the recipient of partnership income within the scope of section 736(a) of the Code. Section 753 of the Code provides that the amount includible in the gross income of a successor in interest of a deceased partner under section 736(a) of the Code shall be considered income in respect of a decedent under section 691 of the Code.

The payments to the decedent's estate which were attributable to the collection of the firm's accounts receivable must be considered distributive share payments within the scope of section 736(a) of the Code, and hence income in respect of a decedent under section 753 of the Code. Consequently the value of the estate's right to receive them had to be excluded from its basis for the partnership interest acquired from the decedent, by reason of section 1.742–1 of the regulations. (Also see section 1014(c) of the Code.)

Accordingly, where the collection of accounts receivable represents income in respect of a decedent, the provisions of section 743 of the Code may not be applied so as to give the estate of a deceased member of a personal service partnership the benefit of an adjustment to the basis of the partnership's accounts receivable existing at the date of the decedent's death.

PROBLEM

D is a one-third general partner in the DEF partnership. Both D and the partnership are cash method, calendar year taxpayers. D dies at a time when the partnership has earned $15,000 for the current year, and his share of the untaxed and undistributed partnership income for the year is $5,000. Under all of the sale or liquidation agreements described below, D is to be paid $30,000 for his interest, which includes his share of income. Immediately prior to D's death, the DEF partnership has the following balance sheet:

Assets	**A.B.**	**F.M.V.**	**Partners' Capital**	**A.B.**	**F.M.V.**
Cash	$ 9,000	$ 9,000	D	$3,000	$30,000
Cash (not yet in D, E, and F's income)	15,000	15,000	E	3,000	30,000
Receivables for services	0	45,000	F	3,000	30,000
Depreciable § 1245 property	0	3,000			
Goodwill	0	18,000			
	$24,000	$90,000		$9,000*	$90,000

* The $9,000 basis does not include the $15,000 not previously taken into income.

Assume, alternatively, that D's interest: (1) passes to his estate; (2) is subject to a buy-out agreement at his death; (3) is liquidated by the partnership (which is a services partnership); or (4) is liquidated by the partnership in which capital is a material income-producing factor. Under each alternative, consider the following questions:

(a) Does the partnership's taxable year close as to D's estate?

(b) What is the amount included in D's gross estate?

(c) To what extent does the interest included in D's gross estate constitute income in respect of a decedent?

(d) What outside basis does D's estate take in the partnership interest immediately following D's death?

D. CONSEQUENCES OF A SALE OR LIQUIDATION OF A DECEASED PARTNER'S INTEREST AT DEATH

Code: Review §§ 691(a), 736 and other sections dealing with liquidations; 741, 751 and other sections dealing with sales; 1014(c).

Regulations: §§ 1.736–1(b)(3).

The preceding sections of this chapter involved the special problems raised by the death of a partner. This section adds nothing new but provides you with an opportunity to review much of the material covered in Chapters 6 through 8, to combine it with the concept of IRD, and to put it all together in solving the problems below. The problems disregard any consideration of income earned by the partnership at the death of the decedent's death by assuming that the date of death is immediately after the end of the partnership year.

PROBLEMS

In each of the problems below, the ABC partnership has three equal partners, A, B, and C and the following balance sheet:

Assets	A.B.	F.M.V.	Partners' Capital	A.B.	F.M.V.
Cash	$60,000	$ 60,000	A	$30,000	$ 45,000
Receivables	0	15,000	B	30,000	45,000
Inventory	15,000	30,000	C	30,000	45,000
Goodwill	15,000	30,000			
	$90,000	$135,000		$90,000	$135,000

1. Partner A dies on the first day of the current year and under a buy-sell agreement his executor sells his interest to D for $45,000. What result to A's estate if:

(a) the partnership has made a § 754 election?

(b) the partnership has made no § 754 election?

(c) the partnership has made no § 754 election but the executor elects under § 732(d)?

2. Partner A dies on the first day of the current year and, in an agreement arranged prior to his death, Services Partnership liquidates A's general partnership interest for $45,000 of cash. What result to A's estate if:

(a) there is a specific provision in the agreement that $10,000 is for A's interest in the goodwill and either a § 754 or a § 732(d) election is in effect?

(b) same as (a), above, but neither a § 754 nor a § 732(d) election is in effect?

(c) the agreement is silent as to goodwill but either a § 754 or a § 732(d) election is in effect?

(d) the agreement is silent as to goodwill and neither a § 754 nor a § 732(d) election is in effect?

(e) the agreement is silent as to goodwill and neither a § 754 nor a § 732(d) election is in effect and the partnership is one in which capital is a material income-producing factor?

3. Prepare the partnership's balance sheet after the liquidation in Problem 2(a), above. See Reg. § 1.734–2(b)(1).

PART THREE

C CORPORATIONS

CHAPTER 10

THE C CORPORATION AS A TAXABLE ENTITY

A. THE CORPORATE INCOME TAX

Code: §§ 11(a), (b)(1) & (2); 63(a). Skim §§ 199(a), (b), (c); 243(a); 1201(a); 1211(a); 1212(a)(1).

Students are often surprised to learn that a study of corporate taxation devotes very little time to the determination of a corporation's tax liability. The reason is that the concepts used in making that determination already should have been mastered in the basic federal income tax course. Those same broad principles—gross income, deductions, assignment of income, timing and characterization—apply in computing the taxable income of a C corporation, and we only need to pause briefly to discuss the rate structure and a few other special rules applicable to C corporations.

Rates. A C corporation, like an individual, is a separate taxable entity for federal income tax purposes. The corporation selects its own taxable year and method of accounting, computes its taxable income under applicable principles of the tax law and otherwise is generally treated like any other taxable person. The corporate rates are found in Section 11, which provides a limited number of brackets for lower income corporations but becomes an essentially flat rate tax for more profitable companies. The maximum corporate rate is 35 percent on a corporation's taxable income in excess of $10,000,000.[1] For corporate income under $10,000,000 the rates are as follows:[2]

Taxable Income	Rate
0 to $50,000	15%
$50,001 to $75,000	25%
$75,001 to $10,000,000	34%

The simple schedule above is modified, however, to prevent the most profitable corporations from enjoying the benefits of the lower graduated rates. Section 11(b) imposes an additional five percent tax on taxable income in excess of $100,000 up to a maximum increase of $11,750, which is the amount of tax savings from the lower rates on the first $75,000 of taxable income. This rate "bubble" in effect creates a 39 percent marginal bracket on taxable income between $100,000 and $335,000. In addition,

1. I.R.C. § 11(b).

2. Id.

corporations with taxable income in excess of $15,000,000 must increase their tax by the lesser of three percent of the excess, or $100,000. As a result of this second (double?) bubble, corporations with taxable income over $18,333,333 are taxed at a flat 35 percent rate on all their income.

To prevent doctors, lawyers, entertainers and other incorporated service providers from taking advantage of the lower marginal corporate rates, Section 11(b)(2) denies the benefit of those rates to any "qualified personal service corporation" as defined in Section 448(d)(2). Incorporated service businesses are thus subject to a 35 percent flat rate tax on all their taxable income. In general, a "qualified personal service corporation" is a corporation substantially engaged in the performance of services in the fields of health, law, engineering, architecture, accounting, actuarial science, performing arts, or consulting, if substantially all of the corporation's stock is held (directly or indirectly) by employees performing services for the corporation, retired employees, or the estates of employees or retirees.[3]

Determination of Taxable Income. Section 63(a) defines taxable income as "gross income minus the deductions allowed by this chapter." In the case of a corporation, this amount generally is determined by applying the same principles and Code sections applicable to individuals. A few differences, primarily attributable to the distinct status of the corporation as an artificial business entity, are worth mentioning.

First, because a corporation has no "personal" expenses, it is not entitled to any personal or dependency exemptions and, unlike an individual, it receives no standard deduction. Corporations thus are not concerned with distinguishing between "above-the-line" deductions allowable in reaching adjusted gross income and "below-the-line" itemized deductions or in applying the Section 67 two percent of adjusted gross income floor to "miscellaneous itemized deductions" or the Section 68 overall limitation on itemized deductions.

In addition, most of the personal deductions allowed to individuals are not available to corporations. For example, a corporation is not entitled to a medical expense deduction under Section 213 or a spousal support deduction under Section 215. Moreover, Section 212, which allows a deduction for certain expenses incurred for the production of income or maintenance of income-producing property or for tax advice, is expressly applicable only to individuals. Corporations need not worry however, because virtually all of their ordinary expenses in the pursuit of profit are deductible under Section 162.

On the other hand, certain *limitations* on the deductibility of personal expenses of individuals do not apply to corporations. For example, Section 165(c), which limits the deductibility of nonbusiness losses; Section 166(d), which characterizes nonbusiness bad debts as short-term capital losses; and Section 183(a), which limits deductions for activities not motivated by profit, are among a number of restrictive sections that do not apply to C

3. I.R.C. § 448(d)(2).

corporations. This is because it is generally assumed that all of a corporation's activities are motivated by the pursuit of profit.[4]

By virtue of their unique status, corporations are entitled to one important deduction not available to individuals. To prevent multiple taxation as earnings wend their way through a chain of corporations, corporate shareholders generally are entitled to deduct 70 percent (or, in some cases, 80 or 100 percent) of the dividends they receive from other corporations. The effect of the 70 percent dividends received deduction is that corporations are subject to tax at a maximum rate of 10.5 percent on dividends—an amount derived by applying the top 35 percent corporate rate to the 30 percent includable portion of the dividends.

The remaining differences in the treatment of corporations and individuals are the result of a conscious legislative choice to treat them differently. For example, the percentage limitation on corporate charitable deductions is 10 percent of taxable income as compared to an overall 50 percent limit on individual charitable contributions.[5] The at-risk limitations in Section 465 and the passive loss limitations in Section 469, which are aimed at tax shelter activities of individual taxpayers, generally do not apply to C corporations.[6] And publicly traded corporations may not deduct more than $1 million per year for otherwise reasonable compensation paid to certain high-level corporate executives.[7]

Another significant difference relates to the treatment of corporate capital losses. Corporations may deduct capital losses only to the extent of capital gains during the taxable year. Although the excess may not be applied against ordinary income, it may be carried back for three years and carried forward for five years. By contrast, individuals are permitted to deduct capital losses to the extent of capital gains, and up to $3,000 of excess losses may be deducted against ordinary income. Unused capital losses may be carried forward indefinitely by an individual taxpayer.[8]

Deduction for Domestic Production Activities. The stated maximum corporate income tax rate of 35 percent will be reduced by approximately 3 percent in 2010 when the Section 199 deduction for domestic production activities is fully phased in.[9] This generous tax benefit was the centerpiece of the American Jobs Creation Act of 2004, which repealed a longstanding

4. Certain payments made by a corporation to or on behalf of its shareholders may be nondeductible because they are in fact dividends, but their disallowance is the result of the classification of the payments as constructive dividends rather than the "personal" nature of the payments. See Chapter 12E, infra.

5. I.R.C. § 170(b)(2).

6. I.R.C. §§ 465(a)(1); 469(a)(2)(B), (j)(1). See Chapter 3C, supra.

7. I.R.C. § 162(m). This limitation only applies to the chief executive officer and the four other most highly compensated executives. I.R.C. § 162(m)(3). Various types of commissions and performance-based compensation are exempt. I.R.C. § 162(m)(4). Tax advisors have been adept at designing compensation plans to avoid the impact of this provision.

8. I.R.C. §§ 1211, 1212.

9. I.R.C. § 199. The deduction is effective for taxable years beginning after December 31, 2004.

export subsidy ruled illegal by the World Trade Organization.[10] To compensate for the lost tax break, Congress added the deduction, which permits U.S. taxpayers engaged in certain domestic production activities to deduct a specified percentage (3 percent in 2005–2006, 6 percent in 2007–2009, and 9 percent in 2010 and thereafter) of the lesser of their taxable income or "qualified production activities income."[11] The deduction is allowed for purposes of both the regular and alternative minimum taxes and is available to individuals, trusts, partnerships and S corporations as well as domestic C corporations.[12]

Section 199 is a typically complex provision littered with definitions and special rules. In keeping with the "fundamentals" philosophy of the text, the following discussion is limited to a few highlights. "Qualified production activities income," the base on which the deduction is determined, equals a taxpayer's "domestic production gross receipts" reduced by the sum of: (1) the cost of goods sold allocable to those receipts, (2) other allocable expenses, and (3) a ratable portion of other not directly allocable deductions and losses.[13] The key term that unlocks the gate to the deduction is "domestic production gross receipts," which are gross receipts derived from various "production" activities within the United States. "Production" is much broader than just "manufacturing." It includes farming, equipment leasing, licensing of software and films (but not if the film is "pornographic"), construction, production of electricity, natural gas and drinking water, and even some service businesses such as engineering or architecture.[14] As a result, many companies that did not benefit from the repealed export subsidy will qualify for the new deduction.

The statute draws some fine lines in determining what activities qualify for the deduction. Profits from the sale of food and beverages prepared by the taxpayer at a retail establishment, such as restaurants and facilities selling take-out food items, do not qualify,[15] but profits from processing food (e.g., from an in-store bakery in a supermarket) are eligible for the tax break.[16] As explained in the legislative history, "the gross receipts of a meat packing establishment" qualify but "the activities of a master chef who creates a venison sausage for his or her restaurant menu" do not.[17] U.S. companies that roast coffee beans and use them to brew coffee for sale qualify for the deduction on the roasting but not the brewing

10. Another generous provision added by the 2004 legislation created a one-year amnesty for companies to repatriate profits earned outside the United States at a reduced tax rate of 5.25 percent. I.R.C. § 965(a). Technology and pharmaceutical companies with large amount of overseas cash especially benefited from this "tax holiday."

11. I.R.C. § 199(a). The deduction cannot exceed 50 percent of "W–2 wages" (defined as wages and certain elective deferrals, such as contributions to Section 401(k) plans) paid by the taxpayer as an employer during the taxable year. I.R.C. § 199(b).

12. I.R.C. §§ 199(d)(1), (6).

13. I.R.C. § 199(c)(1).

14. I.R.C. § 199(c)(4).

15. I.R.C. § 199(c)(4)(B).

16. H.R. Rep. No. 108–755, 108th Cong., 2d Sess. 13 (2004).

17. Id. at 12.

activity.[18] The Service has been delegated the authority to provide additional guidance through regulations.[19]

The Section 199 deduction was part of a massive tax bill intended by Congress to stimulate the creation of new jobs within the United States. It is already clear that deciphering the intricacies of this new deduction will boost the gross receipts of law and accounting firms, but the definition of "domestic production" does not yet extend to the services provided by tax advisers.

Taxable Year and Accounting Method. Most C corporations have the flexibility to adopt either a calendar year or a fiscal year as their annual accounting period.[20] Certain "personal service corporations" must use a calendar year, however, unless they can show a business purpose for using a fiscal year.[21] For this purpose, a "personal service corporation" is one whose principal activity is the performance of personal services that are substantially performed by "employee-owners" who collectively own more than 10 percent (by value) of the corporation's stock.[22] This generally forces most personal service corporations to use a calendar year, subject to an exception in Section 444 which permits them to elect to adopt or change to a fiscal year with a "deferral period" of not more than three months.[23] As a result, a personal service corporation that otherwise would be required to use a calendar year may elect a taxable year ending September 30, October 31 or November 30. To prevent any tax savings that might result from the use of a fiscal year, personal service corporations making a Section 444 election must make certain minimum distributions (e.g., primarily of compensation) to employee-owners during the portion of the employee's fiscal year that ends on December 31.[24] If these minimum distribution requirements are not met, the electing corporation must defer certain otherwise currently deductible payments (e.g., compensation) to employee-owners.[25] A personal service corporation that establishes a business purpose for a fiscal year is not required to make a Section 444 election and is not subject to these distribution requirements and deduction limitations.[26]

18. Id. at 13.

19. I.R.C. § 199(d)(7). The Service issued preliminary guidance in I.R.S. Notice 2005–14, 2005–7 I.R.B. 1, and detailed regulations on most aspects of § 199 in 2006. See T.D. 9263, 71 Fed. Reg. 31267 (June 1, 2006), as amended by T.D. 9293, 71 Fed. Reg. 61662 (Oct. 19, 2006).

20. See generally I.R.C. § 441. A fiscal year is any period of 12 months ending on the last day of any month other than December. I.R.C. § 441(e).

21. I.R.C. § 441(i)(1). Deferral of income to shareholders is not treated as a business purpose. Id.

22. I.R.C. §§ 269A(b)(1); 441(i)(2). An employee-owner is defined as any employee who owns, on any day during the taxable year, any of the outstanding stock of the corporation after applying certain attribution rules. I.R.C. § 269A(b)(2), as modified by I.R.C. § 441(i)(2).

23. I.R.C. § 444(b)(2). The "deferral period" of a taxable year is the number of months between the beginning of the taxable year elected and the close of the required taxable year that ends within the taxable year elected.

24. See generally I.R.C. § 280H.

25. I.R.C. § 280H(a), (b), (c).

26. I.R.S. Notice 88–10, 1988–1 C.B. 478.

In general, C corporations are required to use the accrual method of accounting.[27] Exemptions are provided for corporations engaged in the farming business, "qualified personal service corporations"[28] and any other corporation whose average annual gross receipts for a three-year measuring period preceding the taxable year do not exceed $5 million.[29]

In addition to these general accounting rules, Section 267 regulates certain transactions between corporations and their shareholders to prevent the acceleration of losses on related party transactions and to preclude timing advantages when the corporation and its owner-employees use different methods of accounting. For example, Section 267(a)(1) provides that losses from sales or exchanges of property between an individual shareholder and a more–than–50–percent–owned corporation may not be deducted.[30] The forced matching rules in Section 267(a)(2) prevent an accrual method corporation from accruing and deducting compensation paid to a cash method owner-employee in the year when the services are performed but deferring payment until the following taxable year to provide the employee with a timing advantage. When an owner-employee owns, directly or indirectly, more than 50 percent of the payor corporation, the corporation's deduction is deferred until such time as the owner-employee includes the amount in income.[31]

Credits. Like any taxpayer engaged in business or investment activities, a corporation is entitled to several valuable tax credits. The most significant is the foreign tax credit, which is available to corporations with income from foreign sources.[32] Others include the rehabilitation and energy credits,[33] the work opportunity credit,[34] and the credit for research expenditures.[35]

B. THE CORPORATE ALTERNATIVE MINIMUM TAX

Code: §§ 55(a), (b)(1)(B) & (2), (c)(1), (d)(2) & (3)(A), (e)(1); 56(a)(1)(A), (c)(1), (g)(1), (2), (3), (4)(A)–(C)(ii), (6); 57(a)(5)(A), (6). Skim § 53.

C Corporations also are potentially subject to the alternative minimum tax ("AMT"), which is designed "to ensure that no taxpayer with substan-

27. I.R.C. § 448(a).

28. This is the same category of corporations that is deprived of the lower graduated rates in Section 11. Substantially all of the activities of the corporation must involve the performance of services in the fields of health, law, engineering, accounting, architecture, actuarial science, performing arts, or consulting, and substantially all of the stock must be held by employees, their estates or their heirs. I.R.C. § 448(d)(2).

29. I.R.C. § 448(b).

30. The loss disallowance applies to transactions between related parties as defined in Section 267(b). A corporation and its more–than–50–percent (measured by value) shareholders are considered related. I.R.C. § 267(b)(2). Percentage ownership is determined after application of attribution rules in Section 267(c).

31. I.R.C. § 267(a)(2). This section also may apply to payments of interest and other deductible expenses. In the case of personal service corporations, the corporation and *any* owner-employee (regardless of the percentage ownership) are treated as related parties for purposes of the forced matching rules in Section 267. Id.

32. I.R.C. § 27.

33. I.R.C. §§ 46–48.

34. I.R.C. § 51.

35. I.R.C. § 41.

tial economic income can avoid significant tax liability by using exclusions, deductions and credits."[1] The AMT generally can be described as a flat rate tax which is imposed on a broader income base than the taxable income yardstick used for the regular corporate tax. But that deceptively simple description only begins to explain a complex statutory scheme that takes many twists and turns before reaching "alternative minimum taxable income," the base that Congress believed was a truer measure of a corporation's economic results.

The corporate AMT is payable only to the extent that it exceeds a corporation's regular tax liability.[2] The AMT generally is 20 percent of the amount by which a corporation's alternative minimum taxable income, as defined in Section 55(b)(2), exceeds a $40,000 exemption amount.[3] "Alternative minimum taxable income" ("AMTI") is the corporation's taxable income, increased by various tax preference items and adjusted to eliminate certain timing benefits (e.g., accelerated cost recovery) that are available under the regular tax.[4] Certain "small" corporations are exempt from the corporate AMT. To qualify for this exemption for a taxable year, a corporation's average annual gross receipts must be $7.5 million or less for all preceding three-taxable-year periods (taking into account only taxable years beginning after 1993).[5] In its first year of existence, a corporation is exempt from the AMT regardless of its gross receipts.[6]

Section 56 lists the principal adjustments made in arriving at a corporation's alternative minimum taxable income.[7] Many are narrow and beyond the scope of this text, but a few adjustments will be familiar to students who have completed the basic income tax course. For example, depreciation on tangible personal property eligible for the 200 percent declining balance method under the regular tax is limited to the 150 percent declining balance method for AMT purposes.[8] A special net operating loss, known as the "alternative minimum tax net operating loss," also must be used in computing alternative minimum taxable income.[9]

1. S. Rep. No. 99–313, 99th Cong., 2d Sess. 518 (1986). See generally Lathrope, The Alternative Minimum Tax (1994).

2. I.R.C. § 55(a).

3. I.R.C. § 55(b), (d)(2). The $40,000 exemption amount is phased out at the rate of 25 cents for each dollar that a corporation's alternative minimum taxable income exceeds $150,000. I.R.C. § 55(d)(3)(A). The exemption is thus fully phased out when a corporation's alternative minimum taxable income reaches $310,000.

4. I.R.C. § 55(b)(2).

5. I.R.C. § 55(e)(1)(A). The $7.5 million limit is reduced to $5 million for the first three-taxable-year period taken into account. I.R.C. § 55(e)(1)(B).

6. I.R.C. § 55(e)(1)(C).

7. Certain specialized adjustments in Section 58 also must be made. I.R.C. § 55(b)(2)(A).

8. I.R.C. § 56(a)(1)(A)(ii). For property placed in service after 1986 but before 1999, AMT depreciation also must be computed using the longer class lives prescribed by the alternative depreciation system of Section 168(g). I.R.C. § 56(a)(1)(A)(i).

9. In general, the AMT net operating loss must be computed in a manner consistent with the adjustments and preferences in the alternative minimum tax scheme. The special net operating loss may not offset more than 90 percent of a corporation's alternative

In extending the AMT concept to corporations, Congress was responding to several highly publicized cases of corporations that reported significant operating profits in their financial statements to shareholders but paid minimal amounts of corporate income tax.[10] In an effort to improve perceptions, Section 56(g) requires an upward AMTI adjustment equal to 75 percent of the amount by which "adjusted current earnings" ("ACE") exceed AMTI determined without regard to this adjustment or AMT net operating losses ("pre–ACE AMTI").[11] The purpose of the ACE adjustment is to reach an even more accurate measure of a corporation's economic performance. ACE is determined by starting with pre–ACE AMTI and making several additional adjustments.[12]

Understanding the final round of ACE adjustments requires a brief introduction to the concept of "earnings and profits." The principal function of earnings and profits is to determine whether distributions paid by C corporations to their shareholders are dividends or a return of capital.[13] The computation of earnings and profits begins with taxable income and requires a number of adjustments which are designed to provide a truer measure of the corporation's economic performance. Consequently, certain amounts that were excluded from gross income for purposes of computing pre–ACE AMTI but that are taken into account in determining a corporation's "earnings and profits" must be included in determining ACE. An example is tax-exempt municipal bond interest, which increases a corporation's wealth but (except for interest on certain private activity bonds) is not included in the AMT base. Similarly, items that are disallowed as deductions in computing earnings and profits are added back for ACE purposes. An example is the 70 percent dividends received deduction for corporate shareholders.[14]

Once ACE is determined, the final step is to increase pre–ACE AMTI by 75 percent of the excess of ACE over pre–ACE AMTI.[15] After this orgy of adjustments, one wonders why Congress did not simply adopt ACE (or earnings and profits, for that matter) as the base for the corporate AMT. The answer presumably is political compromise, a force that has complicated the tax system in general and the alternative minimum tax in particular.

The determination of AMTI requires one more step. Once the required Section 56 adjustments are made, a corporation must increase taxable income by the amount of certain tax preference items, most of which are

minimum taxable income, determined without the net operating loss deduction. I.R.C. § 56(a)(4), (d).

10. See, e.g., Citizens for Tax Justice, "Corporate Taxpayers and Corporate Freeloaders," 29 Tax Notes 947 (Dec. 2, 1985).

11. A negative adjustment also is allowed—i.e., pre–ACE AMTI may be reduced by 75 percent of the excess of pre–ACE AMTI over ACE. I.R.C. § 56(g)(2).

12. I.R.C. § 56(g)(3).

13. See I.R.C. §§ 301; 316; and Chapter 12, infra.

14. See I.R.C. § 243(a). An exception is provided for deductions that qualify for a 100 or 80 percent dividends received deduction, provided that the dividends are paid from earnings that were taxable to the payor. I.R.C. § 56(g)(4)(C)(ii).

15. As noted earlier, if pre–ACE AMTI exceeds ACE, then pre–ACE AMTI is decreased by the difference. See note 11, supra.

very specialized. Some of the more familiar preferences included in Section 57(a) are: (1) the excess of percentage depletion over cost depletion; (2) excess intangible drilling costs; and (3) tax-exempt interest on certain private activity bonds issued after August 7, 1986.

A limited number of credits may be applied against a corporation's alternative minimum tax liability.[16] In addition, a minimum tax credit is allowed against a corporation's *regular* tax liability. The minimum credit was enacted in recognition of the fact that many of the alternative minimum tax adjustments and items of tax preference reflect deferral of tax liability rather than permanent tax avoidance. An adjustment thus is required so that taxpayers do not lose these benefits altogether.[17] In general, Section 53(a) allows a corporation's alternative minimum tax to be credited against regular tax liability (reduced by certain other credits) in later years.[18] The minimum tax credit may be carried over until it is fully used, but it cannot be used as a credit against the alternative minimum tax.[19]

Not surprisingly, the corporate AMT is unpopular in the business community, which has placed complete repeal of this tax high on its wish list of proposed legislation. Advocates of tax simplification also have recommended a phase-out and eventual repeal of both the individual and corporate AMT.[20] Although these proposals have broad support in Congress, the revenue loss from AMT repeal would be substantial, and the best guess is that the AMT will remain part of the corporate tax landscape unless and until it can be given a proper burial as part of a comprehensive overall of the federal tax system.

C. ANTI-AVOIDANCE PENALTY TAXES

The regular and alternative minimum taxes are augmented by two penalty taxes enacted by Congress many years ago to prevent C corporations and their shareholders from avoiding the double tax and the steeply progressive marginal rates historically applicable to individual taxpayers. The penalty taxes limit the opportunity either to accumulate the operating income of a business in a more lightly taxed C corporation or to use the C corporation as a vehicle to reduce the tax burden on personal service and investment income. The accumulated earnings tax is specifically aimed at profitable C corporations that are motivated by tax avoidance to accumulate profits beyond the reasonable needs of their business. The personal holding company tax penalizes closely held corporations with income consisting primarily of dividends, interest, rents and certain other forms of

16. See I.R.C. § 38(c) (regular investment tax credit); § 59(a) (alternative minimum tax foreign tax credit).

17. S. Rep. No. 99–313, supra note 1, at 521.

18. I.R.C. § 53(a), (b), (d)(1)(B).

19. I.R.C. § 53(c).

20. See, e.g., Staff of the Joint Committee on Taxation, Study of the Overall State of the Federal Tax System and Recommendations for Simplification, vol. II, pp. 2–23 (JCS–3–01, April 2001).

passive investment or personal service income if they fail to regularly distribute that income to their shareholders.

The importance of the anti-avoidance penalty taxes is greatly diminished when, as now, the gap between individual and corporate rates is narrowed and the maximum tax rate on most dividends is the same as the long-term capital gains rate. But the accumulated earnings and personal holding company taxes remain in the Code, perhaps in anticipation of some future tax rate revolution, and a brief discussion of their history and operation is appropriate as part of this introduction to Subchapter C.

1. The Accumulated Earnings Tax

Background. For most of our income tax history, the graduated rates applicable to individuals greatly exceeded the essentially flat corporate rates. At one time, the top corporate rate was roughly 50 percent while individuals were taxed at rates ranging up to 88 percent. In the early 1980's, there still was a considerable spread between the 46 percent top corporate rate and the 70 percent marginal rate then applicable to the unearned income of wealthy individuals. This rate gap provided an incentive for taxpayers to accumulate business profits or investment income in a corporation. As Professors Bittker and Eustice once said, "use of a corporation as a temporary or permanent refuge from individual income tax rates has been one of the principal landmarks of our tax landscape."[1]

To illustrate a typical accumulation plan that would have invited the tax collector's scrutiny, consider the goals of Accumulator ("A"), a sole proprietor with a profitable business in the days of the 70 percent individual marginal rates. Tempted by the allure of the lower corporate tax rate, A incorporates his business with a healthy (but permissible) dose of debt and pays himself a hefty (but reasonable) salary. His personal consumption needs are fully satisfied by the salary, the interest payments on the debt, and as many nontaxable fringe benefits as the corporation can legally provide. Any additional profits from the business are left to accumulate in the corporation, where they work to increase the value of A's stock. If A needs more funds or later wishes to retire, he can "cash in" on his accumulated profits by selling some stock or liquidating the company, in either case reporting those profits as favored long-term capital gain. An even more attractive alternative would be to avoid entirely the individual income tax by holding the stock until death, when A's heirs would be entitled to a stepped-up basis under Section 1014. Or A might dispose of the business in a tax-free reorganization, emerging with publicly traded stock, albeit with a low substituted basis, which could be sold or held until A's death.[2]

The accumulated earnings tax was enacted to prevent the use of a C corporation to escape the individual income tax by an unreasonable accu-

1. Bittker & Eustice, Federal Income Taxation of Corporations and Shareholders ¶ 1.02 (5th ed. 1987).

2. See I.R.C. §§ 354; 358; 368.

mulation of earnings. Although not part of its original design, it also serves the broader purpose of inducing corporations to subject their earnings to the double tax by paying dividends when those earnings are not required for the reasonable needs of the business.

For a brief time between 1987 and 1992, the corporate income tax rates exceeded the individual rates—a departure from the historic norm that caused some commentators to propose repeal of the accumulated earnings tax on the ground that it was no longer necessary.[3] Under current law, the top individual and corporate rates are the same, and most dividends received by noncorporate shareholders are taxed at a preferential 15 percent rate. As a result, the accumulated earnings tax is much less significant but not totally irrelevant because its lurking presence still may force some profitable companies to distribute their earnings as dividends.

Operation of the Tax. The accumulated earnings tax is imposed on a corporation "formed or availed of for the purpose of avoiding the income tax with respect to its shareholders * * * by permitting earnings and profits to accumulate instead of being divided or distributed."[4] The tax is levied at a rate of 15 percent on a C corporation's "accumulated taxable income," which is generally defined as taxable income with certain adjustments (e.g., subtracting taxes and dividends paid and adding back the dividends received deduction) to reflect the true dividend paying capacity of the corporation.[5] The rate was reduced from the highest individual marginal income tax rate to 15 percent at the same time that Congress reduced the rate on qualified dividends.

Most corporations, regardless of motives, are entitled to an accumulated earnings credit that in effect permits an accumulation of up to $250,000.[6] Although closely held corporations are the principal target of the tax, Section 532(c) provides that its application is to be determined "without regard to the number of shareholders," and the Tax Court has held that in theory the tax can apply to a publicly traded corporation even where ownership is not concentrated in a small group of shareholders.[7] As a practical matter, however, publicly traded companies are rarely threatened because of the difficulty of proving that they were formed for the proscribed tax avoidance purpose.

The Prohibited Tax Avoidance Purpose. The central issue under the accumulated earnings tax is whether the corporation has been formed or availed of for a tax avoidance purpose. The statutory standard is met if tax avoidance is one of several factors motivating corporate accumulations.[8]

3. See, e.g., Wolfman, "Subchapter C and the 100th Congress," 33 Tax Notes 669, 674 (Nov. 17, 1986).

4. I.R.C. § 532(a).

5. I.R.C. §§ 531; 535.

6. I.R.C. § 535(a), (c). A corporation is only permitted a $150,000 credit if its principal function is the performance of services in the field of health, law engineering, architecture, accounting, actuarial science, performing arts or consulting. I.R.C. § 535(c)(2)(B).

7. Technalysis Corp. v. Commissioner, 101 T.C. 397 (1993).

8. United States v. Donruss, 393 U.S. 297, 89 S.Ct. 501 (1969).

Two statutory presumptions assist in determining the presence of a tax avoidance purpose. First, the fact that corporate earnings and profits are permitted to accumulate "beyond the reasonable needs of the business" is determinative of a tax avoidance purpose unless the corporation proves to the contrary by a "preponderance of the evidence."[9] In addition, the fact that the corporation is "a mere holding or investment company" is prima facie evidence of a tax avoidance purpose.[10] Otherwise, the regulations provide that the presence of the proscribed tax avoidance purpose is determined by all the circumstances of the particular case.[11]

The Reasonable Needs of the Business. The critical question in most accumulated earnings tax cases is whether the corporation accumulated profits beyond the reasonable needs of its business. This is a factual question, and the courts frequently defer to the business judgment of corporate management if the managers have documented their needs carefully in a business plan with economic substance.[12] The regulations provide extensive guidance on what are reasonable and unreasonable corporate accumulations.[13]

"Reasonable needs" include anticipated needs of the business if the corporation has a specific and feasible plan,[14] and the regulations expansively define a corporation's "business" as including not only the one in which the corporation has previously engaged but also "any line of business which it may undertake."[15] In addition, Congress has specifically provided that the term "reasonable needs of the business" encompasses accumulations in the year of a shareholder's death or in any subsequent year to the extent they are necessary to make a stock redemption to pay death taxes under Section 303.[16] The cases are inconsistent as to accumulations for other types of future redemptions.[17]

2. THE PERSONAL HOLDING COMPANY TAX

Background. The accumulated earnings tax was not an entirely effective vehicle to prevent the use of a C corporation to avoid the individual tax rates (when they exceeded the corporate rate) because it is not imposed unless a corporation has accumulations that are motivated at least in part by tax avoidance. Moreover, the accumulated earnings credit may shelter substantial accumulations from the Section 531 tax. In response to these

9. I.R.C. § 533(a).

10. I.R.C. § 533(b).

11. Reg. § 1.533–1(a)(2).

12. See, e.g., Myron's Enterprises v. United States, 548 F.2d 331 (9th Cir.1977).

13. Reg. § 1.537–2(b), (c).

14. Reg. § 1.537–1(b)(1) & (2).

15. Reg. § 1.537–3(a).

16. I.R.C. § 537(a)(2); 537(b)(1). Similarly, reasonable needs are considered to include amounts necessary to redeem stock held by a private foundation that is required to shed its excess business holdings. I.R.C. § 537(a)(3); 537(b)(2). See I.R.C. § 4943.

17. See, e.g., Gazette Publishing Co. v. Self, 103 F.Supp. 779 (E.D.Ark.1952); Wilcox Manufacturing Co. v. Commissioner, 38 T.C.M. 378 (1979); John B. Lambert & Associates v. United States, 212 Ct.Cl. 71 (1976).

shortcomings and to prevent certain other tax avoidance devices, Congress enacted the personal holding company tax.

The original purpose of the personal holding company tax was to prevent taxpayers from avoiding the higher graduated individual tax rates by using devices known as "incorporated pocketbooks," "incorporated talents" and "incorporated properties." These schemes were structured as follows:

1. *Incorporated Pocketbooks.* A high bracket individual would transfer passive investments (e.g., stocks, bonds, rental property) to a corporation in exchange for its stock. The corporation then could take advantage of the lower corporate rates and the dividends received deduction for any dividends that it received. The income could be realized at a later date at capital gain rates through a liquidation of the company or, ideally, the stock could be held until the taxpayer's death when his heirs would take a stepped-up basis.
2. *Incorporated Talents.* A highly compensated individual, such as a movie star, would form a wholly owned corporation and agree to work for the corporation at a small salary. The corporation then would contract out the services of its owner-employee for a substantial sum, and the great bulk of the income would be taxed at the lower corporate rates.[1]
3. *Incorporated Properties.* A taxpayer would transfer both investment property and property which did not generate income, such as a yacht or home, to a corporation. The shareholder then would lease back the property for a nominal amount, and the corporation would attempt to shelter both the rental income and its other income by claiming deductions for depreciation and maintenance on the property.[2]

To combat these plans, Section 541 imposes a penalty tax on the "undistributed personal holding company income" of every "personal holding company." The personal holding company tax is imposed in addition to a corporation's regular income tax. To avoid overlap, personal holding companies are not subject to the accumulated earnings tax.[3]

Personal Holding Company Defined. A personal holding company is generally a closely held corporation (more than 50 percent in value of its stock must be owned by five or fewer individuals, after application of attribution rules) that derives at least 60 percent of its ordinary income from sources such as dividends, interest, rents, capital gains, and certain forms of personal service income.[4] The determination of whether a corpora-

1. See Commissioner v. Laughton, 113 F.2d 103 (9th Cir.1940).

2. Bittker & Eustice, Federal Income Taxation of Corporations and Shareholders ¶ 7.20 (7th ed. 2000).

3. I.R.C. §§ 532(b)(1).

4. The definitions in the Code of "personal holding company," and "personal holding company income" are far more technical, but the generality in the text will suffice for purposes of this overview.

tion is a personal holding company is an objective inquiry that does not depend on whether there is a tax avoidance motive.

Taxation of Personal Holding Companies. Personal holding companies are taxed at a 15 percent rate on their undistributed personal holding company income,[5] which very generally is the corporation's after-tax income less a deduction for dividends paid. The policy is to force a personal holding company to distribute net profits to its shareholders or incur a 15 percent penalty tax at the corporate level in addition to the regular corporate tax. The Code includes various "rescue" provisions that permit a personal holding company facing a penalty tax to avoid the punishment—for example, by distributing a "deficiency dividend" that will be taxable to the distributee shareholders.[6]

D. CORPORATE TAX SHELTERS

The corporate income tax base began to erode in the 1990s as a result of the proliferation of transactions being marketed for the specific purpose of substantially reducing the tax liability of profitable corporations and their high-income executives.[1] Loosely defined as "corporate tax shelters," the common characteristics of these transactions are: (1) realization of tax losses without corresponding economic loss through transactions having questionable economic substance apart from the desire to reduce United States income taxes; (2) realization of income by "tax-indifferent" facilitators, such as foreign affiliates, domestic corporations with soon-to-expire loss carryovers, and tax-exempt organizations; (3) reliance on the literal language or ambiguities in the Internal Revenue Code to support a result that may be technically defensible but is inconsistent with the spirit of the law and well-accepted tax principles; (4) marketing of transactions under a veil of secrecy by entrepreneurial accounting firms and investment banks in exchange for enormous fees; (5) inconsistent treatment for financial accounting and tax purposes of items resulting from the same transaction; and (6) the willingness of corporate managers and their advisors, emboldened by "reasoned" opinions of tax counsel[2] and the knowledge that IRS audits have been reduced, to play "audit roulette" by taking questionable tax return reporting positions with the hope (and expectation?) that they will never be scrutinized. A crisper and perhaps more informative definition has been proposed by Professor Michael Graetz, who has characterized

5. I.R.C. § 541.

6. See I.R.C. § 547.

1. See, e.g., Joint Committee on Taxation, Background and Present Law Relating to Tax Shelters (JCX–19–02), March 19, 2002; Symposium, "Business Purpose, Economic Substance, and Corporate Tax Shelters," 54 SMU L. Rev. 3 (2001); Symposium on Corporate Tax Shelters, Part I, 55 Tax L. Rev. No. 2 (Winter 2002); Part II, 55 Tax L. Rev. No. 3 (Spring 2002).

2. An opinion of counsel assuring a taxpayer that a transaction is "more likely than not" to achieve its intended purpose, ordinarily insulates the taxpayers from various civil penalties. See, e.g., I.R.C. § 6662(a), (d); Reg. § 1.6662–4.

a tax shelter as "a deal done by very smart people that, absent tax considerations, would be very stupid."[3]

An aggressive attack on corporate tax shelters has been proceeding for a number of years on multiple fronts. Developments are ongoing and include legislation, regulations, changes to the rules governing tax practice before the Internal Revenue Service, test cases involving high profile taxpayers, and lawsuits by disgruntled clients against their former tax advisors. Key components of the campaign include: (1) disallowance of tax benefits derived in certain types of "listed" tax avoidance transactions;[4] (2) a heightened disclosure regime, requiring taxpayers to put the Service on notice if they have engaged in "reportable" or "listed" transactions and requiring promoters and tax advisors to "register" corporate tax shelters before the transaction occurs;[5] (3) an enhanced substantial understatement penalty regime for items attributable to corporate tax shelters;[6] (4) stiff no-fault penalties for failure to comply with the tax shelter disclosure requirements;[7] and (5) more rigorous regulation of the conduct of professional advisors who provide opinion letters and participate in the marketing of corporate tax shelters.[8] To bolster this assault, some commentators have gone so far as to propose that public companies be required to compute their taxable income by reference to the income reported for financial accounting purposes, with only limited deviations permitted for valid tax policy reasons.[9]

The Service's early track record in the test cases was mixed but has markedly improved as more courts become persuaded to apply established "common law" doctrines[10] to disallow the intended tax benefits from tax-motivated transactions. Historically, the Tax Court was somewhat more inclined to apply the venerable judicial doctrines than the generalist judges of the courts of appeals,[11] but that trend has been changing as several

3. See, e.g., Tom Herman, "Tax Report," Wall St. J. at A–1 (Feb. 10, 1999).

4. A "listed" transaction is one that the Service formally determines to have a potential for tax avoidance or evasion. The "list" continues to grow, mostly through published notices and other guidance. See, e.g., Notice 2001–17, 2001–9 I.R.B. 730, identifying a contingent liability shelter as a listed transaction.

5. See, e.g., I.R.C. §§ 6011 (taxpayer must disclose reportable transaction); 6111 (organizers and promoters must register potentially illegal shelters with the IRS); 6112 (promoters must maintain lists of clients who purchase potentially illegal tax shelters and, on request, must disclose these client lists to the IRS); and Reg. §§ 1.6011–4; 301.6711–1.

6. I.R.C. §§ 6662(d)(1)(B); 6662A.

7. I.R.C. §§ 6707; 6707A; 6708.

8. See, e.g., 31 U.S. § 330(b), (d) and various implementing changes to Circular 230, which regulates professionals who practice before the Treasury Department (including the IRS).

9. See, e.g., Yin, "Getting Serious About Corporate Tax Shelters: Taking a Lesson from History," 54 SMU L. Rev. 209 (2001).

10. See Chapter 1E1, supra which surveys the sham, economic substance, substance over form, and step transaction doctrines.

11. See, e.g., Coltec Industries, Inc. v. United States, 454 F.3d 1340 (4th Cir. 2006), cert. denied, 127 S.Ct. 1261 (2007); Black & Decker v. United States, 436 F.3d 431 (4th Cir. 2006); Dow Chemical Co. v. United States, 435 F.3d 594 (6th Cir. 2006); United Parcel Service of America, Inc. v. Commis-

circuits have invoked different formulations of the economic substance doctrine to disallow claimed benefits from transactions that meet the literal language of the Code but are found to have no substance or utility apart from the desire to achieve tax savings. Although legislation has been proposed repeatedly to "codify" these doctrines to strengthen the Service's position in court, codification has met with opposition from practitioners and even the Treasury who view the proposal as impractical and over-broad.[12]

Corporate tax shelters continue to be an occasional topic of interest to journalists[13] and tax academics. The media's interest has shifted to sad stories of taxpayers who discovered to their great regret (and expense) that they were misled by tax shelter promoters and their enablers from law and accounting firms. The new disclosure and penalty rules, along with this media coverage, have sent a clear message to promoters and taxpayers alike that overly aggressive behavior may result in serious economic consequences beyond disallowance of the claimed tax benefits. A well advised taxpayer now should know that if a tax savings strategy seems too good to be true, it should be viewed with appropriate skepticism.

E. AFFILIATED CORPORATIONS

Background. For a variety of reasons, business owners often conduct their activities through multiple entities. For example, to insulate a low-risk existing business from potential tort liability, the shareholders of a closely held corporation might form a separate corporation to conduct a new, high-risk activity. Similarly, a holding company with an operating subsidiary might determine that the regulatory requirements of a particular state or country are sufficiently stringent that a planned expansion into that jurisdiction should take place through a new subsidiary. The taxation of multiple corporations under common control is a highly complex topic, raising questions going well beyond the scope of a basic course on business enterprise taxation. The brief discussion that follows merely highlights the rules adopted by the Code to prevent tax avoidance and treat multiple corporations as a single economic unit.

Limits on Multiple Tax Benefits. Multiple corporations under common control also might be formed to save taxes. For example, absent limitations, taxpayers would be motivated to create separate corporations to take advantage of the lower marginal rates in Section 11(b), obtain separate $40,000 exemption amounts in computing the corporate alternative minimum tax, and obtain a myriad of other benefits available to separate taxable entities. Recognizing this incentive and its potential for abuse,

sioner, 254 F.3d 1014 (11th Cir.2001), rev'g 78 T.C.M. 262 (1999).

12. See Chapter 1E, supra.

13. See, e.g., Johnston, Perfectly Legal (2004), for an investigative reporter's perspective on the phenomenon.

Section 1561 denies certain multiple tax benefits to a "controlled group" of corporations under complex ownership tests in Section 1563.

Allocation of Income and Deductions Among Related Taxpayers: Section 482. Related corporations also may have an incentive to reduce their tax liability through transactions, such as sales, service contracts, leases, licensing agreements, and loans, where the corporations deal with each other on terms that are not comparable to arm's length dealings between unrelated taxpayers. The Code has a number of provisions designed to prevent tax avoidance resulting from transactions between related taxpayers. The most prominent statutory watchdog in the corporate setting is Section 482, which empowers the Service to reallocate income, deductions, and other tax items between or among commonly controlled trades or businesses in order to prevent tax evasion or clearly reflect income. The courts have broadly construed Section 482, extending it on occasion to transactions between a corporation and a sole proprietorship conducted by a controlling shareholder.[1]

The applicable standard under Section 482 is that of uncontrolled taxpayers dealing with each other at arm's length.[2] In applying the arm's length standard, the Service compares the results of a transaction between commonly controlled taxpayers with those of a comparable transaction under similar circumstances between uncontrolled taxpayers.[3] Section 482 is most frequently applied to reallocate income to a U.S. parent corporation from a more lightly taxed foreign affiliate.[4]

Consolidated Tax Returns. An "affiliated group" of corporations also may elect to consolidate its results for purposes of determination of tax liability and tax reporting. In broad outline, the effect of what is known as a "consolidated return election" is to treat a group of commonly controlled corporations as a single corporate entity for tax purposes. As a result of the election, the group pays tax on its consolidated taxable income. Intercompany transactions between members of the group, such as sales of property and distributions, generally have no immediate tax consequences.[5]

The ownership test applied to determine whether corporations are affiliated is used frequently in Subchapter C and is worth mentioning at this early juncture. Section 1504(a)(2) generally employs an 80 percent of voting power and value standard to test common corporate ownership. For example, an affiliated group would exist if one corporation held at least 80 percent of the total voting power of the stock in another corporation and also owned at least 80 percent of the total value of the stock of the other

1. See, e.g., Keller v. Commissioner, 77 T.C. 1014 (1981). The Service also has attempted, with mixed success, to apply the assignment of income doctrine to reattribute income between a corporation and its controlling owner-employees. See, e.g., Rubin v. Commissioner, 429 F.2d 650 (2d Cir.1970); Foglesong v. Commissioner, 691 F.2d 848 (7th Cir.1982). See also I.R.C. § 269A.

2. Reg. § 1.482–1(b)(1).

3. Id.; Reg. § 1.482–1(d)(1).

4. See, e.g., Bausch & Lomb Inc. v. Commissioner, 933 F.2d 1084 (2d Cir.1991).

5. Reg. §§ 1.1502–2(a),–13.

corporation. For purposes of this test, certain nonconvertible, nonvoting preferred stock is ignored.

F. RECOGNITION OF THE CORPORATE ENTITY

The premise underlying Subchapter C is that a corporation is an entity separate and apart from its shareholders. In addition to the classification questions discussed in Chapter 1, issues have arisen over the years as to whether an entity organized as a corporation under state law should be respected as such for tax purposes. These cases often involve corporations that are formed to avoid state usury laws or to act as nontaxable agents of a related partnership. The case below is the Supreme Court's most recent pronouncement on this issue.

Commissioner v. Bollinger

Supreme Court of the United States, 1988.
485 U.S. 340, 108 S.Ct. 1173.

■ JUSTICE SCALIA delivered the opinion of the Court.

Petitioner the Commissioner of Internal Revenue challenges a decision by the United States Court of Appeals for the Sixth Circuit holding that a corporation which held record title to real property as agent for the corporation's shareholders was not the owner of the property for purposes of federal income taxation. 807 F.2d 65 (1986). We granted certiorari, 482 U.S. 913, 107 S.Ct. 3183, 96 L.Ed.2d 672 (1987), to resolve a conflict in the courts of appeals over the tax treatment of corporations purporting to be agents for their shareholders. * * *

I.

Respondent Jesse C. Bollinger, Jr., developed, either individually or in partnership with some or all of the other respondents, eight apartment complexes in Lexington, Kentucky. (For convenience we will refer to all the ventures as "partnerships.") Bollinger initiated development of the first apartment complex, Creekside North Apartments, in 1968. The Massachusetts Mutual Life Insurance Company agreed to provide permanent financing by lending $1,075,000 to "the corporate nominee of Jesse C. Bollinger, Jr." at an annual interest rate of eight percent, secured by a mortgage on the property and a personal guaranty from Bollinger. The loan commitment was structured in this fashion because Kentucky's usury law at the time limited the annual interest rate for noncorporate borrowers to seven percent. Ky.Rev.Stat. §§ 360.010, 360.025 (1972). Lenders willing to provide money only at higher rates required the nominal debtor and record title holder of mortgaged property to be a corporate nominee of the true owner and borrower. On October 14, 1968, Bollinger incorporated Creekside, Inc., under the laws of Kentucky; he was the only stockholder. The next day, Bollinger and Creekside, Inc., entered into a written agreement which provided that the corporation would hold title to the apartment complex as Bollinger's agent for the sole purpose of securing financing, and would convey, assign, or encumber the property and disburse the proceeds thereof only as directed by Bollinger; that Creekside, Inc., had no obligation to maintain the property or assume any liability by reason of the execution of promissory notes or otherwise; and that Bollinger would indemnify and hold the corporation harmless from any liability it might sustain as his agent and nominee.

Having secured the commitment for permanent financing, Bollinger, acting through Creekside, Inc., borrowed the construction funds for the apartment complex from Citizens Fidelity Bank and Trust Company. Creekside, Inc., executed all necessary loan documents including the promissory note and mortgage, and transferred all loan proceeds to Bollinger's individual construction account. Bollinger acted as general contractor for the construction, hired the necessary employees, and paid the expenses out of the construction account. When construction was completed, Bollinger obtained, again through Creekside, Inc., permanent financing from Massachusetts Mutual Life in accordance with the earlier loan commitment. These loan proceeds were used to pay off the Citizens Fidelity construction loan. Bollinger hired a resident manager to rent the apartments, execute leases with tenants, collect and deposit the rents, and maintain operating records. The manager deposited all rental receipts into, and paid all operating expenses from, an operating account, which was first opened in the name of Creekside, Inc., but was later changed to "Creekside Apartments, a partnership." The operation of Creekside North Apartments generated losses for the taxable years 1969, 1971, 1972, 1973, and 1974, and ordinary income for the years 1970, 1975, 1976, and 1977. Throughout, the income and losses were reported by Bollinger on his individual income tax returns.

Following a substantially identical pattern, seven other apartment complexes were developed by respondents through seven separate partnerships. For each venture, a partnership executed a nominee agreement with Creekside, Inc., to obtain financing. (For one of the ventures, a different Kentucky corporation, Cloisters, Inc., in which Bollinger had a 50 percent interest, acted as the borrower and titleholder. For convenience, we will refer to both Creekside and Cloisters as "the corporation.") The corporation transferred the construction loan proceeds to the partnership's construction account, and the partnership hired a construction supervisor who oversaw construction. Upon completion of construction, each partnership actively managed its apartment complex, depositing all rental receipts into, and paying all expenses from, a separate partnership account for each apartment complex. The corporation had no assets, liabilities, employees, or bank accounts. In every case, the lenders regarded the partnership as the owner of the apartments and were aware that the corporation was acting as agent of the partnership in holding record title. The partnerships reported the income and losses generated by the apartment complexes on their partnership tax returns, and respondents reported their distributive share of the partnership income and losses on their individual tax returns.

The Commissioner of Internal Revenue disallowed the losses reported by respondents, on the ground that the standards set out in National Carbide Corp. v. Commissioner, 336 U.S. 422, 69 S.Ct. 726, 93 L.Ed. 779 (1949), were not met. The Commissioner contended that *National Carbide* required a corporation to have an arm's-length relationship with its shareholders before it could be recognized as their agent. Although not all respondents were shareholders of the corporation, the Commissioner took the position that the funds the partnerships disbursed to pay expenses should be deemed contributions to the corporation's capital, thereby making all respondents constructive stockholders. Since, in the Commissioner's view, the corporation rather than its shareholders owned the real estate, any losses sustained by the ventures were attributable to the corporation and not respondents. Respondents sought a redetermination in the United States Tax Court. The Tax Court held that the corporations were the agents of the partnerships and should be disregarded for tax purposes. On appeal, the United States Court of Appeals for the Sixth Circuit affirmed. 807 F.2d 65 (1986). We granted the Commissioner's petition for certiorari.

II.

For federal income tax purposes, gain or loss from the sale or use of property is attributable to the owner of the property. * * * The problem we face here is that two different taxpayers can plausibly be regarded as the owner. Neither the Internal Revenue Code nor the regulations promulgated by the Secretary of the Treasury provide significant guidance as to which should be selected. It is common ground between the parties, however, that if a corporation holds title to property as agent for a partnership, then for tax purposes the partnership and not the corporation is the owner. Given agreement on that premise, one would suppose that there would be agreement upon the conclusion as well. For each of respondents' apartment complexes, an agency agreement expressly provided that the corporation would "hold such property as nominee and agent for" the partnership, and that the partnership would have sole control of and responsibility for the apartment complex. The partnership in each instance was identified as the principal and owner of the property during financing, construction, and operation. The lenders, contractors, managers, employees, and tenants—all who had contact with the development—knew that the corporation was merely the agent of the partnership, if they knew of the existence of the corporation at all. In each instance the relationship between the corporation and the partnership was, in both form and substance, an agency with the partnership as principal.

The Commissioner contends, however, that the normal indicia of agency cannot suffice for tax purposes when, as here, the alleged principals are the controlling shareholders of the alleged agent corporation. That, it asserts, would undermine the principle of Moline Properties v. Commissioner, 319 U.S. 436, 63 S.Ct. 1132, 87 L.Ed. 1499 (1943), which held that a corporation is a separate taxable entity even if it has only one shareholder who exercises total control over its affairs. Obviously, *Moline's* separate-entity principle would be significantly compromised if shareholders of closely held corporations could, by clothing the corporation with some attributes of agency with respect to particular assets, leave themselves free at the end of the tax year to make a claim—perhaps even a good-faith claim—of either agent or owner status, depending upon which choice turns out to minimize their tax liability. The Commissioner does not have the resources to audit and litigate the many cases in which agency status could be thought debatable. Hence, the Commissioner argues, in this shareholder context he can reasonably demand that the taxpayer meet a prophylactically clear test of agency.

We agree with that principle, but the question remains whether the test the Commissioner proposes is appropriate. The parties have debated at length the significance of our opinion in National Carbide Corp. v. Commissioner, supra. In that case, three corporations that were wholly owned subsidiaries of another corporation agreed to operate their production plants as "agents" for the parent, transferring to it all profits except for a nominal sum. The subsidiaries reported as gross income only this sum, but the Commissioner concluded that they should be taxed on the entirety of the profits because they were not really agents. We agreed, reasoning first, that the mere fact of the parent's control over the subsidiaries did not establish the existence of an agency, since such control is typical of all shareholder-corporation relationships, id., 336 U.S. at 429–434, 69 S.Ct., at 730–732; and second, that the agreements to pay the parent all profits above a nominal amount were not determinative since income must be taxed to those who actually earn it without regard to anticipatory assignment, id., at 435–436, 69 S.Ct., at 733–734. We acknowledged, however, that there was such a thing as "a true corporate agent . . . of [an] owner-principal," id., at 437, 69 S.Ct., at 734, and proceeded to set forth four indicia and two requirements of such status, the sum of which has become known in the lore of federal income tax law as the "six *National Carbide* factors":

> "[1] Whether the corporation operates in the name and for the account of the principal, [2] binds the principal by its actions, [3] transmits money received to the principal, and [4] whether receipt of income is attributable to the services of employees of the principal and to assets belonging to the principal are some of the relevant considerations in determining whether a true agency exists. [5] If the corporation is a true agent, its relations with its principal must not be dependent upon the fact that it is owned by the principal, if such is the case. [6] Its business purpose must be the carrying on of the normal duties of an agent." Id., at 437, 69 S.Ct., at 734 (footnotes omitted).

We readily discerned that these factors led to a conclusion of nonagency in *National Carbide* itself. There each subsidiary had represented to its customers that it (not the parent) was the company manufacturing and selling its products; each had sought to shield the parent from service of legal process; and the operations had used thousands of the subsidiaries' employees and nearly $20 million worth of property and equipment listed as assets on the subsidiaries' books. Id., at 425, 434, 438, and n. 21, 69 S.Ct., at 728, 732–733, 734, and n. 21.

The Commissioner contends that the last two *National Carbide* factors are not satisfied in the present case. To take the last first: The Commissioner argues that here the corporation's business purpose with respect to the property at issue was not "the carrying on of the normal duties of an agent," since it was acting not as the agent but rather as the owner of the property for purposes of Kentucky's usury laws. We do not agree. It assuredly was not acting as the owner in fact, since respondents represented themselves as the principals to all parties concerned with the loans. Indeed, it was the lenders themselves who required the use of a corporate nominee. Nor does it make any sense to adopt a contrary-to-fact legal presumption that the corporation was the principal, imposing a federal tax sanction for the apparent evasion of Kentucky's usury law. To begin with, the Commissioner has not established that these transactions were an evasion. Respondents assert without contradiction that use of agency arrangements in order to permit higher interest was common practice, and it is by no means clear that the practice violated the spirit of the Kentucky law, much less its letter. It might well be thought that the borrower does not generally require usury protection in a transaction sophisticated enough to employ a corporate agent—assuredly not the normal *modus operandi* of the loan shark. That the statute positively envisioned corporate nominees is suggested by a provision which forbids charging the higher corporate interest rates "to a corporation, the principal asset of which shall be the ownership of a one (1) or two (2) family dwelling." Ky.Rev.Stat. § 360.025(2) (1987)—which would seem to prevent use of the nominee device for ordinary home-mortgage loans. In any event, even if the transaction did run afoul of the usury law, Kentucky, like most States, regards only the lender as the usurer, and the borrower as the victim. See Ky.Rev.Stat. § 360.020 (1987) (lender liable to borrower for civil penalty), § 360.990 (lender guilty of misdemeanor). Since the Kentucky statute imposed no penalties upon the borrower for allowing himself to be victimized, nor treated him as *in pari delictu*, but to the contrary enabled him to pay back the principal without any interest, and to sue for double the amount of interest already paid (plus attorney's fees), see Ky.Rev.Stat. § 360.020 (1972), the United States would hardly be vindicating Kentucky law by depriving the usury victim of tax advantages he would otherwise enjoy. In sum, we see no basis in either fact or policy for holding that the corporation was the principal because of the nature of its participation in the loans.

Of more general importance is the Commissioner's contention that the arrangements here violate the fifth *National Carbide* factor—that the corporate agent's "relations with its principal must not be dependent upon the fact that it is owned by the principal." The Commissioner asserts that this cannot be satisfied unless the corporate agent and its shareholder principal have an "arm's-length relationship" that includes the payment of a fee for agency services. The meaning of *National Carbide*'s fifth factor is, at the risk of understatement, not entirely clear. Ultimately, the relations between a corporate agent and its owner-principal are *always* dependent upon the fact of ownership, in that the owner can cause the relations to be altered or terminated at any time. Plainly that is not what was meant, since on that interpretation all subsidiary-parent agencies would be invalid for tax purposes, a position which the *National Carbide* opinion specifically disavowed. We think the fifth *National Carbide* factor—so much more abstract than the others—was no more and no less than a generalized statement of the concern, expressed earlier in our own discussion, that the separate-entity doctrine of *Moline* not be subverted.

In any case, we decline to parse the text of *National Carbide* as though that were itself the governing statute. As noted earlier, it is uncontested that the law attributes tax consequences of property held by a genuine agent to the principal; and we agree that it is reasonable for the Commissioner to demand unequivocal evidence of genuineness in the corporation-shareholder context, in order to prevent evasion of *Moline*. We see no basis, however, for holding that unequivocal evidence can only consist of the rigid requirements (arm's-length dealing plus agency fee) that the Commissioner suggests. Neither of those is demanded by the law of agency, which permits agents to be unpaid family members, friends, or associates. See Restatement (Second) of Agency §§ 16, 21, 22 (1958). It seems to us that the genuineness of the agency relationship is adequately assured, and tax-avoiding manipulation adequately avoided, when the fact that the corporation is acting as agent for its shareholders with respect to a particular asset is set forth in a written agreement at the time the asset is acquired, the corporation functions as agent and not principal with respect to the asset for all purposes, and the corporation is held out as the agent and not principal in all dealings with third parties relating to the asset. Since these requirements were met here, the judgment of the Court of Appeals is

Affirmed.

■ JUSTICE KENNEDY took no part in the consideration or decision of this case.

G. THE INTEGRATION ALTERNATIVE

The double tax on corporate profits has always been controversial. Economists and corporate finance theorists contend that it creates economic distortions and is inequitable, especially when compared to the pass-through treatment available to businesses that operate as partnerships, limited liability companies, or S corporations. Calls frequently have been made for "integration" of the individual and corporate income taxes into a single comprehensive system,[1] and the federal income tax began to move in

1. See, e.g., McLure, "Integration of the Personal and Corporate Income Taxes: The Missing Element in Recent Tax Reform Proposals," 88 Harv.L.Rev. 532 (1975); Canellos, "Corporate Tax Integration: By Design or By Default?" in Corporate Tax Reform: A Report of the Invitational Conference on Subchapter C 129 (Am. Bar Ass'n Section on Taxation; N.Y. State Bar Ass'n Tax Section, 1988); Graetz & Warren, "Integration of Corporate and Individual Income Taxes: An

that direction by reducing the burden of the double tax with the introduction in 2003 of a preferential 15 percent rate on most dividends received by noncorporate shareholders.[2]

Although many developed countries have adopted an integration model to tax business income,[3] the conventional wisdom is that a fully integrated system in the United States is not realistic in the near term. A separate tax on corporations is a politically popular way to raise revenue. Proponents of the classic double tax system have argued that the concentration of economic power represented by the earnings of at least public companies is an appropriate object of a tax system that purports to be built on principles of fairness and ability to pay. Many closely held businesses are able to avoid the double tax by operating as partnerships or S corporations. Even if they do not qualify for pass-through treatment, virtually all well-advised closely held C corporations have engaged in many "self-help" integration techniques (such as payments of deductible compensation or interest) to avoid the sting of the corporate tax. Moreover, a large of amount of the taxable income of publicly traded corporation is only taxed once because of the significant concentration of stock held by tax-exempt pension funds and charitable endowments.

Despite these practical and political realities, proponents of integration continue to argue that the corporate income tax increases the cost of capital for U.S. corporations. It is said to be an indirect tax on shareholders rather than a cost of doing business that is passed on to consumers. So viewed, the tax violates notions of vertical equity (by uniformly taxing income earned indirectly by dissimilarly situated shareholders) and horizontal equity (because income earned through a C corporation is taxed more heavily than the same item of income earned through a proprietorship, S corporation or partnership).[4] Free-market economists contend that integration would encourage corporate earnings to be more freely distributed to shareholders, who then could decide whether to reinvest in the business instead of leaving that reinvestment decision to corporate managers.

With the ongoing theoretical interest in integration, it is worth pausing to consider how such a system might be implemented. The potential integration models fall into two broad categories. The first, referred to as "full" or "complete" integration, would eliminate the corporate income tax and apply a pass-through taxing system to C corporations and their shareholders. A leading alternative is "partial" integration, which typically contemplates different types of tax relief for dividends paid by a corporation. Variations include giving shareholders a tax credit equal to a percentage of dividends paid or allowing shareholders to exclude from gross income a portion of dividends received during the year. Alternatively, the corpora-

Introduction," 84 Tax Notes 1767 (Sept. 27, 1999).

2. See Chapter 12A2, infra.

3. Among the countries with fully or partially integrated business taxation regimes are Canada, Germany, France, Australia, Italy, and the United Kingdom.

4. See Canellos, supra note 1, at 130–131.

tion could be permitted to deduct some or all of the dividends it pays its shareholders. The excerpts below survey the major integration prototypes.

Excerpt from Canellos, "Tax Integration by Design or by Default?"

Reprinted in Corporate Tax Reform: A Report of the Invitational Conference on Subchapter C 132–35 (American Bar Association, Section of Taxation; New York State Bar Association, Tax Section, 1988.)*

Formal Means for Achieving Integration

If it is determined that there should be some formal integration of corporate and shareholder taxation, the next issue is to choose among the range of techniques for achieving such integration. These techniques differ in terms of whether (1) double taxation is mitigated with respect to both retained and distributed assets; and (2) the actual taxpayer on corporate earnings is the corporation or the shareholder.

The purest form of integration is referred to as full or complete integration, and in effect represents the system of tax applicable to partnerships and S corporations. Under full integration, corporate earnings are attributed on some basis to shareholders who pay tax on them whether or not distributed. In turn, corporate losses flow through to shareholders for deduction by them subject to applicable restrictions on such flow through (such as basis rules, at risk rules, and the new passive loss limitations). The mechanics of existing full integration schemes differ. Thus, in the case of S corporations, the "entity" nature of the corporation predominates more than in the case of partnerships, which under Subchapter K are more often viewed as aggregates. As an example, the basis of corporate assets is generally not affected by sales of the S corporation's stock, whereas Section 754 allows for such an adjustment in the case of sales of partnership interests.

A scheme of complete integration was recommended in the 1977 Treasury Department study entitled "Blueprints for Basic Tax Reform." Under that system, the holder of corporate shares on the first day of the corporation's taxable year would be attributed all the earnings of the corporation for the taxable year. His basis would be increased by any allocated earnings, and would be decreased by distributions and losses. Where shares were sold during the taxable year, the seller would not be taxed on the current year's income, nor would he have any basis increase in respect of such income. Given the premise of "Blueprints" that capital gain and ordinary income would be taxed alike, the exclusion of current year's income was fully offset by the failure to increase basis for current year's income.

"Blueprints" dealt at length with the administrative difficulties of a fully integrated scheme. Thus, the problem of taxing shareholders on amounts not received was to be ameliorated through a system of corporate remittance of a "withholding" tax. This tax was to be considered paid on behalf of shareholders. The audit adjustment problem was to be solved by having the adjustment treated as an income or deduction item attributed to those persons holding shares on the first day of the year in which the adjustment was made. Despite these efforts to grapple with the problems of full integration, "Blueprints" never got off the drawing board. In this respect, it shares the fate of all other schemes for applying a full integration system to corporations in general. In this connection, full integration systems were considered and rejected by Canada and Germany for reasons of theory as well as practicality.

A second system of integration provides for a deemed paid credit for shareholders receiving distributions. The corporation is the initial taxpayer. In essence, tax paid by the corporation on distributed earnings would be attributed to shareholders. Distributions would be "grossed up" and the shareholder would apply the attributed tax as a credit against his tax on the "grossed up" dividend. In effect, this system taxes the shareholder in much the same way in which United States domestic corporations are taxed on distributions from foreign subsidiaries. The credit system has been adopted in many foreign countries and represents the generally prevailing corporate integration system.

The credit system raises a number of serious issues. First, there is the issue whether credit should be allowed only for corporate taxes actually paid. If so, integration has the effect of cutting back on corporate tax preferences such as investment tax credits, as well as possibly eliminating the benefit of foreign tax credits. Second, there is the issue whether tax should be paid by the corporation in connection with distributions (the advance corporation tax in the United Kingdom being an example). Such a tax payment assures that the Treasury will receive tax equal to the credit claimed by shareholders and represents in effect a corporate minimum tax applicable even if preferences would otherwise reduce the effective rate of corporate "mainstream" tax below the rate of attributed credit. A third significant issue is whether the credit should be made available to foreign shareholders in domestic corporations. Such credit has generally not been provided to foreign shareholders in the absence of tax treaties. Indeed, a major advantage of the credit system is the leverage which it provides to the taxing jurisdiction in negotiating favorable treaties with other countries.

A third system of integration reduces the corporate tax on distributed profits. This can be achieved by either a dividends-paid deduction or a split-rate system which taxes distributed earnings at a lower rate than retained earnings. The split-rate system had been used in Germany prior to Germany's adoption of the credit system. A dividends-paid deduction had been recommended in the 1984 Treasury Department Tax Reform Proposals, as well as the House version of the 1986 Act. This system of integration relieves corporate tax on distributed earnings at the corporate level rather than offsetting the second tax otherwise payable by shareholders. It raises some of the same issues discussed above in the case of the credit system. In addition, it raises other serious concerns. First, unless measures are taken to alter this result, a dividends-paid deduction or split-rate system has the effect of allowing corporate earnings to pass untaxed to shareholders who are not taxpayers (e.g., tax-exempt organizations and foreign shareholders). The Treasury Department's tax reform proposals would have sought to recapture some of the tax lost as the result of distributions to foreign shareholders by imposing a special withholding tax on dividends qualifying for the dividends-paid deduction. It acknowledged, however, that such a withholding tax would violate most existing tax treaties.

A final system for achieving integration with respect to distributed earnings is to exclude such distributions from the recipient's income.* This system would permit a shareholder to exclude from income dividends paid from a "previously taxed income" account. Issues raised by this system of integration include whether a selling shareholder should receive a basis increase for undistributed, previously-taxed income allocated to his account; and the allocation of distributions among the categories of previously-taxed income, pre-integration earnings, and earnings accumulated after integration which had not been previously taxed (for example, because of corporate tax preferences).

As this short summary demonstrates, difficult issues must be considered and dealt with in determining which, if any, path to express integration should be taken. Typically, the integration scheme which is adopted is tailored to meet the needs of the particular taxing jurisdiction—its historic tax system, the nature of its capital markets, the role of inward and outward international investment, and other factors. Where integration was adopted, it followed a long period of scholarly analysis and political input. Much of that work has already been undertaken in the United States. Despite these efforts, however, we are no closer to formal integration than we were in the sixties. Indeed, the 1986 Act has gone in the opposite direction by increasing the relative burden of corporate as compared with individual income taxes.

Integration of Individual and Corporate Tax Systems

Report of the Department of the Treasury.
January, 1992.

EXECUTIVE SUMMARY

WHAT IS INTEGRATION AND WHY SHOULD IT BE BENEFICIAL?

Currently, our tax system taxes corporate profits distributed to shareholders at least twice—once at the shareholder level and once at the

* An analysis of this approach is contained in Peel, A Proposal for Eliminating Double Taxation of Corporate Dividends, 39 Tax Lawyer 1 (1985).

corporate level. If the distribution is made through multiple unrelated corporations, profits may be taxed more than twice. If, on the other hand, the corporation succeeds in distributing profits in the form of interest on bonds to a tax-exempt or foreign lender, no U.S. tax at all is paid.

The two-tier system (i.e., imposing tax on distributed profits in the hands of shareholders after taxation at the corporate level) is often referred to as a classical tax system. Over the past two decades, most of our trading partners have modified their corporate tax systems to "integrate" the corporate and shareholder taxes to mitigate the impact of imposing two levels of tax on distributed corporate profits. Most typically, this has been accomplished by providing the shareholder with a full or partial credit for taxes paid at the corporate level.

Integration would reduce three distortions inherent in the classical system:

(a) *The incentive to invest in noncorporate rather than corporate businesses.* Current law's double tax on corporations creates a higher effective tax rate on corporate equity than on non-corporate equity. The additional tax burden encourages "self-help" integration through disincorporation.

(b) *The incentive to finance corporate investments with debt rather than new equity.* Particularly in the 1980's, corporations issued substantial amounts of debt. By 1990, net interest expense reached a postwar high of 19 percent of corporate cash flow.

(c) *The incentive to retain earnings or to structure distributions of corporate profits in a manner to avoid the double tax.* Between 1970 and 1990, corporations' repurchases of their own shares grew from $1.2 billion (or 5.4 percent of dividends) to $47.9 billion (or 34 percent of dividends). By 1990, over one-quarter of corporate interest payments were attributable to the substitution of debt for equity through share repurchases.

These distortions raise the cost of capital for corporate investments; integration could be expected to reduce it. To the extent that an integrated system reduces incentives for highly-leveraged corporate capital structures, it would provide important non-tax benefits by encouraging the adoption of capital structures less vulnerable to instability in times of economic downturn. The Report contains estimates of substantial potential economic gains from integration. Depending on its form, the Report estimates that integration could increase the capital stock in the corporate sector by $125 billion to $500 billion, could decrease the debt-asset ratio in the corporate sector by 1 to 7 percentage points and could produce an annual gain to the U.S. economy as a whole from $2.5 billion to $25 billion.

PROTOTYPES

This Report defines four integration prototypes and provides specifications for how each would work. [The prototypes described are: (1) a dividend exclusion; (2) a shareholder allocation under which all corporate income is allocated to shareholders and taxed in a manner similar to partnership income under current law; (3) a comprehensive business income tax (CBIT); and (4) an imputation credit.] For administrative reasons that the Report details, we have not recommended the shareholder allocation prototype * * *. Simplification concerns led us to prefer the dividend exclusion to any form of the imputation credit prototype.

In the dividend exclusion prototype, shareholders exclude dividends from income because they have already been taxed at the corporate level. Dividend exclusion provides significant integration benefits and requires little structural change in the Internal Revenue Code. When fully phased in, dividend exclusion would cost approximately $13.1 billion per year.

CBIT is, as its name implies, a much more comprehensive and larger scale prototype and will require significant statutory revision. CBIT represents a long-term, comprehensive option for equalizing the tax treatment of debt and equity. It is not expected that implementation of CBIT would begin in the short term, and full implementation would likely be phased in over a period of about 10 years. In CBIT, shareholders and bondholders exclude dividends and interest received from corporations from income, but neither type of payment is deductible by the corporation. Because debt and equity receive identical treatment in CBIT, CBIT better achieves tax neutrality goals than does the dividend exclusion prototype. CBIT is self-financing and would permit lowering the corporate rate to the maximum individual rate of 31 percent on a revenue neutral basis, even if capital gains on corporate stock were fully exempt from tax to shareholders.

POLICY RECOMMENDATIONS

In addition to describing prototypes, the Report makes several basic policy recommendations which we believe should apply to any integration proposal ultimately adopted:

(a) *Integration should not result in the extension of corporate tax preferences to shareholders.* This structure is grounded in both policy and revenue concerns and has been adopted by every country with an integrated system. The mechanism for preventing pass-through of preferences varies; some countries utilize a compensatory tax mechanism and others simply tax preference-sheltered income when distributed (as we recommend in the dividend exclusion prototype). Both of these mechanisms are discussed in the Report.

(b) *Integration should not reduce the total tax collected on corporate income allocable to tax-exempt investors.* Absent this restriction, business profits paid to tax-exempt entities could escape all taxation in an integrated system. This revenue loss would prove difficult to finance and would exacerbate distortions between taxable and tax-exempt investors.

(c) *Integration should be extended to foreign shareholders only through treaty negotiations, not by statute.* This is required to assure that

U.S. shareholders receive reciprocal concessions from foreign tax jurisdictions.

(d) *Foreign taxes paid by U.S. corporations should not be treated, by statute, identically to taxes paid to the U.S. Government.* Absent this limitation, integration could eliminate all U.S. taxes on foreign source profits in many cases.

* * *

OBJECTIVES OF THE REPORT

This Report is not a legislative proposal but rather a source document to begin the debate on the desirability of integration. This Report concludes that integration is desirable and presents a variety of integration mechanisms. A major reform such as integration should be undertaken only after appropriate deliberation and consideration of public comments. In light of the increasing isolation of the United States as one of the few remaining countries with a classical tax system, serious consideration of integration is now appropriate.

* * *

NOTE

In December, 1992, the Treasury Department followed up on its report by publishing a specific proposal for integration based on a dividend exclusion.[1] In March, 1993, the American Law Institute released its "Reporter's Study" of corporate tax integration.[2] Much like the Treasury report, the ALI study criticizes the classical double-tax regime. The ALI's recommended cure is a shareholder imputation credit system generally along the lines discussed in the earlier Canellos excerpt. As summarized in the Reporter's Study:[3]

> The proposed approach would convert the separate corporate income tax into a withholding tax with respect to dividends. Because some dividends will not have borne a corporate tax prior to distribution, an auxiliary dividend withholding tax is necessary to assure that shareholders do not receive tax credits for taxes that have never been paid at the corporate level. No double tax would result, because payments of regular corporate tax would be considered prepayments of the auxiliary tax. On the other hand, certain dividends may be free of corporate tax as a result of deliberately enacted corporate tax preferences that should be passed through to shareholders. Finally, in order to minimize differential treatment of debt and equity, a withholding tax on corporate interest pay-

1. See U.S. Treasury Dept., A Recommendation for Integration of the Individual and Corporate Income Tax Systems (1992).

2. See Warren, "Integration of the Individual and Corporate Income Taxes," Reporter's Study of Corporate Tax Integration (American Law Institute, 1993) (hereinafter "Reporter's Study").

3. Reporter's Study, supra note 2, at 4–5.

ments would be desirable. Four proposals implement this basic system of integration:

1. A withholding tax will be levied on dividend distributions; payments of corporate tax will be fully creditable against the withholding tax.

2. Shareholders will receive a refundable tax credit for the dividend withholding tax.

3. Certain corporate tax preferences can be passed through to shareholders.

4. A withholding tax will be levied on payments of corporate interest; that tax will be fully creditable by and refundable to the recipients of such interest payments.

After this flurry of activity in the early and mid–1990's, the integration debate went back into hibernation. Historically, the business community has not embraced the concept of integration, preferring instead to work within the existing system with its many opportunities to reduce or eliminate the corporate income tax. Corporate lobbyists focused their attention on expanding corporate tax preferences (such as accelerated depreciation, research and development incentives, and targeted tax credits) repealing the corporate alternative minimum tax, and lowering corporate tax rates. Some commentators suggested that corporate managers view integration as a threat to their power base because it would force them to act more as stewards of shareholders interests.[4] It seemed more and more likely that integration would remain a topic for occasional academic discourse rather than a viable political reality.

And then, surprising the skeptics, President George W. Bush revived the integration debate in early 2003 with a bold proposal that became the controversial centerpiece of his first economic stimulus package. The original proposal was reminiscent of the Treasury Department's dividend exclusion prototype. It provided for a 100 percent exclusion for all dividends paid out of income previously taxed at the corporate level. The excerpt below is from a Treasury Department press release explaining the proposal and providing an overview of some of the details. Keep in mind that the description of "current law" is as it was prior to individual taxpayer rate reductions enacted in 2003.

Description of President's Dividend Exclusion Proposal

U.S. Dept. of the Treasury, Jan. 21, 2003.

Eliminate the Double Taxation of Corporate Earnings

Current Law

Income earned by a corporation is taxed at the corporate level, generally at the rate of 35 percent. If the corporation distributes earnings to

4. See, e.g., Arlen & Weiss, "A Political Theory of Corporate Taxation," 105 Yale L. J. 325 (1995).

shareholders in the form of dividends, the income generally is taxed a second time at the shareholder level (at rates as high as 38.6 percent). If a corporation instead retains its earnings, the value of corporate stock will reflect the retained earnings. When shareholders sell their stock, that additional value will be taxed as capital gains (generally at a maximum rate of 20 percent for long-term capital gains). The combined rate of tax on corporate income can be as high as 60 percent, far in excess of rates of tax imposed on other types of income.

Reasons for Change

The double taxation of corporate profits creates significant economic distortions.

- First, double taxation creates a bias in favor of debt as compared to equity, because payments of interest by the corporation are deductible while returns on equity in the form of dividends and retained earnings are not. Excessive debt increases the risks of bankruptcy during economic downturns.
- Second, double taxation of corporate profits creates a bias in favor of unincorporated entities (such as partnerships and limited liability companies), which are not subject to the double tax.
- Third, because dividends are taxed at a higher rate than are capital gains, double taxation of corporate profits encourages a corporation to retain its earnings rather than distribute them in the form of dividends. This lessens the pressure on corporate managers to undertake only the most productive investments because corporate investments funded by retained earnings may receive less scrutiny than investments funded by outside equity or debt financing.
- Fourth, double taxation encourages corporations to engage in transactions such as share repurchases rather than to pay dividends because share repurchase permit the corporation to distribute earnings at reduced capital gains tax rates.
- Fifth, double taxation increases incentives for corporations to engage in transactions for the sole purpose of minimizing their tax liability.

By eliminating double taxation, the proposal will reduce tax-induced distortions that, in the current tax system, encourage firms to use debt rather than equity finance and to adopt noncorporate rather than corporate structures. Because shareholders will be exempt from tax only on distributions of previously taxed corporate income, the proposal will reduce incentives for certain types of corporate tax planning. In addition, the proposal will enhance corporate governance by eliminating the current bias against the payment of dividends. Dividends can provide evidence of a corporation's underlying financial health and enable investors to evaluate more readily a corporation's financial condition. This, in turn, increases the accountability of corporate management to its investors.

Proposal

Overview

The proposal would integrate the corporate and individual income taxes so that corporate earnings generally will be taxed once and only once. Under the proposal, public and private corporations would be permitted to distribute nontaxable dividends to their shareholders to the extent that those dividends are paid out of income previously taxed at the corporate level. The proposal generally would be effective for distributions made on or after January 1, 2003, with respect to corporate earnings after 2000.

To calculate the amount that can be distributed to its shareholders without further tax, a corporation will compute an excludable dividend amount (EDA) for each year. The EDA reflects income of the corporation that has been fully taxed. Thus, for example, a corporation with $100 of income that pays $35 of U.S. income taxes will have an EDA of $65 that can be distributed as excludable dividends.

If an amount would be a dividend under current law, it will be treated as an excludable dividend to the extent of EDA. Excludable dividends will not be taxed to shareholders. If a corporation's distributions during a calendar year exceed its EDA, only a proportionate amount of each distribution will be treated as an excludable dividend. Ordering rules are provided below for distributions that exceed EDA.

The capital gains tax on the sale of stock will be retained. Without further change, this would create an incentive for corporations to distribute previously taxed income as excludable dividends rather than retaining earnings for future investment. This is because excludable dividends would not be taxed to the shareholders but capital gains that represent retained earnings would be taxed to the shareholders when they sell their shares.

To ensure that distributions and retentions of previously taxed earnings are treated similarly, shareholders will be permitted to increase their basis in their shares to reflect that the retained earnings have already been taxed at the corporate level. As an alternative to distributing excludable dividends, corporations generally may allocate throughout the year all or a portion of the EDA to provide these basis increases. The basis increases will not be taxable. The effect of the basis increases will be to reduce the capital gains realized when shareholders sell their stock to the extent that the sales price reflects the corporation's retained, previously taxed earnings.

NOTE

The Bush Administration's proposal received a mixed response from Congress and the business community. Opponents argued that it was too complex, favored the wealthy without providing any immediate economic stimulus, and contributed to the federal budget deficit. Tax-privileged sectors, such as issuers of municipal bonds, banks, insurance companies, and real estate investment trusts, were concerned that their existing tax preferences would be undermined. Tax-exempt shareholders, such as pension funds and charitable foundations, as well as companies that were losing money or able to shelter their income from the corporate income tax, had little to gain from the proposal.

Supporters argued that eliminating the double tax on corporate earnings was a long overdue correction to a flawed system that encouraged excessive corporate debt, discouraged the payment of dividends and, in so doing, contributed to a misallocation of capital by favoring retained earnings over cash payouts. Some proponents predicted that a full dividend exclusion would make corporate managers more accountable to shareholders and increase shareholder confidence in the credibility of corporate earnings reports.

It became clear as the debate raged that the Bush dividend exclusion proposal would not be enacted because of its complexity and revenue effect. The ultimate compromise—a 15 percent maximum rate on both qualified dividends and most long-term capital gains—took a small step toward integrating the corporate and individual income taxes. Dividends qualify for the reduced rate whether or not they are paid out of income previously taxed at the corporate level. Some of the details are discussed in Chapter 12. These reduced rates, however, will expire at the end of 2010 unless Congress acts to make them permanent, ensuring that another debate will commence during or, more likely, shortly after a new President assumes office in 2009.

CHAPTER 11

Formation of a Corporation

A. Introduction to Section 351

Code: §§ 351(a), (c), (d)(1)–(2); 358(a), (b)(1); 362(a), (e); 368(c); 1032(a); 1223(1), (2); 1245(b)(3).

Regulations: §§ 1.351–1(a), (b); 1.358–1(a), –2(b)(2); 1.362–1(a); 1.1032–1(a), (d).

Policy of Section 351. In order to commence business operations, a corporation needs assets. It normally acquires these assets—known as the initial "capital" of a corporation—by issuing shares of stock in exchange for cash or other property, or by borrowing. When a corporation raises its equity capital by issuing stock solely for cash, the tax consequences are routine: the shareholder simply has made a cash purchase and takes a cost basis in the shares acquired.[1] If the corporation issues stock for property other than cash, the exchange would be a taxable event without a special provision of the Code. The shareholder would recognize gain or loss equal to the difference between the fair market value of the stock received and the adjusted basis of the property transferred to the corporation.[2] The exchange also might be taxable to the corporation. Its gain—more theoretical than real—would be the excess of the fair market value of the cash and property received over the corporation's zero basis in the newly issued shares.

A simple example illustrates the possibilities. Assume that A decides to form Venture, Inc. by transferring appreciated property with a value of $100 and a basis of $10 in exchange for Venture stock with a value of $100. A would realize $90 of gain and, in theory, Venture might be said to realize $100 of gain by issuing its stock. If both parties were taxed on this simple transaction, however, corporate formations would be severely impeded. To remove these tax obstacles, Congress long ago decided that routine incorporations should be tax free to the shareholders and the corporation. At the shareholder level, Section 351(a) provides that no gain or loss shall be recognized if property is transferred to a corporation by one or more persons solely in exchange for its stock if the transferor or transferors of property are in "control" of the corporation "immediately after the exchange." Section 351 applies both to transfers to newly formed and preexisting corporations provided that the transferors of property have "control" immediately after the exchange. At the corporate level, Section 1032(a) provides that a corporation shall not recognize gain or loss on the

1. I.R.C. § 1012.

2. I.R.C. § 1001(a).

receipt of money or other property in exchange for its stock (including treasury stock).[3] These general rules are accompanied by special basis provisions and are subject to several exceptions, all of which will be discussed as this chapter unfolds.

The policy of Section 351 is one familiar to nonrecognition provisions. The transfer of appreciated or depreciated property to a corporation controlled by the transferor is viewed as a mere change in the form of a shareholder's investment. Consider, for example, the sole proprietor who decides to incorporate an ongoing business. The proprietor clearly *realizes* gain in a theoretical sense when the assets of the business are exchanged for all of the new corporation's stock. But he has neither "cashed out" nor appreciably changed the nature of his investment. He owns and operates the same business with the same assets, only now in corporate solution. Incorporation does not seem to be the appropriate occasion to impose a tax if the transferred assets have appreciated or to allow a deductible loss if the assets have decreased in value.

This policy is more difficult to defend in the case of a minority shareholder. Consider a taxpayer who exchanges appreciated land with a basis of $40 and a fair market value of $100 for a ten percent stock interest in a newly formed corporation with a total net worth of $1,000. As a result of the exchange, the taxpayer's continuing interest in the land has been significantly reduced, and he now owns a ten percent interest in a variety of other assets. Presumably, the exchange should be taxable and he should recognize $60 of gain. Similarly, if two or more unrelated taxpayers join together and transfer various assets to a new corporation in exchange for its stock, they arguably have changed the form of their investment; each now owns a part of several assets in corporate solution rather than all of the assets previously owned directly. Despite these arguments, Congress chose not to make such fine distinctions, perhaps because its primary goal in enacting Section 351 was to facilitate a wide variety of corporate formations. Section 351 thus is broad enough to embrace transfers of property by a group of previously unrelated persons—provided, of course, that the specific statutory requirements set forth below have been met.[4]

Basic Requirements. The three major requirements to qualify for nonrecognition of gain or loss under Section 351 are as follows:

(1) One or more persons (including individuals, corporations, partnerships and other entities) must transfer "property" to the corporation;

(2) The transfer must be solely in exchange for stock of the corporation; and

3. See Reg. § 1.1032–1(a).

4. But see I.R.C. § 351(e)(1), which disallows nonrecognition in the case of a "transfer of property to an investment company." This provision is intended to preclude a group of taxpayers from achieving a tax-free diversification of their investment portfolio through an exchange with a newly formed investment company. See Reg. § 1.351–1(c) for the details.

(3) The transferor or transferors, as a group, must be in "control" of the corporation "immediately after the exchange."

"Control" for this purpose is defined by Section 368(c) as "the ownership of stock possessing at least 80 percent of the total combined voting power of all classes of stock entitled to vote and at least 80 percent of the total number of shares of all other classes of stock of the corporation." These requirements are not as simple as they may first appear. Section 351 contains several statutory terms of art, each of which has raised issues over the years. Before studying the requirements in detail, however, it is necessary to complete the basic statutory scheme by turning to the corollary rules on basis and holding period.

Shareholder Basis and Holding Period. If Section 351 applies to a transfer, any gain or loss realized by the shareholder is not currently recognized. The policy of nonrecognition requires the preservation of these tax attributes to prevent total forgiveness of the unrecognized gain or forfeiture of any unrecognized loss. This goal is achieved by Section 358(a)(1), which provides that the basis of the stock ("nonrecognition property") received in a Section 351 exchange shall be the same as the basis of the property transferred by the shareholder to the corporation. Returning to the introductory example, if A transfers property to Venture, Inc. with a basis of $10 and a fair market value of $100 for stock with a value of $100 in a transaction governed by Section 351, A's basis in the stock will be $10. Assuming no decrease in the value of the stock, the $90 of gain that went unrecognized on the exchange will be recognized if and when A sells the stock.[5]

In keeping with this policy, Section 1223(1) provides that where a transferor receives property with an "exchanged basis,"[6] such as stock in a Section 351 exchange, the holding period of that property is determined by including the period during which he held the transferred property if the transferred property is a capital asset or a Section 1231 asset; if it is not, the transferor's holding period begins on the date of the exchange.

Tax Consequences to Transferee Corporation. On the corporate side, Section 1032 provides that a corporation does not recognize gain or loss when it issues stock in exchange for money or property. Moreover, a corporation that receives property in exchange for its stock in a Section 351 exchange steps into the shoes of the transferor. Section 362(a) generally prescribes a transferred basis—i.e., the corporation's basis in any property

5. If a shareholder dies without selling the stock, however, his basis will be stepped up (or down) to its fair market value on the date of his death (or six months thereafter, if the alternate valuation date is elected for federal estate tax purposes). I.R.C. § 1014(a). This would be the case, of course, if the shareholder had simply continued to hold the transferred assets out of corporate solution and thus is not inconsistent with the policy of Section 358.

6. See I.R.C. § 7701(a)(44), which defines "exchanged basis property" as property having a basis determined in whole or in part by reference to other property held at any time by the person for whom the basis is to be determined. "Exchanged basis property" is a subspecies of "substituted basis property," which also includes "transferred" (formerly "carryover") basis property. See I.R.C. § 7701(a)(42)–(44).

received in a Section 351 exchange is the same as the transferor's basis, thus preserving the gain or loss inherent in the asset for later recognition by the corporation. And Section 1223(2) provides that if property has a transferred (i.e., carryover) basis to the corporation, the transferor's holding period likewise will carry over.

Limitations on Transfer of Built-in Losses. When controlling shareholders transfer noncash assets to a corporation in a Section 351 exchange, the economic gain or loss inherent in those assets is reflected in both the transferor's stock basis and the transferee corporation's basis in the assets. This potential for duplication of the same economic gain or loss has been a longstanding feature of the Section 351 nonrecognition scheme. When Congress discovered that some U.S. corporations were exploiting these rules by deducting the same losses twice, it did what came naturally and enacted yet another statutory watchdog to limit the recognition of losses. In so doing, it not only curtailed a potentially abusive tax shelter but also adversely affected many other transactions that may not be motivated by tax avoidance.

If property with a net built-in loss is transferred to a corporation in a Section 351 transaction or as a contribution to capital, the transferee corporation's aggregate adjusted basis of such property is limited to the fair market value of the transferred property immediately after the transfer.[7] Transferred property has a "net built-in loss" when the aggregate adjusted basis of the property exceeds its fair market value.[8] If multiple properties are transferred in the same transaction, some with built-in gains and others with built-in losses, the basis limitation only applies when there is a *net* built-in loss.[9] If more than one property with a built-in loss is transferred, the aggregate reduction in basis is allocated among the properties in proportion to their respective built-in losses immediately before the transaction.[10] Alternatively, the shareholder and the corporation may jointly elect to reduce the shareholder's basis in the stock that it receives to its fair market value.[11] If the election is made, the assets continue to have a built-

7. I.R.C. § 362(e)(2). This limitation is applied on a transferor-by-transferor basis rather than to an aggregated group of transferors. Prop. Reg. § 1.362–4(b)(2).

8. Any gain recognized by a transferor that increases the transferee corporation's basis in the transferred property is taken into account in determining whether the transferred property has a "net built-in loss" in the transferee's hands. Prop. Reg. § 1.362–4(b)(4)(ii), –4(d) Example 6.

9. I.R.C. § 362(e)(2)(A)(ii). Similar basis limitation rules apply to transactions where there is an "importation of a net built-in loss," such as a transfer of loss property to a domestic corporation by a person not subject to U.S. tax. See I.R.C. § 362(e)(1). The non-importation rule is designed to prevent the shifting of losses from transferors who are not subject to U.S. tax, such as a foreign person or a domestic tax-exempt entity, to transferees who are taxable and can use the loss. In overlap situations where a transaction is subject to both loss limitation rules, Section 362(e)(2) can apply to the portion of the transaction not described in Section 362(e)(1). Prop. Reg. §§ 1.362–4(b)(3); 1.362–4(d) Example 7.

10. I.R.C. § 362(e)(2)(B); Prop. Reg. § 1.362–4(b)(1).

11. I.R.C. § 362(e)(2)(C). The amount of basis reduction resulting from this election may not be any larger than what is necessary to eliminate the duplication of loss in the transferred assets. Thus, the amount of any

in loss in the hands of the transferee corporation, but the loss will not be duplicated on the disposition of the shareholder's stock.

More to Come. All these basis rules are subject to modifications to be discussed later in this chapter,[12] and both Sections 358 and 362 apply to a variety of corporate transactions other than Section 351. For the moment, however, it is best to ignore these distractions and focus on the policy of continuity of tax characteristics that is an essential corollary to the nonrecognition principle of Section 351.

PROBLEM

A, B, C, D and E, all individuals, form X Corporation to engage in a manufacturing business. X issues 100 shares of common stock. A transfers $25,000 cash for 25 shares; B transfers inventory with a value of $10,000 and a basis of $5,000 for 10 shares; C transfers unimproved land with a value of $20,000 and a basis of $25,000 for 20 shares; D transfers equipment with a basis of $5,000 and a value of $25,000 (prior depreciation taken was $20,000) for 25 shares; and E transfers a $20,000 (face amount and value) installment note for 20 shares. E received the note in exchange for land with a $2,000 basis that he sold last year. The note is payable over a five-year period, beginning in two years, at $4,000 per year plus market rate interest.

(a) What are the tax consequences (gain or loss recognized, basis and holding period in the stock received) to each of the transferors? As to E, see I.R.C. § 453B(a); Reg. § 1.453–9(c)(2).

(b) What are the tax consequences (gain recognized, basis and holding period in each of the assets received) to X Corporation?

(c) Assume all the same facts except that C transfers two parcels of unimproved land (Parcel #1 and Parcel #2), each with a value of $10,000. C's basis in Parcel #1 is $15,000 and C's basis in Parcel #2 is $8,000. What result to C and X Corporation?

(d) There was $5,000 of gain inherent in the inventory transferred by B. If X Corporation later sells the inventory for $10,000, and B sells his stock for $10,000, how many times will that $5,000 of gain be taxed? Is there any justification for this result?

B. REQUIREMENTS FOR NONRECOGNITION OF GAIN OR LOSS UNDER SECTION 351

The introductory problem illustrates that a tax-free exchange is easily accomplished if a group of individuals forms a corporation by transferring

stock basis reduction equals the amount of asset basis reduction that would have been required under Section 362(e)(2) if the election had not been made. Prop. Reg. § 1.362–4(c)(3).

12. See Section C1 of this chapter, infra.

property solely in exchange for common stock. But variations abound in the world of corporate formations, and the desires of the parties for a more complex transaction may conflict with the policy of nonrecognition. This section explores the requirements of Section 351 in more depth and shows that it often is possible, through careful planning, to reconcile these competing objectives.

1. "CONTROL" IMMEDIATELY AFTER THE EXCHANGE

Code: §§ 351(a); 368(c).

Regulations: § 1.351–1(a)(1).

Section 351 applies only if the transferors of property, as a group, "control" the corporation immediately after the exchange. For this purpose, "control" is defined by Section 368(c) as: (1) the ownership of at least 80 percent of the total combined voting power of all classes of stock entitled to vote, and (2) at least 80 percent of the total number of shares of all other classes of stock. The dual standard apparently was designed to ensure that the requisite control would not exist unless the transferors owned more than 80 percent of both the voting power and the total value of the corporation. Both prongs of the "control" test raise potentially thorny definitional questions—e.g., what is "stock entitled to vote?"; how is "voting power" determined? But these questions seldom arise in practice either because the routine corporate formation involves only one class of voting common stock or the transferors of property collectively emerge from the exchange owning 100 percent of all classes of stock.

The requisite control must be obtained by one or more transferors of "property" who act in concert under a single integrated plan. There is no limit on the number of transferors, and some may receive voting stock while others receive nonvoting stock. If the corporation issues more than one class of nonvoting stock, the Service requires that the transferor group must own at least 80 percent of *each* class.[1]

To be part of an integrated plan, the transfers need not be simultaneous. It is sufficient if the rights of the parties are "previously defined" and the agreement proceeds with an "expedition consistent with orderly procedure."[2] More important than timing is whether the transfers are mutually interdependent steps in the formation and carrying on of the business. Thus, it is possible for transfers separated by less than an hour to be considered separately for purposes of the control requirement or for transfers several years apart to be treated as part of an integrated plan.[3]

Finally, the transferors of property must be in control "immediately after the exchange." Momentary control will not suffice if the holdings of the transferor group fall below the required 80 percent as a result of

1. Rev.Rul. 59–259, 1959–2 C.B. 115.

2. Reg. § 1.351–1(a)(1).

3. Compare Henricksen v. Braicks, 137 F.2d 632 (9th Cir.1943), with Commissioner v. Ashland Oil & Refining Co., 99 F.2d 588 (6th Cir.1938).

dispositions of stock in a taxable transaction pursuant to a binding agreement or a prearranged plan.[4] But a voluntary disposition of stock, particularly in a donative setting, should not break control even if the original transferor of property parts with the shares moments after the incorporation exchange.[5]

As illustrated by the case below, the courts have taken a practical approach to this much-litigated issue, focusing less on timing and more on the previously defined rights and obligations of the parties.

Intermountain Lumber Co. v. Commissioner

United States Tax Court, 1976.
65 T.C. 1025.

■ WILES, JUDGE: * * *

[From 1948 until March, 1964, Dee Shook owned a sawmill in Montana, where Milo Wilson had logs processed into rough lumber for a fee. The rough lumber was processed into finished lumber at a separate plant jointly owned by Shook and Wilson. In March, 1964, the sawmill was damaged by fire. Shook and Wilson wanted to replace it with a larger facility, but Shook was financially unable to do so. Shook convinced Wilson to personally coguarantee a $200,000 loan to provide financing and, in return, Wilson insisted on becoming an equal shareholder with Shook in the rebuilt sawmill enterprise.

On May 28, 1964, Shook, Wilson and two other individuals incorporated S & W Sawmill, Inc. ("S & W"). Minutes of the first meeting of shareholders on July 7, 1964, recited in part that "Mr. Shook informed the meeting that a separate agreement was being prepared between he and Mr. Wilson providing for the sale of one-half of his stock to Mr. Wilson." Several days later, Shook transferred his sawmill site to S & W in exchange for 364 shares of S & W common stock. The company also issued one share to each of its four incorporators. No other stock was issued. On the same day, Shook and Wilson entered into "An Agreement for Sale and Purchase of Stock" under which Wilson was to purchase 182 shares of Shook's stock for $500 per share, plus annual interest, to be paid in installments. As each principal payment on the purchase price was made, a proportionate number of shares of stock were to be transferred on the corporate records and delivered to Wilson. A certificate for the 182 shares was placed in escrow. Shook also executed an irrevocable proxy granting Wilson voting rights in the 182 shares.

On August 19, 1964, S & W borrowed $200,000 from an outside lender, in part upon the personal guarantees of Shook and Wilson. On July 1, 1967, the taxpayer in this case, Intermountain Lumber Co. (referred to in the

4. See American Bantam Car Co. v. Commissioner, 11 T.C. 397 (1948), affirmed per curiam, 177 F.2d 513 (3d Cir.1949), cert. denied, 339 U.S. 920, 70 S.Ct. 622 (1950).

5. See D'Angelo Associates, Inc. v. Commissioner, 70 T.C. 121 (1978); Stanton v. United States, 512 F.2d 13 (3d Cir.1975).

opinion as "petitioner"), acquired all the outstanding S & W stock from Shook and Wilson. S & W became a wholly owned subsidiary of Intermountain, and the companies filed consolidated tax returns for the years involved in this controversy.

The specific question before the Tax Court related to the tax basis of S & W's assets for purposes of depreciation claimed on the Intermountain Lumber group's consolidated return. In a role reversal, the Service contended that the transfer of assets to S & W was tax-free under Section 351, requiring S & W to take a transferred basis in the assets under Section 362. In support of a higher cost basis, the taxpayer argued that the incorporation did not qualify under Section 351 because Mr. Shook did not have control immediately after the exchange. Ed.]

OPINION

Section 351 provides, in part, that no gain shall be recognized if property is transferred to a corporation by one or more persons solely in exchange for stock or securities ["or securities" was deleted from the statute in 1989. Ed.] in such corporation and immediately after the exchange such person or persons are in control of the corporation. "Control" is defined for this purpose in section 368(c) as ownership of stock possessing at least 80 percent of the total combined voting power of all classes of stock entitled to vote and at least 80 percent of the total number of shares of all other classes of stock of the corporation.

In this case, respondent is in the unusual posture of arguing that a transfer to a corporation in return for stock was nontaxable under section 351, and Intermountain is in the equally unusual posture of arguing that the transfer was taxable because section 351 was inapplicable. The explanation is simply that Intermountain purchased all stock of the corporation, S & W, from its incorporators, and that Intermountain and S & W have filed consolidated income tax returns for years in issue. Accordingly, if section 351 was applicable to the incorporators when S & W was formed, S & W and Intermountain must depreciate the assets of S & W on their consolidated returns on the incorporators' basis. Sec. 362(a). If section 351 was inapplicable, and the transfer of assets to S & W was accordingly to be treated as a sale, S & W and Intermountain could base depreciation on those returns on the fair market value of those assets at the time of incorporation, which was higher than the incorporators' cost and which would accordingly provide larger depreciation deductions. Secs. 167(g), 1011, and 1012.

Petitioner thus maintains that the transfer to S & W of all of S & W's property at the time of incorporation by the primary incorporator, one Dee Shook, was a taxable sale. It asserts that section 351 was inapplicable because an agreement for sale required Shook, as part of the incorporation transaction, to sell almost half of the S & W shares outstanding to one Milo Wilson over a period of time, thereby depriving Shook of the requisite percentage of stock necessary for "control" of S & W immediately after the exchange.

Respondent, on the other hand, maintains that the agreement between Shook and Wilson did not deprive Shook of ownership of the shares immediately after the exchange, as the stock purchase agreement merely gave Wilson an option to purchase the shares. Shook accordingly was in "control" of the corporation and the exchange was thus nontaxable under section 351.

Respondent has abandoned on brief his contention that Wilson was a transferor of property and therefore a person to also be counted for purposes of control under section 351. Respondent is correct in doing so, since Wilson did not transfer any property to S & W upon its initial formation in July of 1964. Wilson's agreement to transfer cash for corporate stock in March of 1965 cannot be considered part of the same transaction.

Since Wilson was not a transferor of property and therefore cannot be counted for control under section 351, William A. James, 53 T.C. 63, 69 (1969), we must determine if Shook alone owned the requisite percentage of shares for control. This determination depends upon whether, under all facts and circumstances surrounding the agreement for sale of 182 shares between Shook and Wilson, ownership of those shares was in Shook or Wilson.

A determination of "ownership," as that term is used in section 368(c) and for purposes of control under section 351, depends upon the obligations and freedom of action of the transferee with respect to the stock when he acquired it from the corporation. Such traditional ownership attributes as legal title, voting rights, and possession of stock certificates are not conclusive. If the transferee, as part of the transaction by which the shares were acquired, has irrevocably foregone or relinquished at that time the legal right to determine whether to keep the shares, ownership in such shares is lacking for purposes of section 351. By contrast, if there are no restrictions upon freedom of action at the time he acquired the shares, it is immaterial how soon thereafter the transferee elects to dispose of his stock or whether such disposition is in accord with a preconceived plan not amounting to a binding obligation. * * *

After considering the entire record, we have concluded that Shook and Wilson intended to consummate a sale of the S & W stock, that they never doubted that the sale would be completed, that the sale was an integral part of the incorporation transaction, and that they considered themselves to be coowners of S & W upon execution of the stock purchase agreement in 1964. These conclusions are supported by minutes of the first stockholders meeting on July 7, 1964, at which Shook characterized the agreement for sale as a "sale"; minutes of a special meeting on July 15, 1964, at which Shook stated Wilson was to "purchase" half of Shook's stock; the "Agreement for Sale and Purchase of Stock" itself, dated July 15, 1964, which is drawn as an installment sale and which provides for payment of interest on unpaid principal; Wilson's deduction of interest expenses in connection with the agreement for sale, which would be inconsistent with an option; the S & W loan agreement, in which Shook and Wilson held themselves out as the "principal stockholders" of S & W and in which S & W covenanted to equally insure Shook and Wilson for $100,000; the March 1965 stock purchase agreement with S & W, which indicated that Shook and Wilson "*are* to remain *equal* "(emphasis added) shareholders in S & W; the letter of May 1967 from Shook and Wilson to Intermountain, which indicated that Wilson owed Shook the principal balance due on the shares as an unpaid obligation; and all surrounding facts and circumstances leading to corporate formation and execution of the above documents. Inconsistent and self-serving testimony of Shook and Wilson regarding their intent and understanding of the documents in evidence is unpersuasive in view of the record as a whole to alter interpretation of the transaction as a sale of stock by Shook to Wilson.

We accordingly cannot accept respondent's contention that the substance varied from the form of this transaction, which was, of course, labeled a "sale." The parties executed an "option" agreement on the same day that the "agreement for sale" was executed, and we have no doubt that they could and indeed did correctly distinguish between a sale and an option.

The agreement for sale's forfeiture clause, which provided that Wilson forfeited the right to purchase a proportionate number of shares for which timely principal payments were not made, did not convert it into an option agreement. Furthermore, the agreement for sale made no provision for forgiving interest payments on the remaining principal due should principal payments not be made on earlier dates; indeed, it specifically provided that "Interest payment must always be kept current before any delivery of stock is to be made resulting from a payment of principal."

We thus believe that Shook, as part of the same transaction by which the shares were acquired (indeed, the agreement for sale was executed before the sawmill was deeded to S & W), had relinquished when he acquired those shares the legal right to determine whether to keep them. Shook was under an obligation, upon receipt of the shares, to transfer the stock as he received Wilson's principal payments. * * * We note also that the agreement for sale gave Wilson the right to prepay principal and receive all 182 shares at any time in advance. Shook therefore did not own, within the meaning of section 368(c), the requisite percentage of stock immediately after the exchange to control the corporation as required for nontaxable treatment under section 351.

We note also that the basic premise of section 351 is to avoid recognition of gain or loss resulting from transfer of property to a corporation which works a change of form only. See Bittker & Eustice, Federal Income Taxation of Corporations and Shareholders, par. 3.01, p. 3–4 (3d ed. 1971). Accordingly, if the transferor sells his stock as part of the same transaction, the transaction is taxable because there has been more than a mere change in form. * * * In this case, the transferor agreed to sell and did sell 50 percent of the stock to be received, placed the certificates in the possession of an escrow agent, and granted a binding proxy to the purchaser to vote the stock being sold. Far more than a mere change in form was effected.

We accordingly hold for petitioner.

NOTE

The Service has taken a pragmatic (some might say "nuanced") view of the issue in *Intermountain Lumber* when the subsequent disposition of stock, even though pursuant to a prearranged binding commitment, is not taxable. Revenue Ruling 2003–51[1] involved a plan by two corporations, referred to here as X Co. and Y Co., to consolidate certain businesses in a holding company structure. To accomplish that goal, X Co. transferred $40 of business assets to a wholly owned subsidiary, X Sub Co., for X Sub Co. stock (the first transfer). Then, pursuant to a preexisting agreement, X Co. transferred its X Sub Co. stock to Y Sub Co., a subsidiary of Y Co., for stock of Y Sub Co. (the second transfer). At the same time as the second transfer, Y Co. also contributed $30 of cash to Y Sub Co. for additional stock (the third transfer). Finally, Y Sub Co. transferred its own business assets and the $30 it got from Y Co. to X Sub Co. (the fourth transfer). When the dust settled, X Co. and Y Co. owned 40 percent and 60 percent, respectively, of Y Sub Co. and Y Sub Co. owned 100 percent of X Sub Co. The issue in the ruling was the tax results of the first transfer. X Co. clearly would have qualified for nonrecognition of gain under Section 351 on the first transfer but for its preexisting obligation to also make the second transfer. In holding that the first transfer satisfied the "control immediately after the exchange requirement," Revenue Ruling 2003–51 distinguishes between prearranged dispositions of stock that are taxable and those that are nontaxable:

> Treating a transfer of property that is followed by ... *a prearranged sale of the stock* received as a transfer described in § 351 is not consistent with Congress' intent in enacting § 351 to facilitate rearrangement of the transferor's interest in its property. Treating a transfer of property that is followed by *a nontaxable disposition of the stock* received as a transfer described in § 351 is not necessarily inconsistent with the purposes of § 351. Accordingly, the control requirement may be satisfied in such a case, even if the stock received is transferred pursuant to a binding commitment in place upon the transfer of the property in exchange for the stock. (Emphasis added.)

Revenue Ruling 2003–51 also notes that its result is supported by the fact that the transaction could have been rearranged to more directly qualify for nonrecognition under Section 351. For example, X Co. could have contributed the business assets directly to Y Sub Co. for Y Sub Co. stock at the same time as Y Co. contributed the $30 of cash to the subsidiary. Those transfers would have been protected by Section 351. Y Sub Co. could have then transferred its assets to a newly formed X Sub Co. in a second tax-free Section 351 exchange. Thus, Revenue Ruling 2003–51

1. 2003–1 C.B. 938.

concludes that treating X Co.'s first transfer as within Section 351 is not inconsistent with the purposes of that section.

2. TRANSFERS OF "PROPERTY" AND SERVICES

Regulations: § 1.351–1(a)(1), (2).

If the transferors of "property" must have control immediately after the exchange, the question then becomes: what is "property?" Although the term is not specifically defined for purposes of Section 351, it has been broadly construed to include cash, capital assets, inventory, accounts receivable, patents, and, in certain circumstances, other intangible assets such as nonexclusive licenses and industrial know-how.[1]

Section 351(d)(1) specifically provides, however, that stock issued for services shall not be considered as issued in return for property.[2] This rule makes good sense in the case of a promoter of the enterprise or even the company lawyer, each of whom contributes no capital but still receives stock in exchange for services rendered to the corporation. Inasmuch as the stock is compensation for those services, the tax consequences are properly determined under Sections 61 and 83.

Apart from realizing ordinary income, a person who receives stock solely in exchange for services may cause the other parties to the incorporation to recognize gain or loss. The pure service provider is not considered a transferor of property and may not be counted as part of the control group for purposes of qualifying the exchange under Section 351. But if a person receives stock in exchange for both property and services, *all* of his stock is counted toward the 80 percent control requirement.[3]

These rules offer some tempting opportunities for the tax planner. Assume, for example, that Promoter and Investor join forces to form a new corporation. In exchange for his services, Promoter receives 25 percent of the corporation's common stock. In exchange for $500,000 of highly appreciated property, Investor receives the other 75 percent. Investor, as the only transferor of property, does not have control and thus must recognize gain on the transaction unless Promoter somehow can qualify as a transferor of property—a status easily achieved, perhaps, by the mere transfer of $100 in cash.

Life is not so simple in the world of Subchapter C. To prevent such facile maneuvering around the control requirement, the regulations provide that the stock will not be treated as having been issued for property if the primary purpose of the transfer is to qualify the exchanges of the other property transferors for nonrecognition and if the stock issued to the nominal transferor is "of relatively small value" in comparison to the value

1. See, e.g., E.I. Du Pont de Nemours & Co. v. United States, 471 F.2d 1211 (Ct.Cl. 1973); Rev.Rul. 64–56, 1964–1 C.B. 133 (industrial know-how); Rev.Rul. 69–357, 1969–1 C.B. 101 (money is "property").

2. See also Reg. § 1.351–1(a)(1)(i).

3. Reg. § 1.351–1(a)(1)(ii), –1(a)(2) Example (3).

of the stock already owned or to be received for services by the transferor.[4] In other words, the accommodation transfer gambit fails if the value of the property transferred is *de minimis* relative to the stock received for services. This regulation has been interpreted generously by the Service in Revenue Procedure 77–37,[5] which provides that property transferred "will not be considered to be of relatively small value * * * if the fair market value of the property transferred is equal to, or in excess of, 10 percent of the fair market value of the stock already owned (or to be received for services) by * * * [the transferor]."

3. SOLELY FOR "STOCK"

Code: Skim § 351(g).

The final requirement for nonrecognition is that the transfers of property be made "solely" in exchange for "stock" of the controlled corporation. "Stock" generally means an equity investment in the company, and in this context the term has presented relatively few definitional problems. It does not include stock rights or warrants.[1] At one time, Section 351(a) applied to transfers of property solely in exchange for both stock and corporate debt securities, but the term "securities" eventually was deleted. A "security" was construed by the courts as a relatively long-term debt obligation (e.g., a bond or debenture) which provided the holder with a continuing degree of participation in corporate affairs, albeit as a creditor.[2] After the amendment, debt securities received in a Section 351 transaction, along with all forms of nonsecurity debt (e.g., a short-term note), are treated as boot, leaving only stock to qualify as nonrecognition property.

Certain preferred stock with debt-like characteristics, labelled by Section 351(g)(2) as "nonqualified preferred stock," is treated as "other property" (known in tax jargon as "boot") rather than stock for purposes of Sections 351 and 356 (relating to recognition of gain or loss on certain otherwise tax-free corporate acquisitions). "Nonqualified preferred stock" is generally defined as preferred stock[3] with any of the following characteristics: (1) the stockholder has the right to require the issuing corporation or a "related person"[4] to redeem or purchase the stock, (2) the issuer or a

4. Reg. § 1.351–1(a)(1)(ii). See also Estate of Kamborian v. Commissioner, 469 F.2d 219 (1st Cir.1972).

5. 1977–2 C.B. 568, § 3.07.

1. Reg. § 1.351–1(a)(1), last sentence.

2. Camp Wolters Enterprises, Inc. v. Commissioner, 22 T.C. 737 (1954), affirmed, 230 F.2d 555 (5th Cir.1956), cert. denied, 352 U.S. 826, 77 S.Ct. 39 (1956).

3. For this purpose, "preferred stock" is stock which is limited and preferred as to dividends and does not participate in corporate growth to any significant extent. I.R.C. § 351(g)(3)(A). Stock is not treated as participating in corporate growth to any significant extent unless there is a real and meaningful likelihood of the shareholder actually participating in the corporation's earnings and growth. Id. If there is not a real and meaningful likelihood that dividends beyond any limitation or preference will actually be paid, the *possibility* of such payments is disregarded in determining whether stock is limited and preferred as to dividends. Id.

4. Persons are "related" if they bear any of the relationships described in Sections 267(b) or 707(b), such as family members,

related person is required to redeem or purchase the stock, (3) the issuer or a related person has the right to redeem or purchase the stock and, as of the issue date, it is more likely than not that such right will be exercised, or (4) the dividend rate on such stock varies in whole or in part with reference to interest rates, commodity prices, or similar indices.[5] The first three of these categories apply only if the right or obligation with respect to the redemption or purchase of the stock may be exercised within the 20–year period beginning on the issue date of the stock, and such right or obligation is not subject to a contingency which, as of the issue date, makes remote the likelihood of the redemption or purchase.[6]

The effect of Section 351(g) is to treat debt-like preferred stock as boot, resulting in potential recognition of gain (but generally not loss) to the recipient under Section 351(b). A taxpayer is allowed to recognize a loss, however, if only nonqualified preferred stock is received in an exchange.[7] The legislative history indicates that nonqualified preferred stock still will be treated as "stock" for all other purposes until the Treasury provides otherwise in prospective regulations issued under the authority of Section 351(g)(4).[8] This hybrid status as boot for gain recognition purposes but stock for other purposes is more significant in connection with tax-free acquisitive reorganizations, which are covered later in the text.[9]

PROBLEMS

1. Consider whether the following transactions qualify under Section 351:

(a) A and B are unrelated individuals. A forms Newco, Inc. on January 2 of the current year by transferring property with a basis of $10,000 and a value of $50,000 for all 50 shares of Newco common stock. On March 2, in an unrelated transaction, B transfers property with a basis of $1,000 and a value of $10,000 for 10 shares of Newco nonvoting preferred stock (that is not nonqualified preferred stock).

(b) Same as (a), above, except the transfers by A and B were part of a single integrated plan.

(c) Same as (b), above, except A transferred 25 of her 50 shares to her daughter, D, as a gift on March 5 (three days after B's transfer). What if A's gift to D were on January 5?

(d) Same as (b), above, except that two months after B's transfer, A sold 15 shares to E pursuant to a preexisting oral understanding, without which Newco would not have been formed.

controlling shareholders or partners, a corporate affiliate, etc. I.R.C. § 351(g)(3)(B).

5. I.R.C. § 351(g)(2)(A).

6. I.R.C. § 351(g)(2)(B).

7. I.R.C. § 351(g)(1)(B).

8. Staff of Joint Committee on Taxation, General Explanation of Tax Legislation Enacted in 1997, 105th Cong., 1st Sess. 210 (1997).

9. See Chapter 17, infra.

2. Mr. Java ("Java") has operated a chain of Internet cafes as a sole proprietorship over the past few years and is now interested in expanding his horizons and limiting his liability. To do so, he wishes to incorporate, raise $150,000 of additional capital and hire an experienced person to manage the business. He has located Venturer, who is willing to invest $150,000 cash and Manager, who has agreed to serve as chief operating officer if the terms are right.

The parties have decided to join forces and form Java Jyve, Inc. ("Jyve") to expand the cafe business and offer fresh bakery items at every location. Java will transfer assets with an aggregate basis of $50,000 and a fair market value of $200,000 (do not be concerned with the character of the individual assets for this problem); Venturer will contribute $150,000 cash; and Manager will enter into a five-year employment contract. Java would like effective control of the business; Venturer is interested in a guaranteed preferred return on his investment but also wants to share in the growth of the company; and Manager wants to be fairly compensated (she believes her services are worth approximately $80,000 per year) and receive stock in the company, but she can not afford to make a substantial cash investment. All the parties wish to avoid adverse tax consequences.

Consider the following alternative proposals and evaluate whether they meet the tax and non-tax objectives of the parties:

(a) In exchange for their respective contributions, Java will receive 200 shares and Venturer will receive 150 shares of Jyve stock. Manager will agree to a salary of $40,000 per year for five years and will receive 150 shares of Jyve common stock upon the incorporation. (Assume that the value of the stock is $1,000 per share.)

(b) Same as (a), above, except Manager will receive compensation of $80,000 per year and will pay $150,000 for her Jyve stock. Any difference if Manager, unable to raise the cash, gave Jyve her unsecured $150,000 promissory note, at market rate interest, payable in five equal installments, in exchange for her 150 shares?

(c) Same as (a), above, except Manager will pay $1,000 for her 150 shares and the incorporation documents specify that she is receiving those shares in exchange for her cash contribution rather than for future services.

(d) Same as (c), above, except Manager will pay $20,000 cash rather than $1,000.

(e) Same as (d), above, except Manager will receive only 20 shares of stock without restrictions; the other 130 shares may not be sold by Manager for five years and will revert back to the corporation if Manager should cease to be an employee of the company during the five-year period. See I.R.C. § 83. Would you advise Manager to make a § 83(b) election in this situation? What other information would you need?

(f) In general, is there another approach to structuring the formation of Jyve that would harmonize the goals of the founders?

C. TREATMENT OF BOOT

1. IN GENERAL

Code: §§ 351(b); 358(a), (b)(1); 362(a). Skim § 351(g).

Regulations: §§ 1.351–2(a); 1.358–1,–2; 1.362–1.

In the introductory section of this chapter, a simple example illustrated the need for Section 351. Recall that A decided to form Venture, Inc. by transferring appreciated property with a value of $100 and a basis of $10 in exchange for Venture stock with a value of $100. Without a special provision of the Code, A would have recognized a $90 gain on the exchange. But since A received solely stock and owned 100 percent of Venture, the transaction qualified for nonrecognition under Section 351. To preserve the gain that went unrecognized, A took a $10 exchanged basis in the Venture stock under Section 358, and Venture took a $10 transferred basis in the contributed assets under Section 362. If A had received more than one class of stock, the transaction still would have qualified under Section 351, and A would have been required to allocate his aggregate exchanged basis of $10 among the various classes of stock received in proportion to their relative fair market values.[1]

But suppose that A, perhaps motivated by the tax advantages of corporate debt,[2] capitalizes Venture, Inc. with the same $100 asset by taking back common stock with a value of $80 and a corporate note with a value of $20. The transaction fails to qualify under Section 351(a) because A, although clearly in "control" of Venture, has not exchanged his $100 asset "solely" in exchange for stock. A's position is not unlike the real estate investor who, desiring a tax-free like-kind exchange, trades his highly appreciated $500,000 building in exchange for other real estate with a value of $450,000 and $50,000 of cash to even out the deal. The question for both A and the real estate investor becomes: should the receipt of this "boot" require full recognition of their realized gain, or should there be a statutory middle ground?

In the corporate setting, this question is answered by Section 351(b). It provides that if an exchange otherwise would have qualified under Section 351(a) but for the fact that the transferor received "other property or money" in addition to stock, then the transferor's realized gain (if any) must be recognized to the extent of the cash plus the fair market value of the other property received. Translated more concisely, Section 351(b) provides that any gain realized by a transferor on an otherwise qualified Section 351(a) exchange must be recognized only to the extent of the boot received. The gain is characterized by reference to the character of the assets transferred, taking into account the impact of the recapture of

1. Reg. § 1.358–2(b)(2).

2. See Section F of this chapter, infra.

depreciation provisions.[3] Despite the presence of boot, however, no *loss* may be recognized under Section 351(b).[4]

In the example where A receives $80 of stock and a $20 corporate note in exchange for his $100 asset with a $10 basis, Section 351(b) will require A to recognize $20 of his $90 realized gain.[5] This makes sense, of course, because to the extent that A has transferred his asset in exchange for property other than stock, he has changed not merely the form of his investment but the substance as well. To that extent, nonrecognition treatment is inappropriate.

As noted earlier, if a shareholder transfers property in a tax-free Section 351(a) transaction, the unrecognized gain on the transfer will be preserved through an exchanged basis in the transferor's stock and again through a transferred basis in the corporation's assets. But if a shareholder recognizes some gain as a result of the receipt of boot, not all of his realized gain must be accounted for at a later time. To avoid this potential double recognition of gain, the shareholder may increase his basis in the stock, securities and other property received by an amount equal to the gain recognized on the transfer.[6] This higher basis will result in less gain (or more loss) if and when the shareholder later sells the property received from the corporation.

The shareholder's basis in the "nonrecognition property" (i.e., stock) received from the corporation thus equals the basis in the property transferred to the corporation, decreased by the fair market value of any other property and the amount of cash received, and increased by the gain recognized on the transfer. The boot takes a fair market value basis. Since any gain recognized by the shareholder is attributable to the boot, and since his continuing investment is represented by the nonrecognition property, the unrecognized gain inherent in the property transferred to the corporation logically should now be preserved in the nonrecognition property. These goals are achieved by assigning the boot a fair market value basis and allocating the remaining basis to the nonrecognition property.[7]

Applying these rules to our previous example, if A received $80 of Venture, Inc. stock and a $20 note in exchange for his $100 asset with a basis of $10, his recognized gain would be $20—the fair market value of the boot. A's basis in the note would be $20, its fair market value. A's basis in the stock would be determined as follows:

3. See I.R.C. §§ 1245(b)(3); 1250(d)(3). Also relevant is I.R.C. § 1239, which characterizes the recognized gain on the transfer of depreciable property to a corporation as ordinary income if the transferor and certain related parties own more than 50 percent of the value of the transferee corporation's stock.

4. See also I.R.C. § 267(a)(1), disallowing losses on sales or exchanges between related taxpayers, including an individual and a corporation more than 50 percent in value of which is owned by the individual (actually or through attribution rules).

5. This example only addresses the *amount* of A's gain. The *timing* of gain triggered by the receipt of installment boot is considered in Section C2 of the chapter, infra.

6. I.R.C. § 358(a)(1)(B)(ii).

7. I.R.C. § 358(a)(2).

Basis of Asset Transferred	$ 10
Less: Fair Market Value of Note Received	(20)
Plus: Gain Recognized	20
Basis of Stock	$ 10

The arithmetic makes sense. Remember that the value of the Venture stock was $80. By assigning the stock a $10 basis, Section 358 preserves the $70 of realized gain that went unrecognized on the partially tax-free exchange. There is no more gain to be preserved, so it is logical to give the boot a fair market value basis.[8]

At the corporate level, Section 362(a) provides that the corporation's basis in the property received on a Section 351 exchange is the same as the transferor's basis, increased by any gain recognized on the exchange. This rule ensures that any gain or loss not recognized by the shareholder will be reflected in the corporation's basis in the transferred assets. Returning one last time to the example, since A recognized $20 of gain on the exchange, Venture's basis in the transferred asset would be $30 (a $10 transferred basis in A's hands plus $20 gain recognized).

If a transferor exchanges several assets in exchange for stock and boot, the transaction becomes more complex. For purposes of determining the gain recognized (and, if relevant, the character of that gain), it becomes necessary to allocate the boot among the transferred assets. Similar allocations are required to determine the basis of the assets in the hands of the corporation. Although these questions rarely arise in the routine corporate formation, they have titillated tax commentators and caused unnecessary anguish to students of corporate tax.[9] The ruling below is the Service's attempt at an orderly resolution of this problem.

Revenue Ruling 68–55

1968–1 Cum.Bull. 140.

Advice has been requested as to the correct method of determining the amount and character of the gain to be recognized by Corporation *X* under section 351(b) of the Internal Revenue Code of 1954 under the circumstances described below.

Corporation *Y* was organized by *X* and *A*, an individual who owned no stock in *X*. *A* transferred 20*x* dollars to *Y* in exchange for stock of *Y* having a fair market value of 20*x* dollars and *X* transferred to *Y* three separate assets and received in exchange stock of *Y* having a fair market value of 100*x* dollars plus cash of 10*x* dollars.

8. As before, this example only addresses the amount of gain recognized under Section 351(b) and the resulting basis consequences.

9. For the seminal article on boot allocation, see Rabinovitz, "Allocating Boot in Section 351 Exchanges," 24 Tax L.Rev. 337 (1969). For an exhaustive (and exhausting) update, see Cohen & Whitney, "Revisiting the Allocation of Boot in Section 351 Exchanges," 48 Tax Lawyer 959 (1995).

In accordance with the facts set forth in the table below if *X* had sold at fair market value each of the three assets it transferred to *Y*, the result would have been as follows:

	Asset I	**Asset II**	**Asset III**
Character of asset	Capital asset held more than 6 months.	Capital asset held not more than 6 months.	Section 1245 property.
Fair market value	$22*x*	$33*x*	$55*x*
Adjusted basis	40*x*	20*x*	25*x*
Gain (loss)	($18*x*)	$13*x*	$30*x*
Character of gain or loss	Long-term capital loss.	Short-term capital gain.	Ordinary income.

The facts in the instant case disclose that with respect to the section 1245 property the depreciation subject to recapture exceeds the amount of gain that would be recognized on a sale at fair market value. Therefore, all of such gain would be treated as ordinary income under section 1245(a)(1) of the Code.

Under section 351(a) of the Code, no gain or loss is recognized if property is transferred to a corporation solely in exchange for its stock and immediately after the exchange the transferor is in control of the corporation. If section 351(a) of the Code would apply to an exchange but for the fact that there is received, in addition to the property permitted to be received without recognition of gain, other property or money, then under section 351(b) of the Code gain (if any) to the recipient will be recognized, but in an amount not in excess of the sum of such money and the fair market value of such other property received, and no loss to the recipient will be recognized.

The first question presented is how to determine the amount of gain to be recognized under section 351(b) of the Code. The general rule is that each asset transferred must be considered to have been separately exchanged. See the authorities cited in Revenue Ruling 67–192, C.B. 1967–2, 140, and in Revenue Ruling 68–23, which hold that there is no netting of gains and losses for purposes of applying sections 367 and 356(c) of the Code. Thus, for purposes of making computations under section 351(b) of the Code, it is not proper to total the bases of the various assets transferred and to subtract this total from the fair market value of the total consideration received in the exchange. Moreover, any treatment other than an asset-by-asset approach would have the effect of allowing losses that are specifically disallowed by section 351(b)(2) of the Code.

The second question presented is how, for purposes of making computations under section 351(b) of the Code, to allocate the cash and stock received to the amount realized as to each asset transferred in the exchange. The asset-by-asset approach for computing the amount of gain realized in the exchange requires that for this purpose the fair market value of each category of consideration received must be separately allocated to the transferred assets in proportion to the relative fair market values of the transferred assets. See section 1.1245–4(c)(1) of the Income Tax Regulations which, for the same reasons, requires that for purposes of computing the amount of gain to which section 1245 of the Code applies each category of consideration received must be allocated to the properties transferred in proportion to their relative fair market values.

Accordingly, the amount and character of the gain recognized in the exchange should be computed as follows:

	Total	**Asset I**	**Asset II**	**Asset III**
Fair market value of asset transferred	$110*x*	$22*x*	$33*x*	$55*x*
Percent of total fair market value	---------	20%	30%	50%
Fair market value of *Y* stock received in exchange	$100*x*	$20*x*	$30*x*	$50*x*
Cash received in exchange	10*x*	2*x*	3*x*	5*x*
Amount realized	$110*x*	$22*x*	$33*x*	$55*x*
Adjusted basis	---------	40*x*	20*x*	25*x*
Gain (loss) realized	---------	($18*x*)	$13*x*	$30*x*

Under section 351(b)(2) of the Code the loss of 18*x* dollars realized on the exchange of Asset Number I is not recognized. Such loss may not be used to offset the gains realized on the exchanges of the other assets. Under section 351(b)(1) of the Code, the gain of 13*x* dollars realized on the exchange of Asset Number II will be recognized as short-term capital gain in the amount of 3*x* dollars, the amount of cash received. Under sections 351(b)(1) and 1245(b)(3) of the Code, the gain of 30*x* dollars realized on the exchange of Asset Number III will be recognized as ordinary income in the amount of 5*x* dollars, the amount of cash received.

NOTE

Overall understanding of Section 351 may be enhanced by an analysis of the additional results to the shareholder ("X") and the corporation ("Y") in the transaction described in Revenue Ruling 68–55. X's basis in the Y stock received will be an exchanged basis ($40 from Asset I, plus $20 from Asset II, plus $25 from Asset III = $85), increased by its total gain recognized on the transfer ($3 on Asset II, plus $5 on Asset III = $8) and decreased by the fair market value of the boot (including cash) received ($10) for a total basis of $83 ($85 + $8 − 10).

The next question is X's holding period for the stock. X received stock worth $100 together with $10 cash for assets with a value of $110 (Asset I $22, Asset II $33, Asset III $55). Thus, it could be said that 22/110 of the stock was received in exchange for Asset I, 33/110 was received in exchange for Asset II, and 55/110 was received in exchange for Asset III. In that event, each share could be considered to have a split holding period allocated in proportion to the fair market value of the transferred assets.[1]

The next step is a determination of Y's basis in the assets received. In the ruling, Y's basis in those assets will be their adjusted bases in X's hands ($40 for Asset I, plus $20 for Asset II, plus $25 for Asset III) increased by the gain recognized to X (zero on Asset I, plus $3 on Asset II, plus $5 on Asset III) for a total of $93 ($40 + $20 + $25 + $3 + $5). Nothing in the Code, regulations or rulings explains how this basis is allocated among the assets. The underlying premise of Section 362, however, is that any gain or loss which is realized but not recognized by the transferor on the Section 351 transfer will be recognized by the corporation on a later sale. This concept is carried out by giving each separate asset its original transferred basis and then increasing the basis by the amount of gain recognized by the transferor on that asset.[2] On the facts in Revenue Ruling 68–55, Y's basis in Asset I would be $40 (transferred basis) since no gain or loss was recognized on that asset. If Y sells Asset I for its $22 fair market value, it then will recognize the $18 loss realized but not recognized by the transferor. Y's basis in Asset II would be $23 (transferred basis of $20 increased by the $3 of gain recognized on Asset II). Of the $13 of realized gain on Asset II, $3 already has been recognized, and Y will recognize the $10 additional gain if it sells that asset for its fair market value of $33. Finally, Asset III will take a basis of $30 (transferred basis of $25, increased by $5 gain recognized) so that if Y sold the asset for its fair market value of $55, it will recognize the $25 additional realized gain that was not recognized by X.

2. TIMING OF SECTION 351(b) GAIN

Proposed Regulations: § 1.453–1(f)(1)(iii), –(f)(3)(i), (ii), (iii) Example (1).

The preceding discussion concerned the amount of gain recognized by a transferor who receives boot in a Section 351 transaction. What about the timing of that gain? If the boot is cash or other corporate property, the transferor recognizes any Section 351(b) gain immediately upon receipt of the boot. But gain is more typically recognized when a shareholder transfers appreciated property in exchange for a mixture of stock and corporate debt instruments.[1] In that event, the question becomes—*when* must that gain be recognized? And if the gain may be deferred, what is the resulting impact on the shareholder's basis in her stock under Section 358 and the corporation's basis in its assets under Section 362? The answers lie in the relationship between Section 351 and the installment sale rules in Section 453.

1. This approach was adopted by the Service in Rev.Rul. 85–164, 1985–2 C.B. 117. In so ruling, the Service rejected an alternative approach, under which some shares would take a tacked holding period and other shares a holding period commencing as of the date of the exchange. The latter approach would permit a shareholder selling a portion of his holdings to designate shares with the longer holding period.

2. See, e.g., P.A. Birren & Son v. Commissioner, 116 F.2d 718 (7th Cir.1940).

1. For the tax incentives to capitalize a corporation with debt, see Section F of this chapter, infra.

For many years, it was not clear whether a shareholder could defer the reporting of Section 351 gain triggered by the receipt of corporate debt obligations. The Code resolves this question in an analogous context by permitting deferral of gain for installment boot received in a Section 1031 like-kind exchange and certain other corporate nonrecognition transactions.[2] In proposed regulations, the Treasury extended this rule to allow a transferor who receives installment boot in a Section 351(b) transaction to defer gain until payments are received on the corporate debt.[3] The regulations also permit a transferor to immediately increase the basis in any nonrecognition property received (e.g., stock) by the transferor's total potential recognized gain, but they delay the corporation's corresponding Section 362(a) basis increase in its assets until the transferor actually recognizes gain on the installment method.[4]

The operation of the proposed regulations is best illustrated by an example. In a conventional installment sale (i.e., a deferred payment sale not made in conjunction with a nonrecognition provision), Section 453 directs the seller to construct a fraction by dividing the realized gain (known in Section 453 parlance as the "gross profit") by the total principal payments to be received on the sale ("total contract price").[5] The seller then applies the fraction to each payment received to determine the gain recognized in the year of sale and as installment payments are later received. Adopting the facts of our continuing example, assume A sells his appreciated asset ("Gainacre"), which has an adjusted basis of $10 and a fair market value of $100, for $80 cash and a $20 note with market rate interest and principal payable in equal installments over the next five years. A's realized gain is $90. A's total payments received will be $100: $80 in the year of sale and $20 in subsequent years. Under the installment method, 90/100, or 90 percent, of each payment received must be reported as taxable gain.

Now assume that A transfers Gainacre to Venture, Inc., in exchange for 80 shares of Venture stock (worth $80), and a $20 Venture five-year note. A again realizes $90 of gain but recognizes that gain only to the extent of the $20 boot received. For timing purposes, the regulations divide the exchange into two separate transactions: a Section 351(a) nonrecognition exchange to the extent of the stock received by the transferor and an installment sale to the extent of the boot received. The basis of the transferred property is first allocated to the nonrecognition transaction. The regulations implement this bifurcation approach as follows:[6]

2. I.R.C. § 453(f)(6).

3. Prop.Reg. § 1.453-1(f)(3)(ii). Any gain attributable to recapture of depreciation or dispositions of dealer property cannot be deferred. I.R.C. § 453(i), (*l*). See generally Cain, "Taxation of Boot Notes in a 351/453 Transaction," 27 S. Texas L.Rev. 61 (1986); Dentino & Walker, "Impact of the Installment Sales Revision Act of 1980 on Evidences of Indebtedness in a Section 351 Transaction," 9 J.Corp. Tax'n 330 (1983).

4. Prop. Reg. § 1.453-1(f)(3)(ii).

5. I.R.C. § 453(c). For purposes of this and subsequent examples, assume that the property sold is unencumbered and is otherwise eligible for installment sale treatment.

6. Prop.Reg. § 1.453-1(f)(1)(iii); -1(f)(3)(ii).

1. A's basis in Gainacre ($10) is first allocated to the Venture stock ("nonrecognition property")[7] received in the exchange in an amount up to the fair market value of that property. The entire $10 of basis is thus allocated to the $80 of Venture stock received by A.
2. If the transferor's basis in the transferred property exceeds the fair market value of the nonrecognition property received, that "excess basis" is then allocated to the installment portion of the transaction. There is no excess basis to allocate in this example because the Gainacre basis ($10) does not exceed the value of the nonrecognition property (stock worth $80).
3. Section 453 is then applied to the installment portion of the transaction. For this purpose, the "selling price" is the sum of the face value of the installment obligation ($20 here) and the fair market value of any other boot (none here). Where, as here, there are no liabilities, the total contract price is the same as the selling price ($20). The gross profit is the selling price less any "excess basis" allocated to the installment obligation ($20–0 = $20). A's gross profit ratio is thus 20/20, or 100%. To determine his recognized gain, A applies that percentage to any boot received in the year of sale and to payments as they are received on the installment note. A thus recognizes no gain in the year of the exchange; his entire $20 "boot" gain is recognized as the note is paid off over the next five years. Note that the gross profit ratio is normally 100% if the boot received is less than the realized gain.[8]

For purposes of determining a shareholder's basis in the nonrecognition property received in a Section 351/453 transaction, the regulations treat the shareholder as electing out of the installment method.[9] Returning to the example, A's basis in his Venture stock under Section 358 is $10, determined as follows: $10 (A's basis in Gainacre) decreased by $20 (total boot received by A) and increased by $20 (the entire gain A would have recognized if he reported all his gain in the year of sale).

Determining the corporation's basis in the transferred property is more complicated. Adopting what one commentator has called a "roller-coaster basis" approach,[10] the regulations provide that the corporation's

7. The proposed regulations refer to nonrecognition property as "permitted property." Prop.Reg. § 1.453–1(f)(1)(i).

8. If the boot exceeds the transferor's realized gain, then some of the basis of the transferred property must be allocated to the installment portion of the transaction. For example, assume the same transaction, except A's basis in Gainacre is $90 and his realized gain is thus only $10. Although A receives $20 of boot, his recognized gain is limited to $10 under Section 351(b). The proposed regulations again direct A to allocate his basis in Gainacre ($90) to the Venture stock received but only up to the fair market value of that "nonrecognition property" ($80 here). The $10 "excess basis" is allocated to the installment sale, resulting in a gross profit of $10 ($20 selling price less $10 excess basis) and a gross profit ratio of 1/2. A thus must report 1/2 of each payment received on the note as taxable gain.

9. Prop.Reg. § 1.453–1(f)(3)(ii).

10. See Bogdanski, "Closely Held Corporations: Section 351 and Installment 'Boot,'" 11 J.Corp.Tax'n 268 (1984).

basis in the transferred property is the same as the transferor's basis increased by the gain recognized only if, as and when that gain is actually recognized. In the example, Venture initially takes a transferred basis of $10 in Gainacre, and that basis gradually is increased by $20 as Venture pays off the note and A recognizes his deferred gain on the installment method.[11] Query whether this rollercoaster basis approach is appropriate, considering that Venture in effect has incurred a liability in connection with its acquisition of Gainacre. If the teachings of the *Crane* case are followed, it would seem that Venture should be permitted to increase its basis by the full $20 liability notwithstanding that A may defer his boot gain over five years. An immediate step-up in basis of the transferred property would be particularly appealing to the corporation when the property is depreciable real estate with no lurking recapture gain.

PROBLEM

A, B and C form X Corporation by transferring the following assets, each of which has been held long-term:

Transferor	**Asset**	**Adj. Basis**	**F.M.V.**
A	Equipment (all § 1245 gain)	$15,000	$22,000
B	Inventory	7,000	20,000
	Land	13,000	10,000
C	Land	20,000	50,000

In exchange, A receives 15 shares of X common stock (value—$15,000), $2,000 cash and 100 shares of X preferred stock (value—$5,000), B receives 15 shares of X common stock (value—$15,000) and $15,000 cash, and C receives 10 shares of X common stock (value—$10,000), $5,000 cash and X's note for $35,000, payable in two years. None of the transferors is a "dealer" in real estate. Assume that the preferred stock issued to A is not "nonqualified preferred stock."

(a) What are the tax consequences (gain or loss realized and recognized, basis and holding period) of the transfers described above to each shareholder and to X Corporation?

(b) What result to C in (a), above, if instead of land, C transferred depreciable equipment with the same adjusted basis and fair market value as the land and an original cost to C of $50,000? See § 453(i).

D. ASSUMPTION OF LIABILITIES

Code: §§ 357(a)–(c); 358(d). Skim § 357(d).

Regulations: §§ 1.357–1, –2; 1.358–3.

Many corporate formations involve the transfer of encumbered property or the assumption of liabilities by the transferee corporation. In most

11. Id. Suppose Venture sells Gainacre prior to the due date of the note. Should Venture recognize a loss when the note is eventually paid off? See Prop. Reg. § 1.453–1(f)(3)(iii) Example (1).

circumstances, a taxpayer who is relieved of a debt in connection with the disposition of property must include the debt relief in the amount realized even if the debt is nonrecourse. This is the teaching of the celebrated *Crane* case,[1] and the Supreme Court took a similar approach nine years earlier in United States v. Hendler.[2] Interpreting the corporate reorganization provisions, the Court held in *Hendler* that the assumption and subsequent payment of the transferor's liabilities by a transferee corporation constituted boot to the transferor. If that rule applied to a corporate formation, however, many incorporations of a going business would become taxable events to the extent of the liabilities assumed, and the policy of Section 351 would be seriously frustrated.

To prevent this result, Congress promptly responded to *Hendler* by enacting the statutory predecessor of Section 357. Section 357(a) now provides that the assumption of a liability[3] by a transferee corporation in a Section 351 exchange (and several other transactions to be studied later) will neither constitute boot nor prevent the exchange from qualifying under Section 351. Rather than treating the debt relief as boot, the Code postpones the recognition of any gain attributable to the transferred liabilities. This deferral is accomplished by Section 358(d), which reduces the basis in the stock received in the exchange by treating the relieved liabilities as "money received" by the transferor for purposes of determining the shareholder's basis.

Section 357 is subject to two exceptions. The first (Section 357(b)) prevents abuse and the second (Section 357(c)) avoids the tax taboo of a negative basis. Under the Section 357(b) "tax avoidance" exception, the assumption of a liability is treated as boot if the taxpayer's "principal purpose" in transferring the liability was the avoidance of federal income taxes or was not a bona fide business purpose. This essentially factual determination is made after "taking into consideration the nature of the liability and the circumstances in the light of which the arrangement for the assumption or acquisition was made."[4] If an improper purpose exists,

1. Crane v. Commissioner, 331 U.S. 1, 67 S.Ct. 1047 (1947).

2. 303 U.S. 564, 58 S.Ct. 655 (1938).

3. A recourse liability is treated as "assumed" if, based on all the facts and circumstances, the transferee has agreed to, and is expected to, satisfy the liability (or a portion of it), whether or not the transferor has been relieved of the liability. I.R.C. § 357(d)(1)(A). A nonrecourse liability is generally treated as having been assumed by any transferee who takes an asset subject to the liability. I.R.C. § 357(d)(1)(B). If a nonrecourse liability also is secured by other assets not transferred to the corporation, the amount treated as assumed must be reduced by the lesser of the portion of the liability that the owner of the other assets has agreed to and is expected to satisfy, or the fair market value of those other assets. I.R.C. § 357(d)(2).

4. I.R.C. § 357(b)(1). In evaluating whether the business purpose is bona fide, the regulations require both the transferor and the corporation to demonstrate a "*corporate* business reason" (emphasis added) for the assumption of the liabilities when they report a Section 351 transaction on their

all the relieved liabilities, not merely the evil debts, are treated as boot.[5] Section 357(b) was designed to prevent taxpayers from transferring personal obligations to a newly formed corporation or from achieving a "bail out without boot" by borrowing against property on the eve of incorporation and then transferring the encumbered asset to the corporation. Perhaps because the rule is more draconian than necessary, it has been sparingly applied.[6]

The purpose of the second exception is more technical. Section 357(c) provides that if the sum of the liabilities assumed by the corporation exceed the aggregate adjusted bases of the properties transferred by a particular transferor,[7] the excess shall be considered as gain from the sale or exchange of the property.[8] A simple illustration explains the need for this exception. Assume our friend, A, forms Venture, Inc. by transferring a building with an adjusted basis of $30, a fair market value of $100 and an outstanding mortgage of $55. In exchange, Venture issues common stock with a value of $45 and takes the building subject to the $55 mortgage. If Section 357(a) applied, without more, A would recognize no gain on the exchange, but pause to consider his basis in the stock under Section 358. It would be $30 (the basis of the building), less $55 (the liability, treated as boot for basis purposes under Section 358(d)), or a *minus* $25. Although tax scholars have debated the issue, the Code abhors a negative basis.[9] Section 357(c) conveniently avoids that taboo by requiring A to recognize $25 gain (the excess of the $55 liability over his $30 adjusted basis). A's basis then becomes zero, and the Code is not further complicated by the mysteries of algebra.

Section 357(c) is itself subject to an exception. Under general tax principles, a taxpayer who is relieved of a liability that would be deductible if paid directly by the taxpayer does not recognize gain if the debt is discharged because any potential income would be offset by a corresponding deduction upon payment.[10] For example, a lender's discharge of a borrow-

income tax returns. Reg. § 1.351–3(a)(6),–3(b)(7).

5. Reg. § 1.357–1(c).

6. Section 357(b) is accompanied by an odd burden of proof rule providing that in "any suit" where the taxpayer has the burden of proving the absence of an improper purpose, that burden shall not be met unless the taxpayer "sustains such burden by the clear preponderance of the evidence." I.R.C. § 357(b)(2). This standard adds little to the normal burden of proof imposed in tax litigation and has largely been ignored by the courts.

7. Section 357(c) is applied on a transferor-by-transferor basis. Rev.Rul. 66–142, 1966–1 C.B. 66.

8. According to the regulations, the character of the Section 357(c) gain is determined by allocating the gain among the transferred assets in proportion to their respective fair market values. Reg. § 1.357–2(b). As the problems illustrate, this approach can be anomalous insofar as it requires an allocation of gain (for characterization purposes) to an asset with no realized gain.

9. For a contrary view on the viability of a negative basis, see Cooper, "Negative Basis," 75 Harv.L.Rev. 1352 (1962).

10. See I.R.C. § 108(e)(2), which provides that no income shall be realized from the discharge of indebtedness to the extent the payment of the liability would have given rise to a deduction.

er's $1,000 interest expense on a home mortgage is economically equivalent to the lender's transfer of $1,000 cash to the borrower (gross income) and a retransfer of $1,000 cash as interest by the borrower to the lender (offsetting deduction). Taken together, these transactions should not result in any net income to the borrower.[11] In keeping with this approach, Section 357(c)(3) excludes from the term "liabilities," for purposes of determining the excess of liabilities over basis, any obligation that would give rise to a deduction if it had been paid by the transferor[12] or which would be described in Section 736(a).[13] These same types of obligations also are not treated as "liabilities" for purposes of determining the basis of the stock received by the transferor under Section 358.[14]

The origin of this exception is best understood by looking back to the difficulties encountered by cash basis proprietors who incorporated a going business prior to the enactment of Section 357(c)(3). Consider the plight of Accountant ("A"), a cash basis taxpayer whose sole proprietorship consisted of the following assets and liabilities:

Assets	**Adj. Basis**	**F.M.V.**
Cash	$100	$100
Accounts Receivable	0	200
Equipment	50	250
	$150	$550
Liabilities		
Accounts payable		$400

Assume A incorporates his business by transferring all the assets to Newco in exchange for $150 of Newco stock and Newco's assumption of the $400 accounts payable. If the payables are "liabilities" for purposes of Section

11. Cf. I.R.C. § 7872. The example assumes that the interest is deductible "qualified residence interest" under Section 163(h).

12. Excepted from this exception are obligations which, when incurred, resulted in the creation of, or an increase in, the basis of any property—e.g., obligations to pay for small tools purchased on credit. I.R.C. § 357(c)(3)(B). To illustrate, assume cash method Proprietor ("P") buys $100 of small tools on credit, promising to pay the seller in two months. Pending payment of the obligation, P has a $100 basis in the tools (P's cost). One month later, P transfers the tools and the related obligation to a new corporation in a Section 351 transaction. The obligation is appropriately treated as a "liability" for purposes of Section 357(c)—but not to worry because the amount of that liability is offset by P's basis in the transferred tools. In comparison, contingent liabilities that have not yet given rise to a capital expenditure (and thus have not created or increased basis) are not included in determining the amount of liabilities assumed by the transferee. See Rev. Rul. 95–74, infra, p. 477.

13. Section 736(a) applies to payments made to a retiring partner or to a deceased partner's successor in interest in liquidation of that partner's interest in the partnership. See Chapter 8, supra. Section 736(a) payments, like accounts payable of a cash basis taxpayer, have the effect of reducing gross income when paid and thus are appropriately excluded from "liabilities" for purposes of Section 357(c) and 358(d).

14. I.R.C. § 358(d)(2). But see I.R.C. § 358(h), a specialized anti-abuse rule, which generally provides that if the basis of stock received in a Section 351 transaction exceeds its fair market value, that basis must be stepped down (but not below fair market value) by the amount of any liabilities not taken into account under Section 358(d) (e.g., "deductible" or contingent liabilities that do not result in a basis reduction) and assumed by the corporation.

357(c)(1), A recognizes $250 gain—the excess of the $400 liabilities assumed by Newco over the $150 aggregate adjusted basis of the assets transferred to the corporation. A's adjusted basis in the Newco stock would be zero.[15]

The harshness of this result becomes apparent when it is compared to an economically equivalent transaction. Suppose, for example, that A had retained the payables, transferred the $550 in assets to Newco in exchange for $150 of Newco stock and $400 cash and then used the cash to pay his creditors. Although A would recognize $400 gain under Section 351(b), that gain would be offset by the $400 deduction that A would receive on payment of the payables. Alternatively, A could have avoided any gain simply by retaining sufficient assets to pay the deductible accounts payable.

As these examples illustrate, the inclusion of accounts payable as "liabilities" for purposes of Section 357(c) often caused cash basis taxpayers to recognize more gain by having their obligations assumed than they would have recognized if they received equivalent cash boot or withheld sufficient assets to pay the liabilities. Several courts attempted to cure this anomaly by excluding certain deductible liabilities from the scope of Section 357(c), but the cases lacked a uniform rationale.[16] To resolve these ambiguities and halt the litigation, Congress amended Sections 357(c) and 358(d) to provide that deductible obligations no longer would be considered "liabilities" for these limited purposes. Congress also indicated that this exception was not intended to affect either the transferee corporation's tax treatment of the excluded liabilities or the definition of liabilities for any other provision of the Code, including Sections 357(a) and 357(b).[17]

If all else fails, a transferor can avoid recognizing Section 357(c) gain simply by contributing additional cash to the corporation in an amount equal to the excess of assumed liabilities over the aggregate adjusted basis of the other contributed assets. A more intriguing question is whether a cash poor transferor can eliminate the gain by remaining personally liable on the assumed debts or by transferring a personal note to the corporation for the Section 357(c) excess. The courts are confused by these questions, as evidenced by the *Peracchi* case and the Note following.

15. A's basis is derived as follows: $150 (basis in assets transferred by A) minus $400 (liabilities assumed by Newco, treated as "money received" for basis purposes) plus $250 (gain recognized by A). I.R.C. § 358(a)(1), (d)(1).

16. See Focht v. Commissioner, 68 T.C. 223 (1977) ("liability" under Sections 357(c) and 358(d) limited to obligations which, if transferred, cause gain recognition under *Crane* case); Thatcher v. Commissioner, 61 T.C. 28 (1973), reversed in part and affirmed in part 533 F.2d 1114 (9th Cir.1976) (analyze transaction as "ordinary exchange" and give transferor constructive deduction for accounts payable discharged by corporation in same year as transfer to the extent of the lesser of accounts receivable or Section 357(c) gain); Bongiovanni v. Commissioner, 470 F.2d 921 (2d Cir.1972) (Section 357(c) only applies to "tax liabilities"—i.e., liens, mortgages, etc.).

17. Staff of Joint Committee on Taxation, General Explanation of the Revenue Act of 1978, 96th Cong., 1st Sess. 219–220 (1979).

Peracchi v. Commissioner

United States Court of Appeals, Ninth Circuit, 1998.
143 F.3d 487.

■ KOZINSKI, CIRCUIT JUDGE:

We must unscramble a Rubik's Cube of corporate tax law to determine the basis of a note contributed by a taxpayer to his wholly-owned corporation.

The Transaction

The taxpayer, Donald Peracchi, needed to contribute additional capital to his closely-held corporation (NAC) to comply with Nevada's minimum premium-to-asset ratio for insurance companies. Peracchi contributed two parcels of real estate. The parcels were encumbered with liabilities which together exceeded Peracchi's total basis in the properties by more than half a million dollars. As we discuss in detail below, under section 357(c), contributing property with liabilities in excess of basis can trigger immediate recognition of gain in the amount of the excess. In an effort to avoid this, Peracchi also executed a promissory note, promising to pay NAC $1,060,000 over a term of ten years at 11% interest. Peracchi maintains that the note has a basis equal to its face amount, thereby making his total basis in the property contributed greater than the total liabilities. If this is so, he will have extracted himself from the quicksand of section 357(c) and owe no immediate tax on the transfer of property to NAC. The IRS, though, maintains that (1) the note is not genuine indebtedness and should be treated as an unenforceable gift; and (2) even if the note is genuine, it does not increase Peracchi's basis in the property contributed.

The parties are not splitting hairs: Peracchi claims the basis of the note is $1,060,000, its face value, while the IRS argues that the note has a basis of zero. If Peracchi is right, he pays no immediate tax on the half a million dollars by which the debts on the land he contributed exceed his basis in the land; if the IRS is right, the note becomes irrelevant for tax purposes and Peracchi must recognize an immediate gain on the half million. The fact that the IRS and Peracchi are so far apart suggests they are looking at the transaction through different colored lenses. To figure out whether Peracchi's lens is rose-tinted or clear, it is useful to take a guided tour of sections 351 and 357 and the tax law principles undergirding them.

Into the Lobster Pot: Section 351[2]

The Code tries to make organizing a corporation pain-free from a tax point of view. A capital contribution is, in tax lingo, a "nonrecognition"

2. "Decisions to embrace the corporate form of organization should be carefully considered, since a corporation is like a lobster pot: easy to enter, difficult to live in, and painful to get out of." Boris I. Bittker & James S. Eustice, Federal Income Taxation of Corporations and Shareholders ¶ 2.01[3] (6th ed.1997) (footnotes omitted) (hereinafter Bittker & Eustice).

event: A shareholder can generally contribute capital without recognizing gain on the exchange.[3] It's merely a change in the form of ownership, like moving a billfold from one pocket to another. See I.R.C. § 351. So long as the shareholders contributing the property remain in control of the corporation after the exchange, section 351 applies: It doesn't matter if the capital contribution occurs at the creation of the corporation or if—as here—the company is already up and running. The baseline is that Peracchi may contribute property to NAC without recognizing gain on the exchange.

Gain Deferral: Section 358(a)

Peracchi contributed capital to NAC in the form of real property and a promissory note. Corporations may be funded with any kind of asset, such as equipment, real estate, intellectual property, contracts, leaseholds, securities or letters of credit. The tax consequences can get a little complicated because a shareholder's basis in the property contributed often differs from its fair market value. The general rule is that an asset's basis is equal to its "cost." See I.R.C. § 1012. But when a shareholder like Peracchi contributes property to a corporation in a nonrecognition transaction, a cost basis does not preserve the unrecognized gain. Rather than take a basis equal to the fair market value of the property exchanged, the shareholder must substitute the basis of that property for what would otherwise be the cost basis of the stock. This preserves the gain for recognition at a later day: The gain is built into the shareholder's new basis in the stock, and he will recognize income when he disposes of the stock.

The fact that gain is deferred rather than extinguished doesn't diminish the importance of questions relating to basis and the timing of recognition. In tax, as in comedy, timing matters. Most taxpayers would much prefer to pay tax on contributed property years later—when they sell their stock—rather than when they contribute the property. Thus what Peracchi is seeking here is gain deferral: He wants the gain to be recognized only when he disposes of some or all of his stock.

Continuity of Investment: Boot and Section 351(b)

Continuity of investment is the cornerstone of nonrecognition under section 351. Nonrecognition assumes that a capital contribution amounts to nothing more than a nominal change in the form of ownership; in sub-

3. The income tax often operates as a tax on transactions. Regardless of when a taxpayer realizes accretions to his economic wealth, income is usually recognized when a measuring event occurs, such as receipt of a paycheck or the "sale or exchange" of property. But the Code exempts certain sales and exchanges from recognition, such as when a sale is involuntary, or merely a change in the form of ownership, or otherwise warrants nonrecognition. See generally Boris I. Bittker & Lawrence Lokken, Federal Taxation of Income, Estates and Gifts ¶ 44.1.1 (2d ed. 1990) ("The Code contains numerous nonrecognition provisions covering a wide range of transactions that have little in common except that they have elicited a legislative judgment that the taxpayer's realized gain or loss should not be taxed or deducted when the exchange or other event occurs.") Congress has not deemed the organization of a corporation an appropriate event for recognition of income.

stance the shareholder's investment in the property continues. But a capital contribution can sometimes allow a shareholder to partially terminate his investment in an asset or group of assets. For example, when a shareholder receives cash or other property in addition to stock, receipt of that property reflects a partial termination of investment in the business. The shareholder may invest that money in a wholly unrelated business, or spend it just like any other form of personal income. To the extent a section 351 transaction resembles an ordinary sale, the nonrecognition rationale falls apart.

Thus the central exception to nonrecognition for section 351 transactions comes into play when the taxpayer receives "boot"—money or property other than stock in the corporation—in exchange for the property contributed. See I.R.C. § 351(b). Boot is recognized as taxable income because it represents a partial cashing out. It's as if the taxpayer contributed part of the property to the corporation in exchange for stock, and sold part of the property for cash. Only the part exchanged for stock represents a continuation of investment; the part sold for cash is properly recognized as yielding income, just as if the taxpayer had sold the property to a third party.

Peracchi did not receive boot in return for the property he contributed. But that doesn't end the inquiry: We must consider whether Peracchi has cashed out in some other way which would warrant treating part of the transaction as taxable boot.

Assumption of Liabilities: Section 357(a)

The property Peracchi contributed to NAC was encumbered by liabilities. Contribution of leveraged property makes things trickier from a tax perspective. When a shareholder contributes property encumbered by debt, the corporation usually assumes the debt. And the Code normally treats discharging a liability the same as receiving money: The taxpayer improves his economic position by the same amount either way. See I.R.C. § 61(a)(12). NAC's assumption of the liabilities attached to Peracchi's property therefore could theoretically be viewed as the receipt of money, which would be taxable boot. See United States v. Hendler, 303 U.S. 564, 58 S.Ct. 655, 82 L.Ed. 1018 (1938).

The Code takes a different tack. Requiring shareholders like Peracchi to recognize gain any time a corporation assumes a liability in connection with a capital contribution would greatly diminish the nonrecognition benefit section 351 is meant to confer. Section 357(a) thus takes a lenient view of the assumption of liability: A shareholder engaging in a section 351 transaction does not have to treat the assumption of liability as boot, even if the corporation assumes his obligation to pay. See I.R.C. § 357(a).

This nonrecognition does not mean that the potential gain disappears. Once again, the basis provisions kick in to reflect the transfer of gain from the shareholder to the corporation: The shareholder's substitute basis in the stock received is decreased by the amount of the liability assumed by the corporation. See I.R.C. § 358(d), (a). The adjustment preserves the gain for recognition when the shareholder sells his stock in the company, since his taxable gain will be the difference between the (new lower) basis and the sale price of the stock.

Sasquatch and The Negative Basis Problem: Section 357(c)

Highly leveraged property presents a peculiar problem in the section 351 context. Suppose a shareholder organizes a corporation and contributes as its only asset a building with a basis of $50, a fair market value of $100, and mortgage debt of $90. Section 351 says that the shareholder does not recognize any gain on the transaction. Under section 358, the shareholder takes a substitute basis of $50 in the stock, then adjusts it downward under section 357 by $90 to reflect the assumption of liability. This leaves him with a basis of minus $40. A negative basis properly preserves the gain built into the property: If the shareholder turns around and sells the stock the next day for $10 (the difference between the fair market value and the debt), he would face $50 in gain, the same amount as if he sold the property without first encasing it in a corporate shell.[8]

But skeptics say that negative basis, like Bigfoot, doesn't exist. Compare Easson v. Commissioner, 33 T.C. 963, 970, 1960 WL 1347 (1960) (there's no such thing as a negative basis) with Easson v. Commissioner, 294 F.2d 653, 657–58 (9th Cir.1961) (yes, Virginia, there is a negative basis). Basis normally operates as a cost recovery system: Depreciation deductions reduce basis, and when basis hits zero, the property cannot be depreciated farther. At a more basic level, it seems incongruous to attribute a negative value to a figure that normally represents one's investment in an asset. Some commentators nevertheless argue that when basis operates merely to measure potential gain (as it does here), allowing negative basis may be perfectly appropriate and consistent with the tax policy underlying nonrecognition transactions. See, e.g., J. Clifton Fleming, Jr., The Highly Avoidable Section 357(c): A Case Study in Traps for the Unwary and Some Positive Thoughts About Negative Basis, 16 J. Corp. L. 1, 27–30 (1990). Whatever the merits of this debate, it seems that section 357(c) was enacted to eliminate the possibility of negative basis. See George Cooper, Negative Basis, 75 Harv. L.Rev. 1352, 1360 (1962).

Section 357(c) prevents negative basis by forcing a shareholder to recognize gain to the extent liabilities exceed basis. Thus, if a shareholder contributes a building with a basis of $50 and liabilities of $90, he does not receive stock with a basis of minus $40. Instead, he takes a basis of zero and must recognize a $40 gain.

Peracchi sought to contribute two parcels of real property to NAC in a section 351 transaction. Standing alone the contribution would have run afoul of section 357(c): The property he wanted to contribute had liabilities

8. If the taxpayer sells the property outright, his amount realized includes the full amount of the mortgage debt, see Crane v. Commissioner, 331 U.S. 1, 14, 67 S.Ct. 1047, 91 L.Ed. 1301 (1947), and the result is as follows: Amount realized ($10 cash + $90 debt) – $50 Basis = $50 gain.

in excess of basis, and Peracchi would have had to recognize gain to the extent of the excess, or $566,807 * * *.[10]

The Grift: Boosting Basis with a Promissory Note

Peracchi tried to dig himself out of this tax hole by contributing a personal note with a face amount of $1,060,000 along with the real property. Peracchi maintains that the note has a basis in his hands equal to its face value. If he's right, we must add the basis of the note to the basis of the real property. Taken together, the aggregate basis in the property contributed would exceed the aggregate liabilities [including the note at face value, the aggregate basis of the contributed properties would be $2,041,406 and would exceed the $1,548,213 of aggregate liabilities, Eds.].

Under Peracchi's theory, then, the aggregate liabilities no longer exceed the aggregate basis, and section 357(c) no longer triggers any gain. The government argues, however, that the note has a zero basis. If so, the note would not affect the tax consequences of the transaction, and Peracchi's $566,807 in gain would be taxable immediately.[11]

Are Promises Truly Free?

Which brings us (phew!) to the issue before us: Does Peracchi's note have a basis in Peracchi's hands for purposes of section 357(c)?[12] The language of the Code gives us little to work with. The logical place to start is with the definition of basis. Section 1012 provides that "[t]he basis of property shall be the cost of such property...." But "cost" is nowhere defined. What does it cost Peracchi to write the note and contribute it to his corporation? The IRS argues tersely that the "taxpayers in the instant case incurred no cost in issuing their own note to NAC, so their basis in the note was zero." * * * See Alderman v. Commissioner, 55 T.C. 662, 665, 1971 WL 2488 (1971); Rev. Rul. 68–629, 1968–2 C.B. 154, 155.[13] Building

10. Peracchi remained personally liable on the debts encumbering the property transferred to NAC. NAC took the property subject to the debts, however, which is enough to trigger gain under the plain language of section 357(c). See Owen v. Commissioner, 881 F.2d 832, 835–36 (9th Cir.1989).

11. The government does not dispute that the note and the two parcels of real estate were contributed as part of the same transaction for purposes of section 351. Their bases must therefore be aggregated for purposes of section 357(c).

12. Peracchi owned all the voting stock of NAC both before and after the exchange, so the control requirement of section 351 is satisfied. Peracchi received no boot (such as cash or securities) which would qualify as "money or other property" and trigger recognition under 351(b) alone. Peracchi did not receive any stock in return for the property contributed, so it could be argued that the exchange was not "solely in exchange for stock" as required by section 351. Courts have consistently recognized, however, that issuing stock in this situation would be a meaningless gesture: Because Peracchi is the sole shareholder of NAC, issuing additional stock would not affect his economic position relative to other shareholders. See, e.g., Jackson v. Commissioner, 708 F.2d 1402, 1405 (9th Cir.1983).

13. We would face a different case had the Treasury promulgated a regulation interpreting section 357(c). A revenue ruling is entitled to some deference as the stated litigating position of the agency which enforces the tax code, but not nearly as much as a regulation. Ruling 68–629 offers no rationale, let alone a reasonable one, for its holding that it costs a taxpayer nothing to write a

on this premise, the IRS makes Peracchi out to be a grifter: He holds an unenforceable promise to pay himself money, since the corporation will not collect on it unless he says so.

It's true that all Peracchi did was make out a promise to pay on a piece of paper, mark it in the corporate minutes and enter it on the corporate books. It is also true that nothing will cause the corporation to enforce the note against Peracchi so long as Peracchi remains in control. But the IRS ignores the possibility that NAC may go bankrupt, an event that would suddenly make the note highly significant. Peracchi and NAC are separated by the corporate form, and this gossamer curtain makes a difference in the shell game of C Corp organization and reorganization. Contributing the note puts a million dollar nut within the corporate shell, exposing Peracchi to the cruel nutcracker of corporate creditors in the event NAC goes bankrupt. And it does so to the tune of $1,060,000, the full face amount of the note. Without the note, no matter how deeply the corporation went into debt, creditors could not reach Peracchi's personal assets. With the note on the books, however, creditors can reach into Peracchi's pocket by enforcing the note as an unliquidated asset of the corporation.

The key to solving this puzzle, then, is to ask whether bankruptcy is significant enough a contingency to confer substantial economic effect on this transaction. If the risk of bankruptcy is important enough to be recognized, Peracchi should get basis in the note: He will have increased his exposure to the risks of the business—and thus his economic investment in NAC—by $1,060,000. If bankruptcy is so remote that there is no realistic possibility it will ever occur, we can ignore the potential economic effect of the note as speculative and treat it as merely an unenforceable promise to contribute capital in the future.

When the question is posed this way, the answer is clear. Peracchi's obligation on the note was not conditioned on NAC's remaining solvent. It represents a new and substantial increase in Peracchi's investment in the corporation.[14] The Code seems to recognize that economic exposure of the shareholder is the ultimate measuring rod of a shareholder's investment. Cf. I.R.C. § 465 (at-risk rules for partnership investments). Peracchi therefore is entitled to a step-up in basis to the extent he will be subjected to economic loss if the underlying investment turns unprofitable. Cf. HGA Cinema Trust v. Commissioner, 950 F.2d 1357, 1363 (7th Cir.1991) (examining effect of bankruptcy to determine whether long-term note contributed by partner could be included in basis). See also Treas. Reg. § 1.704–1(b)(2)(ii)(c)(1) (recognizing economic effect of promissory note contributed by partner for purposes of partner's obligation to restore deficit capital account).

promissory note, and thus deserves little weight.

14. We confine our holding to a case such as this where the note is contributed to an operating business which is subject to a non-trivial risk of bankruptcy or receivership. NAC is not, for example, a shell corporation or a passive investment company; Peracchi got into this mess in the first place because NAC was in financial trouble and needed more assets to meet Nevada's minimum premium-to-asset ratio for insurance companies.

The economics of the transaction also support Peracchi's view of the matter. The transaction here does not differ substantively from others that would certainly give Peracchi a boost in basis. For example, Peracchi could have borrowed $1 million from a bank and contributed the cash to NAC along with the properties. Because cash has a basis equal to face value, Peracchi would not have faced any section 357(c) gain. NAC could then have purchased the note from the bank for $1 million which, assuming the bank's original assessment of Peracchi's creditworthiness was accurate, would be the fair market value of the note. In the end the corporation would hold a million dollar note from Peracchi—just like it does now—and Peracchi would face no section 357(c) gain.[15] The only economic difference between the transaction just described and the transaction Peracchi actually engaged in is the additional costs that would accompany getting a loan from the bank. Peracchi incurs a "cost" of $1 million when he promises to pay the note to the bank; the cost is not diminished here by the fact that the transferor controls the initial transferee. The experts seem to agree: "Section 357(c) can be avoided by a transfer of enough cash to eliminate any excess of liabilities over basis; and since a note given by a solvent obligor in purchasing property is routinely treated as the equivalent of cash in determining the basis of the property, it seems reasonable to give it the same treatment in determining the basis of the property transferred in a s 351 exchange." Bittker & Eustice ¶ 3.06[4][b].

We are aware of the mischief that can result when taxpayers are permitted to calculate basis in excess of their true economic investment. See Commissioner v. Tufts, 461 U.S. 300, 103 S.Ct. 1826, 75 L.Ed.2d 863 (1983). For two reasons, however, we do not believe our holding will have such pernicious effects. First, and most significantly, by increasing the taxpayer's personal exposure, the contribution of a valid, unconditional promissory note has substantial economic effects which reflect his true economic investment in the enterprise. The main problem with attributing basis to nonrecourse debt financing is that the tax benefits enjoyed as a result of increased basis do not reflect the true economic risk. Here

15. In a similar vein, Peracchi could have first swapped promissory notes with a third party. Assuming the bona fides of each note, Peracchi would take a cost basis in the third party note equal to the face value of the note he gave up. Peracchi could then contribute the third party note to NAC, and (thanks to the added basis) avoid any section 357(c) gain. NAC could then close the circle by giving the third party note back to the third party in exchange for Peracchi's note, leaving Peracchi and NAC in exactly the same position they occupy now. The IRS might attack these maneuvers as step transactions, but that would beg the question: Does the contribution of a shareholder's note to his wholly-owned corporation have any real economic effect, or is it just so much window dressing? If the debt has real economic effect, it shouldn't matter how the shareholder structures the transaction. The only substantive difference between the avoidance techniques just discussed—swapping notes or borrowing from a third party—and the case here is the valuation role implicitly performed by the third party. A bank would not give Peracchi the face value of the note unless his credit warranted it, while we have no assurance that NAC wouldn't do so. We readily acknowledge that our assumptions fall apart if the shareholder isn't creditworthy. Here, the government has stipulated that Peracchi's net worth far exceeds the value of the note, so creditworthiness is not at issue. But we limit our holding to cases where the note is in fact worth approximately its face value.

Peracchi will have to pay the full amount of the note with after-tax dollars if NAC's economic situation heads south. Second, the tax treatment of nonrecourse debt primarily creates problems in the partnership context, where the entity's loss deductions (resulting from depreciation based on basis inflated above and beyond the taxpayer's true economic investment) can be passed through to the taxpayer. It is the pass-through of losses that makes artificial increases in equity interests of particular concern. See, e.g., Levy v. Commissioner, 732 F.2d 1435, 1437 (9th Cir.1984). We don't have to tread quite so lightly in the C Corp context, since a C Corp doesn't funnel losses to the shareholder.[16]

We find further support for Peracchi's view by looking at the alternative: What would happen if the note had a zero basis? The IRS points out that the basis of the note in the hands of the corporation is the same as it was in the hands of the taxpayer. Accordingly, if the note has a zero basis for Peracchi, so too for NAC. See I.R.C. § 362(a).[17] But what happens if NAC—perhaps facing the threat of an involuntary petition for bankruptcy—turns around and sells Peracchi's note to a third party for its fair market value? According to the IRS's theory, NAC would take a carryover basis of zero in the note and would have to recognize $1,060,000 in phantom gain on the subsequent exchange, even though the note did not appreciate in value one bit. That can't be the right result.

Accordingly, we hold that Peracchi has a basis of $1,060,000 in the note he wrote to NAC. The aggregate basis exceeds the liabilities of the properties transferred to NAC under section 351, and Peracchi need not recognize any section 357(c) gain.

Genuine Indebtedness or Sham?

The Tax Court never reached the issue of Peracchi's basis in the note. Instead, it ruled for the Commissioner on the ground that the note is not genuine indebtedness. The court emphasized two facts which it believed supported the view that the note is a sham: (1) NAC's decision whether to collect on the note is wholly controlled by Peracchi and (2) Peracchi missed the first two years of payments, yet NAC did not accelerate the debt. These facts certainly do suggest that Peracchi paid imperfect attention to his

16. Our holding therefore does not extend to the partnership or S Corp context.

17. But see Lessinger v. Commissioner, 872 F.2d 519 (2d Cir.1989). In Lessinger, the Second Circuit analyzed a similar transaction. It agreed with the IRS's (faulty) premise that the note had a zero basis in the taxpayer's hands. But then, brushing aside the language of section 362(a), the court concluded that the note had a basis in the corporation's hands equal to its face value. The court held that this was enough to dispel any section 357(c) gain to the taxpayer, proving that two wrongs sometimes do add up to a right. We agree with the IRS that Lessinger's approach is untenable. Section 357(c) contemplates measuring basis of the property contributed in the hands of the taxpayer, not the corporation. Section 357 appears in the midst of the Code sections dealing with the effect of capital contributions on the shareholder; sections 361 et seq., on the other hand, deal with the effect on a corporation, and section 362 defines the basis of property contributed in the hands of the corporation. Because we hold that the note has a face value basis to the shareholder for purposes of section 357(c), however, we reach the same result as Lessinger.

obligations under the note, as frequently happens when debtor and creditor are under common control. But we believe the proper way to approach the genuine indebtedness question is to look at the face of the note and consider whether Peracchi's legal obligation is illusory. And it is not. First, the note's bona fides are adequate: The IRS has stipulated that Peracchi is creditworthy and likely to have the funds to pay the note; the note bears a market rate of interest commensurate with his creditworthiness; the note has a fixed term. Second, the IRS does not argue that the value of the note is anything other than its face value; nothing in the record suggests NAC couldn't borrow against the note to raise cash. Lastly, the note is fully transferable and enforceable by third parties, such as hostile creditors. On the basis of these facts we hold that the note is an ordinary, negotiable, recourse obligation which must be treated as genuine debt for tax purposes. See Sacks v. Commissioner, 69 F.3d 982, 989 (9th Cir.1995).

The IRS argues that the note is nevertheless a sham because it was executed simply to avoid tax. Tax avoidance is a valid concern in this context; section 357(a) does provide the opportunity for a bailout transaction of sorts. For example, a taxpayer with an unencumbered building he wants to sell could take out a nonrecourse mortgage, pocket the proceeds, and contribute the property to a newly organized corporation. Although the gain would be preserved for later recognition, the taxpayer would have partially cashed out his economic investment in the property: By taking out a nonrecourse mortgage, the economic risk of loss would be transferred to the lender. Section 357(b) addresses this sort of bailout by requiring the recognition of gain if the transaction lacks a business purpose.

Peracchi's capital contribution is not a bailout. Peracchi contributed the buildings to NAC because the company needed additional capital, and the contribution of the note was part of that transaction. The IRS, in fact, stipulated that the contribution had a business purpose. Bailout potential exists regardless of whether the taxpayer contributes a note along with the property; section 357(b), not 357(c), is the sword the Service must use to attack bailout transactions.

Is the note a gift?

The IRS also offers a more refined version of the sham transaction argument: The note was really a gift to NAC because Peracchi did not receive any consideration from the exchange. The IRS admits that the tax deferral resulting from avoiding section 357(c) gain is a benefit to Peracchi. It argues, nonetheless, that this is not enough to make the bargain enforceable because it works no detriment to NAC. This argument would classify all contributions of capital as gifts. A corporation never gives up anything explicitly when it accepts a capital contribution. Instead, the corporation implicitly promises to put the money to good use, and its directors and officers undertake the fiduciary duty to generate the highest possible return on the investment. The contribution of the note was no more a gift than the contribution of $1 million in cash to the corporation would have been; it does not reflect the "detached and disinterested generosity" which characterizes a gift for purposes of federal income taxation. See Commissioner v. Duberstein, 363 U.S. 278, 285, 80 S.Ct. 1190, 4 L.Ed.2d 1218 (1960).

The Aftermath

We take a final look at the result to make sure we have not placed our stamp of approval on some sort of exotic tax shelter. We hold that Peracchi is entitled to a step up in basis for the face value of the note, just as if he contributed cash to the corporation. See I.R.C. § 358. If Peracchi does in fact keep his promise and pay off the note with after tax dollars, the tax result is perfectly appropriate: NAC receives cash, and the increase in basis Peracchi took for the original contribution is justified. Peracchi has less potential gain, but he paid for it in real dollars.

But what if, as the IRS fears, NAC never does enforce the note? If NAC goes bankrupt, the note will be an asset of the estate enforceable for the benefit of creditors, and Peracchi will eventually be forced to pay in after tax dollars. Peracchi will undoubtedly have worked the deferral mechanism of section 351 to his advantage, but this is not inappropriate where the taxpayer is on the hook in both form and substance for enough cash to offset the excess of liabilities over basis. By increasing his personal exposure to the creditors of NAC, Peracchi has increased his economic investment in the corporation, and a corresponding increase in basis is wholly justified.[20]

Conclusion

We hold that Peracchi has a basis of $1,060,000 in the note, its face value. As such, the aggregate liabilities of the property contributed to NAC do not exceed its basis, and Peracchi does not recognize any § 357(c) gain. The decision of the Tax Court is REVERSED. The case is remanded for entry of judgment in favor of Peracchi.

■ FERNANDEZ, CIRCUIT JUDGE, DISSENTING:

Is there something that a taxpayer, who has borrowed hundreds of thousands of dollars more than his basis in his property, can do to avoid taxation when he transfers the property? Yes, says Peracchi, because by using a very clever argument he can avoid the strictures of 26 U.S.C. § 357(c). He need only make a promise to pay by giving a "good," though unsecured, promissory note to his corporation when he transfers the property to it. That is true even though the property remains subject to the encumbrances. How can that be? Well, by preparing a promissory note the taxpayer simply creates basis without cost to himself. * * * Thus he can

20. What happens if NAC does not go bankrupt, but merely writes off the note instead? Peracchi would then face discharge of indebtedness income to the tune of $1,060,000. This would put Peracchi in a worse position than when he started, since discharge of indebtedness is normally treated as ordinary income. Peracchi, having increased his basis in the stock of the corporation by $1,060,000 would receive a capital loss (or less capital gain) to that extent. But the shift in character of the income will normally work to the disadvantage of a taxpayer in Peracchi's situation.

extract a large part of the value of the property, pocket the funds, use them, divest himself of the property, and pay the tax another day, if ever at all.

But as with all magical solutions, the taxpayer must know the proper incantations and make the correct movements. He cannot just transfer the property to the corporation and promise, or be obligated, to pay off the encumbrances. That would not change the fact that the property was still subject to those encumbrances. According to Peracchi, the thaumaturgy that will save him from taxes proceeds in two simple steps. He must first prepare a ritualistic writing—an unsecured promissory note in an amount equal to or more than the excess of the encumbrances over the basis. He must then give that writing to his corporation. That is all.[1] But is not that just a "promise to pay," which "does not represent the paying out or reduction of assets?" Don E. Williams Co. v. Commissioner, 429 U.S. 569, 583, 97 S.Ct. 850, 858, 51 L.Ed.2d 48 (1977). Never mind, he says. He has nonetheless increased the total basis of the property transferred and avoided the tax. I understand the temptation to embrace that argument, but I see no real support for it in the law.

Peracchi says a lot about economic realities. I see nothing real about that maneuver. I see, rather, a bit of sortilege that would have made Merlin envious. The taxpayer has created something—basis—out of nothing.

Thus, I respectfully dissent.

NOTE

An Alternative Rationale. As noted in Judge Kozinski's opinion in *Peracchi*, the Second Circuit reached a similar result in Lessinger v. Commissioner,[1] but its rationale was different. The Second Circuit concluded that a shareholder's basis in his own note equals its face amount because, necessarily, the note's basis to the corporation was face value. While it may lead to an equitable result, this backwards reasoning is not supported by the Code. The following excerpt from a commentary on *Lessinger* illustrates the court's faulty logic:[2]

> Before turning to the court's application of Section 357(c) to the note—a genuinely intriguing question—one should clear the air about the general question of the basis on which Section 357(c) must be focusing. To say that this is the corporation's basis in the

1. What is even better, he need not even make payments on the note until after the IRS catches up with him. I, by the way, am dubious about the proposition that the Tax Court clearly erred when it held that the note was not even a genuine indebtedness.

1. 872 F.2d 519 (2d Cir.1989).

2. Bogdanski, "Shareholder Debt, Corporate Debt: Lessons from *Leavitt* and *Lessinger*", 16 J.Corp.Tax'n 348, 352–53 (1990). For a competing view, see Quiring, "Section 357(c) and the Elusive Basis of the Issuer's Note," 57 Tax Law. 97 (2003), and for the rebuttal, see Bogdanski, "Section 358 and *Crane*—A Reply to My Critics," 57 Tax Law. 905 (2004). See also Lazar, "*Lessinger*, *Peracchi*, and the Emperor's New Clothes; Covering a Section 357(c) Deficit with Invisible (or Nonexistent) Property," 58 Tax Law. 41 (2004).

transferred assets is preposterous. If nothing else, such a reading will in many cases be circular. Section 362(a) gives the corporation a carryover basis in the assets received from the shareholder, increased by any gain recognized by the shareholder on the exchange. The classic instance of recognized gain on a Section 351 exchange is under Section 357(c); thus, one cannot determine a corporation's basis in its assets without first determining the shareholder's gain under Section 357(c). To declare, as the Second Circuit did, that the amount of the gain generally turns on the corporation's basis in its assets leads to an endless circle.

To illustrate, assume a shareholder transfers to a corporation, Blackacre, in which the shareholder has a basis of $30,000, subject to a mortgage of $40,000. To determine the gain under Section 357(c) under the appellate decision in *Lessinger*, one would have to first determine the corporation's basis under Section 362(a). Under the latter section, however, the corporation's basis must reflect the gain under Section 357(c), and thus, one must compute the shareholder's gain in order to determine the corporation's basis. Perhaps the court meant that one should determine the corporation's basis without regard to the debt, or that Section 357(c) looks at different bases depending on whether a shareholder note or hard assets are being transferred, but these are even more thoroughly incredible stretches of the Code language.

Perhaps the Second Circuit was trying to say that Mr. Lessinger should receive "basis credit" for his own note because of his future obligation to transfer cash to the corporation or its creditors. In other contexts, a taxpayer's acceptance of even a nonrecourse liability on the acquisition of property gives rise to a cost basis that includes the amount of the future obligation.[3] If Mr. Lessinger's liability were genuine and enforceable by the corporation's creditors, as the court concluded, he arguably is as much entitled to basis credit as is the purchaser of property financed with nonrecourse debt.

Effect of Shareholder's Continuing Personal Liability. The courts historically have been less sympathetic on a closely related question: whether a shareholder's continuing personal liability on debts transferred to a corporation in a Section 351 transaction causes those debts to be excluded for purposes of Section 357(c). The Tax Court has consistently rejected the notion that transferred liabilities are excluded from the Section 357(c) arithmetic if the transferring shareholder remains personally liable for the debt.[4] The Ninth Circuit once appeared to disagree but later had a change of heart. In Jackson v. Commissioner,[5] that court held that Section 357(c)

3. Parker v. Delaney, 186 F.2d 455 (1st Cir.1950). Cf. Crane v. Commissioner, 331 U.S. 1, 67 S.Ct. 1047 (1947); Commissioner v. Tufts, 461 U.S. 300, 103 S.Ct. 1826 (1983).

4. See, e.g., Smith v. Commissioner, 84 T.C. 889 (1985), affirmed, 805 F.2d 1073 (D.C.Cir.1986); Rosen v. Commissioner, 62 T.C. 11 (1974), affirmed in unpublished opinion, 515 F.2d 507 (3d Cir.1975).

5. 708 F.2d 1402 (9th Cir.1983).

did not apply on an incorporation of a partnership where the taxpayer's share of the partnership's liabilities exceeded his adjusted basis in the transferred partnership interest but the taxpayer remained personally liable on the debts. On these facts, the court reasoned that the corporation had not assumed any liabilities and thus the taxpayer did not have any Section 357(c) gain. This result was criticized by courts and commentators,[6] but it is consistent with the Second Circuit's reasoning in *Lessinger* that taxpayers enjoy no economic benefit (and thus no taxable gain) for the excess of transferred liabilities over basis when they retain genuine personal liability on the debts. In a later case, the Ninth Circuit upheld the Tax Court's finding of Section 357(c) gain on a transfer of encumbered equipment to a controlled corporation where the liabilities exceeded the taxpayer's basis even though the transferor had guaranteed the liabilities and remained personally liable following the transfer.[7] Although the court purported to distinguish its earlier *Jackson* holding as not involving property subject to debt, the two decisions are difficult to reconcile.

In a more recent case,[8] the taxpayers, in connection with the incorporation of their family farming business, contributed assets subject to liabilities that exceeded the aggregate adjusted basis of the transferred assets. The taxpayers remained liable as guarantors on the debts. The Seventh Circuit, affirming the Tax Court, held that the taxpayers recognized Section 357(c) gain on the incorporation and, in so holding, followed the line of cases strictly interpreting the statute. Citing *Peracchi* and *Lessinger*, the taxpayers contended that a strict reading of Section 357(c) was based on "outdated precedent" and urged the court to exercise its equitable power to craft a judicial exception to the plain language of the statute. Both the Tax Court and Seventh Circuit declined the invitation to do so and distinguished the pro-taxpayer cases on the ground that personal guaranties of corporate debt are not the same as incurring debt to the corporation. The court reasoned that a guaranty is not an economic outlay but merely a promise to pay in the future if certain events should occur.

As illustrated in our study of Subchapter K. the uneasy relationship between owner debt, entity debt and basis is raised in many settings.[9] Similar conceptual questions will resurface with varying results in other contexts involving C and S corporations.[10]

Determination of Amount of Liability Assumed. Section 357(d) attempts to clarify the amount and effect of liability assumptions under

6. See, e.g., Estate of Juden v. Commissioner, 865 F.2d 960, 962 (8th Cir.1989); Bogdanski, "Of Debt, Discharge, and Discord": Jackson v. Commissioner, 10 J.Corp.Tax'n 357 (1984).

7. Owen v. Commissioner, 881 F.2d 832 (9th Cir.1989), cert. denied, 493 U.S. 1070, 110 S.Ct. 1113 (1990).

8. Seggerman Farms, Inc. v. Commissioner, 308 F.3d 803 (7th Cir. 2002).

9. See I.R.C. § 752 and Chapter 4D, supra.

10. See, e.g., Section F of this chapter, infra (treatment of shareholder guaranteed debt for purposes of characterizing debt and equity in C corporation's capital structure); Chapter 20D, infra (treatment of shareholder debt and S corporation debt guaranteed by shareholders in determining basis of S corporation stock under Section 1366).

Section 357 and several other provisions covered later in the text. A recourse liability is treated as having been "assumed" if, based on all the facts and circumstances, the transferee has agreed to and is expected to satisfy the liability, whether or not the transferor has been relieved of it.[11] Nonrecourse liabilities generally are treated as having been assumed by a transferee who takes an asset subject to the liability, except the amount is reduced by the lesser of: (1) the amount of such liability which an owner of other assets not transferred to the transferee and also subject to such liability has agreed with the transferee to, and is expected to, satisfy, or (2) the fair market value of those other assets.[12] The purpose of this convoluted exception is to prevent double counting the same liability for basis adjustment purposes.

Section 357(d) was enacted to eliminate a corporate tax shelter that exploited ambiguities in the interpretation of the phrase "transferred subject to a liability" in an earlier version of Section 357.[13] Most of the abusive transactions were used by domestic corporations to overstate the basis of encumbered assets received in transfers from foreign affiliates that were indifferent to any potential Section 357(c) gain triggered by the transfer because they were not subject to U.S. tax. If the plan succeeded, the domestic corporation would benefit from excessive depreciation deductions, tax losses, or reduced gain on a future sale of the asset.[14]

Fortunately, the confusing language in Section 357(d) rarely affects most simple incorporations. But it raises some questions (and offers planning opportunities) that could arise in a purely domestic, non-abusive setting. For example, recourse debt is treated as assumed only if the transferee has agreed and is expected to satisfy it. As one commentator has asked, "expected by whom"—the transferee, the transferor, or both?[15] Without such an agreement and expectation, a liability would not be treated as "assumed," perhaps eliminating a Section 357(c) problem that otherwise might have existed. A similar factual inquiry may be required with nonrecourse debt, which generally is treated as "assumed" unless a third party has pledged other assets as collateral and "has agreed to, and is expected to, satisfy" the obligation.[16]

11. I.R.C. § 357(d)(1)(A). Where more than one person agrees to satisfy a liability, only one of them would be "expected" to satisfy it.

12. I.R.C. § 357(d)(2). See also I.R.C. § 362(d), which limits the basis of property in the hands of the transferee to effectuate a similar policy against double counting.

13. See Staff of Joint Committee on Taxation, Description of Revenue Provisions Contained in the President's Fiscal Year 2000 Budget Proposal 197, JCS–1–99, 106th Cong., 1st Sess. (1999).

14. See Department of Treasury, White Paper, "The Problem of Corporate Tax Shelters: Discussion, Analysis and Legislative Proposals," App. A (July 1, 1999).

15. Bogdanski, "Section 357(d)—Old Can, New Worms," 27 J. Corp. Tax'n 17, 22–23 (2000). See also Banks–Golub, "Recent Amendments to Code Sec. 357: Congress Responds to 'Artificial Basis Creation,'" 78 Taxes 19 (2000).

16. The Service has announced that it is studying these and other complex issues and considering whether to issue regulations specifying the "requirements of an agreement between the transferor and transferee regarding which party will satisfy a liability

As for planning, it has been suggested that Section 357(c) problems could be avoided, at least with respect to recourse debt, if a shareholder who transfers encumbered property to a controlled corporation enters into an agreement with the corporation providing that the shareholder will satisfy the debt. In that event, the debt would not be treated as "assumed" under Section 357(d), and neither Section 357(a) nor Section 357(c) would apply to the transfer.[17] This strategy would be an alternative to contributing a note to the corporation in the amount of the potential Section 357(c) gain.

PROBLEMS

1. A organized X Corporation by transferring the following: inventory with a basis of $20,000 and a fair market value of $10,000 and unimproved land held for several years with a basis of $20,000, a fair market value of $40,000 and subject to a recourse debt of $30,000. In return, A received 20 shares of X stock (fair market value, $20,000) and X took the land subject to the debt.

(a) Assuming no application of Section 357(b), how much gain, if any, does A recognize and what is A's basis and holding period in the stock?

(b) What result in (a), above, if the basis of the land were only $5,000?

(c) In (b), above, what is the character of A's recognized gain under Reg. § 1.357–2(b)? Does this result make sense? How else might the character of A's gain be determined?

(d) In (b), above, what is X Corporation's basis in the properties received from A?

(e) What might A have done to avoid the recognition of gain in (b), above?

2. B organized Y Corporation and transferred a building with a basis of $100,000 and a fair market value of $400,000. The building was subject to a first mortgage of $80,000 which was incurred two years ago for valid business reasons. Two weeks before the incorporation of Y, B borrowed $10,000 for personal purposes and secured the loan with a second mortgage on the building. In exchange for the building, Y Corporation will issue $310,000 of Y common stock to B and will take the building subject to the mortgages.

(a) What are the tax consequences to B on the transfer of the building to Y Corporation?

and how such an agreement must be evidenced." Ann. 2003–37, 2003–1 C.B. 1025.

17. See Bogdanski, supra note 15, at 26–28. In dicta, the Tax Court in Seggerman Farms, Inc. v. Commissioner, 81 T.C.M. 1543 (2001), aff'd 308 F.3d 803 (7th Cir. 2002), indicated that remaining personally liable for the transferred debt and providing a personal guarantee would not be sufficient to satisfy Section 357(d)(1)(A).

(b) What result if B did not borrow the additional $10,000 and, instead, Y Corporation borrowed $10,000 from a bank and gave B $310,000 of Y common stock, $10,000 cash and will take the building subject to the $80,000 first mortgage?

(c) Is the difference in results between (a) and (b), above, justified?

(d) When might there be legitimate business reasons for a corporation assuming a transferor's debt or taking property subject to debt?

E. INCORPORATION OF A GOING BUSINESS

The preceding sections were designed to illustrate the basic requirements and exceptions for qualifying as a tax-free incorporation. For pedagogical reasons, the problems have involved relatively isolated fact patterns, and it has been assumed that the Code and regulations will provide an answer to virtually every question. When a going business is incorporated, however, matters may become more complex. The mix of assets transferred by a sole proprietorship or partnership may include "ordinary income" property, such as accounts receivable and inventory, and the corporation may assume accounts payable, contingent liabilities, and supplies the cost of which was deducted by the transferor prior to the incorporation. Questions arise as to the proper taxpayer to report the receivables and to deduct the payables. In addition, these items potentially raise a broad issue that will recur throughout our study of Subchapter C: to what extent must a nonrecognition provision yield to judicially created "common law" principles of taxation or to more general provisions of the Code?

This section examines the special problems raised by midstream transfers and, in so doing, provides an opportunity to review concepts introduced earlier in the chapter.

Hempt Brothers, Inc. v. United States

United States Court of Appeals, Third Circuit, 1974.
490 F.2d 1172, cert. denied 419 U.S. 826, 95 S.Ct. 44 (1974).

■ ALDISERT, CIRCUIT JUDGE.

[A cash method partnership transferred all its assets, including $662,820 in zero basis accounts receivable, to a newly formed corporation in exchange for all the corporation's stock. Because the exchange qualified under Section 351, the Service contended that the partnership's zero basis in the receivables carried over to the corporation under Section 362, causing the corporation to realize income upon their collection. In an odd reversal of roles, because the statute of limitations had run on earlier years, the corporation contended that the receivables were not "property" within the meaning of Section 351 and that their transfer to the corporation was an assignment of income by the partnership, subjecting the partners to tax when the receivables were transferred or collected and providing the corporation with a cost (i.e., fair market value) basis and no income upon collection. The Court thus was required to address the relationship between Section 351 and the assignment of income doctrine.]

I.

Taxpayer argues here, as it did in the district court, that because the term "property" as used in Section 351 does not embrace accounts receivable, the Commissioner lacked statutory authority to apply principles associated with Section 351. The district court properly rejected the legal interpretation urged by the taxpayer. The definition of Section 351 "property" has been extensively treated by the Court of Claims in E.I. Du Pont de Nemours and Co. v. United States, 471 F.2d 1211, 1218–1219 (Ct.Cl. 1973), describing the transfer of a non-exclusive license to make, use and sell area herbicides under French patents:

> Unless there is some special reason intrinsic to * * * [Section 351] * * * the general word "property" has a broad reach in tax law. * * * For section 351, in particular, courts have advocated a generous definition of "property," * * * and it has been suggested in one capital gains case that nonexclusive licenses can be viewed as property though not as capital assets. * * *
>
> We see no adequate reason for refusing to follow these leads.

We fail to perceive any special reason why a restrictive meaning should be applied to accounts receivables so as to exclude them from the general meaning of "property." Receivables possess the usual capabilities and attributes associated with jurisprudential concepts of property law. They may be identified, valued, and transferred. Moreover, their role in an ongoing business must be viewed in the context of Section 351 application. The presence of accounts receivable is a normal, rather than an exceptional accoutrement of the type of business included by Congress in the transfer to a corporate form. They are "commonly thought of in the commercial world as a positive business asset." As aptly put by the district court: "There is a compelling reason to construe 'property' to include * * * [accounts receivable]: a new corporation needs working capital, and accounts receivable can be an important source of liquidity." Hempt Bros., Inc. v. United States, supra, at 1176. In any event, this court had no difficulty in characterizing a sale of receivables as "property" within the purview of the "no gain or loss" provision of Section 337 as a "qualified sale of property within a 12–month period." Citizens' Acceptance Corp. v. United States, 462 F.2d 751, 756 (3d Cir.1972).

The taxpayer next makes a strenuous argument that "[t]he government is seeking to tax the wrong person."[4] It contends that the assignment

4. We put aside the pragmatic consideration that the transferee-corporate taxpayer raises the argument that the partnership should be taxed at a time when the statute of limitations has presumably run against the transferor partners, who ostensibly are the stockholders of the new corporation.

of income doctrine as developed by the Supreme Court applies to a Section 351 transfer of accounts receivable so that the transferor, not the transferee-corporation, bears the corresponding tax liability. It argues that the assignment of income doctrine dictates that where the right to receive income is transferred to another person in a transaction not giving rise to tax at the time of transfer, the transferor is taxed on the income when it is collected by the transferee; that the only requirement for its application is a transfer of a right to receive ordinary income; and that since the transferred accounts receivable are a present right to future income, the sole requirement for the application of the doctrine is squarely met. In essence, this is a contention that the nonrecognition provision of Section 351 is in conflict with the assignment of income doctrine and that Section 351 should be subordinated thereto. Taxpayer relies on the seminal case of Lucas v. Earl, 281 U.S. 111, 50 S.Ct. 16, 74 L.Ed. 731 (1930), and its progeny for support of its proposition that the application of the doctrine is mandated whenever one transfers a right to receive ordinary income.

On its part, the government concedes that a taxpayer may sell for value a claim to income otherwise his own and he will be taxable upon the proceeds of the sale. Such was the case in Commissioner v. P.G. Lake, Inc., 356 U.S. 260, 78 S.Ct. 691, 2 L.Ed.2d 743 (1958), in which the taxpayer-corporation assigned its oil payment right to its president in consideration for his cancellation of a $600,000 loan. Viewing the oil payment right as a right to receive future income, the Court applied the reasoning of the assignment of income doctrine, normally applicable to a gratuitous assignment, and held that the consideration received by the taxpayer-corporation was taxable as ordinary income since it essentially was a substitute for that which would otherwise be received at a future time as ordinary income.

Turning to the facts of this case, we note that here there was the transfer of accounts receivable from the partnership to the corporation pursuant to Section 351. We view these accounts receivable as a present right to receive future income. In consideration of the transfer of this right, the members of the partnership received stock—a valid consideration. The consideration, therefore, was essentially a substitute for that which would otherwise be received at a future time as ordinary income to the cash basis partnership. Consequently, the holding in *Lake* would normally apply, and income would ordinarily be realized, and thereby taxable, by the cash basis partnership-transferor at the time of receipt of the stock.

But the terms and purpose of Section 351 have to be reckoned with. By its explicit terms Section 351 expresses the Congressional intent that transfers of property for stock or securities will not result in recognition. It therefore becomes apparent that this case vividly illustrates how Section 351 sometimes comes into conflict with another provision of the Internal Revenue Code or a judicial doctrine, and requires a determination of which of two conflicting doctrines will control.

As we must, when we try to reconcile conflicting doctrines in the revenue law, we endeavor to ascertain a controlling Congressional mandate. Section 351 has been described as a deliberate attempt by Congress to facilitate the incorporation of ongoing businesses and to eliminate any technical constructions which are economically unsound.

Appellant-taxpayer seems to recognize this and argues that application of the *Lake* rationale when accounts receivable are transferred would not create any undue hardship to an incorporating taxpayer. "All a taxpayer [transferor] need do is withhold the earned income items and collect them, transferring the net proceeds to the Corporation. Indeed * * * the transferor should retain both accounts receivable and accounts payable to avoid income recognition at the time of transfer and to have sufficient funds with which to pay accounts payable. Where the taxpayer [transferor] is on the cash method of accounting [as here], the deduction of the accounts payable would be applied against the income generated by the accounts receivable."

While we cannot fault the general principle "that income be taxed to him who earns it," to adopt taxpayer's argument would be to hamper the incorporation of ongoing businesses; additionally it would impose technical constructions which are economically and practically unsound. None of the cases cited by taxpayer, including *Lake* itself, persuades us otherwise. In *Lake* the Court was required to decide whether the proceeds from the assignment of the oil payment right were taxable as ordinary income or as long term capital gains. Observing that the provision for long term capital gains treatment "has always been narrowly construed so as to protect the revenue against artful devices," 356 U.S. at 265, 78 S.Ct. at 694, the Court predicated its holding upon an emphatic distinction between a conversion of a capital investment—"income-producing property"—and an assignment of income *per se*. "The substance of what was assigned was the right to receive future income. The substance of what was received was the present value of income which the recipient would otherwise obtain in the future." Ibid., at 266, 78 S.Ct. at 695. A Section 351 issue was not presented in *Lake*. Therefore the case does not control in weighing the conflict between the general rule of assignment of income and the Congressional purpose of nonrecognition upon the incorporation of an ongoing business.

We are persuaded that, on balance, the teachings of *Lake* must give way in this case to the broad Congressional interest in facilitating the incorporation of ongoing businesses. As desirable as it is to afford symmetry in revenue law, we do not intend to promulgate a hard and fast rule. We believe that the problems posed by the clash of conflicting internal revenue doctrines are more properly determined by the circumstances of each case. Here we are influenced by the fact that the subject of the assignment was accounts receivable for partnership's goods and services sold in the regular course of business, that the change of business form from partnership to corporation had a basic business purpose and was not designed for the purpose of deliberate tax avoidance, and by the conviction that the totality of circumstances here presented fit the mold of the Congressional intent to give nonrecognition to a transfer of a total business from a non-corporate to a corporate form.

But this too must be said. Even though Section 351(a) immunizes the transferor from immediate tax consequences, Section 358 retains for the transferors a potential income tax liability to be realized and recognized upon a subsequent sale or exchange of the stock certificates received. As to the transferee-corporation, the tax basis of the receivables will be governed by Section 362.

* * *

Revenue Ruling 95–74

1995–2 Cum.Bull. 36.

ISSUES

(1) Are the liabilities assumed by S in the § 351 exchange described below liabilities for purposes of §§ 357(c)(1) and 358(d)?

(2) Once assumed by S, how will the liabilities in the § 351 exchange described below be treated?

FACTS

Corporation P is an accrual basis, calendar-year corporation engaged in various ongoing businesses, one of which includes the operation of a manufacturing plant (the Manufacturing Business). The plant is located on land purchased by P many years before. The land was not contaminated by any hazardous waste when P purchased it. However, as a result of plant operations, certain environmental liabilities, such as potential soil and groundwater remediation, are now associated with the land.

In Year 1, for bona fide business purposes, P engages in an exchange to which § 351 of the Internal Revenue Code applies by transferring substantially all of the assets associated with the Manufacturing Business, including the manufacturing plant and the land on which the plant is located, to a newly formed corporation, S, in exchange for all of the stock of S and for S's assumption of the liabilities associated with the Manufacturing Business, including the environmental liabilities associated with the land. P has no plan or intention to dispose of (or have S issue) any S stock. S is an accrual basis, calendar-year taxpayer.

P did not undertake any environmental remediation efforts in connection with the land transferred to S before the transfer and did not deduct or capitalize any amount with respect to the contingent environmental liabilities associated with the transferred land.

In Year 3, S undertakes soil and groundwater remediation efforts relating to the land transferred in the § 351 exchange and incurs costs (within the meaning of the economic performance rules of § 461(h)) as a result of those remediation efforts. Of the total amount of costs incurred, a portion would have constituted ordinary and necessary business expenses that are deductible under § 162 and the remaining portion would have constituted capital expenditures under § 263 if there had not been a § 351 exchange and the costs for remediation efforts had been incurred by P. * * *

LAW AND ANALYSIS

Issue 1: * * * The legislative history of § 351 indicates that Congress viewed an incorporation as a mere change in the form of the underlying business and enacted § 351 to facilitate such business adjustments generally by allowing taxpayers to incorporate businesses without recognizing gain. * * * Section 357(c)(1), however, provides that the transferor recognizes gain to the extent that the amount of liabilities transferred exceeds the aggregate basis of the assets transferred.

A number of cases concerning cash basis taxpayers were litigated in the 1970s with respect to the definition of "liabilities" for purposes of § 357(c)(1), with sometimes conflicting analyses and results. * * * In response to this litigation, Congress enacted § 357(c)(3) to address the concern that the inclusion in the § 357(c)(1) determination of certain deductible liabilities resulted in "unforeseen and unintended tax difficulties for certain cash basis taxpayers who incorporate a going business." S.Rep. No. 1263, 95th Cong., 2d Sess. 184–85 (1978), 1978–3 C.B. 482–83.

Congress concluded that including in the § 357(c)(1) determination liabilities that have not yet been taken into account by the transferor results in an overstatement of liabilities of, and potential inappropriate gain recognition to, the transferor because the transferor has not received the corresponding deduction or other corresponding tax benefit. Id. To prevent this result, Congress enacted § 357(c)(3)(A) to exclude certain deductible liabilities from the scope of § 357(c), as long as the liabilities had not resulted in the creation of, or an increase in, the basis of any property (as provided in s 357(c)(3)(B)). * * *

While § 357(c)(3) explicitly addresses liabilities that give rise to deductible items, the same principle applies to liabilities that give rise to capital expenditures as well. Including in the § 357(c)(1) determination those liabilities that have not yet given rise to capital expenditures (and thus have not yet created or increased basis) with respect to the property of the transferor prior to the transfer also would result in an overstatement of liabilities. Thus, such liabilities also appropriately are excluded in determining liabilities for purposes of § 357(c)(1). * * *

In this case, the contingent environmental liabilities assumed by S had not yet been taken into account by P prior to the transfer (and therefore had neither given rise to deductions for P nor resulted in the creation of, or increase in, basis in any property of P). As a result, the contingent environmental liabilities are not included in determining whether the amount of the liabilities assumed by S exceeds the adjusted basis of the property transferred by P pursuant to § 357(c)(1).

Due to the parallel constructions and interrelated function and mechanics of §§ 357 and 358, liabilities that are not included in the determination under § 357(c)(1) also are not included in the § 358 determination of the transferor's basis in the stock received in the § 351 exchange. * * * Therefore, the contingent environmental liabilities assumed by S are not treated as money received by P under § 358 for purposes of determining P's basis in the stock of S received in the exchange.

Issue 2: In Holdcroft Transp. Co. v. Commissioner, 153 F.2d 323 (8th Cir.1946), the Court of Appeals for the Eighth Circuit held that, after a transfer pursuant to the predecessor to § 351, the payments by a transferee corporation were not deductible even though the transferor partnership would have been entitled to deductions for the payments had the partnership actually made the payments. The court stated generally that the expense of settling claims or liabilities of a predecessor entity did not arise as an operating expense or loss of the business of the transferee but was a part of the cost of acquiring the predecessor's property, and the fact that the claims were contingent and unliquidated at the time of the acquisition was not of controlling consequence.

In Rev. Rul. 80–198, 1980–2 C.B. 113, an individual transferred all of the assets and liabilities of a sole proprietorship, which included accounts payable and accounts receivable, to a new corporation in exchange for all of its stock. The revenue ruling holds, subject to certain limitations, that the transfer qualifies as an exchange within the meaning of § 351(a) and that the transferee corporation will report in its income the accounts receivable as collected and will be allowed deductions under § 162 for the payments it makes to satisfy the accounts payable. In reaching these holdings, the revenue ruling makes reference to the specific congressional intent of § 351(a) to facilitate the incorporation of an ongoing business by making the incorporation tax free. The ruling states that this intent would be equally frustrated if either the transferor were taxed on the transfer of the accounts receivable or the transferee were not allowed a deduction for payment of the accounts payable. * * *

The present case is analogous to the situation in Rev. Rul. 80–198. For business reasons, P transferred in a § 351 exchange substantially all of the assets and liabilities associated with the Manufacturing Business to S, in exchange for all of its stock, and P intends to remain in control of S. The costs S incurs to remediate the land would have been deductible in part and capitalized in part had P continued the Manufacturing Business and incurred those costs to remediate the land. The congressional intent to facilitate necessary business readjustments would be frustrated by not according to S the ability to deduct or capitalize the expenses of the ongoing business.

Therefore, on these facts, the Internal Revenue Service will not follow the decision in Holdcroft Transp. Co. v. Commissioner, 153 F.2d 323 (8th Cir.1946). Accordingly, the contingent environmental liabilities assumed from P are deductible as business expenses under § 162 or are capitalized under § 263, as appropriate, by S under S's method of accounting (determined as if S has owned the land for the period and in the same manner as it was owned by P).

HOLDINGS

(1) The liabilities assumed by S in the § 351 exchange described above are not liabilities for purposes of § 357(c)(1) and § 358(d) because the

liabilities had not yet been taken into account by P prior to the transfer (and therefore had neither given rise to deductions for P nor resulted in the creation of, or increase in, basis in any property of P).

(2) The liabilities assumed by S in the § 351 exchange described above are deductible by S as business expenses under § 162 or are capital expenditures under § 263, as appropriate, under S's method of accounting (determined as if S has owned the land for the period and in the same manner as it was owned by P).

LIMITATIONS

The holdings described above are subject to § 482 and other applicable sections of the Code and principles of law, including the limitations discussed in Rev. Rul. 80–198, 1980–2 C.B. 113 (limiting the scope of the revenue ruling to transactions that do not have a tax avoidance purpose). * * *

NOTE

Receivables and Payables. When there is a valid business purpose for the transfer of receivables and payables on the incorporation of a going business, the Service's position is that the transferee corporation (and not the transferor) must report the receivables in income as they are collected and deduct the payables when they are paid.[1] This position is consistent with the Government's position in *Hempt Brothers* that the assignment of income doctrine normally will not override Section 351. But to prevent abuse in situations where receivables are accumulated or payables prepaid in anticipation of the incorporation, the Service has noted the following limitations:[2]

> Section 351 of the Code does not apply to a transfer of accounts receivable which constitute an assignment of an income right in a case such as Brown v. Commissioner, 40 B.T.A. 565 (1939), aff'd 115 F.2d 337 (2d Cir.1940). In *Brown*, an attorney transferred to a corporation, in which he was the sole owner, a one-half interest in a claim for legal services performed by the attorney and his law partner. In exchange, the attorney received additional stock of the corporation. The claim represented the corporation's only asset. Subsequent to the receipt by the corporation of the proceeds of the claim, the attorney gave all of the stock of the corporation to his wife. The United States Court of Appeals for the Second Circuit found that the transfer of the claim for the fee to the corporation had no purpose other than to avoid taxes and held that in such a case the intervention of the corporation would not prevent the attorney from being liable for the tax on the income which resulted from services under the assignment of

1. Rev.Rul. 80–198, 1980–2 C.B. 113. See also Rev.Rul. 95–74, p. 477 supra.

2. Id.

income rule of Lucas v. Earl, 281 U.S. 111, 50 S.Ct. 241 (1930). Accordingly, in a case of a transfer to a controlled corporation of an account receivable in respect of services rendered where there is a tax avoidance purpose for the transaction (which might be evidenced by the corporation not conducting an ongoing business), the Internal Revenue Service will continue to apply assignment of income principles and require that the transferor of such a receivable include it in income when received by the transferee corporation.

Likewise, it may be appropriate in certain situations to allocate income, deductions, credits, or allowances to the transferor or transferee under section 482 of the Code when the timing of the incorporation improperly separates income from related expenses. See Rooney v. United States, 305 F.2d 681 (9th Cir.1962), where a farming operation was incorporated in a transaction described in section 351(a) after the expenses of the crop had been incurred but before the crop had been sold and income realized. The transferor's tax return contained all of the expenses but none of the farming income to which the expenses related. The United States Court of Appeals for the Ninth Circuit held that the expenses could be allocated under section 482 to the corporation, to be matched with the income to which the expenses related. Similar adjustments may be appropriate where some assets, liabilities, or both, are retained by the transferor and such retention results in the income of the transferor, transferee, or both, not being clearly reflected.

Tax Benefit Rule. Even when a transferor contributes Section 351 "property" to a controlled corporation, a problem may arise if the transferor deducted the cost of that property prior to the transfer. Under the tax benefit rule, if an amount has been deducted and a later event occurs that is fundamentally inconsistent with the premise on which the deduction was initially based, the earlier deduction must be effectively "cancelled out" by the recognition of income equal to the amount previously deducted.[3] For example, a taxpayer who pays $1,000 for minor office supplies to be used in his business would deduct that amount when paid on the assumption that those supplies soon would be exhausted. If that taxpayer later incorporates before the supplies are used and receives $1,000 of stock in the exchange, an event has occurred that is inconsistent with the presumption upon which the earlier deduction was based. But recognition of $1,000 of current income on the transfer of the supplies to a controlled corporation in exchange for its stock is also inconsistent with Section 351.

Whether or not the tax benefit rule overrides Section 351 has been unsettled for many years, but the importance of the issues appears to have

3. See Bittker & Lokken, Federal Taxation of Income, Estates and Gifts ¶ 5.7.1 (3d ed. 1999).

diminished. In Nash v. United States,[4] an accrual method taxpayer transferred accounts receivable to a newly formed corporation in exchange for stock. The taxpayer already had included the receivables in income and also had deducted a reserve for bad debts. Applying the tax benefit rule, the Service argued that the taxpayer should be taxed on an amount equal to the previously deducted bad debt reserve because the taxpayer's presumption that some of those debts would turn bad while held in his business had proved erroneous. Although the debts still might become worthless, that event would occur only when they were held by the new corporation—a separate business. The Supreme Court held that the net amount the taxpayer had included in his income as a result of the receivables (i.e., the excess of all accrued receivables over the deducted reserve for bad debts) equalled the value of the stock received for the receivables, so that the earlier deduction for the reserve for bad debts was not inappropriate and did not generate income under the tax benefit rule.

The specific fact pattern addressed in *Nash* is no longer important because accrual method taxpayers are now generally precluded from deducting a reserve for bad debts. Moreover, in a subsequent case, the Supreme Court held that the tax benefit rule applies whenever a later unforeseen event is "fundamentally inconsistent" with the premise underlying a taxpayer's earlier deduction.[5] This broader holding suggests that the Court might uphold application of the tax benefit rule in another factual setting involving a transfer to a newly formed corporation. On the other hand, the Code specifically provides that the depreciation recapture provisions, which are grounded on tax benefit rule principles, do not override Section 351.[6]

PROBLEM

Architect, a cash basis taxpayer, has been conducting a business as a sole proprietorship for several years. Architect decides to incorporate, and on July 1 of the current year he forms Design, Inc., to which he transfers the following assets:

Asset	A.B.	F.M.V.
Accounts Receivable	$ 0	$ 60,000
Supplies	0	20,000
Unimproved Land	60,000	120,000
Total	$60,000	$200,000

The land was subject to contingent environmental liabilities that Architect had not taken into account (i.e., had not deducted or capitalized) for tax purposes at the time of the incorporation. The supplies were acquired nine months ago and their cost was immediately deducted by Architect as an ordinary and necessary business expense.

4. 398 U.S. 1, 90 S.Ct. 1550 (1970). See also Rev.Rul. 78–280, 1978–2 C.B. 139.

5. Hillsboro Nat'l Bank v. Commissioner, 460 U.S. 370, 103 S.Ct. 1134 (1983).

6. See, e.g., I.R.C. § 1245(b)(3).

In exchange, Architect receives 100 shares of Design common stock with a fair market value of $100,000. In addition, Design assumes $70,000 of accounts payable to trade creditors of Architect's sole proprietorship and a $30,000 bank loan incurred by Architect two years ago for valid business reasons, and it assumed the environmental liabilities associated with the land.

Design elects to become a cash method, calendar year taxpayer. During the remainder of the current year, it pays $30,000 of the accounts payable and collects $40,000 of the accounts receivable transferred by Architect. In the following taxable year, Design paid $20,000 in environmental remediation expenses that qualified for a current deduction under Section 162 when the expenses were paid or accrued.

(a) What are the tax consequences (gain or loss recognized, basis and holding period) of the incorporation to Architect and Design, Inc.?

(b) Who will be taxable upon collection of the accounts receivable: Architect, Design or both?

(c) When Design pays the accounts payable assumed from Architect and incurs the environmental remediation costs, may it properly deduct these expenses?

(d) Assume that Architect is in the highest marginal individual tax bracket and Design, Inc. anticipates no significant taxable income for the current year. What result if Architect decides to pay (and deduct) personally all the accounts payable and transfers the accounts receivable to the corporation?

(e) Would your answers be any different if Architect had been an accrual method taxpayer?

(f) Is Design, Inc. limited in its choice of accounting method (i.e., cash or accrual) or taxable year? See §§ 441; 448.

F. CAPITAL STRUCTURE OF A C CORPORATION

1. INTRODUCTION

The organizers of a business venture face a major decision in planning the capital structure of their company. The simplest method of raising corporate capital is by issuing stock in exchange for contributions of money, property or services. Stock—known as "equity" in corporate finance parlance—may be common or preferred, and either type may be issued in various classes with different rights and priorities as to voting, dividends, liquidations, convertibility, and the like. A corporation also may raise capital by borrowing, either from the same insider group that owns the company's stock or from banks and other outside lenders. Corporate debt typically is evidenced by a variety of instruments including bonds, notes and more exotic hybrid securities such as convertible debentures. Although both shareholders and creditors contribute capital, their relationship to the corporation is markedly different. As one early case put it, a shareholder is "an adventurer in the corporate business," taking risk and profit from success, while a creditor, "in compensation for not sharing the profits, is to be paid independently of the risk of success, and gets a right to dip into capital when the payment date arrives."[1]

To some extent, decisions concerning the proper mix of debt and equity are made without regard to tax considerations. Most businesses rely on both short and long-term debt to finance their operations. Quite apart from taxes, traditional corporate finance theorists believed that debt financing contributed to a higher rate of investment return. This conventional wisdom did not go unchallenged. In their well known writings on corporate finance, Professors Modigliani and Miller took the view that, assuming away taxes and other factors, the value of a corporation is unrelated to the amount of debt used in its capital structure.[2] On the other hand, excessive debt has its pitfalls, and CFO's of fiscally conservatively public companies may be reluctant to risk insolvency or a shaky credit rating by loading the corporate balance sheet with liabilities.[3] In short, many factors other than taxes affect corporate financing decisions.

Although the tax system may not always drive financing behavior, it profoundly influences the capital structure of both publicly traded and closely held C corporations. Consider the decision facing A and B, who each plan to invest $100,000 on the formation of closely held Newco, Inc. At first glance, it might seem that issuing any Newco debt to A and B would be a needless exercise. If the investors agree on their respective contributions and the allocation of ownership and voting power, what difference does it make whether they hold stock, bonds or notes? The answer is often found in the Internal Revenue Code, which distinguishes between debt and equity for tax purposes, tipping the scales in favor of issuing a healthy dose of debt. This tax bias toward debt financing is influential both at the time of formation and on later occasions in a corporation's life cycle.

The principal advantage of issuing debt as opposed to equity is avoidance of the "double tax." Even though most dividends now qualify for a preferential tax rate (until that rate expires in 2011), they still are includible in a shareholder's income and are not deductible by the corporation. The earnings represented by these dividends are thus taxed at both the corporate and shareholder levels.[4] But interest paid on corporate debt, while also includible in the recipient's income, is deductible by the corpora-

1. Commissioner v. O.P.P. Holding Corp., 76 F.2d 11, 12 (2d Cir.1935).

2. For a general discussion of the debate, see Klein & Coffee, Business Organization and Finance, Legal and Economic Principles 352–385 (10th ed. 2007).

3. The statement in the text is belied by the surge of debt financing that accompanied the corporate mergers and restructurings of the 1980's and the significant increases in corporate debt in 2001 and beyond. See, e.g., Zuckerman, "Climb of Corporate Debt Trips Analysts' Alarm," Wall St. Journal, Dec. 31, 2001, at C1 (reporting that U.S. corporations were incurring debt at record levels as of the end of 2001). The nontax risks of excessive debt were well documented by the collapse of the junk bond market in the early 1990's and the bankruptcy boom of 2001–2002 (e.g., Enron), but the tax system continues to provide incentives for C corporations to engage in debt-financed acquisitions and stock repurchases.

4. The dividends received deduction provides some additional tax relief for corporate shareholders. See I.R.C. § 243 and Chapter 12F, infra.

tion.[5] Assuming the owners of the business desire some ongoing return on their investment, there is an incentive to distribute earnings with tax-deductible dollars.[6]

Several other features of the tax law reflect a bias in favor of debt over equity. The repayment of principal on a corporate debt is a tax-free return of capital to the lender. If the amount repaid exceeds the lender's basis in the debt, the difference generally is treated as a capital gain under Section 1271. In contrast, when a corporation redeems (i.e., buys back) stock from a shareholder—a transaction quite similar to the repayment of a debt—the entire amount received may be taxed as a dividend if the shareholder or related persons continue to own stock in the corporation.[7]

The issuance of debt at the time of incorporation also may provide a defense against subsequent imposition of the accumulated earnings tax.[8] The obligation to repay a debt at maturity may qualify as a "reasonable business need," justifying an accumulation of corporate earnings,[9] while the same type of accumulation for a redemption of stock normally is not regarded as reasonable for purposes of the accumulated earnings tax.[10]

The choice between debt and equity has significant tax ramifications in many other contexts. For example, the classification of a corporate investment may have an impact on whether transfers of property to a corporation qualify for nonrecognition under Section 351. Complete nonrecognition of gain or loss is available only when the contributing taxpayer receives solely stock. Conversely, taxpayers who wish to recognize gain on the transfer of property to a controlled corporation may attempt to accomplish their objective by taking back boot in the form of installment debt obligations.[11] That goal will be thwarted if the notes are reclassified as stock. Classification of an interest in a corporation also may control the character of a loss if the investment becomes worthless.[12]

The tax distinctions between debt and equity have fueled an ongoing policy debate. The relationship between the favorable tax treatment of debt and the explosive growth in debt-financed corporate acquisitions have captured the public's attention for several decades. But Congress to date has declined to embrace a comprehensive legislative solution to the problems of excessive debt. Instead, it has been content to enact narrowly targeted provisions aimed at isolated abuses that are seen as threats to the integrity of the corporate income tax. The excerpt below from a Congressional study on the income tax aspects of corporate financial structures,

5. I.R.C. § 163(a).

6. But see Andrews, "Tax Neutrality Between Equity Capital and Debt," 30 Wayne L.Rev. 1057 (1984), suggesting that this traditional "simple view" is inadequate because it fails to recognize the opportunity for corporations to raise equity capital by accumulating earnings—a process that redounds to the benefit of shareholders without subjecting them to tax until the earnings are distributed or the shares are sold.

7. I.R.C. § 302. See Chapter 13C, infra.

8. I.R.C. § 531 et seq. See Chapter 10C1, supra.

9. Reg. § 1.537–2(b)(3). Repayment of debt owed to shareholders, however, may be subjected to greater scrutiny. See Smoot Sand & Gravel Corp. v. Commissioner, 241 F.2d 197 (4th Cir.1957), cert. denied 354 U.S. 922, 77 S.Ct. 1383 (1957).

10. See, e.g., Bittker & Eustice, Federal Income Taxation of Corporations and Shareholders ¶ 7.07 (7th ed. 2000).

11. See Section G2 of this chapter, infra.

12. See Section F3 of this chapter, infra.

which predates the reduced tax rate on qualified dividends, offers some general insights into the debt vs. equity policy debate.

Excerpt from Joint Committee on Taxation, Federal Income Tax Aspects of Corporate Financial Structures

101st Cong., 1st Sess. pp. 53–58 (Jan. 18, 1989).

A. Tax Advantage of Debt Versus Equity

The total effect of the tax system on the incentives for corporations to use debt or equity depends on the interaction between the tax treatment at the shareholder and corporate levels.

The case of no income taxes.—In a simple world without taxes or additional costs in times of financial distress, economic theory suggests that the value of a corporation, as measured by the total value of the outstanding debt and equity, would be unchanged by the degree of leverage of the firm. This conclusion explicitly recognizes that debt issued by the corporation represents an ownership right to future income of the corporation in a fashion similar to that of equity. In this simple world there would be no advantage to debt or to equity and the debt-equity ratio of the firm would not affect the cost of financing investment.

Effect of corporate income tax

Tax advantages

Taxes greatly complicate this analysis. Since the interest expense on debt is deductible for computing the corporate income tax while the return to equity is not, the tax at the corporate level provides a strong incentive for debt rather than equity finance.

Table IV–A.—Effect of Debt Financing on Returns to Equity Investment

Item	All-equity corporation	50–percent debt-financed corporation
Beginning Balance Sheet:		
Total assets	$1,000	$1,000
Debt	0	500
Shareholders' equity	1,000	500
Income Statement:		
Operating income	150	150
Interest expense	0	50
Taxable income	150	100
Income tax	51	34
Income after corporate tax	99	66
Return on Equity[1] (percent)	9.9	13.2

1. Return on equity is computed as income after corporate tax divided by beginning shareholders' equity.

The advantages of debt financing can be illustrated by comparing two corporations with $1,000 of assets that are identical except for financial structure: the first is entirely equity financed; while the second is 50–percent debt financed. Both corporations earn $150 of operating income. The all-equity corporation pays $51 in corporate tax [this and later examples assume a 34 percent corporate income tax rate, Ed.] and retains or distributes $99 of after-tax income ($150 less $51). Thus, as shown in Table IV–A, the return on equity is 9.9 percent ($99 divided by $1,000).

The leveraged corporation is financed by $500 of debt and $500 of stock. If the interest rate is 10 percent, then interest expense is $50 (10 percent times $500). Taxable income is $100 after deducting interest expense. The leveraged corporation is liable for $34 in corporate tax (34 percent times $100) and distributes or retains $66 of after-tax income ($100 less $34). Consequently, the return on equity is 13.2 percent ($66 divided by $500). Thus, as shown in Table IV–A, increasing the debt ratio from zero to 50 percent increases the rate of return on equity from 9.9 to 13.2 percent.

This arithmetic demonstrates that a leveraged corporation can generate a higher return on equity (net of corporate income tax) than an unleveraged company or, equivalently, that an unleveraged company needs to earn a higher profit before corporate tax to provide investors the same return net of corporate tax as could be obtained with an unleveraged company. More generally, the return on equity rises with increasing debt capitalization so long as the interest rate is less than the pre-tax rate of return on corporate assets. This suggests that the Code creates an incentive to raise the debt-equity ratio to the point where the corporate income tax (or outstanding equity) is eliminated.

Costs of financial distress

With higher levels of debt the possibility of financial distress increases, as do the expected costs to the firm which occur with such distress. These additional costs include such items as the increase in the costs of debt funds; constraints on credit, expenditure or operating decisions; and the direct costs of being in bankruptcy. These expected costs of financial distress may, at sufficiently high debt-equity ratios, offset the corporate tax advantage to additional debt finance.

Effect of shareholder income tax

The above analysis focuses solely on the effect of interest deductibility at the corporate level. Shareholder-level income taxation may offset to some degree the corporate tax incentive for corporate debt relative to equity.

Shareholder treatment of debt and equity

The conclusion that debt is tax favored relative to equity remains unchanged if interest on corporate debt and returns on equity are taxed at the same effective rate to investors. In this case, the returns to investors on both debt and equity are reduced proportionately by the income tax; the advantage to debt presented by corporate tax deductibility remains. One noteworthy exception exists if the marginal investments on both debt and equity are effectively tax-exempt. Given the previously documented importance of tax-exempt pension funds in the bond and equity markets, this case may be of some importance.

Shareholder level tax treatment of equity

In general, returns to shareholders and debtholders are not taxed the same. Although dividends, like interest income, are taxed currently, equity income in other forms may reduce the effective investor-level tax on equity below that on debt. First, the firm may retain earnings and not pay dividends currently. In general, the accumulation of earnings by the firm will cause the value of the firm's shares to rise. Rather than being taxed currently on corporate earnings, a shareholder will be able to defer the taxation on the value of the retained earnings reflected in the price of the stock until the shareholder sells the stock. Thus, even though the tax rates on interest, dividends, and capital gains are the same [the tax rates were the same for a few years after the Tax Reform Act of 1986; under current law, interest is taxable as ordinary income while long-term capital gains and qualified dividends are taxed at preferential rates, Ed.], the ability to defer the tax on returns from equity reduces the effective rate of individual tax on equity investment below that on income from interest on corporate debt.

Other aspects of capital gain taxation serve to reduce further the individual income tax on equity. Since tax on capital gain is normally triggered after a voluntary recognition event (e.g., the sale of stock), the taxpayer can time the realization of capital gain income when the effective rate of tax is low. The rate of tax could be low if the taxpayer is in a low or zero tax bracket because other income is abnormally low, if other capital losses shelter the capital gain, or if changes in the tax law cause the statutory rate on capital gains to be low. Perhaps most important, the step up in the adjusted tax basis of the stock upon the death of the shareholder may permit the shareholder's heirs to avoid tax completely on capital gains. For all these reasons, the effective rate of tax on undistributed earnings may be already quite low.

Corporations can distribute their earnings to owners of equity in forms that generally result in less tax to shareholders than do dividend distributions. Share repurchases have become an important method of distributing corporate earnings to equity holders. When employed by large publicly traded firms, repurchases of the corporation's own shares permit the shareholders to treat the distribution as a sale of stock (i.e., to obtain capital gain treatment, and recover the basis in the stock without tax). The remaining shareholders may benefit because they have rights to a larger fraction of the firm and may see a corresponding increase in the value of their shares. Thus, less individual tax will generally be imposed on a $100 repurchase of stock than on $100 of dividends. In addition, share repurchases allow shareholders to choose whether to receive corporate distributions by choosing whether to sell or retain shares, so as to minimize tax liability.

Acquisitions of the stock of one corporation for cash or property of another corporation provides a similar method for distributing corporate earnings out of corporate solution with less shareholder tax than through a dividend. The target shareholders generally treat the acquisition as a sale and recover their basis free of tax. For purposes of analyzing the individual tax effect of corporate earnings disbursements, this transaction can be thought of as equivalent to a stock merger of the target with the acquiror followed by the repurchase of the target shareholders' shares by the resulting merged firm. The result is similar to the case of a share repurchase in that cash is distributed to shareholders with less than the full dividend tax, except that two firms are involved instead of one.

Since dividends typically are subject to more tax than other methods for providing returns to shareholders, the puzzle of why firms pay dividends remains. Because dividends are paid at the discretion of the firm, it appears that firms cause their shareholders to pay more tax on equity income than is strictly necessary. Until a better understanding of corporate distribution policy exists, the role of dividend taxation on equity financing decisions remain uncertain.

To summarize, although the current taxation of dividends to investors is clearly significant, there are numerous reasons why the overall individual tax on equity investments may be less than that on interest income from debt. Since the effective shareholder tax on returns from equity may be less than that on debt holdings, the shareholder tax may offset some or all of the advantage to debt at the corporate level.

Interaction of corporate and shareholder taxation

With shareholders in different income tax brackets, high tax rate taxpayers will tend to concentrate their wealth in the form of equity and low tax rate taxpayers will tend to concentrate their wealth in the form of debt. The distribution of wealth among investors with different marginal tax rates affects the demand for investments in the form of debt or equity. The interaction between the demand of investors, and the supply provided by corporations, determines the aggregate amount of corporate debt and equity in the economy.

At some aggregate mix between debt and equity, the difference in the investor-level tax on income from equity and debt may be sufficient to offset completely, at the margin, the apparent advantage of debt at the corporate level. Even if the difference in investor tax treatment of debt and equity is not sufficient to offset completely the corporate tax advantage, the advantage to debt may be less than the corporate-level tax treatment alone would provide.

* * *

Implications for policy

The analysis above suggests that any policy change designed to reduce the tax incentive for debt must consider the interaction of both corporate and shareholder taxes. For example, proposals to change the income tax rates for individuals or corporations will change the incentive for corporate debt. Likewise, proposals to change the tax treatment of tax-exempt entities may alter the aggregate mix and distribution of debt and equity.

In addition, proposals to reduce the bias toward debt over equity, for example, by reducing the total tax on dividends, must confront the somewhat voluntary nature of the dividend tax. Since the payment of dividends by corporations generally is discretionary and other means exist for providing value to shareholders with less tax, corporations can affect the level of shareholder level tax incurred. Until a better understanding of the determinants of corporate distribution behavior exists, the total impact of policies designed to reduce the bias between debt and equity are uncertain.

* * *

NOTE

The traditional tax bias for debt over equity has been weakened as long as qualified dividends are taxed at the same preferential rate as long-term capital gains. The Bush Administration's original proposal to allow a 100 percent shareholder-level exclusion for dividends paid from previously taxed corporate earnings would have largely eliminated the bias and profoundly altered the stakes for future capital structure decisions.

The 15 percent rate on qualified dividends, if it becomes permanent,[1] would be a major step toward neutralizing the debt vs. equity distinction. As long as dividends are taxed at preferential rates, equity investments will be more attractive to taxable investors. Not all shareholders pay taxes, however—e.g., tax-exempt pension funds and charities—and corporations still benefit from the ability to deduct interest paid on corporate debt. It thus seems premature to relegate the discussion of capital structure in this chapter to the recycling bin.

2. Debt vs. Equity

a. GENERAL RULES

Taxpayers have considerable flexibility to structure corporate instruments as debt or equity. In view of the sharply disparate tax treatment of debt and equity, it is hardly surprising that the Service may be unwilling to

1. Unless extended, the preferential rate will expire at the end of 2010.

accept the taxpayer's label as controlling.[1] Form would be elevated over substance if every piece of paper embossed with a corporate seal and bearing the label "debt" were treated as such for tax purposes. To prevent tax avoidance through the use of excessive debt, the Service may recast a purported debt obligation as equity. The tax consequences of a recharacterization can be extremely unpleasant. An interest payment becomes a dividend and the corporation loses its deduction. If and when the note is repaid, the "creditor" finds himself in the role of shareholder, and the "loan repayment" may turn into a taxable dividend instead of a tax-free return of capital.

It is one thing to list the advantages of debt and identify the unfortunate ramifications of reclassification. It is quite another to describe with any precision the process employed by the courts and the Service to determine whether a particular instrument is debt or equity. The case law first approaches the issue by describing a spectrum. At one end is equity, a risk investment with the potential to share in corporate profits. At the other end is debt, evidenced by the corporation's unconditional promise to pay back the contributed funds, with market rate interest, at a fixed maturity date. A pure equity investor—the shareholder—has voting rights and upside potential. A pure debt holder—the creditor—is an outsider with no prospect of sharing in the growth of the enterprise. Many classification controversies involve "hybrid securities" having features common to both debt and equity, and the courts must decide whether these instruments falling in the middle of the spectrum are closer to one end or the other.

Any process that looks at something decidedly gray and tries to determine whether it more closely resembles black or white is bound to be frustrating. And so it is here. The litigated cases are legion and the court decisions have been aptly vilified as a "jungle"[2] and a "viper's tangle."[3] The issue is murky because classification of an obligation as debt or equity traditionally is treated as a question of fact to be resolved by applying vague standards that require the weighing of many factors.[4] In a manner reminiscent of the approach to determining whether an asset is "held primarily for sale to customers," the courts have spewed forth laundry lists of "factors," but it is difficult to discern which are controlling in a given case. Exhaustive research leaves one with the firm conviction that the courts are applying an amorphous and highly unsatisfactory "smell test."

1. The characterization of an instrument at its issuance is binding on the issuer, but not the Service. I.R.C. § 385(c)(1). A holder of an instrument generally is bound by the issuer's characterization unless the holder discloses an inconsistent position on a tax return. I.R.C. § 385(c)(2).

2. Commissioner v. Union Mutual Insurance Co. of Providence, 386 F.2d 974, 978 (1st Cir.1967).

3. Bittker & Eustice, Federal Income Taxation of Corporations and Shareholders ¶ 4.04 (4th ed. 1979).

4. For this reason, the Service ordinarily declines to issue advance rulings on the classification on an instrument as debt or equity. Rev. Proc. 2008–3, § 4.02(1), 2008–1 I.R.B. 118. The courts are divided over whether the debt v. equity question is one of fact or law, or a mixed question of fact and law. See Indmar Products Co., Inc. v. Commissioner, 444 F.3d 771 (6th Cir. 2006).

Synthesizing the decisional morass is a perilous enterprise, but the principal factors enunciated by the courts over the years may be summarized as follows:[5]

Form of the Obligation. Labels are hardly controlling, but the decisions provide some guidance for a corporation that wishes to avoid reclassification of debt as equity. At a minimum, debt instruments should bear the usual indicia of debt—an unconditional promise to pay; a specific term; remedies for a default; and a stated, reasonable rate of interest, payable in all events.[6] Equity characteristics should be avoided. For example, the likelihood of reclassification is far greater with a hybrid instrument that makes payment of interest contingent on earnings or provides the holder with voting rights.[7]

The Debt/Equity Ratio. The debt/equity ratio of a corporation is the ratio of the company's liabilities to the shareholders' equity. The ratio has long been used as a tool to determine whether a corporation is thinly capitalized. Thin capitalization, in turn, creates a substantial risk that what purports to be debt will be reclassified as equity on the theory that no rational creditor would lend money to a corporation with such nominal equity.

The trouble with this attempt at quantification is that the cases are inconsistent as to what constitutes an excessive debt/equity ratio. For example, depending on all the other factors, a debt/equity ratio of 3–to–1, which most would regard as conservative, has been held to be excessive,[8] while ratios of 50–to–1 and higher have been held to be acceptable.[9] Some cases apply different norms for different industries,[10] others ignore the ratio entirely,[11] and some evaluate the ratio in the context of the overall growth prospects of the business.[12]

5. See generally Plumb, "The Federal Income Tax Significance of Corporate Debt: A Critical Analysis and a Proposal," 26 Tax L.Rev. 369 (1971); Stone, "Debt–Equity Distinctions in the Tax Treatment of the Corporation and Its Shareholders," 42 Tulane L.Rev. 251 (1968). For a more contemporary summary, see Hariton, "Essay: Distinguishing Between Equity and Debt in the New Financial Environment," 49 Tax L. Rev. 499 (1994).

6. See Wood Preserving Corp. v. United States, 347 F.2d 117, 119 (4th Cir.1965).

7. See Fellinger v. United States, 363 F.2d 826 (6th Cir.1966).

8. See Schnitzer v. Commissioner, 13 T.C. 43 (1949).

9. See Bradshaw v. United States, 231 Ct.Cl. 144, 683 F.2d 365, 367–68 (1982) (50–to–1 ratio not fatal because corporation was likely to and did in fact pay off debts when due); Baker Commodities, Inc. v. Commissioner, 48 T.C. 374 (1967), affirmed, 415 F.2d 519 (9th Cir.1969), cert. denied, 397 U.S. 988, 90 S.Ct. 1117 (1970) (692–to–1 ratio is acceptable because cash flow and earning power of business could cover payments).

10. Compare Tomlinson v. 1661 Corp., 377 F.2d 291 (5th Cir.1967) (improved real estate; debt traditionally high) with John Lizak, Inc. v. Commissioner, 28 T.C.M. 804 (1969) (construction business less able to carry heavy debt burden).

11. See Gooding Amusement Co. v. Commissioner, 23 T.C. 408, 419 (1954), affirmed, 236 F.2d 159 (6th Cir.1956), cert. denied, 352 U.S. 1031, 77 S.Ct. 595 (1957).

12. See, e.g., Delta Plastics, Inc. v. Commissioner, 85 T.C.M. 940 (2003) (26–to–1 ratio was acceptable because likely success of business would reduce ratio to 4–to–1 within three years).

And how is the debt/equity ratio to be computed? Consider some of the basic questions on which there is disagreement. Is debt limited to shareholder debt or does it include debts to outsiders?[13] Does outside debt include accounts payable to trade creditors or only long-term liabilities? What about shareholder guaranteed debt?[14] In determining "equity," are assets taken into account at their book value (i.e., adjusted basis) or fair market value?[15] The differences in approach can be considerable.

Intent. Some cases have turned on the "intent" of the parties to create a debtor-creditor relationship.[16] "Intent" presumably is not gleaned by a subjective inquiry; it would be meaningless to place the corporate insiders on the witness stand and ask whether they "intended" to be shareholders or creditors. The more reasoned decisions measure "intent" by objective criteria such as the lender's reasonable expectation of repayment, evaluated in light of the financial condition of the company, and the corporation's ability to pay principal and interest.[17] Hindsight also plays a role. For example, if the corporation consistently fails to pay interest or repay debts when they are due, its claim to debtor status may be highly questionable.[18]

Proportionality. In a closely held setting, debt held by the shareholders in the same proportion as their stock holdings normally raises the eyebrows of the Service.[19] The rationale is that if debt is held in roughly the same proportion as stock, the "creditors" have no economic incentive to act like creditors by setting or enforcing the terms of the so-called liability. The unanswered question is whether proportionality, without other negative factors, is sufficient in itself to convert the obligation into stock.[20]

Subordination. If a corporation has borrowed from both shareholders and outside sources, the independent creditors frequently will require that

13. Compare Ambassador Apartments, Inc. v. Commissioner, 50 T.C. 236, 245 (1968), affirmed, 406 F.2d 288 (2d Cir.1969) (consider outside debt) with P.M. Finance Corp. v. Commissioner, 302 F.2d 786, 788 (3d Cir.1962) (consider only shareholder debt).

14. Compare Murphy Logging Co. v. United States, 378 F.2d 222 (9th Cir.1967) (disregard shareholder guaranteed debt) with Plantation Patterns, Inc. v. Commissioner, 462 F.2d 712 (5th Cir.1972), cert. denied, 409 U.S. 1076, 93 S.Ct. 683 (1972) (shareholder guaranteed debt recharacterized as equity contribution by guarantor.)

15. See Nye v. Commissioner, 50 T.C. 203, 216 (1968). In Bauer v. Commissioner, 748 F.2d 1365 (9th Cir.1984), the court computed stockholders' equity by adding together paid-in capital and retained earnings and arrived at outside debt/equity ratios for different years ranging from approximately 2 to 1 to 8 to 1. The Tax Court had determined a ratio for one year of approximately 92 to 1 by limiting shareholders' equity to initial paid-in capital.

16. See Gooding Amusement Co. v. Commissioner, 236 F.2d 159 (6th Cir.1956), cert. denied, 352 U.S. 1031, 77 S.Ct. 595 (1957).

17. Indmar Products Co., Inc. v. Commissioner, supra note 5; Fin Hay Realty Co. v. United States, 398 F.2d 694 (3d Cir.1968); Gilbert v. Commissioner, 248 F.2d 399 (2d Cir.1957).

18. See Slappey Drive Industrial Park v. United States, 561 F.2d 572, 582 (5th Cir.1977); Estate of Mixon v. United States, 464 F.2d 394, 409 (5th Cir.1972).

19. See Charter Wire, Inc. v. United States, 309 F.2d 878, 880 (7th Cir.1962), cert. denied, 372 U.S. 965, 83 S.Ct. 1090 (1963).

20. For a negative view, see Harlan v. United States, 409 F.2d 904, 909 (5th Cir. 1969) (proportionality may be considered but has no significant importance).

the shareholder debt be subordinated to the claims of general creditors. Although subordination of inside debt would appear to be inevitable if significant unsecured outside financing is desired, some courts have regarded it as the smoking pistol.[21] Once again, however, it is difficult to advise a client with any certainty that subordination is fatal per se. The economic realities of closely held corporate life would suggest that it should not be determinative, but it grows in importance when combined with other negative factors such as thin capitalization, proportionality, and failure to pay any dividends.[22]

b. SECTION 385

Code: § 385.

Background. Many years ago, in the course of its deliberations on the Tax Reform Act of 1969, Congress concluded that determined effort was needed to alleviate the uncertainties flowing from the debt/equity case law, especially in light of "the increasing use of debt for corporate acquisition purposes."[1] Frustrated in its attempt to draft precise definitions, Congress delegated the chore to the executive branch by enacting Section 385, which authorizes the Treasury to promulgate such regulations "as may be necessary or appropriate" to determine for all tax purposes whether an interest in a corporation is to be treated as stock or debt. Section 385(b) requires the regulations to set forth "factors" to be taken into account in determining whether a debtor-creditor relationship exists and specifies the following factors which may (but need not) be included in the regulations:

1. Form—i.e., whether the instrument is evidenced by a written, unconditional promise to pay a sum certain on demand or on a specific date in return for an adequate consideration and bears a fixed interest rate.
2. Subordination to any indebtedness of the corporation.
3. The debt/equity ratio.
4. Convertibility into stock.
5. Proportionality—i.e., the relationship between holdings of stock in the corporation and holdings of the purported debt interest being scrutinized.

The Regulations Project. Section 385 was hailed by leading commentators as "perhaps the most important and potentially far-reaching corporate provision added by the Tax Reform Act of 1969,"[2] and the literature was

21. See P.M. Finance Corp. v. Commissioner, 302 F.2d 786, 789–90 (3d Cir.1962); R.C. Owen Co. v. Commissioner, 23 T.C.M. 673, 676 (1964), affirmed, 351 F.2d 410 (6th Cir.1965), cert. denied, 382 U.S. 967, 86 S.Ct. 1272 (1966).

22. See Tyler v. Tomlinson, 414 F.2d 844 (5th Cir.1969).

1. S.Rep. No. 91–552, 91st Cong., 1st Sess. 511 (1969), reprinted in 1969–3 C.B. 423, 511. See also H.R.Rep. No. 91–413, 91st Cong., 1st Sess. 265 (1969), reprinted in 1969–3 C.B. 200, 265.

2. Bittker & Eustice, Federal Income Taxation of Corporations and Shareholders, ¶ 4.05 (3rd ed. 1971).

replete with predictions as to the content of the regulations.[3] In March, 1980, 11 years after Section 385 was enacted, the Treasury issued a lengthy, detailed and controversial set of proposed regulations.[4] "Final" regulations were promulgated in December, 1980,[5] followed by amendments and effective date extensions, but all versions of the regulations were withdrawn in 1983[6] and the project has since been abandoned.

Although a detailed examination of the now long defunct regulations would not be productive, some features are noteworthy if only because they represented a concentrated attempt to bring order out of the chaos. For example, the regulations[7] distinguished straight debt from hybrid instruments, appropriately relegating hybrid securities to second class status. A "hybrid" was defined as an instrument convertible into stock or providing for any contingent payment to the holder.[8] In virtually all cases, hybrids would have been treated as preferred stock for tax purposes, at least if they were not held by independent creditors.[9] Straight debt—defined as anything other than a hybrid instrument[10]—still had a fighting chance of avoiding reclassification if certain other requirements were met.

The concept of proportionality played a central role in the regulatory scheme because "it generally makes little economic difference (aside from tax consequences) whether proportionate shareholder advances are made as debt or equity * * *."[11] Elaborate definitions of proportionality were provided, and special scrutiny was required for instruments held in substantial proportion to equity investments.[12]

Another contribution of the regulations was their precise definition of two debt/equity ratios—"outside" (which took into account *all* liabilities, including those to independent creditors) and "inside" (considering only shareholder debt).[13] Corollary rules provided that assets were to be reflected at adjusted basis rather than fair market value and trade liabilities were to be disregarded.[14] The debt/equity ratio was used to determine whether a corporation's debt was "excessive". A debt was excessive if the

3. Id. at 4–16 to 4–19. See also Recommendations as to Federal Tax Distinction between Corporate Stock and Indebtedness, N.Y. State Bar Association Tax Section Committee on Reorganization Problems, 25 Tax Lawyer 57 (1971).

4. 45 Fed.Reg. 18957 (1980).

5. T.D. 7747 (filed Dec. 29, 1980), 45 Fed.Reg. 86438 (Dec. 31, 1980), known as the "December 29" regulations.

6. T.D. 7920, 48 Fed.Reg. 31054 (July 6, 1983).

7. Unless otherwise indicated, citations which follow are to the December 30, 1981 version of the regulations.

8. Prop.Reg. § 1.385–3(d).

9. Prop.Reg. § 1.385–0(c)(2).

10. Prop.Reg. § 1.385–3(e).

11. T.D. 7747, 45 Fed.Reg. 86438, 86440 (Explanation of Changes), reprinted in 1981–1 C.B. 143.

12. Prop.Reg. § 1.385–6. In general, proportional straight debt instruments were treated as debt only if issued to "independent creditors" or if they were marketable instruments issued by a public company; otherwise they generally were reclassified as equity unless they were: (a) issued for cash or, if issued for property, the stated annual interest rate was "reasonable," and (b) the corporation did not have "excessive debt" at the time the instrument was issued. Prop.Reg. § 1.385–6(a)(3), (e), (g).

13. Prop.Reg. § 1.385–6(g)(4).

14. Prop.Reg. § 1.385–6(h).

instrument's terms and conditions, viewed in combination with the corporation's financial structure, would not have been satisfactory to a bank or other financial institution making ordinary commercial loans.[15] It was not excessive, however, if the outside debt/equity ratio did not exceed 10–to–1 and the inside debt/equity ratio did not exceed 3–to–1.[16] Thus, even proportionate straight debt issued for cash would not be reclassified if it fell within this safe harbor from "excessive debt" and bore a "reasonable" (within specified ranges) interest rate. Variations on these themes abounded.

The regulations were withdrawn because lobbyists convinced the Treasury that they would have a negative impact on particular industries and on small businesses generally.[17] Although some of the regulatory themes ultimately may be adopted by the courts, the Treasury is unlikely to initiate the mobilization that would be required to resurrect this project.

Bifurcation of Instruments. Despite the Treasury's lack of success in implementing the goals of Section 385, Congress has not given up hope. Section 385 was amended to allow (but not require) the Treasury to classify an interest having significant debt and equity characteristics as "in part stock and in part indebtedness."[18] According to the legislative history, bifurcation may be appropriate where a debt instrument provides for payments that are dependent to a significant extent on corporate performance, such as through "equity kickers" (i.e., provisions in a debt instrument that provide the holder with an equity interest in certain circumstances), contingent interest (which is dependent on corporate performance), significant deferral of payment, subordination, or an interest rate high enough to suggest a significant risk of default.[19]

If the Treasury accepts this Congressional challenge (it has not yet done so), several options might be considered. One approach would disallow interest deductions in excess of a specified rate of return to investors on the theory that a higher than normal risk is tantamount to an equity investment. For example, the regulations might specify a reference rate (such as the rate on comparable-term Treasury obligations) that is relatively risk-free and permit interest paid up to that rate to be deductible but deny a deduction for the additional "risk" element because it is more akin to a dividend. Under this type of broad disallowance approach, a corporation that issued a 20–year $100,000 unsecured debt instrument paying 14 percent interest (14,000 per year) at a time when comparable Treasury bonds were yielding 10 percent would be permitted to deduct only $10,000 per year as interest and the remaining $4,000 per year would be a nondeductible dividend.[20]

15. Prop.Reg. § 1.385–6(f)(2).

16. Prop.Reg. § 1.385–6(g)(3).

17. See, e.g., Levin & Bowen, "The Section 385 Regulations Regarding Debt Versus Equity: Is the Cure Worse than the Malady?" 35 Tax Lawyer 1 (1981).

18. I.R.C. § 385(a). This regulatory authority may be exercised on a prospective basis only.

19. H.Rep. No. 101–247, 101st Cong., 1st Sess. 1236 (1989).

20. In narrowly targeted situations, Congress began moving in this direction with

Another option is to limit bifurcation to instruments that provide for a combination of a fixed return and an additional return based on earnings. The regulations might treat the fixed return as interest while classifying the performance-based component as a nondeductible dividend. A closely related alternative, which finds isolated support in the case law, would be to divide one instrument into separate components—i.e., one part as debt and another as equity.[21]

Obligation of Consistency. Section 385(c) provides that a corporate issuer's characterization of an instrument as debt or equity at the time of issuance shall be binding on the issuer and all holders of the interest—but not binding, of course, on the Service. This rule of consistency does not apply, however, to holders who disclose on their tax return that they are treating the interest in a manner inconsistent with the issuer's characterization.

The Future. Perhaps in the 22d century, when the Section 385 regulations are reissued, we will know the Treasury's thinking on these questions.

c. HYBRID INSTRUMENTS

The types of financial instruments available to investors have proliferated. As one commentator has described the reality of today's world of corporate finance, "[i]n exchange for capital, corporations can offer investors any set of rights that can be described by words, subject to any conceivable set of qualifications, and in consideration of any conceivable set of offsetting obligations."[1]

The flexibility afforded corporate issuers has contributed to an array of exotic products that seek "best of both worlds" treatment—i.e., debt for tax purposes and equity for regulatory, financial rating, and accounting purposes. These hybrid instruments have been created and marketed by large financial institutions and Wall Street law firms who have advised corporate issuers that they may deduct the "interest" paid on the purported debt while treating the instruments as equity for financial statement or regulatory purposes.

In the mid–1990's, Wall Street and the Service skirmished over the tax treatment of so-called monthly income preferred securities ("MIPs"), a creation of the large investment bank, Goldman Sachs. A MIP commonly has significant equity features. Typically, the obligation term was 50 to 100 years, the "debt" was subordinated to other corporate indebtedness, and

the legislation enacted in 1989. See, e.g., I.R.C. §§ 163(e)(5), (i). Query whether any broader approach would discriminate against start-up companies or firms engaged in high-risk businesses?

21. Two courts have used this approach with respect to so-called hybrid instruments. See Richmond, Fredericksburg and Potomac R.R. v. Commissioner, 528 F.2d 917 (4th Cir. 1975); Farley Realty Corp. v. Commissioner, 279 F.2d 701 (2d Cir.1960). In most other cases, the courts have applied an all-or-nothing approach.

1. Hariton, "Distinguishing Between Equity and Debt in the New Financial Environment," 49 Tax L.Rev. 499, 501 (1994).

the issuer had the right to defer interest payments for up to five years. On the debt side, the lender was entitled to the repayment of the full amount of his investment and had the rights typically enjoyed by a creditor to enforce the terms of the obligation on a default.[2]

In its reaction to MIPs and similar financing vehicles, the Service noted, with its typical imprecision in this area, that characterization of an instrument for federal tax purposes depends on all the facts and circumstances, with no particular factor being conclusive in deciding whether an instrument is debt or equity.[3] It also announced its "particular interest" in instruments that contain a variety of equity features, including an unreasonably long maturity or the ability to repay the instrument's principal with corporate stock. The pronouncement went on to address both of those factors and included a warning to practitioners about relying on the precedential value of specific cases and rulings. Concerning length of maturity, the Service noted the case law supporting debt characterization for instruments with a 50-year term,[4] but cautioned that even in the case of terms of less than 50 years, debt characterization may not be appropriate for an instrument with significant equity characteristics. The Service also noted that the reasonableness of an instrument's term must include consideration of factors such as an obligation to relend funds and the issuer's ability to satisfy the instrument.[5]

As for the form of payment, the Service has ruled that an instrument may be classified as debt where a holder has the right to be repaid in cash or stock.[6] Thus, if a holder is required to accept payment of principal solely in stock, the instrument does not qualify as debt. Similarly, if an instrument provides a holder with a choice between repayment in cash or stock but is structured to ensure that stock is selected, the instrument will not qualify as debt.[7]

Section 163(*l*) may limit a corporation's interest deduction in the case of debt payable in equity by disallowing a deduction for interest (including accrued original issue discount) paid or accrued on a "disqualified debt instrument," which is generally defined as any corporate debt payable in equity of the issuer or a related party.[8] Debt is treated as payable in stock if a substantial amount of the principal or interest is required either: (1) to be

2. MIPs transactions are described in more detail in Hariton, supra note 1; Sheppard, "News Analysis: Treasury Stands Up to Wall Street," 63 Tax Notes 386 (1994); and Sheppard, "News Analysis: Toward Straightforward Section 385 Guidance," 65 Tax Notes 664 (1994).

3. Notice 94–47, 1994–1 C.B. 357. Notice 94–48, 1994–1 C.B. 357 addresses a variation of the MIPs strategy in which a corporation forms a partnership which issues notes to third-party investors and then purchases newly issued preferred stock of the corporation. Notice 94–48 states that the Service believes the overall substance of the arrangement is simply an issuance of preferred stock by the corporation and suggests different theories for denying the corporation an interest deduction.

4. See Monon Railroad v. Commissioner, 55 T.C. 345 (1970), *acq.* 1973–2 C.B. 3.

5. Notice 94–47, 1994–1 C.B. 357.

6. Rev. Rul. 85–119, 1985–2 C.B. 60.

7. Notice 94–47, supra note 3.

8. I.R.C. § 163(*l*)(2). "Related party" is defined by reference to Sections 267(b) and 707. I.R.C. § 163(*l*)(4).

paid or converted into stock of the issuer or a related party, or (2) to be determined by reference to stock of the issuer or related party.[9] Debt also is treated as payable in stock if the issuer has the option to pay, convert, or determine the amount of principal or interest by reference to its stock or stock of a related party.[10]

Despite all the cautionary notes from the Service and occasional legislation, the financial services industry continues to market a dizzying array of hybrid security "products" that allow public companies to claim interest deductions on their tax returns while avoiding debt classification on their books.[11] Known generically as "trust preferred securities" and labelled with various trademarked acronyms, the standard terms are fairly similar and include maturities of from 20 to 30 years, a fixed interest rate, and a right on the part of the issuer to defer interest payments for up to five years at a time.

3. Character of Gain or Loss on Corporate Investment

Code: §§ 165(g)(1), (2); 166(a), (d), (e); 1244(a)–(c). Skim §§ 1045; 1202.

Regulations: §§ 1.165–5(a)–(c); 1.166–5; 1.1244(a)–1(a), (b).

Since equity and debt securities held by investors are capital assets, gain or loss on the sale of stock, bonds and other debt instruments generally is a capital gain or loss.[1] As discussed below, the Code also includes a few special characterization rules, some to stimulate investment and others to clarify the tax treatment of transactions that technically do not constitute a "sale or exchange."

Gain on Sale of Qualified Small Business Stock. To encourage long-term investment in small start-up companies, Section 1202 permits noncorporate shareholders to exclude from gross income 50 percent of the gain from a sale or exchange of "qualified small business stock" held for more than five years.[2] To qualify its stock for this tax benefit, the issuer must be a C corporation with aggregate gross assets of $50 million or less at the

9. I.R.C. § 163(*l*)(3)(A) & (B).

10. An instrument also is treated as payable in stock if it is part of an arrangement reasonably expected to result in such payment with or by reference to the stock. I.R.C. § 163(*l*)(3)(C). Examples include nonrecourse debt secured principally by the issuer's stock or debt convertible at the holder's option when it is substantially certain the conversion right will be exercised.

11. See Sheppard, "The Nine Lives of Equity–Linked Securities," 92 Tax Notes 597 (Aug. 6, 2001); McKinnon, "Congressional Probe to Examine Enron's Tax–Avoidance Strategies," Wall St. Journal, Feb. 19, 2002, at A6.

1. In some cases, where the original issue discount and market discount rules apply, all or part of the gain on the sale or maturity of a debt instrument may be ordinary income. See generally I.R.C. §§ 1271–1275.

2. I.R.C. § 1202(a)(1). To qualify, the shareholder must be an original issuee of the stock. The exclusion is generally available for up to $10 million of recognized gain per qualifying corporation. § 1202(b)(1). In some cases involving larger investors, higher limits may apply.

time the stock is issued.[3] That's the good news. The bad news is that long-term capital gain from the sale of qualified small business stock—known as "Section 1202 gain"—is taxed at a maximum rate of 28 percent.[4] As a result, the maximum effective rate on a sale of qualified small business stock, after taking into account the 50 percent exclusion, is 14 percent, which is not much better than the generally applicable 15 percent maximum rate.[5]

A more meaningful tax benefit is provided by Section 1045, which allows noncorporate shareholders to elect to defer otherwise taxable gain from a sale of qualified small business stock held for more than six months by rolling over the proceeds into new qualified small business stock within 60 days of the sale.

Worthless Securities. Even the most optimistic taxpayers who embark on a business venture are well advised to anticipate the tax consequences if their endeavor should result in a loss. Sole proprietors, partners (including members of limited liability companies) and shareholders in an S corporation may deduct the losses from their business operations as they are incurred if they materially participate in the activity.[1] But shareholders or creditors of a C corporation normally must be content to recognize a capital loss at the time their investment is sold or becomes worthless. If a loss results from the worthlessness of stock or debt evidenced by a "security" which is a capital asset, the calamity is treated as a hypothetical sale or exchange on the last day of the taxable year in which the loss is incurred.[2]

Debts Not Evidenced by a Security. For noncorporate lenders, the tax consequences of losses sustained on a debt not evidenced by a security are governed by the bad debt deduction rules in Section 166. Business bad debts are ordinary losses, while nonbusiness bad debts are artificially treated as short-term capital losses.[3] When a shareholder who is also an employee loans money to a closely held corporation and later is not repaid, an issue arises over whether the loan was made as an investment or in a trade or business carried on by the taxpayer. The loss almost always is treated as a nonbusiness bad debt on the theory that the dominant motivation for making the loan was to protect the taxpayer's investment in the corporation rather than his employment relationship.[4]

Section 1244 Stock. The general rules on worthless securities and bad debts place corporate investors who suffer losses at a tax disadvantage relative to those who conduct their affairs through other business vehicles. In the case of a small business, this dichotomy makes little sense and may

3. I.R.C. § 1202(c)(1), (d).

4. I.R.C. § 1(h)(4), (7).

5. When Section 1202 was first enacted, the rate differential was six percent. For more bad news, see I.R.C. § 57(a)(7), which requires seven percent of the excluded portion of Section 1202 gain to be treated as a tax preference item under the alternative minimum tax.

1. See generally I.R.C. § 469 for limitations on the timing of losses incurred in a passive activity.

2. See I.R.C. §§ 165(g)(1), (g)(2).

3. I.R.C. § 166(a), (d).

4. United States v. Generes, 405 U.S. 93, 92 S.Ct. 827 (1972).

prove to be particularly unfair to those who are forced into the C corporation form for nontax reasons. In the same legislation that produced the earliest version of Subchapter S, Congress provided some limited relief by enacting Section 1244 in order to "encourage the flow of new funds into small business" by placing small business shareholders on more of a par with proprietors and partners.[5] If certain detailed statutory requirements are met, an individual shareholder may (within limits) treat a loss from the sale, exchange or worthlessness of "Section 1244 stock" as an ordinary loss even if it might otherwise have been treated as a capital loss.

Because Section 1244 was designed to stimulate investment in small businesses, only individual taxpayers and partnerships (but not trusts and estates) who were original issuees of the stock are eligible for ordinary loss treatment.[6] Donees, heirs and other transferees of the original investor will continue to be limited to capital loss treatment under Section 165.

Section 1244 stock may be either common or preferred stock that has been issued for money or property.[7] Stock issued for services thus does not qualify.[8] To prevent the benefits of Section 1244 from extending beyond the small business community, its reach is limited to stock of a "small business corporation," a status achieved if the aggregate amount of money and other property received by the corporation for stock, as a contribution to capital and as paid-in surplus does not exceed $1,000,000.[9] This determination is made at the time the stock is issued, but the $1,000,000 cap includes both amounts received for the newly issued stock and any stock previously issued by the corporation.[10]

Qualification under Section 1244 when the stock is issued does not automatically guarantee that an ordinary loss will be allowed when a loss is realized. Section 1244(c)(1)(C) also requires that, for the five taxable years ending before the year in which the loss was sustained, the corporation must have derived more than 50 percent of its aggregate gross receipts from sources other than passive investment income items (royalties, rents, dividends, interest, annuities and sales or exchanges of stock or securities). The requirement is designed to preclude ordinary loss treatment to shareholders of corporations engaged primarily in investment rather than active

5. H.R.Rep. No. 2198, 85th Cong., 1st Sess. (1958), reprinted in 1959–2 C.B. 709, 711.

6. I.R.C. § 1244(a). A partner qualifies for a Section 1244 ordinary loss only if he was a partner when the partnership acquired the stock. Reg. § 1.1244(a)–1(b)(2). The regulations also provide that ordinary loss treatment is not available to a partner who has received the stock in a distribution from the partnership. Reg. § 1.1244(a)–1(b). Unlike a partnership, an S corporation is not eligible for ordinary loss treatment under Section 1244. Rath v. Commissioner, 101 T.C. 196 (1993).

7. I.R.C. § 1244(c)(1)(B).

8. Reg. § 1.1244(c)–1(d).

9. I.R.C. § 1244(c)(3).

10. Id. See also Reg. § 1.1244(c)–2(b). If the capital receipts exceed $1,000,000, the corporation may designate certain shares as Section 1244 stock provided that the amounts received for such designated stock do not exceed $1,000,000 less amounts received for stock or as capital contributions in prior years.

business activities. If these investment losses had been incurred directly, the taxpayer would have been limited to capital loss treatment and the corporate form should not facilitate an end run around this limitation. If the loss is sustained before the corporation has a five-year measuring period, then the gross receipts test is applied by substituting the taxable years ending before the date of the loss in which the corporation was in existence.[11]

The aggregate amount that may be treated by the taxpayer as an ordinary loss for any one taxable year may not exceed $50,000 or, in the case of married couple filing a joint return, $100,000.[12] In the case of partnerships, the limit is determined separately as to each partner.[13]

Section 1244 is a "no lose" provision in the sense that nothing is lost by passing a corporate resolution declaring that an equity interest is being issued as Section 1244 stock even if the stock ultimately fails to qualify. Although there is no longer a requirement for a formal plan, it generally is regarded as good practice to include a reference to Section 1244 in the corporate resolution approving the issuance of stock in a qualifying corporation, if only to remind the shareholders that ordinary loss treatment is available if that unhappy event should later occur.

PROBLEMS

1. Aristocrat, Baker and Chef have formed Chez Guevara, Inc. ("Chez") to operate a gourmet restaurant and bakery previously operated by Chef as a sole proprietorship. Aristocrat will contribute $80,000 cash, Baker will contribute a building with a fair market value of $80,000 and an adjusted basis of $20,000, and Chef will contribute $40,000 cash and the goodwill from his proprietorship which the parties agree is worth $40,000 and has a zero basis. In return, each of the parties will receive 100 shares of Chez common stock, the only class outstanding.

Chez requires at least $1,800,000 of additional capital in order to renovate the building, acquire new equipment and provide working capital. It has negotiated a $900,000 loan from Friendly National Bank on the following terms: interest will be payable at two points above the prime rate, determined semi-annually, with principal due in ten years and the loan will be secured by a mortgage on the renovated restaurant building.

Evaluate the following alternative proposals for raising the additional $900,000 needed to commence business, focusing on the possibility that the Service will reclassify corporate debt instruments as equity:

(a) Aristocrat, Baker and Chef each will loan Chez $300,000, and each will take back a $300,000 five-year corporate note with variable interest payable at one point below the prime rate, determined annually.

11. I.R.C. § 1244(c)(2)(A).

12. I.R.C. § 1244(b).

13. Reg. § 1.1244(b)–1(a).

(b) Same as (a), above except that each of the parties will take back $300,000 of 10% 20–year subordinated income debentures; interest will be payable only out of the net profits of the business.

(c) Same as (a), above, except that the $900,000 loan from Friendly National Bank will be unsecured but personally guaranteed by Aristocrat, Baker and Chef, who will be jointly and severally liable.

(d) Aristocrat will loan the entire $900,000, taking back a $900,000 corporate note with terms identical to those described in (a), above.

(e) Same as (d), above, except that commencing two years after the incorporation, Chez ceases to pay interest on the notes because of a severe cash flow problem.

2. In view of the confused state of the law, how can a tax advisor plan the capital structure of a corporation to avoid the risk of reclassification of debt as equity. From the standpoint of the tax advisor, is the vagueness of the law in this area preferable to more detailed "bright line" rules in the Code or regulations? Which approach is preferable as a matter of policy?

3. High Technologies, Inc. ("Hi–Tech") is a small semiconductor company owned and operated by Thelma High and Allen Woody. Thelma and Allen formed Hi–Tech three years ago by each contributing $400,000 in exchange for 50 percent of the corporation's common stock. Hi–Tech has been planning a major expansion of its manufacturing facility and has decided to seek outside financing. It recently approached Jennifer Leech about the possibility of her investing $200,000 in Hi–Tech.

After investigating the corporation's financial position, Jennifer has decided to make the investment. Her objectives are to obtain maximum security while at the same time participating in Hi–Tech's potential growth. Jennifer also is concerned about the rapid change in computer technology and would like to plan for the most favorable tax consequences in the unfortunate event that her investment in Hi–Tech becomes worthless. Consider to what extent Jennifer will realize her economic and tax goals if, in the alternative, her investment takes the following forms:

(a) A $200,000 unregistered five-year Hi–Tech note bearing market rate interest.

(b) A $200,000 Hi–Tech registered bond bearing market rate interest.

(c) A $190,000 Hi–Tech registered bond bearing market rate interest and warrants to purchase Hi–Tech common stock at a favorable price.

(d) $200,000 of Hi–Tech common stock.

(e) $200,000 of Hi–Tech convertible preferred stock.

(f) Same as (d), above, except that Thelma and Allen originally capitalized Hi–Tech by each contributing $500,000.

(g) Same as (d), above, except that Jennifer plans to give the Hi–Tech common stock to her son, Peter, as a wedding gift.

(h) Same as (d), above, except that Jennifer and her son, Peter, will purchase the Hi–Tech common stock through Leech Associates, a venture capital partnership.

G. COLLATERAL ISSUES

1. CONTRIBUTIONS TO CAPITAL

Code: §§ 118(a); 362(a)(2), (c).

Regulations: § 1.118–1.

When a shareholder transfers property to a corporation and does not receive stock or other consideration in exchange, the transaction is a contribution to capital. Although Section 351 does not apply to capital contributions, the contributing shareholder does not recognize gain or loss on a contribution of property other than cash to a corporation. Instead, the shareholder may increase the basis in her stock by the amount of cash and the adjusted basis of any contributed property.[1] Contributions to capital by shareholders also are excludable from the gross income of the transferee corporation.[2] The corporation's basis in property received as a nontaxable shareholder contribution to capital is the same as the transferor's basis.[3]

If a sole shareholder transfers property to a corporation, or if all shareholders transfer property in the same proportion as their holdings, the issuance of new stock has no economic significance. After some waffling on the issue,[4] the courts now agree that issuance of stock in these circumstances would be "a meaningless gesture" and consequently have held that such transfers are constructive Section 351 exchanges.[5]

Majority shareholders of a financially distressed corporation may surrender some of their stock back to the company in order to improve its credit rating. The proper tax treatment of a voluntary non-pro rata contribution of stock perplexed the courts for many years, as taxpayers sought to immediately deduct their basis in the surrendered shares as an ordinary loss while the Service contended that the surrender was akin to a contribution to capital. In Commissioner v. Fink,[6] the Supreme Court resolved the question by holding that controlling shareholders do not realize a deductible ordinary loss when they surrender part of their stock

1. Reg. § 1.118–1.

2. I.R.C. § 118(a). Contributions to capital by a nonshareholder (e.g., a transfer of property by a municipality to encourage the corporation to build a facility within the city limits) also are excludable. Reg. § 1.118–1.

3. I.R.C. § 362(a)(2). This rule parallels Section 362(a)(1), which provides that the corporation takes a transferred basis in property received in a Section 351 exchange. For the corporation's basis in property contributed by a nonshareholder, see I.R.C. § 362(c).

4. See, e.g., Abegg v. Commissioner, 429 F.2d 1209 (2d Cir.1970), cert. denied 400 U.S. 1008, 91 S.Ct. 566 (1971).

5. See, e.g., Peracchi v. Commissioner, supra page 458. As *Peracchi* illustrates, applying Section 351 to contributions to capital by a sole shareholder may be significant insofar as it triggers the application of other Code sections, such as Section 357, to the transaction.

6. 483 U.S. 89, 107 S.Ct. 2729 (1987).

without receiving cash or property in return and retain voting control of the corporation. The Court analogized this type of transaction to a shareholder's voluntary forgiveness of a corporate debt owed to the shareholder, which is treated as a contribution to capital. Basis in the shares surrendered may be reallocated to stock retained by the shareholder.

2. INTENTIONAL AVOIDANCE OF SECTION 351

Section 351 is not an elective provision. It applies whenever its requirements are met. Historically, some taxpayers attempted to avoid Section 351 in order to recognize a loss[1] or step up the basis of an asset after recognizing a gain to increase the transferee corporation's cost recovery deductions.[2] When long-term capital gains enjoy a significant tax rate preference, taxpayers have also found it advantageous to freeze appreciation as capital gain on an asset that was about to be converted into "ordinary income" property—e.g., land held for investment that the taxpayer intended to subdivide. In these cases, the tax savings achieved by converting ordinary income into capital gain outweighed the disadvantage of accelerating recognition of part of the gain.

Planning to avoid Section 351 may present as great a challenge as satisfying its requirements. As illustrated by the *Intermountain Lumber* case earlier in the chapter,[3] one potentially successful avoidance strategy is to break control after the exchange by a prearranged disposition of more than 20 percent of the stock. Another possibility is to structure an incorporation transfer as a taxable "sale" rather than a tax-free Section 351 exchange.[4]

To illustrate the sale technique, assume Investor owns undeveloped land with an adjusted basis of $50,000 and a fair market value of $300,000. Investor intends to subdivide the land and sell home sites at an aggregate sales price of $500,000. If he developed the land as an individual, Investor would recognize $450,000 of ordinary income.[5] But with long-term capital gains taxed at a significantly lower rate than ordinary income, Investor may benefit by selling the land to a controlled corporation for $300,000 of corporate installment obligations. He would recognize $250,000 of predevelopment capital gain on the sale, the corporation would take a $300,000 stepped-up basis in the land, and the future ordinary income would be limited to $200,000.

1. Recognition of losses in this manner on a sale between a controlling (more than 50 percent) shareholder and a corporation would be limited by Section 267.

2. But see I.R.C. § 1239, which characterizes gain on sales of property between related taxpayers (e.g., a corporation and a more–than–50–percent shareholder) as ordinary income if the property is depreciable in the hands of the transferee.

3. See p. 436, supra.

4. See generally Bittker & Eustice, Federal Income Taxation of Corporations and Shareholders ¶ 3.14 (7th ed. 2000).

5. For convenience, assume no upward adjustments to basis during the subdivision phase.

The sale strategy was successful in Bradshaw v. United States,[6] where the taxpayer transferred 40 acres of Georgia land in which he had a basis of $8,500 to a new corporation in exchange for $250,000 of unsecured corporate installment notes. The corporation's only other capital was a $4,500 automobile transferred on the same day in exchange for common stock. The court treated the transfer of land as a sale and permitted the taxpayer to report his gain on the installment method.[7] In so doing, the court rejected the Service's claim that the notes were really stock even though it conceded that the corporation was thinly capitalized. A contrary result was reached in Burr Oaks Corp. v. Commissioner,[8] where three taxpayers transferred land to a corporation in exchange for two-year notes with a face amount of $330,000. The corporation's only equity capital was $4,500. The court held that the transfer was a nontaxable Section 351 exchange rather than a sale because the notes, payment of which was dependent on the profitability of an undercapitalized corporation, were really preferred stock.

In the last analysis, resolution of the "Section 351 vs. sale" issue turns on the facts in each case and the court's inclination to reclassify what the taxpayer labels "debt" into what the Service believes to be "equity."[9]

3. Organizational and Start-Up Expenses

Code: §§ 195; 212(3); 248.

Regulations: § 1.248–1(b).

A corporation incurs a variety of expenses in connection with its incorporation. Corporations may elect to deduct currently up to $5,000 of these "organizational expenditures" in the taxable year in which they begin business, but this $5,000 maximum current deduction is reduced by the amount by which total organizational expenditures exceed $50,000.[1] Organizational expenditures that are not currently deductible must be amortized over the 180–month period beginning with the month in which the corporation begins business.[2] A similar rule is provided for "start-up expenditures,"[3] which generally are amounts the corporation incurs after formation but before beginning business operations.

"Organizational expenditures" are defined as expenditures which are: (1) incident to the creation of the corporation, (2) chargeable to capital

6. 683 F.2d 365 (Ct.Cl.1982).

7. The deferral of gain achieved by the taxpayer in *Bradshaw* is foreclosed under current law. Because a shareholder and his wholly owned corporation are "related parties," a later sale of the land by the corporation will accelerate recognition of any gain that otherwise would be deferred on the shareholder's installment sale to the corporation. I.R.C. § 453(e), (f)(1).

8. 365 F.2d 24 (7th Cir.1966), cert. denied, 385 U.S. 1007, 87 S.Ct. 713 (1967). See also Aqualane Shores, Inc. v. Commissioner, 269 F.2d 116 (5th Cir.1959).

9. See Section F of this chapter, supra.

1. I.R.C. § 248(a)(1). Prior to October 22, 2004, Section 248 permitted a corporation to elect to amortize all of its organizational expenditures over a period of sixty months or more beginning with the month in which the corporation commenced business.

2. I.R.C. § 248(a)(2).

3. I.R.C. § 195(b).

account, and (3) of a character which, if expended to create a corporation having a limited life, would be amortizable over that life.[4] Examples include legal fees for drafting the corporate charter and bylaws, fees paid to the state of incorporation, and necessary accounting services.[5] Specifically excluded are the costs of issuing or selling stock and expenditures connected with the transfer of assets to the corporation, presumably because such expenses do not create an asset that is exhausted over the life of the corporation.[6] "Start-up expenditures" are amounts that the corporation could have deducted currently as trade or business expenses if they had been incurred in an ongoing business. Pure capital expenditures, such as costs of acquiring a particular asset, are neither organizational nor start-up expenditures and must be capitalized and added to the basis of the asset.

Whether or not they are borne by the corporation, certain items are considered as expenses of the shareholders and, as such, they may neither be deducted nor amortized by the corporation. For example, expenses connected with the acquisition of stock (e.g., appraisal fees) must be capitalized and added to the shareholder's basis in the stock.[7]

4. I.R.C. § 248(b).

5. Reg. § 1.248–1(b)(2).

6. Reg. § 1.248–1(b)(3)(i). See S.Rep. No. 1622, 83d Cong.2d Sess. 224.

7. See Woodward v. Commissioner, 397 U.S. 572, 90 S.Ct. 1302 (1970); United States v. Hilton Hotels Corp., 397 U.S. 580, 90 S.Ct. 1307 (1970).

CHAPTER 12

NONLIQUIDATING DISTRIBUTIONS

A. INTRODUCTION

1. DIVIDENDS: IN GENERAL

Code: §§ 243(a), (b)(1); 301(a), (c); 316(a); 317(a).

Regulations: §§ 1.301–1(c); 1.316–1(a)(1)–(2).

It was once said that a corporation derives no greater pleasure than through making distributions to its shareholders. As one court observed, "like the 'life-rendering pelican,' [a corporation] feeds its shareholders upon dividends."[1] In the case of a close corporation, however, this colorful marine analogy fails to capture reality. Closely held companies, influenced by the federal tax law, typically resist paying dividends and expend considerable energy to avoid the sting of the double tax. Many public companies retain profits for internal expansion, to finance acquisitions, or to repurchase their own stock.[2] But if an enterprise is successful, the pressure may mount to distribute earnings to the shareholders, and distributions often occur in connection with major changes in a corporation's capital structure, such as liquidations, mergers and recapitalizations. At that point, it becomes necessary to classify the distribution as a taxable dividend, a nontaxable return of capital, or as gain from a sale of the shareholder's stock. Simple as the task may seem, drawing these lines has been a central issue in the taxation of corporations and shareholders. Not surprisingly, the statutory scheme is complex and sometimes even illogical.

Distributions come in many forms. A corporation may distribute its own stock or debt obligations; redeem (i.e., repurchase) stock from its shareholders by distributing cash or property; or distribute its net assets in liquidation of the entire business. The tax consequences of these and other more complex transactions are considered in later chapters.[3] This chapter lays a foundation by examining the corporate and shareholder level tax treatment of nonliquidating (or "operating") distributions of cash or property—distributions loosely referred to as "dividends" by those unfamiliar with Subchapter C. We are about to learn, however, that not all distributions classified as dividends under state law or designated as such in the corporate minutes are dividends for federal tax purposes.

1. Commissioner v. First State Bank of Stratford, 168 F.2d 1004, 1009 (5th Cir.1948), cert. denied, 335 U.S. 867, 69 S.Ct. 137 (1948).

2. For an expanded discussion of the influence of federal tax law on corporate dividend policy, see Section A3 of this chapter, infra.

3. See Chapters 13–15, infra.

Determining the tax consequences of a nonliquidating distribution requires an excursion through several sections of the Code. Section 301 governs the amount and classification to corporate and noncorporate shareholders of distributions of "property" made by a C corporation with respect to its stock.[4] Under Section 301(c)(1), distributions that are "dividends" within the meaning of Section 316 must be included in gross income.[5] In order to prevent multiple taxation, corporate shareholders may deduct 70 percent (or sometimes 80 or 100 percent) of the dividends they receive.[6] Dividends received by noncorporate shareholders are usually taxed at preferential long-term capital gains rates.[7] Distributions that are not dividends are first treated as a recovery of the shareholder's basis in his stock, and any excess over basis is treated as gain from the sale or exchange of the stock.[8]

Section 316(a) defines a "dividend" as any distribution of property made by a corporation to its shareholders out of (1) earnings and profits accumulated after February 28, 1913 ("accumulated earnings and profits") or (2) earnings and profits of the current taxable year ("current earnings and profits"). "Earnings and profits," a term of art to be examined in more detail below, is a concept that attempts to distinguish distributions of corporate profits from returns of capital. Section 316(a) also includes two irrebuttable presumptions: every distribution is deemed to be made out of earnings and profits to the extent that they exist and is deemed to be made from the most recently accumulated earnings and profits.

In testing for dividend status, the regulations look first to current earnings and profits, determined as of the close of the taxable year in which the distribution is made.[9] A distribution out of current earnings and profits is thus a taxable dividend even if the corporation has a historical deficit. This seemingly harsh rule was enacted many years ago as a relief measure to permit corporations with deficits to pay dividends and thus avoid an undistributed profits tax then in effect. Although the tax was later repealed, the "nimble dividend" rule survived without any Congressional

4. Distributions to shareholders in their other capacities (e.g., employee, creditor, lessor) are thus not embraced by Section 301. "Property" is deemed to include money and other corporate assets but not stock in the distributing corporation or rights to acquire stock. I.R.C. § 317(a).

5. See also I.R.C. § 61(a)(7).

6. I.R.C. § 243(a), (b)(1), (c). See Chapter 10A, supra. Potential abuses of the dividends received deduction are policed by an assortment of Code provisions. See Section F of this chapter, infra.

7. I.R.C. § 1(h)(11). See Section A2 of this chapter, infra.

8. I.R.C. § 301(c)(2), (3). The rules in the text apply to distributions by C corporations that do not file a consolidated return. Distributions received by one member of a consolidated group from another member generally are tax-free, but the distributee must reduce its basis in the stock of the payor by the amount of the distribution. See Reg. § 1.1502–13(f)(2)(ii) and Chapter 10D, supra. Distributions by S corporations also are tax-free to the extent of the shareholder's basis, and any excess is treated as gain from a sale of the S corporation stock. § 1368(b). The rules are more complex if an S corporation has accumulated earnings and profits from a time when it was a C corporation. § 1368(c). See Chapter 20E, infra.

9. Reg. § 1.316–1(a)(1).

explanation of why it was still necessary.[10] The rule at least simplifies the inquiry because it is rare for a company to make distributions during a period when it is operating at a loss. Only when distributions exceed current earnings and profits must reference be made to the historical track record of the corporation.

The dual focus in Section 316 on current and accumulated earnings and profits may produce anomalous results because dividend status is determined by reference to the corporation's overall financial success rather than the gain or loss realized by a particular shareholder. To be sure, most dividends represent an increase in the shareholder's wealth rather than a return of capital, but this is not inevitable under the current scheme. For example, the existence of accumulated earnings and profits will cause a distribution to be classified as a dividend even if those profits were earned before the shareholder acquired his stock.

To illustrate, assume that Shareholder forms Corporation with initial paid-in capital of $110. During its first year of operation, Corporation earns $20 and distributes $30 to Shareholder. The distribution consists of a $20 dividend (out of current earnings and profits) and a $10 return of capital, and Shareholder reduces his stock basis by $10 to $100. In year two, assume Corporation earns $50 and makes no distributions, ending the year with $50 of accumulated earnings and profits. At the beginning of year three, Buyer (an individual) acquires all the stock of Corporation for $150, and Shareholder realizes a $50 long-term capital gain. Assume further that Corporation, now wholly owned by Buyer, suffers a $10 loss in year three, causing its accumulated earnings and profits account to decrease to $40. If Corporation breaks even in year four but distributes $30, Buyer is taxed on the entire distribution because it is made from accumulated earnings and profits. But in substance Buyer has received merely a return of capital. After all, he paid $150 for the stock, and the company has since lost $10 while distributing $30 to Buyer, who is understandably surprised to realize $30 of ordinary income even though the value of his investment has declined.

In an academically tidy world, the curious result illustrated above should not occur. Instead, the tax treatment of distributions should depend on the gain or loss realized by the shareholder rather than the corporation's financial track record over time. Ideally, Shareholder should be taxed at ordinary income rates to the extent that the gain on a sale of his stock is attributable to undistributed corporate earnings while he was a shareholder. It then would be unnecessary to tax those earnings again when they are distributed to Buyer, who logically should be treated as receiving a return of capital rather than a $30 dividend.

In the early days of the income tax, taxpayers in Buyer's position argued that distributions out of preacquisition earnings should not be

10. See Bittker & Eustice, Federal Income Taxation of Corporations and Shareholders ¶ 8.02[3] (7th ed. 2000).

taxable since they did not represent any real gain to the shareholder. The Supreme Court put this argument to rest, reasoning:[11]

> Dividends are the appropriate fruit of stock ownership, are commonly reckoned as income, and are expended as such by the stockholder without regard to whether they are declared from the most recent earnings, or from a surplus accumulated from the earnings of the past, or are based upon the increased value of the property of the corporation. The stockholder is, in the ordinary case, a different entity from the corporation, and Congress was at liberty to treat the dividends as coming to him *ab extra*, and as constituting a part of his income when they came to hand.

Despite its conceptual flaws, the present approach is defensible on practical grounds. Since shares in publicly held corporations are traded daily, it would be difficult to determine precisely the corporation's earnings during the period that any particular shareholder held his stock. The current scheme at least ensures that earnings will be taxed to some shareholder, even if that shareholder may not be the theoretically correct one. Moreover, the presumption that distributions are made out of a corporation's earnings and profits to the extent they exist often eliminates the chore of tracing the source of a distribution and considerably simplifies the system.[12]

2. QUALIFIED DIVIDENDS

Code: § 1(h)(11).

For most of our tax history, dividends have been taxed as ordinary income. Relief from multiple taxation has been provided to corporate shareholders by the Section 243 dividends received deduction. From time to time, individual shareholders also have received very modest relief from double taxation, most often in the form of a limited dividend exclusion that ranged from $50 to $400 before it was repealed in 1986.

As previewed in Chapter 10,[1] President George W. Bush made eliminating double taxation of corporate earnings a centerpiece of economic stimulus legislation introduced in early 2003. The eventual compromise

11. Lynch v. Hornby, 247 U.S. 339, 343, 38 S.Ct. 543, 545 (1918).

12. In a 1983 report on Subchapter C reform, the Senate Finance Committee Staff recommended repeal of the earnings and profits limitation and proposed to tax all ordinary distributions as dividends, with limited relief for distributions made to the original contributing shareholder within three years of the contribution. See Staff of the Senate Finance Committee, Preliminary Report on the Reform and Simplification of the Income Taxation of Corporations, 98th Cong., 1st Sess. 77–78 (Comm.Print 98–85, 1983). The proposal was deleted from the staff's final report. See Staff of the Senate Finance Committee, Subchapter C Revision Act of 1985: A Final Report Prepared by the Staff, 99th Cong., 1st Sess. (S.Prt. 99–47, 1985). For some other alternatives to the present scheme, see Andrews, " 'Out of Its Earnings and Profits': Some Reflections on the Taxation of Dividends," 69 Harv.L.Rev. 1403 (1956); Blum, "The Earnings and Profits Limitation on Dividend Income: A Reappraisal," 53 Taxes 68 (1975).

1. See p. 426, supra.

was a rate reduction on certain "qualified dividend income" received by noncorporate shareholders. Effective for eligible dividends received from January 1, 2003 through December 31, 2010, the maximum rate on qualified dividend income is reduced to 15 percent for taxpayers whose ordinary income otherwise would be taxed at higher rates, and to 5 percent for lower-income taxpayers whose ordinary income would be taxed in the 10 or 15 percent marginal brackets. Technically, these rate reductions have been implemented by including "qualified dividend income" within the definition of "net capital gain" in Section 1(h), which provides for the maximum rate on long-term capital gains for noncorporate taxpayers.[2] The dividend rate reduction applies for both the regular tax and the individual alternative minimum tax.

To be eligible for the reduced rates, a dividend must be received from a domestic corporation or a foreign corporation that meets certain criteria.[3] Unlike President Bush's original proposal, a qualified dividend need not be derived from earnings that were taxed at the corporate level. But some income items that are labelled "dividends" do not qualify for the rate reduction. Familiar examples are credit union and money market fund dividends, "dividends" paid on hybrid corporate instruments (e.g., certain types of preferred stock that are treated as debt by the issuing corporation), and payments in lieu of dividends on stock that has loaned as part of a short sale transaction.[4] Corporate payors must identify which dividends are "qualified" on the Form 1099's that they send at the end of the year, but shareholders are responsible for determining if they comply with the holding period requirements discussed below.

To prevent arbitrage opportunities on short-term trades, the common stock with respect to which the dividend was paid must have been held by the taxpayer for more than 60 days in the 121-day period beginning 60 days before the stock's ex-dividend date.[5] The ex-dividend date is the first date on which a share with respect to which a dividend has been declared is sold without the buyer being entitled to the dividend.[6] Without this rule, a taxpayer could acquire stock shortly before becoming entitled to a dividend, sell the stock at a capital loss that could offset short-term capital gain or up to $3,000 of ordinary income if the taxpayer had no capital gains, but still pay tax on the dividend at the preferential rate. Several other rules have been included to prevent opportunistic exploitation of the rate reduction.[7]

2. I.R.C. § 1(h)(11)(A). Although qualified dividends are treated as net capital gain for rate reduction purposes, they are still ordinary income and may not be offset by capital losses without being subject to the $3,000 limitation in Section 1211(b).

3. I.R.C. § 1(h)(11)(B)(ii).

4. I.R.C. § 1(h)(11)(B)(ii).

5. See I.R.C. § 1(h)(11)(b)(iii), which imports, with some modifications, similar holding period limitations on the corporate dividends received deduction and requires a longer holding period (91 days during the 181-day period beginning 90 days before the ex-dividend date) for dividends paid with respect to preferred stock. See I.R.C § 246 and Section F2 of this chapter, infra.

6. Under stock exchange rules, the ex-dividend date is typically three days before the date on which shareholders of record are entitled to receive a declared dividend.

7. See, e.g., I.R.C. § 1(h)(11)(D)(ii), which provides that if an individual taxpayer receives qualified dividend income for one or

3. ECONOMIC IMPACT OF DIVIDEND RATE REDUCTIONS

Factors Influencing Corporate Dividend Policy. The distribution policies of closely held C corporations are largely motivated by the goal of getting corporate profits to the shareholders at the lowest tax cost. For that reason, closely held companies typically have resisted paying dividends, preferring instead to distribute earnings in the form of tax-deductible salary, interest or rent, or to engage in transactions (such as redemptions) where shareholders can bail out earnings at capital gains rates.[1] Dividend policies of publicly traded corporations vary widely. Most "old economy" companies adhere to the tradition of paying quarterly dividends, increasing them at regular intervals and rarely reducing their payouts unless the company is in serious financial difficulty. Many "new economy" companies, such as those in the technology sector, historically opted not to pay dividends, hoping instead to reward investors with increased share prices.

What is it that motivates public companies to pay dividends and to what extent do the tax laws influence corporate dividend policy? These questions have stimulated a lively theoretical debate.[2] One view is that companies pay dividends to serve as a signal to the financial markets of a their profitability and future expectations[3], enhancing shareholder value through their positive impact on the price of the stock. But beginning in the 1980's and continuing through 2003, dividends became less fashionable. In explaining this decline, corporate finance theorists explained that, apart from taxes and transaction costs, shareholders benefit more when a corporation deploys its available cash for business expansion, acquisition of other companies, or repurchases of its own stock. Under this theory, shareholders should be indifferent to a corporation's dividend policy because they reap the same benefit when the stock price increases to reflect undistributed earnings and they are free to generate "homemade dividends" by strategically timed sales of stock.[4] Throughout this debate, there also is much discussion of the different interests of corporate managers and shareholders, and the potential "agency costs" when managers use retained earnings

more dividends that are "extraordinary dividends" as defined in Section 1059, any loss on a later disposition of the stock on which the dividends were paid shall be treated as long-term capital loss to the extent of the dividend even if the stock was held for one year or less, and I.R.C. §§ 1(h)(11)(D)(i) and 163(d)(4)(A), providing that qualified dividend income is excluded from "net investment income" for purposes of the limitations on deduction of investment interest unless the taxpayer elects to have the dividend taxed at ordinary income rates.

1. See Chapters 1D & 11F, supra; Section E of this chapter, infra; and Chapter 13, infra.

2. See generally Hamilton & Booth, Business Basics for Law Students: Essential Concepts and Applications § 12.11 (4th ed. 2006); Klein & Coffee, Business Organization and Finance 395 (10th ed. 2007). For a historical perspective, see Bank, "Is Double Taxation a Scapegoat for Declining Dividends? Evidence from History," 56 Tax L. Rev. 463 (2003).

3. Hamilton, supra note 2, at § 12.12.

4. See, e.g., Modigliani & Miller, "Dividend Policy, Growth, and the Valuation of Shares," 34 J. of Bus. 411 (1961), for an early articulation of the "dividend irrelevance" theory. See also Engler, "A Missing Piece to the Dividend Puzzle: Agency Costs of Mutual Funds," 25 Cardozo L. Rev. 215, 217–220 (2003).

to make suboptimal investments or simply hoard cash.[5] Encouraging dividends is said to counteract this form of managerial empire building and imposes a measure of discipline. Returning the money to investors in the form of dividends, so the argument goes, allows capital to be redirected more efficiently and promotes economic growth.[6]

Impact of Taxes on Dividend Payout. The dividend rate reductions have provided an opportunity for economists to revisit the impact of taxes on corporate dividend policy. The traditional view is that the "double tax" on corporate profits lowers a shareholder's return on investment and encourages corporations to hoard cash, locking in huge stockpiles of capital that could be reinvested more efficiently if it were distributed and redeployed by shareholders. It follows from this thesis that lower tax rates will lead to higher dividends and new investments by the shareholders who receive them. Others contend that dividend tax cuts do not cause corporations to increase their payouts because institutional shareholders, such as pension funds and large charities, don't pay taxes. These contrarians also argue that since most new investments are made by corporations from retained earnings, dividend tax rate reductions are not an effective investment stimulus.

The evidence to date suggests that the 2003 dividend tax cuts did influence corporate behavior and contribute to an increase in payouts by public companies. A dramatic example was Microsoft Corporation's decision to distribute $32 billion as an extraordinary dividend at the end of 2004, use another $30 billion to repurchase stock over the next four years, and raise its modest quarterly dividend.[7] More generally, several studies revealed that dividends rose sharply in the years following the rate reductions.[8] The percentage of public companies paying dividends began to increase in 2003 for the first time in more than two decades; many firms that had been paying regular dividends raised their payouts significantly after the tax cut; and a few companies such as Microsoft paid special one-time dividends.[9] A report issued by Standard and Poors at the end of 2004 supports the view that the combination of tax cuts and shareholder pressure contributed to a surge in dividend payments.[10] In the first 19 months after the dividend tax cut was enacted, companies in the S & P 500 announced 421 dividend increases, with 24 companies paying dividends for the first time.[11] By mid–2004, regular dividend payments by public companies increased by approximately 20 percent and increases continued

5. See, e.g., Easterbrook, "Two Agency–Cost Explanations of Dividends," 74 Am. Econ. Rev. 650 (1984).

6. See Moore & Kerpen, "Show Me the Money! Dividend Payouts after the Bush Tax Cut" (Cato Institute, Oct. 11, 2004).

7. Guth & Thurm, Microsoft to Dole Out its Cash Hoard, Wall St. Journal, July 21, 2004, at A1.

8. Chetty & Saez, "Do Dividend Payments Respond to Taxes? Preliminary Evidence from the 2003 Tax Cut," (NBER Working Paper 10572), available at www.nber.org/papers/w10572.

9. Id.

10. Opdyke, "Tax Cut, Shareholder Pressure Stoke Surge in Stock Dividends," Wall St. Journal, Jan. 18, 2005, at A1.

11. Id.

through 2005, when dividend payments set a record of $203 billion, 12.4 percent more than 2004.[12]

Broader Economic Effects of Rate Reductions. The economic stimulus effects of the dividend and capital gains rate reductions also have been debated, with the usual suspects taking predictable political positions. In arguing for extension of the rate reductions, a 2006 Treasury Department report concluded that the lower rates promoted economic growth by increasing capital in the corporate sector and taking a significant step toward removing taxes from important economic decisions. As proof, the Treasury cited a 40 percent increase in the S & P 500 index between the time the President Bush's dividend proposal was first announced and early 2006. Other positive indicators included growth in real gross domestic product and in employment.[13] The counterpoint response from liberal think tanks was that the dividend tax cuts were not principal contributors to the short-term economic recovery and would not have much value in the long run. Their view was that a modest economic recovery was expected even without tax cuts because of other factors such as a low interest rate environment and healthy corporate profits.[14]

In the last analysis, whether or not the dividend rate cuts will be made permanent or allowed to expire is a political question that will be heavily influenced by the outcome of the 2008 elections (unknown and unpredictable as this edition goes to press) and the health of the general economy. Stay tuned.

B. EARNINGS AND PROFITS

Code: § 312(a), (c), (f)(1), (k)(1)–(3); 316(a). Skim § 312(n).

Regulations: § 1.312–6(a), (b), (d) (first sentence), 1.312–7(b)(1) (first sentence).

The Code makes it clear that distributions are dividends only to the extent that they come from the corporation's earnings and profits, but it curiously does not take the extra step and actually define earnings and profits. Section 312 describes the effects of certain transactions on earnings and profits, and the accompanying regulations provide ample elaboration, but a precise definition of the term is nowhere to be found in the Code or regulations.[1] The function of the earnings and profits concept, however, is

12. See U.S. Dept. of the Treasury, Investing in America's Future: Report of the Department of the Treasury on the Economic Effects of Cutting Dividend and Capital Gains Taxes in 2003 ("2006 Treasury Study"), at 8 (March 14, 2006).

13. 2006 Treasury Study, supra note 12, at 2–3.

14. See, e.g., Aron–Dine & Friedman, The Capital Gain and Dividend Tax Cuts and the Economy, Center on Budget and Policy Priorities (March 27, 2006); Aron–Dine, The Effects of the Capital Gains and Dividend Tax Cuts on The Economy and Revenues, Center on Budget and Policy Priorities (July 12, 2007).

1. For a history of the earnings and profits concept, see Rudick, " 'Dividends' and 'Earnings or Profits' Under the Income Tax

clear: it is a measuring device used to determine the extent to which a distribution is made from a corporation's economic income as opposed to its taxable income or paid-in capital.

The meaning of earnings and profits, which is a phrase peculiar to the tax law, has evolved over the years. It is roughly analogous (but not identical) to the accounting concept of retained earnings (sometimes called "earned surplus") in that neither amount includes initial paid-in capital or subsequent contributions to capital. The primary difference is that retained earnings are decreased by stock distributions and contingency reserves. If earnings and profits were similarly reduced, a company could avoid ever making a taxable distribution simply by ensuring that its distributions were preceded by nontaxable stock dividends or the establishment of reserves for contingencies. Earnings and profits also are not identical to taxable income. The earnings and profits account is intended to measure the economic performance of the corporation. In contrast, taxable income does not provide a true financial picture because that concept is cluttered with a host of policy incentives and relief provisions that bear little or no relationship to the corporation's capacity to pay dividends.

Although earnings and profits can be determined by making adjustments to either retained earnings or taxable income, the traditional approach is to start with a corporation's taxable income and to make adjustments that fall into the four broad categories discussed below. In general, the same accounting method used by the corporation to determine its taxable income is employed in determining earnings and profits.[2]

1. *Certain items excluded from taxable income must be added back.* Items that represent true financial gain but are exempt from tax, such as municipal bond interest, life insurance proceeds and federal tax refunds and otherwise excludable discharge of indebtedness income (unless coupled with a basis reduction under Section 1017) are included in earnings and profits.[3] Contributions to capital and gains that are realized but not recognized for tax purposes (e.g., like-kind exchanges, Section 351 transfers, involuntary conversions under Section 1033) are not added back in computing earnings and profits.[4]

2. *Certain items deductible in determining taxable income must be added back.* Certain deductions and benefits allowed in computing taxable income which do not reflect a real decrease in corporate wealth are not permitted or are restricted in determining earnings and profits. For example, a deductible item that involves no actual expenditure, such as the Section 243 dividends received deduction, must be added back to taxable income in determining earnings and profits. Similarly, the depletion allow-

Law: Corporate Non-Liquidating Distributions," 89 U.Pa.L.Rev. 865 (1941).

2. Reg. § 1.312–6(a).

3. Reg. § 1.312–6(b). In the case of life insurance, the Service has ruled that earnings and profits are increased by the proceeds collected less the aggregate premiums paid by the corporation. Rev.Rul. 54–230, 1954–1 C.B. 114. For discharge of indebtedness income, see I.R.C. § 312(*l*)(1).

4. I.R.C. § 312(f)(1).

ance must be based on the corporation's cost of a depletable asset even if the corporation deducts percentage depletion in computing taxable income.[5]

3. *Certain nondeductible items must be subtracted.* Some items not allowed as deductions in computing taxable income in fact represent actual expenditures that diminish a corporation's capacity to pay dividends. These items reduce earnings and profits. For example, federal income taxes paid during the year by a cash method corporation will reduce earnings and profits,[6] as will losses and expenses disallowed under provisions such as Sections 265 (expenses allocable to tax-exempt income), 267 (losses between related taxpayers) and 274 (travel and entertainment expenses) and charitable contributions in excess of the ten percent corporate limitation. In addition, net operating losses and capital losses in excess of capital gains reduce earnings and profits in the year they are incurred. In order to avoid a double tax benefit, they may not be carried back or forward in determining earnings and profits.

4. *Certain timing adjustments must be made.* Finally, a variety of adjustments are required to override timing rules that allow corporations to artificially defer income or accelerate deductions in computing taxable income.[7] For example, a corporation may not use the generally applicable accelerated cost recovery system (ACRS) of Section 168 in determining earnings and profits. Instead, the cost of depreciable property must be recovered in computing earnings and profits under the alternative depreciation system, which employs the straight line method using specially prescribed and generally longer recovery periods than ACRS.[8] The corporation thus must increase its taxable income by the excess accelerated depreciation allowed for tax purposes.[9] Similarly, if the corporation has elected to expense the cost of eligible property under Section 179, it must amortize that expense ratably over five years in determining earnings and profits.[10] Additional earnings and profits timing rules require a corporation to capitalize otherwise amortizable construction period interest and taxes and to amortize normally deductible mineral exploration costs and intangible drilling expenses over extended time periods.[11]

5. Reg. § 1.312–6(c).

6. Rev.Rul. 70–609, 1970–2 C.B. 78; Webb v. Commissioner, 572 F.2d 135 (5th Cir.1978). A few courts, however, have permitted a cash method corporation to reduce its earnings and profits in the year to which the federal taxes relate even though the taxes have not yet been paid. See e.g., Drybrough v. Commissioner, 238 F.2d 735 (6th Cir.1956).

7. See generally I.R.C. § 312(n). To prevent abuse of the dividends received deduction, the Section 312(n) adjustments do not apply to distributions to any 20 percent or more corporate shareholders. I.R.C. § 301(e). The effect of this rule is to reduce earnings and profits only in determining the amount of any dividend to major corporate shareholders. See Section F5 of this chapter, infra.

8. I.R.C. §§ 312(k)(3)(A); 168(g)(2).

9. The adjusted basis of the property determined under this special provision also is used in determining the impact of a sale or other disposition of property on earnings and profits. I.R.C. § 312(f)(1). In virtually all cases, this rule will cause corporations to have different bases in property for purposes of determining taxable income and earnings and profits.

10. I.R.C. § 312(k)(3)(B).

11. I.R.C. § 312(n)(1), (2).

On the income side, realized gains that are deferred for taxable income purposes under the installment sale method of Section 453 or by the completed contract method of accounting must be currently included in earnings and profits.[12] Moreover, for earnings and profits purposes, gains on the sale of inventory must be reported under the standard first-in-first-out (FIFO) method rather than the last-in-first-out (LIFO) method.[13]

It should be apparent by now that earnings and profits is simply a tax accounting concept designed to better measure a corporation's true financial results. It is an artificial "account" created by the Code—not an actual bank account or liquid fund set aside by the corporation for the payment of dividends. There is no statute of limitations on earnings and profits issues, and a corporation sometimes will face the onerous task of reconstructing many years of financial history in order to determine the tax consequences of a current distribution.[14]

PROBLEM

X Corporation is a cash method, calendar year taxpayer. During the current year, X has the following income and expenses:

Gross profits from sales	$20,000
Salaries paid to employees	10,250
Tax-exempt interest received	3,000
Dividends received from IBM	5,000
Depreciation (X purchased 5–year property in the current year for $14,000; assume the property has a 7–year class life; no § 179 election was made and X elected not to take the special depreciation allowance in § 168(k))	2,800
LTCG on a sale of stock	2,500
LTCL on a sale of stock	5,000
LTCL carryover from prior years	1,000
Estimated federal income taxes paid	800

Determine X's taxable income for the current year and its current earnings and profits.

C. Distributions of Cash

Code: §§ 301(a), (b), (c); 312(a); 316(a).

Regulations: §§ 1.301–1(a), (b); 1.316–2(a)–(c).

The taxation of cash distributions by a corporation with respect to its stock is relatively straightforward. The amount of the distribution is simply

12. I.R.C. § 312(n)(5), (6).

13. I.R.C. § 312(n)(4).

14. Because it usually is an inherently factual question, the Service will not issue a ruling on the amount of a corporation's earnings and profits. Rev.Proc. 2008–3, § 3.01(36), 2008–1 I.R.B. 113.

the amount of money received by the shareholder.[1] That amount is taxable as a dividend to the extent of the distributing corporation's current or accumulated earnings and profits.[2] Amounts distributed in excess of available earnings and profits are first applied against and reduce the basis of the shareholder's stock and, to the extent that they exceed the shareholder's basis, they are treated as gain from the sale or exchange of the stock.[3] The distributing corporation generally is permitted to reduce its earnings and profits by the amount of money distributed, except that earnings and profits may be reduced as a result of a distribution only to the extent they exist.[4] Thus, while a deficit in earnings and profits may result from corporate operations, a deficit may not be created or increased by a distribution.[5]

When there are insufficient current earnings and profits available to cover all cash distributions made during the year, earnings and profits must be allocated to the distributions in order to determine dividend status under the following rules:[6]

(1) First, current earnings and profits, determined as of the end of the year, are prorated among the distributions by using the following formula:[7]

$$\frac{\text{Current E \& P}}{\text{allocated to distribution}} = \frac{\text{Amount of}}{\text{distribution}} \times \frac{\text{Total current E \& P}}{\text{Total distributions}}$$

(2) Next, accumulated earnings and profits are allocated chronologically to distributions (i.e., on a first-come, first-served basis).[8]

(3) If the corporation has a current loss but has accumulated earnings and profits from prior years, it will be necessary to determine the amount of accumulated earnings and profits available on the date of distribution. Unless the loss can be earmarked to a particular period, the current deficit is prorated to the date of the distribution.[9]

Revenue Ruling 74–164, below, and the problem which follows test your ability to understand and apply these principles.

Revenue Ruling 74–164

1974–1 Cum.Bull. 74.

Advice has been requested concerning the taxable status of corporate distributions under the circumstances described below.

1. The same rule applies to corporate and noncorporate distributees. I.R.C. § 301(b).

2. I.R.C. §§ 301(c)(1); 316(a).

3. I.R.C. § 301(c)(2), (3).

4. I.R.C. § 312(a).

5. Id.

6. This allocation method is significant only if there is a change in shareholder interests during the year or on a non pro rata distribution.

7. Reg. § 1.316–2(b), (c) Example.

8. Id.

9. Reg. § 1.316–2(b).

X corporation and *Y* corporation each using the calendar year for Federal income tax purposes made distributions of $15,000 to their respective shareholders on July 1, 1971, and made no other distributions to their shareholders during the taxable year. The distributions were taxable as provided by section 301(c) of the Internal Revenue Code of 1954.

Situation 1.

At the beginning of its taxable year 1971, *X* corporation had earnings and profits accumulated after February 28, 1913, of $40,000. It had an operating loss for the period January 1, 1971 through June 30, 1971, of $50,000 but had earnings and profits for the entire year 1971 of $5,000.

Situation 2.

At the beginning of its taxable year 1971, *Y* corporation had a deficit in earnings and profits accumulated after February 28, 1913, of $60,000. Its net profits for the period January 1, 1971 through June 30, 1971, were $75,000 but its earnings and profits for the entire taxable year 1971 were only $5,000.

Situation 3.

Assume the same facts as in *Situation* 1 except that *X* had a deficit in earnings and profits of $5,000 for the entire taxable year 1971.

Situation 4.

Assume the same facts as in *Situation* 1 except that *X* had a deficit in earnings and profits of $55,000 for the entire taxable year 1971.

Section 301(a) and 301(c) of the Code provides, in part, that: (1) the portion of a distribution of property made by a corporation to a shareholder with respect to its stock which is a dividend (as defined in section 316), shall be included in the shareholder's gross income; (2) the portion of the distribution which is not a dividend shall be applied against and reduce the adjusted basis of the stock; and (3) the portion which is not a dividend to the extent that it exceeds the adjusted basis of the stock and is not out of increase in value accrued before March 1, 1913, shall be treated as gain from the sale or exchange of property.

Section 316(a) of the Code provides that the term "dividend" means any distribution of property made by a corporation to its shareholders out of its earnings and profits accumulated after February 28, 1913, or out of its earnings and profits of the taxable year computed as of the close of the taxable year without diminution by reason of any distribution made during the year, and *without regard to the amount of earnings and profits at the time the distribution was made.*

Section 1.316–2(a) of the Income Tax Regulations provides, in part, that in determining the source of a distribution, consideration should be given first, to the earnings and profits of the taxable year; and second, to the earnings and profits accumulated since February 28, 1913, only in the case where, and to the extent that, the distributions made during the taxable year are not regarded as out of the earnings and profits of that year.

Applying the foregoing principles, in *Situation* 1, the earnings and profits of *X* corporation for the taxable year 1971 of $5,000 and the earnings and profits accumulated since February 28, 1913, and prior to the taxable year 1971, of $40,000 were applicable to the distribution paid by it on July 1, 1971. Thus, $5,000 of the distribution of $15,000 was paid from the earnings and profits of the taxable year 1971 and the balance of $10,000 was paid from the earnings and profits accumulated since February 28, 1913. Therefore, the entire distribution of $15,000 was a dividend within the meaning of section 316 of the Code.

In *Situation* 2 the earnings and profits of *Y* corporation for the taxable year 1971 of $5,000 were applicable to the distribution paid by *Y* corporation on July 1, 1971. *Y* corporation had no earnings and profits accumulated after February 28, 1913, available at the time of the distribution. Thus, only $5,000 of the distribution by *Y* corporation of $15,000 was a dividend within the meaning of section 316 of the Code. The balance of such distribution, $10,000 which was not a dividend, applied against and reduced the adjusted basis of the stock in the hands of the shareholders, and to the extent that it exceeded the adjusted basis of the stock was gain from the sale or exchange of property.

In the case of a deficit in earnings and profits for the taxable year in which distributions are made, the taxable status of distributions is dependent upon the amount of earnings and profits accumulated since February 28, 1913, and available at the dates of distribution. In determining the amount of such earnings and profits, section 1.316–2(b) of the regulations provides, in effect, that the deficit in earnings and profits of the taxable year will be prorated to the dates of distribution.

Applying the foregoing to Situations 3 and 4 the distribution paid by *X* corporation on July 1, 1971, in each situation was a dividend within the meaning of section 316 of the Code to the extent indicated as follows:

Situation #3

Accumulated Earnings and Profits (E & P) 1/1	$40,000	
E & P deficit for entire taxable year ($5,000) Prorate to date of distribution 7/1 (½ of $5,000)	(2,500)	
E & P available 7/1	$37,500	
Distribution 7/1 ($15,000)	(15,000)	taxable as a dividend
E & P deficit from 7/1–12/31	(2,500)	
Accumulated E & P balance 12/31	$20,000	

Situation #4

Accumulated E & P 1/1	$40,000
E & P deficit for entire taxable year ($55,000) Prorate to date of distribution 7/1 (½ of $55,000)	(27,500)
E & P available 7/1	$12,500

Distribution 7/1 ($15,000)	(12,500)	taxable as a dividend
E & P deficit from 7/1–12/31	(27,500)	
Accumulated E & P balance 12/31	$(27,500)	

NOTE

Situations 3 and 4 of Revenue Ruling 74–164 do not consider the possibility of earmarking the entire 1971 deficit (i.e., $5,000 in Situation 3 and $55,000 in Situation 4) to the first half of the year. Under the regulations,[1] if those deficits were sustained in the first half of 1971, the full amount (not just one-half) would reduce the accumulated earnings and profits available to characterize the July 1 distribution as a dividend. This would not affect the result in Situation 3 but it would change Situation 4, where there would be no dividend.

PROBLEM

Ann owns all of the common stock (the only class outstanding) of Pelican Corporation. Prior to the transactions below and as a result of a § 351 transfer, Ann has a $10,000 basis in her Pelican stock. What results to Ann and Pelican in each of the following alternative situations?

(a) In year one Pelican has $5,000 of current and no accumulated earnings and profits and it distributes $17,500 to Ann?

(b) Pelican has a $15,000 accumulated deficit in its earnings and profits at the beginning of year two. In year two Pelican has $10,000 of current earnings and profits and it distributes $10,000 to Ann.

(c) Pelican has $10,000 of accumulated earnings and profits at the beginning of year two and $4,000 of current earnings and profits in year two. On July 1 of year two, Ann sells half of her Pelican stock to Baker Corporation for $15,000. On April 1 of year two, Pelican distributes $10,000 to Ann, and on October 1 of year 2, Pelican distributes $5,000 to Ann and $5,000 to Baker.

(d) Same as (c), above, except that Pelican has a $10,000 deficit in earnings and profits in year 2 as a result of its business operations.

D. DISTRIBUTIONS OF PROPERTY

1. CONSEQUENCES TO THE DISTRIBUTING CORPORATION

a. BACKGROUND: THE GENERAL UTILITIES DOCTRINE

Under the double tax regime of Subchapter C, profits from the sale of appreciated corporate property are taxed twice—first to the corporation when it sells the property and again to the shareholders when the sales

1. Reg. § 1.316–2(b).

proceeds are distributed as dividends. What if a corporation *distributes* appreciated property to its shareholders? The shareholders, of course, receive a taxable dividend to the extent the distribution is out of current or accumulated earnings and profits. Should the distributing corporation also recognize gain—just as if it had sold the property for its fair market value? Or is the corporation entitled to nonrecognition of gain because the property was distributed rather than sold? Does the answer depend on the shareholder's basis in the distributed property? If tax relief is appropriate, should nonliquidating distributions be treated less favorably than liquidating distributions? And what about distributions of loss property? Simple as they may seem, these are among the most controversial questions ever spawned by Subchapter C. The answers will come gradually. The coverage in this chapter is limited to nonliquidating distributions. To set the stage, we begin with a brief history of the rise and fall of what has become known as the *General Utilities* doctrine.

In General Utilities & Operating Co. v. Helvering,[1] the Supreme Court first considered the corporate-level tax consequences of a nonliquidating distribution of appreciated property by a corporation to its shareholders. The facts were straightforward. General Utilities Corporation had located a buyer for corporate property with a value of $1,000,000 and an adjusted basis of $2,000. Hoping to escape the large corporate-level tax that would be imposed on a sale by the corporation, General Utilities distributed the property to its shareholders with an "understanding" (but not a legal commitment) that they would sell the targeted property to the prospective buyer. Four days later, the shareholders sold the property to the buyer on the same terms negotiated by the corporation. The Service contended that the distribution was a taxable event at the corporate level.

By the time the controversy reached the Supreme Court, the government's principal argument was based on the premise that General Utilities had created an indebtedness to its shareholders by declaring a dividend. It went on to contend that using appreciated property to discharge that indebtedness was a taxable event. Apparently confining its decision to these narrow grounds, the Court held that the corporation recognized no gain because the distribution was not a "sale" and the corporation did not discharge indebtedness with appreciated assets.[2] Despite this limited holding, it long was assumed that *General Utilities* stood for the broader

1. 296 U.S. 200, 56 S.Ct. 185 (1935).

2. The government also argued that the subsequent sale by the shareholders of the assets could be attributed to the corporation, but the Court declined to consider that question since it had not been raised below. Ten years later, in Commissioner v. Court Holding Co., 324 U.S. 331, 65 S.Ct. 707 (1945), the government successfully advanced the attribution argument in the context of a liquidating distribution. See Chapter 16B2, infra. In *General Utilities*, the government alternatively contended that a distribution of appreciated property by a corporation in and of itself constitutes a realization event, but the Court did not address this argument. See Bittker & Eustice, Federal Income Taxation of Corporations and Shareholders ¶ 8.20[2] n. 313 (7th ed. 2000).

proposition that a distributing corporation does not recognize gain or loss when it makes a distribution in kind with respect to its stock.[3]

The result in *General Utilities* raised fundamental policy questions that went to the heart of the double tax regime. The decision created a significant and arguably unwarranted tax distinction between a distribution in kind of appreciated property and a sale of that same property by the corporation followed by a distribution of the proceeds to the shareholders. In the case of a sale at the corporate level, the corporation recognizes gain and correspondingly must increase its earnings and profits. On distribution of the sale proceeds, the shareholders also are taxed to the extent of the corporation's earnings and profits. Under *General Utilities*, however, the corporation could distribute the same asset to the shareholders without recognizing gain. To be sure, the shareholders were taxable on the distribution, but the asset appreciation escaped tax at the corporate level, and a noncorporate shareholder took the asset with a fair market value basis.[4] This simple comparison demonstrates that the tax treatment of distributions in kind is critical to the integrity of the double tax regime. Because the *General Utilities* doctrine was incompatible with the double tax, it was criticized by commentators.[5]

Despite these deficiencies, Congress codified *General Utilities* in the 1954 Code by enacting Section 311(a)(2), which provides that a corporation generally does not recognize gain or loss on a nonliquidating distribution of property.[6] This nonrecognition rule was never absolute. Over the years, the courts applied "common law" doctrines, such as assignment of income[7] and the tax benefit rule,[8] and substance over form,[9] to override Section 311(a) and attribute income back to the corporation. Congress also chipped away at the doctrine with various specialized statutory exceptions until 1986, when it repealed *General Utilities* in the context of both nonliquidating and liquidating distributions of appreciated property.[10]

b. CORPORATE GAIN OR LOSS

Code: § 311.

3. See, e.g., Commissioner v. Godley's Estate, 213 F.2d 529, 531 (3d Cir.1954), cert. denied 348 U.S. 862, 75 S.Ct. 86 (1954). Even before the 1954 Code, however, the *General Utilities* nonrecognition rule was subject to judicially-created exceptions, such as the assignment of income doctrine. See S.Rep. No. 1622, 83rd Cong., 2d Sess. 247 (1954).

4. I.R.C. § 301(d).

5. See, e.g., Block, "Liquidations Before and After Repeal of *General Utilities*," 21 Harv.J.Legis. 307 (1984); Blum, "Taxing Transfers of Incorporated Business: A Proposal for Improvement," 52 Taxes 516 (1974); Raum, "Dividends in Kind: Their Tax Aspects," 63 Harv.L.Rev. 593 (1950).

6. Prior to 1987, Section 336 provided a similar nonrecognition rule for liquidating distributions. See Chapter 15B2, infra.

7. See, e.g., Commissioner v. First State Bank of Stratford, 168 F.2d 1004 (5th Cir. 1948), cert. denied, 335 U.S. 867, 69 S.Ct. 137 (1948).

8. Cf. Hillsboro National Bank v. Commissioner, 460 U.S. 370, 103 S.Ct. 1134 (1983).

9. Bush Brothers & Co. v. Commissioner, 668 F.2d 252 (6th Cir.1982); Waltham Netoco Theatres, Inc. v. Commissioner, 401 F.2d 333 (1st Cir.1968). But see Anderson v. Commissioner, 92 T.C. 138 (1989).

10. See also Chapter 15B2, infra.

Although the nonrecognition rule in Section 311(a)(2) remains in the Code, Section 311(b) stands that rule on its head for nonliquidating distributions of appreciated property. If a corporation distributes appreciated property (other than its own obligations) in a nonliquidating distribution, it must recognize gain in an amount equal to the excess of the fair market value of the property over its adjusted basis. If the distributed property is subject to a liability or if the distributee shareholder assumes a liability in connection with the distribution, the fair market value of the distributed property is treated as not less than the amount of the liability.[11] The deceptive "general" rule of Section 311(a)(2) still applies, however, to disallow recognition of loss on a distribution of property that has declined in value. The objective of this statutory regime is to strengthen the corporate income tax by ensuring that appreciated property may not leave corporate solution and take a stepped-up basis in the hands of the distributee shareholder without the imposition of a corporate-level tax on the appreciation.[12]

The *General Utilities* doctrine thus no longer applies to nonliquidating distributions of appreciated property. A later chapter examines the repeal of the doctrine in the area of complete liquidations.[13] Despite what appears to be parallel treatment, some differences between the treatment of liquidating and nonliquidating distributions persist, raising lingering policy issues. For example, a distributing corporation generally may recognize a loss on a liquidating distribution of property with a built-in loss.[14] Should nonliquidating distributions be treated similarly? Is the "general" loss disallowance rule in Section 311(a)(2) an indefensible trap for the uninformed? In considering these questions, one should keep in mind that the double tax regime has not been universally accepted, and some have argued that relief through limited *General Utilities* type exceptions would be appropriate.[15]

c. EFFECT ON THE DISTRIBUTING CORPORATION'S EARNINGS AND PROFITS

Code: § 312(a)(3), (b), (c), (f)(1).

Regulations: § 1.312–3.

Nonliquidating distributions of property have several effects upon the earnings and profits of the distributing corporation. Gain recognized by the corporation on the distribution naturally increases current earnings and profits.[16] Following a property distribution, the distributing corporation

11. I.R.C. § 311(b)(2), incorporating the rule for liquidating distributions in I.R.C. § 336(b).

12. Cf. S.Rep.No. 98–169, 98th Cong., 2d Sess. 177 (1984); H.R.Rep.No. 99–426, 99th Cong., 1st Sess. 282 (1985).

13. See Chapter 15B2, infra.

14. I.R.C. § 336(a), (d).

15. Compare Thompson, "An Analysis of the Proposal to Repeal General Utilities with an Escape Hatch," 31 Tax Notes 1121 (June 16, 1986) with Yin, "General Utilities Repeal: Is Tax Reform Really Going to Pass it By?" 31 Tax Notes 1111 (June 16, 1986).

16. I.R.C. § 312(b)(1), (f)(1). For this purpose and for purposes of determining gain recognized, the adjusted basis of any property

may reduce accumulated earnings and profits (to the extent thereof) under Section 312(a)(3) by the adjusted basis of the distributed property. On a distribution of appreciated property (other than a corporation's own debt obligations), this rule is modified by Section 312(b)(2), which provides that the earnings and profits reduction rule in Section 312(a)(3) is applied by substituting the fair market value of the property for its adjusted basis. This special rule logically allows a corporation distributing appreciated property to make a downward adjustment to accumulated earnings and profits in an amount equal to the full fair market value of the property. The net result of these earnings and profits adjustments—the first relating to the gain recognized on the distribution and the second relating to the effect of the distribution itself—is the same as if the corporation had sold the property (increasing current earnings and profits by the gain recognized) and then distributed cash equal to the fair market value of the property (decreasing accumulated earnings and profits by that amount).

Section 312(c) cryptically adds that "proper adjustment" shall be made for liabilities either assumed by the shareholder or to which the property is subject. Section 1.312–3 of the regulations provides that the "proper adjustment" is a reduction in the Section 312(a)(3) charge to earnings and profits for liabilities assumed or to which the property is subject. This adjustment thus *decreases* the charge to earnings and profits and properly reflects the fact that relief from the liability is an economic benefit to the distributing corporation.

2. CONSEQUENCES TO THE SHAREHOLDERS

Code: §§ 301(a), (b), (c), (d).

The rules governing the shareholder level tax consequences of property distributions are essentially the same as those for cash distributions. The amount of the distribution is the fair market value of the distributed property, reduced by any liabilities assumed by the shareholder or to which the property is subject;[1] that amount is taxed under the now familiar principles in Section 301(c). The shareholder's basis in the distributed property is its fair market value as of the date of the distribution.[2]

3. DISTRIBUTIONS OF A CORPORATION'S OWN OBLIGATIONS

Code: §§ 311(a), (b)(1); 312(a)(2).

Regulations: § 1.301–1(d)(1)(ii).

By virtue of the parenthetical in Section 311(b)(1)(A), "(other than an obligation of such corporation)", the general gain recognition rule does not

is its adjusted basis for purposes of computing earnings and profits. I.R.C. § 312(b), flush language. For example, tangible property depreciated for tax purposes under the accelerated cost recovery system must be depreciated for "E & P" purposes under the § 168(g)(2) alternative depreciation system and thus may have a different "E & P" adjusted basis.

1. I.R.C. § 301(b). The fair market value of the distributed property is determined as of the date of distribution. I.R.C. § 301(b)(3).

2. I.R.C. § 301(d).

apply to distributions by a corporation of its own debt obligations. Consequently, the eroded Section 311(a) continues to govern this situation. At the shareholder level, both the amount of the distribution and the distributee shareholder's basis are equal to the fair market value of the obligation.[1] The distributing corporation's earnings and profits are reduced by the principal amount of the obligation or, in the case of an obligation having original issue discount, by its issue price.[2]

PROBLEM

Zane, an individual, owns all of the outstanding common stock in Sturdley Utilities Corporation. Zane purchased his Sturdley stock seven years ago and his basis is $8,000. At the beginning of the current year, Sturdley had $25,000 of accumulated earnings and profits and no current earnings and profits. Determine the tax consequences to Zane and Sturdley in each of the following alternative situations:

(a) Sturdley distributes inventory ($20,000 fair market value; $11,000 basis) to Zane.

(b) Same as (a), above, except that, before the distribution, Sturdley has no current or accumulated earnings and profits.

(c) Sturdley distributes land ($20,000 fair market value; $11,000 basis) which it has used in its business. Zane takes the land subject to a $16,000 mortgage.

(d) Assume Sturdley has $15,000 of current earnings and profits (in addition to $25,000 of accumulated earnings and profits) and it distributes to Zane land ($20,000 fair market value; $30,000 basis) which it held as an investment. Compare the result if Sturdley first sold the land and then distributed the proceeds.

(e) Assume again that Sturdley has $25,000 of accumulated earnings and profits at the beginning of the current year. Sturdley distributes machinery used in its business ($10,000 fair market value, zero adjusted basis for taxable income purposes, and $2,000 adjusted basis for earnings and profits purposes). The machinery is five-year property and has a seven-year class life, was purchased by Sturdley for $14,000 on July 1 of year one (no § 179 election was made), and the distribution is made on January 1 of year seven. See I.R.C. §§ 168(g)(2), 312(k)(3); Reg. § 1.312–15(d).

E. CONSTRUCTIVE DISTRIBUTIONS

Code: Skim § 7872(a), (c)(1)(C).

Regulations: § 1.301–1(j).

Historically, dividend distributions often combined the worst of all possible worlds from a tax standpoint: they were fully taxable to noncorpo-

1. Reg. §§ 1.301–1(d)(1)(ii), –1(h)(2)(i).

2. I.R.C. § 312(a)(2).

rate shareholders at the highest ordinary income rates but were not deductible by the distributing corporation. To avoid the double tax, closely held C corporations have attempted to distribute earnings in a form that may be deductible at the corporate level. Notable examples include a corporation's payment of: (1) excessive compensation to shareholders or their relatives;[1] (2) expenses paid for the personal benefit of shareholders (e.g., travel or entertainment, legal expenses);[2] (3) excessive rent for corporate use of shareholder property;[3] and (4) interest on shareholder debt that in substance represents equity.[4] If these payments are not what they purport to be—i.e., if they are not *really* salary, rent or interest, etc., or if they are primarily for the personal benefit of shareholders—they risk being reclassified by the Service as a constructive dividend. In that event, the corporate level deduction will be disallowed. Other disguised dividend strategies include labeling what in reality is a distribution as a loan to the shareholder,[5] bargain sales or rentals of corporate property to shareholders[6] and interest free loans.[7]

The constructive dividend area has produced many entertaining controversies involving blatant attempts by taxpayers to milk their corporations while avoiding the double tax. The prototype transaction involves a direct payment or receipt of an economic benefit by the shareholder, and resolution of the issue requires an evaluation of all the facts and circumstances, applying broad standards such as "reasonable compensation;" "shareholder benefit vs. corporate benefit" and "intent."[8] The case and ruling below illustrate some typical fact patterns and issues in this area. They are followed by a Note discussing the changing stakes now that most dividends are taxed at a preferential rate.

Nicholls, North, Buse Co. v. Commissioner

Tax Court of the United States, 1971.
56 T.C. 1225.

[Nicholls, North, Buse Co. ("Nicholls") was a Wisconsin corporation in the food-brokerage and food-packing businesses. All of the Nicholls voting

1. For the legal standards used in making this determination, see, e.g., Exacto Spring Corp. v. Commissioner, 196 F.3d 833 (7th Cir.1999), and compare Charles McCandless Tile Service v. United States, 191 Ct.Cl. 108, 422 F.2d 1336 (1970) with Elliotts, Inc. v. Commissioner, 716 F.2d 1241 (9th Cir.1983).

2. See, e.g., Ashby v. Commissioner, 50 T.C. 409 (1968); Hood v. Commissioner, 115 T.C. 172 (2000).

3. See, e.g., International Artists, Ltd. v. Commissioner, 55 T.C. 94 (1970).

4. See Chapter 11F, supra.

5. See, e.g., Williams v. Commissioner, 627 F.2d 1032 (10th Cir.1980).

6. See, e.g., Honigman v. Commissioner, 466 F.2d 69 (6th Cir.1972).

7. Compare Zager v. Commissioner, 72 T.C. 1009 (1979) with I.R.C. § 7872. See also Rountree Cotton Co. v. Commissioner, 113 T.C. 422 (1999), aff'd by order, 12 Fed.Appx. 641 (10th Cir.2001).

8. See generally, Bittker & Eustice, Federal Income Taxation of Corporations and Shareholders ¶ 8.05 (7th ed. 2000).

common stock was owned by Herbert and Charlotte Resenhoeft, who were married. Herbert served as president and a director of the corporation. Nicholls nonvoting common stock was owned by Herbert, Charlotte and their two sons, Robert and James. James was also an employee of Nicholls.

Herbert Resenhoeft previously had personally owned two boats: *Pea Picker I* and *Pea Picker II*. In 1964, Nicholls acquired a new 52–foot yacht—*Pea Picker III*—at a total cost of $68,290. Nicholls' Board of Directors unanimously approved the purchase of *Pea Picker III* and provided in a corporate resolution that "any expenses incurred in the personal use of the boat are to be borne by H.A. Resenhoeft and an accurate log is to be kept of all business use." During 1964, $1,144.72 was charged to Herbert for personal use of *Pea Picker III*.

Both Robert and James were free to operate *Pea Picker III*, without special permission. Herbert was unable to operate the yacht and had little technical knowledge about yachting. James was the principal operator of *Pea Picker III* and was the family boating enthusiast. In fact, James negotiated Nicholls' purchase of the yacht. During 1964, the use of *Pea Picker III* included personal use by James.

In its original notice of deficiency to Herbert, the Service took the position that he was taxable on $68,878.72, the purchase price for the yacht plus yacht expenses for the year. Later, the Service alternatively argued that Herbert was taxable on a dividend equal to the fair rental value of *Pea Picker III*. Ed.]

The issues with regard to individual petitioner Resenhoeft resolve themselves down to the following: (a) Was there a constructive dividend; (b) may the use of the yacht by James, a stockholder in his own right, be imputed to his father who was in control of the corporation to make the father the recipient of the constructive dividend; and (c) is the measure of the dividend the purchase price of the craft plus actual operating expenses or is the fair rental value of the use of the yacht during the period in question the appropriate measure?

(a) It is well established that any expenditure made by a corporation for the personal benefit of its stockholders, or the making available of corporate-owned facilities to stockholders for their personal benefit, may result in the receipt by the stockholders of a constructive dividend. * * * Upon consideration of all the evidence, including the possible instances of unrecorded personal use, we conclude that *Pea Picker III* was used for business purposes 25 percent and for personal purposes 75 percent of the time in 1964.

(b) Since we have found that there was personal use constituting under some circumstances a dividend, the next question is, to whom was the benefit directed? Resenhoeft has established by convincing evidence that he was not interested in the yacht for his own personal pleasure as a boating enthusiast. He had little knowledge of the workings of such craft, could not operate them himself, and played no direct part in the purchase of *Pea Picker III* or the sale of her predecessor. However, to the extent that he was present on an occasion of personal use, he received a benefit and an argument that others benefited as well is of no avail here. * * * He shared in the friendships and joined in the social activity on board on those occasions.

The question remains, however, whether James' personal use of *Pea Picker III* on occasions when Resenhoeft was not present may nevertheless be attributed to Resenhoeft. The essential elements underlying the taxation of assigned income to the assignor were set down in Helvering v. Horst, 311 U.S. 112 (1940). The Court stated in that case that: "The power to dispose of income is the equivalent of 'ownership' of it and the exercise of that power to procure the payment of income to another is the 'enjoyment' and hence the 'realization' of the income by him who exercises it." In this case Resenhoeft personally owned well over 50 percent of all voting stock and together with his wife owned all of it, and in addition was the president of the company and on the board of directors. It is manifestly clear that it was Resenhoeft's decision that the corporation acquire *Pea Picker III*. Resenhoeft's decision to allow the use of the boat by his sons as they desired and without direct control over either the circumstances of use or the maintenance of appropriate supportive documentation must be given particular emphasis. There is no indication here that information regarding the actual use of the boat, or the type of records maintained, was being kept from Resenhoeft or that he had no way of learning the truth. * * *

The principle of assignment was applied to constructive dividends in Byers v. Commissioner, 199 F.2d 273 (C.A.8, 1952), certiorari denied 345 U.S. 907 (1953). See also Commissioner v. Makransky, 321 F.2d 598 (C.A.3, 1963). We remain unpersuaded that Resenhoeft's purpose in agreeing to the acquisition of a large pleasure craft was only to benefit the corporation. This is particularly so in light of his prior personal ownership of *Pea Picker I* and *II* which were available for the use and benefit of his sons. Once it is understood that Resenhoeft was in complete control of the events, the fact that James, the principle user of the boat for noncorporate purposes, was a mature adult and a shareholder in his own right becomes irrelevant.

(c) Although we have determined that there was a dividend, and that the dividend must be attributed to Resenhoeft, we have yet to ascertain the amount of the dividend. Two standards have been used on different occasions, the first being the initial cost of the facility and the second, the approximate rental value for the period at issue. The standard to be chosen rests on the facts and circumstances of the event rather than on which year (the initial year of purchase or a subsequent year) happens to be before the Court, as was argued by respondent in his briefs. In *Louis Greenspon, supra*, the Court held that continued corporate ownership of farm equipment used by the petitioner shareholder prevented the assessment of a constructive dividend based on the purchase price of the equipment. No determination of a dividend was made based on the rental value since respondent failed to raise that issue. Our holding in *Greenspon* that ownership of the asset is a principal factor has not been altered by subsequent cases involving the year an asset was acquired. Although in some cases subsequent to *Greenspon* we have determined the amount of the dividend to be the acquisition cost, in those cases the evidence clearly pointed to shareholder ownership, * * * or the location of title could not be determined and therefore was presumptively in the shareholder. * * * These cases have not been followed when the title was clearly with the corporation. * * *

In this case, ownership continued to rest with Nicholls. The bill of sale was made in Nicholls' name, Nicholls' principal creditor was informed of the purchase and the yacht's intended devotion to corporate purposes, a license to operate short-wave radio equipment installed on *Pea Picker III* was acquired in the corporate name, registration by U.S. Customs was attempted in the corporate name, registration and licensing was received from the State of Wisconsin in the corporate name, and sales tax was paid by the corporation although a significant savings would have resulted by treating this as a purchase by Resenhoeft. Although a listing in the Lake Michigan Yachting Association catalogue showed James as the owner of the *Pea Picker III*, the association provided no means for noting corporate ownership, and registration in whatever name offered values significant to the corporation as well as to James. Therefore we hold that petitioner has not received a constructive dividend equivalent to the cost of acquisition of *Pea Picker III*.

The issue yet remaining is whether there is another more appropriate measure of the constructive dividend, a dividend which we have already decided Resenhoeft received.

Respondent's alternative theory is that the fair rental value of *Pea Picker III* for the period of use in 1964 is the measure of the dividend received; furthermore, respondent argues that the testimony of the captain in charge of delivering *Pea Picker III* from Florida corroborates the minimum rental value alleged in respondent's amended answer. The amended answer alleged that the fair value was not less than Nicholls' combined depreciation and operating expenses, $4,578.86, of which $1,144.72 concededly was included as income by Resenhoeft at the time he filed his 1964 return. Since we have already determined that Resenhoeft should be charged with 75 percent of the total value of the use of the yacht rather than 100 percent as argued by respondent, the remaining amount actually in dispute is $2,289.42. * * *

Ordinarily, respondent's alternative allegation would be determinative since petitioner has offered no evidence showing that determination to be in error. However, since the theory of a dividend based on rental value comprises a separate issue, involving distinct factual questions, and was raised by the Commissioner for the first time in his amended answer, the rental value suggested by the Commissioner may not be given the presumption it would otherwise be due * * *. Upon Considering all evidence, including the rental value of similar craft used in dissimilar water, we hold that the full rental value of *Pea Picker III* for the period following the shakedown cruise and ending with the final storage of the boat was $4,000. Resenhoeft gained personal benefit and therefore received a constructive dividend from his own use and the use of the craft by his sons equaling 75 percent of the above rental value; of that amount he has voluntarily recognized income to the extent of $1,144.72. We have no reason to believe Nicholls' earnings and profits were insufficient for the payment of a taxable dividend of the amount determined above.

Revenue Ruling 69–630

1969–2 Cum. Bull. 112.

Advice has been requested as to the treatment of a "bargain sale" between two corporate entities controlled by the same shareholder(s).

A, an individual, owns all of the stock of X corporation and all of the stock of Y corporation. In 1967, A caused X to sell certain of its property to Y for less than an arm's length price. It has been determined that such sale had as one of its principal purposes the avoidance of Federal income tax and resulted in a significant understatement of X's taxable income.

Section 482 of the Internal Revenue Code * * * provides authority to distribute, apportion, or allocate gross income, deductions, and credits among related organizations, trades, or businesses if it is necessary in order to clearly reflect the income of such entities or to prevent the evasion of taxes.

Section 482 of the Code applies to bargain sale transactions between brother-sister corporations that result in significant shifting of income. Where an allocation is made under section 482 of the Code as a result of a bargain sale between brother-sister corporations, the amount of the allocation will be treated as a distribution to the controlling shareholder(s) with respect to the stock of the entity whose income is increased and as a capital contribution by the controlling shareholder(s) to the other entity involved in the transaction giving rise to the section 482 allocation.

Accordingly, in the instant case, the income of X for 1967 will be increased under section 482 of the Code to reflect the arm's length price of the property sold to Y. The basis of the property in the hands of Y will also be increased to reflect the arm's length price. * * * Furthermore, the amount of such increase will be treated as a distribution to A, the controlling shareholder, with respect to his stock of X and as a capital contribution by A to Y.

* * *

NOTE

The reduced rate on qualified dividends has changed the stakes and planning agenda in some traditional scenarios. The distinction between compensation and a constructive dividend provides a good illustration. Compensation continues to be taxable at the highest ordinary income rates and is subject to employment taxes equal to 12.4 percent of the social security wage base of $102,000 (in 2008) and a 2.9 percent medicare tax on all wages while dividends are taxed at a maximum rate of 15 percent and are not subject to employment taxes. But compensation and the employer's share of employment taxes are deductible while dividends are not.

Under the "old arithmetic," with wages and dividends taxed at the same ordinary income rate, it almost always was advantageous to classify distributions to shareholder-employees as compensation rather than a dividend so that the corporation could deduct the payment. Under current law, however, as long as dividends are taxable at only 15 percent, there now are situations where the aggregate amount of federal taxes is lower if payments are classified as dividends rather than compensation. Important variables are the corporate and individual tax rates and the impact of employment taxes.[1]

To illustrate, consider first the following simple example in a world where wages are not subject to employment taxes, and all income of C corporations and individuals is taxed at a 35 percent rate except for dividends, which are taxed at 15 percent. Assume that X Corporation has $100,000 of earnings to distribute to A, its only employee and shareholder, and is evaluating whether to classify the distribution as a dividend or compensation. The overall tax results are as follows:

	Compensation	Dividend
X's Taxable Income Before Payment to A	$100,000	$100,000
Corporate Income Tax	0	35,000
Payment to A	100,000	65,000
A's Income Tax	35,000	9,750
Net Amount to A	65,000	55,250

The traditional incentive to classify the distribution as compensation remains in this example, despite the lower tax rate on dividends, because of the continuing negative effect of the double tax when a C corporation taxable at the highest marginal rate (35 percent) pays dividends.

Now assume the same facts, except reflect the reality that A's wages are subject to employment taxes of 12.4 percent on the first $102,000[2] and 2.9 percent on all wages, with half of these taxes paid by X Corp. (which can deduct them) and half by A. Assuming that X Corp. has $100,000 available to pay to A before any corporate-level income or employment taxes, the tax results are as follows:

1. For more extended analysis of these issues and other variables, see Feld, "Dividends Reconsidered," 101 Tax Notes 1117 (Dec. 1, 2003); Jewett, "Characterization of Income: Compensation vs. Dividends," 103 Tax Notes 1501 (June 21, 2004).

2. This is the wage base in effect for 2008.

	Compensation[3]	Dividend
X's Taxable Income Before Payment to A	$100,000	$100,000
Employment Taxes (X's share)	7,106	0
Corporate Income Tax	0	35,000
Payment to A	92,894	65,000
Employment Taxes (A's share)	7,106	0
A's Income Tax	32,512	9,750
Net Amount to A	53,276	55,250

When employment taxes are taken into account, there is a slight overall advantage to dividend classification. As A's compensation rises, however, the benefit of dividend classification will diminish because the 12.4 percent social security tax is only imposed on the first $102,000 of wages. With larger distributions, the traditional bias toward compensation persists because of the negative impact of the double tax.

The incentives also change if the corporation or the shareholder pays tax at lower marginal rates. If the corporation's taxable income falls within the lower rate brackets in Section 11, that reduces the amount of double tax paid and favors a dividend. Alternatively, if the shareholder pays tax on ordinary income at lower rates, that will favor compensation because the relative tax advantage for dividends will not be as great.

F. Anti-Avoidance Limitations on the Dividends Received Deduction

1. In General

Code: §§ 243(a)(1), (3), (c); 246(a)(1), (b)(1), (c); 246A; 1059(a), (b), (c), (d), (e)(1). Skim §§ 243(b)(1); 1059(e)(2), (3), (f).

Dividends received by corporate shareholders are treated more generously for tax purposes than dividends received by individuals. If corporate shareholders were taxed in full on the dividends they receive, corporate profits would be subjected to a minimum of three levels of taxation—once when earned, a second time when received as dividends by the corporate shareholder, and again when distributed to the ultimate noncorporate shareholder. To alleviate this multiple taxation, Section 243 generally permits corporate shareholders to deduct 70 percent of dividends received from other corporations. The deduction is increased to 80 percent if the corporate shareholder owns 20 percent or more (by vote or value) of the distributing corporation[1] and to 100 percent for certain "qualifying" dividends if the payor and recipient corporations are members of the same

3. These computations assume that X has $100,000 available for payment of wages to A before X pays the employer's share of employment taxes (6.2 percent of the first $90,000 of wages plus 1.45% of all wages). A's wages were determined using the following formula: wages ("W") = $100,000 − .0765W.

1. I.R.C. § 243(c).

affiliated group.[2] As a result, a maximum of only 30 percent of dividends received by corporate shareholders are subject to tax, for a maximum effective rate of 10.5 percent.[3] The availability of this deduction has inspired tax advisors to devise techniques to take advantage of the lower effective rate on dividends received by corporate shareholders. This section examines ongoing Congressional efforts to curtail some of these abuses.

2. Special Holding Period Requirements

The dividends received deduction may motivate corporate shareholders to convert capital gain (taxable at the 35 percent maximum corporate rate) to tax sheltered dividend income (taxable at a maximum rate of 10.5 percent). Assume, for example, that Converter Corporation acquires 100 shares of Distributor, Inc. for $5,250 shortly before the stock goes "ex-dividend."[4] Converter holds the stock, collects a $250 dividend, includes only 30% ($75) in income, and then sells the stock for its post-dividend value of $5,000, claiming a short-term capital loss of $250 which is available to offset other capital gains normally taxable at 35 percent. Without any patrolling mechanism, this maneuver enables a corporate shareholder to convert short-term gain into 70 percent sheltered income.

An earlier version of Section 246(c) attempted to close this loophole by denying any dividends received deduction unless the stock was held for more than 15 days (90 days for certain preferred stock), but corporations concocted methods to diminish the risk of loss during this brief 15–day holding period. Congress responded by increasing the holding period in Section 246(c) to more than 45 days during the 91–day period beginning on the date which is 45 days before the stock goes ex-dividend.[5] In the case of certain preferred stock, the required holding period is 90 days during the 181–day period beginning on the date which is 90 days before the ex-dividend date.[6] The 45 or 90–day period is tolled whenever the corporate shareholder diminishes its risk of loss with respect to the stock in any one of several specified manners.[7] As a result, a corporation is not entitled to the dividends received deduction unless it is willing to hold the stock and incur a genuine market risk for the requisite period of time.

2. I.R.C. § 243(a)(3). The term "affiliated group" is generally defined by reference to the rules governing affiliated corporations that file consolidated tax returns. I.R.C. § 243(b)(2). A simple example would be a corporate parent and an 80 percent or more subsidiary. See I.R.C. § 1504(a). A "qualifying dividend" must be paid from earnings and profits accumulated with the payor and recipient corporations are members of the same affiliated group. I.R.C. § 243(b)(1).

3. The 10.5 percent effective rate is derived by multiplying the 30 percent includible portion of the dividends by the 35 percent maximum corporate rate.

4. The "ex-dividend" date is the first date that a buyer of the stock with respect to which a dividend has been declared is not entitled to receive the dividend.

5. I.R.C. § 246(c)(1)(A). For purposes of counting the number of days, the date of disposition but not the date of acquisition is included. I.R.C. § 246(c)(3).

6. I.R.C. § 246(c)(2).

7. I.R.C. § 246(c)(4). See Reg. § 1.246–5.

3. EXTRAORDINARY DIVIDENDS: BASIS REDUCTION

If the dividend to be received is extraordinarily large in relation to the price of the stock, a corporate shareholder may incur a minimal risk of loss even if it holds the stock for more than 45 days. This opportunity was illustrated by a dramatic example of a tax-motivated "dividend stripping" transaction described in a Congressional committee report:[8]

> Chrysler's cumulative preferred stock sells at $36 per share shortly before Chrysler is scheduled to distribute $11.69 per share of back dividends. Corporation X has a short-term capital gain of $1 million, on which it will owe tax of $460,000 [the example uses the pre–1987 46 percent corporate rate.] It buys 85,000 shares of Chrysler preferred for $3,060,000 and holds it for 91 days. When the stock goes ex-dividend, the price drops to $24.31 per share. Assume corporation X eventually sells the stock for $24.31. Corporation X has a capital loss of $11.69 per share, or $993,650, which reduces the tax on its capital gain to $2,921, or by $457,079. It receives a dividend of $993,650, of which 85 percent [now 70 percent.], or $844,603 is excluded. The tax on the rest of the dividend is $68,562. Thus, the transaction saves $457,079 of capital gain tax at a price of $68,562 of dividend tax, a net gain of $388,517. This gain is likely to exceed, by far, whatever economic consequences result from fluctuations in the market value of Chrysler preferred during the 91–day mandatory holding period.

To deter this opportunity for tax arbitrage, Congress enacted Section 1059, which provides that a corporate shareholder receiving an "extraordinary dividend" must reduce its basis in the underlying stock (but not below zero) by the amount of the nontaxed (i.e., deductible) portion of the dividend if the corporation has not held the stock for more than two years before the "dividend announcement date"—i.e., the earliest date when the distributing corporation declares, announces or agrees to the amount or payment of the dividend.[9]

To fully understand the workings of Section 1059, some definitions are in order. An "extraordinary dividend" is defined in terms of the size of the dividend in relation to the shareholder's adjusted basis in the underlying stock. A dividend is extraordinary if it exceeds certain threshold percentages—five percent of the shareholder's adjusted basis in the case of most preferred stock and ten percent of the adjusted basis in the case of any other stock.[10] To prevent easy avoidance of these percentage tests, all dividends received by a shareholder with respect to any shares of stock which have ex-dividend dates within the same period of 85 consecutive days

8. Joint Committee on Taxation, Tax Shelter Proposals and Other Tax–Motivated Transactions, 98th Cong., 2d Sess. 39–40 (1984).

9. I.R.C. § 1059(a)(1), (d)(5). A distribution that otherwise would constitute an extraordinary dividend will not be considered as such if the shareholder has held the stock during the entire existence of the corporation or any predecessor corporation. I.R.C. § 1059(d)(6).

10. I.R.C. § 1059(c)(1), (2).

are combined and treated as one dividend.[11] Under an alternate test, a taxpayer may elect to determine the status of a dividend as extraordinary by reference to the fair market value (rather than the adjusted basis) of the stock as of the day before the ex-dividend date.[12] This election could be beneficial if the stock had appreciated substantially from the time when it was acquired by the shareholder.

The basis reduction required by Section 1059 is only for the "nontaxed portion" of an extraordinary dividend. The "nontaxed portion" is the total amount of the dividend reduced by the taxable portion—i.e., the portion of the dividend includible in gross income after application of the dividends received deduction.[13] The basis reduction generally occurs immediately before any sale or disposition of the stock.[14] If the nontaxed portion of an extraordinary dividend exceeds the shareholder's adjusted basis in the stock, any excess is treated as gain from the sale or exchange of property in the taxable year in which the extraordinary dividend is received.[15]

The general definition of "extraordinary dividend" is broadened in two special situations. Section 1059(e)(1) provides that any amount treated as a Section 301 distribution to a corporate shareholder shall be an extraordinary dividend, irrespective of the shareholder's holding period in the stock or the size of the distribution, if it is a distribution in redemption of stock which is: (1) part of a partial liquidation of the redeeming corporation[16], or (2) is non pro rata as to all shareholders.[17] In addition, a corporate shareholder will recognize immediate gain with respect to any redemption treated as a dividend (in whole or in part) when the nontaxed portion of the dividend exceeds the basis of the shares surrendered if the redemption is treated as a dividend because of the holding of options that are treated as constructively owned by the shareholder under Section 318.[18] This rather obscure provision was enacted in response to a few highly publicized transactions where corporate taxpayers sought to structure sales of stock as "dividend" redemptions in order to shelter their gain through the dividends received deduction.

11. I.R.C. § 1059(c)(3)(A). In addition, all dividends received with respect to a share of stock which have ex-dividend dates during the same period of 365 consecutive days are treated as extraordinary if the aggregate of such dividends exceeds 20 percent of the basis in such stock. I.R.C. § 1059(c)(3)(B). These rules are extended to include dividends received with respect to shares of stock having a substituted basis. I.R.C. § 1059(c)(3)(C).

12. I.R.C. § 1059(c)(4). This option is available only if the taxpayer establishes the fair market value of the stock to the satisfaction of the Commissioner.

13. I.R.C. § 1059(b).

14. I.R.C. § 1059(d)(1)(A). Section 1059(d)(1)(B) provides that in testing for an extraordinary dividend under Section 1059(c)(1), any reduction in basis required by reason of a prior distribution is treated as occurring at the beginning of the ex-dividend date for such distribution.

15. I.R.C. § 1059(a)(2). This treatment avoids the tax taboo of a negative basis. Cf. I.R.C. § 357(c) and Chapter 11D, supra.

16. "Partial liquidation" is defined for this purpose under the tests in Section 302(e). See Chapter 13D, infra.

17. The tax consequences of stock redemptions are covered in Chapter 13, infra.

18. I.R.C. § 1059(e)(1)(A)(iii).

Two other special rules carve out liberalizing exceptions. First, certain distributions between an affiliated group of corporations that qualify for the 100 percent dividends received deduction under Section 243(b)(1) are not treated as extraordinary dividends.[19] Second, special relief is provided for "qualified preferred dividends," which are defined as dividends payable with respect to any share of stock which provides for fixed preferred dividends payable not less than annually and was not acquired with dividends in arrears.[20] A "qualified preferred dividend" is not treated as an extraordinary dividend if the dividends received by the shareholder during the period it owned the stock do not exceed an annualized rate of 15 percent of the lower of (a) the shareholder's adjusted basis or (b) the liquidation preference of the stock, and the stock is held by the shareholder for over five years.[21] The theory for this complex exception is that, unlike the typical extraordinary dividend, a qualified preferred dividend offers no potential for effectively purchasing a dividend that accrued prior to the date on which the stock was acquired.

4. Debt–Financed Portfolio Stock

Corporate shareholders also exploited the dividends received deduction by borrowing funds to acquire dividend paying stock. For example, assume Leverage Corporation borrows $10,000 at 10 percent interest to purchase $10,000 of stock that will pay dividends at an 8 percent annual return ($800 per year). Leverage fully deducts the $1,000 interest expense against ordinary income but only $240 of the $800 dividend received would be taxable if the 70 percent dividends received deduction is available. The deduction thus turns this otherwise uneconomic transaction into a profitable low risk arbitrage maneuver. The interest deduction results in an annual tax savings of $350 ($1,000 × 35%) while the tax owed on the dividends would be $84 if the corporation were in the maximum 35 percent bracket. For an annual outlay of $1,000 in interest and $84 in tax, Leverage receives $800 in income and a tax savings of $350, for a $66 after-tax benefit.

Section 246A precludes this strategy by reducing Leverage's dividends received deduction to the extent the dividends are attributable to "debt-financed portfolio stock." A similar policy is reflected in Section 265(a)(2), which denies a deduction for interest incurred to purchase or carry tax-exempt municipal bonds. Thus, if the "portfolio stock" is entirely debt-financed, Section 246A denies any dividends received deduction. If it is debt-financed in some lesser percentage, then that same percentage of the dividends received deduction is denied.[22] In all events, however, the reduction in the dividends received deduction may not exceed the amount of any

19. I.R.C. § 1059(e)(2).

20. I.R.C. § 1059(e)(3)(C)(i).

21. I.R.C. § 1059(e)(3)(A), (B). If all these requirements are met except for the five year holding period, the exclusion from extraordinary dividend treatment is more limited. I.R.C. § 1059(e)(3)(A)(ii).

22. I.R.C. § 246A(a), (d).

interest deduction allocable to the dividend (i.e., to the borrowed funds directly attributable to the stock).[23]

Stock is "debt-financed" if it is "portfolio stock" that is encumbered by "portfolio indebtedness" during a "base period" prescribed in the statute.[24] "Portfolio stock" is defined as any stock of a corporation unless the corporate shareholder owns either: (1) 50 percent of the total voting power and value of the corporation or (2) at least 20 percent of the total voting power and value and five or fewer corporate shareholders own at least 50 percent of the voting power and value, excluding preferred stock.[25] "Portfolio indebtedness" means any indebtedness directly attributable to the investment in the portfolio stock.[26] This means that the stock must have been purchased with borrowed funds or that the borrowing must be directly traceable to the acquisition, such as where the stock was pledged as security for a subsequently incurred debt in a case where the corporation reasonably could have been expected to sell the stock rather than incur the indebtedness.[27]

To illustrate, assume that Leverage Corporation acquires 100 shares of publicly traded X Corp. stock for $10,000, paying $6,000 cash from corporate funds and borrowing the $4,000 balance. X Corp. pays Leverage an annual dividend of $1,000. The stock is debt-financed to the extent of $4,000. The percentage of debt-financing is thus 40 percent (the "average portfolio indebtedness," as defined by Section 246A(d)). Under the convoluted formula in Section 246A(a), Leverage subtracts 40 percent from 100 percent and then multiplies the result (60 percent here) by the usual 70 percent dividends received deduction percentage, to reach 42 percent. That lower figure is substituted for 70 percent in determining Leverage's Section 243 deduction. When Leverage receives its $1,000 dividend, it may deduct only $420 (rather than the usual $700).

5. SECTION 301(e)

The adjustments to earnings and profits required by Sections 312(k) and 312(n) for depreciation and other timing items frequently result in an increase to a corporation's earnings and profits[28] and may cause earnings and profits to exceed the corporation's taxable income. For example, a corporation that reports a gain on the installment method may not defer the gain for purposes of determining its earnings and profits.[29] The increase in earnings and profits resulting from these adjustments often ensures that a distribution will be fully taxable as a dividend to noncorporate shareholders. Because of the dividends received deduction, this may prove to be a bonanza to a corporate shareholder. The following example

23. I.R.C. § 246A(e).

24. I.R.C. § 246A(c)(1), (d)(4).

25. I.R.C. § 246A(c)(2), (4).

26. I.R.C. § 246A(d)(3)(A).

27. H.R.Rep. No. 98–432, 98th Cong., 2d Sess. 1181 (1984).

28. The purpose of these adjustments is to ensure that a corporation's earnings and profits more accurately reflect its true economic performance. See Section B of this chapter, supra.

29. I.R.C. § 312(n)(5).

from the legislative history illustrates one type of abuse that concerned Congress:[30]

> For example, assume that P Corporation owns 100 percent of the stock of X Corporation, that P's basis in such stock is $200, that P and X file separate income tax returns, and that X has no current or accumulated earnings and profits. Assume further that X sells an asset for a $1,000 installment note, realizing an $800 gain. Finally, assume that X borrows $500 secured by the installment note and distributes the $500 to P. Under [Section 312(n)], absent a special rule, X Corporation's earnings and profits would be increased by the amount of gain on the installment sale, and P would treat the $500 distribution as a dividend. Thus P would include the $500 in income but would likely qualify for a 100–percent dividends received deduction. If P later sold its X stock for $200 (the value of that stock if it is assumed that X will ultimately have a $300 tax liability, in present value terms, on account of the installment sale), it would not recognize gain or loss on the sale. As a result, P would have realized an overall profit of $500.

Section 301(e) prevents the result illustrated above by providing that the adjustments required by Sections 312(k) and 312(n) shall not be made for purposes of determining the taxable income of (and the adjusted basis of stock held by) any "20 percent corporate shareholder."[31] A 20 percent corporate shareholder is any corporation entitled to a dividends received deduction with respect to a distribution that owns, directly or through the Section 318 attribution rules, either (1) stock in the distributing corporation possessing at least 20 percent of the total combined voting power, or (2) at least 20 percent of the total value of all of the distributing corporation's stock, except nonvoting preferred stock.[32]

The general effect of Section 301(e) is to reduce the distributing corporation's earnings and profits in determining the tax consequences of distributions to 20 percent corporate shareholders. This reduction, in turn, may cause a distribution to be treated as a return of capital coupled with a reduction in the basis of the distributing corporation's stock. Without Section 301(e), the same distribution likely would have been a tax-free dividend with no basis reduction. Thus, applying Section 301(e) to the earlier example, X Corporation will have no earnings and profits for purposes of determining the tax consequences of a distribution to P Corporation. In the absence of earnings and profits, $200 of the distribution by X to P will be a return of capital under Section 301(c)(2), and $300 will be taxed to P as gain from the sale or exchange of its X stock under

30. Staff of the Joint Committee on Taxation, General Explanation of the Revenue Provisions of the Deficit Reduction Act of 1984 (hereinafter "1984 Act General Explanation"), 98th Cong., 2d Sess. 183 (1984).

31. I.R.C. § 301(e)(1).

32. I.R.C. § 301(e)(2).

Section 301(c)(3). P's basis in its X stock will be reduced to zero and it will recognize a $200 gain on the later sale of the stock.[33]

PROBLEM

On June 1, Publicly Held Corporation's common stock is selling for $15 per share. On that date, Publicly Held declares a dividend of $1 per share, payable on June 12 to shareholders of record as of June 8. Investor Corporation purchases 1,000 shares of Publicly Held common stock for $15,000 on June 3 (two days before the June 5 ex-dividend date), collects a $1,000 dividend on June 12 and sells the stock for $14,000 on June 15.

(a) What are the tax consequences to Investor Corporation?

(b) What result in (a), above, if Investor sold the stock on December 1, instead of June 15?

(c) What result in (b), above, if Publicly Held had paid a second $1 per share dividend on August 15, and the ex-dividend date was August 5?

(d) What result in (c), above, if the August dividend is $2 per share but Investor holds the Publicly Held stock for 25 months before selling it?

(e) What result if Investor purchased the Publicly Held stock by borrowing $15,000, secured by the stock, and Investor paid $1,200 interest during the year and received $1,000 of dividends?

(f) What result in (e), above, if Investor had borrowed only $7,500 of the $15,000 used to buy the stock and paid $600 interest during the year?

G. USE OF DIVIDENDS IN BOOTSTRAP SALES

TSN Liquidating Corp. v. United States

United States Court of Appeals, Fifth Circuit, 1980.
624 F.2d 1328.

■ RANDALL, CIRCUIT JUDGE:

This case presents the question whether assets distributed to a corporation by its subsidiary, immediately prior to the sale by such corporation of all the capital stock of such subsidiary, should be treated, for federal income tax purposes, as a dividend or, as the district court held, as part of the consideration received from the sale of such capital stock. We hold that on the facts of this case, the assets so distributed constituted a dividend and we reverse the judgment of the district court.

33. 1984 Act General Explanation, supra note 29, at 183.

In 1969, TSN Liquidating Corporation, Inc. ("TSN"), which was then named "Texas State Network, Inc.," owned over 90% of the capital stock of Community Life Insurance Company ("CLIC"), an insurance company chartered under the laws of the State of Maine. In early 1969, negotiations began for the purchase of CLIC by Union Mutual Life Insurance Company ("Union Mutual"). On May 5, 1969, TSN and the other CLIC stockholders entered into an Agreement of Stock Purchase (the "Stock Purchase Agreement") with Union Mutual for the sale of the capital stock of CLIC to Union Mutual. The Stock Purchase Agreement provided that there would be no material adverse change in the business or assets of CLIC prior to the closing "except that as of closing certain shares and capital notes as provided in Section '4.(i).' above will not be a part of the assets of [CLIC]." Since the purchase price of the capital stock of CLIC under the Stock Purchase Agreement was based primarily on the book value (or, in some instances, market value) of those assets owned by CLIC on the closing date, the purchase price would be automatically reduced by the elimination of such shares and notes from the assets of CLIC. On May 14, 1969, as contemplated by the Stock Purchase Agreement, the Board of Directors of CLIC declared a dividend in kind, payable to stockholders of record as of May 19, 1969, consisting primarily of capital stock in small, public companies traded infrequently and in small quantities in the over-the-counter market. On May 20, 1969, the closing was held and Union Mutual purchased substantially all the outstanding capital stock of CLIC, including the shares held by TSN. The final purchase price paid by Union Mutual to the selling stockholders of CLIC was $823,822, of which TSN's share was $747,436. Union Mutual thereupon contributed to the capital of CLIC $1,120,000 in municipal bonds and purchased from CLIC additional capital stock of CLIC for $824,598 in cash paid to CLIC.

In its income tax return for the fiscal year ended July 31, 1969, TSN reported its receipt of assets from CLIC as a dividend and claimed the 85% dividends received deduction available to corporate stockholders pursuant to § 243(a)(1) of the Internal Revenue Code of 1954. TSN also reported its gain on the sale of the capital stock of CLIC on the installment method pursuant to § 453 of the Code. [Under current law, installment sale treatment would not be allowed if the CLIC stock were publicly traded. I.R.C. § 453(k)(2). Ed.] On audit, the Internal Revenue Service treated the distribution of the assets from CLIC to TSN as having been an integral part of the sale by TSN of capital stock of CLIC to Union Mutual, added its estimate ($1,677,082) of the fair market value of the assets received by TSN to the cash ($747,436) received by TSN on the sale, and disallowed the use by TSN of the installment method for reporting the gain on the sale of the capital stock of CLIC since aggregating the fair market value of the distributed assets and the cash resulted in more than 30% of the proceeds from the sale being received in the year of sale. TSN paid the additional tax due as a result of such treatment by the Internal Revenue Service, filed a claim for a refund and subsequently instituted this action against the Internal Revenue Service.

The district court made the following findings of fact in part II of its opinion:

> With regard to the negotiations between CLIC and Union Mutual in early 1969, the Court finds that Union Mutual was interested in purchasing CLIC and proposed a formula for valuing the assets, liabilities, and insurance in force, which, together with an additional amount, would be the price paid for the CLIC stock.
>
> The investment portfolio of CLIC was heavily oriented toward equity investments in closely held over-the-counter securities. At least in the mind of CLIC's officers, the makeup of CLIC's investment portfolio was affecting its ability to obtain licenses in various states. As early as the Spring of 1968, the management and principal stockholders of CLIC had begun to seek a solution to the investment portfolio problem. The Court finds, however, that CLIC had never formulated a definite plan on how to solve its investment portfolio problem.
>
> Union Mutual did not like CLIC's investment portfolio but considered bonds to be more in keeping with insurance industry responsibilities. The management of CLIC regarded the Union Mutual offer as a good one, and tried without success to get Union Mutual to take the entire investment portfolio.
>
> Accordingly, the [Stock Purchase Agreement] required CLIC to dispose some of the investment portfolio assets. Thus, the price that would be paid for the CLIC stock was based upon a formula which valued the assets after excluding certain stocks.
>
> * * *
>
> Plaintiff's disposition of the undesirable over-the-counter stock was necessitated by its sale arrangements with Union Mutual. Plaintiff had no definite plans prior to its negotiations with Union Mutual as to how to get rid of the undesirable stock, when it was to get rid of the undesirable stock, or even that it would definitely get rid of the undesirable stock. Accordingly, the Court finds that the dividend in kind of 14 May 1969 was part and parcel of the purchase agreement with Union Mutual.

TSN Liquidating Corp. v. United States, 77–2 U.S.Tax Cas. ¶ 9741 at 88,523 (N.D.Tex.1977). In part III of its opinion, the district court made the following additional findings:

> Union Mutual was interested in purchasing the stock of an approximately $2 million corporation in order that that corporation might be licensed to do business in other states. As of 30 April 1969, CLIC had assets of $2,115,138. On 14 May 1969, CLIC declared a dividend valued at approximately $1.8 million. As a result of this dividend, CLIC was left with assets totaling approximately $300,000. The final purchase price paid by Union Mutual to the selling shareholders of CLIC was $823,822. In addition,

> Union Mutual contributed $1,120,000 of municipal bonds to the capital of CLIC and purchased additional shares of stock of CLIC for $824,598. Thus, subsequent to closing on 20 May 1969, CLIC was worth $2,400,000. Thus, CLIC was worth $2 million when the [Stock Purchase Agreement] was signed on 5 May 1969 and worth over $2 million immediately after closing.
>
> There was no business purpose served in this case by the dividend declared by CLIC prior to the sale of all its stock to Union Mutual. It is evident that the dividend benefitted the shareholders of CLIC and not CLIC itself. There was no benefit or business purpose in CLIC's declaration of the dividend separate and apart from the sale. The Court finds that the dividend would not, and could not, have been made without the sale.
>
> * * *
>
> What actually happened in the period 5 through 20 May 1969 was that the stockholders received $1.8 million in virtually tax-free stocks, as well as over $800,000 in cash, for a total of approximately $2.6 million. This was certainly a fair price for a corporation valued at the time of sale at $2,115,138, and reflects a premium paid for good will and policies in force, as well as the fact that CLIC was an existing business with licenses in eight or nine states. Hence, a $2 million corporation was sold for $2.6 million including the dividend and the cash.

After noting the time-honored principle that the incidence of taxation is to be determined by the substance of the transaction rather than by its form and the related principle that the transaction is generally to be viewed as a whole and not to be separated into its component parts, the district court held:

> The distribution of assets to [TSN] from its subsidiary, CLIC, immediately prior to [TSN's] disposition of its entire stock interest in CLIC should be treated as a part of the gain from the sale of the stock. Thus, the Court concludes that the in-kind distribution of 14 May 1969 to the stockholders of CLIC is taxable to [TSN] as gain from the sale of its stock. The alleged dividend was merely intented [sic] to be part of the purchase price paid by Union Mutual to CLIC for its stock.

The district court relied for its holding primarily on the cases of Waterman Steamship Corp. v. Commissioner, 430 F.2d 1185 (5th Cir.1970), cert. denied, 401 U.S. 939, 91 S.Ct. 936, 28 L.Ed.2d 219 (1971), and Basic, Inc. v. United States, 549 F.2d 740 (Ct.Cl.1977), all discussed infra.

On appeal, TSN argues that the cases relied upon by the district court are exceptions to what TSN characterizes as the established rule, namely, that assets removed from a corporation by a dividend made in contemplation of a sale of the stock of that corporation, when those assets are in good faith to be retained by the selling stockholders and not thereafter transferred to the buyer, are taxable as a dividend and not as a part of the price paid for the stock for the reason that, in economic reality and in substance, the selling stockholders did not sell and the buyer did not purchase or pay for the excluded assets. The principal cases cited by TSN for its position are Gilmore v. Commissioner, 25 T.C. 1321 (1956), Coffey v. Commissioner, 14 T.C. 1410 (1950), and Rosenbloom Finance Corp. v. Commissioner, 24 B.T.A. 763 (1931). According to TSN, the controlling distinction between the *Coffey* line of cases relied upon by TSN and the *Waterman* line of cases relied upon by the district court is whether the buyer negotiated to acquire and pay for the stock, exclusive of the assets distributed out as a dividend, on the one hand, or whether the buyer negotiated to acquire and pay for the stock, including the assets which were then the subject of a sham distribution designed to evade taxes, on the other hand. In the former case, according to TSN, there is a taxable dividend; in the latter case there is not.

We begin by noting that the district court was certainly correct in its position that the substance of the transaction controls over the form and that the transaction should be viewed as a whole, rather than being separated into its parts. Further, having reviewed the record, we are of the view that the operative facts found so carefully by the district court are entirely accurate (except for the valuation of the distributed assets, as to which we express no opinion). We differ with the district court only in the legal characterization of those facts and in the conclusion to be drawn therefrom. We agree with TSN that this case is controlled by the *Coffey, Gilmore* and *Rosenbloom* cases rather than by the *Waterman* and *Basic* cases relied upon by the district court.

In *Coffey*, the principal case relied upon by TSN, the taxpayers owned the stock of Smith Brothers Refinery Co., Inc. and were negotiating for the sale of such stock. Representatives of the purchasers and representatives of the sellers examined and discussed the various assets owned by Smith Brothers Refinery Co., Inc., and the liabilities of the company, with a view to reaching an agreement upon the fair market value of the stock. During these negotiations, the representatives of the purchasers and of the sellers could not agree upon the value of certain assets (including a contingent receivable referred to as the Cabot payment). The representatives of the purchasers informed the representatives of the sellers that the sellers could withdraw those assets from the assets of the company and that they would buy the stock without those assets being a part of the sale, thereby eliminating the necessity for arriving at a valuation of those assets in determining the value of the stock on a net worth basis. The contract of sale provided that the unwanted assets would be distributed by the corporation as a dividend prior to the sale of the stock. The selling stockholders contended before the tax court, as the Internal Revenue Service does in the case before this court, that the Cabot payment distributed to them as a dividend in kind was "part of the consideration for stock sold and that any profit resulting from its receipt by them is taxable as a capital gain." The tax court rejected that contention because it was contrary to the substance of the transaction:

> We do not agree with petitioners that they received the Cabot payment as part of the consideration for the sale of their stock. The purchasers did not agree to buy their stock and then turn over to them $190,000 and the Cabot payment in consideration therefor. From the testimony above set forth it is apparent that they were not interested in the Cabot payment, did not want it included in the assets of the corporation at the time they acquired its stock, and negotiated with petitioners to acquire stock of a corporation whose assets did not include the unwanted Cabot payment. * * * They received $190,000 for their stock. Under the contract of sale, they did not sell or part with their interest in the Cabot contract. It was expressly reserved by them and was a distribution they received as stockholders by virtue of the reservation.

Coffey, 14 T.C. at 1417, 1418. The tax court held the distribution to be a dividend.

In *Gilmore*, the purchasers of corporate stock did not wish to pay for quick assets owned by the corporation, namely cash on hand and United States bonds, and the parties provided for a presale dividend to exclude them from the assets to be transferred to the purchaser by means of the sale of the corporate stock. The tax court held that the assets distributed to the stockholders by means of a dividend were taxable as a dividend and not as a part of the sales proceeds for the corporate stock:

> It may be true the parties could have reached much the same result and have avoided some tax consequences to the stockholders by casting the transaction in the form of a higher purchase offer that would have included all of the quick assets. But this just was not done. * * * The [purchasers] chose to make this offer, one that "waived" the quick assets after payment of indebtedness. * * * The [purchasers] did not agree to pay the stockholders $6.50 or any other sum from the surplus. They "waived any claim" to the surplus and consented that it "may be paid to the present stockholders." * * *
>
> In *T.J. Coffey, Jr.*, 14 T.C. 1410, a situation similar to the one here was before the Court and we held that the corporate distributions there involved were not a part of the consideration for the sale of stock.

Gilmore, 25 T.C. at 1323, 1324.

In *Rosenbloom*, the sole stockholder of Joseph S. Finch Company was Rosenbloom Finance Corporation. Rosenbloom entered into a contract for the sale of all the capital stock of Joseph S. Finch Company to Shenley Products Company. With respect to the unwanted assets, the contract provided:

> "All other assets of every character whatsoever owned by the Finch Company at the time of the transfer of said shares of stock, as herein provided, shall be transferred to the party of the first

part (petitioner) by dividend distribution, prior to the consummation of the sale of said shares of stock herein provided for."

Rosenbloom, 24 B.T.A. at 769. The board of tax appeals held that the assets distributed to Rosenbloom Finance Corporation by Joseph S. Finch Company should be treated as an ordinary dividend and not as an amount distributed in partial liquidation.

The Internal Revenue Service states that it does not disagree with the holdings in *Coffey, Gilmore* and *Rosenbloom*, but it takes the position that they do not apply in the circumstances of this case. The Internal Revenue Service focuses on the receipt by the selling stockholders of CLIC of investment assets, followed immediately by an infusion by Union Mutual of a like amount of investment assets into CLIC, and says that the reinfusion of assets brings the case before the court within the "conduit rationale" of *Waterman*. In *Waterman*, Waterman Steamship Corporation ("Waterman") was the owner of all the outstanding capital stock of Pan–Atlantic Steamship Corporation ("Pan–Atlantic") and Gulf Florida Terminal Company, Incorporated ("Gulf Florida"). Malcolm P. McLean made an offer to Waterman to purchase all the outstanding capital stock of Pan–Atlantic and Gulf Florida for $3,500,000. Since Waterman's tax basis for the stock of the subsidiaries totaled $700,000, a sale of the capital stock of the subsidiaries for $3,500,000 would have produced a taxable gain of approximately $2,800,000. Because the treasury regulations on consolidated returns provided that the dividends received from an affiliated corporation are exempt from tax, a sale of capital stock of the subsidiaries for $700,000, after a dividend payment to Waterman by the subsidiaries of $2,800,000, would, at least in theory, have produced no taxable gain. The Board of Directors of Waterman rejected McLean's offer, but authorized Waterman's president to submit a counter proposal providing for the sale of all the capital stock in the subsidiaries for $700,000, but only after the subsidiaries paid dividends to Waterman in the aggregate amount of $2,800,000. As finally consummated, the dividends and the sale of the capital stock of the subsidiaries took the following form:

(1) Pan–Atlantic gave a promissory note to Waterman for $2,800,000 payable in 30 days as a "dividend."

(2) One hour later, Waterman agreed to sell all of the capital stock of Pan–Atlantic and Gulf Florida for $700,000.

(3) Thirty minutes later, after the closing of the sale of the capital stock of the subsidiaries had occurred, Pan–Atlantic held a special meeting of its new Board of Directors, and the Board authorized Pan–Atlantic to borrow $2,800,000 from McLean and a corporation controlled by McLean. Those funds were used by Pan–Atlantic promptly to pay off the $2,800,000 note to Waterman (which was not yet due).

In its tax return for the fiscal year involved, Waterman eliminated from income the $2,800,000 received as a dividend from Pan–Atlantic and reported $700,000 as the sales price of the capital stock of the two subsidiaries. Since Waterman's tax basis for the stock was the same as the sales price therefor, no taxable gain was realized on the sale. On audit, the Internal Revenue Service took the position that Waterman had realized a long-term capital gain of $2,800,000 on the sale of the capital stock of the subsidiaries and increased its taxable income accordingly. On appeal from a judgment by the tax court in favor of the taxpayer, the Internal Revenue Service contended that the rules applicable to situations where a regular dividend has been declared are not applicable when the parties contemplate that a purported dividend is to be inextricably tied to the purchase price and where, as was the case before the court, the amount of the dividend is not a true distribution of corporate profits. The Internal Revenue Service argued that the funds were supplied by the buyer of the stock, with the corporation acting as a mere conduit for passing the payment through to the seller. This court agreed with the Internal Revenue Service:

> The so-called dividend and sale were one transaction. The note was but one transitory step in a total, pre-arranged plan to sell the stock. We hold that in substance Pan–Atlantic neither declared nor paid a dividend to Waterman, but rather acted as a mere conduit for the payment of the purchase price to Waterman.

Waterman, 430 F.2d at 1192. The opinion of this court began with this sentence:

> This case involves another attempt by a taxpayer to ward off tax blows with paper armor.

Id. at 1185. The opinion stressed the sham, tax motivated aspects of the transaction:

> Here, McLean originally offered Waterman $3,500,000 for the stock of Pan–Atlantic and Gulf Florida. Waterman recognized that since its basis for tax purposes in the stock was $700,180, a taxable gain of approximately $2,800,000 would result from the sale. It declined the original offer and proposed to cast the sale of the stock in a two step transaction. Waterman proposed to McLean that it would sell the stock of the two subsidiaries for $700,180 after it had extracted $2,800,000 of the subsidiaries' earnings and profits. It is undisputed that Waterman intended to sell the two subsidiaries for the original offering price—with $2,800,000 of the amount disguised as a dividend which would be eliminated from income under Section 1502. Waterman also intended that none of the assets owned by the subsidiaries would be removed prior to the sale. Although the distribution was cast in the form of a dividend, the distribution was to be financed by McLean with payment being made to Waterman through Pan–Atlantic. To inject substance into the form of the transaction, Pan–Atlantic issued its note to Waterman before the closing agreement was signed. The creation of a valid indebtedness however, cannot change the true nature of the transaction. * * *

* * *

> The form of the transaction used by the parties is relatively unimportant, for the true substance and effect of their agreement was that McLean would pay $3,500,000 for all of the assets, rights and liabilities represented by the stock of Pan–Atlantic and Gulf Florida.

Id. at 1194–95. This court concluded its opinion in *Waterman* by cautioning against "giving force to 'a purported [dividend] which gives off an unmistakably hollow sound when it is tapped.' " Id. at 1196 (quoting United States v. General Geophysical Co., 296 F.2d 86, 89 (5th Cir.1961), cert. denied, 369 U.S. 849, 82 S.Ct. 932, 8 L.Ed.2d 8 (1962)). A final footnote to the opinion stated that the decision should not be interpreted as standing for the proposition that a corporation which is contemplating a sale of its subsidiary's stock could not under any circumstances distribute its subsidiaries' profits prior to the sale without having such distribution deemed part of the purchase price. Id. at 1196 n. 21.

In summary, in *Waterman*, the substance of the transaction, and the way in which it was originally negotiated, was that the purchaser would pay $3,500,000 of its money to the seller in exchange for all the stock of the two subsidiaries and none of the assets of those subsidiaries was to be removed and retained by the sellers. In the case before the court, the district court found that Union Mutual did not want and would not pay for the assets of CLIC which were distributed to TSN and the other stockholders of CLIC. Those assets were retained by the selling stockholders. The fact that bonds and cash were reinfused into CLIC after the closing, in lieu of the unwanted capital stock of small, publicly held corporations, does not convert this case from a *Coffey* situation, in which admittedly unwanted assets were distributed by the corporation to its stockholders and retained by them, into a *Waterman* situation, in which the distribution of assets was clearly a sham, designed solely to achieve a tax free distribution of assets ultimately funded by the purchaser. Indeed, the Internal Revenue Service does not argue, in the case before the court, that the transaction was in any respect a sham. Instead, the Service would have us hold that the mere infusion of assets into the acquired company after the closing, assets which are markedly different in kind from the assets that were distributed prior to the closing, should result in the disallowance of dividend treatment for the distribution of the unwanted assets, and the Service cites *Waterman* as authority for that proposition. We view the sham aspect—the hollow sound—of the transaction described in *Waterman* as one of the critical aspects of that decision, and we decline to extend the *Waterman* rule to a case which admittedly does not involve a sham and which, in other important respects, is factually different from *Waterman*.

The Internal Revenue Service also cites *Basic* as authority for the disallowance of dividend treatment for the distribution of the unwanted assets in this case. Basic Incorporated ("Basic") owned all the capital stock of Falls Industries Incorporated ("Falls"), which in turn owned all the stock of Basic Carbon Corporation ("Carbon"). Carborundum Company ("Carborundum") made an initial offer to acquire all the assets of Falls and

Carbon. This offer failed to gel when Basic demanded that Carborundum agree to indemnify Basic for any tax assessments that might become payable on the transaction in excess of those which Basic could anticipate and compute in advance, a proposal that was unacceptable to Carborundum. Carborundum then made a second proposal to acquire directly from Basic the capital stock of Falls and the capital stock of Carbon and requested that Basic transfer the ownership of the capital stock of Carbon from Falls to Basic prior to the transaction. In order to achieve that, Falls distributed the capital stock of Carbon to Basic as a dividend, which put Basic in the position of owning the capital stock of both Falls and Carbon. The sale of such capital stock to Carborundum was then consummated. In its federal income tax return for the year involved, Basic reported dividend income from Falls in the amount of $500,000 as a result of its receipt of the capital stock of Carbon. It thereupon claimed a dividends received deduction in the amount of 85% of the dividend pursuant to § 243(a)(1) of the Code. Finally, it reported a long-term capital gain of $2,300,000 from the sale to Carborundum of the shares of Falls and Carbon. On audit, the Internal Revenue Service determined that the gain from the sale of the shares of capital stock of Falls and Carbon should be increased by the amount of the purported dividend. On those facts, the court of claims held that the distribution of the capital stock of Carbon by Falls to Basic was not a true dividend but was part of the total transaction by which Basic, in substance, sold the capital stock of Falls and Carbon to Carborundum:

> Under the facts and circumstances presented here, plaintiff has not shown that there was a reason for the transfer of the Carbon stock from Falls to Basic aside from the tax consequences attributable to that move. Accordingly, for purposes of taxation, the transfer was not a dividend within the meaning of Section 316(a)(1). Instead, it should be regarded as a transfer that avoided part of the gain to be expected from the sale of the business to Carborundum, and should, therefore, be now taxed accordingly.

Basic, 549 F.2d at 749. Basic was a conduit through which an asset, the capital stock of Carbon, was passed to the buyer. The substance of the transaction was a brief removal of the "dividend" asset (the Carbon stock) on the way to the hands of the waiting buyer. In the case before the court, unlike the situation that obtained in *Basic*, the distributed assets were retained by the stockholders to whom they were distributed, rather than being immediately transferred to the purchaser.

As additional support for its position, the court in *Basic* focused on the absence of a business purpose, viewed from the standpoint of Falls, for the payment of a dividend of a valuable corporate asset, i.e., the capital stock of Carbon, by Falls to Basic. The district court, in the case before this court, applied the same test to the payment of the dividend of the unwanted assets by CLIC to TSN, the controlling stockholder of CLIC, and found that, strictly from the standpoint of CLIC, the dividend was lacking in business purpose and, indeed, could not have taken place apart from the sale and the subsequent infusion of investment assets into CLIC by Union

Mutual. However, it seems to us to be inconsistent to take the position that substance must control over form and that a transaction must be viewed as a whole, rather than in parts, and at the same time to state that the business purpose of one participant in a multi-party transaction (particularly where the participant is a corporation controlled by the taxpayer and is not itself a party to the sale transaction) is to be viewed in isolation from the over-all business purpose for the entire transaction. We agree that the transaction must be viewed as a whole and we accept the district court's finding of fact that the dividend of the unwanted assets was "part and parcel of the purchase arrangement with Union Mutual," motivated specifically by Union Mutual's unwillingness to take and pay for such assets. That being the case, we decline to focus on the business purpose of one participant in the transaction—a corporation controlled by the taxpayer—and instead find that the business purpose for the transaction as a whole, viewed from the standpoint of the taxpayer, controls. The facts found by the district court clearly demonstrate a business purpose for the presale dividend of the unwanted assets which fully explains that dividend. We note that there is no suggestion in the district court's opinion of any tax avoidance motivation on the part of the taxpayer TSN. The fact that the dividend may have had incidental tax benefit to the taxpayer, without more, does not necessitate the disallowance of dividend treatment.

Having concluded that the pre-sale distribution by CLIC to its stockholders (including TSN) of assets which Union Mutual did not want, would not pay for and did not ultimately receive is a dividend for tax purposes, and not part of the purchase price of the capital stock of CLIC, we reverse the judgment of the district court and remand for proceedings consistent with this opinion.

Reversed and remanded.

NOTE

Life is not as simple today as it was when the successful tax plan in *TSN Liquidating* was concocted. Several additional provisions of the Code now must be considered in evaluating the continuing viability of a pre-sale distribution of unwanted assets by a corporate shareholder.

As noted earlier,[1] Section 301(e) requires, solely for purposes of computing the amount of any taxable dividend income to a 20 percent or more corporate shareholder and the shareholder's basis in the stock of the distributing corporation, that the distributing corporation's earnings and profits must be determined without regard to the special adjustments in Sections 312(k) and 312(n). Section 301(e), however, will not necessarily impair the technique used in *TSN Liquidating*; it merely limits the utility of pre-acquisition dividend strips to situations where the distributing corporation has substantial earnings and profits before the required earnings and profits timing adjustments.

1. See Section F5 of this chapter, supra.

A more serious impediment is the possibility of a downward adjustment in the basis of the corporate shareholder's stock as a result of the pre-sale dividend. If TSN had been required to reduce the basis in its CLIC stock by the amount of the dividends received deduction that it was allowed on the distribution, the transaction would have lost its allure. A basis reduction would have placed TSN in the position of trading a dollar of dividend income for a dollar of gain on the subsequent sale of its CLIC stock. Since corporations do not enjoy a capital gains preference, they usually are indifferent to the distinction between ordinary income and capital gain.[2] Does current law cause TSN to suffer a basis reduction as a result of the pre-sale dividend? The answer is no unless the distribution is subject to Section 1059. That section requires a basis reduction for the amount of any "extraordinary dividend" which was not taxed to a corporate shareholder because of the dividends received deduction where the stock has not been held for more than two years before the announcement of the dividend.[3] Because of its size (roughly $1.67 million, according to the facts of the case), the dividend to TSN appears to be "extraordinary" under the tests in Section 1059(c). But TSN nonetheless could have avoided any basis reduction if it had held its CLIC stock for more than two years before the dividend was announced.

One final obstacle must be mentioned in the interests of full disclosure. If TSN and CLIC were affiliated corporations and elected to file a consolidated tax return,[4] TSN would have been required to reduce its basis in the CLIC stock as a result of the dividend. The consolidated return regulations, which treat an "affiliated group" as a single taxpaying entity, logically eliminate intracorporate dividends from the consolidated group's joint gross income.[5] The dividend is considered a mere reshuffling of profits within a single taxpayer which should not generate additional income. The regulations also provide that a parent's basis in the stock of a subsidiary is generally reduced by the full amount of any excluded intercompany dividend.[6] It follows that the strategy employed in *TSN Liquidating* has no appeal in the context of a consolidated group.

Despite these technical hurdles, a pre-sale dividend is still viable if the selling parent corporation has held the stock of a subsidiary for more than two years and the corporations do not file a consolidated return. The Tax Court's decision in Litton Industries, Inc. v. Commissioner[7] illustrates the importance of form and timing to the success of this technique. The issue in *Litton* was whether a $30 million dividend, paid to Litton by a wholly owned subsidiary in the form of a negotiable promissory note five months prior to Litton's sale of the subsidiary's stock to Nestle Corporation, was

2. Other tax attributes, however, might cause TSN to prefer one or the other type of income. For example, if TSN had unused capital losses, it might prefer capital gains on the sale to fully taxable dividend income.

3. I.R.C. § 1059(a). See Section F3 of this chapter, supra.

4. See Chapter 10D, supra.

5. Reg. § 1.1502–13(f)(2)(ii).

6. Reg. § 1.1502–32(b)(2), (3)(v).

7. 89 T.C. 1086 (1987).

truly a dividend rather than part of the proceeds received by Litton on the sale of the stock. The promissory note was later satisfied by Nestle at the same time that it purchased the stock. Dividend treatment was preferable to Litton because of the shelter provided by what was then an 85 percent dividends received deduction.

Distinguishing Waterman Steamship Corp. v. Commissioner[8] (discussed in *TSN Liquidating* at pages 541–551 of the text, supra), the Tax Court held that the payment was a dividend. Favorable (and distinguishing) factors were: (1) unlike *Waterman Steamship*, the dividend and subsequent sale in *Litton* were substantially separated in time (over five months in *Litton* was better than the few hours in *Waterman*); (2) at the time the dividend was declared, no formal action had been taken by the parent to initiate a sale to Nestle and "[t]here was no definite purchaser waiting in the wings with the terms and conditions of sale already agreed upon;"[9] and (3) as in *TSN Liquidating*, the overall transaction was not a sham because a business purpose was served by the dividend. In rejecting the Service's contention that the dividend and subsequent sale of the subsidiary should be treated as one transaction for tax purposes, the court reasoned:[10]

> The term "dividend" is defined in section 316(a) as a distribution by a corporation to its shareholders out of earnings and profits. The parties have stipulated that Stouffer had earnings and profits exceeding $30 million at the time the dividend was declared. This Court has recognized that a dividend may be paid by a note. T.R. Miller Mill Co. v. Commissioner, 37 B.T.A. 43, 49 (1938), affd. 102 F.2d 599 (5th Cir.1939). Based on these criteria, the $30 million distribution by Stouffer would clearly constitute a dividend if the sale of Stouffer had not occurred. We are not persuaded that the subsequent sale of Stouffer to Nestle changes that result merely because it was more advantageous to Litton from a tax perspective.
>
> It is well established that a taxpayer is entitled to structure his affairs and transactions in order to minimize his taxes. This proposition does not give a taxpayer carte blanche to set up a transaction in any form which will avoid tax consequences, regardless of whether the transaction has substance. Gregory v. Helvering, 293 U.S. 465 (1935). A variety of factors present here preclude a finding of sham or subterfuge. Although the record in this case clearly shows that Litton intended at the time the dividend was declared to sell Stouffer, no formal action had been taken and no announcement had been made. There was no definite purchaser waiting in the wings with the terms and conditions of sale already agreed upon. At that time, Litton had not even decided upon the form of sale of Stouffer. Nothing in the record here suggests that there was any prearranged sale agreement, formal or informal, at the time the dividend was declared.

8. 430 F.2d 1185 (5th Cir.1970).

9. 89 T.C. at 1099.

10. Id. at 1099–1100.

Petitioner further supports its argument that the transaction was not a sham by pointing out Litton's legitimate business purposes in declaring the dividend. Although the code and case law do not require a dividend to have a business purpose, it is a factor to be considered in determining whether the overall transaction was a sham. T.S.N. Liquidating Corp. v. United States, 624 F.2d 1328 (5th Cir.1980). Petitioner argues that the distribution allowed Litton to maximize the gross after-tax amount it could receive from its investment in Stouffer. From the viewpoint of a private purchaser of Stouffer, it is difficult to see how the declaration of a dividend would improve the value of the stock since creating a liability in the form of a promissory note for $30 million would reduce the value of Stouffer by approximately that amount. However, since Litton was considering disposing of all or part of Stouffer through a public or private offering, the payment of a dividend by a promissory note prior to any sale had two advantages. First, Litton hoped to avoid materially diminishing the market value of the Stouffer stock. At that time, one of the factors considered in valuing a stock, and in determining the market value of a stock was the "multiple of earnings" criterion. Payment of the dividend by issuance of a promissory note would not substantially alter Stouffer's earnings. Since many investors were relatively unsophisticated, Litton may have been quite right that it could increase its investment in Stouffer by at least some portion of the $30 million dividend. Second, by declaring a dividend and paying it by a promissory note prior to an anticipated public offering, Litton could avoid sharing the earnings with future additional shareholders while not diminishing to the full extent of the pro rata dividend, the amount received for the stock. Whether Litton could have come out ahead after Stouffer paid the promissory note is at this point merely speculation about a public offering which never occurred. The point, however, is that Litton hoped to achieve some business purpose, and not just tax benefits, in structuring the transaction as it did.

Under these facts, where the dividend was declared 6 months prior to the sale of Stouffer, where the sale was not prearranged, and since Stouffer had earnings and profits exceeding $30 million at the time the dividend was declared, we cannot conclude that the distribution was merely a device designed to give the appearance of a dividend to a part of the sales proceeds. In this case, the form and substance of the transaction coincide; it was not a transaction entered into solely for tax reasons, and it should be recognized as structured by petitioner.

PROBLEM

Strap Corporation is the sole shareholder of X, Inc. Strap and X do not file a consolidated return, and Strap has held its X stock for more than two years. Strap has a $150,000 basis in its X stock. Boot is a prospective buyer and is willing to purchase all of the X stock, but he is unable to pay the $500,000 price demanded by Strap even though he believes it to be fair. X has $100,000 cash on hand and an ample supply of earnings and profits. To solve these problems, the parties have agreed on the following plan: Strap Corporation will cause X, Inc. to distribute $100,000 to it as a dividend. Promptly thereafter, Strap will sell its X stock to Boot for $400,000. What are the tax consequences of this plan? What if Strap were an individual rather than a corporation?

CHAPTER 13

REDEMPTIONS AND PARTIAL LIQUIDATIONS

A. INTRODUCTION

Code: §§ 302; 317(b).

Shareholders generally recognize a capital gain or loss on the sale of some or all of their stock. Assume, for example, that A purchased 100 shares of X Corporation stock two years ago for $1,000. If A sells 50 of those shares to B, an unrelated outsider, for $750, he will recognize a $250 long-term capital gain. But what if A made the same sale to the corporation? Should that transaction, known as a redemption, also generate a $250 long-term capital gain? We need more facts to answer the question. If A is one of several X shareholders and owns a small percentage of the corporation's stock, a sale of stock to the corporation may be similar (for tax purposes) to a sale to B. But if X has few shareholders and ample earnings and profits and A is a major shareholder, the transaction begins to resemble a dividend.

To illustrate, assume that A's 100 shares constitute all of X Corporation's outstanding stock. In that event, A's "sale" of 50 shares to the corporation in exchange for $750 cash is indistinguishable from a nonliquidating distribution of $750. Although A has surrendered a stock certificate for 50 shares, his proportionate interest in the corporation remains unchanged. When the smoke clears, A continues to control all corporate decisions and he remains the sole shareholder, entitled to 100 percent of X's net assets upon a liquidation. Yet without altering his interest in the business, A has extracted $750 from the corporate coffers. This is the essence of a dividend! But if the "sale" to X were respected, A would be permitted to use a proportionate amount of his stock basis ($500) to offset an equivalent amount of income, and any resulting gain will be taxed at preferential capital gains rates. If A were permitted to avoid dividend characterization with such ease, proportionate redemption programs by shareholders of closely held corporations quickly would become a national sport whenever the shareholders have a substantial basis in their stock.

These simple examples identify the fundamental problem in determining the shareholder level tax consequences of a redemption. A line must be drawn between redemptions having the effect of a dividend—that is, transactions that enable shareholders to withdraw cash or other property while leaving their proportionate interest intact—and redemptions that resemble sales because they result in a meaningful reduction in the shareholder's proportionate interest. Under prior law, there was only one vague standard to resolve this question. A redemption was treated as an operating distribution and taxed as a dividend to the extent of the corporation's current and accumulated earnings and profits unless it was not "essentially equivalent to a taxable dividend."[1] Cases were resolved by looking to all the facts and circumstances, including the corporation's "business purpose" and the "net effect" of the transaction.[2]

The enactment of Section 302 introduced a commendable degree of certainty in an area where predictions had been precarious. Section 302(a) provides that a redemption will be treated as an "exchange" if it satisfies one of four statutory tests in Section 302(b). "Exchange" status means that the shareholder generally will recognize capital gain or loss to the extent of the difference between the amount of the distribution and the shareholder's basis in the redeemed stock. A redemption falling outside of Section 302(b) is treated under Section 302(d) as a "distribution to which Section 301 applies." Under the rules studied in the preceding chapter, the distribution will be a dividend to the extent of the corporation's current and accumulated earnings and profits, then a return of capital to the extent of the shareholder's basis in the redeemed stock, and finally gain from the sale or exchange of the stock to the extent of any balance.[3]

The tax stakes on a redemption have changed considerably over the years. They are influenced by several variables, such as the type of shareholder (individual or corporate), the shareholder's basis in the redeemed stock, and the applicable tax rates for dividends and capital gains. For most of our tax history, noncorporate shareholders preferred a redemption to be treated as a sale of stock resulting in recovery of the shareholder's basis and recognition of more lightly taxed capital gain. Corporate shareholders prefer dividend treatment because they can shelter most of the distribution if they qualify for the dividends received deduction or completely exclude dividends received from other members of an affiliated group of corporations that file a consolidated tax return.

The 15 percent maximum rate on qualified dividends has altered the stakes for individual shareholders. As long as the dividend and long-term capital gains rates remain the same, the major advantage to treating a redemption as an exchange is the shareholder's ability to recover the basis of the redeemed stock in determining gain or loss. In some cases, this still provides an incentive to qualify a redemption as an exchange, but not as much as when exchange treatment offered both recovery of basis and a

1. Internal Revenue Code of 1939, § 115(g).

2. See Bittker & Eustice, Federal Income Taxation of Corporations and Shareholders ¶ 9.01 (7th ed. 2000). Another line of authority treated a redemption as not "essentially equivalent to a taxable dividend" if it involved a contraction in the corporation's business activities. This test focused on events at the corporate rather than the shareholder level and gave birth to the tax concept known as a "partial liquidation." The remnants of this concept are considered in Section F of this chapter, infra.

3. For the basis consequences when a redemption is treated as a Section 301 distribution, see Section C4 of this chapter, infra.

significant capital gains rate preference (as compared to dividends) and hardly at all where a noncorporate shareholder's stock basis is nominal. In special situations, such as where a shareholder has excess capital losses that will offset capital gains but not qualified dividends, or on a deferred payment redemption where installment sale reporting under Section 453 would benefit the shareholder, exchange treatment also will be preferable.

Whether a redemption is treated as an exchange or a Section 301 distribution at the shareholder level, the tax consequences to the distributing corporation of a distribution of property in a redemption are governed by Section 311. The distributing corporation recognizes gain on a distribution of appreciated property, but it may not recognize loss on a distribution of property that has declined in value.[4]

Section 302(b) is thus the nerve center for determining the shareholder-level tax consequences of a redemption and the principal focus of this chapter. Three of the four statutory tests (Sections 302(b)(1)–(3)) examine whether there has been a sufficient reduction in the shareholder's ownership interest in the corporation to justify treating the redemption as an exchange. To obtain a more accurate measure, the shareholder's interest before and after the redemption is determined after application of the constructive ownership rules in Section 318.[5] Section 302(b)(4) shifts the focus to the corporate level and provides exchange treatment for any distribution that qualifies as a "partial liquidation" under Section 302(e) because it involves a genuine contraction of the distributing corporation's business.

Redemptions are used to accomplish a variety of corporate and shareholder planning objectives. In the case of closely held corporations, a redemption may be the vehicle for a shift of corporate control or for the buyout of a dissatisfied or deceased shareholder. Stock redemptions by publicly traded companies also have become increasingly common transactions for corporations with spare cash that they prefer to distribute rather than reinvest in the business. Keep these contexts in mind in studying the somewhat mechanical aspects of Section 302 at the beginning of this chapter. Later sections explore some of the planning opportunities provided by Section 302.

B. CONSTRUCTIVE OWNERSHIP OF STOCK

Code: §§ 302(c)(1); 318.

Regulations: § 1.318–1(a), (b), –2, –3(a), (b), –4.

Any system that purports to measure the change in a shareholder's proportionate interest in a corporation would be ineffective if it failed to

4. I.R.C. § 311(a), (b). For the details and the effect of a redemption on the distributing corporation's earnings and profits, see Section E of this Chapter, infra.

5. I.R.C. § 302(c)(1).

consider the holdings of closely related shareholders. Returning to our introductory example, assume that A and his daughter, D, each own 50 of the 100 outstanding shares of X Corporation and A sells 30 of his shares to the corporation for $450. A's actual percentage ownership drops from 50 percent (50 out of 100 shares) to 29 percent (20 out of 70 shares). Has he substantially reduced his proportionate interest? Looking only to A's *actual* ownership, the reduction is substantial, but the remaining shares are owned by a close relative. With appropriate skepticism, the drafters of the Code concluded that in determining stock ownership for purposes of the Section 302(b) tests for exchange treatment, an individual taxpayer or entity should be considered as owning stock owned by certain family members and related entities under elaborate attribution rules set forth in Section 318.[1]

Section 318 is one of several sets of constructive ownership rules in the Internal Revenue Code[2] and applies only when it is expressly made applicable by another provision of the Code.[3] Its principal role is in the redemption area, where it treats a taxpayer as "owning" stock that is actually owned by various related parties. The attribution rules in Section 318 fall into the following four categories.

1. *Family Attribution.* An individual is considered as owning stock owned by his spouse, children, grandchildren and parents. Siblings and in-laws are not part of the "family" for this purpose, and there is no attribution from a grandparent to a grandchild.[4]

2. *Entity to Beneficiary Attribution.* Stock owned by or for a partnership or estate is considered as owned by the partners or beneficiaries in proportion to their beneficial interests.[5] A person ceases to be a "beneficiary" of an estate for this purpose when she receives all property to which she is entitled (e.g., a specific bequest) and the possibility that she must return the property to satisfy claims is remote.[6] Stock owned by a trust (other than a qualified employees' trust) is considered as owned by the beneficiaries in proportion to their actuarial interests in the trust. In the case of grantor trusts, stock is considered owned by the grantor or other person who is taxable on the trust income.[7] Stock owned by a corporation is considered owned proportionately (comparing the value of the shareholder's stock to the value of all stock) by a shareholder who owns, directly or through the attribution rules, 50 percent or more in value of that corporation's stock.[8]

3. *Beneficiary to Entity Attribution.* Stock owned by partners or beneficiaries of an estate is considered as owned by the partnership or

1. I.R.C. § 302(c)(1).

2. Other constructive ownership provisions include Sections 267(c), 341(e)(8), and 544.

3. Section 318(b) contains a partial list of cross references to sections applying Section 318.

4. I.R.C. § 318(a)(1). Cf. I.R.C. § 318(a)(5)(B).

5. I.R.C. § 318(a)(2)(A).

6. Reg. § 1.318–3(a).

7. I.R.C. § 318(a)(2)(B).

8. I.R.C. § 318(a)(2)(C).

estate.[9] All stock owned by a trust beneficiary is attributed to the trust except where the beneficiary's interest is "remote" and "contingent." Grantor trusts are considered to own stock owned by the grantor or other person taxable on the income of the trust.[10] All the stock owned by a 50 percent or more shareholder of a corporation is attributed to the corporation.[11]

4. *Option Attribution.* A person holding an option to acquire stock is considered as owning that stock.[12]

These general rules are supplemented by a set of "operating rules" in Section 318(a)(5), which generally authorize chain attribution (e.g., parent to child to child's trust) except that there can be no double family attribution (e.g., no attribution from parent to child to child's spouse) or "sidewise" attribution (e.g., stock attributed to an entity from a partner, beneficiary or shareholder may not be reattributed from that entity to another partner, beneficiary or shareholder).[13] In addition, option attribution takes precedence over family attribution where both apply.[14] For Section 318 purposes, an S corporation is treated as a partnership, and S corporation shareholders are treated like partners.[15]

The problems below test your ability to apply the attribution rules in some typical factual contexts.

PROBLEMS

1. Wham Corporation has 100 shares of common stock outstanding. Twenty-five shares are owned by Grandfather, 20 shares are owned by Mother (Grandfather's Daughter), 15 shares are owned by Mother's Daughter, 10 shares are owned by Mother's adopted Son, and the remaining 30 shares are owned by Grandmother's estate, of which Mother is a 50% beneficiary. One of Mother's cousins is the other beneficiary of the estate. Mother also has an option to purchase 5 of Son's shares. How much Wham stock do Grandfather, Mother's Daughter and Grandmother's estate own after application of § 318?

2. All the 100 shares of Xerxes Corporation are owned by Partnership, in which A, B, C and D (all unrelated to each other) are equal partners. W, A's wife, owns all of the 100 shares of Yancy Corporation.

9. I.R.C. § 318(a)(3)(A).

10. I.R.C. § 318(a)(3)(B). Contingent interests are considered remote if the actuarial value of the interest is 5 percent or less of the value of the trust property, assuming the trustee exercises maximum discretion in favor of the beneficiary.

11. I.R.C. § 318(a)(3)(C).

12. I.R.C. § 318(a)(4). "Options" have been interpreted to include warrants and convertible debentures. Rev.Rul. 68–601, 1968–2 C.B. 124. Even options that are exercisable after the lapse of a fixed period of time are considered as options from the time they are granted. Rev.Rul. 89–64, 1989–1 C.B. 91.

13. I.R.C. § 318(a)(5)(A), (B), (C).

14. I.R.C. § 318(a)(5)(D).

15. I.R.C. § 318(a)(5)(E). This rule applies for purposes of attributing stock to and from the S corporation, but not for determining constructive ownership of stock in the S corporation. Id.

(a) How many shares, if any, of Xerxes Corporation are owned by A, W and M (W's mother)?

(b) How many shares, if any, of Xerxes are owned by Yancy? Would Yancy constructively own any shares of Xerxes if W owned only 10 percent of Yancy?

(c) How many shares, if any, of Yancy are owned by Partnership, B, C, D and Xerxes?

C. REDEMPTIONS TESTED AT THE SHAREHOLDER LEVEL

1. SUBSTANTIALLY DISPROPORTIONATE REDEMPTIONS

Code: § 302(b)(2).

Regulations: § 1.302–3.

The virtue of Section 302(b)(2) is its certainty. If a shareholder's reduction in voting stock as a result of a redemption satisfies three mechanical requirements, the redemption will be treated as an exchange. To qualify as "substantially disproportionate," a redemption must satisfy the following requirements:

1. Immediately after the redemption, the shareholder must own (actually and constructively) less than 50 percent of the total combined voting power of all classes of stock entitled to vote,[1]
2. The percentage of total outstanding voting stock owned by the shareholder immediately after the redemption must be less than 80 percent of the percentage of total voting stock owned by the shareholder immediately before the redemption,[2] and
3. The shareholder's percentage ownership of common stock (whether voting or nonvoting) after the redemption also must be less than 80 percent of the percentage of common stock owned before the redemption.[3] If there is more than one class of common stock, the 80 percent test is applied by reference to fair market value.[4]

1. I.R.C. § 302(b)(2)(B).

2. I.R.C. § 302(b)(2)(C). This requirement may be expressed by the following formula:

$$\frac{\text{Voting shares owned after redemption}}{\text{Total voting shares outstanding after redemption}} \text{ must be less than: } .80 \times \frac{\text{Voting shares owned before redemption}}{\text{Total voting shares outstanding before redemption}}$$

3. I.R.C. § 302(b)(2)(C).

4. The common stock cutback test is applied on an aggregate rather than a class-by-class basis. Thus, if a shareholder's aggregate reduction in all classes of common stock (measured by value) meets the percentage tests in Section 302(b)(2)(C), the redemption will be treated as an exchange even if the shareholder continues to own 100 percent of one class of outstanding common stock. Rev. Rul. 87–88, 1987–2 C.B. 81.

The attribution rules of Section 318 are applicable in measuring stock ownership for purposes of all these percentage tests.

To illustrate, assume Redeemer owns 60 percent of the common stock of a corporation which has only one class of stock outstanding. A redemption which reduces Redeemer's stock interest to a percentage below 48 percent would satisfy Section 302(b)(2). Below that level, Redeemer would own less than 50 percent of the corporation's total combined voting power, and his percentage of voting stock after the redemption (below 48 percent) would be less than 80 percent of his percentage of voting stock before the redemption (60 percent).

The regulations elaborate on the operation of Section 302(b)(2). Stock with voting rights only upon the happening of a specific event (e.g., a default in a payment of dividends on preferred stock) is not considered voting stock until the event occurs.[5] A redemption of solely nonvoting stock will never satisfy Section 302(b)(2) because there will not be a sufficient reduction in the shareholder's interest in voting stock. But if a redemption qualifies as substantially disproportionate under Section 302(b)(2), a simultaneous redemption of nonvoting preferred stock (which is not Section 306 stock)[6] will be treated as an exchange.[7] The Service also has ruled that a redemption of voting preferred stock from a shareholder owning no common stock (either directly or by way of attribution) may qualify under Section 302(b)(2), even though the shareholder can not satisfy the 80 percent test relating to common stock.[8]

The substantially disproportionate redemption safe harbor does not apply to any redemption made pursuant to a plan which has the purpose or effect of a series of redemptions that, taken together, result in a distribution that is not substantially disproportionate with respect to the /shareholder.[9] This statutory application of the step transaction doctrine is the subject of the ruling that follows.

Revenue Ruling 85–14

1985–1 Cum.Bull. 83.

ISSUE

Should qualification under section 302(b)(2) of the Internal Revenue Code of a redemption of one shareholder be measured immediately after that redemption, or after a second redemption of another shareholder that followed soon after the first redemption, under the following facts?

FACTS

X, a corporation founded by *A*, is engaged in an ongoing business. As of January 1, 1983, *X*'s sole class of stock, voting common stock, was held by

5. Reg. § 1.302–3(a).

6. See Chapter 14C, infra.

7. Reg. § 1.302–3(a).

8. Rev.Rul. 81–41, 1981–1 C.B. 121.

9. I.R.C. § 302(b)(2)(D).

A, B, C, and *D,* who are unrelated to each other. *A* owned 1,466 shares, *B* owned 210 shares, *C* owned 200 shares, and *D* owned 155 shares of *X* stock. *A* was president and *B* was vice-president of *X.*

X has a repurchase agreement with all *X* shareholders, except *A.* This agreement provides that if any such shareholder ceases to be actively connected with the business operations of *X,* such shareholder must promptly tender to *X* the then-held *X* shares for an amount equal to the book value of such stock. *X* has a reciprocal obligation to purchase such shares at book value within 6 months of such shareholder's ceasing to be actively connected with *X*'s business operations.

On January 1, 1983, *B* informed *A* of *B*'s intention to resign as of March 22, 1983. Based on this information, *A* caused *X* to adopt a plan of redemption and to redeem 902 shares of *A*'s *X* stock, on March 15, 1983, for which *A* received 700*x* dollars. Thus, *A* then held 564 shares of the 1129 shares (49.96 percent) of the *X* stock still outstanding, temporarily yielding majority control over the affairs of *X* until *B* ceased to be a shareholder. On March 22, 1983, *B* resigned from *X* and, in accordance with the *X* stock purchase agreement, *X* redeemed for cash all of *B*'s shares within the next 6 months, thus leaving 919 shares of *X* stock outstanding, restoring majority control to *A.*

LAW AND ANALYSIS

Section 302(a) of the Code provides that if a corporation redeems its stock and if one of the paragraphs of subsection (b) applies, then such redemption will be treated as a distribution in part or full payment in exchange for the stock.

Section 302(b)(2) of the Code provides that a redemption will be treated as an exchange pursuant to section 302(a) if the redemption is substantially disproportionate with respect to the shareholder, but that this paragraph will not apply unless immediately after the redemption the shareholder owns less than 50 percent of the total combined voting power of all classes of stock entitled to vote.

Under section 302(b)(2)(C) of the Code, one of the requirements for the distribution to be substantially disproportionate is that the ratio that the voting stock of the corporation owned by the shareholder immediately after the redemption bears to all the voting stock of the corporation at such time, is less than 80 percent of the ratio that the voting stock of the corporation owned by the shareholder immediately before the redemption bears to all the voting stock of the corporation at such time.

Section 302(b)(2)(D) of the Code, in dealing with a series of redemptions, provides that section 302(b)(2) is not applicable to any redemption made pursuant to a plan the purpose or effect of which is a series of redemptions resulting in a distribution which (in the aggregate) is not substantially disproportionate with respect to the shareholder.

The percentage provisions contained in sections 302(b)(2)(B) and 302(b)(2)(C) of the Code provide "safe harbor" exchange treatment. Examined separately, the transaction that occurred on March 15, 1983, would qualify as a substantially disproportionate redemption because (i) *A*'s ownership of *X*'s voting stock immediately after the redemption was less than 50 percent of the total combined voting power of all the *X* stock and (ii) *A*'s ownership of *X*'s voting stock was reduced from 72.18 percent to 49.96 percent, which meets the 80 percent requirement of section 302(b)(2)(C). However, if *A*'s redemption is considered to be part of a section 302(b)(2)(D) series of redemptions which included *X*'s redemption of *B*'s shares, then *A*'s redemption would not constitute a substantially disproportionate redemption because (i) *A*'s ownership of *X*'s voting stock after the redemptions exceeded 50 percent of the total combined voting power of *X* and (ii) *A*'s ownership of *X*'s voting stock after the redemptions was reduced from 72.18 percent to 61.37 percent, which does not meet the 80 percent requirement of section 302(b)(2)(C).

Section 1.302–3(a) of the Income Tax Regulations states that whether or not a plan described in section 302(b)(2)(D) of the Code exists will be determined from all the facts and circumstances.

In the present situation, although *A* and *B* had no joint plan, arrangement, or agreement for a series of redemptions, the redemption of *A*'s shares was causally related to the redemption of *B*'s shares in that *A* saw an apparent opportunity to secure exchange treatment under section 302(b)(2) of the Code by temporarily yielding majority control over the affairs of *X*.

Nothing in section 302(b)(2)(D) of the Code or in the legislative history of this section * * * indicates that the existence of a plan depends upon an agreement between two or more shareholders. Thus, a "plan" for purposes of section 302(b)(2)(D) need be nothing more than a design by a single redeemed shareholder to arrange a redemption as part of a sequence of events that ultimately restores to such shareholder the control that was apparently reduced in the redemption.

Under the facts and circumstances here, section 302(b)(2)(D) of the Code requires that the redemptions of *A* and *B* be considered in the aggregate. Accordingly, *A*'s redemption meets neither the 50 percent limitation of section 302(b)(2)(B) nor the 80 percent test of section 302(b)(2)(C). Thus, the redemption of *A*'s shares was not substantially disproportionate within the meaning of section 302(b)(2).

HOLDING

Under the facts of this ruling, qualification under section 302(b)(2) of the Code of *A*'s redemption should not be measured immediately after that redemption, but, instead, should be measured after *B*'s redemption that followed soon after *A*'s redemption.

2. Complete Termination of a Shareholder's Interest

a. WAIVER OF FAMILY ATTRIBUTION

Code: § 302(b)(3), (c).

Regulations: § 1.302–4.

The theory of the substantially disproportionate safe harbor is that exchange rather than dividend treatment is appropriate when a distribution in redemption causes a significant reduction in the shareholder's interest in the corporation's voting stock. This policy applies with even greater force in the case of a complete termination of a shareholder's interest, which qualifies for exchange treatment under Section 302(b)(3). For shareholders of a closely held family corporation, however, the attribution rules present a substantial roadblock to a complete termination. Even if all of the stock of a retiring shareholder is redeemed, she will continue to be treated as a 100 percent owner if her children or other related parties hold the remaining shares.

To provide relief where the redeemed shareholder is willing to cut the corporate cord, Section 302(c)(2) eases the path toward a complete termination by waiving the family attribution rules if certain conditions are met. This attribution amnesty is a useful planning tool for shareholders of family corporations, permitting a shareholder to achieve a complete termination even though the remaining shares are held by close relatives. The waiver applies, however, only to *family* attribution; the entity and option attribution rules remain fully applicable.

Waiver of the family attribution rules is available only if immediately after the distribution the redeemed shareholder retains no "interest" in the corporation (other than as a creditor). The ban extends to interests as an officer, director or employee. Section 302(c)(2)(A) also includes a "ten year look forward" rule, under which the shareholder may not retain or acquire (other than by bequest or inheritance) any of the forbidden interests in the corporation "other than an interest as a creditor."[1] To prevent anticipatory bailouts, Section 302(c)(2)(B) provides a "ten year look back" rule, under which the family attribution rules may not be waived if during the ten years preceding the redemption either: (1) the redeemed shareholder acquired any of the redeemed stock from a "Section 318" relative or (2) any such close relative acquired stock from the redeemed shareholder. Neither of these exceptions applies, however, if "tax avoidance" was not one of the principal purposes of the otherwise tainted transfer.[2]

The materials that follow illustrate how the Service and the courts have interpreted these intricate requirements.

1. This rule is enforced by requiring the redeemed shareholder to file a form in which the shareholder agrees to notify the Service of any acquisition of a forbidden interest within ten years from the redemption and to retain such records as may be necessary to permit enforcement of this rule by the Service. The normal three year statute of limitations is extended to one year after the shareholder gives notice of acquisition of a forbidden interest in order to permit the Service to make a retroactive assessment of a deficiency. I.R.C. § 302(c)(2)(A).

2. See generally Kuntz, "Stock Redemptions Following Stock Transfers—An Expanding 'Safe Harbor,' Under Section 302(c)(2)(B)," 58 Taxes 29 (1980).

Lynch v. Commissioner

United States Court of Appeals, Ninth Circuit, 1986.
801 F.2d 1176.

■ CYNTHIA HOLCOMB HALL, CIRCUIT JUDGE:

The Commissioner of the Internal Revenue Service (Commissioner) petitions for review of a Tax Court decision holding that a corporate redemption of a taxpayer's stock was a sale or exchange subject to capital gains treatment. The Commissioner argues that the taxpayer held a prohibited interest in the corporation after the redemption and therefore the transaction should be characterized as a dividend distribution taxable as ordinary income. We agree with the Commissioner and reverse the Tax Court.

I

Taxpayers, William and Mima Lynch, formed the W.M. Lynch Co. on April 1, 1960. The corporation issued all of its outstanding stock to William Lynch (taxpayer). The taxpayer specialized in leasing cast-in-place concrete pipe machines. He owned the machines individually but leased them to the corporation which in turn subleased the equipment to independent contractors.

On December 17, 1975 the taxpayer sold 50 shares of the corporation's stock to his son, Gilbert Lynch (Gilbert), for $17,170. Gilbert paid for the stock with a $16,000 check given to him by the taxpayer and $1,170 from his own savings. The taxpayer and his wife also resigned as directors and officers of the corporation on the same day.

On December 31, 1975 the corporation redeemed all 2300 shares of the taxpayer's stock. In exchange for his stock, the taxpayer received $17,900 of property and a promissory note for $771,920. Gilbert, as the sole remaining shareholder, pledged his 50 shares as a guarantee for the note. In the event that the corporation defaulted on any of the note payments, the taxpayer would have the right to vote or sell Gilbert's 50 shares.

In the years immediately preceding the redemption, Gilbert had assumed greater managerial responsibility in the corporation. He wished, however, to retain the taxpayer's technical expertise with cast-in-place concrete pipe machines. On the date of the redemption, the taxpayer also entered into a consulting agreement with the corporation. The consulting agreement provided the taxpayer with payments of $500 per month for five years, plus reimbursement for business related travel, entertainment, and automobile expenses.[2] In February 1977, the corporation and the taxpayer mutually agreed to reduce the monthly payments to $250. The corporation never withheld payroll taxes from payments made to the taxpayer.

2. The corporation leased or purchased a pickup truck for the taxpayer's use in 1977. If someone at the corporation needed the truck, the taxpayer would make it available to him.

After the redemption, the taxpayer shared his former office with Gilbert. The taxpayer came to the office daily for approximately one year; thereafter his appearances dwindled to about once or twice per week. When the corporation moved to a new building in 1979, the taxpayer received a private office.

In addition to the consulting agreement, the taxpayer had other ties to the corporation. He remained covered by the corporation's group medical insurance policy until 1980. When his coverage ended, the taxpayer had received the benefit of $4,487.54 in premiums paid by the corporation. He was also covered by a medical reimbursement plan, created the day of the redemption, which provided a maximum annual payment of $1,000 per member. Payments to the taxpayer under the plan totaled $96.05.

II

We must decide whether the redemption of the taxpayer's stock in this case is taxable as a dividend distribution under 26 U.S.C. § 301 or as long-term capital gain under 26 U.S.C. § 302(a). Section 302(a) provides that a corporate distribution of property in redemption of a shareholder's stock is treated as a sale or exchange of such stock if the redemption falls within one of four categories described in section 302(b). If the redemption falls outside of these categories, then it is treated as a dividend distribution under section 301 to the extent of the corporation's earnings and profits.[4]

Section 302(b)(3) provides that a shareholder is entitled to sale or exchange treatment if the corporation redeems all of the shareholder's stock. In order to determine whether there is a complete redemption for purposes of section 302(b)(3), the family attribution rules of section 318(a) must be applied unless the requirements of section 302(c)(2) are satisfied. Here, if the family attribution rules apply, the taxpayer will be deemed to own constructively the 50 shares held by Gilbert (100% of the corporation's stock) and the transaction would not qualify as a complete redemption within the meaning of section 302(b)(3).

Section 302(c)(2)(A) states in relevant part:

> In the case of a distribution described in subsection (b)(3), [the family attribution rules in] section 318(a)(1) shall not apply if—
>
> (i) immediately after the distribution the distributee has no interest in the corporation (including an interest as officer, director, or employee), other than an interest as a creditor * * *.

The Commissioner argues that in every case the performance of post-redemption services is a prohibited interest under section 302(c)(2)(A)(i), regardless of whether the taxpayer is an officer, director, employee, or independent contractor.

4. On the date of the redemption, W.M. Lynch Co. had accumulated earnings and profits of $315,863, and had never paid a dividend.

The Tax Court rejected the Commissioner's argument, finding that the services rendered by the taxpayer did not amount to a prohibited interest in the corporation. In reaching this conclusion, the Tax Court relied on a test derived from Lewis v. Commissioner, 47 T.C. 129, 136 (1966) (Simpson, J., concurring):

> Immediately after the enactment of the 1954 Code, it was recognized that section 302(c)(2)(A)(i) did not prohibit office holding per se, but was concerned with a retained financial stake in the corporation, such as a profit-sharing plan, or in the creation of an ostensible sale that really changed nothing so far as corporate management was concerned. Thus, in determining whether a prohibited interest has been retained under section 302(c)(2)(A)(i), we must look to whether the former stockholder has either retained a financial stake in the corporation or continued to control the corporation and benefit by its operations. In particular, where the interest retained is not that of an officer, director, or employee, we must examine the facts and circumstances to determine whether a prohibited interest has been retained under section 302(c)(2)(A)(i).

Lynch v. Commissioner, 83 T.C. 597, 605 (1984) (citations omitted).

After citing the "control or financial stake" standard, the Tax Court engaged in a two-step analysis. First, the court concluded that the taxpayer was an independent contractor rather than an employee because the corporation had no right under the consulting agreement to control his actions.[5] Id. at 606. Second, the court undertook a "facts and circumstances" analysis to determine whether the taxpayer had a financial stake in the corporation or managerial control after the redemption. Because the consulting agreement was not linked to the future profitability of the corporation, the court found that the taxpayer had no financial stake. *Id.* at 606–07. The court also found no evidence that the taxpayer exerted control over the corporation. Id. at 607. Thus, the Tax Court determined that the taxpayer held no interest prohibited by section 302(c)(2)(A)(i).

III

We review the decisions of the Tax Court on the same basis as decisions in civil bench trials in district courts, * * * The Tax Court's interpretation of what constitutes a prohibited interest under section 302(c)(2)(A)(i) is a question of law reviewed de novo.

We reject the Tax Court's interpretation of section 302(c)(2)(A)(i). An individualized determination of whether a taxpayer has retained a financial stake or continued to control the corporation after the redemption is inconsistent with Congress' desire to bring a measure of certainty to the

5. Finding that the taxpayer was not an employee obviated the need to decide whether the parenthetical language in section 302(c)(2)(A)(i) prohibited employment relationships per se. See Seda v. Commissioner, 82 T.C. 484, 488 (1984) (court stated that "section 302(c)(2)(A)(i) may not prohibit the retention of all employment relationships").

tax consequences of a corporate redemption. We hold that a taxpayer who provides post-redemption services, either as an employee or an independent contractor, holds a prohibited interest in the corporation because he is not a creditor.

The legislative history of section 302 states that Congress intended to provide "definite standards in order to provide certainty in specific instances." S.Rep. No. 1622, 83d Cong., 2d Sess. 233, reprinted in 1954 U.S.Code Cong. & Ad.News 4017, 4621, 4870. "In lieu of a factual inquiry in every case, [section 302] is intended to prescribe specific conditions from which the taxpayer may ascertain whether a given redemption" will qualify as a sale or be treated as a dividend distribution. H.R.Rep.No. 1337, 83d Cong.2d Sess. 35, reprinted in 1954 U.S.Cong. & Ad.News 4017, 4210. The facts and circumstances approach created by the Tax Court undermines the ability of taxpayers to execute a redemption and know the tax consequences with certainty.

The taxpayer's claim that the Senate rejected the mechanical operation of the House's version of section 302 is misleading. The Senate did reject the House bill because the "definitive conditions" were "unnecessarily restrictive." S.Rep.No.1622, 83d Cong., 2d Sess. 44, reprinted in 1954 U.S.Code Cong. & Ad.News 4621, 4675. However, the Senate's response was to add paragraph (b)(1) to section 302, which reestablished the flexible, but notoriously vague, "not essentially equivalent to a dividend" test. This test provided that all payments from a corporation that were not essentially equivalent to a dividend should be taxed as capital gains. The confusion that stemmed from a case-by-case inquiry into "dividend equivalence" prompted the Congress to enact definite standards for the safe harbors in section 302(b)(2) and (b)(3). The Tax Court's refusal to recognize that section 302(c)(2)(A)(i) prohibits *all* noncreditor interests in the corporation creates the same uncertainty as the "dividend equivalence" test.

The problem with the Tax Court's approach is apparent when this case is compared with Seda v. Commissioner, 82 T.C. 484 (1984). In *Seda*, a former shareholder, at his son's insistence, continued working for the corporation for two years after the redemption. He received a salary of $1,000 per month. The Tax Court refused to hold that section 302(c)(2)(A)(i) prohibits the retention of employment relations per se, despite the unequivocal language in the statute.[6] Id. at 488. Instead, the court applied the facts and circumstances approach to determine whether the former shareholder retained a financial stake or continued to control the corporation. The Tax Court found that the monthly payments of $1,000 constituted a financial stake in the corporation. Id. This result is at odds with the holding in *Lynch* that payments of $500 per month do *not* constitute a financial stake in the corporation. Compare Lynch, 83 T.C. at 606–07 with Seda, 82 T.C. at 488. The court also found in *Seda* no evidence that the former shareholder had ceased to manage the corporation. 82 T.C.

6. Eight of the seventeen Tax Court judges who reviewed *Seda* concurred in the result but would have classified all officer, director, or employee relationships as prohibited interests under section 302(c)(2)(A)(i).

at 488. Again, this finding is contrary to the holding in *Lynch* that the taxpayer exercised no control over the corporation after the redemption, even though he worked daily for a year and shared his old office with his son. Compare Lynch, 83 T.C. at 607 with Seda, 82 T.C. at 488. *Seda* and *Lynch* thus vividly demonstrate the perils of making an ad hoc determination of "control" or "financial stake."

A recent Tax Court opinion further illustrates the imprecision of the facts and circumstances approach. In Cerone v. Commissioner, 87 T.C. 1 (1986), a father and son owned all the shares of a corporation formed to operate their restaurant. The corporation agreed to redeem all of the father's shares in order to resolve certain disagreements between the father and son concerning the management of the business. However, the father remained an employee of the corporation for at least five years after the redemption, drawing a salary of $14,400 for the first three years and less thereafter. The father claimed that he was entitled to capital gains treatment on the redemption because he had terminated his interest in the corporation within the meaning of section 302(b)(3).

Even on the facts of *Cerone*, the Tax Court refused to find that the father held a prohibited employment interest per se. * * * Instead, the Tax Court engaged in a lengthy analysis, citing both *Seda* and *Lynch*. The court proclaimed that *Lynch* reaffirmed the rationale of *Seda*, even though *Lynch* involved an independent contractor rather than an employee. After comparing the facts of *Seda* and *Cerone*, the Tax Court eventually concluded that the father in *Cerone* held a financial stake in the corporation because he had drawn a salary that was $2,400 per year more than the taxpayer in *Seda* and had been employed by the corporation for a longer period after the redemption. *Cerone*, slip op. at 53. However, the Tax Court was still concerned that prohibited interest in *Seda* might have been based on the finding in that case that the taxpayer had both a financial stake *and* continued control of the corporation. The Tax Court, citing *Lynch*, held that the "test is whether he retained a financial stake *or* continued to control the corporation." * * * Thus, the Tax Court found that the father in *Cerone* held a prohibited interest because he had a financial stake as defined by *Seda*.

Although the Tax Court reached the correct result in *Cerone*, its approach undermines the definite contours of the safe harbor Congress intended to create with sections 302(b)(3) and 302(c)(2)(A)(i). Whether a taxpayer has a financial stake according to the Tax Court seems to depend on two factors, length of employment and the amount of salary. Length of employment after the redemption is irrelevant because Congress wanted taxpayers to know whether they were entitled to capital gains treatment on the date their shares were redeemed. * * * As for the amount of annual salary, the Tax Court's present benchmark appears to be the $12,000 figure in *Seda*. Salary at or above this level will be deemed to be a financial stake in the enterprise, though the $6,000 annual payments in this case were held not to be a financial stake. There is no support in the legislative history of section 302 for the idea that Congress meant only to prohibit service contracts of a certain worth, and taxpayers should not be left to speculate as to what income level will give rise to a financial stake.

In this case, the taxpayer points to the fact that the taxpayers in *Seda* and *Cerone* were employees, while he was an independent contractor. On appeal, the Commissioner concedes the taxpayer's independent contractor status. We fail to see, however, any meaningful way to distinguish *Seda* and *Cerone* from *Lynch* by differentiating between employees and independent contractors. All of the taxpayers performed services for their corporations following the redemption. To hold that only the employee taxpayers held a prohibited interest would elevate form over substance. The parenthetical language in section 302(c)(2)(A)(i) merely provides a subset of prohibited interests from the universe of such interests, and in no way limits us from finding that an independent contractor retains a prohibited interest. Furthermore, the Tax Court has in effect come to ignore the parenthetical language. If employment relationships are not prohibited interests per se, then the taxpayer's status as an employee or independent contractor is irrelevant. What really matters under the Tax Court's approach is how the taxpayer fares under a facts and circumstances review of whether he has a financial stake in the corporation or managerial control.[7] Tax planners are left to guess where along the continuum of monthly payments from $500 to $1000 capital gains treatment ends and ordinary income tax begins.

Our holding today that taxpayers who provide post-redemption services have a prohibited interest under section 302(c)(2)(A)(i) is inconsistent with the Tax Court's decision in Estate of Lennard v. Commissioner, 61 T.C. 554 (1974). That case held that a former shareholder who, as an independent contractor, provided post-redemption accounting services for a corporation did not have a prohibited interest. The Tax Court found that "Congress did not intend to include independent contractors possessing no financial stake in the corporation among those who are considered as retaining an interest in the corporation for purposes of the attribution waiver rules." Id. at 561. We disagree. In the context of *Lennard*, the Tax Court appears to be using financial stake in the sense of having an equity interest or some other claim linked to the future profit of the corporation. Yet, in cases such as *Seda* and *Cerone*, the Tax Court has found that fixed salaries of $12,000 and $14,400, respectively, constitute a financial stake. Fees for accounting

7. The Tax Court's focus on managerial control or a financial stake originated with Judge Simpson's concurrence in *Lewis*, 47 T.C. at 136–38. His interpretation of section 302(c)(2)(A) is supported by Bittker, Stock Redemptions and Partial Liquidations Under the Internal Revenue Code of 1954, 9 Stan. L.Rev. 13, 33 n. 72 (1956). Professor Bittker argues that Congress' goal was to ensure that taxpayers who transferred only ostensible control or maintained a financial stake in the corporation did not receive the benefit of capital gains treatment. He is no doubt correct. However, the means selected by Congress to achieve this goal do not allow for an individualized determination of control and financial stakes. Instead, section 302(c)(2)(A)(i) operates mechanically: the taxpayer must sever all but a creditor's interest to avoid the family attribution rules and thereby receive capital gains treatment. Nowhere in the legislative history of section 302(c) does Congress intimate that courts may use a flexible facts and circumstances test to determine the existence of managerial control or a financial stake.

services could easily exceed these amounts, and it would be irrational to argue that the definition of financial stake varies depending on whether the taxpayer is an employee or an independent contractor. In order to avoid these inconsistencies, we conclude that those who provide post-redemption services, whether as independent contractors or employees, hold an interest prohibited by section 302(c)(2)(A)(i) because they are more than merely creditors.

In addition, both the Tax Court and the Commissioner have agreed that taxpayers who enter into management consulting contracts after the redemption possess prohibited interests. Chertkof v. Commissioner, 72 T.C. 1113, 1124–25 (1979), *aff'd*, 649 F.2d 264 (4th Cir.1981); Rev.Ruling 70–104, 1970–1 C.B. 66 (1970). Taxpayers who provide such services are, of course, independent contractors. However, unlike the Commissioner's opinion in Rev. Ruling 70–104 that all management consulting agreements are prohibited interests, the Tax Court applies the financial stake or managerial control test. In *Chertkof*, the court found that because the services provided under the contract "went to the essence" of the corporation's existence, the taxpayer had not effectively ceded control. 72 T.C. at 1124. Here, the Tax Court distinguished *Chertkof* on the ground that the taxpayer did not retain control of the corporation, but instead provided only limited consulting services. *Lynch*, 83 T.C. at 608. We believe that any attempt to define prohibited interests based on the level of control leads to the same difficulties inherent in making a case-by-case determination of what constitutes a financial stake.[8]

IV

Our decision today comports with the plain language of section 302 and its legislative history. See Gardner & Randall, Distributions in Redemption of Stock: Changing Definitions for a Termination of Interest, 8 J. Corp. Tax'n 240, 247–48 (1981); Marusic, The Prohibited Interest of I.R.C. Section 302(c)(2)(A)(i) After Seda and Lynch, 65 Neb.L.Rev. 486, 502, 518–19 (1986); Rose, The Prohibited Interest of Section 302(c)(2)(A), 36 Tax L.Rev. 131, 145–49 (1981). Taxpayers who wish to receive capital gains treatment upon the redemption of their shares must completely sever all noncreditor interests in the corporation.[9] We hold that the taxpayer, as an

8. Determining the existence of control is particularly difficult in the context of a family-held corporation. The exercise of control often will not be obvious because a parent may influence a child, and hence corporate decisionmaking, in myriad ways. Our rule that the provision of services is a prohibited interest eliminates the need to make a speculative inquiry into whether the parent still controls the corporation after the redemption. Of course, no rule could or should prohibit post-redemption parent-child communication concerning the management of the corporation.

9. Our definition of a prohibited interest still leaves an open question as to the permissible scope of a creditor's interest under section 302(c)(2)(A)(i). See, e.g., Treas. Reg. § 1.302–4(d) (a creditor's claim must not be subordinate to the claims of general creditors or in any other sense proprietary, i.e., principal payments or interest rates must not be contingent on the earnings of the corporation).

The taxpayer argues that some creditor relationships might result in an "opportunity to influence" as great or greater than any

independent contractor, held such a noncreditor interest, and so cannot find shelter in the safe harbor of section 302(c)(2)(A)(i). Accordingly, the family attribution rules of section 318 apply and the taxpayer fails to qualify for a complete redemption under section 302(b)(3). The payments from the corporation in redemption of the taxpayer's shares must be characterized as a dividend distribution taxable as ordinary income under section 301.

Reversed.

Revenue Ruling 59–119

1959–1 Cum.Bull. 68.

A stock redemption agreement between the corporation and the instant shareholder provides that a total of 350*x* dollars will be paid to such shareholder for all his stock interest in the corporation, 100*x* dollars to be paid on the closing date and 250*x* dollars to be paid by the corporation within eight years, payable in quarter-annual installments. The corporation executed an installment judgment note to the shareholder and the judgment note and shares of stock of the corporation to be redeemed are retained by an escrow holder as security for installment payments due. In the event the installment and interest payments are in default, then pursuant to the agreement the escrow holder, upon notice from the taxpayer, may sell the stock of the corporation held by him at public or private sale to satisfy such obligations, however, in no event will the taxpayer become the purchaser of said stock at such sale.

The stock redemption agreement also states that so long as the corporation owes funds to such shareholder it will not, without first receiving the written consent of the shareholder, declare dividends; pay salaries in excess of a certain amount to officers; sell its assets except in the ordinary course of business; or engage in a reorganization, recapitalization, merger, consolidation or liquidation.

Because of the substantial sums due the shareholder, because he plans to reside permanently in another state and will be far removed from the base of operations of the corporation, and pursuant to the advice of persons skilled in creditor protection matters, he considers it advisable to have a member of the law firm representing him serve on the board of directors of the corporation. Therefore, the instant shareholder and the remaining shareholders, all related, entered into a second agreement whereby a nominee of his law firm will serve on the board of directors as long as the corporation is indebted to the shareholder. Such nominee will be paid *x* dollars by the corporation for each meeting he attends and such additional sums as determined in the sole discretion of the instant shareholder for

officer, director, or employee relationship. He cites Rev.Ruling 77–467, 1977–2 C.B. 92 which concluded that a taxpayer who leased real property to a corporation, after the corporation redeemed his shares, held a creditor's interest under section 302(c)(2)(A)(i). While the taxpayer here may be correct in his assessment of a creditor's "opportunity to influence" a corporation, he overlooks the fact that Congress specifically allowed the right to retain such an interest.

other services which may be reasonably necessary to determine that his interests as a creditor are being protected in accordance with the agreements.

The sole purpose of this arrangement is to protect the shareholder as a creditor by determining that the aforementioned conditions are being met rather than running the risk of having to engage in extended litigation at some future date if it is then determined that the conditions of the stock redemption agreement were violated.

* * *

According to the agreement in question, the remaining shareholders and the instant shareholder will appoint, indirectly through the law firm representing such shareholder, a member of that law firm to serve on the board of directors of the corporation. Such a nominee director will be acting solely on the taxpayer's behalf and, therefore, will in effect be his agent. The fact that the nominee director will receive remuneration for his service from someone other than the taxpayer does not make him any less the taxpayer's agent, for the source of remuneration to an agent is only one factor to be considered in determining whether an agency exists between two parties. Such an appointment of an agent to the board of directors is contrary to the condition prescribed in section 302(c)(2) of the Code. For the purposes of section 302(c)(2), it is immaterial whether an interest in the corporation is asserted directly or through an agent.

The fact that the director is a "limited" director in that his only duty will be to determine whether the conditions set forth in the stock redemption agreement are being observed is not material, for section 302(c)(2) of the Code does not make any exception for such directors. Furthermore, that section of the Code does not make an exception for a director whose power is limited because he is a minority member of a board.

In view of the foregoing, it is held that the agreement between the instant shareholder and the remaining shareholders of the corporation, under which a nominee is appointed to serve on the board of directors of the corporation, violates the condition prescribed in section 302(c)(2)(A)(i) of the Code. Accordingly, in the event of such an agreement, the redemption of the taxpayer's stock of the corporation shall be treated as a distribution of property to which section 301 of the Code applies.

However, if the taxpayer-shareholder designates a representative of his law firm to attend the board of director's meetings of the corporation solely for the purposes of determining whether the provisions of the agreement described above have been complied with, and not in the capacity of a director, officer or employee, or advisor, such action will not adversely affect section 302(c)(2) of the Code.

Revenue Ruling 77–293

1977–2 Cum.Bull. 91.

Corporation *X* had 120 shares of common stock outstanding, all of which were owned by *A*, its president. *A*'s son, *B*, had been employed by *X* for many years as its vice-president and general assistant to the president. Realizing that the future successful operation of *X* required a thorough knowledge of its operation, products lines, and customer needs, *A* had trained and supervised *B* in all phases of the business so that upon *A*'s retirement *B* would be able to assume responsibility for managing the business.

As part of *A*'s plan to retire from the business and to give ownership of the business to *B*, *A* gave 60 shares of *X* stock to *B* as a gift, and not as consideration for past, present, or future services. Shortly thereafter, *A* resigned and *B* assumed the position of chairman of the board and president of *X*. *X* redeemed the remaining 60 shares of stock owned by *A* in exchange for property. Immediately after the redemption, *A* was not an officer, director, or employee of *X* and no longer had any interest in *X*. *A*'s gift of stock to *B* was for the purpose of giving *B* complete ownership and control of *X*. The earnings and profits of *X* exceeded the amount of the distribution in redemption of the *X* stock.

* * *

In the instant case, neither section 302(b)(1) of the Code nor section 302(b)(2) applies since *A*, through the constructive ownership rules of section 318(a), owned 100 percent of the stock of *X* both before and after the redemption. Therefore, there was no meaningful reduction under section 302(b)(1) or a substantially disproportionate reduction under section 302(b)(2) of *A*'s stock ownership.

Section 302(c)(2)(A) of the Code provides that for purposes of section 302(b)(3), 318(a)(1) will not apply if (i) immediately after the distribution the distributee has no interest in the corporation (including an interest as an officer, director, or employee), other than an interest as a creditor, (ii) the distributee does not acquire any such interest (other than stock acquired by bequest or inheritance) within ten years from the date of such distribution, and (iii) the distributee files an agreement to notify the district director of any acquisition of any such interest in the corporation. However, pursuant to section 302(c)(2)(B)(ii), the provisions of section 302(c)(2)(A) are not applicable if any person owns (at the time of the distribution) stock the ownership of which is attributable to the distributee under section 318(a) and such person acquired any stock in the corporation, directly or indirectly, from the distributee within the ten-year period ending on the date of the distribution, unless such stock so acquired from the distributee is redeemed in the same transaction. However, section 302(c)(2)(B)(ii) will not apply if the disposition by the distributee did not have as one of its principal purposes the avoidance of Federal income tax.

The structure and legislative history of section 302 of the Code make it clear that the purpose of section 302(c)(2)(B) is not to prevent the reduction of capital gains through gifts of appreciated stock prior to the redemption of the remaining stock of the transferor, but to prevent the withdrawal of earnings at capital gains rates by a shareholder of a family controlled corporation who seeks continued control and/or economic interest in the corporation through the stock given to a related person or the stock he retains. Application of this provision thus prevents a taxpayer from bailing out earnings by transferring part of the taxpayer's stock to such a related person and then qualifying the redemption of either the taxpayer's stock or the transferee's stock as a complete termination of interest by virtue of the division of ownership thus created and the availability of the attribution waiver provisions.

Tax avoidance within the meaning of section 302(c)(2)(B) of the Code would occur, for example, if a taxpayer transfers stock of a corporation to a spouse in contemplation of the redemption of the remaining stock of the corporation and terminates all direct interest in the corporation in compliance with section 302(c)(2)(A), but with the intention of retaining effective control of the corporation indirectly through the stock held by the spouse. Another example, which would generally constitute tax avoidance within the meaning of this provision, is the transfer by a taxpayer of part of the stock of a corporation to a spouse in contemplation of the subsequent redemption of the transferred stock from the spouse. * * *

Whether one of the principal purposes of an acquisition or disposition of stock is tax avoidance within the meaning of section 302(c)(2)(B) of the Code can be determined only by an analysis of all of the facts and circumstances of a particular situation. Here, the gift of *X* stock by *A* was to *B* who is active and knowledgeable in the affairs of the business of *X* and who intends to control and manage the corporation in the future. The gift of stock was intended solely for the purpose of enabling *A* to retire while leaving the business to *B*. Therefore, the avoidance of Federal income tax will not be deemed to have been one of the principal purposes of the gift of stock from *A* to *B*, notwithstanding the reduction of the capital gains tax payable by *A* as a result of the gift of appreciated stock prior to the redemption.

Accordingly, if *A* files the agreement specified in section 302(c)(2)(A)(iii) of the Code, the redemption by *X* of its stock from *A* qualifies as a termination of interest under section 302(b)(3).

Rev.Rul. 57–387, 1957–2 C.B. 225, is modified to the extent that it contains implications to the contrary concerning the reduction of the capital gains tax.

NOTE

Ten–Year–Look–Forward Rule. The prohibition on retaining or acquiring any post-redemption "interest" (other than as a creditor or by bequest or inheritance) in the corporation is one of the major hurdles to utilizing Section 302(c)(2).[1] Until the Ninth Circuit's decision in *Lynch*, the courts generally rejected the Service's strict view that *any* performances of ser-

1. See generally Rose, "The Prohibited Interest of Section 302(c)(2)(A)," 36 Tax L.Rev. 131 (1981).

vices, with or without compensation, constitutes a forbidden corporate interest.[2]

The results are mixed in the many other factual contexts arising under the ten-year look-forward rule. The Service has ruled that a prohibited interest is obtained if the redeemed shareholder becomes a custodian under the Uniform Gifts to Minors Act or a voting trustee of corporate stock during the restricted ten year period.[3] But if the shareholder becomes executor of a deceased shareholder's estate and can vote the stock held by the estate, the protection of Section 302(c)(2) is still available by virtue of the exception for stock acquired by bequest or inheritance.[4] In Revenue Ruling 72–380,[5] the Service ruled that since a redeemed shareholder may reacquire a direct stock interest by bequest or inheritance, it was reasonable to permit "acquisition under identical circumstances of the significantly lesser interest embodied in the * * * right of an executor to vote stock in an estate * * *."[6] In Revenue Ruling 79–334[7] the same reasoning was applied to an appointment by will of a previously redeemed shareholder as a trustee of a trust. The ruling concludes that a redeemed shareholder may waive family attribution even though, as trustee, he can vote stock of the corporation in which he once had an interest.

Deferred Payment Redemptions. In the area of deferred payment redemptions, the Service and the courts have disagreed over what constitutes a complete termination of a shareholder's interest or the acquisition of a forbidden proprietary interest for purposes of the waiver of family attribution exception. The regulations provide that to be considered a creditor, the rights of the redeemed shareholder must not be greater than necessary to enforce the claim. An obligation may be treated as proprietary if it is subordinated to claims of general creditors, if payments of principal depend upon corporate earnings, or if the interest rate fluctuates with the corporation's success.[8] Acquisition of corporate property as a result of enforcement of rights as a creditor does not run afoul of Section 302(c)(2) unless the redeemed shareholder acquires stock in the corporation, its parent corporation, or a subsidiary.[9]

The standards applied by the courts to credit redemptions are not as

2. Compare Rev.Rul. 56–556, 1956–2 C.B. 177 and Rev.Rul. 59–119, 1959–1 C.B. 68 with Estate of Lennard v. Commissioner, 61 T.C. 554 (1974), nonacq. 1978–2 C.B. 3, and Lewis v. Commissioner, 47 T.C. 129 (1966).

3. Rev.Rul. 81–233, 1981–2 C.B. 83; Rev.Rul. 71–426, 1971–2 C.B. 173.

4. I.R.C. § 302(c)(2)(A)(ii).

5. 1972–2 C.B. 201.

6. An executor who also becomes an officer of the corporation acquires a prohibited interest and loses Section 302(c)(2)'s protection. Rev.Rul. 75–2, 1975–1 C.B. 99.

7. 1979–2 C.B. 127.

8. Reg. § 1.302–4(d). A shareholder's ability to defer gain on a credit redemption under the installment method is a separate issue. First, the redemption must be treated as an exchange rather than a dividend. In addition, Section 453(k)(2)(A) denies use of the installment method for sales of stock or securities which are traded on an established securities market. This provision thus limits the tax advantage of deferral on a credit redemption to redemptions of stock in closely held corporations.

9. Reg. § 1.302–4(e).

rigid. In Dunn v. Commissioner,[10] a redemption agreement provided for postponement of principal and interest payments on corporate notes given in payment for the shareholder's stock if such payments would violate financial requirements in the corporation's franchise agreement with General Motors. The court concluded that the postponement provision did not require the notes to be classified as equity or give the shareholder an interest in the corporation other than as a creditor. In Estate of Lennard v. Commissioner,[11] the court found that a subordinated demand note, which was paid approximately three months after issuance, did not represent a proprietary interest in the corporation.

The Service has specific guidelines for granting a favorable ruling under Section 302. For example, it ordinarily will not rule on the tax consequences of a redemption of stock for notes when the note payment period extends beyond 15 years.[12] Nor will a ruling be issued under Section 302(b) if the shareholder's stock is held in escrow or as security for payments on corporate notes given as consideration for the redeemed stock because of the possibility that the stock may be returned to the shareholder as a result of a default by the corporation.[13]

Once again, however, the courts have been far more lenient. For example, in Lisle v. Commissioner[14] the Tax Court found a Section 302(b)(3) complete termination where the redeemed shareholders were to be paid for their stock over a 20 year period, the shareholders retained their voting rights pursuant to a security agreement, the stock was held in escrow and could be returned to the shareholders and the shareholders continued to serve as corporate directors and officers. The court concluded that the shareholders were directors and officers in name only and that, based upon the facts present in the case, the security provisions were not inconsistent with a finding that the transaction qualified as a complete redemption.

Other Post–Redemption Interests. Finally, the Service will permit a redeemed shareholder to lease property to the corporation on an arms length basis provided that the rental payments are not dependent on corporate earnings or subordinated to the claims of the corporation's general creditors.[15]

Retention of Multiple Interests. A shareholder of a closely held corporation often will retain several different types of interests after a redemption. This raises the question of whether, in determining if the shareholder has retained a prohibited financial stake, do we look to each separate economic relationship, or to the totality of continuing interests? In Hurst v. Commis-

10. 615 F.2d 578 (2d Cir.1980).

11. Note 2, supra.

12. Rev.Proc. 2008–3, § 4.01(20), 2008–1 I.R.B. 118, 113.

13. Id. at § 3.01(31), 2008–1 I.R.B. 113.

14. 35 T.C.M. 627 (1976). The issue in *Lisle* was whether there was a complete termination of the shareholder's interest. The case did not involve a waiver of family attribution issue.

15. Rev.Rul. 77–467, 1977–2 C.B. 92.

sioner,[16] the Tax Court rejected the Service's argument that multiple interests taken together can constitute a prohibited interest and concluded that each interest must be analyzed separately. The taxpayers in *Hurst* were a husband and wife who owned stock in two corporations ("A" and "B").[17] Mr. and Mrs. Hurst each were stockholders of A but only Mr. Hurst owned stock of B. To implement retirement and succession planning, they first sold their A stock to B. B then redeemed 90 percent of Mr. Hurst's B stock, and he sold the remaining 10 percent to his son and two unrelated parties. Both the redemption and sale provided for a 15–year payment term and the corporation's payment obligation was secured by the redeemed or sold B stock. The Hursts continued to own B's corporate headquarters, which they leased back to B; and Mrs. Hurst (remember, she was not a B shareholder) continued as a B employee. All the various agreements (stock purchase, redemption, lease, and employment contract) were cross-collateralized by Mr. Hurst's B stock.

The principal issue was whether the redemption of Mr. Hurst's B stock qualified as a complete termination under Section 302(b)(3) after application of the waiver of family attribution rules in Section 302(c). The Tax Court rejected the Service's arguments that the "total number of related obligations resulting from the transaction gave the [taxpayers] a prohibited interest" that was tantamount to a financial stake in the company's continued success. It held that Mr. Hurst did not retain any prohibited interests by virtue of the 15–year promissory notes (they were not tied to the corporation's financial performance, and using the stock as collateral was consistent with common practice), the lease (it had a fixed rent that was reasonable), or his wife's employment agreement (she owned no B stock, her compensation was not related to the corporation's financial performance, and there was no evidence that she was acting as a surrogate manager for her husband).

Although it involved taxable years before the effective date of the dividend rate reduction, *Hurst* is a good example of why, even apart from basis recovery, characterization still can matter under the current rate regime. Redemptions of closely held stock in the typical "family business" setting are frequently funded with installment notes. If the redemption is treated as an exchange under Section 302, installment sale reporting under Section 453 is available, but there is immediate gain recognition if the distribution is a dividend.

b. WAIVER OF ATTRIBUTION BY ENTITIES

Section 302(c)(2) only permits waiver of the *family* attribution rules and requires the "distributee" to file an agreement promising to notify the Service of the acquisition of a forbidden interest within the ten year period following the redemption. What if the redeemed shareholder is a trust,

16. 124 T.C. 16 (2005).

17. The corporations were S corporations that formerly had been C corporations and, because they had accumulated earnings and profits from their C corporation days, the dividend vs. exchange issue was significant for tax purposes. See Chapter 20G, infra.

estate or other entity that completely terminates its *actual* interest in the corporation but continues to own shares attributed to a beneficiary from a related family member which then are reattributed from the beneficiary to the entity?[1] May the entity waive family attribution or is the waiver opportunity limited to individual shareholders?

At one time, the Service contended that only individuals could waive family attribution.[2] The Tax Court disagreed, however, holding that an estate or trust that completely terminated its actual interest in a redemption could waive family attribution from a family member to a beneficiary.[3] One appellate court, rejecting what it called a "crabbed reading" of the Code, even held that an entity could waive attribution from a beneficiary to the entity.[4] The problem with these decisions was that they did not prevent the beneficiary from acquiring an interest in the corporation during the ten years after the redemption or require an agreement from the beneficiary to notify the Service if such a forbidden interest were acquired.

Technical as it may seem, this issue was of considerable interest to shareholders of closely held corporations and their estate planners. The Service's rigid position often was an impediment to a redemption of the stock of an estate or trust where family members of the beneficiaries continued to own shares of the company. In the midst of continuing litigation, Congress enacted a special rule for waiver by entities, incorporating appropriate safeguards to preclude the beneficiaries from reacquiring an interest.[5] The Joint Committee on Taxation explained the rule as follows:[6]

> The Act permits an entity to waive the family attribution rules if those through whom ownership is attributed to the entity join in the waiver. Thus, a trust and its beneficiaries may waive family attribution to the beneficiaries if, after the redemption, neither the trust nor the beneficiaries hold an interest in the corporation, do not acquire such an interest within the 10–year period, and join in the agreement to notify the IRS of any acquisi-

1. For example, assume Mother's Estate, of which Father is the sole beneficiary, owns 50 of the 100 outstanding shares of X Corporation stock. The other 50 shares are owned by Child. If X redeems Estate's 50 shares, Estate continues to constructively own Child's 50 shares, which are attributed from Child to Father via family attribution and then reattributed from Father to Estate. May Estate break the family attribution chain in order to qualify the redemption as a complete termination?

2. Rev.Rul. 59–233, 1959–2 C.B. 106, Rev.Rul. 68–388, 1968–2 C.B. 122.

3. See Crawford v. Commissioner, 59 T.C. 830 (1973); Johnson Trust v. Commissioner, 71 T.C. 941 (1979); but see Metzger Trust v. Commissioner, 76 T.C. 42 (1981), affirmed, 693 F.2d 459 (5th Cir.1982).

4. Rickey v. United States, 592 F.2d 1251 (5th Cir.1979). This remarkable example of "flexible" statutory construction was sharply criticized. See Andrews, "Comment: Estate Waiver of the Estate–Beneficiary Attribution Rules in Nonliquidating Redemptions Under Section 302 and Related Matters: The *Rickey* Case in the Fifth Circuit," 35 Tax L.Rev. 147 (1979).

5. I.R.C. § 302(c)(2)(C).

6. Staff of Joint Committee on Taxation, General Explanation of the Tax Equity and Fiscal Responsibility Act of 1982, 98th Cong.2d Sess. 146–47 (1982).

tion. The entity and beneficiaries are jointly and severally liable in the event of an acquisition by any of them within the 10–year period and the statute of limitations remains open to assess any deficiency. The tax increase is a deficiency in the entity's tax but may be asserted as a deficiency against any beneficiary liable under the rules. Congress intended that the tax will be collected from a beneficiary only when it cannot be assessed against or collected from the entity, such as when the entity no longer exists or has insufficient funds. Further, it was intended that the tax will be assessed and collected from the beneficiary whose acquisition causes the deficiency before it is asserted against any other beneficiary.

Under the Act, only family attribution under Section 318(a)(1) may be waived by an entity and its beneficiaries. The waiver rules are not extended to waivers of attribution to and from entities and their beneficiaries (secs. 318(a)(2) and 318(a)(3)). The Act thus is intended to overrule Rickey v. United States, 592 F.2d 1251 (5th Cir.1979). Congress intended that the Act should not be construed to provide any inference as to whether the *Rickey* decision adopts a proper construction of prior law. Nor was any inference intended as to whether the other cases extending the waiver rules for family attribution to entities adopt a proper construction of prior law.

Certain anti-avoidance rules applicable where the redeemed stock was acquired by the distributee from a related party or a related party at the time of the redemption owns stock acquired from the distributee are extended to the entity and affected beneficiaries.

3. Redemptions Not Essentially Equivalent to a Dividend

Code: § 302(b)(1).

Regulations: § 1.302–2.

United States v. Davis

Supreme Court of the United States, 1970.
397 U.S. 301, 90 S.Ct. 1041, rehearing denied, 397 U.S. 1071, 90 S.Ct. 1495 (1970).

■ Mr. Justice Marshall delivered the opinion of the Court.

In 1945, taxpayer and E.B. Bradley organized a corporation. In exchange for property transferred to the new company, Bradley received 500 shares of common stock, and taxpayer and his wife similarly each received 250 such shares. Shortly thereafter, taxpayer made an additional contribution to the corporation, purchasing 1,000 shares of preferred stock at a par value of $25 per share.

The purpose of this latter transaction was to increase the company's working capital and thereby to qualify for a loan previously negotiated through the Reconstruction Finance Corporation. It was understood that the corporation would redeem the preferred stock when the RFC loan had been repaid. Although in the interim taxpayer bought Bradley's 500 shares and divided them between his son and daughter, the total capitalization of the company remained the same until 1963. That year, after the loan was fully repaid and in accordance with the original understanding, the company redeemed taxpayer's preferred stock.

In his 1963 personal income tax return taxpayer did not report the $25,000 received by him upon the redemption of his preferred stock as income. Rather, taxpayer considered the redemption as a sale of his preferred stock to the company—a capital gains transaction under § 302 of the Internal Revenue Code of 1954 resulting in no tax since taxpayer's basis in the stock equaled the amount he received for it. The Commissioner of Internal Revenue, however, did not approve this tax treatment. According to the Commissioner, the redemption of taxpayer's stock was essentially equivalent to a dividend and was thus taxable as ordinary income under §§ 301 and 316 of the Code. Taxpayer paid the resulting deficiency and brought this suit for a refund. The District Court ruled in his favor, 274 F.Supp. 466 (D.C.M.D.Tenn.1967), and on appeal the Court of Appeals affirmed. 408 F.2d 1139 (C.A.6th Cir.1969).

The Court of Appeals held that the $25,000 received by taxpayer was "not essentially equivalent to a dividend" within the meaning of that phrase in § 302(b)(1) of the Code because the redemption was the final step in a course of action that had a legitimate business (as opposed to a tax avoidance) purpose. That holding represents only one of a variety of treatments accorded similar transactions under § 302(b)(1) in the circuit courts of appeals. We granted certiorari, 396 U.S. 815 (1969), in order to resolve this recurring tax question involving stock redemptions by closely held corporations. We reverse.

I

The Internal Revenue Code of 1954 provides generally in §§ 301 and 316 for the tax treatment of distributions by a corporation to its shareholders; under those provisions, a distribution is includable in a taxpayer's gross income as a dividend out of earnings and profits to the extent such earnings exist. There are exceptions to the application of these general provisions, however, and among them are those found in § 302 involving certain distributions for redeemed stock. The basic question in this case is whether the $25,000 distribution by the corporation to taxpayer falls under that section—more specifically, whether its legitimate business motivation qualifies the distribution under § 302(b)(1) of the Code. Preliminarily, however, we must consider the relationship between § 302(b)(1) and the rules regarding the attribution of stock ownership found in § 318(a) of the Code.

Under subsection (a) of § 302, a distribution is treated as "payment in exchange for the stock," thus qualifying for capital gains rather than ordinary income treatment, if the conditions contained in any one of the four paragraphs of subsection (b) are met. In addition to paragraph (1)'s "not essentially equivalent to a dividend" test, capital gains treatment is available where (2) the taxpayer's voting strength is substantially diminished, [or] (3) his interest in the company is completely terminated. * * * [T]axpayer admits that paragraphs (2) and (3) do not apply. Moreover, taxpayer agrees that for the purposes of §§ 302(b)(2) and (3) the attribution rules of § 318(a) apply and he is considered to own the 750 outstanding shares of common stock held by his wife and children in addition to the 250 shares in his own name.

Taxpayer, however, argues that the attribution rules do not apply in considering whether a distribution is essentially equivalent to a dividend under § 302(b)(1). According to taxpayer, he should thus be considered to own only 25 percent of the corporation's common stock, and the distribution would then qualify under § 302(b)(1) since it was not pro rata or proportionate to his stock interest, the fundamental test of dividend equivalency. See Treas.Reg. 1.302–2(b). However, the plain language of the statute compels rejection of the argument. In subsection (c) of § 302, the attribution rules are made specifically applicable "in determining the ownership of stock for purposes of this section." Applying this language, both courts below held that § 318(a) applies to all of § 302, including § 302(b)(1)—a view in accord with the decisions of the other courts of appeals, a longstanding treasury regulation,[6] and the opinion of the leading commentators.[7]

Against this weight of authority, taxpayer argues that the result under paragraph (1) should be different because there is no explicit reference to stock ownership as there is in paragraphs (2) and (3). Neither that fact, however, nor the purpose and history of § 302(b)(1) support taxpayer's argument. The attribution rules—designed to provide a clear answer to what would otherwise be a difficult tax question—formed part of the tax bill that was subsequently enacted as the 1954 Code. As is discussed further, infra, the bill as passed by the House of Representatives contained no provision comparable to § 302(b)(1). When that provision was added in the Senate, no purpose was evidenced to restrict the applicability of § 318(a). Rather, the attribution rules continued to be made specifically applicable to the entire section, and we believe that Congress intended that they be taken into account wherever ownership of stock was relevant.

Indeed, it was necessary that the attribution rules apply to § 302(b)(1) unless they were to be effectively eliminated from consideration with regard to §§ 302(b)(2) and (3) also. For if a transaction failed to qualify under one of those sections solely because of the attribution rules, it would according to taxpayer's argument nonetheless qualify under § 302(b)(1). We cannot agree that Congress intended so to nullify its explicit directive. We conclude, therefore, that the attribution rules of § 318(a) do apply; and, for the purposes of deciding whether a distribution is "not essentially

6. See Treas.Reg. 1.302–2(b).

7. See B. Bittker & J. Eustice, Federal Income Taxation of Corporations and Shareholders 292 n. 32 (2d ed. 1966).

equivalent to a dividend'' under § 302(b)(1), taxpayer must be deemed the owner of all 1,000 shares of the company's common stock.

II

After application of the stock ownership attribution rules, this case viewed most simply involves a sole stockholder who causes part of his shares to be redeemed by the corporation. We conclude that such a redemption is always ''essentially equivalent to a dividend'' within the meaning of that phrase in § 302(b)(1)[8] and therefore do not reach the Government's alternative argument that in any event the distribution should not on the facts of this case qualify for capital gains treatment.[9]

The predecessor of § 302(b)(1) came into the tax law as § 201(d) of the Revenue Act of 1921, 42 Stat. 228:

> ''A stock dividend shall not be subject to tax but if after the distribution of any such dividend the corporation proceeds to cancel or redeem its stock at such time and in such manner as to make the distribution and cancellation or redemption essentially equivalent to the distribution of a taxable dividend, the amount received in redemption or cancellation of the stock shall be treated as a taxable dividend * * *.''

Enacted in response to this Court's decision that pro rata stock dividends do not constitute taxable income, Eisner v. Macomber, 252 U.S. 189 (1920), the provision had the obvious purpose of preventing a corporation from avoiding dividend tax treatment by distributing earnings to its shareholders in two transactions—a pro rata stock dividend followed by a pro rata redemption—that would have the same economic consequences as a simple dividend. Congress, however, soon recognized that even without a prior stock dividend essentially the same result could be effected whereby any corporation, ''especially one which has only a few stockholders, might be able to make a distribution to its stockholders which would have the same effect as a taxable dividend.'' H.R.Rep. No. 1, 69th Cong., 1st Sess., 5. In order to cover this situation, the law was amended to apply ''(whether or not such stock was issued as a stock dividend)'' whenever a distribution in redemption of stock was made ''at such time and in such manner'' that it was essentially equivalent to a taxable dividend. Revenue Act of 1926, § 201(g), 44 Stat. 11.

This provision of the 1926 Act was carried forward in each subsequent revenue act and finally became § 115(g)(1) of the Internal Revenue Code of 1939. Unfortunately, however, the policies encompassed within the general

8. Of course, this just means that a distribution in redemption to a sole shareholder will be treated under the general provisions of § 301, and it will only be taxed as a dividend under § 316 to the extent that there are earnings and profits.

9. The Government argues that even if business purpose were relevant under § 302(b)(1), the business purpose present here related only to the original investment and not at all to the necessity for redemption. Under either view, taxpayer does not lose his basis in the preferred stock. Under Treas. Reg. 1.302–2(c) that basis is applied to taxpayer's common stock.

language of § 115(g)(1) and its predecessors were not clear, and there resulted much confusion in the tax law. At first, courts assumed that the provision was aimed at tax avoidance schemes and sought only to determine whether such a scheme existed. * * * Although later the emphasis changed and the focus was more on the effect of the distribution, many courts continued to find that distributions otherwise like a dividend were not "essentially equivalent" if, for example, they were motivated by a sufficiently strong nontax business purpose. See cases cited n. 2, supra. There was general disagreement, however, about what would qualify as such a purpose, and the result was a case-by-case determination with each case decided "on the basis of the particular facts of the transaction in question." Bains v. United States, 289 F.2d 644, 646, 153 Ct.Cl. 599, 603 (1961).

By the time of the general revision resulting in the Internal Revenue Code of 1954, the draftsmen were faced with what has aptly been described as "the morass created by the decisions." Ballenger v. United States, 301 F.2d 192, 196 (C.A.4th Cir.1962). In an effort to eliminate "the considerable confusion which exists in this area" and thereby to facilitate tax planning, H.R.Rep. No. 1337, 83d Cong., 2d Sess., 35, the authors of the new Code sought to provide objective tests to govern the tax consequences of stock redemptions. Thus, the tax bill passed by the House of Representatives contained no "essentially equivalent" language. Rather, it provided for "safe harbors" where capital gains treatment would be accorded to corporate redemptions that met the conditions now found in §§ 302(b)(2) and (3) of the Code.

It was in the Senate Finance Committee's consideration of the tax bill that § 302(b)(1) was added, and Congress thereby provided that capital gains treatment should be available "if the redemption is not essentially equivalent to a dividend." Taxpayer argues that the purpose was to continue "existing law," and there is support in the legislative history that § 302(b)(1) reverted "in part" or "in general" to the "essentially equivalent" provision of § 115(g)(1) of the 1939 Code. According to the Government, even under the old law it would have been improper for the Court of Appeals to rely on "a business purpose for the redemption" and "an absence of the proscribed tax avoidance purpose to bail out dividends at favorable tax rates." * * * However, we need not decide that question, for we find from the history of the 1954 revisions and the purpose of § 302(b)(1) that Congress intended more than merely to re-enact the prior law.

In explaining the reason for adding the "essentially equivalent" test, the Senate Committee stated that the House provisions "appeared unnecessarily restrictive, particularly, in the case of redemptions of preferred stock which might be called by the corporation without the shareholder having any control over when the redemption may take place." S.Rep. No. 1622, 83d Cong., 2d Sess., 44. This explanation gives no indication that the purpose behind the redemption should affect the result.[10] Rather, in its more detailed technical evaluation of § 302(b)(1), the Senate Committee reported as follows:

> "The test intended to be incorporated in the interpretation of paragraph (1) is in general that currently employed under section 115(g)(1) of the 1939 Code. Your committee further intends that in applying this test for the future * * * the inquiry will be devoted solely to the question of whether or not the transaction by its nature may properly be characterized as a sale of stock by the redeeming shareholder to the corporation. For this purpose the presence or absence of earnings and profits of the corporation is not material. Example: X, the sole shareholder of a corporation having no earnings or profits causes the corporation to redeem half of its stock. Paragraph (1) does not apply to such redemption notwithstanding the absence of earnings and profits." S.Rep. No. 1622, supra, at 234.

The intended scope of § 302(b)(1) as revealed by this legislative history is certainly not free from doubt. However, we agree with the Government that by making the sole inquiry relevant for the future the narrow one whether the redemption could be characterized as a sale, Congress was apparently rejecting past court decisions that had also considered factors indicating the presence or absence of a tax-avoidance motive.[11] At least that is the implication of the example given. Congress clearly mandated that pro rata distributions be treated under the general rules laid down in §§ 301 and 316 rather than under § 302, and nothing suggests that there should be a different result if there were a "business purpose" for the redemption. Indeed, just the opposite inference must be drawn since there would not likely be a tax-avoidance purpose in a situation where there were no earnings or profits. We conclude that the Court of Appeals was therefore wrong in looking for a business purpose and considering it in deciding whether the redemption was equivalent to a dividend. Rather, we agree with the Court of Appeals for the Second Circuit that "the business purpose of a transaction is irrelevant in determining dividend equivalence" under § 302(b)(1). Hasbrook v. United States, 343 F.2d 811, 814 (1965).

10. See Bittker & Eustice, supra, n. 7, at 291: "It is not easy to give § 302(b)(1) an expansive construction in view of this indication that its major function was the narrow one of immunizing redemptions of minority holdings of preferred stock."

11. This rejection is confirmed by the Committee's acceptance of the House treatment of distributions involving corporate contractions—a factor present in many of the earlier "business purpose" redemptions. In describing its action, the Committee stated as follows:

> "Your committee, as did the House bill, separates into their significant elements the kind of transactions now incoherently aggregated in the definition of a partial liquidation. Those distributions which may have capital-gain characteristics *because they are not made pro rata* among the various shareholders would be subjected, at the shareholder level, to the separate tests described in [§§ 301 to 318]. On the other hand, those distributions characterized by what happens solely at the corporate level by reason of the assets distributed would be included as within the concept of a partial liquidation." S.Rep. No. 1622, supra, at 49. (Emphasis added.)

Taxpayer strongly argues that to treat the redemption involved here as essentially equivalent to a dividend is to elevate form over substance. Thus, taxpayer argues, had he not bought Bradley's shares or had he made a subordinated loan to the company instead of buying preferred stock, he could have gotten back his $25,000 with favorable tax treatment. However, the difference between form and substance in the tax law is largely problematical, and taxpayer's complaints have little to do with whether a business purpose is relevant under § 302(b)(1). It was clearly proper for Congress to treat distributions generally as taxable dividends when made out of earnings and profits and then to prevent avoidance of that result without regard to motivation where the distribution is in exchange for redeemed stock.

We conclude that that is what Congress did when enacting § 302(b)(1). If a corporation distributes property as a simple dividend, the effect is to transfer the property from the company to its shareholders without a change in the relative economic interests or rights of the stockholders. Where a redemption has that same effect, it cannot be said to have satisfied the "not essentially equivalent to a dividend" requirement of § 302(b)(1). Rather, to qualify for preferred treatment under that section, a redemption must result in a meaningful reduction of the shareholder's proportionate interest in the corporation. Clearly, taxpayer here, who (after application of the attribution rules) was the sole shareholder of the corporation both before and after the redemption, did not qualify under this test. The decision of the Court of Appeals must therefore be reversed and the case remanded to the District Court for dismissal of the complaint.

It is so ordered.

■ MR. JUSTICE DOUGLAS, with whom THE CHIEF JUSTICE and MR. JUSTICE BRENNAN concur, dissenting.

I agree with the District Court, 274 F.Supp. 466, and with the Court of Appeals, 408 F.2d 1139, that respondent's contribution of working capital in the amount of $25,000 in exchange for 1,000 shares of preferred stock with a par value of $25 was made in order for the corporation to obtain a loan from the RFC and that the preferred stock was to be redeemed when the loan was repaid. For the reasons stated by the two lower courts, this redemption was not "essentially equivalent to a dividend," for the bona fide business purpose of the redemption belies the payment of a dividend. As stated by the Court of Appeals:

> "Although closely-held corporations call for close scrutiny under the tax law, we will not, under the facts and circumstances of this case, allow mechanical attribution rules to transform a legitimate corporate transaction into a tax avoidance scheme." 408 F.2d, at 1143–1144.

When the Court holds it was a dividend, it effectively cancels § 302(b)(1) from the Code. This result is not a matter of conjecture, for the Court says that in the case of closely held or one-man corporations a redemption of stock is "always" equivalent to a dividend. I would leave such revision to the Congress.

Revenue Ruling 85–106

1985–2 Cum.Bull. 116.

ISSUE

Is a redemption of nonvoting preferred stock not essentially equivalent to a dividend within the meaning of section 302(b)(1) of the Internal Revenue Code when there is no reduction in the percentage of voting and nonvoting common stock owned by the redeemed shareholder, and when the redeemed shareholder continues to have an undiminished opportunity to act in concert with other shareholders as a control group, under the circumstances described below?

FACTS

Corporation *X* had outstanding three classes of stock consisting of 100 shares of voting common stock, 100 shares of nonvoting common stock, and 50 shares of nonvoting 9 percent cumulative preferred stock. The fair market value of each share of common stock was approximately half the fair market value of each share of preferred stock. The voting common stock was held as follows:

Shareholders	***Shares***
A	19
B	19
C	18
Minority shareholders	44
Total	100

None of the minority shareholders owned more than five shares. None of the holders of the voting common stock were related within the meaning of section 318(a) of the Code. The combined voting power of *A, B*, and *C* was sufficient to elect a majority of the board of directors of *X*.

The nonvoting common stock and the preferred stock were held (directly and indirectly) in approximately the same proportions as the common stock. *C* held no nonvoting common stock or preferred stock directly, but was the sole remaining beneficiary of a trust, *T*, which owned 18 percent of both the nonvoting common stock and the preferred stock.

The trustees of *T* decided that it would be in the best interests of that trust if most of the *X* preferred stock held by *T* could be converted into cash. After negotiation, *X* redeemed six shares of preferred stock for its fair market value of 6*x* dollars. Following this redemption, *T* continued to hold three shares of preferred stock, and 18 percent of the nonvoting common stock. Under section 318(a)(3)(B) of the Code, *T* is also considered to own the voting common stock owned by its sole beneficiary, *C*.

LAW AND ANALYSIS

Section 302(a) of the Code provides, in part, that if a corporation redeems its stock, and if section 302(b)(1), (2), (3), or (4) applies, such redemption will be treated as a distribution in part or full payment in exchange for the stock.

* * *

The lack of any reduction in *T*'s 18 percent vote prevented this redemption from qualifying under section 302(b)(2) of the Code, and the lack of complete termination of interest prevented it from qualifying under section 302(b)(3). The question remains whether the redemption should be considered not essentially equivalent to a dividend so as to qualify under section 302(b)(1). Under section 1.302–2(b) of the Income Tax Regulations, this determination depends upon the facts and circumstances of each case.

In United States v. Davis, 397 U.S. 301 (1970), 1970–1 C.B. 62, the Supreme Court of the United States held that in order to qualify under section 302(b)(1) of the Code, a redemption must result in a meaningful reduction of the shareholder's proportionate interest in the corporation, and that, for this purpose, the attribution rules of section 318 apply.

In determining whether a reduction in interest is "meaningful", the rights inherent in a shareholder's interest must be examined. The three elements of a shareholder's interest that are generally considered most significant are: (1) the right to vote and thereby exercise control; (2) the right to participate in current earnings and accumulated surplus; and (3) the right to share in net assets on liquidation. Rev.Rul. 81–289, 1981–2 C.B. 82.

In applying the above principles, it is significant that (as a result of section 318(a)(3)(B) of the Code) the redemption did not reduce *T*'s percentage of the vote in *X*. It is true that *T* reduced its percentage interest in current earnings, accumulated surplus, and net assets upon liquidation, and reduced the fair market value of its ownership in *X*. However, when the redeemed shareholder has a voting interest (either directly or by attribution), a reduction in voting power is a key factor in determining the applicability of section 302(b)(1) of the Code.

It is also true that *T* was not the largest shareholder. *A* and *B* each held slightly larger voting interests, and larger interests measured by fair market value. *T*, however, was not in the position of a minority shareholder isolated from corporate management and control. Compare Rev.Rul. 75–512, where the majority of the redeeming corporation's voting stock was held by a shareholder unrelated (within the meaning of section 318(a)) to the redeemed trust. Also compare Rev.Rul. 76–385, 1976–2 C.B. 92, where the redeemed shareholder's total interest was *de minimis*.

In the present situation, a significant aspect of *T*'s failure to reduce voting power is the fact that the redemption leaves unchanged *T*'s potential (by attribution from *C*) for participating in a control group by acting in concert with *A* and *B*. Compare Rev.Rul. 76–364, 1976–2 C.B. 91, where a reduction in voting interest was found meaningful in itself when it caused the redeemed shareholder to give up a potential for control by acting in concert with one other shareholder. In addition, the Tax Court has indicated significance for this factor of potential group control (*Johnson Trust*, at 947). See also Bloch v. United States, 261 F.Supp. 597, 611–612 (S.D.Tex. 1966), aff'd per curiam, 386 F.2d 839 (5th Cir.1967), where, in finding that "the distributions in question were essentially equivalent to a dividend," the court noted that there was no change in the redeemed shareholder's potential for exercising control "by aligning himself with one or more of the other stockholders."

Although there was a reduction of *T*'s economic interest in *X*, such reduction was not sufficiently large to result in a meaningful reduction of *T*'s interest. The absence of any reduction of *T*'s voting interest in *X* (through *C*) and *T*'s potential (through *C*) for control group participation are compelling factors in this situation.

In Himmel v. Commissioner, 338 F.2d 815 (2d Cir.1964), dealing with a similar question, a decision was reached permitting the applicability of section 302(b)(1) of the Code. That case, however, was decided prior to the decision of the Supreme Court in *Davis*. Thus, *Himmel* fails to reflect the development in the law represented by the *Davis* limitation on section 302(b)(1) applicability where there is no meaningful reduction of the shareholder's proportionate interest in the corporation. Thus, pursuant to *Davis*, it is proper to view *Himmel* as incorrect to the extent it conflicts with the position contained in this revenue ruling.

HOLDING

The redemption of nonvoting preferred stock held by *T* does not qualify as a redemption under section 302(b)(1) of the Code, under the facts of this ruling when there is no reduction in the percentage of voting and nonvoting common stock owned by *T*, and when *T* continues to have an undiminished opportunity to act in concert with other shareholders as a control group. Since the redemption does not otherwise qualify under section 302(b), it is not a distribution in part or full payment for the stock under section 302(a). Consequently, under section 302(d), the redemption will be treated as a distribution of property to which section 301 applies.

NOTE

The Meaningful Reduction Standard. In interpreting the "meaningful reduction" standard of *Davis*, the Service's rulings have considered the effect of the redemption on the redeemed shareholder's voting power, rights to participate in current and future corporate earnings, and rights to share in net assets on liquidation.[1] As illustrated by Revenue Ruling 85–106, if the shareholder has a voting interest, the key factor in measuring dividend equivalence is the reduction in the shareholder's voting power as

1. See, e.g., Rev. Rul. 81–289, 1981–2 C.B. 82.

opposed to other important economic rights. Whether such a reduction is "meaningful" is essentially a question of fact, but some guidelines have emerged from published rulings. For example, in Revenue Ruling 75–502,[2] the Service ruled that a shareholder's reduction of voting common stock ownership from 57 percent to 50 percent was meaningful where the remaining stock was held by a single unrelated shareholder. The ruling also states that a lesser reduction would not have qualified under Section 302(b)(1) because the shareholder would have continued to have "dominant voting rights."[3]

Turning to minority shareholders, the Service held in Revenue Ruling 75–512[4] that a reduction of common stock ownership from 30 percent to 24.3 percent—a near-miss under the substantially disproportionate redemption safe harbor—was meaningful because the redeemed shareholder experienced a reduction in three significant rights: voting, earnings, and assets on liquidation. A reduction in common stock ownership from 27 percent to 22 percent also was held to be meaningful where the remaining shares were owned by three unrelated shareholders because the redeemed shareholder lost the ability to control the corporation in concert with only one other shareholder.[5]

The Section 302 regulations also focus upon the effect of the redemption upon the shareholder's control of corporate affairs. Thus, pro rata redemptions of a corporation's single class of stock do not qualify for exchange treatment, and the redemption of all of one class of stock also fails if all outstanding classes of stock are held proportionately.[6] Any redemption of stock from a shareholder owning only nonvoting preferred stock, however, is not essentially equivalent a dividend since the shareholder does not have control over whether the redemption occurs.[7] The Service also has ruled that a redemption of publicly traded common stock that reduces a shareholder's interest from .0001118 percent to .0001081 percent qualifies for exchange treatment since such a shareholder cannot exercise control over corporate affairs.[8] The same reasoning should apply to redemptions by closely held companies of stock held by minority shareholders who reduce their percentage interests, even if the reduction is slight. But a pro rata redemption of stock in a publicly traded corporation will not satisfy the "meaningful reduction" standard even if the shareholder owns only small noncontrolling interest in the corporation.[9]

Suppose that under state law a simple majority of a corporation's outstanding shares can control day-to-day corporate activities through the board of directors but extraordinary corporate action, such as a merger or

2. 1975–2 C.B. 111.

3. Id.

4. 1975–2 C.B. 112.

5. Rev. Rul. 76–364, 1976–2 C.B. 91.

6. Reg. § 1.302–2(b).

7. Reg. § 1.302–2(a). In Rev.Rul. 77–426, 1977–2 C.B. 87, a redemption of five percent of the outstanding preferred stock from a shareholder owning all of the preferred stock (and only preferred stock) qualified for exchange treatment under Section 302(b)(1).

8. Rev.Rul. 76–385, 1976–2 C.B. 92.

9. Rev.Rul. 81–289, 1981–2 C.B. 82.

liquidation, requires approval by two-thirds of the shares. Should a redemption in which a shareholder loses control of extraordinary corporate action but retains control of routine matters (e.g. a reduction to 60% voting control) qualify for exchange treatment under Section 302(b)(1)? In Wright v. United States,[10] the Eighth Circuit determined that such a redemption is not essentially equivalent to a dividend because of the loss of two-thirds control of the corporation. In Revenue Ruling 78–401,[11] the Service takes a more restrictive view of the application of Section 302(b)(1) to these facts. The ruling concludes that if extraordinary corporate action is not "imminent," the retention of day-to-day control of corporate activities is a "predominant factor" and the redemption does not result in a meaningful reduction in the shareholder's interest. It is unclear what position the Service would take if a merger or similar corporate transaction were contemplated or what evidence would substantiate the likelihood of corporate action.

Family Discord. One of the more titillating issues to arise under Section 302(b)(1) involves whether the Section 318(a)(1) family attribution rules should be ignored when there is evidence of family discord between the redeemed shareholder and related continuing shareholders. A typical factual context in which this "family fight" question arises is well illustrated in the following introduction to a leading Tax Court decision:[12]

> Petitioner Michael N. Cerone * * * and his son Michael L. Cerone * * * owned and operated the Stockade Cafe * * * each owning 50 percent of the stock of the corporation. The father and son had a volatile relationship and frequently disagreed over management decisions. Over the years their disagreements became more serious, and finally they decided one of them should buy the other's interest in the business. Petitioner did not think he could run the business alone, so it was decided that the corporation would redeem all of his stock. After the redemption, petitioner worked at the Stockade Cafe for several years, but he did not exercise any control over the corporation. This case involves the tax treatment of the payments or distributions petitioner received for his stock.

If the family attribution rules applied to the above fact pattern, the redemption of the father's 50 percent stock interest would not qualify under Section 302(b)(1) because he continued to own 100 percent of the company through attribution from his son. If the attribution chain could be broken, however, the father's reduction of his interest from 50 percent to zero would be "meaningful" and the redemption would qualify for ex-

10. 482 F.2d 600 (8th Cir.1973).

11. 1978–2 C.B. 127.

12. Cerone v. Commissioner, 87 T.C. 1 (1986). See also the colorful introduction to the Fifth Circuit's opinion in Metzger Trust v. Commissioner, 693 F.2d 459 (5th Cir.1982) ("We decide today a story driven by tensions as old as Genesis but told in the modern lexicon of the tax law. It is the story of David who built a business and left it in the charge of his eldest son Jacob to be shared with Jacob's two sisters Catherine and Cecilia, of their alienation and resulting quarrel with the tax collectors.")

change treatment under Section 302(b)(1) even if he failed to meet the specific requirements for waiver of family attribution under Section 302(c).[13]

After its victory in United States v. Davis, the Service consistently rejected attempts by taxpayers to break the chain of family attribution by proving family hostility.[14] Most courts to consider the question agree that the attribution rules apply without regard to family squabbles. Although the First Circuit once held that family discord might "negate the presumption" of the attribution rules,[15] the Tax Court and the Fifth Circuit have refused to allow family discord to nullify the attribution rules in applying Section 302(b)(1).[16]

More recently, the Tax Court has suggested that family discord may be relevant in testing for dividend equivalency under Section 302(b)(1) *after* the attribution rules have been applied. In Cerone v. Commissioner,[17] the court summarized its view of the proper role of family hostility:[18]

> Although we [have] rejected the * * * argument that family discord could preclude application of the attribution rules, we nonetheless noted that family discord does have a role, albeit a limited one, in testing for dividend equivalence under section 302(b)(1). We reasoned that under *United States v. Davis*, supra, the proper analysis is as follows: First, the attribution rules are plainly and straightforwardly applied. Second, a determination is made whether there has been a reduction in the stockholder's proportionate interest in the corporation. If not, the inquiry ends because, if there is no change in the stockholder's interest, dividend equivalency results. If there has been a reduction, then all the facts and circumstances must be examined to see if the reduction was meaningful under *United States v. Davis*, supra. It is at this point, *and only then*, that family hostility becomes an appropriate factor for consideration. * * *.

4. Basis Consequences

If a redemption is treated as a sale, the basis of the redeemed stock is taken into account in determining the shareholder's gain or loss. If a

13. See Section C2 of this chapter, supra. Mr. Cerone was unable to waive family attribution under Section 302(c) because he retained a prohibited employment relationship with the corporation after the redemption. 87 T.C. at 29–33.

14. See, e.g., Rev.Rul. 80–26, 1980–1 C.B. 66.

15. Haft Trust v. Commissioner, 510 F.2d 43 (1st Cir.1975), vacating and remanding 61 T.C. 398 (1973).

16. Cerone v. Commissioner, supra note 12; Metzger Trust v. Commissioner, 76 T.C. 42 (1981), affirmed, 693 F.2d 459 (5th Cir.1982), cert. denied, 463 U.S. 1207, 103 S.Ct. 3537 (1983); Haft Trust v. Commissioner, 61 T.C. 398 (1973), vacated and remanded, 510 F.2d 43 (1st Cir.1975).

17. Supra note 12.

18. 87 T.C. at 22. See also Henry T. Patterson Trust v. United States, 729 F.2d 1089 (6th Cir.1984) (percentage reduction from 97 to 93 percent, after applying attribution rules, is meaningful under *Davis* in view of hostility.)

redemption is treated as a dividend, the regulations provide that the shareholder's basis in the redeemed stock does not disappear but may be added to the basis of the shareholder's retained stock. If the shareholder no longer owns any stock after the redemption, the basis of the redeemed stock may be added to the basis of stock held by family members or entities whose stock was attributed to the redeemed shareholder under Section 318. The regulations have never been specific about how this basis shift should be allocated when there is more than one related shareholder.[1]

In 2002, the Service issued proposed regulations that would have changed these straightforward rules as applied to simple redemptions and several other transactions where the rules of Section 302 are implicated.[2] The proposed regulations generally would have treated "dividend redemptions" as triggering a deferred loss, in the amount of the shareholder's basis in the redeemed stock, that is recognized and characterized at the time of the redemption but not "taken into account" (i.e., deducted) until a later date specified by the regulations.[3] These complex rules were designed to combat abusive corporate tax shelter transactions (well beyond the scope of our coverage) that exploited the current regulatory rule, usually by shifting basis from a foreign shareholder not subject to U.S. tax to a related U.S. taxpayer who then utilized the additional basis to increase loss or reduce taxable gain.[4] The proposed regulations were widely criticized, however, and ultimately withdrawn by the Service, which announced that it would continue to study various approaches to the basis consequences of dividend-equivalent redemptions.[5]

PROBLEMS

1. Megahurtz Enterprises, Inc. ("Inc.") is a closely-held C corporation formed 20 years ago by Adam and Bea Hurtz, who are husband and wife, and Bea's wealthy uncle, C.D. Rom, to develop and manufacture multimedia entertainment products for personal computers. Inc. has 10,000 shares of common stock and 1,000 shares of nonvoting preferred stock outstanding. At Inc.'s formation, each of the founding shareholders contributed cash in exchange for Inc. common stock, which was the only class outstanding at the time. About ten years ago, when Inc. needed more paid-in capital, Adam Hurtz and C.D. Rom made additional cash contributions in exchange for 1,000 shares of nonvoting preferred stock. Inc. has been a very profitable company and had $4 million of accumulated earnings and profits as of the beginning of the current year. Inc. also has substantial cash on hand and is in a position to borrow additional cash if necessary to finance a stock repurchase.

1. Reg. § 1.302–2(c), providing for "proper adjustment of the remaining stock."

2. REG–150313–01, 67 Fed. Reg. 64331–64345 (Oct. 18, 2002).

3. Prop. Reg. § 1.302–5(a).

4. See Notice 2001–45, 2001–33 I.R.B. 129.

5. I.R.S. Ann. 2006–30, 2006–19 I.R.B. 879.

Five years ago, Adam and Bea began making gifts of some of their Inc. common stock to their son, Dan, and to a trust for the benefit of Dan's two children. Dan's wife, Hilary, serves as Trustee of the trust. Dan Hurtz has been active in the family business for several years and is currently serving as vice-president.

C.D. Rom died last month, and his substantial Inc. holdings are now held by his estate, the co-executors of which are Bea Hurtz and Local Bank. C.D.'s will bequeathed $200,000 cash (2% of his estate) to Bea and the residue to his children.

As of the beginning of the current year, Inc.'s common and preferred shares were held as follows:

Common Stockholders	**Shs.**	**Adj. Basis**	**F.M.V.**
C.D. Rom Estate	8,000	$8,000,000	$ 8,000,000
Adam Hurtz	800	80,000	800,000
Bea Hurtz	800	80,000	800,000
Dan Hurtz	300	30,000	300,000
Childrens' Trust	100	10,000	100,000
	10,000	$8,200,000	$10,000,000
Preferred Stockholders			
C.D. Rom Estate	500	50,000	50,000
Adam Hurtz	500	50,000	50,000
	1,000	$ 100,000	$ 100,000

Inc. is considering a redemption of all of its preferred stock. In addition, Adam and Bea are contemplating retirement and ultimately wish to shift ownership of Inc. to Dan and his family, and the Rom Estate wishes to diversify its holdings. Evaluate the tax consequences of the following alternative proposals to meet some or all of these goals:

(a) Inc. redeems 6,000 of the Rom Estate's common stock for $6 million cash and all of the Estate's preferred stock for $50,000 cash.

(b) Inc. redeems Bea's 800 common shares for $800,000 cash but Bea continues to serve as an Inc. director.

(c) Same as (b), above, except that six months after the redemption of Bea's stock, Inc. also redeems 4,200 shares from the Estate for $4.2 million.

(d) Inc. only redeems its preferred stock, distributing $50,000 to each preferred shareholder.

2. Incorporate the basic facts of Problem 1, above, but now assume that Inc. never issued any preferred stock and that C.D. Rom's holdings were completely terminated in an earlier unrelated transaction, leaving 2,000 shares of common stock outstanding, held as follows:

Shareholders	Shs.	Adj. Basis	F.M.V.
Adam Hurtz	800	$ 80,000	$ 800,000
Bea Hurtz	800	80,000	800,000
Dan Hurtz	300	30,000	300,000
Childrens' Trust	100	10,000	100,000
	2,000	$200,000	$2,000,000

Using these new assumptions, evaluate the tax consequences of the following alternative transactions:

(a) Inc. redeems Bea's 800 shares for cash.

(b) Same as (a), above, except that Bea neglects to file the agreement required by § 302(c)(2)(A)(iii). What is the purpose of this agreement?

(c) Same as (a), above, except Bea remains as a director of Inc.

(d) Adam and Bea each transfer 400 common shares to Dan as a gift. Inc. then redeems the balance of Adam and Bea's shares, distributing to each $50,000 cash and a $350,000 20–year Inc. note, paying market rate interest and secured by the corporation's assets. Adam and Bea will resign as officers and directors, but Bea will continue to serve as a part-time consultant for Inc. in connection with new product development. Bea expects to earn $50,000 per year in consulting fees.

3. Assume the same basic facts as in Problem 2, above, except that Bea Hurtz dies, and her 800 shares of Inc. common stock are valued at $800,000 for federal estate tax purposes. Adam is the sole beneficiary of her estate.

(a) What are the tax consequences under § 302 if Inc. redeems the 800 shares held by Bea's estate for $800,000 cash.

(b) Same as (a), above, except that all of Adam's shares are redeemed at the same time, leaving Dan and his childrens' trust as the only remaining Inc. shareholders.

4. Finally, incorporate the basic facts of Problem 2, above, except assume that Adam and Bea (who each still own 800 shares) are brother and sister, Dan (who still owns 300 shares) is Adam's son, and the remaining 100 shares are owned by Cousin, who has no § 318 relationship to the other shareholders. Determine whether the following alternative redemptions are not essentially equivalent to a dividend under § 302(b)(1).

(a) Inc. redeems 100 shares from Adam.

(b) Inc. redeems 200 shares from Dan.

(c) Inc. redeems 10 shares from Cousin.

D. REDEMPTIONS TESTED AT THE CORPORATE LEVEL: PARTIAL LIQUIDATIONS

Code: § 302(b)(4), (e).

Section 302(b)(4) provides exchange treatment for redemptions of stock held by noncorporate shareholders if the distribution qualifies as a "partial liquidation." Under Section 302(e)(1), a distribution is treated as in partial liquidation if it is pursuant to a plan, occurs within the taxable year in which the plan is adopted or the succeeding taxable year, and is "not essentially equivalent to a dividend." Although the "not essentially equivalent to a dividend" standard mirrors the language in Section 302(b)(1), the two provisions have a very different focus. For partial liquidation purposes, dividend equivalency is determined at the corporate rather than the shareholder level. Thus, while a pro rata redemption could never escape dividend classification under Section 302(b)(1), any redemption that results in a genuine contraction of the corporation's business may qualify for exchange treatment as a partial liquidation if the distribution is made to a shareholder other than a C corporation. The legislative history of the predecessor of Section 302(e) explains the corporate contraction standard:[1]

> The general language of the proposed draft would include within the definition of a partial liquidation the type of cases involving the contraction of the corporate business. Such as for example, cases which hold that if the entire floor of a factory is destroyed by fire, the insurance proceeds received may be distributed pro rata to the shareholders without the imposition of a tax at the rates applicable to the distribution of a dividend, if the corporation no longer continues its operations to the same extent maintained by the destroyed facility. Voluntary bona fide contraction of the corporate business may of course also qualify to the same extent as under existing law. In addition to the general definition of what constitutes a partial liquidation, your committee's bill provides a rule to indicate one type of distribution that will in any event constitute a partial liquidation. Under this rule, if a corporation is engaged in two or more active businesses which has [sic] been carried on for at least 5 years, it may distribute the assets of either one of the businesses in kind, or the proceeds of their sale.

The amorphous corporate contraction doctrine is a perilous yardstick for the tax planner.[2] Recognizing the need for greater certainty, Congress has provided a safe harbor in Section 302(e)(2), which assures partial liquidation status if the distribution consists of the assets of a "qualified trade or business" or is attributable to the termination of such a trade or business, and immediately after the distribution the corporation continues to conduct another qualified trade or business. To be "qualified," a trade or business must have been actively conducted throughout the five-year period

1. S.Rep. No. 1622, 83d Cong., 2d Sess. 49 (1954). See Imler v. Commissioner, 11 T.C. 836 (1948) (the "contraction-by-fire" case referred to in the Senate Report).

2. For the Service's ruling policy on whether a distribution qualifies as a corporate contraction, see Rev.Proc. 2008–3, § 4.01(21), 2008–1 C.B. 116 (ordinarily no ruling unless distribution results in a 20 percent or greater reduction in gross revenue, net fair market value of assets, and employees).

ending on the date of the distribution and must not have been acquired by the distributing corporation in a taxable transaction during that period.[3] The active trade or business that the corporation continues to conduct must have a similar five-year business history. The "active" business requirement is designed to patrol against the accumulation of earnings in the form of investment assets, such as real estate or securities, followed by prompt bailout distributions masquerading as corporate contractions.[4]

A distribution may qualify as a partial liquidation even if the shareholders do not actually surrender any stock.[5] If the other requirements of either the general corporate contraction doctrine or the statutory safe harbor are met, the transaction will be treated as a constructive redemption of stock.[6]

Distributions to corporate shareholders do not qualify for partial liquidation treatment even if all the other statutory requirements are met.[7] For purposes of determining whether a shareholder is corporate or noncorporate, stock held by a partnership, estate, or trust (but not an S corporation) is treated as if held proportionately by the partners or beneficiaries.[8] S corporations are thus treated as corporate shareholders and do not qualify for exchange treatment on a partial liquidation under Section 302(b)(4).

At first glance, it might seem that C corporation shareholders would welcome their eviction from the partial liquidation safe harbor because distributions that otherwise would give rise to taxable capital gain would become dividends sheltered by the dividends received deduction. But Congress was not acting in a spirit of generosity. Rather, it was attempting to put an end to several widely publicized acquisition techniques that used the partial liquidation as a vehicle for obtaining the best of all tax worlds: a stepped-up basis for selected assets of the acquired corporation along with the preservation of favorable tax attributes (e.g., earnings and profits deficits, loss and credit carryovers, etc.)—all at little or no tax cost.[9]

Congress inflicted further punishment on corporate shareholders when it enacted restrictions to prevent abuse of the dividends received deduction.[10] Any amount treated as a dividend to a corporate shareholder under Section 301 is an "extraordinary dividend" under Section 1059 if it is a distribution in redemption of stock which is part of a partial liquidation of the redeeming corporation, regardless of the shareholder's holding period

3. I.R.C. § 302(e)(3).

4. For the definition of an active trade or business, see Reg. § 1.355–3(b), (c), which govern corporate divisions under Section 355. See Chapter 18B, infra.

5. Fowler Hosiery Co. v. Commissioner, 301 F.2d 394 (7th Cir.1962); Rev.Rul. 90–13, 1990–1 C.B. 65.

6. See Rev.Rul. 77–245, 1977–2 C.B. 105, for the method of computing the tax consequences of a partial liquidation.

7. I.R.C. § 302(b)(4).

8. I.R.C. § 302(e)(5).

9. See, e.g., Henderson, "Federal Tax Techniques for Asset Redeployment Transactions," 37 Tax L.Rev. 325 (1982); Ginsburg, "Taxing Corporate Acquisitions," 38 Tax L.Rev. 171 (1983).

10. See Chapter 12F, supra.

or the size of the distribution.[11] As a result, a corporate shareholder that receives a dividend in a transaction treated as a partial liquidation must reduce its basis in the stock of the redeeming corporation by the portion of the dividend that was not taxed because of the dividends received deduction.[12]

Revenue Ruling 79–184

1979–1 Cum.Bull. 143.

Advice has been requested whether the sale by a parent corporation of all the stock of a wholly owned subsidiary and the distribution of the sales proceeds by the parent to its shareholders qualifies as a distribution in partial liquidation within the meaning of section 346(a)(2) of the Internal Revenue Code of 1954 [now Section 302(e). Ed.].

Corporation *P* owned all of the single class of outstanding stock of Corporation *S* for many years, during which time each had been engaged in the active conduct of a trade or business.

Pursuant to a plan, *P* sold all of the stock of *S* to an unrelated party for cash and distributed the proceeds of the sale pro rata to its shareholders in redemption of part of their *P* stock.

Section [302(e)(1)] of the Code provides, in part, that a distribution will be treated as a partial liquidation of a corporation if it is not essentially equivalent to a dividend, is in redemption of a part of the stock of the corporation pursuant to a plan, and occurs within the taxable year in which the plan is adopted or within the succeeding taxable year. Section 1.346–1(a)(2) of the Income Tax Regulations provides that a distribution resulting from a genuine contraction of the corporate business is an example of a distribution that will qualify as a partial liquidation under section [302(e)(1)].

Generally, for purposes of section [302(e)] of the Code, the business that is terminated or contracted must be operated directly by the corporation making the distribution. See *H.L. Morgenstern*, 56 T.C. 44 (1971). However, Rev.Rul. 75–223, 1975–1 C.B. 109, provides that when a parent corporation liquidates a wholly owned subsidiary and distributes the subsidiary's assets, or the proceeds from the sale of those assets, to its shareholders, the fact that the distributions were attributable to assets used by the subsidiary rather than directly by the parent will not prevent the distribution from qualifying as a "genuine contraction of the corporate business" to the parent within the meaning of section 1.346–1(a)(2) of the regulations. The basis for this holding is that under section 381 a parent corporation that liquidates a subsidiary under section 332 (when section 334(b)(1) applies) inherits attributes (for example, earnings and profits) of

11. I.R.C. § 1059(e)(1).

12. I.R.C. § 1059(a), (b). If the non-taxed portion of the dividend exceeds the shareholder's basis in the redeemed stock, the excess is treated as gain from a sale or exchange of the stock. I.R.C. § 1059(a)(2).

the liquidated subsidiary so that after the liquidation of the subsidiary the parent is viewed as if it had always operated the business of the liquidated subsidiary.

However, when a parent corporation distributes the stock of its subsidiary, as in *Situation 3* of Rev.Rul. 75–223, section 381 of the Code does not apply to integrate the past business results of the subsidiary with those of the parent. Therefore, distribution by the parent of subsidiary's stock does not result in the parent corporation taking into account the past operations of the subsidiary. Thus, there is no analogy between a distribution of stock of the subsidiary and a distribution of the assets of a liquidated subsidiary or the proceeds of a sale of such assets. A distribution of the stock of the subsidiary under such circumstances is a corporate separation, governed by section 355, and not a corporate contraction.

Similarly, as in the present case, where *P* sells all of the stock of its wholly owned subsidiary, *S*, and distributes the proceeds to its shareholders, there is no basis for attributing the business activities of *S* to *P*. It is well established that a corporation is a legal entity separate and distinct from its shareholders. New Colonial Ice Co. v. Helvering, 292 U.S. 435 (1934), XIII–1 C.B. 194 (1934); Moline Properties, Inc. v. Commissioner, 319 U.S. 436 (1943), 1943 C.B. 1011. Although the assets of *P* are reduced by the subsequent distribution of the sale proceeds, the sale by *P* of the *S* stock is not in and of itself sufficient to effect a contraction of the business operations of *P* within the contemplation of section 346(a)(2) of the Code. Rather, the overall transaction has the economic significance of the sale of an investment and distribution of the proceeds.

Accordingly, the distribution by *P* to its shareholders of the proceeds of the sale of the *S* stock does not qualify as a distribution in partial liquidation within the meaning of section [302(e)(1)] of the Code, and the distribution will be treated as a distribution by *P* of property taxable to the *P* shareholders under section 301 by reason of section 302(d). See section 1.302–2(b) of the regulations, which provides that all distributions in pro rata redemption of a part of the stock of a corporation generally will be treated as distributions under section 301 if the corporation has only one class of stock outstanding.

PROBLEM

Alpha Corporation operates a book publishing business ("Books") and a bar exam review course ("Cram") as divisions (i.e., not as separately incorporated entities). Alpha's single class of common stock outstanding is owned in equal shares by Michael, Pamela (Michael's wife) and Iris Corporation. Neither Michael nor Pamela owns any stock in Iris. Alpha also owns all of the stock of Beta Corporation, a separately incorporated company which is engaged in the beta processing business, and it directly owns a diversified securities portfolio.

What are the shareholder level tax consequences of the following alternative transactions:

(a) Alpha has operated Books and Cram for more than five years and it distributes the assets of Books to its three equal shareholders in redemption of 50 shares from each shareholder. Any different result if the redemption is made without an actual surrender of shares?

(b) Is there a different result in (a), above, if Alpha had purchased Books three years ago for cash? If so, why should that matter? What if Alpha acquired Books three years ago in a tax-free reorganization?

(c) What if all the assets of Books were destroyed by fire and Alpha distributes one-half of the insurance proceeds equally to its three shareholders in redemption of an appropriate number of shares of stock and retains the remaining proceeds to carry on its book publishing business on a somewhat smaller scale?

(d) Same as (a), above, except that Alpha distributes the assets of Books to Michael in redemption of all of his stock.

(e) Same as (a), above except that Alpha distributes the assets of Books to Iris in redemption of all of its Alpha stock.

(f) Alpha distributes the securities portfolio to its three equal shareholders in redemption of 20 shares from each shareholder.

(g) Alpha sells all of its Beta stock and distributes the proceeds pro rata to the shareholders in redemption of 20 shares from each.

(h) Same as (g), above, except that Alpha liquidates Beta and then distributes the assets of Beta's business, which Beta has operated for more than five years.

E. CONSEQUENCES TO THE DISTRIBUTING CORPORATION

1. DISTRIBUTIONS OF APPRECIATED PROPERTY IN REDEMPTION

Code: § 311.

In the preceding chapter, the story of the decline of the *General Utilities* doctrine began to unfold.[1] The assault on *General Utilities* in the redemption setting gained momentum when Congress discovered that several insurance companies were redeeming large amounts of their own stock by distributing appreciated securities while avoiding recognition of gain at the corporate level.[2] Congress curtailed this perceived abuse by enacting a rule that required a corporation to recognize gain on a distribution of appreciated property in a redemption as if the property had been sold for its fair market value. Partial liquidation distributions, however, continued to qualify for nonrecognition at the corporate level, and numer-

1. See Chapter 12D1, supra.

2. See S.Rep. No. 91–552, 91st Cong., 1st Sess. 279, reprinted in 1969–3 C.B. 423,-600.

ous exceptions demonstrated that Congress was not yet ready to give *General Utilities* a proper burial.[3]

Corporate takeover specialists were quick to exploit these remaining vestiges of the *General Utilities* doctrine. Through carefully orchestrated transactions, they sought to convert a direct sale of property by a corporation, normally a taxable event to the seller, into a tax-free distribution.[4] After several of these schemes were publicized, Congress responded by further narrowing the opportunity for nonrecognition on nonliquidating distributions of appreciated property in redemption.[5] The final demise of *General Utilities* in the redemption context came with the Tax Reform Act of 1986. In adopting Section 311(b), which also applies to nonliquidating distributions, Congress repealed all the remaining exceptions that had provided for nonrecognition of gain to the distributing corporation. As a result, a corporation distributing property in redemption of stock (including a partial liquidation) always recognizes gain but may not recognize loss.

2. Effect on Earnings and Profits

Code: § 312(n)(7).

The effect of a stock redemption on the distributing corporation's earnings and profits initially depends upon the tax consequences of the redemption at the shareholder level. If the redemption is treated as a distribution to which Section 301 applies, the distributing corporation adjusts its earnings and profits in the same manner as on other nonliquidating distributions—i.e., earnings and profits are decreased by the amount of cash and the principal amount of any obligations, and by the greater of the adjusted basis or the fair market value of any property distributed.[1] In addition, the corporation always recognizes gain and correspondingly increases its current earnings and profits on a distribution of appreciated property, and it reduces current earnings and profits by any taxes paid on that gain.[2]

If a redemption (including a partial liquidation) is treated as an exchange to the redeemed shareholder, the effect on earnings and profits is more complex. In that situation, Section 312(n)(7) provides that the part of the distribution in redemption that is properly chargeable to earnings and profits shall be an amount which does not exceed the ratable share of the corporation's accumulated earnings and profits attributable to the redeemed stock. For purposes of Section 312(n)(7), accumulated earnings and profits include any current earnings and profits available at the time of the

3. See I.R.C. § 311(d)(2) (pre–1982).

4. See Henderson, "Federal Tax Techniques for Asset Redeployment Transactions," 37 Tax L.Rev. 325 (1982). The Service's attack or this strategy was rejected in Esmark, Inc. v. Commissioner, 90 T.C. 171 (1988), aff'd, 886 F.2d 1318 (7th Cir.1989).

5. For a description of some of the abuses at which the 1982 changes were directed, see Staff of Joint Committee on Taxation, General Explanation of Tax Equity and Fiscal Responsibility Act of 1982, 97th Cong., 2d Sess. 125 (1982).

1. I.R.C. § 312(a), (b).

2. I.R.C. § 311(b); 312(b).

redemption. The current earnings and profits available at that time are determined after they first have been applied to characterize as dividends any Section 301 distributions made during the year. If the corporation is unable to show the actual current earnings and profits as of the date of the redemption, then current earnings and profits are allocated to the date of distribution on a pro rata basis.[3] Congress also expressed its intention that earnings and profits never would be reduced by more than the amount of the redemption.[4]

To illustrate the operation of this rule, assume that X Corporation has 1,000 shares of common stock outstanding, and that A and B each acquire 500 of these shares at issuance at a price of $20 per share. Assume further that X is a profitable business that holds $100,000 of net assets, consisting of $50,000 cash and $50,000 of appreciated real property, and X has $50,000 of accumulated earnings and profits. If X distributes $50,000 cash to A in redemption of A's 500 shares, Section 312(n)(7) reduces X's earnings and profits by $25,000—the ratable share of X's $50,000 earnings and profits attributable to A's 50 percent stock interest that was redeemed. The remaining $25,000 of the distribution is charged to X's capital account and, after the redemption, X would have $25,000 of remaining accumulated earnings and profits. The following excerpt from the legislative history of the Tax Reform Act of 1984 explains the operation of this rule in the case of a corporation with a more complex capital structure:[5]

> If a corporation has more than one class of stock outstanding, its earnings and profits generally should be allocated among the different classes in determining the amount by which a redemption of all or a part of one class of stock reduces earnings and profits. However, earnings and profits generally should not be allocated to preferred stock which is not convertible and which does not participate to any significant extent in corporate growth. Therefore, a redemption of such preferred stock should result in a reduction of the capital account only, unless the distribution includes dividend arrearages, which will reduce earnings and profits.
>
> Similarly, priorities legally required as between different classes of stock should be taken into account in allocating earnings and profits between classes. For example, assume that corporation X has 1,000 shares of class A common stock and 1,000 shares of class B common stock. Both classes are $10 par value stock and were issued at the same time at a price of $20. The class A common has a preference as to dividends and liquidating distributions in a 2:1 ratio to the class B common, and only the class B common has voting rights. Assume further that Corporation X

3. Rev. Rul. 74–338, 1974–2 C.B. 101; Baker v. United States, 460 F.2d 827 (8th Cir. 1972).

4. S.Rep. No. 98–169, 98th Cong., 2d Sess. 202 (1984).

5. Staff of Joint Committee on Taxation, General Explanation of the Tax Reform Act of 1984, 98th Cong., 2d Sess. 181 (1984).

holds net assets worth $210,000 and has current and accumulated earnings and profits of $120,000. If X distributes $140,000 in cash in redemption of all of the class A common, earnings and profits should be reduced by $80,000 and capital account by $60,000.

PROBLEM

X Corporation has 200 shares of common stock outstanding. A and B, who are unrelated, each acquired 100 shares of X upon their issuance at a price of $1,000 per share, and they each thus have an adjusted basis of $100,000 in their X stock. At the beginning of the current year, X has $120,000 of accumulated earnings and profits, no current earnings and profits, and a net worth of $400,000. What are the tax consequences to X if it distributes $200,000 cash to A in redemption of A's 100 shares and the redemption qualifies for exchange treatment under Section 302(a)?

3. Stock Reacquisition Expenses

Code: § 162(k).

Amounts paid to acquire stock generally must be capitalized as part of the stock's basis.[1] The capitalization requirement applies to the original purchase price of the stock as well as to acquisition expenses, such as brokerage commissions and legal fees.[2] Some older authority held, however, that expenses incurred by a corporation to repurchase its stock, in limited circumstances, might be ordinary and necessary expenses deductible under Section 162.[3] In the midst of the frenzy of hostile corporate takeovers in the 1980's, Congress became concerned that corporate expenditures incurred to fend off unwanted corporate suitors by purchasing their shares—so-called "greenmail" payments—were being characterized as deductible business expenses.[4] Section 162(k)(1) was enacted to make it clear that all expenditures by a corporation incurred in purchasing its own stock, whether representing amounts paid for the stock, a premium paid in excess of the stock's value, or expenses connected with the purchase, are nondeductible, nonamortizable capital expenditures.[5] Section 162(k)(2) contains exceptions for interest payments deductible under Section 163, and several more specialized situations. In 1996, Congress broadened the scope of Section 162(k)(1) by extending its application to any "reacquisition" of stock regardless of whether the transaction is technically treated as a redemption under Subchapter C.

1. I.R.C. §§ 263(a), 1012.

2. Reg. § 1.263(a)–2(c), (e). See Woodward v. Commissioner, 397 U.S. 572, 90 S.Ct. 1302 (1970); United States v. Hilton Hotels Corp., 397 U.S. 580, 90 S.Ct. 1307 (1970).

3. Five Star Manufacturing Co. v. Commissioner, 355 F.2d 724 (5th Cir.1966). See generally Note, "Deductibility of Stock Redemption Expenses and the Corporate Survival Doctrine," 58 So.Cal.L.Rev. 895 (1985).

4. S.Rep. No. 99–313, 99th Cong., 2d Sess. 223 (1986).

5. Id.

One difficult interpretive problem under the Section 162(k) disallowance rule revolves around the question of what amounts are paid to shareholders "in connection with" a redemption of stock. The legislative history states that while the phrase "in connection with" is to be construed broadly, it is not intended to deny a deduction for "otherwise deductible amounts paid in a transaction which has no nexus with the redemption other than being proximate in time or arising out of the same circumstances."[6] The Conference Report goes on to expand upon this standard:[7]

> For example, if a corporation redeems a departing employee's stock and makes a payment to the employee in discharge of the corporation's obligations under an employment contract, the payment in discharge of the contractual obligation is not subject to disallowance under this provision. Payments in discharge of other types of contractual obligations, in settlement of litigation, or pursuant to other actual or potential legal obligations or rights, may also be outside the intended scope of the provision to the extent it is clearly established that the payment does not represent consideration for the stock or expenses related to its acquisition, and is not a payment that is a fundamental part of a "standstill" or similar agreement.
>
> The conferees anticipate that, where a transaction is not directly related to a redemption but is proximate in time, the Internal Revenue Service will scrutinize the transaction to determine whether the amount purportedly paid in the transaction is reasonable. Thus, even where the parties have countervailing tax interests, the parties' stated allocation of the total consideration between the redemption and the unrelated transaction will be respected only if it is supported by all the facts and circumstances.
>
> However, the conferees intend that agreements to refrain from purchasing stock of a corporation or other similar types of "standstill" agreements in all events will be considered related to any redemption of the payee's stock. Accordingly, payments pursuant to such agreements are nondeductible under this provision provided there is an actual purchase of all or part of the payee's stock. The conferees intend no inference regarding the deductibility of payments under standstill or similar agreements that are unrelated to any redemption of stock owned by the payee.

The most controversial interpretive issue to arise since the enactment of Section 162(k) involves the deductibility of loan fees and related expenses incurred by corporations that have engaged in leveraged stock repurchase transactions. The courts have disagreed on the scope of the disallowance rule in this setting. The Ninth Circuit upheld the deductibility of various fees incurred to finance a stock redemption in a case where a public corporation sought to amortize $4 million in loan fees incurred in

6. H.R.Rep. No. 841, 99th Cong., 2d Sess. II—168 (1986).

7. Id. at II—168–69.

connection with a leveraged buyout designed to enable the company to go private.[8] The Service had disallowed the deductions, contending that the fees were stock redemption expenses subject to disallowance under Section 162(k). The court reasoned that Section 162(k) did not extend to financing costs because the borrowing was a transaction separate from the redemption. In so holding, the court rejected the Service's view that the disallowance rule extended to all costs (other than interest expenses, which is specifically excepted by statute) directly or indirectly related to a stock redemption, including financing fees. The Tax Court has taken a contrary view, holding that fees paid to an investment banking firm to obtain loans to finance a stock repurchase as part of a leveraged buyout were not deductible because they were incurred "in connection with redemption of stock."[9] The court agreed with the Service's broader view of Section 162(k), finding that the various steps taken to effect a leveraged buyout were integrated.

Congress eventually interceded, settling the controversy with a "technical correction" that amended Section 162(k) to make it clear that amounts properly allocable to indebtedness on which interest is deductible may be amortized over the term of the loan even if the debt is incurred by a corporation to repurchase its stock.[10]

F. REDEMPTION PLANNING TECHNIQUES

1. BOOTSTRAP ACQUISITIONS

Revenue Ruling 75–447

1975–2 Cum.Bull. 113.

Advice has been requested as to the Federal income tax consequences, in the situations described below, of the redemption by a corporation of part of its stock.

Situation 1

Corporation *X* had outstanding 100 shares of voting common stock of which *A* and *B* each owned 50 shares. In order to bring *C* into the business with an equal stock interest, and pursuant to an integrated plan, *A* and *B* caused *X* to issue, at fair market value, 25 new shares of voting common stock to *C*. Immediately thereafter, as part of the same plan, *A* and *B* caused *X* to redeem 25 shares of *X* voting common stock from each of them. Neither *A, B,* nor *C* owned any stock of *X* indirectly under section 318 of the Internal Revenue Code of 1954.

8. In re Kroy (Europe) Ltd., 27 F.3d 367 (9th Cir.1994).

9. Fort Howard Corp. v. Commissioner, 103 T.C. 345 (1994).

10. I.R.C. § 162(k)(2)(ii).

Situation 2

Corporation *X* had outstanding 100 shares of voting common stock of which *A* and *B* each owned 50 shares. In order to bring *C* into the business with an equal stock interest, and pursuant to an integrated plan, *A* and *B* each sold 15 shares of *X* voting common stock to *C* at fair market value and then caused *X* to redeem five shares from both *A* and *B*. Neither *A*, *B*, nor *C* owned any stock of *X* indirectly under section 318 of the Code.

Section 302(b)(2) of the Code states that section 302(a), which provides for treating a redemption of stock as a distribution in part or full payment in exchange for the stock, will apply if the distribution is substantially disproportionate with respect to the shareholder. * * *

In Zenz v. Quinlivan, 213 F.2d 914 (6th Cir.1954), a sole shareholder of a corporation, desiring to dispose of her entire interest therein, sold part of her stock to a competitor and shortly thereafter sold the remainder of her stock to the corporation for an amount of cash and property approximately equal to its earned surplus. The Government contended that the redemption was a dividend on the grounds that the result was the same as if the steps had been reversed, that is, as if the stock had been redeemed first and the sale of stock to the competitor had followed. The United States Court of Appeals rejected the Government's contention and held that the purchase of the stock by the corporation (when coupled with the sale of stock to the competitor) was not a dividend to the selling shareholder and that the proceeds should be treated as payment for the stock surrendered under the provisions of the Internal Revenue Code of 1939.

Rev.Rul. 55–745, 1955–2 C.B. 223, states that in situations similar to that in *Zenz*, the amount received by the shareholder from the corporation will be treated as received in payment for the stock surrendered under section 302(a) of the Code since the transaction when viewed as a whole results in the shareholder terminating his interest in the corporation within the meaning of section 302(b)(3).

In determining whether the "substantially disproportionate" provisions of section 302(b)(2) of the Code have been satisfied in *Situation 1* and in *Situation 2*, it is proper to rely upon the holding in *Zenz* that the sequence in which the events (that is, the redemption and sale) occur is irrelevant as long as both events are clearly part of an overall plan. Therefore, in situations where the redemption is accompanied by an issuance of new stock (as in *Situation 1*), or a sale of stock (as in *Situation 2*), and both steps (the sale, or issuance, of stock, as the case may be, and the redemption) are clearly part of an integrated plan to reduce a shareholder's interest, effect will be given only to the overall result for purposes of section 302(b)(2) and the sequence in which the events occur will be disregarded.

Since the *Zenz* holding requires that effect be given only to the overall result and proscribes the fragmenting of the whole transaction into its component parts, the computation of the voting stock of the corporation owned by the shareholder *immediately before* the redemption for purposes of section 302(b)(2)(C)(ii) of the Code should be made before any part of the transaction occurs. Likewise, the computation of the voting stock of the corporation owned by the shareholder *immediately after* the redemption for purposes of section 302(b)(2)(C)(i) should be made after the whole transaction is consummated. Making the immediately before and the immediately after computations in this manner properly reflects the extent to which the shareholder involved in each situation actually reduces his stock holdings as a result of the whole transaction.

Therefore, for purposes of the computations required by section 302(b)(2)(C) of the Code, *A* and *B*, in *Situation 1*, will each be viewed as having owned 50 percent (50/100 shares) of *X* before the transaction and 33⅓ percent (25/75 shares) immediately thereafter. In *Situation 2, A* and *B* will each be viewed as having owned 50 percent (50/100 shares) of *X* before the transaction and 33⅓ percent (30/90 shares) immediately thereafter. Furthermore, in each situation, the result would be the same if the redemption had preceded the issuance, or sale, of stock.

Accordingly, in both *Situations 1* and *2*, the requirements of section 302(b)(2) of the Code are satisfied. Therefore, the amounts distributed to *A* and *B* in both situations are distributions in full payment in exchange for the stock redeemed pursuant to section 302(a).

NOTE

The classic bootstrap acquisition is a transaction where the buyer purchases all or part of the stock of the target corporation in conjunction with a redemption of some of the selling shareholder's stock. In Zenz v. Quinlivan,[1] which is discussed in Revenue Ruling 75–447, the sole shareholder of a corporation sold part of her stock for cash and, three weeks later, the corporation redeemed her remaining shares. The combined sale and redemption structure was used because the buyer wanted to minimize future dividend exposure by reducing the corporation's earnings and profits. The seller's agenda was to be taxed on both the sale and redemption at then favorable capital gains rates and avoid dividend treatment on the redemption.

The Service argued that the redemption would have been a dividend to the target's shareholder if the distribution had preceded the sale and should not be treated any differently where the parties orchestrated a different order of events. The Sixth Circuit disagreed. Finding that the taxpayer intended from the outset to terminate her entire interest in the corporation, it held that the redemption qualified as an exchange rather than a dividend. The Service subsequently acquiesced to the result in *Zenz* and extended its reasoning to substantially disproportionate redemptions in Revenue Ruling 75–447.

In the case of a noncorporate shareholder, *Zenz* and its progeny have far less significance as long as qualified dividends are taxed at preferential

1. 213 F.2d 914 (6th Cir. 1954).

capital gains rates. In a combined sale and redemption transaction, a noncorporate seller ordinarily will suffer no tax disadvantage if the distribution in redemption is characterized as a dividend. The distinction still matters, however, to corporate shareholders. As discussed in Chapter 12,[2] corporate sellers who are seeking to extract liquid assets prior to a sale of stock normally prefer a pre-sale dividend for two reasons: (1) the availability of the dividends received deduction, and (2) corporate capital gains are not taxed at preferential rates.

PROBLEM

Strap is the sole shareholder of Target Corporation. Boot is a prospective buyer and is willing to purchase all of the Target stock, but Boot is unable to pay the $500,000 price demanded by Strap even though he believes it to be fair. Target has $100,000 cash on hand. Should Strap and Boot structure Boot's acquisition of Target along the lines of the *Zenz* case? Is there a better alternative? What additional facts would you like to know? (Compare to *TSN Liquidating* and the problem on page 554, supra.)

2. BUY-SELL AGREEMENTS

a. IN GENERAL

Code: §§ 101(a); 264(a)(1); skim § 2703.

Closely held corporations frequently use buy-sell stock purchase agreements to ensure continuity of the business, to satisfy economic and tax goals when a shareholder dies or retires, and to resolve shareholder disputes. There are two basic forms of buy-sell agreements. Under a "cross-purchase" agreement, the departing shareholder or the shareholder's estate sells stock to the continuing shareholders. Under the more commonly employed "entity-purchase" agreement, the corporation redeems the departing shareholder's stock, funding the redemption with available cash, borrowed funds, an installment note, or the proceeds of a corporate-owned life insurance policy. The obligation to buy (or sell) may be mandatory or optional, as the parties agree, and is triggered by certain events specified in the agreement. The most common trigger event is a shareholder's death. Other typical trigger events are retirement or disability.

Buy-sell provisions frequently are part of a more comprehensive shareholders' agreement that includes restrictions on the transfer of stock, rights of first refusal to the corporation in the event a shareholder wishes to sell, and provisions to determine the value of any stock purchased pursuant to the agreement. Some primitive agreements set the price based on "book value," an accounting concept that often bears little or no relationship to the economic value of the company. More sophisticated agreements will use a formula based on earnings or provide for an appraisal mechanism on the occurrence of a trigger event.

2. See Chapter 12G, infra.

A goal of many buy-sell agreements for closely-held family businesses is to establish the federal estate tax valuation of the stock upon a shareholder's death. A decedent's gross estate generally includes all property held by the decedent, valued either at the date of death or six months thereafter (the alternate valuation date).[1] In the case of unlisted stock, which cannot be valued by market quotations, fair market value is determined by taking into account a variety of factors, including the corporation's net worth, its earnings history and dividend-paying capacity, and the value of stock of publicly traded companies in the same line of business.[2] If stock is subject to an option or contract to purchase, such as a buy-sell agreement, the regulations provide that the agreement will establish the value if it represents a bona fide business arrangement and is not a device to pass the stock to the natural objects of the decedent's bounty for less than adequate and full consideration.[3] But if the decedent was free to dispose of the stock during his lifetime without price restrictions, "little weight" is given to the price set at death by the option or contract.[4] The courts agree that maintaining control of a closely held business constitutes a bona fide business purpose but they require a separate examination of whether a restriction or option constitutes a "testamentary device."[5]

For buy-sell agreements entered into or substantially modified after October 8, 1990, Congress has added some statutory restrictions on the valuation of property subject to an option or contract to purchase. Section 2703(a) provides that the value of any property for estate, gift and generation-skipping tax purposes shall be determined without regard to (1) any option, agreement or other right to acquire or use property at a price less than the fair market value of the property, disregarding the option agreement or right, or (2) any restriction on the right to sell or use such property. Under this general rule, the effect of a buy-sell agreement on valuation would be disregarded. Section 2703(b), however, provides an exception for any option, agreement, right or restriction which satisfies the standards of the regulations (bona fide business arrangement and not a testamentary device) and has terms "comparable to similar arrangements entered into by persons in an arm's length transaction." In adding this comparability standard, Congress intended the taxpayer to show that the agreement was one that could have been obtained in an arm's length bargain with an unrelated party, considering such factors as the term of the agreement, the present value of the affected property, and its expected value at the time of exercise.[6] In noting that this standard would not be

1. I.R.C. §§ 2031; 2032.

2. I.R.C. § 2031(b); Reg. § 20.2031–2(f)(2). See also Rev. Rul. 59–60, 1959–1 C.B. 237.

3. Reg. § 20.2031–2(h). For the buy-sell agreement price to be binding, the decedent's estate must be obligated to sell the decedent's stock; the buyer either must be obligated to buy the decedent's interest or have an option to do so; and the price specified must have been fair at the time the agreement was made. Id.

4. Id.

5. See, e.g., St. Louis County Bank v. United States, 674 F.2d 1207 (8th Cir.1982).

6. Senate Finance Committee Explanation of Revenue Provisions, 1991 Budget Reconciliation Bill (Oct. 13, 1990), 101st Cong., 2d Sess. 68 (1990).

met "by showing isolated comparables but requires a demonstration of the general practice of unrelated parties," the Senate Finance Committee stated that expert testimony—e.g., by an appraiser familiar with the industry—would be evidence of such general practice.[7]

Even with the enactment of Section 2703, drafters of buy-sell agreements still have some flexibility in their use of valuation methodologies. For example, the Conference Report accompanying the 1990 Act states that a buy-sell agreement should not be disregarded merely because its terms differ from those used by another similarly situated company.[8] Noting that general business practice may recognize more than one valuation methodology, even within the same industry, the conferees went on to state that "[i]n such situations, one of several generally accepted methodologies may satisfy the standard contained in the conference agreement."[9]

Section 2703 has not resulted in the demise of buy-sell agreements to fix estate tax valuation. It merely places a greater premium on an evidentiary showing that the arrangement is bona fide and not merely a tax-avoidance device to transfer a family business to the next generation for less than adequate and full consideration.

As developed in the next section of the text, buy-sell agreements also may raise constructive dividend issues if they are not properly structured and implemented. With most dividends now taxed at 15 percent, these issues may or may not be important depending on other variables, such as the shareholder's stock basis, the need for capital gains to absorb otherwise unavailable capital losses, and the shareholder's other tax characteristics.

b. CONSTRUCTIVE DIVIDEND ISSUES

Revenue Ruling 69–608

1969–2 Cum.Bull. 42.

Advice has been requested as to the treatment for Federal income tax purposes of the redemption by a corporation of a retiring shareholder's stock where the remaining shareholder of the corporation has entered into a contract to purchase such stock.

Where the stock of a corporation is held by a small group of people, it is often considered necessary to the continuity of the corporation to have the individuals enter into agreements among themselves to provide for the disposition of the stock of the corporation in the event of the resignation, death, or incapacity of one of them. Such agreements are generally reciprocal among the shareholders and usually provide that on the resignation, death, or incapacity of one of the principal shareholders, the remaining shareholders will purchase his stock. Frequently such agreements are

7. Id. See also Reg. § 25.2703–1.

8. H.Rep. No. 101–964, 101st Cong., 2d Sess. 157 (1990).

9. Id. See also Reg. § 25.2703–1(b)(4).

assigned to the corporation by the remaining shareholder and the corporation actually redeems its stock from the retiring shareholder.

Where a corporation redeems stock from a retiring shareholder, the fact that the corporation in purchasing the shares satisfies the continuing shareholder's executory contractual obligation to purchase the redeemed shares does not result in a distribution to the continuing shareholder provided that the continuing shareholder is not subject to an existing primary and unconditional obligation to perform the contract and that the corporation pays no more than fair market value for the stock redeemed.

On the other hand, if the continuing shareholder, at the time of the assignment to the corporation of his contract to purchase the retiring shareholder's stock, is subject to an unconditional obligation to purchase the retiring shareholder's stock, the satisfaction by the corporation of his obligation results in a constructive distribution to him. The constructive distribution is taxable as a distribution under section 301 of the Internal Revenue Code of 1954.

If the continuing shareholder assigns his stock purchase contract to the redeeming corporation prior to the time when he incurs a primary and unconditional obligation to pay for the shares of stock, no distribution to him will result. If, on the other hand, the assignment takes place after the time when the continuing shareholder is so obligated, a distribution to him will result. While a pre-existing obligation to perform in the future is a necessary element in establishing a distribution in this type of case, it is not until the obligor's duty to perform becomes unconditional that it can be said a primary and unconditional obligation arises.

The application of the above principles may be illustrated by the situations described below.

Situation 1

A and *B* are unrelated individuals who own all of the outstanding stock of corporation *X*. *A* and *B* enter into an agreement that provides in the event *B* leaves the employ of *X*, he will sell his *X* stock to *A* at a price fixed by the agreement. The agreement provides that within a specified number of days of *B*'s offer to sell, *A* will purchase at the price fixed by the agreement all of the *X* stock owned by *B*. *B* terminates his employment and tenders the *X* stock to *A*. Instead of purchasing the stock himself in accordance with the terms of the agreement, *A* causes *X* to assume the contract and to redeem its stock held by *B*. In this case, *A* had a primary and unconditional obligation to perform his contract with *B* at the time the contract was assigned to *X*. Therefore, the redemption by *X* of its stock held by *B* will result in a constructive distribution to *A*. See William J. and Georgia K. Sullivan v. United States of America, 244 F.Supp. 605 (1965), affirmed, 363 F.2d 724 (1966), certiorari denied, 387 U.S. 905, 87 S.Ct. 1683 (1967), rehearing denied, 388 U.S. 924, 87 S.Ct. 2104 (1967).

Situation 2

A and *B* are unrelated individuals who own all of the outstanding stock of corporation *X*. An agreement between them provides unconditionally that within ninety days of the death of either *A* or *B*, the survivor will purchase the decedent's stock of *X* from his estate. Following the death of *B*, *A* causes *X* to assume the contract and redeem the stock from *B*'s estate.

The assignment of the contract to *X* followed by the redemption by *X* of the stock owned by *B*'s estate will result in a constructive distribution to *A* because immediately on the death of *B*, *A* had a primary and unconditional obligation to perform the contract.

Situation 3

All of the stock of *X* corporation was owned by a trust that was to terminate in 1968. Individuals *A* and *B* were the beneficiaries of the trust. Since *B* was the trustee of the trust, he had exclusive management authority over *X* through his control of the board of directors. In 1966, *A* paid to *B* the sum of 25*x* dollars and promised to pay an additional 20*x* dollars to *B* in 1969 for *B*'s interest in the corpus and accumulations of the trust plus *B*'s agreement to resign immediately as supervisor of the trust and release his control over the management of the corporation. The actual transfer of the stock held in trust was to take place on termination of the trust in 1968. In 1969, *X* reimbursed *A* for the 25*x* dollars previously paid to *B*, paid 20*x* dollars to *B*, and received the *X* stock held by *B*.

For all practical purposes, *A* became the owner of *B*'s shares in 1966. Although naked legal title to the shares could not be transferred until the trust terminated in 1968, *B* did transfer all of his beneficial and equitable ownership of the *X* stock to *A* in exchange for an immediate payment by *A* of 25*x* dollars and an unconditional promise to pay an additional 20*x* dollars upon termination of the trust. The payment by *X* of 20*x* dollars to *B* and 25*x* dollars to *A* in 1969 constituted a constructive distribution to *A* in the amount of 45*x* dollars. See Schalk Chemical Company v. Commissioner, 32 T.C. 879 (1959), affirmed 304 F.2d 48 (1962).

Situation 4

A and *B* owned all of the outstanding stock of *X* corporation. *A* and *B* entered into a contract under which, if *B* desired to sell his *X* stock, *A* agreed to purchase the stock or to cause such stock to be purchased. If *B* chose to sell his *X* stock to any person other than *A*, he could do so at any time. In accordance with the terms of the contract, *A* caused *X* to redeem all of *B*'s stock in *X*.

At the time of the redemption, *B* was free to sell his stock to *A* or to any other person, and *A* had no unconditional obligation to purchase the stock and no fixed liability to pay for the stock. Accordingly, the redemption by *X* did not result in a constructive distribution to *A*. See S.K. Ames, Inc. v. Commissioner, 46 B.T.A. 1020 (1942), acquiescence, C.B. 1942–1, 1.

Situation 5

A and *B* owned all of the outstanding stock of *X* corporation. An agreement between *A* and *B* provided that upon the death of either, *X* will redeem all of the *X* stock owned by the decedent at the time of his death. In the event that *X* does not redeem the shares from the estate, the agreement provided that the surviving shareholder would purchase the unredeemed shares from the decedent's estate. *B* died and, in accordance with the agreement, *X* redeemed all of the shares owned by his estate.

In this case *A* was only secondarily liable under the agreement between *A* and *B*. Since *A* was not primarily obligated to purchase the *X* stock from the estate of *B*, he received no constructive distribution when *X* redeemed the stock.

Situation 6

B owned all of the outstanding stock of *X* corporation. *A* and *B* entered into an agreement under which *A* was to purchase all of the *X* stock from *B*. *A* did not contemplate purchasing the *X* stock in his own name. Therefore, the contract between *A* and *B* specifically provided that it could be assigned by *A* to a corporation and that, if the corporation agreed to be bound by the terms, *A* would be released from the contract.

A organized *Y* corporation and assigned the stock purchase contract to it. *Y* borrowed funds and purchased all of the *X* stock from *B* pursuant to the agreement. Subsequently *Y* was merged into *X* and *X* assumed the liabilities that *Y* incurred in connection with the purchase of the *X* stock and subsequently satisfied these liabilities.

The purchase by *Y* of the stock of *X* did not result in a constructive distribution to *A*. Since *A* did not contemplate purchasing the *X* stock in his own name, he provided in the contract that it could be assigned to a corporation prior to the closing date. *A* chose this latter alternative and assigned the contract to *Y*. *A* was not personally subject to an unconditional obligation to purchase the *X* stock from *B*. See Arthur J. Kobacker and Sara Jo Kobacker, et al. v. Commissioner, 37 T.C. 882 (1962), acquiescence, C.B. 1964 2, 6. Compare Ray Edenfield v. Commissioner, 19 T.C. 13 (1952), acquiescence, C.B. 1953–1, 4.

Situation 7

A and *B* owned all of the outstanding stock of *X* corporation. An agreement between the shareholders provided that upon the death of either, the survivor would purchase the decedent's shares from his estate at a price provided in the agreement. Subsequently, the agreement was rescinded and a new agreement entered into which provided that upon the death of either *A* or *B, X* would redeem all of the decedent's shares of *X* stock from his estate.

The cancellation of the original contract between the parties in favor of the new contract did not result in a constructive distribution to either *A* or *B*. At the time *X* agreed to purchase the stock pursuant to the terms of the new agreement, neither *A* nor *B* had an unconditional obligation to purchase shares of *X* stock. The subsequent redemption of the stock from the estate of either pursuant to the terms of the new agreement will not constitute a constructive distribution to the surviving shareholder.

PROBLEM

A, B and C, who are unrelated, each own one-third of Y Corporation's outstanding common stock. The shareholders have entered into a cross-purchase agreement under which they agree that the two surviving shareholders will purchase the Y stock owned by the estate of the first shareholder to die. Y purchased a life insurance policy on the life of each shareholder and has continued to pay the annual premiums. Y is the beneficiary under the policies. B died this year, and Y used the proceeds from the policy on B's life to completely redeem the stock held by B's estate. What will be the tax consequences of these events to A, C and Y?

c. REDEMPTIONS INCIDENT TO DIVORCE

Regulations: § 1.1041–2(a), (b), (c), (d).

Arnes v. United States

United States Court of Appeals, Ninth Circuit, 1992.
981 F.2d 456.

■ HUG, CIRCUIT JUDGE:

The issue in this case is whether a taxpayer must recognize for income tax purposes the gain that she realized when, pursuant to a divorce settlement, a corporation redeemed her half of the stock in the corporation, the remaining stock of which was owned by her former husband. The district court, ruling on cross-motions for summary judgment, held that Section 1041 of the Internal Revenue Code of 1986 (I.R.C.) relieved the taxpayer of having to recognize the gain, and awarded the taxpayer a refund of $53,053 for 1988. * * * We affirm.

I.

Joann Arnes, the Taxpayer–Appellee, married John Arnes in 1970. In 1980, they formed a corporation, "Moriah," to operate a McDonald's franchise in Ellensburg, Washington. That corporation issued 5,000 shares of stock in the joint names of John Arnes and Joann Arnes. In 1987, the couple agreed to divorce. McDonald's Corporation required 100% ownership of the equity and profits by the owner/operator, and informed John Arnes that there should be no joint ownership of the restaurant after the divorce.

Joann and John Arnes entered into an agreement to have their corporation redeem Joann Arnes' 50 percent interest in the outstanding stock for $450,000. The corporation would pay that money to Joann Arnes by forgiving a debt of approximately $110,000 that she owed the corporation, by making two payments of $25,000 to her during 1988, and by paying the remainder of approximately $290,000 to her in monthly installments over ten years beginning in February 1988. The agreement was incorporated into the decree of dissolution of the marriage, dated January 7, 1988. Joann Arnes surrendered her 2,500 shares to the corporation on December

31, 1987, and the corporation cancelled her stock certificate on May 4, 1988, then issuing another 2,500 shares to John Arnes.

On her federal income tax return for 1988, Joann Arnes reported that she sold her stock in Moriah on January 2, 1988, for a price of $450,000, and that her basis was $2,500, resulting in a profit of $447,500. She received $178,042 in 1988 as part of the sales price. Using an installment method, she treated $177,045 as long-term capital gain and the remainder as recovery of a portion of her basis.

On December 27, 1989, she filed a timely claim for refund of $53,053 for 1988 on the ground that she was not required to recognize any gain on the transfer of her stock because the transfer was made pursuant to a divorce instrument. The IRS did not allow the claim for refund, and Joann Arnes initiated this suit.

The district court found that the redemption of Joann Arnes' stock in Moriah was required by a divorce instrument, and that John Arnes had benefitted from the transaction because it was part of the marital property settlement, which limited future community property claims that Joann Arnes might have brought against him. The court, in applying the IRS regulations, found that, although Joann transferred her stock directly to Moriah, the transfer was made on behalf of John and should have been treated as having been made to John. Therefore, the transfer qualified for nonrecognition of gain pursuant to the I.R.C. exemption for transfers made to spouses or former spouses incident to a divorce settlement. See 26 U.S.C. § 1041 (1988). Summary judgment was granted in favor of Joann Arnes.

The Government appeals. Meanwhile, in order to insure that the capital gain will be taxed, the Government has asserted a protective income tax deficiency against John Arnes, who has contested the deficiency by filing a petition with the Tax Court. His case is pending but not before this court. The Government maintains that, although Joann Arnes is the appropriate party to be taxed for the gain, John Arnes should be taxed if the district court's ruling is upheld. If neither John nor Joann is taxed, the $450,000 used to redeem Joann's appreciated stock apparently will be taken out of the corporation tax-free.

* * *

III.

The Government contends that the gain resulting from Moriah's redemption of Joann Arnes' stock does not qualify for exemption under section 1041, which is limited to transfers made directly to one's spouse or former spouse, or transfers made into trust for that person. Joann Arnes' transfer to Moriah, the Government contends, is outside the scope of the exemption. Joann Arnes contends that her transfer of stock to Moriah should be considered a transfer to John, resulting in a benefit to John, and absolving her of the obligation to bear the burden of any resulting tax.

* * *

The purpose of [Section 1041] is to defer the tax consequences of transfers between spouses or former spouses. See H.R.Rep. No. 432, Pt. II, 98th Cong., 2d Sess. 1491 (1984), reprinted in 1984 U.S.Code Cong. & Admin.News 697, 1134 ("a husband and wife are a single economic unit"). Property received in such a transfer is excluded from the recipient's gross income. The recipient's basis is then equal to the transferor's basis. 26 U.S.C. § 1041(b)(2) (1988). Later, when the recipient transfers the property to a third party, the gain or loss must be recognized.

After section 1041 was enacted, the Treasury Department published a temporary regulation to implement the statute. Temp. Treas. Reg. § 1.1041–1T (1992). The regulation explains that in certain cases a transfer of property to a third party "on behalf of" a spouse or former spouse should be treated as a transfer to the spouse or former spouse. Id. at Q–9, A–9. One example supplied in the regulation is the case where the transfer to the third party is required by a divorce or separation instrument. Such a transfer of property will be treated as made directly to the nontransferring spouse (or former spouse) and the nontransferring spouse will be treated as immediately transferring the property to the third party. The deemed transfer from the nontransferring spouse (or former spouse) to the third party is not a transaction that qualifies for nonrecognition of gain under section 1041. Temp.Treas.Reg. § 1.1041–1T, A–9 (1992).

The example suggests that the tax consequences of any gain or loss arising from the transaction would fall upon the nontransferring spouse for whose benefit the transfer was made, rather than upon the transferring spouse. Consistent with the policy of the statute, which is to defer recognition until the property is conveyed to a party outside the marital unit, the regulation seems to provide for shifting the tax burden from one spouse to the other, where appropriate.

Thus, a transfer by a spouse to a third party can be treated as a transfer to the other spouse when it is "on behalf of" the other spouse. Whether the redemption of Joann's stock can be construed as a transfer to John, pursuant to the regulation example in A–9, depends upon the meaning of "on behalf of." The district court interpreted the regulation as meaning that a transfer was made "on behalf of" John Arnes if he received a benefit from the transfer. The court then concluded that John did receive a benefit, because the transfer was part of the marital property agreement which settled any future community property claims that Joann Arnes could have asserted against John.

Although no case is directly on point, many tax cases concern transfers made on behalf of other persons. Generally, a transfer is considered to have been made "on behalf of" someone if it satisfied an obligation or a liability of that person. If an employer pays an employee's income tax, that payment is income to the employee. See Old Colony Trust Co. v. Commissioner, 279 U.S. 716, 729–31, 49 S.Ct. 499, 504, 73 L.Ed. 918 (1929). If a corporation assumes a shareholder's bank note in exchange for stock, the shareholder receives a taxable constructive dividend. Schroeder v. Commissioner, 831 F.2d 856, 859 (9th Cir.1987).

In *Schroeder*, the taxpayer borrowed money from a bank to buy stock in the corporation. The corporation later redeemed part of that stock, assumed the taxpayer's bank note, and forgave a debt owed by the taxpayer to the corporation. At the time that the taxpayer borrowed the money from the bank, he owned no part of the corporation and had no authority to act on behalf of the corporation. See id. at 859–60 & n. 7. The taxpayer had the primary obligation to repay the loan, and the corporation's assumption of the loan relieved the taxpayer of that obligation. We held that the redemption of Schroeder's stock was a taxable constructive dividend. Id. at 859.

The Government argues that the Arnes stock transfer is more properly analogized to Holsey v. Commissioner, 258 F.2d 865 (3d Cir.1958), where the Third Circuit held that a shareholder who owned fifty percent of the stock in a corporation did not receive a taxable benefit when the corporation redeemed the other fifty percent of the stock. The court found that the redemption "did not discharge any obligation of [the taxpayer] and did not benefit him in any direct sense," although the result was that the shareholder gained control of the company. Id. at 868.

John Arnes had an obligation to Joann Arnes that was relieved by Moriah's payment to Joann. That obligation was based in their divorce property settlement, which called for the redemption of Joann's stock. Although John and Joann were the sole stockholders in Moriah, the obligation to purchase Joann's stock was John's, not Moriah's. Furthermore, John personally guaranteed Moriah's note to Joann. Under Washington law, Joann could sue John for payment without suing Moriah. See Wash.Rev.Code Ann. § 62A.3–416(1) (West 1979). Thus, John was liable, with Moriah, for the payments due Joann.

We hold that Joann's transfer to Moriah did relieve John of an obligation, and therefore constituted a benefit to John. Joann's transfer of stock should be treated as a constructive transfer to John, who then transferred the stock to Moriah. The $450,000 was paid to Joann by Moriah on behalf of John. The transfer of $450,000 from the corporate treasury need not escape taxation, if we hold, as we do, that Joann is not required to recognize any gain on the transfer of her stock, because it is subject to section 1041. The tax result for Joann is the same as if she had conveyed the property directly to John.

The Government argues that because Joann transferred her stock to the corporation, rather than to John, the exception in section 1041 should not apply. The corporation cancelled Joann's stock and agreed to pay Joann $450,000. As a result, no asset with a carryover basis exists. John received an additional 2,500 shares from the corporation after Joann's shares were cancelled, but he did not carry over Joann's basis, because the transfer was not made directly to him. Under this literal application of the statute, Joann's gain, from the appreciation of the stock, would not be recognized by John if he were to dispose of his stock. Although John became the sole owner of the corporation as a result of the transfer, the net worth of the corporation was depleted, because the corporation incurred the debt of $450,000 to Joann. As the Government puts it, before the stock redemption, John owned half of a corporation worth $900,000; after the redemption, he owned all of a corporation worth $450,000. John has realized no gain; the value of his stock is still in the corporation, and the redemption did not increase the value of John's stock. In contrast, Joann received cash (and debt forgiveness) for her transfer of stock.

We reject the Government's application of the statute. The regulations, particularly as explained by Question and Answer 9, in Temp. Treas. Reg. § 1.1041–1T, demonstrate that the statute is meant to apply to situations such as this one, where a transfer is made on behalf of one's former spouse.

Finally, the Government points to one other example in the Temporary Treasury Regulations interpreting section 1041. Question 2 describes a situation in which a corporation wholly owned by one spouse sells property to the other spouse. That sale is not subject to the exemption rule of section 1041. See Temp. Treas. Reg. § 1.1041–1T(a), Q–2, A–2, ex. 3 (1992). The example does not apply to the Arnes transaction because Moriah was owned one-half each by John and Joann.

The judgment of the district court is AFFIRMED.

NOTE

Tax Consequences to Nontransferor Spouse. The Ninth Circuit found that the disposition of Mrs. Arnes' stock was not a redemption but rather a sale to Mr. Arnes in a tax-free transaction under Section 1041. What then are the tax consequences to Mr. Arnes, who was not a party to the case? Assuming that Moriah was a C corporation with sufficient earnings and profits, Mr. Arnes would appear to have a $450,000 constructive dividend (taxable, under current law, at a maximum rate of 15 percent but with no recovery of basis) under the Ninth Circuit's characterization of the transaction. But appearances can be deceiving. Mr. Arnes took his controversy to the Tax Court, which held in a reviewed decision that he did not have a constructive dividend because he was not primarily and unconditionally obligated to acquire his wife's stock.[1] The court supported its decision with the following example from Revenue Ruling 69–608:[2]

> A and B owned all the outstanding stock of X corporation. An agreement between A and B provided that upon the death of either, X will redeem all the X stock owned by the decedent at the time of death. In the event that X does not redeem the shares from the estate, the agreement provided that the surviving shareholder would purchase the unredeemed shares from the decedent's estate.

1. Arnes v. Commissioner, 102 T.C. 522 (1994). See also Blatt v. Commissioner, 102 T.C. 77 (1994) (wife taxable on redemption; no Section 1041 transfer because redemption did not satisfy any legal obligation of husband and wife was not acting "on behalf of" husband at time of acquisition); Hayes v. Commissioner, 101 T.C. 593 (1993) (redemption of wife's stock was a constructive dividend to husband where husband had a primary and unconditional obligation to purchase that stock; no Section 1041 issue before the court).

2. See supra p. 611.

> B died and, in accordance with the agreement, X redeemed all of the shares owned by his estate.
>
> In this case A was only secondarily liable under the agreement between A and B. Since A was not primarily obligated to purchase the X stock from the estate of B he received no constructive distribution when X redeemed the stock.

As a result, neither Mr. nor Mrs. Arnes was taxable on the transaction—the dreaded "whipsaw" result that the Service was trying to avoid.

Which result was more favorable overall for the taxpayers—the Ninth Circuit's or the Tax Court's? Remember that it is usually desirable in a marital dissolution setting for the parties to plan to reduce their overall tax liability. In a concurring opinion in *Arnes*, Tax Court Judge Beghe offered this observation:[3]

> Hewing to the bright line rules of Rev. Rul. 69–608 * * * in the marital dissolution context will reduce the tax costs of divorce for the owners of small businesses held and operated in corporate form. If the shareholder spouses can negotiate their separation agreement with the assurance that the redemption will be tax free to the remaining shareholder and a capital gain transaction to the terminating shareholder, the overall tax costs will ordinarily be less than if the terminating spouse qualifies for nonrecognition under Section 1041, but the remaining spouse suffers a dividend tax. This will leave a bigger pie to be divided in setting the consideration for the share to be redeemed.

Confusion in the Courts: Inconsistent Standards. The Ninth Circuit held that Mrs. Arnes was not taxable under Section 1041 because her transfer was "on behalf of" her husband within the meaning of the Section 1041 regulations. But the Tax Court held that Mr. Arnes did not have a constructive dividend because the corporation did not satisfy his "primary and unconditional" obligation to acquire his wife's stock. So neither spouse was taxed and the Service was whipsawed because different standards were applied to the transferor and nontransferor spouse to determine the tax consequences of the same transaction.

The Tax Court has revisited this issue, but its multiple and conflicting opinions in Read v. Commissioner[4] only added to the confusion. The fact pattern in *Read* was fairly typical. Prior to their marital dissolution, Mr. and Mrs. Read owned virtually all the stock of Mulberry Motor Parts, Inc. ("MMP"), a C corporation. Mrs. Read ("W") agreed to sell her MMP stock to Mr. Read ("H") for cash and a promissory note bearing market rate interest unless H elected to cause MMP or its separate employee stock ownership plan to buy the stock on the same terms. H elected to have MMP redeem W's stock. Although W reported the interest paid by MMP on the promissory note as income, neither W nor H reported any taxable gain on the redemption. Fearing a whipsaw, the Service issued deficiency notices to

3. 102 T.C. at 541.

4. 114 T.C. 14 (2000).

both parties. But it ultimately aligned itself with W by arguing in the Tax Court that H had received a constructive dividend from MMP in the full amount of the principal and interest payments received by W.

The Tax Court majority viewed the central issue to be whether W's transfer of MMP stock to MMP was made "on behalf of H" so that W was entitled to nonrecognition of gain under the Section 1041 regulations.[5] W argued that the regulations squarely applied to her situation, while H, seeking to avoid a constructive dividend, relied on established case law in arguing that he should not be taxed because he never had a "primary and unconditional obligation" to purchase W's stock.

The Tax Court majority sided with W, holding for the first time that application of the venerable "primary and unconditional" standard to the nontransferor spouse was inappropriate in divorce-related redemptions. Instead, the majority based its decision on the Section 1041 regulations in holding that W's transfer of MMP stock to MMP was a transfer made "on behalf of" H. The court found that H's election to have MMP redeem W's stock caused W to be acting as H's representative in connection with the redemption. In light of these holdings, the majority sustained the deficiencies asserted against H, noting that H had "indicated" that he would be taxable if the court found that W was entitled to nonrecognition under Section 1041. Because it found H's "indication" as tantamount to a concession, the Tax Court majority offered no analysis of the proper standard to be applied to the nonredeeming spouse. As discussed earlier in this Note, however, the Tax Court previously had applied the "primary and unconditional" standard in holding that a nontransferor spouse does not invariably receive a constructive dividend in a divorce-related redemption.

Nine judges joined the majority opinion in *Read*; six of the nine wrote a concurring opinion with more extensive analysis of the unfavorable tax consequences to H. Seven judges dissented in four separate opinions. Despite differences in emphasis, the essence of the dissents was that the majority should not have discarded the "primary and unconditional" standard in the divorce setting.

Regulations to the Rescue. Reacting to the confusion in the courts, the Service amended the Section 1041 regulations to provide greater certainty in determining the tax consequences of divorce-related redemptions. Unlike the Tax Court majority in *Read*, the regulations seek to harmonize the well recognized "primary and unconditional obligation" standard for constructive dividends with the policy of Section 1041.

The threshold question posed by the regulations is whether a divorce-related redemption results in a constructive distribution to the nontransferor spouse under applicable tax law. For this purpose, "applicable tax law" means the primary and unconditional obligation standard.[6] If the redemption does result in a constructive distribution, the redeemed stock is deemed to have been transferred by the transferor spouse to the non-

5. See Reg. § 1.1041–1T(c), Q & A–9.

6. Reg. § 1.1041–2(a), (d) Examples 1 & 3.

transferor spouse in a tax-free Section 1041 transaction (provided the requirements of Section 1041 are otherwise met), and then retransferred by the nontransferor spouse to the redeeming corporation.[7] The tax consequences of the deemed redemption are then determined under Section 302.[8] As a result, the transferor spouse has no gain or loss on the deemed transfer of stock to the nontransferor spouse, and the nontransferor spouse most likely has a constructive dividend.[9]

If the redemption does not result in a constructive distribution—e.g., because it does not satisfy a primary and unconditional obligation of the nontransferor spouse—the regulations respect the form of the transaction.[10] That means that the corporation is treated as having redeemed stock directly from the transferor spouse in a transaction in which the nontransferor spouse is not a party. As a result, Section 1041 does not apply, the transferor spouse's tax treatment is determined under Section 302 (likely a capital gain), and the nontransferor spouse is not taxed.[11]

The regulations provide a "special rule" permitting spouses to depart from "applicable tax law" and treat a divorce-related redemption as either taxable to the transferor spouse (even if it would have been a constructive dividend to the nontransferor spouse under applicable tax law) or as a constructive distribution to the nontransferor spouse and a tax-free Section 1041 transfer to the transferor spouse (even in the absence of a primary and unconditional obligation).[12] This rule is consistent with the general policy allowing the parties to a divorce to negotiate and ultimately determine the tax consequences of divorce-related transactions (e.g., spousal and child support payments, property transfers, dependency exemptions) as long as they treat the transactions consistently. To utilize the special rule, the parties must memorialize their intent in a written agreement prior to the date on which the nontransferor spouse files his or her first timely filed federal income tax return for the year that includes the date of the stock redemption but no later than the due date of the return (including extensions).[13]

If the regulations had applied to the redemption in the *Arnes* case and the parties had not elected to utilize the special rule, which spouse would have been taxed?

Planning. In light of these permissive regulations, how should the parties plan a divorce-related redemption? For example, how should a redemption be structured if the parties wish to minimize their overall joint tax liability and preserve more dollars for the family? What is the best advice to a transferor or nontransferor spouse who wishes to avoid tax on the redemption? In what circumstances would the parties wish to invoke

7. Reg. § 1.1041–2(a)(2),–2(b)(2).

8. Reg. § 1.1041–2(b)(2).

9. Whether or not the constructive distribution is a dividend depends on whether the corporation has earnings and profits and whether any of the tests for exchange treatment in Section 302 are met (unlikely in the typical fact pattern).

10. Reg. § 1.1041–2(a)(1).

11. Reg. § 1.1041–2(b)(1).

12. Reg. § 1.1041–2(c).

13. Reg. § 1.1041–2(c)(3).

the "special rule?" Is it still possible, either through separate or joint planning, to structure a redemption so that neither spouse is taxed? Do the regulations eliminate all legal controversies over the proper tax treatment of divorce-related redemptions?

G. REDEMPTIONS THROUGH RELATED CORPORATIONS

Code: § 304 (except § 304(b)(3)(C), (D), (b)(4)).

Regulations: § 1.304–2(a), (c) Examples (1) & (3), –3(a).

Section 304 is an intricate statutory watchdog designed to prevent an end run around Sections 301 and 302. Despite its complexity, the basic purpose of Section 304—to prevent controlling shareholders from claiming basis recovery and capital gain treatment on transactions that result in a "bailout" of corporate earnings without a significant reduction in control—can be illustrated by a simple example. Assume that Shareholder A owns all of the common stock (the only class outstanding) of X Corporation and Y Corporation, and both corporations have ample earnings and profits. Having read the *Davis* case, A knows that a redemption of either her X or Y stock will result in a dividend and no recovery of basis. But what if A sells some of her X shares to Y or vice versa? Because this is a "sale" rather than a redemption or a distribution, A hopes to extract cash while enjoying exchange treatment, but in substance A's "sale" is indistinguishable from a dividend. Section 304 ensures this result by requiring shareholder sales involving "brother-sister" and "parent-subsidiary" corporations to satisfy one of the tests in Section 302 in order to qualify for capital gain status and recovery of basis.

Section 304 is yet another area where the tax stakes are less significant as long as dividends and long-term capital gains are taxed at the same preferential rates. As with conventional redemptions and other transactions to be studied later in this text, the importance of dividend classification will depend on variables such as the basis of the stock and the type of shareholder (individual vs. corporate) involved.

Brother–Sister Acquisitions. Section 304(a)(1) applies when one or more persons who are in "control" of each of two corporations transfer stock of one corporation (the "issuing corporation") to the other (the "acquiring corporation") in exchange for cash or other property.[1] "Control" for this purpose is defined as at least 50 percent ownership of either the corporate voting power or of the total value of all classes of stock.[2]

1. For this purpose, "property" does not include stock of the acquiring corporation. I.R.C. § 317(a). See Bhada v. Commissioner, 892 F.2d 39 (6th Cir.1989).

2. I.R.C. § 304(c)(1). In determining control, the Section 318 attribution rules are applicable with certain modifications relating to shareholder-corporation attribution. I.R.C. § 304(c)(3). In the case of a corporation with more than one class of stock, the value prong of the "control" test is applied to the aggregate value of all classes of stock, not class-by-class. Rev.Rul. 89–57, 1989–1 C.B. 90. Thus, a shareholder who owns 50 percent or more

If Section 304(a)(1) applies, Congress devised an intricate method to test the "sale" for dividend equivalence. Returning to the example, when A sells X Corporation stock to Y Corporation for cash, she is treated as having received a distribution of cash in redemption of Y stock (Y being the "acquiring corporation").[3] This hypothetical distribution is then tested under Section 302(b) standards to determine whether A may treat the transaction as an exchange. Dividend equivalence is tested by reference to A's stock ownership of X (the "issuing corporation"—i.e., the company whose stock is sold) before and after the transaction.[4]

In the example, A owned 100 percent of the X stock before the sale to Y. After the sale, A continued to own 100 percent of the stock directly and constructively by virtue of her ownership of Y. Since the sale does not reduce A's interest in X, it fails to satisfy any of the Section 302(b) tests for exchange treatment and thus will be treated as a Section 301 distribution from Y to A. In determining the amount of the distribution that is a dividend, Section 304(b)(2) requires the transaction to be treated as a dividend to A by Y (the "acquiring corporation") to the extent of its earnings and profits and then by X (the "issuing corporation") to the extent of its earnings and profits. Thus, the earnings and profits of both corporations are available to characterize the distribution to A as a dividend.[5]

Parent–Subsidiary Acquisitions. Section 304(a)(2) applies similar principles when a controlled subsidiary acquires stock of its parent from a shareholder of the parent in return for property. The parent-subsidiary relationship is defined by the same 50 percent "control" test described above.[6] The "property" used to make the acquisition is treated as a distribution in redemption of the parent's stock for purposes of testing dividend equivalency under Section 302.[7] If the redemption fails to qualify as an exchange and thus is treated as a Section 301 distribution, the amount and source of any dividend is first determined by reference to the earnings and profits of the acquiring (subsidiary) corporation and then, if necessary, by the earnings and profits of the issuing (parent) corporation.[8] If the constructive redemption is treated as an exchange, the selling shareholders recognize gain or loss under normal tax principles.

of the value of all the corporation's stock has "control" even if that shareholder owns less than 50 percent of a particular class.

3. To the extent that the distribution is treated as a distribution to which Section 301 applies, A is treated as having transferred the X stock to Y (the acquiring corporation) in exchange for Y stock in a tax-free Section 351(a) transaction, and then Y is treated as having redeemed the Y stock that it (hypothetically) issued in the deemed Section 351 transaction. I.R.C. § 304(a)(1). If the distribution is treated as an exchange under Section 302(a), Y is treated as purchasing the stock of X. See S. Rep. No. 99–313, 99th Cong., 2d Sess. 1048 (1986). These deemed transactions are relevant in determining the basis consequences to the parties. See infra notes 11–12 and accompanying text.

4. I.R.C. § 304(b)(1). Once again, modified Section 318 corporation-to-shareholder (and vice versa) attribution rules apply in measuring the effect of this hypothetical transaction on A's interest in X. Id.

5. I.R.C. § 304(b)(2).

6. I.R.C. § 304(c)(1).

7. I.R.C. § 304(b)(1).

8. I.R.C. § 304(b)(2).

If a transaction is both a brother-sister and a parent-subsidiary acquisition, the parent-subsidiary rules take precedence.[9] But because the attribution rules transform most actual brother and sister corporations into a constructive parent and subsidiary, the regulations provide that an actual brother-sister relationship takes precedence over a constructive parent-subsidiary affiliation, causing Section 304(a)(1) to govern acquisitions by related nonsubsidiary corporations.[10]

Collateral Tax Consequences. In the basic Section 304(a)(1) brother-sister acquisition where the amount paid is treated as a Section 301 distribution, A is deemed to have transferred the X stock to Y in exchange for Y stock in a Section 351(a) transaction. Y thus takes a transferred basis from A in the X stock under Section 362, and A's basis in the Y stock received in the deemed Section 351 exchange is equal to A's basis in the X stock that A actually transferred to X.[11] A's basis in the Y stock is decreased on the subsequent deemed distribution of Y stock only if part of the distribution is applied against the Y stock's basis under Section 301(c)(2). The reduction in earnings and profits resulting from any dividend logically should follow the ordering rules in Section 304(b)(2)—i.e., first reduce the acquiring corporation's earnings and profits insofar as they are the source of the dividend and then, if necessary, reduce the issuing corporation's earnings and profits.

If Section 304(a)(1) applies and A's sale of X Corporation stock to Y Corporation is treated as an exchange under Section 302(a), Y is treated as having acquired the X stock by purchase and it thus takes a cost basis under Section 1012, and A's original basis in his Y stock remains unchanged. The theory, based on various fictional transactions (i.e., A is deemed to receive Y stock in exchange for X stock and then Y is deemed to redeem that Y stock from A for cash or other property) is that A "sold" Y stock (to Y) with a basis equal to the basis of the X stock actually transferred by A to Y. As in any actual sale or exchange, the basis of the (hypothetical) Y stock "sold" by A is fully recovered in determining gain or loss on the sale, and thus A's basis in her Y stock is the same as it was before the transaction.[12]

In the brother-sister scenario where the redemption is treated as an exchange, any reduction of earnings and profits is limited by Section 312(n)(7) to an amount not in excess of the redeemed stock's ratable share of earnings and profits.[13] The more difficult question is *which* corporation's earnings and profits? The Code and regulations are silent on this technical

9. I.R.C. § 304(a)(1).

10. Reg. § 1.304–2(c) Example (1).

11. I.R.C. § 304(a)(1). See Reg. § 1.304–2(a) and (c) Example (1), which reaches this result using a different approach based on the statute before it was amended in 1997. Proposed regulations incorporating these amendments were issued in 2002 but withdrawn in 2006 to permit the Treasury to conduct a more deliberate study. See I.R.S. Ann. 2006–30, 2006–19 I.R.B. 879.

12. Cf. Reg. § 1.304–2(c) Example 3, which reaches the same result using an outmoded approach that preceded statutory amendments to Section 304 made in 1997.

13. See Section E2 of this chapter, supra.

teaser. Possibilities include the acquiring corporation's (the transaction is treated as a constructive redemption of acquiring corporation stock and the distributed "property" comes from that entity), the issuing corporation's (the redemption is tested by reference to its stock), neither (the transaction is simply a purchase, not a reduction of either corporation's wealth), or both (pro rata?).[14] One defensible answer is that the required reduction should be made first to the acquiring corporation's earnings and profits and, if necessary, then to the issuing corporation's earnings and profits.

The collateral tax consequences of a parent-subsidiary acquisition are also not entirely settled. If the constructive redemption of the parent's stock is treated as a dividend, the selling shareholder's basis in the parent stock transferred to the subsidiary is added to the basis in the shareholder's remaining parent stock under the regulations.[15] The subsidiary takes a cost basis in the parent stock that it acquires.[16] Tracking Section 304(b)(2), it is logical to first reduce the acquiring subsidiary's earnings and profits to the extent they are the source of the dividend and then move on, if necessary, to reduce the parent's earnings and profits. If the redemption is treated as an exchange, the selling shareholder recovers his basis in the transferred parent stock and recognizes capital gain or loss under normal tax principles. The subsidiary takes a cost basis in the acquired parent stock. If the constructive redemption is treated as an exchange, Section 312(n)(7) again should apply, but it is unclear which corporation's earnings and profits are reduced, leaving taxpayers to apply any reasonable approach.

Coordination with Section 351. Enactment of an intricate statute such as Section 304 inevitably whets the appetite of tax lawyers. Consider the sole shareholder of a profitable company with a desire for cash and a distaste for dividends at a time when dividends were taxed at much higher rates than capital gains. Assume that the shareholder borrows against his stock for valid business reasons and then contributes the stock to a newly formed holding company in exchange for the holding company's stock plus its assumption of the shareholder's liability. Or assume that the shareholder transferred all the stock of the operating company to a wholly owned holding company in exchange for additional stock of the holding company plus cash. Are the tax consequences of these transactions determined under Section 351? Or should they be governed by Section 304? Initially, the courts disagreed on which provision should control in these overlap situations.[17]

14. See Bittker & Eustice, Federal Income Taxation of Corporations and Shareholders ¶ 9.24[4] (7th ed. 2000).

15. Reg. § 1.304–3(a).

16. Cf. Rev.Rul. 80–189, 1980–2 C.B. 106; Broadview Lumber Co. v. United States, 561 F.2d 698 (7th Cir.1977).

17. Compare Gunther v. Commissioner, 92 T.C. 39 (1989), affirmed, 909 F.2d 291 (7th Cir.1990); Commissioner v. Haserot, 355 F.2d 200 (6th Cir.1965) and Haserot v. Commissioner, 46 T.C. 864 (1966), affirmed sub nom. Commissioner v. Stickney, 399 F.2d 828 (6th Cir.1968) with Coates Trust v. Commissioner, 480 F.2d 468 (9th Cir.1973), cert. denied, 414 U.S. 1045, 94 S.Ct. 551 (1973).

In an effort to strengthen the anti-bailout objectives of Subchapter C, Congress settled the overlap issue by providing that Section 304 generally will take precedence.[18] The Joint Committee on Taxation explained the amendment as follows:[19]

> The Act extends the anti-bailout rules of sections 304 * * * to the use of corporations, including holding companies, formed or availed of to avoid such rules. Such rules are made applicable to a transaction that otherwise qualifies as a tax-free incorporation under section 351.
>
> Section 351 generally will not apply to transactions described in section 304. Thus, section 351, if otherwise applicable, will generally apply only to the extent such transaction consists of an exchange of stock for stock in the acquiring corporation. However, section 304 will not apply to debt incurred to acquire the stock of an operating company and assumed by a controlled corporation acquiring the stock since assumption of such debt is an alternative to a debt-financed direct acquisition by the acquiring company. This exception for acquisition indebtedness applies to an extension, renewal, or refinancing of such indebtedness. The provisions of section 357 (other than sec. 357(b)) and Section 358 apply to such acquisition indebtedness provided they would be applicable to such transaction without regard to section 304. In applying these rules, indebtedness includes debt to which the stock is subject as well as debt assumed by the acquiring company.

* * *

This rule, like several other anti-bailout measures in Subchapter C, is much less significant as long as dividends and long-term capital gains are taxed at the same low rate.

Niedermeyer v. Commissioner

United States Tax Court, 1974.
62 T.C. 280, affirmed per curiam 535 F.2d 500 (9th Cir.1976), cert. denied 429 U.S. 1000, 97 S.Ct. 528 (1976).

■ STERRETT, JUDGE: * * *

[In 1966, the taxpayers, Bernard and Tessie Niedermeyer, owned 22.58% of the common stock of American Timber & Trading Co., Inc. ("AT&T"). They also owned 125 of the 2,136 outstanding shares of AT&T preferred stock. Two of the taxpayers' sons, Bernard, Jr. and Walter, owned 67.91% of the common stock of AT&T.

Lents Industries ("Lents") was another corporation controlled by the Niedermeyer family. In 1966, the taxpayers and their sons, Bernard, Jr.

18. I.R.C. § 304(b)(3).

19. Staff of Joint Committee on Taxation, General Explanation of Tax Equity and Fiscal Responsibility Act of 1982, 98th Cong., 2d Sess. 142–43 (1982).

and Walter, did not own any stock of Lents, but three other sons (Ed, Linus and Thomas) each owned 22⅓% of the Lents common stock.

On September 8, 1966, the taxpayers sold their AT&T stock to Lents for $174,975.12, but they retained all their preferred stock until December 28, 1966, when they contributed the preferred to a family foundation. After this contribution, the taxpayers ceased to have any interest in AT&T. Since the time of their sale of AT&T common stock, neither of the taxpayers was an officer, director or employee of the company.

The Niedermeyer family had long been active in the business of manufacturing special wood products in Oregon. During 1963, a family dispute arose between Bernard, Jr. and his brothers, Ed, Linus and Thomas. The brothers had been partners in Niedermeyer–Martin Co., another wood product enterprise, but the dispute caused the partnership to incorporate. During the mid–1960's, Bernard, Jr., as controlling shareholder of AT&T, refused to allow AT&T to do any business with Niedermeyer–Martin Co., which became a competitor. The acquisition by Lents of the taxpayers' common stock in AT&T was part of an effort by Ed, Linus and Thomas Niedermeyer to gain control of AT&T.

On their joint federal income tax return for 1966, the taxpayers reported a long-term capital gain of $168,321.58 on the sale of their AT&T common stock to Lents. The Commissioner determined that the entire proceeds of the sale were taxable as ordinary income because the transaction was covered by Section 304(a) and was essentially equivalent to a dividend. Ed.]

OPINION

The ultimate question to be decided in this case is whether petitioners realized a capital gain or received a dividend on the sale of their AT&T common stock to Lents in 1966. The resolution of this question depends on whether the sale in question was a redemption through the use of a related corporation under the provisions of section 304(a)(1) and, if so, whether the distribution by Lents to petitioners is to be treated as in exchange for the redeemed stock under the provisions of section 302(a) or as of property to which section 301 applies.

Section 304(a)(1) provides, in pertinent part, that, if one or more persons are in "control" of each of two corporations and if one of those corporations acquires stock in the other corporation from the person or persons in control, then the transaction shall be treated as a distribution in redemption for purposes of section 302. Section 304(c)(1) defines the term "control" as "the ownership of stock possessing at least 50 percent of the total combined voting power of all classes of stock entitled to vote, or at least 50 percent of the total value of shares of all classes of stock." Section 304(c)[(3)] then states that the constructive ownership of stock rules contained in section 318(a) shall apply for the purpose of determining "control," except that the 50–percent limitations of sections 318(a)(2)(C) and 318(a)(3)(C) shall be disregarded for such purpose.

It is clear that by its terms section 304(a)(1) applies to the factual situation of this case. Prior to the transaction here in question, petitioners, husband and wife, together actually owned 1,083.117 shares out of the 4,803.083 outstanding shares of AT&T common stock, its only class of stock entitled to vote. Two of petitioners' sons owned 3,263.072 shares. Thus a total of 4,346.189 shares, or 90.49 percent, of the outstanding voting stock of AT&T was actually or constructively owned by petitioners. Three of petitioners' other sons owned 48 out of 72 shares, or 67 percent, of the outstanding stock of Lents, the ownership of such stock being constructively attributable to petitioners. Consequently, under section 304(c)(1), either petitioner, or both, are regarded as the person or persons in control of both AT&T and Lents prior to the transaction in question. Accordingly, under section 304(a)(1) the transaction in which Lents acquired petitioners' AT&T common stock must be treated as a redemption. The fact that neither petitioner actually owned stock in the acquiring corporation is of no concern here. * * *

Petitioners object to the applicability of section 304 on the ground that the attribution rules of section 318(a) should not be applied in this case. They base this position upon what they term the "bad blood" exception to the attribution rules as applied in Estate of Arthur H. Squier, 35 T.C. 950 (1961). In *Squier*, a case under section 302 involving the question of whether a distribution was essentially equivalent to a dividend, this Court decided that, based in part on a "sharp cleavage" between the executor of the taxpayer estate and members of the Squier family, and notwithstanding the attribution rules, the redemption in fact resulted in a crucial reduction of the estate's control over the corporation. The Court held that the distribution there was not essentially equivalent to a dividend and implicit in this conclusion was the belief that the attribution rules were not conclusive in all events in determining whether there had been a significant change of control which would allow the conclusion that the distribution was not essentially equivalent to a dividend. We note that in Robin Haft Trust, 61 T.C. 398 (1973), this Court decided that, in light of United States v. Davis, 397 U.S. 301 (1970), the rationale of *Squier* was no longer applicable to section 302(b)(1).

Besides here, as was not the case with *Squier*, no evidence was adduced to show that there were any disputes or cleavage between petitioners and any of their sons. The falling out was apparently between petitioners' sons. Apparently, petitioners would have us infer from the disagreements between Bernard E. Niedermeyer, Jr., majority shareholder of AT&T, and three other of their sons, who together were majority shareholders of Lents, that petitioners did not in fact control either corporation. We are unwilling to make this assumption and consequently petitioners' argument fails on its facts.

Moreover, we are of the opinion that the "control" test of sections 304(a)(1) and 304(c) requires that the attribution rules be applied in every case. Congress expressly indicated that the attribution rules of section 318 are to be applied in determining "control" for section 304 purposes. Section

304(c)(2) states that "Section 318(a) (relating to the constructive ownership of stock) *shall* apply for purposes of determining control under paragraph (1)." (Emphasis supplied.) Under section 304(c)(1) "control" is defined only as the ownership (either actually or constructively) of certain amounts of stock. Through the use of precise rules of attribution Congress intended to remove the uncertainties existing under prior law, which had no specific statutory guidance for constructive ownership of stock in the area of corporate distributions and adjustments, in the administration of the provisions where attribution was deemed appropriate. H.Rept. No. 1337, to accompany H.R. 8300 (Pub.L. No. 591), 83d Cong., 2d Sess., p. A96 (1954). See also *Coyle v. United States*, supra at 490. We think the attribution rules require, through their employment in section 304, that petitioners be treated as in actual control of both AT&T and Lents, notwithstanding any "bad blood" between petitioners' sons.

Petitioners assert that even though the sale is to be treated as a distribution in redemption of Lents' stock under section 304(a)(1), they are entitled to treat the distribution as in full payment in exchange for their stock under section 302(a) by meeting one of the tests contained in section 302(b). The determination under section 302(b) is to be made by reference to the issuing corporation's stock, here the AT&T stock, except that the 50–percent limitations of sections 318(a)(2)(C) and 318(a)(3)(C) are to be disregarded in applying the attribution rules of section 318(a). Sec. 304(b)(1).

Section 302(b) sets forth certain conditions under which a redemption of stock shall be treated as an exchange. If none of those conditions are met, section 302(d) provides that the distribution will then be treated as one to which section 301 applies. Petitioners do not contend that section 302(b)(2) or 302(b)(4) is applicable but they argue that the transaction in question meets the test of either section 302(b)(1) or 302(b)(3).

The test of section 302(b)(1) requires that the redemption be "not essentially equivalent to a dividend." To meet the test of nondividend equivalency the redemption must, after application of the attribution rules of section 318(a) to the stock ownership interests as they existed both before and after the redemption, result in "a meaningful reduction of the shareholder's proportionate interest in the corporation." *United States v. Davis*, supra at 313. In resolution of the question of dividend equivalency, the fact that the transaction in issue may have had a bona fide business purpose is no longer relevant. *United States v. Davis*, supra at 312. Furthermore, the applicability of the attribution rules in section 302(b)(1) is not affected by any "bad blood" between petitioners' sons. *Robin Haft Trust*, supra at 402–403.

As stated above, prior to the redemption petitioners owned, either actually or constructively, 90.49 percent of the outstanding common stock of AT&T. After the redemption, petitioners actually owned no AT&T common stock, although they did own 125 shares out of 2,136 outstanding shares of that corporation's preferred stock. However, petitioners constructively owned 82.96 percent of the outstanding common stock of AT&T

comprised as follows: 3,055.221 shares actually owned by their son Bernard E. Niedermeyer, Jr., 207.851 shares actually owned by their son Walter E. Niedermeyer, and 67 percent of the 1,083.117 shares, or 725.688 shares, actually owned by Lents and constructively owned by their sons E. C., L. J., and T.J. Niedermeyer. Sec. 318(a)(5)(A). We do not think a reduction in ownership of the AT&T common stock from 90.49 percent to 82.96 percent constitutes a meaningful reduction of petitioners' proportionate interest in AT&T in the instant case. See Friend v. United States, 345 F.2d 761, 764 (C.A.1, 1965); Stanley F. Grabowski Trust, 58 T.C. 650, 659 (1972); *Fehrs Finance Co.*, supra at 185–186. With such a small change in a high percentage interest, petitioners' control and ownership of AT&T is essentially unaltered and cannot be considered to have undergone a meaningful reduction. An 82.96–percent interest clearly is sufficient to dominate and control the policies of the corporation.

Petitioners next assert, under several theories, that they terminated their interest in AT&T as contemplated in section 302(b)(3). The test provided therein allows the redemption to be treated as an exchange "if the redemption is in complete redemption of all of the stock of the corporation owned by the shareholder." Unless the conditions of section 302(c)(2) are satisfied to exempt petitioners from application of the family attribution rules of section 318(a)(1), these rules apply in their entirety in determining whether there has been a redemption of petitioners' complete stock interest in AT&T.

Petitioners sold all their AT&T common stock to Lents on September 8, 1966, and contributed all their AT&T preferred stock to the Niedermeyer Foundation on December 28, 1966. On September 24, 1968, petitioners filed an amended return for the calendar year 1966 to which was attached the agreement called for in section 302(c)(2)(A)(iii).

It is clear that, if they are to meet the requirements of the test of section 302(b)(3), petitioners must show that they completely terminated their stock interest in AT&T and in so doing they must be able to effect a waiver of the family attribution rules of section 318(a)(1) through use of section 302(c)(2).

While section 1.302–4(b), Income Tax Regs., states that the agreement specified in section 302(c)(2)(A)(iii) must be attached to a return timely filed for the year in which the distribution occurs, several cases have held that some delay in filing the agreement does not vitiate it, and we find those cases to be applicable here where petitioners filed the agreement upon discovering their inadvertent failure to do so earlier. United States v. G.W. Van Keppel, 321 F.2d 717 (C.A.10, 1963); Georgie S. Cary, 41 T.C. 214 (1963).

However, the fact that a proper agreement was filed alone does not effect a waiver of the family attribution rules unless the other requirements of section 302(c)(2) are satisfied. The only other requirement in question here is that petitioners must have had no interest in AT&T, other than an interest as a creditor, immediately after the distribution referred to in section 302(b)(3). In the instant case, however, petitioners retained their

125 shares of AT&T preferred stock, at least until December 28, 1966, after the redemption of all their AT&T common stock on September 8, 1966.

Petitioners contend that ownership of these 125 shares of AT&T preferred stock until December 28, 1966, does not prevent application of the exemption provided in section 302(c)(2) and consequently qualification under section 302(b)(3) as having completely terminated their stock interest in AT&T. Petitioners make the following arguments to show that the AT&T preferred stock retained until December 28, 1966, was not the retention of an interest other than that of a creditor and implicitly was not the retention of a stock interest in AT&T: (1) The preferred stock was actually debt; (2) a de minimis rule should be applied; (3) the relinquishment of their preferred stock interest in AT&T on December 28, 1966, was "immediately after" the sale of their AT&T common stock on September 8, 1966; and (4) at the time of the sale of their AT&T common stock they intended to donate their AT&T preferred stock to charity before the year's end.

While citing no cases in their support, petitioners first argue here that the characteristics of the AT&T preferred stock are those commonly associated with debt instruments. We do not agree. A number of factors have been considered in resolution of this question of fact, see O.H. Kruse Grain & Milling v. Commissioner, 279 F.2d 123, 125–126 (C.A.9, 1960), affirming a Memorandum Opinion of this Court; Wilbur Security Co., 31 T.C. 938, 948 (1959), affd. 279 F.2d 657 (C.A.9, 1960); however, we see no useful purpose in reciting all the factors but will confine discussion herein only to those we think relevant.

While it is true that the preferred stockholders had no right to participate in the management of the corporation, such fact is not so uncharacteristic of preferred stock rights as to be conclusive, standing alone, of the question at hand. John Kelley Co. v. Commissioner, 326 U.S. 521, 530 (1946). We think that the following facts are indicative of the equity flavor of the preferred stock: There was no unconditional obligation to pay a principal sum certain on or before a fixed maturity date; the timing of preferred "dividends" was discretionary with the corporate directors; upon liquidation the preferred stockholders would be paid "from the money and/or property available for distribution to shareholders," which indicates to us that the preferred stock was subordinated in priority to the general creditors; AT&T's articles of amendment to the articles of incorporation used the terms "dividends," "preferred stock," and "shareholders" with reference to the instruments in question; and the preferred stock was created during a reorganization by a transfer of earned surplus to AT&T's capital account.

We think petitioners' second argument attempting to interject a de minimis rule allowing the retention of some small stock interest while qualifying under section 302(b)(3) is wholly without merit. Section 302(b)(3) clearly requires no less than a complete termination of all petitioners' stock interest in the corporation.

Petitioners next assert that they had no interest in AT&T "immediately after the distribution," as the phrase is used in section 302(c)(2)(A)(i), because the December 28, 1966, contribution should be considered to have occurred immediately after the September 8, 1966, redemption. We assume petitioners believe that if they satisfy this requirement of having no interest "immediately after" the redemption, they will also satisfy the requirement in section 302(b)(3) of having completely terminated their stock interest in AT&T. While we express no opinion on petitioners' apparent belief, we think the words "immediately after" must be given their ordinary meaning and that consequently December 28 cannot be considered "immediately after" September 8. Cf. Commissioner v. Brown, 380 U.S. 563, 570–571 (1965).

Petitioners' final argument to satisfy the requirements of sections 302(b)(3) and 302(c)(2)(A)(i) is that, at the time of the transfer of their AT&T common stock to Lents, they intended to donate their remaining AT&T preferred stock to charity by the end of 1966. Petitioners did in fact contribute their 125 shares of AT&T preferred stock to the Niedermeyer Foundation on December 28, 1966.

While petitioners' contention in this regard is not entirely clear, their argument appears to be that the September 8, 1966, transfer was but one step in a plan to terminate completely their interest in AT&T, the final step in such plan being their December 28, 1966, contribution of their remaining preferred stock. The only case cited by petitioners, Arthur D. McDonald, 52 T.C. 82 (1969), involved the question of whether a plan, calling for the redemption of that taxpayer's E & M preferred stock which was followed by a reorganization in which the taxpayer exchanged his E & M common stock for Borden stock, resulted in a distribution with respect to the preferred stock, which was essentially equivalent to a dividend under section 302(b)(1). The Court concluded that, after completion of the plan, the taxpayer's direct interest in E & M was terminated and consequently the redemption was not essentially equivalent to a dividend. Petitioners have not urged, and we consider it wise since the attribution rules would frustrate them, that their intention to donate the AT&T preferred stock by year's end shows that the redemption comes within the provisions of section 302(b)(1). Rather, they apparently contend that their intentions to donate the AT&T preferred stock constituted a plan to terminate their interest in AT&T which, with use of section 302(c)(2)(A), satisfies the requirements of section 302(b)(3).

Where redemptions were executed pursuant to a plan to terminate one's interest in a corporation, it has been held that dividend equivalency may be avoided where the individual redemptions are component parts of a single sale or exchange of an entire stock interest. In Re Lukens' Estate, 246 F.2d 403 (C.A.3, 1957), reversing 26 T.C. 900 (1956); Jackson Howell, 26 T.C. 846 (1956), affd. 247 F.2d 156 (C.A.9, 1957); Carter Tiffany, 16 T.C. 1443 (1951).[4] Where there is a plan which is comprised of several steps, one

4. The cited cases were decided under the "essentially equivalent to the distribution of a taxable dividend" standard of sec. 115(g)(1), I.R.C. 1939. Sec. 29.115–9, Regs.

involving the redemption of stock that results in a complete termination of the taxpayer's interest in a corporation, section 302(b)(3) may apply. Otis P. Leleux, 54 T.C. 408 (1970); Estate of Oscar L. Mathis, 47 T.C. 248 (1966). However, the redemption must occur as part of a plan which is firm and fixed and in which the steps are clearly integrated. *Otis P. Leleux*, supra at 418.

We regard the evidence presented on petitioners' behalf as too insubstantial to prove the existence of such a plan. Petitioner Bernard E. Niedermeyer's self-serving statement during the trial that at the time of transfer of the AT&T common stock on September 28, 1966, he intended to donate the AT&T preferred stock to charity by year's end, and petitioners' prior history of contributions do not establish to us a firm and fixed plan in which all the steps are clearly integrated.

The plan certainly was not in writing and there was no evidence of communication of petitioners' asserted donative intention to the charity or to anyone. One of petitioners' sons testified that Lents acquired petitioners' AT&T common stock in an attempt to gain control of AT&T. However, no mention at all was made by this son of any desire on petitioners' part to terminate their total interest in AT&T. Petitioners could easily have changed their minds with regard to any intent to donate the preferred stock. Clearly petitioners' decision to donate the preferred stock has not been shown to be in any way fixed or binding. * * * We note that *Arthur D. McDonald*, supra, cited by petitioners, involved a written plan which was fixed as to its terms and apparently binding. By the above discussion we do not mean to indicate that all such plans need to be in writing, absolutely binding, or communicated to others, but we do think that the above-mentioned factors, all of which are lacking here, tend to show a plan which is fixed and firm.

Since petitioners have not established that the redemption is to be treated as an exchange under section 302(a), the proceeds are to be treated as a distribution of property to which section 301 applies and as a dividend as determined by the respondent.

Decision will be entered for the respondent.

PROBLEMS

1. The *Niedermeyer* case is a good example of a tax planning blunder. It illustrates the need for sensitivity to provisions such as § 304. In reading the case, make sure you can answer the following questions:

111, provided that "a cancellation or redemption by a corporation of all of the stock of a particular shareholder, so that the shareholder ceases to be interested in the affairs of the corporation, does not effect a distribution of a taxable dividend." Under present law, sec. 302(b)(1) would now appear applicable if completion of the plan results in a meaningful reduction in the taxpayer's proportionate interest in the corporation.

(a) Why did § 304 apply to the sale by the taxpayers of their AT&T common stock to Lents?

(b) Given that § 304 applies, how do you test the "redemption" to determine if the taxpayers have a dividend?

(c) Why were the taxpayers unable to waive family attribution and qualify for "sale" treatment under § 302(b)(3)?

(d) How could they have avoided this unfortunate result?

2. Bail Corporation and Out Corporation each have 100 shares of common stock outstanding. Claude owns 80 shares of Bail stock (with a basis of $40,000, or $500 per share) and 60 shares of Out stock (with a basis of $9,000, or $150 per share.) The remaining Bail and Out shares are owned by one individual who is not related to Claude. Bail has no current or accumulated earnings and profits. Out has no current and $5,000 of accumulated earnings and profits. Determine the tax consequences to the various parties in each of the following alternative transactions:

(a) Claude sells 20 of his Out shares, in which he has a $3,000 adjusted basis, to Bail for $4,000.

(b) Claude sells all of his Out shares to Bail for $12,000.

(c) Same as (a), above, except that Claude receives $3,000 and one share of Bail stock (fair market value—$1,000) for his 20 Out shares.

(d) Same as (a), above, except that Claude receives one share of Bail stock (fair market value—$1,000) and Bail takes the 20 Out shares subject to a $3,000 liability that Claude incurred to buy the 20 shares of Out stock.

3. Is Section 304 still necessary?

H. REDEMPTIONS TO PAY DEATH TAXES

Code: § 303(a), (b)(1)–(3), (c). Skim § 6166.

When a shareholder of a closely held corporation dies, it often is necessary to liquidate all or part of the decedent's stock to raise cash to pay death taxes and other expenses. Since the shares are not readily marketable and the family as a whole may be unwilling to risk loss of control, a redemption may be an important component of the decedent's estate plan. Since the basis of the stock normally will have been stepped-up to its fair market value at the decedent's death,[1] a redemption qualifying for exchange treatment can be accomplished virtually tax-free—a once-in-a-lifetime opportunity for a painless withdrawal of corporate earnings. Section 303, one of several income and estate tax provisions offering relief for

1. I.R.C. § 1014(a). This assumes that the current estate tax is not repealed, and the Section 1022 carryover basis regime enacted in 2001 never goes into effect.

owners of closely held businesses,[2] makes it possible to avoid dividend treatment and achieve full recovery of basis on a redemption even if the transaction does not come within one of the Section 302(b) tests.

The purpose of Section 303 is to remove any income tax impediments to a redemption when an estate faces a liquidity problem. If several detailed requirements are met, distributions in redemption are treated as a sale or exchange rather than a dividend up to the sum of federal and state death taxes and allowable funeral and administrative expenses.[3] Curiously, however, the estate is not required to use (or even need) the redemption proceeds to pay taxes and expenses.

To qualify under Section 303, the value of the redeemed stock must be included in determining the decedent's gross estate for federal estate tax purposes.[4] The other principal requirements relate to the relationship of the decedent's holdings in the corporation to his total gross estate and the timing of the distribution.

Relationship of Stock to Decedent's Estate. Congress concluded that income tax relief was justified only when a decedent's holdings in the corporation represented a substantial portion of his gross estate. Section 303(b)(2) requires that the value of all the stock of the distributing corporation included in the decedent's gross estate must exceed 35 percent of the total gross estate less certain expenses deductible for federal estate tax purposes. A special rule permits the stock of two or more corporations to be aggregated for purposes of this 35 percent test if 20 percent or more in value of each such corporation's total outstanding stock is included in the gross estate. For purposes of the 20 percent requirement, stock held by the decedent's surviving spouse as community property, or held with the decedent prior to death in joint tenancy, tenancy-by-the-entirety, or tenancy-in-common, is treated as if it were included in determining the value of the decedent's gross estate.[5] If a decedent's holdings are close to the 35 percent mark, it may be desirable to engage in various lifetime and post-mortem maneuvers to ensure that Section 303 will be available.[6]

Timing of the Redemption. Section 303 applies only to amounts distributed within a reasonable time after the decedent's death. The redemption must occur within 90 days after the expiration of the three year assessment period for federal estate taxes.[7] If the estate becomes embroiled in a controversy with the Service and files a petition for redetermination of estate tax with the Tax Court, the period is extended to 60 days after the

2. E.g., I.R.C. §§ 302(c)(2) (waiver of family attribution when testing redemptions), 2032A (estate tax valuation of certain real property), 6166 (extension of time to pay estate tax). Section 303 contains no "closely held" business requirement, but the vast majority of Section 303 redemptions involve close corporations.

3. I.R.C. § 303(a).

4. Id.

5. I.R.C. § 303(b)(2)(B).

6. See Kahn, "Closely Held Stocks—Deferral and Financing of Estate Tax Costs through Sections 303 and 6166," 35 Tax Lawyer 639, 676–681 (1982).

7. I.R.C. § 303(b)(1)(A). See I.R.C. § 6501(a).

Tax Court's decision becomes final.[8] A further extension is provided if the estate is eligible and elects to pay estate taxes in installments over the extended period (up to 15 years) provided by Section 6166.[9] But if the redemption occurs more than four years after death, the amount that can qualify for Section 303 treatment is limited to the lesser of unpaid death taxes and administrative expenses immediately before the distribution or death taxes and expenses actually paid during the one year period beginning on the date of distribution.[10]

Eligible Shareholders. Although Section 303 is most commonly used by the decedent's estate, other shareholder-beneficiaries sometimes are eligible for its benefits if their interest "is reduced directly (or through a binding obligation to contribute) by any payment" of death taxes or administrative expenses.[11] In the normal case where the decedent's will provides that taxes and expenses are payable out of the residuary estate, specific legatees of stock (including a spouse receiving a bequest eligible for the unlimited marital deduction) are not eligible to use Section 303.

Distributions of Appreciated Property. The most likely asset for a Section 303 redemption is cash, but a corporation that distributes appreciated property to redeem its shares must recognize gain under the now familiar rule in Section 311(b).

PROBLEM

George died last year and his gross estate for federal estate tax purposes is $2,000,000. George's estate expects to incur a total of $100,000 of death taxes and allowable deductions for expenses and losses under §§ 2053 and 2054. George's gross estate includes stock in X Corporation (fair market value—$200,000) and Y Corporation (fair market value—$400,000). The fair market value of all of the outstanding X and Y stock is $1,400,000 and $1,600,000, respectively. George's wife, Adele, also owns $200,000 of X stock. (She and George held a total of $400,000 of X stock as tenants-in-common during his life.)

If Y Corporation redeems shares from George's estate, will the redemption qualify for exchange treatment under § 303?

8. I.R.C. § 303(b)(1)(B).

9. I.R.C. § 303(b)(1)(C).

10. I.R.C. § 303(b)(4).

11. I.R.C. § 303(b)(3).

CHAPTER 14

STOCK DIVIDENDS AND SECTION 306 STOCK

A. INTRODUCTION

Code: Skim §§ 305; 306; 317(a).

It should be evident by now that Subchapter C has been the backdrop for a continuing cops and robbers saga. The goals of the robbers are clear enough, even if their methods may be a bit obscure. When they ran out of ideas to avoid the double tax, the robbers historically shifted their focus to bailing out corporate earnings at the least tax cost. The cops were quick to respond, but they sometimes lacked direction and even were known to engage in isolated acts of police brutality. Nowhere does this drama have a richer history than in the area of stock dividends and Section 306 stock. But for many of these skirmishes, the operative word may now be "history," at least as long as dividends and long-term capital gains are taxed at the same preferential rate.

The evolving plot is best appreciated by first putting the underlying transactions into perspective. A stock dividend is simply a distribution of stock (or rights to acquire stock)[1] by a corporation to some or all of its shareholders. If the distributed stock is of the same class as the shareholder's underlying holdings, a stock dividend is similar to what is known as a "stock split." The only difference is that a stock dividend requires the corporation to transfer an appropriate amount from retained earnings to paid-in capital while a stock split merely increases the number of outstanding shares without any adjustment to the corporate capital account.[2] A stock dividend, however, need not be of the same class of stock as the shareholder's existing interest in the corporation. Preferred stock may be distributed with respect to common or vice versa, and more complex capital structures present the opportunity for countless variations.

1. I.R.C. § 305(d)(1) defines the term "stock" to include rights to acquire such stock.

2. Apart from the financial accounting distinctions, the line of demarcation between a stock dividend and a stock split usually is drawn by the relationship of the number of shares distributed to the previously outstanding shares. To better inform shareholders, the rules of the New York Stock Exchange provide that a distribution of less than 25 percent of the shares outstanding prior to the distribution will be a stock dividend. Larger distributions (e.g., distributions of one share for each share held) are labelled splits. New York Stock Exchange Company Manual, § 703.02.

Stock dividends accomplish a variety of business objectives. Some public companies periodically pay small "common on common" stock dividends instead of cash ostensibly to provide their shareholders with some tangible evidence of their interest in corporate earnings while allowing the corporation to retain cash for use in the business. Although these distributions may have an incidental impact on the price of the stock, they are more of a shareholder public relations gesture than an event of any financial consequence. Stock splits often are prompted by a desire to increase the number of outstanding shares and thus reduce the price per share in an attempt to increase the marketability (and market value) of the stock on a listed exchange.

The business objectives may be different in the case of a closely held corporation. In that setting, stock distributions frequently are a vehicle to shift corporate control.[3] To illustrate, assume that all the outstanding stock of Family Corporation is owned by Mrs. Older and has a fair market value of $1,000 per share. Mr. Younger, Older's son, has been employed by Family for several years and Older expects to gradually shift control of the business to Younger. Older's plan faces several obstacles. Gifts of Family common stock to Younger may not be feasible because Older is unwilling to part with that much wealth or the gift tax liability may be prohibitive. Younger also may not be able to afford a significant purchase of stock from his mother because the current price of Family common stock is too high.

As an alternative, Family might distribute a new class of preferred stock to Older. The preferred stock could be structured with dividend rights and a liquidation preference so that its value absorbs most of the net worth of the company, leaving the common stock with only nominal value. The distribution of preferred stock to Older will be tax-free[4] and, since the value of the common stock will be substantially reduced, Older more easily may shift control to Younger through gifts or even sales of common stock.[5]

The tax consequences of the stock distribution to Older in our example are governed by Section 305, which remains significant in the current tax rate environment. Section 305(a) generally provides that gross income does not include a distribution of stock by a corporation to its shareholders with respect to its stock. This exclusion, however, is subject to various exceptions, the most important of which are found in Section 305(b). Consequently, the applicability of the Section 305(b) exceptions is the critical inquiry in analyzing the tax consequences of a stock distribution. These exceptions are examined more closely in the next section of this chapter. It is sufficient for now to note that the preferred stock distribution to Older is

3. A recapitalization frequently is an alternative method for making adjustments to the corporation's capital structure. In certain situations, a recapitalization may provide more favorable income tax results. See Chapter 17C1, infra.

4. I.R.C. § 305(a). The preferred stock, however, would be Section 306 stock assuming Family has earnings and profits. See Section C of this chapter, infra.

5. But see I.R.C. § 2701 et seq., which limits the estate planning advantages of this strategy.

not a taxable stock dividend. What do you suppose is the rationale for that result?

Lest we forget the cops and robbers saga, there is one other aspect of the previous example to consider. Recall that Older owns 100 percent of the outstanding Family common stock, and Family makes a tax-free distribution of a new class of preferred stock to Older. Assume further that Family has ample earnings and profits. If Older retained her common stock rather than giving it to her son, the preferred stock distribution historically provided her with an opportunity for tax avoidance. She could sell the preferred stock to Facilitator for cash and, after a short period of time, the corporation could redeem the preferred stock, paying Facilitator an appropriate premium for the shares. When the dust settled, this series of transactions had virtually the same economic effect as a cash distribution by Family to Older: Older has cash in hand, Family's corporate treasury has been depleted, and Older still owned 100 percent of the company. But the tax consequences appeared to be dramatically different. Rather than being stuck with a taxable dividend, Older hoped to enjoy "sale" treatment on the disposition of the preferred stock to Facilitator. A sale enabled Older to recover her basis in the preferred stock and to recognize a long-term capital gain to the extent the amount realized on the sale exceeded her basis.[6] A closer examination reveals that this potential loophole (is it still?) was closed by Section 306, which was the legislative response to Older's tax avoidance plan—the so-called "preferred stock bailout." In our simple example, the preferred stock will bear the taint of "Section 306 Stock," and Section 306(a)(1) will characterize Older's amount realized on the sale to Facilitator as ordinary (dividend?) income.[7] The last section of this chapter explores the details of Section 306 and evaluates its continuing significance.

B. TAXATION OF STOCK DIVIDENDS UNDER SECTION 305

Code: §§ 305(a), (b), (c), (d); 307; 312(d)(1)(B), (f)(2); 1223(4).

Regulations: §§ 1.305–1; –2; –3(a), (b), (c); (e) Examples (1), (2), (3), (4), (8), (10) and (11); –4; –5(a); –6; –7(a); 1.307–1.

The current scheme for taxing stock distributions is a distant cousin of statutes fashioned during the infancy of the income tax and is the product of a checkered legislative history. The Revenue Act of 1916 provided that a "stock dividend shall be considered income, to the amount of its cash value."[1] In 1920, the Supreme Court considered the constitutionality of this

6. This assumes that Older had a long-term holding period in the Family common stock, which could be tacked in determining the holding period of the preferred. I.R.C. § 1223(5).

7. I.R.C. § 306(a)(1)(A), (c)(1)(A). Prior to the enactment of Section 306 as part of the 1954 Code, the Service argued that in substance these transactions were equivalent to a cash distribution. The argument met with sporadic success. Compare Chamberlin v. Commissioner, discussed at p. 649 infra, with Rosenberg v. Commissioner, 36 T.C. 716 (1961).

1. Revenue Act of 1916, § 2(a). In Towne v. Eisner, 245 U.S. 418, 38 S.Ct. 158 (1918), the Supreme Court concluded that a

provision in Eisner v. Macomber.[2] Mrs. Macomber, a common shareholder of a corporation with no other class of stock outstanding, received a proportionate distribution of additional common stock. The Supreme Court held that the distribution was not taxable because it did not constitute "income" within the meaning of the 16th Amendment to the Constitution. Although the Court's constitutional commentary has been discredited,[3] the result in *Macomber* is eminently logical and has been codified in Section 305(a). Whatever reshuffling may occur in the corporation's capital account, a common-on-common stock dividend does little more than crowd the shareholder's safe deposit box (or brokerage account) with additional stock certificates (or book entry shares) evidencing the same ownership interest held before the distribution.

An obedient Congress swiftly responded to the Supreme Court's interpretation of the 16th Amendment with a primitive declaration that stock dividends "shall not be subject to tax."[4] The stock dividend terrain remained calm until the Supreme Court generated a minor tremor in 1936 with its decision in Koshland v. Helvering.[5] Corinne Koshland, a shareholder who owned cumulative nonvoting preferred stock, received a distribution of voting common stock. She subsequently disposed of her preferred stock and asserted that she was entitled to use the stock's full cost basis in determining her gain. Since the prior common stock distribution was received tax-free, the Service contended that a proportionate amount of Mrs. Koshland's basis in her preferred shares should be allocated to the common, thereby increasing the gain on the disposition of her preferred stock. The Supreme Court agreed with the shareholder's contention and in the course of its opinion shed additional light on the meaning of Eisner v. Macomber:[6]

> Although *Eisner v. Macomber* affected only the taxation of dividends declared in the same stock as that presently held by the taxpayer, the Treasury gave the decision a broader interpretation which Congress followed in the Act of 1921. Soon after the passage of that Act, this court pointed out the distinction between a stock dividend which worked no change in the corporate entity, the same interest in the same corporation being represented after the distribution by more shares of precisely the same character, and such a dividend where there had either been changes of corporate identity or a change in the nature of the shares issued as dividends whereby the proportional interest of the stockholder after the distribution was essentially different from his former interest. Nevertheless the successive statutes and Treasury regulations

stock dividend was not "income" or "dividends" under the Revenue Act of 1913.

2. 252 U.S. 189, 40 S.Ct. 189 (1920).

3. See Bittker & Eustice, Federal Income Taxation of Corporations and Shareholders ¶ 8.40[1] (7th ed. 2000).

4. Revenue Act of 1921, § 201(d).

5. 298 U.S. 441, 56 S.Ct. 767 (1936).

6. 298 U.S. at 445–46, 56 S.Ct. at 769–70. In Helvering v. Gowran, 302 U.S. 238, 58 S.Ct. 154 (1937), the Court held that a shareholder took a zero basis in preferred shares received as a nontaxable distribution on common stock.

respecting taxation of stock dividends remained unaltered. We give great weight to an administrative interpretation long and consistently followed, particularly when the Congress, presumably with that construction in mind, has reenacted the statute without change. The question here, however, is not merely of our adopting the administrative construction but whether it should be adopted if in effect it converts an income tax into a capital levy.

We are dealing solely with an income tax act. Under our decisions the payment of a dividend of new common shares, conferring no different rights or interests than did the old—the new certificates, plus the old, representing the same proportionate interest in the net assets of the corporation as did the old—does not constitute the receipt of income by the stockholder. On the other hand, where a stock dividend gives the stockholder an interest different from that which his former stock holdings represented he receives income. The latter type of dividend is taxable as income under the Sixteenth Amendment. Whether Congress has taxed it as of the time of its receipt, is immaterial for present purposes.

Koshland at least educated Congress on the subtleties of taxing stock dividends, but the legislators were not yet up to the task of devising a precise statutory solution. Instead, they tossed the ball back into the judiciary's court by providing in the Revenue Act of 1936 that a distribution of stock or rights to acquire stock was not to be treated as a dividend to the extent it did "not constitute income to the shareholder within the meaning of the Sixteenth Amendment to the Constitution."[7] The Supreme Court declined the invitation to reconsider *Eisner v. Macomber*, preferring to develop a "proportionate interest test", under which a stock dividend was taxable if it increased a shareholder's proportionate interest in the corporation.[8]

It was back to the drawing board, however, with the enactment of the Internal Revenue Code of 1954. Seeking a simple approach, Congress enacted the predecessor of current Section 305, largely as an expression of dissatisfaction with the proportionate interest test. A far more elaborate system was adopted in the Tax Reform Act of 1969. The following excerpt of legislative history describes the 1954 Code provisions and explains the 1969 amendments.

7. Revenue Act of 1936, § 115(f)(1). This test was carried over to the 1939 Code.

8. See the legislative history in the text at pp. 643–647, infra. See also Helvering v. Sprouse, 318 U.S. 604, 63 S.Ct. 791 (1943), where the Supreme Court decided that a pro rata distribution of nonvoting common stock to a shareholder owning voting common stock was nontaxable because it did not change the proportionate interests of the shareholders, and Strassburger v. Commissioner, 318 U.S. 604, 63 S.Ct. 791 (1943), where the Court held that a distribution of cumulative nonvoting preferred stock to the corporation's sole shareholder was not taxable because "[b]oth before and after the event he owned exactly the same interest in the net value of the corporation as before." Id. at 607, 63 S.Ct. at 792.

Excerpt From Senate Finance Committee Report on Tax Reform Act of 1969

S.Rep. No. 91–552, 91st Cong., 1st Sess. 150–54 (1969).

Present law.—In its simplest form, a stock dividend is commonly thought of as a mere readjustment of the stockholder's interest, and not as income. For example, if a corporation with only common stock outstanding issues more common stock as a dividend, no basic change is made in the position of the corporation and its stockholders. No corporate assets are paid out, and the distribution merely gives each stockholder more pieces of paper to represent the same interest in the corporation.

On the other hand, stock dividends may also be used in a way that alters the interests of the stockholders. For example, if a corporation with only common stock outstanding declares a dividend payable at the election of each stockholder, either in additional common stock or in cash, the stockholder who receives a stock dividend is in the same position as if he received a taxable cash dividend and purchased additional stock with the proceeds. His interest in the corporation is increased relative to the interests of stockholders who took dividends in cash.

Present law (sec. 305(a)) provides that if a corporation pays a dividend to its shareholders in its own stock (or in rights to acquire its stock), the shareholders are not required to include the value of the dividend in income. There are two exceptions to this general rule. First, stock dividends paid in discharge of preference dividends for the current or immediately preceding taxable year are taxable. Second, a stock dividend is taxable if any shareholder may elect to receive his dividend in cash or other property instead of stock.

These provisions were enacted as part of the Internal Revenue Code of 1954. Before 1954 the taxability of stock dividends was determined under the "proportionate interest test," which developed out of a series of Supreme Court cases, beginning with Eisner v. Macomber, 252 U.S. 189 (1920) [T.D. 3010, C.B. 3, 25]. In these cases the Court held, in general, that a stock dividend was taxable if it increased any shareholder's proportionate interest in the corporation. The lower courts often had difficulty in applying the test as formulated in these cases, particularly where unusual corporate capital structures were involved.

Soon after the proportionate interest test was eliminated in the 1954 Code, corporations began to develop methods by which shareholders could, in effect, be given a choice between receiving cash dividends or increasing their proportionate interests in the corporation in much the same way as if they had received cash dividends and reinvested them in the corporation. The earliest of these methods involves dividing the common stock of the corporation into two classes, A and B. The two classes share equally in earnings and profits and in assets on liquidation. The only difference is that the class A stock pays only stock dividends and class B stock pays only cash dividends. The market value of the stock dividends paid on the class A stock is equated annually to the cash dividends paid on the class B stock.

Class A stock may be converted into class B stock at any time. The stockholders can choose, either when the classes are established, when they purchase new stock, or through the convertibility option whether to own class A stock or class B stock.

In 1956, the Treasury Department issued proposed regulations which treated such arrangements as taxable (under sec. 305(b)(2)) as distributions subject to an election by the stockholder to receive cash instead of stock. In recent years, however, increasingly complex and sophisticated variations of this basic arrangement have been created. In some of these arrangements, the proportionate interest of one class of shareholders is increased even though no actual distribution of stock is made. This effect may be achieved, for example, by paying cash dividends on common stock and increasing by a corresponding amount the ratio at which convertible preferred stock or convertible debentures may be converted into common stock. Another method of achieving this result is a systematic periodic redemption plan, under which a small percentage, such as 5 percent, of each shareholder's stock may be redeemed annually at his election. Shareholders who do not choose to have their stock redeemed automatically increase their proportionate interest in the corporation.

On January 10, 1969, the Internal Revenue Service issued final regulations under which a number of methods of achieving the effect of a cash dividend to some shareholders and a corresponding increase in the proportionate interest of other shareholders are brought under the exceptions in section 305(b), with the result that shareholders who receive increases in proportionate interest are treated as receiving taxable distributions.

General reasons for change.—The final regulations * * * do not cover all of the arrangements by which cash dividends can be paid to some shareholders and other shareholders can be given corresponding increases in proportionate interest. For example, the periodic redemption plan described above is not covered by the regulations, and the committee believes it is not covered by the present statutory language (of sec. 305(b)(2)).

Methods have also been devised to give preferred stockholders the equivalent of dividends on preferred stock which are not taxable as such under present law. For example, a corporation may issue preferred stock for $100 per share which pays no dividends, but which may be redeemed in 20 years for $200. The effect is the same as if the corporation distributed preferred stock equal to 5 percent of the original stock each year during the 20–year period in lieu of cash dividends. The committee believes that dividends paid on preferred stock should be taxed whether they are received in cash or in another form, such as stock, rights to receive stock, or rights to receive an increased amount on redemption. Moreover, the committee believes that dividends on preferred stock should be taxed to the recipients whether they are attributable to the current or immediately preceding taxable year or to earlier taxable years.

Explanation of provisions.—The bill continues (in sec. 305(b)(1)) the provision of present law that a stock dividend is taxable if it is payable at the election of any shareholder in property instead of stock.

The bill provides (in sec. 305(b)(2)) that if there is a distribution or series of distributions of stock which has the result of the receipt of cash or other property by some shareholders and an increase in the proportionate interests of other shareholders in the assets or earnings and profits of the corporation, the shareholders receiving stock are to be taxable (under sec. 301).

For example, if a corporation has two classes of common stock, one paying regular cash dividends and the other paying corresponding stock dividends (whether in common or preferred stock), the stock dividends are to be taxable.

On the other hand, if a corporation has a single class of common stock and a class of preferred stock which pays cash dividends and is not convertible, and it distributes a pro rata common stock dividend with respect to its common stock, the stock distribution is not taxable because the distribution does not have the result of increasing the proportionate interests of any of the stockholders.

In determining whether there is a disproportionate distribution, any security convertible into stock or any right to acquire stock is to be treated as outstanding stock. For example, if a corporation has common stock and convertible debentures outstanding, and it pays interest on the convertible debentures and stock dividends on the common stock, there is a disproportionate distribution, and the stock dividends are to be taxable (under section 301). In addition, in determining whether there is a disproportionate distribution with respect to a shareholder, each class of stock is to be considered separately.

The committee has added two provisions to the House bill (secs. 305(b)(3) and (4)) which carry out more explicitly the intention of the House with regard to distributions of common and preferred stock on common stock, and stock distributions on preferred stock. The first of these provides that if a distribution or series of distributions has the result of the receipt of preferred stock by some common shareholders and the receipt of common stock by other common shareholders, all of the shareholders are taxable (under sec. 301) on the receipt of the stock.

The second of the provisions added by the committee (sec. 305(b)(4)) provides that distributions of stock with respect to preferred stock are taxable (under sec. 301). This provision applies to all distributions on preferred stock except increases in the conversion ratio of convertible preferred stock made solely to take account of stock dividends or stock splits with respect to the stock into which the convertible stock is convertible.

The bill provides (in section 305(b)(5)) that a distribution of convertible preferred stock is taxable (under sec. 301) unless it is established to the satisfaction of the Secretary or his delegate that it will not have the result of a disproportionate distribution described above. For example, if a corporation makes a pro rata distribution on its common stock of preferred stock convertible into common stock at a price slightly higher than the market price of the common stock on the date of distribution, and the period during which the stock must be converted is 4 months, it is likely that a distribution would have the result of a disproportionate distribution. Those stockholders who wish to increase their interests in the corporation would convert their stock into common stock at the end of the 4–month period, and those stockholders who wish to receive cash would sell their stock or have it redeemed. On the other hand, if the stock were convertible for a period of 20 years from the date of issuance, there would be a likelihood that substantially all of the stock would be converted into common stock, and there would be no change in the proportionate interest of the common shareholders.

The bill provides (in sec. 305(c)) that under regulations prescribed by the Secretary or his delegate, a change in conversion ratio, a change in redemption price, a difference between redemption price and issue price, a redemption treated as a section 301 distribution, or any transaction (including a recapitalization) having a similar effect on the interest of any shareholder is to be treated as a distribution with respect to each shareholder whose proportionate interest is thereby increased. The purpose of this provision is to give the Secretary authority to deal with transactions that have the effect of distributions, but in which stock is not actually distributed.

The proportionate interest of a shareholder can be increased not only by the payment of a stock dividend not paid to other shareholders, but by such methods as increasing the ratio at which his stock, convertible securities, or rights to stock may be converted into other stock, by decreasing the ratio at which other stock, convertible securities, or rights to stock can be converted into stock of the class he owns, or by the periodic redemption of stock owned by other shareholders. It is not clear under present law to what extent increases of this kind would be considered distributions of stock or rights to stock. In order to eliminate uncertainty, the committee has authorized the Secretary or his delegate to prescribe regulations governing the extent to which such transactions shall be treated as taxable distributions.

For example, if a corporation has a single class of common stock which pays no dividends and a class of preferred stock which pays regular cash dividends, and which is convertible into the common stock at a conversion ratio that decreases each year to adjust for the payment of the cash dividends on the preferred stock, it is anticipated that the regulations will provide in appropriate circumstances that the holders of the common stock will be treated as receiving stock in a disproportionate distribution (under sec. 305(b)(2)).

It is anticipated that the regulations will establish rules for determining when and to what extent the automatic increase in proportionate interest accruing to stockholders as a result of redemptions under periodic redemption plan are to be treated as taxable distributions. A periodic redemption plan may exist, for example, where a corporation agrees to redeem a small percentage of each common shareholder's stock annually at the election of the shareholder. The shareholders whose stock is redeemed receive cash, and the shareholders whose stock is not redeemed receive an automatic increase in their proportionate interests. However, the committee does not intend that this regulatory authority is to be used to bring isolated redemptions of stock under the disproportionate distribution rule (of sec. 305(b)(2)). For example, a 30 percent stockholder would not be treated as receiving a constructive dividend because a 70 percent stockholder causes a corporation to redeem 15 percent of its stock from him.

NOTE

Collateral Tax Consequences. The collateral tax consequences of a stock distribution (e.g., basis, holding period, and effect on earnings and profits) depend upon whether or not the distribution is taxable to the shareholders. Taxable distributions are governed by the rules in Section 301. The amount of the distribution is the fair market value of the stock.[1] The shareholder takes a fair market value basis in the distributed stock, and his holding period runs from the date of the distribution.[2] The distributing corporation recognizes no gain or loss under Section 311(a)(1), and it may reduce its earnings and profits by the fair market value of the distributed stock.[3]

If a stock distribution is nontaxable under Section 305(a), the shareholder must allocate the basis in the stock held prior to the distribution between the old and new stock in proportion to the relative fair market values of each on the date of distribution,[4] and the holding period of the old shares may be tacked on in determining the holding period of the distributed stock.[5] The distributing corporation recognizes no gain or loss on the distribution of its stock[6], and it may not reduce its earnings and profits.[7]

Stock Rights Distributions. Section 305 also governs distributions of stock rights (sometimes called warrants). Public companies occasionally issue rights to acquire additional stock at a favorable price as a means of raising equity capital.[8] Like stock dividends generally, rights distributions are not taxable unless they come within one of the Section 305(b) exceptions.[9] In the case of a nontaxable rights distribution, Section 307(a) generally requires an allocation of basis between the underlying stock and the rights in proportion to their relative fair market values on the date of the distribution.[10] In most cases, however, such an allocation is unneces-

1. Reg. § 1.305–1(b)(1). This rule also applies to corporate shareholders. Reg. § 1.301–1(d)(1)(ii). In the case of noncorporate shareholders, taxable stock dividends may be "qualified" and thus eligible for the 15 percent maximum rate under Section 1(h)(11).

2. Reg. § 1.301–1(h).

3. Reg. § 1.312–1(d).

4. I.R.C. § 307(a); Reg. § 1.307–1.

5. I.R.C. § 1223(4).

6. I.R.C. § 311(a)(1).

7. I.R.C. § 312(d)(1)(B).

8. See, e.g., Rev.Rul. 72–71, 1972–1 C.B. 99, which is the Service's ruling on a complex rights offering by American Telephone and Telegraph Co.

9. See I.R.C. § 305(d)(1), which treats rights as "stock" for purposes of Section 305.

10. But the regulations permit this allocation only if the rights are exercised (in which event the basis allocated to the rights

sary because of an administrative convenience exception in Section 307(b), which provides that the rights shall take a zero basis if their fair market value is less than 15 percent of the value of the stock with respect to which they were distributed. Taxpayers with time on their hands (or the incentive to make an allocation) may elect to use the allocation method prescribed in Section 307(a).[11] Taxable rights distributions are treated as Section 301 distributions; as such, their value (if any) is a dividend to the extent of the distributing corporation's earnings and profits.

PROBLEMS

1. Hill Corporation is organized with two classes of voting common stock: Class A and Class B. Shares in each class of stock have an equal right to Hill's assets and earnings and profits. Frank owns 100 shares of Class A stock, and Fay and Joyce each own 50 shares of Class B stock.

Assuming that Hill Corporation has ample earnings and profits, determine whether the following distributions are taxable under § 301 or excludable under § 305(a):

(a) A pro rata distribution of nonconvertible preferred stock to both classes of shareholders.

(b) A pro rata distribution of Class A stock on Class A and Class B on Class B. The Class B shareholders also are given the option to take cash in lieu of additional Class B shares. Joyce exercises this option.

(c) A pro rata distribution of Class A stock on Class A and a cash distribution on Class B.

(d) Assume that Class B is a class of nonconvertible preferred stock which pays regular cash dividends and Hill distributes Class B stock to the Class A shareholder.

(e) Same as (d), above, except that Hill distributes a class of nonconvertible preferred stock which has rights to assets and earnings and profits subordinate to those of the existing Class B stock (i.e., "junior" nonconvertible preferred stock) to the Class A shareholder.

(f) Assume that Hill has only one class of common stock outstanding and also has issued a series of 10 percent debentures convertible into common stock at the rate of one share of common stock for each $1,000 debenture. Hill makes an annual interest payment to the debenture holders and one month later distributes a "common on common" stock dividend to the common shareholders without adjusting the conversion ratio on the debentures.

is added to the cost of the new stock acquired) or sold. If the rights simply lapse, the shareholder recognizes no loss but the basis returns to the underlying stock. Reg. § 1.307–1(a).

11. I.R.C. § 307(b)(2).

(g) Same as (f), above, except that the debentures are convertible preferred stock. The corporation declares a one-for-one split on the common stock (i.e., each shareholder receives one new share of common stock for each old share) and the conversion ratio of the preferred is doubled.

(h) Assume again that Class A and Class B are both classes of voting common stock. Hill makes a pro rata distribution of Class A on Class A and a distribution of newly issued shares of nonconvertible preferred stock on Class B.

(i) Same as (h), above, except that the preferred stock which is distributed is convertible into Class B stock over 20 years at Class B's market price on the day of the distribution.

2. Z Corporation has one class of common stock outstanding, held by unrelated individuals A (500 shares), B (300 shares) and C (200 shares). Will § 305(c) create any tax problems if Z agrees to redeem annually 50 shares of stock at the election of each shareholder, and A makes such an election for two consecutive years?

C. SECTION 306 STOCK

1. THE PREFERRED STOCK BAILOUT

As previewed earlier in the chapter, Section 306 is one of several anti-bailout provisions in Subchapter C that are much less significant as long as dividends and long-term capital gains of noncorporate taxpayers are taxed at the same preferential rates. The specific target of Section 306 was the preferred stock bailout, a device used by shareholders in the "good old days" to withdraw corporate earnings at very favorable capital gains rates. In the classic transaction, a profitable C corporation would make a tax-free distribution of preferred stock to its common shareholders, who then sold the preferred stock to an accommodating investor (often an insurance company) and reported long-term capital gain on the sale. A few years later, the corporation redeemed the preferred stock from the investor. The net effect was the receipt of cash by the shareholders with no reduction of their proportionate interest in the corporation.

In Chamberlin v. Commissioner,[1] the Service contended that the preferred stock dividend was taxable as ordinary income on these facts. The Sixth Circuit disagreed, using language dear to the hearts of taxpayers ("[t]he general principle is well settled that a taxpayer has the legal right to decrease the amount of what otherwise would be his taxes, or altogether avoid them, by means which the law permits"). The court found that the preferred stock dividend was legally paid, the buyer made a bona fide investment, the subsequent redemption was a distribution to the investor (not the common shareholders), and nothing in the statute permitted the

1. 207 F.2d 462 (6th Cir. 1953), cert. denied, 347 U.S. 918, 74 S.Ct. 516 (1954).

taxpayer's gain on the sale of the preferred stock to be taxed as ordinary income.

The *Chamberlin* case was decided under the 1939 Code. Left unchecked, the court's endorsement of the preferred stock bailout would have encouraged other closely held corporations to engage in similar profitable end runs around the distribution rules. Although the result in *Chamberlin* might have been overturned in subsequent litigation, the Treasury wisely sought a prompt legislative solution. The central issue facing the drafters of the 1954 Code was whether to attack the bailout by taxing all "preferred on common" stock dividends or to defer the punishment until the shareholder disposed of stock with bailout potential.

Common shareholders who receive a proportionate preferred stock dividend have not increased their interest in the corporation. They simply have a tax opportunity which they may choose to forego for nontax reasons. For example, there may be valid business reasons (e.g., a shift of control from older to younger generation shareholders) for a preferred stock dividend. Recognizing these and other nontax objectives served by preferred stock dividends, Congress concluded that the *receipt* of the dividend was not the appropriate occasion for punitive action.[2] Instead, it chose to label stock with bailout potential as "Section 306 stock" and to require a shareholder to report ordinary income rather than capital gain when Section 306 stock is sold or redeemed. In the case of a sale, the ordinary income amount is generally determined by the amount that would have been a dividend at the time of the stock distribution if cash rather than stock had been distributed.[3] In the case of a redemption, the ordinary income amount is determined at the time of the cash distribution.[4] Other operational and planning aspects of Section 306 are examined below.

Now that dividends and long-term capital gains are taxed at the same low rate, the advantages to be achieved from a bailout of corporate earnings at "capital gains rates" have diminished considerably. As with redemptions and a few other classic bailout transactions to be studied later, the only remaining tax advantages to noncorporate shareholders of a sale rather than a dividend are recovery of stock basis and, in special situations, the ability to offset capital gains (but not qualified dividends) with capital losses. Section 306 nonetheless remains in the Code, in semi-hibernation until the distinction between dividends and capital gains is restored to its former glory, or until Congress decides that it is no longer necessary.

2. THE OPERATION OF SECTION 306

a. SECTION 306 STOCK DEFINED

Code: § 306(c)–(e).

Regulations: §§ 1.306–3(a)–(c), (e).

The definition of Section 306 stock is consistent with the original antibailout objectives of the statute. The principal category is stock distributed

2. S.Rep. No. 1622, 83rd Cong., 2d Sess. 46 (1954).

3. I.R.C. § 306(a)(1).

4. I.R.C. § 306(a)(2). See Section C2b of this chapter, infra.

to a shareholder as a tax-free stock dividend under Section 305(a)—other than "common on common."[1] Ordinarily, this is preferred stock distributed to common shareholders by a corporation with earnings and profits. As the *Chamberlin* case illustrates, preferred stock is the primary vehicle for a bailout because it can be sold without diminishing the shareholder's control or right to share in future corporate growth. "Common" stock is excepted because it lacks bailout potential; it may not be sold without diminishing the shareholder's control and interest in corporate growth.[2]

Although the Service has not defined "common stock" for Section 306 purposes, its published rulings focus on whether a sale of the stock would cause a reduction of the shareholder's equity position in the company. The fundamental inquiry is thus whether the stock has a realistic and unrestricted opportunity to participate in the growth of corporate equity.[3] If stock has either a limited right to dividends or to assets upon liquidation, it is not "common" stock for Section 306 purposes.[4] But voting common stock that is subject to the issuing corporation's first refusal right to purchase the stock at net book value whenever a shareholder wishes to make a transfer is common stock because, upon a transfer, the shareholder will part with some or all of his interest in the future growth of the corporation vis a vis other shareholders.[5]

Congress also concluded that a tax-free stock dividend issued by a corporation with no current or accumulated earnings and profits for the year of the distribution has limited bailout potential. If cash instead of stock had been distributed, the shareholder would not have realized ordinary income whenever the distributing corporation has no earnings and profits. Consequently, Section 306 stock does not include stock which would not have been treated as a dividend at the time of distribution if cash had been distributed in lieu of the stock.[6]

To prevent an easy purge of the taint, Section 306 stock includes stock with a transferred or substituted basis.[7] This category encompasses stock received as a gift which takes a Section 1015 transferred basis, or stock received in exchange for Section 306 stock in a tax-free Section 351 transaction.[8] But the exorcist prevails when stock passes from a decedent and thus qualifies for a date-of-death basis under Section 1014. In that

1. I.R.C. § 306(c)(1)(A).

2. See Walter, " 'Preferred Stock' and 'Common Stock': The Meaning of the Terms and the Importance of the Distinction for Tax Purposes," 5 J.Corp.Tax'n 211 (1978).

3. See, e.g., Rev.Rul. 75–222, 1975–1 C.B. 105; Rev.Rul. 79–163, 1979–1 C.B. 131.

4. Rev. Rul. 79–163, supra note 3.

5. Rev. Rul. 76–386, 1976–2 C.B. 95; see also Rev. Rul. 81–91, 1981–1 C.B. 123.

6. I.R.C. § 306(c)(2).

7. I.R.C. § 306(c)(1)(C).

8. In this situation, the old Section 306 stock remains tainted in the hands of the corporation, and the newly issued stock, whatever its class, also is Section 306 stock by virtue of its substituted basis under Section 358. See Rev.Rul. 77–108, 1977–1 C.B. 86.

event, the Section 306 taint is buried along with the decedent and her old basis.

An important but more specialized category is stock (which is not common stock) received in a tax-free corporate reorganization or division when the effect of the transaction is substantially the same as the receipt of a stock dividend or when the stock is received in exchange for Section 306 stock. For example, preferred stock received by the shareholders of the target (i.e., acquired) corporation in a tax-free merger may be a prime candidate for Section 306 classification. This aspect of Section 306 is considered in a later chapter.[9]

The final category of Section 306 stock was added by Congress to thwart the use of a holding company to bail out earnings. Assume, for example, that Schemer holds only common stock in Profitable Co. Finding that Section 306 presents a substantial roadblock to a bailout, Schemer organizes Holding Co., exchanging her Profitable common stock for newly issued Holding common and preferred stock in a tax-free Section 351 transaction. At one time, the Holding preferred stock would not have been Section 306 stock because Holding had no earnings and profits at the time of its incorporation. This offered shareholders the very bailout opportunity that Congress was trying to prevent! Schemer could sell the Holding preferred stock to an institutional investor, recovering her basis and realizing a capital gain, and the stock later could be redeemed by the corporation—all without losing any of her control or share in the growth of Profitable.

Section 306(c)(3) blocks this maneuver by characterizing the preferred stock of Holding Co. (i.e., preferred stock acquired in a Section 351 exchange) as Section 306 stock if the receipt of money instead of the stock would have been treated as a dividend to any extent. Of course, Holding Co. has no earnings and profits so that a distribution of cash would not have been a dividend. To make the statute achieve its objective, Section 306(c)(3)(A) borrows the rules of Section 304 (relating to redemptions through the use of affiliated corporations). In our example, the Holding Co. preferred would be Section 306 stock if Profitable Co. has any current or accumulated earnings and profits. This is because a cash payment by Holding Co. for the Profitable common stock would have resulted in a dividend to Schemer under Section 304(a)(1). In effect, this means that we look to the earnings and profits of the original corporation (Profitable Co.) in determining whether the receipt of cash would have been a dividend.[10]

b. DISPOSITIONS OF SECTION 306 STOCK

Code: § 306(a).

Regulations: § 1.306–1.

The tax consequences of a disposition of Section 306 stock vary depending on whether the stock is sold or redeemed. On a sale of Section

9. See Chapter 17B5, infra.

10. In testing for the effect of a dividend, the Section 318 attribution rules apply without regard to the 50 percent limitation in Sections 318(a)(2)(C) and 318(a)(3)(C). I.R.C. § 306(c)(4).

306 stock, the amount realized is treated as dividend income to the extent of the stock's "ratable share" of the amount that would have been a dividend if the corporation had distributed cash in an amount equal to the fair market value of the stock at the time of the distribution.[11] This rule requires the shareholder to look back to the time of distribution and determine to what extent a cash distribution would have emanated from the corporation's current or accumulated earnings and profits at that time.[12] The balance, if any, of the amount realized is treated as a reduction of the basis of the Section 306 stock, and any excess is treated as gain from the sale or exchange of the stock.[13] Although the ordinary income amount is treated as a dividend received from the corporation to allow noncorporate shareholder to qualify for the preferred rates under Section 1(h), it is not clear if corporate shareholders are eligible for the Section 243 dividends received deduction, or whether the corporation is entitled to reduce its earnings and profits when Section 306 stock is sold.[14] No loss may be recognized if the shareholder's adjusted basis in the stock exceeds the amount realized, and any unrecovered basis must be allocated back to the stock with respect to which the Section 306 stock was distributed.[15]

A shareholder who receives a nontaxable stock dividend of Section 306 stock that later is redeemed by the corporation has used two steps to achieve what could have been accomplished in a single transaction: the withdrawal of cash from the corporation. To reflect that reality and treat the transactions as a single event, Section 306(a)(2) provides that the amount realized on a redemption of Section 306 stock is treated as a Section 301 distribution, taxable as a dividend (likely a qualified dividend) to the extent of the current or accumulated earnings and profits in the year

11. I.R.C. §§ 306(a)(1)(A), (a)(1)(D).

12. I.R.C. § 306(a)(1)(A). This provision also applies to other nonredemption "dispositions" such as certain pledges of Section 306 stock where the pledgee can only look to the stock as security (an unlikely scenario), but it does not apply to charitable contributions of Section 306 stock. Reg. § 1.306–1(b)(1); Rev.Rul. 57–328, 1957–2 C.B. 229. For charitable deduction purposes, however, a taxpayer who contributes appreciated Section 306 stock to a qualified donee must reduce the fair market value of the donated stock by the amount that would have not have been long-term capital gain if the stock had been sold rather than donated. See I.R.C. § 170(e)(1)(A); Pescosolido v. Commissioner, 91 T.C. 52 (1988). It appears that the treatment of Section 306(a)(1) ordinary income as a dividend and thus, if "qualified," part of "adjusted net capital gain" under Section 1(h)(11), does not permit a donor-shareholder from escaping the reduction rule in Section 170 because the gain technically is not "long-term capital gain." Perhaps the Treasury will specify otherwise if and when it issues regulations under the authority of Section 306(a)(1)(D).

13. I.R.C. § 306(a)(1)(B).

14. Section 306(a)(1)(D) provides that any amount treated as ordinary income on a sale of Section 306 stock shall be treated as a dividend "[f]or purposes of section 1(h)(11) and such other provisions as the Secretary shall specify * * *." As of early 2008, the Treasury had not yet "specified" and, until it does, it appears that corporate shareholders may not claim the dividends received deduction, and no earnings and profit reduction is authorized on a sale of Section 306 stock.

15. I.R.C. § 306(a)(1)(C); Reg. § 1.306–1(b)(2) Example (3).

of redemption.[16] The balance of the distribution, if any, is treated as a reduction of basis and then capital gain under the rules generally applicable to nonliquidating distributions.[17]

c. DISPOSITIONS EXEMPT FROM SECTION 306

Code: § 306(b).

Regulations: § 1.306–2.

Section 306 is aimed only at bailouts, and not every disposition of Section 306 stock presents that opportunity. For example, a shareholder who sells her entire interest in a corporation (including her Section 306 stock) is not withdrawing corporate earnings while preserving control. She is engaging in a transaction that easily could have qualified for capital gain treatment irrespective of any prior stock dividend. Section 306(b)(1) thus provides that the punitive general rule of Section 306(a) shall not apply to nonredemption dispositions if the shareholder completely terminates her interest in the corporation and does not dispose of the stock to a related person within the Section 318 attribution rules.[18] A similar exception is provided for redemptions of Section 306 stock that result in a complete termination of the shareholder's interest under Section 302(b)(3) or qualify as a partial liquidation under Section 302(b)(4).[19]

Other exempt dispositions include: (1) redemptions of Section 306 stock in a complete liquidation;[20] (2) dispositions that are treated as nonrecognition transactions, such as tax-free Section 351 transfers, contributions to capital and the like;[21] and (3) distributions coupled with subsequent dispositions or redemptions of Section 306 stock if the taxpayer satisfies the Service that either: (a) the distribution and subsequent disposition or redemption, or (b) in the case of a prior or simultaneous disposition of the underlying common stock, just the disposition or redemption, was not made pursuant to a plan having tax avoidance as one of its principal purposes.[22] Examples of "no tax avoidance" transactions include an isolated sale of preferred stock by a minority shareholder who owns both common and preferred,[23] or a sale of a portion of a minority shareholder's preferred stock coupled with a sale of the same or a greater portion of the shareholder's underlying common stock.[24]

Although Section 306 is aimed primarily at closely held companies, the Service's hard line position is that holders of Section 306 stock issued by

16. I.R.C. § 306(a)(2).

17. See I.R.C. § 301(c)(2), (3).

18. For purposes of determining whether there has been a complete termination, the Section 318 attribution rules apply. I.R.C. § 306(b)(1)(A)(iii).

19. I.R.C. § 306(b)(1)(B).

20. I.R.C. § 306(b)(2).

21. I.R.C. § 306(b)(3).

22. I.R.C. § 306(b)(4).

23. Reg. § 1.306–2(b)(3).

24. But see Fireoved v. United States, 462 F.2d 1281 (3d Cir.1972), where the court denied Section 306(b)(4) relief to a similar disposition because the taxpayer retained effective control of the corporation pursuant to its bylaws.

public companies are not automatically entitled to relief under the "no tax avoidance" exception in Section 306(b)(4).[25]

PROBLEMS

1. In year one, Argonaut Corporation distributed nonconvertible nonvoting preferred stock worth $1,000 to each of its two unrelated equal common shareholders, Jason and Vera. The Argonaut common stock owned by each of the shareholders had a basis of $2,000 prior to the distribution and a value of $3,000 immediately after the distribution. At the time of the distribution, Argonaut had $2,000 of earnings and profits. In year three, Argonaut had $3,000 of earnings and profits.

(a) What are the tax consequences to Jason, Vera and Argonaut of the distribution of preferred stock in year one?

(b) What results to Vera and Argonaut if Vera sells her preferred stock to Carl, an unrelated party, for $1,000 in year three?

(c) Same as (b), above, except that Vera sells her preferred stock to Carl for $1,750?

(d) Same as (b), above, except that Argonaut had no earnings and profits at the time of the distribution of the preferred stock?

(e) What results if Jason gives his preferred stock to his grandson, Claude, and Claude later sells the stock for $1,000? What if Jason dies and bequeaths his preferred stock to Claude?

(f) What result if Jason contributes his preferred stock to a public charity?

(g) What results to Jason and Argonaut if in year three the corporation redeems half of Jason's common stock for $5,000 and all of his preferred stock for $1,500?

(h) Same as (g), above, except the corporate bylaws require unanimous shareholder agreement for corporate action, and the bylaws may be amended only with the concurrence of more than 75 percent of the shareholders.

(i) Same as (g), above, except that Argonaut has no accumulated or current earnings and profits in year three.

2. Zapco Corporation has 100 shares of common stock outstanding all of which are owned by Sam Shifty. Zapco has an ample supply of current and accumulated earnings and profits.

(a) If Sam forms Holding Co. by transferring 50 Zapco shares in exchange for 100 shares of Holding common stock and 100 shares of Holding preferred stock, will any of the Holding shares be Section 306 stock?

25. Rev. Rul. 89–63, 1989–1 C.B. 90, revoking Rev. Rul. 56–116, 1956–1 C.B. 164.

(b) What result if Zapco were owned equally (50 shares each) by Sam Shifty and Selma Zap, who is unrelated to Sam, and the two shareholders form Holding Co. by transferring all their Zapco stock with Sam taking back 100 shares of Holding Co. common stock and Selma taking back 50 shares of Holding Co. preferred stock and 50 shares of Holding Co. common stock?

3. Is Section 306 still necessary?

CHAPTER 15

Complete Liquidations

A. Introduction

We have been present at the creation of a corporation and nurtured the corporate entity as it engaged in distributions, redemptions, partial liquidations and maneuvers to mitigate the double tax. This chapter shifts the focus to the end of a C corporation's life cycle.

A few definitions are in order to set the stage. The Code does not define "complete liquidation," but the regulations provide that liquidation status exists for tax purposes "when the corporation ceases to be a going concern and its activities are merely for the purpose of winding up its affairs, paying its debts, and distributing any remaining balance to its shareholders."[1] Legal dissolution under state law is not required for the liquidation to be complete, and a transaction will be treated as a liquidation even if the corporation retains a nominal amount of assets to pay any remaining debts and preserve its legal existence.[2]

Liquidations often are preceded by a sale of substantially all of a corporation's assets and a distribution of the sales proceeds to the shareholders in exchange for their stock. Alternatively, the buyer of a corporate business may acquire all the stock of the target company and either keep the old corporation alive or cause it to be liquidated. But liquidations do not necessarily involve sales. The corporation simply may distribute its assets in kind to the shareholders, who either may sell the assets or continue to operate the business outside of corporate solution. Or a parent corporation may wish to rearrange its holdings by liquidating or selling the stock of a subsidiary.

All these transactions raise challenging tax issues at the shareholder and corporate levels. Historically, individual shareholders have hoped to emerge from a complete liquidation or the sale of a profitable corporate business by realizing a capital gain on their stock and, on an installment sale, by deferring recognition of the gain until cash payments are received. At the corporate level, the goals generally have been to avoid recognition of gain on a distribution or sale of assets while providing the shareholders (in a liquidation) or the purchaser (in an acquisition) with a fair market value basis in the distributed or acquired assets. At one time, most of these objectives could be met with careful planning, but liquidations became far

1. Reg. § 1.332–2(c). This regulation technically applies only to the liquidation of a subsidiary, but it has long been assumed to apply also to ordinary liquidations.

2. See, e.g., Rev.Rul. 54–518, 1954–2 C.B. 142.

more expensive after the Tax Reform Act of 1986. This chapter surveys the current landscape, considering first the general shareholder and corporate level tax consequences of complete liquidations and then turning to the special problems raised on the liquidation of a subsidiary. Later chapters will consider the closely related topic of taxable acquisitions of corporate assets or stock, tax-free acquisition techniques known as corporate reorganizations, and the carryover of tax attributes following an acquisition.[3]

B. COMPLETE LIQUIDATIONS UNDER SECTION 331

1. CONSEQUENCES TO THE SHAREHOLDERS

Code: §§ 331; 334(a); 346(a); 453(h)(1)(A)–(B).

Regulations: §§ 1.331–1(a), (b), (e); 1.453–11(a)(1), (2)(i), (3), –11(d).

The complete liquidation of a corporation presents an opportunity to revisit several policy issues that recur throughout the study of Subchapter C. Consider the appropriate tax consequences to Owner, a sole shareholder of X Corporation, who desires to liquidate X and continue to operate its business as a proprietorship. Assume that X has been profitable and has ample earnings and profits at the time of its liquidation. From Owner's standpoint, should the liquidation be treated as: (1) a nonrecognition transaction akin to an incorporation, (2) a dividend distribution, (3) an exchange of the stock for the distributed assets or (4) some combination of the above?

If Owner continues to operate the business as a sole proprietorship, the liquidation results in a mere change in the form of his investment. Since Congress granted nonrecognition treatment to Owner when he transferred the business into corporate solution, is it not also appropriate to treat the transfer of those assets back into Owner's hands as a tax-free event? This analogy has a superficial appeal but Congress has never seriously considered it except in very limited situations.[1] Nonrecognition is inconsistent with the double tax regime of Subchapter C because it would facilitate the tax-free bailout of earnings and profits. Moreover, many complete liquidations involve the sale of a business followed by a distribution of the cash proceeds to the shareholders. Cash distributions do not lend themselves to a nonrecognition regime because it is impossible to assign money the substituted basis that would be necessary to preserve the shareholder's gain for recognition at a later time. Similarly, any attempt to preserve the liquidated corporation's earnings and profits in the hands of its former shareholders would be cumbersome and inconsistent with the termination of the corporation.

A stronger case can be made for treating a liquidating distribution as a dividend to the extent of the corporation's remaining earnings and profits.

3. See Chapters 16, 17, and 19, infra.

1. See, e.g., I.R.C. § 332, discussed in Section C of this chapter, infra.

Because earnings and profits disappear on a complete liquidation, this is the last chance to tax a shareholder's withdrawal of corporate profits as ordinary income. By triggering the distribution rules of Sections 301 and 316, this approach would focus on the source of the liquidating distribution rather than the shareholder's relationship to his investment. Dividend treatment, however, is inconsistent with Section 302, which treats a distribution in redemption as an exchange if the shareholder completely terminates or substantially reduces his interest in the corporation. Why should a complete termination of the interests of all the shareholders be treated any less favorably? Moreover, if liquidating distributions were treated as dividends to the extent of the corporation's earnings and profits, a shareholder's stock basis might never be recovered.

The redemption analogy suggests a third approach, which would treat a complete liquidation as a sale of stock by the shareholder. This solution is imperfect, if only because it ignores the disappearance of the earnings and profits account, a clean sweep that does not occur on a sale of stock. But after a period of waffling,[2] Congress opted to treat liquidations as exchanges, an approach that permits shareholders to avoid the dividend sting and be taxed at capital gains rates. Congress concluded that the dividend threat was "preventing liquidation of many corporations" because of the high tax cost it imposed and therefore was generating only minimal revenue.[3] It regarded exchange treatment as "consistent with the entire theory of the [Code]" and as "the only method * * * which can be easily administered."[4]

The Congressional policy is codified in Section 331(a), which provides that amounts received by a shareholder in complete liquidation are treated as full payment in exchange for the shareholder's stock. The vast majority of shareholders who hold their stock as a capital asset will recognize capital gain or loss in an amount equal to the difference between (1) the money and the fair market value of the property received and (2) the shareholder's adjusted basis in the stock surrendered. Section 334(a) provides that the shareholder's basis in property distributed by a corporation in a complete liquidation that is taxable at the shareholder level shall be the fair market value of the property at the time of the distribution.

Computation of a shareholder's gain or loss on a complete liquidation is ordinarily a straightforward affair. The shareholder's amount realized is the money and the fair market value of all other property received from the liquidating corporation. If a shareholder assumes corporate liabilities or receives property subject to a liability in a liquidating distribution, the amount realized is limited to the value of the property received, net of

2. Liquidations were first treated as exchanges in the Revenue Act of 1924. Congress changed its mind briefly from 1934 to 1936 and then reinstated the present system.

3. H.R.Rep. No. 2475, 74th Cong., 2d Sess. (1936), reprinted in 1939–1 (Part 2) C.B. 667, 674.

4. S.Rep. No. 368, 68th Cong., 1st Sess. (1924), reprinted in 1939–1 (Part 2) C.B. 266, 274.

liabilities. In keeping with the principles of the *Crane* case, however, it is assumed that the distributee shareholder will pay the liabilities and he thus obtains a full fair market value basis in the property under Section 334(a).

Shareholders who hold several blocks of stock with different bases and acquisition dates must compute their gain or loss separately for each block rather than on an aggregate basis.[5] This method generally makes a difference, however, only when some shares are held long-term and others short-term; otherwise, the tax consequences will be identical whether the shareholder uses a share-by-share or an aggregate approach.[6]

The timing of a shareholder's gain or loss on a complete liquidation raises thornier questions. A liquidating corporation often is unable to distribute all of its property at one time or within the same taxable year. Recognizing these practical constraints, Section 346(a) defines a complete liquidation to include a series of distributions occurring over a period of time if they are all pursuant to a plan of complete liquidation. Shareholders normally prefer to treat these "creeping complete" liquidations as open transactions so they can defer reporting any gain until the amounts received exceed their stock basis.[7] This cost recovery approach has been sanctioned by the Service in the liquidation context[8] even though it would appear to be foreclosed by Section 453, which requires ratable basis recovery as payments are received even in cases where the selling price cannot be readily ascertained.[9] Since liquidating distributions are treated as payments in exchange for the shareholders' stock, Section 453 technically seems to apply and, if so, shareholders wishing to defer their gain should be required to use the installment method, allocating each distribution between recovery of basis and taxable gain.[10] But taxpayers who wish to use

5. Reg. § 1.331–1(e). For example, assume that Shareholder ("S") holds 60 shares of X, Inc. stock long-term with a $30,000 basis and 40 shares short-term with a $50,000 basis. If S receives $100,000 in complete liquidation of X, he must allocate the amount realized ratably between the two blocks as follows:

Long–Term 60 shares		**Short–Term 40 shares**	
A.R.	$60,000	A.R.	$40,000
A.B.	30,000	A.B.	50,000
LTCG	$30,000	STCL	$10,000

6. For the problems of valuation of the liquidating distribution and handling contingent claims, see Bittker & Eustice, Federal Income Taxation of Corporations & Shareholders ¶ 10.03[2] (7th ed. 2000).

7. See, e.g., Burnet v. Logan, 283 U.S. 404, 51 S.Ct. 550 (1931). Cf. I.R.C. § 453(d) (installment method applies unless taxpayer elects out of Section 453).

8. Rev.Rul. 68–348, 1968–2 C.B. 141, amplified by Rev.Rul. 85–48, 1985–1 C.B. 126.

9. See I.R.C. § 453(j)(2); Reg. § 15A.453–1(c). See also S.Rep. No. 96–1000, 96th Cong., 2d Sess. 24 (1980), reprinted in 1980–2 C.B. 494, 506–507. But see Rev.Rul. 85–48, supra note 8, where the Service continued to sanction open transaction reporting of gain on a liquidation notwithstanding the limits imposed by Section 453.

10. Cf. Reg. § 1.453–11(d), which appears to support the position taken in the text but only when the liquidating corporation distributes an installment obligation described in Section 453(h). See infra notes 11–13 and accompanying text. Installment sale reporting is not available if the stock of the liquidating corporation is publicly traded. See I.R.C. § 453(k)(2), requiring current inclusion of gain on deferred payment dispositions of stock or securities traded on an established securities market. If open transaction report-

the cost recovery approach are not likely to be challenged in light of the Service's longstanding position in published rulings.

A different issue is presented when a liquidating corporation sells certain assets for installment obligations and then distributes the obligations in complete liquidation. In that situation, shareholders who receive the installment obligations may be able to defer part of their Section 331(a) gain on the liquidation by using the installment method of reporting under Section 453. Installment sale reporting is accomplished by treating the shareholders' receipt of payments on the distributed installment obligations as if they were received in exchange for the shareholder's stock.[11] To qualify for this treatment, the obligations must have been acquired by the corporation in respect of a sale or exchange of property during the 12–month period beginning on the date a plan of complete liquidation is adopted and the liquidation must be completed within that 12–month period.[12] Installment obligations arising from the sale of inventory or other "dealer" property by the corporation are eligible for installment sale treatment in the hands of the distributee shareholders only if the obligation resulted from a bulk sale—i.e., the sale was to one person in one transaction and involves substantially all of the property attributable to a trade or business of the corporation.[13] Installment sale reporting is not available, however, if the stock of the liquidating corporation is publicly traded,[14] or if the shareholder elects out of Section 453.[15]

PROBLEM

A owns 100 shares of Humdrum Corporation which he purchased several years ago for $10,000. Humdrum has $12,000 of accumulated earnings and profits. What are the tax consequences to A on the liquidation of Humdrum Corporation in the following alternative situations:

(a) Humdrum distributes $20,000 to A in exchange for his stock?

ing is still generally available to liquidating distributions, this restriction should not apply when a shareholder of a public company receives a series of distributions straddling two or more taxable years. See also I.R.C. § 453(d), which permits a taxpayer to "elect out" of installment sale treatment. In the case of a liquidation, an election out would require the shareholder to report his entire gain in the year of the first distribution except, perhaps, where the value of future distributions is unascertainable. See Reg. § 15A.453–1(d).

11. I.R.C. § 453(h)(1)(A); Reg. § 1.453–11. A shareholder who receives liquidating distributions that include installment obligations in more than one taxable year must reasonably estimate the gain attributable to distributions received in each taxable year based on the best available information and allocate his stock basis pro rata over all payments to be received. When the exact amount of gain is subsequently determined, any adjustment is made in the taxable year in which that determination is made. Alternatively, the shareholder may file an amended return for the earlier year. I.R.C. § 453(h)(2); Reg. § 1.453–11(d).

12. Id. See Reg. § 1.453–11(c).

13. I.R.C. § 453(h)(1)(B); Reg. § 1.453–11(c)(4).

14. I.R.C. § 453(k)(2); Reg. § 1.453–11(a)(2)(i). But if a nonpublicly traded liquidating corporation distributes an installment obligation arising from a corporate-level sale of publicly traded stock, the obligation generally qualifies for installment sale reporting under Section 453(h). Reg. § 1.453–11(c)(2).

15. I.R.C. § 453(d).

(b) What result in (a), above, if A receives $10,000 in the current year (year one) and $10,000 in year two? Would there be any problem if Humdrum does not adopt a formal plan of complete liquidation in year one?

(c) Humdrum distributes $8,000 cash and an installment obligation with a face and fair market value of $12,000, payable $1,000 per year for 12 years with market rate interest. The installment obligation was received by Humdrum two months ago, after the adoption of the plan of liquidation, on the sale of a capital asset. Would the result be different if Humdrum's stock were publicly traded? See I.R.C. § 453(k).

(d) Same as (c), above, except the installment obligation was received two years ago and no payments have yet been made.

(e) What result in (a), above, if two years later, A is required to pay a $5,000 judgment against Humdrum in his capacity as transferee of the corporation? Compare this with the result if the judgment had been rendered and paid by the corporation prior to the liquidation. See Arrowsmith v. Commissioner, 344 U.S. 6, 73 S.Ct. 71 (1952).

2. CONSEQUENCES TO THE LIQUIDATING CORPORATION

Code: § 336(a), (b), (c), (d). Skim § 267(a)(1), (b), (c).

It should come as no surprise at this juncture that Subchapter C requires property distributions by corporations to their shareholders to be analyzed at both the corporate and shareholder levels. Earlier chapters have chronicled the gradual erosion of the *General Utilities*[1] doctrine, under which a corporation generally did not recognize gain on nonliquidating distributions of appreciated property. We have seen that recognition of gain (but not loss) is now the statutory norm in the nonliquidation setting.[2] Should the same rules apply to liquidating distributions and sales of assets by a liquidating corporation? Once again, a brief historical interlude is appropriate before considering the current answers to what was once a much debated question.

a. BACKGROUND

Although the *General Utilities* case involved a distribution of appreciated property by an ongoing business, the doctrine also applied to liquidating distributions. Until the enactment of the 1986 Code, a corporation generally did not recognize gain or loss on the distribution of property in complete liquidation.[3] Prior to the 1954 Code, however, sales of assets by a liquidating corporation were fully taxable.

1. General Utilities & Operating Co. v. Helvering, 296 U.S. 200, 56 S.Ct. 185 (1935); see Chapters 12D1 and 13E1, supra.

2. I.R.C. § 311(a), (b).

3. I.R.C. § 336(a) (pre–1987). This general nonrecognition rule was subject to various exceptions, such as the statutory recapture of depreciation provisions and the judicially created tax benefit rule and as-

To illustrate the disparate tax treatment of liquidating distributions and sales under the pre–1954 regime, assume that A is the sole shareholder of Target Corporation ("T") and has a $100,000 basis in her T stock. T's only asset is a parcel of undeveloped land ("Gainacre") with a fair market value of $400,000 and a zero adjusted basis. Purchaser ("P") wishes to acquire Gainacre for $400,000 cash. If T distributed Gainacre to A in complete liquidation, it recognized no gain under the *General Utilities* doctrine, and A took Gainacre with a $400,000 fair market value basis. On a sale of Gainacre to P for $400,000 following the liquidation, A thus would recognize no gain. If, instead, T had sold Gainacre directly to P, it would have recognized $400,000 gain under the pre–1954 regime. In either case, A recognized gain on the liquidation of T, measured by the difference between the amount of the distribution and her $100,000 adjusted basis in the T stock.

The different tax results of these economically equivalent transactions prompted savvy taxpayers to "postpone" sales of corporate assets until after a liquidation in order to avoid a corporate-level tax. The ignorant did what came naturally—and often was a practical necessity for large corporations with many assets and shareholders—by selling assets at the corporate level prior to the liquidation. With such high tax stakes, the courts were called upon to determine who *in substance* made the sale—an inquiry that engendered some anomalous results, as evidenced by the two Supreme Court decisions that follow.

Commissioner v. Court Holding Co.

Supreme Court of the United States, 1945.
324 U.S. 331, 65 S.Ct. 707.

■ MR. JUSTICE BLACK delivered the opinion of the Court.

An apartment house, which was the sole asset of the respondent corporation, was transferred in the form of a liquidating dividend to the corporation's two shareholders. They in turn formally conveyed it to a purchaser who had originally negotiated for the purchase from the corporation. The question is whether the Circuit Court of Appeals properly reversed the Tax Court's conclusion that the corporation was taxable under § 22 of the Internal Revenue Code for the gain which accrued from the sale. The answer depends upon whether the findings of the Tax Court that the whole transaction showed a sale by the corporation rather than by the stockholders were final and binding upon the Circuit Court of Appeals.

It is unnecessary to set out in detail the evidence introduced before the Tax Court or its findings. Despite conflicting evidence, the following findings of the Tax Court are supported by the record:

signment of income doctrine. See, e.g., Hillsboro National Bank v. Commissioner, 460 U.S. 370, 103 S.Ct. 1134 (1983).

The respondent corporation was organized in 1934 solely to buy and hold the apartment building which was the only property ever owned by it. All of its outstanding stock was owned by Minnie Miller and her husband. Between October 1, 1939 and February, 1940, while the corporation still had legal title to the property, negotiations for its sale took place. These negotiations were between the corporation and the lessees of the property, together with a sister and brother-in-law. An oral agreement was reached as to the terms and conditions of sale, and on February 22, 1940, the parties met to reduce the agreement to writing. The purchaser was then advised by the corporation's attorney that the sale could not be consummated because it would result in the imposition of a large income tax on the corporation. The next day, the corporation declared a "liquidating dividend," which involved complete liquidation of its assets, and surrender of all outstanding stock. Mrs. Miller and her husband surrendered their stock, and the building was deeded to them. A sale contract was then drawn, naming the Millers individually as vendors, and the lessees' sister as vendee, which embodied substantially the same terms and conditions previously agreed upon. One thousand dollars, which a month and a half earlier had been paid to the corporation by the lessees, was applied in part payment of the purchase price. Three days later, the property was conveyed to the lessees' sister.

The Tax Court concluded from these facts that, despite the declaration of a "liquidating dividend" followed by the transfers of legal title, the corporation had not abandoned the sales negotiations; that these were mere formalities designed "to make the transaction appear to be other than what it was" in order to avoid tax liability. The Circuit Court of Appeals drawing different inferences from the record, held that the corporation had "called off" the sale, and treated the stockholders' sale as unrelated to the prior negotiations.

There was evidence to support the findings of the Tax Court, and its findings must therefore be accepted by the courts. Dobson v. Commissioner, 320 U.S. 489; Commissioner v. Heininger, 320 U.S. 467; Commissioner v. Scottish American Investment Co., 323 U.S. 119. On the basis of these findings, the Tax Court was justified in attributing the gain from the sale to respondent corporation. The incidence of taxation depends upon the substance of a transaction. The tax consequences which arise from gains from a sale of property are not finally to be determined solely by the means employed to transfer legal title. Rather, the transaction must be viewed as a whole, and each step, from the commencement of negotiations to the consummation of the sale, is relevant. A sale by one person cannot be transformed for tax purposes into a sale by another by using the latter as a conduit through which to pass title. To permit the true nature of a transaction to be disguised by mere formalisms, which exist solely to alter tax liabilities, would seriously impair the effective administration of the tax policies of Congress.

It is urged that respondent corporation never executed a written agreement, and that an oral agreement to sell land cannot be enforced in

Florida because of the Statute of Frauds, Comp.Gen.Laws of Florida, 1927, vol. 3, § 5779. But the fact that respondent corporation itself never executed a written contract is unimportant, since the Tax Court found from the facts of the entire transaction that the executed sale was in substance the sale of the corporation. The decision of the Circuit Court of Appeals is reversed, and that of the Tax Court affirmed.

It is so ordered.

United States v. Cumberland Public Service Co.

Supreme Court of the United States, 1950.
338 U.S. 451, 70 S.Ct. 280.

■ MR. JUSTICE BLACK delivered the opinion of the Court.

A corporation selling its physical properties is taxed on capital gains resulting from the sale. There is no corporate tax, however, on distribution of assets in kind to shareholders as part of a genuine liquidation. The respondent corporation transferred property to its shareholders as a liquidating dividend in kind. The shareholders transferred it to a purchaser. The question is whether, despite contrary findings by the Court of Claims, this record requires a holding that the transaction was in fact a sale by the corporation subjecting the corporation to a capital gains tax.

Details of the transaction are as follows. The respondent, a closely held corporation, was long engaged in the business of generating and distributing electric power in three Kentucky counties. In 1936 a local cooperative began to distribute Tennessee Valley Authority power in the area served by respondent. It soon became obvious that respondent's Diesel-generated power could not compete with TVA power, which respondent had been unable to obtain. Respondent's shareholders, realizing that the corporation must get out of the power business unless it obtained TVA power, accordingly offered to sell all the corporate stock to the cooperative, which was receiving such power. The cooperative refused to buy the stock, but countered with an offer to buy from the corporation its transmission and distribution equipment. The corporation rejected the offer because it would have been compelled to pay a heavy capital gains tax. At the same time the shareholders, desiring to save payment of the corporate capital gains tax, offered to acquire the transmission and distribution equipment and then sell to the cooperative. The cooperative accepted. The corporation transferred the transmission and distribution systems to its shareholders in partial liquidation. The remaining assets were sold and the corporation dissolved. The shareholders then executed the previously contemplated sale to the cooperative.

Upon this sale by the shareholders, the Commissioner assessed and collected a $17,000 tax from the corporation on the theory that the shareholders had been used as a mere conduit for effectuating what was really a corporate sale. Respondent corporation brought this action to recover the amount of the tax. The Court of Claims found that the method by which the stockholders disposed of the properties was avowedly chosen in order to reduce taxes, but that the liquidation and dissolution genuinely ended the corporation's activities and existence. The court also found that at no time did the corporation plan to make the sale itself. Accordingly it found as a fact that the sale was made by the shareholders rather than the corporation, and entered judgment for respondent. One judge dissented, believing that our opinion in Commissioner v. Court Holding Co., 324 U.S. 331, required a finding that the sale had been made by the corporation. Certiorari was granted, 338 U.S. 846, to clear up doubts arising out of the *Court Holding Co.* case.

Our *Court Holding Co.* decision rested on findings of fact by the Tax Court that a sale had been made and gains realized by the taxpayer corporation. There the corporation had negotiated for sale of its assets and had reached an oral agreement of sale. When the tax consequences of the corporate sale were belatedly recognized, the corporation purported to "call off" the sale at the last minute and distributed the physical properties in kind to the stockholders. They promptly conveyed these properties to the same persons who had negotiated with the corporation. The terms of purchase were substantially those of the previous oral agreement. One thousand dollars already paid to the corporation was applied as part payment of the purchase price. The Tax Court found that the corporation never really abandoned its sales negotiations, that it never did dissolve, and that the sole purpose of the so-called liquidation was to disguise a corporate sale through use of mere formalisms in order to avoid tax liability. The Circuit Court of Appeals took a different view of the evidence. In this Court the Government contended that whether a liquidation distribution was genuine or merely a sham was traditionally a question of fact. We agreed with this contention, and reinstated the Tax Court's findings and judgment. Discussing the evidence which supported the findings of fact, we went on to say that "the incidence of taxation depends upon the substance of a transaction" regardless of "mere formalisms," and that taxes on a corporate sale cannot be avoided by using the shareholders as a "conduit through which to pass title."

This language does not mean that a corporation can be taxed even when the sale has been made by its stockholders following a genuine liquidation and dissolution.[3] While the distinction between sales by a corporation as compared with distribution in kind followed by shareholder sales may be particularly shadowy and artificial when the corporation is closely held, Congress has chosen to recognize such a distinction for tax purposes. The corporate tax is thus aimed primarily at the profits of a

3. What we said in the *Court Holding Co.* case was an approval of the action of the Tax Court in looking beyond the papers executed by the corporation and shareholders in order to determine whether the sale there had actually been made by the corporation. We were but emphasizing the established principle that in resolving such questions as who made a sale, fact-finding tribunals in tax cases can consider motives, intent, and conduct in addition to what appears in written instruments used by parties to control rights as among themselves. See, e.g., Helvering v. Clifford, 309 U.S. 331, 335–337; Commissioner of Internal Revenue v. Tower, 327 U.S. 280.

going concern. This is true despite the fact that gains realized from corporate sales are taxed, perhaps to prevent tax evasions, even where the cash proceeds are at once distributed in liquidation.[4] But Congress has imposed no tax on liquidating distributions in kind or on dissolution, whatever may be the motive for such liquidation. Consequently, a corporation may liquidate or dissolve without subjecting itself to the corporate gains tax, even though a primary motive is to avoid the burden of corporate taxation.

Here, on the basis of adequate subsidiary findings, the Court of Claims has found that the sale in question was made by the stockholders rather than the corporation. The Government's argument that the shareholders acted as a mere "conduit" for a sale by respondent corporation must fall before this finding. The subsidiary finding that a major motive of the shareholders was to reduce taxes does not bar this conclusion. Whatever the motive and however relevant it may be in determining whether the transaction was real or a sham, sales of physical properties by shareholders following a genuine liquidation distribution cannot be attributed to the corporation for tax purposes.

The oddities in tax consequences that emerge from the tax provisions here controlling appear to be inherent in the present tax pattern. For a corporation is taxed if it sells all its physical properties and distributes the cash proceeds as liquidating dividends, yet is not taxed if that property is distributed in kind and is then sold by the shareholders. In both instances the interest of the shareholders in the business has been transferred to the purchaser. Again, if these stockholders had succeeded in their original effort to sell all their stock, their interest would have been transferred to the purchasers just as effectively. Yet on such a transaction the corporation would have realized no taxable gain.

Congress having determined that different tax consequences shall flow from different methods by which the shareholders of a closely held corporation may dispose of corporate property, we accept its mandate. It is for the trial court, upon consideration of an entire transaction, to determine the factual category in which a particular transaction belongs. Here as in the *Court Holding Co.* case we accept the ultimate findings of fact of the trial tribunal. Accordingly the judgment of the Court of Claims is

Affirmed.

■ MR. JUSTICE DOUGLAS took no part in the consideration or decision of this case.

NOTE

The difficulties faced by the courts in reconciling the results in *Court Holding* and *Cumberland* influenced Congress to extend the *General Utili-*

4. It has also been held that where corporate liquidations are effected through trustees or agents, gains from sales are taxable to the corporation as though it were a going concern. See, e.g., First National Bank v. United States, 10 Cir., 86 F.2d 938, 941; Treas.Reg. 103, § 19.22(a)–21.

ties doctrine to liquidating sales. Under the 1954 Code version of Section 337, a corporation generally did not recognize gain or loss on a sale of property pursuant to a plan of complete liquidation except for recapture of depreciation and a few other items.[1] Aptly named the "anti-*Court Holding*" provision, old Section 337 usually ensured that the tax consequences of liquidating sales and distributions were the same regardless of the form of the transaction. In either case, the corporation generally did not recognize gain or loss, while the buyer (or distributee shareholder) took a fair market value basis in the acquired or distributed assets. As a result, the principal tax cost of a complete liquidation or taxable disposition of assets by a liquidating corporation was the capital gain recognized at the shareholder level.

Shortly after this extension of the *General Utilities* doctrine, reformers began calling for its repeal.[2] Imposing a tax at the shareholder level, they argued, did not justify exempting a liquidating corporation from tax on the disposition of its appreciated property. Until the 1980's, however, support for repeal was limited to the academic community and a handful of principled practitioners. "The General," it was said, had the loyal backing of the troops—battalions of legislators and their business constituents who looked askance at the double tax.[3] A principal justification for retaining the *General Utilities* doctrine was that it provided relief from the double taxation of corporate earnings by partially integrating the corporate and individual taxes.[4] More specialized pleaders focused on the adverse impact of the double tax on the "largely inflationary gains" on long-held assets of small "Mom and Pop" businesses.[5]

Despite these arguments, the movement for legislative reform gained momentum in the 1980's.[6] Eventually, the House of Representatives included *General Utilities* repeal, along with a permanent exception for certain closely held corporations, in its version of the 1986 tax reform legislation.[7]

1. I.R.C. § 337 (pre-1987).

2. See, e.g., Lewis, "A Proposed New Treatment for Corporate Distributions and Sales in Liquidations," 86th Cong., 1st Sess., House Committee on Ways and Means, 3 Tax Revision Compendium 1643 (1959).

3. We are indebted to the late Professor Walter Blum for the military analogy. See Blum, "Behind the *General Utilities* Doctrine, or Why Does the General Have So Much Support from the Troops," 62 Taxes 292 (1984).

4. See, e.g., Nolan, "Taxing Corporate Distributions of Appreciated Property: Repeal of the *General Utilities* Doctrine and Relief Measures," 22 San Diego L.Rev. 97 (1985). For an excellent survey and critique of the arguments for retaining *General Utilities*, see Yin, "General Utilities Repeal: Is Tax Reform Really Going to Pass it By?" 31 Tax Notes 1111 (June 11, 1986).

5. See, e.g., "Reform of Corporate Taxation," Hearing before the Committee on Finance, United States Senate, 98th Cong., 1st Sess. 148, 151, 153–157, 174–176, 185, 268–270 (Oct. 24, 1983).

6. See Staff of the Senate Finance Committee, The Subchapter C Revision Act of 1985: A Final Report Prepared by the Staff, 99th Cong., 1st Sess. 6–8, 42–44, 52–54, 59–68 (S.Prt. 99–47, 1985), recommending repeal of the *General Utilities* doctrine except for liquidating distributions or sales of certain long-held (over five years) assets by closely held corporations with under $2 million in assets.

7. H.R. 3838, 99th Cong., 1st Sess. (1985), §§ 331–335.

The House Ways and Means Committee report summarized the rationale for repeal in the liquidation setting:[8]

> The committee believes that the *General Utilities* rule, even in the more limited form in which it exists today, produces many incongruities and inequities in the tax system. First, the rule may create significant distortions in business behavior. Economically, a liquidating distribution is indistinguishable from a nonliquidating distribution; yet the Code provides a substantial preference for the former. A corporation acquiring the assets of a liquidating corporation is able to obtain a basis in assets equal to their fair market value, although the transferor recognizes no gain (other than possibly recapture amounts) on the sale. The tax benefits may make the assets more valuable in the hands of the transferee than in the hands of the present owner. The effect may be to induce corporations with substantial appreciated assets to liquidate and transfer their assets to other corporations for tax reasons, when economic considerations might indicate a different course of action. Accordingly, the *General Utilities* rule may be responsible, at least in part, for the dramatic increase in corporate mergers and acquisitions in recent years. The committee believes that the Code should not artificially encourage corporate liquidations and acquisitions, and believes that repeal of the *General Utilities* rule is a major step towards that goal.
>
> Second, the *General Utilities* rule tends to undermine the corporate income tax. Under normally applicable tax principles, nonrecognition of gain is available only if the transferee takes a carryover basis in the transferred property, thus assuring that a tax will eventually be collected on the appreciation. Where the *General Utilities* rule applies, assets generally are permitted to leave corporate solution and to take a stepped-up basis in the hands of the transferee without the imposition of a corporate-level tax. Thus, the effect of the rule is to grant a permanent exemption from the corporate income tax.

The Senate had originally included *General Utilities* repeal in its version of the 1986 bill, but that provision was later dropped, reportedly because of concerns over its adverse impact on corporate entrepreneurs.[9] In reconciling the two bills, the Conference Committee adopted the House's approach. To the surprise of even the tax reformers, the conferees went beyond the earlier proposals by eliminating any permanent exceptions for closely held corporations and providing only limited transitional relief. The General, so it seemed, had been deserted by the troops once the battle went behind closed doors. Against that background we turn to the current corporate-level tax treatment of liquidating distributions and sales.

8. H.R.Rep. No. 99–426, 99th Cong., 1st Sess. 281 (1985).

9. See Yin, supra note 4, at 1112–1113.

b. LIQUIDATING DISTRIBUTIONS AND SALES

The current version of Section 336(a) is the reverse of its 1954 Code predecessor. The general rule requires a liquidating corporation to recognize gain or loss on the distribution of property in complete liquidation as if the property were sold to the distributee at its fair market value. If the distributed property is subject to a liability or the distributee shareholder assumes a liability in connection with the distribution, the fair market value of the property is treated as being not less than the amount of the liability.[1] In strengthening the double tax regime of Subchapter C, Congress greatly increased the tax cost of a complete liquidation. Whenever a corporation makes a liquidating distribution of appreciated property, gain generally will be recognized at the corporate level and the distribution also will be a taxable event to the shareholders.[2]

Once Congress required a liquidating corporation to recognize gain or loss on liquidating distributions, it took the next logical step by conforming the tax treatment of liquidating sales. With the repeal of former Section 337, a corporation generally must recognize gain or loss on any sale of its assets pursuant to a complete liquidation plan.[3]

c. LIMITATIONS ON RECOGNITION OF LOSS

The general rule in Section 336(a) differs in one important respect from the rules in Section 311 governing nonliquidating distributions. It allows the distributing corporation to recognize loss as well as gain. Moreover, although Section 267 disallows losses on sales of property by a corporation to a "related" party (e.g., a controlling shareholder), it does not disallow them on liquidating distributions to related parties.[4] This license to recognize corporate-level losses quickly rattled the Congressional nervous system. To prevent taxpayers from recognizing losses "in inappropriate situations" or inflating the amount of loss actually sustained on a liquidation, the Tax Reform Act of 1986 added the two separate limitations in Section 336(d).[5]

Distributions to Related Persons. Section 336(d)(1) partially reinstates the policy of Section 267 by providing that no loss shall be recognized by a liquidating corporation on the distribution of property to a Section 267 related person if either: (1) the distribution is not pro rata among the

1. I.R.C. § 336(b). Cf. I.R.C. § 7701(g); Commissioner v. Tufts, 461 U.S. 300, 103 S.Ct. 1826 (1983), rehearing denied, 463 U.S. 1215, 103 S.Ct. 3555 (1983).

2. The general rule is subject to two exceptions. Nonrecognition of gain or loss is preserved for: (1) distributions in complete liquidation of a controlled—i.e., 80 percent—subsidiary (I.R.C. § 337, see Section C2 of this chapter, infra), and (2) distributions in certain tax-free reorganizations (I.R.C. § 336(c), see Chapter 17B5b, infra).

3. A corporation that sells or distributes stock in an 80 percent or more subsidiary may elect under Section 336(e), however, to treat the sale as a disposition of the subsidiary's assets and ignore any gain or loss on the sale or distribution of the stock. See also I.R.C. § 338(h)(10) and Chapter 16C3, infra.

4. I.R.C. § 267(a)(1).

5. See H.R.Rep. No. 99–841, 99th Cong., 2d Sess. II–200 (1986).

shareholders, or (2) the distributed property was acquired by the liquidating corporation in a Section 351 transaction or as a contribution to capital within the five-year period ending on the date of the distribution. These restrictions thus initially focus on the recipient of the loss property. For this purpose, related persons usually will be shareholders who own directly, or through the Section 267 attribution rules, more than 50 percent in value of the stock of the distributing corporation.[6]

Neither the statute nor the legislative history explains when a distribution is "not pro rata" among the shareholders. Congress presumably intended to single out situations where a majority shareholder receives an interest in loss property that is disproportionate to his stock interest in the corporation.[7] The legislative history provides scant illumination of the rationale for this rule. The conferees merely expressed an intent to restrict the ability of taxpayers to recognize losses in "inappropriate situations."[8] Perhaps Congress believed that it was necessary to apply the loss disallowance policy of Section 267 to liquidating distributions where the parties exercised a measure of control by targeting distributions of loss property to majority shareholders—but at the same time concluded that pro rata liquidating distributions were less likely to be motivated by tax avoidance.[9]

The rationale for limiting losses on distributions of recently contributed property to a related party is easier to discern—or at least it was before Congress imposed limitations on the transfer of built-in losses in Section 351 transactions.[10] Before the enactment of Section 362(e)(2), taxpayers could duplicate a single economic loss for tax purposes by transferring property with a built-in loss to a corporation in a Section 351 transaction or as a contribution to capital. For example, assume Sole Shareholder ("Sole") transferred Lossacre (adjusted basis—$1,000; fair market value—$500) to her wholly owned X Corporation ("X") in exchange for $500 of X stock in a Section 351 nonrecognition transaction. Under prior law, Sole took a $1,000 exchanged basis in her new X stock,[11] and X took Lossacre with a $1,000 transferred basis.[12] Assume further that, three years later, when Lossacre had the same basis and value, X liquidated, distributing Lossacre and its other assets to Sole. Without an "outbound" limitation, both Sole Shareholder and the corporation would recognize a $500 loss on the liquidation—two losses for the price of none considering that, when the

6. I.R.C. § 267(b)(2), (c).

7. For example, assume X Corporation has a net worth of $1,000 and is owned 75% by A and 25% by five unrelated shareholders. X distributes Lossacre (value—$750; basis $1,000) to A and $250 cash to the other shareholders. Since Lossacre was not distributed to the shareholders in proportion to their respective stock interests, the distribution is not pro rata and X may not recognize its $250 loss.

8. H.R.Rep. No. 99–841, supra note 5, at II–200.

9. Even if the distribution is pro rata, however, losses may be disallowed if the asset distributed to a related person is "disqualified property" within the meaning of Section 336(d)(1)(B). See text accompanying notes 14–18, infra.

10. See I.R.C. § 362(e)(2) and Chapter 11A, infra.

11. I.R.C. § 358(a).

12. I.R.C. § 362(a).

smoke cleared, Sole still owned Lossacre.[13] The same technique was effective for controlling shareholders who owned less than 100 percent of the corporation if on liquidation they received their pro rata share of each corporate asset.[14]

Section 336(d)(1)(A)(ii) attacks this form of "stuffing" with a rule that extends Section 267 principles to pro rata liquidating distributions of "disqualified property" to a related person. "Disqualified property" is defined as any property acquired by the liquidating corporation during the five-year period preceding the distribution in a Section 351 transaction or as a contribution to capital.[15] Section 362(e)(2), however, now imposes a similar limitation on duplication of losses for "inbound" transfers of built-in losses in Section 351 transactions. Applying that limitation to the above example, Sole would still take a $1,000 exchanged basis in her X stock, but X's basis in Lossacre would be limited to its $500 fair market value at the time it was transferred to X. As a result, on its liquidation three years later, X would have no recognized loss and Section 336(d) would not apply.

In its haste to adopt an inbound loss limitation rule, Congress may not have paused to ask whether the outbound limitations in Section 336(d)(1) should be modified. One answer that may explain the continuing existence of Section 336(d)(1) is that it does not exclusively target *duplication* of losses. It also applies to liquidating distributions of loss property to related persons that are not pro rata or are of "disqualified property," even if the loss was realized while the property was held by the corporation. Although the policy for such a limitation is difficult to defend in the context of a complete liquidation, the Code often limits losses when property is transferred between corporations and shareholders as well as in other related party transactions.[16]

Losses With Tax Avoidance Purpose. Section 336(d)(2) prevents the duplication of *precontribution* built-in losses even on certain distributions to minority shareholders. This limitation applies only if the distributing corporation acquired property in a Section 351 transaction or as a contribution to capital as part of a plan the principal purpose of which was to recognize loss by the corporation on a liquidating sale, exchange or distribution of the property. In that event, Section 336(d)(2) limits the corporation's deductible loss to the amount that accrued after the corporation

13. Of course, Sole will now hold Lossacre with a stepped-down fair market value basis of $500, but she will have benefitted from two losses without ever having disposed of the property.

14. As noted previously, corporate-level losses on non pro rata ("bullet") distributions to controlling shareholders are disallowed under Section 336(d)(1)(A)(i).

15. I.R.C. § 336(d)(1)(B). The term also includes any property the adjusted basis of which is determined in whole or in part by reference to the adjusted basis of property acquired in a Section 351 transaction or as a contribution to capital—e.g., like-kind property received in a Section 1031 transaction in exchange for property acquired by the corporation in a Section 351 transaction. Id.

16. See, e.g., I.R.C. § 351(b)(2) (no loss on transfers to controlled corporations even if transferor receives boot); § 267(a)(1) (disallowance of losses in related party transactions); § 1015(1) (donee's basis for loss reduced for gifts of built-in loss property).

acquired the property. Precontribution losses are disallowed by a basis step-down rule which requires the corporation to reduce its basis (but not below zero) in the affected property by the amount of built-in loss in the property at the time it was acquired by the corporation.[17]

Section 336(d)(2) is reinforced by a provision that treats any contribution of property after the date that is two years before the adoption of the plan of liquidation as part of a forbidden plan to recognize loss, except as the Treasury may provide in regulations.[18] Congress provided extensive guidance on the operation of this two-year presumption and the escape hatches that it expects to be included in future regulations. For example, although a contribution made more than two years prior to the adoption of a liquidation plan might be made with a prohibited purpose, the Conference Report states that in those circumstances the basis step-down rule in Section 336(d)(2) would apply only "in the most rare and unusual cases."[19] The legislative history also directed the Treasury to issue regulations generally providing that even contributions of property within the period covered by the presumption should be disregarded "*unless* there is no clear and substantial relationship between the contributed property and the conduct of the corporation's current or future business enterprises."[20] A "clear and substantial relationship" generally would include a requirement of a corporate business purpose for placing the property in the particular corporation to which it was contributed as compared to retaining the property outside that corporation.[21] If the contributed property has a built-in loss at the time of contribution that is "significant" relative to the built-in corporate gain at that time, "special scrutiny of the business purpose would be appropriate."[22]

Since the loss limitation rule of Section 362(e)(2) effectively disallows most precontribution losses by stepping down the basis of property when it is acquired, the role of Section 336(d)(2) has been greatly reduced. Section 362(e)(2) applies to transfers after October 22, 2004, and so contributions of loss property before that date will be monitored exclusively by Section 336(d)(2). Even after the effective date of Section 362(e)(2), there still will be situations where the inbound rule will not step down the basis of built-in loss property—e.g., where the corporation holds some properties with built-in losses that are subject to Section 336(d)(2) but the inbound stepdown rule did not apply because the aggregate basis of all properties transferred in a Section 351 transaction did not exceed their aggregate fair market value. Query, however, whether an outbound loss limitation rule is

17. The built-in loss is the excess of the adjusted basis of the property immediately after its acquisition over its fair market value at that time. I.R.C. § 336(d)(2)(A).

18. I.R.C. § 336(d)(2)(B)(ii).

19. H.R.Rep. No. 99–841, supra note 5, at 200. See also Staff of the Joint Committee on Taxation, General Explanation of the Tax Reform Act of 1986 ("1986 Act General Explanation"), 100th Cong., 1st Sess. 343 (1987).

20. H.R.Rep. No. 99–841, supra note 5, at II–201.

21. 1986 Act General Explanation, supra note 19, at 343.

22. Id.

still necessary in this situation? Perhaps the best explanation is traditional Congressional paranoia regarding abuse of tax losses.

In short, Section 336(d)(2) still may operate to prevent recognition of a loss but only in very limited circumstances. We must wait and see if Congress decides to revisit these questions in its next tax bill.

Overlap Situations. If both Section 336(d)(1) and Section 336(d)(2) apply to the same transaction, the harsher rule in Section 336(d)(1) (which disallows the entire loss rather than just the precontribution built-in loss) takes precedence.[23]

PROBLEM

All the outstanding stock of X Corporation is owned by Ivan (60 shares) and Flo (40 shares), who are unrelated. X has no liabilities and the following assets:

Asset	Adj. Basis	F.M.V.
Gainacre	$100,000	$400,000
Lossacre	800,000	400,000
Cash	200,000	200,000

Unless otherwise indicated, assume that each asset has been held by X for more than five years.

On January 1 of the current year, X adopted a plan of complete liquidation. What are the tax consequences to X on the distribution of its assets pursuant to the liquidation plan in each of the following alternatives?

(a) X distributes each of its assets to Ivan and Flo as tenants-in-common in proportion to their stock interests (i.e., Ivan takes a 60% interest and Flo a 40% interest in each asset).

(b) Same as (a), above, except X distributes Lossacre and the cash to Ivan and Gainacre to Flo.

(c) Same as (b), above, except X distributes Gainacre and the cash to Ivan and Lossacre to Flo.

(d) Same as (a), above, except X acquired Lossacre as a contribution to capital four years ago, and X was not required to reduce its basis under § 362(e). Is the result different if Lossacre had a value of $1,000,000 and a basis of $800,000 at the time it was contributed to the corporation?

(e) What result on the distributions in (c), above (i.e., Gainacre and cash to Ivan, Lossacre to Flo) if Lossacre, which had no relationship to X's business operations, was transferred to X by Ivan and Flo in a § 351 transaction 18 months prior to the adoption of the liquidation plan, when Lossacre had a fair market value of

23. 1986 Act General Explanation, supra note 19, at 342, n. 86.

$700,000 and an adjusted basis of $800,000? Assume, alternatively, that § 362(e)(2) did and did not apply to the contribution of Lossacre to X.

(f) Now assume that Ivan and Flo own 80% and 20%, respectively, of X, which was formed with Ivan contributing Gainacre and Lossacre (same adjusted basis and fair market values as in introductory facts above) and Flo contributing $200,000 cash. Assume further that Lossacre is § 336(d)(1) "disqualified property," § 362(e)(2) applied to Ivan's contributions to X but § 336(d)(2) does not apply to the liquidating distribution of Lossacre because there was no "plan" for X to recognize loss on that property. Pursuant to a liquidation plan, X distributes each of the assets to the two shareholders in proportion to their stock interests.

(g) Same as (f), above, except assume that § 362(e)(2) applied to Ivan's contributions to X and § 336(d)(2) applies to Lossacre because there was a "plan" by X to recognize loss in that property.

C. LIQUIDATION OF A SUBSIDIARY

1. CONSEQUENCES TO THE SHAREHOLDERS

Code: §§ 332; 334(b)(1)(A); 1223(1).

Regulations: §§ 1.332–1, –2, –5.

Nonrecognition treatment is inappropriate on an ordinary complete liquidation because it would permit individual shareholders to achieve a tax-free bailout as they watch the corporation's earnings and profits account disappear from the scene. Different policy considerations come into play when a parent corporation liquidates a controlled subsidiary. Since the assets of the subsidiary remain in corporate solution, the liquidation is a mere change in form that should not be impeded by the imposition of a tax. The subsidiary's tax attributes, including its earnings and profits, can be inherited by the parent without administrative burdens. Moreover, the subsidiary could have paid tax-free dividends to the parent under Section 243 or the consolidated return rules. All these factors, together with a desire to encourage the simplification of corporate structures, influenced Congress to adopt a nonrecognition scheme by enacting the statutory predecessor of Section 332.

Section 332 provides that a parent corporation recognizes no gain or loss on the receipt of property in complete liquidation of an 80 percent or more subsidiary if certain conditions are met. In that event, the parent takes the distributed assets with a transferred basis under Section

334(b)(1)[1] and inherits the subsidiary's earnings and profits and other tax attributes under Section 381(a)(1).[2]

To qualify under Section 332, the subsidiary must distribute property to its parent in complete cancellation or redemption of its stock pursuant to a plan of liquidation, and the liquidation must meet two formal requirements, one relating to control and the other to timing.

Control. Under Section 332(b)(1), the parent must own at least 80 percent of the total voting power of the stock of the subsidiary and 80 percent of the total value of all outstanding stock of the subsidiary from the date of adoption of the plan of complete liquidation and at all times thereafter until the parent receives the final distribution.[3] This condition normally is not a problem if the subsidiary is wholly owned, but any significant minority ownership creates a risk that the transaction will run afoul of the control requirement. Indeed, a parent corporation sometimes is motivated to intentionally violate the 80 percent tests in order to avoid Section 332 and recognize a loss on its stock in the subsidiary.[4] Conversely, an aspiring parent that does not meet the 80 percent control test may seek to qualify a liquidation under Section 332 by acquiring more stock of the subsidiary or causing the subsidiary to redeem stock held by minority shareholders shortly before the liquidation. As illustrated by the *Riggs* case, below, this strategy may trigger a controversy with the Service over when the liquidation plan was adopted.

Timing. Section 332 includes two timing alternatives. "One-shot" liquidations qualify if the subsidiary distributes all of its assets within one taxable year[5] even if it is not the same year in which the liquidation plan is adopted.[6] Where the distributions span more than one taxable year, the plan must provide that the subsidiary will transfer all of its property within three years after the close of the taxable year in which the first distribution

1. If the liquidating subsidiary is not subject to U.S. tax with respect to the distributed property (e.g., because it is a foreign corporation) and the distributee parent is subject to U.S. tax (e.g., it is a domestic corporation), the distributee's aggregate adjusted basis of the distributed property, if it otherwise would exceed its fair market value, must be limited to the lesser fair market value. I.R.C. § 334(b)(1)(B). The purpose of this limitation is to prevent importation of tax losses into the U.S. tax system through the liquidation of a foreign subsidiary. See Chapter 11A, supra, for a similar rule for incorporation transactions.

2. The parent's basis in the stock of a subsidiary is not taken into account in determining the tax consequences of a Section 332 liquidation and disappears from the scene. This creates the possibility that the parent may be deprived of a loss on its investment in the subsidiary even though it must inherit a low carryover basis in its assets.

3. The stock ownership requirements are derived from Section 1504(a)(2), which sets forth rules for determining whether a corporation is a member of an "affiliated group." For purposes of the stock ownership requirement, most nonconvertible preferred stock is disregarded. I.R.C. § 1504(a)(4). Reg. § 1.332–2(a), which states that the test is whether the parent owns at least 80 percent of the subsidiary's total combined voting power and 80 percent of all other classes of stock (except nonvoting stock limited and preferred as to dividends), does not reflect legislative changes to Section 332(b)(1).

4. See Commissioner v. Day & Zimmermann, Inc., 151 F.2d 517 (3d Cir.1945).

5. I.R.C. § 332(b)(2); Reg. § 1.332–3. In this situation, the adoption by the shareholders of the resolution authorizing the distributions in liquidation is considered an adoption of a "plan" of liquidation even though it may not specify the time for completing the transfers.

6. Rev.Rul. 71–326, 1971–2 C.B. 177.

is made.[7] Failure to meet the deadline will cause the liquidation to be retroactively disqualified.[8]

Minority Shareholders. Nonrecognition under Section 332 is only granted to the controlling parent corporation. It is not available to minority shareholders, who must determine their gain or loss in the normal manner under Section 331(a) unless the liquidation also qualifies as a tax-free reorganization—a rare situation that will be explored in a later chapter.[9]

George L. Riggs, Inc. v. Commissioner

United States Tax Court, 1975.
64 T.C. 474.

■ DRENNEN, JUDGE: Respondent determined a deficiency in petitioner's income tax for the taxable year ended March 31, 1969, in the amount of $589,882.28.

The sole issue for determination is whether the plan of liquidation of Riggs–Young Corp., a subsidiary of the petitioner, was adopted subsequent to the time when petitioner owned at least 80 percent of the outstanding stock of Riggs–Young, thereby rendering section 332, I.R.C. 1954, applicable to the liquidation so that the gain to petitioner thereon is not to be recognized.

FINDINGS OF FACT

[George L. Riggs, Inc., referred to throughout the opinion as "petitioner," was a holding company which as of December, 1967, owned approximately 35.6 percent (2,432 out of 6,840 shares) of the nonvoting preferred stock and 72.13 percent (8,047 out of 11,156 shares) of the common stock of The Standard Electric Time Co. ("Standard"). Standard owned 90 percent of the outstanding stock of a Delaware subsidiary and 99.5 percent of a California subsidiary. The corporations were in the business of manufacturing and marketing electric clocks and signal devices. Standard was the manufacturing arm of the business, and the two subsidiaries handled marketing.

On December 13, 1967, Frances Riggs–Young, the president of Standard and controlling shareholder of petitioner, notified all of Standard's shareholders that the company and its subsidiaries would be seeking approval for a sale of substantially all of the operating assets of the companies. In connection with the sale, Standard changed its name to Riggs–Young Corporation. The sales were consummated on December 29, 1967. In February, 1968, Riggs–Young (formerly Standard) redeemed all of

7. I.R.C. § 332(b)(3); Reg. § 1.332–4.

8. Id. To allow the Service to assert deficiencies for the early distributions in the event of a retroactive disqualification, the parent is required to file a waiver of the normal three year statute of limitations and may be asked to post a bond in order to protect the Commissioner's ability to collect past due taxes.

9. Reg. § 1.332–5. See Chapter 17B1, infra.

its preferred stock. On April 17, 1968, the directors of Riggs–Young approved the liquidation of the Delaware and California subsidiaries, and authorized Riggs–Young to offer to redeem common stock from all of its shareholders with the exception of petitioner and Frances Riggs–Young. The stated purpose of this tender offer was to eliminate the minority shareholders and provide them with the opportunity to receive cash for their stock. The Tax Court also found that counsel to petitioner and the related subsidiaries "recognized the desirability of petitioner's owning 80 percent of the common stock of Riggs–Young (1) to permit the filing of consolidated returns, and (2) to permit the possible further liquidation of Riggs–Young under section 332 of the Code to simplify the corporate structure." 64 T.C. at 480. The letter informing shareholders of the redemption offer stated that "If this offer is accepted by substantially all of the stockholders to whom it is directed, the Directors will consider liquidation and final dissolution of the Corporation." 64 T.C. at 479.

At the time of its redemption offer, petitioner owned 72.13 percent of Riggs–Young's common stock. The remaining shares were owned by members of the Riggs family, related trusts and a small group of unrelated minority shareholders.

The tender offer was made on April 26, 1968 and expired on May 28, 1968. During this period, owners of 2,738 shares of common stock tendered their shares for redemption. As a result of these redemptions, petitioner owned at least 80 percent of Riggs–Young's common stock on May 9, 1968, and its ownership increased to 95.6 percent by May 28. On June 20, 1968, the directors and shareholders of Riggs–Young approved a plan of complete liquidation and dissolution of the corporation. Between June and December, 1968, when the liquidation was completed, Riggs–Young made distributions to petitioner in excess of $2.2 million.

Petitioner realized a gain of $2,168,975 from the liquidation of Riggs–Young, representing the difference between the liquidating distributions and petitioner's $42,465 basis in its Riggs–Young stock. The gain was reported on petitioner's tax return but not recognized under the authority of Section 332. Ed.]

OPINION

The only question for decision is whether petitioner owned at least 80 percent of the outstanding stock of its subsidiary, Riggs–Young Corp., at the time Riggs–Young Corp. adopted a plan of liquidation within the meaning of section 332, I.R.C. 1954, so that the gain realized by petitioner on the liquidation of Riggs–Young is not to be recognized by virtue of that section. The vital question is when did Riggs–Young adopt a plan of liquidation within the meaning of section 332.

Respondent argues that the plan of liquidation was adopted on December 27, 1967, when about 90 percent of the stock of Riggs–Young (then Standard) was voted in favor of selling substantially all of the assets of Riggs–Young and its two subsidiaries, Delaware and California, to SET; or not later than about April 17, 1968, when the board of directors of Riggs–

Young voted to liquidate Delaware and California and to make an offer to purchase all of the common stock of Riggs–Young then outstanding with the exception of the stock owned by petitioner and Frances Riggs–Young.[2]

On the other hand petitioner contends that the plan of liquidation of Riggs–Young was first adopted when it was formally adopted by vote of the stockholders on June 20, 1968, or at the earliest when counsel for petitioner recommended to petitioner in the early days of June 1968 that it liquidate Riggs–Young. Petitioner also contends that section 332 is an elective section and a taxpayer, by taking appropriate steps, can render that section applicable or inapplicable.

The parties are in agreement that by May 9, 1968, petitioner was the owner of at least 80 percent of the outstanding stock of Riggs–Young.

Section 332(a) of the Code provides as a general rule: "No gain or loss shall be recognized on the receipt by a corporation of property distributed in complete liquidation of another corporation." Subsection (b) of section 332 establishes certain requirements which must be satisfied before subsection (a) becomes applicable. The only requirement of subsection (b) which is in issue in this case is whether petitioner, which received property from Riggs–Young in liquidation, was, on the date of the adoption of the plan of liquidation, the owner of at least 80 percent of the stock of Riggs–Young, the liquidating corporation.

Nowhere in the pertinent statute is the phrase "the date of the adoption of the plan of liquidation" defined. However, in attempting to define this phrase for purposes of the provision of [1954 Code] section 337, the regulations of the Commissioner provide:

> Ordinarily the date of the adoption of a plan of complete liquidation by a corporation is the date of adoption by the shareholders of the resolution authorizing the distribution of all the assets of the corporation (other than those retained to meet claims) in redemption of all of its stock. * * * [Sec. 1.337–2(b), Income Tax Regs.; accord, Virginia Ice & Freezing Corp., 30 T.C. 1251 (1958).]

The date of this shareholder resolution should ordinarily be considered the date of the adoption of the plan of liquidation for purposes of section 332. See sec. 332(b)(2).

This Court has noted, in interpreting section 112(b)(6), I.R.C. 1939 (the predecessor of section 332, I.R.C. 1954), that although the adoption of the plan of liquidation "need not be evidenced by formal action of the corporation or the stockholders. * * * even an informal adoption of the plan to liquidate presupposes some kind of definitive determination to achieve dissolution." Distributors Finance Corp., 20 T.C. 768, 784 (1953).

2. Respondent specifically does not rely on the "end-result" or "step-transaction" theory in this case. * * *

The mere general intention to liquidate is not the adoption of a plan of liquidation. City Bank of Washington, 38 T.C. 713 (1962).

Based on the evidence introduced in the case at bar, we must conclude that a plan for the liquidation of Riggs–Young had not been adopted prior to the critical date of May 9, 1968.

Respondent, in an effort to show that the plan of liquidation of Riggs–Young was informally adopted on December 27, 1967, or no later than April 1968, alludes to actions and statements made in connection therewith taken between December 1967 and June 1968. Petitioner offered the testimony of persons involved in those actions to explain what the parties had in mind in taking those actions and making the statements which cast a quite different light on the reasons therefor. This testimony was creditable and not shaken by cross-examination. In light of such evidence, we cannot agree with respondent's inference that these actions constituted an informal adoption of a plan of liquidation of Riggs–Young prior to May 9, 1968.

Respondent argues that the letter dated December 13, 1967, sent to the common shareholders of Standard (Riggs–Young) notifying them of the proposed sale of its assets and that the corporation was contemplating an offer to purchase the common shares held by all shareholders other than petitioner if the sale was approved, clearly indicates that the shareholders at the meeting on December 27, 1967, intended to approve not only the sale of the assets, but also the liquidation of Standard (Riggs–Young).

We believe this infers too much. As petitioner points out, the use of the word "contemplated" shows the acquisition of the common stock of the minority shareholders was merely a possibility about which a final decision had not been made. In any event, from the possibility of a tender offer to the minority shareholders, we cannot conclude, ipso facto, that a plan for the liquidation had been adopted. Petitioner explained that the possibility of this tender offer was made known to the shareholders in order to avoid any possible disclosure problem with the securities law and to apprise the shareholders, from a fairness standpoint, of eventual possibilities resulting from the sale. This explanation is reasonable.

Respondent next points to the fact that on February 23, 1968, all of the 6,840 shares of preferred stock of Riggs–Young were called for redemption as additional evidence that a definite decision to liquidate the corporation had been made. We believe petitioner adequately explained that this redemption was based on sound business reasons. The preferred stock had a par value of $25 per share and a cumulative dividend of 8 percent. This stock was subject to redemption at the option of Riggs–Young upon payment of the par value and any accumulated dividend. The testimony of Norman Vester, a director of Riggs–Young and president of Security National Bank which was cotrustee of Riggs Trust, and Roger Stokey, the attorney for petitioner, Riggs–Young, and Frances Riggs–Young, reveal that the redemption of the preferred stock was motivated by the desire to eliminate the excessive burden of a cumulative dividend of 8 percent and to reduce the number of shareholders with whom Riggs–Young and National

Security Bank, as cotrustee of the majority shareholder, would have to deal. Both Vester and Stokey testified that as of January 19, 1968, the date the board of directors of Riggs–Young voted to redeem the preferred stock, no decision had been made to liquidate the corporation, and, therefore, no plan had been adopted.

Respondent next claims that a letter dated April 23, 1968, from Stokey to Scott C. Jordan categorically shows that a plan to liquidate Riggs–Young had been adopted prior to the date of the letter. Stokey's letter was in response to a letter from Jordan on behalf of Frances Riggs–Young inquiring whether she could participate in the tender offer that was about to be made to the minority shareholders of Riggs–Young. In his letter, Stokey said that Frances Riggs–Young might run some tax risks if she accepted a tender offer by Riggs–Young, apparently basing this statement on his belief that the amount she received from a tender offer might be taxed to her at ordinary income rates. As a result of this potential risk, Stokey stated in the letter: "Accordingly, we are arranging for her to receive her money in a liquidation."

Respondent perceives this statement by Stokey as a clear indication that a plan of liquidation of Riggs–Young had been adopted by a definite decision by April 23, 1963. We cannot so conclude. Stokey testified that "we," referred to as arranging the liquidation, meant Stokey and another member of his law firm, William Gorham. This letter merely shows that the attorneys involved in these transactions were contemplating the possibility of a liquidation of Riggs–Young. It in no way proves that the directors or shareholders of the corporation had made a definite decision or informally adopted a plan of liquidation.

Finally, respondent views the letter dated April 26, 1968, drafted by Frances Riggs–Young as president of Riggs–Young, which contained the tender offer to the common shareholders, other than petitioner and Frances Riggs–Young, as an additional indication of a prior adoption of a plan to liquidate. In this letter, Frances Riggs–Young did state that if substantially all of the shareholders accepted the offer, the directors of the corporation would consider liquidation and final dissolution of Riggs–Young.

Stokey testified that Gorham and he inserted, in this April 26 letter, the reference to the possible consideration of liquidating Riggs–Young. He also candidly admitted that he had undoubtedly discussed the possibility of liquidation of Riggs–Young at some prior point with Frances Riggs–Young, but hastened to add that he neither recommended liquidation at this time nor did she direct steps be taken to liquidate. Further, Stokey testified that he would never have recommended liquidation of Riggs–Young if petitioner had failed to achieve the 80–percent ownership.

Petitioner contends that the tender offer to the minority shareholders was made solely for business considerations and not with an eye toward the eventual liquidation of Riggs–Young. Vester and Stokey both testified that since the assets of Riggs–Young had been exchanged for cash, the primary purpose of the tender offer was to eliminate minority shareholders who might have different investment objectives for this cash than the majority shareholder. The bank, as trustee of Riggs, did not want to have to deal with a large group of minority shareholders. Furthermore, Stokey testified that Frances Riggs–Young desired to have the minority shareholders, many of whom were former employees of Standard, receive cash for their stock rather than have them remain locked in as minority shareholders of a personal holding company.

Stokey testified that another objective of the tender offer was to increase petitioner's ownership of Riggs–Young to 80 percent thereby enabling them to file a consolidated return. According to petitioner, the ultimate liquidation of Riggs–Young was not motivated by tax considerations and the sole advantage to be achieved from the liquidation was the simplification of petitioner's corporate structure. Petitioner alleges that Riggs–Young could have been kept in existence without any tax disadvantage. In fact the liquidation of Riggs–Young actually resulted in a tax disadvantage to Frances Riggs–Young personally since she had to pay capital gains tax on her share of the liquidation proceeds. She was a wealthy woman in her seventies and not in need of these funds and could have left this money in corporate solution until her death to enable it to receive a stepped-up basis for the beneficiaries of her estate.

We believe petitioner's explanations of why the actions were taken and the statements were made are true and that the considerations mentioned were taken into account in making the decisions that followed. While the motives enumerated by petitioner do not directly negate the notion that a liquidation may have been contemplated, discussed, or even intended prior to May 9, 1968, they do serve to sufficiently undermine the conclusions drawn by respondent from the actions and statements to offset any presumptions that respondent's inferences are correct. Without more concrete evidence than we have before us, we cannot agree with respondent that a plan of liquidation of Riggs–Young was adopted within the meaning of section 332 prior to May 9, 1968. Lacking such a finding, we believe the date on which the resolution to liquidate was actually adopted by the shareholders should be controlling.

The very most that can be gleaned from the evidence favorable to respondent's contention is that there may have been a general intent on the part of petitioner's advisers somewhere along the line prior to May 9, 1968, to liquidate Riggs–Young when and if petitioner achieved 80–percent ownership of Riggs–Young stock as a result of the tender offer. However, the formation of a conditional general intention to liquidate in the future is not the adoption of a plan of liquidation. *City Bank of Washington*, supra.

A mere intent by a taxpayer-corporation to liquidate a subsidiary prior to meeting the 80–percent requirement of section 332 should not be tantamount to the adoption of a plan of liquidation for the subsidiary at the point in time when that intent is formulated or manifested. Such a result would thwart the congressional intent of section 332 and prior judicial interpretations of this section and its predecessor.

The predecessor of section 332, I.R.C. 1954, was section 112(b)(6), first enacted in 1935. The purpose of section 112(b)(6) was to encourage the simplification of corporation structures and allow the tax-free liquidation of a subsidiary. * * *

* * *

Based on legislative history of [Section 112(b)(6) of the 1939 Code] and prior judicial decisions, we conclude that section 332 is elective in the sense that with advance planning and properly structured transactions, a corporation should be able to render section 332 applicable or inapplicable. The Commissioner in his regulations has conceded corporations this power in a seemingly analogous situation. See sec. 1.337–2(b), Income Tax Regs.

Such power of planning presupposes some right to forethought and the accompanying intent to achieve the desired goal. It would be a logical inconsistency equivalent to a "Catch–22" to say that a corporation has the power to control the application of this section, but that once the corporation formulates the intent to do so (assuming that at or subsequent to the time the intent was formed, it owned less than the required 80 percent but enough stock to cause the liquidation of the subsidiary), it has adopted a plan of liquidation and has precluded itself from the section.

A basic tenet of our tax laws is that a taxpayer has the legal right to decrease or altogether avoid his taxes by means which the law permits. Gregory v. Helvering, 293 U.S. 465 (1935); Daniel D. Palmer, 62 T.C. 684 (1974). At most, petitioner did no more than follow this prerogative.

The shareholders of Riggs–Young formally adopted the plan of liquidation of the corporation on June 20, 1968. Stokey testified that based on the records contained in his office diary, he did not discuss definite liquidation of the corporation with the corporate officers prior to June 4, 5, or 6, 1968. He concluded that he recommended liquidation on either the 4th or 5th of June 1968, and that a definite decision to liquidate was probably made on June 6, 1968. The testimony of Vester corroborates these statements of Stokey. We recognize that the adoption of a plan of liquidation need not be evidenced by formal action of the corporation or shareholders, *Distributors Finance Corp.*, supra. In this case, however, we find on the evidence that the plan of liquidation was adopted when the formal action was taken on June 20, 1968. Furthermore, even if it can be said that a plan of liquidation was adopted when Stokey first recommended it to the management, see *Distributors Finance Corp.*, supra, this occurred in June 1968 and would satisfy the requirements of section 332.

Respondent has cited and relied on Rev.Rul. 70–106, 1970–1 C.B. 70, as supportive of his position. This Court is not bound by a revenue ruling. Andrew A. Sandor, 62 T.C. 469 (1974). In addition, we find the facts of this case are greatly dissimilar to those contained in the ruling. The ruling assumes a prior agreement between the minority and majority shareholders concerning the redemption of the minority stockholders' stock. The ruling concludes that the liquidation plan was adopted when this agreement was reached. In the case at bar, there is no evidence of an agreement between the minority and majority shareholders prior to the tender offer. *Madison Square Garden Corp.*, supra at 624 n. 4. Since this revenue ruling is inapplicable, proper judicial restraint dictates that we do not comment on the validity or invalidity of the ruling as limited to the facts contained therein. Ronald C. Packard, 63 T.C. 621 (1975).

Decision will be entered for the petitioner. Reviewed by the Court.

2. Consequences to the Liquidating Subsidiary

Code: §§ 336(d)(3); 337(a), (b)(1), (c), (d). Skim §§ 381(a)(1), (c)(2), (3); 453B(d); 1245(b)(3); 1250(d)(3).

Regulations: § 1.332–7.

Distributions of Property. A liquidating corporation generally recognizes gain or loss on distributions of property in a complete liquidation.[1] A major exception to this general rule is contained in Section 337,[2] which provides that a liquidating subsidiary does not recognize gain or loss on distributions of property to its parent[3] in a complete liquidation to which Section 332 applies. A nonrecognition rule makes sense in this context because the subsidiary's tax attributes, including the built-in gain or loss in its assets, can be preserved in the hands of the parent. Section 334(b)(1) implements this policy by providing that the parent takes a transferred basis in property received from a subsidiary in a Section 332 liquidation. In keeping with this carryover of tax attributes theme, the depreciation recapture provisions do not override Section 337,[4] and recapture potential continues to lurk in the distributed property through the definition of "recomputed basis" in Section 1245 and "additional depreciation" in Section 1250.[5] A liquidating subsidiary likewise does not recognize gain or loss on the distribution of installment obligations if Section 332 applies,[6] and the parent will take a transferred basis in the obligations under Section 334(b)(1).

Distributions to Minority Shareholders. The nonrecognition rule in Section 337(a) is limited to distributions of property by a liquidating subsidiary to "the 80–percent distributee"—i.e., the parent corporation. Distributions to minority shareholders are treated in the same manner as a distribution in a nonliquidating redemption. Accordingly, the distributing corporation will recognize gain but not loss. Recognition of gain is appropriate because minority shareholders do not inherit any built-in gain in the distributed property through a transferred basis but instead take a fair

1. I.R.C. § 336(a).

2. This "new" Section 337 is not to be confused with its 1954 Code counterpart, "old" Section 337, which provided for nonrecognition of gain or loss on certain liquidating sales. Old timers wish Congress had avoided confusion by retiring old Section 337's number and placing it on a monument in "old" Yankee Stadium.

3. Section 337(a) refers to the parent as "the 80–percent distributee," which is defined in Section 337(c) as a corporation that meets the 80 percent stock ownership requirements specified in Section 332(b).

4. I.R.C. §§ 1245(b)(3); 1250(d)(3).

5. I.R.C. §§ 1245(a)(2); 1250(b)(1), (3). Issues of depreciation recapture on real estate have waned because virtually all depreciable real property placed in service after 1986 must be depreciated under the straight line method. I.R.C. § 168(b)(3).

6. I.R.C. § 453B(d)(1).

market value basis under Section 334(a). Distributions of loss property are another matter. In order to prevent a controlled subsidiary from recognizing losses (but not gains) by "bullet" distributions of loss property to minority shareholders, Section 336(d)(3) provides that no loss shall be recognized to a subsidiary on a distribution of property to minority shareholders in a Section 332 liquidation.

Transfer of Property to Satisfy Indebtedness of Subsidiary to Parent. Section 337 applies only to liquidating *distributions.* If a subsidiary is indebted to its parent, a transfer of property to satisfy the debt normally would be a taxable event rather than a nontaxable distribution governed by Section 337(a), causing the subsidiary to recognize gain or loss and the parent to take a fair market value basis in the distributed property. The disparate treatment of distributions in complete liquidation and transfers of property to satisfy intercorporate indebtedness might tempt a subsidiary to distribute appreciated property as part of the liquidation while simultaneously using loss property to extinguish any indebtedness to the parent. Section 337(b)(1) prevents this ploy by providing that any transfer of property in satisfaction of a subsidiary's debt to its parent shall be treated as a distribution, subjecting the transfer to the general nonrecognition rule of Section 337(a). As a necessary corollary, Section 334(b)(1) provides that the parent takes a transferred basis in the distributed property.

Distributions to Tax–Exempt and Foreign Parents. Ever vigilant, Congress was concerned that taxpayers might turn the deferral provided by Section 337 into a permanent exemption from the corporate-level tax. Consider the following possibility. A and B, the sole shareholders of highly appreciated X Corporation, wish to sell the business and avoid at least one level of tax. They sell all their stock to tax-exempt Charity, Inc. and recognize gain on the sale or, if they are philanthropic, they could donate the stock to Charity and take a charitable deduction. Charity now owns 100 percent of the X stock but it does not wish to operate the business. Charity wishes to liquidate X in a tax-free transaction at both the corporate and shareholder levels under Sections 332 and 337(a). Although Charity must take a transferred basis in the property distributed by X, no tax ever would be collected on the subsequent sale of those assets because Charity is exempt from tax.

This technique might have been vulnerable under the step transaction and other judicial doctrines, but Congress decided to attack it from within the Code. Section 337(b)(2) thus provides that the general corporate-level nonrecognition rule for liquidations of a subsidiary shall not apply where the parent is a tax-exempt organization. Nonrecognition is restored, however, if the distributed property is used by the tax-exempt parent in an "unrelated trade or business" immediately after the distribution.[7] In that event, there is no loophole to plug because the tax-exempt organization is

7. Exempt organizations may be taxable on income from an "unrelated business"—i.e., a regularly carried on trade or business activity that is not substantially related to the organization's exempt purposes. See I.R.C. § 511 et seq.

subject to tax on its unrelated business income.[8] A similar rule requires recognition of corporate-level gain in the case of a liquidating distribution to a parent that is a foreign corporation, except as the Treasury may provide in regulations. The legislative history indicates that the regulations should permit nonrecognition if the appreciation on the distributed property is not being removed from the U.S.'s taxing jurisdiction prior to recognition.[9] In both situations where the subsidiary recognizes gain or loss, the parent takes a fair market value basis in the distributed assets.[10]

PROBLEMS

1. P, Inc. ("P") owns 90 percent of the outstanding stock of S, Inc. ("S"). Individual ("I") owns the remaining 10 percent of S. P's basis in its S stock is $3,000. I's basis in his S stock is $200. S has accumulated earnings and profits of $2,000 and the following assets:

Asset	Adjusted Basis	Fair Market Value
Land	$3,000	$8,000
Equipment	2,500	1,000
Inventory	100	1,000

S wishes to liquidate and distribute all of its assets to its shareholders. What are the tax consequences to P, S and I in the following alternative situations?

(a) S distributes the inventory to I and the other assets to P.

(b) S distributes the equipment to I and the other assets to P. How might S improve this result?

(c) What result in (b), above, if P's basis in its S stock were $30,000 and S had a $30,000 basis in the land?

(d) Is (c), above, a situation where P might wish to avoid the application of § 332? Why? How might this be accomplished? Consider in this regard the § 332 qualification requirements and how a parent might assure that they are not met.

2. Child Corporation has 100 shares of common stock outstanding. Mother Corporation owns 75 shares (basis—$1,000) and Uncle, an individual who recently inherited his stock, owns 25 shares (basis—$3,000). Child has no earnings and profits, a $10,000 net operating loss carryover and the following assets (all held long-term):

8. If the tax-exempt parent later disposes of the distributed property or ceases to use it in an unrelated trade or business, any gain not recognized on the earlier liquidation becomes taxable as unrelated business income. I.R.C. § 337(b)(2)(B)(ii).

9. H.R.Rep. No. 99–841, 99th Cong., 2d Sess. II–202 (1986).

10. I.R.C. § 334(b)(1)(A).

Asset	Adjusted Basis	Fair Market Value
Cash	$2,000	$2,000
Installment Note	1,000	4,000
Land	100	1,000
Equipment (all § 1245 gain)	100	1,000
Total	$3,200	$8,000

What are the tax consequences in the following alternative situations, disregarding the impact of any tax paid by Child as a result of its liquidating distributions?

(a) Child adopts a plan of complete liquidation and distributes $2,000 cash to Uncle and all its remaining assets to Mother.

(b) Child distributes $2,000 cash to Uncle in redemption of his 25 shares. One week later, it adopts a plan of complete liquidation and distributes its remaining assets to Mother pursuant to the plan. What are Mother and Child trying to accomplish through this reunion?

3. Parent Corporation ("P") owns all the stock of Subsidiary Corporation ("S"). P has a $1,000 basis in its S stock and also holds S bonds with a basis and face amount of $1,000. S has the following assets:

Asset	Adjusted Basis	Fair Market Value
Inventory	$10,000	$ 1,000
Land	200	10,000
	$10,200	$11,000

P intends to liquidate S, but before adopting a formal plan S distributes the inventory in satisfaction of its outstanding $1,000 debt to P. On the next day, S liquidates, distributing the land to P. Why did P and S structure the transactions in this manner? Will they achieve their tax objectives?

CHAPTER 16

Taxable Corporate Acquisitions

A. Introduction

There are many ways to structure a corporate acquisition. In the preceding chapter, we previewed one method: a sale by the target corporation[1] of all its assets followed by a distribution of the proceeds of sale to the shareholders in complete liquidation of the target.[2] An alternative is a sale by the shareholders of their stock in the target corporation. In either case, the business can be acquired in exchange for cash, notes, stock or bonds of the acquiring corporation, other property, or any combination of consideration. In an asset acquisition, the acquiring corporation may purchase the assets directly, drop them down to a controlled subsidiary or cause a subsidiary to make the acquisition. In a stock acquisition, the target may stay alive as a subsidiary of the acquiring corporation or liquidate. Variations abound on these basic formats.

Although we quickly will turn our attention to the tax consequences of corporate acquisitions, it may be useful at the outset to consider a few nontax factors that may influence the form of a transaction. Stock acquisitions are usually simpler to execute than asset acquisitions. To sell its assets, the target must prepare conveyance documents for many different items of property, give notice to creditors in compliance with local bulk sales laws, and incur sales or other local transfer taxes. In a stock acquisition, however, it is unnecessary to transfer any of the target's assets; instead, the acquiring corporation simply buys the target's stock directly from the T shareholders. A stock purchase thus may be desirable (or even essential) if the target holds certain nonassignable assets, such as a favorable lease or employment contract, or has valuable rights under state law that might be jeopardized if the corporation were dissolved. On the

1. In discussing acquisitions in this and later chapters, the acquired corporation generally will be called the "target," or "T," and the corporate purchaser will be called the "acquiring corporation," or "P." By using the term "target," we do not necessarily mean to suggest that the acquisition is a hostile takeover.

2. A target corporation that sells all or most of its assets usually will liquidate and distribute the proceeds to its shareholders. Alternatively, T could stay alive as an investment company after the sale. If T is closely held, staying alive likely would cause it to be classified as a personal holding company. For the perils of personal holding company status, see Chapter 10C, infra. For the possibility of a sale of assets by a C corporation followed by a conversion to S corporation status, see Chapter 20F, infra.

other hand, a stock acquisition may expose the buyer to liabilities of the target that may be unknown or contingent at the time of the transaction. This threat normally can be minimized by warranties and indemnity provisions in the stock purchase agreement. But some buyers still prefer to avoid the risk altogether by buying the assets and not assuming any burdens that might be connected with the corporate entity. The presence of unwanted assets, the unwillingness of minority shareholders of the target to sell their stock, and the requirements of regulatory agencies and local corporate and securities law are additional nontax factors that may influence the choice of form.

The principal tax issues raised on a corporate acquisition are best introduced by revisiting the simple example from the preceding chapter. Recall that A is the sole shareholder of Target Corporation ("T") and has a $100,000 basis in her T stock. T's only asset is a parcel of undeveloped land ("Gainacre") with a fair market value of $400,000 and a zero adjusted basis. Purchaser, Inc. ("P") wishes to acquire the land for $400,000 cash. Consider three simple methods of structuring the acquisition:

(1) *Liquidation of T Followed by Shareholder Sale of Assets.* T distributes Gainacre to A in complete liquidation and then A sells Gainacre to P for $400,000.

(2) *Sale of T Assets Followed by Liquidation.* T sells Gainacre to P for $400,000 and then liquidates, distributing the after-tax proceeds of sale to A.

(3) *Sale of T Stock.* A sells her T stock to P for $400,000 and P either keeps T alive as a wholly owned subsidiary or causes T to liquidate and distribute Gainacre to P.

Under any of these methods, one would expect A to recognize gain equal to the difference between her amount realized on the liquidation or sale of stock and the $100,000 adjusted basis in her T stock. In addition, T has $400,000 of corporate-level gain inherent in Gainacre. Should that gain also be recognized and, if so, should P (directly or indirectly through its ownership of T stock) take Gainacre with a $400,000 fair market value basis? If T does recognize gain, who bears the economic burden of the corporate-level tax? Alternatively, can the transaction be structured so that T's gain is deferred through a zero transferred basis in the land? Or, perish the thought, might T's gain be permanently forgiven, with P (or T, if it is still alive), taking Gainacre with a $400,000 cost basis? To what extent do (or should) the answers to these questions depend on the form of the transaction? And how are they affected if the seller is not an individual but a corporation that owns 100 percent of the T stock?

The after-tax economic outcome of these transactions may differ radically depending on the structure selected by the parties. The remainder of this chapter fills in the details, first considering asset acquisitions and then stock acquisitions.

B. ASSET ACQUISITIONS

1. TAX CONSEQUENCES TO THE PARTIES

A taxable asset acquisition occurs when a purchaser ("P"), which may be an individual or a business entity such as a corporation or partnership, acquires the assets of a target corporation ("T") in exchange for cash, notes, other property, or a mix of such consideration, and the acquisition does not qualify as a tax-free reorganization under Section 368.[1] Following the sale of its assets, T normally liquidates and distributes the sales proceeds to its shareholders, but the shareholders may choose to keep T alive and cause it to reinvest the proceeds. Under the corporate laws of most states, an asset acquisition also may be accomplished more efficiently by a cash merger of T into P (or a subsidiary of P). On the merger, T's shareholders receive cash or notes (or a combination) from P, and T's assets and liabilities automatically transfer to P (or its subsidiary). The Service views such a "cash merger" as if T sold its assets to P and then completely liquidated.[2]

To illustrate the tax consequences of the most basic asset acquisition methods, return again to the example of A, the sole shareholder (stock basis—$100,000) of T, whose only asset is appreciated Gainacre (basis—zero; fair market value—$400,000). Assume that C corporations and individuals are taxed at a flat 35 percent rate, with a 15 percent preferential rate for capital gains recognized by individual taxpayers.[3]

Liquidation of T Followed by Shareholder Sale of T Assets. If T distributes Gainacre to A in complete liquidation, it recognizes $400,000 gain under Section 336(a) and incurs a tax liability of $140,000 (35% × $400,000). A bears the economic burden of the tax and is obligated to pay it because T has no assets after it liquidates. A recognizes $160,000 gain on the liquidation ($400,000 distribution less $140,000 corporate-level tax less $100,000 basis in T stock) and incurs a shareholder-level capital gains tax of $24,000 (15% × $160,000). A takes Gainacre with a $400,000 basis under Section 334(a) and recognizes no further gain on a sale of Gainacre to P for its fair market value. When the smoke clears, the total corporate and shareholder-level tax on the liquidation and sale is $164,000, leaving A with $236,000. P takes Gainacre with a $400,000 cost basis and, if P is a corporation, it does not succeed to the tax attributes (e.g., earnings and profits, net operating losses, etc.) of T.

Sale of T Assets Followed by Liquidation. The result is identical if T sells Gainacre to P and then liquidates. T recognizes $400,000 gain on the sale, pays a corporate-level tax of $140,000, distributes the $260,000 net

1. See Chapter 17B, infra.

2. Rev.Rul. 69–6, 1969–1 C.B. 104.

3. These assumptions approximate the actual rates in effect as this edition went to press in early 2008 and ignore the impact of any state taxes.

proceeds to A in complete liquidation, and A again recognizes $160,000 gain under Section 331(a) and incurs a $24,000 capital gains tax. P takes Gainacre with a $400,000 cost basis and does not succeed to any of T's tax attributes.

Sale of T Assets Not Followed by Liquidation. If T does not liquidate after selling Gainacre to P, T once again recognizes $400,000 gain and incurs $140,000 in corporate-level tax, but A does not recognize gain if T retains and reinvests the $260,000 net proceeds. Keeping T alive defers and may permanently eliminate any tax at the shareholder level. For example, if A holds the T stock until her death, A's heirs will take a stepped-up basis in the stock under Section 1014 and then may liquidate the corporation without paying a shareholder-level tax. This "no liquidation" strategy may have some appeal if A is elderly and her estate is on the verge of obtaining a stepped-up basis in the T stock, but it is rarely desirable if the liquidation will be postponed for many years. First, the double tax on corporate earnings must be navigated if A wants access to T's earnings.[4] Moreover, if T no longer conducts an ongoing business, it likely will be classified as a "personal holding company."[5] As such, it will be required to distribute its net investment income annually to A or face a penalty tax equal to 15 percent of any undistributed income.[6] In many situations, keeping T alive may be more expensive than liquidating, although not as expensive as it was before the tax rate on qualified dividends was reduced to 15 percent.

Conversion to S Corporation. If T chooses to stay alive, it could avoid some of the problems just described by becoming an S corporation. For example, T's income would pass through to its shareholders and be subject to only one level of tax, albeit at slightly higher marginal rates for some high-bracket individual shareholders. But as an S corporation, T would face other obstacles. To name just two, an S corporation that was once a C corporation may lose its S status or be subject to a special corporate-level tax if it has Subchapter C earnings and profits and significant passive investment income.[7]

2. ALLOCATION OF PURCHASE PRICE

Code: § 1060. Skim § 197.

Regulations: §§ 1.338–6(a), (b), (c)(1); 1.1060–1(a)(1).

Background. The parties to an asset acquisition typically negotiate and agree upon a purchase price based on the value of the target corporation as

4. Dividends received by T, however, would qualify for the 70 percent dividends received deduction under Section 243(a), and corporate-level *regular* tax could be avoided altogether by investing the sales proceeds in tax-exempt municipal bonds. But unless it qualifies for the small corporation exception, T still may be subject to the corporate alternative minimum tax even if it is able to shelter its investment income from the regular tax. See, e.g., I.R.C. § 56(g) and Chapter 10B, supra.

5. See § 541 et seq. and Chapter 10C2, infra.

6. I.R.C. § 541.

7. See I.R.C. §§ 1362(d)(3); 1375; Chapter 20B and 20F, infra.

a going concern. For tax purposes, however, a sale of the assets of a going business for a lump sum is treated as a sale of each individual asset rather than of a single capital asset.[1] This fragmentation approach requires the parties to allocate the purchase price among the various tangible and intangible assets that have been sold. The allocation is used to determine the amount and character of the seller's gain or loss, and the buyer's cost basis in each asset for purposes of computing depreciation and amortization deductions and gain or loss on a subsequent disposition.

The parties historically had adverse interests when it came to allocating the purchase price among the assets. Buyers wished to allocate as much as possible to inventory, depreciable property and amortizable intangibles with the shortest recovery periods, and they resisted allocations to land and nondepreciable goodwill. Sellers, by contrast, benefitted by allocating a larger portion of the purchase price to assets yielding a capital gain and less to ordinary income assets. If the seller is a C corporation, these conflicts have diminished with the elimination of a corporate capital gains rate preference. But buyers are still motivated to allocate basis to assets that provide depreciation or amortization deductions over the shortest possible recovery period, and corporate sellers with unused capital losses still prefer capital gains over ordinary income.

The parties may include a negotiated purchase price allocation in their written agreement. Because buyers and sellers historically had adverse interests, negotiated allocations usually were respected by the Service. Indeed, the Service and some courts generally did not permit a party to take a tax reporting position inconsistent with an agreed allocation unless the contract was unenforceable because of mistake, undue influence, fraud or duress.[2] More often than not, however, agreements of sale did not contain any purchase price allocation, allowing the parties to go their separate ways and possibly "whipsaw" the government in the process by taking inconsistent positions. A typical controversy involved the tension between a covenant not to compete and goodwill. Amounts paid by the buyer that are attributable to a covenant by the seller not to compete with the buyer for a stated period of time result in ordinary income to the seller and, before enactment of Section 197, the payments were amortizable by the buyer over the life of the covenant. Payments for goodwill, on the other hand, could not be depreciated or amortized by the buyer before Section 197 was added to the Code, and gain on the sale of goodwill was capital gain to the seller. Thus, sellers preferred allocations to goodwill, while buyers, craving deductions, preferred allocations to a covenant not to compete.

Even without a covenant not to compete, some of the most contentious allocation controversies have involved the amount properly attributable to

1. Williams v. McGowan, 152 F.2d 570 (2d Cir.1945).

2. Commissioner v. Danielson, 378 F.2d 771 (3d Cir.1967), cert. denied, 389 U.S. 858, 88 S.Ct. 94 (1967). Other courts, using a more lenient standard, permitted a party to override a contractual allocation by a showing of "strong proof" that the agreement should not be respected. See, e.g., Ullman v. Commissioner, 264 F.2d 305 (2d Cir.1959).

goodwill and the going concern value of an acquired business. The allocation is critical to a buyer who pays a premium—i.e., an amount that exceeds the fair market value of the target's identifiable tangible and intangible assets. At one time, the Service permitted the "proportionate" method of allocation, under which the value of each acquired asset (including intangibles such as goodwill) was determined, and then the aggregate purchase price was allocated in proportion to the relative fair market value of each asset. The proportionate method often had the effect of shifting any premium paid for the business toward depreciable and amortizable assets and away from nondepreciable goodwill. The future tax benefits that resulted from this buyer-friendly allocation method were a stimulus to the corporate takeover mania of the 1980's.

Under another valuation approach, known as the residual method, each tangible and intangible asset (excluding goodwill and going concern value) is valued first. If the overall price paid for the business exceeds the aggregate fair market value of these assets, the excess ("residue") is allocated to goodwill and going concern value. The impact of the residual method is to allocate more of the total purchase price to goodwill and going concern value as compared to the proportionate method. In the case of a "bargain purchase," where the price paid for the business is less than the fair market value of T's assets, nothing is allocated to goodwill and the amount allocated to the identifiable assets (other than cash, cash equivalents and marketable securities) is proportionately reduced.

Congress first moved to regulate purchase price allocations in connection with stock purchases that are treated as asset acquisitions under Section 338 by directing the Treasury to prescribe regulations governing allocation of basis among the target's assets.[3] Not unexpectedly, the regulations mandated use of the residual method. Eventually, Congress extended this approach to asset acquisitions by enacting Section 1060, which includes reporting requirements to protect the Service from being whipsawed. Congress took another step toward certainty with the enactment of Section 197, which requires the cost of most acquired intangible assets, including a covenant not to compete, to be amortized over 15 years. Because a buyer's ability to amortize intangible assets and the timing of that amortization affects the economic stakes of a purchase price allocation, an overview of Section 197 is useful before turning to the specific requirements of Section 1060.

Amortization of Intangibles: Section 197. Section 197 permits taxpayers to amortize many intangible assets ratably over a 15–year period, regardless of their actual "useful life" or recovery period under prior law. Amortizable "Section 197 intangibles" include information bases, customer and subscription lists, patient files, know-how, licenses, franchises, trade names and, notably, goodwill, going concern value and covenants not to compete entered into in connection with an acquisition of all or a substantial part of a trade or business.[4] Some of these assets, such as goodwill and

3. I.R.C. § 338(b)(5). See Section C2 of this chapter, infra.

4. I.R.C. § 197(c)(1), (d).

going concern value, were not amortizable at all under prior law, while others were being written off over periods considerably shorter than 15 years. Amortization under Section 197 is available, however, only for acquired intangibles; it is generally not permitted for assets that are created by the taxpayer.[5]

Section 197 puts to rest many of the most contested tax issues in the area of business acquisitions. Litigated disputes abounded under prior law, including one case in which the Supreme Court held that "customer-based" intangibles (primarily subscriber lists) acquired by a publisher on the purchase of a newspaper were amortizable if they had an ascertainable value and a determinable useful life.[6] Rejecting the Service's argument that such intangibles were "nondepreciable per se," the Court concluded that eligibility for amortization turned on whether the asset was capable of being valued and whether that value diminished over time.[7] The Court's approach, and the factual controversies that it necessarily engendered, are now largely moot with the enactment of Section 197.

Allocation of Purchase Price Under Section 1060. The ability of the parties to make strategical purchase price allocations has been reduced with the enactment of Section 197 and the Section 1060 basis allocation rules. Section 1060 applies to any "applicable asset acquisition," defined as any transfer (direct or indirect) of assets which constitute a "trade or business" in the hands of either the buyer or the seller, and the purchaser's basis in the purchased assets is determined wholly by reference to the consideration paid for the assets.[8] This broad definition goes well beyond the typical corporate asset acquisition, extending to sales of sole proprietorships and partnership interests.

Section 1060 requires the buyer and seller to allocate the total consideration received or paid for a business among the various transferred assets using the residual method previewed above.[9] For this purpose, "consideration received" is the seller's aggregate amount realized from the sale of its assets determined under general tax principles, and "consideration paid" is the buyer's aggregate cost of purchasing the assets that is properly taken into account in determining basis.[10] Thus, liabilities assumed by the buyer or to which the transferred property is subject generally are included in total consideration. Aggregate consideration is then allocated among the assets using a refined version of the residual method that places all "acquisition date assets" into one of seven classes and allocates the consideration among those classes in priority order.[11] In general, the amount allocated to an asset (except for the last "residual" category) may

5. I.R.C. § 197(c)(2).

6. Newark Morning Ledger Co. v. United States, 507 U.S. 546, 113 S.Ct. 1670 (1993).

7. Id. at 565–570, 113 S.Ct. at 1680–83.

8. I.R.C. § 1060(c); Reg. § 1.1060–1(b)(1).

9. Reg. § 1.1060–1(a)(1).

10. Reg. § 1.1060–1(c)(1).

11. Reg. § 1.1060–1(c)(2). The Section 1060 regulations incorporate by reference the residual method used under Reg. § 1.338–6 for certain stock acquisitions that are treated as asset acquisitions under Section 338. Id.

not exceed its fair market value.[12] Specifically, total consideration is first reduced by cash and cash equivalents (known as "Class I acquisition date assets") transferred by the seller.[13] The remaining consideration is then allocated first to highly liquid assets such as actively traded personal property (e.g., marketable securities), foreign currencies, and certificates of deposit (Class II assets) in proportion to their fair market values, then to accounts receivable, mortgages, and credit card receivables (Class III), then to inventory and other dealer-type property (Class IV), then to all assets other than those in the other classes (Class V—a broad category that includes most tangible assets, such as equipment and real estate), and finally to all Section 197 intangibles except goodwill and going concern value (Class VI). Any remaining consideration, such as in acquisitions where the purchase price includes a "premium" that exceeds the liquidation value of the tangible and intangible assets acquired, is allocated to Class VII, a category limited to goodwill and going concern value.[14]

Effect of Agreement Between the Parties. As first enacted, Section 1060 did not address the question of whether the parties to a transaction should be bound by any written agreement they reach regarding allocation of the purchase price. Concerned that taxpayers might continue to take reporting positions that were inconsistent with their agreements, Congress amended Section 1060 to provide that a written agreement governing the allocation of consideration in an applicable asset acquisition shall be binding on both parties unless the Treasury determines that the allocation (or fair market value) is not appropriate.[15] The regulations provide that a party may refute an agreed allocation or valuation only by proving that the agreement was unenforceable due to mistake, undue influence, fraud or duress.[16] This is the standard long advanced by the Service and applied by the Third Circuit in the *Danielson* case.[17] In holding the parties to their agreement, however, Congress made it clear that it did not intend to restrict the Service's ability to challenge the taxpayers' allocation to any asset by any appropriate appraisal method, particularly where there is a lack of adverse tax interests between the parties.[18] For example, an allocation that departs from the mandated residual method will not be respected even if it is part of a negotiated agreement and it would be reasonable for the Service to make an independent showing of the value of goodwill in order to challenge the taxpayer's valuation of other assets.[19]

12. Reg. § 1.338–6(c)(1).

13. Reg. § 1.338–6(b)(1). In the unusual case where the total consideration to be allocated is less than the amount of Class I assets, then the purchaser must immediately recognize ordinary income to that extent. Id.

14. Reg. § 1.338–6(b)(2).

15. I.R.C. § 1060(a), last sentence.

16. Reg. § 1.1060–1(c)(4).

17. Commissioner v. Danielson, 378 F.2d 771 (3d Cir.1967), cert. denied, 389 U.S. 858, 88 S.Ct. 94 (1967).

18. H.Rep. No. 101–964, 101st Cong., 2d Sess. 1096 (1990). See Reg. § 1.1060–1(c)(4).

19. See generally Staff of the Joint Committee on Taxation, General Explanation of the Tax Reform Act of 1986, 100th Cong., 1st Sess. 355–360 (1987).

Reporting Requirements. The parties to an applicable asset acquisition must attach a statement (Form 8594) to their tax returns, reporting information concerning the amount of the total sales price and how it was allocated among the various asset classes.[20] The purchaser also must report any collateral agreements related to an acquisition, such as covenants not to compete, employment agreements, licenses, leases and the like.[21]

C. Stock Acquisitions

1. Background

In a taxable stock acquisition, the purchaser ("P") buys the stock of a target corporation ("T") from T's shareholders for cash or a combination of cash, notes and other consideration. A taxable stock acquisition may be structured as a reverse triangular merger, in which P forms a wholly owned transitory subsidiary ("S"), and S merges into T under state law, with T's shareholders receiving cash and debt obligations of P. When the dust settles, T is a wholly owned subsidiary of P.

Acquisitions of public companies are almost always stock acquisitions. They are sometimes launched when P begins acquiring T stock in the open market.[1] The next step may be a cash tender offer to T's shareholders or a friendly merger negotiated with T's management. If P succeeds in acquiring control of T, the final step is usually a "back-end" merger where recalcitrant minority shareholders are squeezed out of the picture, sometimes for the same price originally offered to tendering shareholders or perhaps on less attractive terms.[2]

Whether the transaction is structured as a direct stock purchase or a reverse triangular cash merger,[3] T's shareholders recognize gain or loss on the sale of their stock, measured by the difference between their amount realized and stock basis, and P takes a cost basis in the T stock it acquires.

20. I.R.C. § 1060(b). See Reg. § 1.1060–1(e).

21. Reg. § 1.1060–1(e). Section 1060(e) also provides that where a person owns at least 10 percent of the value of an entity immediately before a transaction and transfers both an interest in the entity and enters into an employment contract, covenant not to compete, royalty, lease or other agreement with the buyer, the parties must report information concerning the transaction as the Service may require. In determining whether a person is a 10 percent owner, the Section 318 attribution rules shall apply. I.R.C. § 1060(e)(2)(B).

1. P may purchase up to five percent of T's stock without any requirement for public disclosure under the federal securities laws. Securities Exchange Act of 1934, § 13(d), 15 U.S.C.A. § 78m(d) (1981).

2. Squeeze outs are facilitated by the modern corporate laws of Delaware and other states where many public companies are incorporated. See, e.g., Del.Corp.Law § 251. For a good basic description of the mechanics, dynamics and economics of corporate takeovers, see Hamilton & Booth, Business Basics for Law Students, ch. 13 (4th ed. 2006).

3. A reverse triangular cash merger is treated for tax purposes as if P purchased T stock directly from the shareholders. Transitory "S" is disregarded. See Rev.Rul. 73–427, 1973–2 C.B. 301; Rev.Rul. 79–273, 1979–2 C.B. 125.

T shareholders who receive notes generally may report their gain on the installment method if the T stock is not publicly traded.[4] The more difficult conceptual questions relate to the tax consequences to T and the impact of a stock acquisition on the basis of T's assets and T's other tax attributes. Should a stock acquisition be treated as if it were a taxable asset acquisition coupled with a liquidation of T, or should the form of the transaction control? Should the parties be permitted to select which treatment they would prefer?

Not surprisingly, Congress has exhibited considerable hyperactivity in answering these questions. The *Kimbell–Diamond* case, which follows, is the best place to begin describing the evolution of the current tax treatment of stock acquisitions.

Kimbell–Diamond Milling Co. v. Commissioner

Tax Court of the United States, 1950.
14 T.C. 74.

■ BLACK, JUDGE.

[In August, 1942, taxpayer's milling plant was destroyed by fire and two months later the taxpayer collected insurance as a reimbursement for its loss. It then purchased for approximately $210,000 cash all the stock of Whaley Mill & Elevator Co. in order to use Whaley's plant and equipment to replace its own destroyed facilities. The purchase price consisted of $120,000 of insurance proceeds and $90,000 of additional funds. The taxpayer's sole intention in purchasing Whaley's stock was to acquire the assets of the company through a prompt liquidation.

Taxpayer liquidated Whaley three days after acquiring the stock. In a prior proceeding, reported at 10 T.C. 7, the Tax Court held that the acquisition of Whaley came within the 1939 Code predecessor of § 1033 so that the taxpayer's gain on the involuntary conversion was not recognized. Since the taxpayer's acquisition of the Whaley stock qualified under § 1033, its basis was $110,000 (the sum of the $20,000 adjusted basis of the destroyed assets and the $90,000 of additional funds that were paid in addition to the insurance proceeds). The assets of Whaley acquired by the taxpayer in the liquidation had an adjusted basis to Whaley of more than $300,000; the depreciable assets represented about $140,000 of this total.

The central dispute in the case was over the taxpayer's basis for depreciation in the assets acquired in the Whaley liquidation. After addressing a procedural issue, the Court proceeded to discuss the merits. Note

4. I.R.C. § 453(k)(2). Installment sales of very large blocks of stock may be affected by Section 453A, which imposes what amounts to an annual interest charge on a seller's tax liability that has been deferred by the installment method. In general, this provision applies only if the face amount of the seller's installment receivables during the taxable year exceed $5 million.

that this case arose under the 1939 Code, which did not contain former § 334(b)(2) or present § 338. Ed.]

* * *

OPINION

Having decided the issue of *res judicata* against petitioner, we must now determine the question of petitioner's basis in Whaley's assets on the merits. Petitioner argues that the acquisition of Whaley's assets and the subsequent liquidation of Whaley brings petitioner within the provisions of [the predecessor of § 332] and, therefore, by reason of [the predecessor of § 334(b)(1)], petitioner's basis in these assets is the same as the basis in Whaley's hands. In so contending, petitioner asks that we treat the acquisition of Whaley's stock and the subsequent liquidation of Whaley as separate transactions. It is well settled that the incidence of taxation depends upon the substance of a transaction. Commissioner v. Court Holding Co., 324 U.S. 331. It is inescapable from petitioner's minutes set out above and from the "Agreement and Program of Complete Liquidation" entered into between petitioner and Whaley, that the only intention petitioner ever had was to acquire Whaley's assets.

We think that this proceeding is governed by the principles of Commissioner v. Ashland Oil & Refining Co., 99 Fed.(2d) 588, certiorari denied, 306 U.S. 661. In that case the stock was retained for almost a year before liquidation. Ruling on the question of whether the stock or the assets of the corporation were purchased, the court stated:

> The question remains, however, whether if the entire transaction, whatever its form, was essentially in intent, purpose and result, a purchase by Swiss of property, its several steps may be treated separately and each be given an effect for tax purposes as though each constituted a distinct transaction. * * * And without regard to whether the result is imposition or relief from taxation, the courts have recognized that where the essential nature of a transaction is the acquisition of property, it will be viewed as a whole, and closely related steps will not be separated either at the instance of the taxpayer or the taxing authority. Prairie Oil & Gas Co. v. Motter, 10 Cir., 66 F.2d 309; Tulsa Tribune Co. v. Commissioner, 10 Cir., 58 F.2d 937, 940; Ahles Realty Corp. v. Commissioner, 2 Cir., 71 F.2d 150; Helvering v. Security Savings Bank, 4 Cir., 72 F.2d 874. * * *

See also *Koppers Coal Co.*, 6 T.C. 1209 and cases there cited.

We hold that the purchase of Whaley's stock and its subsequent liquidation must be considered as one transaction, namely, the purchase of Whaley's assets which was petitioner's sole intention. This was not a reorganization within section 112(b)(6), and petitioner's basis in these assets, both depreciable and nondepreciable, is, therefore, its cost, or $110,721.74 ($18,921.90, the basis of petitioner's assets destroyed by fire, plus $91,799.84, the amount expended over the insurance proceeds). Since petitioner does not controvert respondent's allocation of cost to the individual assets acquired from Whaley, both depreciable and nondepreciable, respondent's allocation is sustained.

* * *

NOTE

If the stock purchase and subsequent liquidation of the target-subsidiary in *Kimbell–Diamond* had been treated as separate transactions, the buyer would have taken a (higher) transferred basis in the target's assets under Section 334(b)(1). The court looked to the buyer's intent, however, in holding that the stock purchase was merely a transitory step in a transaction that was properly characterized as a purchase of assets. Under this application of the step transaction doctrine, the liquidation was disregarded, and the buyer took a cost basis in the assets.

In the 1954 Code, Congress replaced the elusive intent standard of *Kimbell–Diamond* with a more objective test.[1] If a corporation purchased a controlling (80 percent or more) stock interest in the target corporation and then liquidated the target within a specific period of time, the acquiring corporation was treated as if it had purchased the target's assets. In general, the acquiring corporation took a cost basis in the assets equal to what it paid for the stock rather than the usual transferred basis that results from the liquidation of a controlled subsidiary. Although more "objective" than *Kimbell–Diamond*, the 1954 Code rules were laden with timetables, control and "purchase" requirements and a host of adjustments for cash distributions, liabilities assumed and transactions occurring after the acquisition but prior to the liquidation. Additional problems were created by the requirement that the buyer liquidate the newly acquired target in order to secure a *Kimbell–Diamond* cost basis in the target's assets.[2]

Congress responded to these deficiencies by enacting Section 338, which refines the *Kimbell–Diamond* concept by allowing the acquiring corporation to elect to treat certain stock purchases as asset purchases. Unlike *Kimbell–Diamond* and the prior statutory scheme, Section 338 does not require a corporate buyer of stock to liquidate the target in order to get a cost basis in its assets. This is convenient when the buyer wishes to keep the target alive as a subsidiary. Under current law, a corporation that acquires control (i.e., at least 80 percent) of a target corporation in a transaction that is taxable to the selling shareholders is thus presented with four basic choices. It may: (1) not make the Section 338 election and keep T alive, leaving T's bases in its assets and other tax attributes unaffected; (2) not elect under Section 338, liquidate T tax-free under

1. I.R.C. § 334(b)(2) (pre–1982).

2. For historians and masochists, see Bittker & Eustice, Federal Income Taxation of Corporations and Shareholders ¶ 11.45 (5th ed. 1987).

Section 332 and inherit its asset bases and other tax attributes;[3] (3) make the Section 338 election and treat the transaction as an asset acquisition under which "new T" takes a cost basis in its assets and is purged of all of its prior tax attributes; or (4) make the election and then liquidate T.[4]

Before proceeding further, it is important to keep in mind that *Kimbell–Diamond* and Section 338 originated in the *General Utilities* era, when liquidating distributions and sales generally did not trigger a corporate-level tax. The principal question then confronting a corporate buyer of stock was whether to take a cost basis or a transferred basis in the target's assets. If those assets were appreciated, a well advised corporate buyer would make the Section 338 election in order to step up the basis of the target's assets at little or no corporate-level tax cost. The stakes are vastly different today, where liquidating sales and distributions generally are taxable events. If a stock purchase is treated as an asset acquisition, the target must recognize gain or loss, and one of the parties (buyer or seller, or both) must bear the economic burden of the corporate tax imposed on any gain. Accordingly, the Section 338 election is undesirable in virtually all cases where the target's assets are appreciated because it rarely makes economic sense to elect to pay tax currently in order to step up the basis of assets and avoid tax later. Section 338 nonetheless survives in the 1986 Code, along with reams of intricate regulations, and it remains an attractive option in just a few situations that are discussed below.

2. Operation of Section 338

Code: §§ 338(a), (b) (omit (b)(3)), (d), (e)(1), (2)(A) and (D), (g), (h)(1), (2), (3)(A), (4)(A), (5), (6)(A), (9), (11).

Regulations: §§ 1.338–4(a), (b)(1) & (2), (c), (d)(1), (e), –5(a), (b)(1) & (2), (c), (d)(1), (e)(1)–(3).

Overview of Section 338. Section 338 is a complex statutory mechanism that seeks to equate for tax purposes the purchase of an 80 percent or more interest in the stock of the target corporation with a purchase of the target's assets. In general, the goals are to: (1) ensure that the target and its shareholders bear the same tax burden on a sale of the target's stock that they would have incurred on a sale of its assets followed by a complete liquidation; (2) provide the buyer with a cost basis in the assets of the target; and (3) terminate the tax attributes of the target and start afresh, without regard to whether or not the target is actually liquidated.

To achieve these goals, Section 338 provides that if a purchasing corporation ("P") purchases 80 percent or more of the stock of a target corporation ("T") within 12 months or less, it may elect to treat T as

3. Note that the tax treatment of this method is contrary to *Kimbell–Diamond*, which would have treated a stock purchase followed by a prompt intended liquidation of the target as an asset acquisition, giving P a cost basis in T's assets rather than a transferred basis and, under current law, causing T to recognize gain or loss on the sale.

4. T or P's ability to utilize T's net operating losses in the first two situations may be limited. See I.R.C. §§ 269(b); 382; and Chapter 19, infra.

having sold all of its assets for their fair market value in a single transaction.[1] T must recognize gain or loss on the hypothetical asset sale, after which it returns as a virgin corporation ("new T") with a cost basis in its assets and none of its former tax attributes.[2] If T is liquidated, this cost basis simply carries over to the parent under the rules governing liquidations of a subsidiary.[3]

The contours of Section 338 are easier to explain than its details. The section is littered with anti-avoidance provisions, many of which are aimed at maneuvers that are beyond the scope of this book. Understanding Section 338 is eased by focusing on its fundamentals.

Qualification for Section 338. The Section 338 election is available only to a "purchasing corporation," which is defined as "any corporation which makes a qualified purchase of stock of another corporation."[4] A "qualified stock purchase" is a transaction or series of transactions in which one corporation acquires by "purchase" an 80 percent controlling interest in another corporation during a 12–month "acquisition period."[5] Roughly translated, all of this means that P must buy at least 80 percent of the stock of T within a 12–month period in transactions that are taxable to the sellers.[6]

The Election. If a corporation makes a qualified stock purchase and desires to make the Section 338 election, it must do so no later than the fifteenth day of the ninth month beginning after the month in which the "acquisition date" occurs.[7] The acquisition date is the day within the 12–month acquisition period on which the 80 percent purchase requirement is satisfied.[8] Once made, a Section 338 election is irrevocable.[9] There is no turning back, even with the Commissioner's permission, if the results prove to be undesirable.

Effect of Election: Deemed Sale of Target Assets and Termination of Old Target's Existence. If P makes a qualified stock purchase and follows up with a timely Section 338 election, T is treated as having sold all of its assets at the close of the acquisition date for their "fair market value" in a single transaction and is treated as a new corporation which purchased all of its assets as of the beginning of the day after the acquisition date.[10] As a result, T recognizes gain or loss on this hypothetical sale, just as if it

1. I.R.C. § 338(a).

2. I.R.C. § 338(b).

3. I.R.C. §§ 332; 334(b)(1). See Chapter 15C2, supra.

4. I.R.C. § 338(d)(1).

5. I.R.C. §§ 338(d)(3); 338(h)(1). The requisite stock interest is defined in Section 338(d)(3) by reference to Section 1504(a)(2), which defines "control" as possession of at least 80 percent of the total voting power and 80 percent of the total value of a corporation's stock.

6. "Purchase" is defined to exclude transactions that would not have resulted in the full recognition of gain or loss to the seller (i.e., reorganizations, gifts, bequests, Section 351 transfers) and acquisitions from certain "related persons" within the attribution rules of Section 318. I.R.C. § 318(h)(3).

7. I.R.C. § 338(g)(1).

8. I.R.C. § 338(h)(2).

9. I.R.C. § 338(g)(3).

10. I.R.C. § 338(a).

actually had sold its assets.[11] For purposes of this deemed sale, Section 338 provides that T is not treated as a member of an affiliated group if it otherwise might have been.[12] Although the income realized on the deemed asset sale may not be combined with the income of P or its affiliates for tax purposes, the economic burden of the tax liability resulting from the deemed sale is indirectly borne by P, which will factor it into the price to be paid for the stock. On the day after the deemed sale, T is reincarnated. It returns as a new corporation with no earnings and profits or other tax attributes from its pre-deemed sale era and with a cost basis in the assets that it hypothetically purchased from its former self.[13] If all this talk about deemed transactions seems mysterious, keep in mind that it is simply the mechanism used by the Code to equate purchases of assets and stock when a Section 338 election is made.

Aggregate Deemed Sale Price. In the hypothetical asset sale triggered by a Section 338 election, T is treated as selling its assets for their "aggregate deemed sale price" ("ADSP").[14] In general, ADSP is the sum: of (1) the grossed-up amount realized on the sale to P of P's recently purchased T stock, and (2) the liabilities of old T, including tax liabilities from the deemed sale.[15] "Recently purchased stock" is T stock purchased by P during the 12–month acquisition period and held by P at the time of the qualified stock purchase.[16] Thus, if P purchased all of T's stock during the 12–month acquisition period, the ADSP is the total amount realized by the selling T shareholders plus old T's liabilities. If P purchased less than 100 percent of T's outstanding shares during the 12–month acquisition period, then the concept of "grossed-up" amount realized comes into play. The grossed-up amount realized is an amount equal to the amount realized on the sale to P of P's recently purchased T stock determined as if the selling T shareholders used old T's accounting methods and without regard to costs of sale, divided by the percentage of T stock (by value) attributable to that recently purchased stock, less any selling costs (such as brokerage commissions) incurred by the selling T shareholders in connection with their sale of recently purchased stock that reduce their amount realized.[17] The function of this complex formula in situations where P does not acquire 100 percent of T stock is to approximate the total amount that would have been realized on the sale of T stock if P had purchased all the shares at the same average price that P paid for the shares actually purchased during the acquisition period. To illustrate, if during the 12–

11. See Section B1 of this chapter, supra.

12. I.R.C. § 338(h)(9). This means that losses of P or any P affiliate or losses of a corporate parent or affiliate of T may not be used to shelter gains resulting from T's deemed asset sale, but T may deduct its own net operating losses against the gains from the deemed sale. See Reg. § 1.338–1(f)(3)(iv). A "consolidated deemed sale return" may be filed, however, by all target corporations acquired by a purchasing corporation on the same acquisition date if the targets were members of the same selling consolidated group. I.R.C. § 338(h)(15). Cf. I.R.C. § 338(h)(10) and Section C3 of this chapter, infra.

13. I.R.C. § 338(a)(2).

14. Reg. § 1.338–4(a).

15. Reg. § 1.338–4(b)(1), (d).

16. I.R.C. § 338(b)(6)(A).

17. Reg. § 1.338–4(c)(1).

month acquisition period P purchased 80 percent of T's outstanding stock for $800,000, the grossed-up amount realized on the sale to P of P's recently purchased T stock would be $800,000/.80, or $1,000,000.

Remember that the theory underlying Section 338 is to replicate the tax consequences of an asset acquisition. If P were to purchase all of T's assets, the purchase price would reflect any T liabilities assumed or property transferred subject to liabilities as part of the transaction. Under the principles of the *Crane* case, T's amount realized in such an asset sale would include the amount of those liabilities. In a stock purchase, the amount paid by P for T's stock similarly will take into account the debts and liabilities on T's balance sheet as of the "acquisition date." To properly determine the deemed sale price of T's assets under Section 338, the ADSP is increased by liabilities of old T, including tax liabilities, that properly would be taken into account as amount realized on a disposition by T of its assets to an unrelated purchaser who assumed the liabilities or took assets subject to a liabilities of old T.[18]

Determination of Asset Basis After Deemed Purchase. New T's basis in its assets has been described as a *Kimbell–Diamond* type cost basis, but the actual approach used to determine the aggregate basis and allocate it among T's assets is not quite that simple. The regulations label new T's basis as the "adjusted grossed-up basis" ("AGUB").[19] The AGUB generally is the sum of: (1) the grossed-up basis in P's recently purchased T stock, (2) P's basis in nonrecently purchased T stock (e.g., T stock owned by P before the 12–month acquisition period), and (3) liabilities of new T, including any tax liabilities triggered by the deemed sale.[20] AGUB is similar but not necessarily identical to ADSP. If P holds only recently purchased stock in T and T has no contingent liabilities, the two calculations usually produce the same result.

To illustrate, assume again that during the 12–month acquisition period P purchased 80 percent of T's outstanding stock for $800,000 and assume P does not own any other T stock. In computing ADSP and AGUB, the grossed-up amount realized and the adjusted grossed-up basis are both $1,000,000.[21] But if P owns nonrecently purchased T stock with a per-share basis different than P's basis in its recently purchased stock, the calculation of the ADSP for old T's assets and the AGUB for new T's assets will produce different results.[22] The difference is attributable to the fact that

18. Reg. § 1.338–4(d)(1). General tax principles control the time that liabilities are taken into account. See Reg. § 1.338–4(d)(2). Since determination of the ADSP may depend, in part, on the tax liability triggered by the deemed sale, and old T's tax liability depends on the ADSP, the calculation is potentially circular. The regulations recognize that the determination of ADSP may require trial and error computations. Reg. § 1.338–4(e). They also include examples of a formula to resolve this mathematical teaser. To revisit high school algebra, see Reg. § 1.338–4(g) Examples.

19. Reg. § 1.338–5(a).

20. Reg. § 1.338–5(b)(1).

21. For ADSP, see Reg. § 1.338–4(c); for AGUB, see Reg. § 1.338–5(b), (c).

22. Contingent liabilities that are taken into account in determining a seller's amount realized but are not yet properly included in a purchaser's basis also may be the source of an initial disparity that usually will be cor-

the ADSP formula treats P's nonrecently purchased stock the same as stock that is held by T shareholders other than P, while the AGUB formula uses P's actual basis in its nonrecently purchased T stock. P can make an election to recognize gain on its nonrecently purchased T stock.[23] If such an election is made, the sum of the grossed-up basis in P's recently purchased T stock and P's basis in any nonrecently purchased stock will equal the ADSP.[24] The election, however, requires P to currently recognize gain on its nonrecently purchased T stock, and so it usually is not desirable from a tax standpoint.

Allocation of Adjusted Grossed–Up Basis Among Target Assets. If P makes a Section 338 election, new T's aggregate AGUB is allocated among its assets under regulations promulgated under Section 338(b)(5). These regulations utilize the same seven-class system and reporting requirements previously discussed with respect to basis allocations in asset acquisitions.[25]

Consistency Rules. Section 338 allows a purchasing corporation to take a transferred basis in T's assets (by not making the election) or, at the cost of paying a tax on any gain (or deducting any loss) inherent in the target's assets, to take essentially a fair market value basis in those assets. When Section 338 was enacted, the consistency requirement was designed to ensure that P was put to a choice: it could select one or the other, but not both (or some of each) of these options. To achieve that objective, Section 338(e) was intended to prevent P from acquiring some assets from T or an affiliate of T with a cost basis and other assets with a transferred basis during a "consistency period" that begins one year before the start of the acquisition period and lasts to one year after the acquisition date.[26] Under Section 338(e), if P acquired such an asset it was deemed to make a Section 338 election with respect to T, unless T sold the asset in the ordinary course of its business (e.g., a routine sale of inventory) or P took a transferred basis in the asset.[27] Section 338(f) was designed to ensure that if P makes a qualified stock purchase with respect to T and one or more affiliates (e.g., a wholly owned subsidiary) of T during any consistency period, then all such qualified stock purchases must be treated consistently under Section 338; an election with respect to the first applies to all later qualified stock purchases and if no election is made for the first purchase, none may be made for later ones.

In the final Section 338 regulations, the Treasury significantly narrowed the reach of the consistency period rules because they were designed to patrol against exploitation of the long ago repealed *General Utilities* doctrine. Under the regulations, the asset consistency rules of Section 338(e) generally apply only if P acquires an asset directly from T during the consistency period and T is a subsidiary of another corporation ("S") in a

rected by later adjustments. See, e.g., Reg. § 1.338–5(b)(2)(ii).

23. I.R.C. 338(h)(3). Losses on nonrecently purchased stock are not allowed. Reg. § 1.338–5(d)(3)(iii).

24. See Reg. § 1.338–5(d)(3).

25. See Section C4 of this chapter, supra; Reg. § 1.338–6.

26. I.R.C. § 338(h)(4)(A).

27. I.R.C. § 338(e)(2)(A) and (B).

consolidated group.[28] Under the regulations, the stock consistency rules of Section 338(f) are now limited to preventing avoidance of the asset consistency rules.[29]

Understanding the limited application of the asset consistency period rules requires a very basic knowledge of the consolidated return regulations, which generally permit a parent corporation in a consolidated group to increase the basis for its stock in a subsidiary when the subsidiary recognizes a taxable gain on the sale of one of its assets.[30] The relationship of this rule to Section 338 is best illustrated by the following example provided by the Treasury where P is the purchasing corporation, T is the target and S is T's parent:[31]

> The proposed regulations apply the consistency rules in the context of consolidated groups to prevent acquisitions from being structured to take advantage of the investment adjustment rules. If the consistency rules did not apply in such a case, P could acquire assets from T with a stepped-up basis in the assets, and then acquire the T stock at no additional cost to the S group.
>
> Example. S and T file a consolidated return. S has a $100x basis in the T stock, which has a fair market value of $200x. On January 1, 1993, T sells an asset to P and recognizes $100x of gain. Under § 1.1502–32 [of the consolidated return regulations], S's basis in the T stock is increased from $100x to $200x. On March 1, 1993, S sells the T stock to P for $200x and recognizes no gain or loss.
>
> The consistency rules of the proposed regulations apply to the transaction because T's gain on the asset sale is reflected under § 1.1502–32 in S's basis in the T stock. However, under the proposed regulations, the District Director no longer has the discretion to impose a deemed section 338 election for T. Instead, under proposed [regulation] § 1.338–4(d), P takes a carryover basis in any asset acquired from T. (This is referred to as the carryover basis rule).

Section 338 Election Coupled With Liquidation of T. If P purchases 80 percent or more of T stock, makes a Section 338 election, and then promptly liquidates T, the stock purchase and subsequent liquidation of T are accorded independent significance for tax purposes—i.e., they are not stepped together and treated as an integrated transaction. P is treated as having made a qualified stock purchase rather than a direct acquisition of assets under the *Kimbell–Diamond* doctrine.[32] On the liquidation, P recog-

28. Reg. § 1.338–8(a)(2). The rules are also extended to a few other limited abuse cases that are well beyond the coverage of this text. See Reg. § 1.338–8(a)(3),(4).

29. Reg. § 1.338–8(a)(6).

30. See Reg. § 1.1502–32 and Chapter 12B, infra.

31. See Preamble, Prop. Reg. §§ 1.338–4,–5 (CO–111–90), issued Jan. 14, 1992 (1992–1 C.B. 1000).

32. Reg. § 1.338–3(c)(1)(i). See also Rev.Rul. 90–95, 1990–2 C.B. 67 (stating that "Section 338 replaced the *Kimbell–Diamond* doctrine"). But see Rev. Rul. 2001–46, 2001–

nizes no gain or loss under Section 332, and T recognizes no gain or loss on the distribution of its assets to P under Section 337. In any event, neither P nor T would have any significant realized gain or loss because at least 80 percent of the T stock would have been recently purchased, and any built-in gain on T's assets was recognized as a result of the Section 338 deemed asset sale. After the liquidation, P succeeds to T's fair market value basis in its assets.

Stock Acquisitions Without Section 338 Election. The tax consequences of an acquisition of 80 percent or more of T's stock with no Section 338 election are less complicated. T's shareholders, as always, recognize gain or loss on the sale of their stock. T becomes a subsidiary of P and retains its tax attributes, including the historic basis in its assets, earnings and profits, and the like. If P subsequently liquidates T, or T merges into P or another P subsidiary, neither P nor T recognizes gain or loss, and T's asset bases and other tax attributes carry over to the transferee.[33] Significantly, the initial qualified stock purchase and subsequent liquidation of T (or merger of T into P or a P affiliate) are not treated as an integrated transaction (e.g., as a direct purchase of T's assets by P) even if all the steps were planned from the outset. If the transactions were integrated, T would recognize gain or loss on its assets, a result which is fundamentally inconsistent with P's decision not to make a Section 338 election. The extent to which T (if it stays alive) or P (if it liquidates T) may utilize T's net operating losses after the acquisition is likely to be limited by Section 382, which is examined in a later chapter.[34]

3. ACQUISITION OF STOCK OF A SUBSIDIARY

Section 338(h)(10) Election. The previous discussion assumed that T was not a subsidiary of another corporation. Consider, however, the situation where T is a wholly owned subsidiary of Seller, Inc. ("S"), and P wishes to acquire T. Assume that the value of T's stock (and also its underlying assets) is $400,000; S has a $100,000 basis in its T stock; and T has a $100,000 aggregate basis in its assets. T could sell its assets directly to P for $400,000 in a taxable transaction and then distribute the sales proceeds to S in a tax-free liquidation under Section 332, with the net result being $300,000 of taxable gain to T on the asset sale. Alternatively, T could distribute the assets to S in a tax-free liquidation. S would take the assets with a $100,000 transferred basis under Section 334(b) and recognize $300,000 gain on a sale to P. In either case, S does not recognize gain or loss on its T stock, and P acquires the assets with a $400,000 cost basis. If the disappearance of S's $300,000 gain on its T stock seems inconsistent with the double tax regime, remember that no assets have yet been

2 C.B. 321, infra p. 754, where two-step transactions were integrated for purposes of the tax-free reorganization rules.

33. Rev. Rul. 90–95, supra note 32. See also Reg. § 1.338–2(c)(3)(i), discussed in Chapter 17B1, infra.

34. See Chapter 19, infra, and I.R.C. § 269(b).

distributed out of corporate solution to the shareholders of S, the real people who own the enterprise. The policy is to avoid three levels of tax on what may be a single economic gain.

Now assume that for nontax reasons P must acquire T's stock. Under general tax principles, S would recognize gain or loss on the sale of its T stock and P would take the stock with a cost basis. If P makes a Section 338 election, T also is treated as having sold its assets in a taxable transaction. If P does not elect, the bases of T's assets are unchanged and any built-in gain or loss is preserved. Either way, the result is double *corporate*-level gain, with the potential of a third round of taxation when S distributes the sales proceeds to its shareholders.

Section 338(h)(10) offers relief from this potential triple tax by permitting the parties to ignore S's sale of its T stock and treat the transaction as if it were a sale of T's assets.[1] If a Section 338(h)(10) election is made,[2] the transaction is treated as if old T sold its assets to an unrelated person (new T) while a member of the S consolidated group, and T then distributed its assets (i.e., the proceeds of sale) to S and ceased to exist. In most cases, the final step of the various hypothetical transactions is treated as a tax-free liquidation of T under Sections 332 and 337.[3] The tax consequences of the election are: (1) S recognizes no gain or loss on the sale of its T stock; (2) S inherits T's tax attributes (e.g., earnings and profits);[4] (3) T is treated as having sold its assets for their fair market value in a taxable transaction,[5] and any gain or loss is included on the consolidated return filed by S and its affiliates; and (4) "new T," a subsidiary of P, is treated as having acquired old T's assets for an amount equal to their adjusted grossed-up basis.[6] Two levels of corporate-level gain are thus avoided, and the tax burden of the sale remains with the seller.

Returning to the example, if the parties make a Section 338(h)(10) election, S's $300,000 gain on the sale of its T stock is ignored, and the $300,000 gain on the deemed sale of T's assets[7] is included on the

1. In general, before the transaction T must be a member of "the selling consolidated group." I.R.C. § 338(h)(10)(A). A "selling consolidated group" is any group of corporations which, for the taxable period which includes the transaction, includes T and files a consolidated tax return. I.R.C. § 338(h)(10)(B). A qualified seller also may be any "affiliated group" of corporations (within the meaning of Section 1504) which includes T, whether or not the group files a consolidated return. See generally Reg. § 1.338(h)(10)–1(b)(3).

2. The election must be made jointly by the S group and P. See Reg. § 1.338(h)(10)–1(c)(2).

3. See Reg. § 1.338(h)(10)–1(d).

4. These inherited tax attributes generally are reduced in proportion to the percentage of old T stock held by minority shareholders. Cf. Reg. §§ 1.381(c)(2)–1(c)(2).

5. The deemed sale price is determined under a formula prescribed by the regulations, which refers to the actual purchase price paid by P for the T stock and is adjusted for liabilities of T. See Reg. §§ 1.338(h)(10)–1(d)(3)(i); 1.338–4.

6. I.R.C. § 338(b). The adjusted grossed-up basis for new T's assets is determined under Reg. § 1.338–5 and is allocated among the assets under the approach discussed earlier in this chapter. Reg. § 1.338(h)(10)–1(d)(2).

7. We have assumed for convenience that the deemed sale price equals the $400,000 fair market value of T's assets.

consolidated tax return filed by S and its affiliates. P takes a $400,000 cost basis in the T stock and "new T" takes a $400,000 basis in its assets.

Although the Section 338(h)(10) election is generally desirable because it eliminates two levels of corporate-level gain, it has particular allure when S has a large "outside" gain on its T stock relative to minimal "inside" gain on T's assets. In that scenario, P may purchase T's stock at little or no tax cost to S if the parties make a Section 338(h)(10) election. Of course, the same result could have been achieved if S first liquidated T under Section 332 and sold the assets to P, but this method might not be feasible if P needs to keep T alive as a corporate entity for nontax reasons.

The election also is attractive when S's consolidated group has losses that can be applied to offset any gain recognized by T on the deemed sale of its assets. If Section 338 were elected without an accompanying Section 338(h)(10) election, T must file a separate one day return reporting the income from the deemed sale and it could not offset its gain with any losses from S's other operations. If a Section 338(h)(10) election is made, however, the gain on the deemed sale is reported on S's consolidated return and may be offset by losses of S and its other affiliates.

The regulations extend the availability of the Section 338(h)(10) election to two additional situations. First, they permit the election when T and S are affiliated corporations even if T is not a member of the S consolidated group if S sells stock representing at least 80 percent of the voting power and value of T to P on the "acquisition date."[8] Second, a Section 338(h)(10) election is permitted if T is an S corporation immediately before the acquisition date.[9] If T is an S corporation, the gain on the deemed sale of T's assets is reported on old T's final S corporation return and passes through to T's shareholders, who may make appropriate adjustments to the basis of their T stock.[10] These adjustments will affect the gain or loss recognized by these shareholders on the deemed liquidation of old T, and no additional gain or loss is recognized on the actual stock sale. The taxation of S corporations and their shareholders is examined in Chapter 20.

Section 336(e). Section 336(e) is a close but obscure relative of Section 338(h)(10). In some cases, it is an identical twin. Section 336(e) provides that, upon the promulgation of (still awaited) regulations, a corporation that owns at least 80 percent of the voting power and value of the stock of another corporation may elect to treat a sale, exchange or distribution of that subsidiary's stock as if it were a disposition of the subsidiary's assets. If a Section 336(e) election is made, the parent does not recognize gain or loss on the disposition of the subsidiary's stock. The legislative history of Section 336(e) states that "principles similar to those of Section

8. Reg. §§ 1.338(h)(10)–1(c)(1), –1(b)(3), –1(d)(4).

9. Reg. §§ 1.338(h)(10)–1(c)(1), –1(b)(4), –1(d)(4).

10. Reg. § 1.338(h)(10)–1(d)(5)(i).

338(h)(10)" will be used in determining the operation of the Section 336(e) election.[11]

The overlap between Sections 336(e) and 338(h)(10) is apparent when a parent *sells* the stock of a controlled subsidiary to a corporate purchaser. Section 336(e) is potentially broader, but its scope will remain unclear until regulations are promulgated. Presumably, Section 336(e) could apply even if the buyer were an individual or entity (such as a partnership) that is not qualified to make a Section 338 election. Moreover, Section 336(e) is not confined to sales. It potentially encompasses both liquidating and perhaps even nonliquidating distributions of the stock of a subsidiary.

D. Comparison of Acquisition Methods

A typical student's reaction to this chapter (or indeed the entire course up to now) might be something like this: "After considerable effort, I understand the workings of most Code sections as they are studied, but the course is becoming a conglomeration of random detail." The lament might continue with these questions about taxable corporate acquisitions: "How does it all fit together? Does it matter whether P buys T's assets or stock? What rational buyer ever would make the Section 338 election? Does substance control over form—or form over substance? When does the step transaction doctrine apply?" In short, the understandable plea is—"Give me some perspective!" This section attempts to respond by comparing taxable acquisition methods in a tax planning context, and by providing a comprehensive acquisitions problem.

The repeal of the *General Utilities* doctrine greatly altered the tax economics of corporate acquisitions. Prior to that time, the tax consequences of an asset purchase followed by a complete liquidation, or a stock purchase coupled with a Section 338 election, were essentially the same. T's shareholders recognized a capital gain on their investment; T did not recognize gain or loss on the actual or deemed transfer of its assets except for recapture of depreciation and a few other items; and P (or "new T") obtained a fair market value basis in T's assets. In short, taxable acquisitions involved only a single, shareholder-level tax, which could be deferred if P used installment notes as partial consideration for the purchase.

After *General Utilities* repeal, an asset acquisition requires both T and its shareholders to recognize gain unless T does not liquidate. A stock purchase coupled with a Section 338 election is no better because the deemed asset sale results in full recognition of corporate-level gain. In either case, P obtains a fair market value basis in T's assets—but at the price of an immediate corporate-level tax. Corporate-level tax is avoided, however, if P purchases T's stock and does not elect under Section 338. It is perhaps ironic that, after years of effort to equate the tax treatment of different corporate acquisition methods, we are left with an asymmetrical

11. H.R.Rep. No. 841, 99th Cong., 2d Sess. II–204.

system under which asset acquisitions require two levels of tax with no opportunity for T to defer tax through a transferred basis, while a stock acquisition without a Section 338 election requires only a shareholder-level tax, albeit with the trade-off of a transferred basis in T's assets.[1]

It follows that the preferred alternative for most taxable acquisitions is a stock purchase with no Section 338 election. It is rarely desirable to pay a front-end corporate tax on the gain inherent in T's assets in order to achieve tax savings later from the additional depreciation, amortization and other deductions that would flow from the stepped-up basis in T's assets. The two principal exceptions are: (1) where T has large net operating loss carryovers that would be available to offset the gain recognized on the deemed asset sale;[2] and (2) where T is a subsidiary of another corporation.[3]

The prospect of a two-tier tax also may tilt the method of choice in corporate acquisitions more towards tax-free reorganizations, where neither T nor its shareholders currently recognize gain or loss, but tax attributes at both the corporate and shareholder levels are preserved through transferred and exchanged bases. Acquisitive reorganizations are examined in Chapter 17.

PROBLEMS

1. Target Corporation ("T") is a "C" corporation. T's 1,000 shares of common stock (its only class) are owned by three unrelated individual shareholders as follows:

Shareholder	**No. Shs.**	**Adj. Basis**	**F.M.V.**
A	500	$ 50,000	$ 500,000
B	400	40,000	400,000
C	100	140,000	100,000
	1,000	$230,000	$1,000,000

A and B are in their late 70's and have held their T stock since the company was founded many years ago. C recently inherited her stock.

T has $400,000 of accumulated earnings and profits and the following assets (all held long-term) and liabilities:

1. These lingering discontinuities are discussed in Zolt, "The *General Utilities* Doctrine: Examining the Scope of Repeal," 65 Taxes 819 (1987); Yin, "A Carryover Basis Regime? A Few Words of Caution," 37 Tax Notes 415 (1987); and Lewis, "A Proposal for a Corporate Level Tax on Major Stock Sales," 37 Tax Notes 1041 (1987).

2. These losses are available without limitation to offset the gain on T's deemed asset sale. If P acquired T and did not elect under Section 338, T's NOLs would not be purged but they likely would be limited in the future under Section 382. See Chapter 19, infra.

3. See I.R.C. § 338(h)(10) and Section C3 of this chapter, supra.

Assets	**Adj. Basis**	**F.M.V.**
Cash	$200,000	$ 200,000
Inventory	50,000	100,000
Equipment ($100,000 § 1245 recapture)	100,000	200,000
Building (no recapture)	50,000	300,000
Securities	400,000	300,000
Goodwill	0	200,000
	$800,000	$1,300,000
Liabilities		
Bank loan		300,000
		$ 300,000

T and its shareholders are considering a sale of the business. Purchaser Corporation ("P") is interested in acquiring T. If specific computations are required by your instructor, assume (for computational convenience) that C corporations are taxed on all their income at a flat corporate rate of 35 percent and individuals are taxed at a flat 35 percent rate on ordinary income and a 15 percent rate on long-term capital gains.

What are the tax consequences of the following alternative acquisition methods to T, T's shareholders, and P?

(a) T adopts a plan of complete liquidation, sells all of its assets (except the cash but subject to the bank loan) to P for $800,000 cash, and distributes the after-tax proceeds to its shareholders in proportion to their stock holdings.

(b) T adopts a plan of complete liquidation, distributes all of its assets (subject to the liability) to its shareholders in proportion to their stock holdings, and the shareholders then sell the assets (less any cash but subject to the bank loan) to P for $800,000.

(c) In general, how would the result in (a), above, change if P paid T $200,000 in cash and $600,000 in notes, with market rate interest payable annually and the entire principal payable in five years?

(d) T sells all of its assets (except for the cash but subject to the bank loan) to P as in (a), above, except that T does not liquidate and instead invests the after-tax sales proceeds in a portfolio of publicly traded securities.

(e) P purchases all the stock of T for $800 per share and makes a § 338 election. (Why didn't P pay $1,000 per share for the T stock?)

(f) P purchases all the stock of T for cash but does not make the § 338 election. (Consider generally what P should pay for the T stock.)

(g) Assuming P and T are indifferent to the form of the transaction, would you recommend the acquisition method in (a) (purchase of assets), (e) (purchase of stock with § 338 election) or (f) (purchase of stock without § 338 election), above?

(h) Would your recommendation in (g), above, change if T had $600,000 in net operating loss carryovers?

(i) Assume that T is a wholly-owned subsidiary of S, Inc., and S has a $200,000 adjusted basis in its T stock. What result if T distributes all of its assets (subject to the liability) to S in complete liquidation, and S then sells the assets to P?

(j) Same as (i), above, except P insists that the transaction must be structured as an acquisition of T stock.

2. Should Congress enact legislation that treats taxable asset and stock acquisitions consistently for tax purposes? If so, what are its options and which would you support?

E. TAX TREATMENT OF ACQUISITION EXPENSES

The expenses incurred in connection with a corporate acquisition may be substantial. Both the purchaser ("P") and the target ("T") ordinarily must pay fees to lawyers, accountants and investment bankers. P may incur additional expenses to obtain debt and equity financing, and T may be obligated to secure an opinion stating that the proposed acquisition is "fair" to T and its shareholders. In virtually all cases, the central tax question becomes whether the expenses are currently deductible, amortizable, capitalized and added to the basis of a particular tangible or intangible asset, or treated as a permanent nondepreciable capital expenditure.

The tax treatment of P's expenses are relatively settled. Costs of obtaining debt financing (such as fees for negotiating the loan and drafting loan documents, up-front commitment fees and other fees paid to the lender) generally must be amortized over the term of the loan to which the expenses relate.[1] Likewise, expenses of obtaining equity financing (e.g., to register newly issued stock, prepare offering documents, etc.) are treated as permanent capital expenditures that are neither currently deductible nor amortizable.[2] Costs attributable to the acquisition of particular T assets or T stock (e.g., legal expenses for drafting an acquisition agreement, closing costs, finder's fees) also are capital expenditures and must be added to the basis of the acquired property.[3] If P forms a new subsidiary to carry out the acquisition, the organizational expenses are currently deductible (up to $5,000, but reduced as total expenses exceed $50,000), with any excess over the deductible amount amortizable over 15 years if P elects to apply Section 248. In addition, P may attempt to classify certain expenses related to an acquisition as normal business expenses. Examples would include expenses related to employment agreements, executive compensation and retirement planning, tax planning, and the annual retainer paid to an investment banker that may have helped arrange the acquisition.

1. Rev.Rul. 70–359, 1970–2 C.B. 103; Rev.Rul. 70–360, 1970–2 C.B. 103.

2. Rev.Rul. 69–330, 1969–1 C.B. 51.

3. If P acquires T's stock and makes a Section 338 election, these capital expenditures become part of new T's adjusted grossed-up basis and may be allocated among T's assets in accordance with the rules in Sections 338(b)(5) and 1060. See Reg. § 1.338(b)–1(g)(1).

The tax treatment of T's expenses has been more controversial. Assume for example that the target in a friendly corporate takeover incurs legal, investment banking and other fees, including the cost of obtaining an opinion that the terms of the acquisition are fair to T and its shareholders. Are these expenses currently deductible by T as ordinary and necessary businesses expenses under Section 162 or must they be capitalized? In INDOPCO, Inc. v. Commissioner,[4] the Supreme Court held that investment banking fees and other expenses incurred by a target corporation in a friendly takeover were nondeductible capital expenditures because they produced significant long-term benefits, such as the availability of the acquiring corporation's resources, the opportunity for synergy, and the benefits resulting from the target's transformation from a public company to a wholly owned subsidiary. In ruling for the government, the Court held that the creation or enhancement of a separate or distinct asset was not controlling in resolving capital expenditure classification questions. In so doing, it rejected the taxpayer's reliance on a line of appellate decisions that had interpreted the Court's opinion in Commissioner v. Lincoln Savings & Loan Association[5] as adopting a test under which creation or enhancement of an asset is a prerequisite to capitalization. The Court clarified its earlier decision in *Lincoln Savings*, stating that the creation of a separate and distinct asset may be a sufficient reason for capitalizing an expense but not an essential prerequisite. It noted further that *Lincoln Savings* did not prohibit reliance on "future benefit" as a test for distinguishing an ordinary business expense from a capital expenditure. However, the Court conceded that an "incidental future benefit" may not require capitalization but that the taxpayer's realization of benefits beyond the year in which the expenditure was incurred is an important factor in distinguishing ordinary business expenses from capital expenditures.

Soon after it was decided, commentators began to focus on the potential ripple effect of the Supreme Court's *INDOPCO* decision—specifically whether the Court's reasoning would be imported to deny deductibility of various other expenses. The Service has calmed most of these nerves, first in a series of rulings confirming that the deductibility of many expenditures was not affected by *INDOPCO*,[6] and more recently in extensive regulations.[7]

INDOPCO involved a friendly takeover. Should expenses incurred to resist a hostile takeover be treated differently? The contexts in which this issue arises include both defending against a hostile takeover by a corpo-

4. 503 U.S. 79, 112 S.Ct. 1039 (1992).

5. 403 U.S. 345, 91 S.Ct. 1893 (1971).

6. See Rev. Rul. 95–32, 1995–16 I.R.B. 5 (expenditures by a public utility for the implementation and operation of energy conservation and load management programs are deductible under Section 162); Rev. Rul. 94–77, 1994–2 C.B. 19 (severance payments to employees are generally deductible under Section 162); Rev. Rul. 94–38, 1994–1 C.B. 35 (costs to clean up land and treat groundwater contaminated by taxpayer are deductible under Section 162); Rev. Rul. 94–12, 1994–1 C.B. 36 (incidental repair costs are deductible under Section 162); Rev. Rul. 92–80, 1992–2 C.B. 57 (advertising costs are generally deductible under Section 162).

7. See generally Reg. § 1.263(a)–4, –5.

rate raider and arranging for a taxable acquisition by a more friendly "White Knight" buyer. The cases so far indicate that the tax treatment of such expenditures may depend on the eventual outcome of the transaction. In United States v. Federated Department Stores, Inc.,[8] a corporate taxpayer, faced with a hostile offer, arranged a White Knight transaction and agreed to pay "break-up" fees to the White Knight if their merger fell through. Eventually, the hostile bidder was successful and the break-up fees were paid to the White Knight. The Court held that the fees were currently deductible under either Section 162 or Section 165 (as costs incurred in an abandoned transaction). Distinguishing *INDOPCO*, the court found that the fees were incurred to defend the business against attack and not to restructure the corporation in hopes of some future benefit.

In A.E. Staley Manufacturing Co. v. Commissioner,[9] the Tax Court considered a situation where a corporation incurred $23 million in investment bankers' fees and printing costs to respond to a series of hostile tender offers for its stock. The company's board of directors declined two offers but eventually accepted a third bid. Rejecting the taxpayer's argument that *INDOPCO* was distinguishable because the takeover in *Staley* was hostile, the Tax Court held that the fees and costs were nondeductible because they were incurred in connection with a change in the ownership of the taxpayer that "portended strategic changes * * * with long-term consequences" and were capital in nature.[10] The Tax Court also distinguished *Federated Department Stores* because (1) there was no White Knight transaction that could be treated as abandoned and eligible for a loss deduction, and (2) the taxpayer received significant future benefits as a result of the acquisition.[11] Thus, according to the Tax Court the critical question is not whether the transaction is "friendly" or "hostile" but whether an identifiable loss has been sustained and the costs were incurred to realize future benefits.[12]

On appeal, however, the Seventh Circuit reversed and permitted the target corporation to deduct most of the expenses it incurred in resisting a hostile takeover.[13] The court reasoned that *INDOPCO* did not change the law with respect to costs incurred to defend a business because those expenses were to preserve the status quo, not to produce future benefits. It concluded that most of the expenses incurred by the taxpayer in *A.E. Staley* were related to the defense of its business and corporate policy and thus were currently deductible under Section 162(a). Costs properly allocable to

8. 171 B.R. 603 (S.D.Ohio 1994).

9. 105 T.C. 166 (1995).

10. Id. at 200.

11. Id. at 199.

12. The Service also does not seem to base the tax consequences of the expenditure on whether the takeover was hostile. In Tech. Adv. Memo. 9144042 (July 1, 1991), a target corporation was required to capitalize expenses incurred to thwart a hostile tender offer. On the facts presented (the target incurred expenses in repurchasing its own stock from a corporate raider), the Service reasoned that the taxpayer failed to prove that the expenditure did not confer a long-term benefit.

13. A.E. Staley Manufacturing Co. v. Commissioner, 119 F.3d 482 (7th Cir.1997).

unsuccessful efforts to engage in an alternate transaction to prevent the acquisition, such as a financial restructuring, recapitalization, or joint venture, were held to be deductible losses under Section 165. The court also held that fees paid to evaluate the taxpayer's stock and to facilitate the eventual merger were nondeductible capital expenditures.

If either P or T incurs costs in investigating or attempting to consummate an acquisition that ultimately fails, the transactional costs generally are currently deductible as losses under Section 165.[14]

In 2003, the Service issued lengthy regulations under Section 263 relating to the tax treatment of amounts incurred to acquire, create, or enhance various kinds of intangible assets.[15] The regulations provide guidance on when taxpayers must treat these costs as capital expenditures. They do so by specifying, in extraordinary detail, various categories of rights, privileges and future benefits for which capitalization is required. Particular goals of this regulations project were to bring greater clarity to (some would say "erode" or "discard") the "significant future benefit" standard enunciated by the Supreme Court in Indopco, Inc. v. Commissioner, and to resurrect the more taxpayer-friendly "separate and distinct asset" approach of the Court's earlier *Lincoln Savings* decision. The effect of this new liberalized regime is to presume that outlays related to intangible assets are currently deductible unless these or subsequently issued regulations specifically require capitalization.

The regulations include specific rules on an acquisition of a trade or business, a change in the capital structure of a business entity, and certain other transactions such as Section 351 exchanges.[16] Costs that "facilitate" such transactions must be capitalized.[17] This standard is consistent with the previously discussed case law on the purchaser's acquisition expenses. Transaction costs incurred to defend against a hostile takeover are not viewed as facilitating the acquisition. As a result, they may be currently deducted rather than capitalized.[18] This rule follows the Seventh Circuit's decision in *A.E. Staley*. If an initially hostile acquisition becomes friendly, the taxpayer must bifurcate the costs between those incurred to defend against the hostile takeover and those incurred to facilitate the friendly acquisition, using a "facts and circumstances" standard to draw the line.[19] Costs incurred to thwart a hostile acquisition, such as by merging with a White Knight, must be capitalized even if the taxpayer's overall purpose was to defend against a hostile acquisition.[20] But legal fees paid to seek an injunction against a hostile takeover and investment banking fees to locate a potential White Knight acquirer may be currently deducted.[21] And there's

14. Rev.Rul. 73–580, 1973–2 C.B. 86.

15. Reg. § 1.263(a)–4, –5, T.D. 9107, 69 Fed. Reg. 436 (Jan. 5, 2004).

16. See Reg. § 1.263(a)–5(a). For accounting rules for debt issuance costs that must be capitalized, see Reg. § 1.446–5.

17. Id. Costs that facilitate the acquisition of an intangible generally must be capitalized under Reg. §§ 1.263(a)–4(b)(1)(v), (e).

18. Reg. § 1.263(a)–5(*l*) Example 11.

19. Id. See also Reg. § 1.263(a)–5(*l*) Example 12.

20. Reg. § 1.263(a)–5(*l*) Example 11.

21. Id.

much more, including simplifying conventions (e.g., compensation to employees are treated as amounts that do not facilitate a transaction and thus are currently deductible),[22] de minimis exceptions (transaction costs of $5,000 or less generally do not have to be capitalized),[23] and timing rules.[24]

22. Reg. § 1.263(a)–5(d)(2).

23. Reg. § 1.263(a)–5(d)(3).

24. Reg. § 1.263(a)–5(e).

CHAPTER 17

TAX–FREE CORPORATE REORGANIZATIONS

A. INTRODUCTION

1. HISTORICAL BACKGROUND

Some of the major litigation arising under the early federal income tax laws involved a variety of transactions loosely described as corporate reorganizations. Long before they became distracted by tax considerations, corporate lawyers and investment bankers were busy devising transactions ranging from complicated mergers, acquisitions and recapitalizations to routine changes in the state of incorporation. With the arrival of the income tax, the courts were required to determine whether and to what extent these fundamental changes in the structure of a corporate entity were taxable events.

Working with a pristine statute and an unsophisticated perspective, the Supreme Court became one of the first protectors of the comprehensive tax base. In a series of cases, the Court concluded that even minor changes in the form of a corporate business enterprise (e.g., changing the state of incorporation from New Jersey to Delaware) caused the shareholders to realize gain.[1] While these cases were pending, however, Congress quickly came to the rescue by enacting one of the earliest nonrecognition provisions. Preceding even the forerunner of Section 351, Section 202(b) of the Revenue Act of 1918 provided that no gain or loss would be recognized on the "reorganization, merger or consolidation of a corporation" where a person received "in place of stock or securities owned by him new stock or securities of no greater aggregate par face value."[2]

The rationale for the reorganization provisions reflects the broader policies of nonrecognition. Congress concluded that the tax collector should not impede these diverse transactions because they are mere readjustments of a continuing interest in property, albeit in modified corporate form,[3] and the new property received is "substantially a continuation of the old

1. Marr v. United States, 268 U.S. 536, 45 S.Ct. 575 (1925). See also United States v. Phellis, 257 U.S. 156, 42 S.Ct. 63 (1921); Rockefeller v. United States, 257 U.S. 176, 42 S.Ct. 68 (1921).

2. Pub.L. No. 254, 40 Stat. 1057 (1919).

3. Reg. § 1.368–1(b). See also S.Rep. No. 275, 67th Cong., 1st Sess. (1921), reprinted in 1939–1 (Part 2) C.B. 181, 188–189, where the Senate Finance Committee justified the principal forerunners of the modern nonrecognition provisions on the ground that they would permit businesses to proceed with necessary adjustments and remove "a source of grave uncertainty" in the law.

investment still unliquidated."[4] But to the extent that a shareholder liquidates a corporate investment, recognition of gain or loss *is* appropriate. The 1921 predecessor of the present reorganization regime thus provided that shareholders must recognize their realized gain, if any, to the extent of the "boot" (money and other property) received.[5] Congress soon refined the statutory scheme by making clear what it had suggested in earlier versions: nonrecognition really means deferral rather than total forgiveness of gain or loss. The Revenue Act of 1928 introduced rules for carryover and substituted bases in order to preserve the unrecognized gain or loss for recognition at the time that the shareholder liquidated his investment.[6]

What began as a relatively simple concept has evolved into a vast and challenging body of law that governs some of the most financially significant transactions in the business world. It is important to recognize at the outset that the system you are about to study is not necessarily sensible. Functionally different transactions are lumped together and labelled "reorganizations." At the same time, economically equivalent acquisition methods are tested for reorganization status under sharply different criteria that often place a great premium on the form chosen by the parties. Moreover, determining the tax consequences of a corporate combination or readjustment requires an application of both precise statutory provisions and judicially created "common law" principles of uncertain scope. Analysis is further complicated by the possibility of an overlap between the reorganization provisions and other parts of Subchapter C.

In view of these defects in the reorganization scheme, it is not surprising that commentators long ago called for a complete overhaul of the current system.[7] Some modest reforms have come from the Service through recently issued regulations and rulings. Those pronouncements harmonize some of the requirements of Section 368 and in so doing increase flexibility in structuring tax-free acquisitions. But Congress has not yet fully embraced the simplification movement, and so we must turn to a more detailed examination of provisions that Professors Bittker and Eustice have described as "extraordinarily complex, even for the [Internal Revenue] Code."[8]

2. OVERVIEW OF REORGANIZATIONS

Code: Skim §§ 336(c); 354; 355; 356; 358; 361; 362(b); 368(a)(1), (b), (c); 381(a); 1032.

Regulations: § 1.368–1(a), (b), (c).

The term "reorganization" generally is associated with the rehabilitation of a bankrupt company. Under the Internal Revenue Code, however,

4. Reg. § 1.1002–1(c).

5. Revenue Act of 1921, § 202, Pub.L. No. 98, 42 Stat. 227.

6. Revenue Act of 1928, § 113(a)(6)–(9), Pub.L. No. 562, 45 Stat. 791.

7. See generally Federal Income Tax Project, Subchapter C, American Law Institute (1982); Staff of the Senate Finance Committee, The Subchapter C Revision Act of 1985: A Final Report Prepared by the Staff, 99th Cong., 1st Sess. 50–58 (S.Prt. 99–47, 1985).

8. Bittker & Eustice, Federal Income Taxation of Corporations and Shareholders ¶ 12.01[4] (7th ed. 2000).

"reorganization" is a term of art[1] used to describe corporate combinations or readjustments that fall into the following three broad categories:

(1) *Acquisitive reorganizations*, which are the principal focus of this chapter, are transactions in which one corporation (the "acquiring corporation") acquires the assets or stock of another corporation (the "acquired" or "target" corporation). Included in this category are statutory mergers or consolidations ("A" reorganizations); acquisitions of stock of the target for voting stock of the acquiring corporation ("B" reorganizations); acquisitions of assets of the target for voting stock of the acquiring corporation ("C" reorganizations, sometimes called "practical mergers" because of their similarity to statutory mergers); and several other more complex acquisition techniques involving the use of a subsidiary or multiple steps.

(2) *Divisive reorganizations*, which result in the division of a single corporation into two or more separate entities and which often are preceded by a "D" reorganization. Corporate divisions are considered in Chapter 18.

(3) *Nonacquisitive, nondivisive reorganizations*, which involve adjustments to the corporate structure of a single, continuing corporate enterprise. This residual category includes recapitalizations ("E" reorganizations); changes in identity, form or place of incorporation ("F" reorganizations); certain transfers of substantially all of the assets from one corporation to another, followed by a liquidation of the first corporation (nondivisive "D" reorganizations); and transfers of a corporation's assets to another corporation pursuant to a bankruptcy reorganization plan ("G" reorganizations). Coverage of these transactions is limited to a brief overview at the end of this chapter.

A common organizational thread weaves its way through these diverse categories. First, definitional provisions set forth requirements ranging from the general and very flexible test to qualify as a Type A reorganization to the complex criteria imposed by Section 355 for corporate divisions. To qualify as a reorganization, a transaction also must pass muster under "common law" doctrines developed by the courts to reinforce the rationale for nonrecognition. The principal judicial doctrines are continuity of shareholder proprietary interest, continuity of business enterprise and business purpose. In general, the continuity of interest doctrine requires that a substantial part of the value of the proprietary (i.e., equity) interests in the target corporation must be preserved in the reorganization through an exchange of target stock or assets for stock in the acquiring corporation.[2] For some transactions, the continuity of interest doctrine has been incorpo-

1. See I.R.C. § 368(a)(1); Reg. § 1.368-1(c).

2. Reg. § 1.368-1(e)(1).

rated into the statutory definition of "reorganization." For example, the only permissible consideration in a B reorganization is voting stock of the acquiring corporation.[3] The doctrine assumes far more importance if the statute is imprecise, as with Type A reorganizations, where the Code merely requires a "statutory merger or consolidation" without any elaboration on the permissible consideration.[4] We therefore examine continuity of interest questions primarily in connection with Type A reorganizations—the context in which that doctrine most frequently arises.

The continuity of business enterprise doctrine, as its name implies, focuses on the continuing business operations of the target. This requirement has been incorporated in the regulations[5] and also is considered with "A" reorganizations. Because the business purpose doctrine was first applied and has the greatest importance in the context of a corporate division, it is discussed in Chapter 18. In general, all these requirements must be satisfied in order for a transaction to qualify as a reorganization.[6] To further complicate matters, the Service sometimes applies the step transaction doctrine to corporate reorganizations to convert what in form may be separate nontaxable steps into what in substance is a taxable transaction, or vice versa.[7]

If all these statutory and judicial requirements are met, they unlock the doors to the "operative provisions"—sections of the Code that provide for nonrecognition of gain or loss and that govern collateral matters such as the treatment of liabilities, basis, holding period and carryover of tax attributes.[8] For example, Sections 354 and 356 grant total or partial nonrecognition of gain to the shareholders of the target corporation in an acquisitive reorganization. Section 358, which we encountered earlier in connection with tax-free incorporations, provides a formula for determining the substituted basis of the stock or securities received by these shareholders in a reorganization. At the corporate level, Section 361(a) generally provides for nonrecognition when a corporation transfers its assets in a reorganization and distributes property in a liquidation pursuant to a reorganization plan,[9] and Section 357 generally ensures that the assumption of the target's liabilities is not treated as boot for this purpose. The acquiring corporation is accorded nonrecognition under Section 1032 with respect to stock used to make the acquisition and takes a transferred basis in the target's assets or stock under Section 362(b). In keeping with the continuity of investment principle, the tax attributes of the target corpora-

3. I.R.C. § 368(a)(1)(B).

4. I.R.C. § 368(a)(1)(A).

5. Reg. § 1.368–1(d).

6. Reg. §§ 1.368–1(b); 1.368–2(g). However, since the "E" reorganization involves only a single corporation, there is neither a continuity of interest nor a continuity of business enterprise requirement. Microdot, Inc. v. United States, 728 F.2d 593 (2d Cir. 1984); Golden Nugget, Inc. v. Commissioner, 83 T.C. 28 (1984); Rev.Rul. 82–34, 1982–1 C.B. 59. In addition, the legislative history of the "G" reorganization indicates that both doctrines will be leniently applied in an insolvency situation. See Section C of this chapter, infra.

7. See, e.g., Rev. Rul. 79–250, 1979–2 C.B. 156.

8. See Section B5 of this chapter, infra.

9. See also I.R.C. § 336(c).

tion (e.g., earnings and profits and net operating losses) generally carry over to the acquiring corporation under Section 381, subject to various limitations to patrol abuse.[10]

If a transaction does not qualify as a reorganization, these operative provisions do not apply and the tax consequences of the transaction must be determined under other parts of Subchapter C. For example, an asset acquisition that fails as a Type A or C reorganization ordinarily would be a taxable transaction to the shareholders under the rules considered in Chapters 15 and 16. But it is the rare reorganization that fails. Because of the high stakes involved, taxpayers historically were reluctant to proceed with reorganization transactions without first obtaining the Internal Revenue Service's blessing in the form of an advance ruling or, when time was of the essence, a reliable opinion letter from private counsel.[11] More recently, the Service has declined to grant "comfort rulings" on straightforward acquisitions,[12] but it will rule on transactions presenting a "significant issue."[13] As a result, the Service's administrative guidelines are often tantamount to the law in this area, and taxpayers who disagree with the government's viewpoint must proceed with a transaction at their substantial risk.

B. ACQUISITIVE REORGANIZATIONS

1. TYPE A: STATUTORY MERGERS AND CONSOLIDATIONS

Code: § 368(a)(1)(A). Skim §§ 354(a); 356(a); 357; 358(a); 361; 362(b); 368(a)(2)(C), (b); 381(a)(2); 1032.

Regulations: §§ 1.368–1(d)(1)–(3) & (5) Examples 1–5, (e)(1) & (7) Example 1; –1T(e)(2)(i), (v) Example 1, –2(a), (b)(1)(i), (ii), (iii) Examples 1, 2 & 6, (g).

a. THE MERGER OR CONSOLIDATION REQUIREMENT

In General. The Type A reorganization is defined in the Code as a statutory merger or consolidation. For this purpose, "statutory" refers to a merger or consolidation pursuant to local (usually corporate) law.[1] Under a

10. See Chapter 19, infra.

11. For the Service's administrative guidelines in evaluating reorganizations, see Rev.Proc. 77–37, 1977–2 C.B. 568.

12. Rev. Proc. 90–56, 1990–2 C.B. 639.

13. See Rev. Proc. 2008–3, § 3.01(38), 2008–1 I.R.B. 113. A "significant issue" is one that meets three tests: (1) it is not clearly and adequately addressed by a statute, regulation, judicial decision, tax treaty, or administrative authority; (2) its resolution is not essentially free from doubt; and (3) it is legally significant and germane to determining the major tax consequences of the transaction. Id. If there is a significant issue, the Service will rule on the entire transaction. Id.

1. Russell v. Commissioner, 40 T.C. 810 (1963), affirmed 345 F.2d 534 (5th Cir.1965). The regulations provide that a transaction may qualify as a statutory merger or consolidation without requiring it to be effective under a domestic statute, thus permitting foreign corporations to be parties to Type A reorganizations. Reg. § 1.368–2(b)(iii) Examples 13 & 14.

typical state merger statute, the assets and liabilities of the target corporation are transferred to the acquiring corporation without the need for deeds or bills of sale, and the target dissolves by operation of law.[2] The consideration received by the target's shareholders is specified in a formal agreement of merger between the two companies. The shareholders may receive stock or debt instruments of the acquiring corporation, cash or a combination of all three. A consolidation involves a similar transfer of the assets and liabilities of two corporations to a newly created entity followed by the dissolution of the transferor corporations, and the shareholders of the transferors become shareholders of the new entity by operation of law. Either transaction may require approval by a simple majority or two-thirds vote of the shareholders of both corporations,[3] and under state corporate law dissenting shareholders may be granted the right to sell their target stock at a price determined in an appraisal proceeding.[4]

"Divisive" Mergers. To qualify as a Type A reorganization, a merger must be an acquisitive rather than a divisive transaction. To be "acquisitive," the result of the transaction must be that one corporation acquires the assets of another (target) corporation by operation of law, and the target must cease to exist. By contrast, a "divisive" transaction is one in which a corporation's assets are divided among two or more corporations. In Revenue Ruling 2000–5,[5] the Service relied on this distinction in ruling that a transaction in which T "merged" under state law into P, transferring only some of its assets and liabilities, and T remained in existence, was not a Type A reorganization.[6] Similarly, a transaction where T transferred some of its assets and liabilities to each of two acquiring corporations and then T dissolved, with each T shareholder receiving stock in both acquiring corporations, was not a Type A reorganization even though it was a merger under state corporate law.[7] Although both transactions were called "mergers" under state law, they were divisive rather than acquisitive because T's assets were divided between two corporations, and T's shareholders wound up with stock in two separate companies.[8]

2. See, e.g., Calif. Corp. Code § 1107.

3. As a general rule, most state corporate laws give voting rights to shareholders of the purchasing ("P") and target ("T") corporations. But where the amount of P stock used in the acquisition is less than 20 percent of its outstanding shares, P shareholders usually do not have the right to vote. In an acquisition initiated by a tender offer, there is no formal shareholder vote because T shareholders individually may decide whether or not to sell. Some states, such as Delaware, also do not give P shareholders the right to vote on asset acquisitions not structured as a merger, triangular mergers where a P subsidiary makes the acquisition, stock acquisitions, or certain acquisitions for cash or cash equivalents. See generally Oesterle, Mergers and Acquisitions in a Nutshell (2d ed. 2007).

4. Under Delaware law, for example, dissenting target shareholders have appraisal rights in statutory mergers (even if they do not have voting rights) but not in asset acquisitions. 8 Del. Code §§ 262, 271.

5. 2000–1 C.B. 436 (Situation 1).

6. Id. See also Reg. § 1.368–2(b)(1)(iii) Example 1.

7. Rev. Rul. 2000–5, 2000–1 C.B. 436 (Situation 2).

8. Some divisive transactions also may be tax-free but they must satisfy the requirements of Section 355. See Chapter 18, infra.

Revenue Ruling 2000–5 was the Service's response to a new form of corporate merger statute enacted by the Texas legislature in 1989 to permit divisive mergers.[9] The understandable concern was that permitting such mergers to qualify as Type A reorganizations would be inconsistent with the policy of Section 368 and undermine Section 355, which imposes strict and detailed requirements for corporate divisions to qualify for tax-free treatment.[10] The ruling serves as a reminder that simple compliance with a state corporate merger law does not ensure that a transaction will qualify as a Type A reorganization.

Mergers Involving Disregarded Entities. In a similar response to emerging acquisition techniques, the Service issued regulations addressing mergers between corporations and disregarded entities (such as a single-member limited liability company).[11] The regulations take a common sense approach to the two most typical transactional forms: (1) the merger of a single-member limited liability company ("LLC") with a corporate owner ("X") into an acquiring corporation ("P"), and (2) the merger of a target corporation ("T") into a single-member LLC in exchange for stock of LLC's corporate owner ("P"). In both situations, the LLC is a disregarded entity and thus is treated for tax purposes as a division of its corporate owner unless it elects to be taxed as a separate corporation. The first transaction does not qualify as a Type A reorganization because X's assets and liabilities are divided between X and P as a result of the merger.[12] But a merger of T into a single-member LLC in exchange for stock of the LLC's corporate owner ("P") may qualify as a Type A reorganization if the other requirements (e.g., the continuity of interest doctrine, discussed below) are met and the separate legal existence of T terminates.[13] This favorable result is consistent with the treatment of a disregarded entity as a division of its owner. It is as if T merged directly into P. Permitting statutory mergers into disregarded entities to qualify as Type A reorganizations offers more flexibility by eliminating the need for these transactions to pass muster under the stricter requirements applicable to Type C stock-for-assets acquisitions.[14]

Shareholder and Business Enterprise Continuity Requirements. The Code is strangely silent as to the permissible consideration in a Type A reorganization and the degree to which the target's historic business must be conducted by the acquiring corporation. To fill these gaps and preserve

9. For an analysis and critique of Revenue Ruling 2000–5, see Bank, "Taxing Divisive and Disregarded Mergers," 34 Geo. L. Rev. 1523 (2000).

10. See Chapter 18, infra.

11. See Reg. § 301.7701–2(a) and Chapter 1D2, supra, for a discussion of disregarded entities—familiarly known as "tax nothings." Certain real estate investment trusts and S corporation subsidiaries also may be treated as disregarded entities for tax purposes.

12. Reg. § 1.368–2(b)(1)(iii) Example 6.

13. Reg. § 1.368–2(b)(1)(iii) Example 2.

14. For example, Type C reorganizations require the acquiring corporation to acquire substantially all of the target's properties and to use mostly voting stock and only a limited amount of boot in making the acquisition. See Section B3 of this chapter, infra.

the integrity of the nonrecognition scheme, the courts developed the continuity of proprietary interest and continuity of business enterprise requirements.[15] Both doctrines are examined in the materials that follow.

b. CONTINUITY OF PROPRIETARY INTEREST: QUANTITY AND QUALITY

Southwest Natural Gas Co. v. Commissioner

United States Court of Appeals, Fifth Circuit, 1951.
189 F.2d 332.

■ RUSSELL, CIRCUIT JUDGE.

The correctness of asserted deficiencies for corporate income tax for the year 1941 and of declared value excess profits tax and excess profits tax for 1942 due by Southwest Natural Gas Company depends upon whether a merger of Peoples Gas & Fuel Corporation with the taxpayer, effected in accordance with the laws of Delaware, was a sale, as asserted by the Commissioner, or a "reorganization" within the terms of Section 112(g) [the predecessor of Section 368] of the Internal Revenue Code, as contended by the taxpayer. The parties so stipulated the issue in the Tax Court. That Court upheld the Commissioner's determination. Southwest Natural Gas Company has petitioned this Court for review.

The facts found by the Tax Court (which, as facts, are not challenged) and the grounds for its judgment in law thereon are fully set forth in its published opinion. In substance that Court held that literal compliance with the provisions of a state law authorizing a merger would not in itself effect a "reorganization" within the terms applicable under Internal Revenue Statutes; that the test of continuity of interest was nevertheless applicable; and that the transaction in question did not meet this test. This ruling is assigned as error upon grounds which, while variously stated, require for their maintenance establishment of at least one of the propositions that: if the literal language of the statute is complied with, that is if there is a "statutory merger" duly effected in accordance with state law, the statute requires it be treated as a reorganization; or, at least where such merger has been effected the Tax Court must hold the transaction a reorganization in the absence of a finding that it was not in truth and in substance a merger; or, even if this be not correct, that the facts of this case disclose sufficient "continuity of interest." It is insisted in either view the Tax Court was required to hold under the facts found by it that the transaction in question was in truth a "statutory merger" and hence a "reorganization."

Consideration of the underlying purposes of the terms and provisions of Section 112 of the Internal Revenue Code in its entirety and of this Section (g)(1)(A) as involved here, in particular, as being enacted "to free from the imposition of an income tax purely 'paper profits or losses'

15. The earliest continuity of interest cases involved Type C reorganizations but the doctrine now applies primarily to statutory mergers and consolidations.

wherein there is no realization of gain or loss in the business sense but merely the recasting of the same interests in a different form, the tax being postponed to a future date when a more tangible gain or loss is realized." Commissioner of Internal Revenue v. Gilmore's Estate, 3 Cir., 130 F.2d 791, 794, and thus applicable to transactions which effect only the "readjustment of continuing interest in property under modified corporate forms," clearly discloses, we think, that the accomplishment of a statutory merger does not *ipso facto* constitute a "reorganization" within the terms of the statute here involved. This has been expressly held by the Court of Appeals for the Third Circuit in a well considered opinion, supported by numerous authorities cited. Roebling v. Commissioner, 143 F.2d 810. There is no occasion for elaboration or reiteration of the reasoning and authorities set forth in that opinion. In Bazley v. Commissioner, 331 U.S. 737, 67 S.Ct. 1489, 1491, 91 L.Ed. 1782, the Supreme Court enforced a similar construction with reference to the "re-capitalization" provision of the section. The authorities are clearly to the effect that the terms expressed in the statute are not to be given merely a literal interpretation but are to be considered and applied in accordance with the purpose of Section 112. Thus the benefits of the reorganization provision have been withheld "in situations which might have satisfied provisions of the section treated as inert language, because they were not reorganizations of the kind with which § 112, in its purpose and particulars concerns itself. * * * "

It is thus clear that the test of "continuity of interest" announced and applied by these cited authorities, supra, must be met before a statutory merger may properly be held a reorganization within the terms of Section 112(g)(1)(A), supra. Each case must in its final analysis be controlled by its own peculiar facts. While no precise formula has been expressed for determining whether there has been retention of the requisite interest, it seems clear that the requirement of continuity of interest consistent with the statutory intent is not fulfilled in the absence of a showing: (1) that the transferor corporation or its shareholders retained a substantial proprietary stake in the enterprise represented by a material interest in the affairs of the transferee corporation, and, (2) that such retained interest represents a substantial part of the value of the property transferred.

Among other facts, the Tax Court found that under the merger all of Peoples' assets were acquired by the petitioner in exchange for specified amounts of stock, bonds, cash and the assumption of debts. There was a total of 18,875 shares common stock of Peoples' entitled to participate under the agreement of merger. The stockholders were offered Option A and Option B. The holders of 7,690 of such shares exercised Option B of that agreement and received $30.00 in cash for each share, or a total of $230,700.00. In respect to the stock now involved, the stockholders who exercised Option A, the holders of 59.2 per cent of the common stock received in exchange 16.4 per cent of petitioner's outstanding common stock plus $340,350.00 principal amount of six per cent mortgage bonds (of the market value of 90 per cent of principal), which had been assumed by petitioner in a prior merger and $17,779.59 cash. The 16.4 per cent of the common stock referred to was represented by 111,850 shares having a market value of $5,592.50, or five cents per share, and represented the continuing proprietary interest of the participating stockholders in the enterprise. This was less than one per cent of the consideration paid by the taxpayers.

We think it clear that these and other facts found by the Tax Court find substantial support in the evidence, and the conclusion of the Tax Court that they failed to evidence sufficient continuity of interest to bring the transaction within the requirements of the applicable statute is correct.

The decision of the Tax Court is affirmed.

[The dissenting opinion of Chief Judge Hutcheson has been omitted. Ed.]

Revenue Ruling 66–224

1966–2 Cum.Bull. 114.

Corporation *X* was merged under state law into corporation *Y*. Corporation *X* had four stockholders (*A*, *B*, *C*, *D*), each of whom owned 25 percent of its stock. Corporation *Y* paid *A* and *B* each $50,000 in cash for their stock of corporation *X*, and *C* and *D* each received corporation *Y* stock with a value of $50,000 in exchange for their stock of corporation *X*. There are no other facts present that should be taken into account in determining whether the continuity of interest requirement of section 1.368–1(b) of the Income Tax Regulations has been satisfied, such as sales, redemptions or other dispositions of stock prior to or subsequent to the exchange which were part of the plan of reorganization.

Held, the continuity of interest requirement of section 1.368–1(b) of the regulations has been satisfied. It would also be satisfied if the facts were the same except corporation *Y* paid each stockholder $25,000 in cash and each stockholder received corporation *Y* stock with a value of $25,000.

NOTE

Measuring Continuity of Interest. The continuity of interest doctrine historically required the shareholders of the target corporation to receive a sufficient proprietary interest in the acquiring corporation to justify treating the transaction as a wholly or partially tax-free reorganization rather than a taxable sale.[1] The early cases focused on both the quality of the consideration received by the target's shareholders and the percentage of equity consideration (relative to total consideration) received by those shareholders as a group. For example, in one of the first cases to apply the doctrine, the Supreme Court held that a transaction literally satisfying the definition of a reorganization nonetheless was a taxable sale because the T

1. See generally Bittker & Eustice, Federal Income Taxation of Corporations and Shareholders ¶ 12.21 (7th ed. 2000).

shareholders received only short-term notes of the acquiring corporation.[2] In a later case, the Court held that there was sufficient continuity of interest where the T shareholders received 38 percent nonvoting preferred stock of the acquiring corporation and 62 percent cash.[3]

In evaluating continuity of interest, it is the overall continuity preserved in the transaction that controls, not the continuity of any individual shareholder.[4] All classes of stock, whether voting or nonvoting, provide the requisite continuity while any other consideration (cash, short-term notes, bonds, assumption of liabilities) will fail to meet the test.[5] The lines with respect to the percentage of stock that must be received are not so easily drawn if one refers to the case law,[6] but the Service provided a practical benchmark by declaring that it would rule favorably on a Type A reorganization if P uses at least 50 percent equity consideration in making the acquisition,[7] and an example in the regulations confirms the Service's view that 40 percent continuity is sufficient[8]—a position long advocated by experienced tax advisers and supported by case law.[9] Keep in mind that this "percentage" is the proportion of equity consideration relative to total consideration used by P to acquire T, not the percentage of P stock owned by former T shareholders after the P's acquisition of T. Moreover, overall qualification as a reorganization under this liberal standard does not mean that all T shareholders will be able to defer recognition of their gain. Those receiving nonequity consideration must recognize gain, if any, perhaps as ordinary income, to the extent they receive boot.[10] But if the entire transaction fails to qualify as a reorganization, all the parties (including T), not merely those receiving nonequity consideration, must recognize gain or loss.

These venerable principles have not been altered by the enactment in 1997 of Section 356(e), which treats certain debt-like preferred stock, defined in Section 351(g) as "nonqualified preferred stock," as other property (i.e. boot) for purposes of recognition of gain or loss by the T shareholders in a reorganization. In treating nonqualified preferred stock as boot for gain recognition purposes, Congress was responding to concerns about acquisitive transactions in which T shareholders received a relatively secure instrument labelled as "stock" but bearing many of the characteristics of debt in exchange for a riskier equity investment. In those circumstances, Congress believed it was appropriate to view the new debt-like

2. Pinellas Ice & Cold Storage Co. v. Commissioner, 287 U.S. 462, 53 S.Ct. 257 (1933). See also Helvering v. Minnesota Tea Co., 296 U.S. 378, 56 S.Ct. 269 (1935).

3. John A. Nelson Co. v. Helvering, 296 U.S. 374, 56 S.Ct. 273 (1935).

4. See Rev.Rul. 66–224 at p. 726, supra; Reg. § 1.368–1(e)(1)(i).

5. See, e.g., John A. Nelson Co. v. Helvering, supra note 3.

6. See, e.g., John A. Nelson Co. v. Helvering, supra note 3 (38% redeemable nonvoting preferred sufficient for continuity); Miller v. Commissioner, 84 F.2d 415 (6th Cir.1936) (25% stock sufficient).

7. Rev.Proc. 77–37, 1977–2 C.B. 568. See also Rev. Proc. 86–42, 1986–2 C.B. 722.

8. Reg. § 1.368–1T(e)(2)(v) Example 1.

9. See Ginsburg & Levin, Mergers, Acquisitions and Buyouts ¶ 610.2 (2008 ed.)

10. See Section B5 of this chapter, infra.

preferred stock as taxable consideration because the T shareholder was obtaining a more secure form of investment. Congress indicated, however, that nonqualified preferred stock would continue to be treated as equity under other provisions of the Code, such as Sections 351 and 368, at least until prospective regulations provide otherwise.[11]

Remote Continuity. The continuity of interest test was once interpreted as requiring the T stock or assets acquired in a reorganization to be held directly by the corporation that issues its stock to T shareholders.[12] This "remote continuity" doctrine focused on the requisite link between the former T shareholders and the T business assets after the reorganization. Subsequent amendments to the Code provided more flexibility—for example, by permitting "drop-down" transfers to subsidiaries of the acquiring corporation[13] or allowing a controlled subsidiary to use its parent's stock as consideration in a merger.[14] The regulations go further by permitting successive transfers of T stock or assets among various members of an affiliated group of corporations or, in some cases, to a controlled partnership.[15] In general, these regulations provide that continuity is not broken by a transfer or successive transfer of the acquired T stock or assets to lower-tier subsidiaries provided that the transferor continues to "control" (using the 80 percent tests in Section 368(c)) each transferee[16] and the continuity of business enterprise requirement is satisfied.[17]

When to Measure Continuity of Interest. In determining whether the requisite proprietary interest in the target corporation has been preserved for continuity of interest purposes, the regulations provide that the appropriate measuring date is the last business day before the first date that the contract is a "binding contract" if the merger agreement provides for "fixed consideration."[18] A "binding contract" is an instrument enforceable under applicable law against the parties to it.[19] The presence of conditions outside the parties' control (such as the need for regulatory approval) or the fact that insubstantial terms remain to be negotiated or customary conditions satisfied will not prevent a contract from being "binding."[20] Consideration is "fixed" if the contract recites the number of shares of P stock and the amount of nonstock consideration to be received by T's shareholders,[21] provided the contract does not include contingent adjustments that prevent T's shareholders from being subject to the economic benefits and burdens of ownership of P as of the signing date (e.g., T shareholders are entitled to receive additional consideration if the price of

11. Staff of the Joint Committee on Taxation, General Explanation of Tax Legislation Enacted in 1997, 105th Cong., 1st Sess. 212–213 (1997).

12. See, e.g., Groman v. Commissioner, 302 U.S. 82, 58 S.Ct. 108 (1937); Helvering v. Bashford, 302 U.S. 454, 58 S.Ct. 307 (1938).

13. I.R.C. § 368(a)(2)(C).

14. I.R.C. § 368(a)(2)(D). See Section B4 of this chapter, infra.

15. See, e.g., Reg. §§ 1.368–2(f),–2(k)(1),–2(k)(2) Examples 1–3.

16. Reg. § 1.368–1(k)(1).

17. Reg. § 1.368–1(d)(4), (5).

18. Reg. § 1.368–1T(e)(2)(i).

19. Reg. § 1.368–1T(e)(2)(ii)(A).

20. Reg. 1.368–1T(e)(2)(ii)(B).

21. Reg. § 1.368–1T(e)(2)(iii).

P stock declines by specified amounts during the interval between the signing and deal consummation dates). Without this pro-taxpayer signing date rule, a decline in the value of the acquiring corporation's stock between the date that the merger agreement was signed and the date the transaction was consummated could cause the transaction to fall below the continuity threshold. Under the rule, value fluctuations will not jeopardize qualification as a reorganization and convert the transaction into a taxable asset sale. The policy for the signing date rule is that, if a contract provides for fixed consideration, the T shareholders are properly viewed as being subject to the "economic fortunes" of P as of the date the contract becomes binding.[22]

The regulations elaborate on the basic rule, detailing how continuity of interest is measured if the deal terms are modified before the closing date, how tender offers are handled, and how the rules are applied when an agreement provides for contingent adjustments and escrowed stock arrangements.[23]

c. CONTINUITY BY HISTORIC TARGET SHAREHOLDERS

J.E. Seagram Corp. v. Commissioner

United States Tax Court, 1995.
104 T.C. 75.

OPINION

■ NIMS, JUDGE:

[This case arose out of a 1981 takeover contest for Conoco, Inc. After an unsuccessful attempt to negotiate a friendly takeover, J.E. Seagram Corporation ("Seagram") commenced a cash tender offer for Conoco stock. Two weeks later, E.I DuPont de Nemours and Co. ("DuPont") and Conoco entered into an agreement for a two-step acquisition, under which a DuPont subsidiary ("DuPont Tenderor") commenced a competing tender offer to acquire all of Conoco's stock in exchange for a combination of cash and DuPont stock, to be followed by a merger of Conoco into a DuPont subsidiary. The agreement was subject to several conditions, including the requirement that at least 51 percent of Conoco's stock must be tendered.

When the smoke cleared after the various tender offers expired, Seagram had acquired 32 percent of Conoco stock for cash, and DuPont had acquired 46 percent of Conoco stock for cash. DuPont subsequently acquired the Conoco shares it did not own (including Seagram's holding) in exchange for DuPont stock as part of the tender offer and the merger of Conoco into DuPont Tenderor. When the smoke cleared, approximately 78 percent of the Conoco stock had changed hands for cash in the DuPont and Seagram tender offers, but 54 percent of the Conoco stock (including Seagram's stake) was exchanged for DuPont shares.

22. Reg. § 1.368–1T(e)(2)(i).

23. See Reg. § 1.368–1T(e)(1)(ii)–(iv).

Seagram claimed a loss on its exchange of Conoco stock for DuPont stock. The Service disallowed the loss on the grounds that the transaction constituted a tax-free reorganization. Seagram argued that the exchange of its Conoco stock for DuPont stock was not carried out in pursuance of a reorganization plan, as required by Section 368.

In the first part of its lengthy opinion, the Tax Court held that because DuPont was contractually committed to undertake the merger once it completed its tender offer, the "carefully integrated transactions together constituted a plan of reorganization * * *."

Seagram's second argument was that DuPont's tender offer and merger did not constitute a reorganization because they failed the continuity of interest requirement. The Tax Court's resolution of that issue is set forth below. Ed.]

On the date of the Conoco/DuPont Agreement, July 6, 1981, there were approximately 85,991,896 Conoco shares outstanding. Petitioner is essentially arguing that because it acquired approximately 32 percent of these shares for cash pursuant to its own tender offer, and DuPont acquired approximately 46 percent of these shares for cash pursuant to its tender offer, the combined 78 percent of Conoco shares acquired for cash after the date of the Agreement destroyed the continuity of interest requisite for a valid reorganization. We think petitioner's argument, and the logic that supports it, miss the mark.

* * *

The parties stipulated that petitioner and DuPont, through their wholly owned subsidiaries, were acting independently of one another and pursuant to competing tender offers. Furthermore, there is of course nothing in the record to suggest any prearranged understanding between petitioner and DuPont that petitioner would tender the Conoco stock purchased for cash if petitioner by means of its own tender offer failed to achieve control of Conoco. Consequently, it cannot be argued that petitioner, although not a party to the reorganization, was somehow acting in concert with DuPont, which was a party to the reorganization. If such had been the case, the reorganization would fail because petitioner's cash purchases of Conoco stock could be attributed to DuPont, thereby destroying continuity.

* * *

Respondent points out, correctly we believe, that the concept of continuity of interest advocated by petitioner would go far toward eliminating the possibility of a tax-free reorganization of any corporation whose stock is actively traded. Because it would be impossible to track the large volume of third party transactions in the target's stock, all completed transactions would be suspect. Sales of target stock for cash after the date of the announcement of an acquisition can neither be predicted nor controlled by publicly held parties to a reorganization. A requirement that the identity of the acquired corporation's shareholders be tracked to assume a sufficient number of "historic" shareholders to satisfy some arbitrary minimal percentage receiving the acquiring corporation's stock would be completely unrealistic.

Such a mandate to look only to historic shareholder identity to determine continuity was rejected by the Supreme Court in Helvering v. Alabama Asphaltic Limestone Co., 315 U.S. 179 (1942). In *Alabama Asphaltic*, unsecured noteholders of an insolvent corporation commenced a bankruptcy proceeding against the corporation. The noteholders bought the corporate assets from the trustee and transferred them to a newly formed corporation in exchange for its stock. In discussing these facts, the Supreme Court stated:

> When the equity owners are excluded and the old creditors become the stockholders of the new corporation, it conforms to realities to date their equity ownership from the time when they invoked the processes of the law to enforce their rights of full priority. At that time they stepped into the shoes of the old stockholders. The sale "did nothing but recognize officially what had before been true in fact." * * *
>
> * * *
>
> Some contention, however, is made that this transaction did not meet the statutory standard because the properties acquired by the new corporation belonged at that time to the committee and not to the old corporation. That is true. Yet, the separate steps were integrated parts of a single scheme. Transitory phases of an arrangement frequently are disregarded under these sections of the revenue acts where they add nothing of substance to the completed affair. Gregory v. Helvering, 293 U.S. 465; Helvering v. Bashford, 302 U.S. 454. Here they were no more than intermediate procedural devices utilized to enable the new corporation to acquire all the assets of the old one pursuant to a single reorganization plan. * * *

In reaching this conclusion, the Supreme Court upheld the finding of a valid "A" reorganization by this Court. * * *

In the "integrated" transaction before us petitioner, not DuPont, "stepped into the shoes" of 32 percent of the Conoco shareholders when petitioner acquired their stock for cash via the JES competing tender offer, held the 32 percent transitorily, and immediately tendered it in exchange for DuPont stock. For present purposes, there is no material distinction between petitioner's tender of the Conoco stock and a direct tender by the "old" Conoco shareholders themselves. Thus, the requirement of continuity of interest has been met.

* * *

For the reasons stated in this Opinion, we hold that a loss cannot be recognized by petitioner on its exchange of Conoco stock for DuPont stock, made pursuant to the DuPont–Conoco plan of reorganization. * * *

NOTE

The Historic Shareholder Concept After Seagram. The *Seagram* decision raises several questions about the role of the historic shareholder doctrine in applying the continuity of interest doctrine. In an earlier case,[1] the Tax Court concluded that continuity of interest "must be measured by looking to all the pre-tender offer shareholders" and "held that the sale for cash by more than 80 percent of those shareholders was sufficient to prevent the merger of T into P from meeting the quantitative test" of continuity of interest. Isn't that the very same argument that Seagram made to support recognition of its loss? Wasn't Seagram arguing that the DuPont–Conoco merger failed as a reorganization because 78 percent of the historic Conoco shareholders received cash for their stock?

Perhaps the cases can be reconciled by remembering that the attempts by Seagram and DuPont to acquire Conoco were independent of one another. Would it be reasonable to conclude that Seagram's purchase of Conoco stock was "old and cold" for purposes of the DuPont–Conoco merger, so that it was an "historic" shareholder for purposes of that transaction? Is that what the court meant when it said Seagram "stepped into the shoes" of the Conoco shareholders that it bought out?

Or was the Tax Court concerned with the practical effects of its decision in *Seagram* on the world of corporate acquisitions? It noted the difficulty of tracking third-party transactions and the absence of any control by publicly held corporations over their shareholders as practical considerations supporting its decision. The decision offers tax practitioners some interesting planning options. For example, assume Target Corporation ("T") is owned 60 percent by shareholder A and 40 percent by shareholder B, and Acquiring Corporation ("P") wishes to acquire T in a tax-free merger. Before *Seagram*, it was thought that P could not achieve its goal if A wished to cash out of T. Under *Seagram*, however, if A can find an independent third-party purchaser who is willing to buy A's T stock for cash and who eventually becomes a P shareholder after the merger, each of the party's business and tax objectives may be satisfied with careful planning.[2]

The Historic Shareholder Concept: In Memoriam? The Tax Court's decision in *Seagram* represented a significant erosion of the historic shareholder concept. Regulations issued in 1998 appear to go even further by eliminating the relevance of historic T shareholders except in limited situations. Following *Seagram*, the regulations provide that a "mere disposition" of T stock prior to a potential reorganization to buyers unrelated to T or P will be disregarded in applying the continuity of interest doctrine.[3] To illustrate, assume that A, an individual, owns 100 percent of the stock of

1. Kass v. Commissioner, 60 T.C. 218 (1973).

2. See Bloom, "Taxpayers Have More Planning Flexibility in Reorganizations After *Seagram*—If It Survives," 82 J.Tax'n 334 (1995), for a discussion of this and other post-*Seagram* strategies. See also Willens, "Some Observations on the Tax Court's *Seagram* Decision," 66 Tax Notes 1465 (1995).

3. Reg. § 1.368–1(e)(1)(i).

T, Inc. (value—$100), and T plans to merge into P, Inc. Shortly before the merger is consummated, B, who is unrelated to T or P, purchases all of A's T stock for $100 cash, and then B exchanges her T stock for $50 of P stock and $50 cash furnished by P. Under the regulations, A's sale is disregarded and the continuity of interest requirement is met because B's T stock was exchanged for a sufficient amount of P stock (50 percent of total consideration) to preserve a substantial part of the value of the proprietary interest in T.[4]

Relationship of Continuity of Interest Doctrine to Taxable Stock Acquisitions. The tax-free reorganization rules often overlap with other provisions in Subchapter C. One potential jurisdictional conflict is between the treatment of a qualified stock purchase (e.g., P's purchase of 80 percent or more of T stock) as defined in Section 338 and an acquisitive reorganization. The Service has issued regulations addressing the tax consequences of the transfer of T's assets to P or an affiliate of P following a qualified stock purchase where P does not make a Section 338 election.[5] They provide that the T stock acquired by P in the qualified stock purchase will count for continuity of interest purposes if T later transfers its assets to a P subsidiary ("S"), enabling the second step of the transaction to qualify as a tax-free acquisitive reorganization.[6] As a result, T does not recognize gain on the transfer of its assets, which will take a transferred basis in S's hands.[7]

These regulations reverse the holding in Yoc Heating v. Commissioner,[8] a much discussed old Tax Court case where P bought 85 percent of T's stock for cash and notes and, as part of the same transaction, T subsequently transferred its assets to S, a newly formed P subsidiary and then dissolved. P received additional S stock in exchange for its T stock, and the T minority shareholders received cash in exchange for their T stock. The Tax Court viewed P's purchase of T stock and the subsequent T asset transfer to S as an integrated transaction in which P acquired all of T's assets for cash and notes. Consequently, it held that there was insufficient continuity of interest to qualify the asset transfer as a Section 368 reorganization because the historic shareholders of T did not receive any P stock. The upshot was that S received a cost basis in the T assets rather than the transferred basis it would have taken if the acquisition had qualified as a reorganization. Because the *General Utilities* doctrine was still alive at the

4. Reg. § 1.368–1(e)(6) Example 1(ii). Continuity may not be preserved, however, when the consideration received by A prior to or in connection with the reorganization is in a cash redemption of A's T stock (this usually is a problem only when P furnishes the cash) or if B cashes out the P stock received in the merger in a redemption. See Reg. § 1.368–1(e)(ii),–1(e)(6) Example (5) & (9).

5. Reg. § 1.338–3(d)(1). See Chapter 16C2, supra.

6. Reg. § 1.338–3(d)(2). Similarly, P is treated as a historic T shareholder for purposes of determining whether, immediately after the transfer of T assets, a T shareholder is in "control" of the corporation to which the assets are transferred for purposes of Section 368(a)(1)(D). Reg. § 1.338–3(d)(3). See Section C2 of this chapter, infra.

7. Reg. § 1.338–3(d)(5) Example (iii).

8. 61 T.C. 168 (1973).

time of this transaction, T did not recognize any corporate-level gain or loss as a result of the court's decision.

The Section 338 regulations take the position that the result in *Yoc Heating* is inconsistent with the policy of Section 338, which was intended to preempt the subjective *Kimbell–Diamond* doctrine.[9] The regulations also provide that the operative reorganization provisions applicable to shareholders of the target corporation in an acquisitive reorganization do not apply to minority shareholders of T unless the transfer of T assets is pursuant to a reorganization under generally applicable tax rules without regard to the regulations.[10] To illustrate, assume P buys 85 percent of the stock of T for cash from shareholder A and does not make a Section 338 election. The remaining 15 percent of T is owned by Mrs. K. Shortly thereafter, as part of the same plan, T merges into S, a 100 percent subsidiary of P, and Mrs. K receives P (or S) stock in exchange for her T stock. Under the regulations, the continuity of interest requirement is not met in determining the tax consequences to Mrs. K, who thus recognizes gain or loss with respect to the exchange of her T stock.[11] Why? How can a transaction qualify as a reorganization for some purposes (T's transfer of its assets) but not for others (Mrs. K's exchange of her T stock)?

d. POST–ACQUISITION CONTINUITY

Another aspect of the continuity of interest doctrine relates to the length of time that the target shareholders must hold their stock in the acquiring corporation. For example, assume T merges into P in a tax-free reorganization in which the only consideration is P stock, but shareholders who hold 80 percent of the T stock are legally committed at the time of the merger to sell their P stock to a third party. Does the prearranged sale disqualify the merger as a Type A reorganization because the continuity of interest test is not met. The selling T shareholders will be taxed in either event, of course, although the timing of their gain may be affected if the merger and subsequent stock sale occur in different taxable years, but what about the 20 percent who retain their P stock? And what are the appropriate tax consequences to the target and acquiring corporations?

The Service has never required T's shareholders to maintain continuity of interest in P for any particular period of time after an acquisitive reorganization. But in determining if the continuity of interest requirement has been satisfied, the Service for many years considered sales and other dispositions of stock occurring subsequent to a merger which are part of the same overall "plan."[12] The courts disagreed over whether a pre-merger intent to sell (without any binding commitment) would defeat continuity of interest.[13]

9. See Chapter 16C1, supra.

10. Reg. § 1.338–3(d)(5) Example (v). See also Kass v. Commissioner, supra note 1.

11. Id. See also Reg. § 1.368–1(e)(6) Example 4(ii).

12. Rev. Proc. 77–37, 1977–2 C.B. 568.

13. See, e.g., McDonald's Restaurants of Illinois, Inc. v. Commissioner, 688 F.2d 520 (7th Cir.1982), rev'g 76 T.C. 972 (1981), where the Tax Court treated a post-merger

The regulations resolve the issue by providing that subsequent dispositions of P stock received in a potential reorganization by former T shareholders generally will be disregarded in determining whether the continuity of shareholder interest requirement is met, even if the dispositions were pursuant to a preexisting binding contract.[14] This is consistent with the Service's current position that the continuity of interest requirement is satisfied if a substantial part of the value of the proprietary interest in T is preserved through an exchange for a proprietary interest (i.e., stock) of P. But if the facts demonstrate that T shareholders have sold their P stock for cash to P or a related party (e.g., a P subsidiary) before or after the acquisition, the continuity of interest requirement may not be satisfied.[15] For example, if P reacquired stock that it issued in the reorganization from T shareholders in exchange for cash, the reacquisition would be considered in determining if the continuity of interest requirement was satisfied. But sales of P stock by former T shareholders to outsiders would be ignored, even if the sales were pursuant to a binding commitment entered into prior to the reorganization.[16]

Revenue Ruling 99–58, which follows, is another illustration of the Service's new tolerance toward post-acquisition continuity issues.

Revenue Ruling 99–58

1999–2 Cum. Bull. 701.

ISSUE

What is the effect on continuity of interest when a potential reorganization is followed by an open market reacquisition of P's stock?

FACTS

T merges into P, a corporation whose stock is widely held, and is publicly and actively traded. P has one class of common stock authorized and outstanding. In the merger, T shareholders receive 50 percent common stock of P and 50 percent cash. Viewed in isolation, the exchange would satisfy the continuity of interest requirement of § 1.368–1(e) of the Income Tax Regulations. However, in an effort to prevent dilution resulting from the issuance of P shares in the merger, P's preexisting stock repurchase program is modified to enable P to reacquire a number of its shares equal to the number issued in the acquisition of T. The number of shares repurchased will not exceed the total number of P shares issued and outstanding prior to the merger. The repurchases are made following the

sale of P stock by former T shareholders as a separate transaction because the shareholders were not contractually bound to sell, but the Seventh Circuit found that a pre-merger intent to sell was sufficient to invoke the step transaction doctrine and cause the merger to lack continuity of interest. See also Penrod v. Commissioner, 88 T.C. 1415 (1987) (no binding commitment or pre-merger intent to sell; continuity of interest test satisfied).

14. Reg. § 1.368–1(e)(1)(i), –1(e)(6) Example 1(i).

15. Reg. § 1.368–1(e)(1)(ii), –1(c)(2).

16. See Reg. § 1.368–1(e)(6) Example (4)(i).

merger, on the open market, through a broker for the prevailing market price. P's intention to repurchase shares was announced prior to the T merger, but the repurchase program was not a matter negotiated with T or the T shareholders. There was not an understanding between the T shareholders and P that the T shareholders' ownership of P stock would be transitory. Because of the mechanics of an open market purchase, P does not know the identity of a seller of P stock, nor does a former T shareholder who receives P stock in the merger and subsequently sells it know whether P is the buyer. Without regard to the repurchase program, a market exists for the newly-issued P stock held by the former T shareholders. During the time P undertakes its repurchase program, there are sales of P stock on the open market, which may include sales of P shares by former T shareholders.

LAW AND ANALYSIS

Requisite to a reorganization under the Internal Revenue Code is a continuity of interest as described in § 1.368–1(e). Section 1.368–1(b). The general purpose of the continuity of interest requirement is "to prevent transactions that resemble sales from qualifying for nonrecognition of gain or loss available to corporate reorganizations." Section 1.368–1(e)(1)(i). To achieve this purpose, the regulation provides that a proprietary interest in the target corporation is not preserved to the extent that, "in connection with the potential reorganization, . . . stock of the issuing corporation furnished in exchange for a proprietary interest in the target corporation in the potential reorganization is redeemed." Id. However, for purposes of the continuity requirement, "a mere disposition of stock of the issuing corporation received in the potential reorganization to persons not related . . . to the issuing corporation is disregarded." Id. The regulation provides that all facts and circumstances will be considered in determining whether, in substance, a proprietary interest in the target corporation is preserved.

Under the facts set forth above, continuity of interest is satisfied. There was not an understanding between the T shareholders and P that the T shareholders' ownership of the P shares would be transitory. Further, because of the mechanics of an open market repurchase, the repurchase program does not favor participation by the former T shareholders. Therefore, even if it could be established that P has repurchased P shares from former T shareholders in the repurchase program, any such purchase would be coincidental. The merger and the stock repurchase together in substance would not resemble a sale of T stock to P by the former T shareholders and, thus, the repurchase would not be treated as "in connection with" the merger. Under the facts presented, a sale of P stock on the open market by a former T shareholder during the repurchase program will have the same effect on continuity of interest as a mere disposition to persons not related to P.

HOLDING

Under the facts presented, the open market repurchase of shares through a broker has no effect on continuity of interest in the potential reorganization.

e. CONTINUITY OF BUSINESS ENTERPRISE

Bentsen v. Phinney

United States District Court, Southern District of Texas, 1961.
199 F.Supp. 363.

■ GARZA, DISTRICT JUDGE.

[Rio Development Company was a Texas corporation engaged in the land development business along with two other corporations. All three corporations were controlled by the Bentsen family. The three corporations transferred all their assets, subject to liabilities, to a newly formed life insurance company. The transferor corporations then liquidated, and their shareholders became shareholders of the new insurance company. The parties stipulated that there was a business purpose for the transaction.

After failing to obtain an advance ruling from the Service that their exchange of stock in the land development companies for stock in the insurance company was a tax-free transaction, the taxpayers reported a taxable gain and then took the necessary procedural steps to file a refund suit in federal district court. The taxpayers contended that the transaction qualified as a reorganization, while the Service argued that it failed to meet the requirements of Section 368 because of a lack of continuity of business enterprise. Ed.]

The question for the Court to decide is: Was such corporate transaction a corporate "reorganization", as the term "reorganization" is defined in Section 368(a)(1), Internal Revenue Code of 1954, 26 U.S.C.A. § 368(a)(1), even though Rio Development Company engaged in the land development business and thereafter the new Insurance Company engaged in the insurance business?

The plaintiff taxpayers contend there was a corporate reorganization. The Government, Defendant in this cause, maintains that there was not a corporate reorganization under Section 368(a)(1) of the Internal Revenue Code of 1954, because there was not a continuity of business enterprise before and after the reorganization; and that this is a prerequisite as set out in the Treasury Regulations.

This case is governed by the Internal Revenue Code of 1954, 26 U.S.C., the applicable sections of which provide:

> "§ 368. Definitions relating to corporate reorganizations
>
> "(a) Reorganization.—
>
> "(1) In General.—For purposes of parts I and II and this part, the term 'reorganization' means—
>
> * * *
>
> "(C) the acquisition by one corporation, in exchange solely for all or a part of its voting stock (or in exchange solely for all or a part of the voting stock of a corporation which is in control of the acquiring corporation), of substantially all of the properties of

another corporation, but in determining whether the exchange is solely for stock the assumption by the acquiring corporation of a liability of the other, or the fact that property acquired is subject to a liability, shall be disregarded;

"(D) a transfer by a corporation of all or a part of its assets to another corporation if immediately after the transfer the transferor, or one or more of its shareholders (including persons who were shareholders immediately before the transfer), or any combination thereof, is in control of the corporation to which the assets are transferred; but only if, in pursuance of the plan, stock or securities of the corporation to which the assets are transferred are distributed in a transaction which qualifies under section 354, 355, or 356;"

"Sec. 354. Exchanges of stock and securities in certain reorganizations

"(a) General rule.—

"(1) In General.—No gain or loss shall be recognized if stock or securities in a corporation a party to a reorganization are, in pursuance of the plan of reorganization, exchanged solely for stock or securities in such corporation or in another corporation a party to the reorganization."

It is conceded that the 1939 Internal Revenue Code was the same in this respect as the 1954 Code, and that the corresponding Treasury Regulations issued under the 1939 Code are similar to the corresponding Treasury Regulations issued under the 1954 Code.

The Treasury Regulation states: "Requisite to a reorganization under the Code, are a continuity of business enterprise under the modified corporate form."

The Government contends that since there was a lack of "continuity of the business enterprise", there was not a reorganization as contemplated under the statutes.

The question for this Court to decide is the meaning of "continuity of business enterprise", and whether or not it exists in this case.

The Government takes the position that "continuity of business enterprise" means that the new corporation must engage in the same identical or similar business. Stated in another manner, the Government maintains it is necessary that there must be an identity of type of business before and after the reorganization.

The plaintiff taxpayers have cited to the Court the case of Becher v. Commissioner, 221 F.2d 252 (2d Cir.1955) affirming 22 T.C. 932 (1954), which the Government has tried to distinguish. In this case the taxpayer owned all the stock in a corporation engaged in the sponge rubber and canvass-product manufacturing business. The new corporation engaged in the business of manufacturing upholstered furniture. In that case, the Government took the position that there had been a reorganization and that a cash distribution to the shareholders of the old corporation was taxable as "boot" and was ordinary income to the shareholders. The Government prevailed in that case, and the Court, at 221 F.2d 252, 253, said:

> "* * * but the Tax Court here correctly held that a business purpose does not require an identity of business before and after the reorganization. * * *"

Other cases cited are Pebble Springs Distilling Co. v. Commissioner, 231 F.2d 288 (7th Cir.1956), cert. denied 352 U.S. 836, 77 S.Ct. 56, 1 L.Ed.2d 55 affirming 23 T.C. 196 (1954). There the old corporation had the power to carry on both a whiskey distilling business and a real estate business, but it engaged solely in the real estate business.

Another case cited to the Court is Morley Cypress Trust v. Commissioner, 3 T.C. 84 (1944). In that case the old corporation owned land held for timber and the land was conveyed to a new corporation engaged in the oil business.

The Government tries to distinguish these last two cases by saying that in the Pebble Springs Distilling Co. case the new corporation could engage in the whiskey distilling business if it had wanted to, and that in the Morley Cypress Trust case, after the problem of continuity of business enterprise had been presented, the required continuity could have been found because both the old and the new corporations were actively engaged in exploiting the natural resources of the same land.

The Government also contends that under Texas law an insurance company cannot engage in any business other than that of insurance.

The Morley Cypress Trust case cited above, this Court believes, is the case most like the case before the Court. In the Morley Cypress Trust case the land was held for timber. In this case it was held for development. In the Morley case land was conveyed to a new oil corporation for use in the oil business. In this case, land (plus proceeds from the sale of land) was conveyed to a new corporation to furnish the means to capitalize a new insurance business.

The Government contends that the corresponding Treasury Regulation issued under the 1939 Code was in existence when the 1954 Code was enacted and Congress did not see fit to make any changes; that Treasury Regulations have the force of law when the Code section which they interpret is reenacted after they have once been promulgated, and cites Roberts v. Commissioner, 9 Cir., 176 F.2d 221, 10 A.L.R.2d 186.

The Government has been unable to present the Court with any decision in which the meaning of "continuity of business enterprise" as used in the Treasury Regulations, has been interpreted. Since no Court had upheld the contention made by the Government as to the interpretation to be given said words in the Regulations, it is unfair to say that Congress had an opportunity to make a change in passing the 1954 Code. Congress was not apprised of the meaning that the Government wishes to give to said language in the Regulations, and therefore the rule expressed in Roberts v. Commissioner, supra, is not controlling here.

This Court finds that no court has passed on the question of whether "continuity of business enterprise", as used in the Regulations, means that the new corporation must engage in the identical type of business or a similar business; and it is, therefore, held that this Court is not bound by any Treasury Regulation since it is the province of the Court to decide whether the Treasury Regulation means what the Government contends it means; and whether or not if it means what the Government contends, said Regulation is one that could be promulgated under the appropriate sections of the Internal Revenue Code.

This Court finds that "continuity of business enterprise", as used in the Regulations, does not mean that the new corporation must engage in either the same type of business as the old or a similar business, for if this be the requirement, then said Regulation is without authority.

To qualify as a "reorganization" under the applicable statutes, the new corporation does not have to engage in an identical or similar type of business. All that is required is that there must be continuity of the business activity.

This Court therefore finds that there was a reorganization under the applicable sections of the Internal Revenue Code.

Under the facts stipulated in this case, it is found that there was a continuity of the business activity and all requisites having been complied with, the plaintiff taxpayers have a right to a refund of the income taxes paid on the exchange of stock. The amounts to be refunded by the Government are to be those as stated in the Stipulation.

Revenue Ruling 81–25

1981–1 Cum.Bull. 132.

ISSUE

For a transaction to qualify as a reorganization under section 368(a)(1) of the Internal Revenue Code of 1954, does the continuity of business enterprise requirement apply to the business or business assets of the acquiring (transferee) corporation prior to the reorganization?

LAW AND ANALYSIS

Section 1.368–1(b) of the Income Tax Regulations states that in order for a reorganization to qualify under section 368(a)(1) of the Code there must be continuity of the business enterprise under the modified corporate form.

Rev.Rul. 63–29, 1963–1 C.B. 77, holds that the continuity of business enterprise requirement of section 1.368–1(b) of the regulations was satisfied where a transferee corporation sold its assets and discontinued its business, then acquired the assets of another corporation in exchange for its voting stock, and used the sales proceeds realized from the sale of its assets to expand the business formerly conducted by the acquired corporation. The holding of Rev.Rul. 63–29 is now reflected in the recent amendment to section 1.368–1 (1.368–1(d)) of the regulations, which looks only to the transferor's historic business or historic business assets for determining if the continuity of business enterprise requirement is satisfied.

HOLDING

In a section 368(a)(1) reorganization the continuity of business enterprise requirement does not apply to the business or business assets of the transferee corporation prior to the reorganization.

* * *

NOTE

The continuity of business enterprise doctrine requires P either to continue T's historic business or to use a significant portion of T's historic business assets in a business.[1] This determination is based on all the facts and circumstances, applying the permissive regulations. For example, the continuity of business enterprise doctrine is satisfied in the acquisitive reorganization setting even if P transfers the acquired T assets or stock to controlled P subsidiaries, or in certain cases even to a partnership that is controlled by the P corporate group.[2] Numerous examples in the regulations illustrate how the doctrine is applied to various transactional structures.[3]

f. EXCHANGE OF NET VALUE REQUIREMENT

To prevent transactions that resemble sales from qualifying as tax-free reorganizations, regulations proposed in 2005 add an "exchange of net value" requirement, which primarily affects transactions involving insolvent corporations. These rules require both a surrender and a receipt of net value.[1] A target corporation surrenders net value in an asset transaction if the fair market value of the assets it transfers to the "issuing" (i.e., acquiring) corporation ("P") exceeds the sum of the T liabilities assumed by P and the amount of boot (cash and fair market value of other property) received by T.[2] The purpose of this rule is to ensure that T transfers property in exchange for at least some stock. T receives net value if the fair market value of P's assets exceed the amount of P's liabilities immediately

1. Reg. § 1.368–1(d)(1).

2. Reg. § 1.368–1(d)(4) & (5).

3. Reg. § 1.368–1(d)(5). For a rare case in which a transaction was found to fail the continuity of business enterprise requirement, see Honbarrier v. Commissioner, 115 T.C. 300 (2000), where the acquiring corporation did not continue the target's historic business or use a significant portion of its historic business assets in a business.

1. Prop. Reg. § 1.368–1(b)(1), –(f)(1). The net value requirement applies to all types of reorganizations, except Types E and F. Prop. Reg. § 1.368–1(b)(1).

2. Prop. Reg. § 1.368–1(f)(2)(i).

after the exchange.[3] This rule ensures that T receives stock having value. As a result, T's receipt of worthless stock in exchange for assets will not qualify as a reorganization.

2. TYPE B: ACQUISITIONS OF STOCK SOLELY FOR VOTING STOCK

Code: §§ 368(a)(1)(B), (c). Skim §§ 354(a); 358; 362(b); 368(a)(2)(C); (b); 1032(a).

Regulations: § 1.368–2(c).

In its simplest form, a Type B reorganization is P's acquisition of T stock solely in exchange for P voting stock (or the voting stock of P's parent) provided that P emerges from the transaction with "control" of T.[1] For this purpose, "control" is defined as ownership of 80 percent or more of T's voting power and 80 percent or more of the total number of shares of each class of T's nonvoting stock.[2] When the smoke clears, T remains as a controlled subsidiary of P. A transaction that otherwise qualifies as a B reorganization is not disqualified if P transfers all or part of the T stock it acquires to a controlled subsidiary of P.[3]

Solely for Voting Stock Requirement. P voting stock is the only permissible form of consideration in a Type B reorganization. With a few minor exceptions discussed below, the use of even an insignificant amount of nonvoting stock, debt, or cash will disqualify the transaction. As the courts of appeals have consistently held, albeit with considerably more verbiage,[4] there can be "no boot in a B." But the nagging policy question remains: why should the requirements for a stock-for-stock acquisition be so strict when the acquiring corporation in other types of acquisitive reorganization has the leeway to use from 20 to 50 percent nonequity consideration?

The rigid requirements for a B reorganization have placed considerable pressure on the definition of "voting stock." Although the term is not specifically defined in the Code, "voting stock" has been interpreted to require an unconditional right to vote on regular corporate decisions (election of directors, shareholder proposals, etc.) and not merely extraordinary events such as mergers or liquidations.[5] The class of stock transferred is immaterial provided that it has voting rights. Although the Supreme Court has long held that hybrid equity securities, such as warrants to purchase additional voting stock, do not constitute voting stock, contractual rights to receive additional voting stock may qualify.[6]

3. Prop. Reg. § 1.368–1(f)(2)(ii). These rules are modified for stock acquisitions to reflect the fact that T remains in existence.

1. I.R.C. § 368(a)(1)(B).

2. I.R.C. § 368(c).

3. I.R.C. § 368(a)(2)(C).

4. See, e.g., Chapman v. Commissioner, 618 F.2d 856 (1st Cir.1980) and Heverly v. Commissioner, 621 F.2d 1227 (3d Cir.1980), each rev'g Reeves v. Commissioner, 71 T.C. 727 (1979). In *Reeves*, a decision that has proven to be an aberration, the Tax Court had held that there could be some boot in a B as long as P acquired at least 80 percent of T stock for P voting stock in one transaction.

5. Cf. Reg. § 1.302–3(a).

6. Helvering v. Southwest Consolidated Corp., 315 U.S. 194, 62 S.Ct. 546 (1942); Rev.Rul. 66–112, 1966–1 C.B. 68.

The Service has allowed the parties to a B reorganization some flexibility despite the stringency of the voting stock requirement. For example, the "solely" requirement is not violated if the acquiring corporation issues cash in lieu of fractional shares.[7] The acquiring corporation also may pay the target corporation's expenses (e.g., registration fees, legal and accounting fees and other administrative costs) related to the reorganization, but payment of legal, accounting or other expenses of the target's shareholders will constitute forbidden boot.[8] Certain preferred stock with debt-like characteristics, labelled by Section 351(g) as "nonqualified preferred stock,"[9] is treated as boot for gain recognition purposes but remains "stock" for all other purposes until the regulations are modified and provide to the contrary. Thus, the receipt by target shareholders of nonqualified preferred stock with voting rights (an unlikely occurrence) should not disqualify a transaction as a Type B reorganization, but T shareholders would recognize realized gain to the extent of the value of any nonqualified preferred stock received in exchange for their T stock.[10]

Buying Out Dissenting Shareholders. A particular challenge in planning a B reorganization involves shareholders of the target who insist on receiving cash. If the acquiring corporation pays cash directly to these dissenters, the transaction will violate the solely for voting stock requirement and all the target's shareholders must recognize gain. But the Service permits the target to redeem the shares of dissenters prior to a valid B reorganization provided that the cash does not emanate from the acquiring corporation and continuity of interest requirements are satisfied.[11] Another possible approach might be for the transaction to proceed as a stock-for-stock exchange, followed by a later redemption of the acquiring corporation stock held by the dissenters.[12] If they were truly dissenters, however, one would assume they would have sought some assurance, albeit informal, that the later redemption would occur. In that event, the redemption likely would be part of the original reorganization plan and, if so, the entire transaction would fail.

Creeping Acquisitions. The acquiring corporation is not required to *acquire* "control" of T in a Type B reorganization. It simply must emerge from the reorganization with control, as measured by the 80 percent benchmarks in Section 368(c). It thus is possible for a Type B reorganization to be the culmination of a series of acquisitions of T stock provided, of course, that only voting stock is used as consideration and any earlier acquisitions of T stock for cash, notes or other consideration were "old and cold"—i.e., unrelated to the final stock-for-stock exchange. Whether or not an earlier cash acquisition is unrelated is essentially a factual "step transaction" question. The regulations assume that acquisitions are related

7. Mills v. Commissioner, 39 T.C. 393 (1962), affirmed on other grounds, 331 F.2d 321 (5th Cir.1964); Rev.Rul. 66–365, 1966–2 C.B. 116.

8. Rev.Rul. 73–54, 1973–1 C.B. 187.

9. See Chapter 11B3, supra.

10. I.R.C. § 356(e).

11. Rev.Rul. 55–440, 1955–2 C.B. 226. See also Rev.Rul. 68–285, 1968–1 C.B. 147.

12. See Rev.Rul. 56–345, 1956–2 C.B. 206; Rev.Rul. 57–114, 1957–1 C.B. 122.

if they occur over a short time span (e.g., 12 months) but not if they are separated by very long interval (e.g., 16 years).[13] This leaves a vast middle ground of uncertainty.

Contingent Payments and Escrowed Stock Arrangements. During the negotiations over an acquisitive reorganization, the parties may disagree over the price to be paid for the target corporation. The acquiring corporation may contend that the target's earnings are unpredictable or that the value of the business is clouded by contingent liabilities. The target may counter by producing optimistic earnings projections. A common method of breaking this type of stalemate is through a contingent consideration agreement. The acquiring corporation may issue a specified amount of stock or securities and agree to issue additional shares under specified contingencies. For example, additional shares may be issued to the former target shareholders if the earnings of the target attain certain levels during a specified time period after the acquisition.

There are a variety of methods to handle the payment of contingent consideration. The parties simply may agree that additional shares will be issued on the happening of specified events. The acquiring corporation may issue negotiable certificates of contingent interest. Or the parties may take the formal step of transferring the additional shares to an escrow agent with instructions to issue the shares if certain future events occur.

At one time, the Service contended that contingent rights to acquire additional stock violated the "solely for voting stock" requirement for a Type B (and Type C) reorganization. This position was not sustained by the courts, however, and the Service now concedes that contingent consideration will not disqualify an acquisitive reorganization if certain conditions are met.[14] The Service has issued guidelines for approval of contingent and escrowed stock arrangements. The more important requirements for contingent consideration agreements are:[15] (1) to ensure compliance with the continuity of interest doctrine, only additional stock can be received; (2) the acquiring corporation must issue the stock within five years after the reorganization; (3) the arrangement must be based on a valid business reason, such as a valuation dispute; (4) there is a maximum number of contingent shares that can be issued; (5) at least 50 percent of the maximum number of shares of each class of stock must be issued in the initial distribution; (6) the contingent rights may be neither assignable nor readily marketable; and (7) the events triggering the issuance of additional stock are not within the control of the shareholders. Similar requirements are imposed where the acquiring corporation goes beyond merely promising to issue more stock and actually places the shares in escrow with an independent agent. In addition, escrowed stock must be shown as issued

13. Reg. § 1.368–2(c).

14. See, e.g., Hamrick v. Commissioner, 43 T.C. 21 (1964), acq.; Carlberg v. United States, 281 F.2d 507 (8th Cir.1960). The Service now agrees that contingent consideration is not boot but only if the contingent rights to additional shares are not negotiable. See Rev.Rul. 66–112, 1966–1 C.B. 68.

15. See Rev.Proc. 77–37, 1977–2 C.B. 568, amplified by Rev.Proc. 84–42, 1984–1 C.B. 521.

and outstanding on the acquiring corporation's financial statements, and the target shareholders must be entitled to any dividends paid on the stock and voting rights if, as is required in a Type B reorganization, the escrowed stock has voting rights.[16]

3. TYPE C: ACQUISITIONS OF ASSETS FOR VOTING STOCK

Code: § 368(a)(1)(C), (a)(2)(B), (a)(2)(G); Skim §§ 336(c); 354(a); 356(a); 357; 358(a); 361; 362(b); 368(a)(2)(C), (b); 381(a)(2); 1032(a).

Regulations: § 1.368–2(d).

General Requirements. Type C reorganizations are known as "practical mergers" because their end result is generally the same as a merger. The only difference may be the form of the transaction under local corporate law. In a statutory merger, all the assets and liabilities of the target are absorbed by the acquiring corporation automatically, while an asset acquisition technically requires a "transfer" of assets and liabilities under a negotiated agreement and does not necessarily require the target to sell all of its assets or to liquidate.[1]

Despite their similarities in form, it is far more difficult to qualify as a Type C stock-for-assets exchange than as a Type A statutory merger because of the more stringent consideration requirements. Section 368(a)(1)(C) requires the target to transfer "substantially all" of its properties *solely* in exchange for voting stock of the acquiring corporation. Although "voting stock" has the same meaning for both B and C reorganizations, the term "solely" in Section 368(a)(1)(C) is subject to two important exceptions. First, the assumption of liabilities by the acquiring corporation (or the taking of property subject to liabilities) is not treated as disqualifying boot.[2] Second, a "boot relaxation rule" permits the acquiring corporation to use up to 20 percent boot, but for this purpose the transferred liabilities are considered as cash consideration.[3] A transaction thus can qualify as a Type C reorganization when the consideration consists of a substantial amount of debt relief as long as no other boot is used and sufficient voting stock is transferred to maintain continuity of interest. But a combination of debt relief and other boot likely will spell doom for the transaction.

To illustrate the operation of these rules, assume that Target ("T") has gross assets of $120,000 and liabilities of $30,000. Acquiring Corporation ("A") proposes to acquire all of T's assets in exchange for the assumption of $30,000 of liabilities and $90,000 of A voting stock. The transaction qualifies as a C reorganization because the liabilities are not treated as boot. But if A assumes the $30,000 of liabilities and transfers $80,000 of voting stock and $10,000 of cash, the transaction does not

16. Rev.Proc. 84–42, supra note 15.

1. See, e.g., Cal.Corp.Code § 1100; Del. Code Ann. title 8, § 251 (1979). A liquidation of the target is required in a Type C reorganization, however, unless the Commissioner waives the requirement. I.R.C. § 368(a)(2)(G)(ii).

2. I.R.C. § 368(a)(1)(C).

3. I.R.C. § 368(a)(2)(B).

qualify. The liabilities are treated as "money paid" for purposes of the boot relaxation rule, and thus A has acquired only 66⅔ percent of the $120,000 gross assets of T for voting stock. On these facts, A must use at least $96,000 of voting stock (80 percent of $120,000) in order for the transaction to qualify as a Type C reorganization under the boot relaxation rule. This example illustrates that in the normal situation where T's liabilities exceed 20 percent of the value of its gross assets, no boot may be used.

Substantially All of the Properties. The target also must transfer "substantially all" of its properties. The Service's longstanding administrative benchmark requires a transfer of "assets representing at least 90 percent of the fair market value of the net assets and at least 70 percent of the fair market value of the gross assets held by the target corporation immediately preceding the transfer."[4] These guidelines further provide that "all payments to dissenters and all redemptions and distributions (except for regular, normal distributions) made by the corporation immediately preceding the transfer and which are part of the plan of reorganization will be considered as assets held by the corporation immediately prior to the transfer."[5] Other authorities are not as stringent in defining "substantially all," and it is possible that a complete transfer of *operating* assets may qualify even if the Service's percentage tests are not met.[6] Moreover, the Service has ruled that the "substantially all" test is met when the target corporation sells 50 percent of its historic assets to unrelated parties for cash and then transfers all of its assets, including the sales proceeds, to the acquiring corporation.[7] The key to this favorable ruling is that the overall transaction is not "divisive" because the cash proceeds from the asset sale were not retained by the target or its shareholders.

Liquidation Requirement. Prior to 1984, the target corporation in a C reorganization was not required to distribute its assets (which ordinarily will consist primarily of voting stock of the acquiring corporation) in complete liquidation. Some targets chose to stay alive as a holding company with a fresh set of tax attributes.[8] Others opted to distribute the voting stock acquired in the reorganization while retaining other assets that might trigger adverse tax consequences (e.g., a dividend) if distributed to the shareholders.[9] To prevent these and other perceived abuses, Congress added a new rule requiring the target to distribute all of its assets pursuant to the plan of reorganization unless the Service, pursuant to regulations that it has yet to issue, agrees to waive the distribution requirement.[10] In

4. Rev.Proc. 77–37, § 3.01 1977–2 C.B. 568, 569.

5. Id.

6. See, e.g., Rev.Rul. 57–518, 1957–2 C.B. 253 (nonoperating assets, such as cash, retained to pay liabilities); Commissioner v. First National Bank of Altoona, 104 F.2d 865 (3d Cir.1939) (86% of net worth is "substantially all").

7. Rev. Rul. 88–48, 1988–1 C.B. 117.

8. The tax attributes (e.g., earnings and profits) of the target automatically pass to the acquiring corporation on a Type C reorganization. I.R.C. § 381(a)(2).

9. See Rev.Rul. 73–552, 1973–2 C.B. 116.

10. I.R.C. § 368(a)(2)(G). See Rev.Proc. 89–50, 1989–2 C.B. 631, for representations which ordinarily must be included in a request for the Service to waive the liquidation requirement.

the event of a waiver, however, the legislative history states that the retained assets must be treated as if they had been distributed to the T shareholders and recontributed to the capital of a new corporation.[11]

Creeping Acquisitions. A final issue is the treatment of a transaction where the acquiring corporation has previously purchased some stock of the target and now seeks to assume complete control by acquiring all of T's assets through a liquidation of T. We have seen that a creeping acquisition will not necessarily poison the final stock-for-stock exchange in a B reorganization, at least if the stock previously acquired for cash is "old and cold"—i.e., acquired in an unrelated transaction. For many years, creeping C reorganizations were impeded by the Service's wooden interpretation of the "solely for voting stock" requirement.[12] This longstanding position has been reversed by regulations providing that P's prior ownership of a portion of T stock will not by itself prevent the "solely for voting stock" requirement from being met.[13] The Service finally came to its senses and concluded that a transaction in which P converts an indirect interest in T's assets to a direct interest does not necessarily resemble a taxable sale by T of those properties.

To enforce the statutory continuity of interest rules, the regulations provide that where the Section 368(a)(2)(B) boot relaxation rule applies to the final step of a creeping Type C reorganization, the sum of: (1) the money or other boot distributed to T shareholders other than P and to T's creditors, and (2) the liabilities of T assumed by P, may not exceed 20 percent of the value of all of T's properties.[14] But if P acquires T stock from a shareholder of T or T itself for cash or boot as part of the acquisition, such consideration is counted as boot in applying the boot relaxation rule.[15] To illustrate, assume that in an unrelated transaction P acquired 60 percent of the stock of T for cash. T's assets have a value of $110, and it has $10 of liabilities. Assume T transfers all its assets to P and, in exchange, P assumes the liabilities and transfers to T $30 of P voting stock and $10 of cash, and then T distributes the P voting stock and cash to its shareholders (other than P) and liquidates. This transaction will qualify as a Type C reorganization because the sum of cash paid and liabilities assumed ($20) does not exceed 20 percent of the value of T's assets.[16] If, however, P's cash acquisition of 60 percent of T was not "old and cold"—i.e., was related to the subsequent asset acquisition—the transaction would

11. H.R.Rep. No. 98–861, 98th Cong., 2d Sess. 846 (1984).

12. Rev. Rul. 54–396, 1954–2 C.B. 147 (P, which owned 79 percent of S as result of prior unrelated cash purchase, acquired T's assets in exchange for P voting stock, after which T liquidated and distributed P stock to minority shareholders. The transaction was ruled not to qualify as a Type C reorganization because P acquired only 21 percent of T's assets for voting stock and the remaining 79 percent as a liquidating distribution in exchange for previously held T stock). The Service's position was sustained in Bausch & Lomb Optical Co. v. Commissioner, 267 F.2d 75 (2d Cir.1959).

13. Reg. § 1.368–2(d)(4)(i).

14. Id.

15. Id.

16. Reg. § 1.368–2(d)(4)(ii) Example 1.

not qualify as tax-free because only 30 percent of the consideration used by P was voting stock.[17]

4. TRIANGULAR REORGANIZATIONS*

Code: § 368(a)(1)(B) (first parenthetical) and (C) (first parenthetical), (a)(2)(C), (D) and (E), (b).

Regulations: § 1.368–2(b)(2), (f), (j)(1), (3)–(6).

Background. The three basic types of reorganizations offer limited flexibility if the acquiring corporation desires to operate the target as a wholly owned subsidiary. Assume, for example, that P, Inc. wishes to acquire T, Inc. and keep T's business in a separate corporation for nontax reasons. Although this objective could be met by a Type B reorganization, the stringent "solely for voting stock" requirement might be an insurmountable obstacle if P desired to use nonvoting stock as consideration or if a large number of T shareholders were unwilling to accept any class of P stock. Even the flexible A reorganization may not be feasible from a nontax standpoint. P may not wish to incur the risk of T's unknown or contingent liabilities which would remain P's responsibility even if T's assets were dropped down to a subsidiary. P also may be reluctant to bear the expense and delay of seeking formal approval of its shareholders or unwilling to provide T shareholders with the appraisal rights to which they would be entitled under state law on a direct merger.

To maneuver around these problems, corporate lawyers developed other acquisition methods involving the use of a subsidiary. One approach is for P to acquire T's assets in a qualifying Type A or C reorganization and immediately drop down the acquired assets to a newly created subsidiary. This technique does not solve the hidden liability problem, however, and it may not obviate the need for shareholder approval and appraisal rights.[1] An alternative is for P to transfer its stock to a new subsidiary ("S"), and then cause T to merge directly into S, with the T shareholders receiving P stock and, perhaps, other consideration in exchange for their T stock. Or P could form S and have S acquire substantially all of the assets of T in exchange for P voting stock.

The tax consequences of these and other triangular acquisition techniques have been a major subplot within the reorganization drama. In two early cases, the Supreme Court constructed several large roadblocks by holding that transactions similar to those described above failed to satisfy the continuity of interest doctrine if: (1) T merges into S but T sharehold-

17. Reg. § 1.368–2(d)(4)(ii) Example 2.

* For the early history, see generally Ferguson & Ginsburg, "Triangular Reorganizations," 28 Tax L.Rev. 159 (1973).

1. "Drop downs" also are inconvenient because they usually require an inordinate amount of paperwork (e.g., deeds and other documents of transfer, with accompanying recording fees and transfer taxes) as the assets pass from the parent to the subsidiary.

ers receive P stock in a triangular reorganization, or (2) P makes the acquisition using P stock but drops T or its assets down to a subsidiary.[2]

Over the years, Congress gradually came to recognize that there was no reason to deny tax-free status to "drop downs" or triangular reorganizations that were economically equivalent to the simpler acquisition methods authorized by Section 368. In the 1954 Code, it added Section 368(a)(2)(C), which provides that an otherwise qualifying Type A or C reorganization will not lose its tax-free status merely because the acquiring corporation drops down the acquired assets to a subsidiary and it later added a similar rule for Type B reorganizations. Congress also permitted the acquiring corporation in a B or C reorganization to use voting stock of its parent to make the acquisition. For both drop downs and triangular reorganizations, Section 368(b) now makes it clear that the controlling parent will be a "party" to the reorganization. But the Service persisted in ruling that a merger of the target into a controlled subsidiary of the acquiring corporation was not tax-free when the target shareholders received stock of the parent because the parent was not a "party" to the reorganization and the T shareholder lacked continuity of interest.[3] Once again, Congress responded by adding two new categories of tax-free reorganizations: the Section 368(a)(2)(D) forward triangular merger and the Section 368(a)(2)(E) reverse triangular merger.

Forward Triangular Mergers: Section 368(a)(2)(D). From the time it was authorized as a tax-free reorganization in 1969, the forward triangular merger has become one of the most widely used acquisition techniques. Section 368(a)(2)(D) permits S to acquire T in a statutory merger, using P stock as consideration, provided that: (1) S acquires "substantially all" of the properties of T; (2) no stock of S is used in the transaction; and (3) the transaction would have qualified as a Type A reorganization if T had merged directly into P. In typically perverse fashion, Congress—without expressly articulating its rationale—reached into its bag of requirements and borrowed one from the Type C model ("substantially all of the properties") and another from the Type A model (the tests for permissible consideration). Although the legislative history is obscure, it is now clear that the "could have merged with parent" test merely requires the transaction to pass muster under the continuity of interest doctrine.[4] As a result, T shareholders only must receive at least 50 percent P stock (voting or nonvoting) under the Service's continuity guidelines, allowing the parties the freedom to use up to 50 percent cash and other nonequity consideration. Of course, the T shareholders who receive boot must recognize their realized gain to that extent, but those who receive solely stock will enjoy nonrecognition if the overall transaction qualifies under these liberal standards.

2. Groman v. Commissioner, 302 U.S. 82, 58 S.Ct. 108 (1937); Helvering v. Bashford, 302 U.S. 454, 58 S.Ct. 307 (1938). These cases also suggested that in no event could the T shareholders receive stock in both S and P because the receipt of stock in two separate corporations violated continuity of interest requirements.

3. Rev.Rul. 67–448, 1967–2 C.B. 144.

4. Reg. § 1.368–2(b)(2).

Reverse Triangular Mergers: Section 368(a)(2)(E). Before examining the tax consequences of a reverse triangular merger, the transaction itself must be explained. Suppose P desires to acquire the stock of T in a tax-free reorganization and keep T alive as a subsidiary, but P is unable (or unwilling) to structure the deal as a Type B reorganization because of the "solely for voting stock" requirement. Neither a merger nor an asset acquisition is feasible because T, as a corporate entity, has a number of intangible assets (e.g., grandfather rights under state law; franchises or leases; favorable loan agreements) that would be jeopardized if T were dissolved or it would simply take longer or involve cumbersome regulatory hoops to structure the deal as a merger. One ingenious solution to this dilemma is for P to create S, contributing to it P voting stock, and then for S to merge into T under an agreement providing that T shareholders will receive P stock (and, possibly, other consideration) in exchange for their T stock. A variation on the theme, albeit a rare one, would be to use an existing subsidiary with ongoing business activities. In that event, the reverse merger would result in T's business being augmented by S's, all conducted under the same corporate roof. In either case, when the smoke clears P will own all the stock of T and S will disappear as a result of the merger.

Section 368(a)(2)(E) provides that this type of reverse merger will qualify as a tax-free reorganization if: (1) the surviving corporation (T) holds substantially all of the properties formerly held by both corporations (T and S), and (2) the former T shareholders exchange stock constituting "control" (measured by the 80 percent tests in Section 368(c)(1)) for P voting stock.[5] Once again, Congress borrowed from its bag of requirements and combined tests from Type A (merger), Type B (control) and Type C (substantially all of the properties) reorganizations. The reverse merger is thus less flexible for tax purposes than the forward triangular merger, perhaps reflecting its Type B origins. But there *can* be boot in an "(a)(2)(E)" reorganization; only 80 percent of the T stock must be acquired for P voting stock, and the rest may be obtained for cash or other property—or simply not acquired at all if P is willing to put up with minority shareholders.

Although Congress deserves applause for abandoning the formalisms of the old case law, its piecemeal approach to triangular reorganizations is yet another example of the major flaw in the reorganization scheme. In enacting Sections 368(a)(2)(D) and (E), each with its own distinct requirements, Congress added further embroidery to what already had become a crazy quilt. As the Senate Finance Committee staff lamented in its preliminary report on the reform and simplification of Subchapter C, many of the arcane distinctions in Section 368 "defy rationalization" and "[n]o discernible public policy would so sharply distinguish among the forms of an acquisition that are economically so similar."[6] Congress would be well

5. I.R.C. § 368(a)(2)(E)(ii). See Reg. § 1.368–2(j)(3)(ii).

6. See Staff of the Senate Finance Committee, Preliminary Report on the Reform

advised to move toward a system that would impose consistent requirements on economically equivalent acquisition techniques.[7]

5. MULTI-STEP ACQUISITIONS

Regulations: § 1.338(h)(10)–1T(c)(2).

We have seen that choosing the optimal structure for a corporate acquisition involves a wide range of legal and strategical considerations. From the buyer's perspective, important factors include determining the price to be paid for the target corporation and the mix of consideration to be used. Apart from taxes, other factors driving deal structure are the accounting treatment, regulatory hurdles, stock exchange rules, treatment of employer stock options, and timing, to name just a few.

For all these reasons, it may be desirable for the parties to an acquisition to employ a multi-step structure. For example, acquisitions of public companies may proceed at a quicker pace if the first step does not require regulatory clearance, consents from lenders or others with a contractual relationship to P or T, or actions that could impede the momentum of the deal. A good example of a two-step acquisition is when P makes a tender offer for T's stock at an attractive price and acquires sufficient stock to achieve control (but not 100 percent ownership) of T, enabling P to orchestrate a merger of T into P (or more likely into a P subsidiary), squeezing out the minority shareholders. The details of this and other deal structures are complex and beyond the scope of this text. Our concern here is to what extent the federal tax laws have accommodated the multi-step acquisition phenomenon.

The two rulings below are a reflection of the Service's willingness to apply the step transaction doctrine to multi-step acquisitions.[1] This often results in qualifying the integrated transaction as a tax-free reorganization where the separate steps, if viewed in isolation, would not qualify.

Revenue Ruling 2001–26

2001–1 Cum Bull. 1297.

ISSUE

On the facts described below, is the control-for-voting-stock requirement of § 368(a)(2)(E) of the Internal Revenue Code satisfied, so that a

and Simplification of the Income Taxation of Corporations, 98th Cong., 1st Sess., 26–27, 55–66 (Comm.Print S. 98–95, 1983).

7. See Staff of the Senate Finance Committee: The Subchapter C Revision Act of 1985, A Final Report Prepared by the Staff, 99th Cong., 1st Sess. (S.Prt. 99–47, 1985); Posin, "Taxing Corporate Reorganizations: Purging Penelope's Web," 133 U.Penn.L.Rev. 1335 (1985).

1. See also Rev. Rul. 2001–24, 2001–1 C.B. 1290 (following a forward triangular merger of T into S, a P subsidiary, P may drop down the S stock to another of its controlled subsidiaries); Rev. Rul. 2001–25, 2001–1 C.B. 1291 (following a reverse triangular merger of S, a transitory subsidiary of P, into T, T may sell 50 percent of its operating assets to an unrelated buyer without violating the "substantially all of its properties" requirement of Section 368(a)(2)(E) if it retains the sales proceeds).

series of integrated steps constitutes a tax-free reorganization under §§ 368(a)(1)(A) and 368(a)(2)(E) and § 354 or § 356 applies to each exchanging shareholder?

FACTS

Situation 1. Corporation P and Corporation T are widely held, manufacturing corporations organized under the laws of state A. T has only voting common stock outstanding, none of which is owned by P. P seeks to acquire all of the outstanding stock of T. For valid business reasons, the acquisition will be effected by a tender offer for at least 51 percent of the stock of T, to be acquired solely for P voting stock, followed by a merger of a subsidiary of P into T. P initiates a tender offer for T stock conditioned on the tender of at least 51 percent of the T shares. Pursuant to the tender offer, P acquires 51 percent of the T stock from T's shareholders for P voting stock. P forms S and S merges into T under the merger laws of state A. In the statutory merger, P's S stock is converted into T stock and each of the T shareholders holding the remaining 49 percent of the outstanding T stock exchanges its shares of T stock for a combination of consideration, two-thirds of which is P voting stock and one-third of which is cash. Assume that under general principles of tax law, including the step transaction doctrine, the tender offer and the statutory merger are treated as an integrated acquisition by P of all of the T stock. Also assume that all nonstatutory requirements for a reorganization under §§ 368(a)(1)(A) and 368(a)(2)(E) and all statutory requirements of § 368(a)(2)(E), other than the requirement under § 368(a)(2)(E)(ii) that P acquire control of T in exchange for its voting stock in the transaction, are satisfied.

Situation 2. The facts are the same as in Situation 1, except that S initiates the tender offer for T stock and, in the tender offer, acquires 51 percent of the T stock for P stock provided by P.

LAW AND ANALYSIS

Section 368(a)(1)(A) states that the term "reorganization" means a statutory merger or consolidation. Section 368(a)(2)(E) provides that a transaction otherwise qualifying under § 368(a)(1)(A) will not be disqualified by reason of the fact that stock of a corporation (the "controlling corporation") that before the merger was in control of the merged corporation is used in the transaction, if (1) after the transaction, the corporation surviving the merger holds substantially all of its properties and of the properties of the merged corporation (other than stock of the controlling corporation distributed in the transaction), and (2) in the transaction, former shareholders of the surviving corporation exchanged, for an amount of voting stock of the controlling corporation, an amount of stock in the surviving corporation that constitutes control of such corporation (the "control-for-voting-stock requirement"). For this purpose, control is defined in § 368(c).

In King Enterprises, Inc. v. United States, 418 F.2d 511 (Ct.Cl.1969), as part of an integrated plan, a corporation acquired all of the stock of a target corporation from the target corporation's shareholders for consideration, in excess of 50 percent of which was acquiring corporation stock, and subsequently merged the target corporation into the acquiring corporation. The court held that, because the merger was the intended result of the stock acquisition, the acquiring corporation's acquisition of the target corporation qualified as a reorganization under § 368(a)(1)(A).

Section 354(a)(1) provides that no gain or loss will be recognized if stock or securities in a corporation a party to a reorganization are, in pursuance of the plan of reorganization, exchanged solely for stock or securities in another corporation a party to the reorganization.

Section 356(a)(1) provides that, if § 354 would apply to the exchange except for the receipt of money or property other than stock or securities in a corporate party to the reorganization, the recipient shall recognize gain, but in an amount not in excess of the sum of the money and the fair market value of the other property.

Section 1.368–1(c) of the Income Tax Regulations provides that a plan of reorganization must contemplate the bona fide execution of one of the transactions specifically described as a reorganization in § 368(a) and the bona fide consummation of each of the requisite acts under which nonrecognition of gain is claimed. Section 1.368–2(g) provides that the term plan of reorganization is not to be construed as broadening the definition of reorganization as set forth in § 368(a), but is to be taken as limiting the nonrecognition of gain or loss to such exchanges or distributions as are directly a part of the transaction specifically described as a reorganization in § 368(a).

As assumed in the facts, under general principles of tax law, including the step transaction doctrine, the tender offer and the statutory merger in both Situations 1 and 2 are treated as an integrated acquisition by P of all of the T stock. The principles of King Enterprises support the conclusion that, because the tender offer is integrated with the statutory merger in both Situations 1 and 2, the tender offer exchange is treated as part of the statutory merger (hereinafter the "Transaction") for purposes of the reorganization provisions. Cf. J.E. Seagram Corp. v. Commissioner, 104 T.C. 75 (1995) (treating a tender offer that was an integrated step in a plan that included a forward triangular merger as part of the merger transaction). Consequently, the integrated steps, which result in P acquiring all of the stock of T, must be examined together to determine whether the requirements of § 368(a)(2)(E) are satisfied. Cf. § 1.368–2(j)(3)(i); § 1.368–2(j)(6), Ex. 3 (suggesting that, absent a special exception, steps that are prior to the merger, but are part of the transaction intended to qualify as a reorganization under §§ 368(a)(1)(A) and 368(a)(2)(E), should be considered for purposes of determining whether the control-for-voting-stock requirement is satisfied).

In both situations, in the Transaction, the shareholders of T exchange, for P voting stock, an amount of T stock constituting in excess of 80 percent of the voting stock of T. Therefore, the control-for-voting-stock requirement is satisfied. Accordingly, in both Situations 1 and 2, the

Transaction qualifies as a reorganization under §§ 368(a)(1)(A) and 368(a)(2)(E).

Under §§ 1.368–1(c) and 1.368–2(g), all of the T shareholders that exchange their T stock for P stock in the Transaction will be treated as exchanging their T stock for P stock in pursuance of a plan of reorganization. Therefore, T shareholders that exchange their T stock only for P stock in the Transaction will recognize no gain or loss under § 354. T shareholders that exchange their T stock for P stock and cash in the Transaction will recognize gain to the extent provided in § 356. In both Situations 1 and 2, none of P, S, or T will recognize any gain or loss in the Transaction, and P's basis in the T stock will be determined under § 1.358–6(c)(2) by treating P as acquiring all of the T stock in the Transaction and not acquiring any of the T stock before the Transaction.

HOLDING

On the facts set forth in Situations 1 and 2, the control-for-voting-stock requirement is satisfied in the Transaction, the Transaction constitutes a tax-free reorganization under §§ 368(a)(1)(A) and 368(a)(2)(E), and § 354 or § 356 applies to each exchanging shareholder.

Revenue Ruling 2001–46

2001–2 Cum. Bull. 321.

FACTS

Under the facts described below, what is the proper tax treatment if, pursuant to an integrated plan, a newly formed wholly owned subsidiary of an acquiring corporation merges into a target corporation, followed by the merger of the target corporation into the acquiring corporation?

Situation (1). Corporation X owns all the stock of Corporation Y, a newly formed wholly owned subsidiary. Pursuant to an integrated plan, X acquires all of the stock of Corporation T, an unrelated corporation, in a statutory merger of Y into T (the "Acquisition Merger"), with T surviving. In the Acquisition Merger, the T shareholders exchange their T stock for consideration, 70 percent of which is X voting stock and 30 percent of which is cash. Following the Acquisition Merger and as part of the plan, T merges into X in a statutory merger (the "Upstream Merger"). Assume that, absent some prohibition against the application of the step transaction doctrine, the step transaction doctrine would apply to treat the Acquisition Merger and the Upstream Merger as a single integrated acquisition by X of all the assets of T. Also assume that the single integrated transaction would satisfy the nonstatutory requirements of a reorganization under section 368(a) of the Internal Revenue Code.

Situation (2). The facts are the same as in Situation (1) except that in the Acquisition Merger the T shareholders receive solely X voting stock in exchange for their T stock, so that the Acquisition Merger, if viewed independently of the Upstream Merger, would qualify as a reorganization under section 368(a)(1)(A) by reason of section 368(a)(2)(E).

Section 338(a) provides that if a corporation makes a qualified stock purchase and makes an election under that section, then the target corporation (i) shall be treated as having sold all of its assets at the close of the acquisition date at fair market value and (ii) shall be treated as a new corporation which purchased all of its assets as of the beginning of the day after the acquisition date. Section 338(d)(3) defines a qualified stock purchase as any transaction or series of transactions in which stock (meeting the requirements of section 1504(a)(2)) of one corporation is acquired by another corporation by purchase during a 12–month acquisition period. Section 338(h)(3) defines a purchase generally as any acquisition of stock, but excludes acquisitions of stock in exchanges to which section 351, section 354, section 355, or section 356 applies.

Rev. Rul. 90–95 (1990–2 C.B. 67) (Situation 2), holds that the merger of a newly formed wholly owned domestic subsidiary into a target corporation with the target corporation shareholders receiving solely cash in exchange for their stock, immediately followed by the merger of the target corporation into the domestic parent of the merged subsidiary, will be treated as a qualified stock purchase of the target corporation followed by a section 332 liquidation of the target corporation. As a result, the parent's basis in the target corporation's assets will be the same as the basis of the assets in the target corporation's hands. The ruling explains that even though "the step-transaction doctrine is properly applied to disregard the existence of the [merged subsidiary]," so that the first step is treated as a stock purchase, the acquisition of the target corporation's stock is accorded independent significance from the subsequent liquidation of the target corporation and, therefore, is treated as a qualified stock purchase regardless of whether a section 338 election is made.

Section 1.338–3(d) of the Income Tax Regulations incorporates the approach of Rev. Rul. 90–95 into the regulations by requiring the purchasing corporation (or a member of its affiliated group) to treat certain asset transfers following a qualified stock purchase (where no section 338 election is made) independently of the qualified stock purchase. In the example in section 1.338–3(d)(5), the purchase for cash of 85 percent of the stock of a target corporation, followed by the merger of the target corporation into a wholly owned subsidiary of the purchasing corporation, is treated (other than by certain minority shareholders) as a qualified stock purchase of the stock of the target corporation followed by a section 368 reorganization of the target corporation into the subsidiary. As a result, the subsidiary's basis in the target corporation's assets is the same as the basis of the assets in the target corporation's hands.

Section 368(a)(1)(A) defines the term "reorganization" as a statutory merger or consolidation. Section 368(a)(2)(E) provides that a transaction otherwise qualifying under section 368(a)(1)(A) shall not be disqualified by reason of the fact that stock of a corporation (controlling corporation), which before the merger was in control of the merged corporation, is used in the transaction if (i) after the transaction, the corporation surviving the merger holds substantially all of its properties and the properties of the merged corporation, and (ii) in the transaction, former shareholders of the surviving corporation exchange, for an amount of voting stock of the controlling corporation, an amount of stock in the surviving corporation which constitutes control of such corporation.

In Rev. Rul. 67–274 (1967–2 C.B. 141), Corporation Y acquires all of the stock of Corporation X in exchange for some of the voting stock of Y and, thereafter, X completely liquidates into Y. The ruling holds that because the two steps are parts of a plan of reorganization, they cannot be considered independently of each other. Thus, the steps do not qualify as a reorganization under section 368(a)(1)(B) followed by a liquidation under section 332, but instead qualify as an acquisition of X's assets in a reorganization under section 368(a)(1)(C).

Situation (1). Because of the amount of cash consideration paid to the T shareholders, the Acquisition Merger could not qualify as a reorganization under section 368(a)(1)(A) and section 368(a)(2)(E). If the Acquisition Merger and the Upstream Merger in Situation (1) were treated as separate from each other, as were the steps in Situation (2) of Rev. Rul. 90–95, the Acquisition Merger would be treated as a stock acquisition that is a qualified stock purchase, because the stock is not acquired in a section 354 or section 356 exchange. The Upstream Merger would qualify as a liquidation under section 332.Œ

However, if the approach reflected in Rev. Rul. 67–274 were applied to Situation (1), the transaction would be treated as an integrated acquisition of T's assets by X in a single statutory merger (without a preliminary stock acquisition). Accordingly, unless the policies underlying section 338 dictate otherwise, the integrated asset acquisition in Situation (1) is properly treated as a statutory merger of T into X that qualifies as a reorganization under section 368(a)(1)(A). See King Enterprises, Inc. v. United States, 418 F.2d 511 (Ct.Cl.1969) in a case that predated section 338, the court applied the step transaction doctrine to treat the acquisition of the stock of a target corporation followed by the merger of the target corporation into the acquiring corporation as a reorganization under section 368(a)(1)(A); J.E. Seagram Corp. v. Commissioner, 104 T.C. 75 (1995) (same). Therefore, it is necessary to determine whether the approach reflected in Rev. Rul. 90–95 applies where the step transaction doctrine would otherwise apply to treat the transaction as an asset acquisition that qualifies as a reorganization under section 368(a).

Rev. Rul. 90–95 and section 1.338–3(d) reject the approach reflected in Rev. Rul. 67–274 where the application of that approach would treat the purchase of a target corporation's stock without a section 338 election followed by the liquidation or merger of the target corporation as the purchase of the target corporation's assets resulting in a cost basis in the assets under section 1012. The rejection of step integration in Rev. Rul. 90–95 and section 1.338–3(d) is based on Congressional intent that section 338 "replace any nonstatutory treatment of a stock purchase as an asset purchase under the Kimbell–Diamond doctrine." H.R. Rep. No. 760, 97th Cong., 2d Sess. 536 (1982), 1982–2 C.B. 600, 632. (In Kimbell–Diamond Milling Co. v. Commissioner, * * *, the court held that the purchase of the stock of a target corporation for the purpose of obtaining its assets through a prompt liquidation should be treated by the purchaser as a purchase of the target corporation's assets with the purchaser receiving a cost basis in the assets.)

Rev. Rul. 90–95 and section 1.338–3(d) treat the acquisition of the stock of the target corporation as a qualified stock purchase followed by a separate carryover basis transaction in order to preclude any nonstatutory treatment of the steps as an integrated asset purchase. The policy underlying section 338 is not violated by treating Situation (1) as a single statutory merger of T into X because such treatment results in a transaction that qualifies as a reorganization under section 368(a)(1)(A) in which X acquires the assets of T with a carryover basis under section 362, and does not result in a cost basis for those assets under section 1012. Thus, in Situation (1), the step transaction doctrine applies to treat the Acquisition Merger and the Upstream Merger not as a stock acquisition that is a qualified stock purchase followed by a section 332 liquidation, but instead as an acquisition of T's assets through a single statutory merger of T into X that qualifies as a reorganization under section 368(a)(1)(A). Accordingly, a section 338 election may not be made in such a situation.

Situation (2). Situation (2) differs from Situation (1) only in that the Acquisition Merger, if viewed independently of the Upstream Merger, would qualify as a reorganization under section 368(a)(1)(A) by reason of section 368(a)(2)(E). This difference does not change the result from that in Situation (1). The transaction is treated as a single statutory merger of T into X that qualifies as a reorganization under section 368(a)(1)(A) without regard to section 368(a)(2)(E).

HOLDING

Under the facts presented, if, pursuant to an integrated plan, a newly formed wholly owned subsidiary of an acquiring corporation merges into a target corporation, followed by the merger of the target corporation into the acquiring corporation, the transaction is treated as a single statutory merger of the target corporation into the acquiring corporation that qualifies as a reorganization under section 368(a)(1)(A).

* * *

EFFECT ON OTHER DOCUMENTS

Rev. Rul. 67–274 is amplified and Rev. Rul. 90–95 is distinguished.

NOTE

Experienced tax professionals have come to understand that "the step-transaction doctrine generally applies . . . except when it doesn't."[1] What

1. See Stratton, "Step–Transaction Doctrine Tested Under Corporate Rulings," 93 Tax Notes 332 (Oct. 15, 2001), quoting an I.R.S. official who was quoting an unnamed law professor.

factors in the two rulings above supported application of the doctrine? Was it because the first step was conditioned on the second occurring? Does Revenue Ruling 2001–26 offer any guiding principle for application of the doctrine, or does it simply assume for purposes of analysis that the tender offer and merger should be integrated?

A critical point made in Revenue Ruling 2001–46 is that application of the step transaction doctrine was permissible because it did not violate the policy of Section 338. What policy? Does that suggest that the step transaction doctrine should not be applied to the prototype *Kimbell–Diamond* transaction where P purchases 80 percent or more of T's stock and promptly liquidates T, winding up with direct ownership of its assets? If the step transaction doctrine did apply to this fact pattern, P would take a cost basis in T's assets even though no Section 338 election was made—a result clearly at variance with the policy of Section 338.

What if the first step is a qualified stock purchase under Section 338, and P and S (T's corporate parent) jointly make a Section 338(h)(10) election? In that situation, should the first step be viewed in isolation for tax purposes or should step transaction principles be applied, resulting in reorganization treatment and nullification of the Section 338 election? What if T is not a subsidiary and P unilaterally makes a Section 338 election?[2]

The Service has issued regulations answering some of these questions. They provide that the step transaction doctrine will not apply to a multi-step acquisition if the first step is a qualified stock purchase under Section 338 and the parties to the transaction make a joint Section 338(h)(10) election with respect to that step, whether or not the overall transaction would have qualified as a reorganization.[3] To illustrate, assume that P, Inc. owns all the stock of Y, Inc., a newly formed subsidiary, and S, Inc. owns all the stock of T, Inc. As the first step in P's acquisition of T's assets, Y, Inc. merges into T, with T surviving, and S (T's only shareholder) receives 50 percent P voting stock and 50 percent cash. This step, viewed independently, does not qualify as a reorganization and does constitute a qualified stock purchase. T then merges into P. If P and S do not make a Section 338(h)(10) election, the step transaction doctrine would be applied under the principles of Revenue Ruling 2001–46, and the overall acquisition would be treated as a Section 368 reorganization. But if P and S jointly make a Section 338(h)(10) election, the regulations "turn off" the step transaction doctrine and treat P's acquisition of the T stock in the reverse merger as a qualified stock purchase, causing "old T" to recognize gain or loss on the deemed sale of its assets and "new T"—and then P, after the

2. For some analysis of these and other ramifications of Revenue Ruling 2001–46, see Fowler, "Practical Transactional Aspects of Rev. Rul. 2001–46," 93 Tax Notes 963 (Nov. 12, 2001); Ginsburg & Levin, "Integrated Corporate Acquisitions: Comments on Rev. Rul. 2001–46," 93 Tax Notes 553 (Oct. 22, 2001).

3. Reg. § 1.338(h)(10)–1(c)(2).

merger into P—to take a cost basis in its assets.[4] If, however, the first step does not constitute a qualified stock purchase under Section 338(d)(3)—such as in Situation 2 of Revenue Ruling 2001–46 where the first step, viewed independently, was a section 368 reorganization—then no Section 338(h)(10) election can be made and the overall acquisition will be treated as a reorganization.[5] The regulations do not address a situation where a unilateral Section 338 election is made by the acquiring corporation with respect to the first step.

PROBLEMS

1. Publishing Company, Inc. ("P") is a publicly traded C corporation engaged in the publication of professional textbooks. P has 5 million shares of voting common stock outstanding. The stock is currently trading at $10 per share.

P wishes to acquire control of Target Press, Inc. ("T"), a closely held corporation that is the leading publisher of student study aids for law students. T has 4,000 shares of common stock (its only class) outstanding, held by 10 shareholders each of whom owns 400 shares. T's assets and liabilities are as follows:

Asset	**Adj. Basis**	**Fair Mkt. Value**
Cash	$ 600,000	$ 600,000
Inventory	200,000	1,000,000
Equipment	800,000	1,400,000
Goodwill	0	2,000,000
	$1,600,000	$5,000,000
Liabilities		
Bank Loan		$1,000,000
		$1,000,000

Both P and T have substantial accumulated earnings and profits.

T's board of directors has agreed to sell the business for $4 million. Four of T's shareholders have a very low adjusted basis in their stock and wish to minimize their taxable gain on a sale. One shareholder, Dee Minimis, recently inherited her stock and would not have any significant realized gain. The other shareholders are interested in diversifying their investments and less concerned about the tax liability on a sale.

P does not wish to dilute the interests of its current shareholders by issuing too much voting common stock to acquire T, but P is willing to use a mix of consideration (including newly issued preferred stock) and to assume T's $1,000,000 bank loan. For business reasons, P ultimately wishes to operate T's business through a wholly-owned subsidiary and would prefer to avoid exposure to any unknown T liabilities. Assume that

4. Reg. § 1.338(h)(10)–1(e) Examples 11 and 12.

5. Reg. § 1.338(h)(10)–1(e) Example 14.

any preferred stock used by P to make the acquisition is not "nonqualified preferred stock" within the meaning of Section 351(g).

Various plans are under consideration to complete the acquisition. Consider generally the tax consequences of each of the alternative plans described below, focusing on whether the acquisition will qualify as a tax-free reorganization. Then propose one or more desirable alternatives that are compatible with the objectives of the parties. Unless otherwise indicated, assume in all cases that the consideration to be exchanged for stock or assets of T is valued as of the date that the contract was legally binding.

(a) T merges directly into P, and each T shareholder receives $300,000 of P nonvoting preferred stock and $100,000 of P five-year notes.

(b) Same as (a), above, except four T shareholders (holding 40% of the T stock) each receives $400,000 of P voting common stock and the other six T shareholders each receives $400,000 cash.

(c) Same as (b), above, except that the value of the P stock declined between the time the merger agreement was signed and four months later, when the merger was finalized and, as a result, the four T shareholders holding 40% of the T stock receive only $250,000 of P voting stock.

(d) T merges directly into P, and each T shareholder receives $400,000 of P voting common stock. Pursuant to a binding commitment entered into prior to the merger, six of the former T shareholders (who held 60% of the T stock) sell their new P stock for cash to a third party three weeks after the merger.

(e) Same as (a), above, except shortly after the merger and as part of its original plan, P sells T's assets to an unrelated party at a nice profit and uses the sales proceeds to expand its professional textbook business.

(f) In exchange for their respective 400 shares of T stock, P transfers to each T shareholder $360,000 of P voting preferred stock and $40,000 cash.

(g) P purchases 400 shares of T stock from Dee Minimis for $400,000 cash. Three months later, P transfers $400,000 of P voting preferred stock to each of the nine remaining T shareholders in exchange for their respective 400 shares of T stock.

(h) P acquires all the T assets, and assumes the $1,000,000 liability, in exchange for $3.6 million of P voting common stock (360,000 shares) and $400,000 in P five-year notes. Immediately thereafter, T completely liquidates, distributing the P shares and notes pro rata to its shareholders. P drops down the assets it acquires to S, a newly created subsidiary.

(i) Same as (h), above, except that T retains $400,000 of its cash, P acquires the balance of T's assets, and assumes the liability, for $3.6 million of P voting common stock, and T distributes the P shares and cash pro rata to its shareholders in complete liquidation.

(j) P acquires all the T stock in a reverse triangular merger in which Y–1, a transitory subsidiary of P, merges into T. In the merger, four

T shareholders (holding 40% of the T stock) each receive $400,000 cash and the other six T shareholders each receive $400,000 of P nonvoting preferred stock. T then merges upstream into P.

(k) Same as (j), above, except the second step in the transaction is a merger of T into Y–2, a subsidiary of P.

(l) Same as (k) above, except T is a wholly owned subsidiary of S, Inc. Y–1 merges into T and, in the merger, S, Inc. receives $500,000 cash and $500,000 of P nonvoting stock. P and S jointly make an election under § 338(h)(10).

2. Assume the same basic facts as in Problem 1, above, except that P purchased 10% of T's stock five years ago for cash, and purchased an additional 50% of T's stock one year ago for cash. P now wishes to acquire the remaining 40% of T's stock for P voting stock or, if possible, P nonvoting preferred stock. The T minority shareholders are willing to engage in the transaction if they can avoid recognition of taxable gain. Advise the parties on the best method for structuring the acquisition as a tax-free reorganization.

3. Are the results reached in Problems 1–2, above, rational as a matter of tax policy? Would it be preferable to have uniform tax rules governing all corporate acquisitions?

6. TREATMENT OF THE PARTIES TO AN ACQUISITIVE REORGANIZATION

Up to this point, we have been concentrating on the definition of a reorganization in Section 368. Compliance with those statutory requirements and the judicial doctrines unlocks the gate to the operative provisions, which govern the tax treatment of the target shareholders and corporations that are "a party to a reorganization" and provide for transferred and exchanged bases, tacked holding periods and the carryover of corporate tax attributes such as net operating losses. Section 368(b) broadly defines "a party to a reorganization" to include any corporation resulting from a qualifying reorganization (e.g., the surviving corporation in a consolidation), the acquiring and target corporations in a straight acquisitive reorganization and the parent corporation in a "drop down" or triangular reorganization.

This section summarizes the operative provisions, beginning with the tax consequences to the target's shareholders and security holders and then turning to the treatment of the target and acquiring corporations.

a. CONSEQUENCES TO SHAREHOLDERS AND SECURITY HOLDERS

Code: §§ 354(a); 356(a), (c), (d), (e); 358(a), (b), (d), (f); 368(b). Skim §§ 351(g); 356(a).

Regulations: §§ 1.354–1(a), (b), (d) Example (3), (e); 1.356–1, –3, –4; 1.358–1, –2(a)(1), (a)(2)(i); 1.368–2(f), (g).

Recognition of Gain or Loss. One of the principal benefits of reorganization status is the nonrecognition granted to the shareholders and security holders of the target corporation under Section 354(a). Shareholders are entitled to complete nonrecognition only when they receive solely stock or securities of the acquiring corporation.[1] This invariably occurs in a Type B reorganization, but the target shareholders in a Type A, C or any form of triangular reorganization may receive some boot. In that event, the shareholder must recognize any realized gain to the extent of the money plus the fair market value of any other boot received.[2] For this purpose, boot includes any property other than stock or securities of a party to the reorganization. To prevent a bailout through the use of securities,[3] Section 356(d) provides that if the principal amount of securities received exceeds the principal amount of securities surrendered or if securities are received but none are surrendered, the fair market value of the excess is treated as boot.[4] Consequently, a shareholder holding no securities who receives bonds in connection with a reorganization is treated as having "cashed out" his investment to the extent of the bonds—an appropriate result under the continuity of interest principle. But security holders who change their investment to an equity interest or exchange securities for the same or lesser principal amount have not engaged in a bailout and therefore are entitled to nonrecognition treatment. As might be expected, however, a shareholder or security holder who receives boot may not recognize any realized loss.[5]

Characterization of Gain. Section 356(a)(2) provides that any recognized gain is treated as a dividend to a target shareholder if the exchange "has the effect of the distribution of a dividend." In that event, each T shareholder must treat as a dividend the amount of his recognized gain that is not in excess of that shareholder's ratable share of the corporation's accumulated earnings and profits.[6] Any remaining gain is treated as gain from the sale or exchange of the target stock or securities transferred.

The "boot dividend" issue has been one of the most difficult questions arising under the operative provisions. The Service once contended that dividend treatment was automatic if boot were received,[7] but it later conceded that dividend equivalence should be determined by using the tests applicable to stock redemptions in Section 302(b),[8] treating the boot as if it

1. I.R.C. § 354(a)(1).

2. I.R.C. § 356(a)(1).

3. "Securities" are generally defined to encompass relatively long-term corporate debt instruments but not short-term notes, stock rights or warrants.

4. See I.R.C. § 354(a)(2)(A).

5. I.R.C. § 356(c).

6. Note that the gain is not automatically characterized as ordinary income but, if it has the effect of a dividend, it is treated as a Section 301 distribution subject to the Section 243 dividends received deduction. See Rev.Rul. 72–327 at p. 770, infra. In addition, the earnings and profits of the target corporation are reduced under Section 312(a).

7. See Commissioner v. Bedford's Estate, 325 U.S. 283, 65 S.Ct. 1157 (1945).

8. In applying Section 302(b) principles, the Section 318 attribution rules are applicable. I.R.C. § 356(a)(2). Rev.Rul. 74–515,

were received as a distribution in redemption of the *target* corporation's stock immediately prior to the reorganization exchange.[9] Taxpayers argued, however, that dividend equivalence should be determined by examining the effect of the reorganization exchange as a whole, an approach that ultimately was adopted by the Supreme Court in Commissioner v. Clark.[10] Under the *Clark* test, each T shareholder is treated as initially receiving only P stock instead of the combination of P stock and boot actually received, and then P is treated as having distributed the boot in a redemption of the portion of P stock not actually received by the T shareholder. If this hypothetical redemption meets one of the tests for exchange treatment in Section 302(b), the receipt of boot does not have the effect of a dividend, and the shareholder recognizes capital gain or loss. Otherwise, as previewed above, the recognized gain is a dividend (likely a qualified dividend eligible for the 15 percent maximum rate) to the extent of the shareholder's ratable share of "the corporation's"[11] accumulated earnings and profits, and any remaining gain is capital gain.

Whenever there is a meaningful rate preference for long-term capital gains and dividends are taxable as ordinary income at the highest marginal rates, individual taxpayers will benefit from the Supreme Court's holding in *Clark*.[12] Corporate shareholders, however, ordinarily prefer dividend classification in order to qualify for the dividends received deduction under Section 243.[13] Dividend treatment also may be preferable to the acquiring corporation because it reduces the earnings and profits that are inherited under Section 381 as a result of the reorganization. Finally, dividend classification may be undesirable where shareholders receiving notes from the acquiring corporation wish to report their gain on the installment method. Unless the target stock exchanged by the shareholder is publicly traded,[14] installment sale treatment generally is available if the transaction is treated as a sale but not if the receipt of installment boot is treated as a dividend under Section 356(a)(2).[15]

The boot dividend issue rarely is important to individual shareholders, however, now that dividends and long-term capital gains are taxed at the same preferential rate. Since any amount characterized as a dividend under Section 356(a)(2) may not exceed the shareholder's recognized gain, the shareholder is always entitled to recovery of basis. If the dividend is "qualified," the rate is the same unless the capital gain is short-term (or

1974–2 C.B. 118. See also Wright v. United States, 482 F.2d 600 (8th Cir.1973).

9. See, e.g., Shimberg v. United States, 577 F.2d 283 (5th Cir. 1978), cert. denied, 439 U.S. 1115, 99 S.Ct. 1019 (1979).

10. 489 U.S. 726, 109 S.Ct. 1455 (1989). See also Rev. Rul. 93–61, 1993–2 C.B. 118.

11. The statute is unclear, but the majority view appears to be that the dividend determination should be based on the target corporation's earnings and profits.

12. The Service, as it must, has announced that it will apply the *Clark* approach to an acquisitive reorganization. See Rev. Rul. 93–61, 1993–2 C.B. 118.

13. But see I.R.C. § 1059(e)(1)(B), which treats any amount treated as a dividend on a non pro rata redemption of a corporate shareholder's stock as an "extraordinary dividend." See Chapter 12F3, supra.

14. See I.R.C. § 453(k)(2).

15. See I.R.C. § 453(f)(6); Prop.Reg. § 1.453–1(f)(2).

the stock is not a capital asset), in which case dividend treatment is preferable. Corporate shareholders will continue to prefer dividend classification because of the dividends received deduction, and dividend treatment is preferable to the acquiring corporation because it reduces earnings and profits inherited from the target corporation on the reorganization.

Dividend Within Gain Approach: Policy Aspects. Section 356(a)(2) limits the amount of any boot dividend to the shareholder's recognized gain. This approach has been criticized as a "curious mixing of dividend and sale or exchange concepts" which "permits shareholders with a high basis in their stock * * * to withdraw corporate earnings in a reorganization without dividend consequences."[16] Allowing taxpayers to recover their basis even when a transaction is equivalent to a dividend is inconsistent with the rules applicable to stock redemptions in Section 302 and is difficult to justify.

Basis and Holding Period. Target shareholders determine the basis of nonrecognition property (i.e., the stock or nonboot securities received in the exchange) under Section 358 by reference to their basis in the stock that they relinquished, increased by any gain recognized and reduced by any boot received and liabilities assumed. Any boot (other than cash) received takes a fair market value basis under Section 358(a)(2). This is the same formula used many chapters ago in determining the basis of stock received in a Section 351 exchange. If different types of nonrecognition property are received (e.g., two classes of stock or stock and bonds), the aggregate exchanged basis is allocated among those properties in proportion to their relative fair market values under rules provided in the regulations.[17] The nonrecognition property generally takes a tacked holding period under Section 1223(1) and the holding period of the boot commences on the date of its acquisition.

The transferred basis rule in Section 358 is simple enough to apply when a target shareholder acquired all of her T stock at the same time. But it is not uncommon for a shareholder to have acquired T stock at different times, for different prices. When these multiple "tax lots" of T stock are exchanged in a tax-free reorganization for stock of the acquiring corporation, can T shareholders use the average basis in their T shares to determine the basis for all their new P stock or must they use an approach under which the basis of the P stock received is traced to the basis of the different blocks of T stock surrendered? And does it matter how the shares are held—e.g., in certificates that can be physically identified, or a brokerage account where separate lots may be more difficult or impossible to track?[18]

16. Staff of the Senate Committee on Finance, The Subchapter C Revision Act of 1985: A Final Report Prepared by the Staff, 99th Cong., 1st Sess. 45 (S.Prt. 99–47, 1985). See also Wolfman, "Subchapter C and the 100th Congress," 33 Tax Notes 669, 672 (Nov. 17, 1986).

17. I.R.C. § 358(a)(1); Reg. § 1.358–2(a)(2)(i).

18. Even without a reorganization, similar issues are raised when shares are sold by a taxpayer who acquired lots of that stock on different dates or at different prices. See, e.g., Reg. § 1.1012–1(c), providing that if the

From the standpoint of simplicity and administrative convenience, the average basis method has much to offer even when separate lots are easily identifiable. But to prevent potential tax avoidance and also allow taxpayers some flexibility, the Service has concluded that tracing is the preferable approach.[19] Under the regulations, the basis of the stock received in a reorganization transaction, to the greatest extent possible, must be an allocable portion of the basis of each block of stock surrendered.[20] For example, if a T shareholder exchanges more than one block of a single class of T stock acquired on different dates with different bases, the regulations require the basis of the shares surrendered to be allocated to the shares received in a manner that reflects, to the greatest extent possible, that a share of stock received is in respect of (i.e., traceable to) shares of stock acquired on the same date and at the same price.[21] If a T shareholder is unable to identify and trace the shares surrendered and received, he may designate which shares of of P stock are received in exchange for each block of T stock provided the designation is consistent with the terms of the transaction.[22]

The regulations illustrate the tracing approach in a basic fact pattern with this example of a Type A statutory merger where Corporation X is the target and Corporation Y is the acquiring corporation:[23]

> J, an individual, acquired 20 shares of Corporation X stock on Date 1 for $3 each and 10 shares of Corporation X stock on Date 2 for $6 each. On Date 3, Corporation Y acquires the assets of Corporation X in a reorganization under Section 368(a)(1)(A). Pursuant to the terms of the plan of reorganization, J receives 2 shares of Corporation Y stock for each share of Corporation X stock. Therefore, J receives 60 shares of Corporation Y stock. Pursuant to Section 354, J recognizes no gain or loss on the

shares sold cannot be adequately identified, the earliest of the lots acquired is deemed to be sold first. In the reorganization setting, the cases are inconsistent. Compare, e.g., Arrott v. Commissioner, 136 F.2d 449 (3d Cir. 1943) (average basis) and Bloch v. Commissioner, 148 F.2d 452 (9th Cir. 1945) (tracing permissible).

19. See generally Reg. § 1.358–2.

20. Reg. § 1.358–2(a)(2)(i). For simplicity, the discussion in the text is limited to exchanges of stock in acquisitive reorganizations. The regulations use a similar approach for reorganization exchanges of debt securities. If more than one class of stock or security of the target corporation is exchanged for multiple classes of the acquiring corporation, an additional layer of allocation is required. See, e.g., Reg. § 1.358–2(c) Example 3.

21. Reg. § 1.358–2(a)(2)(i). These regulations also address the more complex situation where stock and securities (e.g., bonds) are received.

22. Reg. § 1.358–2(a)(2)(vii). The designation must be made on or before the date when it is first relevant (e.g., at the time of a sale of the P stock received by the selling shareholder). If no designation is made at the time of a sale or transfer, the taxpayer is treated as selling or transferring the P shares received in respect of the earliest T shares purchased or acquired. Id.

23. Reg. § 1.358–2(c) Example 1. More complex fact patterns are analyzed in thirteen other increasingly mind-numbing examples but, not to worry—somewhere, a reputable company has designed portfolio management software to handle all these basis computations.

exchange. J is not able to identify which shares of Corporation Y stock are received for each share of Corporation X stock.

J has 40 shares of Corporation Y each of which has a basis of $1.50 and is treated as having been acquired on Date 1 and 20 shares of Corporation Y each of which has a basis of $3 and is treated as having been acquired on Date 2. On or before the date on which the basis of a share of Corporation Y stock received becomes relevant, J may designate which of the shares of Corporation Y stock have a basis of $1.50 and which have a basis of $3.

In reorganizations where T shareholders receive shares of stock or securities of more than one class, or boot is received in addition to stock or securities, and the terms of the exchange specify which shares of P stock or securities are received in exchange for a particular share (or class) of T stock or securities, the specification controls for basis purposes if the terms are "economically reasonable."[24] If there is no specification, a pro rata portion of the P stock and securities is treated as received in exchange for each share of T stock and securities surrendered, based on the fair market value of surrendered stock and securities.[25]

b. CONSEQUENCES TO THE TARGET CORPORATION

Code: §§ 336(c); 357(a), (b), (c)(1); 358(a), (b)(1), (f); 361.

Regulations: § 1.357–1(a).

Treatment of the Reorganization Exchange. Without a nonrecognition provision, the target corporation in an acquisitive reorganization would recognize gain or loss on the transfer of its assets and the assumption of its liabilities by the acquiring corporation. If the acquisition qualifies as a reorganization, however, Section 361(a) comes to the rescue by providing that the target recognizes no gain or loss if it exchanges property, pursuant to the reorganization plan, solely for stock or securities in a corporation which also is a party to the reorganization. Section 357(a) offers similar protection by providing that the assumption of the target's liabilities in a reorganization exchange will not be treated as boot nor prevent the exchange from being tax-free under Section 361(a).[1] These rules apply primarily to Type A and C reorganizations and forward triangular mergers. In a Type B stock-for-stock exchange or a reverse triangular merger, no assets are transferred because the target corporation remains intact as a controlled subsidiary of the acquiring corporation.

The target in a Type C reorganization may receive a limited amount of boot without disqualifying the transaction under Section 368.[2] In that

24. Reg. § 1.358–2(a)(2)(ii).

25. Id.

1. As in the Section 351 incorporation area, the general nonrecognition rule in Section 357(a) is subject to an exception in Section 357(b) if the liability assumption is motivated by tax avoidance or lacks a bona fide business purpose. The Section 357(c) exception for liabilities assumed in excess of the basis of the transferred assets only applies to a Type D reorganization.

2. I.R.C. § 368(a)(2)(B). Boot in a Type C reorganization would include any property other than stock or securities of the acquiring

event, the target must recognize any realized gain (but may not recognize loss) on the reorganization exchange to the extent of the cash and the fair market value of the boot that the target does not distribute pursuant to the plan of reorganization.[3] Any transfer by the target of cash or other boot received in the exchange to creditors in connection with the reorganization is treated as a "distribution" pursuant to the reorganization plan.[4] Since the target in a Type C reorganization is generally required to distribute all of its properties pursuant to the plan,[5] gain or loss rarely will be recognized on the exchange.[6]

Section 361(a) only applies to the *receipt* of boot by the target pursuant to the reorganization plan. An acquiring corporation that transfers appreciated boot property to the target as partial consideration for the target's assets must recognize gain under Section 1001 because, to that extent, the transaction is considered to be a taxable exchange.[7] In that event, the target takes the boot property with a fair market value basis.[8]

Treatment of Distributions. Section 361(c) generally provides that a corporation does not recognize gain or loss on the distribution of "qualified property" to its shareholders pursuant to a reorganization plan. "Qualified property" is: (1) stock (or rights to acquire stock) in, or obligations (e.g., bonds and notes) of the distributing corporation, or (2) stock (or rights to acquire stock) in, or obligations of, another party to the reorganization which were received by the distributing corporation in the exchange. Thus, any stock, securities or even short-term notes of the acquiring corporation received by the target in the exchange and then distributed to its shareholders would constitute "qualified property." Section 361(c)(3) makes it clear that a transfer of "qualified property" by a target to its creditors in satisfaction of corporate liabilities is treated as a "distribution" pursuant to the reorganization plan.

If the target distributes an asset other than qualified property, it must recognize gain (but may not recognize loss) in the same manner as if the property had been sold to the distributee at its fair market value.[9] For example, the target would recognize gain on the distribution of an appreciated retained asset (i.e., an asset not acquired in the reorganization) or boot (other than notes of the acquiring corporation) which appreciated between the time it was received and the distribution to shareholders.[10]

corporation (or its parent). See Section B3 of this Chapter, infra.

3. I.R.C. § 361(b)(1), (2).

4. I.R.C. § 361(b)(3). The Service may prescribe regulations as necessary to prevent tax avoidance through abuse of this rule. Id.

5. I.R.C. § 368(a)(2)(G).

6. A rare situation where gain might be recognized is where liabilities of the target are assumed in a transaction to which Section 357(b) or (c) applies.

7. Rev.Rul. 72–327 at p. 770, infra. Section 361(a) does not apply in this situation because it only provides nonrecognition to the *recipient* of distributed boot.

8. I.R.C. § 358(a)(2). See also I.R.C. § 358(f).

9. I.R.C. § 361(c)(1), (2).

10. Since the target takes a fair market value basis in the boot under Section 358(a)(2) at the time of the exchange, it would recognize only post-acquisition appreciation on a later distribution of the boot.

Sales Prior to Liquidation. Before liquidating, the target corporation in a Type C reorganization may sell some of the stock or securities received from the acquiring corporation in order to raise money to pay off creditors. Prior to the Tax Reform Act of 1986, the courts were divided over whether these sales were entitled to nonrecognition treatment.[11] The current version of Section 361 settles the debate by providing that only transfers of "qualified property" (i.e., stock or obligations of the acquiring corporation) or boot directly to creditors will qualify for nonrecognition because they are treated as "distributions" to the shareholders pursuant to the reorganization plan.[12] Sales of property to third parties are thus fully taxable events even if they were necessary to raise money to pay off creditors.

Basis and Holding Period. If the target corporation retains property received from the acquiring corporation, which only could occur in a Type C reorganization where the Commissioner waives the Section 368(a)(2)(G) distribution requirement, it is deemed to have distributed that property to its shareholders, who then are treated as having recontributed the property to a "new" corporation as a contribution to capital.[13] The basis and the holding period of the property in the hands of the "new" corporation depend upon the consequences to the shareholders. If the property is boot to the shareholders, it receives a fair market value basis and no tacked holding period in the hands of either the shareholders or the "new" corporation to which it is constructively recontributed.[14] If the property is nonrecognition property (e.g., stock or securities of the acquiring corporation) to the shareholders, then their exchanged bases and tacked holding periods transfer to the "new" corporation.[15] These rules are irrelevant in the typical Type C reorganization where the target liquidates and distributes the stock, securities and boot received in the transaction, along with any retained assets, to its shareholders. In that event, basis and holding period are determined under the operative provisions governing shareholders and security holders.[16]

c. CONSEQUENCES TO THE ACQUIRING CORPORATION

Code: §§ 362(b); 368(b); 1032. Skim § 362(e)(1).

Regulations: § 1.1032–1.

Recognition of Gain or Loss. The acquiring corporation does not recognize gain or loss on the issuance of its stock or the stock of its parent in an acquisitive reorganization or, for that matter, in any other transaction.[1] To the extent that it may issue securities as consideration for the

11. Compare General Housewares Corp. v. United States, 615 F.2d 1056 (5th Cir.1980) (allowing nonrecognition under former Section 337) with FEC Liquidating Corp. v. United States, 548 F.2d 924 (Ct.Cl.1977) (taxing such gains on the ground that former Section 337 and the reorganization provisions were conceptually incompatible).

12. I.R.C. § 361(b)(3), (c)(3).

13. H.R. Rep. No. 98–861, 98th Cong., 2d Sess. 845–846 (1984).

14. I.R.C. §§ 358(a)(2); 362(a).

15. I.R.C. §§ 358(a)(1); 362(a); 1223(1) and (2).

16. See page 761, supra.

1. I.R.C. § 1032(a). It was once feared that Section 1032 would not apply where a

acquired property, the acquiring corporation recognizes no gain because the acquisition is a "purchase." If the acquiring corporation transfers other "boot" property to make the acquisition, however, it recognizes any realized gain or loss under general tax principles.[2]

Basis and Holding Period: In General. Under Section 362(b), the target assets acquired in a Type A, Type C or forward triangular reorganization take a transferred basis, increased by any gain recognized by the target on the transfer. Since Section 361(a) generally provides that the target does not recognize gain or loss on any exchange of property pursuant to the plan of reorganization, an upward basis adjustment for gain recognized by the target will occur only in the rare Type C reorganization where the target receives boot and does not distribute it to its shareholders or creditors. In the case of a Type B or reverse triangular reorganization, however, the property acquired is corporate stock whose transferred basis is determined by its basis in the hands of the target shareholders.[3] In either case, the property acquired is allowed a tacked holding period under Section 1223(2).

Limit on Importation of Built-in Losses. The effect of the Section 362(b) transferred basis rule is to preserve not only built-in gains but also built-in losses when P acquires T's assets in a tax-free reorganization. This rule made it possible for U.S. corporations to engage in what became known as "basis shift" transactions with U.S. tax-indifferent parties, such as foreign corporations. The primary goal was to shift unrealized economic losses to U.S. taxpayers, who could then realize the losses and shelter their taxable income.

Section 362(e)(1) attempts to block basis-shift shelters by providing that if a net built-in loss is "imported" in a tax-free reorganization, the basis of such loss property in the hands of the transferee corporation is limited to its fair market value immediately after the transaction.[4] A net built-in loss is imported into the United States if the aggregate adjusted basis of the properties received by a domestic transferee corporation from a person not subject to U.S. tax exceeds the fair market value of the transferred properties.[5]

Basis of Target Stock Received in Triangular Reorganizations. Determining the acquiring parent corporation's basis in the stock of a subsidiary acquired in a reverse triangular reorganization raises a tantalizing technical question. Under Section 368(a)(2)(E), the acquiring corporation either

controlled subsidiary acquired property in exchange for its *parent's* stock. The Service has ruled, however, that the subsidiary does not recognize gain or loss in this situation, presumably because such an acquisition is economically indistinguishable from a direct acquisition by the parent followed by a drop down of the assets to the subsidiary. See Rev.Rul. 57–278, 1957–1 C.B. 124. Reg. § 1.1032–2(b).

2. See Rev.Rul. 72–327, at p. 770, infra.

3. See Rev.Proc. 81–70, 1981–2 C.B. 729, which provides an approach for determining this transferred basis when the large number of target shareholders makes precise determination of their bases impossible.

4. I.R.C. § 362(e)(1)(A). For a similar rule limiting the transfer of built-in losses in Section 351 transactions, see I.R.C. § 362(e)(2), discussed in Chapter 11A, infra.

5. I.R.C. § 362(e)(1)(B), (C).

may form a "phantom" subsidiary or use a preexisting operating subsidiary to merge into the target corporation. It ordinarily will transfer voting stock and possibly some boot to the subsidiary which then transfers that property to the target shareholders as the consideration for the acquisition.

In a straight Type B reorganization, the parent determines its basis in the target stock under Section 362(b) by reference to the stock bases of the former target shareholders. In the case of a reverse subsidiary merger, however, Section 358 would appear to require the acquiring corporation to take an exchanged basis—i.e., its basis in the target stock acquired would be the same as its basis in the stock of the disappearing subsidiary. That basis likely would be zero if a phantom subsidiary were used to effect the merger. A similar issue arises in the case of forward triangular merger, where the target merges into a subsidiary formed by the acquiring corporation immediately prior to the reorganization. Since the parent normally forms the subsidiary by transferring its own stock, in which it presumably has a zero basis, it would appear that the parent would retain a zero basis in the stock of the subsidiary even after it absorbs the target.

The Treasury has issued regulations that address the zero basis problem. Those regulations seek to conform the tax consequences of a triangular reorganization with those of a "drop down" transaction in which P acquires T's assets or stock directly and then drops them down to a subsidiary ("S") in a tax-free transaction. To illustrate the operation of the regulations in a forward triangular merger in which T merges into S, a newly formed P subsidiary, the regulations permit P to increase its basis in its S stock by the net basis (assets less liabilities) of T's assets.[6] In a simple transaction where P had no prior basis in its S stock, the net effect is that P's basis in its S stock and S's basis in the acquired T assets will be the same.

In a simple reverse triangular merger where newly formed S merges into T, which survives as a P subsidiary, P's basis in its T stock is adjusted by assuming that T had merged into S in a forward triangular merger, applying the rules discussed above.[7] Thus, in a wholly tax-free reverse merger where 100 percent of the T stock is acquired, P's basis in its T stock would equal T's net basis in its assets plus any preexisting basis that P had in its S stock.

Revenue Ruling 72–327

1972–2 Cum.Bull. 197.

Advice has been requested as to the Federal income tax consequences of the transaction described below:

6. Reg. § 1.358–6(c)(1).

7. Reg. § 1.358–6(c)(2). Additional rules are provided for more specialized situations, such as where S was a preexisting subsidiary, the consideration is mixed, or less than all of T's stock is acquired in a reverse merger. See Reg. § 1.358–6(c)(2)(i)(C), –6(c)(4).

On July 1, 1969, corporation *X* merged into corporation *Y* in a reorganization qualifying under section 368(a)(1)(A) of the Internal Revenue Code of 1954. Pursuant to the reorganization, *M* corporation, a stockholder of *X*, received, in exchange for its *X* stock, *Y* stock having a fair market value of 100*x* dollars plus other property having a fair market value of 40*x* dollars but an adjusted basis in the hands of *Y* of 10*x* dollars. *M* had a basis of 90*x* dollars in its stock of *X*. *M*'s ratable share of the undistributed earnings and profits of *X* accumulated after February 28, 1913, was 30*x* dollars. *M* realized gain of 50*x* dollars (140*x* dollars less 90*x* dollars) on the exchange. Of the 50*x* dollar gain, 40*x* dollars was recognized to *M* pursuant to section 356(a)(1) of the Code. Pursuant to section 356(a)(2) of the Code, 30*x* dollars was treated as a dividend and 10*x* dollars was treated as gain from the exchange of property.

The Federal income tax consequences of the above described transaction are as follows:

(1) The 30*x* dollar gain, treated as a dividend to *M* under section 356(a)(2) of the Code, is eligible for the corporate dividends received deduction provided by section 243(a) of the Code. *M*'s basis in the stock of *Y* is 90*x* dollars. Section 358(a)(1) of the Code. *M*'s basis in the other property received is 40*x* dollars, the fair market value thereof. Section 358(a)(2) of the Code.

(2) Pursuant to section * * * 1001 of the Code, gain is recognized by *Y* in the amount of 30*x* dollars (40*x* dollars minus 10*x* dollars). See, for example, United States v. Thomas Crawley Davis, 370 U.S. 65 (1962), Ct.D.1873, C.B. 1962–2, 15; E.F. Simms v. Commissioner, 28 B.T.A. 988, at 1029 (1933). *Y*'s basis for the assets acquired from *X* is the basis of the assets in the hands of *X*. Section 362(b) of the Code.

(3) No gain or loss is recognized by *X* on the transaction. Section 361[(a) of the Code. Under Section 358(a)(2), *X* takes the other property with a basis of 40*x* dollars, and it recognizes no gain on distribution of the other property under Section 361(c). *X* does not recognize gain on the distribution of the *Y* stock. I.R.C. §§ 336(c); 361(c)(1). Ed.]

(4) *Y*'s earnings and profits are increased by the 30*x* dollar gain that it recognized on the exchange of the other property. Section 312(f)(1) of the Code.

(5) *Y* succeeds to, and takes into account, *X*'s earnings and profits, or deficit in earnings and profits, as of the close of the date of the transaction. Section 381(c)(2) of the Code. In computing the earnings and profits of *X* for purposes of section 381(c)(2) of the Code, account must be taken of the amount of *X*'s earnings and profits properly applicable to the distribution to *M*. Section 1.381(c)(2)–1(c)(1) of the Income Tax Regulations. *X*'s earnings and profits, for purposes of section 381(c)(2) of the Code, are computed as follows:

(a) *X*'s earnings and profits are not increased by reason of the receipt [or distribution] of the other property. Sections 361[(a)] and 312(f)(1) of the Code.

(b) *X*'s earnings and profits are reduced (but not below zero) by 40*x* dollars as a result of the distribution of the other property to *M*. Section 312(a)(3) of the Code. For purposes of determining earnings and profits, *X* [has] a basis of 40*x* dollars (fair market value) in the other property. Section [358(a)(2)] of the Code.

(6) *M*'s earnings and profits are increased by 40*x* dollars, the amount of gain recognized on the transaction. Sections 356(a)(1) and (2) of the Code and section 312(f)(1) of the Code.

PROBLEMS

1. Acquiring Corporation ("A") has 500,000 shares of voting common stock outstanding (value—$10 per share) and $500,000 of accumulated earnings and profits. Target Corporation ("T") has assets with an aggregate adjusted basis of $300,000 and an aggregate fair market value of $500,000, and $100,000 of accumulated earnings and profits. Except as otherwise indicated below, assume that T has no liabilities. T's ten equal shareholders each owns 100 shares of T voting common stock with an adjusted basis of $20,000 and a fair market value of $50,000. Discuss the tax consequences to A, T and T's shareholders of each of the following alternative transactions:

(a) T merges into A in a qualified Type A reorganization. Each T shareholder receives 4,000 shares of A voting common stock (value—$40,000) and A nonvoting preferred stock (not "nonqualified preferred stock") worth $10,000.

(b) Same as (a), above, but instead of the preferred stock each T shareholder receives 20–year market rate interest bearing A notes with a principal amount and fair market value of $10,000.

(c) Same as (b), above, except that two of the shareholders receive all the notes (with a principal amount and fair market value of $100,000), and the remaining eight shareholders each receives voting common stock worth $50,000.

(d) Same as (b), above, except that T had $50,000 of accumulated earnings and profits.

(e) Assume for the remainder of the problem that T has assets with an aggregate fair market value of $600,000, an aggregate adjusted basis of $300,000, and a $100,000 liability. A acquires all T's assets in a qualified Type C reorganization in exchange for A voting stock worth $500,000 and A's assumption of T's $100,000 liability. T immediately distributes the A stock to its shareholders in complete liquidation.

(f) Same as (e), above, except A transfers $500,000 of A voting stock and $100,000 cash to T, which uses the cash to pay off its liability and then distributes the stock to its shareholders in complete liquidation.

(g) Same as (e), above, except A transfers to T $500,000 of A voting stock and investment securities with a basis of $40,000 and a fair market value of $100,000. T sells the securities for $100,000, using the proceeds to pay off its liability, and then liquidates and distributes the A stock to its shareholders.

(h) Same as (e), above, except A transfers $600,000 of its voting stock to T in exchange for all of T's assets and does not assume T's liability. T then sells $100,000 of A voting stock and uses the proceeds to pay off the liability. T then distributes the remaining A stock to its shareholders in complete liquidation.

(i) Same as (h), above, except T transfers $100,000 of A voting stock directly to its creditor in payment of the liability and then distributes the remaining A stock to its shareholders in complete liquidation.

2. Parent Corporation ("P") creates Subsidiary Corporation ("S") by transferring P stock as a preliminary step to acquiring the assets of Target Corporation ("T") in a separate subsidiary. T's shareholders own stock worth $200,000 with a basis of $50,000. T has assets worth $200,000 with a basis of $100,000.

(a) Assuming a valid § 368(a)(2)(D) forward triangular merger, what are the tax consequences to P, S, T and T's shareholders?

(b) Assuming a valid § 368(a)(2)(E) reverse triangular merger, what are the tax consequences to P, S, T and T's shareholders?

(c) What results in (a), above, if the transaction fails to qualify as a reorganization?

(d) What results in (b), above, if the transaction fails to qualify as a reorganization?

C. NONACQUISITIVE, NONDIVISIVE REORGANIZATIONS

1. TYPE E: RECAPITALIZATIONS

a. INTRODUCTION

Code: §§ 368(a)(1)(E); 354; 356; 358; 1032; 1036; 1223(1). Skim §§ 305, 306.

Regulations: §§ 1.301–1(*l*); 1.305–7(c); 1.368–2(e).

A tax-free reorganization sometimes involves only a single corporation undergoing a readjustment to its capital structure. The most common form of nonacquisitive, nondivisive reorganization is the recapitalization, which qualifies as a Type E reorganization if certain requirements are met. Recapitalizations traditionally have been used for a variety of business and tax objectives. A corporation may reshuffle its capital structure by exchanging stock for bonds in order to improve its debt/equity ratio and calm the nerves of creditors or as a condition to borrowing additional funds. Alternatively, it may exchange debt instruments for stock in order to lessen the sting of the double tax by withdrawing earnings in the form of deductible interest rather than nondeductible dividends. For closely held corporations, recapitalizations may be used as a device to shift control among the shareholders.

Because a recapitalization is a nonacquisitive transaction involving only a single corporation, the Service has ruled that neither continuity of proprietary interest nor continuity of business enterprise is required to qualify as a tax-free Type E reorganization.[1] To be tax free, however, a recapitalization must serve a corporate business purpose.[2] The courts have been tolerant in this area, and most of the business objectives set forth in the preceding paragraph are acceptable. In analogous situations, the courts have recognized that it may be unrealistic and impractical to distinguish corporate from shareholder purposes in a closely held corporation.[3] Thus, shareholder objectives germane to the corporation's business have been sufficient to satisfy the business purpose requirement.[4]

b. TYPES OF RECAPITALIZATIONS

Recapitalizations fall into four broad categories depending upon the consideration exchanged. These categories raise different issues and are best examined separately.

Bonds Exchanged for Stock. If a corporation discharges outstanding bonds by issuing preferred stock to the bondholders, the transaction qualifies as a Type E reorganization.[1] The result is the same if a corporation uses common stock to discharge its obligations to the bondholders. Under Section 354(a), the bondholders generally will recognize no gain or loss on the exchange of their debt instruments solely for stock. Section 354(a)(2)(B) creates an exception to nonrecognition to the extent stock received is attributable to accrued and untaxed interest on the bonds. This interest component will be taxed as ordinary income under Section 61.[2] The basis of the stock received in a bonds-for-stock recapitalization will be determined under the familiar rules of Section 358, and the new shareholder will be entitled to a tacked holding period on the stock under Section 1223(1).

1. Rev. Rul. 77–415, 1977–2 C.B. 311; Rev. Rul. 82–34, 1982–1 C.B. 59.

2. Reg. § 1.368–1(b).

3. Lewis v. Commissioner, 176 F.2d 646 (1st Cir.1949); Estate of Parshelsky v. Commissioner, 303 F.2d 14 (2d Cir.1962). But see Reg. § 1.355–2(b)(2), requiring a corporate business purpose in a tax-free division under Section 355.

4. Cf. Rafferty v. Commissioner, 452 F.2d 767 (1st Cir.1971), cert. denied, 408 U.S. 922, 92 S.Ct. 2489 (1972).

1. Reg. § 1.368–2(e)(1). A recapitalization should be distinguished from conversion of a bond into stock pursuant to a conversion privilege in the bond. The Service has held that the latter situation does not constitute a taxable event as long as the bond is converted into stock of the same corporation. Rev.Rul. 72–265, 1972–1 C.B. 222; Rev.Rul. 79–155, 1979–1 C.B. 153.

2. I.R.C. § 354(a)(3)(B).

On the corporate side, matters are fairly routine. Since the corporation is issuing its stock, it initially will be excused from recognizing gain or loss by Section 1032. However, a debtor corporation that transfers its stock in satisfaction of its debt is treated as if it satisfied the debt with an amount of money equal to the fair market value of the transferred stock.[3] Only an insolvent or bankrupt corporation may exclude any resulting discharge of indebtedness income under Section 108 and must make a corresponding reduction in its tax attributes.[4] Thus, a bonds-for-stock recapitalization may result in gross income for the corporation.

Bonds for Bonds. After initially contesting the issue,[5] the Service now concedes that if a creditor exchanges outstanding bonds for newly issued bonds in the same corporation, the transaction qualifies as a Type E reorganization.[6] The bondholder in a bonds-for-bonds exchange generally does not recognize gain or loss unless the bonds received are attributable to accrued and untaxed interest[7] or the principal amount of the bonds received in the exchange exceeds the principal amount of the bonds surrendered.[8] Income attributable to interest will be ordinary in character while gain recognized as a result of receipt of excess bonds generally will be either short- or long-term capital gain.[9] The bondholder's basis in the new bonds will be determined under Section 358 and the new bonds will take a tacked holding period under Section 1223(1).

On the corporate side, the primary concern in a bonds-for-bonds recapitalization will be the discharge of indebtedness rules in Section 108.[10] In addition, a bonds-for-bonds recapitalization may subject the corporation and bondholders to the intricate original issue discount provisions.[11]

Stock for Stock. The regulations provide three examples of stock-for-stock exchanges which qualify as reorganizations. Two examples involve exchanges of outstanding preferred stock for common stock and the third involves an exchange of outstanding common for preferred.[12] Thus, virtually all equity-for-equity exchanges will qualify as Type E reorganizations.[13]

3. I.R.C. § 108(e)(8).

4. See I.R.C. § 108(a)(1)(A), (a)(1)(B), (b).

5. See I.T. 2035, III–1 C.B. 55 (1924); Commissioner v. Neustadt's Trust, 131 F.2d 528, 530 (2d Cir.1942), affirming 43 B.T.A. 848 (1941), nonacq. 1941–1 C.B. 17, nonacq. withdrawn, acq. 1951–1 C.B. 2.

6. See I.T. 4081, 1952–1 C.B. 65; Rev. Rul. 77–415, 1977–2 C.B. 311.

7. I.R.C. § 354(a)(2)(B). Cf. I.R.C. § 354(a)(3)(B).

8. I.R.C. §§ 354(a)(2)(A), 356(a)(1), (d).

9. I.R.C. §§ 354(a)(3)(A), 356(a)(1). See Rev.Rul. 71–427, 1971–2 C.B. 183.

10. See I.R.C. § 108(e)(10).

11. In particular, see I.R.C. §§ 163(e), 1272–1275. See Bittker & Eustice, Federal Income Taxation of Corporations and Shareholders ¶ 12.27[4][c] (7th ed. 2000).

12. Reg. § 1.368–2(e)(2)–(4).

13. It is unlikely that a conversion of preferred stock into common stock in the same corporation, or vice versa, pursuant to a conversion privilege in the stock would be a taxable event under the theory of Rev.Rul. 72–265, 1972–1 C.B. 222, which deals with convertible debt instruments. Rev.Rul. 77–238, 1977–2 C.B. 115, however, holds that conversion of stock in furtherance of a corporate business purpose pursuant to a privilege contained in the corporation's certificate of incorporation is a recapitalization under Section 368(a)(1)(E).

In addition, exchanges of common stock in a corporation for common stock in the same corporation or preferred stock for preferred stock will qualify for nonrecognition under Section 1036.[14]

Sections 354 and 356 govern the shareholder level tax consequences of a stock-for-stock recapitalization. The shareholders will recognize gain to the extent they receive boot in the exchange, and the gain will be characterized as gain from the exchange of the stock unless the transaction has "the effect of the distribution of a dividend."[15] The shareholders' basis in the stock received in the exchange will be determined under Section 358 and will take a tacked holding period under Section 1223(1). The corporation will be entitled to nonrecognition under Section 1032 on the exchange of its stock.

Sections 305 and 306 also may come into play in a stock-for-stock recapitalization. The regulations provide that a recapitalization will be deemed to result in a distribution to which Section 305(c) applies if it is (1) pursuant to a plan to periodically increase a shareholder's proportionate interest in the assets or earnings and profits of the corporation or (2) with respect to preferred stock with dividend arrearages and the preferred shareholder increases his proportionate interest in the corporation as a result of the exchange.[16] The second alternative essentially precludes recapitalizations designed to remedy preferred stock dividend arrearages by taxing them under Sections 305(c) and (b)(4).[17]

Stock received in a recapitalization constitutes "Section 306 stock" under Section 306(c)(1)(B) if: (1) it is not common stock, (2) it was received pursuant to a plan of reorganization, (3) on its receipt gain or loss was not recognized to any extent under Sections 354 and 356, and (4) the effect of the transaction was substantially the same as the receipt of a stock dividend or the stock was received in exchange for Section 306 stock. The regulations provide a cash substitute test for determining whether the transaction has the effect of a dividend.[18] If cash received in lieu of the stock obtained in the recapitalization would have been a dividend under Section 356(a)(2), the transaction has substantially the same effect as a dividend. Thus, if the shareholders exchange common stock for common stock and a proportionate amount of preferred stock, the preferred shares will be Section 306 stock.

14. Section 1036 also applies to exchanges between two individual stockholders. Reg. § 1.1036–1(a).

15. I.R.C. § 356(a)(2). See Rev.Rul. 84–114, 1984–2 C.B. 90.

16. Reg. § 1.305–7(c). A preferred shareholder's proportionate interest increases if the greater of the fair market value or liquidation preference of the stock received in the exchange exceeds the issue price of the preferred stock surrendered. In such an exchange, the amount considered distributed to the preferred shareholder under Section 305(c) is the lesser of (1) the greater of the fair market value or liquidation preference of the preferred stock received over the issue price of the preferred stock surrendered or (2) the amount of the dividend arrearages.

17. Reg. § 1.305–5(d) Example (1). See also Reg. § 1.305–3(e) Example (12); Reg. § 1.305–5(d) Examples (2), (3) and (6).

18. Reg. § 1.306–3(d).

Stock Exchanged for Bonds. If a recapitalization requires a shareholder to surrender stock in exchange for bonds or a combination of a new class of stock and bonds, the shareholder's investment has been fundamentally altered to the extent that new debt replaces old equity. This type of recapitalization thus is far less likely to qualify for nonrecognition of gain and may raise the specter of a bailout.

Whether or not a transaction qualifies as a recapitalization, the regulations treat an exchange of old stock solely for new bonds in the same corporation as a redemption of the stock that must be tested for dividend equivalency under the familiar principles in Sections 301 and 302.[19] An exchange of old stock for a combination of new stock and bonds may qualify as a Type E reorganization, but the bonds will constitute boot, with any recognized gain limited to the lesser of the fair market value of the bonds or the shareholder's realized gain on the surrendered stock.[20] If the bonds are issued pro rata to all shareholders, the gain is likely to be a dividend to the extent of the shareholder's ratable share of earnings and profits,[21] but the gain may qualify as a capital gain if the bonds are not issued pro rata.

A more intriguing question, albeit less so as long as dividends are taxed at preferential rates, is whether an exchange of old stock for a combination of new stock and bonds by a corporation with substantial earnings and profits is tantamount to a "securities bailout," triggering dividend income under Section 301 to the extent of the full fair market value of the bonds received. In the venerable case of Bazley v. Commissioner,[22] the Supreme Court, interpreting prior law, held that such a transaction was not a recapitalization but a dividend distribution. *Bazley* involved a pro rata exchange of common stock for common stock and bonds. Later cases have offered some hope for qualifying a stock-for-stock-and-bonds exchange under Section 368(a)(1)(E) if the exchange is not pro rata.[23] Several tax problems remain for an exchanging shareholder even if the transaction constitutes a Type E reorganization. The rules in Section 356(a)(2) and (d) will likely result in characterization of gain as a dividend to the extent of the fair market value of bonds received and the corporation's earnings and profits. Even if the shareholder does not realize a gain on the exchange, the regulations suggest that a stock-for-stock-and-bonds recapitalization may be separately analyzed with the receipt of bonds being treated simply as a Section 301 distribution.[24] Stock-for-bonds exchanges also may give rise to original issue discount.[25]

19. Reg. § 1.354–1(d) Example (e); § 1.301–1(*l*). See Chapter 13B, supra.

20. I.R.C. § 354(a)(2)(A)(ii), (d).

21. I.R.C. § 356(a)(2).

22. 331 U.S. 737, 67 S.Ct. 1489 (1947).

23. See Seide v. Commissioner, 18 T.C. 502 (1952).

24. Reg. § 1.301–1(*l*). Reg. § 1.354–1(d) Example (3) provides that if a shareholder surrenders all of his stock solely for bonds, the tax consequences of the exchange are determined under Section 302 whether or not the transaction is a recapitalization under Section 368(a)(1)(E).

25. See I.R.C. §§ 163(e), 1272–1275. See generally Bittker & Eustice, Federal Income Taxation of Corporations and Shareholders ¶ 12.27[5][d] (7th ed. 2000).

PROBLEMS

1. Recap Corporation has $100,000 of accumulated earnings and profits and makes a pro rata distribution to each of its ten shareholders of new common voting stock worth $20,000 and new callable preferred stock worth $10,000 in exchange for each shareholder's old common voting stock worth $30,000. Assume that the new Recap preferred stock is not "nonqualified preferred stock."

(a) What are the tax consequences to the shareholders on the exchange?

(b) What result when Recap calls the preferred stock?

(c) What result if a shareholder sells his preferred stock?

(d) What result if Recap had a deficit in its earnings and profits account at the time of the distribution but it foresaw future potential profits?

2. The ten equal shareholders of Shuffle Corporation each have a $10,000 basis in their Shuffle common voting stock which has a $50,000 fair market value. Shuffle has $250,000 of earnings and profits. What result if the ten shareholders each transfer all their common voting stock in return for common voting stock worth $25,000 and bonds worth $25,000.

3. Leverage Corporation has 8% interest bonds outstanding with a face amount of $1,000,000 and a fair market value of $800,000. It redeems these bonds and issues new 12% interest bonds with a fair market value and a face amount of $800,000.

(a) Will the transaction qualify as a reorganization?

(b) What result in (a), above, if 12% interest bearing bonds with a face amount of $800,000 are redeemed for 8% interest bonds with a face amount of $1,000,000 and both sets of bonds have the same fair market value of $800,000?

2. NONDIVISIVE TYPE D REORGANIZATIONS

Code: §§ 368(a)(1)(D), (a)(2)(H); 354(b); 381(a)(2). Skim §§ 331; 336; 354(a); 356(a); 358; 361; 1032.

Introduction. Type D reorganizations come in two basic forms. The "divisive D" involves a transfer by one corporation of some of its assets to a newly formed controlled subsidiary followed by a distribution of the stock of the subsidiary in a corporate division that qualifies under Section 355. This is examined in Chapter 18 along with the other aspects of corporate divisions. The second form of Type D reorganization is "nondivisive." It involves the transfer by one corporation of all or part of its assets to another corporation controlled[1] immediately after the transfer by the transferor or its shareholders (or any combination) provided that the stock

1. For this purpose, "control" is measured by the 50 percent test in Section 304(c) rather than the 80 percent benchmark in Section 368(c). I.R.C. § 368(a)(2)(H).

or securities of the controlled corporation are distributed in a transaction that qualifies under Section 354. Section 354(b) requires the first corporation to transfer "substantially all" of its assets to the controlled corporation, and the stock, securities and other properties that it receives, as well as other properties of the transferor, must be distributed pursuant to the plan of reorganization.

The "nondivisive" D reorganization has always been an odd character in the reorganization alphabet. It historically was invoked by the Service as a weapon to attack the liquidation-reincorporation transaction, a technique utilized by taxpayers in the days when the *General Utilities* doctrine and a capital gains preference worked in tandem to encourage bailouts of corporate earnings at capital gains rates without any corporate-level tax. To appreciate why, consider a gambit that might have been used in the "good old days" by Profit Corp., a family company with $800,000 of accumulated earnings and profits and a $2 million net worth, consisting of $1.5 million of operating assets and $500,000 of investment securities. Assume the shareholders wish to extract the securities from corporate solution without the sting of a dividend but otherwise continue operating their business in a new corporation with fresh tax attributes (e.g., no earnings and profits) and no immediate exposure to the accumulated earnings tax.

One classic plan to accomplish these objectives was for the Profit Corp. shareholders to liquidate the corporation, retain the investment securities and, after an appropriate interval, reincorporate the operating assets under Section 351. Alternatively, Profit Corp. might transfer its operating assets to a new subsidiary in exchange for its stock and then liquidate, distributing the new stock and the investment securities to the shareholders. Whatever the format, the basic objective was to achieve what were then the tax benefits of a liquidation: capital gains at the shareholder level, nonrecognition at the corporate level, a step-up in basis of the assets in the reincorporated enterprise, and a fresh start for the earnings and profits account. The Service countered by arguing, with limited success, that the transaction was a reorganization coupled with the receipt of boot that should be taxed as a dividend.[2]

A liquidation-reincorporation rarely makes sense under current law if its form is respected for tax purposes. The liquidation will trigger corporate-level gain under Section 336 and significantly raise the tax cost of the strategy. Indeed, if the classic liquidation-reincorporation were carried out, it is now *taxpayers* who may prefer to characterize the transactions as a reorganization. Although they would recognize dividend income to the extent of the boot received, the good news is that noncorporate shareholders likely will qualify for the preferential qualified dividend rate, and the ongoing corporation would avoid recognizing gain on its assets because the asset bases would carry over to the transferee. The liquidation-reincorporation strategy may retain its vitality, however, in a few limited situations,

2. See, e.g., Davant v. Commissioner, 366 F.2d 874 (5th Cir.1966), cert. denied, 386 U.S. 1022, 87 S.Ct. 1370 (1967).

such as when the corporation has losses to shelter the gains resulting from the distribution of appreciated assets, where the appreciation in the corporation's assets is negligible, or where the corporation has losses that it is trying to accelerate without removing the loss assets from corporate solution.

All–Cash D Reorganizations. The Service is studying whether to alter its approach to nonacquisitive, nondivisive Type D reorganizations, and the changed stakes in liquidation-reincorporation transactions after *General Utilities* repeal. In a much discussed private ruling,[3] it considered a transaction where a corporation owned equally by two unrelated corporate shareholders (A and B) sold all its assets for installment notes in an amount equal to the fair market value of the assets to a new corporation (Newco) owned 90 percent by B and 10 percent by C, Inc., which was unrelated to A and B. In holding that Newco took a cost basis in the acquired assets (which is what it wanted for purposes of determining § 197 amortization deductions on acquired goodwill), the ruling inferred that the transaction was not a D reorganization despite the presence of substantial (but not identical) overlapping ownership of the two corporations. But if Newco had issued some stock as consideration for the assets, the literal statutory requirements for a D reorganization would have been satisfied and, if so, Newco would not have taken a cost basis in the acquired assets.

The ruling created a commotion among many high priests of the mergers and acquisitions tax bar. Some argued that such a transaction could qualify as a D reorganization even though Newco issued no stock or securities because, in similar cases of overlapping ownership, the Service and the courts had held that issuance of stock was an unnecessary under what is known as the "meaningless gesture" doctrine. Others argued that the statutory language would not permit such a result if no stock or securities were issued.[4]

Temporary regulations issued in December 2006 begin to sort out this esoteric issue.[5] They provide that an acquisitive transaction can qualify as a Type D reorganization even where no stock of the transferee corporation is issued and distributed in the transaction when the same person or persons own, directly and indirectly, all of the stock of the transferor and transferee corporations in "identical proportions."[6] For this purpose, an individual and all members of his family having a relationship described in Section 318(a)(1) are treated as one individual.[7] In addition, the distribution requirement under Sections 368(a)(1)(D) and 354(b)(1)(B) is treated as satisfied in the absence of any issuance of stock or securities where there is a de minimis variation in shareholder identity or proportionality of owner-

3. P.L.R. 20551018 (Dec. 23, 2005).

4. See, e.g., "Attorneys Question Ruling That Transaction Wasn't a D Reorganization," 111 Tax Notes 241 (April 10, 2006); Schler, Letter to the Editor, "More on the 'All Cash D' Reorganization," 111 Tax Notes 383 (April 17, 2006).

5. For a good overview of these regulations, see Willens, "IRS Clarifies Contours of D Reorganizations," 114 Tax Notes 227 (Jan. 15, 2007).

6. Reg. § 1.368–2T(*l*)(2)(i).

7. Reg. § 1.368–2T(*l*)(2)(ii).

ship in the transferor and transferee corporations.[8] In these "cash only" D reorganizations, the regulations deem the transferee to have issued a nominal share of stock in addition to the actual consideration exchanged, and the transferor corporation is deemed to have distributed that share to its shareholders and, as appropriate, to have further transferred it to the extent necessary to reflect the actual ownership of the two corporations.[9]

In proposing these regulations, the Service noted that they were a reasonable interpretation of the statute given the history of D reorganizations and how they have been interpreted by the courts, but no inference is to be drawn regarding the law prior to their effective date of December 19, 2006. The Service also announced that it is continuing its "broad study" of issues related to acquisitive reorganizations.[10]

3. TYPE F: MERE CHANGE IN IDENTITY, FORM, OR PLACE OF ORGANIZATION

Code: §§ 368(a)(1)(F); 381(b). Skim §§ 331; 351; 354(a); 356(a); 358; 361; 1032.

A Type F reorganization is defined by the Code as "a mere change in identity, form, or place of organization of one corporation, however effected." An example would be a merger of a closely held New York corporation into a newly formed Delaware corporation with the same shareholders in order to take advantage of Delaware corporate law in anticipation of a public offering of the company's stock.[1] Over fifty years ago a noted commentator stated that the Type F reorganization "is so little relied upon by taxpayers that this part of the statute has indeed perished through lack of use."[2] It has survived calls for repeal, however, and experienced a brief renaissance before resuming its historical role as a relatively dead letter in the tax-free reorganization alphabet.[3]

The resurgence of interest in the Type F reorganization was the result of attempts by taxpayers to carry back the post-acquisition losses of corporations which previously had been operated as an affiliated corporate group to pre-acquisition years of an acquired corporation. Since Section 381(b) only permits such a carryback of net operating losses in an F reorganization, the shareholders argued that the fusion of affiliated corporations qualified as an F reorganization. Although the language of the applicable statute implied that an F reorganization was limited to structur-

8. Reg. § 1.368–2T(*l*)(3)(iii).

9. Reg. § 1.368–2T(*l*)(3)(i). This rule does not apply to a transaction that otherwise would qualify as a Section 368(a)(2)(D) triangular reorganization. Reg. § 1.368–2T(*l*)(3)(iv).

10. T.D. 9303, 71 F.R. 75879 (Dec. 19, 2006).

1. See, e.g., Rev. Rul. 96–29, 1996–1 C.B. 50.

2. Paul, Studies in Federal Taxation 82 (3d Ed. 1940). But see Pugh, "The F Reorganization: Reveille for a Sleeping Giant?" 24 Tax L.Rev. 437 (1969).

3. F reorganization issues occasionally resurface, usually in specialized situations. See, e.g., Rev. Rul. 2003–19, 2003–1 C.B. 468. See also Prop. Reg. § 1.368–2(m), where the Service for the first time specifies the requirements to qualify as an F reorganization.

al changes in a single corporation, the Commissioner, in his attempt to combat the liquidation-reincorporation bailout device, bolstered the argument that the F reorganization also applied to the merger of two or more active corporations. In the *Davant* case, the Commissioner asserted and the Court accepted the argument that an F reorganization could involve two operating corporations.[4] The Commissioner's argument, together with a ruling in which the Service acknowledged that a reorganization meeting the definition of an F reorganization and some other type of reorganization would be treated as an F reorganization for purposes of Section 381(b),[5] opened the floodgates. The only remaining question was how far shareholders could push combinations of operating corporations into the F reorganization category.[6] In the 1970's, the Service conceded that a combination of active corporations under common control could qualify as an F reorganization if there was a complete continuity of shareholder and proprietary interests.[7] But Congress later slammed the door shut by limiting F reorganization status to a single operating corporation through the addition of the words "of one corporation" to Section 368(a)(1)(F). The Type F reorganization thus once again was relegated to its prior role as a minor provision governing reincorporations in another state and other merely formal changes. The following legislative history explains that amendment:[8]

> Present law
>
> A reorganization includes "a mere change in identity, form, or place of organization" (an F reorganization). Generally, present law requires a transferor corporation's taxable year to be closed on the date of a reorganization transfer and precludes a post-reorganization loss from being carried back to a taxable year of the transferor. However, F reorganizations are excluded from these limitations in recognition of the intended scope of such reorganizations as embracing only formal changes in a single operating corporation.
>
> * * *
>
> Conference agreement
>
> The conference agreement limits the F reorganization definition to a change in identity, form, or place of organization of a single operating corporation.

4. Davant v. Commissioner, 366 F.2d 874 (5th Cir.1966), cert. denied 386 U.S. 1022, 87 S.Ct. 1370 (1967). Actually the Commissioner made the argument at the trial court level, 43 T.C. 540 (1965), and it was adopted by the appellate court in its opinion.

5. Rev.Rul. 57–276, 1957–1 C.B. 126.

6. Compare Movielab, Inc. v. United States, 204 Ct.Cl. 6, 494 F.2d 693 (1974), and Stauffer's Estate v. Commissioner, 403 F.2d 611 (9th Cir.1968), with Berger Machine Products, Inc. v. Commissioner, 68 T.C. 358 (1977), and Romy Hammes, Inc. v. Commissioner, 68 T.C. 900 (1977).

7. See Rev.Rul. 75–561, 1975–2 C.B. 129.

8. H.R.Rep. No. 97–760, 97th Cong., 2d Sess. 540–41 (1982), reprinted in 1982–2 C.B. 634–35.

This limitation does not preclude the use of more than one entity to consummate the transaction provided only one operating company is involved. The reincorporation of an operating company in a different State, for example, is an F reorganization that requires that more than one corporation be involved.

4. TYPE G: INSOLVENCY REORGANIZATIONS

Code: §§ 368(a)(1)(G); 354(b). Skim §§ 354; 355; 356.

Excerpt from Report of Senate Finance Committee on Bankruptcy Tax Bill of 1980

S. Rep. No. 96–1035, 96th Cong., 2d Sess. 34–38, reprinted in 1980–2 Cum.Bull. 620, 637.

Present Law

Definition of reorganization

A transfer of all or part of a corporation's assets, pursuant to a court order in a proceeding under chapter X of the Bankruptcy Act (or in a receivership, foreclosure, or similar proceeding), to another corporation organized or utilized to effectuate a court-approved plan may qualify for tax-free reorganization treatment under special rules relating to "insolvency reorganizations" (secs. 371–374 of the Internal Revenue Code).

These special rules for insolvency reorganizations generally allow less flexibility in structuring tax-free transactions than the rules applicable to corporate reorganizations as defined in section 368 of the Code. Also, the special rules for insolvency reorganizations do not permit carryover of tax attributes to the transferee corporation, and otherwise differ in important respects from the general reorganization rules.[1] While some reorganizations under chapter X of the Bankruptcy Act may be able to qualify for nonrecognition treatment under Code section 368, other chapter X reorganizations may be able to qualify only under the special rules of sections 371–374 and not under the general reorganization rules of section 368.

Triangular reorganizations

In the case of an insolvency reorganization which can qualify for nonrecognition treatment only under the special rules of Code sections 371–374, the stock or securities used to acquire the assets of the corpora-

1. Under present law, it is not clear to what extent creditors of an insolvent corporation who receive stock in exchange for their claims may be considered to have "stepped into the shoes" of former shareholders for purposes of satisfying the nonstatutory "continuity of interest" rule, under which the owners of the acquired corporation must continue to have a proprietary interest in the acquiring corporation. Generally, the courts have found the "continuity of interest" test satisfied if the creditors' interests were transformed into proprietary interests prior to the reorganization (e.g., Helvering v. Alabama Asphaltic Limestone Co., 315 U.S. 179 (1942); Treas.Reg. § 1.371–1(a)(4)). It is unclear whether affirmative steps by the creditors are required or whether mere receipt of stock is sufficient.

tion in bankruptcy must be the acquiring corporation's own stock or securities. This limitation generally precludes corporations in bankruptcy from engaging in so-called triangular reorganizations, where the acquired corporation is acquired for stock of the parent of the acquiring corporation. By contrast, tax-free triangular reorganizations generally are permitted under the general rules of Code section 368.

Transfer to controlled subsidiary

In the case of an insolvency reorganization which can qualify for nonrecognition treatment only under the special rules of Code sections 371–374, it is not clear under present law whether and to what extent the acquiring corporation may transfer assets received into a controlled subsidiary. In the case of other corporate reorganizations, the statute expressly defines the situations where transfers to subsidiaries are permitted (Code sec. 368(a)(2)(C)).

Carryover of tax attributes

In the case of an insolvency reorganization which can qualify for nonrecognition treatment only under the special rules of Code sections 371–374, court cases have held that attributes (such as net operating losses) of the corporation in bankruptcy do not carry over to the new corporation. In the case of other corporate reorganizations, however, specific statutory rules permit carryover of tax attributes to the surviving corporation (Code sec. 381).

Reasons for change

The committee believes that the provisions of existing Federal income tax law which are generally applicable to tax-free corporate reorganizations should also apply to reorganizations of corporations in bankruptcy or similar proceedings, in order to facilitate the rehabilitation of financially troubled businesses.

Also, the committee believes that a creditor who exchanges securities in a corporate reorganization (including an insolvency reorganization) should be treated as receiving interest income on the exchange to the extent the creditor receives new securities, stock, or any other property for accrued but unpaid interest on the securities surrendered.

Explanation of provisions

Section 4 of the bill generally conforms the tax rules governing insolvency reorganizations with the existing rules applicable to other corporate reorganizations. These provisions are the same as section 4 of the House bill.

Definition of reorganization

In general

The bill adds a new category—"G" reorganizations—to the general Code definition of tax-free reorganizations (sec. 368(a)(1)). The new category includes certain transfers of assets pursuant to a court-approved reorganization plan in a bankruptcy case under new title 11 of the U.S. Code, or in a receivership, foreclosure, or similar proceeding in a Federal or State court.

* * *

In order to facilitate the rehabilitation of corporate debtors in bankruptcy, etc., these provisions are designed to eliminate many requirements which have effectively precluded financially troubled companies from utilizing the generally applicable tax-free reorganization provisions of present law. To achieve this purpose, the new "G" reorganization provision does not require compliance with State merger laws (as in category "A" reorganizations), does not require that the financially distressed corporation receive solely stock of the acquiring corporation in exchange for its assets (category "C"), and does not require that the former shareholders of the financially distressed corporation control the corporation which receives the assets (category "D").

The "G" reorganization provision added by the bill requires the transfer of assets by a corporation in a bankruptcy or similar case, and the distribution (in pursuance of the court-approved reorganization plan) of stock or securities of the acquiring corporation in a transaction which qualifies under sections 354, 355, or 356 of the Code. This distribution requirement is designed to assure that either substantially all of the assets of the financially troubled corporation, or assets which consist of an active business under the tests of section 355, are transferred to the acquiring corporation.

"Substantially all" test

The "substantially all" test in the "G" reorganization provision is to be interpreted in light of the underlying intent in adding the new "G" category, namely, to facilitate the reorganization of companies in bankruptcy or similar cases for rehabilitative purposes. Accordingly, it is intended that facts and circumstances relevant to this intent, such as the insolvent corporation's need to pay off creditors or to sell assets or divisions to raise cash, are to be taken into account in determining whether a transaction qualifies as a "G" reorganization. For example, a transaction is not precluded from satisfying the "substantially all" test for purposes of the new "G" category merely because, prior to a transfer to the acquiring corporation, payments to creditors and asset sales were made in order to leave the debtor with more manageable operating assets to continue in business.[5]

5. Because the stated intent for adding the new "G" category is not relevant to interpreting the "substantially all" test in the case of other reorganization categories, the comments in the text as to the appropriate interpretation of the "substantially all" test in the context of a "G" reorganization are not intended to apply to, or in any way to affect interpretations under present law of, the "substantially all" test for other reorganization categories.

Relation to other provisions

A transaction which qualifies as a "G" reorganization is not to be treated as also qualifying as a liquidation under section 332, an incorporation under section 351, or a reorganization under another category of section 368(a)(1) of the Code.[6]

A transaction in a bankruptcy or similar case which does not satisfy the requirements of new category "G" is not thereby precluded from qualifying as a tax-free reorganization under one of the other categories of section 368(a)(1). For example, an acquisition of the stock of a company in bankruptcy, or a recapitalization of such a company, which transactions are not covered by the new "G" category, can qualify for nonrecognition treatment under sections 368(a)(1)(B) or (E), respectively.

Continuity of interest rules

The "continuity of interest" requirement which the courts and the Treasury have long imposed as a prerequisite for nonrecognition treatment for a corporate reorganization must be met in order to satisfy the requirements of new category "G". Only reorganizations—as distinguished from liquidations in bankruptcy and sales of property to either new or old interests supplying new capital and discharging the obligations of the debtor corporation—can qualify for tax-free treatment.

It is expected that the courts and the Treasury will apply to "G" reorganizations continuity-of-interest rules which take into account the modification by P.L. 95–598 of the "absolute priority" rule. As a result of that modification, shareholders or junior creditors, who might previously have been excluded, may now retain an interest in the reorganized corporation.

For example, if an insolvent corporation's assets are transferred to a second corporation in a bankruptcy case, the most senior class of creditor to receive stock, together with all equal and junior classes (including shareholders who receive any consideration for their stock), should generally be considered the proprietors of the insolvent corporation for "continuity" purposes. However, if the shareholders receive consideration other than stock of the acquiring corporation, the transaction should be examined to determine if it represents a purchase rather than a reorganization.

Thus, short-term creditors who receive stock for their claims may be counted toward satisfying the continuity of interest rule, although any gain or loss realized by such creditors will be recognized for income tax purposes.

6. However, if a transfer qualifying as a "G" reorganization also meets the requirements of section 351 or qualifies as a reorganization under section 368(a)(1)(D) of the Code, the "excess liability" rule of section 357(c) applies if any former shareholder of the transferor corporation receives consideration for his stock, but does not apply if no former shareholder of the transferor corporation receives any consideration for his stock (i.e., if the corporation is insolvent). This rule parallels present law, under which insolvency reorganizations under sections 371 or 374 are excluded from the application of section 357(c).

Triangular reorganizations

The bill permits a corporation to acquire a debtor corporation in a "G" reorganization in exchange for stock of the parent of the acquiring corporation rather than for its own stock.

In addition, the bill permits an acquisition in the form of a "reverse merger" of an insolvent corporation (i.e., where no former shareholder of the surviving corporation receives any consideration for his stock) in a bankruptcy or similar case if the former creditors of the surviving corporation exchange their claims for voting stock of the controlling corporation which has a value equal to at least 80 percent of the value of the debt of the surviving corporation.

Transfer to controlled subsidiary

The bill permits a corporation which acquires substantially all the assets of a debtor corporation in a "G" reorganization to transfer the acquired assets to a controlled subsidiary without endangering the tax-free status of the reorganization. This provision places "G" reorganizations on a similar footing with other categories of reorganizations.

Carryover of tax attributes

Under the bill, the statutory rule generally governing carryover of tax attributes in corporate reorganizations (Code sec. 381) also applies in the case of a "G" reorganization. This eliminates the so-called "clean slate" doctrine.

"Principal amount" rule; "boot" test

Under the bill, "G" reorganizations are subject to the rules governing the tax treatment of exchanging shareholders and security holders which apply to other corporate reorganizations.

Accordingly, an exchanging shareholder or security holder of the debtor company who receives securities with a principal amount exceeding the principal amount of securities surrendered is taxable on the excess, and an exchanging shareholder or security holder who surrenders no securities is taxed on the principal amount of any securities received. Also, any "boot" received is subject to the general dividend-equivalence test of Code section 356.

Treatment of accrued interest

Under the bill, a creditor exchanging securities in any corporate reorganization described in section 368 of the Code (including a "G" reorganization) is treated as receiving interest income on the exchange to the extent the security holder receives new securities, stock, or any other property attributable to accrued but unpaid interest (including accrued original issue discount) on the securities surrendered. This provision, which reverses the so-called *Carman* rule, applies whether or not the exchanging security holder realizes gain on the exchange overall. Under this provision, a security holder which had previously accrued the interest (including original issue discount) as income recognizes a loss to the extent the interest is not paid in the exchange.

Example

The reorganization provisions of the bill are illustrated in part by the following example.

Assume that Corporation A is in a bankruptcy case commenced after December 31, 1980. Immediately prior to a transfer under a plan of reorganization, A's assets have an adjusted basis of $75,000 and a fair market value of $100,000. A has a net operating loss carryover of $200,000. A has outstanding bonds of $100,000 (on which there is no accrued but unpaid interest) and trade debts of $100,000.

Under the plan of reorganization, A is to transfer all its assets to Corporation B in exchange for $100,000 of B stock. Corporation A will distribute the stock, in exchange for their claims against A, one-half to the security holders and one-half to the trade creditors. A's shareholders will receive nothing.

The transaction qualifies as a reorganization under new section 368(a)(1)(G) of the Code, since all the creditors are here treated as proprietors for continuity of interest purposes. Thus, A recognizes no gain or loss on the transfer of its assets to B (Code sec. 361). B's basis in the assets is $75,000 (sec. 362), and B succeeds to A's net operating loss carryover (sec. 381).

Under the bill, the pro-rata distribution of B stock to A's creditors does not result in income from discharge of indebtedness [But see I.R.C. § 108(e)(8), which now makes stock-for-debt exchanges subject to Section 108. Ed.]

Assume the same facts as above except that B also transfers $10,000 in cash, which is distributed by A to its creditors. Although A would otherwise recognize gain on the receipt of boot in an exchange involving appreciated property, the distribution by A of the $10,000 cash to those creditors having a proprietary interest in the corporation's assets for continuity of interest purposes prevents A from recognizing any gain (Code sec. 361(b)(1)(A)).[10]

10. See Code sec. 371(a)(2)(A) and Treas.Reg. § 1.371–1(b) for a similar rule relating to distribution of boot to creditors in law.an insolvency reorganization under present

CHAPTER 18

CORPORATE DIVISIONS

A. INTRODUCTION

1. TYPES OF CORPORATE DIVISIONS

Code: Skim §§ 355; 368(a)(1)(D), (c).

The preceding chapter examined acquisitive and nondivisive single-party reorganizations. We now turn to a variety of transactions in which a single corporate enterprise is divided into two or more separate corporations. Section 355 allows a corporation to make a tax-free distribution to its shareholders of stock and securities in one or more controlled subsidiaries. If an intricate set of statutory and judicial requirements are met, neither the distributing corporation nor its shareholders recognize gain or loss on the distribution. Section 355 also unlocks the gate to other provisions which govern the treatment and characterization of boot, and collateral matters such as basis, holding period and carryover of tax attributes.[1] The rationale for nonrecognition is that the division of a business conducted under one corporate shell into separate corporations is not an appropriate taxable event when no significant assets leave corporate solution and the historic shareholders continue to control all the resulting corporations.

The three types of corporate divisions are commonly known as spin-offs, split-offs and split-ups. To illustrate the elements of these transactions, assume that Alex and Bertha each own 50 percent of the stock of Diverse Corporation ("D"), which for many years has operated a winery and a chicken ranch as separate divisions. For reasons to be elaborated below, the shareholders wish to divide the businesses into two separate corporations on a tax-free basis. The division method they choose will be influenced by their nontax goals. The possibilities are:

1. *Spin-off.* Assume that to comply with a new state regulation, D is required to operate the chicken ranch and winery as separate corporations. To accomplish the division, D forms a new corporation, Poultry, Inc., contributing the assets of the chicken ranch. It then distributes the stock of Poultry pro rata to Alex and Bertha, who emerge as equal shareholders in each corporation. Because a spin-off involves a distribution of property to shareholders without the surrender of any stock, it resembles a dividend.

1. See, e.g., I.R.C. §§ 356; 357; 358; 361; 362; 381; 1223(1) and Section D of this chapter, infra.

2. *Split-off.* Alex and Bertha desire to part company, with Alex operating the winery and Bertha the chicken ranch. To help them go their separate ways, D again forms a new corporation, Poultry, Inc., contributing the assets of the chicken ranch. D then distributes the stock of Poultry to Bertha in complete redemption of her D stock. Alex becomes the sole shareholder of D, which now owns only the winery, and Bertha is the sole owner of the chicken ranch. If Alex and Bertha did not want to part company, D could have made a pro rata distribution of Poultry stock in redemption of an appropriate amount of D stock. In either situation, a split-off resembles a redemption because the shareholders have surrendered stock of D.

3. *Split-up.* To comply with a new state regulation, D is required to terminate its corporate existence and divide up its two businesses. The fission is accomplished by D forming Vineyard, Inc. and Poultry, Inc., contributing the winery assets to Vineyard and the chicken ranch assets to Poultry. D then distributes the stock of the two new corporations pro rata to Alex and Bertha in exchange for all their D stock. Because D has distributed all of its assets and dissolved, this transaction resembles a complete liquidation. If the objectives of the parties had been different (e.g., Alex and Bertha wanted to sever their relationship), the transaction could have been effected by distributing the Vineyard stock to Alex and the Poultry stock to Bertha.

As these examples demonstrate, spin-offs, split-offs and split-ups can be classified for tax purposes in two different ways: as a tax-free corporate division or as the taxable transaction that each method resembles. In order to qualify as tax free to the shareholders, the division must satisfy the requirements of Section 355 and its accompanying judicial doctrines. In general, Section 355 allows a corporation with one or more businesses that have been actively conducted for five years or more to make a tax-free distribution of the stock of a controlled subsidiary (or subsidiaries) provided that the transaction is being carried out for a legitimate business purpose and is not being used principally as a device to bail out earnings and profits. In the absence of Section 355, a spin-off likely would be treated as a dividend under Section 301; a split-off would be tested for dividend equivalency under the redemption rules in Section 302; and a split-up would be treated as a complete liquidation under Section 331.

There is one more piece to this introduction to the puzzle. In each of the examples above, Diverse Corporation was required to engage in a preliminary step in order to accomplish its division. Because its two businesses were operated as divisions under one corporate roof rather than as separately incorporated subsidiaries, D had to drop one or more of those businesses into a separate corporate shell before proceeding with the distribution to its shareholders. If that distribution satisfies the tests in Section 355, the initial transfer of assets by D to its new subsidiary (or subsidiaries) will constitute a divisive Type D reorganization.[2] As such, the transfer of assets will be tax free to D under Section 361(a), the assumption of liabilities will be governed by Section 357 and the basis of the transferred assets will carry over to the new subsidiary under Section 362(b).[3] Creation of a new subsidiary, however, is not a condition to qualifying for nonrecognition of gain under Section 355. If its requirements are met, Section 355 applies to distributions of stock of preexisting corporations as well as to new subsidiaries created solely to carry out the division.[4]

2. Non-Tax Motives for Corporate Divisions

Many different strategic and economic considerations can lead a company to the decision that its business should be divided. Some of the more routine motives include resolution of shareholder disputes, insulation of one business from the risks and creditors of another, and compliance with a regulatory decree.

In the world of publicly traded companies, one of the most common motives for a division is the desire to separate the distributing and controlled corporations so they each can devote their attention to a single line of business. In the parlance of Wall Street, focusing the old and new corporations on a single business allows investors to have a "pure play" on a particular industry. For example, a corporation engaged in the transportation, energy and real estate businesses might transfer the latter two businesses to newly formed corporations and then distribute all shares of the new entities to the distributing corporation's shareholders to create three companies, each with a single focus. The theory underlying this maneuver is that a more narrowly focused company will have greater success than a conglomerate by virtue of its ability to devote more energy and attention to the single enterprise. This renewed vigor, so the theory goes, will be derived in part from an increased incentive for corporate managers to perform. Because their performance (or at least the perception of their performance) will be reflected more directly in the stock value of a narrowly focused company than in the stock value of a conglomerate, the managers will be more accountable to shareholders. In addition, proponents of corporate divisions expect the resulting streamlined companies to benefit from the freedom of corporate managers to pursue growth opportunities that they otherwise would feel constrained to pursue.

Another common motive for a corporate division is the desire to increase market recognition of the value of a particular business. Executives of a corporation engaged in several lines of business often believe that stock market analysts fail to appreciate the collective value of the corporation's businesses. To overcome this problem, corporate managers often decide to place a particular business in an independent company in the

2. The initial transaction also would qualify for nonrecognition under Section 351, but Section 368(a)(1)(D) and its accompanying operative provisions take precedence if the transfer of assets is followed by a Section 355 distribution.

3. See Section D of this chapter, infra.

4. I.R.C. § 355(a)(2)(C).

hope that "the market" will recognize the value of that business (and perhaps also the value of the distributing corporation's remaining businesses) more clearly. Increased recognition of value, it is hoped, will attract more capital for both the old and new corporations and increase returns to shareholders. There is evidence to support the view that a corporate division will lead to increased recognition of shareholder value. Certain studies of corporate divisions have concluded that, following an initial period of investor uncertainty, the stocks of both distributing and controlled corporations that have engaged in a spin-off generally outperform the market.[1] This increase in stock value may be attributable in part to the fact that, following a spin-off, distributing and controlled corporations frequently are seen as attractive candidates for a corporate acquisition.

Yet another agenda driving some corporate divisions may be an acquiring corporation's need to pay down debt incurred in making an acquisition by selling off some of the target's businesses or, conversely, for a potential target to better position itself for an acquisition by shedding businesses that depress its value. Congress's desire to curb deferral of corporate-level tax in connection with these break-up acquisition strategies has contributed to much of the complexity of Section 355.

Alternatives exist to achieve many of the goals of a corporate division. For example, a corporation simply could sell the assets of an unwanted business. Similarly, if the business is conducted through a subsidiary, the parent could sell the subsidiary's stock. Because the selling corporation generally is taxed on the sale and its shareholders are taxed a second time when the sale proceeds are distributed, however, a sale often is not tax efficient. In contrast, the parties to a properly structured spin-off incur no current tax, and the distributing corporation might even recoup its investment in a pre-existing subsidiary at far less tax cost than in a sale. Before the distribution, more value also can be extracted from the controlled corporation by having it pay a large dividend that likely will be eligible for the dividends received deduction provided by Section 243.[2]

Another alternative is for a corporation to issue tracking stock (sometimes referred to as alphabet or letter stock). The issuer pays dividends on tracking stock based on the performance of a particular division or subsidiary. The stock is listed and traded separately from the issuer's other shares, giving the illusion that there are shares outstanding in two distinct corporations. In theory, tracking stock allows for market recognition of the value of a business and provides incentives for corporate managers in the same way as a spin-off, but it allows the issuing corporation to retain control of the business in question. Issuing tracking stock also does not involve the tax cost of a sale of the business. Tracking stock does not offer

1. See, e.g., P. Cusatis, J. Miles and R. Woolridge, Restructuring Through Spinoffs: The Stock Market Evidence, 33 J. Financial Economics 293 (1993).

2. See Chapter 12A, supra. The distributing corporation's dividends received deduction will be disallowed if the distributing corporation does not hold the controlled corporation's stock for a sufficient period of time. See I.R.C. § 246(c); Chapter 12F2, supra.

all the advantages of a spin-off, however, such as the ability to insulate one business from potential liabilities associated with another. It also may give rise to undesirable administrative and political issues, such as the necessity of satisfying two distinct groups of shareholders.

3. Historical Background of Section 355

To better understand the technical requirements for a tax-free corporate division, it is helpful to look back at the historical background of Section 355. The early income tax provisions governing spin-offs were elegantly simple but dangerously naive. Interpreted literally, they permitted a corporation to transfer all or part of its assets to a newly formed subsidiary and then to make a tax-free distribution of the stock of that subsidiary to its shareholders as part of a plan of reorganization.[1] The tax avoidance potential of this blanket exemption from the dividend rules was enormous, and the judiciary swiftly responded by curtailing the use of a spin-off as a bailout device. In Gregory v. Helvering, which follows, the Supreme Court made one of its earliest contributions to the common law of taxation[2] and paved the way toward the enactment of a comprehensive statutory solution to the problem of corporate divisions.

Gregory v. Helvering

Supreme Court of the United States, 1935.
293 U.S. 465, 55 S.Ct. 266.

■ Mr. Justice Sutherland delivered the opinion of the Court.

Petitioner in 1928 was the owner of all the stock of United Mortgage Corporation. That corporation held among its assets 1,000 shares of the Monitor Securities Corporation. For the sole purpose of procuring a transfer of these shares to herself in order to sell them for her individual profit, and, at the same time, diminish the amount of income tax which would result from a direct transfer by way of dividend, she sought to bring about a "reorganization" under § 112(g) of the Revenue Act of 1928, c. 852, 45 Stat. 791, 818, set forth later in this opinion. To that end, she caused the Averill Corporation to be organized under the laws of Delaware on September 18, 1928. Three days later, the United Mortgage Corporation transferred to the Averill Corporation the 1,000 shares of Monitor stock, for which all the shares of the Averill Corporation were issued to the petitioner. On September 24, the Averill Corporation was dissolved, and liquidated by distributing all its assets, namely, the Monitor shares, to the petitioner. No other business was ever transacted, or intended to be transacted, by that company. Petitioner immediately sold the Monitor shares for $133,333.33. She returned for taxation as capital net gain the sum of

1. See, e.g., Revenue Act of 1924, P.L. No. 176, § 203(c), 43 Stat. 253, 256.

2. See Blum, "Motive, Intent, and Purpose in Federal Income Taxation," 34 U.Chi. L.Rev. 485 (1967); Chirelstein, "Learned Hand's Contribution to the Law of Tax Avoidance," 77 Yale L.J. 440 (1968).

$76,007.88, based upon an apportioned cost of $57,325.45. Further details are unnecessary. It is not disputed that if the interposition of the so-called reorganization was ineffective, petitioner became liable for a much larger tax as a result of the transaction.

The Commissioner of Internal Revenue, being of opinion that the reorganization attempted was without substance and must be disregarded, held that petitioner was liable for a tax as though the United corporation had paid her a dividend consisting of the amount realized from the sale of the Monitor shares. In a proceeding before the Board of Tax Appeals, that body rejected the commissioner's view and upheld that of petitioner. 27 B.T.A. 223. Upon a review of the latter decision, the circuit court of appeals sustained the commissioner and reversed the board, holding that there had been no "reorganization" within the meaning of the statute. 69 F. (2d) 809. Petitioner applied to this court for a writ of certiorari, which the government, considering the question one of importance, did not oppose. We granted the writ.

Section 112 of the Revenue Act of 1928 deals with the subject of gain or loss resulting from the sale or exchange of property. Such gain or loss is to be recognized in computing the tax, except as provided in that section. The provisions of the section, so far as they are pertinent to the question here presented, follow:

"Sec. 112. (g) *Distribution of stock on reorganization.*—If there is distributed, in pursuance of a plan of reorganization, to a shareholder in a corporation a party to the reorganization, stock or securities in such corporation or in another corporation a party to the reorganization, without the surrender by such shareholder of stock or securities in such a corporation, no gain to the distributee from the receipt of such stock or securities shall be recognized * * *.

"(i) *Definition of reorganization.*—As used in this section * * *.

"(1) The term 'reorganization' means * * * (B) a transfer by a corporation of all or a part of its assets to another corporation if immediately after the transfer the transferor or its stockholders or both are in control of the corporation to which the assets are transferred, * * *."

It is earnestly contended on behalf of the taxpayer that since every element required by the foregoing subdivision (B) is to be found in what was done, a statutory reorganization was effected; and that the motive of the taxpayer thereby to escape payment of a tax will not alter the result or make unlawful what the statute allows. It is quite true that if a reorganization in reality was effected within the meaning of subdivision (B), the ulterior purpose mentioned will be disregarded. The legal right of a taxpayer to decrease the amount of what otherwise would be his taxes, or altogether avoid them, by means which the law permits, cannot be doubted. * * * But the question for determination is whether what was done, apart from the tax motive, was the thing which the statute intended. The reasoning of the court below in justification of a negative answer leaves little to be said.

When subdivision (B) speaks of a transfer of assets by one corporation to another, it means a transfer made "in pursuance of a plan of reorganization" [§ 112(g)] of corporate business; and not a transfer of assets by one corporation to another in pursuance of a plan having no relation to the business of either, as plainly is the case here. Putting aside, then, the question of motive in respect of taxation altogether, and fixing the character of the proceeding by what actually occurred, what do we find? Simply an operation having no business or corporate purpose—a mere device which put on the form of a corporate reorganization as a disguise for concealing its real character, and the sole object and accomplishment of which was the consummation of a preconceived plan, not to reorganize a business or any part of a business, but to transfer a parcel of corporate shares to the petitioner. No doubt, a new and valid corporation was created. But that corporation was nothing more than a contrivance to the end last described. It was brought into existence for no other purpose; it performed, as it was intended from the beginning it should perform, no other function. When that limited function had been exercised, it immediately was put to death.

In these circumstances, the facts speak for themselves and are susceptible of but one interpretation. The whole undertaking, though conducted according to the terms of subdivision (B), was in fact an elaborate and devious form of conveyance masquerading as a corporate reorganization, and nothing else. The rule which excludes from consideration the motive of tax avoidance is not pertinent to the situation, because the transaction upon its face lies outside the plain intent of the statute. To hold otherwise would be to exalt artifice above reality and to deprive the statutory provision in question of all serious purpose.

Judgment affirmed.

NOTE

The Board of Tax Appeals was more tolerant in its evaluation of Mrs. Gregory's maneuver. Adopting a strict constructionist approach, the Board reasoned that "[a] statute so meticulously drafted must be interpreted as a literal expression of the taxing policy, and leaves only the small interstices for judicial consideration."[1] On appeal to the Second Circuit, Judge Learned Hand—in one of his most famous pronouncements on tax avoidance—agreed that "[a]ny one may so arrange his affairs that his taxes shall be as low as possible; he is not bound to choose that pattern which will best pay the Treasury; there is not even a patriotic duty to increase one's taxes."[2] But he quickly eschewed literalism in favor of the big picture, reasoning that "the meaning of a sentence may be more than that of the separate words, as a melody is more than the notes, and no degree of particularity can ever obviate recourse to the setting in which all appear,

1. Gregory v. Commissioner, 27 B.T.A. 223, 225 (1932).

2. Helvering v. Gregory, 69 F.2d 809, 810 (2d Cir.1934).

and which all collectively create."[3] The Supreme Court's opinion was a less stylish but equally forceful reaffirmation that the language of the Code must be interpreted in light of its purpose.

Gregory v. Helvering has ramifications that go far beyond corporate divisions. It is one of the earliest articulations of the substance over form and step transaction doctrines. However amorphous they may be, those doctrines serve as a brooding omnipresence in the responsible tax advisor's conscience. When the system works properly (not always the reality), they also thwart the schemes of aggressive tax avoiders who rely on a literal interpretation of the Code to wreak havoc with its intended purpose. As we will see later in the chapter, the narrower business purpose doctrine emanating from *Gregory* also survives as one of the major requirements for qualification as a tax-free corporate division.[4]

While *Gregory* was pending, Congress saw the light and repealed the tax-free spin-off provision involved in that case. Curiously, split-ups (and, for a time, split-offs) continued to qualify for nonrecognition if they did not run afoul of the limitations in *Gregory*.[5] Congress ultimately realized, however, that not every spin-off is a bailout device, and in 1951 it enacted the statutory forerunner of Section 355 to remove any impediment to corporate divisions "undertaken for legitimate business purposes."[6] In general, the new statute granted nonrecognition to spin-offs that were pursuant to a plan of reorganization unless one of the corporate parties to the reorganization did not intend "to continue the active conduct of a trade or business" or "the corporation whose stock is distributed was used principally as a device for the distribution of earnings and profits * * *."[7] The contours of the present Section 355 thus were being shaped: to qualify as tax free, a spin-off had to be motivated by a genuine business purpose and consist of the separation of one or more active trades or businesses in a transaction that was not being used principally as a bailout device.

With the enactment of Section 355 in the 1954 Code, Congress finally provided a comprehensive statutory scheme governing all three types of corporate divisions.[8] At the same time, the business purpose and continuity of interest doctrines were preserved as independent nonstatutory requirements.

4. OVERVIEW OF SECTION 355

Code: §§ 355(a), (b), (c); 368(c).

Regulations: § 1.355–1(b).

Before becoming immersed in technical details, it is important to recall the purpose of Section 355. Congress intended to provide tax-free status to

3. Id.

4. See Section C1 of this chapter, infra.

5. For the history of corporate divisions before the 1954 Code, see Bittker & Eustice, Federal Income Taxation of Corporations and Shareholders ¶ 11.01 (7th ed. 2000).

6. S.Rep. No. 781, 82d Cong., 1st Sess. (1951), reprinted in 1951–2 C.B. 458, 499.

7. Revenue Act of 1951, ch. 521, § 317(a), 65 Stat. 493, amending Internal Revenue Code of 1939, § 112(b)(11).

8. The statute does not explicitly refer to spin-offs, split-offs and split-ups, but Section 355(a)(2) makes it clear that Section 355 applies to all three forms of corporate divisions. The different forms continue to be significant if the transaction fails the Section 355 tests.

corporate divisions serving legitimate business needs. At the same time, it included safeguards to patrol against the bailout of earnings and profits. A more recent Congressional concern has been to prevent taxpayers from using divisions to avoid corporate-level gain on transactions that are more akin to sales than mere changes in form. Most of the statutory and judicial requirements are directed at these broad objectives. But their precise meaning and scope are not always clear, and the waters have been muddied further by piecemeal changes made over the years to address real and perceived abuses.

a. STATUTORY AND JUDICIAL REQUIREMENTS

A corporate division will qualify as tax free to the shareholders and the distributing corporation if it satisfies the requirements discussed below.

Control. One corporation (the "distributing corporation," or "D") must distribute to its shareholders (with respect to their stock) or to security holders (in exchange for their securities) the stock or securities of a corporation that D "controls" immediately before the distribution (the "controlled corporation," or "C").[1] For this purpose, "control" is defined by Section 368(c), which requires ownership of 80 percent of the total combined voting power and 80 percent of the total number of shares of all other classes of stock.

Distribution of All Stock or Securities. D must distribute all the stock or securities of C that it holds or, alternatively, an amount of stock sufficient to constitute "control" within the meaning of Section 368(c).[2] If any stock or securities of C are retained, D also must establish to the satisfaction of the Service that the retention is not pursuant to a plan having tax avoidance as one of its principal purposes.[3]

Active Trade or Business Requirement. Immediately after the distribution, both D and C—or in a split-up, both controlled corporations—must be engaged in, or treated as engaged (through a subsidiary) in, a trade or business that has been actively conducted throughout the five-year period ending on the date of the distribution.[4] That business must not have been acquired within the five-year predistribution period in a transaction in which gain or loss was recognized in whole or in part (e.g., a sale of assets taxable to the seller).[5] Moreover, the distributing corporation must not have purchased a controlling stock interest in a corporation conducting the business in a taxable transaction during the five-year predistribution

1. I.R.C. § 355(a)(1)(A).

2. I.R.C. § 355(a)(1)(D).

3. I.R.C. § 355(a)(1)(D)(ii); Rev. Proc. 96–30, 1996–1 C.B. 696. See also Rev.Rul. 75–469, 1975–2 C.B. 126; Rev.Rul. 75–321, 1975–2 C.B. 123.

4. I.R.C. § 355(a)(1)(C); (b).

5. I.R.C. § 355(b)(2)(C).

period.[6] In applying these rules, all members of D's and C's "separated affiliated group" (generally, subsidiaries in which the parent owns 80 percent of the voting power and total value) are treated as one corporation.[7]

Not A "Device." The division must not be used "principally as a device for the distribution" of the earnings and profits of either D or C. The "mere fact" that stock or securities of either corporation are sold after the distribution is not to be considered as evidence of a device unless the sales were pursuant to a prearranged plan.[8]

Judicial Limitations: Business Purpose and Continuity of Interest. In addition to the statutory tests, the regulations incorporate three judicially created limitations. Nonrecognition is available only if the distribution is carried out for an independent corporate business purpose[9] and the shareholders prior to the division maintain adequate continuity of interest in D and C, and continuity of business enterprise is maintained after the distribution.[10]

All these requirements are applied without regard to the form the parties choose to accomplish the division. Thus, a distribution may qualify as tax-free under Section 355 irrespective of whether it is pro rata and whether or not the distributee shareholder surrenders stock in the distributing corporation or the distribution is preceded by the formation of a new controlled corporation in a Type D reorganization.[11]

This list of basic Section 355 requirements does not tell the entire story. Several other specialized provisions may cause D to recognize gain on its distribution of C stock even though D's shareholders qualify for tax-free treatment.[12]

b. TAXATION OF THE PARTIES

Section 355 provides total shareholder-level nonrecognition only where the distributing corporation distributes stock or securities of a controlled corporation.[13] Stock rights or warrants are not treated as "stock or securities" for this purpose and thus constitute taxable boot under Section 356.[14] In the case of a distribution of securities (e.g., long-term notes, bonds, debentures), if the principal amount of securities of the controlled corporation received by the distributee exceeds the principal amount of the

6. I.R.C. § 355(b)(2)(D). The active trade or business test also will be violated if the distributee shareholder is a corporation that acquired control of the distributing corporation within the five-year predistribution period. Id.

7. I.R.C. § 355(b)(3). This rule applies to distributions made after May 17, 2006. See Section B of this chapter, infra, for the details and ramifications.

8. I.R.C. § 355(a)(1)(B).

9. Reg. § 1.355–2(b).

10. Reg. § 1.355–2(c), –1(b).

11. I.R.C. § 355(a)(2).

12. See Section E of this chapter, infra.

13. I.R.C. § 355(a)(1). For this purpose, "nonqualified preferred stock," as defined in section 351(g)(2), received in a distribution with respect to stock other than nonqualified preferred stock is not treated as "stock or securities"—i.e., it will be boot. I.R.C. § 355(a)(3)(D).

14. Reg. § 1.355–1(b).

distributing corporation's securities surrendered in connection with the distribution, the value of the excess is treated as boot.[15] If securities of the controlled corporation are received and no securities of the parent are surrendered, the entire value of the securities received is treated as boot.[16] In addition, any stock of a controlled corporation acquired in a taxable transaction within the five years preceding the distribution constitutes boot.[17] The distribution of boot does not necessarily disqualify a transaction under Section 355, but it will cause the distributee shareholder to recognize any realized gain, normally as a qualified dividend taxable at preferential capital gains rates, to the extent of the boot received.[18] At the corporate level, the distributing corporation generally does not recognize gain on the distribution of stock or securities of its subsidiary but may recognize gain on the distribution of appreciated boot or in certain situations where a divisive transaction is used to facilitate the sale of a subsidiary.[19]

The principal hurdles to achieving nonrecognition under Section 355 are the active trade or business and business purpose requirements and the "device" limitation. The government's interpretation of these tests has evolved over the years and currently is reflected in extensive regulations, which have largely supplanted the case law and are a principal focus of this chapter.

B. THE ACTIVE TRADE OR BUSINESS REQUIREMENT

Code: § 355(a)(1)(C), (b)(1), (2), (3)(A) & (B).

Regulations: § 1.355–3(a)(1)(i), (b)(1), (2), (3).

Lockwood's Estate v. Commissioner

United States Court of Appeals, Eighth Circuit, 1965.
350 F.2d 712.

■ VOGEL, CIRCUIT JUDGE.

The single question involved in this review of an unreported decision of the Tax Court of the United States, entered August 26, 1964, is whether the "spin-off" of part of the business conducted by the Lockwood Grader Corporation of Gering, Nebraska, (hereinafter Lockwood) through the organization of a new corporation, Lockwood Graders of Maine, Inc. (hereinafter Maine, Inc.) was tax-free to petitioners, recipients of the stock of Maine, Inc., under 26 U.S.C.A. § 355 (Int.Rev.Code). The government

15. I.R.C. §§ 355(a)(3)(A)(i); 356(d)(2)(C).

16. I.R.C. §§ 355(a)(3)(A)(ii); 356(d)(2)(C).

17. I.R.C. § 355(a)(3)(B). See Edna Louise Dunn Trust v. Commissioner, 86 T.C. 745 (1986).

18. I.R.C. §§ 355(a)(4)(A); 356. See Section C of this Chapter, infra, for a more detailed explanation of the treatment of boot and the other operative provisions that accompany Section 355.

19. I.R.C. § 355(c), (d).

contended that the spin-off was not tax-free since the requirements of § 355(b)(2)(B) relating to the conducting of an active business for five years prior to the date of distribution had not been met. The government apparently conceded and the Tax Court found that the petitioners had met all other requirements to qualify under § 355 for tax-free treatment. The Tax Court upheld the government's contention and petitioners appeal.

The now deceased Thorval J. Lockwood, * * * and his wife Margaret were the sole stockholders of Lockwood and had been so since its incorporation under Nebraska law in 1946. Lockwood's predecessor, Lockwood Graders, was a partnership formed in 1935 for the purpose of producing and selling a portable potato sorting machine invented by the decedent. Starting in the early spring of each year Thorval and Margaret drove to Alabama and worked their way north through Missouri to North Dakota for the purpose of selling Lockwood products. The equipment was sold in "all of the potato growing areas of the United States" but primarily in the biggest growing areas such as North Dakota, Idaho and Colorado.

From 1946 to 1951, inclusive, Lockwood operated its business of manufacturing and selling wash lines, potato machinery, parts and supplies to potato shippers in the potato growing areas. Though Lockwood continued to have its principal place of business at Gering, Nebraska, branches were opened, as the business expanded, in Grand Forks, North Dakota; Antigo, Wisconsin; Monte Vista, Colorado; and Rupert, Idaho. These branches performed both manufacturing and sales functions. In 1952, under a reorganization plan, these branches were separately incorporated to promote greater efficiency and to properly provide for expansion. Assets of Lockwood were exchanged for all of the stock of each new corporation and the stock so exchanged was passed without consideration to Thorval and Margaret as sole stockholders of Lockwood. The reorganization plan, among other things, was specifically designed to make use of the tax-free provisions of what is now § 355.

In the early 1950's Lockwood and the other controlled corporations changed the nature of their business somewhat by selling to individual farmers as well as to potato suppliers. Lockwood had previously dealt primarily in grading equipment but at this time it began to manufacture and sell field equipment such as harvesting pieces, bin holders and vine beaters as well.

Beginning as early as 1947 Lockwood began to make some sporadic and relatively inconsequential sales in the northeastern part of the United States. From 1949 to 1955 the primary sales of products and parts in that part of the country were made to Gould & Smith, Inc., a retailer of farming and industrial equipment, of Presque Isle, Maine (although there are no records of sales made to them in 1952). Such sales were found to be of a relatively small volume by the Tax Court. On November 15, 1954, Lockwood established a branch office in Presque Isle, Maine, from which to handle Lockwood products. On March 1, 1956, pursuant to the 1951 plan for reorganization, the Maine branch office was incorporated under the laws of Maine with its principal place of business at Presque Isle, Maine.

Maine, Inc., was a wholly owned subsidiary of Lockwood. On incorporating, Lockwood transferred to Maine, Inc., $23,500 in assets consisting of petty cash totalling $150.00, accounts receivable totalling $4,686.67, automobiles and trucks worth $1,100, shop equipment worth $295.00, office furniture and fixtures worth $81.60, and inventory worth $17,186.73. In return for these assets Maine, Inc., issued all of its stock, 235 shares at $100.00 par value, to Lockwood. On March 31, 1956, Lockwood distributed 162 of these shares of Maine, Inc., to Thorval and 73 of them to Margaret. This distribution gave rise to the controversy here involved.

The Tax Court held this distribution to be outside of § 355. According to the Tax Court there was:

> "* * * the absence of evidence that the *Maine business* was actively conducted during the months between March 31, 1951, and August 1953—a span of time totaling over 40 per cent of the requisite five-year period [required by § 355(b)(2)(B).]" (Emphasis supplied.)

The Tax Court found that the Maine business was not actively and continuously conducted until August 1953, at which time a Lockwood salesman traveled to Maine and personally solicited orders from farmers and businessmen other than Gould & Smith. We do not disagree with the factual finding of the Tax Court as to the active conduct of Lockwood's business in Maine prior to the incorporation of Maine, Inc. However, the Tax Court, for reasons set out below, erred in looking only at the business performed by Lockwood in Maine to determine if the five-year active business requirement had been met prior to the incorporation of Maine, Inc. Nothing in the language of § 355 suggests that prior business activity is only to be measured by looking at the business performed in a geographical area where the controlled corporation is eventually formed. In this case, when the entire Lockwood market is viewed, it can be seen that Lockwood was engaged in active business as required by § 355 for the five years prior to the incorporation of Maine, Inc. Since its incorporation Maine, Inc., has carried on the same kind of manufacturing and selling business previously and concurrently performed by Lockwood. Thus all § 355 prerequisites are met and the Tax Court erred in determining this was not a tax-free transfer.

At this point it would be helpful to look at the evolvement of what is now § 355. Prior to 1924 a distribution to stockholders pursuant to a spin-off was taxed as a dividend. From 1924 to 1932, however, the revenue acts changed position and provided spin-offs could be tax-free. From 1934 to 1950 tax-free spin-offs were again abolished since this device was being used as a method for distributing earnings and profits, which would otherwise be taxable dividends, through the issuance of stock in the controlled corporation. Such stock could be disposed of at the more favorable capital gain rates. Because of the usefulness of the spin-off device in the achievement of corporate growth and flexibility, Congress again accorded it tax-free status in 1951. At that time certain conditions were imposed to prevent any abuse from using this device. In 1954 the tax-free spin-off was continued as § 355 of the Code with additional tax avoidance safeguards which included the five-year active business requirement involved in this case.

As stated by the Second Circuit in Bonsall v. Commissioner, 2 Cir., 1963, 317 F.2d 61, at page 65:

> "* * * Only long application may completely clarify the difficult terminology of section 355."

With this we agree. However, certain things have become clear since the enactment of § 355 in 1954. After much controversy it has been determined that tax-free treatment will not be denied to a transaction under § 355 merely because it represents an attempt to divide a single trade or business. See United States v. Marett, 5 Cir., 1963, 325 F.2d 28; Coady v. Commissioner, 33 T.C. 771, affirmed per curiam, 6 Cir., 1961, 289 F.2d 490. The Commissioner has acceded to the holdings of Marett and Coady in Rev.Rule 64–147, 1964–1, Cum.Bull. 136, even though the Commissioner had previously insisted, in § 1.355–1(a) of the Income Tax Regulations, that two or more existing businesses had to be actively operated the five years prior to distribution.

* * *

Respondent in the instant case, although claiming to accept the single business interpretation, points to the language of § 355(b)(1) and argues, as did the government in Coady, that the word "*and*" in that section means that, in determining whether or not the active business requirement was met, one has to look at both the business done by the distributing corporation (Lockwood) *and* the business done as such by the controlled corporation (Maine, Inc.) and its predecessors in Maine. Contrary to the government's position, once it has been ascertained that two or more trades or businesses are not required for § 355 to apply, the crucial question becomes whether or not the two corporations existing after distribution are doing the same type of work and using the same type of assets previously done and used by the prior *single* existing business. § 355(b)(1) has no relevance to respondent's point once it has been determined that only a single business is required.

Here the five years of prior activity we are concerned with involve the prior overall activity of Lockwood. Previous to 1956 Lockwood had carried on *in toto* what Maine, Inc., would later carry on in part in the northeast. We are not concerned with the prior activity of Lockwood in the northeast only, for Congress has never intimated that such a geographical test should be applied and we are not about to apply such a test now. A perusal of the House and Senate Reports indicates conclusively that at no time did the House or the Senate contemplate any kind of geographic test in applying the five-year active business requirement. The facts clearly show that Lockwood, in fact, was actively conducting the trade or business involved five years prior to the distribution period.

One case, Patricia W. Burke v. Commissioner, 1964, 42 T.C. 1021, did discuss the past business of a controlled corporation as performed in a limited geographical area in finding the prerequisites of § 355 had been met. That case did not, however, hold that there was in fact a geographical test. Further, at page 1028 that court set out what we believe to be the test:

> "* * * as long as the business which is divided has been actively conducted for 5 years before the distribution and the resulting businesses are actively conducted after the division, the active business requirements of the statute are met. Cf. also H. Grady Lester, 40 T.C. 947 (1963)."

Since there is no Congressional intent evidenced to the contrary, the test, restated, is not whether active business had been carried out in the geographic area later served by the controlled corporation but, simply, whether the distributing corporation, for five years prior to distribution, had been actively conducting the type of business now performed by the controlled corporation without reference to the geographic area. In the instant case the facts are abundantly clear that Lockwood had been actively engaged in the type of business later carried on by Maine, Inc., if one refers to a national rather than just the northeastern market.

It was mentioned earlier in this opinion that beginning in 1950 Lockwood began to sell field equipment as well as grading equipment. The respondent apparently does not contend, nor do we find, that Lockwood so changed its business as to be engaged in a new business that had been active for only two years prior to the incorporation of Maine, Inc. Lockwood meets the requirements of an existing five-year active business as set out by the Conference Committee in Conference Report No. 2543 at page 5298 of 3 U.S.C.Cong. & Adm.News, 1954:

> "It is the understanding of the managers on the part of the House, in agreeing to the active business requirements of section 355 and of section 346 (defining partial liquidations), that a trade or business which has been actively conducted throughout the 5–year period described in such sections will meet the requirements of such sections, even though such trade or business underwent change during such 5–year period, for example, *by the addition of new*, or the dropping of old, *products*, changes in production capacity, and the like, provided the changes are not of such a character as to constitute the acquisition of a new or different business." (Emphasis supplied.)

In § 1.355–4(b)(3) of the Income Tax Regulations the Commissioner specifically adopts the above-quoted portion of the Committee Report.

The respondent contends:

> "If the taxpayers' argument prevails, then any corporation with a five-year history could distribute any of its assets regardless of when they were acquired and regardless of what kind of business they are in after the division, as long as the distributing corporation is in an active business. In other words, taxpayer argues that the five-year history rule requires that only the

business of the distributing corporation have a five-year history. For instance, suppose a large manufacturing corporation with a ten-year life acquired some data processing machines in order to better control its inventory and work-in-process flow. If taxpayers' argument is correct, a year later this corporation could transfer all the data processing equipment to a new corporation in exchange for its stock, spin off the stock and claim a tax-free distribution under Section 355 since the manufacturing corporation had more than a five-year life and the data processing business, once an integral part of the original business, was being actively conducted after the spin-off. Moreover, the same logic would allow the spin-off of real estate owned by the manufacturing corporation and used in its business."

The fears of the government are unfounded. The example of the manufacturing company is more closely akin to the Bonsall case, supra, and is factually distinguishable from the instant case. Here Lockwood had not just recently acquired that part or segment of its business that was spun off. Rather, what was spun off was a part of the business Lockwood had always performed in the past and which it has continued to perform since the distribution. If Lockwood had, just before distribution, acquired or opened up a new or entirely different aspect of its business unrelated to prior activities and had spun this off to the controlled corporation, a different result might ensue. In Bonsall the distributing company, a dealer in floor covering materials, attempted to assert a tax-free spin-off occurred when a rental business of *de minimis* proportions was transferred to a subsidiary with the stock of the subsidiary being distributed to the distributor's shareholders. The Second Circuit held at page 64 of 317 F.2d:

"There is ample support for the factual determination that Albany Linoleum [the distributing company therein] was not actively conducting a real-estate rental business. * * * the portion of its income realized from real estate rentals was minute. * * * No activity appeared beyond a few casual conversations with prospective tenants. Moreover, most of the floor-space of the two buildings combined was occupied by the floor-covering business. Only a very small part was available for rental, and an even smaller part actually leased. The continuing rental to Armstrong Cork Co. which provided most of the rental income appeared to be an accommodation to a large supplier of the floor-covering business and thus an adjunct to it, rather than indicative of an independent business, for the Tax Court found that the premises were let at less than fair rental value over the five-year period. Finally, no separate records of rental income and expenses were kept. Absence of such records is at least probative of the fact that the managers of Albany Linoleum did not regard it as engaged in an independent rental business. The Tax Court was plainly justified in concluding that the small amount of rental activity was merely an incidental part of the sole business of the corporation—wholesale floor-coverings. * * *"

Thus it is clear that in respondent's example and in Bonsall the business sought to be spun off was not actively engaged in for five years prior to distribution, which is not the situation in the instant case. Here, what was spun off was merely an integral part of what had been Lockwood's primary and only business from its inception.

Further, it should be remembered that even if the five-year active business requirement is met, there is further protection in § 355 against spin-offs being used for mere tax avoidance, which would be contrary to Congressional intent. § 355(a)(1)(B) will only allow a tax-free spin-off transaction where "* * * the transaction was not used principally as a device for the distribution of the earnings and profits of the distributing corporation or the controlled corporation or both * * *." Under this section, the government and the courts have great latitude in preventing the abuses which the respondent fears will happen by finding for petitioners in this case. Cf. Gregory v. Helvering, 1935, 293 U.S. 465, 55 S.Ct. 266, 79 L.Ed. 596. Herein the respondent does not contend that the purpose of the spin off was designed primarily for tax avoidance. No earnings and profits were in fact distributed to Thorval and Margaret. The Tax Court stated that:

> "* * * we do not view the distribution as running afoul of the congressional purpose behind section 355, * * *."

This being so, and since petitioners otherwise complied with § 355, the decision of the Tax Court will be reversed. The transaction herein involved cannot be treated as a taxable distribution of dividends.

Revenue Ruling 2003–38

2003–1 Cum. Bull. 811.

ISSUE

Whether the creation by a corporation engaged in the retail shoe store business of an Internet web site on which the corporation will sell shoes at retail constitutes an expansion of the corporation's business rather than the acquisition of a new or different business under § 1.355–3(b)(3)(ii) of the Income Tax Regulations.

FACTS

Corporation D has operated a retail shoe store business, under the name "D," since Year 1 in a manner that meets the requirements of § 355(b) of the Internal Revenue Code. D's sales are made exclusively to customers who frequent its retail stores in shopping malls and other locations. D's business enjoys favorable name recognition, customer loyalty, and other elements of goodwill in the retail shoe market. In Year 8, D creates an Internet web site and begins selling shoes at retail on the web site. To a significant extent, the operation of the web site draws upon D's experience and know-how. The web site is named "D.com" to take advantage of the name recognition, customer loyalty, and other elements of goodwill associated with D and the D name and to enhance the web site's chances for success in its initial stages. In Year 10, D transfers all of the web site's assets and liabilities to corporation C, a newly formed, wholly owned subsidiary of D, and distributes the stock of C pro rata to D's shareholders. Apart from the issue of whether the web site is considered an expansion of D's business and therefore entitled to share the business's five-year history at the time of the distribution in Year 10, the distribution meets all the requirements of § 355.

LAW

Section 355(a) provides that a corporation may distribute stock and securities in a controlled corporation to its shareholders and security holders in a transaction that will not cause the distributees to recognize gain or loss, provided that, among other requirements, (i) each of the distributing corporation and controlled corporation is engaged, immediately after the distribution, in the active conduct of a trade or business, (ii) each trade or business has been actively conducted throughout the five-year period ending on the date of the distribution, and (iii) neither trade or business was acquired in a transaction in which gain or loss was recognized, in whole or in part, within the five-year period. Sections 355(b)(1)(A), 355(b)(2)(B), and 355(b)(2)(C).

In determining whether an active trade or business has been conducted by a corporation throughout the five-year period preceding the distribution, the fact that a trade or business underwent change during the five-year period (for example, by the addition of new or the dropping of old products, changes in production capacity, and the like) shall be disregarded, provided that the changes are not of such a character as to constitute the acquisition of a new or different business. Section 1.355–3(b)(3)(ii). In particular, if a corporation engaged in the active conduct of one trade or business during that five-year period purchased, created, or otherwise acquired another trade or business in the same line of business, then the acquisition of that other business is ordinarily treated as an expansion of the original business, all of which is treated as having been actively conducted during that five-year period, unless that purchase, creation, or other acquisition effects a change of such character as to constitute the acquisition of a new or different business. Id.

In Example (7) of § 1.355–3(c), corporation X had owned and operated a department store in the downtown area of the City of G for six years before acquiring a parcel of land in a suburban area of G and constructing a new department store. Three years after the construction, X transferred the suburban store and related business assets to new subsidiary Y and distributed the Y stock to X's shareholders. Citing § 1.355–3(b)(3)(i) and (ii), the example concludes that X and Y both satisfy the requirements of § 355(b).

In Example (8) of § 1.355–3(c), corporation X had owned and operated hardware stores in several states for four years before purchasing the assets of a hardware store in State M where X had not previously conducted business. Two years after the purchase, X transferred the State M store and related business assets to new subsidiary Y and distributed the Y stock to X's shareholders. Citing § 1.355–3(b)(3)(i) and (ii), the example concludes that X and Y both satisfy the requirements of § 355(b).

Rev. Rul. 2003–18, 2003–7 I.R.B. 467, concludes that the acquisition by a dealer engaged in the sale and service of brand X automobiles of a franchise (and the assets needed) to sell and service brand Y automobiles is an expansion of the brand X business and does not constitute the acquisition of a new or different business under § 1.355–3(b)(3)(ii) because (i) the product of the brand X automobile dealership is similar to the product of the brand Y automobile dealership, (ii) the business activities associated with the operation of the brand X automobile dealership (i.e., sales and service) are the same as the business activities associated with the operation of the brand Y automobile dealership, and (iii) the operation of the brand Y automobile dealership involves the use of the experience and know-how that the dealer developed in the operation of the brand X automobile dealership.

ANALYSIS

The product of the retail shoe store business and the product of the web site are the same (shoes), and the principal business activities of the retail shoe store business are the same as those of the web site (purchasing shoes at wholesale and reselling them at retail). Selling shoes on a web site requires some know-how not associated with operating a retail store, such as familiarity with different marketing approaches, distribution chains, and technical operations issues. Nevertheless, the web site's operation does draw to a significant extent on D's existing experience and know-how, and the web site's success will depend in large measure on the goodwill associated with D and the D name. Accordingly, the creation by D of the Internet web site does not constitute the acquisition of a new or different business under § 1.355–3(b)(3)(ii). Instead, it is an expansion of D's retail shoe store business. Therefore, each of D and C is engaged in the active conduct of a five-year active trade or business immediately after the distribution. See Rev. Rul. 2003–18 and § 1.355–3(c), Examples (7) and (8).

HOLDING

The creation by a corporation engaged in the retail shoe store business of an Internet web site that sells shoes at retail constitutes an expansion of the retail shoe store business rather than the acquisition of a new or different business under § 1.355–3(b)(3)(ii).

Revenue Ruling 2007–42

2007–2 Cum. Bull. 44.

ISSUE(S)

Under the facts described below, is a corporation (D) that owns a membership interest in a limited liability company (LLC) classified as a partnership for Federal tax purposes engaged in the active conduct of a trade or business for purposes of § 355(b) of the Internal Revenue Code?

FACTS

Situation 1.

LLC is a domestic limited liability company that has been classified as a partnership for Federal tax purposes since its date of organization. For more than five years, LLC has owned several commercial office buildings that are leased to unrelated third parties. LLC has one class of membership interests outstanding. For more than five years, D has owned a 33 1/3–percent membership interest in LLC, and has owned all the stock of a subsidiary (C), a corporation that has been engaged for more than five years in the active conduct of a trade or business that is unrelated to D's activities.

LLC continuously seeks additional properties to expand its rental business. When a property is located, LLC negotiates its purchase and financing and determines whether renovations or alterations are necessary to make the building suitable for rental. LLC periodically repaints and refurbishes its existing properties.

Pursuant to the terms of its leases, LLC provides day-to-day upkeep and maintenance services for its office buildings. These services include trash collection, ground maintenance, electrical and plumbing repair, and insect control. Additionally, LLC advertises for new tenants, verifies information contained in lease applications, negotiates leases, handles tenant complaints, prepares eviction notices and warnings for delinquent tenants, collects rent, and pays all expenses, including gas, water, sewage, electricity and insurance for the office buildings. LLC also maintains financial and accounting records to reflect income and expenses relating to each of its rental properties as well as LLC's general expenses.

The above described activities of LLC have been conducted for more than five years. The employees of LLC perform all management and operational functions with respect to LLC's rental business. Neither D nor any other member of LLC performs services with respect to LLC's business.

For a valid business purpose, D proposes to distribute all its C stock pro rata to D's shareholders in a transaction intended to satisfy the requirements of § 355.

Except for the issue of whether D is engaged in the active conduct of a trade or business under § 355(b), the transaction will otherwise meet all the requirements of § 355.

Situation 2.

The facts are the same as Situation 1 except that D owns a 20–percent membership interest in LLC.

LAW AND ANALYSIS

Section 355(a) provides that, under certain circumstances, a corporation may distribute stock or securities in a corporation it controls to its shareholders or security holders in a transaction that is nontaxable to such shareholders or security holders. Sections 355(a)(1)(C) and 355(b) require that both the distributing and controlled corporations be engaged, immediately after the distribution, in the active conduct of a trade or business that has been actively conducted throughout the five-year period ending on the date of distribution.

Section 1.355–3(b)(2)(ii) of the Income Tax Regulations, in defining trade or business for purposes of § 355, provides that a corporation is treated as engaged in a trade or business immediately after the distribution if a specific group of activities are being carried on by the corporation for the purpose of earning income or profit, and the activities included in such group include every operation that forms a part of, or a step in, the process of earning income or profit. Such group of activities ordinarily must include the collection of income and the payment of expenses.

Section 1.355–3(b)(2)(iii) provides that the determination whether a trade or business is actively conducted will be made from all the facts and circumstances. Generally, for a trade or business to be actively conducted, the corporation is required itself to perform active and substantial management and operational functions. Generally, activities performed by the corporation itself do not include activities performed by persons outside the corporation, including independent contractors. A corporation may, however, satisfy the active trade or business test through the activities that it performs itself, even though some of its activities are performed by others.

Under § 1.355–3(b)(2)(iv), the active conduct of a trade or business does not include the holding of property for investment purposes. It also does not include the ownership and operation (including leasing) of property used in a trade or business, unless the owner performs significant services with respect to the operation and management of the property.

The fact that a partnership engages in activities that would constitute the active conduct of a trade or business if conducted by a corporation does not necessarily mean that each partner in the partnership is considered to be engaged in the active conduct of a trade or business for purposes of § 355(b). In such a case, the determination of whether a partner is considered to be engaged in the active conduct of a trade or business must be based on the requirements of § 355 and the regulations thereunder taking into account the activities of the partner (if any), the partner's interest in the partnership, and the activities of the partnership.

Rev. Rul. 92–17, 1992–1 C.B. 142, considers whether D, a corporate general partner in a limited partnership, is engaged in the active conduct of a trade or business within the meaning of § 355(b). For more than five years, D owned a 20–percent interest in LP, a limited partnership that owned several commercial office buildings leased to unrelated third parties. D's officers performed active and substantial management functions with respect to LP, including the significant business decision-making of the partnership, and regularly participated in the overall supervision, direction, and control of LP's employees in operating LP's rental business. concludes that D is engaged in the active conduct of a trade or business within the meaning of § 355(b). Rev. Rul. 2002–49, 2002–2 C.B. 288, reaches a similar conclusion where D and another corporation (X) each own a 20–percent interest in a member-managed LLC that is classified as a partnership for Federal tax purposes and D and X jointly manage the LLC's business.

By comparison, § 1.368–1(d)(4)(iii)(B), regarding the continuity of business enterprise requirement applicable to corporate reorganizations, provides that the issuing corporation will be treated as conducting a business of a partnership if members of the qualified group, in the aggregate, own an interest in the partnership representing a significant interest in that partnership business. Those regulations indicate that a one-third interest in the partnership represents a significant interest in the partnership business, and a corporation that owns such interest but does not perform active and substantial management functions for the business of the partnership is nevertheless treated as conducting the business of the partnership.

In Situation 1, D is engaged in the active conduct of LLC's rental business for purposes of § 355(b) because D owns a significant interest in LLC and LLC performs the required activities that constitute an active trade or business under the regulations.

In Situation 2, D is not engaged in the active conduct of LLC's rental business for purposes of § 355(b) because D neither owns a significant interest in LLC nor performs active and substantial management functions for LLC.

HOLDING

In Situation 1, D is engaged in the active conduct of a trade or business for purposes of § 355(b).

In Situation 2, D is not engaged in the active conduct of a trade or business for purposes of § 355(b).

EFFECT ON OTHER REVENUE RULINGS

Rev. Rul. 92–17 is modified to the extent it indicated that a partner must perform management functions in order for the partner to be treated as engaged in the active conduct of the trade or business of the partnership.

NOTE

Although the anti-bailout objective of the active business requirement is clear enough, this multifaceted test has engendered many controversies. The *Lockwood* case is typical of the Commissioner's unsuccessful early efforts to apply the test strictly. The Service has since retreated on many previously contentious issues and most of these changes of heart are reflected in the regulations and in comprehensive proposed regulations issued in 2007 that, when finalized, will profoundly influence the interpretation of the active trade or business requirement.[1] The proposed regulations were issued in response to the enactment of Section 355(b)(3), which substantially revised the active trade or business requirement for corporations that utilize complex structures such as subsidiaries and partnerships to conduct their activities. They also incorporate and "upgrade" several decades of rulings and cases. This Note surveys the settled and lingering questions, incorporating selectively the proposed regulations.

Trade or Business: In General. Both the distributing and the controlled corporation (or the controlled corporations in the case of a split-up) must be engaged immediately after the distribution in a trade or business with a five-year history. The regulations treat a corporation as being engaged in a trade or business if:[2]

> * * * a specific group of activities are being carried on by the corporation for the purpose of earning income or profit, and the activities included in such group include every operation that forms a part of, or a step in, the process of earning income or profit. Such group of activities ordinarily must include the collection of income and the payment of expenses.

The regulations go on to create a dichotomy between the active conduct of a trade or business and passive investment activities. Although the determination of whether a trade or business is "actively conducted" is a factual question turning on all the facts and circumstances, active business status generally requires the corporation to itself perform active and substantial management and operational functions.[3] For this purpose, the activities performed by persons outside the corporation, such as independent contractors, generally are not taken into account.[4] To preclude a tax-free separation of passive investment assets, "active conduct" does not include the holding of property for investment (e.g., raw land or portfolio securities) or the ownership and operation (including leasing) of real or personal property used in the owner's trade or business unless the owner performs significant management services with respect to the property.[5]

Treatment of Affiliated Groups. A corporation historically was treated as actively conducting a trade or business if it did so directly (e.g., through a division) or if "substantially all"[6] of its assets consisted of the stock or

1. See REG–123365–03, 2007–1 C.B. 1357.

2. Reg. § 1.355–3(b)(2)(ii).

3. Reg. § 1.355–3(b)(2)(iii). Under the proposed regulations, some of the corporation's activities, however, can be performed by others, such as employees, shareholders, affiliated corporations, and partnerships in which the corporation is a partner. Prop. Reg. § 1.355–3(b)(2)(iii).

4. Reg. § 1.355–3(b)(2)(iii). Activities performed by independent contractors, however, are considered if the corporation itself performs a sufficient quantity of active management and operational functions. See Rev. Rul. 73–234, 1973–1 C.B. 180; Prop. Reg. § 1.355–3(b)(2)(iii).

5. Reg. § 1.355–3(b)(2)(iv).

6. For advance ruling purposes, "substantially all" was 90 percent of the fair market value of a corporation's gross assets.

securities of one or more "controlled"[7] corporations each of which was engaged in the active conduct of a trade or business.[8] As a result, a holding company that did not directly conduct any business activities still could satisfy the active trade or business test if substantially all of its assets consisted of stock or securities of a controlled corporation that itself conducted an active trade or business. In some situations, however, the holding company was forced to orchestrate cumbersome predistribution maneuvers by relocating active businesses within the corporate group in order to satisfy the "substantially all" requirement and qualify a distribution under Section 355.[9]

To simplify corporate division planning for affiliated groups, Congress added Section 355(b)(3), which eliminates the "substantially all" test and provides that, for purposes of determining whether a corporation is engaged in the active conduct of a trade or business, all members of that corporation's separate affiliated group ("SAG") are treated as one corporation.[10] A corporation's SAG is the affiliated group determined under the rules used for consolidated tax returns in Section 1504(a) as if such corporation were the "common parent."[11] Roughly translated, this means that the distributing or controlled corporation will be treated as meeting the active trade or business test if any lower-tier affiliate in its SAG is so engaged. This rule simplifies planning for corporations with complex structures but, as discussed below, it also has a ripple effect on other aspects of the active trade or business test.

Vertical Divisions of a Single Integrated Business. Suppose a corporation wishes to divide a single trade or business that has been operated for

See Rev. Proc. 96–30, § 4.03(5), 1996–1 C.B. 696; Rev. Proc. 77–37, § 3.04, 1977–2 C.B. 68.

7. "Control" for this purpose was measured by the 80 percent tests for voting power and total shares of all other classes of stock in Section 368(c).

8. I.R.C. § 355(b)(2)(A) (pre–2008).

9. See, e.g., Rev. Rul. 74–79, 1974–1 C.B. 81, where a holding company's assets consisted solely of the stock of four subsidiaries (W, X, Y and Z) of equal size, only two of which (W and X) conducted active businesses. The holding company wished to distribute all the stock of W to its shareholders, but the distribution would not satisfy the active business requirement because, after it occurred, only one-third (far less than "substantially all") of its assets—the stock of X—would consist of an active trade or business. It could qualify, however, by causing X to liquidate tax-free prior to the distribution of W stock and then conducting X's active business directly as a division.

10. I.R.C. § 355(b)(3)(A). This amendment generally applies to distributions occurring after May 27, 2006. The proposed regulations apply this single-entity approach in testing for active trade or business status immediately after a distribution and also throughout the five-year predistribution period. Prop. Reg. § 1.355–3(b)(3).

11. Under Section 1504(a), an affiliated group is one or more chains of "includible corporations" connected through stock ownership with a "common parent." At least 80 percent of the total voting power and 80 percent of the total value of the stock of each of the includible corporations (other than the common parent) must be owned by one or more of the other corporations, and the common parent must satisfy the 80 percent tests with respect to at least one of the other includible corporations. For purposes of the SAG definition in Section 355(b)(3), the rule in Section 1504(b) that disregards "nonincludible" corporations (e.g., a foreign corporation or an insurance company, among others) does not apply. I.R.C. § 355(b)(3)(A).

more than five years? Does Section 355 require two separate predistribution trades or businesses, each with its own five-year history, or may one existing business be divided in two? After several defeats,[12] the Service acknowledged that Section 355 can apply to the separation of a single business. Thus, assuming the other statutory and judicial requirements are met, a corporation engaged in an integrated business at one location may transfer half of its assets to a new subsidiary and distribute the stock of the subsidiary to a 50 percent shareholder in a tax-free split-off.[13] Similarly, as illustrated by the *Lockwood* case, a separation of activities in the same line of business conducted at different locations can be accomplished tax-free if one of the locations does not have a five-year history. The current regulations look to the character of the activity and commonality of functions in determining whether geographically dispersed operations constitute a single integrated business.[14]

Horizontal Divisions. The treatment of horizontal (sometimes called "functional") divisions—i.e., separations of certain distinct functions of a single business enterprise—was once uncertain, but they are now authorized by the active trade or business regulations. To illustrate the issue, assume that a manufacturer of high technology equipment wishes to spin off its research and development function for valid business reasons. The Service once maintained that such support activities did not constitute a separate trade or business because they did not independently produce income.[15] The regulations now sanction some types of horizontal divisions, as illustrated in the following example:[16]

> For the past eight years, corporation X has engaged in the manufacture and sale of household products. Throughout this period, X has maintained a research department for use in connection with its manufacturing activities. The research department has 30 employees actively engaged in the development of new products. X transfers the research department to new subsidiary Y and distributes the stock of Y to X's shareholders. After the distribution, Y continues its research operations on a contractual basis with several corporations, including X. X and Y both satisfy the requirements of section 355(b). * * * The result in this example is the same if, after the distribution, Y continues its research operations but furnishes its services only to X. * * *

12. See Coady v. Commissioner, 33 T.C. 771 (1960), affirmed per curiam 289 F.2d 490 (6th Cir.1961) (single construction business divided into two businesses to resolve shareholder dispute); United States v. Marett, 325 F.2d 28 (5th Cir.1963) (food manufacturer operating at three factories spun off one factory opened eight months before the distribution).

13. See, e.g., Reg. § 1.355–3(c) Examples (4) & (5); Prop. Reg. § 1.355–3(d) Examples 14 & 15.

14. See Reg. § 1.355–3(c) Example 7, which permits a nine-year old department store to spin off a suburban branch constructed three years ago where, after the distribution, each store has its own manager and is operated independently.

15. Reg. § 1.355–1(c)(3) (pre–1989).

16. Reg. § 1.355–3(c) Example (9). See also Prop. Reg. § 1.355–3(d) Example 16, which reaches the same conclusion provided the research department has significant assets and goodwill.

Similarly, if a company that has processed and sold meat products for more than five years separates the sale and processing functions, the active business test is satisfied.[17]

The regulations make it clear that the functional separation in the example above satisfies the active business test whether the research department subsequently provides services only to the business from which it was separated or also to other customers. The example reflects the Service's abandonment of any requirement that an active business must "independently" produce income. But even if the active business test is met, tax-free treatment for a functional division is still not assured. The transaction also must have a corporate business purpose, and it must not run afoul of the "device" limitation. As we will discover shortly, the regulations provide that the same functional separations that pass muster under the active business test may present "evidence" of a prohibited bailout device.[18]

Expansion of a Trade or Business. To satisfy the active business test, both the distributing and distributed (i.e., controlled) corporations—or both distributed corporations in a split-up—must have actively conducted businesses for the five years prior to the distribution.[19] In addition, those businesses must not have been acquired within the five-year predistribution period in a transaction in which gain or loss was recognized by the seller, and must not have been conducted by a corporation the control (i.e., 80 percent) of which was acquired by the distributing or any distributee corporation in a taxable transaction during that five-year period.[20] A purpose of these requirements is to prevent a corporation from using Section 355 to avoid the dividend provisions of Subchapter C by temporarily investing its earnings in a business that it plans to spin off to its shareholders.

The five-year rules have spawned controversies over whether a particular activity is a separate business requiring its own five-year history or simply part of an integrated business which has been active for more than five years. For example, a recently opened suburban branch store may be treated as an integral part of an ongoing department store business with a more than five-year history.[21] On the other hand, businesses with clearly distinct products or services (e.g., a chicken ranch and a winery) are considered to be separate.[22] As *Lockwood* and Revenue Ruling 2003–38 illustrate, similar issues arise in the case of a diversification or expansion of

17. Reg. § 1.355–3(c) Example (10). See also Prop. Reg. § 1.355–3(d) Example 17.

18. See Reg. § 1.355–2(d)(2)(iv)(C).

19. I.R.C. § 355(b)(2)(B).

20. I.R.C. § 355(b)(2)(C)–(D); Reg. § 1.355–3(b)(1)–(5). For this purpose, a "taxable transaction" is one in which gain or loss was recognized in whole or in part by the seller. If a business is acquired in a tax-free reorganization, its previous history carries over (along with its tax attributes) for purposes of the five-year rule.

21. Reg. § 1.355–3(c) Example (7).

22. See, e.g., Rev.Rul. 56–655, 1956–2 C.B. 214 (retail appliance branch and retail furniture branch considered separate businesses); Rev.Rul. 56–451, 1956–2 C.B. 208 (metal industry magazine separate from magazine to serve electrical industry).

a business within the five-year predistribution period. In rulings and regulations, the Service has offered helpful guidance on this question, suggesting that a new activity in the same line of business will be treated as an expansion of the original business unless the "purchase, creation, or other acquisition effects a change of such a character as to constitute the acquisition of a new or different business."[23] This interpretation permits a corporation to accumulate funds and use them to create or purchase the assets of a business, or buy the stock of a corporation conducting the business, and promptly spin off that business to its shareholders provided the "new" activity is in the same line of business that the distributing corporation historically conducted.[24]

Real Estate. The Service has consistently maintained that the holding of vacant investment land does not constitute an actively conducted business and that separation of owner-occupied real estate will be subject to "careful scrutiny."[25] Real estate qualifies as an active business only if the owner performs "significant services with respect to the operation and management of the property."[26] Thus, the Service will not approve the spin-off of vacant land or mineral rights on ranch land, even if development activities are imminent.[27] But it will sanction the separation of an office building substantially leased (10 of 11 floors) to outsiders and actively managed by the lessor.[28] More recently, the Service has ruled that a real estate investment trust's rental activities can constitute an active trade or business if, for example, the REIT provides significant services to its tenants.[29] Even if the active business hurdle is surmounted, however, separations of real estate may be vulnerable under the "device" and business purpose tests.[30]

Limit on Taxable Acquisitions Within Five–Year Predistribution Period. A trade or business does not qualify for purposes of the predistribution

23. Reg. § 1.355–3(b)(3)(ii). See also Rev. Rul. 2002–49, 2002–2 C.B. 288, where a corporation that actively conducted a commercial real estate business in conjunction with another unrelated corporation through a limited liability company in which each corporation held a 20 percent interest continued to engage in the same trade or business (and did not acquire a new or different business) after it acquired the remaining 80 percent of the LLC in a taxable transaction.

24. The proposed regulations endorse this approach and make it clear that a corporation can expand an existing active trade or business by acquiring not only assets but also enough stock (at least 80 percent of the voting power and value) in another corporation in the same line of business to qualify the new subsidiary as a member of the acquiring corporation's "separate affiliated group." Prop. Reg. § 1.355–3(b)(3)(ii), –3(d)(2) Examples 18 & 20.

25. Reg. § 1.355–3(b)(2)(iv).

26. Id.

27. Reg. § 1.355–3(c) Examples (2) and (3). See also Prop. Reg. § 1.355–3(d) Example 13.

28. Reg. § 1.355–3(c) Example (12). Compare Reg. § 1.355–3(c) Example (13), where the separation of a two-story office building did not qualify where the distributing corporation occupied the ground floor and half of the second floor in the conduct of its banking business and rented the remaining area as storage space. See also Prop. Reg. § 1.355–3(d) Examples 11 & 12.

29. Rev. Rul. 2001–29, 2001–1 C.B. 1348.

30. See, e.g., Reg. § 1.355–2(d)(2)(iv)(C).

business history requirement if it was acquired within the five years preceding the distribution in a transaction in which gain or loss was recognized in whole or in part.[31] Although the statute is not crystal clear, it obviously means gain or loss recognized by seller—e.g., a taxable acquisition in which the buyer takes a cost rather than a carryover basis.[32] Tax-free acquisitions, such as liquidations of a controlled subsidiary, do not disqualify the acquired trade or business nor do acquisitive reorganizations even if the target shareholders recognize some gain because they receive boot.[33] The active trade or business requirement also is not met if within the five-year predistribution period the distributing corporation acquires control, measured by the 80 percent tests in Section 368(c), of a corporation conducting the trade or business in a taxable transaction.[34] The proposed regulations, however, treat stock acquisitions that result in the acquired corporation becoming a member of a separate affiliated group as if they were asset acquisitions because, once the acquisition occurs, the corporations are treated as a single corporation.[35]

Activities Conducted by a Partnership or LLC. With the issuance of Revenue Ruling 2007–42,[36] the Service has clarified when a corporate partner is considered to be engaged in the active conduct of a trade or business by attributing to it the activities performed by a partnership in which it holds an interest. Prior rulings held that a corporate partner could be treated as engaged in the active conduct of a trade or business of the partnership if the corporation itself or through its officers performed active and substantial functions for the partnership's business,[37] even if another partner also performed active and substantial management functions. Revenue Ruling 2007–42 goes further and attributes to a member that owns a "significant interest" (at least one-third) in an LLC's capital and profits the trade or business of the LLC even if the corporate member does not itself directly conduct any activities relating to the LLC's business.[38]

31. I.R.C. § 355(b)(2)(C).

32. See Bittker & Eustice, Federal Income Taxation of Corporations and Shareholders ¶ 11.05[2][a] (7th ed. 2000). The proposed regulations elaborate in great detail. See Prop. Reg. § 1.355–3(b)(4).

33. Bittker & Eustice, supra note 32.

34. I.R.C. § 255(b)(2)(D)(ii). In addition, if control of a corporation conducting the trade or business is acquired by a corporate distributee shareholder within the five-year period preceding the distribution in a transaction in which gain or loss is recognized, the active trade or business requirement is not met. I.R.C. § 355(b)(2)(D)(i). For an explanation of this cryptic rule and related roadblocks to using corporate divisions to avoid corporate-level gain on the sale of a business, see Section E1 of this chapter, infra.

35. Prop. Reg. § 1.355–3(b)(4)(iv)(F). If this regulation becomes final, the applicability of Section 355(b)(2)(D) will be limited to situations where D acquires stock constituting "control" of C as measured by the Section 368(c) tests (voting power and other classes of stock) but not the type of control measured by Section 1504(a) (voting power and value) that would cause C to become part of D's separate affiliated group.

36. Supra p. 807.

37. Rev. Rul. 92–17, 1992–1 C.B. 142; Rev. Rul. 2002–49, 2002–2 C.B. 288. See also Prop. Reg. § 1.355–3(b)(2)(v)(C), which requires the corporate partner to own a "meaningful" interest (at least 20 percent is meaningful based on prior rulings) in the partnership.

38. See also Prop. Reg. § 1.355–3(b)(2)(v)(B), –3(d)(2) Example 23.

C. JUDICIAL AND STATUTORY LIMITATIONS

1. BUSINESS PURPOSE

Regulations: § 1.355–2(b).

Background. The business purpose doctrine originated in Gregory v. Helvering[1] and rapidly assumed its role as one of the first "common law" principles of federal taxation. The doctrine has become an increasingly important limitation under Section 355 even though it is never mentioned in the Code. The business purpose and device limitations are conceptually linked, each focusing on the taxpayer's motivation for the transaction. It is appropriate to consider the business purpose requirement first because the strength or weakness of a corporate business purpose is evidence in determining whether a transaction was used principally as a device for distributing earnings and profits.[2] Moreover, the regulations have long provided that the "business purpose requirement is independent of the other requirements under section 355."[3] Thus, a corporate division lacking a business purpose can not be accomplished tax free even if it is not used principally as a device to bail out earnings and profits.[4]

Business Purpose Regulations. The regulations define a corporate business purpose as "a real and substantial non Federal tax purpose germane to the business of the distributing corporation, the controlled corporation or the affiliated group to which the distributing corporation belongs."[5] Valid business purposes include compliance with antitrust and other regulatory decrees, resolution of shareholder disputes, or even amicable partings to permit shareholders to pursue separate business interests.[6] Among other business purposes approved by the courts and the Service over the years are: facilitating a merger of the distributing or controlled corporation;[7] increasing access to credit or new equity investment (such as by enabling either the controlled or distributing corporations to raise capital on more favorable terms through a public offering);[8] resolving labor

1. See p. 793, supra.

2. Reg. § 1.355–2(b)(4), (d)(3)(ii).

3. Reg. § 1.355–2(b)(1).

4. Reg. § 1.355–2(b)(1).

5. Reg. § 1.355–2(b)(2). See also Rev. Proc. 96–30, App. A, 1996–1 C.B. 696, which provided detailed guidelines to be used for ruling purposes in evaluating whether a distribution satisfies the business purpose requirement. But in Rev. Proc. 2003–48, 2003–2 C.B. 86, the Service announced a "no ruling" policy on business purposes issues and deleted the guidelines, which still offer planning guidance. The "no ruling" policy is a pilot program and may be reevaluated by the Service in 2005.

6. Reg. § 1.355–2(b)(5) Examples (1) and (2).

7. Commissioner v. Morris Trust, 367 F.2d 794 (4th Cir.1966); Rev. Proc. 96–30, supra note 5, App. A, §§ 2.07–.08. But see I.R.C. § 355(e) and Section E2 of this chapter, infra.

8. See, e.g., Rev.Rul. 77–22, 1977–1 C.B. 91; Rev.Rul. 85–122, 1985–2 C.B. 118; Rev. Proc. 96–30, supra note 5, App. A, §§ 2.02–.03.

problems;[9] providing an equity interest to a newly-hired key employee;[10] and warding off a hostile takeover.[11]

A pure shareholder purpose, such as personal estate planning, does not suffice under the regulations,[12] but the transaction may pass muster if a shareholder purpose is "so nearly coextensive with a corporate business purpose as to preclude any distinction between them."[13] For example, in Revenue Ruling 2003–52,[14] the Service ruled that the division of a family farm business into two separate corporations, one to grow grain and the other to raise livestock, satisfied the business purpose requirement. The division was motivated by a desire to permit the two principal shareholders (a brother and sister who disagreed over the future direction of the family business) to go their separate ways and devote their undivided attention to the businesses in which they were most involved, and also to promote family harmony and further the estate planning goals of their parents, who also were shareholders. The Service concluded that since the principal motivation for the transaction was to benefit both businesses, the fact that it also facilitated personal estate planning of the shareholders and promoted family harmony was not fatal.

Similarly, the Service found nearly co-extensive corporate and shareholder purposes on a separation of two lines of business of a public company that was motivated by a desire to increase the aggregate trading price of the stock of both businesses after they became separate corporations.[15] In addition to the obvious shareholder benefit, the higher stock prices were found to benefit the distributing corporation in two alternative situations: (1) by enhancing an equity-based employee compensation plan without diluting the interests of existing shareholders by issuing more stock, and (2) by allowing the corporation to use its own (more valuable) stock as partial consideration for future acquisitions with significantly less dilution of existing shareholder interests.[16]

The Service has ruled that the reduction of state and local taxes can be a corporate business purpose.[17] But the regulations make it clear that the reduction of "non Federal" taxes is not an independent corporate business purpose if: (1) the transaction will result in a reduction in both Federal and non Federal taxes because of similarities in the respective laws, and (2) the reduction of Federal taxes is greater than or substantially coextensive with the reduction of non Federal taxes.[18] For example, a spin-off of a subsidiary to enable one or both of the resulting corporations to elect S corporation

9. Olson v. Commissioner, 48 T.C. 855 (1967).

10. Rev. Rul. 88–34, 1988–1 C.B. 115.

11. See Priv. Ltr.Rul. 8819075 (May 13, 1988).

12. Reg. § 1.355–2(b)(2). But see Estate of Parshelsky v. Commissioner, 303 F.2d 14 (2d Cir.1962), where the court held that a shareholder business purpose justified a spin-off even in the absence of a corporate business purpose.

13. Reg. § 1.355–2(b)(2).

14. 2003–1 C.B. 960.

15. Rev. Rul. 2004–23, 2004–1 C.B. 585.

16. Id.

17. Rev.Rul. 76–187, 1976–1 C.B. 97.

18. Reg. § 1.355–2(b)(2).

status is not a business purpose[19] even though the transaction may bear little resemblance to the original bailout evil of Gregory v. Helvering.

A business purpose for a distribution also does not exist if the same corporate objectives can be met through a nontaxable transaction that does not require a distribution of stock of a controlled corporation and which is neither impractical nor unduly expensive.[20] For example, assume that a corporation manufactures both toys and candy through divisions which are not separately incorporated, and the shareholders wish to insulate the candy business from the risks of the toy business. If that goal can be achieved by dropping down the assets of one of the businesses to a new subsidiary, a subsequent distribution of the subsidiary's stock to the parent's shareholders is not carried out for a corporate business purpose.[21]

The fact that Section 355 permits a distributing corporation to avoid corporate-level gain on the distribution of stock of a controlled corporation is not considered by the Service to present such a potential for avoidance of federal taxes that it overrides an otherwise valid corporate business purpose.[22] The Service also has ruled that as long as a distribution is motivated in whole or substantial part by a corporate business purpose at the time it is made, the corporation's later failure to succeed in meeting that purpose will not prevent the distribution from satisfying the business purpose requirement.[23] In addition, continuing relationships for a limited period of time between the distributing and spun-off companies do not necessarily jeopardize the distribution from qualifying under Section 355.[24]

A notable recent addition to the list of acceptable business purposes is known as "fit and focus." The Service has ruled[25] that a software company's spin-off of a paper products business satisfied the business purpose requirement because the distribution was motivated by a desire to allow senior management of the distributing corporation "to concentrate its efforts on the software business, which it believes presents better opportunities for growth and allow the management of the paper products business

19. Reg. § 1.355–2(d)(5) Example (6); see Rev. Proc. 96–30, supra note 5, App. C.

20. Reg. § 1.355–2(b)(3).

21. Reg. §§ 1.355–2(b)(3), 1.355–2(b)(5) Example (3). See also Reg. § 1.355–2(b)(5) Examples (4) and (5).

22. Rev. Rul. 2003–110, 2003–2 C.B. 1083 (corporation used Section 355 to separate its baby food and pesticide businesses to improve a market perception problem arising from the baby food company's affiliation with a pesticide business).

23. Rev. Rul. 2003–55, 2003–1 C.B. 961, where the business purpose for a corporate separation was to facilitate the raising of capital through an initial public offering of the stock of what previously was a wholly owned subsidiary of the distributing corporation. Even though market conditions unexpectedly deteriorated and the public offering was postponed indefinitely, there was a valid business purpose at the time the distribution was made.

24. See Rev. Rul. 2003–75, 2003–2 C.B. 79, where a distribution was made to resolve issues relating to the competition for capital between two businesses (pharmaceuticals and cosmetics) and, after the spin-off, the two companies entered into "transitional" agreements (two years, after which the agreements were to be renegotiated at arm's length for a limited period) relating to information technology, benefits administration, and accounting and tax matters.

25. Rev. Rul. 2003–74, 2003–2 C.B. 77.

to secure for that business the management resources needed for its full development." The ruling also states that the existence of common directors of the distributing and spun-off companies does not necessarily preclude reliance on a "fit and focus" business purpose.

Advance Rulings. In Revenue Procedure 96–30,[26] the Service set forth in great detail the type of information taxpayers must submit in order to obtain an advance ruling in a Section 355 transaction and provided new insight on the Service's approach to the business purpose requirement. The revenue procedure also provided guidelines to be used by the Service in evaluating whether a distribution satisfies the corporate business purpose requirement and a nonexclusive list of valid business purposes. But in 2003, the Service announced a "pilot program" under which it would no longer issue advance rulings on the business purpose requirement and the device limitation.[27] In lieu of guidelines, the Service is releasing more published rulings (many are discussed in the text above) approving a business purpose in a variety of factual contexts.

2. Continuity of Interest

Regulations: § 1.355–2(c).

The regulations require that those persons who historically owned an interest in the enterprise prior to a corporate division must own, in the aggregate, an amount of stock establishing a continuity of interest in each of the modified corporate forms in which the enterprise is conducted after the distribution.[1] This means that one or more of the shareholders of the distributing corporation must emerge from the transaction (in the aggregate) with at least a 50 percent equity interest in each of the corporations that conduct the enterprise after the division.[2] The continuity of interest test overlaps considerably with the device limitation, which patrols against prearranged postdistribution sales as part of its anti-bailout mission. The regulations nonetheless emphasize that continuity of interest is an independent test that must be met in addition to the other Section 355 requirements.[3]

A common divisive transaction involves the breakup of a corporate enterprise to allow feuding shareholders to part company, with each taking a share of the business in the form of stock in separate corporations. The

26. See supra note 5.

27. Rev. Proc. 2003–48, 2003–2 C.B. 86.

1. Reg. § 1.355–2(c)(1).

2. Without explicitly saying so, several examples in the regulations indicate that a 50 percent equity interest, the safe harbor benchmark for Type A reorganizations, is what is needed to "maintain" continuity of interest. See, e.g., Reg. § 1.355–2(c)(2) Example (2); Rev.Proc. 96–30, § 4.06, 1996–19 I.R.B. 8, 18. Although 50 percent continuity historically was required to obtain an advance ruling from the Service, the case law supports a lower percentage, and the regulations on acquisitive reorganizations now confirm that the Service will accept 40 percent continuity for mergers. Reg. § 1.368–1T(e)(2)(iv) Example 1. It follows that 40 percent also should be sufficient for corporate divisions. See Ginsburg & Levin, Mergers, Acquisitions & Buyouts, § 610.2 (2008).

3. Reg. § 1.355–2(c)(1). For a rare published ruling on the application of the continuity of interest doctrine to a spin-off, see Rev.Rul. 79–273, 1979–2 C.B. 125.

regulations acknowledge that this type of transaction, whether structured as a split-off or split-up, satisfies the continuity of interest requirement because the prior owners of the integrated enterprise emerge in the aggregate with all the stock of two corporations that survive the separation. Assume, however, that A and B each own 50 percent of the stock of P, Inc., which is engaged in one business, and P owns all the stock of S, Inc., which is engaged in a different business. If new and unrelated shareholder C purchases all of A's stock in P and P then distributes all the stock of S to B in redemption of B's P stock, the transaction fails the continuity of interest test because the owners of P prior to the distribution (A and B) do not, in the aggregate, own an amount of stock establishing continuity of interest in both P and S after the distribution.[4] Only the historic shareholders of P (i.e., A and B) may be counted for continuity of interest purposes, and the smoking pistol is present if none of those shareholders owns any stock of P after the distribution. As for who qualifies as an historic shareholder, it appears that a shareholder who acquires P stock prior to the time that P decides to engage in a division should qualify even if the acquisition occurred shortly before the distribution.[5] Apparently, even a person who acquired P stock in contemplation of a distribution of S stock will be treated as an historic shareholder if the acquisition was more than two years prior to the distribution.[6]

The shareholders of the distributing corporation also must maintain continuity of interest after the distribution.[7] A post-distribution continuity issue might arise, for example, if shareholders sold more than 50 percent of the stock of either the distributing or controlled corporations shortly after the distribution. Shareholders who committed themselves to sell prior to the distribution or who had a fixed intention to do so are not likely to have maintained continuity of interest, but an unanticipated sale should not be a problem.

3. THE "DEVICE" LIMITATION

Code: § 355(a)(1)(B).

Regulations: § 1.355–2(d).

a. IN GENERAL

Section 355(a)(1)(B) provides that a corporate division may not be "used principally as a device for the distribution of the earnings and

4. Reg. § 1.355–2(c)(2) Example (3).

5. See Kaden & Wolfe, "Spin-offs, Split-offs, and Split-ups: A Detailed Analysis of Section 355," 44 Tax Notes 565, 588–589 (July 31, 1989).

6. Id. at 589. Cf. Rev.Rul. 74–5, 1974–1 C.B. 82, declared obsolete on other grounds by Rev.Rul. 89–37, 1989–1 C.B. 107.

7. This is similar to the recently abandoned post-acquisition continuity requirement for acquisitive reorganizations. See Chapter 17B1, supra. It remains to be seen whether the Service will modify its post-distribution continuity rules in the corporate divisions context. For an extensive discussion of the Section 355 version of the continuity of interest doctrine, see Shores, "Reexamining Continuity of Shareholder Interest in Corporate Divisions," 18 Va. Tax Rev. 473 (1999).

profits'' of the distributing corporation or the controlled subsidiary. The historic mission of this requirement has been to prevent the conversion of ordinary dividend income into preferentially taxed capital gain through a bailout masquerading as a corporate division.[1] This goal is reaffirmed in the regulations, which provide:[2]

> * * * a tax-free distribution of the stock of a controlled corporation presents a potential for tax avoidance by facilitating the avoidance of the dividend provisions of the Code through the subsequent sale or exchange of stock of one corporation and the retention of the stock of another corporation. A device can include a transaction that effects a recovery of basis.

Ever since the device limitation was added to the Code, its meaning and scope have been mired in obscurity. The regulations initially fail to burn off the fog, declaring that ''generally, the determination of whether a transaction was used principally as a device will be made from all of the facts and circumstances.''[3] They go on to offer some guidance by identifying certain ''device'' and ''nondevice'' factors which are ''evidence'' of the presence or absence of a device, but the strength of this ''evidence'' still depends on ''the facts and circumstances.''[4]

The role of the device limitation is diminished but not eliminated as long as dividends and long-term capital gains of noncorporate taxpayers are taxed at the same preferential rate. A ''device'' still may include a transaction that effects a recovery of a shareholder's stock basis. In situations where shareholders have a nominal basis and are indifferent to dividend vs. capital gain treatment, the question remains whether the Service might invoke the device limitation to tax the distributing corporation, which would be required to recognize gain on the distribution if the transaction does not qualify under Section 355, or whether it is sufficient to rely on more targeted corporate-level statutory watchdogs, such as Sections 355(d) and 355(e), which are discussed later in this chapter.[5]

Transactions Ordinarily Not a Device. Notwithstanding the presence or absence of the ''device factors'' to be discussed below, three transactions ''ordinarily'' are not considered a tax avoidance device. Distributions are presumed innocent if:

(1) the distributing and controlled corporations have neither accumulated nor current earnings and profits as of the date of the distribution, taking into account the possibility that a distribution of appreciated property by the distributing corporation as part of a divisive transaction would create earnings and profits if Section 355 did not apply;[6]

1. See, e.g., Rev.Rul. 71–383, 1971–2 C.B. 180.

2. Reg. § 1.355–2(d)(1).

3. Reg. § 1.355–2(d)(1).

4. Reg. § 1.355–2(d)(2)(i), (3)(i).

5. See Section E of this chapter, infra.

6. Reg. § 1.355–2(d)(5)(ii).

(2) in the absence of Section 355, the distribution would qualify as a redemption to pay death taxes under Section 303;[7] and

(3) in the absence of Section 355, the distribution would qualify, with respect to each distributee shareholder, as an exchange redemption under Section 302(a).[8]

Section 303 and Section 302(a)–type redemptions lose the benefit of the presumption, however, if they involve the distribution of stock of more than one controlled corporation and facilitate the avoidance of the dividend provisions of the Code through the subsequent sale or exchange of stock of one corporation and the retention of the stock of another corporation.[9]

Device and Nondevice Factors: In General. The regulations specify three factors that are "evidence" of a device ("device factors") and three factors that are evidence of a nondevice ("nondevice factors"). The device factors are: (1) a pro rata distribution; (2) a subsequent sale or exchange of stock of either the distributing or controlled corporation; and (3) the nature and use of the assets of the distributing and controlled corporations immediately after the transaction.[10] The three nondevice factors are: (1) the corporate business purpose for the transaction; (2) the fact that the distributing corporation is publicly traded and widely held; and (3) the fact that the stock of the controlled corporation is distributed to one or more domestic corporations which would be entitled to a dividends received deduction under Section 243 if Section 355 does not apply to the transaction.[11] The presence of one or more of these factors is not controlling, however, and the "strength" of the evidence depends on the facts and circumstances.[12]

b. DEVICE FACTORS

Pro Rata Distribution. A pro rata distribution—for example, a spin-off—is considered to present the greatest potential for avoidance of the dividend provisions of Subchapter C and thus is more likely to be used principally as a device. As a result, the regulations provide that a pro rata or substantially pro rata distribution is evidence of a device.[13]

Subsequent Sale or Exchange of Stock. A parenthetical clause in Section 355(a)(1)(B) cryptically provides that the "mere fact" that stock or securities of either the distributing or controlled corporations are sold by all or some of the shareholders is not to be construed to mean that the transaction was used principally as a device. But the Service has long contended that a sale of stock of the distributing or controlled corporation

7. Reg. § 1.355–2(d)(5)(iii). See Chapter 13H, supra.

8. Reg. § 1.355–2(d)(5)(iv). For this purpose, the waiver of family attribution rules apply without regard to the ten year look forward rule and the requirement to file a waiver agreement in Sections 302(c)(2)(A)(ii) and (iii). See Chapter 13C, supra.

9. Reg. § 1.355–2(d)(5)(i). For an example, see Reg. § 1.355–2(d)(5)(v) Example (2).

10. Reg. § 1.355–2(d)(2).

11. Reg. § 1.355–2(d)(3).

12. Reg. § 1.355–2(d)(2)(i); –2(d)(3)(i).

13. Reg. § 1.355–2(d)(2)(ii).

shortly after a corporate division is evidence that the transaction was used as a bailout device. The "strength" of the evidence depends upon the percentage of stock disposed of after the distribution, the length of time between the distribution and the subsequent sale and the extent to which the subsequent sale was prearranged.[14]

A subsequent sale or exchange negotiated or agreed upon before the distribution is "substantial evidence" of a device.[15] A sale is always prearranged if it was "pursuant to an arrangement negotiated or agreed upon before the distribution if enforceable rights to buy or sell existed before the distribution."[16] The regulations are more equivocal if a sale was merely discussed by the parties but was "reasonably to be anticipated." In that event, it "ordinarily" will be considered to be previously negotiated or agreed upon.[17] Seemingly ignoring the express language of Section 355(a)(1)(B), the regulations also provide that even in the absence of prior negotiations or agreement, a subsequent sale nonetheless is "evidence of a device."[18] Presumably, the evidence would be fairly weak if the decision to sell were not made until after the distribution.

The perceived bailout abuse of a subsequent sale normally is present only when the selling shareholders cash out their investment. The regulations logically provide that if the shareholders dispose of stock in a subsequent tax-free reorganization in which no more than an "insubstantial" amount of gain is recognized, the transaction will not be treated as a subsequent sale or exchange. Rather, because the shareholders maintain an interest in the continuing enterprise, the stock received in the exchange is treated as equivalent to the stock surrendered.[19] But any sale of the new stock received will be subject to the "subsequent sale" rules and could be evidence of a device.[20]

The Service's reliance on subsequent stock sales (whether or not prearranged) as substantial evidence of a device has always been questionable. To return to the earlier introductory example, assume that Diverse Corporation has actively conducted profitable winery and chicken ranch businesses for more than five years. If Diverse wished to spin off the chicken ranch as Poultry, Inc., it would have no difficulty satisfying the active business test. But what if the spin-off were the prelude to a prearranged sale of the Poultry, Inc. stock by the controlling shareholders? If gain on that sale were taxable to the shareholders at capital gains rates, or even if it merely effected a recovery of part of the shareholders' basis in their Diverse Corp. stock, should the spin-off be viewed principally as a device to bail out Diverse's earnings and profits?

In considering these questions, keep in mind the alternatives available to Diverse. If the corporation simply had sold the chicken ranch assets and distributed the proceeds to its noncorporate shareholders, the distribution

14. Reg. § 1.355–2(d)(2)(iii)(A).

15. Reg. § 1.355–2(d)(2)(iii)(B).

16. Reg. § 1.355–2(d)(2)(iii)(D).

17. Id.

18. Reg. § 1.355–2(d)(2)(iii)(C).

19. Reg. § 1.355–2(d)(2)(iii)(E).

20. Id.

likely would have qualified as a partial liquidation, entitling noncorporate shareholders to exchange (and thus capital gains) treatment.[21] The same result would have occurred if the chicken ranch assets were distributed pro rata to the shareholders and sold shortly thereafter. To be sure, a sale or distribution of the chicken ranch assets by the corporation would have triggered gain at the corporate and shareholder levels.[22] But, historically at least, the principal concern in Section 355 was not with the double taxation of corporate earnings but rather the tax treatment of a distribution to the shareholders. If an economically equivalent transaction (i.e., a partial liquidation) would have qualified for capital gain treatment, it seems anomalous to classify a spin-off followed by a prearranged sale of the same business as a device to convert ordinary dividend income to capital gain. In the last analysis, the correct answer from a policy perspective may be to treat partial liquidation distributions as dividends to noncorporate shareholders. Moreover, even if it is not a device, a distribution followed by a taxable sale is unlikely to satisfy the business purpose test and, if the sale closely follows the distribution but somehow escapes the device limitation, the transaction also may fail the continuity of interest requirement. And, of course, much of this discussion is less important as long as dividends and capital gains of noncorporate taxpayers are taxed at the same preferential rate.

Nature and Use of the Assets. The regulations also enforce the device limitation by taking into account the "nature, kind, amount, and use of the assets of the distributing and the controlled corporations (and corporations controlled by them) immediately after the transaction."[23] Thus, the existence of assets that are not used in an active trade or business, such as cash and other liquid assets that are not related to the reasonable needs of the active business, is evidence of a device.[24] To illustrate, assume that Corporation P spins off Corporation S in order to comply with certain regulatory requirements under state law. As part of the separation, P transfers excess cash (not related to the reasonable needs of P's or S's business) to S and then distributes the S stock pro rata to P's shareholders. The result of this infusion of cash into S is that the percentage of liquid assets not related to the trade or business is substantially greater for S than for P. The regulations view this as suspect, providing in an example that the transfer of cash by P to S is "relatively strong evidence of device."[25] When coupled with the pro rata nature of the distribution, the transaction is considered to have been used principally as a device notwithstanding the "strong business purpose" because there was no business purpose for the infusion of cash into S.[26]

21. See I.R.C. § 302(b)(4), (e). But see Rev.Rul. 75–223, 1975–1 C.B. 109, discussed at p. 599, supra, in which the Service ruled that a distribution of stock of a subsidiary may not qualify as a partial liquidation. See also Morgenstern v. Commissioner, 56 T.C. 44 (1971).

22. See Chapters 15 and 16, supra.

23. Reg. § 1.355–2(d)(2)(iv).

24. Reg. § 1.355–2(d)(2)(iv)(A), (B).

25. Reg. § 1.355–2(d)(4) Example (3).

26. Reg. § 1.355–2(d)(2)(iv)(B); 1.355–2(d)(4) Example (3). Compare Reg. § 1.355–2(d)(4) Example (2), where the transfer of cash and liquid securities from the distribut-

The regulations also consider the relationship between the distributing and controlled corporations and the effect of a sale of one of the businesses on the overall enterprise. Evidence of a device is presented if the distributing or controlled corporation is a business that principally serves the business of the other corporation (a "secondary business") and it can be sold without adversely affecting the business that it serves.[27] Thus, the spin-off of a captive coal mine from a steel manufacturer, a transaction which satisfied the active business test,[28] nonetheless presents evidence of a device if the principal function of the coal mine is to satisfy the requirements of the steel business and the coal mine could be sold without adversely affecting the steel business.[29] The apparent concern here is not so much with the potential for tax avoidance through non-arm's length intercorporate transactions between the separated corporations. That type of abuse is adequately policed by Section 482, which authorizes the Commissioner to allocate income or deductions between or among commonly controlled trades or businesses.[30] What appears to be bothering the Service is the likelihood for avoidance of the dividend provisions of the Code when the "related function" is not truly integral to the business from which it has been separated.

c. NONDEVICE FACTORS

Acknowledging that the corporate business purposes for a transaction may be sufficiently compelling to outweigh any evidence of a device, the regulations provide that the corporate business purpose for a transaction is evidence of nondevice.[31] In keeping with the "sliding scale" approach that pervades the device regulations, the stronger the evidence of device, then the stronger is the business purpose required to prevent determination that the transaction was used principally as a device.[32] The strength of a corporate business purpose, of course, is based on all the facts and circumstances, including but not limited to the importance of achieving the purpose to the success of the business, the extent to which the transaction is prompted by a person not having a proprietary interest in either corporation or by other outside factors beyond the control of the distributing corporation, and the "immediacy of the conditions" prompting the transaction.[33]

ing to the controlled corporation was "relatively weak evidence of device" because after the transfer the two corporations held liquid assets in amounts proportional to the values of their businesses.

27. Reg. § 1.355–2(d)(2)(iv)(C).

28. See Reg. § 1.355–3(c) Example (11).

29. Reg. § 1.355–2(d)(2)(iv)(C). Likewise, the separation of the sales and manufacturing functions will constitute evidence of a device if the principal function of the sales operation after the separation is to sell the output from the manufacturing operation and the sales operation could be sold without adversely affecting the manufacturing operation.

30. See Chapter 10D, infra.

31. Reg. § 1.355–2(d)(3)(ii).

32. Id.

33. Id.

The fact that the distributing corporation is publicly traded and widely held, having no shareholder who directly or indirectly owns more than five percent of any class of stock, also is evidence of nondevice.[34]

Finally, the fact that the stock of the controlled corporation is distributed to a domestic corporate distributee which, without Section 355, would be entitled to the Section 243 dividends received deduction, is evidence of a nondevice.[35]

4. DISQUALIFIED INVESTMENT CORPORATIONS

Section 355(g) was added to the Code to prevent transactions known as "cash-rich split-offs" from qualifying for nonrecognition treatment. The abuse at which Section 355(g) is directed is best illustrated by a simple example. Assume that for more than five years Investor Corp. ("I") has owned a highly appreciated 30 percent interest in Distributing Corp. ("D"). I wishes to accomplish what would appear to be impossible: a sale of its D stock for cash without paying any current tax. D wishes to buy back some of its stock and is willing to assist I plan a tax-efficient disposition. To accomplish these objectives, D transfers a small five-year active trade or business to C Corp. ("C"), a newly formed subsidiary, along with a large amount of cash (or other liquid assets) in exchange for all the C stock. D then redeems I's D stock by distributing its C stock to I in exchange for I's entire holding in D. I then promptly liquidates C (its new cash-rich subsidiary), treating the transaction as a tax-free liquidation under Section 332.[1]

Prior to the enactment of Section 355(g), the transaction described above was likely to qualify as tax-free. The active trade or business test did not require the active business of the controlled corporation to constitute any particular percentage of the overall value of C, and the device test was not violated because the distributee shareholder (I, in the example above) completely terminated its interest in D. This "too good to be true" strategy was employed by several public companies in significant transactions, prompting the Treasury to seek corrective legislation.[2]

Section 355(g) provides that a distribution does not qualify as tax-free if: (1) either the distributing or controlled corporation is, immediately after the transaction, a "disqualified investment corporation," and (2) any person holds, immediately after the transaction, a 50–percent or greater interest (measured by voting power and value) in any disqualified investment corporation but only if such person did not hold such an interest in

34. Reg. § 1.355–2(d)(3)(iii).

35. Reg. § 1.355–2(d)(3)(iv).

1. For a good discussion of the cash-rich split-off strategy, see Willens, "Dividends, Capital Gains, and Spin-offs Affected by Increase, Prevention and Reconciliation Act," 104 J. Tax'n 327 (2006).

2. In one reported transaction, Clorox distributed $2.1 billion in cash and a business worth $740 million to a U.S. subsidiary of a German company in redemption of that subsidiary's 29 percent interest in Clorox.

the corporation immediately before the transaction.[3] D or C is a disqualified investment corporation if the fair market value of its "investment assets" is two-thirds or more of the fair market value of all its assets.[4] Investment assets include cash; corporate stock or securities; partnership interests; debt instruments or other evidences of indebtedness; any option, forward, or futures contract, notional principal contract, or derivative; foreign currency; or any similar asset.[5] Various exceptions and special rules apply to determine a corporation's investment assets and to measure whether a person has a 50–percent–or–greater interest.[6]

If Section 355(g) applies, the transaction is fully taxable at the corporate and shareholder levels, but cash-rich (albeit not as rich) split-offs are still feasible if tainted liquid assets fall below the two-thirds threshold.

PROBLEMS

1. Lemon Corporation has been engaged in the manufacture and sale of computer hardware equipment for ten years at separate facilities in Boston, Massachusetts and San Jose, California. During this same period, Lemon has operated research and development divisions at each location. Lemon's only class of common stock is owned equally by Ms. Micro and Mr. Chips.

Consider whether each of the following alternative transactions qualifies as a tax-free corporate division under Section 355:

(a) As a result of a shareholder dispute, Ms. Micro wishes to say goodbye to Mr. Chips. To enable the shareholders to part company but continue in the computer business, Lemon contributes the assets of its Boston manufacturing and research divisions to a new corporation, Peach, Inc., and distributes all the Peach stock to Mr. Chips in redemption of his Lemon stock. Ms. Micro remains as the sole shareholder of Lemon, which continues to conduct its business in San Jose.

(b) Same as (a), above, except that the Boston facility was opened only three years ago.

(c) Same as (a), above, except that three years ago Lemon acquired all the stock of Peach, Inc., which operated the Boston facility, for cash.

(d) Same as (c), above, except Peach had two classes of stock and Lemon acquired enough stock to constitute control under Section 368(c) but not enough to make Peach a member of Lemon's

3. I.R.C. § 355(g)(1). The provision applies to distributions after May 17, 2006, with certain specialized exceptions.

4. I.R.C. § 355(g)(2)(A)(i). To provide transitional relief, in the case of distributions during the one year following enactment of Section 355(g), the tainted asset threshold was three-fourths. The two-thirds threshold became effective on May 17, 2007.

5. I.R.C. § 355(g)(2)(B)(i).

6. I.R.C. § 355(g)(2)(ii)–(iv); 355(g)(3)–(5).

separate affiliated group under Section 1504(a)(2). (How could this happen?).

(e) Assume again that the Boston and San Jose divisions have been operated by Lemon for ten years. To comply with a court-imposed divestiture order, Lemon transfers the assets of the research divisions to a new corporation, Research, Inc., and distributes all the Research stock pro rata to its two shareholders. After the distribution, Research, Inc. continues to perform services solely for Lemon. Any different result if Research also performed services for other companies?

(f) Same as (e), above, except the purpose of the transaction was to enable the manufacturing and research divisions to maintain different compensation and retirement plans for their employees.

2. Assume the same basic facts as in Problem 1, except that Lemon Corporation operates its computer hardware manufacturing business at only one location. Lemon also owns all the stock of Floppy Disk, Inc., a software manufacturer. Lemon purchased the Floppy Disk stock six years ago for cash. The hardware and software businesses are of approximately equal value, and both Lemon and Floppy Disk have substantial earnings and profits.

Consider whether each of the following alternative transactions qualifies as a tax-free corporate division under Section 355:

(a) To resolve a shareholder dispute, Lemon distributes all the stock of Floppy Disk, Inc. to Mr. Chips in complete redemption of his stock in Lemon.

(b) Same as (a), above, except that shortly before the distribution of Floppy Disk stock to Mr. Chips, Ms. Micro sold all of her Lemon stock to Mr. Modem, who wished to acquire the hardware business but not the software company.

(c) To comply with a state law providing that computer hardware and software businesses may not be conducted by parent and subsidiary corporations, Lemon must spin off or sell its Floppy Disk, Inc. subsidiary. In anticipation of the new law, Lemon's board of directors informally negotiates a sale of Floppy Disk to Suitor, Inc. Before the agreement is reduced to an enforceable writing, Lemon distributes the Floppy Disk stock to Ms. Micro and Mr. Chips. Two months later, the shareholders sell the Floppy Disk stock to Suitor on the same terms negotiated by the Lemon board of directors.

(d) Same as (c), above, except that the Lemon board rejects Suitor's offer and instead distributes the Floppy Disk stock pro rata to the shareholders. Four months later, the shareholders sell their Floppy Disk stock to White Knight, Inc.

(e) Same as (d), above, except the sale by the shareholders is made to Suitor, Inc. on essentially the same terms that had been rejected by the Lemon board of directors.

D. TAX TREATMENT OF THE PARTIES TO A CORPORATE DIVISION

Code: §§ 311(a), (b)(1) & (2); 312(a), (b), (h); 336(c); 355(a)(1)(A), (3), (c); 356; 358(a)–(c); 361; 362(b), (e)(1); 1032. Skim §§ 301; 302; 355(d); 381(a); 1223(1) & (2).

Regulations: §§ 1.312–10; 1.358–2.

1. INTRODUCTION

If the requirements of Section 355 and the accompanying judicial doctrines are satisfied, other provisions come into play to govern the specific tax consequences (e.g., total or partial nonrecognition of gain, basis, holding period, etc.) to the parties. In this section, we consider the tax consequences if a corporate division is preceded by the formation of one or more new corporations in a Type D reorganization, the consequences of the division itself, and the results if the division fails to satisfy the statutory and judicial requirements.

If one or more corporations are formed as a preparatory step to a qualifying corporate division, the formation of the new subsidiary is a Type D reorganization.[1] The parent (distributing) corporation does not recognize gain or loss on the transfer of assets to the controlled corporation,[2] and it takes an exchanged basis in the new stock that it receives[3] and may tack the holding period of any capital assets or Section 1231 property that it exchanges for the stock.[4] The newly formed controlled corporation does not recognize gain on the issuance of its stock[5] and it takes the assets with a transferred basis and a tacked holding period.[6] The earnings and profits of the parent corporation are apportioned between the parent and controlled corporations according to rules provided in the regulations.[7] Section 381, providing for carryover of corporate attributes in certain corporate acquisi-

1. I.R.C. § 368(a)(1)(D). A "divisive" D reorganization involves a transfer by one corporation of part of its assets to another corporation if, immediately after the transfer, the transferor "controls" the transferee and, pursuant to the same plan, stock or securities of the controlled corporation are distributed to the shareholders of the transferor corporation in a transaction that qualifies under Section 355. Id. For this purpose, the fact that the shareholders of the distributing corporation dispose of part or all of their distributed stock, or that the distributing corporation issues additional stock, is not taken into account. I.R.C. § 368(a)(2)(H).

2. I.R.C. § 361(a).

3. I.R.C. § 358(a).

4. I.R.C. § 1223(1).

5. I.R.C. § 1032(a).

6. I.R.C. §§ 362(b); 1223(2).

7. I.R.C. § 312(h); Reg. § 1.312–10(a), (c). In the case of a newly created corporation, this allocation generally is made in proportion to the relative fair market values of the assets retained by the parent corporation and the assets transferred to the controlled corporation. Reg. § 1.312–10(a). In a "proper case," the regulations provide that this allocation should be made in proportion to the "net basis" (after reduction for liabilities) of the transferred and retained assets. Id.

tions, does not apply to divisive reorganizations and thus the parent corporation retains its tax attributes other than the earnings and profits which are allocated to the controlled corporation.

2. Consequences to Shareholders and Security Holders

No Boot Received. If the requirements of Section 355 are met, the shareholders or security holders of the distributing corporation generally do not recognize gain or loss on the distribution of stock or securities of the controlled corporation.[1] The aggregate basis of the stock or securities in the distributing corporation held by the shareholder is allocated among the stock and securities of both the distributing and controlled corporations in proportion to their relative fair market values,[2] and the shareholder's holding period in the stock or securities of the controlled corporation received in the distribution includes the holding period of the stock or securities of the distributing corporation.[3]

Treatment of Boot. As with most other types of reorganizations, the receipt of boot in an otherwise qualifying corporate division does not necessarily spell doom for the transaction but results in the recognition of gain to the shareholder receiving the boot. For this purpose, boot includes cash, any property other than stock or securities of the controlled corporation (e.g., short-term debt obligations, stock rights or warrants), securities of the controlled corporation to the extent that their principal amount exceeds the principal amount of any securities surrendered, any stock of the controlled corporation that was acquired by the distributing corporation in a transaction in which gain or loss was recognized within the five-year period prior to the distribution, and nonqualified preferred stock received in a distribution with respect to stock other than nonqualified preferred stock.[4]

The treatment of boot depends on the form of the division. In the case of a spin-off, the boot is treated as a distribution to which Section 301 applies (without regard to the shareholder's realized gain) and is thus a dividend to the extent of the distributing corporation's current and accumulated earnings and profits and a return of capital to the extent of any balance.[5] In the case of a split-off or split-up, both of which involve an exchange rather than a distribution, Section 356(a)(1) requires the shareholder to recognize any realized gain to the extent of the boot received in the distribution. The characterization of that gain is more problematic. Section 356(a)(2) adopts the same rule used for acquisitive reorganizations

1. I.R.C. § 355(a)(1).

2. I.R.C. § 358(b), (c).

3. I.R.C. § 1223(1).

4. I.R.C. §§ 355(a)(3), (4); 356(a), (b), (d)(2)(C) & (D). For the definition of nonqualified preferred stock, see I.R.C. § 355(g)(2) and Chapter 11B3, supra.

5. I.R.C. § 356(b). For noncorporate shareholders, virtually all such dividends will be "qualified" and thus taxable at the 15 percent maximum rate.

by providing that if the exchange has "the effect of the distribution of a dividend," the gain recognized is treated as a dividend to the extent of the shareholder's ratable share of accumulated earnings and profits of the distributing corporation.[6] The balance of any recognized gain is treated as gain from the exchange of property.[7] Dividend equivalence is tested by applying the "before" and "after" ownership principles of Section 302 (i.e., meaningful reduction of the shareholder's proportionate interest) using an assumption that the shareholder had retained the distributing corporation stock that actually was exchanged for controlled corporation stock and then had received the boot in exchange for distributing corporation stock equal in value to the boot.[8] Whether or not this hypothetical redemption results in a dividend is tested by comparing the shareholder's percentage ownership in the distributing corporation before the transaction with the interest the shareholder would have retained in the distributing corporation if he surrendered only the stock exchanged for the boot. Any loss realized by a shareholder in a Section 355 exchange may not be recognized.[9]

Section 358 again governs the basis of the boot and nonrecognition property received in the distribution. The boot takes a fair market value basis and its holding period commences as of the date of the distribution.[10] The aggregate basis of the nonrecognition property (i.e., stock and securities) is the same as the basis of the stock or securities of the distributing corporation plus any gain recognized and less any cash and the fair market value of any boot property received in the exchange.[11] That aggregate basis is then allocated among the old and new stock or securities (or the new stock or securities, in the case of a split-up) in proportion to their relative fair market values.[12] If the "old stock" was acquired at different times or for different prices, the distributee shareholders generally must trace their bases in the various blocks of old stock (rather than using an average basis) in determining the basis of the new stock under Section 358. If tracing is impossible, the taxpayer may designate how the Section 358 basis is to be allocated among the different lots.[13] The nonrecognition property ordinarily is eligible for a tacked holding period.[14]

6. In one of the many curiosities in the world of reorganizations, neither Section 356(a)(2) nor the applicable regulations refer to *current* earnings and profits.

7. See Reg. § 1.356–1(b)(2).

8. Rev.Rul. 93–62, 1993–2 C.B. 118. See also Commissioner v. Clark, 489 U.S. 726, 109 S.Ct. 1455 (1989), which uses a similar approach in testing for dividend equivalence in acquisitive reorganizations where T shareholders receive boot. See Chapter 17B6a, supra.

9. I.R.C. § 356(c).

10. I.R.C. § 358(a)(2).

11. I.R.C. § 358(a)(1).

12. I.R.C. § 358(b)(2), (c); Reg. § 1.358–2.(a)(2)(i). The Service has never provided any guidance as to the precise date to be used in valuing the corporations for purposes of this allocation. In the case of publicly held companies, the date selected ordinarily is the first day that the stock of the controlled corporation was traded on a listed exchange. For other possibilities, see Bittker & Eustice, Federal Income Taxation of Corporations and Shareholders ¶ 11.12[1] (7th ed. 2000).

13. See Reg. § 1.358–2(a)(2)(i), –2(c) Example 12.

14. I.R.C. § 1223(1).

3. CONSEQUENCES TO THE DISTRIBUTING AND CONTROLLED CORPORATIONS

Nonrecognition of Gain or Loss: General Rules. The tax consequences to the distributing corporation in a Section 355 transaction initially are determined by Section 361(c) if the distribution is preceded by a Type D reorganization and by Section 355(c) if it is not. In either case, the results generally are the same. If a Section 355 transaction occurs in conjunction with certain changes in shareholder ownership, the distributing corporation also may be required to recognize gain under Section 355(d).[1]

If a Section 355 distribution is part of a reorganization plan—i.e., where the distributing corporation first contributes property to the controlled corporation—no gain or loss is recognized if the property is contributed solely in exchange for stock or securities of the controlled corporation.[2] The distributing corporation recognizes gain, however, if the liabilities assumed by the controlled corporation exceed the aggregate adjusted basis of the transferred property or if it otherwise receives boot that is not distributed to shareholders or creditors as part of the reorganization plan.[3]

The distributing corporation also does not recognize gain on the distribution to its shareholders of "qualified property"—i.e., stock or debt obligations of the controlled corporation.[4] Thus, in the typical spin-off or split-off, where the distributing corporation's basis in the stock of the controlled corporation is ordinarily less than its fair market value, no corporate-level gain is recognized on the distribution. Section 311(b), which otherwise might have required gain recognition, is not applicable because it only applies to distributions under Subpart A of Subchapter C (Sections 301–307), and Section 355 is not within that portion of the Code.[5] The same result occurs on a split-up. Section 336, which otherwise might have required the recognition of corporate-level gain on a liquidating distribution, does not apply to distributions that are part of a reorganization.[6] Gain is recognized, however, in the rare case where appreciated boot is distributed in a Section 355 transaction that is part of a reorganization.[7]

If the distribution is not preceded by a Type D reorganization—e.g., where the controlled corporation is not a newly formed subsidiary—Section 355(c) takes over for all forms of divisions,[8] providing generally that the distributing corporation recognizes no gain or loss on any distribution to which Section 355 applies.[9] Gain must be recognized, however, on a

1. See Section E1 of this chapter, infra.

2. I.R.C. §§ 368(a)(1)(D); 361(a).

3. I.R.C. § 361(b). The amount of cash and property that a distributing corporation may distribute to creditors without gain recognition is limited to the aggregate adjusted basis of the assets contributed to the controlled corporation in the Type D reorganization. I.R.C. § 361(b)(3).

4. I.R.C. § 361(c)(1), (2).

5. See also I.R.C. § 361(c)(4).

6. I.R.C. § 361(c)(4); see also § 336(c).

7. I.R.C. § 361(c)(2).

8. Section 355(c)(3) makes it clear that Sections 311 (relating to nonliquidating distributions) and 336 (relating to liquidating distributions) do not apply to a distribution governed by Section 355.

9. I.R.C. § 355(c)(1).

distribution of appreciated property other than "qualified property,"—i.e., other than stock or securities in the controlled corporation.[10] Thus, no gain will be recognized on a distribution of stock or securities of the controlled corporation in a qualifying corporate division even if the recipient shareholder is taxed,[11] but gain is recognized on a distribution of any other appreciated boot.[12]

In all cases, any stock of the controlled corporation that is acquired by the distributing corporation in a taxable transaction within the five-year period preceding the distribution will constitute boot.[13] For example, assume the distributing corporation had owned 90 percent of the stock of a controlled subsidiary for many years and acquired the remaining 10 percent shortly prior to an otherwise qualifying Section 355 distribution. Because the recently acquired stock is treated as boot, it is taxable to the shareholders and any gain accruing during the period between the acquisition and distribution of the stock will be taxable to the distributing corporation.

Recognition of Gain on Certain Disqualified Distributions. The general nonrecognition rule in Section 355(c) does not apply if the distributing corporation makes a "disqualified distribution" of "disqualified stock" within the meaning of Section 355(d). In general, a disqualified distribution is any distribution of stock or securities of a controlled subsidiary ("S") if, immediately after the distribution, any person holds a 50 percent or greater interest in either the distributing corporation or the controlled subsidiary and that interest consists of "disqualified stock," defined generally as any stock acquired by "purchase" within the five-year period preceding the distribution.[14] This rule, which is designed to prevent the use of Section 355 to facilitate the tax-free sale of part of a business following a takeover (and in related transactions), is discussed later in the chapter,[15] as is Section 355(e), which taxes the distributing corporation on distributions of controlled corporation stock in certain situations where as part of a "plan" a 50–percent or greater interest in either the distributing or controlled corporations was acquired within two years before or after the distribution.[16]

Carryover of Tax Attributes. The method of allocating the earnings and profits of the various parties to a corporate division depends on the form of the transaction. If a division is preceded by a Type D reorganization, the earnings and profits of the distributing corporation are allocated between

10. I.R.C. § 355(c)(2). The definition of "qualified property" in Section 355(c)(2)(B) is somewhat narrower than the one used to define the same term in Section 361(c)(2)(B), where "qualified property" includes both rights to acquire stock and nonsecurity debt obligations.

11. The recipient would be taxed, for example, if the principal amount of securities received exceeds the principal amount of any securities surrendered. I.R.C. § 355(a)(3)(A).

12. I.R.C. § 355(c)(2)(A).

13. I.R.C. § 355(a)(3)(B).

14. I.R.C. § 355(d)(2)–(5).

15. See Section E1 of this chapter, infra.

16. See Section E2 of this chapter, infra.

the distributing and controlled corporations in proportion to the relative fair market values of the assets retained by each corporation.[17] If the division is not preceded by a Type D reorganization—e.g., where the stock of a preexisting subsidiary or subsidiaries is distributed—the regulations provide methods for determining the decrease in the distributing corporation's earnings and profits.[18] In no event may any deficit of the distributing corporation be allocated to the controlled corporation.[19]

Earnings and profits are the only tax attributes affected by a corporate division. The carryover rules of Section 381 relating to other tax attributes are not applicable to divisive reorganizations, and thus the tax history of the distributing corporation will remain intact in a spin-off or a split-off. Since a split-up involves the liquidation of the distributing corporation, its tax attributes will disappear as a result of the transaction.[20]

4. CONSEQUENCES OF FAILED DIVISIONS

If a corporate division fails to qualify under Section 355, the tax consequences depend on the form of the transaction. If the defective division is preceded by the formation of a new corporation, that formation still qualifies for nonrecognition—but under Section 351 rather than Section 368(a)(1)(D).[1]

As for the division itself, the distribution of stock or securities in a nonqualifying spin-off is treated as an ordinary distribution to which Section 301 applies. That means it will be a dividend to the extent of current and accumulated earnings and profits and a return of capital to the extent of any balance. If the distribution takes the form of a split-off, it is tested under the stock redemption rules of Section 302. To avoid being subject to Section 301, the redemption thus must come within one of the Section 302(b) tests for exchange treatment.[2] If the failed division is a split-up, the transaction logically should be governed by the complete liquidation rules, allowing the shareholders to recognize capital gain or loss under Section 331(a).[3]

17. I.R.C. § 312(h); Reg. § 1.312–10(a). The regulations also state that in a "proper case" the allocation should be made in proportion to the net bases of the transferred and retained assets.

18. Reg. § 1.312–10(b).

19. Reg. § 1.312–10(c).

20. See Rev.Rul. 56–373, 1956–2 C.B. 217.

1. Although the formation of the new corporation still qualifies for nonrecognition, different operative provisions come into play to govern the transaction. See I.R.C. §§ 351; 358; 362(a); 1032. See Reg. § 1.312–11(a) for the allocation of earnings and profits in these circumstances.

2. If the distribution is pro rata, dividend treatment is thus assured. The distribution of stock in a failed split-off would not qualify for partial liquidation treatment under Section 302(b)(4). See Morgenstern v. Commissioner, 56 T.C. 44 (1971); Rev.Rul. 75–223, 1975–1 C.B. 109.

3. It is possible, however, that certain split-ups may be treated as a reorganization coupled with a dividend. This might occur on a split-up involving a failed division of an operating business from liquid assets in preparation for a sale of the liquid assets. See Bittker & Eustice, Federal Income Taxation of Corporations and Shareholders ¶ 11.15[3] (7th ed. 2000). But it may not matter when dividends and long-term capital gains are taxed at the same rate.

At the corporate level, the distributing corporation will be required to recognize gain on a distribution of appreciated property in a failed spin-off or split-off under Section 311(b). Section 311(a)(2), however, denies recognition of loss on a distribution of property that has declined in value. In a split-up, the distributing corporation will be required to recognize gain or loss under Section 336(a), subject to the limitations on recognition of loss in Section 336(b).

PROBLEM

Father is the sole shareholder of an incorporated department store which he has owned for 15 years. He has a basis of $200,000 in his Store Corporation stock, which is currently worth $2 million. Store has $400,000 of accumulated earnings and profits. Three years ago, Store acquired land in Suburb, where it constructed and then opened a new branch store. The branch has been quite successful and represents $500,000 of the $2 million net worth of Store Corporation. The assets of the branch have a $100,000 basis.

Father recently celebrated his 65th birthday and is exploring some estate planning alternatives. His attorney has suggested that he should have Store Corporation transfer the Suburb store to newly created Branch Corporation in exchange for Branch stock worth $400,000 and Branch securities worth $100,000. Store Corporation, which would be worth $1.5 million after this transaction, then would distribute the Branch stock and securities to Father who in turn would give the Branch stock to his children.

Discuss all the income tax consequences of the above transactions to Father, Store Corporation and Branch Corporation, assuming first that the corporate division totally or partially qualifies under Section 355 and then that it fails to qualify.

E. USE OF SECTION 355 IN CORPORATE ACQUISITIONS

1. LIMITATIONS ON USE OF SECTION 355 IN TAXABLE ACQUISITIONS

a. INTRODUCTION

The repeal of the *General Utilities* doctrine required tax advisors to search for new techniques to avoid corporate-level gain on the sale of all or part of a business. In one common transactional pattern, a corporate buyer of a controlling stock interest in a target corporation may seek to dispose of unwanted pieces of the target, perhaps to help finance the acquisition or maximize overall shareholder value. The tax goal is to consummate those sales without recognizing gain. After Congress blocked several other promising techniques, taxpayers turned to Section 355 to facilitate tax-free sales of unwanted assets in corporate solution. Congress reacted by curtailing the benefits of nonrecognition for certain transactions that previously would have qualified as tax-free divisions. These anti-avoidance limitations, which were previewed earlier in this chapter, are best explained in the context of the transactions at which they were directed.

b. DISPOSITIONS OF RECENTLY ACQUIRED BUSINESSES

Code: § 355(a)(2)(D).

Congress's first line of attack was to amend the active trade or business requirement in Section 355(b)(2)(D) in order to prevent a purchasing corporation ("P") that had recently acquired a controlling stock interest in a target corporation ("T") from disposing of a target subsidiary ("S") without paying a corporate-level tax. To illustrate the prototype transaction at which this rule is aimed, assume that P purchases all the stock of T, which has engaged directly in the active conduct of a trade or business for more than five years. T owns the stock of S, which also has engaged in the active conduct of a trade or business for the requisite five-year period. Both T and S have highly appreciated assets. P does not make a Section 338 election when it purchases T's stock and, as a result, T and S retain their historic asset bases. P intends to dispose of S shortly after the takeover of T.

At one time, the parties could have used a two-step transaction to sell S without recognizing gain. T would first distribute the S stock to P in a tax-free distribution under Section 355.[1] The Service ruled that such a distribution qualified as tax-free and did not violate the active trade or business requirement unless P attempted a bailout by distributing the S stock to its shareholders.[2] P would allocate the cost basis in its T stock under Section 358 between the T stock and the S stock it received in the distribution, obtaining essentially a fair market value basis in the stock of both corporations.[3] After a respectable interval, P then would sell the S stock without recognition of any corporate-level gain by S. Although the new buyer would take a cost basis in the S stock, S would retain its historic lower asset bases. This is noteworthy because the gain inherent in S's assets was not avoided by this technique; it merely was deferred. Moreover, that gain did not accrue while P owned T (and thus indirectly S), and any

1. To avoid problems under the continuity of interest doctrine, P needed to hold the T stock for a respectable period of time (two years was considered safest) to become a "historic" shareholder of T. See Section C2 of this chapter, supra.

2. Rev.Rul. 74–5, 1974–1 C.B. 82. The key to the ruling was that T (the distributing corporation) and S (the controlled corporation) both had been engaged in the active conduct of a trade or business for five years. It did not matter that P (the distributee shareholder of T) had acquired a controlling interest in T in a taxable transaction within the five-year period preceding the distribution.

3. P thus obtained a basis in the S stock that usually was significantly higher than T's basis in the S stock. T's basis would disappear if the spin-off qualified under Section 355. Cf. I.R.C. §§ 332; 336(e); 338(h)(10).

economic gain that did accrue during P's ownership would be taxed on P's sale of the S stock.[4]

Section 355(b)(2)(D) forecloses this strategy by providing that the active trade or business requirement is not met if "control" (measured by the 80 percent tests in Section 368(c)) of the distributing corporation (T) was acquired by a corporate distributee (P) within the five-year period preceding the distribution of stock in the controlled corporation (S). The limitation does not apply, however, if P acquired T in a wholly tax-free transaction, such as an acquisitive reorganization.[5] Distributee corporations that are members of the same affiliated group (as defined in Section 1504(a)) are treated as a single corporate distributee for this purpose.[6]

The principal sanction from denying Section 355 treatment to the above fact pattern is that T must recognize gain on the distribution of its S stock to P. In addition, assuming that T has ample earnings and profits, P has a dividend on receipt of the S stock, but as a corporate parent of T, P likely would be entitled to a 100 percent dividends received deduction.[7] P would obtain a fair market value basis in the distributed S stock[8] and thus recognize no further gain on the subsequent sale. But in the likely event that the buyer of the S stock does not make a Section 338 election, the gain inherent in S's assets is preserved through their transferred bases, raising the specter of yet another corporate-level tax.[9]

c. DIVISIVE TRANSACTIONS IN CONNECTION WITH CERTAIN CHANGES OF OWNERSHIP

Code: § 355(c), (d).

The active business requirement disqualifies a divisive transaction if P acquires a controlling stock interest in T within the five years preceding

4. Of course, T could not have sold its S stock without recognizing at least one level of gain. Query whether P should be able to avoid gain on a sale of a piece of T's business when T could not have done so. On the other hand, no corporate-level gain was recognized when T's shareholders sold all their T stock to P and no Section 338 election was made. Query why T or P should not be able to sell S without corporate-level gain provided that gain is preserved through transferred asset bases.

5. I.R.C. § 355(b)(2)(D)(ii); see also Rev. Rul. 89–37, 1989–1 C.B. 107.

6. Thus, if in the example P had two existing wholly owned subsidiaries (X and Y) and each acquired 50 percent of the T stock for cash, a distribution by T of its S stock within five years after the acquisition would not qualify under Section 355 because X and Y, as members of the same affiliated group, are treated as a single corporation that acquired a controlling stock interest in T within five years preceding the distribution.

7. I.R.C. § 243(a)(3), (b). If P, T and S were members of a consolidated group, the dividend would be deferred and P's basis in its T stock would be reduced by the amount of the distribution. Reg. §§ 1.1502–14(a)(1), 1.1502–32(b)(2).

8. I.R.C. § 301(d).

9. This double *corporate*-level tax could be avoided if T sold its S stock directly to the new buyer, and the parties jointly made an election under Section 338(h)(10). In that event, T could ignore the gain on the sale of its S stock but S would recognize gain on a deemed sale of its assets, and "new S" would obtain a stepped-up basis in those assets. See Chapter 17C3, supra. Query why the result is worse in a comparable transaction caught by the Section 355(b)(2)(D) trap?

the distribution of S stock.[10] The requirement does not apply, however, in some other situations that offer promising avenues of escape from corporate-level tax in ostensibly divisive transactions that are really sales. For example, if P did not acquire a controlling stock interest in T, the active business limitation would not preclude essentially the same transaction described in the example above. This opportunity may be illustrated through a simple fact pattern in which four unrelated corporations (A, B, C and D) each purchase a portion of the stock of T with the ultimate objective of winding up with different pieces of T's business that are conducted through separate T subsidiaries. After waiting two years to establish their status as historic shareholders for continuity of interest purposes, A, B and C could exchange their T stock for stock of the desired T subsidiary in a split-off that would qualify under Section 355.[11] All of this could be accomplished without waiting five years after the acquisition of T because no single corporate distributee acquired a controlling stock interest in T. The five-year holding period requirement also does not apply to acquisitions of a controlling interest in T through a partnership or by any other noncorporate purchaser. A variety of other avoidance techniques quickly revealed that Congress had not successfully curtailed the use of Section 355 to avoid corporate-level gain on essentially acquisitive transactions.

The Treasury might have attacked a Section 355 transaction that was inconsistent with *General Utilities* repeal by exercising its authority to issue regulations under Section 337(d).[12] Instead, it returned to Congress for a more comprehensive solution. The result is Section 355(d), which imposes a corporate-level tax on divisive transactions in connection with certain changes of ownership.

Because Section 355(d) attempts to reach such a wide range of transactions, its operation is complex. Very generally, Section 355(d) requires recognition of gain by the distributing corporation (but not the distributee shareholders) on a "disqualified distribution" of stock or securities of a controlled corporation regardless of whether the distribution is part of a reorganization.[13] A "disqualified distribution" is any Section 355 distribution if, immediately after the distribution, any person holds "disqualified stock" in either the distributing corporation or any distributed controlled corporation constituting a 50 percent or greater interest (measured by total combined voting power or value) in such corporation.[14] "Disqualified stock"

10. I.R.C. § 355(b)(2)(D).

11. For this purpose, it is assumed that all relevant business of T have a five-year history; the business purpose requirement can be satisfied; and the parties could structure the transaction to avoid the step transaction doctrine.

12. Section 337(d) grants the Service authority to promulgate regulations to prevent circumvention of the purposes of certain amendments made by The Tax Reform Act of 1986 (i.e., repeal of the *General Utilities* doctrine) through the use of any provision of the Code or regulations.

13. This is technically accomplished by removing the stock or securities of the controlled corporation from the category of "qualified property" under Sections 361(c)(2) and 355(c)(2). I.R.C. § 355(d)(1). As a result, the distributing corporation must recognize gain as if the stock and securities were appreciated boot.

14. I.R.C. § 355(d)(2).

is: (1) any stock in either the distributing corporation or any controlled corporation acquired after October 9, 1990 by purchase during the five-year period before the distribution, and (2) any stock in any controlled corporation received in a distribution attributable to stock in the distributing corporation described in (1).[15]

In effect, Section 355(d) creates a five-year statutory predistribution continuity of interest test. If violated, the test requires the distributing corporation to recognize gain on the distribution of stock or securities of a subsidiary to a person who ends up with 50 percent or more of the stock of the subsidiary. Section 355(d) also includes aggregation and attribution rules to prevent easy avoidance of the 50 percent or more ownership test.[16]

2. Dispositions of Unwanted Assets in Conjunction With Tax-Free Reorganizations

As discussed earlier in this chapter, a corporate division may be used as the vehicle for a tax-free spin-off of unwanted assets in preparation for an acquisition of the rest of the target corporation's business. Consider a typical scenario. An attractive takeover candidate ("T"), engaged in two different businesses, is approached by a motivated buyer ("P") whose interest is limited to only one of those businesses. To facilitate the transaction and maximize shareholder value, T spins off the unwanted business to its shareholders and then is acquired by P in a tax-free acquisitive reorganization. Should the spin-off qualify under Section 355? What if T spins off the wanted business ("Newco") to its shareholders, who then exchange their Newco stock for P stock? Should the form of the transaction make any difference? These and other scenarios present a challenge to the target corporation's tax advisor and provide the student of Subchapter C with an opportunity to relate the requirements for a tax-free corporate division to the acquisitive reorganization concepts encountered in the previous chapter.

In Commissioner v. Morris Trust,[1] the Fourth Circuit held that a spin-off of an unwanted business followed by a prearranged merger of the parent "distributing" corporation with an unrelated acquiring corporation qualified as tax-free—specifically, a Type D reorganization coupled with a Section 355 corporate division, and a Section 368 Type A acquisitive reorganization. The Service ultimately blessed the *Morris Trust* form of transaction[2] and even acknowledged that a spin-off to prepare for an acquisition of a separate business was a valid Section 355 business purpose,[3] but it was less receptive to other transactional patterns despite their economic similarity. For example, a spin off of unwanted assets followed by

15. I.R.C. § 355(d)(3). See I.R.C. § 355(d)(5)(B) for the details on the "purchase" requirement.

16. See I.R.C. §§ 355(d)(7) and (8).

1. 367 F.2d 794 (4th Cir.1966).

2. Rev. Rul. 68–603, 1968–2 C.B. 148. See also Rev. Rul. 70–434, 1970–2 C.B. 83 (Type B reorganization followed spin-off of unwanted business).

3. Rev. Proc. 96–30, 1996–1 C.B. 696.

a Type C reorganization or a forward triangular merger was likely to be treated as an integrated transaction, with the unfortunate result that the unwanted assets would be considered in determining whether P transferred substantially all of its properties in the subsequent reorganization. If the unwanted assets were a substantial part of P's overall business, the acquisition would not qualify as a reorganization, and the spin-off also was unlikely to qualify under Section 355.[4]

Other transactional forms also were vulnerable to challenge under the step transaction doctrine. For example, if P contributed the assets of a *wanted* business with a five-year history to newly created S, retained another (unwanted) business, distributed the S stock to its shareholders, and then S was acquired by an unrelated corporation ("X") in an attempted tax-free reorganization, the Service took the position that neither the spin-off nor the reorganization qualified for tax-free treatment. If the steps were prearranged, S was disregarded and P was treated as having made a taxable sale of the wanted assets to X and having distributed the consideration received from X to P's shareholders as a dividend.[5] If P was publicly traded and S was an "old and cold" (i.e., not newly formed) subsidiary, however, the Service ruled that a spin-off of S stock followed by X's acquisition of S in a Type A or Type B reorganization did qualify as tax-free if no formal negotiations with respect to the subsequent acquisition took place prior to the spin-off.[6]

After repeal of the *General Utilities* doctrine, Congress became concerned (some might say paranoid) that Section 355 was being used to avoid corporate-level gain on the sale of a business. Section 355(d), discussed earlier in this chapter, was an early response. To further narrow the scope of Section 355, Congress followed up by enacting Section 355(e), which virtually eliminates the time-tested *Morris Trust* technique.[7] The legislative

4. See, e.g., Helvering v. Elkhorn Coal Co., 95 F.2d 732 (4th Cir.1937), cert. denied, 305 U.S. 605, 59 S.Ct. 65 (1938). But see Rev. Rul. 2003–79, 2003–2 C.B. 80, where distributing corporation ("D") engaged in two businesses ("X" and "Y") of equal size. To facilitate an acquisition of business "X" by acquiring corporation ("P"), D contributed the wanted X assets to a new controlled corporation ("C"), distributed the C stock to its shareholders in a valid Section 355 spin-off, and then P acquired all of C's assets in exchange for P voting stock, and C liquidated. The Service ruled that the acquisition of C's assets qualified as a Type C reorganization even though, under *Elkhorn Coal*, P's acquisition of the same properties from D would have failed the "substantially all of the properties" requirement if D had retained the wanted business and spun-off the unwanted business to C before the attempted reorganization. In so ruling, the Service, citing Congressional intent, held that it was appropriate to consider the controlled corporation as independent of the distributing corporation in determining if the "substantially all" requirement of Section 368(a)(1)(C) is satisfied. The ruling is further evidence that the form of a transaction often matters in Subchapter C and that the Service is willing to turn off the step transaction doctrine when the overall policy of the Code dictates a more formalistic analysis.

5. Rev. Rul. 70–225, 1970–1 C.B. 80.

6. Rev. Rul. 96–30, 1996–1 C.B. 36.

7. See also I.R.C. § 355(f), which disqualifies a transaction in its entirety under Section 355 when one member of an affiliated corporate group makes a distribution to another member if the distribution is part of a plan or series of related transactions to which Section 355(e) applies.

history explains that where new shareholders acquire ownership of a business in connection with a spin-off, the transaction more closely resembles a taxable corporate-level disposition of the portion of the business that is acquired rather than a tax-free division among existing shareholders.[8]

Section 355(e) is a typically complex anti-avoidance provision and this discussion is limited to an overview. It requires the distributing (parent) corporation to recognize gain as if it had sold the stock of the distributed controlled subsidiary for its fair market value on the date of the distribution if, as part of a "plan" or series of related transactions, one or more persons acquire[9] (directly or indirectly) a 50–percent or greater interest in either the distributing or controlled corporation within two years before or after the distribution.[10] Put differently (and, one hopes, more coherently), the distributing corporation (but not its shareholders) must recognize corporate-level gain on an otherwise tax-free spin-off if "pursuant to a plan" stock of either the distributing or controlled corporation is acquired and the historic shareholders of the distributing corporation do not retain more than 50 percent (by vote and value) of both corporations. Significantly (and inexplicably), neither the distributing nor controlled corporations may adjust the basis of their assets or stock to reflect this recognition of Section 355(e) gain.

Section 355(e) applies only if the transaction is part of a "plan" (or a series of related transactions) to acquire the requisite 50 percent or greater interest in the target. For this purpose, if one or more persons directly or indirectly acquire a 50–percent or greater interest in the distributing corporation or any controlled corporation during the four-year period beginning two years before the distribution, the acquisition is presumed to be pursuant to a plan unless the taxpayer establishes that such a plan did not exist.[11] Whether or not a prohibited "plan" exists is based on all the facts and circumstances.[12]

The regulations provide considerable flexibility in making this factual determination.[13] In the case of acquisitions (other than public offerings) of the distributing or controlled corporation after a distribution, the distribution and acquisition will be considered as part of a plan only if there was an agreement, understanding, arrangement, or substantial negotiations re-

8. S.Rept. No. 105–33, 105th Cong., 1st Sess. 139–140 (1997).

9. Acquisitions, for this purpose, are not limited to cost basis purchase transactions but also can include tax-free acquisitions. Certain acquisitions that do not involve a shift in control are disregarded. I.R.C. § 355(e)(3)(A). If the assets rather than the stock of either corporation are acquired, the shareholders of the acquiring corporation are deemed to have acquired the target stock for purposes of determining whether the gain-triggering shift of control has occurred. I.R.C. § 355(e)(3)(B).

10. I.R.C. § 355(e)(1), (2). Technically, this result occurs because the stock or securities in the controlled corporation is not treated as "qualified property" for purposes of Section 355(c)(2) or Section 361(c)(2), and thus gain is recognized on the distribution under Section 311(b).

11. I.R.C. § 355(e)(2)(B).

12. Reg. § 1.355–7(b)(1).

13. See generally Reg. § 1.355–7.

garding the acquisition or a similar acquisition (collectively referred to below as "Talks") at some time during the two year period preceding the distribution.[14] Although not labelled as a safe harbor, this "two year lookback rule" operates as a security blanket in many situations, especially in light of the narrow definitions of several critical terms. An "agreement, understanding or arrangement," for example, is generally considered to exist only if the parties have reached a common understanding on most of the significant terms of the transaction.[15] "Substantial negotiations" exist only if the significant economic terms of the acquisition have been discussed at the highest levels (directors, officers, shareholders, or their representatives).[16] In short, for a plan to exist, the dealings must have reached a fairly advanced stage.

The regulations go on to provide that, even though the existence of Talks between the parties within the two years preceding the distribution "tend to show" that the distribution and acquisition are part of a plan, all the facts and circumstances still must be considered, and the existence of a corporate business purpose (apart from facilitating the acquisition) will help the taxpayer rebut the statutory presumption.[17] Further comfort is available from nine safe harbors.[18] A key factor under most of these safe harbors is whether there were bilateral Talks during a specified time period. For example, if the acquisition occurred more than six months after the distribution and there were no Talks during the period commencing one year before and ending six months after the distribution, the transactions are not considered part of a plan if the distribution was motivated by a substantial business purpose other than facilitating the acquisition.[19] If a transaction does not fit within any of the safe harbors, the regulations include a list of "plan" and "nonplan" factors to consider in determining whether a plan exists.[20]

In summary, Section 355(e) obliterates many typical "planned" *Morris Trust* transactions but leaves open the possibility that a spin-off followed by an acquisition will continue to qualify under Section 355 if there was a valid business purpose and Talks with potential acquirers did not occur prior to the distribution and within six months thereafter. On the other hand, the existence of an agreement, understanding or negotiations to sell either the distributing or controlled corporations at the time of the spin-off likely will doom the transaction. In an ironic twist, Section 355(e) would not have changed the tax-free treatment in the actual *Morris Trust* transaction, because the distributing corporation's shareholders received 54 percent of the equity of the acquiring corporation as part of the transaction and thus the "control shift" required to trigger Section 355(e) would not have occurred. As a practical matter, Section 355(e) does not apply when

14. Reg. § 1.355–7(b)(2).

15. Reg. § 1.355–7(h)(1)(i).

16. Reg. § 1.355–7(h)(1)(iv).

17. Reg. § 1.355–7(b)(2).

18. Reg. § 1.355–7(d).

19. Reg. § 1.355–7(d)(1).

20. Reg. § 1.355–7(b)(3) & (4).

the equity value of the distributing corporation after the spin-off exceeds that of the acquiring corporation.

PROBLEM

Leisure, Inc. is a publicly held corporation that operates a chain of motels and manufactures leisure apparel. Each business has roughly the same net worth and has been operated by Leisure for over five years. Denim Corporation wishes to acquire the apparel business but is not interested in the motels. Leisure would like to dispose of the apparel business, preferably in a tax-free reorganization, and it will continue to operate the motel business for the indefinite future. Consider the tax consequences of the following alternative plans for carrying out the objectives of the parties:

(a) Leisure will transfer the motel assets to a newly formed subsidiary, Motel, Inc., and distribute the Motel stock pro rata to the Leisure shareholders. Leisure then will transfer the assets and liabilities of the apparel business to Denim in exchange for Denim voting stock (representing less than 50 percent of the total outstanding voting stock of Denim after the acquisition), and then Leisure will liquidate, distributing the Denim stock pro rata to its shareholders.

(b) Same as (a), above, except that after the spin-off, Leisure merges into Denim. Under the terms of the merger, Leisure shareholders receive Denim nonvoting preferred stock.

(c) What result if Leisure transfers the apparel business to a new corporation, Cords, Inc., and then distributes the Cords stock pro rata to the Leisure shareholders. Leisure continues to operate the motel business, but Cords, Inc. merges into Denim, Inc., and the Cords shareholders receive Denim voting stock.

(d) Same as (c), above, except that after the merger, the Denim voting stock received by Cords shareholders represents more than 50 percent of the total outstanding stock of Denim.

(e) Same as (b), above, except that the merger of Leisure into Denim occurred one year after the spin-off. What factors are relevant in determining whether the transaction was part of a "plan" to acquire Leisure?

(f) Same as (b), above, except that the business purpose for the spin-off was unrelated to any acquisition of the apparel business, and the merger of Leisure into Denim occurred three years after the spin-off.

(g) Is § 355(e) necessary? How did the typical *Morris Trust* transaction violate the policy of Subchapter C?

CHAPTER 19

CARRYOVERS OF CORPORATE TAX ATTRIBUTES

A. INTRODUCTION

Code: § 381(a). Skim § 381(c).

The Internal Revenue Code contains a comprehensive statutory scheme governing the carryover of various corporate "tax attributes" (such as earnings and profits, net operating losses, and capital loss carryforwards) on corporate acquisitions and other major transactions involving a change of ownership of a corporation. As always, some brief historical background helps to put the current law into perspective.

Prior to 1954, the Code contained few rules regulating the carryover of corporate tax attributes. The Supreme Court merely followed the lead of lower courts[1] in holding that a corporation's earnings and profits could not be eliminated by means of a reorganization but that instead the acquiring corporation inherited the target's earnings and profits along with its assets.[2] Because any other approach would have allowed a profitable corporation to use a reorganization to sweep its earnings and profits account clean and diminish future dividends, the Court's decision was no more surprising than the reaction of the tax bar to the proposition that corporate attributes could survive a reorganization. They assumed, or at least hoped, that an acquiring corporation could inherit negative as well as positive tax attributes in a tax-free reorganization or liquidation. If that assumption proved true, profitable corporations could acquire the assets of their unprofitable brethren solely to succeed to the target's earnings and profits deficit and net operating losses (NOLs). The acquiring corporation thus could assure itself that future distributions would be sheltered by the newly acquired earnings and profits deficit and that future income would be effectively exempt from tax because of the newly acquired NOLs.

The Supreme Court responded by holding that earnings and profits deficits did *not* survive a reorganization[3] and that NOLs could be used only by the corporate entity that incurred them.[4] But tax advisors were not to be

1. See, e.g., Commissioner v. Sansome, 60 F.2d 931 (2d Cir.1932), cert. denied, 287 U.S. 667, 53 S.Ct. 291 (1932).

2. Commissioner v. Munter, 331 U.S. 210, 67 S.Ct. 1175 (1947).

3. Commissioner v. Phipps, 336 U.S. 410, 69 S.Ct. 616 (1949).

4. New Colonial Ice Co. v. Helvering, 292 U.S. 435, 54 S.Ct. 788 (1934). But see Helvering v. Metropolitan Edison, 306 U.S. 522, 59 S.Ct. 634 (1939), where the Court

outdone. Shortly after these decisions, several reorganizations which followed a similar pattern appeared on the scene. Loss Corp., a corporation with NOLs but no current income to absorb them, would acquire the assets of Profit Corp., a successful company, in a tax-free reorganization. In the process, the Profit Corp. shareholders would receive more than enough Loss Corp. stock to control the continuing and expanded Loss Corp. Since Loss Corp. technically was the surviving entity, it retained its NOLs, which then were used to offset the gains generated by the new business. Once again, the Supreme Court was forced to respond to a device involving trafficking in tax attributes. In Libson Shops, Inc. v. Koehler,[5] the Court decided that even if a loss corporation survives a reorganization, NOLs incurred prior to the transaction only could be used to offset post-acquisition gains if they were generated by substantially the same *business* as well as the same entity which had incurred the losses.

With the arrival of the 1954 Internal Revenue Code, the case law regulating the carryover of tax attributes was replaced by a comprehensive statutory scheme.[6] The principal provisions are: (1) Section 381, which generally provides that a target corporation's tax attributes follow its assets in tax-free reorganizations (other than B and E reorganizations) and tax-free liquidations of a subsidiary; (2) Sections 382 and 383, which restrict the carryforward of net operating losses and certain other losses and credits following a substantial change of ownership; (3) Section 384, which limits the use of loss carryforwards to offset certain gains following a corporate acquisition; and (4) Section 269, which allows the Secretary to disallow deductions, credits or other allowances in certain situations where one corporation's stock or assets were acquired for the principal purpose of obtaining the specific deductions, credits or allowances in question. This chapter first considers the general carryover rules and limitations in Section 381 and then turns to the more specialized limitations on loss carryforwards.

B. SECTION 381 CARRYOVER RULES

Code: § 381(a), (b). Skim § 381(c).

General Carryover Rules. Section 381(a) provides that in a tax-free liquidation of a subsidiary or a reorganization (other than a Type B or E reorganization), the acquiring corporation shall "succeed to and take into account" some 26 specified attributes of the target,[1] including earnings and profits, NOLs, accounting and depreciation methods and capital loss, in-

held that these attributes did follow the target's assets in certain mergers.

5. 353 U.S. 382, 77 S.Ct. 990 (1957).

6. Some commentators and courts have suggested that the *Libson Shops* doctrine survived the 1954 Code, but Congress intended specifically not to incorporate the doctrine into the new statutory scheme governing limitations on net operating loss carryforwards. H.R.Rep. No. 99–841, 99th Cong., 2d Sess. II–194 (1986).

1. I.R.C. § 381(c)(1)–(26).

vestment credit and charitable contribution carryovers.[2] In Type B stock-for-stock acquisition and Type E recapitalization, the acquired or recapitalized corporation remains intact after the transaction and thus no carryover mechanism is necessary. In a triangular reorganization where substantially all of the target's assets are transferred to a subsidiary of the issuing corporation, the subsidiary is the "acquiring corporation" and succeeds to the target's attributes.[3]

Earnings and Profits Deficits. Left unchecked, Section 381 would subject the revenue to some of the same abuses already discussed. As we have seen, one promising tax avoidance strategy is presented where Profit Corp. acquires Loss Corp.'s assets in a reorganization and inherits its earnings and profits deficit and NOL carryovers. To some extent, this abuse is limited by Section 381 itself. Section 381(c)(2) restricts Profit Corp.'s ability to rid itself of its own current or accumulated earnings and profits through a simple acquisition of Loss Corp. by providing that an earnings and profits deficit inherited from Loss Corp. may not be applied against any earnings and profits of Profit Corp. that existed prior to the acquisition. Loss Corp.'s deficit therefore only can be used to offset post-acquisition accumulated earnings and profits. If a distribution is made in a post-acquisition year in which there are current earnings and profits, any offsetting accumulated deficit acquired from Loss Corp. is irrelevant in any event, since the distribution will be deemed to come from the current earnings and profits of the taxable year and then from Profit Corp.'s own pre-acquisition accumulated earnings and profits.[4]

Net Operating Losses. Even though Profit Corp. receives little benefit from Loss Corp.'s earnings and profits deficit, Loss's NOL carryovers still might be used to eliminate Profit's own tax liability. Section 381(c)(1) provides complex rules governing the carryover of NOLs, but it does not prevent them from being misused by Profit Corp. Instead, Section 382, which is discussed later in this chapter, is the designated policing agent in this situation.

Rather than Profit Corp. acquiring the assets and tax attributes of Loss Corp., Loss might acquire Profit's assets in a Type A or C reorganization, maintaining Loss's earnings and profits deficit and NOLs without assistance from Section 381, and then might use those negative tax attributes to offset Profit's past and future income. If Profit's shareholders receive sufficient Loss Corp. stock to control the combined company, the transaction in substance is identical to the acquisition of Loss Corp. by Profit. The benefits of this transaction also are limited by both Sections 381(b) and 382. Section 381(b)(3) generally provides that an acquiring

2. Cf. I.R.C. § 312(h)(2), which requires a "proper allocation" of earnings and profits between the acquiring corporation and the target if less than 100 percent of the assets are acquired in a Type C or Type D reorganization.

3. Reg. § 1.381(a)–1(b)(2).

4. I.R.C. § 381(c)(2)(B). See Chapter 12, supra. Thus, an acquired earnings and profits deficit will do no more than prevent undistributed current earnings and profits from becoming accumulated earnings and profits in a subsequent year.

corporation may not carry back an NOL incurred after the acquisition to a taxable year of a profitable target corporation.[5] In one of the few cases interpreting the NOL limitation, the Ninth Circuit has held that Section 381(b)(3) does not limit the carryback of an NOL to a pre-acquisition year of a target corporation which merges into a newly formed subsidiary of the acquiring corporation in a forward triangular reorganization.[6] The court concluded that to deny a carryback in this situation would exalt form over substance and would not present the complex accounting problem that motivated Congress to enact the Section 381(b)(3) NOL carryback limitation.

C. LIMITATIONS ON NET OPERATING LOSS CARRYFORWARDS: SECTION 382

1. INTRODUCTION

Code: Skim § 382(a), (b)(1), (g)(1), (i)(1).

Before examining the Section 382 limitations on carryovers of corporate NOLs, it is helpful to review the concept of a net operating loss. In general, a net operating loss, often identified by its "NOL" monogram, is the excess of business deductions allowed by the Code over the taxpayer's gross income in a single taxable period.[1] A net operating loss ordinarily may be carried back to the two taxable years preceding the loss year and may be carried forward to the 20 following years.[2] An NOL carryback reduces the taxpayer's taxable income in the earlier year and typically results in a refund. Carryforwards serve as deductions in the subsequent years to which they are carried and reduce the tax due for those periods. NOLs first must be carried to the earliest available year and, to the extent not used, are then carried forward to the next available taxable periods.[3] Net operating losses thus stand as an exception to the annual taxable year concept. The purpose of the carryover scheme is to serve as an averaging device that ameliorates the harsh consequences that would result for a business taxpayer with a fluctuating economic track record. As the Supreme Court has described NOL carryovers, "[t]hey were designed to permit a taxpayer to set off its lean years against its lush years, and to strike something like an average taxable income computed over a period longer than one year."[4] All of this works smoothly in the corporate setting if the owners of the entity are unchanged during the 23–year carryover period. Section 382 addresses the problems that arise if the ownership of a loss corporation changes at a time that the company has unexpired net operating losses.

5. Because these allocation problems do not exist in a Section 332 liquidation of a subsidiary or a Type E or Type F reorganization, the Section 381(b)(3) limitation does not apply to those transactions.

6. Bercy Industries, Inc. v. Commissioner, 640 F.2d 1058 (9th Cir.1981).

1. See generally I.R.C. § 172.

2. I.R.C. § 172(b)(1)(A).

3. I.R.C. § 172(b).

4. United States v. Foster Lumber Co., 429 U.S. 32, 97 S.Ct. 204 (1976).

A profitable company seeking tax savings may be tempted to acquire a corporation with NOL carryovers to use those deductions to shelter its taxable income. To illustrate, assume that Mr. Loser forms Loss Co. to engage in the manufacture and sale of passing fads. The company is initially capitalized with $1,000,000, all represented by Mr. Loser's equity investment. Despite Loser's high hopes, Loss Co. incurs $999,999 in deductible expenses in the first two years of its operation and never earns a cent. At the end of two years, the company has nothing left except $1 in its checking account and a $999,999 NOL deduction that is useless because Loss Co. has no income to offset. At that point, the company is worth $1 plus the value, if any, of its deductions. If Loss Co. is liquidated, the sad story ends. If Loser infuses new property or cash into the corporation to keep the business afloat, then Loss Co. may deduct its loss carryforwards against any future income as long as Loser continues to own a controlling interest in the company.

But what if Profit Co., shopping around for tax deductions, learns of Loss Co.'s difficulties? If Profit wishes to acquire Loss, it has many options. It could: (1) acquire all of Loss Co.'s assets (i.e., $1) in exchange for Profit Co. stock in an acquisitive Type A or C tax-free reorganization, as a result of which Profit Co. would inherit all of Loss Co.'s tax attributes (i.e., its $999,999 NOL deduction);[5] (2) acquire the stock of Loss Co. in either a taxable purchase, a tax-free Type B reorganization, or reverse triangular merger, and later liquidate Loss Co. under Section 332, thereby inheriting its NOL carryforwards;[6] (3) acquire Loss Co.'s stock and then transfer its own assets into Loss Co. in a Section 351 exchange; in that case Loss Co., now a wholly owned subsidiary of Profit Co., can operate the Profit business while retaining its own NOLs; or (4) Loss Co. can acquire the assets of Profit Co. in an acquisitive tax-free reorganization by exchanging enough Loss Co. stock to give the Profit Co. shareholders virtually 100 percent ownership of Loss Co. The Profit Co. shareholders then will own Loss Co., which will own all of old Profit Co.'s assets plus a $999,999 NOL carryforward.

Is something wrong here? If Loss Co. lost money, should its NOLs be available to offset Profit's future income or should the use of those NOLs be limited to offsetting later income earned by Loss? Should Profit be able to avoid tax on $999,999 of its future income by acquiring (or being acquired by) the corporate shell of an unsuccessful business?

After pondering these questions for many years, Congress enacted ineffective legislation in the 1954 Code aimed at limiting the use of NOL carryforwards in the corporate acquisitions setting. Amendments followed in 1976, but they were so unappealing that their effective date was delayed four times until 1986, when they were discarded completely in favor of a

5. I.R.C. § 381(a)(2).

6. I.R.C. § 381(a)(1). If the liquidation occurs immediately after a Type B reorganization, it would be treated as a Type C reorganization. See Rev.Rul. 67–274, 1967–2 C.B. 141. In addition, if Profit Co. acquires the Loss Co. stock and files a consolidated return, the availability of Loss Co.'s losses will be limited by the consolidated return regulations. See Section E3 of this chapter, infra.

new Section 382.[7] The current statutory scheme is the outgrowth of decades of study, most notably the Subchapter C Project of the American Law Institute and the Senate Finance Committee staff's Subchapter C study.[8]

When applicable, Section 382 limits the use of a loss corporation's NOL carryforwards when there is a change of ownership of more than 50 percent of the stock of that company over a period of three years or less.[9] Stating this general rule in the language of the Code, the loss limitations are triggered only after an "ownership change,"[10] which is either an "owner shift involving a 5-percent shareholder", or an "equity structure shift,"[11] coupled with a more than 50 percent increase in the stock ownership of "5-percent shareholders" which occurs during a three-year "testing period".[12] If Section 382 is triggered, it limits the use by a "new loss corporation" of any NOLs of an "old loss corporation" for any "post-change year" (i.e., any year after the ownership change).[13] In general, the taxable income of a new loss corporation that may be offset by preacquisition NOLs is limited to the value of the old loss corporation's stock on the date of the ownership change multiplied by a prescribed "long-term tax-exempt rate."[14] These and many other statutory terms will be explained in detail later in the chapter.

The rationale of Section 382 is to allow a loss company's NOLs to offset only the future income generated by that company's business. If the section is triggered by an ownership change, its limitations apply in two different ways. First, if the Loss Co. business is not continued (or substantially all of its assets are not used) for at least two years after the change of ownership, all of its NOLs are disallowed.[15] Second, if the Loss Co. business is continued or if its assets are used for at least two years, the losses are allowable only to the extent of the income generated from the old Loss Co.'s assets. Because the transactions that trigger Section 382 may involve the combining of a loss company with a profitable company, it may be impossible to determine exactly what part of the combined company's income is generated by the Loss Co.'s business or assets. Section 382 solves this problem by adopting a method to approximate Loss Co.'s income. It irrebuttably assumes that the return on Loss Co.'s equity will be the rate of

7. See generally Jacobs, "Tax Treatment of Corporate Net Operating Losses and Other Tax Attribute Carryovers," 5 Va. Tax Rev. 701 (1986).

8. See American Law Institute, Federal Income Tax Project, Subchapter C (1986); Staff of the Senate Finance Committee, The Subchapter C Revision Act of 1985: A Final Report Prepared by the Staff, 99th Cong., 1st Sess. 32–35, 55–56, 68–71 (S.Prt. 99–47, 1985); Eustice, "Alternatives for Limiting Loss Carryovers," 22 San Diego L.Rev. 149 (1985).

9. I.R.C. § 382(g)(1), (i).

10. I.R.C. § 382(a), (g), (k)(3).

11. I.R.C. § 382(g), (k)(7).

12. I.R.C. § 382(g), (i), (k)(7).

13. I.R.C. § 382(a), (d)(2). The "new loss corporation" is the successor to Loss Co. in a merger or asset acquisition; it is Loss Co. itself in a stock acquisition. See I.R.C. § 382(k)(3). The "old loss corporation" is Loss Co. prior to the ownership change. I.R.C. § 382(k)(2).

14. I.R.C. § 382(b)(1).

15. I.R.C. § 382(c).

return payable on long-term tax-exempt bonds. Thus, in any year, Loss Co.'s NOLs can be used by the combined company only to the extent of the value of old Loss Co. multiplied by an assumed return on equity known as the long-term tax-exempt rate.[16] These basic rules are augmented by attribution rules, technical adjustments and a swarm of anti-avoidance provisions that give new dimension to Congressional paranoia.

Our study of Section 382 begins with an examination of the ownership change requirement and then turns to the effect of such a change on the ability to use Loss Co.'s NOL carryforwards.

2. THE OWNERSHIP CHANGE REQUIREMENTS

Code: § 382(g), (i), (k), (*l*)(3) & (4). See § 318.

In General. Since the economic burden of corporate losses falls on the individuals who were shareholders when the corporation was losing money, the Section 382 limitations do not intercede as long as those individuals continue as shareholders. After all, they suffered through the losses, so it is only fair to give them the benefit of the accompanying tax deductions. Consequently, Section 382 applies only if there is an "ownership change," which occurs if the percentage of Loss Co. stock owned by one or more "5–percent shareholders" increases by more than 50 percentage points[1] during the three-year "testing period."[2] Thus, if Profit Co. purchases 51 percent or more of Loss Co.'s stock within a three-year period, or if Loss Co. is acquired in a corporate reorganization and its ownership changes by more than 50 percent, the loss limitations will apply. Similarly, if ten unrelated individuals each purchase six percent of the Loss Co. stock, Section 382 applies.

These various types of ownership changes are divided by the statute into two categories: an "owner shift involving a 5–percent shareholder" and an "equity structure shift."[3] An "owner shift" generally occurs upon any change in the stock ownership (either an increase or a decrease) of any 5–percent or more shareholder (e.g., the taxable purchases illustrated above).[4] An "equity structure shift" includes tax-free reorganizations, certain public offerings and reorganization-type transactions such as cash mergers.[5]

Owner Shift Involving 5–Percent Shareholder. An owner shift involving a 5–percent shareholder is any change in stock ownership (increase or decrease) that affects the percentage of stock owned by any person who is a 5–percent shareholder before or after the change.[6] Most owner shifts are

16. I.R.C. § 382(b)(1).

1. I.R.C. § 382(g)(1).

2. Id. I.R.C. § 382(i)(1).

3. I.R.C. § 382(g)(2), (3).

4. I.R.C. § 382(g)(2).

5. I.R.C. § 382(g)(3). Regulations designating taxable reorganization-type transactions as equity structure shifts have not yet been issued. See Reg. § 1.382–2T(e)(2)(ii).

6. I.R.C. § 382(g)(2). A 5–percent shareholder is defined as any person holding 5 percent or more of the stock of the loss corporation at any time during the three year testing period. I.R.C. § 382(k)(7).

purchases. Thus, if Profit Co. purchases 10 percent of Loss Co. stock from one shareholder, an owner shift has occurred. Apart from purchases, owner shifts can occur as a result of Section 351 exchanges, redemptions, issuances of stock, or recapitalizations.[7] However, the statute specifically excludes owner shifts as a result of a gift, death or divorce transfer.[8] Changes in proportionate ownership attributable solely to fluctuations in the market value of different classes of stock also are disregarded, except to the extent provided in regulations.[9]

Keep in mind that a single "owner shift" is not enough to trigger Section 382; there also must be a more than 50 percent change in ownership of Loss Co.[10] And while a more than 50 percentage point change in ownership is an essential ingredient in the Section 382 recipe, it is not the only one. Here is where the "5–percent shareholder" concept enters the scene. Consider, for example, the consequences of a simple 50 percent change in ownership rule to a publicly traded company that has loss carryforwards. Those NOLs might be limited as a result of random public trading if more than 50 percent of the company's shares happened to change hands during a three-year period. To preclude such a result, the type of "owner shift" required to trigger Section 382 occurs only if the percentage of stock of Loss Co. owned by one or more "5–percent shareholders" increases by the requisite 50 percent.[11]

A rule that only counted the increased ownership of 5–percent shareholders might be easily circumvented. For example, a shareholder who held Loss Co. stock while the losses were incurred might sell four percent interests to 25 equal purchasers rather than to a single individual. In so doing, the owner would avoid selling any of his stock to a 5–percent shareholder despite an obvious sale and purchase of tax benefits. To assure that the loss limitations apply in these circumstances, Section 382 generally treats all less than 5–percent shareholders as a single 5–percent shareholder.[12] Thus, the sales to 25 four percent shareholders in the example are treated as sales to a single 5–percent shareholder, and the Section 382 limits apply because that 5–percent shareholder's ownership shifts from zero percent to 100 percent. But in the earlier publicly traded example, the group of less than 5–percent shareholders always would have held 100 percent both before and after the transfers, and thus Section 382 would not apply. Unfortunately, not all "owner shifts" are the result of such simple purchases. The problems at the end of this section explore some of these additional complications.

Equity Structure Shifts. Recall that Section 382 first must be triggered by either an "owner shift involving a 5–percent shareholder" or an "equity structure shift,"[13] either of which must result in an "ownership change."

7. Reg. § 1.382–2T(e)(1).
8. I.R.C. § 382(*l*)(3)(B).
9. I.R.C. § 382(*l*)(3)(C).
10. I.R.C. § 382(g)(1).
11. I.R.C. § 382(g)(1)(A).
12. I.R.C. § 382(g)(4)(A).
13. I.R.C. § 382(g)(1).

An "equity structure shift" is defined to include tax-free reorganizations[14] and certain taxable "reorganization-type" transactions, public offerings and similar transactions.[15] Consequently, if there is a shift in the ownership of Loss Co. stock in a reorganization, which when combined with any other stock transfers within the three-year period results in a more than 50 percent change of ownership, such an equity structure shift will bring the Section 382 limitations into play.[16]

Special Rules for Determining Change in Ownership. In determining whether a change in ownership has occurred, reorganizations involve some special complications. In a Type A or C reorganization, the acquiring company that inherits the loss is probably an entirely different company from Loss Co. In that event, what ownership is tested under Section 382? This question is answered indirectly by Section 382(k), which defines the "loss corporation" affected by Section 382 as the corporation entitled to use the loss after the ownership change. Thus, in a Type A statutory merger or a Type C stock-for-assets reorganization involving a loss corporation and another corporation, the limits apply to the survivor. In order to determine the extent of ownership change that has occurred, the ownership of the surviving corporation must be compared to the pre-reorganization ownership of the old Loss Co. In effect, the statute looks at the pre- and post-reorganization ownership of whatever company possesses the losses—whether this is the acquiring corporation or the target. For example, if Loss Co. is merged into Profit Co., Section 382 requires a comparison of the ownership of pre-merger Loss Co. and post-merger Profit Co. If the pre-merger Loss Co. shareholders own at least 50 percent of the post-merger Profit Co. (defined as "new loss corporation")[17] an ownership change within the meaning of Section 382(g) will not have occurred. On the other hand, if Loss Co. acquires the stock (in a Type B reorganization or reverse triangular merger) or assets (in a Type A or C reorganization, or a forward triangular merger) of Profit Co. in exchange for Loss Co. stock, Section 382 will apply unless at least 50 percent of the post-reorganization Loss Co. stock continues to be owned by the pre-reorganization Loss Co. shareholders.

In order to assure proper results in the context of the fusion of two corporations, one more special rule is required. All shareholders who own less than five percent of a company's stock generally are treated as a single 5-percent shareholder. In a reorganization, there may be at least two groups of less than 5-percent shareholders—in our examples, the shareholders of Loss Co. and those of Profit Co. If these two groups were treated as a single shareholder, virtually all reorganizations of publicly held compa-

14. I.R.C. § 382(g)(3)(A). Some reorganizations are excluded from the definition of "equity structure shift." Section 382(g)(3)(A) excludes a Type D or G reorganization, unless the requirements of Section 354(b)(1) are met, and a Type F reorganization.

15. I.R.C. § 382(g)(3)(B). The regulations have not yet identified the reorganization-type transactions covered by this rule. See Reg. § 1.382–2T(e)(2)(ii).

16. The regulations acknowledge that any equity structure shift affecting a 5-percent shareholder is also an owner shift. Reg. § 1.382–2T(e)(2)(iii).

17. I.R.C. § 382(k)(3).

nies would escape Section 382. For example, assume that Loss Co. and Profit Co. are both public companies, with no shareholder owning stock of both and no individual owning (directly or indirectly) five percent of either company. If Profit Co. acquires the Loss Co. assets in a merger pursuant to which the old Loss Co. shareholders receive enough Profit Co. stock to become, as a group, 15 percent shareholders of Profit Co., it would appear that Section 382 should apply because the Profit Co. shareholders went from zero to 85 percent ownership of the "new loss corporation." But if all less–than–5–percent shareholders of Loss Co. and Profit Co. are treated as a single shareholder, 100 percent ownership of Loss Co. has remained within the exclusive ownership of that "single" shareholder—i.e., the group of less than 5–percent shareholders owned all of Loss Co. and all of Profit Co. and still owns all of Profit Co. In order to assure that Section 382 will apply in this and similar situations, the statute segregates public shareholders by providing that the group of less than 5–percent shareholders of Profit Co. and the group of less than 5–percent shareholders of Loss Co. are treated as separate shareholders.[18] In the example, ownership of Loss Co. by the Profit Co. shareholders will have increased from zero to 85 percent and Section 382 therefore will apply.

Attribution Rules. The rules outlined above are buttressed by a set of attribution rules that borrows from and expands upon the attribution regime of Section 318.[19] In general, they treat all stock as owned by individuals, and only actual or constructive ownership by individuals is relevant in testing whether an ownership change has taken place under Section 382. As illustrated by the *Garber Industries* case, which follows, the attribution rules can raise challenging issues of statutory interpretation even in the simplest family settings.

Garber Industries Holding Co. v. Commissioner

United States Tax Court, 2005.
124 T.C. 1.

■ HALPERN, J.

By notice of deficiency dated June 21, 2001, respondent determined deficiencies in petitioner's Federal income taxes for petitioner's 1997 and 1998 taxable (calendar) years in the amounts of $4,916 and $301,835, respectively. The parties have settled all issues save one, leaving for our decision only the question of whether a 1998 stock sale between siblings that increased one sibling's percentage ownership of petitioner by more than 50 percentage points resulted in an ownership change for purposes of section 382, triggering that section's limitation on net operating loss (NOL) carryovers. That issue turns on the interpretation of section 382(*l*)(3)(A)(i), a matter of first impression for this Court.

18. I.R.C. § 382(g)(4)(B)(i).

19. I.R.C. § 382(*l*)(3).

Unless otherwise indicated, all section references are to the Internal Revenue Code in effect for 1998, and all Rule references are to the Tax Court Rules of Practice and Procedure. For the sake of convenience, all percentages are rounded to the nearest full percent.

FINDINGS OF FACT

* * *

At the time of petitioner's incorporation in December 1982, Charles M. Garber, Sr. (Charles), and his brother, Kenneth R. Garber, Sr. (Kenneth) (collectively, sometimes, the Garber brothers), owned 68 percent and 26 percent, respectively, of petitioner's common stock. The spouses, children, and other siblings of the Garber brothers owned the remaining shares of such stock. The Garber brothers' parents, who are deceased, never owned any of petitioner's stock.

On or about July 10, 1996, petitioner underwent a reorganization described in section 368(a)(1)(D) (the reorganization). Pursuant to the reorganization, petitioner canceled Charles's original stock certificate for 3,492.85 shares and issued a new certificate to him for 386 shares. As a result, Charles's percentage ownership of petitioner decreased from 68 percent to 19 percent, and Kenneth's percentage ownership of petitioner increased from 26 percent to 65 percent.

On April 1, 1998, Kenneth sold all of his shares in petitioner to Charles (the 1998 transaction). As a result of the 1998 transaction, Charles's percentage ownership of petitioner increased from 19 percent to 84 percent.

On its 1998 consolidated Federal income tax return, petitioner claimed an NOL deduction in the amount of $808,935 for regular tax purposes and $728,041 for alternative minimum tax (AMT) purposes. As one of the adjustments giving rise to the deficiencies here in question, respondent adjusted the amount of petitioner's 1998 NOL deduction, for both regular tax and AMT purposes, to $121,258 pursuant to section 382(b). Petitioner assigns error to that adjustment.

OPINION

I. Substantive Law

A. Overview of Section 382

Section 382(a) limits the amount of "pre-change losses" that a corporation (referred to as a loss corporation) may use to offset taxable income in the taxable years or periods following an ownership change. "Pre-change losses" include NOL carryovers to the taxable year in which the ownership change occurs and any NOL incurred during that taxable year to the extent such NOL is allocable to the portion of the year ending on the date of the ownership change. Sec. 382(d)(1). An ownership change is deemed to have occurred if, on a required measurement date (a testing date), the aggregate percentage ownership interest of one or more 5–percent shareholders of the loss corporation is more than 50 percentage points greater than the lowest percentage ownership interest of such shareholder(s) during the (generally) 3–year period immediately preceding such testing date (the testing period). Sec. 382(g)(1) and (2), (i); sec. 1.382–2(a)(4), Income Tax Regs.

B. Determining Stock Ownership for Purposes of Section 382

Section 382(*l*)(3)(A) provides that, with certain exceptions, the constructive ownership rules of section 318 apply in determining stock ownership. Under the first of those exceptions, set forth in section 382(*l*)(3)(A)(i), the family attribution rules of section 318(a)(1) and (5)(B) do not apply; instead, an individual and all members of his family described in section 318(a)(1) (spouse, children, grandchildren, and parents) are treated as one individual.

C. Regulations

The family aggregation rule of section 382(*l*)(3)(A)(i) is further addressed in section 1.382–2T(h)(6), Temporary Income Tax Regs., 52 Fed. Reg. 29686 (Aug. 11, 1987). Paragraph (h)(6)(ii) of that section repeats the general rule that, for purposes of section 382, an individual and all members of his family described in section 318(a)(1) are treated as one individual.[6] Paragraph (h)(6)(iv) provides further that, if an individual may be treated as a member of more than one family under paragraph (h)(6)(ii), such individual will be treated as a member of the family with the smallest increase in percentage ownership (to the exclusion of all other families).

II. Arguments of the Parties

A. Petitioner's Argument

Petitioner argues that, although siblings are not family members described in section 318(a)(1), Charles and Kenneth are nonetheless members of the same family when such determination is made by reference to their parents and grandparents. That is, as sons, they are both members of each family consisting of a parent and that parent's family members described in section 318(a)(1). Similarly, as grandsons, they are both members of each family consisting of a grandparent and that grandparent's family members described in section 318(a)(1). Accordingly, petitioner argues, Charles and Kenneth are treated as one individual under section 382(*l*)(3)(A)(i), with the result that transactions between them are disregarded for purposes of section 382.

B. Respondent's Argument

Respondent maintains that the family aggregation rule applies solely with reference to living individuals. Under that view, inasmuch as none of

6. The family aggregation rule does not apply, however, to any family member who, without regard to aggregation, would not be a 5–percent shareholder. Sec. 1.382–2T(h)(6)(iii), Temporary Income Tax Regs., 52 Fed.Reg. 29686 (Aug. 11, 1987). That exception in turn does not apply if the loss corporation has actual knowledge of such family member's stock ownership. *Id.*; sec. 1.382–2T(k)(2), Temporary Income Tax Regs., *supra* at 29694.

the parents and grandparents of the Garber brothers was alive at the commencement of the 3–year testing period immediately preceding the 1998 transaction, from that point forward there was no individual, within the meaning of section 382(*l*)(3)(A)(i), whose family members (as described in section 318(a)(1)) included both Charles and Kenneth. It follows, respondent argues, that Charles and Kenneth are not treated as one individual for purposes of section 382 and that the 1998 transaction resulted in an ownership change with respect to petitioner under section 382.

III. Analysis

A. General Principles of Statutory Construction

As a general matter, if the language of a statute is unambiguous on its face, we apply the statute in accordance with its terms, without resort to extrinsic interpretive aids such as legislative history. * * * Accordingly, our initial inquiry is whether the language of section 382(*l*)(3)(A)(i) is so plain as to permit only one reasonable interpretation insofar as the question presented in this case is concerned. * * *. That threshold determination must be made with reference to the context in which such language appears. Id.

B. Language of Section 382(*l*)(3)(A)(I)

Section 382(*l*)(3)(A)(i) provides as follows:

> (A) Constructive ownership.—Section 318 (relating to constructive ownership of stock) shall apply in determining ownership of stock, except that—
>
> (i) paragraphs (1) and (5)(B) of section 318(a) shall not apply and an individual and all members of his family described in paragraph (1) of section 318(a) shall be treated as 1 individual for purposes of applying this section * * *

Respondent apparently would limit our textual analysis to a single word. According to respondent, Charles and Kenneth are not common members of any individual's family under section 382(*l*)(3)(A)(i) "[b]ecause the commonly used meaning of the term 'individual' does not include a deceased parent". We believe respondent's focus is too narrow. As stated by the Court of Appeals for the Fifth Circuit:

> However, even apparently plain words, divorced from the context in which they arise and in which their creators intended them to function, may not accurately convey the meaning the creators intended to impart. It is only, therefore, within a context that a word, any word, can communicate an idea.

Leach v. FDIC, 860 F.2d 1266, 1270 (5th Cir.1988). In our view, the question is not whether the noun "individual", standing alone, typically denotes a living person—typically it does. The question, rather, is whether the language of section 382(*l*)(3)(A)(i) as a whole definitively establishes, one way or the other, that the identification of a (living) individual whose family members are aggregated thereunder must be made, as respondent maintains (or need not be made, as petitioner maintains), coincident with the determination of stock ownership under section 382 (i.e., on a testing date or at any point during a testing period). Stated negatively, is the language of section 382(*l*)(3)(A)(i) so plain as to preclude either party's position, as so identified?

We are satisfied that the language of section 382(*l*)(3)(A)(i) can variably (and reasonably) be interpreted as being consistent with each party's position in this case. That is, there is nothing in the language of the statute that would make either party's position patently untenable. While a rule attributing stock owned by an individual on a measurement date to members of his family presupposes that the individual is alive, the same need not be said of a rule (such as that contained in section 382(*l*)(3)(A)(i)) that identifies (by reference to an individual) the members of a family that, on some measurement date, are to be treated as a single shareholder. By the same token, the language of section 382(*l*)(3)(A)(i) certainly does not *compel* the conclusion that the individual whose family members are so aggregated need not be alive on that measurement date. Because the answer to our inquiry is not apparent from the face of the statute, we may look beyond the language of section 382(*l*)(3)(A)(i) for interpretive guidance.

C. Legislative History of Section 382(*l*)(3)(A)(I)

Congress enacted the family aggregation rule of section 382(*l*)(3)(A)(i) as part of its overhaul of section 382 included in the Tax Reform Act of 1986, * * * The rule first appeared in the conference committee bill. The conference committee report that accompanied that bill (the 1986 conference report) does not address the temporal aspect of family aggregation identified above: "The family attribution rules of sections 318(a)(1) and 318(a)(5)(B) do not apply, but an individual, his spouse, his parents, his children, and his grandparents are treated as a single shareholder." H. Conf. Rept. 99–841 (Vol.II), at II–182 (1986), 1986–3 C.B. (Vol.4) 1, 182.[10]

D. Other Considerations

1. Family Aggregation Under Pre–1986 Act Section 382

a. General Structure of the Statute

Prior to the amendment of section 382 by the 1986 Act, section 382 contained separate rules for ownership changes resulting from purchases and redemptions, see former sec. 382(a), and those resulting from corporate reorganizations, see former sec. 382(b). Under the "purchase" rules of former section 382(a), ownership changes were ascertained by reference to the holdings of the 10 largest shareholders at the end of the corporation's

10. As noted *supra* part I.B., the members of an individual's family described in sec. 318(a)(1) (to which sec. 382(*l*)(3)(A)(i) refers) are his spouse, children, grandchildren, and parents. Regarding the possible significance of the conferees' reference to "grandparents" in lieu of "grandchildren", see *infra* part III.E.4.

taxable year (as compared to their holdings at the beginning of such taxable year or the preceding taxable year). Former sec. 382(a)(1) and (2).

b. Family Attribution and Aggregation

Intrafamily sales were excluded from the operation of former section 382(a) by means of stock attribution (as opposed to shareholder aggregation) rules. Specifically, purchases of stock from persons whose stock ownership would be attributed to the purchaser under the family attribution rules of section 318 were ignored for purposes of determining whether an ownership change by "purchase" had occurred. See former sec. 382(a)(3) and (4). Although family members were potentially subject to aggregation for purposes of determining the 10 largest shareholders at year-end, that rule applied only if loss corporation stock owned by one was attributed to the other under the family attribution rules of section 318. Former sec. 382(a)(2) and (3). For that reason, the aggregation rule of former section 382(a)(2), unlike the aggregation rule of section 382(*l*)(3)(A)(i), necessarily applied as of the date on which stock ownership was measured (in the case of former section 382(a)(2), at year end). Accordingly, no inference can be drawn from former section 382(a)(2) as to whether, as respondent maintains, the identification of the individuals whose family members are aggregated under section 382(*l*)(3)(A)(i) occurs as of the date on which stock ownership is measured.

2. Practical Consequences of Each Party's Interpretation of Section 382(*l*)(3)(A)(I)

a. Petitioner's Interpretation

Under petitioner's interpretation of section 382(*l*)(3)(A)(i), an individual would be aggregated with (and therefore could, without any section 382 consequences, sell loss corporation shares to) not only his spouse, children, grandchildren, and parents, but also his siblings, nephews, nieces, grandparents, in-laws, great-grandchildren, aunts, uncles, first cousins, and great-grandparents.[12] It is difficult to believe that Congress intended to expand the scope of exempted intrafamily sales so significantly (as compared to both the then-existing version of section 382, see *supra* part III.D.1.b., and the House and Senate versions of revised section 382, see *supra* note 9) with nary a mention of that objective in the 27 pages devoted to section 382 in the 1986 conference report.

12. As a member of each parent's family (i.e., in his capacity as a child of those parents), an individual would be aggregated with his parents' children (his siblings), grandchildren (his nephews and nieces), and parents (his grandparents). As a member of his spouse's family (i.e., in his capacity as her spouse), an individual would be aggregated with his spouse's parents (his mother- and father-in-law). As a member of each child's family (i.e., in his capacity as a parent of those children), an individual would be aggregated with each child's spouse (his sons- and daughters-in-law) and grandchildren (his great-grandchildren). As a member of each grandparent's family (i.e., in his capacity as a grandchild of those grandparents), an individual would be aggregated with his grandparents' children (his aunts and uncles), grandchildren (his first cousins), and parents (his great-grandparents). See secs. 382(*l*)(3)(A)(i), 318(a)(1).

b. Respondent's Interpretation

Respondent's interpretation of section 382(*l*)(3)(A)(i) is perhaps even more troubling than petitioner's. First, it has the potential for being just as expansive as petitioner's interpretation.[13] More importantly, respondent's interpretation leads to arbitrary distinctions. As relevant to this case, respondent would have us believe that the ability of siblings to sell loss corporation shares among themselves without any section 382 consequences is wholly dependent on the continued good health of their parents. We see no rational basis for Congress's having drawn a distinction in this context between siblings whose parents happen to be living and those whose parents happen to be deceased; the former are no more related than the latter.

E. A Third Interpretation

1. Introduction

Our own analysis of the legislative evolution of section 382(*l*)(3)(A)(i) leads us to believe that both parties have erroneously interpreted that provision. For the reasons discussed below, we conclude that Congress most likely intended the aggregation rule of section 382(*l*)(3)(A)(i) to apply solely from the perspective of individuals who are shareholders (as determined under the *attribution* rules of section 382(*l*)(3)(A)) of the loss corporation.[14] In practical terms, our conclusion dictates that we sustain respondent's determination in this case, even though we disagree with his interpretation of the statute.

2. 1986 Act Revisions to Section 382

a. Relevant Fundamental Changes to the Statute

Among other things, section 621(a) of the 1986 Act replaced the "purchase" rules of former section 382(a) with the concept of the "owner shift", defined broadly to include any change in the respective ownership of the stock of a corporation. Sec. 382(g)(2)(A). The occurrence of an owner shift involving a 5–percent shareholder, see sec. 382(g)(2)(B), (k)(7), is one of two occasions for opening the corporation's stock transfer books to determine whether the aggregate percentage ownership interest of one or more such shareholders has increased by more than 50 percentage points within the relevant "lookback" (testing) period.[15] See sec. 382(g)(1), (i). While the owner shift "trigger" presupposes some type of transaction in the stock of the loss corporation, see H. Conf. Rept. 99–841 (Vol.II), supra at II–174, 1986–3 C.B. (Vol.4) at 174, the requisite increase in stock

13. Respondent's interpretation of the statute differs from petitioner's in that respondent would require that the relevant parent, spouse, child, or grandparent of the individual in question be living when stock ownership is measured. See *supra* note 12.

14. In other words, composite shareholders are to be constructed only around individuals who directly or indirectly (through an entity or by means of an option) own shares of the loss corporation.

15. The other such occasion is the occurrence of an equity structure shift (in general, most corporate reorganizations). See sec. 382(g)(1), (3).

ownership within the resulting testing period need not be attributable to a purchase, redemption, or, indeed, any transaction in which shares actually change hands, see sec. 382(g)(1)(A) and (B).

b. Consequences for Family Attribution: Changes in Family Status

Under a system in which an increase in one's percentage ownership of a corporation need not be associated with a transaction in which shares actually change hands, a straightforward application of the family attribution rules of section 318(a) could produce "artificial" ownership increases; i.e., ownership increases solely attributable to changes in family status. For instance, under the attribution rules, the ownership percentage of an individual who marries the sole shareholder of a loss corporation would thereby increase from zero to 100 percent. If the wedding occurred during a testing period (which could be triggered, for instance, by the subsequent issuance of a relatively small number of additional shares to a key employee), then the increase in the nonshareholder spouse's deemed ownership percentage would result in an ownership change. A similar result presumably would occur if the shareholder legally adopted someone during a testing period. See sec. 318(a)(1)(B).

c. House Bill Provision Regarding Changes in Family Status

The House version of revised section 382 provided that the family attribution rule of section 318(a)(1) would apply "by assuming that the family status as of the close of the testing period was the same as the family status as of the beginning of the testing period". H.R. 3838, 99th Cong., 1st Sess. sec. 321(a) (1985) (provision designated as sec. 382(n)(3)(A)). Although the report of the Committee on Ways and Means accompanying the House bill provides no additional insight, see H. Rept. 99–426, at 266 (1985), 1986–3 C.B. (Vol.2) 1, 266, the practical effect of that provision would have been to eliminate the possibility that a change in family status during a testing period could, in and of itself, contribute to an ownership change.[17] The conference committee, in addition to substituting family aggregation for family attribution, dropped the provision in the House bill regarding changes in family status.[18]

d. Observations

In the context of the parties' arguments in this case, the conference committee's excision of the House bill provision regarding changes in family status is somewhat puzzling. Specifically, under each party's inter-

17. Returning to our marriage hypothetical, under the House bill's provision, the couple's relationship on the testing date would have been deemed to be the same as it was at the beginning of the testing period (i.e., not married), with the result that the nonshareholder spouse's ownership percentage would have been deemed to be zero throughout the testing period.

18. The Senate version of the bill contained no such provision, providing instead for the application of the family attribution rules of sec. 318 without modification. H.R. 3838, 99th Cong., 2d Sess. sec. 621(a) (1986) (provision designated as sec. 382(k)(3)(A)).

pretation of section 382(*l*)(3)(A)(i), the family aggregation rule adopted by the conferees would produce the same "artificial" ownership increases that the House bill provision eliminated in the context of attribution. In terms of our marriage hypothetical, the addition of the shareholder spouse to the nonshareholder spouse's family unit during the testing period would increase the ownership percentage of that family unit by 100 percentage points during that period. If, however, the family aggregation rule applies solely from the perspective of shareholders of the loss corporation, there would be no separate family unit headed by the nonshareholder spouse in our hypothetical and, consequently, (1) no increase in ownership attributable to the marriage, and (2) no need for the remedial provision contained in the House bill. Under that interpretation of the family aggregation rule, the conference committee's excision of the House bill's family status provision makes perfect sense.[19]

3. Revisiting the Language of the Statute

That our interpretation of section 382(*l*)(3)(A)(i) provides a cogent explanation for the conference committee's action is of no consequence if a plain reading of the statute does not permit that interpretation. See *supra* part III.A. The use of the term "individual" in section 382(*l*)(3)(A)(i), however, does not preclude a contextual interpretation pursuant to which the set of individuals contemplated by Congress (i.e., individuals who own shares of the loss corporation) is smaller than the universe of all possible individuals (i.e., all living beings). More importantly, we are satisfied that our interpretation proceeds from an entirely natural reading of the statute. Given a stock ownership rule that operates by reference to an individual and other persons who are defined in terms of their relationship to that individual, it is hardly a stretch to surmise that the rule presupposes the shareholder status of the referenced individual.

4. Revisiting the 1986 Conference Report

Having concluded that our interpretation of section 382(*l*)(3)(A)(i) does not do violence to the plain language of the statute, we return to the legislative history to determine whether it is any more supportive of our view than it is of the views of the parties. As indicated above, see *supra* part III.C. and note 10, the 1986 conference report contradicts the statutory language by including an individual's grandparents (rather than his grandchildren) among the family members who are aggregated for purposes of section 382. If that disconnect were attributable to a simple typographical error, one might reasonably expect that the subsequently issued report of the Joint Committee on Taxation explaining the 1986 Act (the so-called

19. We recognize that, even if the family aggregation rule were *not* limited to shareholders, the "tiebreaker" rule of sec. 1.382–2T(h)(6)(iv), Temporary Income Tax Regs., 52 Fed.Reg. 29686, would preclude the artificial ownership increase illustrated above by treating the shareholder spouse as a member of his own family rather than that of the nonshareholder spouse. See *supra* part I.C. Of course, that regulation was not in existence when the conference committee acted on H.R. 3838. Accordingly, it is not relevant to our analysis of such committee action. Regarding the remedial effect of the regulation under our interpretation of the family aggregation rule, see *infra* part III.E.5.

Blue Book) would point out the error. See, e.g., Staff of Joint Comm. on Taxation, General Explanation of Tax Legislation Enacted in the 104th Congress at 81 n. 59 (J. Comm. Print 1996), (noting that the conference report accompanying H.R. 3448, the bill eventually enacted as the Small Business Job Protection Act of 1996, mistakenly refers to the lessee rather than the lessor in the context of new section 168(i)(8)). The Blue Book for the 1986 Act, however, retains the reference in the 1986 conference report to "grandparents" in the context of section 382(*l*)(3)(A)(i). Staff of Joint Comm. on Taxation, General Explanation of the Tax Reform Act of 1986 at 311 (J. Comm. Print 1987).

As is the case with the conference committee's excision of the family status provision of the House bill, see *supra* part III.E.2.d., the substitution of "grandparents" for "grandchildren" in the 1986 conference report makes perfect sense if the family aggregation rule applies solely from the perspective of individuals who are shareholders of the loss corporation. Section 318(a)(1) (to which section 382(*l*)(3)(A)(i) refers) is phrased in terms of the family members (spouse, children, grandchildren, and parents) *from whom* shares are attributed. The converse of that rule is that shares owned by an individual are attributed *to* that individual's spouse, parents, grandparents, and children. The substitution of "grandparents" for "grandchildren" in the 1986 conference report (reiterated in the 1986 Blue Book) therefore suggests that Congress intended individuals to be aggregated with the same family members to whom their shares would otherwise be attributed under section 318(a)(1), which in turn suggests that Congress intended the family aggregation rule to apply from the perspective of individuals who are shareholders of the loss corporation.[20]

5. Revisiting the Regulations

Having concluded that our interpretation of the family aggregation rule (1) does not violate the plain meaning rule, and (2) arguably finds support in the legislative history of section 382(*l*)(3)(A)(i), we would nonetheless be hard pressed to adopt that interpretation if it were inconsistent with respondent's 17–year–old "legislative" regulations. See, e.g., Chevron U.S.A., Inc. v. Natural Res. Def. Council, Inc., 467 U.S. 837, 843–844, 104 S.Ct. 2778, 81 L.Ed.2d 694 (1984); see also sec. 382(m) (directing the Secretary to "prescribe such regulations as may be necessary or appropriate to carry out the purposes of this section"). As is the case with the statute, see *supra* part III.E.3., the language of the relevant regulation presents no such obstacle. See sec. 1.382–2T(h)(6), Temporary Income Tax Regs, *supra* at 29686.

Nor does our interpretation of the statute render superfluous the "tiebreaker" rule of paragraph (h)(6)(iv) of the above-cited regulation. See *supra* note 19. To the contrary, that rule serves the useful purpose of precluding purely "vicarious" ownership increases that could otherwise

20. We do not mean to suggest that sec. 382(*l*)(3)(A)(i) should be interpreted as incorporating a modified version of sec. 318(a)(1) (i.e., one that substitutes grandparents for grandchildren); such an interpretation presumably would violate the plain meaning rule. See *supra* part III.A.

occur under our interpretation of the statute (as well as those of the parties). For instance, if a husband and wife each own shares of a loss corporation, and the husband purchases additional shares from his mother, the ownership percentage of the family unit centered on the wife would increase as a result of the otherwise exempt transaction.[21] The tiebreaker rule precludes that result by treating the wife as a member of the family unit centered on her husband rather than a member of the family unit centered on her, since such inclusion would result in the smallest increase (zero) in percentage ownership.[22] See *supra* part I.C.; *supra* note 21.

IV. Conclusion

We hold that the family aggregation rule of section 382(*l*)(3)(A)(i) applies solely from the perspective of individuals who are shareholders (as determined under the attribution rules of section 382(*l*)(3)(A)) of the loss corporation. Inasmuch as an individual shareholder's family consists solely of his spouse, children, grandchildren, and parents for these purposes, sibling shareholders are not aggregated under section 382(*l*)(3)(A)(i) if none of their parents and grandparents is a shareholder of the loss corporation.[23] Since Kenneth and Charles were not children or grandchildren of an individual shareholder of petitioner at any relevant time, they are not aggregated for purposes of applying section 382 to the facts of this case. It follows that Charles's purchase of shares from Kenneth in 1998 resulted in an ownership change with respect to petitioner as contemplated in section 382(g).

PROBLEMS

1. Loss Co. has 100 shares of common stock outstanding and is owned equally by Shareholders 1 through 25, who are not related to one another.

21. Since the purchased shares would be included in the holdings of the family unit centered on the husband both before and after the sale, the percentage ownership of the husband-centric family unit would remain unchanged. However, since the purchased shares would not be included in the holdings of the family unit centered on the wife until after the sale, the percentage ownership of the wife-centric family unit would increase as a result of the sale. A similar result would occur if the purchaser's child (rather than his wife) were a shareholder.

22. As is the case with changes in family status, see *supra* note 16, this problem did not arise under former sec. 382(a), since the "vicarious" ownership increase would not have been attributable to a purchase by the wife. See former sec. 382(a)(1)(B)(i).

23. We recognize that our interpretation of the statute suggests a distinction between siblings who are the children or grandchildren of a shareholder and those who are not, a distinction that is arguably just as arbitrary as the distinctions resulting from respondent's interpretation of the statute. See *supra* part III.D.2.b. That problem would not arise if the tiebreaker rule of sec. 1.382–2T(h)(6)(iv), Temporary Income Tax Regs., *supra* at 29686, were inapplicable in any instance in which such application would have the effect of exempting a transaction (such as a sale between siblings) that otherwise would have increased the percentage ownership of the purchaser's family unit. Cf. sec. 1.382–4(d)(6)(i), Income Tax Regs. (rules treating an option as exercised do not apply if a principal purpose of the option is to avoid an ownership change by having it treated as exercised); T.D. 9063, 2003–2 C.B. 510, 511 (discussing the need for additional regulations dealing with changes in family composition in the context of sec. 382).

Loss Co. has assets worth $1,000,000 and net operating loss carryovers of $8,000,000. Will the Section 382 loss limitations apply in the following situations?

(a) All shareholders sell their stock to Ms. Julie ("J")?

(b) Shareholders 1 through 13 sell their stock to J?

(c) Shareholders 1 through 12 sell their stock to J?

(d) What result in (c), above, if Loss Co. redeems the stock of Shareholders 13 and 14 two years later?

(e) What result in (c), above, if Shareholder 13 sells his stock to New Shareholder 26?

(f) What result in (e), above, if Shareholder 14 also sells her stock to New Shareholder 26?

(g) What result if Shareholders 1 through 25 sell their stock to New Shareholders 26 through 50?

2. Loss Co. is owned 40 percent by Bill and 60 percent by the general public. Loss Co.'s stock is worth $10,000,000. Loss Co. acquires all the assets of Gain Co. (net worth—$10,500,000) in a Type C reorganization in exchange for $10,500,000 worth of Loss Co. voting stock. If no shareholders of Gain Co. owned any Loss Co. stock prior to the transaction, has there been an ownership change?

3. Whale Co. and Minnow Co. (which has loss carryovers) are both publicly held companies, neither of which has any 5-percent shareholder. Whale Co. purchases all the stock of Minnow Co. for cash. Does § 382 apply?

3. RESULTS OF AN OWNERSHIP CHANGE

Code: § 382(a)–(f), (h), (*l*)(1) & (4).

In General. If an ownership change occurs, the Section 382 loss limitations then must be applied. Before considering any further details, the function of the limitations must be examined. We have seen that Congress designed Section 382 to prevent taxpayers from selling and purchasing tax deductions. If that were the only relevant consideration, the rest would be easy—whenever there is an ownership change, simply eliminate all loss carryforwards. But our study of Subchapter C has revealed one other salient factor—a corporation is treated as a separate entity for tax purposes. Although the individual shareholder may bear the ultimate burden or reap the ultimate benefit of a corporation's losses or profits, it is the corporation itself that is the focus of the corporate income tax.

In Section 382, Congress has adopted a principle of "neutrality" toward a loss company. While the Section 382 limitations restrict trafficking in deductions, they permit the purchaser of a loss corporation to use that corporation's net operating losses to offset the old loss corporation's own subsequent income. What Section 382 seeks to prevent is the use of a corporation's losses to offset another taxpayer's income after an ownership change. It is from this policy that the two limitations in Section 382 directly flow.

Continuity of Business Enterprise Limit. The first limit is found in Section 382(c),[1] which incorporates the continuity of business enterprise doctrine[2] by disallowing all net operating loss carryovers if the old loss corporation business is not continued for at least two years after the ownership change.[3] As described in the reorganization regulations, continuity of business enterprise requires either that the historic business of the loss corporation be continued for at least two years or that a significant portion of its assets are used in some other business carried on by the new loss corporation.[4] As a result, a corporation that runs afoul of this first limit in the second year following an ownership change may be required to amend its tax return for the earlier year and remove any inherited NOL deductions that had been applied against taxable income.

The Section 382 Limitation. A second, more complex limitation is "the Section 382 limitation," under which losses can be used in any "post-change year" only to the extent of the value of the old loss corporation multiplied by the "long-term tax-exempt rate."[5] To illustrate, assume Loss Co. has a value of $200,000 and has losses of $800,000 at a time when the long-term tax-exempt rate is 6 percent. After an ownership change, New Loss Co. may use its loss carryforwards only to the extent of $200,000 multiplied by 6 percent, or $12,000 per year.

The theory of this limit is to allow the loss carryforwards to offset any income earned by the old loss business. But since many of the acquisitions that will trigger the limit involve combining a loss business with some other more profitable enterprise, it is impossible to determine exactly how much income will be generated by the old company. To solve this problem, Section 382 irrebuttably presumes that the old loss business will generate income on its assets at a predetermined rate—the long-term tax-exempt rate. Because the amount of available loss carryforwards depends on the value of the old loss company, the greater the value (and cost) of that company, the more loss carryforwards may be used each year. Although the object of this limit is to defer the use of loss carryforwards by limiting the amount that can be used in any one year, the deferral will turn into a complete disallowance if the losses cannot be used before their expiration under Section 172.

Carryforwards of Unused Limitation. The Section 382 limitation results in some further complexity if it exceeds a corporation's taxable

1. This limitation is inapplicable to the extent of any built-in gains or gains resulting from a Section 338 election as well as any Section 382(b)(2) carryovers related to such gains. See I.R.C. § 382(c)(2) and page 870, infra.

2. See Chapter 17B1d, supra.

3. I.R.C. § 382(c)(1).

4. Reg. § 1.368–1(d).

5. I.R.C. § 382(b)(1), (f). "Post-change year" is any taxable year ending after the "change date"—i.e., in the case of an owner shift, the date on which the shift occurs and, in the case of an equity structure shift, the date of the reorganization. I.R.C. § 382(d)(2), (j).

income in a given post-change year. To illustrate, if Loss Co. in the example above, with a value of $200,000, had at least $12,000 of taxable income (disregarding its NOL carryover), the full $12,000 of NOLs that were available in each year after the change of ownership would be used. But if the combined taxable income of the new loss company were only $4,000, the full amount available under the Section 382(b)(1) limitation would not be utilized. In that situation, the $8,000 of available but unused NOLs may be carried forward and the limitation in the following year would be $20,000 (the sum of the regular $12,000 limitation plus the $8,000 carryover).[6]

Mid–Year Ownership Change. Another special rule applies if the "change date"[7] occurs on a date other than the last day of a year. In that event, the Section 382 limitation for the portion of the year after the change is a prorated amount derived by applying a ratio of the remaining days in the year to the total days in the year.[8] Thus, if the change occurs two-thirds of the way through the year, the limitation for that year is one-third of what otherwise would be available—i.e., $12,000 × ⅓, or $4,000 in the example above.[9]

The Long–Term Tax–Exempt Rate. Returning to the basic Section 382 limitation, recall that it is the value of the old loss corporation multiplied by the long-term tax-exempt rate. The use of this measure to predict the expected return on Loss Co.'s assets is the product of substantial Congressional debate.[10] Loss Co. presumably can generate earnings on its assets at a rate at least equal to the higher federal long-term taxable rate. Indeed, if it could not do so some other way, Loss Co. simply could sell its assets and invest the proceeds in long-term federal obligations. Use of the lower tax-exempt rate to predict Loss Co.'s earnings is intended to offset the fact that the amount against which this rate is applied will exceed the real value of Loss Co.'s income-generating assets. How so? Because under Section 382(e)(1), the value of Loss Co. is the value of its stock immediately before the ownership change. Since Loss Co. has loss carryforwards to offset any income it earns in the near future, that income will be essentially tax-free. Loss Co.'s after-tax return will equal its before-tax profit, and the value of its stock will reflect not only the value of its income-generating assets but also the fact that the income which is generated will be tax free.

The Value of the Company. The second component of the Section 382 limitation is the value of the stock of the old loss corporation immediately preceding the ownership change.[11] Congress included several special rules

6. I.R.C. § 382(b)(2).

7. I.R.C. § 382(j).

8. I.R.C. § 382(b)(3)(B).

9. In addition, the limitation is inapplicable to the days of the year prior to the change date. I.R.C. § 382(b)(3)(A).

10. The long-term tax-exempt rate is defined by Section 382(f) as the highest federal long-term rate determined under Section 1274(d) in effect for the three-month period ending with the month of the ownership change, adjusted to reflect differences between returns on long-term taxable and tax-exempt obligations.

11. I.R.C. § 382(b)(1), (e)(1). For purposes of determining the value of the loss corporation, all stock is counted, even preferred stock that would be ignored in deter-

to guard against predictable efforts to abuse this rule by inflating the value of the loss company.

One obvious technique to increase the available NOLs after an ownership change would be for the shareholders to increase the value of the loss company just prior to the change by contributing cash or other property to the corporation. Congress attacked this maneuver with an "anti-stuffing" rule, under which the value of any pre-change capital contribution received by the loss company as part of a plan to increase the Section 382 limitation is disregarded.[12] Any contribution received within two years before an ownership change is generally treated as part of such a plan.[13]

Even without "stuffing" in anticipation of a planned ownership change, shareholders of a loss company may be tempted to transfer cash or income-producing investments to the company. If there is a later ownership change, the allowable losses then would be greater; and if there is not a change, the investment income could be accumulated tax-free at the corporate level because it would be offset by the loss carryforwards. If the shareholders do not wish to transfer portfolio investments to the loss company, they at least might be tempted to prevent the company's profits (assuming it later becomes profitable) from being taken out of the company in order to reinvest these profits in portfolio investments which can accumulate tax-free at the corporate level and be available to increase the Section 382 limit in the event of a subsequent ownership change.

These possibilities did not go unnoticed by an ever suspicious Congress. If at least one-third of a loss corporation's assets consist of nonbusiness (i.e., investment) assets, the value of the corporation for purposes of Section 382 includes only the percentage of its actual net value that represents the percentage of its gross assets which are business assets.[14] To illustrate, if Loss Co. has $2,000,000 of investment assets, $3,000,000 of business assets and $1,000,000 of debt, it has a net value of $4,000,000, but only 60 percent of that value is taken into account for purposes of the Section 382 limitation because only 60 percent of its gross assets are business assets.[15]

If taxpayers are unable to increase useable NOLs by inflating the value of the loss corporation prior to an ownership change, they might be tempted to at least enable a profitable corporation to more easily avail itself

mining whether an ownership change has occurred. I.R.C. §§ 382(e)(1), (k)(6)(A); 1504(a)(4).

12. I.R.C. § 382(*l*)(1).

13. I.R.C. § 382(*l*)(1)(B). Exempted from this presumption are any contributions to be specified in regulations. The Conference Report instructs the Treasury that the regulations should generally exempt contributions only if they occurred prior to the accrual of the losses or if they were contributions of necessary operating capital. H.R.Rep. No. 99–841, 99th Cong., 2d Sess. II–182.

14. I.R.C. § 382(*l*)(4).

15. When it applies, Section 382(*l*)(4) specifically requires that the value of the loss corporation shall be reduced by the excess of the value of its nonbusiness assets over an amount of the corporation's debt which bears the same ratio to all the company's debt which the nonbusiness assets bear to all the company's assets. I.R.C. § 382(*l*)(4)(A). See § 382(*l*)(4)(D). The net result is as described in the text above.

of these losses by decreasing the value of the loss corporation after an ownership change. To illustrate, assume Loss Co. has a value of $1,000,000 and loss carryforwards of $1,000,000 and the tax-exempt rate is 6 percent. Profit Co. could acquire Loss Co. for $1,000,000 and use loss carryforwards at the rate of $60,000 per year, which probably would be enough only to offset Loss Co.'s own income. But what if Profit Co. pays $510,000 for 51 percent of Loss Co., and then Loss Co. redeems the remaining 49 percent of its outstanding shares? Loss Co.'s value has decreased by 49 percent (the amount paid to redeem its stock), and its revenues presumably will decrease by the same 49 percent. Profit Co. will have paid only $510,000, but the smaller New Loss Co. may deduct its loss carryovers to the extent of 6 percent times $1,000,000, or $60,000 per year. Once again, Congress cuts off a promising strategy at the pass. Section 382(e)(2) provides that if a redemption or other corporate contraction occurs in connection with an ownership change, the value of the loss corporation is determined only after taking the redemption or contraction into account.[16]

Limit on Built-in Losses. Finally, a corporation generally is subject to the Section 382 limitations only if it has loss carryforwards. A prospective buyer of deductions might be tempted to avoid the section by simply acquiring an asset that did not have the carryforwards themselves but rather the ability to produce them. Specifically, instead of acquiring a corporation that had loss carryforwards, a taxpayer could acquire a corporation that had substantial unrealized losses and other deductions built into its assets. Assuming a buyer is in the market for deductions, a company with assets having an aggregate basis of $1,000,000 and a value of $100,000 may be as attractive as a company with a $900,000 loss carryforward. Once the company is acquired, the profitable company could sell those assets and use the losses against its own profits.

In its eternal race to stay one step ahead of the taxpayer, Congress has extended the limitations in Section 382 to certain built-in unrealized losses and deductions that economically accrue prior to an ownership change but are not recognized until after the change.[17] If a corporation has assets whose aggregate bases exceed their total value—i.e., a "net unrealized built-in loss"[18]—then any built-in losses which are recognized within five years[19] of an ownership change are treated as loss carryforwards of the old loss corporation and are subject to the Section 382 deduction limits.[20] Depreciation, amortization or depletion deductions during the five-year recognition period are treated as recognized built-in losses for purposes of this rule unless the corporation establishes that such amounts are not attributable to the excess of the adjusted basis over the fair market value of

16. The legislative history suggests that the "in connection with" standard should be broadly construed to include any redemption that is contemplated at the time of the ownership change. See H.R.Rep. No. 99–841, supra note 13, at II–187.

17. I.R.C. § 382(h)(1)(B).

18. I.R.C. § 382(h)(3)(A).

19. This is known as the "recognition period." I.R.C. § 382(h)(7).

20. I.R.C. § 382(h)(1)(B).

the asset on the change date.[21] To the extent that the new loss corporation establishes that a loss recognized during the five-year period accrued after the ownership change, the loss may be deducted without limitation.[22] Even if the new loss company is unable to establish when any particular loss was accrued, the total amount of loss subject to this rule may not exceed the net unrealized loss built into the old loss corporation's assets.[23] A special de minimis rule provides that a corporation's net unrealized built-in loss is considered to be zero if it does not exceed the lesser of (1) 15 percent of the fair market value of the assets of the corporation, or (2) $10 million.[24]

Special Rules for Built-in Gains. On occasion, Congress is as eager to be fair as it is to be vigilant. In that spirit, the Section 382 limitation is increased to reflect built-in gains and other income items that accrued prior to the ownership change but are recognized within five years after the change. If on the change date the aggregate fair market value of a loss corporation's assets exceeds the aggregate adjusted basis of those assets—i.e., the corporation has a "net unrealized built-in gain"[25]—the Section 382 limitation is increased by any built-in gain (up to total net unrealized built-in gain) which is recognized during the five-year "recognition period" following an ownership change.[26] As a result, the new loss company can use its loss carryforwards (in addition to otherwise allowable post-change losses) to offset any built-in gains which it recognizes either on a disposition of an asset of the old loss corporation[27] or because of a Section 338 election made with respect to the loss corporation.[28] The corporation must be able to prove that the built-in gains accrued prior to the change date;[29] and the total increase in the Section 382 limitation may not exceed the net unrealized built-in gain as of the change date.[30] Once again, a de minimis rule provides that net unrealized built-in gains do not increase the Section 382 limitation if they do not exceed the lesser of (1) 15 percent of the fair

21. I.R.C. § 382(h)(2)(B). For example, depreciation deductions attributable to capital improvements made with respect to an asset after the change date would not be subject to the limitation.

22. I.R.C. § 382(h)(2)(B)(i).

23. I.R.C. § 382(h)(1)(B)(ii).

24. I.R.C. § 382(h)(3)(B)(i). For purposes of this test, cash, cash equivalents and marketable securities with a value not substantially different from their bases generally are disregarded. § 382(h)(3)(B)(ii).

25. I.R.C. § 382(h)(3)(A).

26. I.R.C. § 382(h)(1).

27. Id. If a taxpayer sells a built-in gain asset prior to or during the recognition period in an installment sale under Section 453, the provisions of Section 382(h) continue to apply to gain recognized from the sale (including a disposition of the installment obligations) after the recognition period. I.R.S. Notice 90–27, 1990–1 C.B. 336.

28. I.R.C. § 382(h)(1)(C). If an ownership change and Section 338 qualified stock purchase occur simultaneously, the target is treated as selling its assets to itself ("new T") at the close of the acquisition date. I.R.C. § 338(a). In that situation, the Section 382 limit does not apply to the Section 338 deemed sale gain because the losses do not carry over to a "post-change year." I.R.C. § 382(a), (d)(2). When an ownership change takes place prior to a qualified stock purchase (i.e., a creeping qualified stock purchase), Section 382(h)(1)(C) provides special rules when the Section 382(h)(3)(B) de minimis threshold is not satisfied and the corporation's built-in gains are considered to be zero.

29. I.R.C. § 382(h)(2)(A).

30. I.R.C. § 382(h)(1)(A)(ii).

market value of the corporation's assets, or (2) $10 million.[31]

PROBLEMS

1. Loss Co. has net operating loss carryforwards of $10,000,000. It has assets worth $10,000,000 and liabilities of $2,000,000. Profit Co. is a publicly held company worth $100,000,000.

(a) On January 1, 2006, Profit Co. acquires all of the Loss Co. assets in a merger of Loss Co. into Profit Co. where Loss Co. shareholders receive Profit Co. stock worth $8,500,000. The long-term tax-exempt rate at that time is 5 percent. Assuming the Loss Co. business is continued, to what extent can Profit Co. deduct Loss Co.'s loss carryforwards in 2006?

(b) What result in (a), above, if Profit Co. instead purchases all of the Loss Co. stock for $8,500,000?

(c) What result in (a), above, if Profit Co.'s taxable income, disregarding any loss carryforward, is $300,000 in 2006?

(d) What result in (a), above, if Profit Co. discontinues the Loss Co. business and disposes of its assets in 2006?

(e) What result in (a), above, if the merger occurs on June 30, 2006? Assume the date is halfway through each corporation's taxable year.

2. Loss Co. has loss carryforwards of $10,000,000. It has the following assets, all of which have been held for more than two years unless otherwise indicated:

Asset	**Adj. Basis**	**F.M.V.**
Equipment	$2,000,000	$4,500,000
Land	6,000,000	3,000,000
IBM stock	2,000,000	2,000,000
Cash	500,000	500,000

Loss Co. has liabilities of $2,000,000. Profit Co. is a publicly held company worth $100,000,000. On January 1, 2006, Profit Co. acquires all of the Loss Co. assets in exchange for Profit Co. stock worth $8,500,000. The long-term tax-exempt rate is 5 percent.

(a) Assuming that the business conducted by Loss Co. is continued, to what extent can Profit Co. deduct Loss Co.'s loss carryforwards in 2006?

(b) What result in (a), above, if the stock and cash had been contributed to the capital of Loss Co. in November, 2005?

(c) What result in (a), above, if the IBM stock had a value and basis of $5,000,000?

31. I.R.C. § 382(h)(3)(B).

(d) What result in (c), above, if IBM were a wholly owned subsidiary of Loss Co.?

(e) What result in (a), above, if Profit Co. acquires 70 percent of the Loss Co. stock for Profit Co. stock on January 1 and the IBM stock and the cash are distributed to Joe, a 30 percent shareholder of Loss Co., on March 1 in redemption of all of his stock?

(f) Will the result in (a), above, change if Profit Co. sells the equipment in February? Would the answer be different if the land had a basis of zero?

(g) Assume in (a), above, that the land had a basis of $8,000,000 and that Profit Co. sells the land for $3,000,000 two years later. Is the loss deductible? What if Profit Co. sells the land for $2,700,000?

D. Limitations on Other Tax Attributes: Section 383

Code: § 383.

Section 383 is a brief section that is easily mastered if one understands the operation of Section 382. It essentially calls for the Treasury to issue regulations that will adopt the principles of Section 382 (i.e., the continuity of business enterprise requirement and ownership change rules coupled with limitations) to limit corporate attributes other than loss carryforwards. Section 383 applies to the Section 39 carryforward of the general business credit,[1] the Section 53 carryforward of the alternative minimum tax credit,[2] and the Section 904(c) carryforward of the foreign tax credit.[3] Section 383 also calls for regulations to employ Section 382 principles to limit capital loss carryforwards of a loss company.[4] In addition, the regulations must provide that any permitted use of a capital loss carryforward in any year will reduce the Section 382 limitation on loss carryforwards for that year.[5]

E. Other Loss Limitations

1. Acquisitions Made to Evade Tax: Section 269

Code: § 269.

If a corporation surmounts the hurdles of Section 382, it still may find its losses limited by Section 269. The subjective approach of Section 269 is fundamentally different from the objective tests of Section 382. Section 269 applies to a transaction only if the principal purpose of the acquisition was "evasion or avoidance of Federal income tax by acquiring the benefit of a

1. I.R.C. § 383(a)(2)(A).

2. I.R.C. § 383(a)(2)(B).

3. I.R.C. § 383(c).

4. I.R.C. § 383(b).

5. I.R.C. § 383(b). For regulations implementing Section 383, see Reg. § 1.383–1.

deduction, credit, or other allowance" which the taxpayer otherwise might not enjoy. Section 269(a) potentially applies to Type A and C reorganizations and forward triangular mergers and to Type B reorganizations or stock purchases where the acquiring corporation previously owned less than 50 percent of the target.[1] Section 269(b) applies to liquidations which occur within two years after a corporation makes a stock purchase which would have qualified for a Section 338 election but only if no such election was made.[2]

If Section 269 applies, the Commissioner has the power to deny any "deduction, credit or allowance." In theory, Section 269 thus has a potentially broader reach than Section 382. Although Congress has indicated that Section 269 should not be applied to a transaction where carryovers were limited by the prior versions of Section 382,[3] the proposed regulations make it clear that current Sections 382 and 383 do not limit the Service's ability to invoke Section 269.[4] Thus, if a tax avoidance device or scheme is detected, Section 269 can deny even those NOLs that otherwise slip by the limits of Section 382. It is expected, however, that Section 269 will be applied more sparingly now that the objective limits on loss carryovers have been strengthened.

2. LIMITATIONS ON USE OF PREACQUISITION LOSSES TO OFFSET BUILT-IN GAINS: SECTION 384

Code: § 384.

Section 384 restricts an acquiring corporation from using its preacquisition losses to offset built-in gains of an acquired corporation. The policy and operation of Section 384 can best be illustrated by an example. Assume that Loss Corporation ("L") has $100,000 of net operating loss carryforwards. At the beginning of the current year, profitable Target Corporation ("T") merges into L in a tax-free Type A reorganization. L and T are owned by unrelated individual shareholders, and the merger does not result in a Section 382 ownership change to L. T's only asset, Gainacre, has a value of $200,000 and an adjusted basis of $125,000 which will transfer to L under Section 362(b). Assume that L sells Gainacre for $200,000 shortly after the merger, realizing a $75,000 gain.

Unless Section 269 or Section 382 applied, L could apply its preacquisition losses to shelter any gains recognized on the disposition of the assets acquired from T. Thus, L could use its net operating loss carryforwards to offset the $75,000 gain on the sale of Gainacre. Because it was not clear that Section 269 would effectively deter this strategy, Congress became

1. I.R.C. § 269(a)(2).

2. See Chapter 16C2, supra.

3. See, e.g., S.Rep. No. 94–938, 94th Cong., 2d Sess. 206 (1976), reprinted in 1976–3 C.B. (Part 1) 244; S.Rep. No. 1622, 83d Cong., 2d Sess. 284 (1954).

4. Reg. § 1.269–7 provides that Section 269 may be applied to disallow a deduction, credit or other allowance when the item is limited or reduced under Section 382 or 383. The fact that an item is limited under Section 382(a) or 383 is relevant to the determination of whether the principal purpose of the acquisition is evasion or avoidance of federal tax.

concerned that loss corporations would become vehicles for "laundering" the built-in gains of profitable target companies. Section 384—yet another attack on the real and perceived abuses flowing from corporate acquisitions—is the legislative response. Its purpose is to preclude a corporation from using its preacquisition losses to shelter built-in gains of another (usually, a target) corporation which are recognized within five years of an acquisition of the gain corporation's assets or stock. In the example above, L would be prevented from using its preacquisition net operating loss as a deduction against the $75,000 "recognized built-in gain" on the disposition of Gainacre.

Section 384 is triggered in two situations: (1) stock acquisitions, where one corporation acquires "control" (defined by reference to the 80–percent–of–vote–and–value benchmark in Section 1504(a)(2)) of another corporation, and (2) asset acquisitions in an acquisitive Type A, C or D reorganization, if either corporation is a "gain corporation"—i.e., a corporation having built-in gains.[1] As originally enacted, Section 384 applied only when a loss corporation acquired the stock or assets of a gain corporation, but Congress later expanded the provision to apply regardless of which corporation acquired the other. If applicable, Section 384(a) provides that the corporation's income, to the extent attributable to "recognized built-in gains," shall not be offset by any "preacquisition loss" other than a preacquisition loss of the gain corporation. This punishment occurs during any "recognition period taxable year," which is any taxable year within the five-year period beginning on the "acquisition date."[2]

Understanding the operation of Section 384 requires a mastery of its glossary, much of which is borrowed from Section 382. The essential terms are as follows:

(1) The "acquisition date" is the date on which control is acquired, in the case of a stock acquisition, or the date of the transfer, in the case of an asset acquisition.[3]

(2) A "preacquisition loss" is any net operating loss carryforward to the taxable year in which the acquisition date occurs and the portion of any net operating loss for the taxable year of the acquisition to the extent the loss is allocable to the period before the acquisition date.[4]

1. I.R.C. § 384(a), (c)(4) and (5). Section 384 does not displace any of the other Code provisions limiting loss carryovers—e.g., Sections 269, 382, and certain provisions in the consolidated return regulations. Congress has indicated that the limitations of Section 384 apply independently of and in addition to the limitations of Section 382. Staff of the Joint Committee on Taxation, Description of the Technical Corrections Bill of 1988, 100th Cong., 2d Sess. 421 (1988). In contrast to Section 269, the application of Section 384 is not dependent on the subjective intent of the acquiring corporation.

2. See I.R.C. §§ 384(c)(8); 382(h)(7). The Section 384 limitation also applies to any "successor" corporation to the same extent it applied to its predecessor. I.R.C. § 384(c)(7).

3. I.R.C. § 384(c)(2).

4. I.R.C. § 384(c)(3)(A). In the case of a corporation with a net unrealized built-in loss, as defined by Section 382(h)(1)(B), the term "preacquisition loss" also includes any

(3) A "recognized built-in gain" is any gain recognized on the disposition of any asset during the five-year recognition period except to the extent that the gain corporation (in the case of an acquisition of control) or the acquiring corporation (in the case of an asset acquisition) establishes that the asset was not held by the gain corporation on the acquisition date, or that the gain accrued after the acquisition date.[5] Income items recognized after the acquisition date but attributable to prior periods are also treated as recognized built-in gain.[6] This definition should be familiar; it is similar to the definition of the same term in Section 382(h)(2)(A) except that the burden of proof is different. Under Section 382, the burden is on the taxpayer to establish that the asset was held by the old loss corporation before the change date and the recognized gain does not exceed the appreciation in the asset on that date. Under Section 384, it is presumed that a gain recognized during the recognition period is a built-in gain unless the corporation establishes that the asset was not held on the acquisition date or that the recognized gain exceeds the built-in gain at the time of the acquisition.

(4) The amount of recognized built-in gain for any taxable year is limited to the "net unrealized built-in gain" reduced by recognized built-in gains for prior years in the recognition period which, but for Section 384, would have been offset by preacquisition losses.[7] For this purpose, the definition of "net unrealized built-in gain" is borrowed from Section 382(h)(3), substituting the acquisition date for the ownership "change date."[8] Thus, it is the excess of the aggregate fair market value of the assets of the "gain corporation" over the aggregate adjusted bases of those assets, except that the net unrealized built-in gain will be deemed to be zero unless it is greater than the lesser of (1) 15 percent of the fair market value of the corporation's assets other than cash and certain marketable securities or (2) $10 million.[9]

The limitations in Section 384(a) do not apply to the preacquisition loss of any corporation that was a member of the same "controlled group" that included the gain corporation at all times during the five-year period ending on the acquisition date. For this purpose, the definition of controlled group is borrowed from Section 1563 (as modified to generally require more than 50 percent common ownership of both voting power and value).[10]

built-in loss recognized during the five-year recognition period. I.R.C. § 384(c)(3)(B).

5. I.R.C. § 384(c)(1)(A).

6. I.R.C. § 384(c)(1)(B).

7. I.R.C. § 384(c)(1)(C).

8. I.R.C. § 384(c)(8).

9. I.R.C. §§ 384(c)(8); 382(h)(3)(B).

10. I.R.C. § 384(b). The common control testing period would be shortened if the gain corporation was not in existence for the full five-year preacquisition date period by substituting its period of existence. I.R.C. § 384(b)(3).

As if the foregoing rules were not enough, Section 384(f) authorizes the Treasury to promulgate regulations as may be necessary to carry out the anti-abuse mission of the section.[11]

PROBLEM

Gain Corp., which is wholly owned by individual A, has the following assets and no liabilities:

Asset	Adj. Basis	F.M.V.
Inventory	$150,000	$300,000
Machinery	300,000	200,000
Gainacre	100,000	350,000

Loss Corp., which is wholly owned by unrelated individual B, has $500,000 in net operating loss carryforwards.

Unless otherwise indicated below, assume that Loss Corp. acquired all the assets of Gain Corp. in a tax-free Type A reorganization on January 1, 2005. After the acquisition, B owned 80% and A owned 20% of the Loss Corp. stock. To what extent, if any, may Loss Corp. use its preacquisition net operating loss carryforwards against the gains recognized in the following alternative transactions?:

(a) Loss Corp. sells Gainacre for $500,000 in 2006.

(b) Same as (a), above, except that Loss Corp. acquired all of Gain Corp.'s stock from A for cash (not making a § 338 election) on January 1, 2005, after which it liquidated Gain Corp. under § 332.

(c) Same as (a), above, except Loss Corp. also sells the inventory for $400,000 in 2006.

(d) Instead of (a)–(c), above, Loss Corp. sells Gainacre for $900,000 in 2011.

(e) Same as (a), above, except that Loss Corp. has no net operating loss carryforwards at the time of the acquisition but its only asset is Lossacre, which had a fair market value of $300,000 and an adjusted basis of $500,000. In 2006, Loss Corp. sells Lossacre for $200,000 at the same time that it sells Gainacre for $500,000.

3. CONSOLIDATED RETURN RULES

C corporations generally determine their taxable income and tax liability without regard to the income and losses of other affiliated entities. The consolidated return rules are an exception to this separate entity principle. Section 1501 permits an "affiliated group of corporations" to elect to file a consolidated tax return in which their separate taxable income and losses are aggregated.[1] An "affiliated group" is defined as a chain of corporations

11. As of early 2008, no regulations had been issued.

1. See generally, Chapter 10E, supra.

linked by specific levels of stock ownership. The common parent of the group must own at least 80 percent of the total voting power and value of at least one corporation in the chain, and every corporation in the chain must be 80 percent owned (based on voting power and value) by other members of the group.[2]

When computing the consolidated taxable income or loss of an affiliated group of corporations, each member of the group first determines its separate taxable income or loss.[3] The separate taxable income or loss figures of the members of the group are then combined, and the Section 11 tax rates are applied to the aggregate figure to arrive at the group's tax liability.

Because the consolidated return rules permit aggregation of the separate taxable income and loss of the members, the potential exists for one member of the group to offset its taxable income with the losses of another member. For example, without a specific limitation, a profitable corporation could acquire the requisite ownership of a corporation with a large net operating loss, the two corporations could elect to file a consolidated return, and the joint tax liability of the corporate family would be reduced as the net operating losses of one member are deducted against the income of the other. A multi-layer of statutes and regulations limit the use of net operating losses by corporations filing a consolidated return. First, all of the statutory limitations on the use of NOLs studied earlier in this chapter (i.e., Sections 382, 383, 384 and 269) potentially apply to a consolidated group.[4] If any loss somehow should survive these statutory gatekeepers, the consolidated return regulations contain an additional rule to patrol abuse: the "separate return limitation year" ("SRLY") limitation.[5] The operation of these rules should be familiar because they reflect many of the same policies embodied in the generally applicable statutory limitations.

The SRLY limitation is designed to prevent the use by an affiliated group of net operating losses arising in a separate return limitation year of a member of the group. A separate return limitation year is a taxable year in which the member filed either its own separate tax return or filed as part of another affiliated group.[6] In general, the aggregate net operating losses of a member of an affiliated group arising in separate return years only may be carried over and used to offset the aggregate consolidated income attributable to that member.[7] Thus, if a profitable corporation ("P") acquires a target corporation ("T") with large net operating losses,

2. I.R.C. § 1504(a)(1), (2). In general, preferred stock is not counted for purposes of the ownership tests and certain corporations subject to special tax regimes, such as tax-exempt and foreign corporations, are not permitted to be part of an affiliated group. I.R.C. § 1504(a)(4), (b).

3. Reg. §§ 1.1502–2, 1.1502–11(a)(1), 1.1502–12.

4. See Reg. § 1.1502–90 through Reg. § 1.1502–99, which apply Section 382 to a consolidated group of corporations.

5. The regulations also include limitations on the use of built-in losses and capital loss carryovers and carrybacks. See Reg. §§ 1.1502–15; 1.1502–22(c), (d). These items are also subject to the SRLY limitation.

6. Reg. § 1.1502–1(e), (f).

7. Reg. § 1.1502–21(c).

and the two corporations file a consolidated tax return, preacquisition losses and built-in losses of T may not be used to reduce the post-acquisition tax liability on consolidated taxable income attributable to P.

The regulations include an important exception that restricts the application of the SRLY limitation. Generally, the SRLY limitation does not apply in any case where a corporation becomes a member of a consolidated group (where the limitation otherwise would apply) within six months of the change date of a Section 382(g) change of ownership.[8] As a result, in many acquisitions the SRLY limitation relinquishes jurisdiction over NOLs to Section 382.[9]

8. Reg. § 1.1502–21(g)(1) & (2).

9. A similar rules applies in the case of recognized built-in losses. See Reg. § 1.1502–15(g).

PART FOUR

S CORPORATIONS

CHAPTER 20

S CORPORATIONS AND THEIR SHAREHOLDERS*

A. INTRODUCTION

We have seen that a C corporation's net income is subject to tax at rates ranging from 15 to 35 percent,[1] and those earnings are taxed again when distributed as dividends to individual shareholders.[2] Although many techniques have been devised to avoid the double tax, it nonetheless remains the principal feature distinguishing the taxation of incorporated and unincorporated businesses. We also have seen that partnerships and limited liability companies are treated for tax purposes as conduits whose income and deductions pass through to the partners or members as they are realized, with the various items retaining their original character in the process.[3] Because income is taxed at the partner level, partnership distributions of cash and property generally do not produce any additional tax liability.[4]

Taxpayers have long sought to obtain the state law benefits of the corporate form (limited liability, centralized management, etc.) without the sting of the double tax. Congress attempted to accommodate this desire in 1958 when it enacted Subchapter S, which then permitted the shareholders of a "small business corporation" to elect to avoid a corporate level tax in most situations. The stated purpose of Subchapter S was to permit a business to select its legal form "without the necessity of taking into account major differences in tax consequence."[5]

As originally adopted, Subchapter S was a modified corporate scheme of taxation rather than a partnership-like pass-through regime. This early version was a strange hybrid of corporate and partnership concepts, laden with complexity. In these formative years, an electing small business necessarily depended on skilled lawyers and accountants to avoid Subchapter S's many technical traps. Calls for reform began with a 1969 Treasury Department study, which in general proposed a liberalization of the eligibility requirements and the adoption of a conduit approach more closely

* See generally Eustice and Kuntz, Federal Income Taxation of Subchapter S Corporations (4th ed. 2001).

1. I.R.C. § 11.

2. I.R.C. §§ 61(a)(7), 301.

3. I.R.C. § 702(a), (b). See Chapter 1B2, supra.

4. I.R.C. § 731(a).

5. S.Rep. No. 1983, 85th Cong., 2d Sess. § 68 (1958), reprinted in 1958–3 C.B. 922.

conforming to the tax treatment of partnerships.[6] Congress gradually relaxed the eligibility requirements through piecemeal legislation, most notably the Subchapter S Revision Act of 1982.[7] The 1982 Act greatly reduced the tax disparities between Subchapter S corporations and partnerships by replacing the modified corporate structure of Subchapter S with a statutory scheme which is similar but not identical to the tax treatment of partnerships and partners under Subchapter K. The Act also introduced the terminology now used in the Code. Electing small business corporations are called "S corporations" while other corporations are known as "C corporations."[8]

Subsequent legislation further liberalized the Subchapter S eligibility requirements and eliminated technical traps for corporations seeking to elect and maintain S corporation status. As a result of these reforms, the tax differences between partnerships and S corporations have narrowed, making operation as an S corporation a viable, albeit less flexible, alternative for some closely held businesses. But significant differences in tax treatment remain between S corporations and unincorporated businesses. For example, Subchapter S status is available only for corporations that satisfy the statutory definition of "small business corporation" in Section 1361(b). This definition restricts eligibility to corporations with 100 or fewer shareholders; prohibits more than one class of stock; and limits the types of permissible shareholders. Moreover, partners' bases in their partnership interests are increased by their share of partnership liabilities,[9] while debts incurred by an S corporation have no effect on the bases of the corporation's shareholders in their stock. This difference may have an impact upon the ability of investors to utilize losses generated by the enterprise and the treatment of distributions.[10] Subchapter K also offers partners more flexibility in determining their individual tax results from partnership operations. Partnership allocations of specific items of income or deduction to a particular partner will be respected as long as the allocation has substantial economic effect, while shareholders of an S corporation are required to report a pro rata share of each corporate item.[11]

For a brief time, the inverted rate structure introduced by the Tax Reform Act of 1986 expanded the role of S corporations by reducing the top individual rate below the maximum rate for C corporations and broadening the corporate tax base. As a result, many closely held businesses requiring the corporate form and able to meet the eligibility requirements chose to operate as S corporations. The current maximum individual rate on ordinary income now equals the top corporate rate. More importantly, the emergence of the limited liability company, with its far greater flexibility,

6. See U.S. Treasury Department, Technical Explanation of Treasury Tax Reform Proposals: Hearings Before the House Comm. on Ways and Means, 91st Cong., 1st Sess. 5228–5275 (April 22, 1969).

7. Pub.L. No. 97–354 (1982), reprinted in 1982–2 C.B. 702.

8. I.R.C. § 1361(a).

9. I.R.C. § 752(a).

10. See also I.R.C. § 469, limiting the current deductibility of losses from certain passive activities.

11. Compare I.R.C. § 704(b)(2) with I.R.C. §§ 1366(a) & 1377(a).

and the Service's willingness to allow any unincorporated business entity to elect partnership status for tax purposes, have profoundly influenced the choice of entity decision.[12] At least for newly formed businesses, many predicted that these developments would threaten to send S corporations to the sidelines, despite the more liberal eligibility requirements introduced by Congress. Many existing S corporations remain on the scene, however, and the S corporation tax regime and governance structure are relatively simple and familiar. In fact, S corporations became the most common corporate entity type in 1997 and, for the taxable year 2003, 61.9 percent of all corporations filing tax returns were S corporations.[13] Thus, S corporations continue to be an important option for investors and a study of the fundamentals of Subchapter S is essential for a comprehensive understanding of business enterprise taxation. It also is instructive to compare the provisions of Subchapters S and K and to consider which of these pass-through taxation models is preferable from a policy standpoint.[14]

B. ELIGIBILITY FOR S CORPORATION STATUS

Code: § 1361.

Eligibility to make a Subchapter S election is limited to a "small business corporation," defined in Section 1361(b) as a domestic corporation[1] which is not an "ineligible corporation" and which has: (1) no more than 100 shareholders, (2) only shareholders who are individuals, estates, and certain types of trusts and tax-exempt organizations, (3) no nonresident alien shareholders, and (4) not more than one class of stock. The 100–shareholder limit disqualifies publicly traded corporations from S status, and the one-class-of-stock rule shuts the door to corporations with complex capital structures. Significantly, however, a "small business corporation" need not be small when measured by income or value as a going concern, and some very large enterprises operate as S corporations.

Some remaining aspects of the S corporation eligibility requirements are summarized below.

Ineligible Corporations and Subsidiaries. An "ineligible corporation" may not qualify as a "small business corporation."[2] Certain types of corporations, such as banks and insurance companies, are "ineligible" because they are governed by other specialized tax regimes.[3] At one time, any corporation that was a member of an "affiliated group" also was ineligible to be an S corporation—a rule that effectively precluded S corporations from owning 80 percent or more of the stock of another C or S

12. See Chapter 1C, supra.

13. Luttrell, "S Corporation Returns, 2003," at http://irs.gov/pub/irs-soi/03scorp.pdf.

14. See Section H of this chapter, infra.

1. I.R.C. § 1361(b)(1). A domestic corporation is defined as a corporation created or organized in the United States or under the laws of the United States or of any state or territory. Reg. §§ 1.1361–1(c); 301.7701–5.

2. I.R.C. § 1361(b)(1).

3. I.R.C. § 1361(b)(2).

corporation.[4] Under current law, S corporations may hold subsidiaries under certain conditions. C corporation subsidiaries generally are permitted,[5] and a parent-subsidiary relationship between two S corporations also is allowed if the parent elects to treat its offspring as a "qualified subchapter S subsidiary" ("QSSS"), which generally is defined as a 100 percent owned domestic corporation that is not an "ineligible corporation."[6] If this QSSS election is made, the subsidiary is disregarded for tax purposes, and all of its assets, liabilities, income, deductions, and credits are treated as belonging to its S parent.[7] The regulations provide detailed procedures to govern revocation and other terminations of a QSSS election. In general, they treat a terminating event as a deemed incorporation of a new subsidiary that is governed by general tax principles.[8]

Number of Shareholders. Congress has made S corporations more widely available by gradually increasing the number of permissible shareholders. The current 100–shareholder limit[9] is nearly triple an earlier 35–shareholder cap. For purposes of this limit, a husband and wife (and their estates) are counted as one shareholder regardless of their form of ownership.[10] If stock is jointly owned (e.g., as tenants in common or joint tenants) by other than a husband and wife, each joint owner is considered a separate shareholder.[11] In the case of a nominee, guardian, custodian, or agent holding stock in a representative capacity, the beneficial owners of the stock are counted toward the 100–shareholder limit.[12]

In addition to the special rule for a husband and wife, all the members of a "family" (and their estates) are treated as a single shareholder for purposes of the 100–shareholder limit.[13] A family is defined as the lineal descendants (and their spouses and former spouses) of a common ancestor who is no more than six generations removed from the youngest generation shareholder as of the later of the date the S election is made, the earliest date that a family member holds stock in the corporation, or October 22, 2004.[14]

Eligible Shareholders. Congress also has gradually expanded the eligible S corporation shareholder pool. Once limited to individuals who were

4. I.R.C. § 1361(b)(2)(A) (pre–1997).

5. I.R.C. § 1504(b)(8). The S parent, however, may not join in a consolidated return with the C corporation. See Chapter 10D for a brief discussion of consolidated returns.

6. I.R.C. § 1361(b)(3)(B). For election procedures, see Reg. § 1.1361–3(a).

7. I.R.C. § 1361(b)(3)(A). See Reg. § 1.1361–4(a)(1). If a subsidiary was in existence and had a prior tax history, the QSSS election triggers a deemed liquidation of the subsidiary under Sections 332 and 337 as of the day before the election is effective. Reg. § 1.1361–4(a)(2).

8. See Reg. § 1.1361–5(b).

9. I.R.C. § 1361(b)(1)(A).

10. I.R.C. § 1361(c)(1)(A)(i); Reg. § 1.1361–1(e)(2).

11. I.R.C. § 1.1361–1(e)(2).

12. Reg. § 1.1361–1(e)(1).

13. I.R.C. § 1361(c)(1)(A)(ii). If a husband and wife are part of a family they are counted as part of that family. I.R.C. § 1361(c)(1)(B)(i).

14. I.R.C. § 1361(c)(1)(B). Adopted children and foster children are treated as children by blood. I.R.C. § 1361(c)(1)(C). A spouse is considered to be of the same generation as the individual to whom the spouse is married. I.R.C. § 1361(c)(1)(B)(ii).

U.S. citizens or resident aliens, the permissible shareholder list now also includes decedent's and bankruptcy estates,[15] certain types of trusts discussed in more detail below,[16] qualified pension trusts, and charitable organizations that are exempt from tax under Section 501(c)(3).[17] A corporation still may not make an S election if any of its shareholders are C corporations, partnerships, ineligible trusts, or nonresident aliens.[18]

When Subchapter S was first enacted, trusts were not eligible shareholders, primarily because of Congress's desire for a relatively simple one-tier corporate tax regime where all beneficial owners were clearly identifiable. In response to the pleas of tax advisors to closely held businesses, Congress gradually relented by permitting various widely used types of trusts to be S corporation shareholders if certain conditions are met. Under current law, the trusts that are permissible shareholders include:

(1) Voting trusts, in which case each beneficial owner is treated as a separate shareholder;[19]

(2) Grantor trusts—i.e., domestic trusts treated for tax purposes as owned by their grantor—provided the grantor is an individual who is a U.S. citizen or resident.[20] An example would be the commonly used revocable living trust created to provide for continuity of asset management in the event of the grantor's disability and to avoid probate administration on death. For purposes of the 100–shareholder limit, the deemed owner of the trust is treated as the shareholder.[21]

(3) Former grantor trusts that continue as testamentary trusts, but only for the two-year period following the grantor's death.[22] The former deemed owner's estate is treated as the S corporation shareholder.[23]

(4) Testamentary trusts that receive S corporation stock under the terms of a will, but again only for the two-year period after the date of transfer of the stock to the trust.[24] The testator's estate continues to be treated as the S corporation shareholder.[25]

(5) Qualified Subchapter S trusts ("QSSTs"), defined generally as trusts all of the income of which is actually distributed or must be distributed currently to one individual who is a U.S. citizen or

15. I.R.C. §§ 1361(b)(1)(B), (c)(3).

16. See infra text accompanying notes 19–34.

17. I.R.C. §§ 1361(b)(1)(B), (c)(6). The trade-off for tax-exempt pension trusts and Section 501(c)(3) organizations is that their interest in the S corporation is treated as an interest in an "unrelated trade or business," and any net income is generally taxable at the trust or corporate rates. I.R.C. § 512(e)(1).

18. I.R.C. § 1361(b)(1)(B).

19. I.R.C. § 1361(c)(2)(A)(iv), (B)(iv).

20. I.R.C. § 1361(c)(2)(A)(i). Foreign grantor trusts are not eligible shareholders. I.R.C. § 1361(c)(2)(A), flush language.

21. I.R.C. § 1361(c)(2)(B)(i).

22. I.R.C. § 1361(c)(2)(A)(ii).

23. I.R.C. § 1361(c)(2)(B)(ii).

24. I.R.C. § 1361(c)(2)(A)(iii).

25. I.R.C. § 1361(c)(2)(B)(iii).

resident.[26] A QSST may only have one current income beneficiary, who must elect QSST status and, as a result, is treated as the owner for tax purposes of the portion of the trust consisting of the S corporation stock with respect to which the election was made.[27] Among other things, the QSST definition permits a Qualified Terminable Interest Property ("QTIP") Trust,[28] the most widely used type of estate tax marital deduction trust created for the benefit of a surviving spouse, to hold S corporation stock.

(6) Electing small business trusts ("ESBTs"), a statutory creation that potentially expands the usefulness of S corporations in estate planning for a family business. All the beneficiaries of an ESBT must be individuals or estates who are eligible S corporation shareholders, or charitable organizations holding contingent remainder interests.[29] The beneficial interests in an ESBT must have been acquired by gift or bequest, not purchase,[30] and the trust must elect ESBT status to qualify as an S corporation shareholder.[31] Each potential current beneficiary of the trust is treated as a shareholder for purposes of the 100–shareholder limit,[32] but the trust's pro rata share of S corporation income is taxable to the trust at the highest individual marginal rates under rules specially designed for this purpose.[33] The significance of the ESBT category is that it permits inter vivos and testamentary trusts with more than one beneficiary—e.g., a "sprinkling" trust where the trustee has discretion to determine whether and how much income or corpus to distribute among several beneficiaries—to qualify as an S corporation shareholder.

The legislative history of the rule treating a family as one shareholder for the 100–shareholder limit explains that the rule applies to family members who own stock directly as well as those who are shareholders because they are beneficiaries of a QSST or ESTB.[34]

One-Class-of-Stock Requirement. An S corporation may issue both stock and debt, but it may not have more than one class of stock.[35] The purpose of this rule is to simplify the allocation of income and deductions among an S corporation's shareholders and prevent "special allocations" and their potential for income shifting. The one-class-of-stock requirement

26. I.R.C. § 1361(d).

27. Id.

28. See I.R.C. § 2056(b)(7).

29. I.R.C. § 1361(e)(1)(A)(i). Charitable remainder trusts, however, may not be S corporation shareholders. I.R.C. § 1361(e)(1)(B)(iii). See also Rev. Rul. 92–48, 1992–1 C.B. 301.

30. I.R.C. § 1361(e)(1)(A)(ii).

31. I.R.C. § 1361(e)(1)(A)(iii). Trusts that already have made a QSST election or are wholly exempt from tax do not qualify as ESBTs. I.R.C. § 1361(e)(1)(B).

32. I.R.C. § 1361(c)(2)(B)(v). If there are no potential current income beneficiaries, then the trust is treated as the shareholder for that period. Id.

33. I.R.C. § 641(d).

34. H.Rep. No.108–755, 108th Cong., 2d Sess. 34 (2004).

35. I.R.C. § 1361(b)(1)(D).

has spawned many controversies over its history, but the issuance of final regulations has resolved the most contentious issues.

An S corporation generally is treated as having one class of stock if all of its outstanding shares confer identical rights to distributions and liquidation proceeds.[36] Significantly, differences in voting rights among classes of common stock are disregarded, permitting an S corporation to issue both voting and nonvoting common stock.[37] In determining whether outstanding stock confers identical rights to distribution and liquidation proceeds, the regulations look to the corporate charter, articles of incorporation, bylaws, applicable state law, and binding shareholders' agreements.[38]

Commercial contractual arrangements, such as leases, employment agreements, or loan agreements, are disregarded in determining whether a second class of stock is present unless a principal purpose of the agreement is to circumvent the one class of stock requirement.[39] For example, differences in salary or fringe benefits paid to employee-shareholders under compensation agreements will not result in a second class of stock if the agreements are not designed to circumvent the requirement.[40] Bona fide agreements to redeem or purchase stock at the time of death, divorce, disability or termination of employment also are disregarded in determining whether an S corporation has a second class of stock.[41] Other shareholder buy-sell, stock transfer and redemption agreements are disregarded in determining whether a corporation's outstanding shares confer identical distribution and liquidation rights unless: (1) a principal purpose of the agreement is to circumvent the one-class-of-stock requirement, and (2) the purchase price under the agreement is significantly in excess of or below the fair market value of the stock. Agreements that provide for a purchase or redemption of stock at book value or at a price between book value and fair market value satisfy the purchase price standard.[42]

Unless the straight debt safe harbor applies,[43] any instrument, obligation or arrangement issued by a corporation (other than outstanding stock) is treated as a second class of stock if: (1) it constitutes equity under general tax principles, and (2) a principal purpose of issuing or entering

36. Reg. § 1.1361–1(*l*)(1). "Outstanding stock" generally does not include stock that is subject to a substantial risk of forfeiture under Section 83 unless the holder has made the Section 83(b) election. Reg. § 1.1361–1(*l*)(3).

37. I.R.C. § 1361(c)(4); Reg. § 1.1361–1(*l*)(1).

38. Reg. § 1.1361–1(*l*)(2)(i).

39. Reg. § 1.1361–1(*l*)(2)(i).

40. Reg. § 1.1361–1(*l*)(2)(v) Examples (3) & (4). Any distributions (actual, constructive or deemed) that differ in timing or amount are given appropriate tax treatment. For example, even though an employment agreement does not result in a second class of stock, excessive compensation paid under the agreement is not deductible. Reg. § 1.1361–1(*l*)(2)(i), (v) Example (3).

41. Reg. § 1.1361–1(*l*)(2)(iii)(B).

42. Reg. § 1.1361–1(*l*)(2)(iii)(A). A good faith determination of fair market value is respected unless it is substantially in error and was not determined with reasonable diligence. Id. A determination of book value is respected if it is determined in accordance with generally accepted accounting principles or used for any substantial nontax purpose. Reg. § 1.1361–1(*l*)(2)(iii)(C).

43. See I.R.C. § 1361(c)(5) and notes 47–54, infra, and accompanying text.

into the instrument, obligation or arrangement is to circumvent the distribution and liquidation rights of outstanding shares or the limitation on eligible shareholders.[44] Safe harbors from reclassification are provided for short-term unwritten advances to the corporation that do not exceed $10,000 and obligations held proportionately among the shareholders.[45] The existence of various corporate instruments that give holders the right to acquire stock (e.g., call options or warrants) also may create a second class of stock depending upon whether the right is substantially certain to be exercised by the holder.[46]

Straight Debt Safe Harbor. The interaction of the one-class-of-stock limitation with the debt vs. equity classification issues encountered under Subchapter C[47] historically presented some knotty problems for S corporations with outstanding debt. In the formative years of Subchapter S, the Service adopted a practice of reclassifying nominal S corporation debt owed to shareholders as a second class of stock, causing the corporation to lose its S status.[48] This threat has diminished considerably by a safe harbor provision in Section 1361(c)(5) under which "straight debt" is not treated as a disqualifying second class of stock. "Straight debt" is defined as any written unconditional promise to pay on demand or on a specified date a sum certain in money if: (1) the interest rate and payment dates are not contingent on profits, the borrower's discretion or similar factors; (2) the instrument is not convertible (directly or indirectly) into stock; and (3) the creditor is an individual (other than a nonresident alien), an estate or trust that would be a qualifying shareholder in an S corporation, or a person that is actively and regularly engaged in the business of lending money.[49] The fact that an obligation is subordinated to other debt of the corporation does not prevent it from qualifying as straight debt.[50]

Obligations that qualify as straight debt are not classified as a second class of stock even if they would be considered equity under general tax principles and they generally are treated as debt for other purposes of the Code.[51] Thus, interest paid or accrued on straight debt is treated as such by the corporation and the recipient and does not constitute a distribution governed by Section 1368.[52] But if a straight debt instrument bears an unreasonably high rate of interest, the regulations provide than an "appropriate" portion may be recharacterized and treated as a payment that is

44. Reg. § 1.1361–1(*l*)(4)(ii)(A).

45. Reg. § 1.1361–1(*l*)(4)(ii)(B).

46. Reg. § 1.1361–1(*l*)(4)(iii). Exceptions are provided for certain call options in connection with loans or to employees and independent contractors. If the strike price of a call option is at least 90 percent of its fair market value at its issuance, it is not substantially certain to be exercised. Reg. § 1.1361–1(*l*)(4)(iii)(B)–(C).

47. See generally I.R.C. § 385 and Chapter 11F, infra.

48. The courts, however, usually were not receptive to this argument. See, e.g., Portage Plastics Co. v. United States, 486 F.2d 632 (7th Cir.1973).

49. I.R.C. § 1361(c)(5)(B).

50. Reg. § 1.1361–1(*l*)(5)(ii).

51. I.R.C. § 1361(c)(5)(A); Reg. § 1.1361–1(*l*)(5)(iv).

52. Id.

not interest.[53] If a C corporation has outstanding debt obligations that satisfy the straight debt definition but may be classified as equity under general tax principles, the safe harbor ensures that the obligation will not be treated as a second class of stock if the C corporation elects to convert to S status. The conversion and change of status also is not treated as an exchange of the debt instrument for stock.[54]

PROBLEM

Unless otherwise indicated, Z Corporation ("Z") is a domestic corporation which has 120 shares of voting common stock outstanding. In each of the following alternative situations, determine whether Z is eligible to elect S corporation status:

(a) Z has 99 unrelated individual shareholders, each of whom owns one share of Z stock. The remaining 21 shares are owned by A and his brother, B, as joint tenants with right of survivorship.

(b) Same as (a), above, except that A and B are married and own 11 of the 21 shares as community property. The remaining 10 shares are owned 5 by A as her separate property and 5 by B as his separate property.

(c) In (b), above, assume that the shareholders of Z elected S corporation status. What will be the effect on Z's election if one year later A dies and bequeaths her interest in Z stock to F, her long-time friend?

(d) Same as (a), above, except that the remaining 21 shares are held by a voting trust which has three beneficial owners.

(e) Same as (a), above, except that the remaining 21 shares are owned by a revocable living trust created by an individual, the income of which is taxed to the grantor under § 671.

(f) Same as (a), above, except that the remaining 21 shares are owned by a testamentary trust under which the surviving spouse has the right to income for her life, with the remainder passing to her children. The trust is a "qualified terminable interest trust" (see § 2056(b)(7)).

(g) Assume Z has 100 individual shareholders and forms a partnership with two other S corporations, each of which also have 100 individual shareholders, for the purposes of jointly operating a business. Z's one-third interest in this partnership is its only asset.

(h) Z has 100 shares of Class A voting common stock and 50 shares of Class B nonvoting common stock outstanding. Apart from the differences in voting rights, the two classes of common stock have equal rights with regard to dividends and liquidation distributions. Z also has an authorized but unissued class of nonvoting stock

53. Id. Such a reclassification does not result in a second class of stock.

54. Reg. § 1.1361–1(*l*)(5)(v).

which would be limited and preferred as to dividends. The Class A common stock is owned by four individuals and the Class B common stock is owned by E and F (a married couple) as tenants-in-common.

(i) Same as (h), above, except that Z enters into a binding agreement with its shareholders to make larger annual distributions to shareholders who bear heavier state income tax burdens. The amount of the distributions is based on a formula that will give the shareholders equal after-tax distributions.

(j) Z has four individual shareholders each of whom own 100 shares of Z common stock for which each paid $10 per share. Each shareholder also owns $25,000 of 15–year Z bonds. The bonds bear interest at 3% above the prime lending rate established by the Chase Manhattan Bank, adjusted quarterly, and are subordinated to general creditors of Z.

C. ELECTION, REVOCATION AND TERMINATION

Code: §§ 1362 (omit (e)(5)–(6)); 1378. Skim §§ 444(a), (b), (c)(1), (e); 7519(a), (b), (d)(1), (e)(4).

Electing S Corporation Status. An otherwise eligible corporation may elect S corporation status under Section 1362 if all the shareholders consent.[1] Once made, an election remains effective until it is terminated under Section 1362(d).[2] An election is effective as of the beginning of a taxable year if it is made either during the preceding taxable year or on or before the fifteenth day of the third month of the current taxable year.[3] If the election is made during the first 2½ months of the year, the S corporation eligibility requirements must have been met for the portion of the taxable year prior to the election, and all shareholders at any time during the pre-election portion of the year must consent to the election.[4] If the eligibility requirements are not met during the pre-election period or if any shareholder who held stock during that period does not consent, the election does not become effective until the following taxable year.[5] In some cases, however, such as where an election is technically invalid because of the corporation's inadvertence or failure to obtain all the requisite share-

1. I.R.C. § 1362(a). For rules and procedures on shareholders' consent to an S election, see Reg. § 1.1362–6.

2. I.R.C. § 1362(c). See generally Reg. § 1.1362–2.

3. I.R.C. § 1362(b)(1). Elections made not later than 2 months and 15 days after the first day of the taxable year are deemed made during the year even if the year is shorter than 2 months and 15 days. I.R.C. § 1362(b)(4). For rules on how to count months and days for this purpose, see Reg. § 1.1362–6(a)(2)(ii). For the Service's authority to treat a late election as timely if there was reasonable cause for the tardiness, see I.R.C. § 1362(b)(5). See Rev. Proc. 2004–48, 2004–2 C.B. 172, supplemented by Rev. Proc. 2007–62, 2007–41 I.R.B. 786, for the procedures to obtain relief for a late election.

4. I.R.C. § 1362(b)(2).

5. I.R.C. § 1362(b)(2)(B).

holder consents on time, the Service may grant dispensation and waive the defect if there is reasonable cause.[6]

Revocation of Election. An S corporation election may be revoked if shareholders holding more than one-half of the corporation's shares (including nonvoting shares) consent to the revocation.[7] The revocation may specify a prospective effective date.[8] If a prospective effective date is not specified, a revocation made on or before the fifteenth day of the third month of the taxable year is effective on the first day of the taxable year and a revocation made after that date is effective on the first day of the following taxable year.[9]

Termination of Election. Apart from revocation, an S corporation election may be terminated if the corporation ceases to satisfy the definition of a small business corporation or, in certain circumstances, if the corporation earns an excessive amount of passive investment income.[10] The first ground for termination is easily illustrated. Terminating events include: (1) exceeding 100 shareholders; (2) issuance of a second class of stock; or (3) transfer of stock to an ineligible shareholder. In all those cases, the corporation will cease to be a small business corporation and its S corporation election will terminate on the day after the disqualifying event.[11] To prevent or cure transfers that may jeopardize a corporation's S corporation status, the shareholders will be well advised at the outset to enter into an agreement restricting stock transfers.

The limitation on passive investment income is more complex. Under Section 1362(d)(3), an election to be an S corporation will terminate if for three consecutive taxable years the corporation's "passive investment income" exceeds 25 percent of its gross receipts and the corporation has Subchapter C earnings and profits.[12] A termination triggered by excess passive investment income is effective beginning on the first day of the taxable year following the three year testing period.[13] It is important to note that the Subchapter C earnings and profits requirement has the effect of rendering this limitation inapplicable to a corporation that has always been an S corporation or which has been purged of its earnings and profits.[14] Passive investment income generally is defined as gross receipts

6. I.R.C. § 1362(f). An ineffective election to treat (1) a subsidiary as a qualified subchapter S subsidiary or (2) a family as one shareholder may also be salvaged under Section 1362(f).

7. I.R.C. § 1362(d)(1)(B). See Reg. § 1.1362–2(a).

8. I.R.C. § 1362(d)(1)(D).

9. I.R.C. § 1362(d)(1)(C). If the revocation is effective on a day other than the first day of a taxable year (e.g., because a prospective date is selected in the middle of the year), the taxable year will be an "S termination year," and the corporation will be taxed pursuant to rules in Section 1362(e). See Reg. § 1.1362–3 and infra text accompanying notes 19–21.

10. I.R.C. § 1362(d)(2), (3).

11. I.R.C. §§ 1361(b)(1)(A)–(D); 1362(d)(2)(B).

12. See Reg. § 1.1362–2(c). Prior years in which the corporation was not an S corporation are not considered for purposes of the passive investment income component of this test. I.R.C. § 1362(c)(3)(A)(iii)(II).

13. I.R.C. § 1362(d)(3)(A)(ii).

14. An S corporation, however, may acquire earnings and profits under Section 381 in a corporate acquisition.

from royalties, rents, dividends, interest, and annuities,[15] but it does not include gains on the disposition of property, or dividends received by an S corporation from a C corporation subsidiary to the extent they are attributable to earnings and profits of the subsidiary that are derived from the active conduct of a trade or business.[16] For purposes of the overall gross receipts definition, gross receipts from sales or exchanges of stock or securities are considered only to the extent of gains.[17] Gross receipts on the disposition of capital assets other than stock or securities are taken into account only to the extent of the excess of capital gains over capital losses from such dispositions.[18]

When an S corporation election terminates during the S corporation's taxable year, the corporation experiences an "S termination year," which is divided into two short years: an S short year and a C short year.[19] Income, gains, losses, deductions and credits for an S termination year generally may be allocated between the two short years on a pro rata basis or the corporation may elect to make the allocation under its normal accounting rules.[20] The corporation's tax liability for the short taxable year as a C corporation is then computed on an annualized basis.[21]

Inadvertent Terminations. If an S corporation election is terminated, the corporation generally is not eligible to make another election for five taxable years unless the Treasury consents to an earlier election.[22] Section 1362(f) provides relief if a termination is caused by the corporation ceasing to be a small business corporation or by excessive passive investment income. The corporation will be treated as continuing as an S corporation and the terminating event will be disregarded if: (1) the Service determines that the termination was inadvertent, (2) the corporation takes steps within a reasonable time to rectify the problem, and (3) the corporation and its shareholders agree to make whatever adjustments are required by the Service.[23] The corporation has the burden of establishing that under the relevant facts and circumstances the Commissioner should determine that the termination was inadvertent. Under the regulations, inadvertence may be established by showing that the terminating event was not reasonably within the control of the corporation and was not part of a plan to terminate the election, or that the event took place without the knowledge of the corporation notwithstanding its due diligence to prevent the termi-

15. I.R.C. § 1362(d)(3)(C)(i). The statute also contains rules for certain specialized items. See I.R.C. § 1362(d)(3)(C)(ii)–(v).

16. I.R.C. § 1362(d)(3)(C)(iv).

17. I.R.C. § 1362(d)(3)(B)(ii).

18. I.R.C. § 1362(d)(3)(B)(i).

19. I.R.C. § 1362(e)(1). The C short year begins on the first day the termination is effective. I.R.C. § 1362(e)(1)(B).

20. See Reg. § 1.1362–3. To use normal accounting rules, an election must be filed by all persons who are shareholders during the S short year and all persons who are shareholders on the first day of the C short year. I.R.C. § 1362(e)(3). The pro rata allocation method may not be used in an S termination year if there is a sale or exchange of 50 percent or more of the stock in the corporation during the year. I.R.C. § 1362(e)(6)(D). For more rules on taxing an S termination year, see I.R.C. § 1362(e)(6).

21. I.R.C. § 1362(e)(5)(A).

22. I.R.C. § 1362(g).

23. I.R.C. § 1362(f).

nation.[24] For example, if a corporation in good faith determines that it has no Subchapter C earnings and profits but the Service later determines on audit that the corporation's S election terminated because it had excessive passive investment income for three consecutive years while it also had accumulated earnings and profits, it may be appropriate for the Service to find that the termination was inadvertent.

Taxable Year of an S Corporation. To preclude S corporations from using fiscal years to achieve a deferral of the shareholders' tax liability, S corporations must use a "permitted year," which is defined as either a calendar year or an accounting period for which the taxpayer establishes a business purpose.[25] The Service has ruled that the business purpose requirement may be satisfied if the desired tax accounting period coincides with a "natural business year"[26] and has quantified the concept with the same 25–percent test applicable to partnerships seeking to use a natural business fiscal year.[27] Under this test, a natural business year exists if 25 percent or more of the S corporation's gross receipts for the selected 12–month period are earned in the last two months. This 25–percent test must be met in each of the preceding three 12–month periods that correspond to the requested fiscal year.[28]

Section 1378 makes it clear that tax deferral for shareholders does not constitute a business purpose for a fiscal year. The legislative history also identifies several factors which generally do not support a claim of business purpose:[29]

> The conferees intend that (1) the use of a particular year for regulatory or financial accounting purposes; (2) the hiring patterns of a particular business, e.g., the fact that a firm typically hires staff during certain times of the year; (3) the use of a particular year for administrative purposes, such as the admission or retirement of partners or shareholders, promotion of staff, and compensation or retirement arrangements with staff, partners, or shareholders; and (4) the fact that a particular business involves the use of price lists, model year, or other items that change on an annual basis ordinarily will not be sufficient to establish that the business purpose requirement for a particular taxable year has been met.

Fiscal Year Election. Congress has modified these strict taxable year requirements by allowing S corporations to elect to adopt, retain or change to a fiscal year under certain conditions, including the payment of an entity-level tax designed to represent the value of any tax deferral to the shareholders that would result from the use of the fiscal year. The rules

24. Reg. § 1.1362–4(b).

25. I.R.C. § 1378(b). See Reg. § 1.1378–1.

26. Rev.Proc. 74–33, 1974–2 C.B. 489.

27. Rev.Proc. 2006–46; §§ 2.02, 2.06, 5.07; 2006–2 C.B. 859. See Chapter 3A3, supra.

28. If the taxpayer does not have the required period of gross receipts, it cannot establish a natural business year under the revenue procedure. Rev. Proc. 2006–46, supra note 27.

29. H.R.Rep. No. 99–841, 99th Cong., 2d Sess. II–319 (1986).

governing the fiscal year election and the required entity-level payment are found in Sections 444 and 7519 and are similar to the rules applicable to partnerships.[30]

Section 444 permits a newly formed S corporation to elect to use a taxable year other than the calendar year required by Section 1378 provided that the year elected results in no more than a three-month deferral of income to the shareholders.[31] An election and the Section 7519 payment is not required, however, for any S corporation that has established a business purpose for a fiscal year under Section 1378(b)(2).[32]

The trade-off for a Section 444 fiscal year election is that the corporation must make a "required payment" under Section 7519 for any taxable year for which the election is in effect. The mechanics of the required payment are annoyingly complex, but the concept is clear. An electing S corporation must pay and keep "on deposit" an amount roughly approximating the value of the tax deferral that the shareholders would have achieved from the use of a fiscal year. Thus, if an S corporation whose shareholders all used calendar years elected a fiscal year ending September 30, the corporation would be required to pay a tax that supposedly equalled the tax benefit from the three months deferral received by the shareholders.[33] Under a de minimis rule, no payment is required if the amount due is less than $500,[34] and a payment made in one year generates a balance "on deposit" that may be used in subsequent years.[35]

PROBLEM

Snowshoe, Inc. ("Snowshoe"), a ski resort located in Colorado, was organized by its four individual shareholders (A, B, C and D) and began operations on October 3 of the current year. A owns 300 shares of Snowshoe voting common stock and B, C and D each own 100 shares of Snowshoe nonvoting common stock. Each share of common stock has equal rights with respect to dividends and liquidation distributions. Consider the following questions in connection with the election and termination of Snowshoe's S corporation status:

(a) If the shareholders wish to elect S corporation status for Snowshoe's first taxable year, who must consent to the election? What difference would it make if, prior to the election, B sold her stock to her brother, G? What difference would it make if B is a partnership which, prior to the election, sold its stock to H, an individual?

30. See Chapter 3A3, supra.

31. I.R.C. § 444(a), (b)(1). S corporations formed or electing prior to 1987 also were permitted to retain a taxable year that was the same as the entity's last taxable year beginning in 1986. I.R.C. § 444(b)(3).

32. See I.R.S. Notice 88–10, 1988–1 C.B. 478.

33. We say "supposedly" because the Section 7519 "required payment" is determined mechanically, without regard to amounts actually deferred by the shareholders. See I.R.C. §§ 7519(b), (c) and (d) for the details.

34. I.R.C. § 7519(a)(2).

35. I.R.C. § 7519(b)(2), (e)(4).

(b) What is the last day an effective Subchapter S election for Snowshoe's first taxable year is permitted?

(c) If the shareholders elect S corporation status, what taxable year will Snowshoe be allowed to select?

In the following parts of the problem, assume that Snowshoe elected S corporation status during its first taxable year.

(d) Can A revoke Snowshoe's Subchapter S election without the consent of B, C or D?

(e) If C sold all of his stock to Olga, a citizen of Sweden living in Stockholm, what effect would the sale have on Snowshoe's status as an S corporation?

(f) Same as (e), above, except that C only sold five shares to Olga and had no idea that the sale might adversely affect Snowshoe's S corporation status.

(g) Would it matter if Snowshoe's business is diversified and 45% of its gross receipts come from real estate rentals, dividends and interest?

D. TREATMENT OF THE SHAREHOLDERS

Code: §§ 1363(b), (c); 1366(a)–(e); 1367. Skim §§ 1366(f); 1371(b); 1377.

1. PASS–THROUGH OF INCOME AND LOSSES: BASIC RULES

Entity Treatment. Although an S corporation is generally exempt from tax,[1] it nonetheless must determine its gross income,[2] deductions and other tax items in order to establish the amounts which pass through to the shareholders. Like a partnership, an S corporation computes its "taxable income" in the same manner as an individual except that certain deductions unique to individuals (e.g., personal exemptions, alimony, medical and moving expenses) are not allowed.[3] In addition, deductions normally available only to corporations, such as the dividends received deduction, are not allowed,[4] but an S corporation may elect to deduct and amortize its organizational expenses under Section 248.[5] Finally, a wide variety of items, ranging from charitable contributions and capital gains to depletion, must be separately computed in order to preserve their special tax character for purposes of the pass-through to the shareholders.[6] Thus, an S corporation is not entitled to any charitable deduction, but corporate

1. For the few limited exceptions, see Section F of this chapter, infra.

2. Section 1366(c) provides that a shareholder's pro rata share of the S corporation's gross income is used to determine the shareholder's gross income.

3. I.R.C. § 1363(b)(2).

4. S.Rep. No. 97–640, 97th Cong., 2d Sess. 15 (1982), reprinted in 1982–2 C.B. 718, 724.

5. I.R.C. § 1363(b)(3).

6. I.R.C. §§ 1363(b)(1); 1366(a)(1)(A).

charitable gifts may pass through to the shareholders without regard to the normal 10 percent limit on corporate contributions.

Although an S corporation is not a *taxable* entity, it is treated as an entity for various purposes. For example, tax elections affecting the computation of items derived from an S corporation (e.g., to defer recognition of gain on an involuntary conversion under Section 1033) generally are made at the corporate level.[7] Likewise, limitations on deductions (e.g., the dollar limitation under Section 179 on expensing the cost of certain recovery property) apply at the corporate level and often at the shareholder level as well.[8] And like a partnership, an S corporation is treated as an entity for filing tax returns and other procedural purposes.[9]

Pass–Through of Income and Deductions. Once the S corporation's tax items have been identified, the next step is to determine the manner in which they pass through to the shareholders. The pass-through scheme applicable to S corporations will have a familiar ring to a student who has endured the rigors of Subchapter K. First, income and deductions are characterized at the corporate level.[10] Section 1366(a)(1)(A) provides that items which may have potentially varying tax consequences to the individual shareholders must be separately reported. The most common separately stated items are capital and Section 1231 gains and losses, dividends taxed as net capital gain, interest and other types of "portfolio income" under the Section 469 passive loss limitations, tax-exempt interest, charitable contributions, investment interest, foreign taxes, intangible drilling expenses and depletion on oil and gas properties.[11] Thus, Section 1231 gains and losses do not fall into any corporate hotchpot; rather, they pass through and are aggregated with each shareholder's other Section 1231 gains and losses in order to determine their ultimate character. All the nonseparately stated items are aggregated and the resulting lump sum passes through as ordinary income or loss.

The timing of the shareholders' income and the allocation of pass-through items also is virtually a mirror image of the partnership rules. The shareholders of an S corporation take into account their respective pro rata shares of income, deductions and other separately stated items on a pro rata, per share daily basis.[12] These items are reported in the shareholder's taxable year in which the corporation's taxable year ends.[13] For example, if an S corporation with a natural business year uses a fiscal year ending

7. I.R.C. § 1363(c)(1).

8. See, e.g., I.R.C. § 179(d)(8).

9. I.R.C. § 6037. Cf. I.R.C. §§ 6221–6255.

10. I.R.C. § 1366(b). See Reg. § 1.1366–1(b). If shareholders are utilizing an S corporation for the principal purpose of converting ordinary income to capital gain or capital loss into ordinary loss on the sale or exchange of property, the regulations generally provide for the character of the gain or loss to be determined at the shareholder level. Reg. § 1.1366–1(b)(2), (3).

11. See generally Reg. § 1.1366–1(a)(2). See also Rev.Rul. 84–131, 1984–2 C.B. 37, where the Service ruled that a shareholder's share of an S corporation's investment interest is a separately stated item.

12. I.R.C. § 1366(a)(1). See § 1377(a)(1) for the method of determining each shareholder's "pro rata share."

13. I.R.C. § 1366(a)(1).

January 31, 2009, the shareholders will report the respective pass-through items on their 2009 calendar year tax returns, thus achieving a healthy deferral of any gains or an unfortunate delay in recognizing any losses. A deceased shareholder's Subchapter S items are allocated on a daily basis between the shareholder's final income tax return and the initial return of the decedent's estate.[14]

Basis Adjustments. Section 1367 requires S corporation shareholders to increase the basis of their stock by their respective shares of income items (including tax-exempt income) and to reduce basis (but not below zero) by losses, deductions, and non-deductible expenses which do not constitute capital expenditures, and by tax-free distributions under Section 1368. Under the Code's ordering rules, basis is first increased by current income items, then decreased by distributions, and finally decreased (to the extent permitted) by any losses for the year.[15] Any additional losses in excess of a shareholder's stock basis must be applied to reduce the shareholder's basis (again, not below zero) in any corporate indebtedness to the shareholder.[16] If the basis of both stock and debt is reduced, any subsequent upward adjustments must first be applied to restore the basis in the indebtedness to the extent that it was previously reduced before increasing the basis of the stock.[17] These basis adjustments are generally made as of the close of the S corporation's taxable year unless a shareholder disposes of stock during the year, in which case the adjustments with respect to the transferred stock are made immediately prior to the disposition.[18]

2. Loss Limitations

a. IN GENERAL

Section 1366(d) limits the amount of losses or deductions that may pass through to a shareholder to the sum of the shareholder's adjusted basis in the stock plus his adjusted basis in any indebtedness of the corporation to the shareholder. Losses disallowed because of an inadequate basis may be carried forward indefinitely and treated as a loss in any subsequent year in which the shareholder has a basis in either stock or debt.[1] A special rule also provides that if a shareholder's stock is transferred under Section 1041 to a spouse or former spouse incident to a divorce, any suspended loss or deduction may be carried forward indefinitely by the transferee-spouse.[2] As illustrated by the *Harris* case, which follows this Note, one of the most litigated issues to arise under Subchapter S has involved the determination of a shareholder's basis in S corporation stock and debt for purposes of applying the general loss limitation rules in Section 1366(d).

14. Id. See also Reg. § 1.1366–1(a)(1).

15. I.R.C. §§ 1366(d)(1)(A); 1368(d), last sentence. For other details on stock and debt basis adjustments, see Reg. § 1.1367–1, –2.

16. I.R.C. § 1367(b)(2)(A).

17. I.R.C. § 1367(b)(2)(B).

18. Reg. § 1.1367–1(d)(1).

1. I.R.C. §§ 1366(d)(2)(A), 1366(a)(1).

2. I.R.C. § 1366(d)(2)(B).

Losses that pass through to a shareholder of an S corporation also may be restricted by the at-risk limitations in Section 465 and the passive activity loss limitations in Section 469.[3] The at-risk rules are applied on an activity-by-activity basis, except that activities constituting a trade or business generally are aggregated if the taxpayer actively participates in the management of the trade or business and at least 65 percent of the losses are allocable to persons actively engaged in the management of the trade or business.[4] The passive activity loss limitations cast a wider net and may delay an investor's ability to deduct legitimate start-up losses passing through from a new business operating as an S corporation unless the investor also materially participates in the activity.[5]

Harris v. United States

United States Court of Appeals, Fifth Circuit, 1990.
902 F.2d 439.

■ GARWOOD, CIRCUIT JUDGE:

Facts and Proceedings Below

In June 1982, Taxpayers contracted with Trans–Lux New Orleans Corporation to purchase for $665,585 cash a New Orleans pornographic theater that they intended to convert into a wedding hall. The Taxpayers' obligations under the contract were conditioned on their being able to secure from a third party a loan for not less than $600,000 repayable in fifteen to twenty years.[1] Shortly before this time, Taxpayers had contacted John Smith (Smith), a real estate loan officer with Hibernia National Bank (Hibernia), to discuss the possibility of obtaining financing for the impending acquisition. Smith orally committed to lend Taxpayers $700,000.[2]

Subsequently, to shield themselves from the potential adverse publicity that could follow from the purchase of the pornographic theater, as well as to limit their personal liability and enhance their chances of qualifying for industrial revenue bonds to finance the theater's renovation, in July 1982 Taxpayers formed Harmar (Harmar), a Louisiana corporation, which elected to be taxed pursuant to Subchapter S of the Internal Revenue Code, to purchase and operate the subject property. Harris and Martin each initially contributed $1,000 to the corporation, receiving its stock in return, and

3. See generally Chapter 3C2 and 3C3, supra. These limitations apply on a shareholder-by-shareholder basis rather than at the corporate level. I.R.C. §§ 465(a)(1)(A); 469(a)(2)(A).

4. I.R.C. § 465(c)(3)(B).

5. I.R.C. § 469(c)(1).

1. As part of the contract, Taxpayers deposited with the seller $32,500, all of which was to be applied to the purchase price. In the event Taxpayers were unable to procure the loan, the purchase contract called for their deposit to be refunded.

2. Smith asserted in his deposition that he did not know the purpose of the borrowed funds in excess of the purchase price, but he surmised that the money was intended for improvements to the theater. No written loan commitment was ever issued.

each also loaned Harmar $47,500 to satisfy operating expenses. Harris and Martin were the sole shareholders of Harmar, each owning half of its stock.

The purchase of the theater closed on November 1, 1982, and the theater was conveyed to Harmar on that date. Hibernia furnished the $700,000 necessary to close the transaction. In borrowing the funds necessary to acquire the subject property, Harmar executed two promissory notes payable to Hibernia for $350,000 each, each dated November 1, 1982. One of these notes was secured by a $50,322.09 Hibernia certificate of deposit in Harris' name and another $304,972.49 certificate of deposit in the name of his wholly-owned corporation, Harris Mortgage Corporation. Harmar secured the other note, in accordance with its collateral pledge agreement, by its $3,000,000 note (which was unfunded apart from the $700,000) and its collateral mortgage on the theater, each executed by Harmar in favor of Hibernia and dated November 1, 1982. Under the terms of the collateral pledge agreement executed by Harmar in reference to the $3,000,000 note and mortgage, the mortgage secured "not only" Harmar's $350,000 note to Hibernia, "but also any and every other debts, liabilities and obligations" (other than consumer credit debt) of Harmar to Hibernia whether "due or to become due, or whether such debts, liabilities and obligations" of Harmar "are now existing or will arise in the future." Thus, the collateral mortgage secured the full $700,000 loan from Hibernia. Additionally, Taxpayers each executed personal continuing guarantees of Harmar indebtedness in the amount of $700,000 in favor of Hibernia. Smith testified in his deposition that the transaction was structured so that half the loan, as represented by one of the $350,000 notes, would be primarily secured by the certificates of deposit and the other half, represented by the other $350,000 note, primarily by the mortgage on the property purchased, with the entire amount also secured by Taxpayers' individual guarantees.

On its income tax return for the year ending December 31, 1982, Harmar reported a net operating loss of $104,013. Pursuant to [the predecessor of Section 1366], Taxpayers each claimed half of the loss as a deduction on their 1982 individual returns,[5] concluding that their bases in Harmar were in fact greater than Harmar's net operating loss for that year and that they therefore were entitled to deduct the entire loss on their personal returns. On audit, the Internal Revenue Service (IRS) found to the contrary and determined that Harris and Martin each had a basis of $1,000 in his Harmar stock and an adjusted basis in Harmar's indebtedness to each of them as shareholders of $47,500. Pursuant to I.R.C. [§ 1366(d)], the IRS limited Taxpayers' deductions of the net operating loss to what it considered to be their bases in Harmar, $48,500 each. The IRS's disallowance of a portion of the deductions claimed by Taxpayers[6] resulted in additional tax liability, including interest, for Martin of $3,150.58 and for

5. Harris and Martin claimed deductions for Harmar's loss of $52,006 and $52,007, respectively.

6. The IRS disallowed $4,506 of Harris' deduction and $4,507 of Martin's.

Harris of $1,280. Taxpayers paid the tax in dispute and now appeal the district court's summary judgment dismissing their suit for refund.

Discussion

Taxpayers contend on appeal that in determining the deduction allowable for Harmar's net operating loss, the IRS should have included in Taxpayers' bases in their Harmar stock the full value of the $700,000 Hibernia loan they guaranteed. I.R.C. [§ 1366] permits a Subchapter S shareholder to deduct from his personal return a proportionate share of his corporation's net operating loss to the extent that the loss does not exceed the sum of the adjusted basis of his Subchapter S corporation stock and any corporate indebtedness to him. See section [1366(d)(1)]. To arrive at their basis figure, Taxpayers seek to recast the transaction in question. They in essence urge that we disregard the form of the Hibernia loan—one from Hibernia to Harmar—in favor of what Taxpayers consider as the substance of the transaction—a $700,000 loan from Hibernia to them, the $700,000 proceeds of which they then equally contributed to Harmar's capital account. As evidence of their view of the substance of the transaction, Taxpayers point to the deposition testimony of Smith indicating that Hibernia looked primarily to Taxpayers, rather than to Harmar, for repayment of the loan, and they call attention to the $700,000 guarantees they each provided Hibernia as well as the $355,294.58 in certificates of deposit that Harris pledged to Hibernia as part of the November 1, 1982 loan transaction.

In its summary judgment memorandum, the district court declared that Brown v. Commissioner, 706 F.2d 755 (6th Cir.1983), was "on all fours" with the instant case and therefore resolved it. In *Brown*, the Sixth Circuit rejected shareholders' substance over form argument in ruling that the shareholders' guarantees of loans to their Subchapter S corporation could not increase their bases in their stock in the corporation unless the shareholders made an economic outlay by satisfying at least a portion of the guaranteed debt. Id. at 757. Without such an outlay, the *Brown* court concluded that " 'the substance matched the form' " of the transaction before it. Id. at 756. The reasoning of *Brown* was followed by the Fourth Circuit in Estate of Leavitt v. Commissioner, 875 F.2d 420 (4th Cir.1989), *aff'g*, 90 T.C. 206 (1988). There, the court, affirming the en banc Tax Court, held that shareholder guarantees of a loan to a Subchapter S corporation did not increase shareholders' stock basis because such guarantees had not "cost" shareholders anything and thus did not constitute an economic outlay. *Leavitt*, 875 F.2d at 422 & n. 9.[7] In reaching this conclusion, the Fourth Circuit affirmed as not clearly erroneous a finding of the Tax Court that the loan, in form as well as in substance, was made to

7. In reasoning that the shareholders had not increased their stock bases as a result of their guarantees, the court turned to I.R.C. § 1012, which defines basis of property as its cost. Id. at 422 n. 9. Cost of property, in turn, is defined in the Treasury Regulations as the "amount paid for such property in cash or other property." 26 C.F.R. § 1.1012–1(a).

the corporation rather than to the shareholders.[8] Id. at 424. The court rejected appellants' suggestion that it employ the debt/equity principles espoused in Plantation Patterns, Inc. v. Commissioner, 462 F.2d 712 (5th Cir.1972), in determining whether the shareholders had actually made an economic outlay,[9] instead choosing to employ a debt/equity analysis only after making a finding that an economic outlay had occurred. *Leavitt*, 875 F.2d at 427. The *Leavitt* court reasoned that the legislative history of section [1366] limiting the basis of a Subchapter S shareholder to his corporate investment or outlay could not be circumvented through the use of debt/equity principles. Id. at 426 & n. 16. See generally Bogdanski, Shareholder Guarantees, Interest Deductions, and S Corporation Stock Basis: The Problems with Putnam, 13 J.Corp.Tax'n 264, 268–89 (1986).

Taxpayers press this Court to follow the contrary holding of Selfe v. United States, 778 F.2d 769 (11th Cir.1985). There, the Eleventh Circuit ruled that a shareholder's guaranty of a Subchapter S corporation loan could result in an increase in equity or debt basis even though the shareholder had not satisfied any portion of the obligation. *Selfe*, 778 F.2d at 775. The court remanded the case to the district court for it to employ debt/equity principles in determining if the loan in question was in substance one to the shareholder rather than to the corporation. Id.

The courts have uniformly ruled that a shareholder must make an economic outlay to increase his Subchapter S corporation stock basis. Taxpayers assert that if we look beyond the form of the transaction at what they contend is its substance—a loan from Hibernia to them, which in turn they contributed to Harmar as capital—we must find that a $700,000 outlay occurred and that their stock bases therefore correspondingly increased. They contend that use of debt/equity principles will lead us to such a conclusion.

Ordinarily, taxpayers are bound by the form of the transaction they have chosen; taxpayers may not in hindsight recast the transaction as one that they might have made in order to obtain tax advantages. * * * The IRS, however, often may disregard form and recharacterize a transaction by looking to its substance. Higgins v. Smith, 308 U.S. 473, 60 S.Ct. 355, 357, 84 L.Ed. 406 (1940). The Tax Court has recognized an exception to the rule that a taxpayer may not question a transaction's form in cases such as

8. The court noted that the loan in question had been made by the bank directly to the corporation, the loan payments were made by the corporation directly to the bank, and neither the corporation nor the shareholders reported the payments as constructive dividends. Id.

Under *Leavitt*, the presumption is that the form will control and that presumption will not be surmounted absent the shareholder's satisfying the higher standard applicable to a taxpayer's seeking to disavow the form he selected and recast a transaction. See Bowers, Building Up an S Shareholder's Basis through Loans and Acquisitions, J. Tax'n S Corp., Fall 1989, at 22, 29.

9. In *Plantation Patterns*, this Court considered whether a Subchapter C corporation could deduct interest payments made on its debt and whether its shareholders had resulting dividend income. The Court, using a debt/equity analysis, affirmed a Tax Court finding that a corporation's interest payments on debentures were constructive dividends and could not be deducted as interest payments. Id. at 723–24. * * *

this one in which the shareholder argues that guaranteed corporate debt should be recast as an equity investment on the shareholder's part. Blum v. Commissioner, 59 T.C. 436, 440 (1972).

In this case we find that the transaction as structured did not lack adequate substance or reality and that an economic outlay justifying the basis claimed by Taxpayers never occurred.

The summary judgment evidence reflects that the parties to this transaction intended that the Hibernia loan be one to the corporation. Each of the two $350,000 promissory notes was executed by and only in the name of Harmar. The notes have been renewed and remain in the same form, namely notes payable to Hibernia in which the sole maker is Harmar. Hibernia, an independent party, in substance earmarked the loan proceeds for use in purchasing the subject property to which Harmar took title, Harmar contemporaneously giving Hibernia a mortgage to secure Harmar's debt to Hibernia. The bank sent interest due notices to Harmar, and all note payments were made by checks to Hibernia drawn on Harmar's corporate account. Harmar's books and records for all years through the year ended December 31, 1985, prepared by its certified public accountant, reflect the $700,000 loan simply as an indebtedness of Harmar to Hibernia. They do not in any way account for or reflect any of the $700,000 as a capital contribution or loan by Taxpayers to Harmar, although they do reflect the $1,000 capital contribution each Taxpayer made and Harmar's indebtedness to Taxpayers for the various cash advances Taxpayers made to it. The Harmar financial statements for the year ended December 31, 1986, are the first to show any contributed capital attributable to the Hibernia loan. Further, Hibernia's records showed Harmar as the "borrower" in respect to the $700,000 loan and the renewals of it. Harmar's 1982 tax return, which covered August 15 through December 31, 1982, indicates that Harmar deducted $12,506 in interest expenses. Because only the Hibernia loan generated such expenses for that period, it is reasonably inferable that the deduction corresponded to that loan. The 1982 Harmar return showed no distribution to Taxpayers, as it should have if the $700,000 Hibernia loan on which Harmar paid interest was a loan to the Taxpayers. Further, the return shows the only capital contributed as $2,000 and the only loan from stockholders as $68,000, but shows other indebtedness of $675,000. In short, Harmar's 1982 income tax return is flatly inconsistent with Taxpayers' present position. Moreover, there is no indication that Taxpayers treated the loan as a personal one on their individual returns by reporting Harmar's interest payments to Hibernia as constructive dividend income. In sum, the parties' treatment of the transaction, from the time it was entered into and for years thereafter, has been wholly consistent with its unambiguous documentation and inconsistent with the way in which Taxpayers now seek to recast it. Hibernia was clearly an independent third party, and the real and bona fide, separate existence of Harmar is not challenged. The parties did what they intended to do, and the transaction as structured did not lack adequate reality or substance.

Moreover, if the transaction is to be "recast," it is by no means clear that it should be recast in the form sought by Taxpayers, namely as a cash loan to them from Hibernia followed by their payment of the cash to Harmar as a contribution to its capital, and Harmar's then using the cash to purchase the building. Such recasting does not account for Hibernia's mortgage on the building. In any event, if the transaction is to be recast, why should it not be recast as a loan by Hibernia to Taxpayers, with the Taxpayers using the funds to themselves purchase the building, giving Hibernia a mortgage on the building to secure their debt to it, and then transferring the building, subject to the mortgage, to Harmar as a contribution to capital? Presumably in that situation Taxpayers' bases in their Harmar stock would be reduced by the amount of the debt secured by the mortgage under I.R.C. § 358(d). See Wiebusch v. Commissioner, 59 T.C. 777, aff'd per curiam "on the basis of the opinion of the Tax Court," Wiebusch v. Commissioner, 487 F.2d 515 (8th Cir.1973).[15] While section 358(d) likely does not affect stockholder basis in the debt of the Subchapter S corporation to the stockholder, Taxpayers have not sought to recast the transaction as a loan by Hibernia to them followed by their loan of the proceeds to Harmar; indeed even after Harmar's books were rearranged starting with the year ending December 31, 1986, the books do not show any indebtedness in this respect of Harmar to Taxpayers and do continue to show Harmar as owing the money in question to Hibernia. There is simply no evidence of Harmar indebtedness to Taxpayers in respect to these funds.

Taxpayers' guarantees and Harris' pledge of certificates of deposit do not undermine the intent of the parties that Harmar be the borrower in this transaction. It certainly is not difficult to fathom that a careful lender to a new, small, closely held corporation such as Harmar would seek personal guarantees from all of its shareholders. See Bogdanski, supra, at 269. Moreover, the wholly unperformed guarantees do not satisfy the requirement that an economic outlay be made before a corresponding increase in basis can occur. See generally *Underwood*, 535 F.2d at 312. In the same light, Harris' pledge to Hibernia of some $355,000 in certificates of deposit of his (and Harris Mortgage Corporation) does not provide such an outlay.[16]

We conclude that the transaction must be treated as it purports to be and as the parties treated it—namely as a loan by Hibernia to Harmar, all

15. See also Megaard, No Stock Basis for Shareholder Guarantee of S Corporation Debt, 15 J.Corp.Tax'n 340 (1989). Megaard explains that "[u]nder Section 358(d), the assumption by a corporation of its shareholder's debt is treated as money received which reduces the shareholder's basis in the stock." Id. at 349. Cf. id. at 350 ("Having the corporation's assets encumbered by the shareholder's personal debt runs the risk of a basis reduction under Section 358 should the Service argue that the transaction was a purchase by the shareholder of the * * * assets followed by a contribution of the assets to the corporation subject to the debt.").

16. Taxpayers would have us, in effect, convert this pledge to Hibernia into a $700,000 cash contribution made to Harmar by Taxpayers equally. But that did not happen. Taxpayers do not contend that the certificates of deposit were contributed to Harmar's capital.

payments on which through the relevant time have been made by Harmar to Hibernia. For any funds or other assets Taxpayers have actually provided to Harmar as loans or contributions, Taxpayers are, of course, entitled to basis additions as of the time such contributions or loans were furnished by them to Harmar, but they are not entitled to a 1982 basis addition for Hibernia's 1982 $700,000 loan to Harmar, notwithstanding that it was also secured by Taxpayers' execution of guarantees and Harris' pledge to Hibernia of his and Harris Mortgage Corporation's certificates of deposit in the total face amount of some $355,000.

Conclusion

There was no genuine dispute as to any material fact necessary to sustain the Government's summary judgment motion. The district court's judgment is correct and it is therefore

Affirmed.

NOTE

In *Harris*, the Fifth Circuit joined several other circuits[1]and the Tax Court[2] in holding that the guarantee of an S corporation's loan by its shareholders may not be treated as an additional investment in the corporation which will increase the shareholders' bases for purposes of the loss limitation rule in Section 1366(d). In conflict with this line of authority is the Eleventh Circuit's decision in Selfe v. United States.[3] In *Selfe*, the court reasoned that debt-equity principles under Subchapter C were applicable in determining whether a shareholder-guaranteed debt should be characterized as a capital contribution. In remanding the case for a determination of whether the shareholder's guarantee amounted to either an equity investment or a shareholder loan to the corporation, the court directed the district court to apply the principles of *Plantation Patterns*, a Subchapter C case discussed in *Harris*.

Despite the seeming conflict among the circuits, the Supreme Court has declined to add this fascinating tax issue to its docket.[4]

b. SUBCHAPTER S LOSSES AND SECTION 362(e)(2)

Code: § 362(e)(2)

The rules for allocating and characterizing gains and losses that are inherent in property contributed to a partnership (''precontribution gains

1. Brown v. Commissioner, 706 F.2d 755 (6th Cir.1983); Estate of Leavitt v. Commissioner, 875 F.2d 420 (4th Cir.1989), cert. denied, 493 U.S. 958, 110 S.Ct. 376 (1989); Uri v. Commissioner, 949 F.2d 371 (10th Cir.1991); Sleiman v. Commissioner, 187 F.3d 1352 (11th Cir. 1999); Grojean v. Commissioner, 248 F.3d 572 (2001); Maloof v. Commissioner, 456 F.3d 645 (6th Cir. 2006).

2. Estate of Leavitt v. Commissioner, 90 T.C. 206 (1988); Hitchins v. Commissioner, 103 T.C. 711 (1994).

3. 778 F.2d 769 (11th Cir.1985).

4. The Court denied the taxpayer's petition for certiorari in the *Estate of Leavitt* case, supra note 1.

and losses") are one of the principal features of the Subchapter K partnership tax regime. Under Section 704(c)(1)(A), precontribution gains and losses generally must be taxed to the contributing partner, and Section 724 prevents partners from gaining a tax advantage by converting precontribution ordinary income into capital gain and precontribution capital loss into ordinary loss. Other provisions buttress these rules by preventing shifting of precontribution gains and losses through partnership distributions and dispositions of partnership interests.[1] In short, Subchapter K has an array of provisions designed to ensure that a partner who contributes property with a precontribution gain will be taxed on that gain and that precontribution losses may not be shifted to other partners.[2]

Subchapter S is relatively primitive compared to its Subchapter K cousin in the treatment of precontribution gains and losses. Under Section 1377, precontribution gains and losses are taxed like any other gain or loss under a per-share, per-day allocation method.[3] Precontribution gains and losses in an S corporation are thus routinely shifted to other shareholders.

Congress decided to attack various schemes by taxpayers to duplicate losses by way of transactions involving corporations. Section 362(e)(2) was one of the provisions enacted to curb those abuses. That section provides that if a shareholder transfers property with an aggregate built-in loss to a corporation in a Section 351 transaction, the corporation's basis in the property must be reduced to the fair market value of such property.[4] If more than one asset is contributed, the basis reduction is allocated among the property in proportion to their respective built-in losses immediately before the transaction.[5] As an alternative to reducing the property's basis, the shareholder and the corporation may elect to reduce the basis of the stock that was received for the property to the stock's fair market value immediately after the transfer.[6]

Section 362(e)(2) potentially will defer or limit precontribution losses in an S corporation, sometimes in a very unusual way. For example, assume that an individual decides to form an S corporation by contributing property with a $20,000 basis and $12,000 fair market value for all of the corporation's stock in a Section 351 exchange. Under Section 362(e)(2), the property's basis will be reduced to $12,000 and the precontribution loss in the property will disappear. If the corporation were to sell the property for $12,000, there would be no gain or loss recognized by the corporation. The shareholder's basis in the stock, however, would still be $20,000 so the loss would remain in the shares. The timing of the loss, however, would be deferred until the shareholder either liquidates the corporation or sells the stock. Alternatively, assume that the shareholder and the corporation elect to reduce the basis of the shareholder's stock to $12,000. In that case, the

1. I.R.C. §§ 704(c)(1)(B); 737; 751(a).

2. Section 704(c)(1)(C) prevents a shift of precontribution losses to other partners, even a transferee partner.

3. The regulations hold out the possibility of attacking plans to alter the character of precontribution gains and losses in an S corporation. See Reg. § 1.1366–1(b)(2) & (3).

4. I.R.C. § 362(e)(2)(A).

5. I.R.C. § 362(e)(2)(B).

6. I.R.C. § 362(e)(2)(C).

basis of the property in the corporation would remain at $20,000. If the corporation were to sell the property, it would recognize its $8,000 loss, which would pass through to the shareholder. The shareholder's stock basis would then be reduced by the loss down to $4,000, putting the shareholder in a position where a sale of the stock for its $12,000 fair market value would result in an $8,000 gain. Over time, the shareholder would report an $8,000 loss and an $8,000 gain, the net result being that the loss essentially disappeared. Finally, assume that the shareholder also contributed property with a $10,000 built-in gain to the S corporation at the same time as the transfer of the property with the built-in loss. In that case, no reduction in the basis of the loss property or the stock would be required under Section 362(e)(2) because the two properties that were transferred did not have an aggregate built-in loss.

It is hard to believe that Congress considered the effects on Subchapter S when it enacted Section 362(e)(2). That section now lurks as a trap for those who either receive poor advice or are not initiated in the ways of Subchapters C and S. Until Congress fixes this problem, taxpayers planning a new venture involving property with a built-in loss will be well advised to consider structuring the venture as a limited liability company or partnership governed by Subchapter K. Alternatively, another strategy for preserving a built-in loss in property would be to offer to make the property available to an S corporation through a leasing arrangement.

3. Sale of S Corporation Stock

Code: § 1(h).

The tax consequences of a sale of S corporation stock are determined by regulations promulgated under the "look-through" rules of Section 1(h). In general, S corporation stock is treated as a capital asset that gives rise to capital gain or loss on sale. Unlike the more complex approach taken by Subchapter K to the sale of a partnership interest, Subchapter S historically has not required selling shareholders to characterize a portion of their gain or loss on a stock sale by reference to the types of assets (e.g., ordinary income property) held by the corporation at the time of the sale. When Congress enacted the Section 1(h) capital gains rate regime, however, it authorized the Service to prescribe appropriate regulations to apply the various maximum capital gains rates to the sale of interests in pass-through entities.[1]

The Section 1(h) regulations apply a partial capital gains "look-through" rule for sales and exchanges of interests in an S corporation.[2] Shareholders who sell S corporation stock held for more than one year may recognize collectibles gain (taxable at a maximum rate of 28 percent) and residual capital gain, which is generally taxable at a maximum rate of 15 percent.[3] The selling shareholder's share of collectibles gain is defined as

1. I.R.C. § 1(h)(9).

2. Reg. § 1.1(h)–1.

3. Reg. § 1.1(h)–1(a). In limited situations (e.g., where a transaction is governed by

the amount of the net collectibles gain (but not net collectibles loss) that would be allocated to that shareholder if the S corporation transferred all of its collectibles in a fully taxable transaction immediately before the transfer of the stock.[4] The selling shareholder's residual capital gain is the amount of long-term capital gain or loss that the shareholder would recognize on the sale of the stock ("pre-look-through capital gain or loss") minus the partner's share of collectibles gain.[5] The look-through rules do not extend to other corporate assets, such as inventory or depreciable real estate, that would generate ordinary income, or to real estate that would produce unrecaptured (i.e., 25-percent) Section 1250 gain on a corporate-level sale. What is the policy justification for this "pick and choose" look-through approach for S corporations?

The regulations illustrate these rules with the following example.[6] Assume that X, Inc., which always has been an S corporation and is owned equally by individuals A, B, and C, invests in antiques. After they were purchased, the antiques appreciated in value by $300. A owned one-third of the X stock and has held the stock for more than one year. A's adjusted basis in the X stock is $100. If A were to sell all of the X stock to T for $150, A would recognize $50 of pre-look-through long-term capital gain. If X were to sell all of the antiques in a fully taxable transaction immediately before the transfer to T, A would be allocated $100 of collectibles gain on account of the sale. Therefore, A will recognize $100 of collectibles gain on account of the collectibles held by X. The difference between A's pre-look-through capital gain or loss ($50) and the collectibles gain ($100) is A's residual long-term capital gain or loss on the sale of the X stock. Thus, A will recognize $100 of collectibles gain and $50 of residual long-term capital loss on the sale of A's X stock.

PROBLEMS

1. S Corporation is a calendar year taxpayer which elected S corporation status in its first year of operation. S's common stock is owned by A (200 shares with a $12,000 basis) and B (100 shares with a $6,000 basis). During the current year, S will have the following income and expenses:

Business income	$92,000
Tax-exempt interest	1,000
Salary expense	44,000
Depreciation	8,000
Property taxes	7,000
Supplies	4,000

provisions of Subchapter C that treat gain on a sale or redemption of stock as ordinary income), shareholders also may recognize ordinary income on a sale of their S corporation stock. See, e.g., I.R.C. §§ 304, 306.

4. Reg. § 1.1(h)–1(b)(2)(ii). A shareholder's share of collectibles gain is limited to the amount attributable to the portion of the stock transferred that was held for more than one year.

5. Reg. § 1.1(h)–1(c).

6. Reg. § 1.1(h)–1(f) Example 4.

Interest expense paid on a margin account maintained with S Corp.'s stock broker	6,000
Gain from the sale of equipment held for two years:	
§ 1245 gain	7,000
§ 1231 gain	12,000
STCG from the sale of AT&T stock	7,500
LTCG from the sale of Chrysler stock held for two years	15,000
LTCL from the sale of investment real estate held for two years	9,000
Bribe of government official	6,000
Recovery of a bad debt previously deducted	4,500

(a) How will S Corporation, A and B report these events? Compare § 704(b)(2) and (c).

(b) What is A's basis in his S stock at the end of the current year?

(c) Whose accounting method will control the timing of income and deductions?

(d) If S realizes a gain upon an involuntary conversion, who makes the election under § 1033 to limit recognition of gain?

(e) Would it matter if the equipment would have been property described in § 1221(1) if held by A?

2. D, E and F each own one-third of the outstanding stock of R Corporation (an S corporation). During the current year, R will have $120,000 of net income from business operations. The net income is realized at a rate of $10,000 per month. Additionally, in January of this year R sold § 1231 property and recognized a $60,000 loss.

(a) Assume D's basis in her R stock at the beginning of the year is $10,000. If D sells one-half of her stock to G midway through the year for $25,000, what will be the tax results to D and G?

(b) What difference would it make in (a), above, if D sold all of her stock to G for $50,000?

3. The Ace Sporting Goods Store (an S corporation) is owned by Dick and Harry. Dick and Harry each own one-half of Ace's stock and have a $2,000 basis in their respective shares. At incorporation, Dick loaned $4,000 to Ace and received a five year, 12% note from the corporation.

(a) If Ace has an $8,000 loss from business operations this year, what will be the results to Dick and Harry? Do you have any suggestions for Harry? Would it matter if on December 15 Ace borrowed $4,000 from its bank on a full recourse basis? What if Dick and Harry personally guaranteed the loan? Compare §§ 752(a) and 722.

(b) If Ace has $6,000 of net income from business operations next year, what will be the results to Dick and Harry?

(c) What difference would it make in (a), above, if the $8,000 loss was made up of $2,000 of losses from business operation and a $6,000 long-term capital loss? See Reg. § 1.704–1(d)(2).

(d) What would be the effect in (a), above, if Ace's S corporation status was terminated at the end of the current year?

E. DISTRIBUTIONS TO SHAREHOLDERS

Code: §§ 311(b); 1368; 1371(a)(1), (c), (e); Skim § 301(a), (b) and (d).

S Corporations Without Earnings and Profits. If an S corporation has no accumulated earnings and profits, distributions to shareholders are treated as a tax-free return of capital which is first applied to reduce the shareholder's stock basis.[1] Any distribution in excess of basis is treated as gain from the sale or exchange of property—capital gain if the stock is a capital asset.[2] Virtually all S corporations formed after 1982 do not generate earnings and profits[3] and are governed by this simple regime. This basic taxing pattern for distributions by S corporations also governs any distribution of property to which Section 301(c) would apply.[4] Thus, the tax consequences of transactions characterized as Section 301 distributions by other Code provisions, such as Sections 302 (redemptions) and 305 (stock dividends), are determined under Section 1368.

S Corporations With Earnings and Profits. S corporations with earnings and profits present more challenging problems because of the need to harmonize the Subchapter S rules with the corporation's prior C history. Distributions by a C corporation to its shareholders are taxable as dividends to the extent of the corporation's current and accumulated earnings and profits.[5] Some S corporations may have accumulated earnings and profits attributable to prior years when they were governed by Subchapter C. In addition, an S corporation may have inherited the earnings and profits of another company in a corporate acquisition subject to Section 381. In all these cases, the undistributed earnings have not been taxed at the shareholder level and represent an irresistible temptation for a tax-free bailout. There is no free lunch, however, and it thus becomes necessary to identify those distributions which should be taxed at the shareholder level because they are made out of accumulated earnings and profits.

The drafters of the 1982 Act devised a new tax concept—the "accumulated adjustments account" ("AAA")—to serve as the reference point for determining the source of distributions by an S corporation with accumulated earnings and profits. The AAA represents the post–1982 undistributed net income of the corporation. It begins at zero and is increased and decreased annually in a manner similar to the adjustment of the basis in a shareholder's stock.[6] Any distribution by an S corporation with accumulat-

1. I.R.C. § 1368(b)(1).

2. I.R.C. § 1368(b)(2).

3. I.R.C. § 1371(c)(1). An S corporation formed after 1982 may generate earnings and profits for any year in which it is not an S corporation and may acquire earnings and profits under Section 381 in a corporate acquisition. See Chapter 19B, supra.

4. I.R.C. § 1368(c). See Section G of this Chapter, infra.

5. I.R.C. §§ 301(c)(1), 316.

6. I.R.C. § 1368(e)(1)(A); Reg. § 1.1368–2. Unlike a shareholder's basis,

ed earnings and profits is treated as a tax-free return of capital to the extent it does not exceed the AAA.[7] A distribution in excess of the AAA is treated as a dividend to the extent of accumulated earnings and profits,[8] and any portion of the distribution still remaining after both the AAA and accumulated earnings and profits are exhausted is treated first as a recovery of basis and then as gain from the sale of property.[9]

One might reasonably ask at this point: what is the purpose of this statutory scheme? The answer is more straightforward than it first appears. The function of the AAA is to identify the source of distributions by those few S corporations with accumulated earnings and profits. It permits the corporation to make a tax-free distribution of the net income recognized during its S corporation era which already was taxed at the shareholder level. Only after these previously taxed earnings are exhausted will a distribution be considered as emanating from accumulated earnings and profits.[10]

Distributions of Appreciated Property. At the shareholder level, the Section 1368 distribution rules make no distinction between distributions of cash and other property. At the corporate level, however, an S corporation that distributes appreciated property (other than its own obligations) recognizes gain in the same manner as if the property had been sold to the shareholder at its fair market value.[11] This familiar rule, borrowed from Subchapter C, applies to liquidating and nonliquidating distributions of property by an S corporation.[12] The gain is not taxed to the corporation but, like other corporate-level income, it passes through to the distributee shareholder, who takes a fair market value basis in the distributed property.[13] The shareholder's basis in his S corporation stock is reduced by the

however, the AAA is not increased by tax-exempt income items and is not decreased for expenses related to tax-exempt income. The adjustments also may result in a negative AAA. Reg. § 1.1368–2(a)(3)(ii). In addition, no adjustment is made for federal taxes attributable to any taxable year in which the corporation was a C corporation. Id.

7. I.R.C. § 1368(c)(1). Except to the extent provided in regulations, the AAA is allocated proportionately among distributions if the distributions exceed the AAA. See Reg. § 1.1368–2(b), (c).

8. I.R.C. § 1368(c)(2).

9. I.R.C. § 1368(c)(2), (3). For lots of details about the AAA, see Reg. § 1.1368–2.

10. In lieu of these rules, an S corporation may elect, with the consent of all shareholders who have received distributions during the year, to treat distributions as a dividend to the extent of accumulated earnings and profits. I.R.C. § 1368(e)(3); Reg. § 1.1368–1(f)(2). There normally is little incentive to make this election. One possible motivation would be to enable the corporation to sweep its Subchapter C earnings and profits account clean and thus avoid the corporate level tax and possible termination of S corporation status that would result from the co-existence of Subchapter C earnings and profits and excessive passive investment income. See I.R.C. § 1375. A similar election is provided during a post-termination transition period. I.R.C. § 1371(e)(2).

11. I.R.C. § 311(b). An S corporation may not recognize loss, however, on a distribution of property that has declined in value. I.R.C. § 311(a).

12. See I.R.C. § 1371(a), which provides that, except as otherwise provided in Subchapter S, the provisions of Subchapter C apply to S corporations and their shareholders. For more on the coordination of Subchapters S and C, see Section G of this chapter, infra.

13. I.R.C. § 301(d)(1).

fair market value (not the adjusted basis) of the distributed property.[14] These rules are required to prevent the appreciation from escaping tax through a distribution which is tax-free at both the corporate and shareholder levels followed by a tax-free sale by the shareholder, who would take the property with a fair market value basis.

PROBLEMS

1. Ajax Corporation is a calendar year taxpayer which was organized two years ago and elected S corporation status for its first taxable year. Ajax's stock is owned one-third by Dewey and two-thirds by Milt. At the beginning of the current year, Dewey's basis in his Ajax shares was $3,000 and Milt's basis in his shares was $5,000. During the year, Ajax will earn $9,000 of net income from operations and have a $3,000 long-term capital gain on the sale of 100 shares of Exxon stock. What results to Dewey, Milt and Ajax in the following alternative situations?

(a) On October 15, Ajax distributes $5,000 to Dewey and $10,000 to Milt.

(b) On October 15, Ajax distributes $8,000 to Dewey and $16,000 to Milt.

(c) Ajax redeems all of Dewey's stock on the last day of the year for $20,000. What result to Dewey?

(d) On October 15, Ajax redeems one-fourth of Dewey's stock for $5,000 and one-fourth of Milt's stock for $10,000.

(e) Ajax distributes a parcel of land with a basis of $9,000 and a fair market value of $8,000 to Dewey and a different parcel with a basis of $13,000 and fair market value of $16,000 to Milt.

(f) On October 15, Ajax distributes its own notes to Dewey and Milt. Dewey receives an Ajax five year, 12% note with a face amount and fair market value of $8,000 and Milt receives an Ajax five year, 12% note with a face amount and fair market value of $16,000.

2. P Corporation was formed in 1981 by its two equal shareholders, Nancy and Opal, and elected S corporation status at the beginning of the current year. On January 1, Nancy had a $1,000 basis in her P stock and Opal had a $5,000 basis in her stock. P has $6,000 of accumulated earnings and profits from its prior C corporation operations and has the following results from operations this year:

Gross Income	$32,000
Long-term capital gain	4,000
Salary Expense	18,000
Depreciation	8,000

What are the tax consequences to Nancy, Opal and P Corporation in the following alternative situations.

14. I.R.C. §§ 1367(a)(2)(A), 1368.

(a) On November 1, P distributes $5,000 to Nancy and $5,000 to Opal.

(b) Same as (a), above, except that P distributes $10,000 to Nancy and $10,000 to Opal.

(c) What difference would it make in (a), above, if P also received $4,000 of tax-exempt interest during the year and distributed $2,000 of the interest to Nancy and $2,000 to Opal?

(d) During the current year P makes no distributions. On January 1 of next year Nancy sells her P stock to Rose for $6,000. If P breaks even on its operations next year, what will be the result to Rose if P distributes $6,000 to each of its shareholders next February 15?

(e) During the current year P makes no distributions. Nancy and Opal revoke P's Subchapter S election effective January 1 of next year. Assume P Co. has $5,000 of earnings and profits next year. What results to Nancy and Opal if P distributes $7,000 to each of them on August 1 of next year?

3. How do the tax rules governing distributions of appreciated property by an S corporation differ from the rules governing similar distributions by partnerships? Why? Which approach is preferable?

F. TAXATION OF THE S CORPORATION

Code: §§ 1363; 1374; 1375.

The major benefit of a Subchapter S election is the elimination of tax at the corporate level. But this immunity from tax is not absolute. As part of its continuing mission to patrol abuse, Congress has provided that in certain limited situations an S corporation may be subject to tax under Section 1374 on certain built-in gains inherent in corporate property and under Section 1375 on a portion of its passive investment income.

Tax on Certain Built-in Gains: Section 1374. When Congress repealed the *General Utilities* doctrine, it recognized that the shareholders of a C corporation might elect S corporation status in order to avoid the corporate-level tax imposed under the new statutory scheme.[1] For example, assume Liquidating Co. is a C corporation, holds highly appreciated assets, and is owned by shareholders A and B, who also would realize large taxable gains if they sell their stock or liquidate the company. If A and B cause Liquidating Co. to sell its assets and liquidate, or to distribute its assets in complete liquidation, Liquidating Co. will be taxed on its gains and A and B also will be taxed on their stock gains.[2] If Liquidating Co. qualified as a "small business corporation," A and B could elect S corporation status in order to reduce the double-tax burden on the sale or liquidation. The company then could sell its assets and the gains would pass through to A and B, whose stock bases would be correspondingly increased. The effect of

1. See Chapters 12D, 13E and 15B2, supra.

2. See I.R.C. §§ 331; 336; 1001(a).

the S corporation/liquidation strategy would be to avoid the full impact of the double tax.

Section 1374 blocks this opportunity by taxing an S corporation that has a "net recognized built-in gain" at any time within ten years of the effective date of its S corporation election.[3] At the outset, two important limitations on this tax should be noted. First, Section 1374 applies only if the corporation's S election was made after December 31, 1986.[4] Second, it does not apply to a corporation that always has been subject to Subchapter S.[5]

In general, Section 1374 is designed to tax an S corporation on the net gain that accrued while it was subject to Subchapter C if that gain is subsequently recognized on sales, distributions and other dispositions of property within a ten-year "recognition period" beginning with the first taxable year in which the corporation was an S corporation. For this purpose, any gain recognized during the recognition period, including income from "ripe" items such as cash-basis accounts receivable or Section 453 installment obligations, is a "recognized built-in gain" unless the corporation establishes either that it did not hold the asset at the beginning of its first S taxable year or the recognized gain exceeds the gain inherent in the asset at that time.[6] Conversely, any loss recognized during the recognition period, including deductible items attributable to the corporation's pre-S life, is a "recognized built-in loss" to the extent that the S corporation establishes that it held the asset at the beginning of its first S year and the loss does not exceed the loss inherent in the asset at that time.[7] Since the taxpayer has the burden of proof under these definitions, a C corporation making an S election should obtain an independent appraisal of its assets to establish their value on the relevant date in order to avoid being taxed on gain arising under the S regime and to benefit from the losses that accrued during the corporation's C years.

The Section 1374 tax is computed by applying the highest rate applicable to C corporations (currently 35 percent) to the S corporation's "net recognized built-in gain," which is defined as the corporation's taxable income computed by taking into account only recognized built-in gains and losses but limited to the corporation's taxable income computed generally as if it were a C corporation.[8] The purpose of the taxable income limitation is to ensure that Section 1374 does not tax the corporation on more income

3. I.R.C. § 1374(a), (d)(7).

4. Tax Reform Act of 1986, P.L. No. 99–514, 99th Cong., 2d Sess. § 633(b) (1986).

5. I.R.C. § 1374(c)(1). This exemption may not apply, however, if the S corporation had a "predecessor" that was a C corporation. Id. This could occur, for example, where a C corporation was acquired by the S corporation in a tax-free reorganization.

6. I.R.C. § 1374(d)(3), (5)(A).

7. I.R.C. § 1374(d)(4), (5)(B).

8. I.R.C. § 1374(b)(1), (d)(2). Taxable income, as defined in Section 63(a), is modified by disregarding certain deductions (e.g., the dividends received deduction) and net operating losses. I.R.C. §§ 1374(d)(2)(A)(ii); 1375(b)(1)(B). Net operating loss and capital loss carryforwards from prior years as a C corporation are taken into account in computing the amount subject to tax under Section 1374. I.R.C. § 1374(b)(2).

than it actually realizes during the taxable year. To prevent taxpayers from avoiding the tax by manipulating the timing of post-conversion losses, Section 1374(d)(2)(B) provides that any net recognized built-in gains not taxed because of the taxable income limitation are carried forward and treated as recognized built-in gain in succeeding years in the recognition period.[9] Finally, the amount of net recognized built-in gain taken into account for any taxable year may not exceed the net unrealized built-in gain at the time the corporation became an S corporation reduced by any net recognized built-in gains which were subject to Section 1374 in prior taxable years.[10]

The Section 1374 tax easily could be avoided if it applied only to built-in gains recognized on the disposition of assets that were held by the S corporation at the beginning of its first S taxable year. For example, assume that a C corporation converting to S status holds an asset (Oldacre) with a built-in gain which it subsequently exchanges for property of like kind (Newacre) in a Section 1031 nonrecognition transaction. The gain inherent in Oldacre is preserved in Newacre's exchanged basis under Section 1031(d). If the corporation disposes of Newacre within ten years after switching to S status, the Section 1374 tax should apply to the built-in "C gain" even though Newacre was not held on the first day that the corporation was subject to Subchapter S. Section 1374(d)(6) ensures this result by providing that an asset taking an exchanged basis from another asset held by the corporation at the time it converted to S status shall be treated as having been held as of the beginning of the corporation's first S year. In the above example, the built-in gain inherent in Oldacre on the conversion from C to S status is recognized under Section 1374 if the corporation disposes of Newacre at a gain during the recognition period.

Section 1374(d)(8) is another testament to Congress's protective attitude toward the double tax. It ensures that built-in gain in assets acquired by an S corporation from a C corporation in a tax-free reorganization does not escape a corporate level tax. For this purpose, the recognition period commences as of the date the asset is acquired rather than on the beginning of the first taxable year for which the corporation was an S corporation.[11]

Tax advisors began to plot strategies to reduce the impact of Section 1374 soon after it was enacted. For example, it was suggested that the tax might be avoided if an S corporation sold an asset with built-in gain during the 10–year recognition period on the installment method but delayed receipt of any payments (and thus any recognized gain) until after the recognition period had expired.[12] Not surprisingly, the Service has ex-

9. The carryover rule applies only to corporations that elected S status on or after March 31, 1988. I.R.C. § 1374(d)(2)(B).

10. I.R.C. § 1374(c)(2), (d)(1).

11. I.R.C. § 1374(d)(8). See Section G of this chapter, infra, for an overview of the tax consequences when an S corporation is the acquiring or target corporation in a tax-free reorganization.

12. See, e.g., Taggart, "Emerging Tax Issues in Corporate Acquisitions," 44 Tax L.Rev. 459, 481 (1989).

pressed its displeasure with this gambit. The regulations provide that the built-in gain rules will continue to apply to income recognized under the installment method during taxable years ending after the expiration of the recognition period. The gain, when recognized, will be subject to tax under Section 1374.[13]

Tax on Passive Investment Income. When it widened the gates to Subchapter S, Congress became concerned that a C corporation with earnings and profits might make an S election and redeploy substantial amounts in liquid assets yielding passive investment income such as dividends and interest. Left unchecked, this strategy would enable a profitable C corporation to move to the single-tax regime of Subchapter S and pass through the investment income to its shareholders, who might delay, perhaps forever, paying any shareholder-level tax on the Subchapter C earnings and profits. This plan had particular allure when a C corporation sold all of its operating assets and was seeking an alternative to the shareholder-level tax that would be imposed under Section 331 on a distribution of the proceeds in complete liquidation.[14]

The Code includes two weapons to foil the Subchapter S/passive income ploy. As discussed earlier, an S corporation with accumulated earnings and profits from its prior life as a C corporation will lose its S status if it has passive investment income that exceeds 25 percent of its gross receipts for three consecutive taxable years.[15] In addition, even before its S status is terminated, the corporation will be subject to a corporate-level tax under Section 1375. The tax, which equals 35 percent of the corporation's "excess net passive income," is imposed if an S corporation has earnings and profits from a taxable year prior to its S election and more than 25 percent of the corporation's gross receipts for the taxable year consist of "passive investment income."

For purposes of the Section 1375 tax, "passive investment income" is defined as gross receipts from royalties, rents, dividends, interest, and annuities.[16] Gains on the disposition of property, interest earned on obligations acquired from the sale of inventory, the gross receipts of certain lending and finance institutions, and dividends received from a C corporation subsidiary that are derived from the active conduct of a trade or business, are not passive investment income.[17] To prevent easy manipulation of the gross receipts test, only the excess of gains over losses from dispositions of capital assets (other than stock and securities) is included in overall gross receipts, and gross receipts from the sales or exchanges of stock or securities are taken into account only to the extent of gains.[18] The term "stock or securities" is interpreted expansively and includes stock

13. Reg. § 1.1374–4(h)(1). For the relationship of this rule to other aspects of Section 1374, see Reg. § 1.1374–4(h)(2)–(5).

14. See Chapter 16B1, supra.

15. I.R.C. § 1362(d)(3). See Section C of this chapter, supra.

16. I.R.C. §§ 1375(b)(3); 1362(d)(3)(C)(i).

17. I.R.C. § 1362(d)(3)(C)(ii)–(iv).

18. I.R.C. §§ 1375(b)(3); 1362(d)(3)(B); 1222(9).

rights, warrants, debentures, partnership interests, and "certificates of interest" in profit-sharing arrangements.[19]

The computation of the Section 1375 tax is a technician's dream (and a student's nightmare?). The base for the Section 1375 tax, "excess net passive income," is a percentage of the corporation's "net passive income," which is generally equal to passive investment income less deductions directly connected with the production of such income.[20] To arrive at excess net passive income, net passive income is multiplied by a ratio, which has a numerator equal to the excess of passive investment income over 25 percent of gross receipts for the year, and a denominator equal to passive investment income for the year.[21] There is one final caveat: excess net passive income cannot exceed the corporation's taxable income for the year computed with the special changes described in Section 1374(d)(4).[22]

An example may help control the pollution. Assume that X Corporation made a Subchapter S election last year and will have accumulated earnings and profits from prior C corporation operations at the end of its current taxable year, in which X has $50,000 of income from its regular business operations and $35,000 of business deductions. X also receives $15,000 of interest income and $10,000 of dividends and incurs $5,000 of expenses directly related to the production of the investment income.

Is X subject to the Section 1375 tax? The corporation will have Subchapter C earnings and profits at the close of its taxable year and more than 25 percent of its gross receipts are passive investment income ($25,000 out of $75,000 of gross receipts), so the tax is potentially applicable. X's net passive income is $20,000 ($25,000 of passive investment income less directly connected expenses), and it will have $5,000 of excess net passive income ($20,000 of net passive income multiplied by a ratio having $6,250 as the numerator ($25,000 of passive investment income reduced by 25 percent of gross receipts) and $25,000 as the denominator (passive investment income)). Since excess net passive income does not exceed X's taxable income as determined under Section 1374(d)(4), the corporation's tax liability will be $1,750 ($5,000 × 35 percent).

Section 1375(d) offers one avenue for relief from the Section 1375 tax. The tax may be waived if the S corporation establishes to the satisfaction of the Service that it determined, in good faith, that it had no earnings and profits at the close of a taxable year and, within a reasonable period after discovering earnings and profits, they were distributed. The addition of an "anti-blunder" provision to this complex area is a welcome sign and one hopes the Service will be merciful in its administration of Section 1375(d).

Congress also considered the interaction of Sections 1374 and 1375 with the provisions taxing the shareholders of an S corporation. Any Section 1374 tax is treated as a loss (characterized according to the built-in gain subject to tax) sustained by the S corporation which will pass through

19. See Reg. § 1.1362–2(c)(4)(ii)(B)(3).

20. I.R.C. § 1375(b)(2).

21. I.R.C. § 1375(b)(1)(A).

22. I.R.C. § 1375(b)(1)(B).

to the shareholders, and each item of passive investment income is reduced by its proportionate share of the Section 1375 tax.[23]

It is important to keep the application of Sections 1374 and 1375 in perspective. A new corporation making a Subchapter S election generally does not have to be concerned with either provision. Section 1374(c)(1) will protect the corporation from the Section 1374 tax and, since the corporation's activities will not generate earnings and profits,[24] Section 1375 cannot apply to the corporation. Therefore, Sections 1374 and 1375 normally will not play a role in deciding whether to utilize a partnership or an S corporation for a new venture.

Additional considerations come into play if a C corporation is considering a move to a single tax regime. An operating C corporation must consider the impact of Sections 1374 and 1375 on a possible Subchapter S election. Weighed against these penalty provisions is the fact that a shift from C corporation status to partnership status requires a liquidation of the corporation, which may result in significant current corporate and shareholder tax liability.[25] The immediate tax cost of moving to a partnership format may be significant enough to tip the balance in favor of a Subchapter S election and force an accommodation with Sections 1374 and 1375, if planning cannot successfully eliminate their impact.

PROBLEMS

1. Built-in Corporation ("B") was formed in 2000 as a C corporation. The shareholders of B elected S corporation status effective as of January 1, 2004, when it had no Subchapter C earnings and profits and the following assets:

Asset	Adj. Basis	F.M.V.
Land	$30,000	$20,000
Building	10,000	35,000
Machinery	15,000	30,000

For purposes of this problem, disregard any cost recovery deductions that may be available to B. Consider the shareholder and corporate level tax consequences of the following alternative transactions:

(a) B sells the building for $50,000 in 2005; its taxable income for 2005 if it were not an S corporation would be $75,000.

(b) Same as (a), above, except that B's taxable income for 2005 if it were not an S corporation would be $20,000.

(c) Same as (a), above, except that B also sells the machinery for $40,000 in 2006, when it would have substantial taxable income if it were not an S corporation.

23. I.R.C. § 1366(f)(2), (3).

24. I.R.C. § 1371(c)(1).

25. See I.R.C. §§ 331, 336, 1001.

(d) B trades the building for an apartment building in a tax-free § 1031 exchange and then sells the apartment building for $50,000 in 2005, when it would have substantial taxable income if it were not an S corporation.

(e) B sells the building for $90,000 in 2014.

2. S Corporation elected S corporation status beginning in 2001 and will have Subchapter C earnings and profits at the close of the current taxable year. This year, S expects that its business operations and investments will produce the following tax results:

Gross income from operations	$75,000
Business deductions	60,000
Tax-exempt interest	23,000
Dividends	12,000
Long-term capital gain from the sale of investment real property	35,000

(a) Is S Corporation subject to the § 1375 tax on passive investment income? If so, compute the amount of tax.

(b) Same as (a), above, except that S receives an additional $5,000 of tax-exempt interest.

3. The San Diego Bay Boat Storage and Marina Corporation ("Bay") was formed in 1999 as a C corporation and has substantial accumulated earnings and profits. Bay's business consists of three primary activities. About one-third of Bay's gross receipts are derived from marine service and repair work conducted by its two mechanics. Another one-third of Bay's total receipts come from the rental of berths to boat owners. Berthing fees vary depending upon the size of the particular boat. A boat owner renting a berth from Bay must pay a separate charge to have Bay's employees launch or haul out his boat. However, if given advance notice, Bay employees will fuel an owner's boat, charging only for the fuel. The remainder of bay's receipts come from dry storage of boats. Owners pay $200 per month for dry storage in Bay's warehouse where a Bay employee is on duty 24 hours a day. For this fee, Bay employees will launch, fuel (with a charge for fuel) and haul out the boat whenever requested by the owner. Bay's mechanics also will perform a free engine analysis every other year for owners of power boats in dry storage.

Bay is considering the possibility of making a Subchapter S election and has requested your advice concerning any problems which it may have. What difference would it make if Bay were a newly formed corporation?

G. Coordination With Subchapter C

Code: §§ 1371; 1372.

It is important to remember that an S corporation is still a corporation for many tax purposes. It is organized in the same manner as other corporations, and it may engage in most of the transactions and experience the corporate adjustments encountered throughout this text. After incorporating or escaping from Subchapter C, S corporations may make nonliquidating distributions of property or stock, engage in redemptions, or acquire other businesses in either taxable or tax-free transactions. They may sell their assets and liquidate, be acquired by another corporation, or divide up into two or more separate corporations. The tax consequences of these and other events in an S corporation's life cycle are determined by a patchwork quilt of Code sections pieced together from Subchapters C and S. The resulting product provides a challenging opportunity to study the uneasy relationship between a double tax regime and a pass-through scheme.

Section 1371(a) begins the statutory snake dance with the deceptively simple general rule that the provisions of Subchapter C apply to an S corporation and its shareholders. This broad admonition is subject to two related exceptions. First, any provision in the Code specifically applicable to S corporations naturally will apply. Second, if the provisions of Subchapter C are "inconsistent with" Subchapter S, the S rules are controlling. Reliable authority is sparse on precisely how Congress intended to harmonize the rules, but the Service gradually has offered guidance. The details are best raised in the context of specific transactions.

Formation of a Corporation. All the basic rules studied in connection with the formation of a C corporation apply to newly formed S corporations.[1] Shareholders who comprise the founding 80 percent or more "control" group do not recognize gain or loss on the transfer of property to the corporation if the requirements of Section 351(a) are met, but realized gain is recognized to the extent the shareholder receives boot[2] or if the transferred liabilities exceed the shareholder's basis for the transferred property.[3] Shareholders determine their basis in stock, debt obligations and other boot received under Section 358. The corporation takes a transferred basis in any contributed assets under Section 362(a). Organizational expenditures may be deducted and amortized if the corporation elects to do so under Section 248, and the benefit of the deductions passes through to the shareholders.

Several other formation issues, most relating to the "small business corporation requirements," are unique to S corporations. To qualify for the S election, the corporation must be mindful of the 100–shareholder limit and the prohibition against certain types of shareholders (e.g., nonresident aliens, partnerships). As for capital structure, an S corporation is limited to one class of stock and thus may not issue preferred stock, but it is free to issue debt, preferably in a form that qualifies for the straight debt safe harbor.[4] Unlike a corporation facing the double tax, an S corporation has no particular incentive to issue pro rata debt to its shareholders.[5]

1. See generally Chapter 11, supra.
2. I.R.C. § 351(b).
3. I.R.C. § 357(c).
4. I.R.C. § 1361(c)(5).
5. See Chapter 11F, supra. For the advantages and disadvantages of issuing debt in the S corporation setting, see Eustice &

S Corporations as Shareholders. At one time, an S corporation in its capacity as a shareholder of another corporation was treated as an individual for purposes of Subchapter C. The purpose of this rule was to ensure that an S corporation would not qualify for the Section 243 dividends received deduction, which is designed to prevent double taxation at the corporate level and thus should not be available to a pass-through entity.[6] As drafted, however, the rule had a ripple effect on other transactions, leading Congress to repeal it and clarify the tax consequences of many of the transactions discussed below. The legislative history includes a reminder that S corporations, like individuals, may not claim a dividends received deduction or treat any item of income or deduction in a manner inconsistent with the treatment accorded to individual taxpayers.[7]

Distributions and Liquidating Sales. As discussed earlier,[8] Subchapter S generally preempts Subchapter C in determining the tax consequences of nonliquidating distributions. Section 1368 specifically provides that it shall apply to any distribution to which Section 301(c) otherwise would apply. This means that Section 1368 is the reference point not only for routine nonliquidating distributions but also other transactions, such as dividend-equivalent redemptions and taxable stock distributions, which are classified under Subchapter C as distributions to which Section 301 applies.[9] We have seen that an S corporation recognizes gain under Section 311(b) on a distribution of appreciated property but, unless Section 1374 applies, that gain is not taxed at the corporate level. Instead, the gain passes through to the shareholders, who may increase their stock basis by their respective shares of the gain.

In the case of liquidating distributions and sales, Subchapter C reassumes center stage. Liquidating distributions generally trigger recognition of gain or loss to an S corporation under Section 336 in the same manner as if the corporation were subject to Subchapter C. Sales of assets pursuant to a plan of complete liquidation also are taxable. In either case, however, these gains will pass through to the shareholders and be subject to a single shareholder-level tax unless Section 1374 intercedes. An S corporation also may make a liquidating sale on the installment method. Under certain conditions, these installment obligations may be distributed without triggering corporate-level gain (unless Section 1374 applies), and the shareholders may use the installment method to report the gain.[10] The *character* of the shareholder's gain in this situation is not determined by reference to

Kuntz, Federal Income Taxation of S Corporations ¶ 6.03[1] (4th ed. 2001).

6. See, e.g., S.Rep. No. 640, 97th Cong., 2d Sess. 15, reprinted in 1982–2 C.B. 718, 724–725.

7. See H.R. Rep. 104–737, 104th Cong., 2d Sess. 56 (1996).

8. See Section E of this chapter, supra.

9. See, e.g., I.R.C. §§ 302(d); 305(b). Section 306 is unlikely to apply in the S setting, however, because an S corporation may not issue preferred stock.

10. See I.R.C. § 453B(h). To qualify for corporate-level nonrecognition, the S corporation must distribute the obligation in complete liquidation. In addition, the obligations must result from sales of assets (other than nonbulk sales of inventory) during the 12–month period following the adoption of the liquidation plan. See I.R.C. § 453(h).

their stock, which ordinarily would be a capital asset, but rather "in accordance with the principles of Section 1366(d)"[11]—i.e., as if the corporate-level gain on the sale of the asset had been passed through to the shareholders.[12]

Subchapter C also governs the shareholder-level consequences of a complete liquidation. An S corporation shareholder treats distributions in complete liquidation as in full payment in exchange for the stock under Section 331. Although liquidating distributions and sales result in only one level of tax to an S corporation and its shareholders,[13] variations between the shareholder's stock basis and the corporation's basis in its assets may have an impact on the character of the shareholder's gain or loss. For example, assume A owns all of the stock of S, Inc. (an S corporation with no prior C history) and has a $2,000 basis in her S stock. Assume S owns one ordinary income asset which has a $10,000 fair market value and a $1,000 adjusted basis. If S sells the asset, it will recognize $9,000 of ordinary income. The gain passes through to A, and her stock basis is increased by $9,000, to $11,000, under Section 1367. When S liquidates and distributes $10,000 cash to A, she recognizes a $1,000 long-term capital loss. Alternatively, if the ordinary income asset had a $2,000 basis, S would recognize $8,000 of ordinary income on its sale which would pass through to A, increasing her stock basis to $10,000. When S liquidates and distributes $10,000 cash to A, she would recognize no additional gain or loss.

Taxable Acquisitions of S Corporations. An acquisition of an S corporation may be structured as either a purchase of stock from the shareholders or a purchase of assets from the corporation. The method chosen affects not only the amount, character and timing of gain but also may have an impact on the tax status of the S corporation and perhaps even the acquiring party if it also is an S corporation.

An asset acquisition often is preferable because the purchaser will obtain a cost basis in the S corporation's assets at the cost of only a shareholder-level tax.[14] For example, assume P, Inc. wishes to acquire T, Inc. (an S corporation with no prior C history). If P purchases T's assets, any gain or loss recognized by T on the sale will pass through to its shareholders, and P will obtain a cost basis in the assets. T's shareholders will increase their stock basis by any gain recognized on the sale under Section 1367, thus avoiding a second tax on the same economic gain when T liquidates.

11. I.R.C. § 453B(h).

12. Thus, if the installment sale would have given rise to ordinary income, that character will pass through to the shareholders when they collect the installment obligations.

13. This is because the corporate-level gain on a liquidating distribution or sale results in upward basis adjustments to the shareholder's stock under Section 1367. A double tax would be imposed, however, if Section 1374 applies.

14. Once again, this assumes that the corporation has no built-in gains that would be taxed under Section 1374. In contrast, an acquisition of assets from a C corporation generates tax at both the corporate and shareholder levels if the target liquidates. See Chapter 16B, supra.

If P is a C corporation and purchases a controlling interest in the T stock, the T shareholders recognize gain or loss on the sale, and P takes a cost basis in the stock it acquires. T's S election will terminate, however, because an S corporation may not have any C corporation shareholders.[15] If P does not make a Section 338 election, T retains its historic bases in its assets, and as a new C corporation it will face the prospect of a corporate-level tax on any built-in gain. If P makes a Section 338 election to obtain a cost basis in T's assets, T—which loses its S status on the acquisition—must pay a corporate-level tax as a result of the deemed asset sale.[16] If P and T make a joint Section 338(h)(10) election, the regulations provide that old T (still considered an S corporation at this point) recognizes gain or loss on the deemed sale of its assets and then is deemed to have distributed those assets in complete liquidation. The gain or loss on the deemed asset sale passes through to T's shareholders, with resulting basis adjustments to their T stock. Those adjustments then may be taken into account in determining the shareholders' gain or loss under Section 331 on the deemed complete liquidation of old T.[17]

Taxable Acquisitions by S Corporations. When the purchasing corporation ("P") is an S corporation, the primary concern usually is the preservation of P's S status. If P purchases the assets of T, the mix of consideration used in the transaction must be tailored to the S corporation eligibility requirements. P thus should avoid using its own stock or hybrid debt in order to avoid running afoul of the 100–shareholder limit or the prohibition against having more than one class of stock.[18]

When an S corporation acquires the stock of T, the acquisition will not necessarily result in a loss of the acquiring corporation's S status because S corporations may have controlled C corporation subsidiaries. In addition, an acquiring S corporation is eligible to make a Section 338 election, which will trigger immediate recognition of all T's gains and losses. Finally, if an S corporation acquires 80 percent or more of T's stock and liquidates T, the liquidation will be tax free to both corporations under Sections 332 and 337. Following that liquidation, however, any of T's built-in gains while it was a C corporation may later be subject to tax under Section 1374 upon a subsequent disposition.[19]

Tax–Free Reorganizations. An S corporation may be either the target or the acquiring corporation in a tax-free acquisitive reorganization. Looking first to situations where an S corporation is the target, it will lose its S status if it remains in existence as an 80 percent or more subsidiary following a tax-free acquisition of its stock by a C corporation in a Type B reorganization or reverse triangular merger. If an S corporation-target's assets are acquired in a merger or Type C reorganization, the transaction

15. I.R.C. §§ 1362(d)(2); 1361(b)(1)(B). After 1996, two or more S corporations may have a parent-subsidiary relationship in which case they are treated as one S corporation for tax purposes. I.R.C. § 1361(b)(3).

16. T's S election terminates when P acquires T's stock, and its short C year includes the day of the terminating event. Thus, the gain on the deemed asset sale must be reported on a one-day return for old T's "short C year." See I.R.C. §§ 1362(e)(1)(B); 338(a)(1). The economic burden of the corporate-level tax is borne by P unless it is reflected in the price paid for the stock.

17. See Reg. § 1.338(h)(10)–1.

18. See generally I.R.C. § 1361(b).

19. As to built-in gains, see I.R.C. § 1374(d)(8); Reg. § 1.1374–8.

may proceed on a tax-free basis, and the target will terminate its existence as a result of the merger or the liquidation that necessary must follow a Type C reorganization.

If an S corporation is the acquiring corporation in a tax-free reorganization, it necessarily must issue new stock to the target shareholders. Whatever form of acquisition is used, care must be exercised to avoid termination of the election by exceeding the 100–shareholder limit or inheriting an ineligible shareholder. Now that S corporations may have subsidiaries, a Type B stock-for-stock acquisition, once impossible without losing S status, is now a feasible alternative. Similarly, acquisition of the assets of a C corporation in a Type A or C reorganization should not adversely affect the acquirer's S election, but the earnings and profits from the target's C years could jeopardize the acquiring corporation's S status or subject it to the Section 1375 tax if it has substantial passive investment income.[20] Moreover, an S corporation that is the acquiring corporation in a Type A or C reorganization or a forward triangular merger will inherit the target's tax attributes, including its earnings and profits, under Section 381, and its accumulated adjustments account if the target is an S corporation with a prior C history.[21] Finally, any assets acquired from a C corporation in a tax-free reorganization trigger a new ten-year recognition period for purposes of the Section 1374 tax on built-in gains.[22]

Corporate Divisions. An S corporation may divide itself into separate corporations in a transaction that is tax-free at both the corporate and shareholder levels if all the requirements of Section 355 are met. Even when S corporations were not permitted to have subsidiaries, the Service was tolerant in this area, ignoring the transitory nature of a subsidiary formed in preparation for a division.[23] After the division, the new corporation (or corporations, in the case of a split-up) may immediately make an S election.[24]

PROBLEMS

1. Hi–Flying Co. is an aggressive growth company which was formed as a C corporation many years ago to develop new innovative technology. Hi–Flying has been successful and expects to receive inquiries concerning possible taxable and tax-free takeovers in the next few years. Can Hi–Flying's shareholders improve their tax situation in a future takeover by making an S election? In general, if Hi–Flying makes an S election, would you advise a potential corporate purchaser desiring a cost basis in Hi–Flying's assets to structure its acquisition as a purchase of stock or assets?

2. Target Corporation ("T") is a C corporation which has substantially appreciated assets and is a takeover candidate being pursued by several suitors. Purchasing Corporation ("P") has a Subchapter S election in effect and is considering making a bid for T. Consider the tax consequences of the following acquisition offers by P:

20. I.R.C. § 1362(b)(3); 1375.

21. For rules on AAA carryovers, see Reg. § 1.1368–2(d)(2).

22. I.R.C. § 1374(d)(8).

23. See, e.g., G.C.M. 39678 (1987).

24. For other issues, such as how to divide up the accumulated adjustments account, see Eustice & Kuntz, supra note 5, at ¶ 12.10.

(a) P will offer to purchase T's stock for cash or a combination of cash and P notes.

(b) P will acquire T in a Type C reorganization.

H. COMPENSATION ISSUES

S corporation shareholders also commonly serve as officers, directors and employees of their corporation. Individuals with this multiple status may have a choice as to whether to withdraw cash as compensation or as a shareholder distribution. Payments of salary are deductible by the corporation as a business expense (with the benefit of the deduction passing through to the shareholders), and are includible in the employee's gross income. Employee wages also are subject to various federal and state employment taxes imposed on both the employer and the employee (e.g., federal social security and medicare taxes).[1] Distributions, by contrast, generally may be received tax-free by shareholders to the extent of their stock basis, but they do not give rise to a deduction at the corporate level.

Because the payment of salaries to shareholders usually results in a tax "wash" in the case of a profitable corporation (the compensation deduction reduces the operating income that passes through to the shareholders), the *income* tax consequences of salaries and distributions may be identical.[2] The escalating employment tax base has influenced some S corporation shareholders to avoid this additional federal levy by foregoing salaries in lieu of larger shareholder distributions. The *Radtke* case, below, is one court's hostile reaction to this maneuver.

Joseph Radtke, S.C. v. United States

United States District Court, Eastern District of Wisconsin, 1989.
712 F.Supp. 143, affirmed 895 F.2d 1196 (7th Cir.1990).

ORDER

■ TERENCE T. EVANS, DISTRICT JUDGE.

* * *

FACTS

None of the facts are disputed.

Joseph Radtke received his law degree from Marquette University in 1978. The Radtke corporation was incorporated in 1979 to provide legal

1. In 2008, for example, both the employer and employee must pay social security ("FICA") taxes of 6.2% of the first $102,000 of an employee's taxable wages. I.R.C. §§ 3101; 3111; 3121. An additional medicare tax of 1.45%, again payable by both the employer and employee, is imposed on all of an employee's wages. I.R.C. § 3121(b). See generally Raby & Raby, "New Incentives for Avoiding SE and FICA Tax," 81 Tax Notes 1389 (Oct. 14, 1998).

2. The tax results are more complex, however, if the S corporation has losses for the taxable year. See Eustice & Kuntz, Federal Income Taxation of S Corporations ¶ 11.02[2] (4th ed. 2001).

services in Milwaukee. Mr. Radtke is the firm's sole incorporator, director, and shareholder. In 1982, he also served as the unpaid president and treasurer of the corporation, while his wife Joyce was the unpaid and nominal vice-president and secretary. The corporation is an electing small business corporation, otherwise known as a subchapter S corporation. This means that it is not taxed at the corporate level. All corporate income is taxed to the shareholder, whether or not the income is distributed.

In 1982, Mr. Radtke was the only full-time employee of the corporation, though it employed a few other persons on a piece-meal and part-time basis. Under an employment contract executed between Mr. Radtke and his corporation in 1980, he received "an annual base salary, to be determined by its board of directors, but in no event shall such annual salary be less than $0 per year * * *. Employee's original annual base salary shall be $0." This base salary of $0 continued through 1982, a year in which Mr. Radtke devoted all of his working time to representing the corporation's clients.

Mr. Radtke received $18,225 in dividends from the corporation in 1982. Whenever he needed money, and whenever the corporation was showing a profit—that is, when there was money in its bank account—he would do what was necessary under Wisconsin corporate law to have the board declare a dividend, and he would write a corporate check to himself.

Mr. Radtke paid personal income tax on the dividends in 1982. The Radtke corporation also declared the $18,225 on its form 1120S, the small business corporation income tax return. But the corporation did not file a federal employment tax form (Form 941) or a federal unemployment tax form (Form 940). In other words, it did not deduct a portion of the $18,225 for Social Security (FICA) and unemployment compensation (FUTA). The IRS subsequently assessed deficiencies as well as interest and penalties. The Radtke corporation paid the full amount that IRS demanded under FUTA—$366.44—and it also paid $593.75 toward the assessed FICA taxes, interest, and penalties. Then the corporation sued here after a fruitless claim for refunds.

DISCUSSION

* * *

The Radtke corporation acknowledges that wages are subject to FICA and FUTA taxes, but it argues that the Internal Revenue Code nowhere treats a shareholder-employee's dividends as wages for the purpose of employment taxes. The government, on the other hand, contends that "since Joseph Radtke performed substantial services for Joseph Radtke,

S.C., and did not receive reasonable compensation for such services other than 'dividends', the 'dividends' constitute 'wages' subject to federal employment taxes." The government does not allege that the Radtke corporation is a fiction that somehow failed to comply with Wisconsin statutes governing corporations.

The Federal Insurance Contributions Act defines "wages" as "all remuneration for employment," with various exceptions that are not relevant to this dispute. 26 U.S.C. § 3121(a). Similarly, the Federal Unemployment Tax Act defines "wages" as "all remuneration for employment," with certain exceptions that are not relevant. 26 U.S.C. § 3306(b). (Dividends are not specifically excepted in either act, and "remuneration" is not defined.) Mr. Radtke was clearly an "employee" of the Radtke corporation, as the plaintiff concedes. *See* 26 U.S.C. §§ 3121(d) and 3306(i). Likewise, his work for the enterprise was obviously "employment." *See* 26 U.S.C. §§ 3121(b) and 3306(c).

According to the Radtke corporation, not all "income" can be characterized as "wages." I agree. See Royster Company v. United States, 479 F.2d 387, 390 (4th Cir.1973) (free lunches did not constitute "wages" subject to FICA and FUTA); Central Illinois Public Service Co. v. United States, 435 U.S. 21, 25, 98 S.Ct. 917, 919, 55 L.Ed.2d 82 (1978) (reimbursement for lunches not "wages" subject to withholding tax; Court says in dicta that dividends are not wages).

At the same time, however, I am not moved by the Radtke corporation's connected argument that "dividends" cannot be "wages." Courts reviewing tax questions are obligated to look at the substance, not the form, of the transactions at issue. Transactions between a closely held corporation and its principals, who may have multiple relationships with the corporation, are subject to particularly careful scrutiny. Whether dividends represent a distribution of profits or instead are compensation for employment is a matter to be determined in view of all the evidence.

In the circumstances of this case—where the corporation's only director had the corporation pay himself, the only significant employee, *no* salary for substantial services—I believe that Mr. Radtke's "dividends" were in fact "wages" subject to FICA and FUTA taxation. His "dividends" functioned as remuneration for employment.

It seems only logical that a corporation is required to pay employment taxes when it employs an employee. See Automated Typesetting, Inc. v. United States, 527 F.Supp. 515, 519 (E.D.Wis.1981) (corporation liable for employment taxes on payments to officers who performed more than nominal services for corporation); C.D. Ulrich, Ltd. v. United States, 692 F.Supp. 1053, 1055 (D.Minn.1988) (discussing case law defining who is an "employee"; court refuses to enjoin IRS from collecting employment taxes from S corporation that paid dividends but no salary to sole shareholder and director, a certified public accountant who worked for the firm). See also Rev.Rul. 73–361, 1973–2 C.B. 331 (stockholder-officer who performed substantial services for S corporation is "employee," and his salary is subject to FICA and FUTA tax); Rev.Rul. 71–86, 1971–1 C.B. 285 (president and sole stockholder of corporation is "employee" whose salary is subject to employment taxes, even though he alone fixes his salary and determines his duties).

An employer should not be permitted to evade FICA and FUTA by characterizing *all* of an employee's remuneration as something other than "wages." Cf. Greenlee v. United States, 87–1 U.S.T.C. Para. 9306 (corporation's interest-free loans to sole shareholder constituted "wages" for FICA and FUTA where loans were made at shareholder's discretion and he performed substantial services for corporation). This is simply the flip side of those instances in which corporations attempt to disguise profit distributions as salaries for whatever tax benefits that may produce. See, e.g., Miles–Conley Co. v. Commissioner, 173 F.2d 958, 960–61 (4th Cir.1949) (corporation could not deduct from its gross income excessive salary paid to president and sole stockholder).

Accordingly, the plaintiff's motion for summary judgment is DENIED, and the defendant's motion for summary judgment is GRANTED. The plaintiff is ORDERED to pay the remaining deficiency on its 1982 FICA taxes along with the assessed interest, penalties, and fees.

NOTE

Subsequent Developments. In accord with *Radtke* are Fred R. Esser, P.C. v. United States,[1] Dunn & Clark, P.A. v. Commissioner,[2] and Spicer Accounting Inc. v. United States.[3] A contrary result was reached in Davis v. United States,[4] where the court declined to recharacterize S corporation distributions as taxable wages. *Davis* is distinguishable, however, because the shareholders performed only minor services on behalf of the S corporation.

Fringe Benefits. Fringe benefits paid by an S corporation to its shareholder-employees also are subject to special treatment. Section 1372 provides that an S corporation shall be treated as a partnership for purposes of employee fringe benefits, and any shareholder owning either more than two percent of the corporation's outstanding stock or more than two percent of the total voting power of all stock will be treated as a partner. As a result, an S corporation seldom can provide benefits, such as a medical reimbursement plan or group-term life insurance, which are deductible by the corporation and excludable from gross income of its shareholder-employees.[5]

1. 750 F.Supp. 421 (D.Ariz.1990).
2. 57 F.3d 1076 (9th Cir.1995).
3. 918 F.2d 90 (9th Cir.1990).
4. 74 AFTR 2d 5618 (D.Colo.1994).
5. For special rules relating to health insurance, see I.R.C. § 162(*l*)(1), (5), and Rev. Rul. 91–26, 1991–1 C.B. 184.

I. TAX POLICY ISSUES: SUBCHAPTER K VS. SUBCHAPTER S*

The check-the-box elective classification regime discussed in Chapter 1 has made it easier for virtually any closely held business to obtain pass-through taxation treatment. This has resurrected the longstanding debate on the most desirable structure for a pass-through system. The excerpt below, from a study by the Joint Committee on Taxation, compares the tax treatment of partnerships and S corporations and surveys the competing views on the need to retain two different pass-through regimes.

Excerpt From Review of Selected Entity Classification and Partnership Tax Issues

Staff of Joint Committee on Taxation (JCS–6–97) 23–25 (April 8, 1997).

Need for multiple sets of rules for pass-through entities

[The issuance of final check-the-box classification regulations raises a set of issues regarding] whether there is a continuing need in the tax law for parallel pass-through systems for general business activities.[42] Although S corporations (and their shareholders) generally are treated similarly to partnerships (and their partners), significant differences exist, some of which favor S corporations while others favor partnerships.

For example, the items of income, gain, loss, deduction or credit of a partnership generally are taken into account by a partner pursuant to the partnership agreement (or in accordance with the partners' interest in the partnership if the agreement does not provide for an allocation) so long as such allocation has substantial economic effect.[43] Because of the one-class-of-stock rule for S corporations (sec. 1361(b)(1)(D)), the items of income, gain, loss, deduction or credit of an S corporation cannot be separately allocated to a particular shareholder, but are taken into account by all the shareholders on a per-share, per-day basis. Thus, partnerships generally are considered to be a more flexible vehicle for purposes of allocating particular entity-level items to investors.

Another important difference making partnerships more flexible than S corporations is the treatment of entity-level debt, for purposes of the owner's basis in his interest. A partner includes partnership-level debt in the basis of his interest (sec. 752), whereas an S corporation shareholder does not (sec. 1367). The amount of the partner's or S corporation share-

* See generally Eustice, "Subchapter S Corporations and Partnerships: A Search for the Pass Through Paradigm (Some Preliminary Proposals)," 39 Tax L.Rev. 345 (1984).

42. Eliminating the two-tier corporate tax system, perhaps through some form of corporate integration, could also minimize the need for multiple sets of rules for pass-through entities, but is beyond the scope of this discussion.

43. Sections 704(a) and (b). The determination of whether an allocation has substantial economic effect is complex (Treas. Reg. sec. 1.704–1(b)(2)).

holder's basis in his interest serves as a limit on the amount of losses that can be passed through (secs. 704(d), 1366(d)), which makes increases in basis for entity-level debt important.

The sale of stock in an S corporation generally results in capital gain or loss to the selling shareholder. The sale of an interest in a partnership also generally gives rise to capital gain or loss, but gives rise to ordinary income to the selling partner to the extent attributable to unrealized receivables and certain inventory items (sec. 751).

The distribution of appreciated property by an S corporation to a shareholder (as a dividend, in redemption of shares, or in liquidation) is treated as a taxable sale of such property. Any gain is allocated to all the shareholders on a per-share, per day basis and increases the shareholder's adjusted bases in their shares. The distributee shareholder then reduces his basis by the amount of the distribution (i.e., fair market value of the distributed property) and takes a fair market value basis in the property. By contrast, the distribution of appreciated property by a partnership to a partner generally is not treated as a taxable sale of the property (sec. 731).

An existing C corporation may elect to be treated as an S corporation on a tax-free basis, subject to certain special rules. Converting C corporations are subject to corporate-level tax on the recapture of LIFO benefits,[44] on certain built-in gains recognized within a 10–year period after conversion,[45] and on certain passive investment income earned while the corporation retains its former C corporate earnings and profits.[46] The conversion of a C corporation to a partnership (or sole proprietorship) is treated as a liquidation of the entity, taxable to both the corporation and its shareholders.

The rules of subchapter C generally apply to an S corporation and its shareholders. Thus, for example, an S corporation may merge into a C corporation (or vice versa) on a tax-free basis. Similar rules do not apply to combinations of C corporations and partnerships.

Individual partners treated as general partners generally are subject to self-employment tax on their distributive shares of partnership income. Shareholders of an S corporation are not subject to self-employment tax on

44. Sec. 1363(d).

45. Section 1374. For a discussion of how section 1374 allows the conversion of a C corporation to S corporation to be treated more favorably than the liquidation of a C corporation into a sole proprietorship or a partnership, despite the economic equivalence of the transactions, see, letter to Chairman Dan Rostenkowski from Ronald A. Pearlman, Chief of Staff of the Joint Committee on Taxation, recommending several simplification proposals, reprinted in Committee on Ways and Means, Written Proposals on Tax Simplification (WMCP 101–27), May 25, 1990, p. 24. In his 1995 and 1997 budget messages to the Congress, President Clinton recommended that section 1374 be repealed for C corporations above a certain size. [Later proposals made by the Clinton administration would have repealed Section 1374 for C-to-S conversions of corporations with a value of more than $5 million at the time of conversion and treated the transaction as a taxable liquidation of the C corporation followed by a contribution of the assets to an S corporation by the recipient shareholders. Ed.]

46. Section 1375.

S corporation earnings, but are subject to payroll tax to the extent they receive salaries or wages from the corporation.

Partnerships, LLCs treated as partnerships, and S corporations may be treated differently for State income or franchise tax purposes.

Continuing utility of S corporations

If an LLC can provide limited liability to all owners and achieve pass-through status as a partnership under the check-the-box regulations (or under the Service's prior revenue rulings on LLCs), the need for S corporations could be questioned. Particularly in light of the growing use of LLCs, it could be argued that the great flexibility of the partnership tax rules outweigh the principal advantage of S corporations: relative simplicity. Thus, it is argued that the rules for S corporations could be repealed without detriment to taxpayers.[47]

Others say the continued existence of subchapter S is worthwhile. A corporate charter is a prerequisite imposed by regulators for some trades or businesses (e.g., for depository institutions or to hold certain licenses), and LLCs may not meet such regulatory requirements. Moreover, the corporate form is a familiar, time-tested format, while the LLC form is new and unfamiliar (particularly where a business undertakes interstate commerce). Subchapter S supporters further point out that the rules of subchapter S are much simpler than the rules of subchapter K.[48] Others point to specific advantages of subchapter S over the partnership tax rules (primarily the ability to convert from C to S corporation status generally without current corporate tax on appreciation, and the availability of tax-free reorganization rules for business combinations and reorganizations). At least until LLC interests are as easily issued in capital markets as traditional corporate stock, the S corporation may continue to be an attractive vehicle in which to start a business, if it is anticipated that it will later go public. Finally, any repeal of subchapter S would require rules providing for the treatment of existing S corporations.[49]

Whether or not it is advisable to retain both the partnership rules and the S corporation rules, some argue that the complexity of either regime is excessive for small businesses, and a new, much simpler pass-through system should be provided for small businesses that would be consistent with the new simplicity for choice of entity under the check-the-box

47. W. Schwidetzky, "Is It Time to Give the S Corporation a Proper Burial?" 15 Virginia Tax Review 591 (1996).

48. However, it must be pointed out that partners of a partnership may opt for a simple, subchapter-S like structure if they so desire. It could be said that the check-the-box regulations expand the appeal of subchapter S, because prior to those regulations, only entities structured as corporations for State law purposes could elect S corporation status, whereas now, a State-law partnership or LLC can be classified as a corporation for tax purposes and elect S status (provided applicable requirements are met).

49. See, for example, the letter of July 25, 1995, from Leslie B. Samuels, Assistant Treasury Secretary (Tax Policy) to Senator Orin Hatch, suggesting possible legislative proposals to allow S corporations to elect partnership status or to apply the check-the-box regulations to S corporations.

regulations.[50] A significant question, under such an approach, is the definition of a small business, which could depend on the number of owners, the value of the entity's assets, the amount of its gross or net income (if any), or some combination of these or other factors. Related questions involve the treatment of businesses that grow (or fluctuate in size), crossing the definitional line, and the treatment of tax attributes imported from a more complex tax regime. Weighing of simplicity against accuracy of income measurement and allocation would be a factor in designing a simpler regime.

Others would argue that there is nothing inherently complex in the application of the partnership tax rules to most small business transactions. Small businesses today can achieve the effect of a simplified partnership regime for most common business arrangements. Mandating the use of specific rules for small business would deny them the flexibility of present law partnership rules and, it could be argued, would represent a competitive disadvantage relative to larger businesses.

50. American Law Institute, Federal Income Tax Project—Taxation of Pass-Through Entities, Memorandum No. 2 96–105 (Sept. 2, 1996) (G. Yin and D. Shakow, reporters).

APPENDIX

FORM 1065, SCHEDULE K–1

651107

☐ Final K-1 ☐ Amended K-1 OMB No. 1545-0099

Schedule K-1 (Form 1065) **2007**

Department of the Treasury
Internal Revenue Service

For calendar year 2007, or tax year beginning ________, 2007 ending ________, 20____

Partner's Share of Income, Deductions, Credits, etc. ► **See back of form and separate instructions.**

Part I Information About the Partnership

A Partnership's employer identification number

B Partnership's name, address, city, state, and ZIP code

C IRS Center where partnership filed return

D ☐ Check if this is a publicly traded partnership (PTP)

Part II Information About the Partner

E Partner's identifying number

F Partner's name, address, city, state, and ZIP code

G ☐ General partner or LLC member-manager ☐ Limited partner or other LLC member

H ☐ Domestic partner ☐ Foreign partner

I What type of entity is this partner? ________

J Partner's share of profit, loss, and capital:

	Beginning	Ending
Profit	%	%
Loss	%	%
Capital	%	%

K Partner's share of liabilities at year end:

Nonrecourse . . . . $________

Qualified nonrecourse financing . . $________

Recourse . . . . $________

L Partner's capital account analysis:

Beginning capital account . . . . $________

Capital contributed during the year . $________

Current year increase (decrease) . . $________

Withdrawals & distributions . . . $(________)

Ending capital account . . . . $________

☐ Tax basis ☐ GAAP ☐ Section 704(b) book

☐ Other (explain)

Part III Partner's Share of Current Year Income, Deductions, Credits, and Other Items

1	Ordinary business income (loss)	15	Credits
2	Net rental real estate income (loss)		
3	Other net rental income (loss)	16	Foreign transactions
4	Guaranteed payments		
5	Interest income		
6a	Ordinary dividends		
6b	Qualified dividends		
7	Royalties		
8	Net short-term capital gain (loss)		
9a	Net long-term capital gain (loss)	17	Alternative minimum tax (AMT) items
9b	Collectibles (28%) gain (loss)		
9c	Unrecaptured section 1250 gain		
10	Net section 1231 gain (loss)	18	Tax-exempt income and nondeductible expenses
11	Other income (loss)		
12	Section 179 deduction	19	Distributions
13	Other deductions	20	Other information
14	Self-employment earnings (loss)		

*See attached statement for additional information.

For IRS Use Only

For Paperwork Reduction Act Notice, see Instructions for Form 1065. Cat. No. 11394R **Schedule K-1 (Form 1065) 2007**

Schedule K-1 (Form 1065) 2007 Page **2**

This list identifies the codes used on Schedule K-1 for all partners and provides summarized reporting information for partners who file Form 1040. For detailed reporting and filing information, see the separate Partner's Instructions for Schedule K-1 and the instructions for your income tax return.

1. Ordinary business income (loss). You must first determine whether the income (loss) is passive or nonpassive. Then enter on your return as follows:

	Report on
Passive loss	See the Partner's Instructions
Passive income	Schedule E, line 28, column (g)
Nonpassive loss	Schedule E, line 28, column (h)
Nonpassive income	Schedule E, line 28, column (j)
2. Net rental real estate income (loss)	See the Partner's Instructions
3. Other net rental income (loss)	
Net income	Schedule E, line 28, column (g)
Net loss	See the Partner's Instructions
4. Guaranteed payments	Schedule E, line 28, column (j)
5. Interest income	Form 1040, line 8a
6a. Ordinary dividends	Form 1040, line 9a
6b. Qualified dividends	Form 1040, line 9b
7. Royalties	Schedule E, line 4
8. Net short-term capital gain (loss)	Schedule D, line 5, column (f)
9a. Net long-term capital gain (loss)	Schedule D, line 12, column (f)
9b. Collectibles (28%) gain (loss)	28% Rate Gain Worksheet, line 4 (Schedule D instructions)
9c. Unrecaptured section 1250 gain	See the Partner's Instructions
10. Net section 1231 gain (loss)	See the Partner's Instructions
11. Other income (loss)	
Code	
A Other portfolio income (loss)	See the Partner's Instructions
B Involuntary conversions	See the Partner's Instructions
C Sec. 1256 contracts & straddles	Form 6781, line 1
D Mining exploration costs recapture	See Pub. 535
E Cancellation of debt	Form 1040, line 21 or Form 982
F Other income (loss)	See the Partner's Instructions
12. Section 179 deduction	See the Partner's Instructions
13. Other deductions	
A Cash contributions (50%)	See the Partner's Instructions
B Cash contributions (30%)	See the Partner's Instructions
C Noncash contributions (50%)	See the Partner's Instructions
D Noncash contributions (30%)	See the Partner's Instructions
E Capital gain property to a 50% organization (30%)	See the Partner's Instructions
F Capital gain property (20%)	See the Partner's Instructions
G Investment interest expense	Form 4952, line 1
H Deductions—royalty income	Schedule E, line 18
I Section 59(e)(2) expenditures	See the Partner's Instructions
J Deductions—portfolio (2% floor)	Schedule A, line 23
K Deductions—portfolio (other)	Schedule A, line 28
L Amounts paid for medical insurance	Schedule A, line 1 or Form 1040, line 29
M Educational assistance benefits	See the Partner's Instructions
N Dependent care benefits	Form 2441, line 14
O Preproductive period expenses	See the Partner's Instructions
P Commercial revitalization deduction from rental real estate activities	See Form 8582 instructions
Q Pensions and IRAs	See the Partner's Instructions
R Reforestation expense deduction	See the Partner's Instructions
S Domestic production activities information	See Form 8903 instructions
T Qualified production activities income	Form 8903, line 7
U Employer's Form W-2 wages	Form 8903, line 15
V Other deductions	See the Partner's Instructions

14. Self-employment earnings (loss)

Note. *If you have a section 179 deduction or any partner-level deductions, see the Partner's Instructions before completing Schedule SE.*

A Net earnings (loss) from self-employment	Schedule SE, Section A or B
B Gross farming or fishing income	See the Partner's Instructions
C Gross non-farm income	See the Partner's Instructions
15. Credits	
A Low-income housing credit (section 42(j)(5))	See the Partner's Instructions
B Low-income housing credit (other)	See the Partner's Instructions
C Qualified rehabilitation expenditures (rental real estate)	See the Partner's Instructions
D Other rental real estate credits	See the Partner's Instructions
E Other rental credits	See the Partner's Instructions
F Undistributed capital gains credit	Form 1040, line 70; check box a
G Credit for alcohol used as fuel	See the Partner's Instructions
H Work opportunity credit	See the Partner's Instructions
I Welfare-to-work credit	See the Partner's Instructions
J Disabled access credit	See the Partner's Instructions

Code	*Report on*
K Empowerment zone and renewal community employment credit	Form 8844, line 3
L Credit for increasing research activities	See the Partner's Instructions
M New markets credit	See the Partner's Instructions
N Credit for employer social security and Medicare taxes	See the Partner's Instructions
O Backup withholding	Form 1040, line 64
P Other credits	See the Partner's Instructions
16. Foreign transactions	
A Name of country or U.S. possession	Form 1116, Part I
B Gross income from all sources	Form 1116, Part I
C Gross income sourced at partner level	Form 1116, Part I
Foreign gross income sourced at partnership level	
D Passive category	Form 1116, Part I
E General category	Form 1116, Part I
F Other	Form 1116, Part I
Deductions allocated and apportioned at partner level	
G Interest expense	Form 1116, Part I
H Other	Form 1116, Part I
Deductions allocated and apportioned at partnership level to foreign source income	
I Passive category	Form 1116, Part I
J General category	Form 1116, Part I
K Other	Form 1116, Part I
Other information	
L Total foreign taxes paid	Form 1116, Part II
M Total foreign taxes accrued	Form 1116, Part II
N Reduction in taxes available for credit	Form 1116, line 12
O Foreign trading gross receipts	Form 8873
P Extraterritorial income exclusion	Form 8873
Q Other foreign transactions	See the Partner's Instructions
17. Alternative minimum tax (AMT) items	
A Post-1986 depreciation adjustment	See the Partner's Instructions and the Instructions for Form 6251
B Adjusted gain or loss	See the Partner's Instructions and the Instructions for Form 6251
C Depletion (other than oil & gas)	See the Partner's Instructions and the Instructions for Form 6251
D Oil, gas, & geothermal—gross income	See the Partner's Instructions and the Instructions for Form 6251
E Oil, gas, & geothermal—deductions	See the Partner's Instructions and the Instructions for Form 6251
F Other AMT items	See the Partner's Instructions and the Instructions for Form 6251
18. Tax-exempt income and nondeductible expenses	
A Tax-exempt interest income	Form 1040, line 8b
B Other tax-exempt income	See the Partner's Instructions
C Nondeductible expenses	See the Partner's Instructions
19. Distributions	
A Cash and marketable securities	See the Partner's Instructions
B Other property	See the Partner's Instructions
20. Other information	
A Investment income	Form 4952, line 4a
B Investment expenses	Form 4952, line 5
C Fuel tax credit information	Form 4136
D Qualified rehabilitation expenditures (other than rental real estate)	See the Partner's Instructions
E Basis of energy property	See the Partner's Instructions
F Recapture of low-income housing credit (section 42(j)(5))	Form 8611, line 8
G Recapture of low-income housing credit (other)	Form 8611, line 8
H Recapture of investment credit	See Form 4255
I Recapture of other credits	See the Partner's Instructions
J Look-back interest—completed long-term contracts	See Form 8697
K Look-back interest—income forecast method	See Form 8866
L Dispositions of property with section 179 deductions	See the Partner's Instructions
M Recapture of section 179 deduction	See the Partner's Instructions
N Interest expense for corporate partners	See the Partner's Instructions
O Section 453(l)(3) information	See the Partner's Instructions
P Section 453A(c) information	See the Partner's Instructions
Q Section 1260(b) information	See the Partner's Instructions
R Interest allocable to production expenditures	See the Partner's Instructions
S CCF nonqualified withdrawals	See the Partner's Instructions
T Information needed to figure depletion—oil and gas	See the Partner's Instructions
U Amortization of reforestation costs	See the Partner's Instructions
V Unrelated business taxable income	See the Partner's Instructions
W Other information	See the Partner's Instructions

INDEX

References are to Pages

†